# theNewMediaReader

# theNewMediaReader

Edited by Noah Wardrip-Fruin and Nick Montfort

Designed by Michael Crumpton

The MIT Press

Cambridge, Massachusetts

London, England

This book was set in ITC Chapparal, Officina Serif, and
Officina Sans by Michael Crumpton.

Printed and bound in the United States of America.


Library of Congress Cataloging-in-Publication Data

The new media reader / edited by Noah Wardrip-Fruin and Nick Montfort
        p. cm.
    Includes bibliographical references and index.
    ISBN 0-262-23227-8 (hc.: alk. paper)
        1. Telecommunication. 2. Mass media. 3. Computers and
civilization. 4. Internet. I. Wardrip-Fruin, Noah. II. Montfort, Nick.

    TK5102.5 .N48 2003
    302.23—dc21
                            2002026412


10 9 8 7 6 5 4 3 2

# Contents

## Perspectives on New Media: Two Introductions

## I. The Complex, the Changing, and the Indeterminate

## II. Collective Media, Personal Media

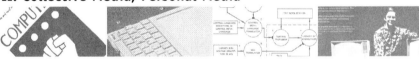

## III. Design, Activity, and Action

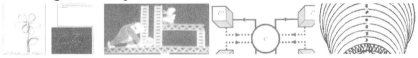

## IV. Revolution, Resistance, and the Launch of the Web

## I. The Complex, the Changing, and the Indeterminate

*Principle of the graph of the Cent Milli...
the arcs and vertices h...*

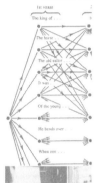

## II. Collective Media, Personal Media

# Contents

## III. Design, Activity, and Action

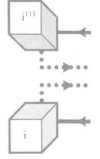

Consultation, *gen*

## IV. Revolution, Resistance, and the Launch of the Web

## Advisors

Espen Aarseth
Mark Bernstein
Chris Bregler
Edward Fox
Cynthia Goodman
Carolyn Guyer
Terry Harpold
N. Katherine Hayles
Carol Hutchins
Henry Jenkins
Carl Machover
Stuart Moulthrop
Christiane Paul
Ken Perlin
Edward A. Shanken
Herman Tavani
Gregory Ulmer
Adrianne Wortzel

# *The New Media Reader,* A User's Manual

## Noah Wardrip-Fruin and Nick Montfort

### Audience

*The New Media Reader* is designed as a foundation for understanding new media. We have selected its contents with three audiences in mind:

### New Media Professionals

The ideas now current in new media are a few of the many put forward during the founding of this field. The selections here reveal where today's important ideas came from and provide a basis for understanding them more deeply. *The New Media Reader* also presents ideas that still await their moment in the sun—ideas from the same visionaries who brought us the mouse, the link, object-oriented programming, and more. Considering how these ideas play out in today's new media environment could be the source of the next big innovation.

### Students and Professors

These selections provide the basis for a wide variety of new media courses, especially for courses that merge theory and application, aesthetics and implementation. They could serve as the sole texts for a course on the history of new media. In other courses, *The New Media Reader* can undergird a syllabus that also contains a selection of current writings, programs, and imagery in the course's area of focus. The materials offered here also represent a wealth of inspiration for final projects and independent studies, and provide a reference for scholars, offering historical works that are hard to access in other ways.

### Readers Seeking to Understand New Media

Whoever may try to understand the computer as new media in our changing world—whether a journalist, a manager, a dentist, or a delivery driver—will find in *The New Media Reader* an introduction to each selection, placing it in context and explaining its importance. These introductions do not assume a reader with a degree in computer science or mathematics—or in literature or philosophy, for that matter.

### Contents

*The New Media Reader* contains three types of material:

### Foundational Writings

The texts in the book part of *The New Media Reader* come from computer scientists, architects, artists, writers, cultural critics—and quite a few people whose defining insights came precisely from working across these categories. These essays range from World War II to the emergence of the World Wide Web. They begin just as digital computing, cybernetic feedback, and the early ideas that led to hypertext and the Internet are emerging into public discussion—and they end as the combined product of these ideas enters into the mainstream of public life. These writings are the most influential encapsulations of new media's most significant concepts and critiques.

### Functioning Programs

On the CD part of *The New Media Reader* are working versions of some of the most important new media artifacts ever created, many of which are extremely difficult to find elsewhere or difficult to get running on modern computers. Included are games, tools, digital art, and more—with selections of academic software, independent literary efforts, and home-computer-era commercial software such as *Karateka,* a famous cinematically-inspired computer game from the creator of *Prince of Persia* and *The Last Express.*

## Digitized Video

Also on the CD are pieces of digitized video, documenting some new media programs of which no operational version exists and documenting important demonstrations of programs. For example, there is a video record of Doug Engelbart's 1968 demonstration, one that fundamentally altered the course of new media. This was the first presentation of the mouse, the word processor, the hyperlink, computer-supported cooperative work, video conferencing, and even a dividing up of the screen that we'd now call non-overlapping "windows." Along more artistic lines, there is also video documentation of interactive artworks by Lynn Hershman and Grahame Weinbren—works that redefined what, and how, new media could *mean*.

## Directions

Reading *The New Media Reader* in the usual way should of course be informative and helpful. Below are two particular suggestions of other ways to apply the concepts and critiques herein.

### Make Something

Understanding new media is almost impossible for those who aren't actively involved in the experience of new media; for deep understanding, actually creating new media projects is essential to grasping their workings and poetics. The ideas described in these selections can open important new creative areas for beginners and professionals alike. The book and CD can also help readers avoid an all-too-common problem in the new media field: the reinvention of the wheel. Instead of rebuilding the same systems with new technologies, those who look to *The New Media Reader* can base their new attempts on the lessons learned from existing work.

### Rethink Something

New media's biggest breakthroughs haven't come by simply expending huge resources to tackle well-understood problems. They have come from moments of realization: that a problem others haven't solved is being formulated in the wrong way, or that a technology has a radically different possible use than its current one, or that the metaphors and structures of one community of practice could combine with the products of another to create a third. That is, breakthroughs have come from thinking across disciplines, from rethinking one area of inquiry with tools and methodologies gained from another—whether in the direction of Ted Nelson's conception of computing in literary terms, or the opposite movement of Raymond Queneau's formulation of storytelling and poetry in algorithmic terms. One of these brought us the Web; the other, digital narrative. There are almost certainly still fundamental contributions like this to be made in new media. Reading *The New Media Reader's* selections against one another can offer a way to begin this type of rethinking.

*The New Media Reader* speaks to articulate the history of a field that has too often gone unheard, both by entrepreneurs seeking to bring the next big thing to the Web and by academics approaching new media from their own discipline. Why the past has been neglected is no mystery: the genealogy of new media is much more obscure than its ecstatic, fully-indexed, online present. What historical documents are available are often found in fragments—on the Web in PDF, in an assortment of anthologies divided by subfields, or in the dusty microfilm files that Vannevar Bush hoped would one day be hooked into the memex. Often when early articles in new media are reprinted they do not include the important illustrations that accompanied the original publications. This anthology, embracing print and digital media, is our effort to uncover and assemble a representative collection of critical thoughts, events, and developments from the computer's humanistic and artistic past, its conception not as an advanced calculator but as a new medium, or as enabling new media. Many of these original insights, even many of the most radical, grew out of an understanding of media that came before as well as a background in what already existed of the new media field. We hope the materials here will help provide such an understanding and offer fuel for inspiration.

Free floating edge links, like the one to the left of this paragraph, point to other chapters based on references that are made in the main text.

**000**

Edge markers like the one to the left of *this* paragraph contain the current page number—and the height of the marker on the page visually indicates the current chapter's position in the book.

Link lines that cross other link lines are shaded differently to help the reader follow the path (◊BB).

◊AA
123

◊BB
123

Numbers and lines that grow out of boxes refer to the content in the boxes (◊99) and (◊AA).

◊99
123

## Key to Special Symbols

Michael Crumpton's design for *The New Media Reader* includes a number of symbols and devices intended to aid in navigating and using this book—to make it easier for readers to find their way among the selections.

### Edge Markers

Just as some dictionaries provide edge tabs to aid the finding of parts of the alphabet, each text reprinted in *The New Media Reader* is represented by a mark on the outer edge of each page which can be seen even with the book closed.

### Link Lines

When a margin note makes reference to a chapter elsewhere in the book, this is represented by a "link line" drawn to the edge of the page. When the reference is instead from the page's main text (see below) the link line originates with an edge link (see below). Link lines are aligned with the edge marker for the appropriate article.

### In-Text Link Indicators

When one of *The New Media Reader's* original texts makes reference to a text elsewhere in the volume, this reference is followed by a diamond symbol "◊" which indicates that a link line to this text appears in the page margin. This sample marker (◊00) refers to the edge link in the upper left of this page. When one of *The New Media Reader's* original texts makes reference to something included, excerpted, or documented on the project's CD, this reference is followed by the symbol "⊗".

◊02
123   The upper number in an edge link tells the chapter number and the lower number is the page number of that chapter.

# Acknowledgments

We offer our thanks to the people at the MIT Press (especially Doug Sery, Michael Sims, and Katherine Innis), those who contributed the introductions (Lev Manovich and Janet Murray), and everyone who gave permission for their materials to be reproduced in the book and on the CD. Authors whose work is included in the volume have also offered much additional assistance, ranging from help with the permissions process to corresponding with us so that we could better introduce their ideas. The contributions of all of these people have made this project possible.

The project's advisors, listed earlier, have contributed inestimable quantities of time and wisdom to make *The New Media Reader* a success, for which we are very grateful. Many other people have also offered valuable assistance, and we thank Ingrid Ankerson, Marcel Benabou, Michael Benedikt, John Boe, Jan Cohen-Cruz, Mary Coppernol, Warren Motte, Celia Pearce, Jeff O'Connell, and Grahame Weinbren for their help as well.

The support of New York University's Center for Advanced Technology and Media Research Laboratory was essential, and we particularly wish to thank directors Ken Perlin and Mike Uretsky, director of operations Clilly Castiglia, founding director Jack Schwartz, and founding program coordinator Cynthia Allen. The libraries of New York University, the University of California at Santa Cruz, Stanford University, MIT, and the University of Pennsylvania, as well as the New York Public Library, provided needed resources. Other help came from the MIT Media Lab, the School of Information Arts and Technologies at the University of Baltimore, the Scholarly Technology Group of Brown University, the Department of Computer and Information Science at the University of Pennsylvania, and the Rhode Island School of Design.

Noah Wardrip-Fruin thanks the PACE program at Long Beach Polytechnic High School (where his first electronic writing project was completed), the Johnston Center for Integrative Studies at the University of Redlands, and the Gallatin School of Individualized Study at New York University for providing the educational environments in which the roots of this project grew. Thanks are also due to many not mentioned elsewhere, including Ben Abrahamse, Kendra Anderson, Janet Allard, Kam Bellamy, Adam Chapman, Hetal Dalal, Gertrude Fruin, Richard Fruin, Norma Grady, Marjetta Geerling, Helene Goodman, Pat Harrigan, Bob Hudspeth, Kirstin Kantner, Nancy Kaplan, Suzanne Kemperman, Nancy Kramer, Kevin Leathers, Marjorie Luesebrink, Bill McDonald, Bella Mirabella, Brion Moss, Yash Owada, Kathy Ogren, Cynthia Beth Rubin, Chris Spain, Stephanie Strickland, Chris Walker, Buford Wardrip, Elma Wardrip, Nathan Wardrip-Fruin, Duane Whitehurst, Kevin Whelan, Tia Winn, and Sara Zatz.

Nick Montfort thanks those, from many different disciplines, who have been his mentors in new media at the University of Texas at Austin, MIT, and Boston University: Michael Benedikt, Justine Cassell, Glorianna Davenport, Edsger W. Dijkstra, Henry Jenkins, Benjamin Kuipers, Janet Murray, Robert Pinsky, Bruce Porter, and John Slatin. He also appreciates the company of his fellow students and of colleagues he has met through the Digital Arts and Culture conference and through IFNYC, and that of others in online communities he has been a part of: BBSs in San Antonio, the Well, Cyborganic, and ifMUD. Exploring the literary and humanistic uses of the computer has been more rewarding thanks to such friends.

Michael Crumpton thanks the guys at BCW design who showed him how to have fun with graphic design and his wife Marjetta for her patience with the crazy life of a freelancer. Last but not least he wants to acknowledge his grandmother Hada Bostelmann whose inspiration and support gave him the world of art and design.

We wish to dedicate this project to our parents: Carolyn and Mark, John and Gena, Nina and Charles and Edward.

# Perspectives on New Media
## Two Introductions

# Inventing
# the Medium

## Janet H. Murray

This is a landmark volume, marking the first comprehensive effort at establishing the genealogy of the computer as an expressive medium.

Although the name of the book is *The New Media Reader,* its subject is the emergence of a single medium, and one which we can define more particularly than by merely by pointing to its novelty. The *digital medium* which we see emerging in these well-selected and contextualized essays may seem plural to us now, because it is so myriad in its forms—virtual reality CAVEs, the Internet, "enhanced" television, videogames. Indeed, like the medium of film 100 years earlier, the computer medium is drawing on many antecedents and spawning a variety of formats. But the term "new media" is a sign of our current confusion about where these efforts are leading and our breathlessness at the pace of change, particularly in the last two decades of the 20th century. How long will it take before we see the gift for what it is—a single new medium of representation, the digital medium, formed by the braided interplay of technical invention and cultural expression at the end of the 20th century? This reader, reflecting the burgeoning of "New Media Studies" throughout academic life and new media practice throughout the world, should help to hasten that change in our thinking.

Here for the first time within a single volume we can trace the cultural helix, the echoing and opposing strands that form the DNA for cyberspace itself. The first two essays establish the pattern, a call and response of fantasist and engineer, philosopher and inventor. Borges (◊01), the storyteller-librarian, and Bush (◊02), the soldier-scientist, speak to us out of the same midcentury frame of mind, exhausted by war, exhilarated by a dawning sense of globalism. They are both almost viscerally aware of the increased complexity of human consciousness and the failure of linear media to capture the structures of our thought. Borges, one of the first fiction writers to place himself in the

expanded context of a global culture, is fascinated by the arbitrariness of language itself, by the flutter of meaning across cultural boundaries. His fiction evokes a sense of flickering focus, of an individual consciousness constantly reforming itself, of an utterance constantly in the process of translation. Borges confronts us with the "pullulating" moment, when we become aware of all the possible choices we might make, all the ways in which we might intersect one another for good or evil. His imagined Garden of Forking Paths is both a book and landscape, a book that has the shape of a labyrinth that folds back upon itself in infinite regression. It is a dizzying vision, one which will be described again by humanist writers for the rest of the century.

For Vannevar Bush, the scientist, the world is not an imprisoning labyrinth, but a challenging maze, waiting to be solved by an appropriately organized and clever team effort. Like Borges, Bush imagines alternate libraries. But where Borges's visions are playful and subversive of rationalist exploration, Bush dreams of the hyperrational. He is alarmed to discover that the library shelf is no longer an adequate map of knowledge. Book-based organizational structures have been outpaced by the tempo of investigation, and no longer reflect the constantly reformulating disciplinary boundaries of contemporary scholarship. Knowledge is expanding, but human life remains too short. Where Borges is frozen at the crossroads, enraptured by the proliferating paths, Bush is impatiently searching for the shortcuts, the paths forged by the experts who have scouted the territory before us. He wants to follow in their footsteps and to lay down new trails, trails that do not fade. His engineer's commitment to the redemptive machine runs throughout this volume as well.

Bush, of course, is not thinking about the "computer"— and neither is Borges. Instead they are inventing fantasy information structures—a book-garden-maze, a desk-library-machine—that reflect not a new technology but a change in how our minds are working. The change they imagine is made more urgent by the experience of two world wars, wars that made apparent the huge gulf between our technological prowess and our social development, between our complex thinking and our atavistic behavior. In Borges's fable, the protagonist kills a man as a form of information processing, the murdered man being significant only because his name in the newspaper will act as an appropriate coded message.

Bush's example of a representative research subject is the history of bow and arrow technology. He has learned the power of information organization in the context of wartime weapons development, where more knowledge means more power against the enemy.

Central to Borges's story is our discomfort over the narrator's amoral choice, the impersonal, political murder of a man who in alternate "forks" becomes his friend. There is no right side in his warscape; the murderer does not believe in his cause or care which side wins. In the world of the forking path garden, time does not move forward at all, but outward in proliferating possibilities of creation and destruction that make up the totality of human potential. To live in Borges's world is to feel complicity and exhaustion, but also wonder. Bush's view, on the other hand, is moralistic, energetic, and engaged. Implicit in Bush's narrative is the Enlightenment faith in human progress driven by expanded knowledge, the American metaphor of the rich frontier waiting to be conquered by the able trailblazer, the absolute necessity of self-defense. Bush's maze challenges us, but we are smart enough to find our way out. The solution lies in building something, in making something new that will better serve human need. This dichotomy runs through the rest of the century and is echoed throughout this anthology.

All creativity can be understood as taking in the world as a problem. The problem that preoccupies all of the authors in this volume is the pullulating consciousness that is the direct result of 500 years of print culture. One can think of the humanist strand as dramatizing the problem, amplifying our discomfort by denaturalizing the rituals by which we deny it. The disciplinary humanists in this volume, whether artists, theorists, or scholars, are all engaged in foregrounding our cultural confusions, tuning up our sense of existential befuddlement before the scientifically revealed world of the twentieth century. The engineers, on the other hand, put their faith in the invention of the proper instruments, that, like the microscope and telescope before them, will let us focus on the things that baffle and unhinge us so that we can think about them in a systematic way. The right instruments organize not just the outer world but consciousness itself, a phenomenon that is feared by the humanists and embraced by the engineers. The engineers see the central task of our time—finding the key to survival in the atomic age—as a challenge to our intellects. The

world has become more difficult to understand, so we need better ways of thinking about it, more powerful methods of mastering complexity. The library shelf and the chaptered book create both overview and close-up and allow us to move between them without losing our place. What the computer offers us is a more capacious shelf, a finer grained division. The engineers articulate a vision of a new meta-book, a navigable collection of books that will carry us gracefully to the next level of information control and systematic thought, just as the invention of print did 500 years ago. The humanist voices in this survey start off at a greater distance from the material basis of the new medium, and they are often much less hopeful. They find the punch cards of the early information age of little use. They are surveying the wreck of ideologies, coming to terms with the failed promises of print, the horrifying trajectory of the rationalist arrow. They insist that we experience the flickering focus, the slipping away of meaning between the signifier and the signified, that is the intellectual predicament of the second half of the twentieth century.

The authors in this volume line up on both sides of this divide, but they are also facing one another along the braided path. The difference is not so much in what they describe as in their orientation to it. The humanists see the contradictions and limitations of the great systems of thought and it causes them to question the very project of systemized thinking. Such questioning is of their moment but it also is part of a longer tradition of literary and philosophical discourse that articulates the unknowability of life, its tragic dimension, and the absurd and maddening persistence of longing, suffering, need.

The engineers are grounded in a tradition that emphasizes solution and defines the needs it cannot satisfy—and the suffering its solutions can inflict—as outside the domain of the problem. At its worst, the engineering mentality creates efficient killing machines, faster and more deadly arrows. It exults in the ability to "Put-That-There" (◊29), to move weapons around a map with the flick of a magically gloved finger. At its best, it fosters the comic view of the world in which we are resilient enough to problem-solve our way out of our troubles up to the very barrier of mortality itself. At its best, it also celebrates the human capacity to learn and to conceive things that had not been thought of before, things that might make us not just smarter but more creative.

◊01
29
◊02
35
◊03
49
◊04
65
◊05
73
◊07
89
◊08
93
◊11
133
◊12
147
◊16
231
◊21
301
◊24
367
◊26
391
◊30
441

The strands cross one another throughout the period that this anthology delineates, and a single individual often seems to straddle the gap between them. The engineers draw upon cultural metaphors and analogies to express the magnitude of the change, the shape of the as yet unseen medium. The storytellers and theorists build imaginary landscapes of information, writing stories and essays that later become blueprints for actual systems. The engineers pace themselves against an accelerating threat of annihilation by the new war technologies; the humanists imagine the machine as a redemptive environment, welcoming the prospect of cyborg architectures that reconfigure our bodies, our cultures, our selves in hopeful ways. The two traditions come together most energetically in collaborations focused on new structures of learning in which exploration of the computer is motivated by a desire to foster the exploratory processes of the mind itself. Gradually, the braided collaboration gives rise to an emergent form, a new medium of human expression.

By bringing these two strands together in this chronologically arranged collection, the editors invite us to look more closely at the rich interplay of cultural practice and technical innovation. We see the scientific culture articulating a medium that "augments" our humanity, that makes us smarter by pooling our thinking and organizing it at a higher level, and even by facilitating new ways of thinking that are more synthetic and have more power to master complex operations and ideas. Meanwhile the arts are engaged in dicing the language and recombining it randomly, calling attention to the arbitrary nature of the written and spoken signifiers, dramatizing the sense of cultural unraveling after two world wars. Seeing all of these players gathered within the boundaries of this one volume we can almost imagine them in a single room, participating in a kind of quilting bee. In one corner, Borges (◊01), Burroughs (◊07), and the Oulipo (◊12) are busy shredding the outgrown garments of print, while across the room Bush (◊02), Engelbart (◊08, ◊16), and the Xerox PARC collaborators (◊26) are eagerly sewing the fragments together into an intricately patterned, vast, and welcoming quilt. The process begins in mid-century, with the earliest understanding by Turing (◊03), Wiener (◊04), and others of the potential of the computer for symbolic representation and for the capturing of complex interactive systems.

Computer languages were developed that allowed for more powerful manipulation of quantitative and text-based data, supporting large databases, scientific and economic simulations, and research in artificial intelligence. The 1960s were a time of dizzying progress for computer scientists, the period in which the field itself was defined, separated from electrical engineering and mathematics with its own advanced degree programs. It was the time when Licklider (◊05) and others were proposing the Internet, when Weizenbaum (◊24) inadvertently invented the first believable computer-based character, when Nelson (◊11, ◊21, ◊30) coined the word "hypertext" and began his lifelong quest to embody it.

And it was the time when Douglas Englebart, looking about him and seeing that the human race was "in trouble," committed his career to the "augmenting of human intellect." Had Englebart been given the resources to realize more of his "Framework," he might have been the prolific Michaelangelo of the computer renaissance, demonstrating how to do many difficult things with maximum expressivity. As it was, he has been a kind of Leonardo, accomplishing much, indirectly influencing much, but leaving behind the unrealized plans for even more. Englebart did not think of the computer as merely improving human thinking, but as transforming the processes of our institutions in a more profound way. The "augmented institution" as he saw it would change not into a "bigger and faster snail" but would become a new species, like a cat, with new sensory abilities and entirely new powers. The evolutionary metaphor is an expression of awe at the magnitude of the shift, a way of sharing the shiver of terror at the unfamiliar rush of mind-power that makes us wonder if we might be capable of outthinking our very humanity.

By the end of the 1960s the engineers had a good understanding of the potential of the computer. They were supporting large databases, experimenting with on-screen images and game-like interaction, establishing networked systems that could be accessed by remote terminals with multiple users sharing the same mainframe, and building large-scale simulation systems. Although the machines themselves were slow and of little capacity by current standards, and were primarily used for number crunching, they had been developed well enough to make concrete Turing's vision of a universal machine. A decade before the development of "multimedia" and at the point when "hypertext" was just a concept, the sheer representational power of the computer was apparent to those who were leading its development. They realized that the whole of the medium was much more than the sum of the various enabling technologies.

As I have argued elsewhere, the awe-inspiring representational power of the computer derives from its four defining qualities: its procedural, participatory, encyclopedic, and spatial properties. The most obvious property of the new medium, the one most clearly needed by the post-war world, was its encyclopedic capacity. The digital computer is simply the largest medium human beings have ever invented, the one capable of holding the most information. In the 1960s much of that memory was on tape or punch cards, and dependent on linear reading. In the succeeding decades it reached dizzying thresholds of random access availability, with exponential increases becoming the norm. But the deeper encyclopedic potential of binary representation itself was clear from Turing's time. If the computer is a universal machine, capable of representing anything, then can it represent all of human knowledge? Like other capacious technologies (print, moving images) which the computer contains, it calls forth our desire to get everything in one place, to get, as William Faulkner once described the aspiration of the novelist, the whole world in one sentence.

Furthermore, the computer can present itself to us as a place, one which we enter and do not wish to leave. This enveloping quality derives from the spatial property of the medium, its capability for embodying dimensionality. That is, we can place things within it in assigned locations, both actual (as registers within the machines) and, more importantly, symbolic (as on a Web "site," or in a dungeon under a trap door within a fantasy environment). These locations are more than merely labels because we can navigate by them, and they will be consistent relative to one another. This spatial quality made the early text-based dungeon games like *Adventure* ⊗ and *Zork* enormously successful. This spatializing quality is based upon the other two properties of the digital medium, the two most basic and defining attributes: its processing power, which allows

us to specify procedures which will be not merely recorded but executed; and its participatory quality, which allows it to receive input, to allow manipulation of its processes and data by the user. The creation of the illusion of space within the machine, which can be achieved with only a text-based display, is the result of its capacity for accepting navigational commands from us and then responding according to its programming in a consistent manner that reinforces our notion of space. That is, we can program the responses of the computer to simulate any space we can imagine, displaying "north" and "south" or "left" and "right" appropriately so that the participating user will form a reliable mental map of the symbolically represented territory. But even though this "spatial" property is derivative of the procedural and participatory properties, it is so fundamental to the way we experience the world, and so desirable a means of representing the world, that we have to think about it as a property in itself. It is not accidental that we refer to information in digital networks as existing in "cyberspace," or that the first computer game to be massively distributed by network was a text-based exploration of a virtual cave.

Together the two properties of encyclopedic capacity and spatial navigability create the experience of enclosure in explorable, extensive spaces. These can be fictional landscapes, like Borges's labyrinthine garden, or they can be information spaces, like Bush's memex machine. The sense of following a trail is the same in both cases, and it is a sense that creates the pleasurable experience of immersion, of moving within a capacious, consistent, enveloping digital environment rather than just looking at it.

But the more fundamental properties, the procedural and participatory foundation of the computer, are the ones that provide the basis for what we think of as the defining experience of the digital medium, its "interactivity." Although this word is often used loosely it can be thought of as encompassing these two properties, and also the pleasure of agency, the sense of participating in a world that responds coherently to our participation. We do something with the computer—whether it is shooting at a fantasy enemy or manipulating words or images or moving from one Web site to another—and it processes our input and responds in a way that makes sense to us. Because of the interactive nature of the medium, the computer environment is not just immersive, it is animated. This effect was clear from the introduction of the computer workstation in the 1960s, when the new conversational structure of programmer and processor, keyboard and display, connected in real time provoked playful applications like the therapist Eliza ⊗ or the dungeon and dragon of *Adventure* ⊗. Both of these inventions took advantage of the streamlined interactivity of the new environments. They elicited engagement from an interactor, and they responded to that engagement in a way that made clear the animating rules of the computer's world.

The invention of Eliza is particularly instructive. Unlike early hypertext systems that were developed in answer to the vision of the memex, Eliza far exceeded expectations. Eliza's persuasiveness, her existence not as a program but as a perceived human being, as a character capable of inspiring theatrical belief, came as a shock to Joseph Weizenbaum. Turing had called for a similar system as a test of the powers of the computer to simulate a human being in free conversation, but Weizenbaum was offended by such confusions and dismayed to have inadvertently created a program that was mistakenly believed to have passed the Turing test. The widespread confusion over Eliza's potential as a real rather than a simulated and comic therapist, and Weizenbaum's attempts to straighten people out, were symptoms of the gap between our new ability to make digital artifacts and our inability to understand what we were making. Weizenbaum came to terms with his creation only after he was able to describe it in literary terms. His secretary who thought Eliza was a real therapist and his computer scientist friends who were charmed by her despite their understanding of the code were not deluded; they were merely engaging in the willing suspension of disbelief, as Coleridge had pointed out that theater goers do. But he missed the importance of this event: the discovery of a new literary medium, like the play or the novel or the sonnet—a medium that consisted of the writing of procedural rules and the engagement of an improvising interactor with the rule-governed system.

With the invention of Eliza, the computer had reached an important milestone: it had achieved the illusion of life through the rules of behavior. But it was not until the 1980s that practice became self-conscious enough to allow for a serious discourse about digital artifacts. For while computer scientists were laying down the technical foundation for such

immersive and interactive environments, humanists were expanding our theoretical grasp of technologies of representation. Cultural critics and communications researchers, responding to the growth of television in the 1950s and its expansion in the 1960s, focused our attention on the media experience itself as a subject of analysis and encouraged a new interest in analyzing the varieties of media experiences. Newer media such as photography, radio, film, and television could now be seen in the longer history that stretched back beyond the printing press to oral composition and the invention of writing. Marshall McLuhan (◊13) in particular brought interest in media to the forefront with his playful and insightful aphoristic writings. Like the computer scientists who were inventing the foundational technologies of the coming Internet, McLuhan saw media as "extensions of man," a means to augment our powers of perception and communication. He celebrated this change, but he did so in the tone of an old testament prophet, acknowledging the threatening as well as the thrilling aspects of this new communicative power. Other critics were more distrustful, seeing the mass media as the means by which the existing power structures maintain the status quo. The basis of the much of the popular and academic discourse on the media of later decades begins in the 1960s with this fascination with, and distrust of, television. As a result digital enthusiasts often described their efforts as remediating the dangers of television (for example, in allowing two-way instead of only one-way communication), and digital skeptics condemned the new medium as amplifying the destructive powers of television (for example, in exercising even greater holding power over consumers, further alienating them from the "real" world).

The technophobic response to computers, which was strong throughout the period covered here, was also an important part of the story, and it should continue to be so. The augmenting of human intellect remains an uncertain and even a perilous activity. Hitler's genocidal efficiency was made possible by sophisticated information processing. The census tools he relied on are mere crayon scratches compared with those a tyrant could now command to automate the knowledge of everything from our reading habits to our DNA. Surveillance can now be extended not just inside the walls of our houses but inside our brain where we can witness the retrieval of a memory almost neuron by neuron.

◊13
193

New media in any age are always distrusted media. Prometheus is a hero to some and a transgressor to others, and both are right. Fire warms and fire burns. It remains to be seen which of the anti-technological voices from the second half of the twentieth century will be of lasting importance. The technophobic response is most clearly useful when it spurs us to question the uses to which we put technology and to guard against the dangers of abuse. It is perhaps less persuasive when arguing the abandonment of a medium—whether it is print, photography, television, or computers—or when it argues for the cultural or moral superiority of one means of expression over another, regardless of the content. But the anxieties aroused by a new medium are real, and worthy of attending to. The critics of technology are an important part of the development of a new medium because they challenge us to identify more clearly what we find so compelling about it, why we are so drawn to shape this new clay into objects that have not existed before.

Throughout the 1970s the humanities expanded its critical vocabulary and sophistication in understanding the process of representation, applying the same focused analysis to mass communication and cultural rituals (such as advertising posters and sports events) as had formerly been directed toward great works of literature. And as the postwar babies came into maturity, eager to understand and transcend the destructive history of the 20th century, ideology itself became an important subject of study, especially its embodiment in cultural artifacts within both high and low culture. The political insights of the 1960s combined with the methodologies of semiotics and its successors were applied to every aspect of human society, including the discourses of humanism itself—with devastating results. The great pillars of knowledge and social coherence were exposed as tyrannical at worst, delusional at best. All was ideology, and at the bottom of these vast nested pyramids of ideological representation was language itself, which was left to point at nothing real beyond our own consciousness, nothing external beyond our shared hallucinations. The signifiers of cultural discourse by which we defined our lives—faith, love, gender, family, nation, morality—pointed at one another in a dizzyingly infinite regression. In short, for humanists of the late 20th century the tools of analysis were increasing, but the content of the

analysis was disorienting. We understood how human beings constructed meaning better than we had ever done before; but we no longer could believe in anything that we asserted. This condition, which came to be thought of as postmodernism, was one that called for new forms of artistic expression that simultaneously utilized and distanced themselves from the great traditions of cultural expression. It was the age of the put-on, an ironic age in which even the most exuberant expressions had a bitter aftertaste, and much of the most ambitious work possessed a cold derisive quality, a sense that everything had been said before and that it was all lies. Academic discourse was infected with word-play that substituted allusion for assertion as its prevalent rhetorical style.

For the computer scientists, on the other hand, the 1970s were a time of great earnestness and exhilarating possibilities as the computer was coming into its own as a new medium of representation. But while educational innovators like Alan Kay (◊26) and Seymour Papert (◊28) were celebrating the computer as a new and powerful tool for the active construction of meaning, artists and humanists were celebrating deconstruction, finding evidence in high and low culture throughout the world of the inevitable unraveling of meaning. All throughout the 1970s while university-based researchers were enjoying the new Internet technologies, and the computer was growing as a vehicle for connection and imaginative engagement—the discourse of humanism was growing increasingly fragmented and distrustful of the constructive imagination.

Of course the humanists were not inventing the postmodern condition—they were merely chronicling it, registering and giving form to the cultural anxiety caused by the loss of faith in the great human meta-narratives of sacred and secular salvation. At the heart of the most ironic deconstruction of outworn conventions was a celebration of expressivity itself, a delight in throwing off the monolithic straightjacket in favor of an antic, mutable series of costumes, of foregoing the longing for the end of the story in order to revel in the possibilities of the middle. What was missing was a form that could contain so many middles and such a sustained refusal of an ending.

The 1980s marked the beginning of the shift. For many humanists a key component of this change was provided by Deleuze and Guattari (◊27) who, without thinking of computers at all, offered a metaphor for intellectual discourse that served as a bridge for many humanists to the otherwise alien world of the machine. The two philosophers suggested a new model of textual organization to replace the ideologically suspect hierarchies of the old print-based world. The new ideal of form was the rhizome—an erudite word for a very down to earth thing: a potato root system. It was as if Deleuze and Guattari had dug beneath the forking path garden of Borges (which after all was still a hierarchy of sorts) and come up with an even more profound labyrinth, but one that offers the hope of knowability and a metaphor of healthy growth. The potato root system has no beginning, no end, and grows outward and inward at the same time. It forms a pattern familiar to computer scientists: a network with discrete interconnected nodes. Here was a way out of the pullulating paralysis, one that went beyond the subversion of all existing hierarchies. Here was a way of constructing something new. The humanist project of shredding culture had found a radical new pattern of meaning, a root system that offered a metaphor of growth and connection rather than rot and disassembly.

The gift of this metaphor at the beginning of the 1980s coincided with the introduction of the first personal computers and the introduction of word processing software, bringing a new accessibility of computational power to those outside the computer lab. At the more privileged educational institutions, the 1980s brought gifts of equipment and grant money that allowed for hitherto unprecedented collaborations between engineers and humanists. George Landow at Brown University, Gregory Crane at Harvard, Larry Friedlander at Stanford, and others gained access to sophisticated computational systems and began applying them to the representation of networked knowledge systems, working in fields such as Victorian culture, Ancient Greece, and Shakespeare. In North Carolina, J. David Bolter (◊47), Michael Joyce (◊42), and John Smith invented Storyspace, a hypertext system specifically designed for storytelling, which greatly expanded the use of computers in the humanities. With the arrival of HyperCard and similar notecard-based systems the personal computer came into usefulness throughout the educational system as a location for the creation of educational resources by teachers and students, rivaling the development of textbooks. These authoring environments

and applications programs of the 1980s marked a new era in the expressiveness of the medium, by opening up the encyclopedic and spatial properties of the computer to wider communities of practices, communities composed not of programmers but of artists, writers, and educators.

While the academically-rooted experiments with hypertext took their course and found their enthusiastic but relatively small audiences, the video game was growing into a entertainment form to rival movies and television. Video games were successful because, as Brenda Laurel (◊38) pointed out, they exploited the computer's capacity to "represent action in which humans could participate." The videogame also won over the young to the new medium and developed an expanding vocabulary of engagement, including ever more detailed and intricate elaboration on the theme of the violent contest as well as increasing interest in creating detailed, immersive, expressive story worlds.

The expansion of practice was accompanied by another mark of a maturing medium, the moment at which computer practice became widespread enough to become an object of study in itself. Sherry Turkle (◊34) offered the foundational view of the psychosocial dynamics of the digital medium, calling it a "second self" upon which we projected consciousness, and an "evocative object" which had tremendous "holding power" over the interactor. The first online communities were forming and began to display the complex social relationships so well captured in the account by Morningstar and Farmer (◊46) of Lucasfilm's Habitat.  The conflict between player killing and community building in that world was mirrored by the conflict between those, like Richard Stallman (◊36), who wanted a distributed, cooperative open programming community and the commercial influences, now personified by Microsoft, who wanted to standardize development on closed, centrally controlled systems. The computer began to emerge as a noticeable entity in the social world, with its utopian and dystopian promises now the subject of explicit policy debates.

The 1980s also marked the beginning of our understanding of interactive design as a new field of study, the beginning of the self-conscious creation of digital artifacts not by small teams of researchers but by a newly defined profession. Apple established guidelines for its graphical user interface, allowing multiple developers to use the same conventions for the same functions. The original focus of design, building on the industrial design insights of Donald Norman and others, placed emphasis on the "interface." Shneiderman (◊33), Laurel (◊38), and Winograd (◊37) moved the emphasis to the human actor and the shaping of the interaction. This change was marked by the movement of the field from Computer Human Interface to Human Computer Interaction, from CHI (which is still the designation of the special interest group of the ACM which holds the central meeting in the field) to HCI (which is what universities now teach and give degrees in).

The humanities and arts became more visible to the engineers as computers became more available to the humanists. The spatial property of the medium brought forth a new interest in architecture; the participatory property provoked interest in improvisational theater. The teams who produced new application software, new educational environments, and new "multimedia" games became intentionally interdisciplinary. As they struggled to understand one another's conflicting design criteria, new academic programs arose to educate professionals for a rapidly morphing field.

By the end of the 1980s the computer had emerged as an everyday tool for business, education, and entertainment. But it was primarily a desktop tool, networked to a few co-workers perhaps. Those who were using the Internet on a regular basis were mostly using it for email or for the uploading and downloading of files between home and office machines or perhaps among a small circle of close collaborators. This was to change dramatically with the invention of the World Wide Web, which is the subject of the final essay in this anthology.

It is fitting that this chronicle of joint invention ends with Tim Berners-Lee (◊54), who is both inventor and culture hero. Berners-Lee set out to solve a technical problem of information flow, to simplify the communication of the worldwide community of physics. He changed the model of communication from passing around containers of information (streaming bits identified by filename) to passing around viewable documents (Web pages). By displaying the documents on the screen and at a distance, he opened up the possibility of a true global library, an ultimate Alexandria. He also, somewhat inadvertently, opened up a new marketplace. The World Wide Web stands at the

crossroads of many of the strands within this volume, combining Stallman's passion for open standards with Negroponte's (◊23) enchantment with "bits" (replacing "atoms") as a global commodity. It is the best embodiment so far of the encyclopedic, labyrinthine fantasies of the memex and the potato garden. It allows for previously unimaginable levels of surveillance—webcams operating 24/7 in the service of science, tourism, exhibitionism, policing, stalking, and even pure whimsy, monitoring, for instance, the state of a coffee pot in a lab halfway around the world. The Web also provides participatory experiences with such ease of availability that gaming is often described in the press as a threat to productivity in the office and to learning from kindergarten through college. And over the horizon is a faster connection, a bigger data pipe, a more elegantly designed indexing, retrieval, and display system, a more tactile interface, a more complete convergence of entertainment media into interactive TV and of museums, libraries, universities into a single digital information source. The title of one active current field of design could stand as summary for the whole effort at the turn of the 21st century: we are moving toward a world of *ubiquitous computing*. And a key enabling technology behind this change is the coherent transmission of information across multiple platforms with standardized protocols like those that now underlie the Web.

But as important as Tim Berners-Lee's technical work is his role as culture hero of the information age. Instead of commercializing his invention, Berners-Lee established an open Web standard, administered in the interest of uniting all the worlds' information sources into ever larger and more coherent units. Berners-Lee's grand gesture of renunciation (as it is often described) is a counter-fable to the one with which this anthology begins. The spy in the forking garden is a tool of the meaning machine, bound to transmit messages at any cost (messages that carry no meaning to him) in obedience to the prevailing social order, the order of competition to the death. The Berners-Lee fable, on the other hand, celebrates a refusal to commodify the message, an affirmation of meaning over money, of world cooperation over global competition. It offers a way out of the pullulating, paralyzed consciousness of meaningless. It offers a fulfillment in part of Bush's vision. In the world of structured Web pages, we agree on metadata that will link one bit of information with its counterpart across the globe, annotated by another hand. We make multiple patterns and change them kaleidoscopically to express many views of the same data, the same object, the same event. The promise of the Web, not as it is, but as it could be, is like that of the book before it: it will allow us to say more complicated things to more people with greater understanding. The promise is that we will not be crushed by our own knowledge, as the writers at the beginning of this period anticipated, because we will organize it together in a vast distributed and synchronized effort. We will not be mere prisoners of the labyrinth, nor even trail-blazers: we will be the makers of the labyrinth, the gods of our own machines.

Perhaps the most amazing thing in all these essays is the record of perseverance. What would make us engage with machines for fifty years despite their core stupidity, their 0s and 1s and their propensity to crash, their maddening literalness and oblivious torpor? Why do we struggle to make them coherent and expressive despite all that can be said of their inhuman rigidity and still primitive state? Why do human beings choose at this time in our cultural history to communicate with one another by making complex artifacts out of electrical impulses? For the same reason that we couldn't put down the stylus or the whittling knife. We

are drawn to a new medium of representation because we are pattern makers who are thinking beyond our old tools. We cannot rewind our collective cognitive effort, since the digital medium is as much a pattern of thinking and perceiving as it is a pattern of making things. We are drawn to this medium because we need it to understand the world and our place in it.

To return to Bush's speculations: now that we have shaped this a new medium of expression, *how may we think?* We may, if we are lucky and mindful enough, learn to think together by building shared structures of meaning. How will we escape the labyrinth of deconstructed ideologies and self-reflective signs? We will, if we are lucky enough and mindful enough, invent communities of communication at the widest possible bandwidth and smallest possible granularity.

We need not imagine ourselves stranded somewhere over the evolutionary horizon, separated from our species by the power of our own thinking. The machine like the book and the painting and the symphony and the photograph is made in our own image, and reflects it back again. The task is the same now as it ever has been, familiar, thrilling, unavoidable: we work with all our myriad talents to expand our media of expression to the full measure of our humanity.

# New Media from Borges to HTML

## Lev Manovich

### The New Media Field: a Short Institutional History

The appearance of *The New Media Reader* is a milestone in the history of a new field that, just a few years ago, was somewhat of a cultural underground. Before taking up the theoretical challenge of defining what new media actually is, as well as discussing the particular contributions this reader makes to answering this question, I would like very briefly to sketch the history of the field for the benefit of whose who are newcomers to it.

If we are to look at any modern cultural field sociologically, measuring its standing by the number and the importance of cultural institutions devoted to it such as museum exhibitions, festivals, publications, conferences, and so on, we can say that in the case of new media (understood as computer-based artistic activities) it took about ten years for it to move from cultural periphery to the mainstream. Although SIGGRAPH in the United States and Ars Electronica in Austria had already acted as annual gathering places of artists working with computers since the late 1970s, the new media field began to take real shape only in the end of the 1980s. Around that time new institutions devoted to the production and support of new media art were founded in Europe: ZKM in Karlsruhe (1989), New Media Institute in Frankfurt (1990), and ISEA (Inter-Society for the Electronic Arts) in the Netherlands (1990). (Jeffrey Shaw was appointed to be director of the part of ZKM focused on visual media while the Frankfurt Institute was headed by Peter Weibel.) In 1990 as well, Intercommunication Center in Tokyo began its activities in new media art (it moved into its own building in 1997). Throughout the 1990s, Europe and Japan remained the best places to see new media work and to participate in high-level discussions of the new field. Festivals such as ISEA, Ars Electronica, and DEAF have been required places of pilgrimage for interactive installation artists, computer musicians, choreographers working with computers, media curators, critics, and, since the mid-1990s, net artists.

As was often the case throughout the twentieth century, countries other than the United States were first to critically engage with new technologies developed and deployed in the United States. There are a few ways to explain this phenomenon. Firstly, the speed with which new technologies are assimilated in the United States makes them "invisible" almost overnight: they become an assumed part of the everyday existence, something which does not seem to require much reflection. The slower speed of assimilation and the higher costs involved give other countries more time to reflect upon new technologies, as it was the case with new media and the Internet in the 1990s. In the case of the Internet, by the end of the 1990s it became as commonplace in the United States as the telephone, while in Europe the Internet still remained a phenomenon to reflect upon, both for economic reasons (U.S. subscribers would pay a very low monthly flat fee; in Europe they had to pay by the minute) and for cultural reasons (a more skeptical attitude towards new technologies in many European countries slowed down their assimilation). So when in the early 1990s the Soros Foundation set up contemporary art centers throughout the Eastern Europe, it wisely gave them a mandate to focus their activities on new media art, both in order to support younger artists who had difficulty getting around the more established "art mafia" in these countries and also in order to introduce the general public to the Internet.

Secondly, we can explain the slow U.S. engagement with new media art during the 1990s by the very minimal level of the public support for the arts there. In Europe, Japan, and Australia festivals for media and new media art such as the ones I mentioned above, commissions for artists to create such work, exhibition catalogs and other related cultural activities were funded by the governments. In the United States the lack of government funding for the arts left only two cultural players which economically could have supported creative work in new media: anti-intellectual, market- and cliché-driven commercial mass culture and equally commercial art culture (i.e., the art market). For different reasons, neither of these players would support new media art nor would foster intellectual discourse about it. Out of the two, commercial culture (in other words, culture designed for mass audiences) has played a more progressive role in adopting and experimenting with new media, even though for obvious reasons the content of commercial new media products has had severe limits. Yet without commercial culture we would not have computer games using artificial intelligence; network-based multimedia (including various Web plug-ins which enable distribution of music, moving images and 3-D environments over the Web); sophisticated 3-D modeling; animation and rendering tools; database-driven Web sites; CD-ROMs, DVDs, and other storage formats; and most other advanced new media technologies and forms.

The 1990s the U.S. art world proved to be the most conservative cultural force in contemporary society, lagging behind the rest of the cultural and social institutions in dealing with new media technologies. (In the 1990s a standard joke at new media festivals was that a new media piece requires two interfaces: one for art curators and one for everybody else.) This resistance is understandable given that the logic of the art world and the logic of new media are exact opposites. The first is based the romantic idea of authorship which assumes a single author, the notion of a one-of-a-kind art object, and the control over the distribution of such objects which takes place through a set of exclusive places: galleries, museums, auctions. The second privileges the existence of potentially numerous copies; infinitely many different states of the same work; author-user symbiosis (the user can change the work through interactivity); the collective; collaborative authorship; and network distribution (which bypasses the art system distribution channels). Moreover, exhibition of new media requires a level of technical sophistication and computer equipment which neither U.S. museums nor galleries were able to provide in the 1990s. In contrast, in Europe generous federal and regional funding allowed not only for mountings of sophisticated exhibitions but also for the development of a whole new form of art: the interactive computer installation. It is true that after many years of its existence, the U.S. art world learned how to deal with and in fact fully embraced video installation—but video installations require standardized equipment and don't demand constant monitoring. Neither is the case with interactive installations or even with Web pieces. While in Europe equipment-intensive forms of interactive installation have flourished throughout the 1990s, the U.S. art world has taken the easy way out by focusing on "net art," i.e., Web-based pieces whose

exhibition does not require much resources beyond an off-the-shelf computer and a net connection.

All this started to change with increasing speed by the end of the 1990s. Various cultural institutions in the United States finally began to pay attention to new media. The first were education institutions. Around 1995 universities and art schools, particularly on the West Coast, began to initiate programs in new media art and design as well as open faculty positions in these areas; by the beginning of the new decade, practically every university and art school on the West Coast had both undergraduate and graduate programs in new media. A couple of years later museums such as Walker Art Center begun to mount a number of impressive online exhibitions and started to commission online projects. The 2000 Whitney Biannual included a room dedicated to net art (even though its presentation conceptually was ages behind the presentation of new media in such places as Ars Electronica Center in Linz, Intercommunication Center in Tokyo, or ZKM in Germany). Finally in 2001, both the Whitney Museum in New York and the San Francisco Museum of Modern art (SFMOMA) mounted large survey exhibitions of new media art (*Bitstreams* at the Whitney, *010101: Art in Technological Times* at SFMOMA). Add to this a constant flow of conferences and workshops mounted in such bastions of American Academia as the Institute for Advanced Studies in Princeton; fellowships in new media initiated by such prestigious funding bodies as the Rockefeller Foundation and Social Science Research Council (both begun in 2001); book series on new media published by such well-respected presses as the MIT Press. What ten years ago was a cultural underground became an established academic and artistic field; what has emerged from on-the-ground interactions of individual players has solidified, matured, and acquired institutional forms.

Paradoxically, at the same time as the new media field started to mature (the end of the 1990s), its very reason for existence came to be threatened. If all artists now, regardless of their preferred media, also routinely use digital computers to create, modify, and produce works, do we need to have a special field of new media art? As digital and network media rapidly become an omnipresent in our society, and as most artists came to routinely use these new media, the field is facing a danger of becoming a ghetto whose participants would be united by their fetishism of latest computer technology, rather than by any deeper conceptual, ideological or aesthetic issues—a kind of local club for photo enthusiasts. I personally do think that the existence of a separate new media field now and in the future makes very good sense, but it does require a justification—something that I hope the rest of this text, by taking up more theoretical questions, will help to provide.

## Software Design and Modern Art: Parallel Projects

Ten years after the appearance of the first cultural institutions solely focused on new media, the field has matured and solidified. But what exactly is new media? And what is new media art? Surprisingly, these questions remain not so easy to answer. The book you are now holding in your hands does provide very interesting answers to these questions; it also provides the most comprehensive foundation for the new media field, in the process redefining it in a very productive way. In short, this book is not just a map of the field as it already exists but a creative intervention into it.

The particular selections and their juxtaposition this book re-define new media as parallel tendencies in modern art and computing technology after the World War II. Although the editors of the anthology may not agree with this move, I would like to argue that eventually this parallelism changes the relationship between art and technology. In the last few decades of the twentieth century, modern computing and network technology materialized certain key projects of modern art developed approximately at the same time. In the process of this materialization, the technologies overtook art. That is, not only have new media technologies—computer programming, graphical human-computer interface, hypertext, computer multimedia, networking (both wired-based and wireless)—actualized the ideas behind projects by artists, they have also extended them much further than the artists originally imagined. As a result these technologies themselves have become the greatest art works of today. The greatest hypertext is the Web itself, because it is more complex, unpredictable and dynamic than any novel that could have been written by a single human writer, even James Joyce. The greatest interactive work is the interactive human-computer interface itself: the fact that the user can easily change everything which appears on her screen, in the

process changing the internal state of a computer or even commanding reality outside of it. The greatest avant-garde film is software such as Final Cut Pro or After Effects which contains the possibilities of combining together thousands of separate tracks into a single movie, as well as setting various relationships between all these different tracks—and it thus it develops the avant-garde idea of a film as an abstract visual score to its logical end, and beyond. Which means that those computer scientists who invented these technologies—J. C. R. Licklider (◊05), Douglas Engelbart (◊08. ◊16), Ivan Sutherland (◊09), Ted Nelson (◊11, ◊21, ◊30), Seymour Papert (◊28), Tim Berners-Lee (◊54), and others—are the important artists of our time, maybe the only artists who are truly important and who will be remembered from this historical period.

To prove the existence of historical parallelism, *The New Media Reader* positions next to each of the key texts by modern artists that articulate certain ideas those key texts by modern computer scientists that articulate similar ideas in relation to software and hardware design. Thus we find next to each other a story by Jorge Luis Borges (1941) (◊01) and an article by Vannevar Bush (1945) (◊02) which both contain the idea of a massive branching structure as a better way to organize data and to represent human experience.

The parallelism between texts by artists and by computer scientists involves not only the ideas in the texts but also the form of the texts. In the twentieth century artists typically presented their ideas either by writing manifestos or by creating actual art works. In the case of computer scientists, we either have theoretical articles that develop plans for particular software and/or hardware designs or more descriptive articles about already created prototypes or the actual working systems. Structurally manifestos correspond to the theoretical programs of computer scientists, while completed artworks correspond to working prototypes or systems designed by scientists to see if their ideas do work and to demonstrate these ideas to colleagues, sponsors and clients. Therefore *The New Media Reader* to a large extent consists of these two types of texts: either theoretical presentations of new ideas and speculations about projects (or types of projects) that would follow from them; or the descriptions of the projects actually realized.

Institutions of modern culture that are responsible for selecting what makes it into the canon of our cultural

◊01 29
◊02 35
◊05 73
◊08 93
◊09 109
◊11 133
◊16 231
◊21 301
◊28 413
◊30 441
◊54 791

memory and what is left behind are always behind the times. It may take a few decades or even longer for a new field which is making an important contribution to modern culture to "make it" into museums, books, and other official registers of cultural memory. In general, our official cultural histories tend to privilege art (understood in a romantic sense as individual products an individual artists) over mass industrial culture. For instance, while modern graphical and industrial designers do have some level of cultural visibility, their names, with the exception of a few contemporary celebrity designers such as Bruce Mau and Philip Stark, are generally not as known as the names of fine artists or fiction writers. Some examples of key contemporary fields that so far have not been given their due are music videos, cinematography, set design, and industrial design. But no cultural field so far has remained more unrecognized than computer science and, in particular, its specific branch of human-computer interaction, or HCI (also called human-computer interface design).

It is time that we treat the people who have articulated fundamental ideas of human-computer interaction as the major modern artists. Not only did they invent new ways to represent any data (and thus, by default, all data which has to do with "culture," i.e. the human experience in the world and the symbolic representations of this experience) but they have also radically redefined our interactions with all of old culture. As the window of a Web browser comes to supplement the cinema screen, museum space, CD player, book, and library, the new situation manifests itself: all culture, past and present, is being filtered through the computer, with its particular human-computer interface. Human-computer interface comes to act as a new form through which all older forms of cultural production are being mediated.

*The New Media Reader* contains essential articles by some of the key interface and software designers in the history of computing so far, from Engelbart to Berners-Lee. Thus in my view this book is not just an anthology of new media but also the first example of a radically new history of modern culture—a view from the future when more people will recognize that the true cultural innovators of the last decades of the twentieth century were interface designers, computer game designers, music video directors and DJs — rather than painters, filmmakers, or fiction writers, whose fields remained relatively stable during this historical period.

## What Is New Media? Eight Propositions

Having discussed the particular perspective adopted by *The New Media Reader* in relation to the larger cultural context we may want to place new media in—the notion of parallel developments in modern art and in computing—I now want to go through other possible concepts of new media and its histories (including a few proposed by the present author elsewhere). Here are eight answers; without a doubt, more can be invented if desired.

### 1 New Media versus Cyberculture

To begin with, we may distinguish between new media and cyberculture. In my view they represent two distinct fields of research. I would define cyberculture as the study of various social phenomena associated with the Internet and other new forms of network communication. Examples of what falls under cyberculture studies are online communities, online multi-player gaming, the issue of online identity, the sociology and the ethnography of email usage, cell phone usage in various communities, the issues of gender and ethnicity in Internet usage, and so on.[1] Notice that the emphasis is on the *social* phenomena; cyberculture does not directly deal with new cultural objects enabled by network communication technologies. The study of these objects is the domain of new media. In addition, new media is concerned with cultural objects and paradigms enabled by all forms of computing and not just by networking. To summarize: cyberculture is focused on the social and on networking; new media is focused on the cultural and computing.

### 2 New Media as Computer Technology Used as a Distribution Platform

What are these new cultural objects? Given that digital computing is now used in most areas of cultural production, from publishing and advertising to filmmaking and architecture, how can we single out the area of culture that specifically owes its existence to computing? In my *The Language of New Media* I begin the discussion of new media by invoking its definition which can be deduced from how the term is used in popular press: new media are the cultural objects which use digital computer technology for distribution and exhibition.[2] Thus, Internet, Web sites, computer multimedia, computer games, CD-ROMs and DVDs, virtual reality, and computer-generated special effects all fall under new media. Other cultural objects which use computing for production and storage but not for final distribution—television programs, feature films, magazines, books and other paper-based publications, etc.—are not new media.

The problems with this definition are three-fold. Firstly, it has to be revised every few years, as yet another part of culture comes to rely on computing technology for distribution (for instance, the shift from analog to digital television; the shift from film-based to digital projection of feature films in movie theatres; e-books, and so on) Secondly, we may suspect that eventually most forms of culture will use computer distribution, and therefore the term "new media" defined in this way will lose any specificity. Thirdly, this definition does not tell us anything about the possible effects of computer-based distribution on the aesthetics of what is being distributed. In other words, do Web sites, computer multimedia, computer games, CD-ROMs, and virtual reality all have something in common because they are delivered to the user via a computer? Only if the answer is at least a partial yes does it makes sense to think about new media as a useful theoretical category.

## 3 New Media as Digital Data Controlled by Software

*The Language of New Media* is based on the assumption that, in fact, all cultural objects that rely on digital representation and computer-based delivery do share a number of common qualities. In the book I articulate a number of principles of new media: numerical representation, modularity, automation, variability, and transcoding. I do not assume that any computer-based cultural object will necessary be structured according to these principles today. Rather, these are tendencies of a culture undergoing computerization that gradually will manifest themselves more and more. For instance, the principle of variability states that a new media cultural object may exist in potentially infinitely many different states. Today the examples of variability are commercial Web sites programmed to customize Web pages for each user as she is accessing the site, or DJs remixes of already existing recordings; tomorrow the principle of

variability may also structure a digital film which will similarly exist in multiple versions.

I deduce these principles, or tendencies, from the basic fact of digital representation of media. New media is reduced to digital data that can be manipulated by software as any other data. This allows automating many media operations, to generate multiple versions of the same object, etc. For instance, once an image is represented as a matrix of numbers, it can be manipulated or even generated automatically by running various algorithms, such as sharpen, blue, colorize, change contrast, etc.

More generally, extending what I proposed in my book, I could say that two basic ways in which computers model reality—through data structures and algorithms—can also be applied to media once it is represented digitally. In other words, given that new media is digital data controlled by particular "cultural" software, it make sense to think of any new media object in terms of particular data structures and/or particular algorithms it embodies.[3] Here are examples of data structures: an image can be thought of as a two-dimensional array $(x, y)$, while a movie can be thought of as a three-dimensional array $(x, y, t)$. Thinking about digital media in terms of algorithms, we discover that many of these algorithms can be applied to any media (such as copy, cut, paste, compress, find, match) while some still retain media specificity. For instance, one can easily search for a particular text string in a text but not for a particular object in an image. Conversely, one can composite a number of still or moving images together but not different texts. These differences have to do with different semiotic logics of different media in our culture: for example, we are ready to read practically any image or a composite of images as being meaningful, while for a text string to be meaningful we require that it obey the laws of grammar. On the other hand, language has a priori discrete structure (a sentence consists of words which consist if morphemes, and so on) that makes it very easily to automate various operations on it (such as search, match, replace, index), while digital representation of images does not by itself allow for automation of semantic operations.

## 4 New Media as the Mix Between Existing Cultural Conventions and the Conventions of Software

As a particular type of media is turned into digital data controlled by software, we may expect that eventually it will fully obey the principles of modularity, variability, and automation. However, in practice these processes may take a long time and they do not proceed in a linear fashion—rather, we witness "uneven development." For instance, today some media are already totally automated while in other cases this automation hardly exists—even though technologically it can be easily implemented.

Let us take as the example contemporary Hollywood film production. Logically we could have expected something like the following scenario. An individual viewer receives a customized version of the film that takes into account her/his previous viewing preferences, current preferences, and marketing profile. The film is completely assembled on the fly by AI software using pre-defined script schemas. The software also generates, again on the fly, characters, dialog, and sets (this makes product placement particularly easy) that are taken from a massive "assets" database.

The reality today is quite different. Software is used in some areas of film production but not in others. While some visuals may be created using computer animation, cinema still centers on the system of human stars whose salaries account for a large percent of a film budget. Similarly, script writing (and countless re-writing) is also trusted to humans. In short, the computer is kept out of the key "creative" decisions, and is delegated to the position of a technician.

If we look at another type of contemporary media—computer games—we will discover that they follow the principle of automation much more thoroughly. Game characters are modeled in 3D; they move and speak under software control. Software also decides what happens next in the game, generating new characters, spaces, and scenarios in response to user's behavior. It is not hard to understand why automation in computer games is much more advanced than in cinema. Computer games are one of the few cultural forms "native" to computers; they began as singular computer programs (before turning into a complex multimedia productions which they are today)—rather than being an already established medium (such as cinema) which is now slowly undergoing computerization.

Given that the principles of modularity, automation, variability and transcoding are tendencies that slowly and unevenly manifest themselves, is there a more precise way to describe new media, as it exists today? *The Language of New Media* analyzes the language of contemporary new media (or, to put this differently, "early new media") as the mix (we can also use software metaphors of "morph" or "composite") between two different sets of cultural forces, or cultural conventions: on the one hand, the conventions of already mature cultural forms (such as a page, a rectangular frame, a mobile point of view) and, on the other hand, the conventions of computer software and, in particular, of HCI, as they have developed until now.

Let me illustrate this idea with two examples. In modern visual culture a representational image was something one gazed at, rather than interacted with. An image was also one continuous representational field, i.e. a single scene. In the 1980s the graphical user interface (GUI) redefined an image as a figure-ground opposition between a non-interactive, passive ground (typically a desktop pattern) and active icons and hyperlinks (such as the icons of documents and applications appearing on the desktop). The treatment of representational images in new media represents a mix between these two very different conventions. An image retains its representational function while at the same time is treated as a set of hot spots ("image-map"). This is the standard convention in interactive multimedia, computer games, and Web pages. So while visually an image still appears as a single continuous field, in fact it is broken into a number of regions with hyperlinks connected to these regions, so clicking on a region opens a new page, or re-starts the game narrative, etc.

This example illustrates how a HCI convention is "superimposed" (in this case, both metaphorically and literally, as a designer places hot spots over an existing image) over an older representational convention. Another way to think about this is to say that a technique normally used for control and data management is mixed with a technique of fictional representation and fictional narration. I will use another example to illustrate the opposite process: how a cultural convention normally used for fictional representation and narration is "superimposed" over software techniques of data management and presentation.

The cultural convention in this example is the mobile camera model borrowed from cinema. In *The Language of New Media* I analyze how it became a generic interface used to access any type of data:

> Originally developed as part of 3D computer graphics technology for such applications as computer-aided design, flight simulators, and computer movie making, during the 1980s and 1990s the camera model became as much of an interface convention as scrollable windows or cut and paste operations. It became an accepted way for interacting with any data which is represented in three dimensions—which, in a computer culture, means literally anything and everything: the results of a physical simulation, an architectural site, design of a new molecule, statistical data, the structure of a computer network and so on. As computer culture is gradually spatializing all representations and experiences, they become subjected to the camera's particular grammar of data access. Zoom, tilt, pan, and track: we now use these operations to interact with data spaces, models, objects and bodies.[4]

To sum up: new media today can be understood as the mix between older cultural conventions for data representation, access, and manipulation and newer conventions of data representation, access, and manipulation. The "old" data are representations of visual reality and human experience, i.e., images, text-based and audio-visual narratives—what we normally understand by "culture." The "new" data is numerical data.

As a result of this mix, we get such strange hybrids as clickable "image-maps," navigable landscapes of financial data, QuickTime (which was defined as the format to represent any time-based data but which in practice is used exclusively for digital video), animated icons—a kind of micro-movies of computer culture—and so on.

As can be seen, this particular approach to new media assumes the existence of historically particular aesthetics that characterize new media, or "early new media," today. (We may also call it the "aesthetics of early information culture.") This aesthetics results from the convergence of historically particular cultural forces: already existing cultural conventions and the conventions of HCI. Therefore, it could not have existed in the past and it unlikely to stay without

changes for a long time. But we can also define new media in the opposite way: as specific aesthetic features which keep re-appearing at an early stage of deployment of every new modern media and telecommunication technology.

## 5 New Media as the Aesthetics that Accompanies the Early Stage of Every New Modern Media and Communication Technology

Rather than reserving the term "new media" to refer to the cultural uses of current computer and computer-based network technologies, some authors have suggested that every modern media and telecommunication technology passes through its "new media stage." In other words, at some point photography, telephones, cinema, and television each were "new media." This perspective redirects our research efforts: rather than trying to identify what is unique about digital computers functioning as media creation, media distribution and telecommunication devices, we may instead look for certain aesthetic techniques and ideological tropes which accompany every new modern media and telecommunication technology at the initial stage of their introduction and dissemination. Here are a few examples of such ideological tropes: new technology will allow for "better democracy;" it will give us a better access to the "real" (by offering "more immediacy" and/or the possibility "to represent what before could not be represented"); it will contribute to "the erosion of moral values"; it will destroy the "natural relationship between humans and the world" by "eliminating the distance" between the observer and the observed.

And here are two examples of aesthetic strategies that seem to often accompany the appearance of a new media and telecommunication technology (not surprisingly, these aesthetic strategies are directly related to ideological tropes I just mentioned). In the mid 1990s a number of filmmakers started to use inexpensive digital cameras (DV) to create films characterized by a documentary style (for instance, *Timecode, Celebration, Mifune*). Rather than treating live action as a raw material to be later re-arranged in post-production, these filmmakers placed premier importance on the authenticity of the actors' performances. DV equipment is small enough to allow a filmmaker to literally be inside the action as it unfolds. In addition to adopting a more intimate filmic approach, a filmmaker can keep shooting for a whole duration of a 60 or 120 minute DV tape as opposed to the standard ten-minute film roll. This gives the filmmaker and the actors more freedom to improvise around a theme, rather than being shackled to the tightly scripted short shots of traditional filmmaking. (In fact the length of *Timecode* exactly corresponds to the length of a standard DV tape.)

These aesthetic strategies for representing the real, which at first may appear to be unique to digital revolution in cinema, are in fact not unique. DV-style filmmaking has a predecessor in an international filmmaking movement that begun in the late 1950s and unfolded throughout the 1960s. Called "direct cinema," "candid" cinema, "uncontrolled" cinema, "observational" cinema, or *cinéma vérité* ("cinema truth"), it also involved filmmakers using lighter and more mobile (in comparison to what was available before) equipment. Like today's "DV realists," the 1960s "direct cinema" proponents avoided tight staging and scripting, preferring to let events unfold naturally. Both then and now, the filmmakers used new filmmaking technology to revolt against the existing cinema conventions that were perceived as being too artificial. Both then and now, the key word of this revolt was the same: "immediacy."

My second example of similar aesthetic strategies re-appearing deals with the development of moving image technology throughout the nineteenth century and the development of digital technologies to display moving images on a computer desktop during the 1990s. In the first part of the 1990s, as computers' speed kept gradually increasing, CD-ROM designers were able to go from a slide show format to the superimposition of small moving elements over static backgrounds and finally to full-frame moving images. This evolution repeats the nineteenth century progression: from sequences of still images (magic lantern slides presentations) to moving characters over static backgrounds (for instance, in Reynaud's Praxinoscope Theater) to full motion (the Lumieres' cinematograph). Moreover, the introduction of QuickTime by Apple in 1991 can be compared to the introduction of the Kinetoscope in 1892: both were used to present short loops, both featured the images approximately two by three inches in size, both called for private viewing rather than collective exhibition. Culturally, the two technologies also functioned similarly: as the latest technological "marvel." If in the early 1890s the public patronized Kinetoscope parlors where peep-hole

machines presented them with the latest invention—tiny moving photographs arranged in short loops; exactly a hundred years later, computer users were equally fascinated with tiny QuickTime movies that turned a computer in a film projector, however imperfect. Finally, the Lumieres' first film screenings of 1895 which shocked their audiences with huge moving images found their parallel in 1995 CD-ROM titles where the moving image finally fills the entire computer screen (for instance, in the *Johnny Mnemonic* computer game, based on the film by the same title). Thus, exactly a hundred years after cinema was officially "born," it was reinvented on a computer screen.

Interesting as they are, these two examples also illustrate the limitations of thinking about new media in terms of historically recurrent aesthetic strategies and ideological tropes. While ideological tropes indeed seem to be reappearing rather regularly, many aesthetic strategies may only reappear two or three times. Moreover, some strategies and/or tropes can be already found in the first part of the nineteenth century while others only made their first appearance much more recently.[5] In order for this approach to be truly useful it would be insufficient to simply name the strategies and tropes and to record the moments of their appearance; instead, we would have to develop a much more comprehensive analysis which would correlate the history of technology with social, political, and economical histories of the modern period.

So far my definitions of new media have focused on technology; the next three definitions will consider new media as material re-articulation, or encoding, of purely cultural tendencies—in short, as ideas rather than technologies.

## 6 New Media as Faster Execution of Algorithms Previously Executed Manually or through Other Technologies

A modern digital computer is a programmable machine. This simply means that the same computer can execute different algorithms. An algorithm is a sequence of steps that need to be followed to accomplish a task. Digital computers execute most algorithms very quickly—however in principle an algorithm, since it is just a sequence of simple steps, can also be executed by a human, although much more slowly. For instance, a human can sort files in a particular order, or count the number of words in a text, or cut a part of an image and paste it in a different place.

This realization gives us a new way to think about both digital computing, in general, and new media in particular as a massive speed-up of various manual techniques that all have already existed. Consider, for instance, the computer's ability to represent objects in linear perspective and to animate such representations. When you move your character through the world in a first person shooter computer game (such as *Quake*), or when you move your viewpoint around a 3D architectural model, a computer re-calculates perspectival views for all the objects in the frame many times every second (in the case of current desktop hardware, frame rates of 80 frames a second are not uncommon). But we should remember that the algorithm itself was codified during the Renaissance in Italy, and that, before digital computers came along (that is, for about five hundred years) it was executed by human draftsmen. Similarly, behind many other new media techniques there is an algorithm that, before computing, was executed manually. (Of course since art has always involved some technology— even as simple as a stylus for making marks on stone—what I mean by "manually" is that a human had to systematically go through every step of an algorithm himself, even if he was assisted by some image making tools.) Consider, for instance, another very popular new media technique: making a composite from different photographs. Soon after photography was invented, such nineteenth century photographers as Henry Peach Robinson and Oscar G. Rejlander were already creating smooth "combination prints" by putting together multiple photographs.

While this approach to thinking about new media takes us away from thinking about it purely in technological terms, it has a number of problems of its own. Substantially speeding up the execution of an algorithm by implementing this algorithm in software does not just leave things as they are. The basic point of dialectics is that a substantial change in quantity (i.e., in speed of execution in this case) leads to the emergence of qualitatively new phenomena. The example of automation of linear perspective is a case in point. Dramatically speeding up the execution of a perspectival algorithm makes possible previously non-existent representational technique: smooth movement through a perspectival space. In other words, we get not only quickly produced perspectival drawings but also computer-generated movies and interactive computer graphics.

The technological shifts in the history of "combination prints" also illustrate the cultural dialectics of trans-formation of quantity into quality. In the nineteenth century, painstakingly crafted "combination prints" represented an exception rather than the norm. In the twentieth century, new photographic technologies made possible photomontage that quickly became one of the basic representational techniques of modern visual culture. And finally the arrival of digital photography via software like Photoshop as well as scanners and digital cameras, in the late 1980s and 1990s, not only made photomontage much more omnipresent than before but it also fundamentally altered its visual characteristics. In place of graphic and hard-edge compositions pioneered by Moholy-Nagy and Rodchenko we now have smooth multi-image composites which use transparency, blur, colorization, and other easily available digital manipulations and which often incorporate typography that is subjected to exactly the same manipulations (thus in post-Photoshop visual culture the type becomes a subset of a photo-based image). To see this dramatic change, it is enough to compare a typical music video from 1985 and a typical music video from 1995: within ten years, the visual aesthetics of photomontage had undergone a fundamental change.

Finally, thinking about new media as speeding up of algorithms which previously were executed by hand foregrounds the use of computers for fast algorithm execution, but ignores two other essential uses: real-time network communication and real-time control. The abilities to interact with or control remotely located data in real time, to communicate with other human beings in real time, and control various technologies (sensors, motors, other computers) in real time constitute the very foundation of our information society—phone communications, Internet, financial networking, industrial control, the use of micro-controllers in numerous modern machines and devices, and so on. They also make possible many forms of new media art and culture: interactive net art, interactive computer installations, interactive multimedia, computer games, real-time music synthesis.

While non-real-time media generation and manipulation via digital computers can be thought of as speeding up of previously existing artistic techniques, *real-time* networking and control seem to constitute qualitatively new phenomena.

When we use Photoshop to quickly combine photographs together, or when we compose a text using a Microsoft Word, we simply do much faster what before we were doing either completely manually or assisted by some technologies (such as a typewriter). However, in the cases when a computer interprets or synthesizes human speech in real time, monitors sensors and modifies programs based on their input in real-time, or controls other devices, again in real-time, this is something which simply could not be done before. So while it is important to remember that, on one level, a modern digital computer is just a faster calculator, we should not ignore its other identity: that of a cybernetic control device. To put this in different way, while new media theory should pay tributes to Alan Turing (◊03), it should not forget about its other conceptual father—Norbert Wiener (◊04).

## 7 New Media as the Encoding of Modernist Avant-Garde; New Media as Metamedia

The approach to new media just discussed does not foreground any particular cultural period as the source of algorithms that are eventually encoded in computer software. In my article "Avant-Garde as Software" I have proposed that, in fact, a particular historical period is more relevant to new media than any other—that of the 1920s (more precisely, the years between 1915 and 1928).[6] During this period the avant-garde artists and designers invented a whole new set of visual and spatial languages and communication techniques that we still use today. According to my hypothesis,

> With new media, 1920s communication techniques acquire a new status. Thus new media does represent a new stage of the avant-garde. The techniques invented by the 1920s Left artists became embedded in the commands and interface metaphors of computer software. In short, the avant-garde vision became materialized in a computer. All the strategies developed to awaken audiences from a dream-existence of bourgeois society (constructivist design, New Typography, avant-garde cinematography and film editing, photo-montage, etc.) now define the basic routine of a post-industrial society: the interaction with a computer. For example, the avant-garde strategy of collage reemerged as a "cut and paste" command, the most basic operation one can perform on any computer data. In another example, the dynamic windows, pull-down menus, and HTML

tables all allow a computer user to simultaneously work with practically unrestricted amount of information despite the limited surface of the computer screen. This strategy can be traced to Lissitzky's use of movable frames in his 1926 exhibition design for the International Art Exhibition in Dresden.

The encoding of the 1920s avant-garde techniques in software does not mean that new media simply quantitatively extends the techniques which already existed. Just as it is the case with the phenomenon of real-time computation that I discussed above, tracing new media heritage in the 1920s avant-garde reveals a qualitative change as well. The modernist avant-garde was concerned with "filtering" visible reality in new ways. The artists were concerned with representing the outside world, with "seeing" it in as many different ways as possible. Of course some artists already began to react to the emerging media environment by making collages and photo-montages consisting of newspaper clippings, existing photographs, pieces of posters, and so on; yet these practices of manipulating existing media were not yet central. But a number of decades later they have moved to the foreground of cultural production. To put this differently, after a century and a half of media culture, already existing media records (or "media assets," to use the Hollywood term) become the new raw material for software-based cultural production and artistic practice. Many decades of analog media production resulted in a huge media archive and it is the contents of this archive—television programs, films, audio recordings, etc.—which became the raw data to be processed, re-articulated, mined and re-packaged through digital software—rather than raw reality. In my article I formulate this as follows:

> New media indeed represents the new avant-garde, and its innovations are at least as radical as the formal innovations of the 1920s. But if we are to look for these innovations in the realm of forms, this traditional area of cultural evolution, we will not find them there. For the new avant-garde is radically different from the old:
>
> 1. The old media avant-garde of the 1920s came up with new forms, new ways to represent reality and new ways to see the world. The new media avant-garde is about new ways of accessing and manipulating information. Its techniques are

hypermedia, databases, search engines, data mining, image processing, visualization, and simulation.

2. The new avant-garde is no longer concerned with seeing or representing the world in new ways but rather with accessing and using in new ways previously accumulated media. In this respect new media is post-media or meta-media, as it uses old media as its primary material.

My concept of "meta-media" is related to a more familiar notion of "postmodernism"—the recognition that by the 1980s the culture became more concerned with reworking already existing content, idioms and style, rather than genially creating new ones. What I would like to stress (and what I think the original theorists of post-modernism in the 1980s have not stressed enough) is the key role played by the material factors in the shift towards postmodernist aesthetics: the accumulation of huge media assets and the arrival of new electronic and digital tools which made it very easy to access and re-work these assets. This is another example of quantity changing into quality in media history: the gradual accumulation of media records and the gradual automation of media management and manipulation techniques eventually recoded modernist aesthetics into a very different postmodern aesthetics.

## 8 New Media as Parallel Articulation of Similar Ideas in Post-WWII Art and Modern Computing

Along with the 1920s, we can think of other cultural periods that generated ideas and sensibilities particularly relevant to new media. In the 1980s a number of writers looked at the connections between Baroque and post-modern sensibilities; given the close link between post-modernism and new media I just briefly discussed, it would be logical if parallels between the Baroque and new media can also be established.[7] It can also be argued that in many ways new media returns us to a pre-modernist cultural logic of the eighteenth century: consider for instance, the parallel between eighteenth-century communities of readers who were also all writers and participants in Internet newsgroups and mailing lists who are also both readers and writers.

In the twentieth century, along with the 1920s, which for me represents the cultural peak of this century (because during this period more radically new aesthetic techniques were prototyped than in any other period of similar duration), the second cultural peak—the 1960s—also seems

to contain many of new media's genes. A number of writers such as Söke Dinkla have argued that interactive computer art (from the 1980s on) further develops ideas already contained in the new art of the 1960s (happenings, performances, installation): active participation of the audience, an artwork as a temporal process rather than as a fixed object, an artwork as an open system.[8] This connection makes even more sense when we remember that some of the most influential figures in new media art (Jeffrey Shaw, Roy Ascott (◊10)) started their art careers in the 1960s and only later moved to computing and networking technologies. For instance, at the end of the 1960s Jeffrey Shaw was working on inflatable structures for film projections and performances which were big enough to contain a small audience inside—something which he later came back to in many of his VR installations, and even more directly in the EVE project.[9]

There is another aesthetic project of the 1960s that also can be linked to new media not only conceptually but also historically, since the artists who pursued this project with computers (such as Manfred Mohr) knew of minimalist artists who during the same decade pursued the same project "manually" (most notably, Sol LeWitt).[10] This project can be called "combinatorics."[11] It involves creating images and/or objects by systematically varying a single parameter or by systematically creating all possible combinations of a small number of elements.[12] "Combinatorics" in computer art and minimalist art of the 1960s led to the creation of remarkably similar images and spatial structures; it illustrates well that the algorithms, this essential part of new media, do not depend on technology but can be executed by humans.

## Four Decades of New Media

Along with the ones I already mentioned, more connections between 1960s cultural imaginations and new media exist. As with another recent important anthology on new media (Randall Packer and Ken Jordan's *Multimedia: From Wagner to Virtual Reality*), *The New Media Reader* contains a number of important texts by the radical artists and writers from the 1960s which have conceptual affinity to the logic of computing technology: those of Allan Kaprow (◊06), William Burroughs (◊07); the Oulipo (◊12) (whose members pursued the combinatorics project in relation to literature), Nam June Paik (◊15) and others. Section I, "The Complex, the

◊05 73
◊08 93
◊09 109
◊11 133
◊16 231
◊21 301
◊26 391
◊29 433
◊30 441
◊33 485
◊34 499
◊34 515
◊38 563

Changing, and the Intermediate" and section II, "Collective Media, Personal Media," present what is to date the most comprehensive set of cultural texts from the 1960s. These ideas particularly resonate with the developments in computing in the same period.

Although modern computing has many conceptual fathers and mothers, from Leibnitz to Ada Lovelace, and its prehistory spans many centuries, I would argue that the paradigm that still defines our understanding and usage of computing was defined in the 1960s. During the 1960s the principles of the modern interactive GUI were given clear articulation (although the practical implementation and refinement of these ideas took place later, in the 1970s at Xerox PARC). The articles by Licklider (◊05), Sutherland (◊09), Nelson (◊11, ◊21, ◊30), and Engelbart (◊08, ◊17) from the 1960s included in the reader are the essential documents of our time; one day the historians of culture will rate them on the same scale of importance as texts by Marx, Freud, and Saussure. (Other key developments that also took place in the 1960s and early 1970s were the Internet, Unix, and object-oriented programming. A number of other essential ideas of modern computing such as networking itself, the use of computers for real-time control, and the graphical interactive display were articulated earlier, in the second part of the 1940s and the first part of the 1950s.)[13]

The first two sections of the reader take us into the end of the 1970s; during the time period covered in section II the key principles of modern computing and the GUI had already been practically implemented and refined by the developers at Xerox PARC but they were not yet commercially available to consumers. The third section, "Design, Activity, and Action," runs from the end of the 1970s into the 1980s. Near the end of this period the Macintosh (released in 1984) popularized the GUI; it also shipped with a simple drawing and painting programs which emphasized the new role of a computer as a creative tool; finally, it was the first inexpensive computer which came with a bit-mapped display. Atari computers made computer-based sound manipulation affordable; computer games achieved a new level of popularity; cinema started to use computers for special effects (*Tron*, released by Disney in 1982, contained seventeen minutes of 3-D computer generated scenes); towards the very end of the decade, Photoshop, which can be called the key software application of postmodernism, was finally released. All these developments of the 1980s created a new set of roles for the modern digital computer: a manipulator of existing media (Photoshop); a media synthesizer (film special effects, sound software); and a new medium (or rather, more than one new media) in its own right (computer games). *The New Media Reader* collects essential articles by computer scientists from the 1980s that articulate ideas behind these new roles of a computer (Bolt (◊29), Shneiderman (◊33), Laurel (◊38) and others).

As computing left the strict realm of big business, the military, the government, and the university and entered society at large, cultural theorists begin to think about its effects, and it is appropriate that *The New Media Reader* also reprints key theoretical statements from the 1980s (e.g., Sherry Turkle (◊34), Donna Haraway (◊35)). I should note here that European cultural theorists reacted to computerization earlier than the Americans: both Jean-François Lyotard's *The Post-Modern Condition* (1979) and Jean Baudrillard's *Simulacra and Simulations* (1981) contain detailed discussions of computing, something which their 1980s American admirers did not seem to notice.

The last section of the reader, "Revolution, Resistance, and the Launch of the Web" continues to weave texts by computer scientists, social researchers, cultural theorists, and critics from the end of the 1980s onward; it also takes us into the early 1990s when the rise of the Web redefined computing one again. If the 1980s gradually made visible the new role of a computer as a media manipulator and an interface to media—the developments which eventually were codified around 1990 in the term "new media"—in the 1990s another role of a digital computer (which was already present since the late 1940s) came to the foreground: that of a foundation for real-time multimedia networking, available not just for selected researchers and the military (as it was for decades) but for millions of people.

In the 1960s we can find strong conceptual connections between computing and radical art of the period, but with the sole exception of Ted Nelson (the conceptual father of hypertext) no computer scientist was directly applying radical political ideas of the times to computer design. In fact these ideas had a strong effect on the field, but it was delayed until the 1970s when Alan Kay (◊26) and his colleagues at Xerox PARC pursued the vision of personal computer workstation that would empower an individual rather than a big organization. In the late 1980s and early 1990s, however, we seem to witness a different kind of parallel between social changes and computer design. Although causally unrelated, conceptually it makes sense that the end of Cold War and the design of the Web took place at exactly the same time. The first development ended the separation of the world into parts closed off from each other, making it a single global system; the second development connected world's computers into a single network. The early Web (i.e., before it came to be dominated by big commercial portals towards the end of the 1990s) also practically implemented a radically horizontal, non-hierarchical model of human existence in which no idea, no ideology, and no value system can dominate the rest—thus providing a perfect metaphor for a new post–Cold-War sensibility.

The emergence of new media studies as a field testifies to our recognition of the key cultural role played by digital computers and computer-enabled networking in our global society. For a field in its infancy, we are very lucky to now have such a comprehensive record of its origins as the one provided by *The New Media Reader;* I believe that its readers will continue to think about both the ideas in its individual texts and the endless connections which can be found between different texts for many years to come.

1. For a good example of cyberculture paradigm, see the Resource Center for Cyberculture Studies, <http://www.com.washington.edu/rccs/>

2. Lev Manovich, *The Language of New Media* (Cambridge: MIT Press, 2001).

3. I don't mean here the actual data structures and algorithms which may be used by particular software—rather, I am thinking of them in a more abstract way: what is the structure of a cultural object and what kind of operations it enables for the user.

4. Manovich, *The Language of New Media,* 80.

5. I believe that the same problems apply to Erkki Huhtamo's very interesting theory of media archeology which is close to the approach presented here and which advocates the study of tropes which accompany the history of modern media technology, both the ones which were realized and the ones which were only imagined.

6. Lev Manovich, "Avant-Garde as Software," in *Ostranenie,* edited by Stephen Kovats (Frankfurt: Campus Verlag, 1999). <http://www.manovich.net/docs/avantgarde_as_software.doc> (Quotations are from the online text.)

7. Norman Klein is currently completing a book entitled *From Vatican to Las Vegas: A History of Special Effects* that is discussing in detail the connections between the treatment of space in the Baroque and in cyberculture.

8. See for instance Söke Dinkla, "From Participation to Interaction: Towards the Origins of Interactive Art," in *Clicking In: Hots Links to a Digital Culture,* edited by Lynn Herhman Leeson (Seattle: Bay Press, 1996).

9. Jeffrey Shaw, ed., *Jeffrey Shaw—A User's Manual* (DAP, 1997).

10. Information on Manfred Mohr can be found online at <http://www.emohr.com/>.

11. Frank Dietrich has used the term "combinatorics"to talk about a particular direction in the early computer art of the 1960s. See Dietrich, Frank, "Visual Intelligence: The First Decade of Computer Art," Computer Graphics, 1985.

12. It is interesting that Sol LeWitt was able to produce works "by hand" which often consisted of more systematic variations of the same elements than similar works done by other artists who used computers. In other words, we can say that Sol LeWitt was better in executing certain minimalist algorithms than the computers of the time.

13. See Paul N. Edwards, *The Closed World: Computers and the Politics of Discourse in Cold War America* (Cambridge: MIT Press, 1997).

# I

## The Complex,
## the Changing,
## and the Indeterminate

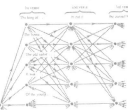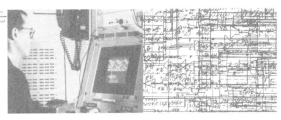

# 01. [Introduction]
# The Garden of Forking Paths

Many of new media's important ideas and influences first appeared in unexpected contexts. Artists and writers have often presaged developments in new media that were invisible to the most esteemed technologists. Ted Nelson and Doug Engelbart, who devised many of new media's most important concepts, have spent most of their careers on the periphery of the field. The Web, the one system that has created the greatest public interest and involvement in new media so far, was initially rejected by the new media community as a giant backward leap both conceptually and technologically. Thus it is fitting to begin this anthology not with some journal article from an established scientist but with the following detective story, written by an Argentine librarian.

To say that Jorge Luis Borges was a librarian, of course, is like saying Wallace Stevens was an insurance executive. It is true but particularly misleading. Borges did head Argentina's National Library for some time, and books and libraries figure prominently in his writing. Borges also may have been the most important figure in Spanish-language literature since Cervantes. But whatever his particular literary rank, he was clearly of tremendous influence, writing intricate poems, short stories, and essays that instantiated concepts of dizzying power.

The concept Borges described in "The Garden of Forking Paths"—in several layers of the story, but most directly in the combination book and maze of Ts'ui Pen—is that of a novel that can be read in multiple ways, a hypertext novel. Borges described this in 1941, prior to the invention (or at least the public disclosure) of the electromechanical digital computer. Not only did he invent the hypertext novel—Borges went on to describe a theory of the universe based upon the structure of such a novel. Then he sketched out, in the actions of the protagonist, one particular existential philosophy which motivates action within this universe, a universe in which everything that is possible does indeed occur in some branch of reality. These matters are all handled in the story alongside issues of race, war, espionage, ancestry, and even the nature of academic discourse about history.

Borges did not ever write a hypertext novel. In fact, although Carlos Fuentes has stated that today's Latin American novel would not exist without Borges, he never wrote a novel at all. He found it sufficient to encode ideas rich enough for treatment in a novel in a format which was smaller than the typical short story, a format he called a "fiction." A hypertext novel (in codex form) was in fact written by another Argentine author, Julio Cortázar. His *Hopscotch*, which has several "expendable" chapters and which invites the reader to read in two different ways, was written in Paris and published in 1963. (It was soon afterwards read by Robert Coover, and led him to experiment with punch-card literature.) Although Cortázar and Borges held different political views, wrote in different styles, and lived far apart, the author of *Hopscotch* was certainly acquainted with Borges's writing. Borges, as editor of *El Sur*, published Cortázar's first story in 1946.

Writers using the computer as a medium have found many types of inspiration in the work of Borges. In structuring works, they have looked not only to "The Garden of Forking Paths" but also to combinatorial ideas and notions of textual infinity found in "The Library of Babel" and "The Book of Sand." Many writers have also found the metafictional workings of Borges's stories, and his symbology (which includes chessboards, mirrors, and mazes) to be inspiring. Not only did Stuart Moulthrop create a hypertextual version of "The Garden of Forking Paths" in 1987 ⊗; he also gave his important hypertext novel set during the Gulf War a title that refers to both American wartime efforts and to Borges: *Victory Garden*.

For new media to exist, a great deal of experimentation and programming had to be undertaken, much of it at a very low level and requiring great technical skill and effort. Borges was no hacker; nor did he specify the hypertext novel in perfect detail. But computers do not function as they do today

◊11
133

◊12
147

Another important predecessor to new media literature is seen in the work of the Oulipo (◊12), a group that constrained their writing processes with algorithms.

The term "hypertext" was coined by Ted Nelson; his essay (◊11) defines the term.

Robert Coover (◊49) became the major advocate for hypertext and electronic literature among authors of literary fiction in print.

Moulthrop's "Forking Paths" ⊗, although never published, is known through discussion in academic literature. Also, see Moulthrop's essay (◊48).

◊48
679

◊49
705

*only* because of the playful labor of hackers or because of planned-out projects to program, develop, and reconfigure systems. Our use of computers is also based on the visions of those who, like Borges—pronouncing this story from the growing dark of his blindness—saw those courses that future artists, scientists, and hackers might take.
—NM

Further Reading

Borges, Jorge Luis. "The Library of Babel," 112–118, and "The Book of Sand," 480–483 in *Collected Fictions*. Trans. Andrew Hurley. New York: Viking, 1998.

Cortázar, Julio. *Hopscotch*. Trans. Gregory Rabassa. New York: Pantheon, 1966. From the Spanish *Rayuela*. Buenos Aires: Editorial Sudamericana, 1963.

Original Publication

Trans. Donald A. Yates. *Labyrinths: Selected Stories & Other Writings*, 19–29. Ed. Donald A. Yates and James E. Irby. New York: New Directions, 1964. From the Spanish "El jardin de senderos que se bifurcan," first published in *El jardin de senderos que se bifurcan*. Buenos Aires: Sur, 1941.

# The Garden of Forking Paths

## Jorge Luis Borges

*For Victoria Ocampo*

On page 22 of Liddell Hart's *History of World War I* you will read that an attack against the Serre-Montauban line by thirteen British divisions (supported by 1,400 artillery pieces), planned for the 24th of July, 1916, had to be postponed until the morning of the 29th. The torrential rains, Captain Liddell Hart comments, caused this delay, an insignificant one, to be sure.

The following statement, dictated, reread and signed by Dr. Yu Tsun, former professor of English at the *Hochschule* at Tsingtao, throws an unsuspected light over the whole affair. The first two pages of the document are missing.

". . . and I hung up the receiver. Immediately afterwards, I recognized the voice that had answered in German. It was that of Captain Richard Madden. Madden's presence in Viktor Runeberg's apartment meant the end of our anxieties and—but this seemed, *or should have seemed*, very secondary to me—also the end of our lives. It meant that Runeberg had been arrested or murdered.[1] Before the sun set on that day, I would encounter the same fate. Madden was implacable. Or rather, he was obliged to be so. An Irishman at the service of England, a man accused of laxity and perhaps of treason, how could he fail to seize and be thankful for such a miraculous opportunity: the discovery, capture, maybe even the death of two agents of the German Reich? I went up to my room; absurdly I locked the door and threw myself on my back on the narrow iron cot. Through the window I saw the familiar roofs and the cloud-shaded six o'clock sun. It seemed incredible to me that that day without premonitions or symbols should be the one of my inexorable death. In spite of my dead father, in spite of having been a child in a symmetrical garden of Hai Feng, was I—now—going to die? Then I reflected that everything happens to a man precisely, precisely *now*. Centuries of centuries and only in the present do things happen; countless men in the air, on the face of the earth and the sea, and all that really is happening is happening to me. . . . The almost intolerable recollection of Madden's horselike face banished these wanderings. In the midst of my hatred and terror (it means nothing to me now to speak of terror, now that I have mocked Richard Madden, now that my throat yearns for the noose) it occurred to me that that tumultuous and doubtless happy warrior did not suspect that I possessed the Secret. The name of the exact location of the new British artillery park on the River Ancre. A bird streaked across the gray sky and blindly I translated it into an airplane and that airplane into many (against the French sky) annihilating the artillery station with vertical bombs. If only my mouth, before a bullet shattered it, could cry out that secret name so it could be heard in Germany. . . . My human voice was very weak. How might I make it carry to the ear of the Chief? To the ear of that sick and hateful man who knew nothing of Runeberg and me save that we were in Staffordshire and who was waiting in vain for our report in his arid office in Berlin, endlessly examining newspapers. . . . I said out loud: *I must flee*. I sat up noiselessly, in a useless perfection of silence, as if Madden were already lying in wait for me. Something—perhaps the mere vain ostentation of proving my resources were nil—made me look through my pockets. I found what I knew I would find. The American watch, the nickel chain and the square coin, the key ring with the incriminating useless keys to Runeberg's apartment, the notebook, a letter which I resolved to destroy immediately (and which I did not destroy), a crown, two shillings and a few pence, the red and blue pencil, the handkerchief, the revolver with one bullet. Absurdly, I took it in my hand and weighed it in order to inspire courage within myself. Vaguely I thought that a pistol report can be heard at a great distance. In ten minutes my plan was perfected. The telephone book listed the name of the only person capable of transmitting the message; he lived in a suburb of Fenton, less than a half hour's train ride away.

I am a cowardly man. I say it now, now that I have carried to its end a plan whose perilous nature no one can deny. I know its execution was terrible. I didn't do it for Germany, no. I care nothing for a barbarous country which imposed upon me the abjection of being a spy. Besides, I know of a man from England—a modest man—who for me is no less great than Goethe. I talked with him for scarcely an hour, but during that hour he was Goethe. . . . I did it because I sensed that the Chief somehow feared people of my race—for the innumerable ancestors who merge within me. I wanted to prove to him that a yellow man could save his armies. Besides, I had to flee from Captain Madden. His hands and his voice could call at my door at any moment. I dressed silently, bade farewell to myself in the mirror, went downstairs, scrutinized the peaceful street and went out. The station was not far from my home, but I judged it wise to take a cab. I argued that in this way I ran less risk of being recognized; the fact is that in the deserted street I felt myself visible and vulnerable, infinitely so. I remember that I told the cab driver to stop a short distance before the main entrance. I got out with voluntary, almost painful slowness; I was going to the village of Ashgrove but I bought a ticket for a more distant station. The train left within a very few minutes, at eight-fifty. I hurried; the next one would leave at nine-thirty. There was hardly a soul on the platform. I went through the coaches; I remember a few farmers, a woman dressed in mourning, a young boy who was reading with fervor the *Annals* of Tacitus, a wounded and happy soldier. The coaches jerked forward at last. A man whom I recognized ran in vain to the end of the platform. It was Captain Richard Madden. Shattered, trembling, I shrank into the far corner of the seat, away from the dreaded window.

From this broken state I passed into an almost abject felicity. I told myself that the duel had already begun and that I had won the first encounter by frustrating, even if for forty minutes, even if by a stroke of fate, the attack of my adversary. I argued that this slightest of victories foreshadowed a total victory. I argued (no less fallaciously) that my cowardly felicity proved that I was a man capable of carrying out the adventure successfully. From this weakness I took strength that did not abandon me. I foresee that man will resign himself each day to more atrocious undertakings; soon there will be no one but warriors and brigands; I give them this counsel: *The author of an atrocious undertaking ought to imagine that he has already accomplished it, ought to impose upon himself a future as irrevocable as the past.* Thus I proceeded as my eyes of a man already dead registered the elapsing of that day, which was perhaps the last, and the diffusion of the night. The train ran gently along, amid ash trees. It stopped, almost in the middle of the fields. No one announced the name of the station. "Ashgrove?" I asked a few lads on the platform. "Ashgrove," they replied. I got off.

A lamp enlightened the platform but the faces of the boys were in shadow. One questioned me, "Are you going to Dr. Stephen Albert's house?" Without waiting for my answer, another said, "The house is a long way from here, but you won't get lost if you take this road to the left and at every crossroads turn again to your left." I tossed them a coin (my last), descended a few stone steps and started down the solitary road. It went downhill, slowly. It was of elemental earth; overhead the banches were tangled; the low, full moon seemed to accompany me.

For an instant, I thought that Richard Madden in some way had penetrated my desperate plan. Very quickly, I understood that that was impossible. The instructions to turn always to the left reminded me that such was the common procedure for discovering the central point of certain labyrinths. I have some understanding of labyrinths:

> 1. An hypothesis both hateful and odd. The Prussian spy Hans Rabener, alias Viktor Runeberg, attacked with drawn automatic the bearer of the warrant for his arrest, Captain Richard Madden. The latter, in self-defense, inflicted the wound which brought about Runeberg's death. (Editor's note.)

not for nothing am I the great grandson of that Ts'ui Pên who was governor of Yunnan and who renounced worldly power in order to write a novel that might be even more populous than the *Hung Lu Meng* and to construct a labyrinth in which all men would become lost. Thirteen years he dedicated to these heterogeneous tasks, but the hand of a stranger murdered him—and his novel was incoherent and no one found the labyrinth. Beneath English trees I meditated on that lost maze: I imagined it inviolate and perfect at the secret crest of a mountain; I imagined it erased by rice fields or beneath the water; I imagined it infinite, no longer composed of octagonal kiosks and returning paths, but of rivers and provinces and kingdoms. . . . I thought of a labyrinth of labyrinths, of one sinuous spreading labyrinth that would encompass the past and the future and in some way involve the stars. Absorbed in these illusory images, I forgot my destiny of one pursued. I felt myself to be, for an unknown period of time, an abstract perceiver of the world. The vague, living countryside, the moon, the remains of the day worked on me, as well as the slope of the road which eliminated any possibility of weariness. The afternoon was intimate, infinite. The road descended and forked among the now confused meadows. A high-pitched, almost syllabic music approached and receded in the shifting of the wind, dimmed by leaves and distance. I thought that a man can be an enemy of other men, of the moments of other men, but not of a country: not of fireflies, words, gardens, streams of water, sunsets. Thus I arrived before a tall, rusty gate. Between the iron bars I made out a poplar grove and a pavilion. I understood suddenly two things, the first trivial, the second almost unbelievable: the music came from the pavilion, and the music was Chinese. For precisely that reason I had openly accepted it without paying it any heed. I do not remember whether there was a bell or whether I knocked with my hand. The sparkling of the music continued.

From the rear of the house within a lantern approached: a lantern that the trees sometimes striped and sometimes eclipsed, a paper lantern that had the form of a drum and the color of the moon. A tall man bore it. I didn't see his face for the light blinded me. He opened the door and said slowly, in my own language: "I see that the pious Hsi P'êng persists in correcting my solitude. You no doubt wish to see the garden?"

I recognized the name of one of our consuls and I replied, disconcerted, "The garden?"

"The garden of forking paths."

Something stirred in my memory and I uttered with incomprehensible certainty, "The garden of my ancestor Ts'ui Pên."

"Your ancestor? Your illustrious ancestor? Come in."

The damp path zigzagged like those of my childhood. We came to a library of Eastern and Western books. I recognized bound in yellow silk several volumes of the Lost Encyclopedia, edited by the Third Emperor of the Luminous Dynasty but never printed. The record on the phonograph revolved next to a bronze phoenix. I also recall a *famille rose* vase and another, many centuries older, of that shade of blue which our craftsmen copied from the potters of Persia . . .

Stephen Albert observed me with a smile. He was, as I have said, very tall, sharp-featured, with gray eyes and a gray beard. He told me that he had been a missionary in Tientsin "before aspiring to become a Sinologist."

We sat down—I on a long, low divan, he with his back to the window and a tall circular clock. I calculated that my pursuer, Richard Madden, could not arrive for at least an hour. My irrevocable determination could wait.

"An astounding fate, that of Ts'ui Pên," Stephen Albert said. "Governor of his native province, learned in astronomy, in astrology and in the tireless interpretation of the canonical books, chess player, famous poet and calligrapher—he abandoned all this in order to compose a book and a maze. He renounced the pleasures of both tyranny and justice, of his populous couch, of his banquets and even of erudition—all to close himself up for thirteen years in the Pavilion of the Limpid Solitude. When he died, his heirs found nothing save chaotic manuscripts. His family, as you may be aware, wished to condemn them to the fire; but his executor—a Taoist or Buddhist monk—insisted on their publication."

"We descendants of Ts'ui Pên," I replied, "continue to curse that monk. Their publication was senseless. The book is an indeterminate heap of contradictory drafts. I examined it once: in the third chapter the hero dies, in the fourth he is alive. As for the other undertaking of Ts'ui Pên, his labyrinth . . ."

"Here is Ts'ui Pên's labyrinth," he said, indicating a tall lacquered desk.

"An ivory labyrinth!" I exclaimed. "A minimum labyrinth."

"A labyrinth of symbols," he corrected. "An invisible labyrinth of time. To me, a barbarous Englishman, has been entrusted the revelation of this diaphanous mystery. After more than a hundred years, the details are irretrievable; but it is not hard to conjecture what happened. Ts'ui Pên must have said once: *I am withdrawing to write a book.* And another time: *I am withdrawing to construct a labyrinth.* Every one imagined two works; to no one did it occur that the book and the maze were one and the same thing. The Pavilion of the Limpid Solitude stood in the center of a garden that was perhaps intricate; that circumstance could have suggested to the heirs a physical labyrinth. Hs'ui Pên died; no one in the vast territories that were his came upon the labyrinth; the confusion of the novel suggested to me that *it* was the maze. Two circumstances gave me the correct solution of the problem. One: the curious legend that Ts'ui Pên had planned to create a labyrinth which would be strictly infinite. The other: a fragment of a letter I discovered."

Albert rose. He turned his back on me for a moment; he opened a drawer of the black and gold desk. He faced me and in his hands he held a sheet of paper that had once been crimson, but was now pink and tenuous and cross-sectioned. The fame of Ts'ui Pên as a calligrapher had been justly won. I read, uncomprehendingly and with fervor, these words written with a minute brush by a man of my blood: *I leave to the various futures (not to all) my garden of forking paths.* Wordlessly, I returned the sheet. Albert continued:

"Before unearthing this letter, I had questioned myself about the ways in which a book can be infinite. I could think of nothing other than a cyclic volume, a circular one. A book whose last page was identical with the first, a book which had the possibility of continuing indefinitely. I remembered too that night which is at the middle of *The Thousand and One Nights* when Scheherazade (through a magical oversight of the copyist) begins to relate word for word the story of *The Thousand and One Nights,* establishing the risk of coming once again to the night when she must repeat it, and thus on to infinity. I imagined as well a Platonic, hereditary work, transmitted from father to son, in which each new individual adds a chapter or corrects with pious care the pages of his elders. These conjectures diverted me; but none seemed to correspond, not even remotely, to the contradictory chapters of Ts'ui Pên. In the midst of this perplexity, I received from Oxford the manuscript you have examined. I lingered, naturally, on the sentence: *I leave to the various futures (not to all) my garden of forking paths.* Almost instantly, I understood: 'the garden of forking paths' was the chaotic novel; the phrase 'the various futures (not to all)' suggested to me the forking in time, not in space. A broad rereading of the work confirmed the theory. In all fictional works, each time a man is confronted with several alternatives, he chooses one and eliminates the others; in the fiction of Ts'ui Pên, he chooses—simultaneously—all of them. *He creates,* in this way, diverse futures, diverse times which themselves also proliferate and fork. Here, then, is the explanation of the novel's contradictions. Fang, let us say, has a secret; a stranger calls at his door; Fang resolves to kill him. Naturally, there are several possible outcomes: Fang can kill the intruder, the intruder can kill Fang, they both can escape, they both can die, and so forth. In the work of Ts'ui Pên, all possible outcomes occur; each one is the point of departure for other forkings. Sometimes, the paths of this labyrinth converge: for example, you arrive at this house, but in one of the possible pasts you are my enemy, in another, my friend. If you will resign yourself to my incurable pronunciation, we shall read a few pages."

His face, within the vivid circle of the lamplight, was unquestionably that of an old man, but with something unalterable about it, even immortal. He read with slow precision two versions of the same epic chapter. In the first, an army marches to a battle across a lonely mountain; the horror of the rocks and shadows makes the men undervalue their lives and they gain an easy victory. In the second, the same army traverses a palace where a great festival is taking place; the resplendent battle seems to them a continuation of the celebration and they win the victory. I listened with proper veneration to these ancient narratives, perhaps less admirable in themselves than the fact that they had been created by my blood and were being restored to me by a man of a remote empire, in the course of a desperate adventure, on a Western isle. I remember the last words, repeated in each version like a secret commandment: *Thus fought the heroes, tranquil their admirable hearts, violent their swords, resigned to kill and to die.*

From that moment on, I felt about me and within my dark body an invisible, intangible swarming. Not the swarming of the divergent, parallel and finally coalescent armies, but a more inaccessible, more intimate agitation that they in some manner prefigured. Stephen Albert continued:

"I don't believe that your illustrious ancestor played idly with these variations. I don't consider it credible that he would sacrifice thirteen years to the infinite execution of a rhetorical experiment. In your country, the novel is a subsidiary form of literature; in Ts'ui Pên's time it was a despicable form. Ts'ui Pên was a brilliant novelist, but he was also a man of letters who doubtless did not consider himself a mere novelist. The testimony of his contemporaries proclaims—and his life fully confirms—his metaphysical and mystical interests. Philosophic controversy usurps a good part of the novel. I know that of all problems, none disturbed him so greatly nor worked upon him so much as the abysmal problem of time. Now then, the latter is the only problem that does not figure in the pages of the *Garden*. He does not even use the word that signifies *time*. How do you explain this voluntary omission?"

I proposed several solutions—all unsatisfactory. We discussed them. Finally, Stephen Albert said to me:

"In a riddle whose answer is chess, what is the only prohibited word?"

I thought a moment and replied, "The word *chess*."

"Precisely," said Albert. "*The Garden of Forking Paths* is an enormous riddle, or parable, whose theme is time; this recondite cause prohibits its mention. To omit a word always, to resort to inept metaphors and obvious periphrases, is perhaps the most emphatic way of stressing it. That is the tortuous method preferred, in each of the meanderings of his indefatigable novel, by the oblique Ts'ui Pên. I have compared hundreds of manuscripts, I have corrected the errors that the negligence of the copyists has introduced, I have guessed the plan of this chaos, I have re-established—I believe I have re-established—the primordial organization, I have translated the entire work: it is clear to me that not once does he employ the word 'time.' The explanation is obvious: *The Garden of Forking Paths* is an incomplete, but not false, image of the universe as Ts'ui Pên conceived it. In contrast to Newton and Schopenhauer, your ancestor did not believe in a uniform, absolute time. He believed in an infinite series of times, in a growing, dizzying net of divergent, convergent and parallel times. This network of times which approached one another, forked, broke off, or were unaware of one

another for centuries, embraces *all* possibilities of time. We do not exist in the majority of these times; in some you exist, and not I; in others I, and not you; in others, both of us. In the present one, which a favorable fate has granted me, you have arrived at my house; in another, while crossing the garden, you found me dead; in still another, I utter these same words, but I am a mistake, a ghost."

"In every one," I pronounced, not without a tremble to my voice, "I am grateful to you and revere you for your re-creation of the garden of Ts'ui Pên."

"Not in all," he murmured with a smile. "Time forks perpetually toward innumerable futures. In one of them I am your enemy."

Once again I felt the swarming sensation of which I have spoken. It seemed to me that the humid garden that surrounded the house was infinitely saturated with invisible persons. Those persons were Albert and I, secret, busy and multiform in other dimensions of time. I raised my eyes and the tenuous nightmare dissolved. In the yellow and black garden there was only one man; but this man was as strong as a statue . . . this man was approaching along the path and he was Captain Richard Madden.

"The future already exists," I replied, "but I am your friend. Could I see the letter again?"

Albert rose. Standing tall, he opened the drawer of the tall desk; for the moment his back was to me. I had readied the revolver. I fired with extreme caution. Albert fell uncomplainingly, immediately. I swear his death was instantaneous—a lightning stroke.

The rest is unreal, insignificant. Madden broke in, arrested me. I have been condemned to the gallows. I have won out abominably; I have communicated to Berlin the secret name of the city they must attack. They bombed it yesterday; I read it in the same papers that offered to England the mystery of the learned Sinologist Stephen Albert who was murdered by a stranger, one Yu Tsun. The Chief had deciphered this mystery. He knew my problem was to indicate (through the uproar of the war) the city called Albert, and that I had found no other means to do so than to kill a man of that name. He does not know (no one can know) my innumerable contrition and weariness.

# 02. [Introduction]
# As We May Think

The blasts that leveled Hiroshima and Nagasaki were produced by one of the most powerful forces of the 20th century: the U.S. military-industrial complex. Vannevar Bush was arguably the man that put this force in motion, and was a primary organizer of the Manhattan Project that produced the bombs themselves. Yet Bush was also deeply troubled by later developments in the Cold War arms race. His vision of how technology could lead toward understanding and away from destruction was a primary inspiration for the postwar research that lead to the development of new media.

◊004
65

Before the war, Bush had been the architect of groundbreaking analog computing projects at MIT. In June 1940 he convinced Franklin Delano Roosevelt to give him funding and political support to create a new kind of collaborative relationship between the military, industry, and academic researchers—without congressional, or nearly any other, oversight. His influence, and the size of this new collaboration, grew phenomenally over the next five years. The result was named the "military-industrial complex" by Dwight Eisenhower, but this structure is perhaps more aptly called the "iron triangle" of self-perpetuating military, industrial, and academic relationships. The iron triangle had a decisive role in the history of new media (funding and shaping many important projects) as well as in Bush's personal history.

As part of the war effort, Bush's organization provided funding for Norbert Wiener to investigate new models for anti-aircraft guns. During this research Wiener formulated his initial thoughts on feedback loops, and began down an intellectual path that eventually led him to coin the term "cybernetics." See Wiener's speech (◊04).

"As We May Think" was published twice in 1945—in the *Atlantic Monthly* and *Life*—first shortly before, and then just after, the U.S. nuclear attacks on Japan. On one level, the technologies it describes now seem amusingly antiquated, as if they could sit alongside ray guns and food pills. But read in a different light, the article seems remarkably cutting-edge. It describes voice interaction, wearable information devices, and wireless data connections that are still part of our near-future vision today. These descriptions, however, are only the preparation for Bush's most famous proposal: the "memex," a "future device for individual use . . . a sort of mechanized private file and library" in the shape of a desk. The memex, as described, uses methods such as microfilm storage, dry photography, and analog computing to give postwar scholars access to a huge, indexed repository of knowledge—any section of which can be called up with a few keystrokes.

The field of information retrieval has been inspired by Bush's vision of simple, elegant information access. New media, however, has been inspired by a different aspect of Bush's vision: the scholar creating links and pathways through this information—associative connections that attempt to partially reflect the "intricate web of trails carried by the cells of the brain." The trails envisioned freely interconnect all the contents of the memex, which include both public documents and personal notes, diagrams, and photographs. Given a memex, a scholar could create her own knowledge tools as connections within reams of information, share these tools, and use complexes of tools to create yet more sophisticated knowledge that could in turn be deployed toward this work. The memex has been envisioned as a means of turning an *information explosion* into a *knowledge explosion*. This remains one of the defining dreams of new media.

◊035
515

Toward the close of the article, Bush also discusses direct connections between human and machinic electrical systems, a basis for more recent cyborg visions. See Donna Harraway's "Cyborg Manifesto" (◊35).

Shortly after "As We May Think" was first published, Doug Engelbart, a young radar technician, came across it in a Red Cross library for U.S. soldiers in the Philippines. Later, with the memex in mind, Engelbart began work that would result in the invention of the mouse, the word processor, the hyperlink, and concepts of new media for which these groundbreaking inventions were merely enabling technologies. Another history-making moment of inspiration is likely to have taken place at the dinner table of Ted Nelson's grandfather, who regularly read aloud from the *Atlantic Monthly*. Nelson, later, couldn't place exactly his first encounter with Bush's essay. He knew, however, that it was a major influence as he made his discovery of the hyperlink (independent of Engelbart's discovery of it), coined the terms "hypertext" and "hypermedia," and wrote books that envisioned personal computing and network publishing (of a more sophisticated sort than now provided by Web technologies) before the first personal computer was even available.

Bush's is the first of many essays in *The New Media Reader* that look not toward but beyond the Web. The documents presented in this volume are useful not only because they contain ideas that were influential. These documents are also useful because they contain ideas that, to many users and producers of new media, are in fact still *new*. Bush's trails are an example of this. Nothing quite like them yet exists on the Web, or in other common new media systems. In addition to one-jump, one-way links, wouldn't it be a pleasure to have trails, capable of connecting through a series of information places in order to help construct a more nuanced map of connections in the reader's mind?

Bush concluded his article by expressing the hope that the applications of science, which had recently been used to "throw masses of people against one another with cruel weapons," could also help the human race "encompass the great record and to grow in the wisdom of race experience." Bush had already helped to speed the world toward both outcomes. Toward the first, by playing an instrumental role in initiating a massive worldwide arms race, whose dangers he saw clearly—he said, shortly after the dropping of the first hydrogen bomb, that it "was a turning point when we entered into the grim world that we are entering right now" (*Endless Frontier*, 364). Toward the second, by fostering and inspiring the research community that would contribute so notably to the "great record" in wartime and postwar years.
—NWF

Bush's wartime efforts had tremendous and lasting outcomes.

As Paul Edwards writes in *The Closed World*, "It would be almost impossible to overstate the long-term effects of this enormous undertaking on American science and engineering. The vast interdisciplinary effort profoundly restructured scientific research communities. It solidified the trend to science-based industries—already entrenched in the interwar years—but it added the new ingredient of massive government funding and military direction." (p. 47)

Further Reading

Bush, Vannevar. *Endless Horizons* Washington, D.C.: Public Affairs Press, 1946.

Edwards, Paul N. *The Closed World: Computers and the Politics of Discourse in Cold War America*. Cambridge: MIT Press, 1996.

Nyce, James and Paul Kahn. *From Memex to Hypertext: Vannevar Bush and the Mind's Machine*. New York: Academic Press, 1991.

Zachary, G. Pascal. *Endless Frontier*. New York: Free Press, 1997.

Original Publication

Text from the *Atlantic Monthly*, 176(1):101–108. (July 1945).
Images from *Life*, 19(11):112–114, 116, 121, 123–124.
(September 1945). The text printed in the *Atlantic Monthly* was
abridged in *Life*.

# As We May Think

## Vannevar Bush

As Director of the Office of Scientific Research and Development,
Dr. Vannevar Bush has coordinated the activities of some six
thousand leading American scientists in the application of science
to warfare. In this significant article he holds up an incentive for
scientists when the fighting has ceased. He urges that men of
science should then turn to the massive task of making more
accessible our bewildering store of knowledge. For years inventions
have extended man's physical powers rather than the powers of his
mind. Trip hammers that multiply the fists, microscopes that
sharpen the eye, and engines of destruction and detection are new
results, but not the end results, of modern science. Now, says Dr.
Bush, instruments are at hand which, if properly developed, will
give man access to and command over the inherited knowledge of
the ages. The perfection of these pacific instruments should be the
first objective of our scientists as they emerge from their war work.
Like Emerson's famous address of 1837 on "The American Scholar,"
this paper by Dr. Bush calls for a new relationship between
thinking man and the sum of our knowledge.

—THE EDITOR [*The Atlantic Monthly*]

This has not been a scientist's war; it has been a war in
which all have had a part. The scientists, burying their old
professional competition in the demand of a common
cause, have shared greatly and learned much. It has been
exhilarating to work in effective partnership. Now, for
many, this appears to be approaching an end. What are the
scientists to do next?

For the biologists, and particularly for the medical scientists,
there can be little indecision, for their war has hardly required
them to leave the old paths. Many indeed have been able to
carry on their war research in their familiar peacetime
laboratories. Their objectives remain much the same.

It is the physicists who have been thrown most violently
off stride, who have left academic pursuits for the making of
strange destructive gadgets, who have had to devise new
methods for their unanticipated assignments. They have
done their part on the devices that made it possible to turn
back the enemy, have worked in combined effort with the
physicists of our allies. They have felt within themselves the
stir of achievement. They have been part of a great team.
Now, as peace approaches, one asks where they will find
objectives worthy of their best.

### 1

Of what lasting benefit has been man's use of science and of
the new instruments which his research brought into
existence? First, they have increased his control of his
material environment. They have improved his food, his
clothing, his shelter; they have increased his security and
released him partly from the bondage of bare existence. They
have given him increased knowledge of his own biological
processes so that he has had a progressive freedom from
disease and an increased span of life. They are illuminating
the interactions of his physiological and psychological
functions, giving the promise of an improved mental health.

Science has provided the swiftest communication between
individuals; it has provided a record of ideas and has enabled
man to manipulate and to make extracts from that record so
that knowledge evolves and endures throughout the life of a
race rather than that of an individual.

There is a growing mountain of research. But there is
increased evidence that we are being bogged down today as
specialization extends. The investigator is staggered by the
findings and conclusions of thousands of other workers—
conclusions which he cannot find time to grasp, much less to
remember, as they appear. Yet specialization becomes increasingly necessary for progress, and the effort to bridge between
disciplines is correspondingly superficial.

Professionally our methods of transmitting and reviewing
the results of research are generations old and by now are
totally inadequate for their purpose. If the aggregate time
spent in writing scholarly works and in reading them could
be evaluated, the ratio between these amounts of time might
well be startling. Those who conscientiously attempt to keep
abreast of current thought, even in restricted fields, by close
and continuous reading might well shy away from an
examination calculated to show how much of the previous
month's efforts could be produced on call. Mendel's concept
of the laws of genetics was lost to the world for a generation
because his publication did not reach the few who were
capable of grasping and extending it; and this sort of
catastrophe is undoubtedly being repeated all about us, as
truly significant attainments become lost in the mass of the
inconsequential.

The difficulty seems to be, not so much that we publish unduly in view of the extent and variety of present day interests, but rather that publication has been extended far beyond our present ability to make real use of the record. The summation of human experience is being expanded at a prodigious rate, and the means we use for threading through the consequent maze to the momentarily important item is the same as was used in the days of square-rigged ships.

But there are signs of a change as new and powerful instrumentalities come into use. Photocells capable of seeing things in a physical sense, advanced photography which can record what is seen or even what is not, thermionic tubes capable of controlling potent forces under the guidance of less power than a mosquito uses to vibrate his wings, cathode ray tubes rendering visible an occurrence so brief that by comparison a microsecond is a long time, relay combinations which will carry out involved sequences of movements more reliably than any human operator and thousands of times as fast—there are plenty of mechanical aids with which to effect a transformation in scientific records.

Two centuries ago Leibnitz invented a calculating machine which embodied most of the essential features of recent keyboard devices, but it could not then come into use. The economics of the situation were against it: the labor involved in constructing it, before the days of mass production, exceeded the labor to be saved by its use, since all it could accomplish could be duplicated by sufficient use of pencil and paper. Moreover, it would have been subject to frequent breakdown, so that it could not have been depended upon; for at that time and long after, complexity and unreliability were synonymous.

Babbage, even with remarkably generous support for his time, could not produce his great arithmetical machine. His idea was sound enough, but construction and maintenance costs were then too heavy. Had a Pharaoh been given detailed and explicit designs of an automobile, and had he understood them completely, it would have taxed the resources of his kingdom to have fashioned the thousands of parts for a single car, and that car would have broken down on the first trip to Giza.

Machines with interchangeable parts can now be constructed with great economy of effort. In spite of much complexity, they perform reliably. Witness the humble typewriter, or the movie camera, or the automobile. Electrical contacts have ceased to stick when thoroughly understood. Note the automatic telephone exchange, which has hundreds of thousands of such contacts, and yet is reliable. A spider web of metal, sealed in a thin glass container, a wire heated to brilliant glow, in short, the thermionic tube of radio sets, is made by the hundred million, tossed about in packages, plugged into sockets—and it works! Its gossamer parts, the precise location and alignment involved in its construction, would have occupied a master craftsman of the guild for months; now it is built for thirty cents. The world has arrived at an age of cheap complex devices of great reliability; and something is bound to come of it.

## 2

A record if it is to be useful to science, must be continuously extended, it must be stored, and above all it must be consulted. Today we make the record conventionally by writing and photography, followed by printing; but we also record on film, on wax disks, and on magnetic wires. Even if utterly new recording procedures do not appear, these present ones are certainly in the process of modification and extension.

Certainly progress in photography is not going to stop. Faster material and lenses, more automatic cameras, finer-grained sensitive compounds to allow an extension of the minicamera idea, are all imminent. Let us project this trend ahead to a logical, if not inevitable, outcome. The camera hound of the future wears on his forehead a lump a little larger than a walnut. It takes pictures 3 millimeters square, later to be projected or enlarged, which after all involves only a factor of 10 beyond present practice. The lens is of universal focus, down to any distance accommodated by the unaided eye, simply because it is of short focal length. There is a built-in photocell on the walnut such as we now have on at least one camera, which automatically adjusts exposure for a wide range of illumination. There is film in the walnut for a hundred exposures, and the spring for operating its shutter and shifting its film is wound once for all when the film clip is inserted. It produces its result in full color. It may well be stereoscopic, and record with two spaced glass eyes, for striking improvements in stereoscopic technique are just around the corner.

The cord which trips its shutter may reach down a man's sleeve within easy reach of his fingers. A quick squeeze, and the picture is taken. On a pair of ordinary glasses is a square of fine lines near the top of one lens, where it is out of the way of ordinary vision. When an object appears in that square, it is lined up for its picture. As the scientist of the future moves about the laboratory or the field, every time he looks at something worthy of the record, he trips the shutter and in it goes, without even an audible click. Is this all fantastic? The only fantastic thing about it is the idea of making as many pictures as would result from its use.

Will there be dry photography? It is already here in two forms. When Brady made his Civil War pictures, the plate had to be wet at the time of exposure. Now it has to be wet during development instead. In the future perhaps it need not be wetted at all. There have long been films impregnated with diazo dyes which form a picture without development, so that it is already there as soon as the camera has been operated. An exposure to ammonia gas destroys the unexposed dye, and the picture can then be taken out into the light and examined. The process is now slow, but someone may speed it up, and it has no grain difficulties such as now keep photographic researchers busy. Often it would be advantageous to be able to snap the camera and to look at the picture immediately.

Another process now in use is also slow, and more or less clumsy. For fifty years impregnated papers have been used which turn dark at every point where an electrical contact touches them, by reason of the chemical change thus produced in an iodine compound included in the paper. They have been used to make records, for a pointer moving across them can leave a trail behind. If the electrical potential on the pointer is varied as it moves, the line becomes light or dark in accordance with the potential.

This scheme is now used in facsimile transmission. The pointer draws a set of closely spaced lines across the paper one after another. As it moves, its potential is varied in accordance with a varying current received over wires from a distant station, where these variations are produced by a photocell which is similarly scanning a picture. At every instant the darkness of the line being drawn is made equal to the darkness of the point on the picture being observed by the photocell. Thus, when the whole picture has been covered, a replica appears at the receiving end.

A scene itself can be just as well looked over line by line by the photocell in this way as can a photograph of the scene. This whole apparatus constitutes a camera, with the added feature, which can be dispensed with if desired, of making its picture at a distance. It is slow, and the picture is poor in detail. Still, it does give another process of dry photography, in which the picture is finished as soon as it is taken.

It would be a brave man who would predict that such a process will always remain clumsy, slow, and faulty in detail. Television equipment today transmits sixteen reasonably good pictures a second, and it involves only two essential differences from the process described above. For one, the record is made by a moving beam of electrons rather than a moving pointer, for the reason that an electron beam can sweep across the picture very rapidly indeed. The other difference involves merely the use of a screen which glows momentarily when the electrons hit, rather than a chemically treated paper or film which is permanently altered. This speed is necessary in television, for motion pictures rather than stills are the object.

Use chemically treated film in place of the glowing screen, allow the apparatus to transmit one picture only rather than a succession, and a rapid camera for dry photography results. The treated film needs to be far faster in action than present examples, but it probably could be.

More serious is the objection that this scheme would involve putting the film inside a vacuum chamber, for electron beams behave normally only in such a rarefied environment. This difficulty could be avoided by allowing the electron beam to play on one side of a partition, and by pressing the film against the other side, if this partition were such as to allow the electrons to go through perpendicular to its surface, and to prevent them from spreading out sideways. Such partitions, in crude form, could certainly be constructed, and they will hardly hold up the general development.

Like dry photography, microphotography still has a long way to go. The basic scheme of reducing the size of the record, and examining it by projection rather than directly, has possibilities too great to be ignored. The combination of optical projection and photographic reduction is already producing some results in microfilm for scholarly purposes, and the potentialities are highly suggestive. Today, with microfilm, reductions by a linear factor of 20 can be employed and still produce full clarity when the material is re-enlarged for examination. The limits are set by the graininess of the film, the excellence of the optical system, and the efficiency of the light sources employed. All of these are rapidly improving.

Assume a linear ratio of 100 for future use. Consider film of the same thickness as paper, although thinner film will certainly be usable. Even under these conditions there would be a total factor of 10,000 between the bulk of the ordinary record on books, and its microfilm replica. The Encyclopoedia Britannica could be reduced to the volume of a matchbox. A

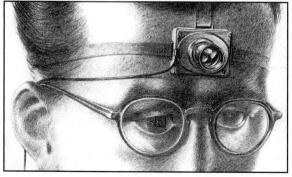

Figure 2.1. A scientist of the future records experiments with a tiny camera fitted with universal-focus lens. The small square in the eyeglass at the left sights the object (*Life* 19(11), p. 112).

library of a million volumes could be compressed into one end of a desk. If the human race has produced since the invention of movable type a total record, in the form of magazines, newspapers, books, tracts, advertising blurbs, correspondence, having a volume corresponding to a billion books, the whole affair, assembled and compressed, could be lugged off in a moving van. Mere compression, of course, is not enough; one needs not only to make and store a record but also be able to consult it, and this aspect of the matter comes later. Even the modern great library is not generally consulted; it is nibbled at by a few.

Compression is important, however, when it comes to costs. The material for the microfilm Britannica would cost a nickel, and it could be mailed anywhere for a cent. What would it cost to print a million copies? To print a sheet of newspaper, in a large edition, costs a small fraction of a cent. The entire material of the Britannica in reduced microfilm form would go on a sheet eight and one-half by eleven inches. Once it is available, with the photographic reproduction methods of the future, duplicates in large quantities could probably be turned out for a cent apiece beyond the cost of materials. The preparation of the original copy? That introduces the next aspect of the subject.

### 3

To make the record, we now push a pencil or tap a typewriter. Then comes the process of digestion and correction, followed by an intricate process of typesetting, printing, and distribution. To consider the first stage of the procedure, will the author of the future cease writing by hand or typewriter and talk directly to the record? He does so indirectly, by talking to a stenographer or a wax cylinder; but the elements are all present if he wishes to have his talk directly produce a typed record. All he needs to do is to take advantage of existing mechanisms and to alter his language.

At a recent World Fair a machine called a Voder was shown. A girl stroked its keys and it emitted recognizable speech. No human vocal chords entered into the procedure at any point; the keys simply combined some electrically produced vibrations and passed these on to a loud-speaker. In the Bell Laboratories there is the converse of this machine, called a Vocoder. The loudspeaker is replaced by a microphone, which picks up sound. Speak to it, and the corresponding keys move. This may be one element of the postulated system.

The other element is found in the stenotype, that somewhat disconcerting device encountered usually at public meetings. A girl strokes its keys languidly and looks about the room and sometimes at the speaker with a disquieting gaze. From it emerges a typed strip which records in a phonetically simplified language a record of what the speaker is supposed to have said. Later this strip is retyped into ordinary language, for in its nascent form it is intelligible only to the initiated. Combine these two elements, let the Vocoder run the stenotype, and the result is a machine which types when talked to.

Our present languages are not especially adapted to this sort of mechanization, it is true.

It is strange that the inventors of universal languages have not seized upon the idea of producing one which better fitted the technique for transmitting and recording speech. Mechanization may yet force the issue, especially in the scientific field; whereupon scientific jargon would become still less intelligible to the layman.

One can now picture a future investigator in his laboratory. His hands are free, and he is not anchored. As he moves about and observes, he photographs and comments. Time is automatically recorded to tie the two records together. If he goes into the field, he may be connected by radio to his recorder. As he ponders over his notes in the evening, he again talks his comments into the record. His typed record, as well as his photographs, may both be in miniature, so that he projects them for examination.

Much needs to occur, however, between the collection of data and observations, the extraction of parallel material from the existing record, and the final insertion of new material into the general body of the common record. For mature thought there is no mechanical substitute. But creative thought and essentially repetitive thought are very different things. For the latter there are, and may be, powerful mechanical aids.

Adding a column of figures is a repetitive thought process, and it was long ago properly relegated to the machine. True, the machine is sometimes controlled by a keyboard, and thought of a sort enters in reading the figures and poking the corresponding keys, but even this is avoidable. Machines have been made which will read typed figures by photocells and then depress the corresponding keys; these are combinations of photocells for scanning the type, electric circuits for sorting the consequent variations, and relay circuits for interpreting the result into the action of solenoids to pull the keys down.

All this complication is needed because of the clumsy way in which we have learned to write figures. If we recorded them positionally, simply by the configuration of a set of dots on a card, the automatic reading mechanism would become comparatively simple. In fact if the dots are holes, we have the punched-card machine long ago produced by Hollorith for the purposes of the census, and now used throughout business. Some types of complex businesses could hardly operate without these machines.

Adding is only one operation. To perform arithmetical computation involves also subtraction, multiplication, and division, and in addition some method for temporary storage of results, removal from storage for further manipulation, and recording of final results by printing. Machines for these purposes are now of two types: keyboard machines for accounting and the like, manually controlled for the insertion of data, and usually automatically controlled as far as the sequence of operations is concerned; and punched-card machines in which separate operations are usually delegated to a series of machines, and the cards then transferred bodily from one to another. Both forms are very useful; but as far as complex computations are concerned, both are still in embryo.

Rapid electrical counting appeared soon after the physicists found it desirable to count cosmic rays. For their own purposes the physicists promptly constructed thermionic-tube equipment capable of counting electrical impulses at the rate of 100,000 a second. The advanced arithmetical machines of the future will be electrical in nature, and they will perform at 100 times present speeds, or more.

Moreover, they will be far more versatile than present commercial machines, so that they may readily be adapted for a wide variety of operations. They will be controlled by a control card or film, they will select their own data and manipulate it in accordance with the instructions thus inserted, they will perform complex arithmetical computations at exceedingly high speeds, and they will record results in such form as to be readily available for distribution or for later further manipulation. Such machines will have enormous appetites. One of them will take instructions and data from a whole roomful of girls armed with simple key board punches, and will deliver sheets of computed results every few minutes. There will always be plenty of things to compute in the detailed affairs of millions of people doing complicated things.

### 4

The repetitive processes of thought are not confined however, to matters of arithmetic and statistics. In fact, every time one combines and records facts in accordance with established logical processes, the creative aspect of thinking is concerned only with the selection of the data and the process to be employed and the manipulation thereafter is repetitive in nature and hence a fit matter to be relegated to the machine. Not so much has been done along these lines, beyond the bounds of arithmetic, as might be done, primarily because of the economics of the situation. The needs of business and the extensive market obviously waiting, assured the advent of mass-produced arithmetical machines just as soon as production methods were sufficiently advanced.

With machines for advanced analysis no such situation existed; for there was and is no extensive market; the users of advanced methods of manipulating data are a very small part of the population. There are, however, machines for solving differential equations—and functional and integral equations, for that matter. There are many special machines, such as the harmonic synthesizer which predicts the tides. There will be many more, appearing certainly first in the hands of the scientist and in small numbers.

If scientific reasoning were limited to the logical processes of arithmetic, we should not get far in our understanding of the physical world. One might as well attempt to grasp the game of poker entirely by the use of the mathematics of probability. The abacus, with its beads strung on parallel wires, led the Arabs to positional numeration and the concept of zero many centuries before the rest of the world; and it was a useful tool—so useful that it still exists.

It is a far cry from the abacus to the modern keyboard accounting machine. It will be an equal step to the arithmetical machine of the future. But even this new machine will not take the scientist where he needs to go. Relief must be secured from laborious detailed manipulation of higher mathematics as well, if the users of it are to free their brains for something more than repetitive detailed transformations in accordance with established rules. A mathematician is not a man who can readily manipulate figures; often he cannot. He is not even a man who can readily perform the transformations of equations by the use of calculus. He is primarily an individual who is skilled in the use of symbolic logic on a high plane, and especially he is a man of intuitive judgment in the choice of the manipulative processes he employs.

All else he should be able to turn over to his mechanism, just as confidently as he turns over the propelling of his car to the intricate mechanism under the hood. Only then will mathematics be practically effective in bringing the growing knowledge of atomistics to the useful solution of the advanced problems of chemistry, metallurgy, and biology. For this reason there still come more machines to handle advanced mathematics for the scientist. Some of them will be sufficiently bizarre to suit the most fastidious connoisseur of the present artifacts of civilization.

## 5

The scientist, however, is not the only person who manipulates data and examines the world about him by the use of logical processes, although he sometimes preserves this appearance by adopting into the fold anyone who becomes logical, much in the manner in which a British labor leader is elevated to knighthood. Whenever logical processes of thought are employed—that is, whenever thought for a time runs along an accepted groove—there is an opportunity for the machine. Formal logic used to be a keen instrument in the hands of the teacher in his trying of students' souls. It is readily possible to construct a machine which will manipulate premises in accordance with formal logic, simply by the clever use of relay circuits. Put a set of premises into such a device and turn the crank, and it will readily pass out conclusion after conclusion, all in accordance with logical law, and with no more slips than would be expected of a keyboard adding machine.

Logic can become enormously difficult, and it would undoubtedly be well to produce more assurance in its use. The machines for higher analysis have usually been equation solvers. Ideas are beginning to appear for equation transformers, which will rearrange the relationship expressed by an equation in accordance with strict and rather advanced logic. Progress is inhibited by the exceedingly crude way in which mathematicians express their relationships. They employ a symbolism which grew like Topsy and has little consistency; a strange fact in that most logical field.

A new symbolism, probably positional, must apparently precede the reduction of mathematical transformations to machine processes. Then, on beyond the strict logic of the mathematician, lies the application of logic in everyday affairs. We may some day click off arguments on a machine with the same assurance that we now enter sales on a cash register. But the machine of logic will not look like a cash register, even of the streamlined model.

So much for the manipulation of ideas and their insertion into the record. Thus far we seem to be worse off than before—for we can enormously extend the record; yet even in its present bulk we can hardly consult it. This is a much larger matter than merely the extraction of data for the purposes of scientific research; it involves the entire process by which man profits by his inheritance of acquired knowledge. The prime action of use is selection, and here we are halting indeed. There may be millions of fine thoughts, and the account of the experience on which they are based, all encased within stone walls of acceptable architectural form; but if the scholar can get at only one a week by diligent search, his syntheses are not likely to keep up with the current scene.

Selection, in this broad sense, is a stone adze in the hands of a cabinetmaker. Yet, in a narrow sense and in other areas, something has already been done mechanically on selection. The personnel officer of a factory drops a stack of a few thousand employee cards into a selecting machine, sets a code in accordance with an established convention, and produces in a short time a list of all employees who live in Trenton and know Spanish. Even such devices are much too slow when it comes, for example, to matching a set of fingerprints with one of five million on file. Selection devices of this sort will soon be speeded up from their present rate of reviewing data at a few hundred a minute.

Figure 2.2. Supersecretary of the coming age, the machine contemplated here would take dictation, type it automatically and even talk back if the author wanted to review what he had just said. It is somewhat similar to the Voder seen at the New York World's Fair. Like all machines suggested by the diagrams in this article, it is not yet in existence (*Life* 19(11), p. 114).

By the use of photocells and microfilm they will survey items at the rate of a thousand a second, and will print out duplicates of those selected.

This process, however, is simple selection: it proceeds by examining in turn every one of a large set of items, and by picking out those which have certain specified characteristics. There is another form of selection best illustrated by the automatic telephone exchange. You dial a number and the machine selects and connects just one of a million possible stations. It does not run over them all. It pays attention only to a class given by a first digit, then only to a subclass of this

given by the second digit, and so on; and thus proceeds rapidly and almost unerringly to the selected station. It requires a few seconds to make the selection, although the process could be speeded up if increased speed were economically warranted. If necessary, it could be made extremely fast by substituting thermionic-tube switching for mechanical switching, so that the full selection could be made in one one-hundredth of a second. No one would wish to spend the money necessary to make this change in the telephone system, but the general idea is applicable elsewhere.

Take the prosaic problem of the great department store. Every time a charge sale is made, there are a number of things to be done. The inventory needs to be revised, the salesman needs to be given credit for the sale, the general accounts need an entry, and, most important, the customer needs to be charged. A central records device has been developed in which much of this work is done conveniently. The salesman places on a stand the customer's identification card, his own card, and the card taken from the article sold— all punched cards. When he pulls a lever, contacts are made through the holes, machinery at a central point makes the necessary computations and entries, and the proper receipt is printed for the salesman to pass to the customer.

But there may be ten thousand charge customers doing business with the store, and before the full operation can be completed someone has to select the right card and insert it at the central office. Now rapid selection can slide just the proper card into position in an instant or two, and return it afterward. Another difficulty occurs, however. Someone must read a total on the card, so that the machine can add its computed item to it. Conceivably the cards might be of the dry photography type I have described. Existing totals could then be read by photocell, and the new total entered by an electron beam.

The cards may be in miniature, so that they occupy little space. They must move quickly. They need not be transferred far, but merely into position so that the photocell and recorder can operate on them. Positional dots can enter the data. At the end of the month a machine can readily be made to read these and to print an ordinary bill. With tube selection, in which no mechanical parts are involved in the switches, little time need be occupied in bringing the correct card into use—a second should suffice for the entire operation. The whole record on the card may be made by magnetic dots on a steel sheet if desired, instead of dots to be observed optically, following the scheme by which Poulsen long ago put speech on a magnetic wire. This method has the advantage of simplicity and ease of erasure. By using photography, however one can arrange to project the record in enlarged form and at a distance by using the process common in television equipment.

One can consider rapid selection of this form, and distant projection for other purposes. To be able to key one sheet of a million before an operator in a second or two, with the possibility of then adding notes thereto, is suggestive in many ways. It might even be of use in libraries, but that is another story. At any rate, there are now some interesting

from subclass to subclass. It can be in only one place, unless duplicates are used; one has to have rules as to which path will locate it, and the rules are cumbersome. Having found one item, moreover, one has to emerge from the system and re-enter on a new path.

The human mind does not work that way. It operates by association. With one item in its grasp, it snaps instantly to the next that is suggested by the association of thoughts, in accordance with some intricate web of trails carried by the cells of the brain. It has other characteristics, of course; trails that are not frequently followed are prone to fade, items are not fully permanent, memory is transitory. Yet the speed of

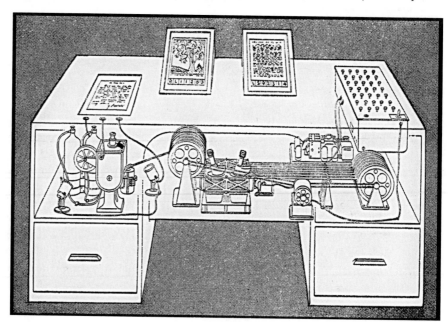

Figure 2.3. Memex in the form of a desk would instantly bring files and material on any subject to the operator's fingertips. Slanting translucent viewing screens magnify supermicrofilm filed by code numbers. At left is a mechanism which automatically photographs longhand notes, pictures and letters, then files them in the desk for future reference (*Life* 19(11), p. 123).

combinations possible. One might, for example, speak to a microphone, in the manner described in connection with the speech controlled typewriter, and thus make his selections. It would certainly beat the usual file clerk.

## 6

The real heart of the matter of selection, however, goes deeper than a lag in the adoption of mechanisms by libraries, or a lack of development of devices for their use. Our ineptitude in getting at the record is largely caused by the artificiality of systems of indexing. When data of any sort are placed in storage, they are filed alphabetically or numerically, and information is found (when it is) by tracing it down

action, the intricacy of trails, the detail of mental pictures, is awe-inspiring beyond all else in nature.

Man cannot hope fully to duplicate this mental process artificially, but he certainly ought to be able to learn from it. In minor ways he may even improve, for his records have relative permanency. The first idea, however, to be drawn from the analogy concerns selection. Selection by association, rather than indexing, may yet be mechanized. One cannot hope thus to equal the speed and flexibility with which the mind follows an associative trail, but it should be possible to beat the mind decisively in regard to the permanence and clarity of the items resurrected from storage.

Consider a future device for individual use, which is a sort of mechanized private file and library. It needs a name, and, to coin one at random, "memex" will do. A memex is a device in which an individual stores all his books, records, and communications, and which is mechanized so that it may be consulted with exceeding speed and flexibility. It is an enlarged intimate supplement to his memory.

It consists of a desk, and while it can presumably be operated from a distance, it is primarily the piece of furniture at which he works. On the top are slanting translucent screens, on which material can be projected for convenient reading.

There is a keyboard, and sets of buttons and levers. Otherwise it looks like an ordinary desk.

In one end is the stored material. The matter of bulk is well taken care of by improved microfilm. Only a small part of the interior of the memex is devoted to storage, the rest to mechanism. Yet if the user inserted 5000 pages of material a day it would take him hundreds of years to fill the repository, so he can be profligate and enter material freely.

Most of the memex contents are purchased on microfilm ready for insertion. Books of all sorts, pictures, current periodicals, newspapers, are thus obtained and dropped into place. Business correspondence takes the same path. And there is provision for direct entry. On the top of the memex is a transparent platen. On this are placed longhand notes, photographs, memoranda, all sorts of things. When one is in place, the depression of a lever causes it to be photographed onto the next blank space in a section of the memex film, dry photography being employed.

There is, of course, provision for consultation of the record by the usual scheme of indexing. If the user wishes to consult a certain book, he taps its code on the keyboard, and the title page of the book promptly appears before him, projected onto one of his viewing positions. Frequently-used codes are mnemonic, so that he seldom consults his code book; but when he does, a single tap of a key projects it for his use. Moreover, he has supplemental levers. On deflecting one of these levers to the right he runs through the book before him, each page in turn being projected at a speed which just allows a recognizing glance at each. If he deflects it further to the right, he steps through the book 10 pages at a time; still further at 100 pages at a time. Deflection to the left gives him the same control backwards.

A special button transfers him immediately to the first page of the index. Any given book of his library can thus be called up and consulted with far greater facility than if it were taken from a shelf. As he has several projection positions, he can leave one item in position while he calls up another. He can add marginal notes and comments, taking advantage of one possible type of dry photography, and it could even be arranged so that he can do this by a stylus scheme, such as is now employed in the telautograph seen in railroad waiting rooms, just as though he had the physical page before him.

## 7

All this is conventional, except for the projection forward of present-day mechanisms and gadgetry. It affords an immediate step, however, to associative indexing, the basic idea of which is a provision whereby any item may be caused at will to select immediately and automatically another. This is the essential feature of the memex. The process of tying two items together is the important thing.

When the user is building a trail, he names it, inserts the name in his code book, and taps it out on his keyboard. Before him are the two items to be joined, projected onto adjacent viewing positions. At the bottom of each there are a number of blank code spaces, and a pointer is set to indicate one of these on each item. The user taps a single key, and the items are permanently joined. In each code space appears the code word. Out of view, but also in the code space, is inserted a set of dots for photocell viewing; and on each item these dots by their positions designate the index number of the other item.

Thereafter, at any time, when one of these items is in view, the other can be instantly recalled merely by tapping a button below the corresponding code space. Moreover, when numerous items have been thus joined together to form a trail, they can be reviewed in turn, rapidly or slowly, by deflecting a lever like that used for turning the pages of a book. It is exactly as though the physical items had been gathered together from widely separated sources and bound together to form a new book. It is more than this, for any item can be joined into numerous trails.

The owner of the memex, let us say, is interested in the origin and properties of the bow and arrow. Specifically he is studying why the short Turkish bow was apparently superior to the English long bow in the skirmishes of the Crusades.

He has dozens of possibly pertinent books and articles in his memex. First he runs through an encyclopedia, finds an interesting but sketchy article, leaves it projected. Next, in a history, he finds another pertinent item, and ties the two together. Thus he goes, building a trail of many items. Occasionally he inserts a comment of his own, either linking it into the main trail or joining it by a side trail to a particular

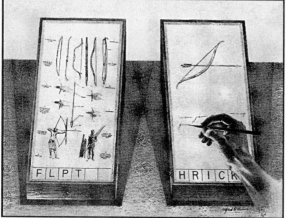

Figure 2.4. Memex in use is shown here. On one transparent screen the operator of the future writes notes and commentary dealing with reference material which is projected on the screen at left. Insertion of the proper code symbols at the bottom of right-hand screen will tie the new item to the earlier one after notes are photographed on supermicrofilm (*Life* 19(11), p. 124).

item. When it becomes evident that the elastic properties of available materials had a great deal to do with the bow, he branches off on a side trail which takes him through textbooks on elasticity and tables of physical constants. He inserts a page of longhand analysis of his own.

Thus he builds a trail of his interest through the maze of materials available to him.

And his trails do not fade. Several years later, his talk with a friend turns to the queer ways in which a people resist innovations, even of vital interest. He has an example, in the fact that the outraged Europeans still failed to adopt the Turkish bow.

In fact he has a trail on it. A touch brings up the code book. Tapping a few keys projects the head of the trail. A lever runs through it at will, stopping at interesting items, going off on side excursions. It is an interesting trail, pertinent to the discussion. So he sets a reproducer in action, photographs the whole trail out, and passes it to his friend for insertion in his own memex, there to be linked into the more general trail.

## 8

Wholly new forms of encyclopedias will appear, ready made with a mesh of associative trails running through them, ready to be dropped into the memex and there amplified. The lawyer has at his touch the associated opinions and decisions of his whole experience, and of the experience of friends and authorities. The patent attorney has on call the millions of issued patents, with familiar trails to every point of his client's interest. The physician, puzzled by a patient's reactions, strikes the trail established in studying an earlier similar case, and runs rapidly through analogous case histories, with side references to the classics for the pertinent anatomy and histology. The chemist, struggling with the synthesis of an organic compound, has all the chemical literature before him in his laboratory, with trails following the analogies of compounds, and side trails to their physical and chemical behavior. The historian, with a vast chronological account of a people, parallels it with a skip trail which stops only on the salient items, and can follow at any time contemporary trails which lead him all over civilization at a particular epoch. There is a new profession of trail blazers, those who find delight in the task of establishing useful trails through the enormous mass of the common record. The inheritance from the master becomes, not only his additions to the world's record, but for his disciples the entire scaffolding by which they were erected.

Thus science may implement the ways in which man produces, stores, and consults the record of the race. It might be striking to outline the instrumentalities of the future more spectacularly, rather than to stick closely to methods and elements now known and undergoing rapid development, as has been done here. Technical difficulties of all sorts have been ignored, certainly, but also ignored are means as yet unknown which may come any day to accelerate technical progress as violently as did the advent of the thermionic tube. In order that the picture may not be too commonplace, by reason of sticking to present-day patterns, it may be well to mention one such possibility, not to prophesy but merely to suggest, for prophecy based on extension of the known has substance, while prophecy founded on the unknown is only a doubly involved guess.

All our steps in creating or absorbing material of the record proceed through one of the senses—the tactile when we touch keys, the oral when we speak or listen, the visual when we read. Is it not possible that some day the path may be established more directly?

We know that when the eye sees, all the consequent information is transmitted to the brain by means of electrical vibrations in the channel of the optic nerve. This is an exact analogy with the electrical vibrations which occur in the cable of a television set: they convey the picture from the photocells which see it to the radio transmitter from which it is broadcast. We know further that if we can approach that cable with the proper instruments, we do not need to touch it; we can pick up those vibrations by electrical induction and thus discover and reproduce the scene which is being transmitted, just as a telephone wire may be tapped for its message.

The impulses which flow in the arm nerves of a typist convey to her fingers the translated information which reaches her eye or ear, in order that the fingers may be caused to strike the proper keys. Might not these currents be intercepted, either in the original form in which information is conveyed to the brain, or in the marvelously metamorphosed form in which they then proceed to the hand?

By bone conduction we already introduce sounds: into the nerve channels of the deaf in order that they may hear. Is it not possible that we may learn to introduce them without the present cumbersomeness of first transforming electrical vibrations to mechanical ones, which the human mechanism promptly transforms back to the electrical form? With a couple of electrodes on the skull the encephalograph now produces pen-and-ink traces which bear some relation to the electrical phenomena going on in the brain itself. True, the record is unintelligible, except as it points out certain gross misfunctioning of the cerebral mechanism; but who would now place bounds on where such a thing may lead? In the outside world, all forms of intelligence whether of sound or sight, have been reduced to the form of varying currents in an electric circuit in order that they may be transmitted. Inside the human frame exactly the same sort of process occurs. Must we always transform to mechanical movements in order to proceed from one electrical phenomenon to another? It is a suggestive thought, but it hardly warrants prediction without losing touch with reality and immediateness.

Presumably man's spirit should be elevated if he can better review his shady past and analyze more completely and objectively his present problems. He has built a civilization so complex that he needs to mechanize his records more fully if he is to push his experiment to its logcal conclusion and not merely become bogged down part way there by overtaxing his limited memory. His excursions may be more enjoyable if he can reacquire the privilege of forgetting the manifold things he does not need to have immediately at hand, with some assurance that he can find them again if they prove important.

The applications of science have built man a well-supplied house, and are teaching him to live healthily therein. They have enabled him to throw masses of people against one another with cruel weapons. They may yet allow him truly to encompass the great record and to grow in the wisdom of race experience. He may perish in conflict before he learns to wield that record for his true good. Yet, in the application of science to the needs and desires of man, it would seem to be a singularly unfortunate stage at which to terminate the process, or to lose hope as to the outcome.

# 03. [Introduction]
# Computing Machinery and Intelligence

Early computers were viewed purely as number-crunchers. From their paper-tape input to their numeric output, they used their symbol-manipulation powers to calculate, producing tables of figures for artillery targeting or to help construct the atomic bomb. It wasn't obvious, early on, that computers could usefully manipulate words. The leap into language made possible a huge range of applications: email, word processing, voice recognition, and even the simple ability to click "OK."

A small amount of early computing actually was text processing, although of a highly mathematical sort. The British Colossus computers, built starting in 1943 with the help of Cambridge mathematician Alan Turing, worked to decrypt encoded language. That might have been one experience that led computer pioneer Turing (who also devised the mathematical abstraction called the "Turing machine," a theoretical, formally-described machine that can solve any computable problem) to write this groundbreaking essay. Turing's essay is well known for setting forth the "Turing test." Instead of asking if a computer can think, Turing replaced that question with one that could be answered: can a computer, communicating over a teleprinter, fool a person into believing it is human? The Turing test has inspired the annual Loebner Prize competition for chatterbots that started in 1991, but it has often been derided as useless for computer science. It's important to recall that Turing offered it to the philosophers who read the journal *Mind*, not to computer scientists, as a way of challenging their notion of intelligence and of how it could be defined phenomenologically. Computer scientists are quite likely to remember this paper as anticipating the field of artificial intelligence. Others will think of it as provocative for predicting a thinking computer within fifty years. Turing put forth another interesting idea in this article, however: that actual human-computer dialog, using language, could take place. At the beginning of the 1950s, some billing systems were being developed for use by businesses, and these did suggest that the computer could act as scribe. These systems fit boilerplate language around what were basically mathematical operations. Turing's paper was important not just in describing a "thinking" machine, but in describing an essentially linguistic computer that could converse fluidly.

Turing's description of a verbal computer was one inspiration for early programmers to forge into new media, pushing computing into territory beyond that of numbers and calculation. Using computers to manipulate words made possible not just the mundane yet important word processor, but also modern programming languages and operating systems, today's Web, and all sorts of databases that store text. While readers of Turing's paper were bristling at the idea of a thinking computer, a more subtle idea was being portrayed in the example conversations quoted: that computing machinery could be engineered to operate on language.

—NM

Even the prescient Vannevar Bush (◊02) envisioned machines like microfiche readers, rather than computers, doing the work of textual storage and retrieval for researchers.

◊02 35

49

◊08 93

◊09 109

The Association for Computing Machinery's most prestigious award for technical contributions in the field, offered annually since 1966, is called the Turing Award. The winners include Ivan Sutherland (◊09) in 1988 "for his pioneering and visionary contributions to computer graphics, starting with Sketchpad . . ." and Douglas Engelbart (◊08, ◊16) in 1997, "for an inspiring vision of the future of interactive computing and the invention of key technologies to help realize this vision."

◊16 231

◊24 367

The first convincing conversational computer program was Joseph Weizenbaum's Eliza running the *Doctor* script ⊗. Also, see Weizenbaum's essay (◊24).

The Turing machine, developed by Turing in order to precisely discuss the nature of computation, is an abstract computer that has a tape, upon which symbols from a finite alphabet (e.g., 0 and 1) can be written and read. The machine is in one of a finite number of states at any point in a computation, and its next state is determined by the input from the tape and the rules corresponding to its current state. While the Turing machine is extremely simple, it is also extremely general. For any algorithm that can be computed at all, there is a Turing machine that can compute it; thus the machine is *universal*, in the sense discussed in the following selection.

Soon after Turing's paper appeared, in 1952, Grace Murray Hopper programmed the first compiler, and computer languages began to take shape. This move paved the way for English-like high-level languages like FORTRAN and, later, COBOL, which Hopper developed. Unfortunately, Turing, whose codebreaking help may have been decisive in England's success against German U-boats, was arrested in 1952 for homosexuality and sentenced under his country's laws to regular injections of estrogen. Turing was unable to see the rise of the artificial intelligence field, and the widespread use of language in computing, as he committed suicide two years after his arrest.

Further Reading

Bolter, J. David. *Turing's Man: Western Culture in the Computer Age.* Chapel Hill: University of North Carolina Press, 1984.

Hodges, Andrew. *Turing.* New York: Routledge, 1999.

Original Publication

*Mind: A Quarterly Review of Psychology and Philosophy* 59(236): 433–460. October 1950.

# Computing Machinery and Intelligence

## Alan Turing

## 1 The Imitation Game

I propose to consider the question, "Can machines think?" This should begin with definitions of the meaning of the terms "machine" and "think." The definitions might be framed so as to reflect so far as possible the normal use of the words, but this attitude is dangerous. If the meaning of the words "machine" and "think" are to be found by examining how they are commonly used it is difficult to escape the conclusion that the meaning and the answer to the question, "Can machines think?" is to be sought in a statistical survey such as a Gallup poll. But this is absurd. Instead of attempting such a definition I shall replace the question by another, which is closely related to it and is expressed in relatively unambiguous words.

The new form of the problem can be described in terms of a game which we call the "imitation game." It is played with three people, a man (A), a woman (B), and an interrogator (C) who may be of either sex. The interrogator stays in a room apart from the other two. The object of the game for the interrogator is to determine which of the other two is the man and which is the woman. He knows them by labels X

and Y, and at the end of the game he says either "X is A and Y is B" or "X is B and Y is A." The interrogator is allowed to put questions to A and B thus:

C: Will X please tell me the length of his or her hair?

Now suppose X is actually A, then A must answer. It is A's object in the game to try and cause C to make the wrong identification. His answer might therefore be "My hair is shingled, and the longest strands, are about nine inches long."

In order that tones of voice may not help the interrogator the answers should be written, or better still, typewritten. The ideal arrangement is to have a teleprinter communicating between the two rooms. Alternatively the question and answers can be repeated by an intermediary. The object of the game for the third player (B) is to help the interrogator. The best strategy for her is probably to give truthful answers. She can add such things as "I am the woman, don't listen to him!" to her answers, but it will avail nothing as the man can make similar remarks.

We now ask the question, "What will happen when a machine takes the part of A in this game?" Will the interrogator decide wrongly as often when the game is played like this as he does when the game is played between a man and a woman? These questions replace our original, "Can machines think?"

## 2 Critique of the New Problem

As well as asking, "What is the answer to this new form of the question," one may ask, "Is this new question a worthy one to investigate?" This latter question we investigate without further ado, thereby cutting short an infinite regress.

The new problem has the advantage of drawing a fairly sharp line between the physical and the intellectual capacities of a man. No engineer or chemist claims to be able to produce a material which is indistinguishable from the human skin. It is possible that at some time this might be done, but even supposing this invention available we should feel there was little point in trying to make a "thinking machine" more human by dressing it up in such artificial flesh. The form in which we have set the problem reflects this fact in the condition which prevents the interrogator from seeing or touching the other competitors, or hearing their voices. Some other advantages of the proposed criterion may be shown up by specimen questions and answers. Thus:

Q: Please write me a sonnet on the subject of the Forth Bridge.

A: Count me out on this one. I never could write poetry.

Q: Add 34957 to 70764.

A: (Pause about 30 seconds and then give as answer) 105621.

Q: Do you play chess?

A: Yes.

Q: I have K at my K1, and no other pieces. You have only K at K6 and R at R1. It is your move. What do you play?

A: (After a pause of 15 seconds) R-R8 mate.

The question and answer method seems to be suitable for introducing almost any one of the fields of human endeavour that we wish to include. We do not wish to penalise the machine for its inability to shine in beauty competitions, nor to penalise a man for losing in a race against an aeroplane. The conditions of our game make these disabilities irrelevant. The "witnesses" can brag, if they consider it advisable, as much as they please about their charms, strength or heroism, but the interrogator cannot demand practical demonstrations.

The game may perhaps be criticised on the ground that the odds are weighted too heavily against the machine. If the man were to try and pretend to be the machine he would clearly make a very poor showing. He would be given away at once by slowness and inaccuracy in arithmetic. May not machines carry out something which ought to be described as thinking but which is very different from what a man does? This objection is a very strong one, but at least we can

say that if, nevertheless, a machine can be constructed to play the imitation game satisfactorily, we need not be troubled by this objection.

It might be urged that when playing the "imitation game" the best strategy for the machine may possibly be something other than imitation of the behaviour of a man. This may be, but I think it is unlikely that there is any great effect of this kind. In any case there is no intention to investigate here the theory of the game, and it will be assumed that the best strategy is to try to provide answers that would naturally be given by a man.

## 3 The Machines Concerned in the Game

The question which we put in §1 will not be quite definite until we have specified what we mean by the word "machine." It is natural that we should wish to permit every kind of engineering technique to be used in our machines. We also wish to allow the possibility than an engineer or team of engineers may construct a machine which works, but whose manner of operation cannot be satisfactorily described by its constructors because they have applied a method which is largely experimental. Finally, we wish to exclude from the machines men born in the usual manner. It is difficult to frame the definitions so as to satisfy these three conditions. One might for instance insist that the team of engineers should be all of one sex, but this would not really be satisfactory, for it is probably possible to rear a complete individual from a single cell of the skin (say) of a man. To do so would be a feat of biological technique deserving of the very highest praise, but we would not be inclined to regard it as a case of "constructing a thinking machine." This prompts us to abandon the requirement that every kind of technique should be permitted. We are the more ready to do so in view of the fact that the present interest in "thinking machines" has been aroused by a particular kind of machine, usually called an "electronic computer" or "digital computer." Following this suggestion we only permit digital computers to take part in our game.

This restriction appears at first sight to be a very drastic one. I shall attempt to show that it is not so in reality. To do this necessitates a short account of the nature and properties of these computers.

It may also be said that this identification of machines with digital computers, like our criterion for "thinking," will only be unsatisfactory if (contrary to my belief), it turns out that digital computers are unable to give a good showing in the game.

There are already a number of digital computers in working order, and it may be asked, "Why not try the experiment straight away? It would be easy to satisfy the conditions of the game. A number of interrogators could be used, and statistics compiled to show how often the right identification was given." The short answer is that we are not asking whether all digital computers would do well in the game nor whether the computers at present available would do well, but whether there are imaginable computers which would do well. But this is only the short answer. We shall see this question in a different light later.

## 4 Digital Computers

The idea behind digital computers may be explained by saying that these machines are intended to carry out any operations which could be done by a human computer. The human computer is supposed to be following fixed rules; he has no authority to deviate from them in any detail. We may suppose that these rules are supplied in a book, which is altered whenever he is put on to a new job. He has also an unlimited supply of paper on which he does his calculations. He may also do his multiplications and additions on a "desk machine," but this is not important.

If we use the above explanation as a definition we shall be in danger of circularity of argument. We avoid this by giving an outline of the means by which the desired effect is achieved. A digital computer can usually be regarded as consisting of three parts:

> (i) Store.
>
> (ii) Executive unit.
>
> (iii) Control.

The store is a store of information, and corresponds to the human computer's paper, whether this is the paper on which he does his calculations or that on which his book of rules is printed. In so far as the human computer does calculations in his head a part of the store will correspond to his memory.

The executive unit is the part which carries out the various individual operations involved in a calculation. What these individual operations are will vary from machine to machine. Usually fairly lengthy operations can be done such as "Multiply 3540675445 by 7076345687" but in some

machines only very simple ones such as "Write down 0" are possible.

We have mentioned that the "book of rules" supplied to the computer is replaced in the machine by a part of the store. It is then called the "table of instructions." It is the duty of the control to see that these instructions are obeyed correctly and in the right order. The control is so constructed that this necessarily happens.

The information in the store is usually broken up into packets of moderately small size. In one machine, for instance, a packet might consist of ten decimal digits. Numbers are assigned to the parts of the store in which the various packets of information are stored, in some systematic manner. A typical instruction might say—

> Add the number stored in position 6809 to that in 4302 and put the result back into the latter storage position.

Needless to say it would not occur in the machine expressed in English. It would more likely be coded in a form such as 6809430217. Here 17 says which of various possible operations is to be performed on the two numbers. In this case the operation is that described above, *viz.* "Add the number. . . ." It will be noticed that the instruction takes up 10 digits and so forms one packet of information, very conveniently. The control will normally take the instructions to be obeyed in the order of the positions in which they are stored, but occasionally an instruction such as

> Now obey the instruction stored in position 5606, and continue from there

may be encountered, or again

> If position 4505 contains 0 obey next the instruction stored in 6707, otherwise continue straight on.

Instructions of these latter types are very important because they make it possible for a sequence of operations to be repeated over and over again until some condition is fulfilled, but in doing so to obey, not fresh instructions on each repetition, but the same ones over and over again. To take a domestic analogy. Suppose Mother wants Tommy to call at the cobbler's every morning on his way to school to see if her shoes are done, she can ask him afresh every morning. Alternatively she can stick up a notice once and for all in the hall which he will see when he leaves for school and which tells him to call for the shoes, and also to destroy the notice when he comes back if he has the shoes with him.

The reader must accept it as a fact that digital computers can be constructed, and indeed have been constructed, according to the principles we have described, and that they can in fact mimic the actions of a human computer very closely.

The book of rules which we have described our human computer as using is of course a convenient fiction. Actual human computers really remember what they have got to do. If one wants to make a machine mimic the behaviour of the human computer in some complex operation one has to ask him how it is done, and then translate the answer into the form of an instruction table. Constructing instruction tables is usually described as "programming." To "programme a machine to carry out the operation A" means to put the appropriate instruction table into the machine so that it will do A.

An interesting variant on the idea of a digital computer is a "digital computer with a random element." These have instructions involving the throwing of a die or some equivalent electronic process; one such instruction might for instance be, "Throw the die and put the resulting number into store 1000." Sometimes such a machine is described as having free will (though I would not use this phrase myself). It is not normally possible to determine from observing a machine whether it has a random element, for a similar effect can be produced by such devices as making the choices depend on the digits of the decimal for $\pi$.

Most actual digital computers have only a finite store. There is no theoretical difficulty in the idea of a computer with an unlimited store. Of course only a finite part can have been used at any one time. Likewise only a finite amount can have been constructed, but we can imagine more and more being added as required. Such computers have special theoretical interest and will be called infinitive capacity computers.

The idea of a digital computer is an old one. Charles Babbage, Lucasian Professor of Mathematics at Cambridge from 1828 to 1839, planned such a machine, called the Analytical Engine, but it was never completed. Although Babbage had all the essential ideas, his machine was not at that time such a very attractive prospect. The speed which would have been available would be definitely faster than a human computer but something like 100 times slower than the Manchester machine, itself one of the slower of the modern machines. The storage was to be purely mechanical, using wheels and cards.

The fact that Babbage's Analytical Engine was to be entirely mechanical will help us to rid ourselves of a superstition. Importance is often attached to the fact that modern digital computers are electrical, and that the nervous system also is electrical. Since Babbage's machine was not electrical, and since all digital computers are in a sense equivalent, we see that this use of electricity cannot be of theoretical importance. Of course electricity usually comes in where fast signalling is concerned, so that it is not surprising that we find it in both these connections. In the nervous system chemical phenomena are at least as important as electrical. In certain computers the storage system is mainly acoustic. The feature of using electricity is thus seen to be only a very superficial similarity. If we wish to find such similarities we should look rather for mathematical analogies of function.

## 5 Universality of Digital Computers

The digital computers considered in the last section may be classified amongst the "discrete state machines." These are the machines which move by sudden jumps or clicks from one quite definite state to another. These states are sufficiently different for the possibility of confusion between them to be ignored. Strictly speaking there are no such machines. Everything really moves continuously. But there are many kinds of machine which can profitably be *thought of* as being discrete state machines. For instance in considering the switches for a lighting system it is a convenient fiction that each switch must be definitely on or definitely off. There must be intermediate positions, but for most purposes we can forget about them. As an example of a discrete state machine we might consider a wheel which clicks round through 120° once a second, but may be stopped by a lever which can be operated from outside; in addition a lamp is to light in one of the positions of the wheel. This machine could be described abstractly as follows. The internal state of the machine (which is described by the position of the wheel) may be $q_1$, $q_2$ or $q_3$. There is an input signal $i_0$ or $i_1$ (position of lever). The internal state at any moment is determined by the last state and input signal according to the table

Last State

$$q_1 \quad q_2 \quad q_3$$

Input

$$\begin{array}{c} i_0 \\ \\ i_1 \end{array} \begin{array}{ccc} q_2 & q_3 & q_1 \\ \cdot \\ q_1 & q_2 & q_3 \end{array}$$

The output signals, the only externally visible indication of the internal state (the light), are described by the table

State $\quad q_1 \quad q_2 \quad q_3$

Output $o_0 \quad o_0 \quad o_1$

This example is typical of discrete state machines. They can be described by such tables provided they have only a finite number of possible states.

It will seem that given the initial state of the machine and the input signals it is always possible to predict all future states. This is reminiscent of Laplace's view that from the complete state of the universe at one moment of time, as described by the positions and velocities of all particles, it should be possible to predict all future states. The prediction which we are considering is, however, rather nearer to practicability than that considered by Laplace. The system of the "universe as a whole" is such that quite small errors in the initial conditions can have an overwhelming effect at a later time. The displacement of a single electron by a billionth of a centimetre at one moment might make the difference between a man being killed by an avalanche a year later, or escaping. It is an essential property of the mechanical systems which we have called "discrete state machines" that this phenomenon does not occur. Even when we consider the actual physical machines instead of the idealised machines, reasonably accurate knowledge of the state at one moment yields reasonably accurate knowledge any number of steps later.

As we have mentioned, digital computers fall within the class of discrete state machines. But the number of states of which such a machine is capable is usually enormously large. For instance, the number for the machine now working at Manchester is about $2^{165,000}$, i.e. about $10^{50,000}$. Compare this with our example of the clicking wheel described above, which had three states. It is not difficult to see why the number of states should be so immense. The computer

includes a store corresponding to the paper used by a human computer. It must be possible to write into the store any one of the combinations of symbols which might have been written on the paper. For simplicity suppose that only digits from 0 to 9 are used as symbols. Variations in handwriting are ignored. Suppose the computer is allowed 100 sheets of paper each containing 50 lines each with room for 30 digits. Then the number of states is $10^{100 \times 50 \times 30}$, i.e. $10^{150,000}$. This is about the number of states of three Manchester machines put together. The logarithm to the base two of the number of states is usually called the "storage capacity" of the machine. Thus the Manchester machine has a storage capacity of about 165,000 and the wheel machine of our example about 1.6. If two machines are put together their capacities must be added to obtain the capacity of the resultant machine. This leads to the possibility of statements such as "The Manchester machine contains 64 magnetic tracks each with a capacity of 2560, eight electronic tubes with a capacity of 1280. Miscellaneous storage amounts to about 300 making a total of 174,380."

Given the table corresponding to a discrete state machine it is possible to predict what it will do. There is no reason why this calculation should not be carried out by means of a digital computer. Provided it could be carried out sufficiently quickly the digital computer could mimic the behaviour of any discrete state machine. The imitation game could then be played with the machine in question (as B) and the mimicking digital computer (as A) and the interrogator would be unable to distinguish them. Of course the digital computer must have an adequate storage capacity as well as working sufficiently fast. Moreover, it must be programmed afresh for each new machine which it is desired to mimic.

This special property of digital computers, that they can mimic any discrete state machine, is described by saying that they are *universal* machines. The existence of machines with this property has the important consequence that, considerations of speed apart, it is unnecessary to design various new machines to do various computing processes. They can all be done with one digital computer, suitably programmed for each case. It will be seen that as a consequence of this all digital computers are in a sense equivalent.

We may now consider again the point raised at the end of §3. It was suggested tentatively that the question, "Can machines think?" should be replaced by "Are there imaginable digital computers which would do well in the imitation game?" If we wish we can make this superficially more general and ask "Are there discrete state machines which would do well?" But in view of the universality property we see that either of these questions is equivalent to this, "Let us fix our attention on one particular digital computer C. Is it true that by modifying this computer to have an adequate storage, suitably increasing its speed of action, and providing it with an appropriate programme, C can be made to play satisfactorily the part of A in the imitation game, the part of B being taken by a man?"

## 6 Contrary Views on the Main Question

We may now consider the ground to have been cleared and we are ready to proceed to the debate on our question, "Can machines think?" and the variant of it quoted at the end of the last section. We cannot altogether abandon the original form of the problem, for opinions will differ as to the appropriateness of the substitution and we must at least listen to what has to be said in this connection.

It will simplify matters for the reader if I explain first my own beliefs in the matter. Consider first the more accurate form of the question. I believe that in about fifty years' time it will be possible to programme computers with a storage capacity of about $10^9$ to make them play the imitation game so well that an average interrogator will not have more than 70 per cent. chance of making the right identification after five minutes of questioning. The original question, "Can machines think?" I believe to be too meaningless to deserve discussion. Nevertheless I believe that at the end of the century the use of words and general educated opinion will have altered so much that one will be able to speak of machines thinking without expecting to be contradicted. I believe further that no useful purpose is served by concealing these beliefs. The popular view that scientists proceed inexorably from well-established fact to well-established fact, never being influenced by any unproved conjecture, is quite mistaken. Provided it is made clear which are proved facts and which are conjectures, no harm can result. Conjectures are of great importance since they suggest useful lines of research.

I now proceed to consider opinions opposed to my own.

## (1) The Theological Objection

Thinking is a function of man's immortal soul. God has given an immortal soul to every man and woman, but not to any other animal or to machines. Hence no animal or machine can think.

I am unable to accept any part of this, but will attempt to reply in theological terms. I should find the argument more convincing if animals were classed with men, for there is a greater difference, to my mind, between the typical animate and the inanimate than there is between man and the other animals. The arbitrary character of the orthodox view becomes clearer if we consider how it might appear to a member of some other religious community. How do Christians regard the Moslem view that women have no souls? But let us leave this point aside and return to the main argument. It appears to me that the argument quoted above implies a serious restriction of the omnipotence of the Almighty. It is admitted that there are certain things that He cannot do such as making one equal to two,[1] but should we not believe that He has freedom to confer a soul on an elephant if He sees fit? We might expect that He would only exercise this power in conjunction with a mutation which provided the elephant with an appropriately improved brain to minister to the needs of this soul. An argument of exactly similar form may be made for the case of machines. It may seem different because it is more difficult to "swallow". But this really only means that we think it would be less likely that He would consider the circumstances suitable for conferring a soul. The circumstances in question are discussed in the rest of this paper. In attempting to construct such machines we should not be irreverently usurping His power of creating souls, any more than we are in the procreation of children: rather we are, in either case, instruments of His will providing mansions for the souls that He creates.

However, this is mere speculation. I am not very impressed with theological arguments whatever they may be used to support. Such arguments have often been found unsatisfactory in the past. In the time of Galileo it was argued that the texts, "And the sun stood still ... and hasted not to go down about a whole day" (Joshua x. 13) and "He laid the foundations of the earth, that it should not move at any time" (Psalm cv. 5) were an adequate refutation of the Copernican theory. With our present knowledge such an argument appears futile. When that knowledge was not available it made a quite different impression.

## (2) The "Heads in the Sand" Objection

"The consequences of machines thinking would be too dreadful. Let us hope and believe that they cannot do so."

This argument is seldom expressed quite so openly as in the form above. But it affects most of us who think about it at all. We like to believe that Man is in some subtle way superior to the rest of creation. It is best if he can be shown to be *necessarily* superior, for then there is no danger of him losing his commanding position. The popularity of the theological argument is clearly connected with this feeling. It is likely to be quite strong in intellectual people, since they value the power of thinking more highly than others, and are more inclined to base their belief in the superiority of Man on this power.

I do not think that this argument is sufficiently substantial to require refutation. Consolation would be more appropriate: perhaps this should be sought in the transmigration of souls.

## (3) The Mathematical Objection

There are a number of results of mathematical logic which can be used to show that there are limitations to the powers of discrete-state machines. The best known of these results is known as *Gödel's* theorem,[2] and shows that in any sufficiently powerful logical system statements can be formulated which can neither be proved nor disproved within the system, unless possibly the system itself is inconsistent. There are other, in some respects similar, results due to *Church, Kleene, Rosser,* and *Turing.* The latter result is the most convenient to consider, since it refers directly to machines, whereas the others can only be used in a comparatively indirect argument: for instance if Gödel's theorem is to be used we need in addition to have some means of describing logical systems in terms of machines, and machines in terms of logical systems. The result in question refers to a type of machine which is essentially a digital computer with an infinite capacity. It states that there are certain things that such a machine cannot do. If it is rigged up to give answers to questions as in the imitation game, there will be some questions to which it will either give a wrong answer, or fail to give an answer at all however much time is allowed for a reply. There may, of course, be many such questions, and questions which cannot be answered by one machine may be satisfactorily answered by another. We are of course supposing for the present that the questions are of the kind

to which an answer "Yes" or "No" is appropriate, rather than questions such as "What do you think of Picasso?" The questions that we know the machines must fail on are of this type, "Consider the machine specified as follows. . . . Will this machine ever answer 'Yes' to any question?" The dots are to be replaced by a description of some machine in a standard form, which could be something like that used in §5. When the machine described bears a certain comparatively simple relation to the machine which is under interrogation, it can be shown that the answer is either wrong or not forthcoming. This is the mathematical result: it is argued that it proves a disability of machines to which the human intellect is not subject.

The short answer to this argument is that although it is established that there are limitations to the powers of any particular machine, it has only been stated, without any sort of proof, that no such limitations apply to the human intellect. But I do not think this view can be dismissed quite so lightly. Whenever one of these machines is asked the appropriate critical question, and gives a definite answer, we know that this answer must be wrong, and this gives us a certain feeling of superiority. Is this feeling illusory? It is no doubt quite genuine, but I do not think too much importance should be attached to it. We too often give wrong answers to questions ourselves to be justified in being very pleased at such evidence of fallibility on the part of the machines. Further, our superiority can only be felt on such an occasion in relation to the one machine over which we have scored our petty triumph. There would be no question of triumphing simultaneously over *all* machines. In short, then, there might be men cleverer than any given machine, but then again there might be other machines cleverer again, and so on.

Those who hold to the mathematical argument would, I think, mostly be willing to accept the imitation game as a basis for discussion. Those who believe in the two previous objections would probably not be interested in any criteria.

## (4) The Argument from Consciousness

This argument is very well expressed in *Professor Jefferson's* Lister Oration for 1949, from which I quote.

> Not until a machine can write a sonnet or compose a concerto because of thoughts and emotions felt, and not by the chance fall of symbols, could we agree that machine equals brain—that is, not only write it but know that it had written it. No mechanism could feel (and not merely artificially signal, an easy

contrivance) pleasure at its successes, grief when its valves fuse, be warmed by flattery, be made miserable by its mistakes, be charmed by sex, be angry or depressed when it cannot get what it wants.

This argument appears to be a denial of the validity of our test. According to the most extreme form of this view the only way by which one could be sure that a machine thinks is to *be* the machine and to feel oneself thinking. One could then describe these feelings to the world, but of course no one would be justified in taking any notice. Likewise according to this view the only way to know that a *man* thinks is to be that particular man. It is in fact the solipsist point of view. It may be the most logical view to hold but it makes communication of ideas difficult. A is liable to believe "A thinks but B does not" whilst B believes "B thinks but A does not." Instead of arguing continually over this point it is usual to have the polite convention that everyone thinks.

I am sure that Professor Jefferson does not wish to adopt the extreme and solipsist point of view. Probably he would be quite willing to accept the imitation game as a test. The game (with the player B omitted) is frequently used in practice under the name of *viva voce* to discover whether some one really understands something or has "learnt it parrot fashion." Let us listen in to a part of such a *viva voce:*

> Interrogator: In the first line of your sonnet which reads "Shall I compare thee to a summer's day," would not "a spring day" do as well or better?
>
> Witness: It wouldn't scan.
>
> Interrogator: How about "a winter's day"? That would scan all right.
>
> Witness: Yes, but nobody wants to be compared to a winter's day.
>
> Interrogator: Would you say Mr. Pickwick reminded you of Christmas?
>
> Witness: In a way.
>
> Interrogator: Yet Christmas is a winter's day, and I do not think Mr. Pickwick would mind the comparison.
>
> Witness: I don't think you're serious. By a winter's day one means a typical winter's day, rather than a special one like Christmas.

And so on. What would Professor Jefferson say if the sonnet-writing machine was able to answer like this in the *viva voce?* I do not know whether he would regard the machine as "merely artificially signalling" these answers, but if the answers were as satisfactory and sustained as in the above passage I do not think he would describe it as "an easy contrivance." This phrase is, I think, intended to cover such devices as the inclusion in the machine of a record of someone reading a sonnet, with appropriate switching to turn it on from time to time.

In short then, I think that most of those who support the argument from consciousness could be persuaded to abandon it rather than be forced into the solipsist position. They will then probably be willing to accept our test.

I do not wish to give the impression that I think there is no mystery about consciousness. There is, for instance, something of a paradox connected with any attempt to localise it. But I do not think these mysteries necessarily need to be solved before we can answer the question with which we are concerned in this paper.

## (5) Arguments from Various Disabilities

These arguments take the form, "I grant you that you can make machines do all the things you have mentioned but you will never be able to make one to do X". Numerous features X are suggested in this connection. I offer a selection:

> Be kind, resourceful, beautiful, friendly (§6(5)), have initiative, have a sense of humour, tell right from wrong, make mistakes (§6(5)), fall in love, enjoy strawberries and cream (§(5)), make some one fall in love with it, learn from experience (§7), use words properly, be the subject of its own thought (§6(5)), have as much diversity of behaviour as a man, do something really new (§6(6)). (Some of these disabilities are given special consideration as indicated by the section numbers.)

No support is usually offered for these statements. I believe they are mostly founded on the principle of scientific induction. A man has seen thousands of machines in his lifetime. From what he sees of them he draws a number of general conclusions. They are ugly, each is designed for a very limited purpose, when required for a minutely different purpose they are useless, the variety of behaviour of any one of them is very small, etc., etc. Naturally he concludes that these are necessary properties of machines in general. Many of these limitations are associated with the very small storage capacity of most machines. (I am assuming that the idea of storage capacity is extended in some way to cover machines other than discrete-state machines. The exact definition does not matter as no mathematical accuracy is claimed in the present discussion.) A few years ago, when very little had been heard of digital computers, it was possible to elicit much incredulity concerning them, if one mentioned their properties without describing their construction. That was presumably due to a similar application of the principle of scientific induction. These applications of the principle are of course largely unconscious. When a burnt child fears the fire and shows that he fears it by avoiding it, I should say that he was applying scientific induction. (I could of course also describe his behaviour in many other ways.) The works and customs of mankind do not seem to be very suitable material to which to apply scientific induction. A very large part of space-time must be investigated, if reliable results are to be obtained. Otherwise we may (as most English children do) decide that everybody speaks English, and that it is silly to learn French.

There are, however, special remarks to be made about many of the disabilities that have been mentioned. The inability to enjoy strawberries and cream may have struck the reader as frivolous. Possibly a machine might be made to enjoy this delicious dish, but any attempt to make one do so would be idiotic. What is important about this disability is that it contributes to some of the other disabilities, *e.g.* to the difficulty of the same kind of friendliness occurring between man and machine as between white man and white man, or between black man and black man.

The claim that "machines cannot make mistakes" seems a curious one. One is tempted to retort, "Are they any the worse for that?" But let us adopt a more sympathetic attitude, and try to see what is really meant. I think this criticism can be explained in terms of the imitation game. It is claimed that the interrogator could distinguish the machine from the man simply by setting them a number of problems in arithmetic. The machine would be unmasked because of its deadly accuracy. The reply to this is simple. The machine (programmed for playing the game) would not attempt to give the *right* answers to the arithmetic problems. It would deliberately introduce mistakes in a manner calculated to confuse the interrogator. A mechanical fault would probably show itself through an unsuitable decision as

to what sort of a mistake to make in the arithmetic. Even this interpretation of the criticism is not sufficiently sympathetic. But we cannot afford the space to go into it much further. It seems to me that this criticism depends on a confusion between two kinds of mistake. We may call them "errors of functioning" and "errors of conclusion." Errors of functioning are due to some mechanical or electrical fault which causes the machine to behave otherwise than it was designed to do. In philosophical discussions one likes to ignore the possibility of such errors; one is therefore discussing "abstract machines." These abstract machines are mathematical fictions rather than physical objects. By definition they are incapable of errors of functioning. In this sense we can truly say that "machines can never make mistakes." Errors of conclusion can only arise when some meaning is attached to the output signals from the machine. The machine might, for instance, type out mathematical equations, or sentences in English. When a false proposition is typed we say that the machine has committed an error of conclusion. There is clearly no reason at all for saying that a machine cannot make this kind of mistake. It might do nothing but type out repeatedly "0=1." To take a less perverse example, it might have some method for drawing conclusions by scientific induction. We must expect such a method to lead occasionally to erroneous results.

The claim that a machine cannot be the subject of its own thought can of course only be answered if it can be shown that the machine has *some* thought with *some* subject matter. Nevertheless, "the subject matter of a machine's operations" does seem to mean something, at least to the people who deal with it. If, for instance, the machine was trying to find a solution of the equation $x^2 - 40x - 11 = 0$ one would be tempted to describe this equation as part of the machine's subject matter at that moment. In this sort of sense a machine undoubtedly can be its own subject matter. It may be used to help in making up its own programmes, or to predict the effect of alterations in its own structure. By observing the results of its own behaviour it can modify its own programmes so as to achieve some purpose more effectively. These are possibilities of the near future, rather than Utopian dreams.

The criticism that a machine cannot have much diversity of behaviour is just a way of saying that it cannot have much storage capacity. Until fairly recently a storage capacity of even a thousand digits was very rare.

The criticisms that we are considering here are often disguised forms of the argument from consciousness. Usually if one maintains that a machine *can* do one of these things, and describes the. kind of method that the machine could use, one will not make much of an impression. It is thought that the method (whatever it may be, for it must be mechanical) is really rather base. Compare the parenthesis in Jefferson's statement quoted in §5(4).

## (6) Lady Lovelace's Objection

Our most detailed information of Babbage's Analytical Engine comes from a memoir by *Lady Lovelace.* In it she states, "The Analytical Engine has no pretensions to *originate* anything. It can do *whatever we know how to order it* to perform" (her italics). This statement is quoted by *Hartree* (p.70) who adds: "This does not imply that it may not be possible to construct electronic equipment which will 'think for itself', or in which, in biological terms, one could set up a conditioned reflex, which would serve as a basis for 'learning.' Whether this is possible in principle or not is a stimulating and exciting question, suggested by some of these recent developments. But it did not seem that the machines constructed or projected at the time had this property."

I am in thorough agreement with Hartree over this. It will be noticed that he does not assert that the machines in question had not got the property, but rather that the evidence available to Lady Lovelace did not encourage her to believe that they had it. It is quite possible that the machines in question had in a sense got this property. For suppose that some discrete-state machine has the property. The Analytical Engine was a universal digital computer, so that, if its storage capacity and speed were adequate, it could by suitable programming be made to mimic the machine in question. Probably this argument did not occur to the Countess or to Babbage. In any case there was no obligation on them to claim all that could be claimed.

This whole question will be considered again under the heading of Learning Machines (§7).

A variant of Lady Lovelace's objection states that a machine can "never do anything really new." This may be parried for a moment with the saw, "There is nothing new under the sun." Who can be certain that "original work" that he has done was not simply the growth of the seed planted in him by teaching, or the effect of following well-known general principles. A better variant of the objection says that a machine can never "take us by surprise." This statement is a more direct challenge and can be met directly. Machines take me by surprise with great frequency. This is largely because I do not do sufficient calculation to decide what to expect them to do, or rather because, although I do a calculation, I do it in a hurried, slipshod fashion, taking risks. Perhaps I say to myself, "I suppose the voltage here ought to be the same as there: anyway let's assume it is." Naturally I am often wrong, and the result is a surprise for me for by the time the experiment is done these assumptions have been forgotten. These admissions lay me open to lectures on the subject of my vicious ways, but do not throw any doubt on my credibility when I testify to the surprises I experience.

I do not expect this reply to silence my critic. He will probably say that such surprises are due to some creative mental act on my part, and reflect no credit on the machine. This leads us back to the argument from consciousness, and far from the idea of surprise. It is a line of argument we must consider closed, but it is perhaps worth remarking that the appreciation of something as surprising requires as much of a "creative mental act" whether the surprising event originates from a man, a book, a machine or anything else.

The view that machines cannot give rise to surprises is due, I believe, to a fallacy to which philosophers and mathematicians are particularly subject. This is the assumption that as soon as a fact is presented to a mind all consequences of that fact spring into the mind simultaneously with it. It is a very useful assumption under many circumstances, but one too easily forgets that it is false. A natural consequence of doing so is that one then assumes that there is no virtue in the mere working out of consequences from data and general principles.

## (7) Argument from Continuity in the Nervous System

The nervous system is certainly not a discrete-state machine. A small error in the information about the size of a nervous impulse impinging on a neuron, may make a large difference to the size of the outgoing impulse. It may be argued that, this being so, one cannot expect to be able to mimic the behaviour of the nervous system with a discrete-state system.

It is true that a discrete-state machine must be different from a continuous machine. But if we adhere to the conditions of the imitation game, the interrogator will not be able to take any advantage of this difference. The situation can be made clearer if we consider some other simpler continuous machine. A differential analyser will do very well. (A differential analyser is a certain kind of machine not of the discrete-state type used for some kinds of calculation.) Some of these provide their answers in a typed form, and so are suitable for taking part in the game. It would not be possible for a digital computer to predict exactly what answers the differential analyser would give to a problem, but it would be quite capable of giving the right sort of answer. For instance, if asked to give the value of $\pi$ (actually about 3.1416) it would be reasonable to choose at random between the values 3.12, 3.13, 3.14, 3.15, 3.16 with the probabilities of 0.05, 0.15, 0.55, 0.19, 0.06 (say). Under these circumstances it would be very difficult for the interrogator to distinguish the differential analyser from the digital computer.

## (8) The Argument from Informality of Behaviour

It is not possible to produce a set of rules purporting to describe what a man should do in every conceivable set of circumstances. One might for instance have a rule that one is to stop when one sees a red traffic light, and to go if one sees a green one, but what if by some fault both appear together? One may perhaps decide that it is safest to stop. But some further difficulty may well arise from this decision later. To attempt to provide rules of conduct to cover every eventuality, even those arising from traffic lights, appears to be impossible. With all this I agree.

From this it is argued that we cannot be machines. I shall try to reproduce the argument, but I fear I shall hardly do it justice. It seems to run something like this. "If each man had a definite set of rules of conduct by which he regulated his life he would be no better than a machine. But there are no such rules, so men cannot be machines." The undistributed middle is glaring. I do not think the argument is ever put quite like this, but I believe this is the argument used nevertheless. There may however be a certain confusion between "rules of conduct" and "laws of behaviour" to cloud the issue. By "rules of conduct" I mean precepts such as "Stop if you see red lights," on which one can act, and of which one can be conscious. By "laws of behaviour" I mean laws of nature as applied to a man's body such as "if you pinch him he will squeak." If we substitute "laws of behaviour which regulate his life" for "laws of conduct by which he regulates his life" in the argument quoted the undistributed middle is no longer insuperable. For we believe that it is not only true that being regulated by laws of behaviour implies being some

sort of machine (though not necessarily a discrete-state machine), but that conversely being such a machine implies being regulated by such laws. However, we cannot so easily convince ourselves of the absence of complete laws of behaviour as of complete rules of conduct. The only way we know of for finding such laws is scientific observation, and we certainly know of no circumstances under which we could say, "We have searched enough. There are no such laws."

We can demonstrate more forcibly that any such statement would be unjustified. For suppose we could be sure of finding such laws if they existed. Then given a discrete-state machine it should certainly be possible to discover by observation sufficient about it to predict its future behaviour, and this within a reasonable time, say a thousand years. But this does not seem to be the case. I have set up on the Manchester computer a small programme using only 1000 units of storage, whereby the machine supplied with one sixteen figure number replies with another within two seconds. I would defy anyone to learn from these replies sufficient about the programme to be able to predict any replies to untried values.

## (9) The Argument from Extra-Sensory Perception

I assume that the reader is familiar with the idea of extra-sensory perception, and the meaning of the four items of it, *viz.* telepathy, clairvoyance, precognition and psycho-kinesis. These disturbing phenomena seem to deny all our usual scientific ideas. How we should like to discredit them! Unfortunately the statistical evidence, at least for telepathy, is overwhelming. It is very difficult to rearrange one's ideas so as to fit these new facts in. Once one has accepted them it does not seem a very big step to believe in ghosts and bogies. The idea that our bodies move simply according to the known laws of physics, together with some others not yet discovered but somewhat similar, would be one of the first to go.

This argument is to my mind quite a strong one. One can say in reply that many scientific theories seem to remain workable in practice, in spite of clashing with E.S.P.; that in fact one can get along very nicely if one forgets about it. This is rather cold comfort, and one fears that thinking is just the kind of phenomenon where E.S.P. may be especially relevant.

A more specific argument based on E.S.P. might run as follows:

"Let us play the imitation game, using as witnesses a man who is good as a telepathic receiver, and a digital computer. The interrogator can ask such questions as "What suit does the card in my right hand belong to?" The man by telepathy or clairvoyance gives the right answer 130 times out of 400 cards. The machine can only guess at random, and perhaps gets 104 right, so the interrogator makes the right identification." There is an interesting possibility which opens here. Suppose the digital computer contains a random number generator. Then it will be natural to use this to decide what answer to give. But then the random number generator will be subject to the psycho-kinetic powers of the interrogator. Perhaps this psycho-kinesis might cause the machine to guess right more often than would be expected on a probability calculation, so that the interrogator might still be unable to make the right identification. On the other hand, he might be able to guess right without any questioning, by clairvoyance. With E.S.P. anything may happen.

If telepathy is admitted it will be necessary to tighten our test up. The situation could be regarded as analogous to that which would occur if the interrogator were talking to himself and one of the competitors was listening with his ear to the wall. To put the competitors into a "telepathy-proof room" would satisfy all requirements.

## 7 Learning Machines

The reader will have anticipated that I have no very convincing arguments of a positive nature to support my views. If I had I should not have taken such pains to point out the fallacies in contrary views. Such evidence as I have I shall now give.

Let us return for a moment to Lady Lovelace's objection, which stated that the machine can only do what we tell it to do. One could say that a man can "inject" an idea into the machine, and that it will respond to a certain extent and then drop into quiescence, like a piano string struck by a hammer. Another simile would be an atomic pile of less than critical size: an injected idea is to correspond to a neutron entering the pile from without. Each such neutron will cause a certain disturbance which eventually dies away. If, however, the size of the pile is sufficiently increased, the disturbance caused by such an incoming neutron will very likely go on and on increasing until the whole pile is destroyed. Is there a corresponding phenomenon for minds, and is there one for machines? There does seem to be one for the human mind. The majority of them seem to be "sub-critical," i.e. to correspond in this analogy to piles of sub-critical size. An

idea presented to such a mind will on average give rise to less than one idea in reply. A smallish proportion are super-critical. An idea presented to such a mind may give rise to a whole "theory" consisting of secondary, tertiary and more remote ideas. Animals minds seem to be very definitely sub-critical. Adhering to this analogy we ask, "Can a machine be made to be super-critical?"

The "skin of an onion" analogy is also helpful. In considering the functions of the mind or the brain we find certain operations which we can explain in purely mechanical terms. This we say does not correspond to the real mind: it is a sort of skin which we must strip off if we are to find the real mind. But then in what remains we find a further skin to be stripped off, and so on. Proceeding in this way do we ever come to the "real" mind, or do we eventually come to the skin which has nothing in it? In the latter case the whole mind is mechanical. (It would not be a discrete-state machine however. We have discussed this.)

These last two paragraphs do not claim to be convincing arguments. They should rather be described as "recitations tending to produce belief."

The only really satisfactory support that can be given for the view expressed at the beginning of §6, will be that provided by waiting for the end of the century and then doing the experiment described. But what can we say in the meantime? What steps should be taken now if the experiment is to be successful?

As I have explained, the problem is mainly one of programming. Advances in engineering will have to be made too, but it seems unlikely that these will not be adequate for the requirements. Estimates of the storage capacity of the brain vary from $10^{10}$ to $10^{15}$ binary digits. I incline to the lower values and believe that only a very small fraction is used for the higher types of thinking. Most of it is probably used for the retention of visual impressions. I should be surprised if more than $10^9$ was required for satisfactory playing of the imitation game, at any rate against a blind man. (Note—The capacity of the *Encyclopaedia Britannica*, 11th edition, is $2 \times 10^9$.) A storage capacity of $10^7$ would be a very practicable possibility even by present techniques. It is probably not necessary to increase the speed of operations of the machines at all. Parts of modern machines which can be regarded as analogues of nerve cells work about a thousand times faster than the latter. This should provide a "margin of safety" which could cover losses of speed arising in many ways. Our problem then is to find out how to programme these machines to play the game. At my present rate of working I produce about a thousand digits of programme a day, so that about sixty workers, working steadily through the fifty years might accomplish the job, if nothing went into the waste-paper basket. Some more expeditious method seems desirable.

In the process of trying to imitate an adult human mind we are bound to think a good deal about the process which has brought it to the state that it is in. We may notice three components,

(a) The initial state of the mind, say at birth,

(b) The education to which it has been subjected,

(c) Other experience, not to be described as education, to which it has been subjected.

Instead of trying to produce a programme to simulate the adult mind, why not rather try to produce one which simulates the child's? If this were then subjected to an appropriate course of education one would obtain the adult brain. Presumably the child-brain is something like a note-book as one buys it from the stationers. Rather little mechanism, and lots of blank sheets. (Mechanism and writing are from our point of view almost synonymous.) Our hope is that there is so little mechanism in the child-brain that something like it can be easily programmed. The amount of work in the education we can assume, as a first approximation, to be much the same as for the human child.

We have thus divided our problem into two parts. The child-programme and the education process. These two remain very closely connected. We cannot expect to find a good child-machine at the first attempt. One must experiment with teaching one such machine and see how well it learns. One can then try another and see if it is better or worse. There is an obvious connection between this process and evolution, by the identifications

Structure of the child-machine = Hereditary material

Changes of the child-machine = Mutations

Natural selection = Judgment of the experimenter

One may hope, however, that this process will be more expeditious than evolution. The survival of the fittest is a slow method for measuring advantages. The experimenter, by the exercise of intelligence, should be able to speed it up. Equally important is the fact that he is not restricted to random mutations. If he can trace a cause for some weakness he can probably think of the kind of mutation which will improve it.

It will not be possible to apply exactly the same teaching process to the machine as to a normal child. It will not, for instance, be provided with legs, so that it could not be asked to go out and fill the coal scuttle. Possibly it might not have eyes. But however well these deficiencies might be overcome by clever engineering, one could not send the creature to school with out the other children making excessive fun of it. It must be given some tuition. We need not be too concerned about the legs, eyes, etc. The example of Miss *Helen Keller* shows that education can take place provided that communication in both directions between teacher and pupil can take place by some means or other.

We normally associate punishments and rewards with the teaching process. Some simple child-machines can be constructed or programmed on this sort of principle. The machine has to be so constructed that events which shortly preceded the occurrence of a punishment-signal are unlikely to be repeated, whereas a reward-signal increased the probability of repetition of the events which led up to it. These definitions do not presuppose any feelings on the part of the machine. I have done some experiments with one such child-machine, and succeeded in teaching it a few things, but the teaching method was too unorthodox for the experiment to be considered really successful.

The use of punishments and rewards can at best be a part of the teaching process. Roughly speaking, if the teacher has no other means of communicating to the pupil, the amount of information which can reach him does not exceed the total number of rewards and punishments applied. By the time a child has learnt to repeat "Casabianca" he would probably feel very sore indeed, if the text could only be discovered by a "Twenty Questions" technique, every "NO" taking the form of a blow. It is necessary therefore to have some other "unemotional" channels of communication. If these are available it is possible to teach a machine by punishments and rewards to obey orders given in some language, *e.g.* a symbolic language. These orders are to be transmitted through the "unemotional" channels. The use of this language will diminish greatly the number of punishments and rewards required.

Opinions may vary as to the complexity which is suitable in the child-machine. One might try to make it as simple as possible consistently with the general principles. Alternatively one might have a complete system of logical inference "built in."[3] In the latter case the store would be largely occupied with definitions and propositions. The propositions would have various kinds of status, *e.g.* well-established facts, conjectures, mathematically proved theorems, statements given by an authority, expressions having the logical form of proposition but not belief-value. Certain propositions may be described as "imperatives." The machine should be so constructed that as soon as an imperative is classed as "well-established" the appropriate action automatically takes place. To illustrate this, suppose the teacher says to the machine, "Do your homework now." This may cause "Teacher says 'Do your homework now'" to be included amongst the well-established facts. Another such fact might be, "Everything that teacher says is true." Combining these may eventually lead to the imperative, "Do your homework now," being included amongst the well-established facts, and this, by the construction of the machine, will mean that the homework actually gets started, but the effect is very satisfactory. The processes of inference used by the machine need not be such as would satisfy the most exacting logicians. There might for instance be no hierarchy of types. But this need not mean that type fallacies will occur, any more than we are bound to fall over unfenced cliffs. Suitable imperatives (expressed *within* the systems, not forming part of the rules *of* the system) such as "Do not use a class unless it is a subclass of one which has been mentioned by teacher" can have a similar effect to "Do not go too near the edge."

The imperatives that can be obeyed by a machine that has no limbs are bound to be of a rather intellectual character, as in the example (doing homework) given above. Important amongst such imperatives will be ones which regulate the order in which the rules of the logical system concerned are to be applied. For each stage when one is using a logical system, there is a very large number of alternative steps, any of which one is permitted to apply, so far as obedience to the rules of the logical system is concerned. These choices make the difference between a brilliant and a footling reasoner, not the difference between a sound and a fallacious one. Propositions leading to imperatives of this kind might be "When Socrates is mentioned, use the syllogism in Barbara" or "If one method has been proved to be quicker than another, do not use the slower method." Some of these may

be "given by authority," but others may be produced by the machine itself, *e.g.* by scientific induction.

The idea of a learning machine may appear paradoxical to some readers. How can the rules of operation of the machine change? They should describe completely how the machine will react whatever its history might be, whatever changes it might undergo. The rules are thus quite time-invariant. This is quite true. The explanation of the paradox is that the rules which get changed in the learning process are of a rather less pretentious kind, claiming only an ephemeral validity. The reader may draw a parallel with the Constitution of the United States.

An important feature of a learning machine is that its teacher will often be very largely ignorant of quite what is going on inside, although he may still be able to some extent to predict his pupil's behaviour. This should apply most strongly to the later education of a machine arising from a child-machine of well-tried design (or programme). This is in clear contrast with normal procedure when using a machine to do computations: one's object is then to have a clear mental picture of the state of the machine at each moment in the computation. This object can only be achieved with a struggle. The view that "the machine can only do what we know how to order it to do,"[4] appears strange in face of this. Most of the programmes which we can put into the machine will result in its doing something that we cannot make sense of at all, or which we regard as completely random behaviour. Intelligent behaviour presumably consists in a departure from the completely disciplined behaviour involved in computation, but a rather slight one, which does not give rise to random behaviour, or to pointless repetitive loops. Another important result of preparing our machine for its part in the imitation game by a process of teaching and learning is that "human fallibility" is likely to be omitted in a rather natural way, *i.e.* without special "coaching." (The reader should reconcile this with the point of view in §6(5).) Processes that are learnt do not produce a hundred per cent. certainty of result; if they did they could not be unlearnt.

It is probably wise to include a random element in a learning machine (see §4). A random element is rather useful when we are searching for a solution of some problem. Suppose for instance we wanted to find a number between 50 and 200 which was equal to the square of the sum of its digits, we might start at 51 then try 52 and go on until we got a number that worked. Alternatively we might choose numbers at random until we got a good one. This method has the advantage that it is unnecessary to keep track of the values that have been tried, but the disadvantage that one may try the same one twice, but this is not very important if there are several solutions. The systematic method has the disadvantage that there may be an enormous block without any solutions in the region which has to be investigated first. Now the learning process may be regarded as a search for a form of behaviour which will satisfy the teacher (or some other criterion). Since there is probably a very large number of satisfactory solutions the random method seems to be better than the systematic. It should be noticed that it is used in the analogous process of evolution. But there the systematic method is not possible. How could one keep track of the different genetical combinations that had been tried, so as to avoid trying them again?

We may hope that machines will eventually compete with men in all purely intellectual fields. But which are the best ones to start with? Even this is a difficult decision. Many people think that a very abstract activity, like the playing of chess would be best. It can also be maintained that it is best to provide the machine with the best sense organs that money can buy, and then teach it to understand and speak English. This process could follow the normal teaching of a child. Things would be pointed out and named, etc. Again I do not know what the right answer is, but I think both approaches should be tried.

We can only see a short distance ahead, but we can see plenty there that needs to be done.

Bibliography

Samuel Butler, Erewhon, London, 1865. Chapters 28, 24, 25, *The Book of the Machines*.

Alonzo Church, An Unsolvable Problem of Elementary Number Theory *American J. of Math.*, 58 (1936), 345–363.

K. Gödel, Über formal unentscheidbare Sätze der Principia Mathematica und verwandter Systeme, I, *Monatshefte für Math. und Phys.*, (1931), 173–189.

D. R. Hartree, *Calculating Instruments and Machines*, New York, 1949.

S. C. Kleene, General Recursive Functions of Natural Numbers *American J. of Math.*, 57 (1935), 153–173 and 219–244.

G. Jefferson, *The Mind of Mechanical Man*, Lister Oration for 1949 British Medical Journal, vol. i (1949), 1105–1121.

Countess of Lovelace, Translator's notes to an article on Babbage's Analytical Engine *Scientific Memoir* (ed. by R. Taylor), vol. 3 (1842), 691–731.

Bertrand Russell, *History of Western Philosophy*, London 1940.

A. M. Turing, On Computable Numbers, with an Application to the Entscheidungsproblem, *Proc. London Math. Soc.* (2), 42 (1937), 230–265.

Notes

1. Possibly this view is heretical. St. Thomas Aquinas (Summa Theologica, quoted by Bertrand Russell, 1, 480) states that God cannot make a man to have no soul. But this may not be a real restriction on His powers, but only a result of the fact that men's souls are immortal, and therefore indestructible.

2. Authors' names in italics refer to the Bibliography.

3. Or rather "programmed in" for our child-machine will be programmed in a digital computer. But the logical system will not have to be learnt.

4. Compare Lady Lovelace's statement (§5(6)), which does not contain the word "only."

# 04. [Introduction]
# Men, Machines, and
# the World About

Norbert Wiener began working toward *cybernetics* while engaged in a World War II research project. This project, like the atomic bomb, was funded and organized by Vannevar Bush's (◊02) academic/industrial/military "iron triangle." In response to the dropping of the bomb and other horrors of the war, Wiener decided that a new type of scientist was required, a scientist engaged with the consequences of scientific work (as Wiener argued eloquently in the open letter "A Scientist Rebels"). In the following selection, first delivered as an address to the New York Academy of Medicine and Science, Wiener explained some of the history and concepts of his new cybernetic science, while simultaneously attempting to be the new scientist for which he had called.

Cybernetics is perhaps most immediately recognized for bringing the "cyber" prefix into English usage in terms like "cyborg" and "cyberspace." Other, less immediately obvious terms were also introduced into common speech by Wiener's writings on cybernetics—including "feedback," "input," and "output." These words had existed in English, but for very narrow technical purposes—for the description of engineering problems, the description of machines. Now they are used to describe human interchanges, as when one asks for "feedback" from a colleague on an idea.

Cyberneticists sought to create an overarching study of "communication and control in the animal and machine." The work of the cyberneticists was extremely influential, redefining the object of study for many scientists and technologists. Before cybernetics, technology was largely defined in terms of mechanics. Studies involved movements of power and accompanying observable, physical changes such as one might have found inside Vannevar Bush's memex: its operations of request, recording, calculation, and display moving like an intricate jukebox or clockwork. When "communication and control" became the object of study, the ground shifted. Communication and control involve power differentials and have physical manifestations, to be sure, but are more akin to the workings of a digital computer: most observable, not with a voltage meter or the gaze of the naked eye, but from the inside, from within the system. And these systems tend to overflow the boundaries of any single object. As a result some previous studies of isolated objects seemed outmoded in a cybernetic context, while cybernetics created a framework for studying communication and control systems that spread across multiple entities. The first of these studied, and perhaps the defining case of cybernetics, was the subject of the WWII research project on which Wiener worked: the system of a bomber, an anti-aircraft gun, and the human operators of each.

As Katherine Hayles points out, this type of study has the effect of eroding liberal humanist ideas of subjectivity. That is to say, if we humans are simply parts of systems—our skins not boundaries but permeable membranes, our actions measured as behavior rather than by introspection—the autonomous, sufficient "self" begins to seem an illusion. This anticipates some poststructuralist positions, and echoes, in some ways, Zen Buddhism. However, anticipating many U.S. reactions to poststructuralism and Zen, Wiener did not embrace this thought.

Wiener's devotion to social justice—to becoming a scientist engaged with the social outcomes of his work—is particularly notable in the McCarthyite context of the 1950s. After World War II Wiener refused to take any military funding for his work, and his figure of the new scientist has become an important model for many. Since 1987, Computer Professionals for Social Responsibility (notable opponents of "Star Wars" space weapons and proponents of ethics in high technology contexts) has given a yearly Wiener Award to recognize outstanding contributions toward "social responsibility in computing technology."

*As Heinz von Foerster writes in volume four of Wiener's* Collected Works *(800):*

A quick comparison of curricula offered in departments of electrical engineering in the early fifties with today's will convince even the skeptic of the significance of [these] ideas: although then almost all that was taught was "power," today almost all that is taught is "communication."

For more on the cyborg, see the next selection by J. C. R. Licklider (◊05) and Donna Harraway's manifesto (◊35). For more on cyberspace, see the article by Chip Morningstar and F. Randall Farmer on (◊46).

◊10
127

◊15
227

◊17
247

◊27
405

◊35
515

In *How We Became Posthuman,* Hayles states, "Writing in the years immediately preceding and following World War II, Wiener anticipated some aspects of poststructuralist theories. He questioned whether humans, animals, and machines have any 'essential' qualities that exist in themselves, apart from the web of relations that constituted them in discursive and communicative fields" (91). See the selections from Gilles Deleuze and Felix Guattari (◊27) and Donna Harraway (◊35) for poststructuralist treatments of selfhood. While Zen finds selflessness to be a root of compassion, which in cases such as Vietnamese Nobel Laureate Thich Naht Hanh's leads to direct action, selflessness has often seemed nihilistic to U.S. thinkers—removing the basis for traditional constructions of social justice and life's meaning. It is a question, perhaps, of a small conception of self as opposed to a large one—not that our hand is not part of us, but that much more is.

"Communication and control" is in some ways synonymous with "interactivity." While cybernetics (and even its prefix-progeny such as "cyberspace") may seem anachronistic at the present moment, new media's focus on interactivity is unflagging. From this perspective, the foundational and ongoing importance of cybernetics cannot be overstated. This is true not only in the engineering areas of new media, but also in the arts. Some consider Roy Ascott's "The Construction of Change" (◊10) to be the founding document of new media art—and in that essay Ascott takes cybernetics as his explicit subject. An important early exhibition of new media art was Jasia Reichardt's *Cybernetic Serendipity.* And Jack Burnham and Les Levine's concept of "Software" art (◊17) was, in many ways, constructed as a reaction to the influence of cybernetic concepts on new media art. In the same period, particularly via the influence of John Cage, the arts were also bringing concepts of Zen Buddhism to public consciousness. Nam June Paik (◊15), often considered the first video artist and the first to use television as an art object, considered his work cybernetic and was a close associate of Cage's.
—NWF

From *"A Scientist Rebels,"* an open letter by Wiener to a research scientist, published in The Atlantic Monthly *in January 1947:*

[When] you turn to me for information concerning controlled missiles, there are several considerations which determine my reply. In the past, the comity of scholars has made it a custom to furnish scientific information to any person seriously seeking it. However, we must face these facts: The policy of the government itself during and after the war, say in the bombing of Hiroshima and Nagasaki, has made it clear that to provide scientific information is not a necessarily innocent act, and may entail the gravest consequences. One therefore cannot escape reconsidering the established custom of the scientist to give information to every person who may inquire of him. The interchange of ideas which is one of the great traditions of science must of course receive certain limitations when the scientist becomes an arbiter of life and death.

Further Reading

Wiener, Norbert. *Cybernetics: or Control and Communication in the Animal and the Machine.* 2nd Ed. Cambridge: MIT Press, 1965. (1st ed. 1948.)

Wiener, Norbert. *The Human Use of Human Beings: Cybernetics and Society,* Da Capo Press, 1988. (Originally published 1950.)

Wiener, Norbert. *Norbert Wiener: Collected Works—Vol. 4: Cybernetics, Science, and Society; Ethics, Aesthetics, and Literary Criticism; Book Reviews and Obituaries.* Ed. P. Masani, Cambridge: MIT Press, 1986.

Computer Professionals for Social Responsibility. <http://www.cpsr.org>

Reichardt, Jasia, ed. *Cybernetic Serendipity: The Computer and the Arts.* Exhibition catalog, distributed in the U.S. as a special issue of *Studio International,* 1969. Exhibition organized by by Jasia Reichardt (with Mark Dowson and Peter Schmidt) at the Institute of Contemporary Arts, Nash House, The Mall, London, August 2–October 20, 1968.

Original Publication

*Medicine and Science,* 13–28, New York Academy of Medicine and Science. Ed. I. Galderston, New York: International Universities Press, 1954.

# Men, Machines, and the World About

## Norbert Wiener

I want to point historically to the various things that got me interested in the problems of man, machines, and the world about, because they are relevant to the various things I shall have to say about the present status of the problem.

There were two converging streams of ideas that brought me into cybernetics. One of them was the fact that in the last war, or when it was manifestly coming, at any rate before Pearl Harbor, when we were not yet in the conflict, I tried to see if I could find some niche in the war effort.

In that particular problem, I looked for something to do, and found it in connection with automatic computing machines. Automatic computing machines, of what is called an analogy sort, in which physical quantities are measured and not numbers counted, had already been made very successfully by Professor Vannevar Bush, but there were certain gaps in the theory.

One of the gaps I can express mathematically by saying that these machines could do ordinary differential equations but not partial differential equations. I shall express it physically by the fact that these machines could work in one dimension, namely, time, but not in any efficient way in two dimensions, or three.

Now, it occurred to me that (a) the use of television had shown us a way to represent two or more dimensions on one device; and (b) that the previous device which measured quantities should be replaced by a more precise sort of device that counted numbers.

These were not only my ideas, but at any rate, they were ideas that I had then, and I communicated them in a memorandum to Vannevar Bush, who was in charge of scientific war planning for the entire country. The report that I gave was, in many ways, not in all, a substantial account of the present situation with automatic computing

machines. Thus, I had already become familiar with the idea of the machine which does its arithmetic by making choices on the basis of previous choices, and these on the basis of previous choices, and so on, according to a schedule furnished to the machine by punched tape, or by magnetized tape, or other methods of the sort.

The other thing which led me to this work was the problem that I actually got put into a war work. It turned out that at that time Professor Bush did not feel that this contribution was immediate enough to have been effective in the last war. So I looked around for another thing, and the great question that was being discussed at that time was antiaircraft defense. It was at the time of the Battle of England and the existence of the United States as a combatant country—the survival of anybody to combat Germany—seemed to depend on antiaircraft defense.

The antiaircraft gun is a very interesting type of instrument. In the First World War, the antiaircraft gun had been developed as a firing instrument, but one still used range tables directly by hand for firing the gun. That meant, essentially, that one had to do all the computation while the plane was flying overhead, and, naturally, by the time you got in position to do something about it, the plane had already done something about it, and was not there.

It became evident—and this was long before the work that I did—by the end of the First World War, and certainly by the period between the two, that the essence of the problem was to do all the computation in advance and embody it in instruments which could pick up the observations of the plane and fuse them in the proper way to get the necessary result to aim the gun and to aim it, not at the plane, but sufficiently ahead of the plane, so that the shell and the plane would arrive at the same time as induction. That led to some very interesting mathematical theories.

I had some ideas that turned out to be useful there, and I was put to work with a friend of mine, Julian Bigelow. Very soon we ran into the following problem: the antiaircraft gun is not an isolated instrument. While it can be fired by radar, the equivalent and obvious method of firing it is to have a gun pointer. The gun pointer is a human element; this human element is joined with the mechanical elements. The actual fire control is a system involving human beings and machines at the same time. It must be reduced, from an engineering point of view, to a single structure, which means either a human interpretation of the machine, or a mechanical interpretation of the operator, or both. We were forced—both for the man firing the gun and for the aviator himself—to replace them in our studies by appropriate machines. The question arose: How would we make a machine to simulate a gun pointer, and what troubles would one expect with the situation?

There is a certain sort of control apparatus used for controlling speed in the governors of steam engines that is used for controlling direction in the ship-steering apparatus, which is called a negative feedback apparatus. In the ship-steering apparatus, the quartermaster who turns the wheel does not move the rudder directly. The rudder is much too heavy in the modern ship for a dozen quartermasters to do that. What he does is to move an element in the steering-engine house which is connected with the tiller of the ship by another element. The difference between the two positions is then conveyed to the steering engines of the two sides of the ship to regulate the admission of steam in the port or starboard steering engine. The steering engine moves the rudder head, the tiller, in such a way as to cancel this interval that has been placed between this moving element and the rudder head, and in doing that it recloses the valves and moves the rudder with the ship. In other words, the rudder is moved by something representing the difference between the commanded position and in its own actual position. That is called negative feedback.

This negative feedback, however, has its diseases. There is a definite pathology to it which was already discussed—you will be rather astonished at the date—in 1868, by the great physicist, Clerk Maxwell, in a paper in the Proceedings of the Royal Society in London. If the feedback of the rudder, or the governor, is too intense, the apparatus will shoot past the neutral position a little further than it was originally past it on one side—will shoot further past it on the other—and will go into oscillation.

Since we thought that the simplest way that we could explain human control was by a feedback, we wondered whether this disease would occur. We went with the following question to our friend, Dr. Arturo Rosenblueth, a physiologist, who was then Cannon's right-hand man in the Harvard Medical School: Is there any nervous disease known in which a person trying to accomplish a task starts swinging

wider and wider, and is unable to finish it? For example, I reach for my cigar. I suppose the ordinary way I control my action is so as to reduce the amount by which the cigar has not yet been picked up. Is that disease of excessive oscillation known?

The answer was most definitely that this disease is known. It has exactly the symptoms named. It occurs in the pathology of the cerebellum, the little brain. It is known as purpose tremor or cerebellar tremor.

Well, that gave us the lead. It looked as if a common pattern could be given to account for human behavior and controlled machine behavior in this case, and that it depended on negative feedback.

That was one of the leads we had. The other lead went back to the study of the automatic controlling machine, the automatic computing machine.

In the first place, automatic computing machinery is of no value except for one thing: its speed. It is more expensive than the ordinary desk machine, enormously more. You do not get anything out of it unless you use it at high speed. But to use a machine at high speed, it is necessary to see that every operation it carries out is carried out at a corresponding speed. If you mix in slow stages with fast stages of the machine, the slow stages always win out. They more nearly govern the behavior of the machine than the fast stages. Therefore, the commands given to a high-speed computing machine cannot be given by hand, while the machine is running. They must be built in in advance to what is called a taping, like punched cards, like punched tape, like magnetic tape, or something of the sort; and your machine must not only control the numbers and their combinations, but the scheduling of operations. Your machine must be a logical machine.

There again we found a great similarity to what a human being was doing. The human nervous system, it is perfectly true, does not exhaust all of human control activity. There is, without any doubt, a control activity in man that goes through hormones, that goes through the blood, and so on. But, as far as the nervous system works, the individual fibers come very near to showing an "all or none" action, that is, they fire or they do not fire; they do not fire halfway. If your individual fibers leading to a given fiber, and connected to it by what is known as a synapse, fire in the proper combination—perhaps at least as many as a certain number—and if certain so-called inhibitory fibers do not interrupt them, the outgoing fibers fire. Otherwise they do not.

This is an operation of connected switching extremely like the connected switching of the automatic computing machine. This led us to another comparison between the nervous system and the computing machine, and led us, furthermore, to the idea that since the nervous system is not only a computing machine but a control machine, that we may make very general control machines, working on the successive switching basis and much more like the control machine part, the scheduling part of a computing machine, than we might otherwise have thought possible.

In particular, it seemed to us a very hopeful thing to make an automatic feedback control apparatus in which the feedback itself was carried out, in large measure, by successive switching operations such as one finds either in the nervous system or in the computing machine.

It was the fusion of these two ideas, each of which has a human or animal side and has a machine side, which led to *Cybernetics*. That book I wrote in response to a request from a French publisher, and I chose the name, for I felt that this particular combination of ideas could not be left too long unbaptized, took it from the Greek word κυβερναν meaning to govern, as essentially the art of the steersman.

From here on, I can go ahead in very many ways. The first thing that I want to say is that the feedback mechanisms are not only well known to occur in the voluntary actions of the human body, but that they are necessary for its very life.

A few years ago, Professor Henderson of Harvard wrote a book entitled *The Fitness of the Environment*. Anybody who has read that book must regard it as very much of a miracle that any organism can live, and particularly a human organism. Man cannot exist over any variety of temperatures. For that matter, there is no active life, certainly not above the boiling point and below the freezing point, and most planets probably do not have temperatures lying in that convenient range. When I say "boiling point" and "freezing point," I mean of water, because water is a very distinct and special sort of chemical substance.

Now, even a fish cannot exist at the boiling point. It can exist at something like our own temperature to something around the freezing point, perhaps a little bit below, but not much below.

We cannot do anything like that. We either have a chill or a fever if we get near it. The temperature at which life is possible does not vary for man for any extended period of time. It certainly does not vary much over ten degrees, and practically varies much less than that. Again, we must live under constant conditions of saltiness of our blood, of urea concentration in our blood, and so on.

How do we do this? The idea goes back to Claude Bernard and was developed very much by Cannon. We are full of what is called homeostatic mechanisms, which are mechanisms like thermostats. A homeostat is a mechanism which keeps certain bodily conditions within a narrow range. One of those homeostats, located partly, at least, in the medulla, regulates temperature. Another one regulates breathing. Another one of them regulates urea concentration. That is the apparatus of the kidneys. There are not only a few, but many, many such controls.

Now, such control is like the house thermostat. The house thermostat, if you remember it, is a piece of apparatus which has a little thermometer in it made of two pieces of metal. It makes a contact at one temperature and breaks it at others, and it regulates the admission of oil to the furnace and the ignition of that oil. The interesting thing is it has its own pathology. Many of you people must know that.

We have a house in which there is a thermostat which some brilliant architect placed in the only room in the house with a fireplace. The result is that if we want to cool the house in winter, we light the fire because we give false information to the thermostat that the house is warm and the thermostat turns out the furnace fire.

I might point out that a similar behavior in the human thermostat might cause chills or might cause fever. I am going to depart a little from the main part of the formal talk, because this thing is medically very interesting.

There are certain diseases—I am not going into a characterization of these, because I am not going to commit myself before so many doctors—in which the production of certain substances, say cells, the density of certain cells in the blood, as in leukemia, in increasing steadily. However, this steady increase is rather a regular thing in the disease. The actual rate of production and destruction of the cells is much, much higher than the rate of increase. That might be due, conceivably, to an independent disease of production or of destruction, but I do not think so, because if these two phenomena give you big quantities that are nearly the same, a relatively small change in one will throw this difference out badly and produce a great irregularity in their difference. That is what would have happened if we had no homeostat. I do not think that is what happens. I think that the regularity of the procedure is an indication that we have a homeostat which is working, but working at the wrong level, as if the spring of the house thermostat were changing. That is an idea which is entirely tentative, but which may have serious consequences for medicine.

There is another side to this which is also interesting. The homeostats in the body that I have spoken of are built into the human body. Can we make a homeostat that is partly in the body and partly outside? The answer is definitely yes.

Dr. Bickford at the Mayo Clinic—and he has been followed in this by Dr. Verzeano in the Cushing Veterans Hospital in Framingham—has made an apparatus which takes the brain waves of the electroencephalogram and divides them up, using the total amount that has passed for a stated time, to inject anesthetic either into the vein or into a mask. The procedure is this: as the patient goes under, the brain waves become less active; the injections become less, as less injection is actually needed to keep the level of unconsciousness. In this way, anesthesia can be kept at a reasonably constant level for hours. Here you have a homeostat which is a manufactured one. I do not believe that this is the last example in medicine. I think that the administration of drugs by homeostats which are monitored by their physiologic consequences is a field which has a great future. However, I say this tentatively.

Now, so far I have been talking about man. Let us go to the machine. Where will we find a case where a homeostatic machine is particularly desirable?

Chemistry is an interesting case in point. A chemical factory is generally full of pipes carrying acids, or alkalis, or explosives—at any rate, substances dangerous to work with. When certain thermometers reach certain readings, and certain pressures have been reached, and so on, somebody turns certain valves. He had better turn the right valves, particularly in something like an oil-cracking plant or atomic energy plant, where we are dealing with radioactive materials.

If he has to turn valves on the basis of readings, then, as in the antiaircraft gun, we can build in in advance the combinations which should turn valves as distinguished

from those which should not. The valves may be turned through amplifiers, through what is essentially computing apparatus, by the reading of the instruments themselves, the instruments or sense organs.

You may say, "Very good, but you have to have a man to provide for emergencies."

By the way, it is extremely desirable not to have people in a factory that is likely to explode. People are expensive to replace, and besides we have certain elementary humanitarian instincts.

The question is: Is a man likely to use better emergency judgment than a machine? The answer is no. The reason for that is this: Any emergency you can think of, you can provide for in your computing and control apparatus. If before the time of the emergency, you cannot think of what to do, during the emergency you are almost certain to make a wrong decision. If you cannot figure out a reasonable course of conduct in advance, you simply do not find that the Lord will give you the right thing to do when the emergency comes. Emergencies are provided for in times of peace. I also mean by that, emergencies like the falling of an atomic bomb, about which I may or may not have something to say later.

Then, for perfectly legitimate or even humanitarian reasons, the automatic control system is coming in in the chemical industry and in other especially dangerous industries. However, the same techniques that make possible the automatic assembly line for automobiles, perhaps one automatic assembly line in the textiles industry, and possibly even in dozens of other industries.

The interesting thing is this: that while the successive orders that you give can be almost indefinitely varied in a machine, the instruments which elaborate successive orders are practically standard, no matter what you are doing. These are two variables: one is the quasihuman hands to which the central machine leads, and the other is the sequence of orders put in.

To change from one set of orders, say, from one make of car to another, or to change from one style of body to another, in an assembly line, it is not necessary to alter the order-giving machine. It is enough to alter the particular taping of that machine.

I suppose a good many of you have seen the movie, *Cheaper by the Dozen*. In that movie, what I consider to be the leading idea of the Gilbraiths is completely missed, as it would be in most movies. The Gilbraiths had the idea that man was not working at anything like his full efficiency in his ordinary operations. They thought that families of a dozen were not had by people simply because of human stupidity in the performance of daily tasks, and that this could be avoided by a better ordering of those tasks. That was the motive behind the large family. That was the motive behind the systematic bringing up of those children.

However, when you have simplified a task by reducing it to a routine of consecutive procedures, you have done the same sort of thing that you need to do to put the task on a tape and run the procedure by a completely automatic machine. The problem of industrial management and the systematic handling of ordinary detail by the Gilbraiths, and so forth, is almost the same problem as the taping of a control machine; so that instead of actually improving the conditions of the worker, their advance has tended to telescope the worker out of the picture. That is a very important thing, because it is a procedure taking place now.

I want to say that we are facing a new industrial revolution. The first industrial revolution represented the replacement of the energy of man and of animals by the energy of the machine. The steam engine was its symbol. That has gone so far that there is nothing that steam and the bulldozer cannot do. There is no rate at which pure pick-and-shovel work can be paid in this country which will guarantee a man's doing it willingly. It is simply economically impossible to compete with a bulldozer for bulldozer work.

The new industrial revolution which is taking place now consists primarily in replacing human judgment and discrimination at low levels by the discrimination of the machine. The machine appears now, not as a source of power, but as a source of control and a source of communication. We communicate with the machine and the machine communicates with us. Machines communicate with one another. Energy and power are not the proper concepts to describe this new phenomenon.

If we, in a small way, make human tasks easier by replacing them with a machine execution of the task, and in a large way eliminate the human element in these tasks, we may find we have essentially burned incense before the machine god. There is a very real danger in this country in bowing down before the brass calf, the idol, which is the gadget. I know a great engineer who never thinks further than the construction of the gadget and never thinks of the question of the integration between the gadget and human beings in society. If we allow things to have a reasonably slow development, then the introduction of the gadget as it naturally comes may hurt us enough to provoke a salutary response. So, we realize we cannot worship the gadget and sacrifice the human being to it, but a situation is easily possible in which we may incur a disaster.

Let us suppose that we get into a full-scale war with Russia. I think that Korea, if nothing else, has shown us that modern war means nothing without the infantry. The trouble of occupying Korea is serious enough. The problem of occupying China and Russia staggers the imagination.

We shall have to prepare to do this, if we go to war, at the same time as we have to keep up an industrial production to feed the Army. I mean feed it with munitions as well as with ordinary food and ordinary equipment, a job second to none in history. We shall have to do a maximum production job with a labor market simply scraped to the bottom, and that means the automatic machine.

A war of that sort would mean that we would be putting a large part of our best engineering talent in developing the machine, within two months, probably. It happens that the people who do this sort of job are there. They are the people who were trained in electronic work in the last war when they worked with radar. We are further on with the automatic machine than we were with radar at Pearl Harbor.

Therefore, the situation is that probably two to three years will see the automatic factory well understood and its use beginning to accelerate production. Five years from now will see in the automatic assembly line something of which we possess the complete know-how, and of which we possess a vast backlog of parts.

Furthermore, social reforms do not get made in war. At the end of such a war, we shall find ourselves with a tremendous backlog of parts and know-how, which is extremely tempting to anybody who wants to make a quickie fortune and get out from under, and leave the rest of the community to pick up the pieces. That may very well happen. If that does happen, heaven help us, because we will have an unemployment compared with which the great depression was a nice little joke.

Well, you see the picture drawing together. I suppose one of the things that you people would like would be consolation. Gentlemen, there is no Santa Claus! If we want to live with the machine, we must understand the machine, we must not worship the machine. We must make a great many changes in the way we live with other people. We must value leisure. We must turn the great leaders of business, of industry, of politics, into a state of mind in which they will consider the leisure of people as their business and not as something to be passed off as none of their business.

We shall have to do this unhampered by slogans which fitted a previous stage in society but which do not fit the present.

We shall have to do this unhampered by the creeping paralysis of secrecy which is engulfing our government, because secrecy simply means that we are unable to face situations as they really exist. The people who have to control situations are as yet in no position to handle them.

We shall have to realize that while we may make the machines our gods and sacrifice men to machines, we do not have to do so. If we do so, we deserve the punishment of idolators. It is going to be a difficult time. It we can live through it and keep our heads, and if we are not annihilated by war itself and our other problems, there is a great chance of turning the machine to human advantage, but the machine itself has no particular favor for humanity.

It is possible to make two kinds of machines (I shall not go into the details): the machine whose taping is determined once and for all, and the machine whose taping is continually being modified by experience. The second machine can, in some sense, learn.

Gentlemen, the moral problem of the machine differs in no way from the old moral problem of magic. The fact that the machine follows the law of Nature and that magic is supposed to be outside of Nature is not an interesting distinction. Sorcery was condemned in the Middle Ages. In those ages certain modern types of gadgeteer would have been hanged or burned as a sorcerer. An interesting thing is that the Middle Ages to a certain extent—oh, I don't mean in its love for the flame, but in its condemnation of the gadgeteer—would have been right; namely, sorcery was not the use of the supernatural, but the use of human power for other purposes than the greater glory of God.

Now, I am not theistic when I say the greater glory of God. I mean by God some end to which we can give a justifiable human value. I say that the medieval attitude is the attitude of the fairy tale in many things, but the attitude of the fairy tale is very wise in many things that are relevant to modern life.

If you have the machine which grants you your wish, then you must pay attention to the old fairy tale of the three wishes, which tells you that if you do make a wish which is likely to be granted, you had better be very sure that it is what you want and not what you think you want.

You know Jacob's story of the monkey's paw, the talisman. An old couple came into possession of this, and learned that it would grant them three wishes. The first wish was for two hundred pounds. Immediately, a man appeared from the factory to say that their boy had been crushed in the machinery, and although the factory recognized no responsibility, they were ready to give a solatium of two hundred pounds.

After this they wished the boy back again, and his ghost appeared.

Then they wished the ghost to go away, and there they were left with nothing but a dead son. That is the story.

This is a piece of folklore; but the problem is quite as relevant to the machine as to any piece of magic.

However, a machine can learn. Here the folklore parallel is to the tale of the fisherman and the genie. You all know the story. The fisherman opens a bottle which he has found on the shore, and the genie appears. The genie threatens him with vengeance for his own imprisonment. The fisherman talks the genie back into the bottle. Gentlemen, when we get into trouble with the machine, we cannot talk the machine back into the bottle.

# 05. [Introduction]
# Man-Computer Symbiosis

◊02
35

73

◊08
93

◊16
247

◊19
277

◊41
599

One arm of the military-industrial complex that Vannevar Bush (◊02) helped to establish is devoted to helping the military use computers more effectively through forward-looking research. This was originally called the Advanced Research Projects Agency (ARPA, now DARPA, the Defense Advanced Research Projects Agency). It was organized to head the military's space program. Leaving his post as vice-president of Bolt Beranek and Newman (BBN) to assume leadership of this agency in 1962 was Joseph Carl Robnett Licklider, who went by the nickname Lick. He had an unusual background, in both engineering and behavioral science. Licklider soon became a force in promoting computer science education, time-sharing systems, interactive computing, and computer networks—and even in promoting more visionary extensions of computing as new media.

By redirecting ARPA funding from companies to universities, Licklider helped to make the iron triangle of industry, the military, and academia as equilaterally triangular as it is today. ARPA funding and Licklider's involvement also led to Ph.D. programs in computer science at MIT, Berkeley, Carnegie Mellon University, and Stanford. (Computer science Ph.D.s were not offered at all before Licklider took over at ARPA.) Licklider was praised by his contemporaries for directing ARPA funding toward projects that were of broad benefit, rather than ones that served exclusively or even primarily military purposes.

In 1962 Licklider addressed a memo to a group he called "Members and Affiliates of the Intergalactic Computer Network." In that document, as at other times in the early 1960s, Licklider encouraged universities to link their computers together so as to benefit from the development of software tools that had already been done on other campuses. Although Licklider left ARPA in 1964, the network he envisioned took shape as ARPAnet under the guidance of Lawrence Roberts. In October 1969, the second ARPAnet node was connected by Doug Engelbart's group at SRI (◊08, ◊16), bringing online the network that would eventually become the Internet.

Licklider's radical vision of human/computer coexistence that appears here was the first influential publication from this visionary and implementer of visions. Writing with Robert W. Taylor in 1968, he began another important article, "The Computer as a Communication Device," with a bold statement: "In a few years, men will be able to communicate more effectively through a machine than face to face." Then the two went on to provide evidence: they had accomplished in two days, during a computer-mediated technical meeting, what usually took a week to hash out. (The authors also collaborated on that article, in fact, from different cities.) The article argued against communication as being a simple one-way process between sender and receiver. An illustration in the article even hinted at the possibility of cyber-romance. Licklider and Taylor put forth the idea of a personal network agent—an "Oliver," or "on-line interactive vicarious expediter and responder." In contrast to some pro-computer political proponents in the 1990s, they were not sanguine about the possibility of a global computer network exacerbating inequality: "Will 'to be on line' be a privilege or a right? If only a favored segment of the population gets a chance to enjoy the advantage of 'intelligence amplification,' the network may exaggerate the discontinuity in the spectrum of intellectual opportunity."

> Lucy Suchman (◊41) makes a related argument for considering computer communication in the context of human communication, which is not a simple series of one-way processes. From a different perspective, Jean Baudrillard (◊19) makes an argument with interesting parallels to that of Licklider and Taylor.

In the details of the article that follows, one can see how Licklider has described a plan for a speech recognition system of the sort Bush had envisioned. Licklider also suggested a need for graphical input and handwriting recognition. Although his prediction that corporate presidents would not need to type has not held true, Licklider was, in general, prescient in that he saw a need—initially in military operations—for quick access to computing to aid in decision-making.

—NM

Further Reading

Hafner, Katie, and Matthew Lyon. *Where Wizards Stay Up Late: The Origins of the Internet.* New York: Touchstone Books, 1998.

Licklider, J. C. R., and Robert W. Taylor. "The Computer as a Communication Device." *Science and Technology,* April 1968. Reprinted in Digital SRC Research Report 61, 7 August 1990. <http://gatekeeper.dec.com/pub/DEC/SRC/research-reports/abstracts/src-rr-061.html>.

Licklider, J. C. R. "Topics for Discussion at Forthcoming Meeting," Memorandum, 23 April 1963. MIT Institute Archives.

Licklider. J. C. R., and Welden Clark. "On-Line Man Computer Communication," *Proceedings Spring Joint Computer Conference* 21:113–128. May 1962.

Original Publication

*IRE Transactions on Human Factors in Electronics,* HFE–1:4–11. March 1960. Reprinted in *Digital SRC Research Report* 61, 7 August 1990. <http://gatekeeper.dec.com/pub/DEC/SRC/research-reports/abstracts/src-rr-061.html>.

# Man-Computer Symbiosis

## J. C. R. Licklider

## Summary

Man-computer symbiosis is an expected development in cooperative interaction between men and electronic computers. It will involve very close coupling between the human and the electronic members of the partnership. The main aims are 1) to let computers facilitate formulative thinking as they now facilitate the solution of formulated problems, and 2) to enable men and computers to cooperate in making decisions and controlling complex situations without inflexible dependence on predetermined programs. In the anticipated symbiotic partnership, men will set the goals, formulate the hypotheses, determine the criteria, and perform the evaluations. Computing machines will do the routinizable work that must be done to prepare the way for insights and decisions in technical and scientific thinking. Preliminary analyses indicate that the symbiotic partnership will perform intellectual operations much more effectively than man alone can perform them. Prerequisites for the achievement of the effective, cooperative association include developments in computer time sharing, in memory components, in memory organization, in programming languages, and in input and output equipment.

# 1 Introduction
## 1.1 Symbiosis

The fig tree is pollinated only by the insect *Blastophaga grossorun*. The larva of the insect lives in the ovary of the fig tree, and there it gets its food. The tree and the insect are thus heavily interdependent: the tree cannot reproduce without the insect; the insect cannot eat without the tree; together, they constitute not only a viable but a productive and thriving partnership. This cooperative "living together in intimate association, or even close union, of two dissimilar organisms" is called symbiosis [27].

"Man-computer symbiosis" is a subclass of man-machine systems. There are many man-machine systems. At present, however, there are no man-computer symbioses. The purposes of this paper are to present the concept and, hopefully, to foster the development of man-computer symbiosis by analyzing some problems of interaction between men and computing machines, calling attention to applicable principles of man-machine engineering, and pointing out a few questions to which research answers are needed. The hope is that, in not too many years, human brains and computing machines will be coupled together very tightly, and that the resulting partnership will think as no human brain has ever thought and process data in a way not approached by the information-handling machines we know today.

## 1.2 Between "Mechanically Extended Man" and "Artificial Intelligence"

As a concept, man-computer symbiosis is different in an important way from what North [21] has called "mechanically extended man." In the man-machine sytems of the past, the human operator supplied the initiative, the direction, the integration, and the criterion. The mechanical parts of the systems were mere extensions, first of the human arm, then of the human eye. These systems certainly did not consist of "dissimilar organisms living together...." There was only one kind of organism—man—and the rest was there only to help him.

In one sense of course, any man-made system is intended to help man, to help a man or men outside the system. If we focus upon the human operator within the system, however, we see that, in some areas of technology, a fantastic change has taken place during the last few years. "Mechanical extension" has given way to replacement of men, to automation, and the men who remain are there more to help than to be helped. In some instances, particularly in large computer-centered information and control systems, the human operators are responsible mainly for functions that it proved infeasible to automate. Such systems ("humanly extended machines," North might call them) are not symbiotic systems. They are "semi-automatic" systems, systems that started out to be fully automatic but fell short of the goal.

Man-computer symbiosis is probably not the ultimate paradigm for complex technological systems. It seems entirely possible that, in due course, electronic or chemical "machines" will outdo the human brain in most of the functions we now consider exclusively within its province. Even now, Gelernter's IBM-704 program for proving theorems in plane geometry proceeds at about the same pace as Brooklyn high school students, and makes similar errors.[12] There are, in fact, several theorem-proving, problem-solving, chess-playing, and pattern-recognizing programs (too many for complete reference [1, 2, 5, 8, 11, 13, 17, 18, 19, 22, 23, 25]) capable of rivaling human intellectual performance in restricted areas; and Newell, Simon, and Shaw's [20] "general problem solver" may remove some of the restrictions. In short, it seems worthwhile to avoid argument with (other) enthusiasts for artificial intelligence by conceding dominance in the distant future of cerebration to machines alone. There will nevertheless be a fairly long interim during which the main intellectual advances will be made by men and computers working together in intimate association. A multi-disciplinary study group, examining future research and development problems of the Air Force, estimated that it would be 1980 before developments in artificial intelligence make it possible for machines alone to do much thinking or problem solving of military significance. That would leave, say, five years to develop man-computer symbiosis and 15 years to use it. The 15 may be 10 or 500, but those years should be intellectually the most creative and exciting in the history of mankind.

## 2 Aims of Man-Computer Symbiosis

Present-day computers are designed primarily to solve preformulated problems or to process data according to predetermined procedures. The course of the computation may be conditional upon results obtained during the computation, but all the alternatives must be foreseen in advance. (If an unforeseen alternative arises, the whole process comes to a halt and awaits the necessary extension of the program.) The requirement for preformulation or predetermination is sometimes no great disadvantage. It is often said that programming for a computing machine forces one to think clearly, that it disciplines the thought process. If the user can think his problem through in advance, symbiotic association with a computing machine is not necessary.

However, many problems that can be thought through in advance are very difficult to think through in advance. They would be easier to solve, and they could be solved faster, through an intuitively guided trial-and-error procedure in which the computer cooperated, turning up flaws in the reasoning or revealing unexpected turns in the solution. Other problems simply cannot be formulated without computing-machine aid. Poincaré anticipated the frustration of an important group of would-be computer users when he said, "The question is not, 'What is the answer?' The question is, 'What is the question?'" One of the main aims of man-computer symbiosis is to bring the computing machine effectively into the formulative parts of technical problems.

The other main aim is closely related. It is to bring computing machines effectively into processes of thinking that must go on in "real time," time that moves too fast to permit using computers in conventional ways. Imagine trying, for example, to direct a battle with the aid of a computer on such a schedule as this. You formulate your problem today. Tomorrow you spend with a programmer. Next week the computer devotes 5 minutes to assembling your program and 47 seconds to calculating the answer to your problem. You get a sheet of paper 20 feet long, full of numbers that, instead of providing a final solution, only suggest a tactic that should be explored by simulation. Obviously, the battle would be over before the second step in its planning was begun. To think in interaction with a computer in the same way that you think with a colleague whose competence supplements your own will require much tighter coupling between man and machine than is suggested by the example and than is possible today.

## 3 Need for Computer Participation in Formulative and Real-Time Thinking

The preceding paragraphs tacitly made the assumption that, if they could be introduced effectively into the thought process, the functions that can be performed by data-processing machines would improve or facilitate thinking and problem solving in an important way. That assumption may require justification.

### 3.1 A Preliminary and Informal Time-and-Motion Analysis of Technical Thinking

Despite the fact that there is a voluminous literature on thinking and problem solving, including intensive case-history studies of the process of invention, I could find nothing comparable to a time-and-motion-study analysis of the mental work of a person engaged in a scientific or technical enterprise. In the spring and summer of 1957, therefore, I tried to keep track of what one moderately technical person actually did during the hours he regarded as devoted to work. Although I was aware of the inadequacy of the sampling, I served as my own subject.

It soon became apparent that the main thing I did was to keep records, and the project would have become an infinite regress if the keeping of records had been carried through in the detail envisaged in the initial plan. It was not. Nevertheless, I obtained a picture of my activities that gave me pause. Perhaps my spectrum is not typical—I hope it is not, but I fear it is.

About 85 per cent of my "thinking" time was spent getting into a position to think, to make a decision, to learn something I needed to know. Much more time went into finding or obtaining information than into digesting it. Hours went into the plotting of graphs, and other hours into instructing an assistant how to plot. When the graphs were finished, the relations were obvious at once, but the plotting had to be done in order to make them so. At one point, it was necessary to compare six experimental determinations of a function relating speech-intelligibility to speech-to-noise ratio. No two experimenters had used the same definition or measure of speech-to-noise ratio. Several hours of calculating were required to get the data into comparable form. When they were in comparable form, it took only a few seconds to determine what I needed to know.

Throughout the period I examined, in short, my "thinking" time was devoted mainly to activities that were essentially clerical or mechanical: searching, calculating, plotting,

transforming, determining the logical or dynamic consequences of a set of assumptions or hypotheses, preparing the way for a decision or an insight. Moreover, my choices of what to attempt and what not to attempt were determined to an embarrassingly great extent by considerations of clerical feasibility, not intellectual capability.

The main suggestion conveyed by the findings just described is that the operations that fill most of the time allegedly devoted to technical thinking are operations that can be performed more effectively by machines than by men. Severe problems are posed by the fact that these operations have to be performed upon diverse variables and in unforeseen and continually changing sequences. If those problems can be solved in such a way as to create a symbiotic relation between a man and a fast information-retrieval and data-processing machine, however, it seems evident that the cooperative interaction would greatly improve the thinking process.

It may be appropriate to acknowledge, at this point, that we are using the term "computer" to cover a wide class of calculating, data-processing, and information-storage-and-retrieval machines. The capabilities of machines in this class are increasing almost daily. It is therefore hazardous to make general statements about capabilities of the class. Perhaps it is equally hazardous to make general statements about the capabilities of men. Nevertheless, certain genotypic differences in capability between men and computers do stand out, and they have a bearing on the nature of possible man-computer symbiosis and the potential value of achieving it.

As has been said in various ways, men are noisy, narrow-band devices, but their nervous systems have very many parallel and simultaneously active channels. Relative to men, computing machines are very fast and very accurate, but they are constrained to perform only one or a few elementary operations at a time. Men are flexible, capable of "programming themselves contingently" on the basis of newly received information. Computing machines are single-minded, constrained by their "pre-programming." Men naturally speak redundant languages organized around unitary objects and coherent actions and employing 20 to 60 elementary symbols. Computers "naturally" speak nonredundant languages, usually with only two elementary symbols and no inherent appreciation either of unitary objects or of coherent actions.

To be rigorously correct, those characterizations would have to include many qualifiers. Nevertheless, the picture of dissimilarity (and therefore potential supplementation) that they present is essentially valid. Computing machines can do readily, well, and rapidly many things that are difficult or impossible for man, and men can do readily and well, though not rapidly, many things that are difficult or impossible for computers. That suggests that a symbiotic cooperation, if successful in integrating the positive characteristics of men and computers, would be of great value. The differences in speed and in language, of course, pose difficulties that must be overcome.

## 4 Separable Functions of Men and Computers in the Anticipated Symbiotic Association

It seems likely that the contributions of human operators and equipment will blend together so completely in many operations that it will be difficult to separate them neatly in analysis. That would be the case if, in gathering data on which to base a decision, for example, both the man and the computer came up with relevant precedents from experience and if the computer then suggested a course of action that agreed with the man's intuitive judgment. (In theorem-proving programs, computers find precedents in experience, and in the SAGE System, they suggest courses of action. The foregoing is not a far-fetched example.) In other operations, however, the contributions of men and equipment will be to some extent separable.

Men will set the goals and supply the motivations, of course, at least in the early years. They will formulate hypotheses. They will ask questions. They will think of mechanisms, procedures, and models. They will remember that such-and-such a person did some possibly relevant work on a topic of interest back in 1947, or at any rate shortly after World War II, and they will have an idea in what journals it might have been published. In general, they will make approximate and fallible, but leading, contributions, and they will define criteria and serve as evaluators, judging the contributions of the equipment and guiding the general line of thought.

In addition, men will handle the very-low-probability situations when such situations do actually arise. (In current man-machine systems, that is one of the human operator's most important functions. The sum of the probabilities of very-low-probability alternatives is often much too large to neglect.) Men will fill in the gaps, either in the problem solution or in the computer program, when the computer has no mode or routine that is applicable in a particular circumstance.

The information-processing equipment, for its part, will convert hypotheses into testable models and then test the models against data (which the human operator may designate roughly and identify as relevant when the computer presents them for his approval). The equipment will answer questions. It will simulate the mechanisms and models, carry out the procedures, and display the results to the operator. It will transform data, plot graphs ("cutting the cake" in whatever way the human operator specifies, or in several alternative ways if the human operator is not sure what he wants). The equipment will interpolate, extrapolate, and transform. It will convert static equations or logical statements into dynamic models so the human operator can examine their behavior. In general, it will carry out the routinizable, clerical operations that fill the intervals between decisions.

In addition, the computer will serve as a statistical-inference, decision-theory, or game-theory machine to make elementary evaluations of suggested courses of action whenever there is enough basis to support a formal statistical analysis. Finally, it will do as much diagnosis, pattern-matching, and relevance-recognizing as it profitably can, but it will accept a clearly secondary status in those areas.

## 5 Prerequisites for Realization of Man-Computer Symbiosis

The data-processing equipment tacitly postulated in the preceding section is not available. The computer programs have not been written. There are in fact several hurdles that stand between the nonsymbiotic present and the anticipated symbiotic future. Let us examine some of them to see more clearly what is needed and what the chances are of achieving it.

### 5.1 Speed Mismatch Between Men and Computers

Any present-day large-scale computer is too fast and too costly for real-time cooperative thinking with one man. Clearly, for the sake of efficiency and economy, the computer must divide its time among many users. Time-sharing systems are currently under active development. There are even arrangements to keep users from "clobbering" anything but their own personal programs.

It seems reasonable to envision, for a time 10 or 15 years hence, a "thinking center" that will incorporate the functions of present-day libraries together with anticipated advances in information storage and retrieval and the symbiotic functions suggested earlier in this paper. The picture readily enlarges itself into a network of such centers, connected to one another by wide-band communication lines and to individual users by leased-wire services. In such a system, the speed of the computers would be balanced, and the cost of the gigantic memories and the sophisticated programs would be divided by the number of users.

## 5.2 Memory Hardware Requirements

When we start to think of storing any appreciable fraction of a technical literature in computer memory, we run into billions of bits and, unless things change markedly, billions of dollars.

The first thing to face is that we shall not store all the technical and scientific papers in computer memory. We may store the parts that can be summarized most succinctly— the quantitative parts and the reference citations—but not the whole. Books are among the most beautifully engineered, and human-engineered, components in existence, and they will continue to be functionally important within the context of man-computer symbiosis. (Hopefully, the computer will expedite the finding, delivering, and returning of books.)

The second point is that a very important section of memory will be permanent: part indelible *memory* and part *published memory*. The computer will be able to write once into indelible memory, and then read back indefinitely, but the computer will not be able to erase indelible memory. (It may also over-write, turning all the 0's into 1's, as though marking over what was written earlier.) Published memory will be "read-only" memory. It will be introduced into the computer already structured. The computer will be able to refer to it repeatedly, but not to change it. These types of memory will become more and more important as computers grow larger. They can be made more compact than core, thin-film, or even tape memory, and they will be much less expensive. The main engineering problems will concern selection circuitry.

In so far as other aspects of memory requirement are concerned, we may count upon the continuing development of ordinary scientific and business computing machines. There is some prospect that memory elements will become as fast as processing (logic) elements. That development would have a revolutionary effect upon the design of computers.

## 5.3 Memory Organization Requirements

Implicit in the idea of man-computer symbiosis are the requirements that information be retrievable both by name and by pattern and that it be accessible through procedure much faster than serial search. At least half of the problem of memory organization appears to reside in the storage procedure. Most of the remainder seems to be wrapped up in the problem of pattern recognition within the storage mechanism or medium. Detailed discussion of these problems is beyond the present scope. However, a brief outline of one promising idea, "trie memory," may serve to indicate the general nature of anticipated developments.

Trie memory is so called by its originator, Fredkin [10], because it is designed to facilitate retrieval of information and because the branching storage structure, when developed, resembles a tree. Most common memory systems store functions of arguments at locations designated by the arguments. (In one sense, they do not store the arguments at all. In another and more realistic sense, they store all the possible arguments in the framework structure of the memory.) The trie memory system, on the other hand, stores both the functions and the arguments. The argument is introduced into the memory first, one character at a time, starting at a standard initial register. Each argument register has one cell for each character of the ensemble (e.g., two for information encoded in binary form) and each character cell has within it storage space for the address of the next register. The argument is stored by writing a series of addresses, each one of which tells where to find the next. At the end of the argument is a special "end-of-argument" marker. Then follow directions to the function, which is stored in one or another of several ways, either further trie structure or "list structure" often being most effective.

The trie memory scheme is inefficient for small memories, but it becomes increasingly efficient in using available storage space as memory size increases. The attractive features of the scheme are these: 1) The retrieval process is extremely simple. Given the argument, enter the standard initial register with the first character, and pick up the address of the second. Then go to the second register, and pick up the address of the third, etc. 2) If two arguments have initial characters in common, they use the same storage space for those characters. 3) The lengths of the arguments need not be the same, and need not be specified in advance. 4) No room in storage is reserved for or used by any argument until it is actually stored. The trie structure is created as the items are introduced into the memory. 5) A function can be used as an argument for another function, and that function as an argument for the next. Thus, for example, by entering with the argument, "matrix multiplication," one might retrieve the entire program for performing a matrix multiplication on the computer. 6) By examining the storage at a given level, one can determine what thus-far similar items have been stored. For example, if there is no citation for Egan, J. P., it is but a step or two backward to pick up the trail of Egan, James. . . .

The properties just described do not include all the desired ones, but they bring computer storage into resonance with human operators and their predilection to designate things by naming or pointing.

## 5.4 The Language Problem

The basic dissimilarity between human languages and computer languages may be the most serious obstacle to true symbiosis. It is reassuring, however, to note what great strides have already been made, through interpretive programs and particularly through assembly or compiling programs such as FORTRAN, to adapt computers to human language forms. The "Information Processing Language" of Shaw, Newell, Simon, and Ellis [24] represents another line of rapprochement. And, in ALGOL and related systems, men are proving their flexibility by adopting standard formulas of representation and expression that are readily translatable into machine language.

For the purposes of real-time cooperation between men and computers, it will be necessary, however, to make use of an additional and rather different principle of communication and control. The idea may be highlighted by comparing instructions ordinarily addressed to intelligent human beings with instructions ordinarily used with computers. The latter specify precisely the individual steps to take and the sequence in which to take them. The former present or imply something about incentive or motivation, and they supply a criterion by which the human executor of the instructions will know when he has accomplished his task. In short: instructions directed to computers specify courses; instructions directed to human beings specify goals.

Men appear to think more naturally and easily in terms of goals than in terms of courses. True, they usually know something about directions in which to travel or lines along which to work, but few start out with precisely formulated itineraries. Who, for example, would depart from Boston for Los Angeles with a detailed specification of the route? Instead, to paraphrase Wiener, men bound for Los Angeles try continually to decrease the amount by which they are not yet in the smog.

Computer instruction through specification of goals is being approached along two paths. The first involves problem-solving, hill-climbing, self-organizing programs. The second involves real-time concatenation of preprogrammed segments and closed subroutines which the human operator can designate and call into action simply by name.

Along the first of these paths, there has been promising exploratory work. It is clear that, working within the loose constraints of predetermined strategies, computers will in due course be able to devise and simplify their own procedures for achieving stated goals. Thus far, the achievements have not been substantively important; they have constituted only "demonstration in principle." Nevertheless, the implications are far-reaching.

Although the second path is simpler and apparently capable of earlier realization, it has been relatively neglected. Fredkin's trie memory provides a promising paradigm. We may in due course see a serious effort to develop computer programs that can be connected together like the words and phrases of speech to do whatever computation or control is required at the moment. The consideration that holds back such an effort, apparently, is that the effort would produce nothing that would be of great value in the context of existing computers. It would be unrewarding to develop the language before there are any computing machines capable of responding meaningfully to it.

## 5.5 Input and Output Equipment

The department of data processing that seems least advanced, in so far as the requirements of man-computer symbiosis are concerned, is the one that deals with input and output equipment or, as it is seen from the human operator's point of view, displays and controls. Immediately after saying that, it is essential to make qualifying comments, because the engineering of equipment for high-speed introduction and extraction of information has been excellent, and because some very sophisticated display and control techniques have been developed in such research laboratories as the Lincoln Laboratory. By and large, in generally available computers, however, there is almost no provision for any more effective, immediate man-machine communication than can be achieved with an electric typewriter.

Displays seem to be in a somewhat better state than controls. Many computers plot graphs on oscilloscope screens, and a few take advantage of the remarkable capabilities, graphical and symbolic, of the charactron display tube. Nowhere, to my knowledge, however, is there anything approaching the flexibility and convenience of the pencil and doodle pad or the chalk and blackboard used by men in technical discussion.

### 1) Desk-Surface Display and Control

Certainly, for effective man-computer interaction, it will be necessary for the man and the computer to draw graphs and pictures and to write notes and equations to each other on the same display surface. The man should be able to present a function to the computer, in a rough but rapid fashion, by drawing a graph. The computer should read the man's writing, perhaps on the condition that it be in clear block capitals, and it should immediately post, at the location of each hand-drawn symbol, the corresponding character as interpreted and put into precise type-face. With such an input-output device, the operator would quickly learn to write or print in a manner legible to the machine. He could compose instructions and subroutines, set them into proper format, and check them over before introducing them finally into the computer's main memory. He could even define new symbols, as Gilmore and Savell [14] have done at the Lincoln Laboratory, and present them directly to the computer. He could sketch out the format of a table roughly and let the computer shape it up with precision. He could correct the computer's data, instruct the machine via flow diagrams, and in general interact with it very much as he would with another engineer, except that the "other engineer" would be a precise draftsman, a lightning calculator, a mnemonic wizard, and many other valuable partners all in one.

### 2) Computer-Posted Wall Display

In some technological systems, several men share responsibility for controlling vehicles whose behaviors interact. Some information must be presented simultaneously to all the men, preferably on a common grid,

to coordinate their actions. Other information is of relevance only to one or two operators. There would be only a confusion of uninterpretable clutter if all the information were presented on one display to all of them. The information must be posted by a computer, since manual plotting is too slow to keep it up to date.

The problem just outlined is even now a critical one, and it seems certain to become more and more critical as time goes by. Several designers are convinced that displays with the desired characteristics can be constructed with the aid of flashing lights and time-sharing viewing screens based on the light-valve principle.

The large display should be supplemented, according to most of those who have thought about the problem, by individual display-control units. The latter would permit the operators to modify the wall display without leaving their locations. For some purposes, it would be desirable for the operators to be able to communicate with the computer through the supplementary displays and perhaps even through the wall display. At least one scheme for providing such communication seems feasible.

The large wall display and its associated system are relevant, of course, to symbiotic cooperation between a computer and a team of men. Laboratory experiments have indicated repeatedly that informal, parallel arrangements of operators, coordinating their activities through reference to a large situation display, have important advantages over the arrangement, more widely used, that locates the operators at individual consoles and attempts to correlate their actions through the agency of a computer. This is one of several operator-team problems in need of careful study.

### 3) Automatic Speech Production and Recognition

How desirable and how feasible is speech communication between human operators and computing machines? That compound question is asked whenever sophisticated data-processing systems are discussed. Engineers who work and live with computers take a conservative attitude toward the desirability. Engineers who have had experience in the field of automatic speech recognition take a conservative attitude toward the feasibility. Yet there is continuing interest in the idea of talking with computing machines. In large part, the interest stems from realization that one can hardly take a military commander or a corporation president away from his work to teach him to type. If computing machines are ever to be used directly by top-level decision makers, it may be worthwhile to provide communication via the most natural means, even at considerable cost.

Preliminary analysis of his problems and time scales suggests that a corporation president would be interested in a symbiotic association with a computer only as an avocation. Business situations usually move slowly enough that there is time for briefings and conferences. It seems reasonable, therefore, for computer specialists to be the ones who interact directly with computers in business offices.

The military commander, on the other hand, faces a greater probability of having to make critical decisions in short intervals of time. It is easy to overdramatize the notion of the ten-minute war, but it would be dangerous to count on having more than ten minutes in which to make a critical decision. As military system ground environments and control centers grow in capability and complexity, therefore, a real requirement for automatic speech production and recognition in computers seems likely to develop. Certainly, if the equipment were already developed, reliable, and available, it would be used.

In so far as feasibility is concerned, speech production poses less severe problems of a technical nature than does automatic recognition of speech sounds. A commercial electronic digital voltmeter now reads aloud its indications, digit by digit. For eight or ten years, at the Bell Telephone Laboratories, the Royal Institute of Technology (Stockholm), the Signals Research and Development Establishment (Christchurch), the Haskins Laboratory, and the Massachusetts Institute of Technology, Dunn [6], Fant [7], Lawrence [15], Cooper [3], Stevens [26], and their co-workers, have demonstrated successive generations of intelligible automatic talkers. Recent work at the Haskins Laboratory has led to the development of a digital code, suitable for use by computing machines, that makes an automatic voice utter intelligible connected discourse [16].

The feasibility of automatic speech recognition depends heavily upon the size of the vocabulary of words to be recognized and upon the diversity of talkers and accents with which it must work. Ninety-eight percent correct recognition of naturally spoken decimal digits was demonstrated several years ago at the Bell Telephone Laboratories and at the Lincoln Laboratory [4], [9]. To go a step up the scale of vocabulary size, we may say that an automatic recognizer of clearly spoken alpha-numerical characters can almost surely be developed now on the basis of existing knowledge. Since untrained operators can read at least as rapidly as trained ones can type, such a device would be a convenient tool in almost any computer installation.

For real-time interaction on a truly symbiotic level, however, a vocabulary of about 2000 words, e.g., 1000 words of something like basic English and 1000 technical terms, would probably be required. That constitutes a challenging problem. In the consensus of acousticians and linguists, construction of a recognizer of 2000 words cannot be accomplished now. However, there are several organizations that would happily undertake to develop an automatic recognizer for such a vocabulary on a five-year basis. They would stipulate that the speech be clear speech, dictation style, without unusual accent.

Although detailed discussion of techniques of automatic speech recognition is beyond the present scope, it is fitting to note that computing machines are playing a dominant role in the development of automatic speech recognizers. They have contributed the impetus that accounts for the present optimism, or rather for the optimism presently found in some quarters. Two or three years ago, it appeared that automatic recognition of sizeable vocabularies would not be achieved for ten or fifteen years; that it would have to await much further, gradual accumulation of knowledge of acoustic, phonetic, linguistic, and psychological processes in speech communication. Now, however, many see a prospect of accelerating the acquisition of that knowledge with the aid of computer processing of speech signals, and not a few workers have the feeling that sophisticated computer programs will be able to perform well as speech-pattern recognizes even without the aid of much substantive knowledge of speech signals and processes. Putting those two considerations together brings the estimate of the time required to achieve practically significant speech recognition down to perhaps five years, the five years just mentioned.

References

[1] A. Bernstein and M. deV. Roberts, "Computer versus chess-player," *Scientific American,* vol. 198, pp. 96–98; June, 1958.

[2] W. W. Bledsoe and I. Browning, "Pattern Recognition and Reading by Machine," presented at the Eastern Joint Computer Conf., Boston, Mass., December, 1959.

[3] F. S. Cooper, et al., "Some experiments on the perception of synthetic speech sounds," *J. Acoust. Soc. Amer.,* vol. 24, pp. 597–606; November, 1952.

[4] K. H. Davis, R. Biddulph, and S. Balashek, "Automatic recognition of spoken digits," in W. Jackson, *Communication Theory,* Butterworths Scientific Publications, London, Eng., pp. 433–441; 1953.

[5] G. P. Dinneen, "Programming pattern recognition," *Proc. WJCC,* pp. 94–100; March, 1955.

[6] H. K. Dunn, "The calculation of vowel resonances, and an electrical vocal tract," *J. Acoust. Soc. Amer.,* vol. 22, pp. 740–753; November, 1950.

[7] G. Fant, "On the Acoustics of Speech," paper presented at the Third Internatl. Congress on Acoustics, Stuttgart, Ger.; September, 1959.

[8] B. G. Farley and W. A. Clark, "Simulation of self-organizing systems by digital computers." *IRE Trans. on Information Theory,* vol. IT-4, pp. 76–84; September, 1954.

[9] J. W. Forgie and C. D. Forgie, "Results obtained from a vowel recognition computer program," *J. Acoust. Soc. Amer.,* vol. 31, pp. 1480–1489; November, 1959.

[10] E. Fredkin, "Trie memory," *Communications of the ACM,* Sept. 1960, pp. 490–499.

[11] R. M. Friedberg, "A learning machine: Part I," *IBM J. Res. & Dev.,* vol. 2, pp. 2–13; January, 1958.

[12] H. Gelernter, "Realization of a Geometry Theorem Proving Machine." Unesco, NS, ICIP, 1.6.6, Internatl. Conf. on Information Processing, Paris, France; June, 1959.

[13] P. C. Gilmore, "A Program for the Production of Proofs for Theorems Derivable Within the First Order Predicate Calculus from Axioms," Unesco, NS, ICIP, 1.6.14, Internatl. Conf. on Information Processing, Paris, France; June, 1959.

[14] J. T. Gilmore and R. E. Savell, "The Lincoln Writer," Lincoln Laboratory, M. I. T., Lexington, Mass., Rept. 51–58; October, 1959.

[15] W. Lawrence, et al., "Methods and Purposes of Speech Synthesis," Signals Res. and Dev. Estab., Ministry of Supply, Christchurch, Hants, England, Rept. 56/1457; March, 1956.

[16] A. M. Liberman, F. Ingemann, L. Lisker, P. Delattre, and F. S. Cooper, "Minimal rules for synthesizing speech," *J. Acoust. Soc. Amer.,* vol. 31, pp. 1490–1499; November, 1959.

[17] A. Newell, "The chess machine: an example of dealing with a complex task by adaptation," *Proc. WJCC,* pp. 101–108; March, 1955.

[18] A. Newell and J. C. Shaw, "Programming the logic theory machine." *Proc. WJCC,* pp. 230–240; March, 1957.

[19] A. Newell, J. C. Shaw, and H. A. Simon, "Chess-playing programs and the problem of complexity," *IBM J. Res. & Dev.,* vol. 2, pp. 320–335; October, 1958.

[20] A. Newell, H. A. Simon, and J. C. Shaw, "Report on a general problem-solving program," Unesco, NS, ICIP, 1.6.8, Internatl. Conf. on Information Processing, Paris, France; June, 1959.

[21] J. D. North, "The rational behavior of mechanically extended man," Boulton Paul Aircraft Ltd., Wolverhampton, Eng.; September, 1954.

[22] O. G. Selfridge, "Pandemonium, a paradigm for learning," *Proc. Symp. Mechanisation of Thought Processes,* Natl. Physical Lab., Teddington, Eng.; November, 1958.

[23] C. E. Shannon, "Programming a computer for playing chess," *Phil. Mag.,* vol. 41, pp. 256–275; March, 1950.

[24] J. C. Shaw, A. Newell, H. A. Simon, and T. O. Ellis, "A command structure for complex information processing," *Proc. WJCC,* pp. 119–128; May, 1958.

[25] H. Sherman, "A Quasi-Topological Method for Recognition of Line Patterns," Unesco, NS, ICIP, H.L.5, Internatl. Conf. on Information Processing, Paris, France; June, 1959.

[26] K. N. Stevens, S. Kasowski, and C. G. Fant, "Electric analog of the vocal tract," *J. Acoust. Soc. Amer.,* vol. 25, pp. 734–742; July, 1953.

[27] *Webster's New International Dictionary,* 2nd ed., G. and C. Merriam Co., Springfield, Mass., p. 2555; 1958.

# 06. [Introduction]
# "Happenings" in
# the New York Scene

The "Happenings" are a touchstone for nearly every discussion of new media as it relates to interactivity in art.

The term "Happening" has been used to describe many performances and events, organized by Allan Kaprow and others during the 1950s and 1960s, including a number of theatrical productions that were traditionally scripted and invited only limited audience interaction (e.g., applause). Yet however interactive the various events actually were, the *idea of interaction* associated with Happenings was profoundly inspiring and has remained so for decades. Kaprow wrote in the essay below, "Some of us will probably become famous. It will be an ironic fame fashioned largely by those who have never seen our work." And, in fact, many more came into contact with Happenings through the writing about them than through the actual experience of them. Perhaps the Happenings achieved such fame, beyond those who participated directly, because they reflected and provoked a desire to break down distinctions between creator and audience—a desire and activity now central for many new media practitioners.

Once we have put aside the question of whether the original Happenings were actually interactive, we may turn to the consideration, more thought-provoking in a new media context, of how we can learn from the contrasts between this and other models of interactivity. While we might compare Kaprow's statements with obviously-dissimilar models (such as menu-driven species of interaction), it is arguably more interesting to ask how this model of interactive performance compares with that of other performance models, such as Augusto Boal's (◊22). For example, Kaprow discusses increasing the responsibility of the observer, and then abolishing the audience altogether, with the artist remaining the organizing force. Boal similarly speaks of abolishing the distinction between actor and spectator (in his performances the "protagonist" becomes a turn-taking role), and makes organization of the performance activity a community function as well. However, the work Kaprow reports does not necessarily employ interaction in the service of something besides the creation of a new experience and type of attention—while Boal's work is analytically and politically motivated, hoping to recognize and practice opportunities for action against oppression. In both cases the interactive method comes from outside the community, and because the organizing principles are not within the audience's sphere of influence, one might next ask whether interactivity of either of these sorts actually goes beyond what Jean Baudrillard (◊19) calls "reversibility"—processes like sending letters to the editor to the newspaper—and rearranges communication in a fundamental way.

In parallel, Kaprow's insight into the cultural moment from which Happenings sprang may help us put related new media technology developments into context. For example, a useful connection can be drawn between Kaprow's anti-hierarchical formulation of art and Nelson's anti-hierarchical formulation of computing. Kaprow's Happenings seem to have their closest new media relative in Myron Krueger's (◊25) "responsive environments"—a body of work heralded as art by some, as technology by others, and as neither by powerful groups in each field. Yet Krueger's work, like Kaprow's, has been enormously influential. Perhaps this ambivalence and influence is the mark of true "intermedia" work—a term coined by Fluxus artist Dick Higgins to describe work of this cultural moment, work which was greeted with ecstasy and rejected with horror as it threatened to overflow, and even wash away, the boundaries between disciplines that the "total forms" (such as opera) had only subsumed and reinforced.

—NWF

*Regina Cornwell, "From the Analytical Engine to Lady Ada's Art" (51–52):*

Allan Kaprow's use of the term *happening* in 1959 was picked up by the media and the art world and applied to various performances and events. He spoke of increasing the "'responsibility' of the observer" and finally eliminating the audience altogether as each individual present would become part of the event organized by an artist. Yoko Ono, identified with Fluxus, produced a number of works that demanded participation from her audience. For instance, in her *Cut Piece*, performed in 1965 at New York's Carnegie Recital Hall and elsewhere, she invited her audience to come forward, pick up scissors, and cut off a piece of her clothing as she sat placidly on the stage floor facing them. This work appears as a script in Ono's book, *Strip Tease Show*. There, and in other books, such as *Grapefruit* (1964), she bids her readers to participate by following instructions, either imaginatively or in fact.

◊19
277

◊22
339

◊25
377

*Söke Dinkla, "From Participation to Interaction" (283, 289–290):*

Kaprow's Happenings make abundantly clear that not every form of participation per se implies a higher responsibility for the visitor and thus a less authoritarian role of the artist. Rather, participation is located along a fragile border between emancipatory act and manipulation. The decisive factor in judging the receptive situation is how active the unprepared viewer becomes within a certain framework of action and without specific instructions. . . .

The widespread judgment that interactive intercourse with computer systems prepares the ground for an emancipation from the media context, via the development from 'passive' to 'active' reception, is being euphorically defended by referring to the participatory art of the sixties. But the role of the performers and the leader of Happenings has also shown that neither the authoritative role of the artist nor the notion of work has been abandoned completely. These concepts will remain a principle in interactive art, too. They are delegated to the program and automatized. The *artistic material* of interactive art is the *automatized dialogue* between program and user. Interactive artworks provide a critical analysis of the automatized communication that is replacing interhuman relationships in more and more social fields. Thus the distribution of power between user and system is not just a technological issue but a social and political issue as well.

Further Reading

Cornwell, Regina. "From the Analytical Engine to Lady Ada's Art," *Iterations: The New Image*. Ed. Timothey Druckrey. New York: International Center of Photography, dist. MIT Press, 1993.

Dinkla, Söke. "From Participation to Interaction: Toward the Origins of Interactive Art." *Clicking In: Hot Links to a Digital Culture*. Ed. Lynn Hershman Leeson. Seattle: Bay Press, 1996.

Kaprow, Allan. *Assemblage, Environments, & Happenings*. New York: Harry N. Abrams, 1966.

Original Publication

*Art News* 60(3):36–39,58–62. 1961. Reprinted in Allan Kaprow, *Essays on the Blurring of Art and Life*. Ed. Jeff Kelley. Berkeley: University of California Press, 1993.

# "Happenings" in the New York Scene

## Allan Kaprow

If you haven't been to the Happenings, let me give you a kaleidoscope sampling of some of their great moments. Everybody is crowded into a downtown loft, milling about, like at an opening. It's hot. There are lots of big cartons sitting all over the place. One by one they start to move, sliding and careening drunkenly in every direction, lunging into one another, accompanied by loud breathing sounds over four loudspeakers. Now it's winter and cold and it's dark, and all around little blue lights go on and off at their own speed while three large brown gunnysack constructions drag an enormous pile of ice and stones over bumps, losing most of it, and blankets keep falling over everything from the ceiling. A hundred iron barrels and gallon wine jugs hanging on ropes swing back and forth, crashing like church bells, spewing glass all over. Suddenly, mushy shapes pop up from the floor and painters slash at curtains dripping with action. A wall of trees tied with colored rags

advances on the crowd, scattering everybody, forcing them to leave. There are muslin telephone booths for all with a record player or microphone that tunes you in to everybody else. Coughing, you breathe in noxious fumes, or the smell of hospitals and lemon juice. A nude girl runs after the racing pool of a searchlight, throwing spinach greens into it. Slides and movies, projected over walls and people, depict hamburgers: big ones, huge ones, red ones, skinny ones, flat ones, etc. You come in as a spectator and maybe you discover you're caught in it after all, as you push things around like so much furniture. Words rumble past, whispering, dee-daaa, baroom, love me, love me; shadows joggle on screens; power saws and lawn mowers screech just like the I.R.T. at Union Square. Tin cans rattle and you stand up to see or change your seat or answer questions shouted at you by shoeshine boys and old ladies. Long silences when nothing happens, and you're sore because you paid $1.50 contribution, when bang! there you are facing yourself in a mirror jammed at you. Listen. A cough from the alley. You giggle because you're afraid, suffer claustrophobia, talk to someone nonchalantly, but all the time you're there, getting into the act. . . . Electric fans start, gently wafting breezes of New-Car smell past your nose as leaves bury piles of a whining, burping, foul, pinky mess.

So much for the flavor. Now I would like to describe the nature of Happenings in a different manner, more analytically—their purpose and place in art.

Although widespread opinion has been expressed about these events, usually by those who have never seen them, they are actually little known beyond a small group of interested persons. This small following is aware of several different kinds of Happenings. There are the sophisticated, witty works put on by the theater people; the very sparsely abstract, almost Zen-like rituals given by another group (mostly writers and musicians); and those in which I am most involved, crude, lyrical, and very spontaneous. This kind grew out of the advanced American painting of the last decade, and those of us involved were all painters (or still are). There is some beneficial exchange among the three, however.

In addition, outside New York there is the Gutai group in Osaka; reported activity in San Francisco, Chicago, Cologne, Paris, and Milan; and a history that goes back through Surrealism, Dada, Mime, the circus, carnivals, the traveling saltimbanques, all the way to medieval mystery plays and processions. Of most of this we know very little; only the spirit has been sensed. Of what *I* know, I find that I have decided philosophical reservations. Therefore, the points I make are intended to represent, not the views of all those who create works that might be generically related, or even of all those whose work I admire, but of those whose works I feel to be the most adventuresome, fruitfully open to applications, and the most challenging of any art in the air at present.

Happenings are events that, put simply, happen. Though the best of them have a decided impact—that is, we feel, "here is something important"—they appear to go nowhere and do not make any particular literary point. In contrast to the arts of the past, they have no structured beginning, middle, or end. Their form is open-ended and fluid; nothing obvious is sought and therefore nothing is won, except the certainty of a number of occurrences to which we are more than normally attentive. They exist for a single performance, or only a few, and are gone forever as new ones take their place.

These events are essentially theater pieces, however unconventional. That they are still largely rejected by devotees of the theater may be due to their uncommon power and primitive energy, and to their derivation from the rites of American Action Painting. But by widening the concept "theater" to include them (like widening the concept "painting" to include collage), we can see them against this basic background and understand them better.

To my way of thinking, Happenings possess some crucial qualities that distinguish them from the usual theatrical works, even the experimental ones of today. First, there is the *context*, the place of conception and enactment. The most intense and

essential Happenings have been spawned in old lofts, basements, vacant stores, natural surroundings, and the street, where very small audiences, or groups of visitors, are commingled in some way with the event, flowing in and among its parts. There is thus no separation of audience and play (as there is even in round or pit theaters); the elevated picture-window view of most playhouses is gone, as are the expectations of curtain openings and *tableaux vivants* and curtain closings. . . .

The sheer rawness of the out-of-doors or the closeness of dingy city quarters in which the radical Happenings flourish is more appropriate, I believe, in temperament and un-artiness, to the materials and directness of these works. The place where anything grows up (a certain kind of art in this case), that is, its "habitat," gives to it not only a space, a set of relationships to the various things around it, and a range of values, but an overall atmosphere as well, which penetrates it and whoever experiences it. Habitats have always had this effect, but it is especially important now, when our advanced art approaches a fragile but marvelous life, one that maintains itself by a mere thread, melting the surroundings, the artist, the work, and everyone who comes to it into an elusive, changeable configuration.

If I may digress a moment to bring this point into focus, it may reveal why the "better" galleries and homes (whose decor is still a by-now-antiseptic neoclassicism of the twenties) dessicate and prettify modern paintings and sculpture that had looked so natural in their studio birthplace. It may also explain why artists' studios do not look like galleries and why when an artist's studio does, everyone is suspicious. I think that today this organic connection between art and its environment is so meaningful and necessary that removing one from the other results in abortion. Yet the artists who have made us aware of this lifeline deny it; for the flattery of being "on show" blinds them to every insensitivity heaped upon their suddenly weakened offerings. There seems no end to the white walls, the tasteful aluminum frames, the lovely lighting, fawn gray rugs, cocktails, polite conversation. The attitude, I mean the worldview, conveyed by such a fluorescent reception is in itself not "bad." It is unaware. And being unaware, it can hardly be responsive to the art it promotes and professes to admire.

Happenings invite us to cast aside for a moment these proper manners and partake wholly in the real nature of the art and (one hopes) life. Thus a Happening is rough and sudden and often feels "dirty." Dirt, we might begin to realize, is also organic and fertile, and everything, including the visitors, can grow a little in such circumstances.

To return to the contrast between Happenings and plays, the second important difference is that a Happening has no plot, no obvious "philosophy," and is materialized in an improvisatory fashion, like jazz, and like much contemporary painting, where we do not know exactly what is going to happen next. The action leads itself any way it wishes, and the artist controls it only to the degree that it keeps on "shaking" right. A modern play rarely has such an impromptu basis, for plays are still *first written*. A Happening is *generated* in action by a headful of ideas or a flimsily jotted-down score of "root" directions.

A play assumes that words are the almost absolute medium. A Happening frequently has words, but they may or may not make literal sense. If they do, their sense is not part of the fabric of "sense" that other nonverbal elements (noise, visual stuff, action) convey. Hence, they have a brief, emergent, and sometimes detached quality. If they do not make sense, then they are heard as the *sound* of words instead of the meaning conveyed by them. Words, however, need not be used at all: a Happening might consist of a swarm of locusts being dropped in and around the performance space. This element of chance with respect to the medium itself is not to be expected from the ordinary theater.

Indeed, the involvement in chance, which is the third and most problematical quality found in Happenings, rarely occurs in the conventional theater. When it does, it is usually a marginal benefit of interpretation. In the present work, chance (in conjunction with improvisation) is a deliberately employed mode of operating that penetrates the whole composition and its character. It is the vehicle of the spontaneous. And it is the clue to understanding how control (the setting up of chance techniques) can effectively produce the opposite quality of the unplanned and apparently uncontrolled. I think it can be demonstrated that much contemporary art, which counts upon inspiration to yield that admittedly desirable verve or sense of the unselfconscious, is by now getting results that appear planned and academic. A loaded brush and a mighty swing always seem to hit the ball to the same spot.

Chance then, rather than spontaneity, is a key term, for it implies risk and fear (thus reestablishing that fine nervousness so pleasant when something is about to occur). It also better names a method that becomes manifestly unmethodical if one considers the pudding more a proof than the recipe.

Traditional art has always tried to make it good every time, believing that this was a truer truth than life. Artists who directly utilize chance hazard failure, the "failure" of being less artistic and more lifelike. The "Art" they produce might surprisingly turn out to be an affair that has all the inevitability of a well-ordered middle-class Thanksgiving dinner (I have seen a few remarkable Happenings that were "bores" in this sense). But it could be like slipping on a banana peel, or going to heaven.

If a flexible framework with the barest limits is established by selecting, for example, only five elements out of an infinity of possibilities, almost anything can happen. And something always does, even things that are unpleasant. Visitors to a Happening are now and then not sure what has taken place, when it has ended, even when things have gone "wrong." For when something goes "wrong," something far more "right," more revelatory, has many times emerged. This sort of sudden near-miracle presently seems to be made more likely by chance procedures.

If artists grasp the import of that word *chance* and accept it (no easy achievement in our culture), then its methods needn't invariably cause their work to reduce to either chaos or a bland indifference, lacking in concreteness and intensity, as in a table of random numbers. On the contrary, the identities of those artists who employ such techniques are very clear. It is odd that when artists give up certain hitherto privileged aspects of the self, so that they cannot always "correct" something according to their taste, the work and the artist frequently come out on top. And when they come out on the bottom, it is a very concrete bottom!

The final point I should like to make about Happenings as against plays is implicit in all the discussion—their impermanence. Composed so that a premium is placed on the unforeseen, a Happening cannot be reproduced. The few performances given of each work differ considerably from one another; and the work is over before habits begin to set in. The physical materials used to create the environment of Happenings are the most perishable kind: newspapers, junk, rags, old wooden crates knocked together, cardboard cartons cut up, real trees, food, borrowed machines, etc. They cannot last for long in whatever arrangement they are put. A Happening is thus fresh, while it lasts, for better or worse.

Here we need not go into the considerable history behind such values embodied in the Happenings. Suffice it to say that the passing, the changing, the natural, even the willingness to fail are familiar. They reveal a spirit that is at once passive in its acceptance of what may be and affirmative in its disregard of security. One is also left exposed to the quite marvelous experience of being surprised. This is, in essence, a continuation of the tradition of Realism.

The significance of the Happening is not to be found simply in the fresh creative wind now blowing. Happenings are not just another new style. Instead, like American art of the late 1940s, they are a moral act, a human stand of great urgency, whose professional status as art is less a criterion than their certainty as an ultimate existential commitment.

It has always seemed to me that American creative energy only becomes charged by such a sense of crisis. The real weakness of much vanguard art since 1951 is its complacent assumption that art exists and can be recognized and practiced. I am not so sure whether what we do now is art or something not quite art. If I call it art, it is because I wish to avoid the endless arguments some other name would bring forth. Paradoxically, if it turns out to be art after all, it will be so in spite of (or because of) this larger question.

But this explosive atmosphere has been absent from our arts for ten years, and one by one our major figures have dropped by the wayside, laden with glory. If tense excitement has returned with the Happenings, one can only suspect that the pattern will be repeated. These are our greenest days. Some of us will become famous, and we will have proven once again that the only success occurred when there was a lack of it.

Such worries have been voiced before in more discouraging times, but today is hardly such a time, when so many are rich and desire a befitting culture. I may seem therefore to throw water on a kindly spark when I touch on this note, for we customarily prefer to celebrate victories without ever questioning whether they are victories indeed. But I think it is necessary to question the whole state of American success, because to do so is not only to touch on what is characteristically American and what is crucial about Happenings but also partly to explain America's special strength. And this strength has nothing to do with success.

Particularly in New York, where success is most evident, we have not yet looked clearly at it and what it may imply— something that, until recently, a European who had earned it did quite naturally. We are unable to accept rewards for being artists, because it has been sensed deeply that to be one means to live and work in isolation and pride. Now that a new haut monde is demanding of us art and more art, we find ourselves running away or running to it, shocked and guilty, either way. I

must be emphatic: the glaring truth, to anyone who cares to examine it calmly, is that nearly all artists, working in any medium from words to paint, who have made their mark as innovators, as radicals in the best sense of that word, have, once they have been recognized and paid handsomely, capitulated to the interests of good taste. There is no overt pressure anywhere. The patrons of art are the nicest people in the world. They neither wish to corrupt nor actually do so. The whole situation is corrosive, for neither patrons nor artists comprehend their role; both are always a little edgy, however abundantly smiles are exchanged. Out of this hidden discomfort there comes a stillborn art, tight or merely repetitive at best and at worst, chic. The old daring and the charged atmosphere of precarious discovery that marked every hour of the lives of modern artists, even when they were not working at art, vanishes. Strangely, no one seems to know this except, perhaps, the "unsuccessful" artists waiting for their day. . . .

To us, who are already answering the increasing telephone calls from entrepreneurs, this is more than disturbing. We are, at this writing, still free to do what we wish, and are watching ourselves as we become caught up in an irreversible process. Our Happenings, like all the other art produced in the last decade and a half by those who, for a few brief moments, were also free, are in no small part the expression of this liberty. In our beginning some of us, reading the signs all too clearly, are facing our end.

If this is close to the truth, it is surely melodrama as well, and I intend the tone of my words to suggest that quality. Anyone moved by the spirit of tough-guyism would answer that all of this is a pseudo-problem of the artists' own making. They have the alternative of rejecting fame if they do not want its responsibilities. Artists have made their sauce; now they must stew in it. It is not the patrons' and the publicists' moral obligation to protect the artists' freedom.

But such an objection, while sounding healthy and realistic, is in fact European and old-fashioned; it sees the creator as an indomitable hero who exists on a plane above any living context. It fails to appreciate the special character of our mores in America, and this matrix, I would maintain, is the only reality within which any question about the arts may be asked.

The tough answer fails to appreciate our taste for fads and "movements," each one increasingly equivalent to the last in value and complexion, making for that vast ennui, that anxiety lying so close to the surface of our comfortable existence. It does not account for our need to "love" everybody (our democracy) that must give every dog his bone and compels everyone known by no one to want to be addressed by a nickname. This relentless craving loves everything destructively, for it actually hates love. What can anyone's interest in this kind of art or that marvelous painter possibly mean then? Is it a meaning lost on the artist?

Where else can we see the unbelievable but frequent phenomenon of successful radicals becoming "fast friends" with successful academicians, united only by a common success and deliberately insensitive to the fundamental issues their different values imply? I wonder where else but here can be found that shutting of the eyes to the question of purpose. Perhaps in the United States such a question could not ever before exist, so pervasive has been the amoral mush.

This everyday world affects the way art is created as much as it conditions its response—a response the critic articulates for the patron, who in turn acts upon it. Melodrama, I think, is central to all of this.

Apart from those in our recent history who have achieved something primarily in the spirit of European art, much of the positive character of America can be understood by the word *melodrama*: the saga of the Pioneer is true melodrama, the Cowboy and the Indian; the Rent Collector, Stella Dallas, Charlie Chaplin, the Organization Man, Mike Todd are melodrama. And now the American Artist is a melodramatic figure. Probably without trying, we have been able to see profoundly what we are all about through these archetypal personages. This is the quality of our temperament that a classically trained mind would invariably mistake for sentimentality.

But I do not want to suggest that avant-garde artists produce even remotely sentimental works; I am referring more to the hard and silly melodrama of their lives and almost farcical social position, known as well as the story of George Washington and the Cherry Tree, which infuses what they do with a powerful yet fragile fever. The idea is partly that they will be famous only after they die, a myth we have taken to heart far more than the Europeans, and far more than we care to admit. Half-consciously, though, there is the more indigenous dream that the adventure is everything; the tangible goal is not important. The Pacific coast is farther away than we thought, Ponce de Leon's Fountain of Youth lies beyond the next everglade, and the next, and the next . . . meanwhile let's battle the alligators.

What is not melodramatic, in the sense I am using the word, but is disappointing and tragic, is that today vanguard artists are given their prizes very quickly instead of being left to their adventure. Furthermore, they are led to believe, by no one in particular, that this was the thing they wanted all the while. But in some obscure recess of their mind, they assume they must now die, at least spiritually, to keep the myth intact. Hence, the creative aspect of their art ceases. To all intents and purposes, they are dead and they are famous.

In this context of achievement-and-death, artists who make Happenings are living out the purest melodrama. Their activity embodies the myth of nonsuccess, for Happenings cannot be sold and taken home; they can only be supported. And because of their intimate and fleeting nature, only a few people can experience them. They remain isolated and proud. The creators of such events are adventurers too, because much of what they do is unforeseen. They stack the deck that way.

By some reasonable but unplanned process, Happenings, we may suspect, have emerged as an art that can function precisely as long as the mechanics of our present rush for cultural maturity continue. This situation will no doubt change eventually and thus will change the issues I address here.

But for now there is this to consider, the point I raised earlier: some of us will probably become famous. It will be an ironic fame fashioned largely by those who have never seen our work. The attention and pressure of such a position will probably destroy most of us, as they have nearly all the others. We know no better than anyone else how to handle the metaphysics and practice of worldly power. We know even less, since we have not been in the slightest involved with it. That I feel it necessary, in the interests of the truth, to write this article, which may hasten the conclusion, is even more fatefully ironic. But this is the chance we take; it is part of the picture. . . .

Yet I cannot help wondering if there isn't a positive side, too, a side also subject to the throw of the dice. To the extent that a Happening is not a commodity but a brief event, from the standpoint of any publicity it may receive, it may become a state of mind. Who will have been there at that event? It may become like the sea monsters of the past or the flying saucers of yesterday. I shouldn't really mind, for as the new myth grows on its own, without reference to anything in particular, the artist may achieve a beautiful privacy, famed for something purely imaginary while free to explore something nobody will notice.

# 07. [Introduction]
# The Cut-Up Method of Brion Gysin

There is nothing new under the sun. Here, William Burroughs—adding machine fortune heir, junkie, killer of his wife, most challenging and complex of the Beat writers—describes a technique itself based on earlier experiments of the surrealists, which in turn had their origins centuries before, in techniques of very literal "cut and paste" editing. It is quite fitting that Burroughs invoked computing pioneer John von Neumann in tracing the uses of the cut-up method, for these techniques have been employed in many aspects of new media, in computer literary practice as well as game theory. That they are not novel should not deter writers from use of these techniques. Although drawing words out of a hat to form a poem may be old hat, it can still be an effective technique for textual production. It can also suggest different techniques which are genuinely new.

There have been plenty of "surrealist" poetry generators available on the Web for years. Their invocation of surrealism is misleading. Generating texts directly for readers by means of computer-approximated randomness is not what the Surrealists or Burroughs meant to suggest. Burroughs indicates, rather, that randomness and recombination can be used by an author as an intermediate step in composition. The surrealists were uninterested in tossing dice unless the throw might help to coax something up from the unconsciousness. It is only in juxtaposition with our personal and social ghosts, as Italo Calvino writes, that randomly-retrieved words resonate.

Those using the cut-up method should note that it is hardly incompatible with the process of revision. In fact, this very article was substantially revised and expanded by Burroughs between its first appearance in 1961 and its publication in a 1978 book that he and Brion Gysin edited. In the much shorter original article, Burroughs wrote that "The cut-up method was used in *Naked Lunch* without the author's full awareness of the method he was using. . . . Subsequently I used the method with awareness scissors in *Minutes to Go* and *The Exterminator*." He encouraged cut-up creators to "Cut paper cut film cut tape" and to employ "Scissors or switch blade as preferred."

Although the claim was made that the book *The Policeman's Beard is Half Constructed* was generated by computer alone, few who have studied the text (and the program that purportedly generated it, *Racter*) believe this claim. Rather, it seems certain that *Racter* was loaded with special, additional templates to generate a draft, which was then edited into its published shape by a human editor. A similar method was used without dissimulation by Charles O. Hartman, who has written computer programs, had them programmatically mangle texts, and then has gone on to use the texts in creating poems. More recently, free software has been used to generate metrical, rhymed sonnets. These are descendants of the traditional poetic cut-up form, the cento, cross-bred with Burroughs's cut-up technique and the combinatorial and procedural methods of the Oulipo (◊12).
—NM

**Further Reading**

Beiles, Sinclair, William Burroughs, Gregory Corso, and Brion Gysin. *Minutes to Go.* Paris: Two Cities Editions, 1960.

Burroughs, William S. "The Invisible Generation." *The Ticket That Exploded,* 205–217. New York: Grove Press, 1967.

Calvino, Italo. "Cybernetics and Ghosts." *The Uses of Literature,* 3–27. New York: Harcourt Brace Jovanovich, 1986.

Gnoetry. <http://www.beardofbees.com/gnoetry.html>

Hartman, Charles O. *The Virtual Muse: Experiments in Computer Poetry.* Hanover, N.H.: Wesleyan University Press, 1996.

Odier, Daniel. *The Job: Interviews with William S. Burroughs.* New York: Penguin, 1989.

Burroughs's article was published just before Ted Nelson (◊11) coined the term "hypertext" in a famous piece which also imagined decomposing and rearranging the traditional hierarchical text.

89
◊11
133

◊12
147

*Italo Calvino, "Cybernetics and Ghosts" (20,22):*

The relationship between combinatorial play and the unconscious in artistic activity lies at the heart of one of the most convincing aesthetic theories currently in circulation, a formula that draws upon both psychoanalysis and the practical experience of arts and letters. . . . Literature is a combinatorial game that pursues the possibilities implicit in its own material, independent of the personality of the poet, but it is a game that at a certain point is invested with an unexpected meaning, a meaning that is not patent on the linguistic plane on which we were working but has slipped in from another level, activating something that on that second level is of great concern to the author or his society. The literature machine can perform all the permutations possible on a given material, but the poetic result will be the particular effect of one of these on a man endowed with consciousness and an unconscious, that is, an empirical and historical man. It will be the shock that occurs only if the writing machine is surrounded by the hidden ghosts of the individual and his society.

Original Publication

*A Casebook on the Beat,* 105–106. Ed. Thomas Parkinson. New York: Crowell, 1961. This text is from William S. Burroughs and Brion Gysin, *The Third Mind,* 29–33. New York: Viking, 1978. This text was revised and enlarged by Burroughs from his six paragraphs in *A Casebook on the Beat.*

Ellipses are from the text as published in *The Third Mind.*

# The Cut-Up Method of Brion Gysin
## William S. Burroughs

At a surrealist rally in the 1920s Tristan Tzara the man from nowhere proposed to create a poem on the spot by pulling words out of a hat. A riot ensued wrecked the theater. André Breton expelled Tristan Tzara from the movement and grounded the cut-ups on the Freudian couch.

In the summer of 1959 Brion Gysin painter and writer cut newspaper articles into sections and rearranged the sections *at random. Minutes to Go* resulted from this initial cut-up experiment. *Minutes to Go* contains unedited unchanged cut ups emerging as quite coherent and meaningful prose.

The cut-up method brings to writers the collage, which has been used by painters for fifty years. And used by the moving and still camera. In fact all street shots from movie or still cameras are by the unpredictable factors of passers by and juxtaposition cut-ups. And photographers will tell you that often their best shots are accidents ... writers will tell you the same. The best writing seems to be done almost by accident but writers until the cut-up method was made explicit—all writing is in fact cut ups. I will return to this point—had no way to produce the accident of spontaneity. You can not *will* spontaneity. But you can introduce the unpredictable spontaneous factor with a pair of scissors.

The method is simple. Here is one way to do it. Take a page. Like this page. Now cut down the middle and cross the middle. You have four sections: 1   2   3   4 ... one two three four. Now rearrange the sections placing section four with section one and section two with section three. And

you have a new page. Sometimes it says much the same thing. Sometimes something quite different—cutting up political speeches is an interesting exercise—in any case you will find that it says something and something quite definite. Take any poet or writer you fancy. Here, say, or poems you have read over many times. The words have lost meaning and life through years of repetition. Now take the poem and type out selected passages. Fill a page with excerpts. Now cut the page. You have a new poem. As many poems as you like. As many Shakespeare Rimbaud poems as you like. Tristan Tzara said: "Poetry is for everyone." And André Breton called him a cop and expelled him from the movement. Say it again: "Poetry is for everyone." Poetry is a place and it is free to all cut up Rimbaud and you are in Rimbaud's place. Here is a Rimbaud poem cut up.

> Visit of memories. Only your dance and your voice house. On the suburban air improbable desertions ... all harmonic pine for strife.

> The great skies are open. Candor of vapor and tent spitting blood laugh and drunken penance.

> Promenade of wine perfume opens slow bottle.

> The great skies are open. Supreme bugle burning flesh children to mist.

Cut-ups are for everyone. Anybody can make cut ups. It is experimental in the sense of being *something to do.* Right here write now. Not something to talk and argue about. Greek philosophers assumed logically that an object twice as heavy as another object would fall twice as fast. It did not occur to them to push the two objects off the table and see how they fall. Cut the words and see how they fall.

Shakespeare Rimbaud live in their words. Cut the word lines and you will hear their voices. Cut-ups often come through as code messages with special meaning for the cutter. Table tapping? Perhaps. Certainly an improvement on the usual deplorable performance of contacted poets through a medium. Rimbaud announces himself, to be followed by some excruciatingly bad poetry. Cutting Rimbaud's words and you are assured of good poetry at least if not personal appearance.

All writing is in fact cut-ups. A collage of words read heard overhead. What else? Use of scissors renders the process explicit and subject to extension and variation. Clear classical prose can be composed entirely of rearranged cut-ups. Cutting and rearranging a page of written words introduces a new dimension into writing enabling the writer to turn images in cinematic variation. Images shift sense under the scissors smell images to sound sight to sound sound to kinesthetic. This is where Rimbaud was going with his color of vowels. And his "systematic derangement of the senses." The place of mescaline hallucination: seeing colors tasting sounds smelling forms.

The cut-ups can be applied to other fields than writing. Dr Neumann in his *Theory of Games and Economic Behavior* introduces the cut-up method of random action into game and military strategy: assume that the worst has happened and act accordingly. If your strategy is at some point determined . . . by random factor your opponent will gain no advantage from knowing your strategy since he can not predict the move. The cut-up method could be used to advantage in processing scientific data. How many discoveries have been made by accident? We can not produce accidents to order. The cut-ups could add new dimension to films. Cut gambling scene in with a thousand gambling scenes all times and places. Cut back. Cut streets of the world. Cut and rearrange the word and image in films. There is no reason to accept a second-rate product when you can have the best. And the best is there for all. "Poetry is for everyone" . . .

Now here are the preceding two paragraphs cut into four sections and rearranged:

ALL WRITING IS IN FACT CUT-UPS OF GAMES AND ECONOMIC BEHAVIOR OVERHEARD? WHAT ELSE? ASSUME THAT THE WORST HAS HAPPENED EXPLICIT AND SUBJECT TO STRATEGY IS AT SOME POINT CLASSICAL PROSE. CUTTING AND REARRANGING FACTOR YOUR OPPONENT WILL GAIN INTRODUCES A NEW DIMENSION YOUR STRATEGY. HOW MANY DISCOVERIES SOUND TO KINESTHETIC? WE CAN NOW PRODUCE ACCIDENT TO HIS COLOR OF VOWELS. AND NEW DIMENSION TO FILMS CUT THE SENSES. THE PLACE OF SAND. GAMBLING SCENES ALL TIMES COLORS TASTING SOUNDS SMELL STREETS OF THE WORLD. WHEN YOU CAN HAVE THE BEST ALL: "POETRY IS FOR EVERYONE" DR NEUMANN IN A COLLAGE OF WORDS READ HEARD INTRODUCED THE CUT-UP SCISSORS RENDERS THE PROCESS GAME AND MILITARY STRATEGY, VARIATION CLEAR AND ACT ACCORDINGLY. IF YOU POSED ENTIRELY OF REARRANGED CUT DETERMINED BY RANDOM A PAGE OF WRITTEN WORDS NO ADVANTAGE FROM KNOWING INTO WRITER PREDICT THE MOVE. THE CUT VARIATION IMAGES SHIFT SENSE ADVANTAGE IN PROCESSING TO SOUND SIGHT TO SOUND. HAVE BEEN MADE BY ACCIDENT IS WHERE RIMBAUD WAS GOING WITH ORDER THE CUT-UPS COULD "SYSTEMATIC DERANGEMENT" OF THE GAMBLING SCENE IN WITH A TEA HALLUCINATION: SEEING AND PLACES. CUT BACK. CUT FORMS. REARRANGE THE WORD AND IMAGE TO OTHER FIELDS THAN WRITING.

# 08. [Introduction]
# From *Augmenting Human Intellect*
## *A Conceptual Framework*

Douglas Engelbart invented many of the defining features of the computer interfaces we work with each day, including the mouse, the window, and the word processor. He helped establish the Internet, made the first serious investigation of computer-supported cooperative work, first demonstrated videoconferencing and mixed text/graphic displays, created structured programming editors and used remote procedure calls in the 1960s, and independently invented the hyperlink at the same time the idea was being hatched by Ted Nelson (◊11).

In short, Engelbart is one of the great inventors of the 20th century. Unfortunately, in addition to being largely unrecognized, he is also one of the most misunderstood figures in new media. Few who know him as "the inventor of the mouse" realize that Engelbart's inventions have never been widely used to pursue the goals that motivated his work in the first place. His inventions to date represent only the first steps of an unfulfilled vision, one summed up in the title of this report, "Augmenting Human Intellect." In 1988, in *A History of Personal Workstations*, Engelbart told the story of his decision to pursue this path:

> I was doing odd-job electrical engineering work at Ames Research Laboratory in Mountain View, California, with the National Advisory Committee for Aeronautics (NACA, forerunner of NASA). For several months I had been devoting most of my spare time to searching for professional goals; for some reason I wanted to invest the rest of my heretofore aimless career toward making the most difference in improving the lot of the human race. . . .

> Suddenly, up through all of this delightful, youthful abstraction bobbed the following clear realization: The complexity of the human situation was steadily increasing. Along with the increasing complexity had come a general increase in the urgency associated with the more critical problems. . . .

> FLASH–1: The difficulty of mankind's problems was increasing at a greater rate than our ability to cope. (We are in trouble.)

> FLASH–2: Boosting mankind's ability to deal with complex, urgent problems would be an attractive candidate as an arena in which a young person might try to "make the most difference." (Yes, but there's that question of what does the young electrical engineer do about it? Retread for a role as educator, research psychologist, legislator, . . . ? Is there any handle there that an electrical engineer could . . . ?)

> FLASH–3: Ahah—graphic vision surges forth of me sitting at a large CRT console, working in ways that are rapidly evolving in front of my eyes (beginning from memories of the radar-screen consoles I used to service).

> The imagery of FLASH–3 evolved within a few days to a general information environment where the basic concept was a document that would include mixed text and graphic portrayals on the CRT. The imagery carried on to extensions of the symbology and methodology that we humans could employ to do our heavy thinking. There were also images of other people at consoles attached to the same computer complex, simultaneously working in a collaboration mode that would be much closer and more effective than we had ever been able to accomplish.

> Within weeks I had committed my career to "augmenting the human intellect" (188–189).

*In Engelbart's view, essentially all humans are already augmented. (For example, a typewriter makes the process of writing faster.) He dubbed this augmentation, in the context of which he proposed to do his work, the H-LAM/T system. H-LAM/T stands for "Human using Language, Artifacts, Methodology, in which he is Trained." Each of these terms is explained in section II.A of the report:*

1. *Artifacts—physical objects designed to provide for human comfort, for the manipulation of things or materials, and for the manipulation of symbols.*

2. *Language—the way in which the individual parcels out the picture of his world into the concepts that his mind uses to model that world, and the symbols that he attaches to those concepts and uses in consciously manipulating the concepts ("thinking").*

3. *Methodology—the methods, procedures, strategies, etc., with which an individual organizes his goal-centered (problem-solving) activity.*

4. *Training—the conditioning needed by the human being to bring his skills in using Means 1, 2, and 3 to the point where they are operationally effective.*

**94**

Within the H-LAM/T system, Engelbart discusses the augmented human's repertoire of capabilities as a "toolkit"—a discussion of the human in mechanical terms that recalls Norbert Wiener's formulations of cybernetics (◊04).

Engelbart's report proposed to make improvements to the artifacts of this system as enabled by unanticipated new technology opportunities—and then simultaneously pursuing new opportunities for evolving our language and methodologies concurrently with the new artifacts. Because Engelbart, in 1962, could only speculate about effective augmentation means (in ways that were remarkably correct), he also included examples of de-augmentation. One of the most amusing, which an illustration is included here, is that of de-augmenting the writing process.

Engelbart quit his job, earned a Ph.D., went to work at the Stanford Research Institute (SRI), and began to pursue funding for his augmentation research program. Two years after joining SRI (in 1959) he had partial support for his time. The next year he was full-time on augmentation, and in 1962 he filed the historic report excerpted here—the first major fruit of FLASH–3.

Some of the most stirring, most prescient sections of Engelbart's report are told in the style of a "graphic vision" (that is, in the style of science fiction) and are narrated in the second person. Other styles found in the report include a relatively standard reporting style, personal reflection on his modes of working, a speculative voice, and a dense investigation of the human augmentation system. The last of these is the most challenging to read; serious students and practitioners of new media will benefit from reading Engelbart's entire report ⊗. The excerpts here represent some of the most useful starting points for this work.

These excerpts are situated within the report's overall framework. The first excerpt combines a general introduction to the report with a vision of "process augmentation" for an architect (offered before Nicholas Negroponte's famous *The Architecture Machine* and its follow-up *Soft Architecture Machines*, ◊23). The second excerpt includes Engelbart's discussion of Vannevar Bush's "As We May Think" (◊02) and of experiments Engelbart undertook along memex lines using paper notecards. (These experiments may remind one of Xerox PARC's Notecards system, or of a passage found in Walter Benjamin's *Reflections* that is well-loved by hypertext theorists: "And today the book is already, as the present mode of scholarly production demonstrates, an outdated mediation between two different filing systems. For everything that matters is to be found in the card box of the researcher who wrote it, and the scholar studying it assimilates it into his own card index" (78).) Finally, a portion of Engelbart's second-person narration of future technology is included. Rather than also excerpt the dead-on specification for what we would come to know as the word processor, these selections include powerful descriptions of capabilities most computers still do not have, 40 years later. Some of these capabilities relate closely to today's research—including the Fisheye Views generalized by George Furnas and link types (which enable links to play a greater variety of informational roles than being jump markers). Since Engelbart, link types have been investigated by many working in hypertext. While they have failed to gain the popularity that the monolithic link of the Web has gained, they may come into more popular use if the W3C's XLink or a related standard is successful.

More discussion of Engelbart's work, and its history, is included in this volume's introduction to his 1968 paper with William English, "A Research Center for Augmenting Human Intellect." (◊16)
—NWF

*Although this report is obscure when compared to Engelbart's widely-adopted inventions, Engelbart considers the conceptual framework outlined here his most significant contribution to the field of new media. As he discusses in* A History of Personal Workstations:

[W]hat I came to realize is that there is only one, clearly dominant factor that underlies essentially every cause for any uniqueness that I might list for historical record. It isn't a technology, it isn't a science, and it isn't a marketing or business model ... It is what I call my "Framework." My Framework is based upon an intuitive conviction, implanted in my head (apparently permanently) over 30 years ago, that the gains in human knowledge-work capability that we will achieve by properly harnessing this new technology will be very large. Metaphorically, I see the augmented organization or institution of the future as changing, not as an organism merely to be a bigger and faster snail, but to achieve such new levels of sensory capability, speed, power, and coordination as to become a new species—a cat.

Further Reading

Bardini, Thierry. *Bootstrapping*. Stanford, Calif.: Stanford University Press, 2000.

Furnas, George. "Generalized Fisheye Views." *Human Factors in Computing Systems,* 16–23. CHI '86 Conference Proceedings, 1986.

Goldberg, Adele, ed. *A History of Personal Workstations*. New York: ACM Press History Series, 1988.

Halasz, Frank, Thomas Moran, and Randall Trigg. "NoteCards in a Nutshell." *CHI+GI'87 Conference Proceedings*, 345–365. 1987.

Original Publication

Excerpted from Summary Report AFOSR–3223 under Contract AF 49(638)–1024, SRI Project 3578 for Air Force Office of Scientific Research, Menlo Park, California: Stanford Research Institute, October 1962.

# Augmenting Human Intellect
## A Conceptual Framework

# Douglas Engelbart

## I  Introduction

### A  General

By "augmenting human intellect" we mean increasing the capability of a man to approach a complex problem situation, to gain comprehension to suit his particular needs, and to derive solutions to problems. Increased capability in this respect is taken to mean a mixture of the following: more-rapid comprehension, better comprehension, the possibility of gaining a useful degree of comprehension in a situation that previously was too complex, speedier solutions, better solutions, and the possibility of finding solutions to problems that before seemed insoluble. And by "complex situations" we include the professional problems of diplomats, executives, social scientists, life scientists, physical scientists, attorneys, designers—whether the problem situation exists for twenty minutes or twenty years. We do not speak of isolated clever tricks that help in particular situations. We refer to a way of life in an integrated domain where hunches, cut-and-try, intangibles, and the human "feel for a situation" usefully co-exist with powerful concepts, streamlined terminology and notation, sophisticated methods, and high-powered electronic aids.

Man's population and gross product are increasing at a considerable rate, but the *complexity* of his problems grows still faster, and the *urgency* with which solutions must be found becomes steadily greater in response to the increased rate of activity and the increasingly global nature of that activity. Augmenting man's intellect, in the sense defined above, would warrant full pursuit by an enlightened society if there could be shown a reasonable approach and some plausible benefits.

This report covers the first phase of a program aimed at developing means to augment the human intellect. These "means" can include many things—all of which appear to be but extensions of means developed and used in the past to help man apply his native sensory, mental, and motor capabilities—and we consider the whole system of a human and his augmentation means as a proper field of search for practical possibilities. It is a very important system to our society, and like most systems its performance can best be improved by considering the whole as a set of interacting components rather than by considering the components in isolation.

This kind of system approach to human intellectual effectiveness does not find a ready-made conceptual framework such as exists for established disciplines. Before a research program can be designed to pursue such an approach intelligently, so that practical benefits might be derived within a reasonable time while also producing results of long-range significance, a conceptual framework must be searched out—a framework that provides orientation as to the important factors of the system, the relationships among these factors, the types of change among the system factors that offer likely improvements in performance, and the sort of research goals and methodology that seem promising.[*]

In the first (search) phase of our program we have developed a conceptual framework that seems satisfactory for the current needs of designing a research phase. Section II contains the essence of this framework as derived from several different ways of looking at the system made up of a human and his intellect-augmentation means.

The process of developing this conceptual framework brought out a number of significant realizations: that the intellectual effectiveness exercised today by a given human has little likelihood of being intelligence limited—that there are dozens of disciplines in engineering, mathematics, and the social, life, and physical sciences that can contribute

---

[*] Kennedy and Putt (see Ref. 1 in the list at the end of the report) bring out the importance of a conceptual framework to the process of research. They point out that new, multi-disciplinary research generally finds no such framework to fit within, that a framework of sorts would grow eventually, but that an explicit framework-search phase preceding the research is much to be preferred.

improvements to the system of intellect-augmentation means; that any one such improvement can be expected to trigger a chain of coordinating improvements; that until every one of these disciplines comes to a standstill *and* we have exhausted all the improvement possibilities we could glean from it, we can expect to continue to develop improvements in this "human-intellect" system; that there is no particular reason not to expect gains in personal intellectual effectiveness from a concerted system-oriented approach that compare to those made in personal geographic mobility since horseback and sailboat days.

The picture of how one can view the possibilities for a systematic approach to increasing human intellectual effectiveness, as put forth in Section II in the sober and

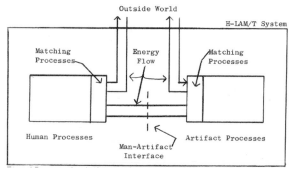

Figure 8.1. Portrayal of the Two Active Domains Within the H-LAM/T System.

*From section II.C.3:* The human and the artifacts are the only physical components of the H-LAM/T system. It is upon their capabilities that the ultimate capability of the system will depend. . . . There are thus two separate domains of activity within the H-LAM/T system: that represented by the human, in which all explicit-human processes occur; and that represented by the arti-facts, in which all explicit-artifact processes occur. In any composite process, there is cooperative interaction between the two domains, requiring interchange of energy (much of it for information exchange purposes only). Figure 8.1 depicts this two-domain concept. . . .

Exchange across this [man-artifact] "interface" occurs when an explicit-human process is coupled to an explicit-artifact process. Quite often these coupled processes are designed for just this exchange purpose, to provide a functional match between other explicit-human and explicit-artifact processes buried within their respective domains that do the more significant things. For instance, the finger and hand motions (explicit-human processes) activate key-linkage motions in the typewriter (couple to explicit-artifact processes). But these are only part of the matching processes between the deeper human processes that direct a given word to be typed and the deeper artifact processes that actually imprint the ink marks on the paper.

general terms of an initial basic analysis, does not seem to convey all of the richness and promise that was stimulated by the development of that picture. Consequently, Section III is intended to present some definite images that illustrate meaningful possibilities derivable from the conceptual framework presented in Section II—and in a rather marked deviation from ordinary technical writing, a good portion of Section III presents these images in a fiction-dialogue style as a mechanism for transmitting a feeling for the richness and promise of the possibilities in one region of the "improvement space" that is roughly mapped in Section II.

The style of Section III seems to make for easier reading. If Section II begins to seem unrewardingly difficult, the reader may find it helpful to skip from Section II-B directly to Section III. If it serves its purpose well enough, Section III will provide a context within which the reader can go back and finish Section II with less effort.

In Section IV (Research Recommendations) we present a general strategy for pursuing research toward increasing human intellectual effectiveness. This strategy evolved directly from the concepts presented in Sections II and III; one of its important precepts is to pursue the quickest gains first, and use the increased intellectual effectiveness thus derived to help pursue successive gains. We see the quickest gains emerging from (1) giving the human the minute-by-minute services of a digital computer equipped with computer-driven cathode-ray-tube display, and (2) developing the new methods of thinking and working that allow the human to capitalize upon the computer's help. By this same strategy, we recommend that an initial research effort develop a prototype system of this sort aimed at increasing human effectiveness in the task of computer programming.

To give the reader an initial orientation about what sort of thing this computer-aided working system might be, we include below a short description of a possible system of this sort. This illustrative example is not to be considered a description of the actual system that will emerge from the program. It is given only to show the general direction of the work, and is clothed in fiction only to make it easier to visualize.

Let us consider an "augmented" architect at work. He sits at a working station that has a visual display screen some three feet on a side; this is his working surface, and is controlled by a computer (his "clerk") with which he can communicate by means of a small keyboard and various other devices.

He is designing a building. He has already dreamed up several basic layouts and structural forms, and is trying them out on the screen. The surveying data for the layout he is working on now have already been entered, and he has just coaxed the "clerk" to show him a perspective view of the steep hillside building site with the roadway above, symbolic representations of the various trees that are to remain on the lot, and the service tie points for the different utilities. The view occupies the left two-thirds of the screen. With a "pointer," he indicates two points of interest, moves his left hand rapidly over the keyboard, and the distance and elevation between the points indicated appear on the right-hand third of the screen.

Now he enters a reference line with his "pointer," and the keyboard. Gradually the screen begins to show the work he is doing—a neat excavation appears in the hillside, revises itself slightly, and revises itself again. After a moment, the architect changes the scene on the screen to an overhead plan view of the site, still showing the excavation. A few minutes of study, and he enters on the keyboard a list of items, checking each one as it appears on the screen, to be studied later.

Ignoring the representation on the display, the architect next begins to enter a series of specifications and data—a six-inch slab floor, twelve-inch concrete walls eight feet high within the excavation, and so on. When he has finished, the revised scene appears on the screen. A structure is taking shape. He examines it, adjusts it, pauses long enough to ask for handbook or catalog information from the "clerk" at various points, and readjusts accordingly. He often recalls from the "clerk" his working lists of specifications and considerations to refer to them, modify

them, or add to them. These lists grow into an ever-more-detailed, interlinked structure, which represents the maturing thought behind the actual design.

Prescribing different planes here and there, curved surfaces occasionally, and moving the whole structure about five feet, he finally has the rough external form of the building balanced nicely with the setting and he is assured that this

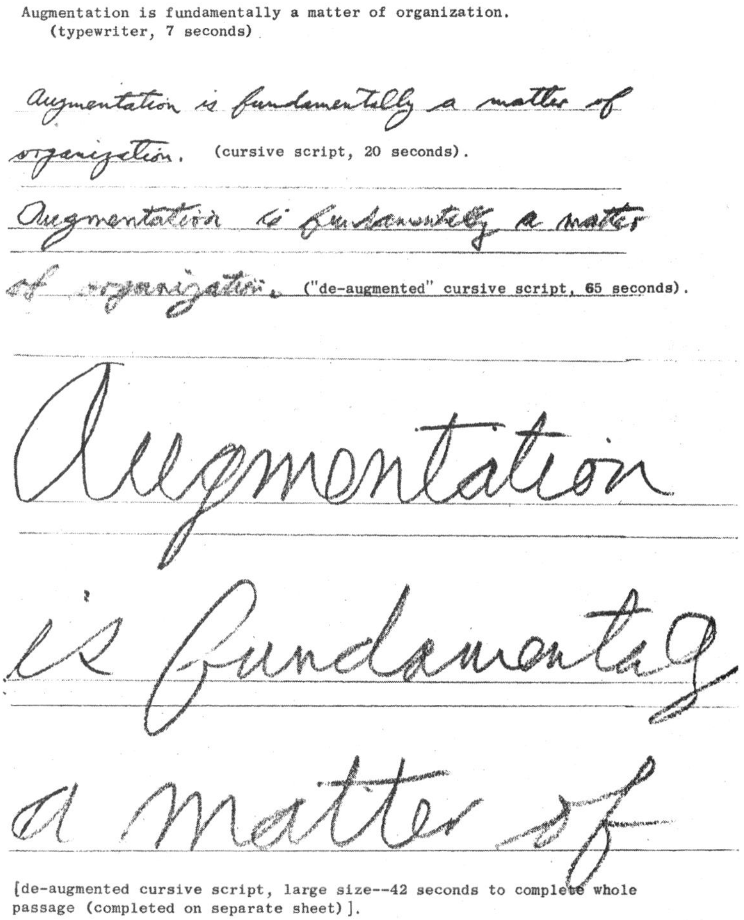

Figure 8.2. Experimental Results of Tying a Brick to a Pencil to "De-Augment" the Individual

*From section II.C.4:* Brains of equal power to ours could have evolved in an environment where the combination of artifact materials and muscle strengths were so scaled that the neatest scribing tool (equivalent to a pencil) possible had a shape and mass as manageable as a brick would be to us—assuming that our muscles were not specially conditioned to deal with it. We fastened a pencil to a brick and experimented. Figure 8.2 shows the results, compared with typewriting and ordinary pencil writing. . . . How would our civilization have matured if this had been the only manual means for us to use in graphical manipulation of symbols? For one thing, the record keeping that enables the organization of commerce and government would probably have taken a form so different from what we know that our social structure would undoubtably have evolved differently. . . .

form is basically compatible with the materials to be used as well as with the function of the building.

Now he begins to enter detailed information about the interior. Here the capability of the "clerk" to show him any view he wants to examine (a slice of the interior, or how the structure would look from the roadway above) is important. He enters particular fixture designs, and examines them in a particular room. He checks to make sure that sun glare from the windows will not blind a driver on the roadway, and the "clerk" computes the information that one window will reflect strongly onto the roadway between 6 and 6:30 on midsummer mornings.

Next he begins a functional analysis. He has a list of the people who will occupy this building, and the daily sequences of their activities. The "clerk" allows him to follow each in turn, examining how doors swing, where special lighting might be needed. Finally he has the "clerk" combine all of these sequences of activity to indicate spots where traffic is heavy in the building, or where congestion might occur, and to determine what the severest drain on the utilities is likely to be.

All of this information (the building design and its associated "thought structure") can be stored on a tape to represent the "design manual" for the building. Loading this tape into his own "clerk," another architect, a builder, or the client can maneuver within this "design manual" to pursue whatever details or insights are of interest to him—and can append special notes that are integrated into the "design manual" for his own or someone else's later benefit.

In such a future working relationship between human problem-solver and computer "clerk," the capability of the computer for executing mathematical processes would be used whenever it was needed. However, the computer has many other capabilities for manipulating and displaying information that can be of significant benefit to the human in nonmathematical processes of planning, organizing, studying, etc. Every person who does his thinking with symbolized concepts (whether in the form of the English lan-guage, pictographs, formal logic, or mathematics) should be able to benefit significantly.

## B  Objective of the Study

The objective of this study is to develop a conceptual framework within which could grow a coordinated research and development program whose goals would be the

following: (1) to find the factors that limit the effectiveness of the individual's basic information-handling capabilities in meeting the various needs of society for problem solving in its most general sense; and (2) to develop new techniques, procedures, and systems that will better match these basic capabilities to the needs, problems, and progress of society. We have placed the following specifications on this framework:

> (1) That it provide perspective for both long-range basic research and research that will yield practical results soon.

> (2) That it indicate what this augmentation will actually involve in the way of changes in working environment, in thinking, in skills, and in methods of working.

> (3) That it be a basis for evaluating the possible relevance of work and knowledge from existing fields and for assimilating whatever is relevant.

> (4) That it reveal areas where research is possible and ways to assess the research, be a basis for choosing starting points, and indicate how to develop appropriate methodologies for the needed research.

Two points need emphasis here. First, although a conceptual framework has been constructed, it is still rudimentary. Further search, and actual research, are needed for the evolution of the framework. Second, even if our conceptual framework did provide an accurate and complete basic analysis of the system from which stems a human's intellectual effectiveness, the explicit nature of future improved systems would be highly affected by (expected) changes in our technology or in our understanding of the human being.

. . .

## III  Examples and Discussion

### A  Background
### 2  Comments Related to [Vannevar] Bush's Article

There are many significant items in the article, but the main ones upon which we shall comment here will be those relative to the use and implications of his Memex. The associative trails whose establishment and use within the files he describes at some length provide a beautiful example of a new capability in symbol structuring that derives from new artifact-process capability, and that provides new ways to develop and portray concept structures. Any file is a symbol structure whose purpose is to represent a variety of concepts and concept structures in a way that makes them maximally available and useful to the needs of the human's mental-structure development—within the limits imposed by the capability of the artifacts and human for jointly executing processes of symbol-structure manipulation. The Memex allows a human user to do more conveniently (less energy, more quickly) what he could have done with relatively ordinary photographic equipment and filing systems, but he would have had to spend so much time in the lower-level processes of manipulation that his mental time constants of memory and patience would have rendered the system unusable in the detailed and intimate sense which Bush illustrates.

The Memex adds a factor of speed and convenience to ordinary filing-system (symbol-structuring) processes that would encourage new methods of work by the user, and it also adds speed and convenience for processes not generally used before. Making it easy to establish and follow the associative trails makes practical a new symbol-structuring process whose use can make a significant difference in the concept structuring and basic methods of work. It is also probable that clever usage of associative-trail manipulation can augment the human's process structuring and executing capabilities so that he could successfully make use of even more powerful symbol-structure manipulation processes utilizing the Memex capabilities. An example of this general sort of thing was given by Bush where he points out that the file index can be called to view at the push of a button, which implicitly provides greater capability to work within more sophisticated and complex indexing systems.

Note, too, the implications extending from Bush's mention of one user duplicating a trail (a portion of his structure) and giving it to a friend who can put it into his Memex and integrate it into his own trail (structure). Also note the "wholly new forms of encyclopedia," the profession of "trail blazers," and the inheritance from a master including "the entire scaffolding" by which such additions to the world's record were erected. These illustrate the types of changes in the ways in which people can cooperate intellectually that can emerge from the augmentation of the individuals. This type of change represents a very significant part of the potential value in pursuing research directly on the means for making individuals intellectually more effective

## 3 Some Possibilities with Cards and Relatively Simple Equipment

A number of useful new structuring processes can be made available to an individual through development and use of relatively simple equipment that is mostly electromechanical in nature and relatively cheap. We can begin developing examples of this by describing the hand-operated, edge-notched card system that I developed and used over the past eight years.

### a An Existing Note and File System

The "unit records" here, unlike those in the Memex example, are generally scraps of typed or handwritten text on IBM-card-sized edge-notchable cards. These represent little "kernels" of data, thought, fact, consideration, concepts, ideas, worries, etc., that are relevant to a given problem area in my professional life. Each such specific problem area has its notecards kept in a separate deck, and for each such deck there is a master card with descriptors associated with individual holes about the periphery of the card. There is a field of holes reserved for notch coding the serial number of a reference from which the note on a card may have been taken, or the serial number corresponding to an individual from whom the information came directly (including a code for myself, for self-generated thoughts).

None of the principles of indexing or sorting used here is new: coordinate-indexing descriptors with direct coding on edge-notched cards, with needle-sort retrieval. Mainly what is new is the use of the smaller units of information, in restricted-subject sets (notedecks) so that I gain considerable flexibility in the manipulations of my thought products at the level at which I actually work in my minute-by-minute struggle with analytical and formulative thought. Not only do my own thoughts produce results in this fashion, but when I digest the writings of another person, I find generally anyway that I have extracted from his structure and integrated into my own a specific selection of facts, considerations, ideas, etc. Often these different extracted items fit into different places in my structure, or become encased in special substructures as I modify or expand his concepts. Extracting such items or kernels and putting each on its own notecard helps this process considerably—the role or position of each such item in the growth of the note structure is independent, and yet if desired all can quickly be isolated and extracted by simple needle sorting on the reference-number notching field.

These notecards represent much more than just an in formation file. They provide a workspace for me, in which I can browse, make additions or corrections, or build new sets of thought kernels with a good deal of freedom. I can leave notes with suggestions or questions for myself that will drop out at an appropriate later time. I can do document-reference searches with good efficiency, too, by needle sorting for notes within relevant descriptor categories. Any notecard with relevant notes on it points to the original source (by the source serial number, which I always write, together with the page, at the top of the card). When I am in the process of developing an integrated writeup covering some or all of the notedeck's material, I can quickly needle out a set of cards relevant to the topic under consideration at the moment— with all other cards in one pile to the side—and I need do a very minimum of hand searching or stacking in special little category piles. If I utilize specific information from another person, I can register my acknowledgment in my draft writeup merely by writing in the source serial number that is at the top of the notecard—it is a straightforward clerical job for a secretary later to arrange footnote entries and numbering.

## b  Comments on the System

First, let me relate what has been described to the special terms brought out in previous sections. The writing contained on each notecard is a small-sized symbol structure, representing or portraying to me a small structure of concepts. The notches on the edges of the cards are symbols that serve to tie these card-sized symbol substructures into a large symbol structure (the notedeck). One aspect of the structure is the physical grouping of the cards at a given time—which happens to be the only aspect of the over-all structuring that my human capabilities can make direct use of—and in this respect I can execute processes which produce restructuring (that is, physical regrouping) that helps me considerably to perceive and assimilate the concepts of worth to me. This restructuring is effected by composite processes involving me, a master code card, a sorting needle, and a work surface. I can add to the symbol structure by executing other composite processes which involve me, writing instruments (pen, pencil, or typewriter), a master code card, and a card notcher.

If my mental processes were more powerful, I could dispense with the cards, and hold all of the card-sized concept structures in my memory, where also would be held the categorization linkages that evolved as I worked (with my feet up on the artifacts and my eyes closed). As it is, and as it probably always will be no matter how we develop or train our mental capabilities, I want to work in problem areas where the number and interrelationship complexity of the individual factors involved are too much for me to hold and manipulate within my mind. So, my mind develops conscious sets of concepts, or recognizes and selects them from what it perceives in the work of others, and it directs the organization of an external symbol structure in which can be held and portrayed to the mind those concepts I cannot (reliably) remember or whose manipulations I cannot visualize. The price I pay for this "augmentation" shows up in the time and energy involved in manipulating artifacts to manipulate symbols to give me this artificial memory and visualization of concepts and their manipulation.

## c  Associative-Linking Possibilities

But let us go further with discussing specific examples of means for augmenting our intellects. In using the edge-notched-card system described, I found several types of structuring which that system could not provide, but which would both be very useful and probably obtainable with reasonably practical artifact means. One need arose quite commonly as trains of thought would develop on a growing series of notecards. There was no convenient way to link these cards together so that the train of thought could later be recalled by extracting the ordered series of notecards. An associative-trail scheme similar to that out lined by Bush for his Memex could conceivably be implemented with these cards to meet this need and add a valuable new symbol-structuring process to the system. Straightforward engineering development could provide a mechanism that would be able to select a specific card from a relatively large deck by a parallel edge-notch sort on a unique serial number notched into each card, and the search mechanism could be set up automatically by a hole sensing mechanism from internal punches on another card that was placed in the sensing slot. An auxiliary notching mechanism could automatically give succeeding serial-number encoding to new notecards as they are made up.

Suppose that one wants to link Card B to Card A, to make a trail from A to B. He puts Card B into a slot so that the edge-notched coding of the card's serial number can automatically be sensed, and slips Card A under a hole-punching head which duplicates the serial-number code of Card B in the coding of the holes punched in a specific zone on Card A. Later, when he may have discovered Card A, and wishes to follow this particular associative trail to the next card, he aligns that zone on Card A under a hole-sensing head which reads the serial number for Card B therein and automatically sets up the sorting mechanism. A very quick and simple human process thus initiates the automatic extraction of the next item on the associative trail. It's not unreasonable to assume that establishing a link would take about three seconds, and tracing a link to the next card about three to five seconds.

There would still be descriptor-code notching and selection to provide for general grouping classifications—and we can see that the system could really provide a means for *working within* the structure of the contained information.

## d An Experiment Illustrating Usage and Further System Possibilities

I once tried to use my cards, with their separate little "concept packets," in the process of developing a file memo outlining the status and plans of a research project. I first developed a set of cards upon each of which I described a separate consideration, possibility, or specification about the memo—in the disorderly sequence in which they occurred to me as my thoughts about the basic features of the memo evolved. Right off the bat I noticed that there were two distinct groups—some ideas were about what the memo ought to accomplish, what time period it should cover, when it should be finished, what level and style of presentation should be used, etc., and some ideas were about the subject of the memo. As more thoughts developed, I found that the latter group also divided into ideas representing possible content and those representing possible organization.

I separated the cards into three corresponding groups (which I shall call Specification, Organization, and Content), and began to organize each of them. I started with the Specification group (it being the "highest" in nature), and immediately found that there were several types of notes within that group just as there had been in the total group. Becoming immediately suspicious, I sorted through each of the other two main groups and found similar situations in each. In each group there was finally to emerge a definite set of statements (product statements) that represented that

group's purpose—e.g., the specifications currently accepted for the design of the memo—and some of the cards contained candidate material for this. But there were also considerations about what these final statements might include or exclude or take into account, or conditions under which inclusion or modification might be relevant, or statements that were too bulky or brief or imprecise to be used as final statements.

It became apparent that the final issuance from my work, the memo itself, would represent but one facet of a complex symbol structure that would grow as the work progressed— a structure comprising three main substructures, each of which had definite substructuring of its own that was apparent. I realized that I was being rather philosophically introspective with all of this analysis, but I was curious as to the potential value of future augmentation means in allowing me to deal explicitly with these types of structuring. So I went ahead, keeping the groups and sub-groups of cards separated, and trying to organize and develop them.

I found rather quickly that the job of extracting, rearranging, editing, and copying new statements into the cards which were to represent the current set of product statements in each grouping was rather tedious. This brought me to appreciate the value of some sort of copying device with which I could transfer specified strings of words from one card to another, thus composing new statements from fragments of existing ones. This type of device should not be too hard to develop and produce for a price that a professional man could justify paying, and it would certainly facilitate some valuable symbol-structuring processes.

I also found that there would have been great value in having available the associative-trail marking and following processes. Statements very often had implicit linkages to other statements in the same group, and it would have been very useful to keep track of these associations. For instance, when several consideration statements bore upon a given product statement, and when that product statement came to be modified through some other consideration, it was not always easy to remember why it had been established as it had. Being able to fish out the other considerations linked to that statement would have helped considerably.

Also, trial organizations of the statements in a group could be linked into trial associative trails, so that a number of such organizations could be constructed and considered without copying that many sets of specially ordered statements. Any of the previously considered organizations could be reconstructed at will.

In trying to do flexible structuring and restructuring within my experiment, I found that I just didn't have the means to keep track of all of the kernel statements (cards) and the various relationships between them that were important—at least by means that were easy enough to leave time and thought capacity enough for me to keep in mind the essential nature of the memo-writing process. But it was a very provocative experience, considering the possibilities that I sensed for the flexible and powerful ways in which I could apply myself to so universal a design task if I but had the necessary means with which to manipulate symbol structures.

It would actually seem quite feasible to develop a unit-record system around cards and mechanical sorting, with automatic trail-establishment and trail-following facility, and with associated means for selective copying or data transfer, that would enable development of some very powerful methodology for everyday intellectual work. It is plain that even if the equipment (artifacts) appeared on the market tomorrow, a good deal of empirical research would be needed to develop a methodology that would capitalize upon the artifact process capabilities. New concepts need to be conceived and tested relative to the way the "thought kernels" could be knitted together into working structures, and relative to the conceptual presentations which become available and the symbol-manipulation processes which provide these presentations. "Such an approach would present useful and interesting research problems, and could very likely produce practical and significant results (language, artifacts, methodology) for improving the effectiveness of professional problem solvers. However, the technological trends of today foretell the obsolescence of such electromechanical information-handling equipment." Very likely, by the time good augmentation systems could be developed, and the first groups of users began to prove them out so that they could gain more widespread acceptance, electronic data-processing equipment would have evolved much further and become much more prevalent throughout the critical-problem domains of our society where such ideas would first be adopted. The relative limitations of the mechanical equipment in providing processes which could be usefully integrated into the system would soon lead to its replacement by electronic computer equipment.

The next set of descriptive examples will involve the use of electronic computers, and their greatly increased flexibility and processing potential will be evident. Research based upon such electronic artifacts would be able to explore language and methodology innovations of a much wider range of sophistication than could research based upon limited and relatively inflexible electromechanical artifacts. In particular, the electronic-based experimental program could simulate the types of processes available from electromechanical artifacts, if it seemed possible (from the vantage of experience with the wide range of augmentation processes) that relatively powerful augmentation systems could be based upon their capabilities—but the relative payoffs for providing even-more-sophisticated artifact capabilities could be assessed too so that considerations of how much to invest in capital equipment versus how much increase in human effectiveness to expect could be based upon some experimental data.

. . .

## III  Examples and Discussion

### B  Hypothetical Description of Computer-Based Augmentation System
### 4  Structuring an Argument

"If we want to go on to a higher-level capability to give you a feeling for how our rebuilt capability hierarchy works, it will speed us along to look at how we might organize these more primitive capabilities which I have demonstrated into some new and better ways to set up what we can call an 'argument.' This refers loosely to any set of statements (we'll call them 'product statements') that represents the product of a period of work toward a given objective. Confused? Well, take the simple case where an argument leads to a single product statement. For instance, you come to a particular point in your work where you have to decide what to do for the next step. You go through some reasoning process—usually involving statements—and come up with a statement specifying that next step. That final statement is the product statement, and it represents the product of the argument or reasoning process which led to it.

"You usually think of an argument as a serial sequence of steps of reason, beginning with known facts, assumptions, etc., and progressing toward a conclusion. Well, we do have to think through these steps serially, and we usually do list the steps serially when we write them out because that is pretty much the way our papers and books have to present them—they are pretty limiting in the symbol structuring they enable us to use. Have you even seen a 'scrambled-text' programmed instruction book? That is an interesting example of a deviation from straight serial presentation of steps.

"Conceptually speaking, however, an argument is not a serial affair. It is sequential, I grant you, because some statements have to follow others, but this doesn't imply that its nature is necessarily serial. We usually string Statement B after Statement A, with Statements C, D, E, F, and so on following in that order—this is a serial structuring of our symbols. Perhaps each statement logically followed from all those which preceded it on the serial list, and if so, then the conceptual structuring would also be serial in nature, and it would be nicely matched for us by the symbol structuring.

"But a more typical case might find A to be an independent statement, B dependent upon A, C and D independent, E depending upon D and B, E dependent upon C, and F dependent upon A, D, and E. See, sequential but not serial? A conceptual network but not a conceptual chain. The old paper and pencil methods of manipulating symbols just weren't very adaptable to making and using symbol structures to match the ways we make and use conceptual structures. With the new symbol-manipulating methods here, we have terrific flexibility for matching the two, and boy, it really pays off in the way you can tie into your work."

This makes you recall dimly the generalizations you had heard previously about process structuring limiting symbol structuring, symbol structuring limiting concept structuring, and concept structuring limiting mental structuring. You nod cautiously, in hopes that he will proceed in some way that will tie this kind of talk to something from which you can get the "feel" of what it is all about. As it turns out, that is just what he intends to do.

"Let's actually work some examples. You help me." And you become involved in a truly fascinating game. Joe tells you that you are to develop an argument leading to statements summarizing the augmentation means so far revealed to you for doing the kind of straight-text work usually done with a pencil and eraser on a single sheet of paper. You unconsciously look for a scratch pad before you realize that he is telling you that you are going to do this the "augmented way" by using him and his system—with artful coaching

from him. Under a bit of urging from him, you begin self-consciously to mumble some inane statements about what you have seen, what they imply, what your doubts and reservations are, etc. He mercilessly ignores your obvious discomfort and gives you no cue to stop, until he drops his hands to his lap after he has filled five frames with these statements (the surplus filled frames disappeared to somewhere—you assume Joe knows where they went and how to get them back).

"You notice how you wandered down different short paths, and criss-crossed yourself a few times?" You nod—depressed, no defense. But he isn't needling you. "Very natural development, just the way we humans always seem to start out on a task for which we aren't all primed with knowledge, method, experience, and confidence—which is to include essentially every problem of any consequence to us. So let's see how we can accommodate the human's way of developing his comprehension and his final problem solution.

"Perhaps I should have stopped sooner—I *am* supposed to be coaching you instead of teasing you—but I had a reason. You haven't been making use of the simple symbol-manipulation means that I showed you—other than the shorthand for getting the stuff on the screens. You started out pretty much the way you might with your typewriter or pencil. I'll show you how you could have been doing otherwise, but I want you to notice first how hard it is for a person to realize how really unquestioning he is about the way he does things. Somehow we implicitly view most all of our methods as just sort of 'the way things are done, that's all.' You knew that some exotic techniques were going to be applied, and you'll have to admit that you were passively waiting for them to be handed to you."

With a non-committal nod, you suggest getting on with it. Joe begins, "You're probably waiting for something impressive. What I'm trying to prime you for, though, is the realization that the impressive new tricks *all* are based upon lots of changes in the little things you do. This computerized system is used over and over and over again to help me do little things—where my methods and ways of handling *little* things are changed until, lo, they've added up and suddenly I can do *impressive* new things."

You don't know. He's a nice enough guy, but he sure gets preachy. But the good side of your character shows through, and you realize that everything so far *has* been about little things—this is probably an important point. You'll stick with him. Okay, so what could you have been doing to use the simple tricks he had shown you in a useful way? Joe picks up the light pen, poises his other hand over the keyset, and looks at you. You didn't need the hint, but thanks anyway, and let's start rearranging and cleaning up the work space instead of just dumping more raw material on it.

With closer coaching now from Joe, you start through the list of statements you've made and begin to edit, re-word, compile, and delete. It's fun—"put that sentence back up here between these two"—and blink, it's done. "Group these four statements, indented two spaces, under the heading 'shorthand,'" and blinko, it's done. "Insert what I say next there, after that sentence." You dictate a sentence to extend a thought that is developing, and Joe effortlessly converts it into an inserted new sentence. Your ideas begin to take shape, and you can continually re-work the existing set of statements to keep representing the state of your "concept structure."

You are quite elated by this freedom to juggle the record of your thoughts, and by the way this freedom allows you to *work* them into shape. You reflected that this flexible cut-and-try process really did appear to match the way you seemed to develop your thoughts. Golly, you could be writing math expressions, ad copy, or a poem, with the same type of

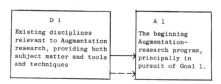

Figure 8.3. Initial Augmentation-Research Program

*From section IV.E:* An integrated set of tools and techniques will represent an art of doing augmentation research. Although no such art exists ready-made for our use, there are many applicable or adaptable tools and techniques to be borrowed from other disciplines. Psychology, computer programming and physical technology, display technology, artificial intelligence, industrial engineering (e.g., motion and time study). management science, systems analysis, and information retrieval are some of the more likely sources. These disciplines also offer initial subject matter for the research. Because this kind of diagramming can help more later on, we represent in Figure 8.3 the situation of the beginning research drawing upon existing disciplines for subject matter and tools and techniques.

The program begins with general dependence upon other, existing disciplines for its subject matter (solid arrow) and its tools and techniques (dashed arrow). Goal 1 has been stated as that of verifying the basic hypothesis that concerted augmentation research can increase the intellectual effectiveness of human problem solvers.

benefit. You were ready to tell Joe that now you saw what he had been trying to tell you about matching symbol structuring to concept structuring—when he moved on to show you a succession of other techniques that made you realize you hadn't yet gotten the full significance of his pitch.

"So far the structure that you have built with your symbols looks just like what you might build with pencil-and-paper techniques—only here the building is so much easier when you can trim, extend, insert, and rearrange so freely and rapidly. But the same computer here that gives us these freedoms with so trivial an application of its power, can just as easily give us other simple capabilities which we can apply to the development and use of different *types* of structure from what we used to use. But let me unfold these little computer tricks as we come to them.

"When you look at a given statement in the middle of your argument structure, there are a number of things you want to know. Let's simplify the situation by saying that you might ask three questions, 'What's this?', 'How come?', and 'So what?' Let's take these questions one at a time and see how some changes in structuring might help a person answer them better.

"You look at a statement and you want to understand its meaning. You are used to seeing a statement portrayed in just the manner you might hear it—as a serial succession of words. But, just as with the statements within an argument, the conceptual relationship among the words of a sentence is not generally serial, and we can benefit in matching better to the conceptual structure if we can conveniently work with certain non-serial symbol-structuring forms within sentences.

"Most of the structuring forms I'll show you stem from the simple capability of being able to establish arbitrary linkages between different substructures, and of directing the computer subsequently to display a set of linked substructures with any relative positioning we might designate among the different substructures. You can designate as many different kinds of links as you wish, so that you can specify different display or manipulative treatment for the different types."

Joe picked out one of your sentences, and pushed the rest of the text a few lines up and down from it to isolate it. He then showed you how he could make a few strokes on the keyset to designate the type of link he wanted established, and pick the two symbol structures that were to be linked by means of the light pen. He said that most links possessed a direction, i.e., they were like an arrow pointing from one substructure to another, so that in setting up a link he must specify the two substructures in a given order.

He went to work for a moment, rapidly setting up links within your sentence. Then he showed you how you could get some help in looking at a statement and understanding it. "Here is one standard portrayal, for which I have established a computer process to do the structuring automatically on the basis of the interword links." A few strokes on the keyset and suddenly the sentence fell to pieces—different parts of it being positioned here and there, with some lines connecting them. "Remember diagramming sentences when you were studying grammar? Some good methods, plus a bit of practice, and you'd be surprised how much a diagrammatic breakdown can help you to scan a complex statement and untangle it quickly.

"We have developed quite a few more little schemes to help at the statement level. I don't want to tangle you up with too much detail, though. You can see, probably, that quick dictionary-lookup helps." He aimed at a term with the light pen and hit a few strokes on the keyset, and the old text jumped farther out of the way and the definition appeared above the diagram, with the defined term brighter than the rest of the diagram. And he showed you also how you could link secondary phrases (or sentences) to parts of the statement for more detailed description. These secondary substructures wouldn't appear when you normally viewed the statement, but could be brought in by simple request if you wanted closer study.

"It proves to be terrifically useful to be able to work easily with statements that represent more sophisticated and complex concepts. Sort of like being able to use structural members that are lighter and stronger—it gives you new freedom in building structures. But let's move on—we'll come back to this area later, if we have time.

"When you look at a statement and ask, 'How come?', you are used to scanning back over a serial array of previously made statements in search of an understanding of the basis upon which this statement was made. But some of these previous statements are much more significant than others to this search for understanding. Let us use what we call 'antecedent links' to point to these, and I'll give you a basic idea of how we structure an argument so that we can quickly track down the essential basis upon which a given statement rests."

You helped him pick out the primary antecedents of the statement you had been studying, and he established links to them. These statements were scattered back through the serial list of statements that you had assembled, and Joe showed you how you could either brighten or underline them to make them stand out to your eye—just by requesting the computer to do this for all direct antecedents of the designated statement. He told you, though, that you soon get so you aren't very much interested in seeing the serial listing of all of the statements, and he made another request of the computer (via the keyset) that eliminated all the prior statements, except the direct antecedents, from the screen. The subject statement went to the bottom of the frame, and the antecedent statements were neatly listed above it.

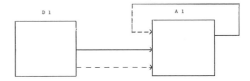

Figure 8.4. Regeneration

*From section IV.F:* We basically recommend A 1 research adhering to whatever formal methodology is required for (a) knowing when an improvement in effectiveness has been achieved, and (b) knowing how to assign *relative* value to the changes derived from two competing innovations.

Beyond this, and assuming dedication to this goal, reasonable maturity, and plenty of energy, intelligence, and imagination, we would recommend turning loose a group of four to six people (or a number of such groups) to develop means that augment their own programming capability. We would recommend that their work begin by developing the capability for composing and modifying simple symbol structures, in the manner pictured in Section III-B-2, and work up through a hierarchy of intermediate capabilities toward the single high-level capability that would encompass computer programming. This would allow their embryonic and free wheeling "art of doing augmentation research" to grow and work out its kinks through a succession of increasingly complex system problems—and also, redesigning a hierarchy from the bottom up somehow seems the best approach.

As for the type of programming to tell them to become good at— tell them, "the kind that you find you have to do in your research." In other words, their job assignment is to develop means that will make them more effective at doing their job. Figure 8.4 depicts this schematically, with the addition to what was shown in Figure 8.3 of a connection that feeds the subject-matter output of their research (augmentation means for their type of programming problems) right back into their activity as improved tools and techniques to use in their research.

Joe then had you designate an order of "importance to comprehension" among these statements, and he rearranged them accordingly as fast as you could choose them. (This choosing was remarkably helped by having only the remainder statements to study for each new choice—another little contribution to effectiveness, you thought.) He mentioned that you could designate orderings under several different criteria, and later have the display show whichever ordering you wished. This, he implied, could be used very effectively when you were building or studying an argument structure in which from time to time you wanted to strengthen your comprehension relative to different aspects of the situation.

"Each primary antecedent can similarly be linked to its primary antecedents, and so on, until you arrive at the statements representing the premises, the accepted facts, and the objectives upon which this argument had been established. When we had established the antecedent links for all the statements in the argument, the question 'So what?' that you might ask when looking at a given statement would be answered by looking for the statements for which the given statement was an antecedent. We already have links to these consequents—just turn around the arrows on the antecedent links and we have consequent links. So we can easily call forth an uncluttered display of consequent statements to help us see why we needed this given statement in the argument.

"To help us get better comprehension of the structure of an argument, we can also call forth a schematic or graphical display. Once the antecedent-consequent links have been established, the computer can automatically construct such a display for us." So, Joe spent a few minutes (with your help) establishing a reasonable set of links among the statements

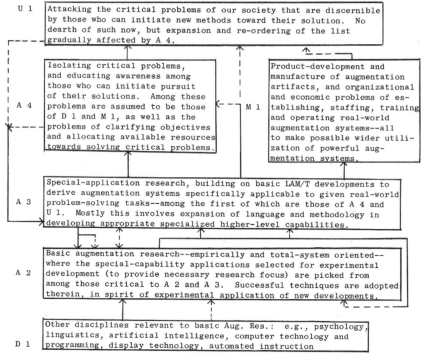

Figure 8.5. A Total Program

Suggested relationships among the major activities involved in achieving the stated objective (essentially, of significantly boosting human power in A 4 and U 1). Solid lines represent subject information or artifacts used or generated within an activity, and dashed lines represent special tools and techniques for doing the activity in the box to which they connect. Subject product of an activity (output solid) can be used as working material (input solid) or as tools and techniques (input dashed). Tools and techniques as used or needed in an activity (output dashed) can be used as either to work on (input solid) or as tools and techniques to work with (input dashed).

you had originally listed. Then another keyed-in request to the computer, and almost instantaneously there appeared a network of lines and dots that looked something like a tree—except that sometimes branches would fuse together. "Each node or dot represents one of the statements of your argument, and the lines are antecedent-consequent links. The antecedents of one statement always lie above that statement—or rather, their nodes lie above its node. When you get used to using a network representation like this, it really becomes a great help in getting the feel for the way all the different ideas and reasoning fit together—that is, for the conceptual structuring."

Joe demonstrated some ways in which you could make use of the diagram to study the argument structure. Point to any node, give a couple of strokes on the keyset, and the corresponding statement would appear on the other screen—and that node would become brighter. Call the antecedents forth on the second screen, and select one of special interest—deleting the others. Follow back down the antecedent trail a little further, using one screen to look at the detail at any time, and the other to show you the larger view, with automatic node-brightening indication of where these detailed items fit in the larger view.

"For a little embellishment here, and to show off another little capability in my repertoire, let me label the nodes so that you can develop more association between the nodes and the statements in the argument. I can do this several ways. For one thing, I can tell the computer to number the statements in the order in which you originally had them listed, and have the labelling done automatically." This took him a total of five strokes on the keyset, and suddenly each node was made into a circle with a number in it. The statements that were on the second screen now each had its respective serial number sitting next to it in the left margin. "This helps you remember what the different nodes on the network display contain. We have also evolved some handy techniques for constructing abbreviation labels that help your memory quite a bit.

"Also, we can display extra fine-structure and labelling detail within the network in the specific local area we happen to be concentrating upon. This finer detail is washed out as we move to another spot with our close attention, and the coarser remaining structure is compressed, so that there is room for our new spot to be blown up. It is a lot like using zones of variable magnification as you scan the structure—higher magnification where you are inspecting detail, lower magnification in the surrounding field so that your feel for the whole structure and where you are in it can stay with you."

## 5 General Symbol Structuring

"If you are tangling with a problem of any size—whether it involves you for half an hour or two years—the entire collection of statements, sketches, computations, literature sources, and source extracts that is associated with your work would in our minds constitute a single symbol structure. There may be many levels of substructuring between the level of individual symbols and that represented by the entire collection. You and I have been working with some of the lower-ordered substructures—the individual statements and the multistatement arguments—and have skimmed through some of the ways to build and manipulate them. The results of small arguments are usually integrated in a higher level

network of argument or concept development, and these into still higher-level networks, and so on. But at any such level, the manner in which the interrelationship between the kernels of argument can be tagged, portrayed, studied and manipulated is much the same as those which we have just been through.

"Substructures that might represent mathematical or formal-logic arguments may be linked right in with substructures composed of the more informal statements. Substructures that represent graphs, curves, engineering drawings, and other graphical forms can likewise be integrated. One can also append special substructures, of any size, to particular other substructures. A frequent use of this is to append descriptive material—something like footnotes, only much more flexible. Or, special messages can be hung on that offer ideas such as simplifying an argument or circumventing a blocked path—to be uncovered and considered at some later date. These different appended substructures can remain invisible to the worker until such time as he wants to flush them into view. He can ask for the cue symbols that indicate their presence (identifying where they are linked and what their respective types are) to be shown on the network display any time he wishes, and then call up whichever of them he wishes. If he is interested in only one type of appended substructure, he can request that only the cues associated with that type be displayed.

"You should also realize that a substructure doesn't have to be a hunk of data sitting neatly distinct within the normal form of the larger structure. One can choose from a symbol structure (or substructure, generally) any arbitrary collection of its substructures, designate any arbitrary structuring among these and any new substructures he wants to add, and thus define a new substructure which the computer can untangle from the larger structure and present to him at any time. The associative trails that Bush suggested represent a primitive example of this. A good deal of this type of activity is involved during the early, shifting development of some phase of work, as you saw when you were collecting tentative argument chains. But here again, we find ever more delightful ways to make use of the straightforward-seeming capabilities in developing new higher-level capabilities—which, of course, seem sort of straightforward by then, too.

"I found, when I learned to work with the structures and manipulation processes such as we have outlined, that I got rather impatient if I had to go back to dealing with the serial-statement structuring in books and journals, or other ordinary means of communicating with other workers. It is rather like having to project three-dimensional images onto two-dimensional frames and to work with them there instead of in their natural form. Actually, it is much closer to the truth to say that it is like trying to project n-dimensional forms (the concept structures, which we have seen can be related with many many nonintersecting links) onto a one-dimensional form (the serial string of symbols), where the human memory and visualization has to hold and picture the links and relationships. I guess that's a natural feeling, though. One gets impatient any time he is forced into a restricted or primitive mode of operation—except perhaps for recreational purposes.

"I'm sure that you've had the experience of working over a journal article to get comprehension and perhaps some special-purpose conclusions that you can integrate into your own work. Well, when you ever get handy at roaming over the type of symbol structure which we have been showing here, and you turn for this purpose to another person's work that is structured in this way, you will find a terrific difference there in the ease of gaining comprehension as to what he has done and why he has done it, and of isolating what you want to use and making sure of the conditions under which you can use it. This is true even if you find his structure left in the condition in which he has been working on it—that is, with no special provisions for helping an outsider find his way around. But we have learned quite a few simple tricks for leaving appended road signs, supplementary information, questions, and auxiliary links on our working structures—in such a manner that they never get in our way as we work—so that the visitor to our structure can gain his comprehension and isolate what he

wants in marvelously short order. Some of these techniques are quite closely related to those used in automated-instruction programming—perhaps you know about 'teaching machines?'

"What we found ourselves doing, when having to do any extensive digesting of journal articles, was to type large batches of the text verbatim into computer store. It is so nice to be able to tear it apart, establish our own definitions and substitute, restructure, append notes, and so forth, in pursuit of comprehension, that it was generally well worth the trouble. The keyset shorthand made this reasonably practical. But the project now has an optical character reader that will convert our external references into machine code for us. The references are available for study in original serial form on our screens, but any structuring and tagging done by a previous reader, or ourselves, can also be utilized.

"A number of us here are using the augmented systems for our project research, and we find that after a few passes through a reference, we very rarely go back to it in its original form. It sits in the archives like an orange rind, with most of the real juice squeezed out. The contributions from these references form sturdy members of our structure, and are duly tagged as to source so that acknowledgment is always implicitly noted. The analysis and digestion that any of us makes on such a reference is fully available to the others. It is rather amazing how much superfluous verbiage is contained in those papers merely to try to make up for the pitifully sparse possibilities available for symbol structuring in printed text."

Reference

1. Kennedy, J. L. and Putt, G. H., "Administration of Research in a Research Corporation," RAND Corporation Report P-847 (20 April 1956).

# 09. [Introduction]
# Sketchpad
## A Man-Machine Graphical Communication System

The Sketchpad ⊗ system—created by Ivan Sutherland on a computer built for developing military radar—is the graphical ancestor of today's human-computer interaction and computer graphics, and much of new media in general. In the early 1960s this system not only let people draw on a computer display, it also embodied a crucial conceptual step: considering the screen as more than a poor replacement for a piece of paper.

Sketchpad's most familiar features to us today are the basic vocabulary of computer drawing—tools such as rubber-band lines (that start with one point, and change the size and direction of the line segment until the next point is defined) and circles that are drawn based on their own constraints, so that the path of drawing need not be anything like a circle. These features made Sketchpad the first direct-manipulation interface (◊33), the first interface to use constraints, and (as Susan Brennan argues) the first *conversational* interface.

But something we rarely consider about computer drawings, something which Sketchpad first demonstrated, is that these images are *objects*, and, as such, can be manipulated, constrained, instantiated, represented iconically, copied, and recursively operated upon, even recursively merged. Because Sketchpad implemented all of these things, it laid the foundation for modern object-oriented programming and graphic user interfaces.

Sutherland describes how the building up of objects and constraints within Sketchpad can allow work on cantilever and arch bridge designs, with appropriate force calculations; how linkages can be used to produce simple computer animations; and how electrical circuit diagrams can be drawn and reused. In this way, through their work process, users can assemble complex objects out of previous constructions, from their personal library of objects. When changes are made to improve or otherwise alter earlier work, these changes are propagated automatically. While Vannevar Bush had suggested a similar strategy with scholarly information (◊02), and basic code-reuse was certainly not new to programmers, Sutherland implemented this in the area of *dynamic media*. Alan Kay (◊26) followed up on these ideas, creating the object-oriented programming language Smalltalk and user-empowering media environment of the Dynabook—but in our current new media landscape these aspects of Sutherland's creation are seldom as fully realized.
—NWF

Sketchpad also moved beyond paper by allowing the user to work at any of 2000 levels of magnification—enabling the creation of projects that, in physical media, would either be unweildly large or require detail work at an impractically small size.

### Further Reading

Baecker Ronald M., Jonathan Grudin, William A. S. Buxton, and Saul Greenberg. "A Historical and Intellectual Perspective." *Readings in Human-Computer Interaction: Toward the Year 2000*. 2d ed. San Mateo, Calif.: Morgan Kaufman, 1995.

Brennan, Susan E. "Conversation as Direct Manipulation: An Iconoclastic View." *The Art of Human-Computer Interface Design* 393–404, edited by Brenda Laurel. Reading, Mass.: Addison Wesley, 1990.

Nelson, Theodor H. "Sutherland's Sketchpad." *Computer Lib/Dream Machines*, page DM23. Self-published, 1974.

◊02 35

**109**

In "Conversation as Direct Manipulation" Susan Brennan writes: "Appropriately enough, the first great conversational human/computer interface was also the first great direct manipulation one. Ivan Sutherland's Sketchpad enabled a user and a computer 'to converse rapidly through the medium of line drawings.' This style of interaction was primarily graphical, yet it exhibited some of the important features of human conversation. A user conversed with Sketchpad by pointing. The system responded by updating the drawing immediately, so that the relationship between the user's action and the graphical display was clear. In fact, because the feedback was so timely and relevant, it could be considered analogous to *backchannels*, or secondary speech in human/human communication" (394–395). Of course, while Brennan identifies salient aspects of conversation in Sketchpad, she is writing in the technological era when "conversation" was necessarily a metaphor for interaction. Conversational agents today implement conversation in a more literal way by allowing multimodal conversations based on speech and similar to those found in human-human discourse.

◊26 391

◊33 485

Figure 9.1. TX-2 operating area—Sketchpad in use. On the display can be seen part of a bridge similar to those of Figure 9.15. The Author is holding the light pen. The push buttons "draw," "move," etc., are on the box in front of the Author. Part of the bank of toggle switches can be seen behind the Author. The size and position of the part of the total picture seen on the display are controlled by the four black knobs just above the tables.

Original Publication

*American Federation of Information Processing Societies (AFIPS) Conference Proceedings* 23:329–246. Spring Joint Computer Conference, 1963.

# Sketchpad
## A Man-Machine Graphical Communication System
## Ivan E. Sutherland

## I Introduction

The Sketchpad system makes it possible for a man and a computer to converse rapidly through the medium of line drawings. Heretofore, most interaction between man and computers has been slowed down by the need to reduce all communication to written statements that can be typed; in the past, we have been writing letters to rather than conferring with our computers. For many types of communication, such as describing the shape of a mechanical part or the connections of an electrical circuit, typed statements can prove cumbersome. The Sketchpad system, by eliminating typed statements (except for legends) in favor of line drawings, opens up a new area of man-machine communication.

### An Introductory Example

To understand what is possible with the system at present let us consider using it to draw the hexagonal pattern in Figure 9.4. We will issue specific commands with a set of push buttons, turn functions on and off with switches, indicate position information and point to existing drawing parts with the light pen, rotate and magnify picture parts by turning knobs, and observe the drawing on the display system. This equipment as provided at Lincoln Laboratory's TX-2 computer[1] is shown in Figure 9.1. When our drawing is complete it may be inked on paper, as were all the drawings in this paper, by a PACE plotter.[15]

If we point the light pen at the display system and press a button called "draw," the computer will construct a straight line segment which stretches like a rubber band from the initial to the present location of the pen as shown in Figure 9.2. Additional presses of the button will produce

additional lines, leaving the closed irregular hexagon shown in Figure 9.3A.

To make the hexagon regular, we can inscribe it in a circle. To draw the circle we place the light pen where the center is to be and press the button "circle center," leaving behind a center point. Now, choosing a point on the circle (which fixes the radius) we press the button "draw" again, this time getting a circle arc whose angular length only is controlled by light pen position as shown in Figure 9.2.

Next we move the hexagon into the circle by pointing to a corner of the hexagon and pressing the button "move" so that the corner follows the light pen, stretching two rubber band line segments behind it. By pointing to the circle and terminating, we indicate that the corner is to lie on the circle. Each corner is in this way moved onto the circle at roughly equal spacing as shown in Figure 9.3D.

We have indicated that the vertices of the hexagon are to lie on the circle, and they will remain on the circle throughout our further manipulations. If we also insist that

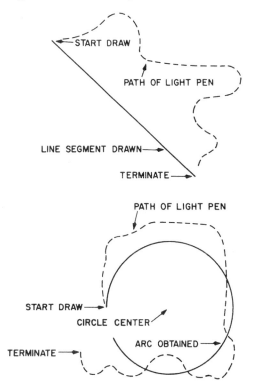

Figure 9.2. Steps for drawing straight lines and circle arcs.

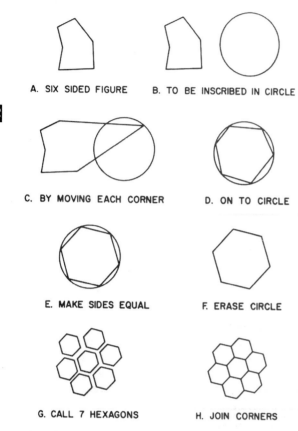

A. SIX SIDED FIGURE     B. TO BE INSCRIBED IN CIRCLE

C. BY MOVING EACH CORNER     D. ON TO CIRCLE

E. MAKE SIDES EQUAL     F. ERASE CIRCLE

G. CALL 7 HEXAGONS     H. JOIN CORNERS

Figure 9.3. Illustrative example, see text.

new sheet we assemble, by pressing a button to create each hexagon as an "instance" or subpicture, six hexagons around a central seventh in approximate position as shown in Figure 9.3G. A subpicture may be positioned with the light pen, rotated or scaled by turning the knobs, or fixed in position by a termination signal, but its internal shape is fixed.

By pointing to the corner of one hexagon, pressing a button, and then pointing to the corner of another hexagon, we can fasten those corners together, because these corners have been designated as attachment points. If we attach two corners of each outer hexagon to the appropriate corners of the inner hexagon, the seven are uniquely related, and the computer will reposition them as shown in Figure 9.3H. An entire group of hexagons, once assembled, can be treated as a symbol. An "instance" of the entire group can be called up on another "sheet of paper" as a subpicture and assembled with other groups or with single hexagons to make a very large pattern.

## Interpretation of Introductory Example

In the introductory example above we used the light pen both to position parts of the drawing and to point to existing parts. We also saw in action the very general *subpicture*, *constraint*, and *definition copying* capabilities of the system.

### Subpicture

The original hexagon might just as well have been anything else: a picture of a transistor, a roller bearing, or an airplane wing. Any number of different symbols may be drawn, in terms of other simpler symbols if desired, and any symbol may be used as often as desired.

### Constraint

When we asked that the vertices of the hexagon lie on the circle we were making use of a basic relationship between picture parts that is built into the system. Basic relationships (atomic constraints) to make lines vertical, horizontal, parallel, or perpendicular; to make points lie on lines or circles; to make symbols appear upright, vertically above one another or be of equal size; and to relate symbols to other drawing parts such as points and lines have been included in the system. Specialized constraint types may be added as needed.

### Definition Copying

We made the sides of the hexagon be equal in length by pressing a button while pointing to the side in question. Had we defined a composite operation such as to make two lines

the sides of the hexagon be of equal length, a regular hexagon will be constructed.

With Sketchpad we can say, in effect, make *this* line equal in length to *that* line, pointing to the lines with the light pen. The computer satisfies all existing conditions (if it is possible) whenever we turn on a toggle switch. This done, we have a complete regular hexagon inscribed in a circle. We can erase the entire circle by pointing to any part of it and pressing the "delete" button. The completed hexagon is shown in Figure 9.3F.

To make the hexagonal pattern in Figure 9.4 we wish to attach a large number of hexagons together by their corners, and so we designate the six corners of our hexagon as attachment points by pointing to each and pressing a button. We now file away the basic hexagon and begin work on a fresh "sheet of paper" by changing a switch setting. On the both parallel and equal in length, we could have applied it just as easily.

## Implications of Introductory Example

As we have seen, a Sketchpad drawing is entirely different from the trail of carbon left on a piece of paper. Information about how the drawing is tied together is stored in the computer as well as the information which gives the drawing its particular appearance. Since the drawing is tied together, it will keep a useful appearance even when parts of it are moved. For example, when we moved the corners of the hexagon onto the circle, the lines next to each corner were automatically moved so that the closed topology of the hexagon was preserved. Again, since we indicated that the corners of the hexagon were to lie on the circle, they remained on the circle throughout our further manipulations.

As well as storing how the various parts of the drawing are related, Sketchpad stores the structure of the subpictures used. For example, the storage for the hexagonal pattern of Figure 9.4 indicates that this pattern is made of smaller patterns which are in turn made of smaller patterns which are composed of single hexagons. If the master hexagon is changed, the entire appearance but not the structure of the hexagonal pattern will be changed. For example, if we change the basic hexagon into a semicircle, the fish scale pattern shown in Figure 9.4 instantly results.

## Sketchpad and the Design Process

Construction of a drawing with Sketchpad is *itself* a model of the design process. The locations of the points and lines of the drawing model the variables of a design, and the geometric constraints applied to the points and lines of the drawing model the design constraints which limit the values of design variables. The ability of Sketchpad to satisfy the geometric constraints applied to the parts of a drawing models the ability of a good designer to satisfy all the design conditions imposed by the limitations of his materials, cost, etc. In fact, since designers in many fields produce nothing themselves but a drawing of a part, design conditions may well be thought of as applying to the drawing of a part rather than to the part itself. When such design conditions are added to Sketchpad's vocabulary of constraints, the computer will be able to assist a user not only in arriving at a nice looking drawing, but also in arriving at a sound design.

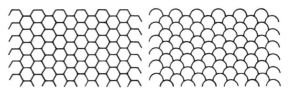

Figure 9.4. Hexagonal lattice with half hexagon and semicircle as basic elements.

## Present Usefulness

As more and more applications have been made, it has become clear that the properties of Sketchpad drawings make them most useful in four broad areas:

*For Storing and Updating Drawings*

Each time a drawing is made, a description of that drawing is stored in the computer in a form that is readily transferred to magnetic tape. A library of drawings will thus develop, parts of which may be used in other drawings at only a fraction of the investment of time that was put into the original drawing.

*For Gaining Scientific or Engineering Understanding of Operations That Can Be Described Graphically*

A drawing in the Sketchpad system may contain explicit statements about the relations between its parts so that as one part is changed the implications of this change become evident throughout the drawing. For instance, Sketchpad makes it easy to study mechanical linkages, observing the path of some parts when others are moved.

*As a Topological Input Device for Circuit Simulators, etc.*

Since the storage structure of Sketchpad reflects the topology of any circuit or diagram, it can serve as an input for many network or circuit simulating programs. The additional effort required to draw a circuit completely from scratch with the Sketchpad system may well be recompensed if the properties of the circuit are obtainable through simulation of the circuit drawn.

*For Highly Repetitive Drawings*

The ability of the computer to reproduce any drawn symbol anywhere at the press of a button, and to recursively include subpictures within subpictures makes it easy to produce drawings which are composed of huge numbers of parts all similar in shape.

## II  Ring Structure

The basic *n*-component element structure described by Ross[10] has been somewhat expanded in the implementation of Sketchpad so that all references made to a particular *n*-component element or block are collected together by a string of pointers which originates within that block. For example, not only may the end points of a line segment be found by following pointers in the line block (*n*-component element), but also all the line segments which terminate on a particular point may be found by following a string of pointers which starts within the point block. This string of pointers closes on itself; the last pointer points back to the first, hence the name "ring." The ring points both ways to

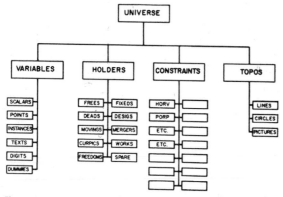

Figure 9.5. Generic structure. The n-component elements for each point or line, etc., are collected under the generic blocks "lines," "points," etc., shown.

make it easy to find both the next and the previous member of the ring in case, as when deleting, some change must be made to them.

## Basic Operations

The basic ring structure operations are:

1. Inserting a new member into a ring at some specified location on it, usually first or last.

2. Removing a member from a ring.

3. Putting all the members of one ring, in order, into another at some specified location in it, usually first or last.

4. Performing some auxiliary operation on each member of a ring in either forward or reverse order.

These basic ring structure operations are implemented by short sections of program defined as MACRO instructions in the compiler language. By suitable treatment of zero and one member rings, the basic programs operate without making special cases.

Subroutines are used for setting up new *n*-component elements in free spaces in the storage structure. As parts of the drawing are deleted, the registers which were used to represent them become free. New components are set up at the end of the storage area, lengthening it, while free blocks are allowed to accumulate. Garbage collection periodically compacts the storage structure by removal of the free blocks.

## Generic Structure, Hierarchies

The main part of Sketchpad can perform basic operations on any drawing part, calling for help from routines specific to particular types of parts when that is necessary. For example, the main program can show any part on the display system by calling the appropriate display subroutine. The big power of the clear-cut separation of the general and the specific is that it is easy to change the details of specific parts of the program to get quite different results without any need to change the general parts.

In the data storage structure the separation of general and specific is accomplished by collecting all things of one type together in a ring under a generic heading. The generic heading contains all the information which makes this type of thing different from all other types of things. Thus the data storage structure itself contains all the specific information. The generic blocks are further gathered together under super-generic or generic-generic blocks, as shown in Figure 9.5.

## Expanding Sketchpad

Addition of new types of things to the Sketchpad system's vocabulary of picture parts requires only the construction of a new generic block (about 20 registers) and the writing of appropriate subroutines for the new type. The subroutines might be easy to write, as they usually are for new constraints, or difficult to write, as for adding ellipse capability, but at least a finite, well-defined task faces one to add a new ability to the system. Without a generic structure it would be almost impossible to add the instructions required to handle a new type of element.

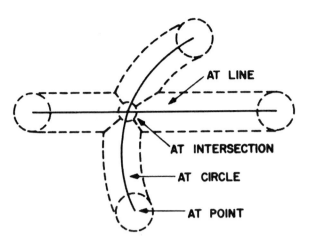

AT LINE

AT INTERSECTION

AT CIRCLE

AT POINT

Figure 9.6. Areas in which pen must lie to "aim at" existing drawing parts (solid lines).

## III  Light Pen

In Sketchpad the light pen* is time shared between the functions of coordinate input for positioning picture parts on the drawing and demonstrative input for pointing to existing picture parts to make changes. Although almost any kind of coordinate input device could be used instead of the light pen for positioning, the demonstrative input uses the light pen optics as a sort of analog computer to remove from consideration all but a very few picture parts which happen to fall within its field of view, saving considerable program time. Drawing systems using storage display devices of the Memotron type may not be practical because of the loss of this analog computation feature.

*The reader unacquainted with light pens should refer to the paper on Man-Machine Console Facilities by Stotz.[12]

### Pen Tracking

To initially establish pen tracking,* the Sketchpad user must inform the computer of an initial pen location. This has come to be known as "inking-up" and is done by "touching" any existing line or spot on the display, whereupon the tracking cross appears. If no picture has yet been drawn, the letters INK are always displayed for this purpose. Sketchpad uses loss of tracking as a "termination signal" to stop drawing. The user signals that he is finished drawing by flicking the pen too fast for the tracking program to follow.

### Demonstrative Use of Pen

During the 90% of the time that the light pen and display system are free from the tracking chore, spots are very rapidly displayed to exhibit the drawing being built, and thus the lines and circles of the drawing appear. The light pen is sensitive to these spots and reports any which fall within its field of view. Thus, a table of the picture parts seen by the light pen is assembled during each complete display cycle. At the end of a display cycle this table contains all the picture parts that could even remotely be considered as being "aimed at."

The one-half inch diameter field of view of the light pen, although well suited to tracking, is relatively large for pointing. Therefore, the Sketchpad system will reject any seen part which is further from the center of the light pen than some small minimum distance; about 1/8 inch was found to be suitable. For every kind of picture part some method must be provided for computing its distance from the light pen center or indicating that this computation cannot be made.

After eliminating all parts seen by the pen which lie outside the smaller effective field of view, the Sketchpad system considers objects topologically related to the ones actually seen. End points of lines and attachment points of instances (subpictures) are especially important. One can thus aim at the end point of a line even though only the line is displayed. Figure 9.6 outlines the various regions within which the pen must lie to be considered aimed at a line segment, a circle arc, their end points, or their intersection.

### Pseudo Pen Location

When the light pen is aimed at a picture part, the exact location of the light pen is ignored in favor of a "pseudo pen location" exactly on the part aimed at. If no object is aimed at, the pseudo pen location is taken to be the actual pen location. The pseudo pen location is displayed as a bright dot which is used as the "point of the pencil" in all drawing operations. As the light pen is moved into the areas outlined in Figure 9.6 the dot will lock onto the existing parts of the drawing, and any moving picture parts will jump to their new locations as the pseudo pen location moves to lie on the appropriate picture part.

With just the basic drawing creation and manipulation functions of "draw," "move," and "delete," and the power of the pseudo pen location and demonstrative language programs, it is possible to make fairly extensive drawings. Most of the

115

constructions normally provided by straight edge and compass are available in highly accurate form. Most important, however, the pseudo pen location and demonstrative language give the means for entering the topological properties of a drawing into the machine.

## IV  Display Generation

The display system, or "scope," on the TX-2 is a ten bit per axis electrostatic deflection system able to display spots at a maximum rate of about 100,000 per second. The coordinates of the spots which are to be seen on the display are stored in a large table so that computation and display may proceed independently. If, instead of displaying each spot successively, the display program displays them in a random order or with interlace, the flicker of the display is reduced greatly.

### Marking of Display File

Of the 36 bits available to store each display spot in the display file, 20 give the coordinates of that spot for the display system, and the remaining 16 give the address of the $n$-component element which is responsible for adding that spot to the display. Thus, all the spots in a line are tagged with the ring structure address of that line, and all the spots in an instance (subpicture) are tagged as belonging to that instance. The tags are used to identify the particular part of the drawing being aimed at by the light pen.

If a part of the drawing is being moved by the light pen, its display spots will be recomputed as quickly as possible to show it in successive positions. The display spots for such moving parts are stored at the end of the display file so that the display of the many nonmoving parts need not be disturbed. Moving parts are made invisible to the light pen.

### Magnification of Pictures

The shaft position encoder knobs below the scope (see Figure 9.1) are used to tell the program to change the display scale factor or the portion of the page displayed. The range of magnification of 2000 available makes it possible to work, in effect, on a 7-inch square portion of a drawing about 1/4 mile on a side.

For a magnified picture, Sketchpad computes which portion(s) of a curve will appear on the display and generates display spots for those portions only. The "edge detection" problem is the problem of finding suitable end points for the portion of a curve which appears on the display.

In concept the edge detection problem is trivial. In terms of program time for lines and circles the problem is a small

fraction of the total computational load of the system, but in terms of program logical complexity the edge detection problem is a difficult one. For example, the computation of the intersection of a circle with any of the edges of the scope is easy, but computation of the intersection of a circle with all four edges may result in as many as eight intersections, some pairs of which may be identical, the scope corners. Now which of these intersections are actually to be used as starts of circle arcs?

### Line and Circle Generation

All of Sketchpad's displays are generated from straight line segments, circle arcs, and single points. The generation of the lines and circles is accomplished by means of the difference equations:

$$x_i = x_{i-1} + \Delta x$$
$$y_i = y_{i-1} + \Delta y \tag{1}$$

for lines, and

$$x_i = x_{i-2} + \tfrac{2}{R}(y_{i-1} - y_c)$$
$$y_i = y_{i-2} - \tfrac{2}{R}(x_{i-1} - x_c) \tag{2}$$

for circles, where subscripts $i$ indicate successive display spots, subscript $c$ indicates the circle center, and $R$ is the radius of the circle in Scope Units. In implementing these difference equations in the program, the fullest possible use is made of the coordinate arithmetic capability of the TX-2 so that both the $x$ and $y$ equation computations are performed in parallel on 18 bit subwords. Even so, about $3/4$ of the total Sketchpad computation time is spent in line and circle generation. A vector and circle generating display would materially reduce the computational load of Sketchpad.

For computers which do only one addition at a time, the difference equations:

$$x_i = x_{i-1} + \tfrac{1}{R}(y_{i-1} - y_c)$$
$$y_i = y_{i-1} - \tfrac{1}{R}(x_i - x_c) \tag{3}$$

should be used to generate circles. Equations (3) approximate a circle well enough and are known to close exactly both in theory and when implemented, because the x and y equations are dissimilar.

### Digits and Text

Text, to put legends on a drawing, is displayed by means of special tables which indicate the locations of line and circle segments to make up the letters and numbers. Each piece of text appears as a single line of not more than 36 equally spaced characters which can be changed by typing. Digits to display the value of an indicated scalar at any position and in any size and rotation are formed from the same type face as text. It is possible to display up to five decimal digits with

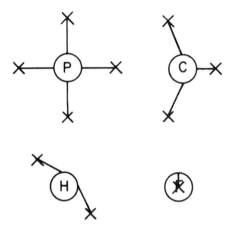

Figure 9.7. Display of constraints.

sign; binary to decimal conversion is provided, and leading zeros are suppressed.

Subpictures, whose use was seen in the introductory example above, are each represented in storage as a single *n*-component element. A subpicture is said to be an "instance" of its "master picture." To display an instance, all of the lines, text, etc. of its master picture must be shown in miniature on the display. The instance display program makes use of the line, circle, number, and text display programs and *itself* to expand the internal structure of the instance.

## Display of Abstractions

The usual picture for human consumption displays only lines, circles, text, digits, and instances. However, certain very useful abstractions which give the drawing the properties desired by the user are represented in the ring structure storage. For example, the fact that the start and end points of a circle arc should be equidistant from the circle's center point is represented in storage by a "constraint" block. To make it possible for a user to manipulate these abstractions, each abstraction must be able to be seen on the display if desired. Not only does displaying abstractions make it

possible for the human user to know that they exist, but also makes it possible for him to aim at them with the light pen and, for example, erase them. To avoid confusion, the display for particular types of objects may be turned on or off selectively by toggle switches. Thus, for example, one can turn on display of constraints as well as or instead of the lines and circles which are normally seen.

If their selection toggle switch is on, constraints are displayed as shown in Figure 9.7. The central circle and code letter are located at the average location of the variables constrained. The four arms of a constraint extend from the top, right side, bottom, and left side of the circle to the first, second, third, and fourth variables constrained, respectively. If fewer than four variables are constrained, excess arms are omitted. In Figure 9.7 the constraints are shown applied to "dummy variables," each of which shows as an X.

Another abstraction that can be displayed if desired is the value of a set of digits. For example, in Figure 9.8 are shown three sets of digits all displaying the same scalar value, −5978. The digits themselves may be moved, rotated, or changed in size, without changing the value displayed. If we wish to change the value, we point at its abstract display, the # seen in Figure 9.8. The three sets of digits in Figure 9.8 all display the same value, as indicated by the lines connecting them to the #; changing this value would make all three sets of digits change. Constraints may be applied independently to either the position of the digits or their value as indicated by the two constraints in the figure.

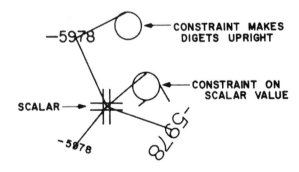

Figure 9.8. Three sets of digits displaying the same scalar value.

## V  Recursive Functions

In the process of making the Sketchpad system operate, a few very general functions were developed which make no reference at all to the specific types of entities on which they operate. These general functions give the Sketchpad system the ability to operate on a wide range of problems. The motivation for making the functions as general as possible came from the desire to get as much result as possible from the programming effort involved. For example, the general function for expanding instances makes it possible for Sketchpad to handle any fixed geometry subpicture. The power obtained from the small set of generalized functions in Sketchpad is one of the most important results of the research.

In order of historical development, the recursive functions in use in the Sketchpad system are:

1. Expansion of instances, making it possible to have subpictures within subpictures to as many levels as desired.

2. Recursive deletion, whereby removal of certain picture parts will remove other picture parts in order to maintain consistency in the ring structure.

3. Recursive merging, whereby combination of two similar picture parts forces combination of similarly related other picture parts, making possible application of complex definitions to an object picture.

### Recursive Deleting

*If a thing upon which other things depend is deleted, the dependent things must be deleted also.* For example, if a point is to be deleted, all lines which terminate on the point must also be deleted. Otherwise, since the n-component elements for lines contain no positional information, where would these lines end? Similarly, deletion of a variable requires deletion of all constraints on that variable; a constraint must have variables to act on.

### Recursive Merging

*If two things of the same type which are independent are merged, a single thing of that type results, and all things which depended on either of the merged things depend on the result\* of the merger.* For example, if two points are merged, all lines which previously terminated on either point now terminate on the single resulting point. In Sketchpad, if a thing is being moved with the light pen and the termination flick of the pen is given while aiming at another thing of the same type, the two things will merge. Thus, if one moves a point to another point and terminates, the points will merge, connecting all lines which formerly terminated on either. This makes it possible to draw closed polygons.

*If two things of the same type which do depend on other things are merged, the things depended on by one will be forced to merge, respectively, with the things depended on by the other. The result\* of merging two dependent things depends, respectively, on the results\* of the mergers it forces.* For example, if two lines are merged, the resultant line must refer to only two end points, the results of merging the pairs of end points of the original lines. All lines which terminated on any of the four original end points now terminate on the appropriate one of the remaining pair. More important and useful, all constraints which applied to any of the four original end points now apply to the appropriate one of the remaining pair. This makes it possible to speak of line segments as being parallel even though (because line segments contain no numerical information to be constrained) the

\*The "result" of a merger is a single thing of the same type as the merged things.

parallelism constraint must apply to their end points and not to the line segments themselves. If we wish to make two lines both parallel and equal in length, the steps outlined in Figure 9.9 make it possible. More obscure relationships between dependent things may be easily defined and applied. For example, constraint complexes can be defined to make line segments be collinear, to make a line be tangent to a circle, or to make the values represented by two sets of digits be equal.

### Recursive Display of Instances

The block of registers which represents an instance is remarkably small considering that it may generate a display of any complexity. For the purposes of display, the instance block makes reference to its master picture. The instance will appear on the display as a figure geometrically similar to its master picture at a location, size, and rotation indicated by the four numbers which constitute the "value" of the instance. The value of an instance is considered numerically as a four dimensional vector. The components of this vector are the coordinates of the center of the instance and its actual size as it appears on the drawing times the sine and cosine of the rotation angle involved.

In displaying an instance of a picture, reference is made to the master picture to find out what picture parts are to be shown. The master picture referred to may contain instances, however, requiring further reference, and so on until a picture is found which contains no instances. At each stage in the recursion, any picture parts displayed must be relocated so that they will appear at the correct position, size and rotation on the display. Thus, at each stage of the recursion, some transformation is applied to all picture parts before displaying them. If an instance is encountered, the transformation represented by its value must be adjoined to the existing transformation for display of parts within it. When the expansion of an instance within an instance is finished, the transformation must be restored for continuation at the higher level.

## Attachers and Instances

Many symbols must be integrated into the rest of the drawing by attaching lines to the symbols at appropriate

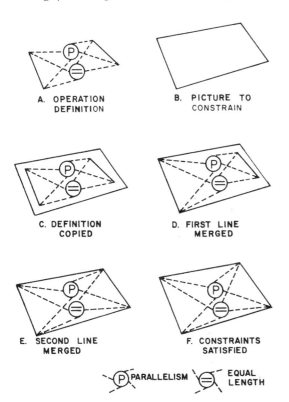

A. OPERATION
   DEFINITION

B. PICTURE TO
   CONSTRAIN

C. DEFINITION
   COPIED

D. FIRST LINE
   MERGED

E. SECOND LINE
   MERGED

F. CONSTRAINTS
   SATISFIED

(P) PARALLELISM    (=) EQUAL
                       LENGTH

Figure 9.9. Applying a two-constraint definition to turn a quadrilateral into a parallelogram.

points, or by attaching the symbols directly to each other. For example, circuit symbols must be wired up, geometric patterns made by fitting shapes together, or mechanisms composed of links tied together appropriately. An instance may have any number of attachment points, and a point may serve as attacher for any number of instances. The light pen has the same affinity for the attachers of an instance that it has for the end point of a line.

An "instance-point" constraint, shown with code T in Figure 9.10C, is used to relate an instance to each of its attachment points. An instance-point constraint is satisfied only when the point bears the same relationship to the instance that a master point in the master picture for that instance bears to the master picture coordinate system.

Any point may be an attacher of an instance, but the point must be designated as an attacher in the master drawing of the instance. For example, when one first draws a resistor, the ends of the resistor must be designated as attachers if wiring is to be attached to instances of it. At each level of building complex pictures, the attachers must be designated anew. Thus of the three attachers of a transistor it is possible to select one or two to be the attachers of a flip-flop.

## VI  Building a Drawing, the Copy Function

At the start of the Sketchpad effort certain ad hoc drawing functions were programmed as the atomic operations of the system. Each such operation, controlled by a push button, creates in the ring structure a specific set of new drawing parts. For example, the "draw" button creates a line segment and two new end points (unless the light pen happens to be aimed at a point in which case only one new point need be created). Similarly, there are atomic operations for drawing circles, applying a horizontal or vertical constraint to the end points of a line aimed at, and for adding a "point-on-line" constraint whenever a point is moved onto a line and left there.

The atomic operations described above make it possible to create in the ring structure new picture components and relate them topologically. The atomic operations are, of course, limited to creating points, lines, circles, and two or three types of constraints. Since implementation of the copy function it has become possible to create in the ring structure any predefined combination of picture parts and constraints at the press of a button. The recursive merging function makes it possible to relate the copied set of picture parts to any existing parts. For example, if a line segment and its two end points are copied into the object picture, the action of the "draw" button may be exactly duplicated in every respect. Along with the copied line, however, one might copy as well a constraint, Code H, to make the line horizontal as shown in Figure 9.10A, or two constraints to make the line both horizontal and three inches long, or any other variation one cares to put into the ring structure to be copied.

When one draws a definition picture to be copied, certain portions of it to be used in relating it to other object picture parts are designated as "attachers." Anything at all may be designated: for example, points, lines, circles, text, even constraints! The rules used for combining points when the "draw" button is pressed are generalized so that:

For copying a picture, the last-designated attacher is left moving with the light pen. The next-to-last-designated attacher is recursively merged with whatever object the pen is aimed at when the copying occurs, if that object is of like type. Previously designated attachers are recursively merged with previously designated object picture parts, if of like type, until either the supply of designated attachers or the supply of designated object picture parts is exhausted. The last-designated attacher may be recursively merged with any other object of like type when the termination flick is given.

Normally only two designated attachers are used because it is hard to keep track of additional ones.

If the definition picture consists of two line segments, their four end points, and a constraint, Code M, on the points which makes the lines equal in length, with the two lines designated as attachers as shown in Figure 9.10B, copying enables the user to make any two lines equal in length. If the pen is aimed at a line when "copy" is pushed, the first of the two copied lines merges with it (taking its position and never actually being seen). The other copied line is left moving with the light pen and will merge with whatever other line the pen is aimed at when termination occurs. Since merging is recursive, the copied equal-length constraint, Code M, will apply to the end points of the desired pair of object picture lines.

### Copying Instances

As we have seen above, the internal structure of an instance is entirely fixed. The internal structure of a copy, however, is entirely variable. An instance always retains its identity as a

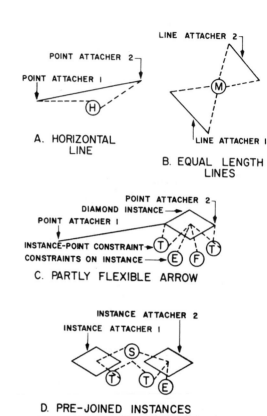

Figure 9.10. Definition pictures to be copied, see text.

single part of the drawing; one can only delete an entire instance. Once a definition picture is copied, however, the copy loses all identity as a unit; individual parts of it may be deleted at will.

One might expect that there was intermediate ground between the fixed-internal-structure instance and the loose-internal-structure copy. One might wish to produce a collection of picture parts, some of which were fixed internally and some of which were not. *The entire range of variation between the instance and the copy can be constructed by copying instances.*

For example, the arrow shown in Figure 9.10C can be copied into an object picture to result in a fixed-internal-structure diamond arrowhead with a flexible tail. As the definition in Figure 9.10C is set up, drawing diamond-arrowheaded lines is just like drawing ordinary lines. One aims the light pen where the tail is to end, presses "copy," and moves off with an arrowhead following the pen. The diamond arrowhead in this case will not rotate (constraint Code E), and will not change size (constraint Code F).

Copying pre-joined instances can produce vast numbers of joined instances very easily. For example, the definition in Figure 9.10D, when repetitively copied, will result in a row of joined, equal size (constraint Code S) diamonds. In this case the instances themselves are attachers. Although each press of the "copy" button copies two new instances into the object picture, one of these is merged with the last instance in the growing row. In the final row, therefore, each instance carries all constraints which are applied to either of the instances in the definition. This is why only one of the instances in Figure 9.10D carries the erect constraint, Code E.

## VII  Constraint Satisfaction

The major feature which distinguishes a Sketchpad drawing from a paper and pencil drawing is the user's ability to specify to Sketchpad mathematical conditions on already drawn parts of his drawing which will be automatically satisfied by the computer to make the drawing take the exact shape desired. The process of fixing up a drawing to meet new conditions applied to it after it is already partially complete is very much like the process a designer goes through in turning a basic idea into a finished design. As new requirements on the various parts of the design are thought of, small changes are made to the size or other properties of parts to meet the new conditions. By making Sketchpad able to find new values for variables which satisfy the conditions imposed, it is hoped that designers can be relieved of the need of much mathematical detail. The effort expended in making the definition of constraint types as general as possible was aimed at making design constraints as well as geometric constraints equally easy to add to the system.

### Definition of a Constraint Type

Each constraint type is entered into the system as a generic block indicating the various properties of that particular constraint type. The generic block tells how many variables are constrained, which of these variables may be changed in order to satisfy the constraint, how many degrees of freedom are removed from the constrained variables, and a code letter for human reference to this constraint type.

The definition of what a constraint type does is a subroutine which will compute, for the existing values of the variables of a particular constraint of that type, the error

introduced into the system by that particular constraint. For example, the defining subroutine for making points have the same $x$ coordinate (to make a line between them vertical) computes the difference in their $x$ coordinates. What could be simpler? The computed error is a scalar which the constraint satisfaction routine will attempt to reduce to zero by manipulation of the constrained variables. The computation of the error may be non-linear or time dependent, or it may involve parameters not a part of the drawing such as the setting of toggle switches, etc.

When the one pass method of satisfying constraints to be described later on fails, the Sketchpad system falls back on the reliable but slow method of relaxation[11] to reduce the errors indicated by various computation subroutines to smaller and smaller values. For simple constructions such as the hexagon illustrated in Figure 9.3, the relaxation procedure is sufficiently fast to be useful. However, for complex systems of variables, especially directly connected instances, relaxation is unacceptably slow. Fortunately it is for just such directly connected instances that the one pass method shows the most striking success.

### One Pass Method

Sketchpad can often find an order in which the variables of a drawing may be re-evaluated to completely satisfy all the conditions on them in just one pass. For the cases in which the one pass method works, it is far better than relaxation: it gives correct answers at once; relaxation may not give a correct solution in any finite time. Sketchpad can find an order in which to re-evaluate the variables of a drawing for most of the common geometric constructions. Ordering is also found easily for the mechanical linkages shown in Figures 9.13 and 9.14. Ordering cannot be found for the bridge truss problem in Figure 9.15.

The way in which the one pass method works is simple in principle and was easy to implement as soon as the nuances of the ring structure manipulations were understood. To visualize the one pass method, consider the variables of the drawing as places and the constraints relating variables as passages through which one might pass from one variable to another. Variables are adjacent to each other in the maze formed by the constraints if there is a single constraint which constrains them both. Variables are totally unrelated if there is no path through the constraints by which to pass from one to the other.

Suppose that some variable can be found which has so few constraints applying to it that it can be re-evaluated to completely satisfy all of them. Such a variable we shall call a "free" variable. As soon as a variable is recognized as free, the constraints which apply to it are removed from further consideration, because the free variable can be used to satisfy them. Removing these constraints, however, may make adjacent variables free. Recognition of these new variables as free removes further constraints from consideration and may make other adjacent variables free, and so on throughout the maze of constraints. The manner in which freedom spreads is much like the method used in Moore's algorithm[8] to find the shortest path through a maze. Having found that a collection of variables is free, Sketchpad will re-evaluate them in reverse order, saving the first-found free variable until last. In re-evaluating any particular variable, Sketchpad uses only those constraints which were present when that variable was found to be free.

## VIII  Examples and Conclusions

The examples in this section were all taken from the library tape and thus serve to illustrate not only how the Sketchpad system can be used, but also how it actually has been used so

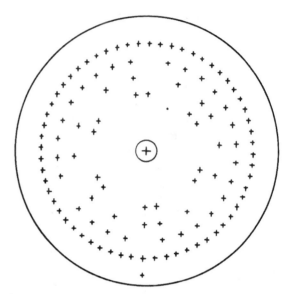

Figure 9.12. Binary coded decimal encoder for clock. Encoder was plotted exactly 12 inches in diameter for direct use as a layout.

Figure 9.11. Zig-Zag for delay line.

far. We conclude from these examples that Sketchpad drawings can bring invaluable understanding to a user. For drawings where motion of the drawing, or analysis of a drawn problem is of value to the user, Sketchpad excels. For highly repetitive drawings or drawings where accuracy is required, Sketchpad is sufficiently faster than conventional techniques to be worthwhile. For drawings which merely communicate with shops, it is probably better to use conventional paper and pencil.

### Patterns

The instance facility enables one to draw any symbol and duplicate its appearance anywhere on an object drawing at the push of a button. This facility made the hexagonal

pattern we saw in Figure 9.4 easy to draw. It took about one half hour to generate 900 hexagons, including the time taken to figure out how to do it. Plotting them takes about 25 minutes. The drafting department estimated it would take two days to produce a similar pattern.

The instance facility also made it easy to produce long lengths of the zig-zag pattern shown in Figure 9.11. As the figure shows, a single "zig" was duplicated in multiples of five

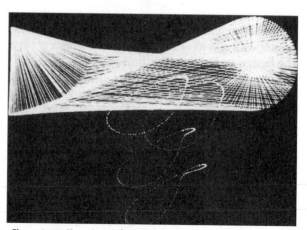

Figure 9.13. Three bar linkage. The paths of four points on the central link are traced. This is a 15 second time exposure of a moving Sketchpad drawing.

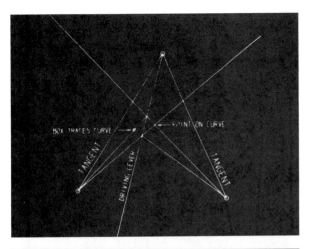

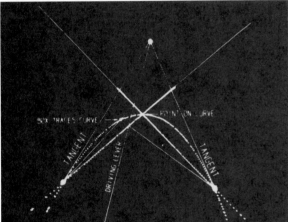

Figure 9.14. Conic drawing linkage. As the "driving lever" is moved, the point shown with a box around it (in A) traces a conic section. This conic can be seen in the time exposure (B).

## Linkages

By far the most interesting application of Sketchpad so far has been drawing and moving linkages. The ability to draw and then move linkages opens up a new field of graphical manipulation that has never before been available. It is remarkable how even a simple linkage can generate complex motions. For example, the linkage of Figure 9.13 has only three moving parts. In this linkage a central ⊥ link is suspended between two links of different lengths. As the shorter link rotates, the longer one oscillates as can be seen in the multiple exposure. The ⊥ link is not shown in Figure 9.13 so that the motion of four points on the upright part of the ⊥ may be seen. These are the four curves at the top of the figure.

To make the three bar linkage, an instance shaped like the ⊥ was drawn and given 6 attachers, two at its joints with the other links and four at the places whose paths were to be observed. Connecting the ⊥ shaped subpicture onto a linkage composed of three lines with fixed length created the picture shown. The driving link was rotated by turning a knob below the scope. Total time to construct the linkage was less than 5 minutes, but over an hour was spent playing with it.

A linkage that would be difficult to build physically is shown in Figure 9.14A. This linkage is based on the complete quadrilateral. The three circled points and the two lines which extend out of the top of the picture to the right and left are fixed. Two moving lines are drawn from the lower circled points to the intersections of the long fixed lines with the driving lever. The intersection of these two moving lines (one must be extended) has a box around it. It can be shown theoretically that this linkage produces a conic section which passes through the place labeled "point on curve" and is tangent to the two lines marked "tangent." Figure 9.14B shows a time exposure of the moving point in many positions. At first, this linkage was drawn and working in 15 minutes. Since then we have rebuilt it time and again until now we can produce it from scratch in about 3 minutes.

## Dimension Lines

To make it possible to have an absolute scale in drawings, a constraint is provided which forces the value displayed by a set of digits to indicate the distance between two points on the drawing. This distance-indicating constraint is used to make the number in a dimension line correspond to its length. Putting in a dimension line is as easy as drawing any

and three, etc. Five hundred zigs were generated in a single row. Four such rows were plotted one-half inch apart to be used for producing a printed circuit delay line. Total time taken was about 45 minutes for constructing the figure and about 15 minutes to plot it.

A somewhat less repetitive pattern to be used for encoding the time in a digital clock is shown in Figure 9.12. Each cross in the figure marks the position of a hole. The holes are placed so that a binary coded decimal (BCD) number will indicate the time. Total time for placing crosses was 20 minutes, most of which was spent trying to interpret a pencil sketch of their positions.

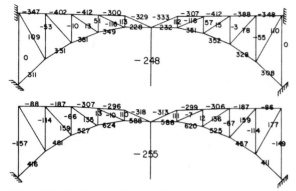

Figure 9.15. Cantilever and arch bridges. The numbers indicate the forces in the various members as computed by Sketchpad. Central load is not exactly vertical.

other line. One points to where one end is to be left, copies the definition of the dimension line by pressing the "copy" button, and then moves the light pen to where the other end of the dimension line is to be. The first dimension line took about 15 minutes to construct, but that need never be repeated since it is a part of the library.

### Bridges

One of the largest untapped fields for application of Sketchpad is as an input program for other computation programs. The ability to place lines and circles graphically, when coupled with the ability to get accurately computed results pictorially displayed, should bring about a revolution in computer application. By using Sketchpad's relaxation procedure we were to demonstrate analysis of the force distribution in the members of a pin connected truss.

A bridge is first drawn with enough constraints to make it geometrically accurate. These constraints are then deleted and each member is made to behave like a bridge beam. A bridge beam is constrained to maintain constant length, but any change in length is indicated by an associated number. Under the assumption that each bridge beam has a cross-sectional area proportional to its length, the numbers represent the forces in the beams. The basic bridge beam definition (consisting of two constraints and a number) may be copied and applied to any desired line in a bridge picture by pointing to the line and pressing the "copy" button.

Having drawn a basic bridge shape, one can experiment with various loading conditions and supports to see what the effect of making minor modifications is. For example, an arch bridge is shown in Figure 9.15 supported both as a three-hinged arch (two supports) and as a cantilever (four

supports). For nearly identical loading conditions the distribution of forces is markedly different in these two cases.

### Artistic Drawings

Sketchpad need not be applied exclusively to engineering drawings. For example, the girl "Nefertite" shown in Figure 9.16 can be made to wink by changing which of the three types of eyes is placed in position on her otherwise eyeless face. In the same way that linkages can be made to move, a stick figure could be made to pedal a bicycle or Nefertite's hair could be made to swing. The ability to make moving drawings suggests that Sketchpad might be used for making animated cartoons.

### Electrical Circuit Diagrams

Unfortunately, electrical circuits require a great many symbols which have not yet been drawn properly with Sketchpad and therefore are not in the library. After some time is spent working on the basic electrical symbols it may be easier to draw circuits. So far, however, circuit drawing has proven difficult.

The circuits of Figure 9.17 are parts of an analog switching scheme. You can see in the figure that the more complicated circuits are made up of simpler symbols and circuits. It is

Figure 9.16. Winking girl, "Nefertite," and her component parts.

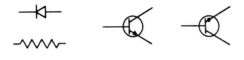

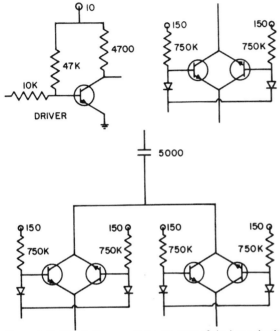

Figure 9.17. Circuit diagrams. These are parts of the large circuit mentioned in the text.

linkage examples, we were able to gain an understanding of the behavior of a linkage as well as its appearance. In the bridge examples we got design answers which were worth far more than the computer time put into them. If we had had a circuit simulation program connected to Sketchpad so that we would have known whether the circuit we drew worked, it would have been worth our while to use the computer to draw it. We are as yet a long way from being able to produce routine drawings economically with the computer.

## Future Work

The methods outlined in this paper generalize nicely to three dimensional drawing. In fact, the work reported in "Sketchpad III" by Timothy Johnson[3] will let the user communicate solid objects to the computer. Johnson is completely bypassing the problem of converting several two dimensional drawings into a three dimensional shape. Drawing will be directly in three dimensions from the start. No two dimensional representation will ever be stored.

Work is also proceeding in direct conversion of photographs into line drawings. Roberts reports a computer program[9] able to recognize simple objects in photographs well enough to produce three dimensional line drawings for them. Roberts is storing his drawings in the ring structure described here so that his results will be compatible with the three dimensional version of Sketchpad.

Major improvements to Sketchpad of the same order and power as the existing definition copying capability can be foreseen. At present Sketchpad is able to add defined relationships to an existing object drawing. A method should be devised for defining and applying changes which involve removing some parts of the object drawing as well as adding new ones. Such a capability would permit one to define, for example, what rounding off a corner means. Then, one could round off any corner by pointing to it and applying the definition.

very difficult, however, to plan far enough ahead to know what composites of circuit symbols will be useful as subpictures of the final circuit. The simple circuits shown in Figure 9.17 were compounded into a big circuit involving about 40 transistors. Including much trial and error, the time taken by a new user (for the big circuit not shown) was ten hours. At the end of that time the circuit was still not complete in every detail and he decided it would be better to draw it by hand after all.

## Conclusions

The circuit experience points out the most important fact about Sketchpad drawings. It is only worthwhile to make drawings on the computer if you get something more out of the drawing than just a drawing. In the repetitive patterns we saw in the first examples, precision and ease of constructing great numbers of parts were valuable. In the

Notes and Acknowledgements

This paper is based in part on a thesis submitted to the Department of Electrical Engineering, M.I.T., in partial fulfillment of the requirements for the Degree of Doctor of Philosophy.

Lincoln Laboratory is operated with the support of the U.S. Army, Navy, and Air Force.

The author is indebted to Professors Claude E. Shannon, Marvin Minsky and Steven A. Coons of the Massachusetts Institute of Technology for their help and advice throughout the course of this research.

The author also wishes to thank Douglas T. Ross and Lawrence G. Roberts for their help and answers to his many questions.

Bibliography

1. Clark, W. A., Frankovich, J. M., Peterson, H. P., Forgie, J. W., Best, R. L., Olsen, K. H., "The Lincoln TX-2 Computer," Technical Report 6M-4968, Massachusetts Institute of Technology, Lincoln Laboratory, Lexington, Mass., April 1, 1957, *Proceedings of the Western Joint Computer Conference,* Los Angeles, California, February 1957.

2. Coons, S. A., *Notes on Graphical Input Methods,* Memorandum 8436-M-17, Dynamic Analysis and Control Laboratory, Massachusetts Institute of Technology, Department of Mechanical Engineering, Cambridge, Mass., May 4, 1960.

3. Johnson, T. E., "Sketchpad III, Three Dimensional Graphical Communication with a Digital Computer," *Proceedings of the Spring Joint Computer Conference,* Detroit, Michigan, May 21–23, 1963.

4. Johnston, L. E., *A Graphical Input Device and Shape Description Interpretation Routines,* Memorandum to Prof. Mann, Massachusetts Institute of Technology, Department of Mechanical Engineering, Cambridge, Mass., May 4, 1960.

5. Licklider, J. C. R., "Man-Computer Symbiosis," *I.R.E. Trans. on Human Factors in Electronics,* vol. HFE, pp. 4–10, March 1960.

6. Licklider, J. C. R., and Clark, W., "On-line Man-Computer Communication," *Proceedings of the Spring Joint Computer Conference,* San Francisco, California, May 1–3, 1962, vol. 21, pp. 113–128.

7. Loomis, H. H. Jr., Graphical Manipulation Techniques Using the Lincoln TX-2 Computer, Group Report 51G-0017, Massachusetts Institute of Technology, Lincoln Laboratory, Lexington, Mass., November 10, 1960.

8. Moore, E. F., "On the Shortest Path Through a Maze," *Proceedings of the International Symposium on the Theory of Switching,* Harvard University, Harvard Annals, vol. 3, pp. 285–292, 1959.

9. Roberts, L. G., *Machine Perception of Three Dimensional Solids,* Ph.D. Thesis, Massachusetts Institute of Technology, Electrical Engineering Department, Cambridge, Mass., February 1963.

10. Ross, D. T., Rodriguez, J. E., "Theoretical Foundations for the Computer-Aided Design System," *Proceedings of the Spring Joint Computer Conference,* Detroit, Michigan, May 21–23, 1963.

11. Southwell, R. V., *Relaxation Methods in Engineering Science,* Oxford University Press, 1940.

12. Stotz, R., "Man-Machine Console Facilities for Computer-Aided Design," *Proceedings of the Spring Joint Computer Conference,* Detroit, Michigan, May 21–23, 1963, (this issue).

13. Vanderburgh, A. Jr., *TX-2 Users Handbook,* Lincoln Manual No. 45, Massachusetts Institute of Technology, Lincoln Laboratory, Lexington, Mass., July 1961.

14. Walsh, J. F., and Smith, A. F., "Computer Utilization," *Interim Engineering Report 6873-IR-10 and 11,* Electronic Systems Laboratory, Massachusetts Institute of Technology, Cambridge, Mass., pp. 57–70, November 30, 1959.

15. *Handbook for Variplotter Models 205S and 205T,* PACE, Electronic Associates Incorporated. Long Branch, New Jersey, June 15, 1959.

# 10. [Introduction]
# The Construction of Change

◊04
65

◊06
83

127

In 1961, while the Happenings Allan Kaprow reported on were creating a stir in New York (◊06), in London Roy Ascott was remaking art (and art education) in view of Wiener's cybernetics (◊04). The essay reprinted here is Ascott's first publication on the subject, and one of the first writings to advocate this connection between cybernetics and art, making it a founding document for the fusion of procedural technology and aesthetics/design that is new media. Through the rest of the 1960s the connection between "cybernetics and art" would continue to be an area of focus, in these words. More generally, artistic interest continues to this day in conception, information, behavior, and interaction.

While the Happening is viewed by some as the paradigmatic example of artistic interaction, others (as discussed in the introduction to Kaprow's essay) would disagree with this characterization. Frank Popper, in his influential *Art of the Electronic Age*, redraws the bounds of this debate by underscoring a distinction between *participation* and *interaction*:

> In the artistic context, "participation" meant in the 1960s, and still means today, an involvement on both the contemplative (intellectual) and the behavioural level. It differed from traditional attitudes towards the spectator by this double invitation and by its political and social implications. Besides being invited to participate through the devices specific to the plastic arts, the spectator was often encouraged to take part in events resembling a ritual ceremony or tribal feast.
>
> The term "interaction" has a more recent history in this area and refers to a still more comprehensive involvement. Here the artist tries to stimulate a two-way interaction between his works and the spectator, a process that becomes possible only through the new technological devices that create a situation in which questions by the user/spectator are effectively answered by the art work itself. A global network is the usual form taken by these works, requiring equally global involvement from the spectator. The projects again have important social implications, though they are far less directly "political" than those of the 1960s. They tend to address more immediately daily problems or environmental issues, and can have a distinctly "scientific" flavour.
>
> Thus, the term *participation*, in the context of contemporary art, refers to a relationship between a spectator and an already existing open-ended art work, whereas the term "interaction" implies a two-way interplay between an individual and an artificial intelligence system. (8)

Popper's distinction can be a useful one, especially if we are willing to adopt for its purposes a much broader definition of artificial intelligence than is traditional in computer science. At the same time, however, it is instructive to note that Ascott's later works do not fit neatly into Popper's dichotomy. In the 1980s Ascott became a pioneer and primary articulator of *telematic* art, in which an artist creates a system for communication and collaboration between physically dispersed individuals. Such cases are clearly not what Popper calls participation, and yet they are also not cases in which "questions by the user/spectator are effectively answered by the art work itself." Instead they are answered, in a sense, by the other user/spectators, through the context created by the artist—a "global network" of a rather different sort. Telematic art, in fact, might potentially be defined as work that attempts both Popper's participation and interaction. Further, telematic art remains fully consistent with the framework Ascott presented in 1964—of art as an investigation of behavior, of creating situations for exploring behavior.

Ascott's exercises in the second portion of this essay can be read as dematerialized art (along the lines of Yoko Ono's instructions) or as a straightforward report of the embodied work he was carrying out at the Ealing School of Art—and either reading may be useful.
—NWF

Some have argued that Ascott's essay is the first to be published on new media art. Whether one agrees with this assertion or not, it is almost certainly the first published on education in these subjects. Consider how it compares to the classroom reports of Michael Joyce (◊42) and Robert Coover (◊49), and the imaginary classroom conjured by Seymour Papert (◊28).

◊28
413

◊42
613

◊49
705

Further Reading

Popper, Frank. *Art of the Electronic Age.* New York: Harry N. Abrams, 1993.

Ascott, Roy, ed. *Reframing Consciousness: Art and Consciousness in the Post-Biological Era.* Exeter: Intellect, 1999.

Deitz, Steve, ed. *Telematic Connections: The Virtual Embrace.* Online and CD-ROM catalog produced by Carl DiSalvo for a traveling exhibition, organized by Independent Curators International (ICI), New York, curated by Steve Dietz, copresented online by the Walker Art Center, Minneapolis, 2001. <http://telematic.walkerart.org>

Shanken, Edward A., ed. *Is There Love in the Telematic Embrace? Visionary Theories of Art, Technology, and Consciousness by Roy Ascott.* Berkeley: University of California Press, 2001.

Original Publication

*Cambridge Opinion 41 (Modern Art in Britain).* 37–42, 1964.

# The Construction of Change

## Roy Ascott

### Art and Didactics

While the creative process demands acts of synthesis which defy verbal description and which only the work of art itself can define, there are some aspects of artistic activity which can be examined and set down rationally. They are both empirical and analytical and involve forays into unfamiliar conceptual territories. Very often scientific ideas can reinforce or extend what is uncovered. To discuss what one is *doing* rather than the artwork which results, to attempt to unravel the loops of creative activity, is, in many ways, a behavioural problem. The fusion of art, science and personality is involved. It leads to a consideration of our total relationship to a work of art, in which physical moves may lead to conceptual moves, in which Behaviour relates to Idea.

Art, for me, is largely a matter of freely developing ideas and creating forms and structures which embody them. Whatever ideas I may pursue, and in the art the entire universe is open to investigation and reconstruction, Behaviour is an important reference in my considerations of space, time and form. I make structures in which the relationships of parts are not fixed and may be changed by the intervention of a spectator. As formal relationships are altered, so the ideas they stand for are extended. I am conscious of the spectator's role. Once positioned to a work he may become totally involved—physically as well as intellectually or emotionally. To project my ideas I set limits within which he may behave. In response to behavioural clues in a construction (to push, pull, slide back, open, peg-in, for example) the participant becomes responsible for the extension of the artwork's meaning. He becomes a decision-maker in the symbolic world which confronts him. My *Change Paintings* and kinetic constructions are not intended only to discuss and project ideas, but as analogues of ideas—structures which are subject to change and human intervention in the way that ideas themselves are. It is predominantly the experience of Change and the concept of power which lies behind our control and prediction of events which holds my attention at present.

In trying to clarify the relationship between art, science and behaviour, I have found myself able to become involved in a teaching situation without compromising my own work. The two activities, creative and pedagogic, interact, each feeding back to the other. Both, I believe, are enriched. The didactics of art, set against the discoveries of science, have concerned many artists in the past. It is useful to turn to the writings of, for example, Leonardo, Seurat or Paul Klee, but they cannot go all the way towards dealing with problems and experiences that face us today.

All art is, in some sense, didactic: every artist is, in some way, setting out to instruct. For, by instruction, we mean to give direction, and that is precisely what all great art does. Art shapes life. It is a force; only the aesthete makes a refuge of it. Through his work the artist learns to understand his existence. Through culture it informs, art becomes a force for change in society. It seems to me that one should be highly conscious of the didactic and social role of one's art today. Society is in a state of enormous transition. The most extensive changes in our environment can be attributed to science and technology. The artist's moral responsibility demands that he should attempt to understand these changes. Some real familiarity with scientific thought is indispensable to him. It is not enough to accept our condition, or simply to enjoy it. Acceptance can only lead to a "murderous easy-goingness," as Thomas Mann has described it. "It would need a new society if art is again to become innocent and harmless."

Culture regulates and shapes society. The artist functions socially on a symbolic level. He acts out the role of the free man par excellence. Having chosen the symbolic field within which he will act, and setting for himself material limitations with which he is familiar, he sets out to discover the unknown. He stakes everything on finding the unfamiliar, the unpredictable. His intellectual audacity is matched only by the vital originality of the forms and structures he creates. Symbolically he takes on responsibility for absolute power and freedom, to shape and create his world. He demonstrates, perhaps ritualistically, man's "capacity to create what is to be . . . man's highest merit, after all, is to control circumstances as far as possible" (Goethe). In this context the artist's activity is as significant as the artwork he produces.

Creative leaps are taken in science also. Science seeks to reduce the unpredictable to measurable limits. While it may have a symbolic or ritualistic function, it is generally see to operate in the practical works in consort with practical power. By prediction, it reduces our anxiety of the unknown future. By control, it reduces the contingent nature of events and orders them to our advantage. By comparison, the artist plays, but it is play "in deep seriousness" (Mann). The culture to which art contributes, although it works without practical power, is responsible to a considerable extent for the direction in which society moves. The artist's activity serves to set before his fellow men the symbolic pattern of an existence in which, given absolute choice and responsibility and the power to take incalculable risks, the world and his own identity are shaped to his will. it stands for that optimum of control and creativity to which man's practical life constantly aspires.

## Science and a Discipline for Art

Culture has been well defined as "the sum of all the learned behaviours that exist in a given locality." The work of art occupies a pivotal point between two sets of behaviour, the artist's and the spectator's. it is essentially a matrix, the substance *between*. It neither exists for itself nor by itself. Consequently the artist would do well to examine with some precision the nature of the special activity which gives rise to his own art. "An organism is most efficient when it knows its own internal order." He might direct his attention to those sciences which measure behaviour, scrutinise biological processes and explore the internal systems of communication and self-regulation. He may ask how the human organism interacts with its environment: what relation knowledge has to perception. A consistent and thorough enquiry might lead to the forming of a discipline. But the behavioural sciences alone could hardly constitute the total backbone to one's art. Some real understanding of the world to which we respond and with which we have commerce must be obtained. Traditionally the artist relies on visual observation, intuitive judgement and day to day experience for this. But to fully orientate himself in the modern world the artist must turn to science as a tool and reference. I recommend that he turn to Cybernetics.

Science as a whole works on many fronts—too many highly specialised fields, in fact, for the artist to consult them all, except casually. Cybernetics however is essentially *integrative*, drawing many disparate sciences together. It ranges over many territories of scientific enquiry. It is a co-ordinator of science, as Art is the co-ordinator of experience. Cybernetic method may be characterised by a tendency to exteriorise its concepts in some solid form; to produce models in hardware of the natural or artificial system it is discussing. It is concerned with what things *do*, how they do them and with the process within which they behave. It takes a dynamic view of life not unlike that of the artist. Phenomena are studied in so far as they do something or are part of something which is being done. The identity we give to what we perceive is always relative, yet it presupposes a whole. Everything changes ceaselessly; we investigate our world best by seeing first the system or process before evaluating the "thing." Cybernetics is concerned with the behaviour of the environment, its regulation and the structure which reveals the organisation of its parts. "Control and communication in animal and machine" is a proper study for the artist.

Linked to technology, Cybernetics is responsible for unprecedented changes in the human condition. Cybernation is bringing about a total industrial revolution which will have far reaching social consequences. This science of control and communication is leading to new concepts of urban planning, production, shelters, transport and learning methods. The ball has started to roll. The artist cannot ignore this creative force which is changing his world. Moreover, Cybernetics deals with concepts of information, perception, translation, logic and chance which are singularly relevant to his art.

And man's relationship to his environment has changed. As a result of cybernetic efficiency, he finds himself becoming more and more predominantly a Controller and less an Effecter. The machine, largely self-regulating and highly adaptive, stands between man and his world. It extends his perception into furthest space and deep into the finest particles of matter; physical labour is replaced by accurate, tireless automata; in many situations the machine can gather required information, store, process and act on it more swiftly and reliably than Man himself can. He perceives the world through the excellent artificial systems he has devised. Cybernetics is not only changing our world, it is presenting us with qualities of experience and modes of perception which radically alter our conception of it.

Science can inform a discipline for art, then, not to produce a scientific work but to substantiate our empirical findings and intuitions with clear analysis and reason. The final stage is beyond theory; only creative synthesis can produce that co-ordinating matrix for ideas which is art.

To praise science, however, is not to praise a spurious scientism; I mean that tendency in Art to use images and notations found in the *products* of science with no understanding of the concepts behind them:—a "scientific" style; a romanticism of machines and laboratories, micro-photographs and unidentified cross-sections; the furniture of science, the props. This attitude is often accompanied by a sentimental nostalgia for the past. To ignore the theory, the process, the demonstration must be a contradiction of science and, indeed, of a forward-reaching art. Anti-science in art is equally to be criticised. It is an attitude which derives from a fear of the vitality of modern life, its technological advance, its scientific daring. It is hostile to reason and clarity of purpose, it is irresponsible and vague.

Great art symbolises our will to shape and change the world and also puts forward the particular aspirations of its time. What is our symbol of faith? We may find that it will embody a concept of power realised in our capacity for highly adaptive control, subtlety of communication, and the boldness of our investigation and planning at the most complex biological and environmental levels.

## A Groundcourse for Art

But no matter what our aspirations or intentions in art, we must prepare a discipline, a groundwork for creative activity. When I emphasise that my art and didactics are one, I am suggesting that the artist's discipline and experience can be usefully extended to the student. One can help him to win an outlook and to construct the groundwork for his own unique creative identity. But one artist is not enough. A wide diversity of artists and scientists, suitably co-ordinated, must confront the student. He, in turn, must be sufficiently uninhibited to respond. Out of the flux a many sided organism can evolve.

Such an organism, so to speak, is in the course of evolution at a London art school (Ealing School of Art). This two year "Groundcourse" (initiated and directed by Roy Ascott) is a microcosm of a total process of art education which would stretch from general secondary education to the graduate levels of professional art and design training and it occupies the pivotal point in it. It takes students from the secondary school and prepares them for a subsequent professional training. I would like to describe the Groundcourse, very broadly. My collaborators on the course have included a deliberately varied selection of painters, sculptors, designers, and scientists.[1] Each one has expanded his own given area of teaching with ideas fresh from his studio or study. These areas interact and suggest new fields of study and the need for new kinds of personalities. Ideas grow and exercises proliferate as teachers discuss and dissect each other's attitudes and pedagogic methods. So many exercises and methods of presenting them are thrown up in this creative milieu, even in the course of one week, that it would be impossible to list them here. I shall describe the general areas of study and a few examples of specific problems students may be set.

The First year course has many facets. Empirical enquiry in response to precise questions is balanced by scientific study; irrational acts by logical procedures. At the core is a concept of power, the will to shape and change. Cybernetics and behavioural sciences are studied regularly.

The new student's preconceptions of the nature of art and his own limitations ("art is Van Gogh"; "art is what my teacher said it was to get me through GCE"; "I am no good at colour"; "I am the class clown"; "I am thick, but good at patterns and posters") must first be severely shaken and opened up to his close scrutiny. His disorientation is contrived within an environment which is sometimes unexpectedly confusing, where he is faced with problems which seem absurd, aimless or terrifying.

The nature of drawing is questioned. Example 1. Draw the room in reverse perspective. What information is lost? If any, find a way of adding it to your drawing. 2. Time-drawing of the model. Draw her hair in three seconds, face in three minutes, left hand thumb nail in three hours, legs in six seconds, right ankle in two days. 3. Draw her with acute earache. 4. Draw the room using only rubbings from surfaces in it. Copy the drawing precisely with line and tone.

The values of perspective, mechanical and architectural drawing are practised and tested against problems of space—scanning and design.

Perception studies examine the modes of human perception, their co-ordination and include the search for visual/plastic equivalents. Surface gesture, mark, colour, volume are investigated, always within some context. Example 1. Imagine you wake up one morning to find that you are a sponge. Describe visually your adventures during the day. 2. List the sense-data of an umbrella or a hot water bottle. Visually restructure the parts to form a new entity. Ask your neighbour to identify it. 3. If fifteen ragged criss-cross lines stand for a cough, how would you draw the BBC time signal? 4. Use only solid shapes to discuss your perception of: a bottle of ink; fish and chips; a police siren; ice hockey. 5. Show how zebras disguise themselves. 6. Invent a typewriter-bird and show the kind of tree within which it could most successfully hide.

In the workshop the student acquires skills in joining, moulding, separating, transforming wood, metals, and various transparent, reflective and flexible materials. Example 1. Make a sculpture in plaster of interlocking units, such that when a key piece is removed, the rest falls apart. Allot colours to the separate pieces, (a) to indicate the key, (b) to facilitate reassembly. 2. Using only wood, sheet aluminium, string and panel pins, construct analogues of: a high pitched scream, the taste of ice cream; a football match. Kinetic structures are built and studies. Concepts can be formed and developed by visual means. This might be seen as the third leg in the learning process, where, for some reason, verbal or numerical systems are inadequate. Unlike the latter symbolic systems, however, the visual ABC and syntax have to be reinvented for every problem. In visual terms students set

about analysing and inventing games, logical propositions, idea sequences, matrices. Visual polemic is induced, codes designed and broken.

Natural growth and form in the context of, say scale, reproduction, simultaneity are analysed with meticulously detailed drawings. Example 1. Analyse and dissect a section of a pomegranate. Discuss with precise drawing its three-dimensional cellular structure. 2. Examine a plant in minute detail; design a new plant based upon the principles of growth you have observed. 3. Discuss visually the movements of a hungry, caged lion; a frightened squirrel.

In the light handling class students control a limited environment with lights, coloured filters grids and lenses, moving screens and prefabricated items. A theatre-play situation emerges, in the course of which students rehearse a variety of social and archetypal roles and explore the relationship of illusion to identity in terms of colour and light. The registration of environmental changes on light sensitive paper introduces photography.

Concepts of behaviour, environment, identity find their way into practical classes. Example 1. Draw a man, machine or animal. Cut up the drawing into seven sections (e.g. arm, head, wheel, handle, etc). Put the pieces with every one else's in a box. Pull out another seven at random; construct logically a new entity. Draw the environment in which you might expect to encounter it. 2. Show, with line and colour, the potential function of: the studio door, a water tap, an elephant, the window blind. Attempt to describe what they might have in common. 3. Invent two distinctly different animals; imagine them to mate and draw the offspring. 4. Make the illusion of, say, a bun or sausage, in three dimensions and on paper. Show it being submitted to various events: run over, squeezed dry, soaked in acid, minced, pierced by a shot gun. Measure the real against the metaphoric. 5. Create a world on paper with major and minor structural systems. Show a fault occurring in the minor one; design a repair centre to put it right. 6. Entropy may be described as a constant drift in the universe towards a state of total undifferentiation; pockets of resistance are organising continuously. Discuss this proposition, limiting yourself to six visual elements.

In this first year course the student is bombarded at every point with problems demanding a total involvement for their solution. Ideas are developed within material limitations and in the abstract. For the teachers, the formulation of problems is in itself a creative activity; the above examples give a general indication of the kind of questions they have set.

In the second year the situation changes radically. The general direction is programmed but beyond that students must find their own problems. Students are set the task of acquiring and acting out for a limited period (ten weeks) a totally new personality, which is to be narrowly limited and largely the converse of what is considered to be their normal "selves." They design "calibrators" to read off their responses to situations, materials, tools and people. They equip themselves with handy "mind-maps" for immediate reference to their behaviour pattern as changes in the limitations of space, substance and state occur.

They form groups of six. These sexagonal organisms, whose members are of necessity interdependent and highly conscious of each other's capabilities and limitations, are set the goal of producing out of substances and space in their environment, an *ordered entity*.

The limitations on individual behaviour are severe and unfamiliar. The student who thinks himself "useless" with, say, colour, machine tools, objective drawing, may find himself with the sole responsibility for these things in his group. The shy girl must act out an easy sociability; the aggressive youth must become co-operative. One student may be limited to transporting himself about the school on a trolley; another may not use paper, numbers or adhesive substances.

The subsequent "ordered entities" are as diverse as the composite personalities of the organisms they reflect. Totems, time machines, sense boxes, films, sexagonal cabinets, cages have been produced out of the flux of discussion and activity.

Students are then invited to return to their former personalities. They must make a total visual documentation of the whole process in which they have been engaged. They must search for relationships and ideas unfamiliar to art (i.e.

spatial relationships are familiar). They use, at first, every possible expressive means: film, collage, graphic processes, wood, plaster, metal, cloth, glass, readymades, rubber, paint and so on. They work on a huge scale at one point, and in miniature at another, sometimes with kinetic structures, sometimes with static relationships.

In the process, and reflecting upon their previously contrived limitations of behaviour, they become aware of the flexibility of their responses, their resourcefulness and ingenuity in the face of difficulties. What they assumed to be ingrained in their personalities, they now tend to see as controllable. A sense of creative viability is being acquired.

They move progressively into problems of their own; one set of ideas is preferred to another, exploited and pushed to an extremity of thought or technique. They also begin to chose specific limitations of material within which to work. They are moving towards the point of deciding within which professional field they will act. They are becoming aware of their special creative identity. Analysis and experiment are beginning to lead to synthesis. This is a report of work in progress; it can be little more than a brief summary of an evolving situation. It is difficult to do justice to the vitality and sense of purpose which the course engenders. What has been proposed is not a rigid system but a flexible structure within which every thing can find its place, every individual his way. It is an art which does not eschew science. It enables the student to become aware of himself and the world while enabling him to give dimension and substance to his will to create and change.

Note

1  Kenneth Adams, Anthony Benjamin, Adrian Berg, David Bindman, Dennis Bowen, Bernard Cohen, Harold Cohen, Noel Forster, B French, N Johnson, R B Kitaj, Stephen McKenna, J. Morris, J Nerichov, George Popperwell, Peter Startup, William Suddaby, Brian Wall, Brian Wright.

# 11. [Introduction]
# A File Structure for the Complex, the Changing, and the Indeterminate

Ted Nelson coined the word "hypertext" and developed the concept that goes along with it, one that underpins multimedia computing, electronic literature, and the World Wide Web. However, as the contents of this essay reveal, Nelson's vision was in some ways far different—his thinking much more general, and his proposals significantly more advanced—than the Web's model of hypertext.

The Web's type of "chunk style" hypertext—static links that allow the user to jump from page to page—has been around for decades and has been criticized for just as long. For Nelson, chunk style hypertext is just one subtype of hypertext, a term he introduced to mean "a body of written or pictorial material interconnected in such a complex way that it could not conveniently be presented or represented on paper." The "hyper" in Nelson's neologism does not mean "link" but rather "connotes extension and generality; cf. 'hyperspace.'"

This essay, in addition to introducing the term hypertext, also proposes a specific type of hypertext. Here Nelson's model is of complex, reconfigurable, linked structures of information, which can be manipulated at a granularity much smaller (or larger) than the page. In fact, Nelson's proposed form of hypertext may be almost unrecognizable to the user familiar only with the Web (or chunk-style precursors such as Apple's HyperCard).

While the power of today's Web is unmistakable, its workings should not be mistaken for a definition of hypertext. Rather than think of the Web as a hypertext system, we may do better to think of it as a monumental public publishing space—one that attained critical mass by employing a subset of hypertext concepts, primarily those of the chunk style. In the future the Web, and other information technologies, may become yet more powerful by implementing other elements of Nelson's hypertext visions. For example, the specific type of hypertext that appears in this essay (outlined 30 years before the launch of the Palm Pilot) would finally make personal information managers useful platforms for thinking and working in a networked world, rather than souped-up address books. And the potential for a Web-sized hypertext embodying more of Nelson's concepts, which he considers elsewhere in this volume (◊21, ◊30), is exciting enough that it stimulated speculation for decades before the rise of the Web.
—NWF

A couple of years after this paper was published, Nelson ran into his old college friend, Andries van Dam, at the 1967 Spring Joint Computer Conference. Van Dam was by then a professor at Brown University, and after their meeting Nelson began to travel up from New York to Brown to work with van Dam and others to create one of the first hypertext systems. Nelson called it "Carmody's system" after the young programmer whose name appeared first on the alphabetically credited writeup (see "Further Reading" below). At Brown the system was called HES, for Hypertext Editing System, and marked the beginning of Brown's pioneering research program (which also created the FRESS and Intermedia systems). The Carmody/HES system also stands symbolically at the juncture of the space and information ages. As van Dam noted in his address to the Hypertext '87 conference, the system "was sold by IBM (unbeknownst to me and Ted and others who had worked on it) to the Apollo mission team at the Houston Manned Spacecraft Center and used to produce documentation that went up with Apollo, I'm proud to say."

◊21
301

◊30
441

While some might place the rise of Human-Computer Interaction in the mid–1980s, Nelson was writing about a central theme of HCI—the psychological needs of users—decades before this.

Further Reading

Carmody, Steven, Walter Gross, Theodor H. Nelson, David Rice, and Andries van Dam, "A Hypertext Editing System for the /360." *Pertinent Concepts in Computer Graphics*. Ed. Michael Faiman and Jurg Nievergelt, Urbana: University of Illinois Press, 1969.

Nelson, Ted. "Getting It out of Our System" *Information Retrieval: A Critical Review*, 191–210. Ed. George Schecter, Washington, D.C.: Thompson Books, 1967.

Van Dam, Andries. "Hypertext '87 Keynote Address" *Communications of the ACM* 31(7):887-895. 1988.

Proceedings of the ACM Hypertext conferences. New York: ACM Press, 1987–present.

Original Publication

*Association for Computing Machinery: Proceedings of the 20th
National Conference, 84–100. Ed. Lewis Winner, 1965.*

# A File Structure for the Complex, the Changing, and the Indeterminate

## Theodor H. Nelson

## Summary

The kinds of file structures required if we are to use the
computer for personal files and as an adjunct to creativity
are wholly different in character from those customary in
business and scientific data processing. They need to provide
the capacity for intricate and idiosyncratic arrangements,
total modifiability, undecided alternatives, and thorough
internal documentation.

The original idea was to make a file for writers and
scientists, much like the personal side of Bush's Memex, that
would do the things such people need with the richness they
would want. But there are so many possible specific
functions that the mind reels. These uses and considerations
become so complex that the only answer is a simple and
generalized building-block structure, user-oriented and
wholly general-purpose.

The resulting file structure is explained and examples of
its use are given. It bears generic similarities to list-
processing systems but is slower and bigger. It employs
zippered lists plus certain facilities for modification and
spin-off of variations. This is technically accomplished by
index manipulation and text patching, but to the user it acts
like a multifarious, polymorphic, many-dimensional, infinite
blackboard.

The ramifications of this approach extend well beyond its
original concerns, into such places as information retrieval
and library science, motion pictures and the programming
craft; for it is almost everywhere necessary to deal with deep
structural changes in the arrangements of ideas and things.

I want to explain how some ideas developed and what
they are. The original problem was to specify a computer
system for personal information retrieval and documentation, able to do some rather complicated things in clear
and simple ways. The investigation gathered generality,
however, and has eventuated in a number of ideas. These are
an information structure, a file structure, and a file language,
each progressively more complicated. The information
structure I call zippered lists; the file structure is the ELF, or
Evolutionary List File; and the file language (proposed) is
called PRIDE.

In this paper I will explain the original problem. Then I
will explain why the problem is not simple, and why the
solution (a file structure) must yet be very simple. The file
structure suggested here is the Evolutionary List File, to be
built of zippered lists. A number of uses will be suggested for
such a file, in order to show the breadth of its potential
usefulness. Finally, I want to explain the philosophical
implications of this approach for information retrieval and
data structure in a changing world.

I began this work in 1960, with no help from anybody. Its
purpose was to create techniques for handling personal file
systems and manuscripts in progress. These two purposes
are closely related and not sharply distinct. Many writers
and research professionals have files or collections of notes
which are tied to manuscripts in progress. Indeed, often
personal files shade into manuscripts, and the assembly of
textual notes *becomes* the writing of text without a sharp
break.

I knew from my own experiment what can be done for
these purposes with card file, notebook, index tabs, edge-
punching, file folders, scissors and paste, graphic boards,
index-strip frames, Xerox machine and the roll-top desk. My
intent was not merely to computerize these tasks but to
think out (and eventually program) the *dream* file: the file
system that would have every feature a novelist or absent-
minded professor could want, holding everything he wanted
in just the complicated way he wanted it held, and handling
notes and manuscripts in as subtle and complex ways as he
wanted them handled.

Only a few obstacles impede our using computer-based
systems for these purposes. These have been high cost, little
sense of need, and uncertainty about system design.

The costs are now down considerably. A small computer
with mass memory and video-type display now costs

$37,000; amortized over time this would cost less than a secretary, and several people could use it around the clock. A larger installation servicing an editorial office or a newspaper morgue, or a dozen scientists or scholars, could cost proportionately less and give more time to each user.

The second obstacle, sense of need, is a matter of fashion. Despite changing economies, it is fashionably believed that computers are possessed only by huge organizations to be used only for vast corporate tasks or intricate scientific calculations. As long as people think that, machines will be brutes and not friends, bureaucrats and not helpmeets. But since (as I will indicate) computers could do the dirty work of personal file and text handling, and do it with richness and subtlety beyond anything we know, there *ought* to be a sense of need. Unfortunately, there are no ascertainable statistics on the amount of time we waste fussing among papers and mislaying things. Surely half the time spent in writing is spent physically rearranging words and paper and trying to find things already written; if 95% of this time could be saved, it would only take half as long to write something.

The third obstacle, design, is the only substantive one, the one to which this paper speaks.

Let me speak first of the automatic personal filing system. This idea is by no means new. To go back only as far as 1945, Vannevar Bush, in his famous article "As We May Think,"[1] described a system of this type. Bush's paper is better remembered for its predictions in the field of information retrieval, as he foresaw the spread and power of automatic document handling and the many new indexing techniques it would necessitate. But note his predictions for personal filing:

> Consider a future device for individual use, which is a sort of mechanized private file and library. It needs a name, and, to coin one at random, "memex" will do. A memex is a device in which an individual stores all his books, records, and communications, and which is mechanized so that it may be consulted with exceeding speed and flexibility. It is an enlarged intimate supplement to his memory.
>
> It consists of a desk, and while it can presumably be operated from a distance, it is primarily the piece of furniture at which he works. On the top are slanting translucent screens, on which material can be projected for convenient reading. There is a keyboard,

and sets of buttons and levers. Otherwise it looks like an ordinary desk.

. . . .

> A special button transfers him immediately to the first page of the index. Any given book of his library [and presumably other textual material, such as notes] can thus be called up and consulted with far greater facility than if it were taken from a shelf. As he has several projection positions, he can leave one item in position while he calls up another. He can add marginal notes and comments. . . ."[1] (106–7)

Understanding that such a machine required new kinds of filing arrangements, Bush stressed his file's ability to store related materials in associative trails, lists or chains of documents joined together.

> When the user is building a trail, he names it, inserts the name in his code book, and taps it out on his keyboard. Before him are the two items to be joined, projected onto adjacent viewing positions. At the bottom of each there are a number of blank code spaces, and a pointer is set to indicate one of these on each item. The user taps a single key, and the items are permanently joined.

. . . .

> Thereafter, at any time, when one of these items is in view, the other can be instantly recalled merely by tapping a button below the corresponding code space. Moreover, when numerous items have been thus joined together to form a trail, they can be reviewed in turn, rapidly or slowly, by deflecting a lever like that used for turning the pages of a book. It is exactly as though the physical items had been gathered together from widely separated sources and bound together to form a new book. It is more than this, for any item can be joined into numerous trails.

. . . .

> Thus he goes, building a trail of many items. Occasionally he inserts a comment of his own, either linking it into the main trail or joining it by a side trail to a particular item.[1] (107)

Two decades later, this machine is still unavailable.*

*The Bush Rapid Selector, which he designed[2], is a powerful microfilm instrument, but it is not suited to idiosyncratic personal uses, nor to evolutionary modification, as described hereunder.

The hardware is ready. Standard computers can handle huge bodies of written information, storing them on magnetic recording media and displaying their contents on CRT consoles, which far outshine desktop projectors. But no programs, no file software are standing ready to do the intricate filing job (keeping track of associative trails and other structures) that the active scientist or thinker wants and needs. While Wallace[3] reports that the System Development Corporation has found it worthwhile to give its employees certain limited computer facilities for their own filing systems, this is a bare beginning.

Let us consider the other desideratum, manuscript handling. The remarks that follow are intended to apply to all forms of writing, including fiction, philosophy, sermons, news and technical writing.

The problems of writing are little understood, even by writers. Systems analysis in this area is scanty; as elsewhere, the best doers may not understand what they do. Although there is considerable anecdote and lore about the different physical manuscript and file techniques of different authors, literary tradition demerits any concern with technical systems as detracting from "creativity." (Conversely, technical people do not always appreciate the difficulty of organizing text, since in technical writing much of the organization and phraseology is given, or appears to be.) But in the computer sciences we are profoundly aware of the importance of systems details, and of the variety of consequences for both quality and quantity of work that result from different systems. Yet to design and evaluate systems for writing, we need to know what the process of writing *is*.

There are three false or inadequate theories of how writing is properly done. The first is that writing is a matter of inspiration. While inspiration is useful, it is rarely enough in itself. "Writing is 10% inspiration, 90% perspiration," is a common saying. But this leads us to the second false theory, that "writing consists of applying the seat of the pants to the seat of the chair." Insofar as sitting facilitates work, this view seems reasonable, but it also suggests that what is done while sitting is a matter of comparative indifference; probably not.

The third false theory is that all you really need is a good outline, created on prior consideration, and that if the outline is correctly followed the required text will be produced. For most good writers this theory is quite wrong. Rarely does the original outline predict well what headings and sequence will create the effects desired: the balance of emphasis, sequence of interrelating points, texture of insight, rhythm, etc. We may better call the outlining process *inductive:* certain interrelations appear to the author in the material itself, some at the outset and some as he works. He can only decide which to emphasize, which to use as unifying ideas and principles, and which to slight or delete, by trying. Outlines in general are spurious, made up after the fact by examining the segmentation of a finished work. If a finished work clearly follows an outline, that outline probably has been hammered out of many inspirations, comparisons and tests.**

Between the inspirations, then, and during the sitting, the task of writing is one of rearrangement and reprocessing, and the real outline develops slowly. The original crude or fragmentary texts created at the outset generally undergo many revision processes before they are finished. Intellectually they are pondered, juxtaposed, compared, adapted, transposed, and judged; mechanically they are copied, overwritten with revision markings, rearranged and copied again. This cycle may be repeated many times. The whole grows by trial and error in the processes of arrangement, comparison and retrenchment. By examining and mentally noting many different versions, some whole but most fragmentary, the intertwining and organizing of the final written work gradually takes place.***

Certain things have been done in the area of computer manuscript handling. IBM recently announced its "Administrative Terminal System"[5,6,7,8] which permits the storage of unfinished sections of text in computer memory, permits various modifications by the user, and types up the final draft with page numbers, right justification and headers.

While this is a good thing, its function for manuscripts is cosmetic rather than organizing. Such a system can be used only with textual sections which are already well organized, the visible part of the iceberg. The major and strenuous part of such writing must already have been done.

If a writer is really to be helped by an automated system, it ought to do more than retype and transpose: it should stand

**I understand that this account is reasonably correct for such writers as Tolstoy, Winston Churchill and Katherine Anne Porter. Those who can stick to a prior outline faithfully, like James Fenimore Cooper, tend to be either hacks or prodigies, and don't need this system.

by him during the early periods of muddled confusion, when his ideas are scraps, fragments, phrases, and contradictory overall designs. And it must help him through to the final draft with every feasible mechanical aid—making the fragments easy to find, and making easier the tentative sequencing and juxtaposing and comparing.

It was for these two purposes, taken together—personal filing and manuscript assembly—that the following specifications were drawn up.

Here were the preliminary specifications of the system: It would provide an up-to-date index of its own contents (supplanting the "code book" suggested by Bush). It would accept large and growing bodies of text and commentary, listed in such complex forms as the user might stipulate. No hierarchical file relations were to be built in; the system would hold any shape imposed on it. It would file texts in any form and arrangement desired—combining, at will, the functions of the card file, loose-leaf notebook, and so on. It would file under *an unlimited number of categories*. It would provide for filing in Bush trails. Besides the file entries themselves, it would hold commentaries and explanations connected with them. These annotations would help the writer or scholar keep track of his previous ideas, reactions and plans, often confusingly forgotten.

In addition to these static facilities, the system would have various provisions for change. The user must be able to change both the contents of his file and the way they are arranged. Facilities would be available for the revising and rewording of text. Moreover, changes in the arrangements of the file's component parts should be possible, including changes in sequence, labelling, indexing and comments.

It was also intended that the system would allow index manipulations which we may call *dynamic outlining* (or *dynamic indexing*). Dynamic outlining uses the change in one text sequence to guide an automatic change in another text sequence. That is, changing an outline (or an index) changes the sequence of the main text which is linked with it. This would permit a writer to create new drafts with a relatively small amount of effort, not counting rewordings.

***For a poignant, mordant portrayal of the writer's struggle, the reader is directed to Gorey's *The Unstrung Harp; or, Mr Earbrass Writes a Novel*.

However, because it is necessary to examine changes and new arrangements before deciding to use or keep them, the system must not commit the user to a new version until he is ready. Indeed, the system would have to provide spin-off facilities, allowing a draft of a work to be preserved while its successor was created. Consequently the system must be able to hold several—in fact, many—*different* versions of the same sets of materials. Moreover, these alternate versions would remain indexed to one another, so that however he might have changed their sequences, the user could compare their equivalent parts.

Three particular features, then, would be specially adapted to useful change. The system would be able to sustain changes in the bulk and block arrangements of its contents. It would permit dynamic outlining. And it would permit the spin-off of many different drafts, either successors or variants, all to remain within the file for comparison or use as long as needed. These features we may call *evolutionary*.

The last specification, of course, one that emerged from all the others, was that it should not be complicated.

These were the original desiderata. It was not expected at first that a system for this purpose would have wider scope of application; these jobs seemed to be quite enough. As work continued, however, the structure began to look more simple, powerful and general, and a variety of new possible uses appeared. It became apparent that the system might be suited to many unplanned applications involving multiple categories, text summaries or other parallel documents, complex data structures requiring human attention, and files whose relations would be in continuing change.

Note that in the discussion that follows we will pretend we can simply see into the machine, and not worry for the present about how we can actually see, understand and manipulate these files. These are problems of housekeeping, I/O and display, for which many solutions are possible.

## Elements of the ELF

What was required we may call an *evolutionary file structure*: a file structure that can be shaped into various forms, changed from one arrangement to another in accordance with the user's changing need. It was apparent also that some type of list structure was necessary. Making the file out of lists would allow different categories of personal notes, separate drafts, outlines and master indices all to be handled as lists of some sort; their segments could then be manipulated through automatic handling of index numbers. The resulting file structure I will accordingly call the Evolutionary List File, or ELF, since it is an evolutionary file structure constructed with lists. The system proposed here is not the only ELF possible. It is built upon a specific technique of attaching lists together which has a natural resistance to becoming confused and messy.

As computer-based systems grow in capability and diversity of uses, they tend to become more and more cluttered with niggling complications, hidden passageways, and lurking, detailed interlocks, restrictions, specializations, provisos. These should be forsworn, if possible, in the system under discussion, so that it might be attractive to laymen (including artists and writers) who feel unkindly disposed toward computers. It should readily adapt to their own styles of handling things, imposing few conventions or methods of use. How could this imposition be avoided? And among so many interesting and possible system functions and file relations, how may the users know what connections to make, how may they understand what they are doing, and how may they avoid muddling and losing the things they are working with?

The answer, I think you see, is to choose a *very simple* structure that can be used and compounded in many different ways. The basic arrangement chosen for these purposes is an information structure I will refer to as *zippered lists*. (We might call it permutation-invariant one-for-one inter-list entry-linking, but that is not necessary.)

There are only three kinds of things in the zippered-list ELF, with no predetermined relations among them—no hierarchies, machine-based features or trick exceptions. The system is user-oriented and open-faced, and its clear and simple rules may be adapted to all purposes.

The ELF has three elements: entries, lists and links. An *entry* is a discrete unit of information designated by the user. It can be a piece of text (long or short), a string of symbols, a picture or a control designation for physical objects or operations.

A *list* is an ordered set of entries designated by the user. A given entry may be in any number of lists.

A *link* is a connector, designated by the user, between two particular entries which are in different lists (Figure 11.1). An entry in one list may be linked to only one entry in another list.

On the left we see two zippered lists. Between the entries of list A and those of B are dashed lines, representing the links between the two lists. On the right is the table of links as it might look to a machine. The machine can read this table from right to left or left to right, finding entries in B that correspond to given entries in A, or vice versa. A change in the sequence of either list, or additions to either list, will not change the links that stand between them. Changes in the link structure will occur only if the user specifically

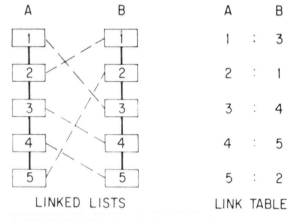

Figure 11.1. Zippered lists: 1-for-1 links between entries are invariant under list permutation.

changes the links, or if he destroys entries which are linked to others.

To be technical, then, two lists are *zippered* if there are any pairwise links between their respective elements, each element is in no more than one link pair, and these links are unaffected by permutation of the lists, remaining affixed to the same pairs of elements. It is not required that the two lists be of the same length, or, even if they are, that all entries have a link to the other list.

## The ELF's File Operations

Zippered lists are an information structure; the Evolutionary List File is a file structure. The ELF described in this paper holds its contents exclusively as zippered (or unzippered) lists. But the file structure must also include a set of operations by which it may be modified. These file operations exist for creating, adjusting or removing the entry, list and link, and for manipulating the sequence relation. An ELF is actually any machine which will, on command, carry out the basic operations on entry, list, link and sequence.

**Entries**  The user may create new entries at any time, putting anything in them that he thinks appropriate. Entries may be combined or divided (unless indivisible, like objects, commands, etc.). Entries may be put in any list, and the same entry may be put in different lists. The user may direct that entries of one list be automatically copied onto another list, without affecting the original list.

**Lists**  The user may create lists and assign entries to them. He may at will make new copies of lists. He may rearrange the sequence of a list, or copy the list and change the sequence of that copy. Lists may be combined; lists may be cut into sublists.

**Links**  The user may create links between entries that are in different lists. Any number of legal links may be created, although the upper limit of links between any two lists is determined by the 1-for-1 rule. When an entry or a list is copied into a list, links will remain between parent and daughter entries. Moreover, after a list-copying operation, the daughter list will have the same links to all other lists as does the parent list.

**Sequences**  The user may put a list in any sequence he wishes. (A copied list will maintain the original sequence until modified.) Sequences may be transferred between lists via the links: if the sequence of A is transferred to B, each entry of A linked to an entry in B takes the sequential position of its linked entry in B.

No definite meaning is assigned to these entities or operations by the system; the user is free to let them mean anything he likes. A list may be a category, trail, index, dialogue, catalogue or poem, and lists may be assembled into larger structures. The ELF may be thought of as a *place*; not a machine, but a piece of stationery or office equipment with many little locations which may be rearranged with regard to one another.****

Note that zippered lists generate only one of various possible Evolutionary List Files. Indeed, the description of the file structure given here is in some ways restrictive: the ELF could take a number of other, closely similar forms and still be much the same thing. For example, it would be

****An ELF might even be constructed out of cards, blocks, sticks and strings, using techniques of puppetry, but this would not be a convenient object.

possible to allow subentries and superentries into the file, to behave and link up like normal entries, even though they contained or were contained in other entries. But the equivalent can be done with the current system. Another possibility would be to allow links other than 1-for-1; these could be modal, the different link-modes having different meanings to the user. Or we might make it an evolutionary *network* file, allowing any two entries to be connected. Or, besides such general changes in the rules, plausible changes and accessory functions for any purposes could be introduced outside the given file structure, even including modifications and widgets to do some of the same things "more easily."

But to the user such complication might render the system far less handy or perspicuous. The ELF, with its associated techniques as described above, is simple and unified. Many tasks can be handled within the file structure. This means it can be of particular benefit to people who want to learn without complications and use it in ways they understand. For psychological, rather than technical reasons, the system should be lucid and simple. I believe that this ELF best meets these requirements.

## Technical Aspects

Since the ELF description above bears some resemblance to the list languages, such as IPL, SLIP, etc., a distinction should be drawn. These list languages[9] are particularly suited to *processing* data, fast and iteratively, whose elements are manipulable in Newell-Shaw-Simon lists. Essentially they may be thought of as organizations of memory which facilitate sequential operations on unpredictably branching or hierarchical data. These data may change far too quickly for human intervention. Evolutionary file structures, and the ELF in particular, are designed to be changed piecemeal by a human individual. While it might be convenient to program an ELF in one of these languages, the low speed at which user file commands need to be executed makes such high-powered implementation unnecessary; the main problem is to keep track of the file's arrangements, not to perform computation on its contents. Although work has been done to accommodate the list-language approach to larger chunks of material than usual,[10] the things people will want to put into an ELF will typically be too big for core memory.

The ELF does in fact share some of the problems of the list languages: not available-storage accounting or garbage collection (concerns associated with organization of fast memory for processing, which may be avoided at slower speeds), but the problems of checkout for disposal (what other lists is an entry on?) and list naming. The former problem is rather straightforwardly solved,[11] p. 164; the latter is complicated in ways we cannot go into here.

The ELF appears to be closest, topologically and in other organizing features, to the Multilist system described by Prywes and Gray.[12] Like that system, it permits putting entries in many different lists at once. However, in current intent[13] that system is firmly hierarchical, and thus somewhat removed from the ELF's scope of application. Another closely related system is the Integrated Data Store of Bachman[14,15,16,17,18]; this is intended as a hardware-software system for disc I/O and storage arrangement, but in its details it seems the ELF's close relative. Each of these systems has a connection logic that might be feasible as a basis for an ELF different from this one. Or, either might prove a convenient programming base for the implementation of this file structure.

Another obvious technical question must be considered. How can the ELF allow "unlimited" copies of entries and lists? By patching techniques, of course. Variant entries and lists can take virtually no space, being modification data plus pointers to the original. When a modified version of a list or entry is created, the machine patches the original with the changes necessary to make the modified version. (Figure 11.2).

## Uses

In the discussion that follows, we will examine various possible applications of zippered lists and the ELF, and postpone discussing the file language they require. Finally we will return to this problem, and describe the file language PRIDE whose additional features are needed to adapt the ELF for the uses originally discussed.

By assigning entries to lists, the ELF may be used as a glorified card file, with separate lists used for categories, trails, etc. This permits extensive cross-indexing by the assignment of one entry to different lists. It permits subsets and sub-sequences for any use to be held apart and examined without disturbing the lists from which they have been drawn, by copying them onto other, new lists. The ELF permits the filing of historical trails or associative (Bush) trails through documents, business correspondence, belles-

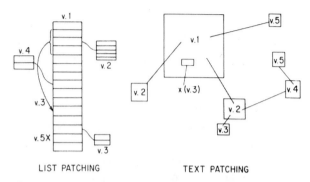

LIST PATCHING                    TEXT PATCHING

Figure 11.2. Spinoff of variants: extra versions need little space.

lettres, case law, treaties, scholarly fields and history, and the mixture of trail with categorical filing.

These are the simple uses; the compound uses are much more interesting. But since we cannot intuitively fit every possible conceptual relationship into zippered lists, imaginative use is necessary. Remember that there is no *correct* way to use the system. Given its structure, the user may figure out any method useful to him. A number of different arrangements can be constructed in the ELF, using only the basic elements of entry, list and link. Zippered lists may be assembled into rectangular arrays, lattices and more intricate configurations. These assemblies of lists may be assigned meaning *in combination* by the user, and the system will permit them to be stored, displayed, taken apart for examination, and corrected, updated, or modified.

By using such combining arrangements on lists composed of text, the file can be self-documenting, with all labelling and documentation kept integrally within the file structure. It is thus possible to incorporate, in a body of information filed in the ELF, various levels of index, summary, explanation and commentary. Many useful ways of listing and linking such documentation are possible. In Figure 11.3 we see some of the ways that documentary lists may be linked together. The lists shown are outline, suboutline, draft, subdraft, summary, commentary and source list. These are not all the possible types of documentary lists; for example, "footnotes" are omitted. The ELF will permit any number of these documentary lists; observe that they can be built on one another, and indefinitely compounded. The system will have no trouble accepting a commentary on a commentary on a subdraft of an outline for a variant list of source materials.

Figure 11.3 shows also how two lists may contain some of the same entries. The dashed line represents linkage between entries, the solid line shows that both lists contain the same entry. This may be useful for creating alternate versions, or, as in this example, the lists containing the same entry may have different purposes. Here, for instance, an entry in the summary is also to be found in the main draft.

This self-documentation feature permits any string of text in the ELF, long or short, to be annotated or footnoted for scholarly or other purposes. Such marginalia can be temporary or permanent, for the private memoranda of an individual or for communication among different persons using the file.

In a like manner, the ELF is capable of storing many texts in parallel, if they are equivalent or linked in some way. For example, instruction manuals for different models of the same machine may be kept in the file as linked lists, and referred to when machines are to be compared, used or fixed. This is of special use to repairmen, project managers and technical writers.

Moreover, the ELF's cross-sequencing feature—the fact that links ignore permutations—permits the collation of very different cognate textual materials for comparison and understanding. In law, this would help in comparing statutes (or whole legal systems); in literature, variorum editions and parodies. Thus such bodies as the Interpreter's Bible and a Total Shakespeare (incorporating Folios, bowdlerizations, satires, and all critical commentary) could be assembled for study.

Let me try to illustrate the possible comprehensiveness and versatility of this file structure as applied to texts. Figure 11.4 shows the different arrangements that might be used by one man—in this case an historian writing a book—to assemble and integrate his intellectual and professional concerns. Although it is impossible to show the links between all the separate entries of these lists—the entries are not themselves discernible in this drawing—it is possible to note the kinds of links between lists. A thin line between lists shows that some links exist; a solid line indicates that some entries of both lists are the same.

Perhaps this looks complicated. In fact, each of the connectors shows an indexing of one body of information to another; this user may query his file in any direction along these links, and look up the parts of one list which are related to parts of another. Therefore the lines mean knowledge and

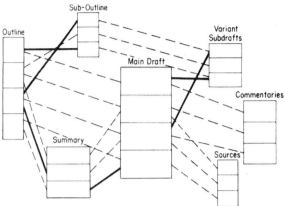

Figure 11.3. All levels of documentation may be contained in the ELF. (Heavy lines indicate that linked entries are identical.)

order. Note that in such uses it is the man's job to draw the connections, not the machine's. The machine is a repository and not a judge.

The ELF may be an aid to the mind in creative tasks, allowing the user to compare arrangements and alternatives with some prior ideal. This is helpful in planning nonlinear assemblages (museum exhibits, casting for a play,) or linear constructions of any kind. Such linear constructions include not only written texts; they can be any complicated sequences of things, such as motion pictures (in the editing stage) and computer programs.

Indeed, computer programming with an on-line display and the ELF would have a number of advantages. Instructions might be interleaved indefinitely without resorting to tiny writing. Moreover, the programmer could keep up work on several variant approaches and versions at the same time, and easily document their overall features, their relations to one another and their corresponding parts. Adding a load-and-go compiler would create a self-documenting programming scratchpad.

The natural shape of information, too, may call for the ELF. For instance, sections of information often arrange themselves naturally in a lattice structure, whose strands need to be separately examined, pondered or tested. Such lattices include PERT networks, programmed instruction sequences, history books, and genealogical records. (The ELF can handle genealogical source documentation and its original text as well.) Indeed, any informational networks that require storage, handling and consideration will fit the ELF; a feature that could have applications in plant layout, social psychology, contingency planning, circuit design and itineraries.

The ELF may, through its mutability, its expansibility, and its self-documentation features, aid in the integration, understanding and channeling of ideas and problems that will not yield to ordinary analysis or customary reductions; for instance, the contingencies of planning, which are only partially Boolean. Often the reason for a so-called Grand Strategy in a setting is that we cannot keep track of the interrelations of particular contingencies. The ELF could help us understand the interrelations of possibilities, consequences, and strategic options. In a logically similar case, evaluating espionage, it might help trace consistencies and contradictions among reports from different spies.

The use of an ELF as the basis for a management information system is not inconceivable. Its evolutionary capability would provide a smooth transition from the prior systems, phasing out old paperwork forms and information channels piecemeal. Beginning with conventional accounting arrays and information flow, and moving through discrete evolutionary steps, the ELF might help restructure an entire corporate system. Numerical subroutining could permit the system to encompass all bookkeeping. The addresses of all transaction papers, zippered to lists of their dates and contents, would aid in controlling shipments, inventory, and cash. The ELF's cross-sequencing feature could be put to concrete uses, helping to rearrange warehouses (and the company library) by directing the printout of new labels to guide physical rearrangement. Inventories, property numbers, and patents could be so catalogued and recatalogued in the ELF. Legal documents, correspondence, company facts, and history could be indexed or filed in historical and category trails. And upper management could add private annotations to

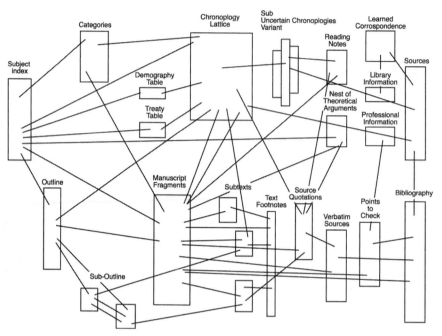

Figure 11.4. ELF's capacity for total filing: hypothetical use by historian. (A thin line indicates the presence of links; a heavy line indicates that some linked entries are identical.)

the public statements, reports and research of both the organization and its competitors, with amendments, qualifications, and inside dope.

## PRIDE

While the ELF as described is expected to be general and useful, the original purposes described at the beginning of this paper call for certain further provisions. Now I would like to describe a desirable file and information handling language that will meet these needs, called the PRIDE (Personalized Retrieval, Indexing, and Documentation Evolutionary) System. Its purpose is to facilitate the use of an ELF. The system described is not yet implemented, nor even fully specified, but let us speak as though it is.

PRIDE includes the ELF operations. However, for safety and convenience nearly every operation has an inverse. The user must be permitted, given a list of what he has done recently, to undo it. It follows that "destroy" instructions must fail safe; if given accidentally, they are to be revocable. For safety's sake, it should take several steps to throw a thing away *completely*. An important option would permit the user to retrace chronologically everything he does on the system.

Most of PRIDE's applications will involve text handling, either as a primary purpose or in the documentation of some other task. Hence a number of features exist for convenient text usage. Text handling commands (for modifying entries) include the equivalents of standard proofreader's marks for insertion, deletion, and switching of sections.

Also for text usage and user comfort, there are certain system non-restrictions. There is no practical restriction on the length of an input entry, and it need follow only the most trivial format conventions. In addition, the machine will interrupt any other PRIDE function to receive input text (inspiration mode). It is necessary that entries of unspecified length be acceptable to the system without fuss or warning. PRIDE does not stipulate fixed record lengths, either for input or storage; any such restrictions would have a psychologically cramping effect. There is no reason the system cannot appear to the user to have no fixed or standard unit lengths; the machine's operating units and sections should not concern him.

Ideally, neither the length of entries, the number of lists, or any other parameter of a file is restricted by anything but the absolute size of all memory. This is a difficult requirement for the programmer. Routinely, however, the system should be able to accept entries thousands of characters long, accept hundreds of entries to a list, and accept hundreds of lists in the file. Otherwise, extraneous consideration by the user of whether there's room to add material or try out an offshoot begins to interfere with the system's use.

Although I have avoided discussing the means by which the user sees his file, PRIDE must, of course, have functions and commands for this purpose. For a CRT these include quick lookup schemes,[19] preferably with moving menus and means of readily changing the hierarchy of lookup structure; as well as visual cuing and mnemonic formats, including cursor maneuvers, overlays and animated wipes and other transitions. But such glamorous features do not reduce the challenge or worth of working through a line printer, or seeking to make the system useful under a batch-processing monitor.

Many instructions aside from those already mentioned will be needed by the user; particular applications will require such operations as text lookup and integer arithmetic. And surely all the uses of the system have not been anticipated. Hence a subroutining facility is to be available, reaching to assembly language or opening into the machine's other languages. This could be used for processing the file's contents (e.g., numbers or character strings), or for creating more convenient combined operations out of the different operations dealing with file structure, input-output and text.

PRIDE is one possible way to make an ELF, or any evolutionary file structure, useful. PRIDE would be a foreground, free-standing language with the primary mission of handling files and manuscripts, as discussed at the beginning, and secondary applications in ordering and documenting other kinds of complex information. Its major use would presumably be in connection with time-shared display and information systems. But such a language is only one suggestion. Actually, there is not much reason that the ELF could not be made a standard file structure for all purposes; unused capabilities would not intrude, but would still be there if unexpectedly wanted. ELF systems could be built into the file capabilities of general utility software. The actual computation involved is relatively trivial, and the ELF could easily be incorporated into I/O routines or data channel languages. Even small-scale hardware implementations are not unthinkable; a control box between a typewriter and a tape recorder, for instance.

All these applications depend, of course, on the system's being actually useful, which is an empirical question. A number of possible applications have been mentioned. But, except as a crutch to man's fallible mind, is there any reason to suppose that the system has any general applicability in principle?

## Philosophy

As "philosophy" I want to speak of two major things. First, complex file structures (like the ELF) make possible the creation of complex and significant new media, the hypertext and hyperfilm. Second, evolutionary file structures (like the ELF) make it possible to keep track of things that have been changing, without our awareness, all along. These include the major categories of human thought, which will go on changing.

Systems of paper have grave limitations for either organizing or presenting ideas. A book is never perfectly suited to the reader; one reader is bored, another confused by the same pages. No system of paper—book or programmed text—can adapt very far to the interests or needs of a particular reader or student.

However, with the computer-driven display and mass memory, it has become possible to create a new, readable medium, for education and enjoyment, that will let the reader find his level, suit his taste, and find the parts that take on special meaning for him, as instruction or entertainment.

Let me introduce the word "hypertext"***** to mean a body of written or pictorial material interconnected in such a complex way that it could not conveniently be presented or represented on paper. It may contain summaries, or maps of its contents and their interrelations; it may contain annotations, additions and footnotes from scholars who have examined it. Let me suggest that such an object and system, properly designed and administered, could have great potential for education, increasing the student's range of choices, his sense of freedom, his motivation, and his intellectual grasp.****** Such a system could grow indefinitely, gradually including more and more of the world's written knowledge. However, its internal file structure would have to be built to accept growth, change and complex informational arrangements. The ELF is such a file structure.

Films, sound recordings, and video recordings are also linear strings, basically for mechanical reasons. But these, too, can now be arranged as non-linear systems—for instance, lattices—for editing purposes, or for display with different emphasis. (This would naturally require computer control, using the ELF or a related system, and various cartridge or re-recording devices.) The hyperfilm—a browsable or vari-sequenced movie—is only one of the possible hypermedia that require our attention.

So much for what we can create afresh with this structure. What about the things that have already been around awhile?

The physical universe is not all that decays. So do abstractions and categories. Human ideas, science, scholarship, and language are constantly collapsing and unfolding. Any field, and the corpus of all fields, is a bundle of relationships subject to all kinds of twists, inversions, involutions, and rearrangement: these changes are frequent but unpredictable. Recall that computers, once a branch of mathematics, are now their own field (but the development of fluid logic indicates a

possible merger with the art of wind instruments). Social relations, psycholinguistics and psychonomics are new fields, even though they rest on no special discoveries; political economy, natural history and social ethics are gone. Within a given area, too, the subheadings of importance are in constant flux. In the social sciences, for instance, the topic headings of the nineteen-thirties now sound quaint.

While the disappearance and up-ending of categories and subjects may be erratic, it never stops; and the meaning of this for information retrieval should be clear. Last week's categories, perhaps last night's field, may be gone today. To the extent that information retrieval is concerned with seeking *true* or *ideal* or *permanent* codes and categories—and even the most sophisticated "role indicator" syntaxes are a form of this endeavor—to this extent, information retrieval seems to me to be fundamentally mistaken. *The* categories are chimerical (or temporal) and our categorization systems must evolve as they do. Information systems must have *built in* the capacity to accept the new categorization systems as they evolve from, or outside, the framework of the old. Not just the new material, but the capacity for new arrangements and indefinite rearrangements of the old, must be possible. In this light, the ELF, indefinitely revisible and unperturbed by changes in overall structural relations, offers some promise.

There is, then, a general rationale. I believe that such a system as the ELF actually ties in better than anything previously used with the actual processes by which thought is progressively organized, whether into stories or hypertext or library categories. Thus it may help integrate, for human understanding, bodies of material so diversely connected that they could not be untangled by the unaided mind. For both logistic and psychological reasons it should be an important adjunct to imaginative, integrating and creative enterprises. It is useful where relationships are unclear; where contingencies and tasks are undefined and unpredictable; where the structures or final outcome it must represent are not yet fully known; where we do not know the file's ultimate arrangement; where we do not know what parts of the file are most important; or where things are in permanent and unpredictable flux. Perhaps this includes more places than we think. And perhaps here, as in biology, the only ultimate structure is change itself.

*****The sense of "hyper-" used here connotes extension and generality; cf. "hyperspace." The criterion for this prefix is the inability of these objects to be comprised sensibly into linear media, like the text string, or even media of somewhat higher complexity. The ELF is a hyperfile.

******I will discuss this idea at length elsewhere.

## Conclusion

This paper has proposed a different kind of structure for handling information.

Essentially it is a file with certain storage provisions which, combined, permit the file's contents to be arranged any-which-way, and in any number of ways at once. A set of manipulation functions permits making changes or keeping track of developments. The file is capable of maintaining many different arrangements at the same time, many of which may be dormant. This makes ordinary measures of efficiency inappropriate; as with high fidelity music systems, enrichment is derived from the lavish use of surplus capacity.

The key ideas of the system are the inter-linking of different lists, regardless of sequence or additions; the re-configurable character of a list complex into any humanly conceivable forms; and the ability to make copies of a whole list, or list complex—in proliferation, at will—to record its sequence, contents or arrangement at a given moment. The Evolutionary List File is a member of the class of evolutionary file structures; and its particular advantages are thought to be psychological, not technical. Despite this file's adaptability to complex purposes, it has the advantage of being conceptually very simple. Its structure is complete, closed, and unified as a concept. This is its psychological virtue. Its use can be easily taught to people who do not understand computers. We can use it to try out combinations that interest us, to make alternatives clear in their details and relationships, to keep track of developments as they occur, to sketch things we know, like or currently require; and it will stand by for modifications. It can be extended for all sorts of purposes, and implemented or incorporated in any programming language.

There are probably various possible file structures that will be useful in aiding creative thought. This one operates, as it were, on lists that hook together sideways, and their copies. There may be many more.

References

1. Bush, Vannevar, "As We May Think." *The Atlantic Monthly,* 176:1 (July, 1945), 101–108.

2. Hirsch, Phil, "The Bush Rapid Selector." *Datamation,* June 1965, 56–57.

3. Wallace, Everett R., "Experience with EDP Support of Individuals' File Maintenance." *Parameters of Information Science: Proceedings of the American Documentation Institute,* v. I (American Documentation Institute, 1964), 259–261.

4. Gorey, Edward, *The Unstrung Harp; or, Mr Earbrass Writes a Novel.* Duell, Sloan and Pearce, N.Y., 1953.

5. International Business Machines Data Processing Division, "The IBM Administrative Terminal System." Company brochure 520–1146.

6. International Business Machines Technical Publications Department, "1440–1460 Administrative Terminal System Application Description." IBM, White Plains, New York.

7. Timberlake, W.D., "Administrative Terminal System" (abstract.) *STWP Proceedings,* May 1965, no page number. New York: Society of Technical Writers and Publishers, 1965.

8. Farrell, Austin C., "Evolution of Automated Writing." *STWP Proceedings,* May 1965, no page numbers. New York: Society of Technical Writers and Publishers, 1965.

9. Bobrow, Daniel G, and Bertram Raphael, "A Comparison of List-Processing Languages." *Comm. ACM* 7:4 (April, 1964), 231–240.

10. Comfort, W.T., "Multiword List Items." *Comm. ACM* 7:6 (June, 1964), 357–362.

11. Weizenbaum, J., "Knotted List Structures." *Comm. ACM* 5:3 (March, 1962), 161–165.

12. Prywes, N.S. and H.J. Gray, "The Multilist System for Real Time Storage and Retrieval." *Proceedings of IFIP Conference,* 1962, 112–116.

13. Prywes, N.S., "Interim Technical Report: The Organization of Files for Command and Control." Moore School of Engineering, March, 1964.

14. Bachman, C.W. and S.B. Williams, "The Integrated Data Store—A General Purpose Programming System for Random Access Memories." *AFIPS Conference Proceedings,* v. 26, 411–422. Spartan Books, 1964.

15. General Electric Computer Department, "I-D-S." Company brochure CPB-425.

16. General Electric Computer Department, "Introduction to Integrated Data Store." Company brochure CPB-1048, 1965.

17. Bachman, Charles W., "Software for Random Access Processing." *Datamation,* April 1965.

18. General Electric Computer Department, "Integrated Data Store: New General Electric Technique for Organizing Business Data." Company publication, January 1965.

19. Corbin, Harold S., and George J. Stock, "On-Line Querying via a Display Console." *Fourth National Symposium on Information Display: Technical Session Proceedings,* 127–154. Society for Information Display, Washington, 1964.

# 12. [Introduction]
# Six Selections by the Oulipo

*A Hundred Thousand Billion Poems* and
"Yours for the Telling" by Raymond Queneau
"A Brief History of the Oulipo" by Jean Lescure
"For a Potential Analysis of Combinatory Literature" by Claude Berge
"Computer and Writer: The Centre Pompidou Experiment" by Paul Fournel
"Prose and Anticombinatorics" by Italo Calvino

Looming over the development of the literary machine in the last century stand the smiling members of the Oulipo (Ouvroir de Littérature Potentielle, Workshop for Potential Literature). The *ouvroir* of the group's name is not a workshop of the Bread Loaf or Bennington sort, but a knitting room, a place where procedural effort produces a tangible textile, or in this case textual, outcome. This knitting circle is not primarily about producing texts, however—it is *potential* literature, not literature, that its members fashion. As François Le Lionnais wrote in the group's first manifesto, an ordinary literary work is the result of rigorous constraints in areas such as vocabulary and syntax, novelistic or dramatic convention, poetic meter and form, and so forth. The idea of *potential literature* is to both analyze and synthesize constraints—drawn from current mathematics as well as from older writing techniques that never entered the literary mainstream. One such technique is the lipogram, in which a certain letter of the alphabet may not be used; another is the palindrome.

Some forms, demonstrated in short Oulipian works, have proven their broader merits. Raymond Queneau's "Un Conte à votre façon" is an application of simple algorithmic techniques to narrative, and is itself the structural model for countless works of hypermedia and more than a hundred Choose-Your-Own-Adventure books. (John Crombie's translation "Yours for the Telling" is included; another translation, by Warren Motte, is called "Story as You Like It.") Systems of lexical or phonetic constraints have proven productive in novels such as George Perec's *La Disparation* (*A Void*), which does not contain the letter e. More elaborate schemas resulted in two stunning works that sit innocently alongside their non-Oulipian fellows as major novels of the past century: Perec's *La Vie mode d'emploi* (*Life a User's Manual*) and Italo Calvino's *Se una notte d'inverno un viaggiatore* (*If on a winter's night a traveler*).

Perhaps the prototypical example of Oulipian potential, however, remains the group's founding text, Queneau's *Cent Mille Milliards de poèmes*, included here in French and in the English translation by Stanley Chapman, *A Hundred Thousand Billion Poems*. (Another English translation of this intricate work has been done by John Crombie: *One Hundred Million Million Poems*.) One sees the *Poems* at any moment as a sonnet. If the reader cuts along the dotted lines as this book invites her to do, one of 10 interchangeable lines of the poem (which fit with the others in terms of the rhyme scheme as well as syntactically and metrically) can be selected to take its place in each of the poem's 14 positions. As described in "Computer and Writer: The Centre Pompidou Experiment," the Oulipians realized that such a system had the potential to define a new type of computer-mediated textuality, producing custom poems in ways that give the reader an enhanced role in the process of literary creation.

Also see the discussion of Queneau's potential poem by Espen Aarseth (◊52).

◊52
761

Italo Calvino, in the essay here about the composition of his story "The Burning of the Abominable House," shows that the computer can be used to do more than spin out practically infinite variations from a set of initial materials. Instead, Calvino's computer takes a very large space of possible stories and narrows it to one. This is a potentially powerful story-production method, and yet the conclusion of Calvino's essay argues that the solution of any algorithm, the narrowing of even the most artfully constructed set of combinatory possibilities, cannot create literature. He states that it is the "'clinamen' which, alone, can make of the text a true work of art." The clinamen is the deviation, the error in the system. In interactive systems, in new media, the most important clinamen can be that which is introduced from outside of the system, by the reader in the company of the reader's personal and cultural experiences. A similar point was made by Calvino in an important lecture he gave in Turin and elsewhere in Italy, "Cybernetics and Ghosts."

The potential that lies within such an understanding of interactive experiences is a reconfiguration of the relationship between reader, author, and text. The playful construction within constraints that the Oulipo defined as the role of the author can become an activity extended to readers, who can take part in the interpretation, configuration, and construction of texts. —NM & NWF

Further Reading

Braffort, Paul. "The Education of Adams (Henry) / ALAMO." *ebr (Electronic Book Review)* 10. Winter 1999/2000. <http://www.altx.com/ebr/ebr10/10bra.htm>

Calvino, Italo. *Se una notte d'inverno un viaggiatore.* Turin: Einaudi, 1979. [*If on a winter's night a traveler,* trans. William Weaver. New York: Harcourt Brace Jovanovich, 1985.]

Calvino, Italo. *Comment j'ai écrit un de mes livres.* Paris: Bibliothèque Oulipienne 20, 1983. ["How I Wrote One of My Books." In *Oulipo Laboratory,* translated by Harry Mathews and Ian White. London: Atlas Press, 1995.]

Calvino, Italo. "Cybernetics and Ghosts." *The Uses of Literature,* 3–27. New York, Harcourt Brace Jovanovich, 1986.

Calvino, Italo. "The Burning of the Abominable House." *Numbers in the Dark,* 176–189. Trans. Tim Parks. New York: Pantheon Books, 1995.

Mathews, Harry, and Alistair Brotchie, eds. *Oulipo Compendium.* London: Atlas Press, 1998.

Motte, Warren F., Jr., ed. and trans. *Oulipo: A Primer of Potential Literature.* Lincoln: University of Nebraska Press, 1986.

Perec, George. *La Vie mode d'emploi.* Paris: Hatchette, 1980. [*Life A User's Manual,* trans. David Bellos. Boston: David Godine, 1987.]

Wittig, Rob, and IN.S.OMNIA. *Invisible Rendezvous: Connection and Collaboration in the New Landscape of Electronic Writing.* Hanover, N.H.: Wesleyan University Press, 1994.

Original Publication

Queneau, Raymond. "100,000,000,000,000 Poems," Trans. Stanley Chapman. *Oulipo Compendium.* Ed. Harry Mathews and Alastair Brotchie. London: Atlas Press, 1998, 15–33. Facing the original French text of *Cent Mille Milliards de poèmes,* Paris: Gallimard, 1961, as corrected in *One Hundred Million Million Poems,* Trans. John Crombie. Paris: Kickshaws, 1983.

Queneau, Raymond. *Yours for the Telling.* Trans. and desgined by John Crombie, graphics by Sheila Bourne. Paris: Kickshaws, 1982. From the French "Un Conte à votre façon." *La Littérature potentielle,* Paris: Gallimard, 1973.

Lescure, Jean, "A Brief History of the Oulipo." In Motte 1986, 32–39. From the French "Petite Histoire pour un tri-centenaire," with four additional paragraphs. *La Littérature potentielle,* Paris: Gallimard, 1973.

Berge, Claude. "For a Potential Analysis of Combinatory Literature." In Motte 1986, 115–125. From the French "Pour une analyse potentielle de la litterature combinatoire." *La Littérature potentielle,* Paris: Gallimard, 1973.

Fournel, Paul "Computer and Writer: The Centre Pompidou Experiment." In Motte 1986, 140–142. From the French "Ordinateur et écrivain." *Atlas de littérature potentielle,* Paris: Gallimard, 1981.

Calvino, Italo. "Prose and Anticombinatorics." In Motte 1986, 143–152. From the French "Prose et anticombinatoire" *Atlas de littérature potentielle,* Paris: Gallimard, 1981.

**To enjoy *A Hundred Thousand Billion Poems* and allow this literary work to function as inteneded, please cut along the lines to allow any of 10 lines to occupy each of the 14 positions in the sonnet. Those too timid to operate on their books may wish to photocopy the pages and cut the photocopies. Cutting out a small gap between each strip will allow the strips to turn and be interchanged most easily.**

# A Hundred

# Thousand

# Billion

# Poems

## Raymond Queneau

Translated by Stanley Chapman

*"Only a machine can appreciate a sonnet*

*written by another machine."*

—Turing

Le roi de la pampa retourne sa chemise

pour la mettre à sécher aux cornes des taureaux

le cornédbîf en boîte empeste la remise

et fermentent de même et les cuirs et les peaux

Je me souviens encor de cette heure exeuquise

les gauchos dans la plaine agitaient leurs drapeaux

nous avions aussi froid que nus sur la banquise

lorsque pour nous distraire y plantions nos tréteaux

Du pôle à Rosario fait une belle trotte

aventures on eut qui s'y pique s'y frotte

lorsqu'on boit du maté l'on devient argentin

L'Amérique du Sud séduit les équivoques

exaltent l'espagnol les oreilles baroques

si la cloche se tait et son terlintintin

Don Pedro from his shirt has washed the fleas

The bull's horns ought to dry it like a bone

Old corned-beef's rusty armour spreads disease

That suede ferments is not at all well known

To one sweet hour of bliss my memory clings

Signalling gauchos very rarely shave

An icicle of frozen marrow pings

As sleeping-bags the silent landscape pave

Staunch pilgrims longest journeys can't depress

What things we did we went the whole darned hog

And played their mountain croquet jungle chess

Southern baroque's seductive dialogue

Suits lisping Spanish tongues for whom say some

The bell tolls fee-less fi-less fo-less fum

Le cheval Parthénon s'énerve sur sa frise

depuis que lord Elgin négligea ses naseaux

le Turc de ce temps-là pataugeait dans sa crise

il chantait tout de même oui mais il chantait faux

Le cheval Parthénon frissonnait sous la bise

du climat londonien où s'ébattent les beaux

il grelottait, le pauvre aux bords de la Tamise

quand les grêlons fin mars mitraillent les bateaux

    La Grèce de Platon à coup sûr n'est point sotte

    on comptait les esprits acérés à la hotte

    lorsque Socrate mort passait pour un lutin

    Sa sculpture est illustre et dans le fond des coques

    on transporte et le marbre et débris et défroques

    Si l'Europe le veut l'Europe ou son destin

The wild horse champs the Parthenon's top frieze

Since Elgin left his nostrils in the stone

The Turks said just take anything you please

And loudly sang off-key without a tone

O Parthenon you hold the charger's strings

The North Wind Bites into his architrave

Th'outrageous Thames a troubled arrow slings

To break a rule Britannia's might might waive

Platonic Greece was not so talentless

A piercing wit would sprightliest horses flog

Socrates watched his hemlock effervesce

*Their* sculptors did *our* best our hulks they clog

With marble souvenirs then fill a slum

For Europe's glory while Fate's harpies strum

Le vieux marin breton de tabac prit sa prise

pour du fin fond du nez exciter les arceaux

sur l'antique bahut il choisit sa cerise

il n'avait droit qu'à une et le jour des Rameaux

Souvenez-vous amis de ces îles de Frise

où venaient par milliers s'échouer les harenceaux

nous regrettions un peu ce tas de marchandise

lorsqu'on voyait au loin flamber les arbrisseaux

On sèche le poisson dorade ou molve lotte

on sale le requin on fume à l'échalote

lorsqu'on revient au port en essuyant un grain

Enfin on vend le tout homards et salicoques

on s'excuse il n'y a ni baleines ni phoques

le mammifère est roi nous sommes son cousin

At snuff no Cornish sailorman would sneeze

His nasal ecstasy beats best Cologne

Upon his old oak chest he cuts his cheese

With cherry-pips his cottage floor is sown

The Frisian Isles my friends are cherished things

Whose ocean still-born herrings madly brave

Such merchandise a melancholy brings

For burning bushes never fish forgave

When dried the terrapin can naught express

Shallots and sharks' fins face the smould'ring log

While homeward thirsts to each quenched glass say yes

Lobsters for sale must be our apologue

On fish-slab whale nor seal has never swum

They're kings we're mammal-cousins hi ho hum

C'était à cinq o'clock qu'il sortait la marquise

pour consommer un thé puis des petits gâteaux

le chauffeur indigène attendait dans la brise

elle soufflait bien fort par-dessus les côteaux

On était bien surpris par cette plaine grise

quand se carbonisait la fureur des châteaux

un audacieux baron empoche toute accise

lorsque vient le pompier avec ses grandes eaux

Du Gange au Malabar le lord anglais zozotte

comme à Chandernagor le manant sent la crotte

le colonel s'éponge un blason dans la main

Ne fallait pas si loin agiter ses breloques

les Indes ont assez sans ça de pendeloques

l'écu, de vair ou d'or ne dure qu'un matin

At five precisely out went La Marquise

For tea cucumber sandwiches a scone

Her native chauffeur waited in the breeze

Which neither time nor tide can long postpone

How it surprised us pale grey underlings

When flame a form to wrath ancestral gave

A darling baron pockets precious Mings

Till firemen come with hose-piped tidal wave

The fasting fakir doesn't smell the less

In Indian summers Englishmen drink grog

The colonel's still escutcheoned in undress

No need to cart such treasures from the fog

The Taj Mahal has trinkets spice and gum

And lessors' dates have all too short a sum

Du jeune avantageux la nymphe était éprise

snob un peu sur les bords des bords fondamentaux

une toge il portait qui n'était pas de mise

des narcisses on cueille ou bien on est des veaux

Quand on prend des photos de cette tour de Pise

d'où Galilée jadis jeta ses petits pots

d'une étrusque inscription la pierre était incise

les Grecs et les Romains en vain cherchent leurs mots

L'esprit souffle et resouffle au-dessus de la botte

le touriste à Florence ignoble charibotte

l'autocar écrabouille un peu d'esprit latin

Les rapports transalpins sont-ils biunivoques?

les banquiers d'Avignon changent-ils les baïoques?

le Beaune et le Chianti sont-ils le même vin?

From playboy Chance the nymph no longer flees

Through snobbish growing round her hemline zone

His toga rumpled high above his knees

One gathers rosebuds or grows old alone

Old Galileo's Pisan offerings

Were pots graffiti'd over by a slave

The leaning linguist cameramaniac sings

Etruscan words which Greece and Rome engrave

Emboggled minds may puff and blow and guess

With gravity at gravity's great cog

On wheels the tourist follows his hostess

With breaking voice across the Alps they slog

Do bank clerks rule their abacus by thumb?

In cognac brandy is Bacardi rum?

Il se penche il voudrait attraper sa valise

que convoitait c'est sûr une horde d'escrocs

il se penche et alors à sa grande surprise

il ne trouve aussi sec qu'un sac de vieux fayots

Il déplore il déplore une telle mainmise

qui se plaît à flouer de pauvres provinciaux

aller à la grand'ville est bien une entreprise

elle effraie le Berry comme les Morvandiaux

Devant la boue urbaine on retrousse sa cotte

on gifle le marmot qui plonge sa menotte

lorsqu'il voit la gadoue il cherche le purin

On regrette à la fin les agrestes bicoques

on mettait sans façon ses plus infectes loques

mais on n'aurait pas vu le métropolitain

He bent right down to pick up his valise

That hordes of crooks felt they'd more right to own

He bent right down and well what did he seize

The thumb- and finger-prints of Al Capone

Oh how oh how he hates such pilferings

Filching the lolly country thrift helped save

He's gone to London how the echo rings

Through homestead hillside woodland rock and cave

The peasant's skirts on rainy days she'd tress

And starve the snivelling baby like a dog

Watching manure and compost coalesce

One misses cricket hearth and croaking frog

Where no one bothered how one warmed one's bum

Yet from the City's pie pulled not one plum

Quand l'un avecque l'autre aussitôt sympathise

se faire il pourrait bien que ce soit des jumeaux

la découverte alors voilà qui traumatise

on espère toujours être de vrais normaux

Et pourtant c'était lui le frère de feintise

qui clochard devenant jetait ses oripeaux

un frère même bas est la part indécise

que les parents féconds offrent aux purs berceaux

Le généalogiste observe leur bouillotte

gratter le parchemin deviendra sa marotte

il voudra retrouver le germe adultérin

Frère je te comprends si parfois tu débloques

frère je t'absoudrai si tu m'emberlucoques

la gémellité vraie accuse son destin

When one with t'other straightaway agrees

The answer is they could be twins full-grown

Replies like this the dumbstruck brain may tease

Normal one aims to be *and* share the throne

And yet 'twas he the beggar Fate just flings

Rejecting ermine to become a knave

The fertile mother changeling drops like kings

In purest cradles tha's how they behave

The genealogist with field and fess

With quill white-collared through his life will jog

To prove mamma an adult with a tress

But *I* can understand you Brother Gog

And let you off from your opinions glum

A wise loaf always knows its humblest crumb

Lorsqu'un jour exalté l'aède prosaïse

pour déplaire au profane aussi bien qu'aux idiots

la critique lucide aperçoit ce qu'il vise

il donne à la tribu des cris aux sens nouveaux

L'un et l'autre a raison non la foule insoumise

le vulgaire s'entête à vouloir des vers beaux

l'un et l'autre ont raison non la foule imprécise

à tous, n'est pas donné d'aimer les chocs verbaux

Le poète inspiré n'est point un polyglotte

une langue suffit pour emplir sa cagnotte

même s'il prend son sel au celte c'est son bien

Barde que tu me plais toujours tu soliloques

tu me stupéfies plus que tous les ventriloques

le métromane à force incarne le devin

Prose took the minstrel's verse without a squeeze

His exaltation shocked both youth and crone

The understanding critic firstly sees

'Ere meanings new to ancient tribes are thrown

They both are right not untamed mutterings

That metred rhyme alone can souls enslave

They both are right not unformed smatterings

That every verbal shock aims to deprave

Poetic licence needs no strain or stress

One tongue will do to keep the verse agog

From cool Parnassus down to wild Loch Ness

Bard I adore your endless monologue

Ventriloquists be blowed *you* strike me dumb

Soliloquies predict great things old chum

Le marbre pour l'acide est une friandise

d'aucuns par-dessus tout prisent les escargots

sur la place un forain de feu se gargarise

qui sait si le requin boulotte les turbots?

Du voisin le Papou suçote l'apophyse

que n'a pas dévoré la horde des mulots?

le gourmet en salade avale le cytise

l'enfant pur aux yeux bleus aime les berlingots

Le loup est amateur de coq et de cocotte

le chat fait un festin de têtes de linotte

chemin vicinal se nourrit de crottin

On a bu du pinard à toutes les époques

grignoter des bretzels distrait bien des colloques

mais rien ne vaut grillé le morceau de boudin

The acid tongue with gourmet's expertise

Licks round carved marble chops on snails full-blown

The showman gargles fire and sword with ease

While sharks to let's say potted shrimps are prone

The roundabout eats profits made on swings

Nought can the mouse's timid nibbling stave

In salads all chew grubs before they've wings

The nicest kids for strickiest toffees crave

The wolf devours both sheep and shepherdess

A bird-brain banquet melts bold Mistress Mog

The country land just thrives on farmyard mess

Whiskey will always wake an Irish bog

Though bretzels take the dols from board-room drum

Fried grilled black pudding's still the world's best yum

Lorsque tout est fini lorsque l'on agonise

lorsque le marbrier astique nos tombeaux

des êtres indécis vous parlent sans franchise

**168**

et tout vient signifier la fin des haricots

On vous fait devenir une orde marchandise

on prépare la route aux pensers sépulcraux

de la mort on vous greffe une orde bâtardise

la mite a grignoté tissus os et rideaux

Le brave a beau crier ah cré nom saperlotte

le lâche peut arguer de sa mine pâlotte

Les croque-morts sont là pour se mettre au turbin

Cela considérant ô lecteur tu suffoques

comptant tes abattis lecteur tu te disloques

toute chose pourtant doit avoir une fin

The marble tomb gapes wide with jangling keys

When masons clutch the breath we hold on loan

Forms shadowy with indecision wheeze

And empty cages show lif'e bird has flown

It's one of many horrid happenings

With sombre thoughts they grimly line the nave

Proud death quite il-le-gi-ti-mate-ly stings

Victorious worms grind all into the grave

It's no good rich men crying Heaven Bless

Or grinning like a pale-faced golliwog

Poor Yorick comes to bury not address

We'll suffocate before the epilogue

Poor reader smile before your lips go numb

The best of all things to an end must come

# Yours for the Telling

## Raymond Queneau

Translated by John Crombie

1 Would you like to read the tale
of the three sprightly peas?

If so, go to 4;

if not, go to 2.

---

2 Would you prefer the tale of
the three tall, lanky beanpoles?

If so, go to 16;

if not, go to 3.

3 Would you rather read the one about the
three rather common or garden shrubs?

If so, go to 17;

if not, go to 21.

4 Once upon a time there were three wee peas
dressed in green dozing cosily in their pod. They
had chubby, moon-shaped faces and breathed through
their funny little nozzles, snoring softly and
euphoniously.

If you'd prefer another description, go to 9;

if this one will do you, proceed to 5.

# Brief History of the Oulipo

## Jean Lescure

History will never question it: the Oulipo was founded by François Le Lionnais. Queneau said it on the radio. Leaves and writings fade, but words remain. On the same occasion, furthermore, Queneau indicated that he himself was the cofounder. On the cause of this foundation, he expressed himself in the following terms

*I had written five or six of the sonnets of the* Cent Mille Milliards de poèmes, *and I was hesitant to continue; in short, I didn't have the strength to continue; the more I went along, the more difficult it was to do naturally* [here I note that the Gallimard edition, p. 116 of the *Entretiens* with Georges Charbonnier, doesn't punctuate this part of the sentence, whereas one wonders if, when pronouncing it, Raymond Queneau didn't put a comma between *do* and *naturally*. So that we don't know whether the author's intended meaning is *it was difficult to do naturally,* which brings us to the very heart of Oulipian thought, or *it was difficult to do, naturally*]. *But* [I continue to quote] *when I ran into Le Lionnais, who is a friend of mine, he suggested that we start a sort of research group in experimental literature. That encouraged me to continue working on my sonnets.*

It must be admitted: this encouragement, the necessity of which was not evident to everyone, didn't appear sufficient to anyone. We have the proof of this in the minutes of the first meeting, on 24 November 1960, minutes which we owe to the invigorating eagerness of Jacques Bens, named from that day forward, and definitively so, provisional secretary. We read therein:

*It would not seem that the composition of poems arising from a vocabulary composed by intersections, inventories, or any other process may constitute an end in itself.*

For the activity of the Oulipo, that goes without saying. As to anyone else's activity, we didn't object that their assigned task be the composition of poems. That day in the basement of the Vrai Gascon, what more necessary task brought together Queval Jean, Queneau Raymond, Lescure Jean, Le Lionnais François, Duchateau Jacques, Berge Claude, and Bens Jacques as is noted in the minutes? (With, moreover, the intention to urge Schmidt Albert-Marie, Arnaud Noël, and Latis to attend the next luncheon.)

We asked ourselves that question. We asked ourselves that question the next day in written form: *Considering that we do not meet merely to amuse ourselves (which is in itself appreciable, surely), what can we expect from our work?*

Obviously, if we were asking ourselves this question, the fact was that we had not yet answered it. Allow me to slip a remark into this vacillation of our early days. This is that of the seven persons meeting on the occasion of the first luncheon, six had attended the ten-day conference organized at Cerisy in September, two months earlier, dedicated to Raymond Queneau, entitled *Une nouvelle défense et illustration de la langue française.* Not all of those six had been friends before the meeting at Cerisy. Some of them had never even met. Those six, plus André Blavier, who would later become a corresponding member of the Oulipo, had already met at Cerisy in the little entry pavilion with the intention of forming a group within the Collège de Pataphysique.[1] During that session, Queval was banned several times, for a total of 297 years, and each time readmitted by popular acclaim. Which of course colored his later career as an Oulipian, condemning him to ban himself unceasingly and equally unceasingly to cede to our objections.

At the time of this first meeting in November of 1960, the Oulipo still called itself the S.L.E., short for *sélitex,* or *séminaire de littérature expérimentale.* It wasn't until a month later, on 19 December 1960, and on the happy initiative of Albert-Marie Schmidt, that this S.L.E. became the Oulipo, or rather the Olipo: *ouvroir de littérature potentielle.* One can therefore legitimately say that during a month there was a

---

**5** Their sleep was dreamless. The fact is that these creatures never deam.

If you'd rather they did dream, go to 6;

if not, go to 7.

**6** They were dreaming. The fact is these little creatures are always deaming, and their nights are quite deliciously oneiric.

If you wish to know what they were dreaming, go to 11;

if it's neither here nor there to you, proceed to 7.

**7** Their cute little tootsies were muffled in cozy socks, and they wore black velvet mittens in bed.

If you'd prefer mittens of another colour, proceed to 8;

if you're happy with black, go to 10.

po oulipo. A potentialoulipo. What important difference did the *oulipo* introduce compared to the stillborn *sélitex*, or S.L.E.? The *li* did not change. Of course, certain people claimed that there was a lot to be said about "li." But our work at Cerisy had convinced us that language only solicited our attention as literature. Thus we kept the *li* of literature. *Séminaire* bothered us in that it conjures up stud farms and artificial insemination; *ouvroir*, on the contrary, flattered the modest taste that we shared for beautiful work and good deeds: out of respect for both fine arts and morals, we consented to join the *ou* to the *li*. There remained the *po*, or the *po* of this *ouli*. The inspiration was general. And the word *expérimental* having seemed to us to base the entire operation on acts and experiments as yet only poorly discernible, we judged it advisable to settle ourselves squarely on an objective notion, on a real fact of every literary being: his potential. (This potential remaining in any case sufficient unto itself, even when the experimental energy of the *littérateurs* would find it lacking.)

It was, finally, the thirteenth of February 1961 that the Private General Secretary to the Baron Vice-Curator of the Collège de Pataphysique, M. Latis, concluded the nomination of this enterprise by suggesting, for the sake of symmetry, that we add the second letter of the word *ouvroir* to the O, which definitely rendered the Olipo the Oulipo.

Our first labors immediately indicated the desire to inscribe the Oulipo within a history. The Oulipo didn't claim to innovate at any price. The first papers dealt with ancient works, works that might serve as ancestors if not as models for the work we wanted to begin. This led us to consider according a good deal of our efforts to an H.L.E., or *Histoire des littératures expérimentales*. Here, we saw the notion of experimentation or exercise reappear; at the same time we were beginning to realize that which distinguished us from the past: potentiality.

But in any case the essential object of our quest was still literature, and François Le Lionnais wrote: *Every literary work begins with an inspiration . . . which must accommodate itself as*

well as possible to a series of constraints and procedures, etc. What the Oulipo intended to demonstrate was that these constraints are felicitous, generous, and are in fact literature itself. What it proposed was to discover new ones, under the name of *structures*. But at that time, we didn't formulate this as clearly.

The position of the Oulipo in regard to literature is determined in memorandum #4, minutes of the meeting on 13 February 1961, in the following form:

*Jean Queval intervened to ask if we are in favor of literary madmen. To this delicate question, F. Le Lionnais replied very subtly:*

*—We are not against them, but the literary vocation interests us above all else.*

*And R. Queneau stated precisely:*

*—The only literature is voluntary literature.*

If I may refer to the henceforth famous dictum in *Odile*, we can add to this notion the considerable consequences resulting from the fact that: *The really inspired person is never inspired, but always inspired.* What does this mean? What? This thing so rare, inspiration, this gift of the gods which makes the poet, and which this unhappy man never quite deserves in spite of all his heartaches, this enlightenment coming from who knows where, is it possible that it might cease to be capricious, and that any and everybody might find it faithful and compliant to his desires? The serious revolution, the sudden change this simple sentence introduced into a conception of literature still wholly dominated by romantic effusions and the exaltation of subjectivity, has never been fully analyzed. In fact, this sentence implied the revolutionary conception of the objectivity of literature, and from that time forward opened the latter to all possible modes of manipulation. In short, like mathematics, literature could be *explored.*

We know that for Queneau, at Cerisy, the origin of language might be traced back to a man who had a stomachache and wanted to express that fact.[2] But as Queneau stated to Charbonnier, *Of course he didn't succeed in*

---

**8** They wore midnight blue velvet mittens in bed.

If you'd prefer mittens of another colour, go back to 7;

if you have no objection to blue, proceed to 10.

**9** Once upon a time there were three wee peas who travelled the open road. In the evening, foot-sore and weary, they would drop off to sleep in no time at all.

If you wish to know what happened next, go back to 5;

if not, proceed to 21.

*expressing this; never could succeed; nobody will ever succeed.*
Since this mysterious origin, the failures of language have
little by little led its users to reflect on this strange tool
which one could consider, which sometimes commands
consideration, without reference to utility.

People noticed that they were language from head to toe.
And that when they thought they had a stomachache, it was
in fact a language-ache. That all of that was more or less
indiscernible. That medicine was fine and dandy, but if we
were suffering in our language, medicine wasn't enough,
although it itself is a language. We started therefore to
explore, or to want to explore, language. We began by relying
on its properties. We let it play by itself. Word games became
the game of words in Queneau, subject of the excellent
Daubercies's doctoral thesis. We directed the games of
language, searched, found, and encouraged certain of its
capacities. We remained attentive to this nature which it
seems to have, or which it constitutes for itself and which, in
turn, constitutes us.

This movement became entirely natural. And this is why I
underlined Queneau's words a little while ago: *the more
difficult it was to do naturally*. It has become so natural that we
forget the punctuation and everyone jumps in.

Let me point out that Lévi-Strauss begins the *Pensée
sauvage* with a remark on nomination, and the expression of
the concrete by the abstract. He quotes two sentences from
Chinook, a very useful language for linguists. These two
sentences use abstract words to designate properties or
qualities of beings or things. Thus, in order to say: *The bad
man killed the unfortunate child*, one will say: *The badness of the
man killed the misfortune of the child*; and to say: *This woman is
using a basket which is too small*, one will say: *She is putting
potentilla roots into the smallness of a shell basket.*

It is clear in this case that the notions of abstract and
concrete are confused and, as Lévi-Strauss says, that "oak" or
"beech" is just as abstract as "tree." But another thing
becomes clear to the wise poet who examines this text. This
is that *the badness of the man killed the misfortune of the child* is

not precisely the same thing as *the bad man killed the
unfortunate child*. In fact, it's not the same thing at all. And
this difference reveals a new concreteness which is not only
that of the thing referred to by the words but also that of the
words themselves. Language is a concrete object.

One can therefore operate on it as on other objects of
science. Language (literary language) doesn't manipulate
notions, as people still believe; it handles verbal objects and
maybe even, in the case of poetry (but can one draw a
distinction between poetry and literature?), sonorous
objects. Just as in painting the dissimulation of the object of
reference by grids of nonfiguration claimed less to annihilate
this object, table, landscape, or face, than to divert attention
toward the painting-object, a certain number of sentences
written today fix the attention of the observer on the
singular object that is literary language, whose significations
because of this multiply indefinitely. Unusual designations
point to the sign rather than to the signified.

A simple example will clarify this: the beginning of *Le
Chiendent:*[3] *A man's silhouette was outlined, simultaneously
thousands*. A realist novelist would have written: *Jules came
along. There was a crowd*. But in writing this, the realist
novelist would only have shown that he was confusing the
concreteness of things with literary concreteness, and that he
was counting on quashing the latter in favor of the former.
He would have claimed to have rendered his sentence wholly
transparent to that which it designates. That is literature
according to Sartre, and transitive language. In literature, the
smallest combination of words secretes perfectly intransitive
properties. The recourse to the abstract in Queneau means
simply the choice of a system of concreteness at once both
very ancient and very new: literature itself.

I don't mean to suggest that this is an absolute discovery.
Queneau knows better than anyone that literature existed
before us. For example, one finds in *Ange Pitou* a description
of a fight that conforms precisely to what we've been
saying. Ange Pitou fights with the seminarist who had
raised him, if memory serves me, and whom he had just

---

**10** All three were dreaming the same dream; for they loved each other tenderly and, old inseparables that they were, always dreamed alike.
If you wish to know their dream, proceed to 11;
if not, go to 12.

**11** They were dreaming they had gone to fetch their soup from the soup kitchen and, upon opening their billy-cans, discovered it to be vetch soup. Sickened with horror, they awoke.
If you wish to know why they awoke sickened with horror,
consult your *Oxford English Dictionary* under "vetch" and draw your own conclusions;
if it's all the same to you, proceed to 12.

found again. The seminarist throws a punch which, says A. Dumas, *Ange Pitou warded off with an eye*. Everything here is concrete in its terms, but the organization of these various concretes is absurd. It's not the world that's being referred to, but literature. But of course, literature is always the world.

It's because we had the profound feeling that we were not an absolute beginning, but rather that we belonged to a tradition, that the Oulipo decided to devote a large share of its work to bringing together texts for an anthology of experimental literature. For there were not only these naive and aleatory illuminations of Alexandre Dumas's sort: other writers systematically sought to transform the constraints of literary rules into sources of inspiration. Hugo's famous *Je rime à dait*[4] is an example of the energetic virtues of rhyme, if not of the work of the greatest of French poets.

Experimentation was thus reintroduced into the Oulipo, not only in order to establish our genealogical tree, the history of our origins, but also to give direction to our exploration. For most of the experiments that one can conduct on language reveal that the field of meanings extends far beyond the intentions of any author. It's a commonplace today that an author understands only very few of the meanings offered by his work. And one can no longer find a single writer provincial enough to explain: *I intended to say that*. . . . When questioned today, the writer responds: *I wanted to* . . . and the description of a machine producing at the discretion of consumers follows. In short, every literary text is literary because of an indefinite quantity of potential meanings.

That involves the objects of literature, and one notices that, from this point of view, all literature is potential. For which the Oulipo rejoices. But as the equating of potentiality and literature would perhaps cause the Oulipo to lose itself in the totality of language, we had to seek a specific potentiality which we intended to use for our purposes. It's not that of literature already written but that of literature which remains to be written.

It was not an easy thing to accomplish. It was even exceedingly difficult. First, we elaborated the following broad definition. *Oulipo: group which proposes to examine in what manner and by what means, given a scientific theory ultimately concerning language (therefore anthropology), one can introduce aesthetic pleasure (affectivity and fancy) therein.* We will never know exactly who came up with this definition, the definitive secretary having generously attributed it to all in his minutes of the 5 April 1961 meeting.[5]

Things could only get worse. And the same day, the Oulipians "slyly" followed this definition with another: *Oulipians: rats who must build the labyrinth from which they propose to escape.*

The storm broke on the twentieth of April.[6] The word "affectivity" unleashed the tempest that Jacques Bens had been brooding for a month. Appealing to a *method*, and a scientific one, the provisional secretary claimed that we could only work from real things, from existing texts. To Albert-Marie Schmidt, who worried that the treatments to which these texts were subjected in order to actualize their potentialities in fact destroyed the latter as such, transforming them into realities, Arnaud answered that we must begin with the concrete, with the material. Oulipian activity applies systematic and predictable treatments to these materials. That's the experimental method. To which Queneau replied: *Our method could be applied to nonexistent acts.* And Lescure Jean going so far as to suggest that the greatest potentiality is that of nonexistence, Bens cried in an aggressive voice: *That's poetic method, not scientific.* Queneau: *Historically, we may consider that the day when the Carolingians began to count on their fingers 6, 8, and 12 to make verse, they accomplished an Oulipian task. Potential literature is that which doesn't yet exist.* With the worst insincerity in the world, Jacques Bens then affirmed that that was precisely what he had been saying: *To get to the potential (in the future), one must begin with that which exists (in the present).* Granted that it's he himself who writes the minutes, he didn't interrupt himself, and he gave himself the last word.

**12** "Eeky-peeky!" they cried as they popped open their optics. "Eeky-peeky! What a ghastly dream we've just dreamed!" "A bad omen," the first pea said. "Amen," said the second pea, "I feel quite glum." "Don't let it upset you so," said the third pea, who was the smartest of the three; "the point is not to mope and fret but to understand, right? Just you listen while I analyse it all . . ."

If you can't wait to know his interpretation of the dream, go to 15;
if you'd rather learn how the other two responded, proceed to 13.

**13** "Come off it!" piped the first pea. "Since when were you able to analyse dreams?" "Yes, since when?" piped the second pea.

If you too wish to know since when, proceed to 14.

if not, proceed to 14 anyway, as you'll not be any the wiser.

It was during the night of 28 August 1961, in the gardens of François Le Lionnais and in the presence of Lady Godiva,[7] that the Oulipians began to understand what they had been trying to do for so long. Le Lionnais expressed himself in these terms: *It is possible to compose texts that have poetic, surrealist, fantastic, or other qualities without having qualities of potential. Now it is these last qualities that are essential for us. They are the only ones that must guide our choice. . . . The goal of potential literature is to furnish future writers with new techniques which can dismiss inspiration from their affectivity. Ergo, the necessity of a certain liberty. Nine or ten centuries ago, when a potential writer proposed the sonnet form, he left, through certain mechanical processes, the possibility of a choice.*

Thus, continues Le Lionnais, *there are two Lipos: an analytic and a synthetic. Analytic lipo seeks possibilities existing in the work of certain authors unbeknownst to them. Synthetic lipo constitutes the principal mission of the Oulipo; it's a question of opening new possibilities previously unknown to authors.*

Finally elaborated, this definition remains the Oulipo's rule. In his conversations with Charbonnier, Queneau returns to it nearly word for word: *The word "potential" concerns the very nature of literature; that is, fundamentally it's less a question of literature strictly speaking than of supplying forms for the good use one can make of literature. We call potential literature the search for new forms and structures that may be used by writers in any way they see fit.*

Finally, and more recently, Le Lionnais: *The Oulipo's goal is to discover new structures and to furnish for each structure a small number of examples.*

As we can see, the rules of the sonnet, which are the Oulipo's bread and butter, remain the perfect example of our aims. But in all of this there is a relatively new way of considering literature, and it is not by chance (and without bad feelings toward the old world) that Queneau writes that we propose to elaborate *a whole arsenal in which the poet may pick and choose, whenever he wishes to escape from that which is called inspiration* (*Entretiens*, p. 154).

History will testify that the Oulipo saved men from the infantile diseases of writers and gave true freedom to the latter, which consists, exercising "their passionate taste for the obstacle,"[8] in finding the springboard of their action in the world itself.

Having understood its mission, the Oulipo happily embarked upon the centuries that awaited it.[9] Barely into the fifth of these, it had astutely mixed the sap which Oulipians were unknowingly making from lipo with the diverse characters of its members. Exercises sometimes illustrated these characters. There were snowballs, isosyntactic, isovocalic, or isoconsonatic poems, anterhymes, lipograms, etc. . . . and numerous proposals for permutations for a combinatory literature.

Bereavements darkened our history. The very dear, very lettered, and very fraternal Albert-Marie Schmidt first, through whose death we lost much of our scholarship, depriving us as well of the most amusing works. Marcel Duchamp, from one of the Americas, became interested in the Oulipo. The Ouvroir flattered itself to count him among its corresponding members. He died an Oulipian.

New ones were born:[10] Georges Perec, Jacques Roubaud, Luc Etienne, Marcel Bénabou, Paul Fournel. And we saw works appear bearing obvious traces of our reflections. By Perec, precisely, *La Disparition*. By Roubaud, whose ∈ invents constraints that will continue to provoke comment. *Zinga 8* by Jacques Duchateau surprised and even astonished me. Raymond Queneau's *Un Conte à votre façon*, a "programmed" story. *Le Petit Meccano poétique n° 00*, modest exercises for beginners.

Although the goal of the Oulipo is not to give birth to literary works, one ought to mention that the work of the best can draw new force from it—and we are delighted to note from *Le Vol d'Icare* that Raymond Queneau is making very good progress.

Each of our centuries having been celebrated by a conference, it's rather satisfying to realize that we have now youthfully passed our first millennium.

---

**14** "Since when?" cried the third pea. "How should I know? The fact is, I analyse them, OK? You'll soon see!"

If you too wish to see, proceed to 15;

if not, proceed likewise to 15, as you won't see a thing.

**15** "OK, let's see!" said his brothers. "I don't care much for your irony," the other replied; "you shan't see a thing. Besides, hasn't your feeling of horror dimmed and even faded quite away since this rather heated exchange began? So why bother to stir up the sink of your leguminous unconscious? Let's go and bathe in the fountain, rather, and greet this bright morning in that state of holy euphoria that is hygiene's own reward!" No sooner said than done. Slipping out of their pod, they rolled downhill and scampered merrily off to the theatre of their ablutions.

If you wish to know what happens at the theatre of their ablutions, proceed to 16;

if not, go to 21.

# For a Potential Analysis of Combinatory Literature

## Claude Berge

When, at twenty years of age, Leibniz published his *Dissertatio de Arte Combinatoria*,[1] he claimed to have discovered a new branch of mathematics with ramifications in logic, history, ethics, and metaphysics. He treated all sorts of combinations therein: syllogisms, juridical forms, colors, sounds; and he announced two-by-two, three-by-three, etc., combinations, which he wrote: com2natio, com3natio, etc. . . . .

In the field of plastic arts, the idea was not entirely new, since Breughel the Elder several years before had numbered the colors of his characters in order to determine their distribution by a roll of the dice; in the field of music, people were beginning to glimpse new possibilities, which were to inspire Mozart in his "Musical Game," a sort of card index that allows anyone to achieve the aleatory composition of waltzes, rondos, and minuets. But what about literature?

One has to wait until 1961 for the expression *combinatory literature* to be used, undoubtedly for the first time, by François Le Lionnais, in the postface to Raymond Queneau's *Cent Mille Milliards de poèmes*. Literature is a known quantity, but combinatorics? Makers of dictionaries and encyclopedias manifest an extreme degree of cowardice when it comes to giving a definition of the latter; one can hardly blame their insipid imprecision, since traditional mathematicians who "feel" that problems are of combinatory nature very seldom are inclined to engage in systematic and independent study of the methods of resolving them.

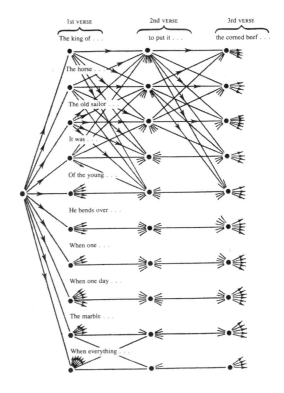

Figure 12.1. Principle of the graph of the *Cent Mille Milliards de poèmes* (not all of the arcs and vertices have been drawn).

In an attempt to furnish a more precise definition, we shall rely on the concept of *configuration*; one looks for a configuration each time one disposes a finite number of objects, and one wishes to dispose them according to certain constraints postulated in advance; Latin squares and finite geometries are configurations, but so is the arrangement of packages of different sizes in a drawer that is too small, or the disposition of words or sentences given in advance (on the condition that the given constraints be sufficiently "crafty" for the problem to be real).[2] Just as arithmetic studies whole numbers (along with the traditional operations), as algebra studies operations in general, as

---

**16** Three tall, lanky beanpoles were watching them.

If you don't much care for the three tall lanky beanpoles, go to 21;

if you like the look of them, proceed to 18.

**17** Three rather common or garden shrubs were watching them.

If you don't care for the three common or garden shrubs, go to 21;

if, contrariwise, they rather take your fancy, proceed to 18.

**18** Observing that they were being ogled, the three sprightly peas, who were very bashful, took to their heels.

If you wish to know what they did next, proceed to 19;

if it's immaterial to you, go to 21.

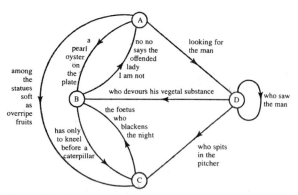

Figure 12.2. The verses corresponding to the arcs arriving at the same point (or leaving from the same point) were chosen in function of a very precise constraint; for example, those that end up at point D contain the word "man"; those leaving from point D have the same grammatical structure, etc. . . . Using this figure, the reader may choose a priori the point of departure and the point of arrival, and look for "the shortest path." He can also construct "Hamiltonian Poems," which correspond to an itinerary in which each point is encountered once and only once. Thus, the Hamiltonian Path BADC gives:

"No no says the offended lady I am not looking for the man who spits in the pitcher."

One can even construct quasi-Eulerian poems, traveling through the figure without passing twice by the same arc, and in maximizing the number of arcs used; fundamental, purely mathematical concepts from the Theory of Graphs furnish thus so many constraints . . . and the number of texts that may be constructed using the same figure is infinite!

analysis studies functions, as geometry studies forms that are rigid and topology those that are not, so combinatorics, for its part, studies configurations. It attempts to demonstrate the existence of configurations of a certain type. And if this existence is no longer open to doubt, it undertakes to count them (equalities or inequalities of counting), or to list them ("listing"), or to extract an "optimal" example from them (the problem of optimization).

It is thus not surprising to learn that a systematic study of these problems revealed a large number of new mathematical concepts, easily transposable into the realm of language, and

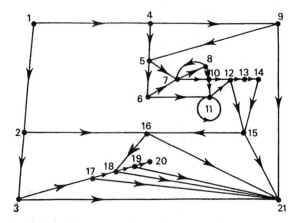

Figure 12.3. Bifurcating graph representing the structure of Raymond Queneau's "A Story as You Like It," ["Yours for the Telling,"] Lettres Nouvelles, July–September 1967. (We owe this sagittal representation to Queneau.)

that the pruritus of combinatorics has wrought its worst on the Oulipian breast.

Although the first complete literary work of frankly combinatory nature is the *Cent Mille Milliards de poèmes*, and although Raymond Queneau and François Le Lionnais are the cofounders of the Oulipo, created simultaneously, it should not be deduced that combinatory literature *is* the Oulipo.

If one dissects Oulipian tendencies with a sharp enough scalpel, three currents become apparent: the first Oulipian vocation is undoubtedly "the search for new structures, which may be used by writers in any way they see fit," which means that we wish to replace traditional *constraints* like the "sonnet" with other linguistic constraints: alphabetical (Georges Perec's poems without e), phonetic (Noël Arnaud's heterosexual rhymes), syntactic (J. Queval's isosyntactic novels), numerical (J. Bens's irrational sonnets), even semantic.

The second Oulipian vocation, apparently unrelated to the first, is research into *methods of automatic transformation* of texts: for example, J. Lescure's S + 7 method.

Finally, the third vocation, the one that perhaps interests us most, is the *transposition* of concepts existing in different

**19** They skedaddled back to their pod, pulled down the lid over themselves and fell fast asleep again.

If you wish to know the sequel, proceed to 20; if not, go to 21.

**20** There is no sequel. The tale is finished. Finished!

**21** In this case too, the tale is finished. Ended!

branches of mathematics into the realm of words: geometry (Le Lionnais's poems which are tangentical among themselves), Boolian algebra (intersection of two novels by J. Duchateau), matrical algebra (R. Queneau's multiplication of texts), etc. . . .

It is within this last current that combinatory literature is situated. Let us sharpen our scalpel a little bit more and cut up a few specimens.

The roughest form, the Stone Age of combinatory literature, it must be noted, is factorial poetry, in which certain elements of the text may be permuted in all possible ways as the reader (or chance) sees fit; the meaning changes, but syntactic correctness is preserved.

As early as the seventeenth century, Harsdörffer published in his *Récréations* factorial couplets like:

*Ehr, Kunst, Geld, Guth, Lob, Weib* und *Kind*

*Man* hat, *sucht, fehlt,* hofft und verschwind[3]

The ten words in *italics* may be permuted in all possible ways by the speaker without altering the rhythm (for they are all monosyllabic); whence 3,628,800 poems, different and grammatically correct (if one changes *sucht* to *Sucht, fehlt* to *Fehl, man* to *Mann*). With *n* words to permute, the number of possibilities would be "*n* factorial," that is, the number:

$$n! = 1 \times 2 \times \ldots \times n$$

This form of poetry seems moreover to have been common during the period when it was called "Protean Poetry" (*Poetices Proteos*), following Julius Caesar Scaliger, who supposedly invented it. Leibniz, in his *Dissertatio*, cites numerous examples in monosyllabic Latin, from Bernhardus

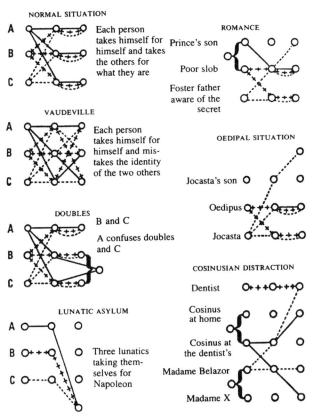

Figure 12.4. Graphs of the Ternary Relation: X Takes Y for Z (paper delivered by Raymond Queneau at the 26 December 1965 meeting of the Oulipo.)

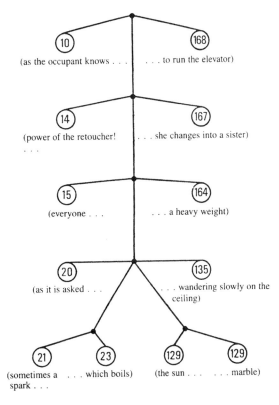

Figure 12.5. Tree representing the embedding of the parentheses in Raymond Roussel, *Nouvelles Impressions d'Afrique,* canto I (the encircled numbers represent the number of the verse wherein the parentheses are opened or closed).

Bauhusius, Thomas Lansius, Johan Philippus Ebelius, Johan Baptistus Ricciolus, etc....

And, as nothing is invented, we must wait until 1965 for Saporta to write and publish a "factorial" novel, whose pages, unbound, may be read in any order, according to the whim of the reader.[4]

Finally, in 1967, the Oulipo stated that it no longer expected any good to come from pure, unbridled chance, and Jacques Roubaud published his collection of poems, ∈ (Gallimard, 1967), wherein the author proposes the reading of the 361 texts that compose it in four different but well-determined orders.

Another more elaborate form of combinatory poetry: Fibonaccian poems. We call thus a text which has been split into elements (sentences, verses, words), and which one recites using only elements that were not juxtaposed in the original text.

This type of poetry is called Fibonaccian because, with $n$ elements, the number of poems one can engender is none other than "Fibonacci's Number":

$$F_n = 1 + \frac{n!}{1!(n-1)} + \frac{(n-1)!}{2!(n-2)!} + \frac{(n-2)!}{3!(n-5)!} + \frac{(n-3)!}{4!(n-7)!} + \cdots$$

Here is an example, whose origin is easily recognizable:

> Feu filant,
>
> déjà sommeillant,
>
> bénissez votre
>
> os
>
> je prendrai
>
> une vieille accroupie
>
> vivez les roses de la vie![5]

Unfortunately, it is difficult to invent texts that lend themselves to such manipulations or rules for intervals that permit the conservation of literary quality.

In the *Cent Mille Milliards de poèmes*, Raymond Queneau introduces ten sonnets, of fourteen verses each, in such a way that the reader may replace

Figure 12.6. Representation by means of a bifurcating arborescence of the preceding system of parentheses.

Figure 12.7. Representation by means of a bifurcating arborescence of another system of parentheses: [( )] {[( )]}.

as he wishes each verse by one of the nine others that correspond to it. The reader himself may thus compose $10^{14}$ = 100,000,000,000,000 different poems, all of which respect all the immutable rules of the sonnet. This type of poetry could be called "exponential," for the number of poems of $n$ verses one can obtain with Queneau's method is given by the exponential function, $10^n$. However, each of the hundred thousand billion poems may also be considered as a line drawn in a graph of the sort indicated in figure 12.1. According to this point of view, it should be noted that the reader advances in a graph *without circuits*; that is, he can never encounter the same verse twice in a reading respecting the direction of the arrows.

For this reason, in 1966 we proposed the dual form, the antipode: that is, poems on graphs *without cocircuits*. Without wishing to define a cocircuit here, let us say that these graphs are characterized by the property that, beginning from a given point, one can always end up at a point determined in advance.

Let us consider the simplified example of figure 12.2.

Other pathway procedures were proposed by Paul Braffort and François Le Lionnais at the 79th meeting of the Oulipo. This principle is also behind Raymond Queneau's "A Story as You Like It" ["Yours for the Telling."] This text, submitted at the Oulipo's 83rd working meeting, draws its inspiration from the instructions given to computers, the reader at each moment disposing of two continuations, according to whether the adventures of the "three alert peas" suit him or not. Presented in the form of a bifurcating graph (figure 12.3), imbrication of circuits becomes apparent, as do converging paths, etc. . . . whose properties might be analyzed in terms of the Theory of Graphs. [See figure 12.4 for additional Queneau graphs.]

Finally, it should be noted that in his *Drailles* (Gallimard, 1968), Jean Lescure travels pleasantly through a graph of order 4:

Feuille de rose porte d'ombre

Ombre de feuille porte rose

Feuille, porte l'ombre d'une rose

Feuille rose à l'ombre d'une porte

Toute rose ombre une porte de feuille

. . .

Another form of literature, which may lend itself to schemas rich in combinatory properties, is what has come to be called the *episodic story*. Since Potocki's famous novel, *Un Manuscrit trouvé à Saragosse*, especially since the episodic novels of Eugène Sue, certain authors have imagined characters who relate adventures in which figure other garrulous heroes who in turn relate other adventures, which leads to a whole series of stories embedded one in the other. In his poems, Raymond Roussel[6] went so far as to embed progressively six sets of parentheses [see figure 12.5].

In order to describe or count the agglomerations of parentheses in a monoid, the Polish logician Lukasiewicz established the bases of a mathematical theory; it is to this theory that we refer in figure 12.6, where we represent the structure of the first canto of Raymond Roussel's *Nouvelles Impressions d'Afrique* by a bifurcating arborescence. It may be remarked that this arborescence is much less complex than that of figure 12.7, for instance . . . which seems to open the door to a new field of research for the Oulipo.

We could not conclude this little inventory without mentioning bi-Latin literature and the work begun within the Oulipo by the author with Jacques Roubaud and Georges Perec. Since Euler, combinatorics has been interested in Latin bi-squares; a *Latin bi-square of order n* is a table of $n \times n$ squares, filled with $n$ different letters and $n$ different numbers, each square containing a letter and a number, each letter figuring only once in each line and each column, each number figuring only once in each line and each column.

A Latin bi-square of order 10 is reproduced in figure 12.8; it is, moreover, an extremely rare specimen, and at the present time only two are known to exist. We thus proposed to write 10 stories (represented by the 10 lines of the table) wherein appear 10 characters (represented by the 10 columns of the table). Each character's attribute is

determined by the letter of the corresponding square; his action is likewise determined by the number of the corresponding square.

These 10 stories contain thus all the possible combinations in the most economical fashion possible. Moreover, they are the result of a century of arduous mathematical research, for Euler conjectured that a Latin bi-square of order 10 could not exist, and we had to wait until 1960 for Bose, Parker, and Shrikhande to prove him wrong. . . .[7]

| Story number | Mr. Demaison | Paul | Mrs. Demaison | Count Bellerval | Archimedes | The goldfish | Destiny | Valerie | Don Diego | Mr. Member |
|---|---|---|---|---|---|---|---|---|---|---|
| 1 | $A_0$ | $G_7$ | $F_8$ | $E_2$ | $J_1$ | $I_5$ | $H_4$ | $B_3$ | $C_4$ | $D_6$ |
| 2 | $H_6$ | $B_1$ | $A_7$ | $G_8$ | $F_2$ | $J_3$ | $I_4$ | $C_3$ | $D_5$ | $E_0$ |
| 3 | $I_5$ | $H_0$ | $C_2$ | $B_7$ | $A_4$ | $G_9$ | $J_3$ | $D_4$ | $E_5$ | $F_1$ |
| 4 | $J_4$ | $I_6$ | $H_1$ | $D_3$ | $C_7$ | $B_8$ | $A_9$ | $E_5$ | $F_0$ | $G_1$ |
| 5 | $B_3$ | $J_6$ | $I_0$ | $H_2$ | $E_4$ | $D_7$ | $C_8$ | $F_9$ | $G_1$ | $A_3$ |
| 6 | $D_2$ | $C_9$ | $J_4$ | $I_1$ | $H_3$ | $F_5$ | $E_7$ | $G_0$ | $A_1$ | $B_4$ |
| 7 | $F_7$ | $E_8$ | $D_9$ | $J_0$ | $I_5$ | $H_6$ | $G_4$ | $A_1$ | $B_2$ | $C_5$ |
| 8 | $C_1$ | $D_2$ | $E_3$ | $F_4$ | $G_5$ | $A_6$ | $B_0$ | $H_7$ | $I_8$ | $J_9$ |
| 9 | $E_1$ | $F_3$ | $G_4$ | $A_5$ | $B_6$ | $C_0$ | $D_1$ | $I_9$ | $J_7$ | $H_8$ |
| 10 | $G_8$ | $A_4$ | $B_5$ | $C_6$ | $D_0$ | $E_1$ | $F_1$ | $J_2$ | $H_9$ | $I_7$ |

Figure 12.8. Specimen of the Latin bi-square of order 10; the letters represent a characteristic attribute: A = violent lover, B = stupid as an ox, C = rascal; etc. . . . The numbers represent the dominant action of the character: 0 = does nothing, 1 = steals and assassinates, 2 = behaves in a strange and inexplicable way; etc. . . .

It is clear that the contribution of combinatorics to the domains of words, rhymes, and metaphors is more complex than it seems, and that it is far from the anagrams of the Rhétoriqueurs or the stammerings of the Protean poets.

# Computer and Writer
## The Centre Pompidou Experiment

## Paul Fournel

When the literary project of the A.R.T.A. was launched, rapid efforts had to be made to establish a basis for a possible agreement between computer science and literary creation.[1] Christian Cavadia entrusted the whole of the project to Paul Braffort (logician, computer scientist, and writer), whose first goal was to educate the public and the writers themselves about this new undertaking.

## Aided Reading

At first, work was brought to bear on preexisting literary material. There are, in fact, a few combinatory or algorithmic works that may be read far more easily with the help of a computer. Here, the machine performs a simple task of selecting and editing.

### Combinatory Literature

The *Cent Mille Milliards de poèmes*[2] by Raymond Queneau furnishes material particularly favorable to this type of experiment. It consists of ten sonnets composed such that each verse of each of them may be combined with any of the other verses in the ten texts, which gives a total of $10^{14}$ sonnets. The printed collection is very prettily conceived, but the manipulation of the strips on which each verse is printed is sometimes tedious.

The computer, though, makes a selection in the corpus in function of the length of the "reader's" name and the time which he takes to type it into the terminal, then prints the sonnet, which bears the double signature of Queneau and his reader.[3]

The author himself may profit from this process: when the combinations are this numerous, he may take soundings of his work. The computer in this case serves as an assistant in the definitive fine-tuning of the text.

## Algorithmic Literature

Same application in the domain of algorithmic literature: Dominique Bourguet has programmed Raymond Queneau's "A Story as You Like It" ["Yours for the Telling"][4] so as to facilitate its reading. In this brief text, the reader is repeatedly invited to choose what follows in the tale through a system of double questions. The elements of narration being very short, the game dominates the reading of the text itself. This is unfortunate, since all of these possible texts have real charm. The computer first of all "speaks" with the reader, proposing the different choices to him, then prints the chosen text "cleanly" and without the questions. The pleasure of play and the pleasure of reading are thus combined.

In the same spirit and according to the same principles, a medieval tale was programmed by Jean-Pierre Enard and Paul Fournel,[5] and the 720 fairy tales of a work group directed by J. P. Balpe will be programmed.

## Aided Creation

After all of this, the relation work→computer→reader must be replaced by other sorts of relations in which the author plays a role (without necessarily stripping the reader of *his* role). Among the different projects submitted by authors to Paul Braffort, one may already find examples of very different types of relations.

### Type 1:
### Author→Computer→Work

In this type, only creation is aided. The computer is an integral part of the drafting process and its work serves to elaborate the definitive text. Italo Calvino proposes lists of characters, constraints, and events to the machine, asking it to determine through progressive refinement who may indeed have done what. The author thus chooses to work on material that the machine allows him to dominate.[6]

### Type 2:
### Author→Computer→Work→Computer→Reader

The computer intervenes on two levels this time. For one of the chapters in the *Princesse Hoppy*, Jacques Roubaud elaborates, with the help of a machine, a chapter which the reader must read with this same machine.[7] He will be called upon to solve a series of enigmas, and the machine will furnish him with clues (inspired by the game of cork-penny) as to his groping progression in the text.

**Type 3:**
**Author→Computer→Reader→Computer→Work**

With this third type we enter into the domain of projects that are more distant and more technically complex. In Marcel Bénabou's "artificial aphorisms," the author furnishes a stock of empty forms and a stock of words destined to fill them; the reader then comes along to formulate a request, and, following this request, the machine combines words and forms to produce aphorisms.[8]

The reader's participation is limited, but it nonetheless necessitates a few elementary flexions in the resultant text. In spite of everything, one may affirm that the author dominates his material in these aphorisms; this is not so in the case of the S.S.A.Y.L.I. (Short Story As You Like It) project.

The goal of this enterprise is to produce diversified short stories in very large quantities according to the precise and various wishes formulated by the reader (he may choose the length, the theme, the decor, the characters, and the style).

Beginning with a few homosyntactic short stories, Paul Braffort and Georges Kermidjian attempt to establish an extremely supple general ossature and a stock of "agms," minimal unities of action or description. Their exact description is in permanent evolution, but one may say, roughly, that they are the intermediary unities between the word and the sentence, which in theory ought to permit one to avoid both the pitfalls of grammar and the feeling of suffocation provoked by sentence types that recur incessantly (as in the work of Sheldon Kline). Each of these agms receives specific attributes which will come into play according to the reader's wishes.

The interest of this project is triple: first, it allows one to produce short stories, and this is nice when one likes producing short stories; second, it enables one to elaborate a particular grammar prudently, step by step; third, it allows one to constitute a stock of agms that may be used on other occasions. But it is a long-term project that is only beginning. It will take patience, work, and time (= money).[9]

# Prose and Anticombinatorics

## Italo Calvino

The preceding examples concerned the use of the computer as an aid to literary creation in the following situations:

The structures chosen by the author are relatively few in number, but the possible realizations are combinatorily exponential.

Only the computer may realize a number (more or less large) of these potentialities.

On the contrary, the assistance of the computer takes on an *anticombinatory* character when, among a large number of possibilities, the computer selects those few realizations compatible with certain constraints.

### Order in Crime

I have been working for some time on a short story (perhaps a novel?) which might begin thus:

#### The Fire in the Cursed House

In a few hours Skiller, the insurance agent, will come to ask for the computer's results, and I have still not introduced the information into the electronic circuits that will pulverize into innumerable impulses the secrets of the Widow Roessler and her shady pension. Where the house used to stand, one of those dunes in vacant lots between the shunting yards and the scrapyards that the periphery of our city leaves behind itself like so many little piles of trash forgotten by the broom, nothing now remains but scattered debris. It might have been a cute little villa beforehand, or just as well nothing other than a ghostly hovel: the reports of the insurance company do not say; now, it has burned from the cellar to the attic, and nothing was found on the charred cadavers of its four inhabitants that might enable one to reconstitute the antecedents of this solitary massacre.

A notebook tells more than these bodies, a notebook found in the ruins, entirely burned except for the cover, which was protected by a sheet of plastic. On the front is written: *Accounts of horrible acts perpetrated in this house,* and on the back there is an index divided into twelve headings, in alphabetical order: To Bind and Gag, To Blackmail, To Drug, To Prostitute, To Push to Suicide, To Rape, To Seduce, To

183

Slander, To Spy Upon, To Stab, To Strangle, To Threaten with a Revolver.

It is not known which of the inhabitants of the house wrote this sinister report, nor what was its intent: denunciation, confession, self-satisfaction, fascinated contemplation of evil? All that remains to us is this index, which gives the names neither of the people who were guilty nor those of the victims of the twelve actions—felonious or simply naughty—and it doesn't even give the order in which they were committed, which would help in reconstituting a story: the headings in alphabetical order refer to page numbers obscured by a black stroke. To complete the list, one would have to add still one more verb: To Set Ablaze, undoubtedly the final act of this dark affair—accomplished by whom? In order to hide or destroy what?

Even assuming that each of these twelve actions had been accomplished by only one person to the prejudice of only one person, reconstituting the events is a difficult task: if the characters in question are four in number, they may represent, taken two by two, twelve different relations for each of the twelve sorts of relations listed. The possible solutions, in consequence, are twelve to the twelfth power; that is, one must choose among solutions whose number is in the neighborhood of eight thousand eight hundred seventy-four billion two hundred ninety-six million six hundred sixty-two thousand two hundred fifty-six. It is not surprising that our overworked police preferred to shelve the dossier, their excellent reasoning being that however numerous were the crimes committed, the guilty died in any case with the victims.

Only the insurance company needs to know the truth, principally because of a fire insurance policy taken out by the owner of the house. The fact that the young Inigo died in the flames only renders the question that much thornier: his powerful family, who undoubtedly had disinherited and excluded this degenerate son, is notoriously disinclined to renounce anything to which it may have a claim. The worst conclusions (included or not in that abominable index) may be drawn about a young man who, hereditary member of the House of Lords, dragged an illustrious title over the park benches that serve a nomadic and contemplative youth as beds, and who washed his long hair in public fountains. The little house rented to the old landlady was the only heritage that remained to him, and he had been admitted into it as sublessee by his tenant, against a reduction of the already modest rent. If he, Inigo, had been both guilty incendiary and victim of a criminal plot carried out with the imprecision and insouciance that apparently characterized his behavior, proof of fraud would relieve the company from payment of damages.

But that was not the only policy that the company was called upon to honor after the catastrophe: the Widow Roessler herself each year renewed a life insurance policy whose beneficiary was her adopted daughter, a fashion model familiar to anyone who leafs through the magazines devoted to *haute couture*. Now Ogiva too is dead, burned along with the collection of wigs that transformed her glacially charming face—how else to define a beautiful and delicate young woman with a totally bald head?—into hundreds of different and delightfully asymmetric characters. But it so happened that Ogiva had a three-year-old child, entrusted to relatives in South Africa, who would soon claim the insurance money, unless it were proved that it was she who had killed (*To Stab? To Strangle?*) the Widow Roessler. And since Ogiva had even thought to insure her wig collection, the child's guardians may also claim this indemnization, except if she were responsible for its destruction.

Of the fourth person who died in the fire, the giant Uzbek wrestler Belindo Kid, it is known that he had found not only a diligent landlady in the Widow Roessler (he was the only paying tenant in the *pension*) but also an astute impresario. In the last few months, the old woman had in fact decided to finance the seasonal tour of the ex–middleweight champion, hedging her bets with an insurance policy against the risk of contract default through illness, incapacity, or accident. Now a consortium of promoters of wrestling matches is claiming the damages covered by the insurance; but if the old lady *pushed him to suicide*, perhaps through *slandering* him, *blackmailing* him, or *drugging* him (the giant was known in international wrestling circles for his impressionable character), the company could easily silence them.

My hero intends to *solve the enigma*, and from this point of view the story belongs thus to the *detective mystery* genre.

But the situation is also characterized by an eminently combinatory aspect, which may be schematized as follows:

4 characters: A, B, C, D.

12 transitive, nonreflexive actions (see list below).

All the possibilities are open: one of the 4 characters may (for example) rape the 3 others or be raped by the 3 others.

One then begins to eliminate the impossible sequences. In order to do this, the 12 actions are divided into 4 classes, to wit:

| | |
|---|---|
| appropriation of will | to incite |
| | to blackmail |
| | to drug |
| appropriation of a secret | to spy upon |
| | to brutally extort a confession from |
| | to abuse the confidence of |
| sexual appropriation | to seduce |
| | to buy sexual favors from |
| | to rape |
| murder | to strangle |
| | to stab in the back |
| | to induce to commit suicide |

## Objective Constraints
### Compatibility between Relations

*For the actions of murder:* If A strangles B, he no longer needs to stab him or to induce him to commit suicide.

It is also improbable that A and B kill each other.

One may then postulate that for the murderous actions the relation of two characters will be possible only once in each permutation, and it will not be reversible.

*For sexual actions:* If A succeeds in winning the sexual favors of B through seduction, he need not resort to money or to rape for the same object.

One may also exclude, or neglect, the reversibility of the sexual rapport (the same or another) between two characters.

One may then postulate that for the sexual acts, the relation of two characters will be possible only once in each permutation, and it will not be reversible.

*For the appropriation of a secret:* If A secures B's secret, this secret may be defined in another relation that follows in the sequence, between B and C, or C and B (or even C and D, or D and C), a sexual relation, or a relation of murder, or of the appropriation of will, or of the appropriation of another secret. After that, A no longer needs to obtain the same secret from B by another means (but he may obtain a different secret by a different means from B or from other characters). Reversibility of the acts of appropriation of a

secret is possible, if there are on both sides two different secrets.

*For the appropriation of will:* If A imposes his will on B, this imposition may provoke a relation between A (or another) and B, or even between B and C (or A), a relation that may be sexual, murderous, the appropriation of a secret, the appropriation of another will. After that, A no longer needs to impose the same will on B by another means (but he may, etc.).

Reversibility is possible, obviously, between two different wills.

### Order of Sequences

In each permutation, after an action of murder has taken place, the victim may no longer commit or submit to any other action.

Consequently, it is impossible for the three acts of murder to occur in the beginning of a permutation, because no characters would then be left to accomplish the other actions. Even two murders in the beginning would render the development of the sequence impossible. One murder in the beginning dictates permutations of 11 actions for 3 characters.

The optimal case is that in which the three acts of murder occur at the end.

The sequences given by the computer must be able to reveal chains of events held together by possible logical links. We have seen that the acts of will and of secret can imply others. In each permutation will be found privileged circuits, to wit:

| appropriation of a secret | of a sexual appropriation | determines an appropriation of will that determines | a murder |
|---|---|---|---|
| | of a muder | | a sexual appropriation |

or:

| | | a murder |
|---|---|---|
| appropriation of a will | leads to | a sexual appropriation that determines, etc. |
| | | an appropriation of a secret |

Each new relation in the chain excludes others.

## Subjective Constraints

Incompatibility of each character with certain actions committed or submitted to. The 12 actions may also be divided according to a second sort of system, classifying them in 4 *subjective categories*.

| acts of physical strength | acts of persuasion | disloyal acts | acts that exploit another's weakness |
|---|---|---|---|
|  |  | to abuse the confidence |  |
|  | to incite |  |  |
| to extort |  |  | to buy good graces |
|  | to seduce |  |  |
| to rape |  | to stab in the back |  |
|  | to induce | | to blackmail |
| to strangle | to commit suicide |  |  |
|  |  | to spy upon | to drug |

—Of A it is known that he is a man of enormous physical strength, but that he is also an almost inarticulate brute.

A cannot submit to acts of physical strength.

A cannot commit acts of persuasion.

—Of B it is known that she is a woman in complete control of herself, with a strong will; she is sexually frigid; she hates drugs and drug addicts; she is rich enough to be interested only in herself.

B cannot submit to acts of persuasion.

B is not interested in acts that exploit another's weakness (she is not interested in buying sexual favors, she does not touch drugs, she has no motive for blackmail).

—Of C it is known that he is a very innocent Boy Scout, that he has a great sense of honor; if he takes drugs, he vomits immediately; his innocence protects him from all blackmail.

C cannot submit to acts that exploit another's weakness.

C cannot commit disloyal acts.

—Of D it is known that she is a terribly mistrustful woman and physically very weak.

D cannot submit to disloyal acts.

D cannot commit acts of strength.

An ulterior complication could be introduced!!!!

Each character could *change* in the course of the story (after certain actions committed or submitted to): each might lose certain incompatibilities and acquire others!!!!!!!!

For the moment, we forgo the exploration of this domain.

## Esthetic Constraints
### (or Subjective on the Part of the Programmer)

The programmer likes order and symmetry. Faced with the huge number of possibilities and with the chaos of human passions and worries, he tends to favor those solutions that are the most harmonious and economical.

He proposes a model, such that:

—each action be perpetrated by one and only one character and have one and only one character as a victim;

—the 12 actions be equally distributed among the 4 characters; that is, each of them perpetrates 3 actions (one on each of the others) and is the victim of 3 actions (each perpetrated by one of the others);

—each of the 3 actions perpetrated by a character belongs to a different (objective) class of actions;

—the same as above for each of the three actions submitted to by any given character;

—between two characters there be no commutativity within the same class of actions (if A kills B, B cannot kill A; likewise, the three sexual relations will occur between differently assorted couples).

Is it possible at the same time to take account of the subjective constraints and of the so-called esthetic constraints?

This is where the computer comes in; this is where the notion of "computer-aided literature" in exemplified.

Let us consider, for instance, 4 characters whom we shall call:

ARNO, CLEM, DANI, BABY

A very simple program permits us to engender selections of 12 misdeeds. Each of these selections might be, in theory, the scenario our hero is trying to reconstitute.

A few examples of such scenarios are given on the next page under the headings SELEC1.

The absurdity of these scenarios is obvious. In fact, the program used is completely *stupid*: it permits a character to commit a misdeed against himself.

The program can be improved in imposing:

—that autocrimes be excluded;

—that each character figure only 3 times as criminal and 3 times as victim.

One then obtains scenarios as shown under the headings SELEC2 on the next page.

This new program comprises obvious inefficiencies.

### SELEC1

| | | |
|---|---|---|
| ARNO | BUYS | CLEM |
| CLEM | EXTORTS A CONFESSION FROM | ARNO |
| ARNO | CONSTRAINS | ARNO |
| ARNO | EXTORTS A CONFESSION FROM | BABY |
| CLEM | RAPES | DANI |
| ARNO | CUTS THE THROAT OF | DANI |
| DANI | CONSTRAINS | BABY |
| BABY | EXTORTS A CONFESSION FROM | ARNO |
| CLEM | POISONS | ARNO |
| DANI | EXTORTS A CONFESSION FROM | CLEM |
| ARNO | ABUSES | ARNO |
| CLEM | EXTORTS A CONFESSION FROM | CLEM |

### SELEC2

| | | |
|---|---|---|
| DANI | POISONS | ARNO |
| BABY | THREATENS | CLEM |
| BABY | SPIES UPON | ARNO |
| CLEM | BLACKMAILS | ARNO |
| CLEM | EXTORTS A CONFESSION FROM | BABY |
| DANI | SEDUCES | BABY |
| DANI | STRANGLES | CLEM |
| ARNO | RAPES | BABY |
| BABY | CUTS THE THROAT OF | DANI |
| ARNO | CONSTRAINS | CLEM |
| ARNO | ABUSES | DANI |
| CLEM | BUYS | DANI |

### SELEC1

| | | |
|---|---|---|
| ARNO | POISONS | ARNO |
| DANI | SEDUCES | DANI |
| BABY | SPIES UPON | CLEM |
| BABY | RAPES | CLEM |
| BABY | EXTORTS A CONFESSION FROM | DANI |
| CLEM | SPIES UPON | ARNO |
| CLEM | THREATENS | CLEM |
| DANI | CONSTRAINS | BABY |
| DANI | EXTORTS A CONFESSION FROM | BABY |
| DANI | EXTORTS A CONFESSION FROM | ARNO |
| CLEM | ABUSES | BABY |
| BABY | BLACKMAILS | ARNO |

### SELEC2

| | | |
|---|---|---|
| ARNO | CONSTRAINS | CLEM |
| CLEM | BLACKMAILS | ARNO |
| DANI | BUYS | ARNO |
| ARNO | CUTS THE THROAT OF | BABY |
| ARNO | EXTORTS A CONFESSION FROM | DANI |
| BABY | RAPES | CLEM |
| CLEM | SEDUCES | BABY |
| DANI | THREATENS | CLEM |
| CLEM | ABUSES | DANI |
| BABY | STRANGLES | DANI |
| BABY | POSIONS | ARNO |
| DANI | SPIES UPON | BABY |

### SELEC1

| | | |
|---|---|---|
| DANI | SEDUCES | ARNO |
| BABY | CONSTRAINS | ARNO |
| ARNO | SPIES UPON | DANI |
| BABY | ABUSES | ARNO |
| CLEM | RAPES | CLEM |
| BABY | CUTS THE THROAT OF | DANI |
| ARNO | STRANGLES | ARNO |
| DANI | BUYS | ARNO |
| ARNO | ABUSES | ARNO |
| DANI | CUTS THE THROAT OF | CLEM |
| DANI | SEDUCES | CLEM |
| ARNO | CONSTRAINS | BABY |

### SELEC2

| | | |
|---|---|---|
| BABY | SPIES UPON | CLEM |
| ARNO | CUTS THE THROAT OF | DANI |
| DANI | STRANGLES | CLEM |
| DANI | THREATENS | ARNO |
| BABY | BLACKMAILS | ARNO |
| DANI | BUYS | BABY |
| CLEM | EXTORTS A CONFESSION FROM | BABY |
| BABY | RAPES | DANI |
| CLEM | CONSTRAINS | DANI |
| ARNO | ABUSES | BABY |
| ARNO | SEDUCES | CLEM |
| CLEM | POISONS | ARNO |

187

Thus, in the first scenario it is not possible for Clem to blackmail Arno who has already been poisoned by Dani. In the second scenario, Baby cannot rape Clem because Arno has already cut the latter's throat, etc. Paul Braffort, who ensures the development in computer science necessary to the progress of our work, has also written a series of programs for selections that progressively account for the *constraints* our story must respect in order to remain "logically" and "psychologically" acceptable.

This clearly demonstrates, we believe, that the aid of a computer, far from *replacing* the creative act of the artist, permits the latter rather to liberate himself from the slavery of a combinatory search, allowing him also the best chance of concentrating on this "clinamen" which, alone, can make of the text a true work of art.

*Brief History of the Oulipo*—Notes

1. The Collège de Pataphysique takes its name from "pataphysics," the discipline proposed by Alfred Jarry, which he defined in his *Gestes et opinions du Docteur Faustroll* (II, viii) as "the science of imaginary solutions." Jarry himself spelled the word with an initial apostrophe, perhaps to suggest *épataphysique,* or "shocking physics." The Collège itself was founded on 11 May 1948, the fiftieth anniversary of *Faustroll;* its principal (if by no means exclusive) function is to promote work on Jarry. Publications of the group include the *Cahiers du Collège de Pataphysique* and the *Dossiers du Collège de Pataphysique.* See Linda Klieger Stillman, *Alfred Jarry* (Boston: Twayne, 1983), 41–42. Several of the founding members of the Oulipo held titles within the Collège de Pataphysique: Queneau, for example, was a Transcendent Satrap; Latis was the Private General Secretary to the Baron Vice-Curator; Noël Arnaud is the Regent of General Pataphysics and the Clinic of Rhetoriconosis, as well as Major Conferant of the Order of the Grande Gidouille. (WM)

2. See Noël Arnaud, "Et naquit l'Ouvroir de Littérature Potentielle," in Jacques Bens, *Oulipo 1960–1963,* 8. (WM)

3. Raymond Queneau's first novel, published by Gallimard in 1933. (WM)

4. In the penultimate quatrain of his "Booz endormi," Victor Hugo rhymes *Jérimadeth* with *se demandait.* As the former place name figures in no known atlas, it has been conjectured that *Jérimadeth* may be read as *je rime à dait,* or "I rhyme with *dait."* (WM)

5. According to Bens's minutes, this meeting took place not on April 5 but on April 17. See *Oulipo 1960–1963,* 42–43. (WM)

6. Again, according to Bens, the date of the meeting was not April 20 but April 28. See *Oulipo 1960–1963,* 45–52. (WM)

7. Lady Godiva was a female tortoise who lived in François Le Lionnais's garden. See *Oulipo 1960–1963,* 71. (WM)

8. Baudelaire, of course.

9. Years become centuries in Oulipospeak. (WM)

10. Let us recall the names of the old ones: Noël Arnaud, Jacques Bens, Claude Berge, Paul Braffort, Jacques Duchateau, François Le Lionnais, Jean Lescure, Raymond Queneau, Jean Queval. Foreign correspondents: André Blavier, Ross Chambers, Stanley Chapman.

*For a Potential Analysis of Combinatory Literature*—Notes

1. *Dissertatio de Arte Combinatoria,* J.-E. Erdmann (1666). It is surprising to note that this very rare work, written in Latin, has never to our knowledge been translated. We owe certain of the references we used in the inventory of combinatory literature to Y. Belaval. Let us also cite another famous mathematician, Leonhard Euler, who suggested principles for a Combinatory Art in his *Lettres à une princesse d'Allemagne sur divers sujets de physique et de philosophie,* Steidel (1770–74), 27.

2. One could mathematize the concept of configuration in defining it as an *application of a set of objects within an abstract finite set provided with a known structure;* for example, a permutation of $n$ objects is a "bijective application of the set of objects within the set ordered 1, 2, . . . , $n$." Nevertheless, we are interested only in those applications that satisfy certain constraints, and the nature of these constraints is too varied to allow us to use this definition as the basis for a general theory.

3. "Honor, Art, Money, Property, Praise, Woman, and Child/One has, seeks, misses, hopes for, and disappears." G. P. Harsdörffer (1607–58), a founder of the "Pegnitz Shepherds," a Nuremberg society, wrote a *Poetischer Trichter* (*Poetic Funnel*) (1647–53) with which one could "pour" the art of poetry into anybody in six hours. See J. G. Robertson, *Outlines of the History of German Literature* (Edinburgh: Blackwood, 1950), 83. (WM)

4. Marc Saporta's *Composition No. 1* (Paris: Seuil, 1962) was published in 1962, not 1965. (WM)

5. The poem Berge has transformed is Ronsard's "Quand vous serez bien vieille":

Quand vous serez bien vieille, au soir, à la chandelle,
Assise auprès du feu, devidant et filant,
Direz, chantant mes vers, en vous esmerveillant:
Ronsard me celebroit du temps que j'estois belle.

Lors vous n'aurez servante oyant telle nouvelle,
Desja sous le labeur à demy sommeillant,
Qui, au bruit de Ronsard, ne s'aille réveillant,
Benissant vostre nom de louange immortelle.

Je seray sous la terre, et, fantosme sans os,
Par les ombres myrteux je prendray mon repos;
Vous serez au fouyer une vieille accroupie,

Regrettant mon amour et vostre fier desdain.
Vivez, si m'en croyez, n'attendez à demain;
Cueillez dés aujourd'hui les roses de la vie.

Humbert Wolfe, in Pierre de Ronsard, *Sonnets for Helen* (London: George Allen and Unwin, 1934), translates the poem as follows:

When you are old, at evening candle-lit
beside the fire bending to your wool,
read out my verse and murmur, "Ronsard writ
this praise for me when I was beautiful."

And not a maid but, at the sound of it,
though nodding at the stitch on broidered stool,
will start awake, and bless love's benefit
whose long fidelities bring Time to school.

I shall be thin and ghost beneath the earth
by myrtle shade in quiet after pain,
but you, a crone, will crouch beside the hearth

Mourning my love and all your proud disdain.
And since what comes tomorrow who can say?
Live, pluck the roses of the world to-day. (WM)

6. See the study Jean Ferry devoted to him in the journal *Bizarre* 34–35 (1964).

7. Work on the literary applications of the Latin bi-square was pursued by Georges Perec; in 1978 it resulted in his *La Vie mode d'emploi*. (WM)

*Computer and Writer: The Centre Pompidou Experiment*—Notes

1. A.R.T.A.: "Atelier de Recherches et Techniques Avancées," or "Workshop of Advanced Studies and Techniques," a group working at the Centre Pompidou. For a time, the Oulipo used A.R.T.A. equipment in their work on computer-aided literature. Personal letter from Paul Fournel to the editor, 5 December 1983. (WM)

2. Gallimard.

3. In the same spirit and using a very similar technique, Michel Bottin programmed the $10^{67}$ poems contained in the XLIst kiss of love of Quirinus Kuhlman.

4. This story is published in Oulipo, *La Littérature potentielle*, Gallimard's "Idées" collection, 277. [It also appears in the present volume (WM).]

5. A prototype of this text may be found in Oulipo, *La Littérature potentielle*, Gallimard's "Idées" collection, 281. [Appearing here as "The Theater Tree: A Combinatory Play." (WM)]

6. See Calvino's "Prose and Anticombinatorics." (WM)

7. See Roubaud's *La Princesse Hoppy ou le conte du Labrador*: Bibliothèque Oulipienne 2 (ch. 1); Bibliothèque Oulipienne 7 (ch. 2); *Change* 38 (1980), 11–29 (chs. 3, 4). (WM)

8. See Bénabou, *Un Aphorisme peut en cacher un autre.* (WM)

9. This paper was presented at the "Writer-Computer" meetings of June 1977.

189

# II
## Collective Media, Personal Media

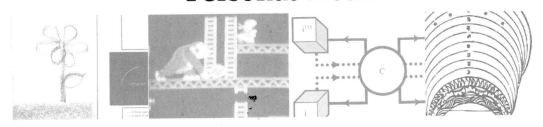

# 13. [Introduction]
# Two Selections by Marshall McLuhan
## The Galaxy Reconfigured
## The Medium Is the Message

Marshall McLuhan's writings on media introduced terms and concepts that are now quite popular, and used in so many contexts that it can be difficult figure out exactly what they were once supposed to mean. McLuhan's exhortation that "the medium is the message" is still repeated, often hollowly. The idea this phrase brought to the foreground in the 1960s—that media themselves overwhelm the importance of their "content"—is now almost an unspoken (and sometimes unexamined) assumption in today's vision of the world and in our understanding of our media ecology. Some of McLuhan's other striking contributions are laid out in the following excerpts from two of his most influential books. After describing how media extend human abilities and the human body itself, McLuhan distinguished between hot and cold media, which assert themselves in different ways and invite different sorts of engagement. McLuhan also argued that the culture was moving (because of our media transition) back toward tribal configurations, as he explained in one of two illustrated collaborations with Quentin Fiore: *War and Peace in the Global Village*—a book whose title gave politicians and pundits another famous phrase.

McLuhan saw his 350-page *The Gutenberg Galaxy,* the concluding chapter of which is presented here, as complementary with *The Singer of Tales* by Albert Bates Lord, a book that sought to describe the practice of oral literature—namely, the Homeric epics. McLuhan's point was to describe how typographic technology caused a shift in Western thought, as a starting point for understanding the current shifts brought about by what he called "electric" or "new" media. The media considered in *Understanding Media,* which appeared two years later, in 1964, include television and radio as well as weapons and clothing—although the digital computer did not earn its own chapter.

*Understanding Media* brought denouncements from those in traditional academic disciplines. Christopher Ricks, in a typical reply, wrote in *McLuhan: Hot & Cool* that "the style is a vicious fog, through which loom stumbling metaphors," and continued by bemoaning McLuhan's artistic taste and his idea that advertisements have artistic merit (215–216). One of Hans Magnus Enzensberger's denunciations of McLuhan is found in ◊18. Another harsh critic of *Understanding Media* — in 1967, at least — was Jean Baudrillard (◊19). But Baudrillard began in the following decades to employ some of McLuhan's terminology and ideas in his own critical writing.

In declaring that popular media should be studied, and on their own terms, McLuhan achieved special fame to complement his popular infamy. Along with the ill-fated quiz show champion Charles Van Doren (whom McLuhan defended as behaving appropriately, with regard to the television medium), McLuhan was one of the first true celebrity academics. He was frequently discussed outside the academy and made a cameo appearance in Woody Allen's *Annie Hall.*

McLuhan appears on the masthead of *Wired* magazine as "patron saint," but McLuhan's irreverence was seen more clearly in *Wired's* spunky and ironic kid brother, the first Web daily, *Suck* ⊗, which ran for almost six years. Although McLuhan's style is not without precedent (his sometimes tentative explorations really continue the original concept of the essay from Montaigne), they are among the first modern academic writings to combine irreverence and serious thought overtly, as seen in McLuhan's intentional misquotation of Shakespeare in the second of the following selections.

McLuhan's comments are not always incisive. In chapter 11 of *Understanding Media,* "Number, Profile of the Crowd," he writes about counting and the use of numbers within language, claiming, oddly enough, that "The computer is strong on contours, weak on digits."

**193**

◊18
259
◊19
277

Lord's book is also of interest to electronic literary creators; it is cited by Janet Murray in *Hamlet on the Holodeck* as describing a form of interactive telling, tailored to the audience, which has implications for the creation of interactive works on the computer.

Stuart Moulthrop's essay (◊48) treats hypertext to a McLuhanesque analysis.

◊48
691

While McLuhan's theories can be applied to the computer in its manipulations of different media or in its appearance as a new medium, the shift he described, from book-culture to a culture of electronic media, has certainly taken place already. Looking at McLuhan's explorations, although they are directed at earlier types of "new media," is sure to aid in understanding our world's further transitions from analog to digital media. Even if McLuhan's exhortations to ignore content completely are not persuasive, it certainly makes sense at times to consider the medium on its own. Besides reminding us of the excitement of transitional times and providing us with useful and powerful ideas for thinking about our media environment, McLuhan also shows us, by example, another significant point: it's important to have fun and to explore new ways of thinking a bit, rather than always asserting, arguing, and sifting the new into old categories—and it helps to not take yourself too seriously. —NM

McLuhan's influence remains strong in today's media writing, among enthusiasts of new media and those who are less ebullient about its prospects. Neil Postman, for instance, writes in *Amusing Ourselves to Death,* "this book is an inquiry into and lamentation about the most significant American cultural fact of the second half of the twentieth century: the decline of the Age of Typography and the ascendancy of the Age of Television. This change-over has dramatically and irreversibly shifted the content and meaning of public discourse, since two media so vastly different cannot accommodate the same ideas. . . . If all of this sounds suspiciously like Marshall McLuhan's aphorism, the medium is the message, I will not disavow the association . . . he spoke in the tradition of Orwell and Huxley—that is, as a prophesier, and I have remained steadfast to his teaching that the clearest way to see through a culture is to attend to its tools for conversation" (8).

Further Reading

Lord, Albert Bates. *The Singer of Tales.* Cambridge: Harvard University Press, 1960.

McLuhan, Marshall, and Quentin Fiore. *The Medium Is the Massage: An Inventory of Effects* New York: Random House, 1967.

McLuhan, Marshall, and Quentin Fiore. *War and Peace in the Global Village: An Inventory of Some of the Current Spastic Situations That Could Be Eliminated by More Feedforward.* New York: McGraw-Hill, 1968.

Postman, Neil. *Amusing Ourselves to Death.* New York: Viking Penguin, 1985

Stearn, Gerald Emanuel, ed. *McLuhan, Hot & Cool: A Primer for the Understanding of & a Critical Symposium with a Rebuttal by McLuhan.* New York: Dial Press, 1967.

Original Publication

"The Galaxy Reconfigured or the Plight of Mass Man in an Individualist Society" from *The Gutenberg Galaxy: The Making of Typographic Man.* Toronto: University of Toronto Press, 1962.

"The Medium Is the Message" from *Understanding Media: The Extensions of Man.* New York: McGraw Hill, 1964.

# The Galaxy Reconfigured
## or the Plight of Mass Man in an Individualist Society

## Marshall McLuhan

The present volume has employed a mosaic pattern of perception and observation up till now. William Blake can provide the explanation and justification of this procedure. *Jerusalem,* like so much of his other poetry, is concerned with the changing patterns of human perception. Book II, chapter 34, of the poem contains the pervasive theme:

> If Perceptive organs vary, Objects of Perception seem to vary:
> If the Perceptive Organs close, their Objects seem to close also.

Determined as he was to explain the causes and effects of psychic change, both personal and social, he arrived long ago at the theme of *The Gutenberg Galaxy:*

> The Seven Nations fled before him: they became what they beheld.

Blake makes quite explicit that when sense ratios change, men change. Sense ratios change when any one sense or bodily or mental function is externalized in technological form:

> The Spectre is the Reasoning Power in Man, & when separated
> From Imagination and closing itself as in steel in a Ratio
> Of the Things of Memory, It thence frames Laws & Moralities
> To destroy Imagination, the Divine Body, by Martyrdoms & Wars.[1]

Imagination is that ratio among the perceptions and faculties which exists when they are not embedded or outered in material technologies. When so outered, each sense and faculty becomes a closed system. Prior to such outering there is entire interplay among experiences. This interplay or synesthesia is a kind of tactility such as Blake sought in the bounding line of sculptural form and in engraving.

When the perverse ingenuity of man has outered some part of his being in material technology, his entire sense ratio is altered. He is then compelled to behold this fragment of himself "closing itself as in steel." In beholding this new thing, man is compelled to become it. Such was the origin of lineal, fragmented analysis with its remorseless power of homogenization:

> The Reasoning Spectre Stands between
> the Vegetative Man & his Immortal Imagination.[2]

Blake's diagnosis of the problem of his age was, like Pope's in *The Dunciad*, a direct confrontation of the forces shaping human perception. That he sought mythical form by which to render his vision was both necessary and ineffectual. For myth is the mode of simultaneous awareness of a complex group of causes and effects. In an age of fragmented, lineal awareness, such as produced and was in turn greatly exaggerated by Gutenberg technology, mythological vision remains quite opaque. The Romantic poets fell far short of Blake's mythical or simultaneous vision. They were faithful to Newton's single vision and perfected the picturesque outer landscape as a means of isolating single states of the inner life.[3]

It is instructive for the history of human sensibility to note how the popular vogue of the Gothic romance in Blake's time later unfolded into a serious esthetic with Ruskin and the French symbolists. This Gothic taste, trite and ridiculous as it first appeared to serious people, was yet a confirmation of Blake's diagnosis of the defects and needs of his age. It was itself a pre-Raphael or pre-Gutenberg quest for a unified mode of perception. In *Modern Painters* (vol. III, p. 91) Ruskin states the matter in a way which entirely dissociates Gothic medievalism from any historical concern about the Middle Ages. He states the matter in a way that won him the serious interest of Rimbaud and Proust:

> A fine grotesque is the expression, in a moment, by a series of symbols thrown together in bold and fearless connection, of truths which it would have taken a long time to express in any verbal way, and of which the connection is left for the beholder to work out for

himself; the gaps, left or overleaped by the haste of the imagination, forming the grotesque character.

For Ruskin, Gothic appeared as an indispensable means of breaking open the closed system of perception that Blake spent his life describing and fighting. Ruskin proceeds (p. 96) to explain Gothic grotesque as the best way of ending the regime of Renaissance perspective and single vision or realism:

> It is with a view (not the least important among many others bearing upon art) to the reopening of this great field of human intelligence, long entirely closed, that I am striving to introduce Gothic architecture into daily domestic use; and to revive the art of illumination, properly so called; not the art of miniature-painting in books, or on vellum, which has ridiculously been confused with it; but of making writing, simple writing, beautiful to the eye, by investing it with the great chord of perfect colour, blue, purple, scarlet, white, and gold, and in that chord of colour, permitting the continual play of the fancy of the writer in every species of grotesque imagination, carefully excluding shadow; the distinctive difference between illumination and painting proper, being, that illumination admits no shadows, but only gradations of pure colour.

The student of Rimbaud will find that it was while reading this part of Ruskin that Rimbaud found his title for *Illuminations*. The technique of vision in the *Illuminations* or "painted slides," (as Rimbaud called them, in English, on his title page) is exactly as Ruskin delineates the grotesque. But even Joyce's *Ulysses* finds anticipatory designation in the same context:

> Hence it is an infinite good to mankind when there is full acceptance of the grotesque, slightly sketched or expressed; and, if field for such expression be frankly granted, an enormous mass of intellectual power is turned to everlasting use, which, in this present century of ours, evaporates in street gibing or vain revelling; all the good wit and satire expiring in daily talk, (like foam on wine,) which in the thirteenth and fourteenth centuries had a permitted and useful expression in the arts of sculpture and illumination, like foam fixed into chalcedony.[4]

Joyce, that is to say, also accepted the grotesque as a mode of broken or syncopated manipulation to permit *inclusive* or simultaneous perception of a total and diversified field. Such, indeed, is symbolism by definition—a collocation, a *parataxis* of components representing insight by carefully established ratios, but without a point of view or lineal connection or sequential order.

Nothing, therefore, could be more remote from Joyce's ratios than the aim of pictorial realism. Indeed, he uses such realism and such Gutenberg technology as part of his symbolism. For example, in the seventh or Aeolus episode of *Ulysses* the technology of the newspaper is made the occasion for introducing all of the nine hundred and more rhetorical figures specified by Quintilian in his *Institutes of Oratory*. The figures of classical rhetoric are archetypes or postures of individual minds. Joyce by means of the modern press translates them into archetypes or postures of collective consciousness. He breaks open the closed system of classical rhetoric at the same time that he cuts into the closed system of newspaper somnambulism. Symbolism is a kind of witty jazz, a consummation of Ruskin's aspirations for the grotesque that would have shocked him a good deal. But it proved to be the only way out of "single vision and Newton's sleep."

Blake had the insights but not the technical resources for rendering his vision. Paradoxically, it was not through the book but through the development of the mass press, especially the telegraph press, that poets found the artistic keys to the world of simultaneity, or of modern myth. It was in the format of the daily press that Rimbaud and Mallarmé discovered the means of rendering the interplay of all the functions of what Coleridge called the "esemplastic" imagination.[5] For the popular press offers no single vision, no point of view, but a mosaic of the postures of the collective consciousness, as Mallarmé proclaimed. Yet these modes of collective or tribal consciousness proliferating in the telegraphic (simultaneous) press, remain uncongenial and opaque to the bookmen locked in "single vision and Newton's sleep."

The principal ideas of the eighteenth century were so crude as to seem risible to the wits of the time. The great chain of Being was in its way as comical as the chains which Rousseau proclaimed in his *Social Contract*. Equally inadequate as an idea of order was the merely visual notion of goodness as a *plenum*: "The best of all possible worlds" was merely a quantitative idea of a bag crammed to the utmost with goodies—an idea which lurked still in the nursery world of R. L. Stevenson. ("The world is so full of a number of things.") But in J. S. Mill's *Liberty* the quantitative idea of truth as an ideal container packed with every possible

opinion and point of view created mental anguish. For the suppression of any possible aspect of truth, any valid angle, might weaken the whole structure. In fact, the stress on the abstract visual evoked as standards of truth the mere matching of object with object. So unconscious were people of this matching theory as being dominant, that when a Pope or a Blake pointed out that truth is a ratio between the mind and things, a ratio made by the shaping imagination, there was nobody to note or comprehend. Mechanical matching, not imaginative making, will rule in the arts and sciences, in politics and education, until our own time.

Earlier, in presenting Pope's prophetic vision of the return of tribal or collective consciousness, the relation to Joyce's *Finnegans Wake* had been indicated. Joyce had devised for Western man individual pass-keys to the collective consciousness, as he declared on the last page of the *Wake*. He knew that he had solved the dilemma of Western individual man faced with the collective or tribal consequences of first his Gutenberg, and next his Marconi, technologies. Pope had seen the tribal consciousness latent in the new mass culture of the book-trade. Language and the arts would cease to be prime agents of critical perception and become mere packaging devices for releasing a spate of verbal commodities. Blake and the Romantics and the Victorians alike became obsessed with the actualization of Pope's vision in the new organization of an industrial economy embedded in a self-regulating system of land, labour, and capital. The Newtonian laws of mechanics, latent in Gutenberg typography, were translated by Adam Smith to govern the laws of production and consumption. In accordance with Pope's prediction of automatic trance or "robo-centrism," Smith declared that the mechanical laws of the economy applied equally to the things of the mind: "In opulent and commercial societies to think or to reason comes to be, like every other employment, a particular business, which is carried on by a very few people, who furnish the public with all the thought and reason possessed by the vast multitudes that labour."[6]

Adam Smith is always faithful to the fixed visual point of view and its consequent separation of faculties and functions. But in this passage Smith does seem to sense that the new role of the intellectual is to tap the collective consciousness of "the vast multitudes that labour." That is to say, the intellectual is no longer to direct individual perception and judgment but to explore and to communicate the massive unconsciousness of collective man. The intellectual is newly cast in the role of a primitive seer, *vates*, or hero incongruously peddling his discoveries in a commercial market. If Adam Smith was reluctant to push his view to this point of the transcendental imagination, Blake and the Romantics felt no qualms but turned literature over to the transcendental arm. Henceforth, literature will be at war with itself and with the social mechanics of conscious goals and motivations. For the matter of literary vision will be collective and mythic, while the forms of literary expression and communication will be individualist, segmental, and mechanical. The vision will be tribal and collective, the expression private and marketable. This dilemma continues to the present to rend the individual Western consciousness. Western man knows that his values and modalities are the product of literacy. Yet the very means of extending those values, technologically, seem to deny and reverse them. Whereas Pope fully faced up to this dilemma in *The Dunciad,* Blake and the Romantics tended to devote themselves to one side of it, the mythic and collective. J. S. Mill, Matthew Arnold, and a great many others devoted themselves to the other side of the dilemma, the problem of individual culture and liberty in an age of mass-culture. But neither side has its meaning alone, nor can the causes of the dilemma be found anywhere but in the total galaxy of events that constitute literacy and Gutenberg technology. Our liberation from the dilemma may, as Joyce felt, come from the new electric technology, with its profound organic character. For the electric puts the mythic or collective dimension of human experience fully into the conscious wake-a-day world. Such is the meaning of the title *Finnegans Wake.* While the old Finn cycles had been tribally entranced in the collective night of the unconscious, the new Finn cycle of totally interdependent man must be lived in the daylight of consciousness.

At this point, *The Great Transformation* by Karl Polanyi, on "the political and economic origins of our time," assumes complete relevance in the mosaic of *The Gutenberg Galaxy.* Polanyi is concerned with the stages by which the Newtonian mechanics invaded and transformed society in the eighteenth and nineteenth centuries, only to encounter a reverse dynamic from within. His analysis of how prior to the eighteenth century "the economic system was absorbed in the social system" is exactly parallel to the situation of literature and the arts up till that time. This was true till the

time of Dryden, Pope, and Swift, who lived to detect the great transformation. Polanyi enables us (p. 68) to face the familiar Gutenberg principle of practical advance and utility by separation of forms and functions:

> As a rule, the economic system was absorbed in the social system, and whatever principle of behavior predominated in the economy, the presence of the market pattern was found to be compatible with it. The principle of barter or exchange, which underlies this pattern, revealed no tendency to expand at the expense of the rest. Where markets were most highly developed, as under the mercantile system, they throve under the control of a centralized administration which fostered autarchy both in the households of the peasantry and in respect to national life. Regulation and markets, in effect, grew up together. The self-regulating market was unknown; indeed the emergence of the idea of self-regulation was a complete reversal of the trend of development.

The principle of self-regulation repeating by reverberation from the Newtonian sphere swiftly entered all the social spheres. It is the principle that Pope mocked in "whatever is is right" and that Swift ridiculed in "the mechanickal operation of the Spirit." It derives from a merely vision image of an uninterrupted chain of Being or a visual *plenum* of the good as "the best of all possible worlds." Granted the merely visual assumptions of lineal continuity or of sequential dependence, the principle of non-interference in the natural order becomes the paradoxical conclusion of applied knowledge.

Through the sixteenth and seventeenth centuries the transformation of mechanization of crafts by the application of visual *method* had proceeded slowly. But it was a procedure of maximal interference with existing non-visual modes. By the eighteenth century the process of applied knowledge had reached such a momentum that it became accepted as a natural process which must not be impeded save at the peril of greater evil: "all partial evil universal good." Polanyi notes (p. 69) this automation of consciousness as follows:

> A further group of assumptions follows in respect to the state and its policy. Nothing must be allowed to inhibit the formation of markets, nor must incomes be permitted to be formed otherwise than through sales. Neither must there be any interference with the adjustment of prices to changed market conditions—

197

whether the prices are those of goods, labor, land, or money. Hence there must not only be markets for all elements of industry, but no measure of policy must be countenanced that would influence the action of these markets. Neither price, nor supply, nor demand must be fixed or regulated; only such policies and measures are in order which help to ensure the self-regulation of the market by creating conditions which make the market the only organizing power in the economic sphere.

The assumptions latent in typographic segmentation, and in applied knowledge by the method of fragmenting of crafts and the specializing of social tasks, these assumptions were the most acceptable in the degree that typography enlarged its markets. The same assumptions presided over the formation of Newtonian space and time and mechanics. So literature, industry, and economics were easily accommodated within the Newtonian sphere. Those who questioned these assumptions were simply denying the facts of science. Now that Newton is no longer synonymous with science, we can meditate on the dilemmas of the self-regulating economy and the hedonistic calculus with light hearts and clear heads. But eighteenth century man was locked into a closed visual system that had enveloped him he knew not how. So he proceeded, robo-centred, to carry out the behests of the new vision.

However, in 1709 Bishop Berkeley had published *A New Theory of Vision*, which revealed the lop-sided assumptions of Newtonian optics. Blake, at least, had understood the Berkeleyan critique and had restored tactility to its prime role as agent of unified perception. Today artists and scientists alike concur in praising Berkeley. But his wisdom was lost on his age that was wrapped in "single vision and Newton's sleep." The hypnotized patient carried out the behests of the abstract visual control. Polanyi observes (p. 71):

> A self-regulating market demands nothing less than the institutional separation of society into an economic and political sphere. Such a dichotomy is, in effect, merely the restatement, from the point of view of society as a whole, of the existence of a self-regulating market. It might be argued that the separateness of the two spheres obtains in every type of society at all times. Such an inference, however, would be based on a fallacy. True, no society can exist without a system of some kind which ensures order in the production and distribution of goods. But that does not imply the existence of separate economic institutions; normally, the economic

order is merely a function of the social, in which it is contained. Neither under tribal, nor feudal, nor mercantile conditions was there, as we have shown, a separate economic system in society. Nineteenth century society, in which economic activity was isolated and imputed to a distinctive economic motive, was, indeed, a singular departure.

> Such an institutional pattern could not function unless society was somehow subordinated to its requirements. A market economy can exist only in a market society. We reached this conclusion on general grounds in our analysis of the market pattern. We can now specify the reasons for this assertion. A market economy must comprise all elements of industry, including labor, land, and money. (In a market economy the last also is an essential element of industrial life and its inclusion in the market mechanism has, as we will see, far-reaching institutional consequences.) But labor and land are no other than the human beings themselves of which every society consists and the natural surroundings in which it exists. To include them in the market mechanism means to subordinate the substance of society itself to the laws of the market.

A market economy "can exist only in a market society." But to exist, a market society requires centuries of transformation by Gutenberg technology; hence, the absurdity in the present time of trying to institute market economies in countries like Russia or Hungary, where feudal conditions obtained until the twentieth century. It is possible to set up modern production in such areas, but to create a market economy that can handle what comes off the assembly lines presupposes a long period of psychic transformation, which is to say, a period of altering perception and sense ratios.

When a society is enclosed within a particular fixed sense ratio, it is quite unable to envisage another state of affairs. Thus, the advent of nationalism was quite unforeseen in the Renaissance, although its causes arrived earlier. The Industrial Revolution was well on the way in 1795, yet, as Polanyi points out (p. 89):

> . . . the generation of Speenhamland was unconscious of what was on its way. On the eve of the greatest industrial revolution in history, no signs and portents were forthcoming. Capitalism arrived unannounced. No one had forecast the development of a machine industry; it came as a complete surprise. For some time England had been actually expecting a permanent recession of foreign trade when the dam burst, and the

old world was swept away in one indomitable surge towards a planetary economy.

That every generation poised on the edge of massive change should later seem oblivious of the issues and the imminent event would seem to be natural enough. But it is necessary to understand the power and thrust of technologies to isolate the senses and thus to hypnotize society. The formula for hypnosis is "one sense at a time." And new technology possesses the power to hypnotize because it isolates the senses. Then, as Blake's formula has it: "They became what they beheld." Every new technology thus diminishes sense interplay and consciousness, precisely in the new area of novelty where a kind of identification of viewer and object occurs. This somnambulist conforming of beholder to the new form or structure renders those most deeply immersed in a revolution the least aware of its dynamic. What Polanyi observes about the insentience of those involved in the expediting of the new machine industry is typical of all the local and contemporary attitudes to revolution. It is felt, at those times, that the future will be a larger or greatly improved version of the *immediate past*. Just before revolutions the image of the immediate past is stark and firm, perhaps because it is the only area of sense interplay free from obsessional identification with new technological form.

No more extreme instance of this delusion could be mentioned than our present image of TV as a current variation on the mechanical, movie pattern of processing experience by repetition. A few decades hence it will be easy to describe the revolution in human perception and motivation that resulted from beholding the new mosaic mesh of the TV image. Today it is futile to discuss it at all.

Looking back to the revolution in literary forms in the later eighteenth century, Raymond Williams writes in *Culture and Society, 1780–1850* (p. 42) that "changes in convention only occur when there are radical changes in the general structure of feeling." Again, "while in one sense the market was specializing the artist, artists themselves were seeking to generalize their skills into the common property of imaginative truth." (p. 43) This can be seen in the Romantics who, discovering their inability to talk to conscious men, began by myth and symbol to address the unconscious levels of dream life. The imaginative reunion with tribal man was scarcely a voluntary strategy of culture.

One of the most radical of new literary conventions of the market society of the eighteenth century was the novel. It had been preceded by the discovery of "equitone prose." Addison and Steele, as much as anybody else, had devised this novelty of maintaining a single consistent tone to the reader. It was the auditory equivalent of the mechanically fixed view in vision. Mysteriously, it is this break-through into equitone prose which suddenly enabled the mere author to become a "man of letters." He could abandon his patron and approach the large homogenized public of a market society in a consistent and complacent role. So that with both sight and sound given homogeneous treatment, the writer was able to approach the mass public. What he had to offer the public was equally a homogenized body of common experience such as the movie finally took over from the novel. Dr. Johnson devoted his *Rambler no. 4* (March 31, 1750) to this theme:

> The works of fiction, with which the present generation seems more particularly delighted, are such as exhibit life in its true state, diversified only by accidents that daily happen in the world, and influenced by passions and qualities which are really to be found in conversing with mankind.

Johnson shrewdly notes the consequences of this new form of social realism, indicating its basic deviation from the forms of book learning:

> The task of our present writers is very different; it requires, together with that learning which is to be gained from books, that experience which can never be attained by solitary diligence, but must arise from general converse and accurate observation of the living world. Their performances have, as Horace expresses it, *plus oneris quantum veniae minus*, little indulgence, and therefore more difficulty. They are engaged in portraits of which every one knows the original, and can detect any deviation from exactness of resemblance. Other writings are safe, except from the malice of learning, but these are in danger from every common reader; as the slipper ill executed was censured by a shoemaker who happened to stop in his way at the Venus of Apelles.

Johnson continues in this vein, pointing out further rivalries between the new novel and the older modes of book learning:

> In the romances formerly written, every transaction and sentiment was so remote from all that passes among

men, that the reader was in very little danger of making any applications to himself; the virtues and crimes were equally beyond his sphere of activity; and he amused himself with heroes and with traitors, deliverers and persecutors, as with beings of another species, whose actions were regulated upon motives of their own, and who had neither faults nor excellencies in common with himself.

But when an adventurer is levelled with the rest of the world, and acts in such scenes of the universal drama, as may be the lot of any other man; young spectators fix their eyes upon him with closer attention, and hope, by observing his behaviour and success, to regulate their own practices, when they shall be engaged in the like part.

For this reason these familiar histories may perhaps be made of greater use than the solemnities of professed morality, and convey the knowledge of vice and virtue with more efficacy than axioms and definitions.

Quite parallel with this extension of the book page into the form of a talking picture of ordinary life, was what Leo Lowenthal mentions in *Popular Culture and Society* (p. 75) as "the crucial shift from Patron to Public," citing the testimony of Oliver Goldsmith's 1759 *Enquiry into the Present State of Polite Learning in Europe:*

> At present the few poets of England no longer depend on the Great for subsistence, they have now no other patrons but the public, and the public, collectively considered, is a good and generous master. . . . A writer of real merit now may easily be rich if his heart be set only on fortune: and for those who have no merit, it is but fit that such should remain in merited obscurity.

Leo Lowenthal's new study of popular literary culture is not only concerned with the eighteenth century and after, but studies the dilemmas of diversion *v.* salvation through art from Montaigne and Pascal to modern magazine iconology. In pointing out how Goldsmith made a great change in criticism by shifting attention to the *experience* of the reader, Lowenthal has broken rich new ground (pp. 107–8):

> But perhaps the most far-reaching change which took place in the concept of the critic was that a two-way function was premised for him. Not only was he to reveal the beauties of literary works to the general public by means of which, in Goldsmith's terms, "even the philosopher may acquire popular applause"; he must also interpret the public back to the writer. In brief, the critic

not only "teaches the vulgar on what part of a character to lay the emphasis of praise," he must also show "the scholar where to point his application so as to deserve it." Goldsmith believed that the absence of such critical mediators explained why wealth rather than true literary fame was the goal of so many writers. The result, he feared, might be that nothing would be remembered of the literary works of his time.

We have observed that Goldsmith, in his endeavor to come to grips with the dilemma of the writer, represented a variety of sometimes conflicting views. We have seen, however, that it was likely to be Goldsmith in his optimistic rather than in his pessimistic vein who set the tone for what was to come. So, too, his view of the "ideal" critic, of his function as one of mediation between the audience and the writer, was to prevail. Critics, writers, and philosophers—Johnson, Burke, Hume, Reynolds, Kames, and the Whartons—all adopted Goldsmith's premise as they began to analyze the experience of the reader.

As the market society defined itself, literature moved into the role of consumer commodity. The public became patron. Art reversed its role from guide for perception into convenient amenity or package. But the producer or artist was compelled, as never before, to study the effect of his art. This in turn revealed to human attention new dimensions of the function of art. As manipulators of the mass market tyrannized over the artist, the artist in isolation achieved new clairvoyance concerning the crucial role of design and of art as a means to human order and fulfilment. Art has become as total in its mandate for human order as the mass markets that created the plateau from which all can now share the awareness of new scope and potential for everyday beauty and order in all aspects of life at once. Retrospectively, it may well prove necessary to concede to the period of mass marketing the creation of the means of a world order in beauty as much as in commodities.

It is quite easy to establish the fact that the same means that served to create the world of consumer abundance by mass production served also to put the highest levels of artistic production on a more assured and consciously controlled basis. And, as usual, when some previously opaque area becomes translucent, it is because we have moved into another phase from which we can contemplate the contours of the preceding situation with ease and clarity. It is this fact that makes it feasible to write *The Gutenberg Galaxy* at all. As we experience the new electronic and organic age with ever stronger indications of its main outlines, the preceding mechanical age becomes quite intelligible. Now that the assembly line recedes before the new patterns of information, synchronized by electric tape, the miracles of mass-production assume entire intelligibility. But the novelties of automation, creating workless and propertyless communities, envelop us in new uncertainties.

A most luminous passage of A. N. Whitehead's classic *Science and the Modern World* (p. 141) is one that was discussed previously in another connection.

> The greatest invention of the nineteenth century was the invention of the method of invention. A new method entered into life. In order to understand our epoch, we can neglect all the details of change, such as railways, telegraphs, radios, spinning machines, synthetic dyes. We must concentrate on the method in itself; that is the real novelty, which has broken up the foundations of the old civilisation. The prophecy of Francis Bacon has now been fulfilled; and man, who at times dreamt of himself as a little lower than the angels, has submitted to become the servant and the minister of nature. It still remains to be seen whether the same actor can play both parts.

Whitehead is right in insisting that "we must concentrate on the method itself." It was the Gutenberg method of homogeneous segmentation, for which centuries of phonetic literacy had prepared the psychological ground, that evoked the traits of the modern world. The numerous galaxy of events and products of that method of mechanization of handicrafts, are merely incidental to the method itself. It is the method of the fixed or specialist point of view that insists on repetition as the criterion of truth and practicality. Today our science and method strive not towards a point of view but to discover how not to have a point of view, the method not of closure and perspective but of the open "field" and the suspended judgment. Such is now the only viable method under electric conditions of simultaneous information movement and total human interdependence.

Whitehead does not elaborate on the great nineteenth century discovery of the method of invention. But it is, quite simply, the technique of beginning at the end of any operation whatever, and of working backwards from that point to the beginning. It is the method inherent in the Gutenberg technique of homogeneous segmentation, but not until the nineteenth century was the method extended from production to consumption. Planned production means that the total process must be worked out in exact stages, backwards, like a detective story. In the first great age of mass production of commodities, and of literature as a commodity for the market, it became necessary to study the consumer's experience. In a word it became necessary to examine the *effect* of art and literature before producing anything at all. This is the *literal* entrance to the world of myth.

It was Edgar Allan Poe who first worked out the rationale of this ultimate awareness of the poetic process and who saw that instead of directing the work to the reader, it was necessary to incorporate the reader in the work. Such was his plan in "the philosophy of composition." And Baudelaire and Valéry, at least, recognized in Poe a man of the Leonardo da Vinci stature. Poe saw plainly that the anticipation of effect was the only way to achieve organic control for the creative process. T. S. Eliot, like Baudelaire and Valéry, gives his entire sanction to Poe's discovery. In a celebrated passage of his essay on *Hamlet*,[7] he writes:

> The only way of expressing emotion in the form of art is by finding an "objective correlative"; in other words, a set of objects, a situation, a chain of events which shall be the formula of that *particular* emotion; such that when the external facts, which must terminate in sensory experience, are given, the emotion is immediately evoked. If you examine any of Shakespeare's more successful tragedies, you will find this exact equivalence; you will find that the state of mind of Lady Macbeth walking in her sleep has been communicated to you by a skilful accumulation of imagined sensory impressions; the words of Macbeth on hearing of his wife's death strike us as if, given the sequence of events, these words were automatically released by the last event in the series.

Poe set this method to work in many of his poems and stories. But it is most obvious in his invention of the detective story in which Dupin, his sleuth, is an artist-esthete who solves crimes by a method of artistic perception. Not only is the detective story the great popular instance of working backwards from effect to cause, it is also the form in which the reader is deeply involved as co-author. Such is also the case in symbolist poetry whose completion of effect from moment to moment requires the reader to participate in the poetic process itself.

201

It is a characteristic chiasmus that waits upon the utmost development of any process that the last phase shall show characteristics opposite to the early phases. A typical example of massive psychic chiasmus or reversal occurred when Western man fought the harder for individuality as he surrendered the idea of unique personal existence. The nineteenth century artists made a mass-surrender of that unique selfhood, that had been taken for granted in the eighteenth century, as the new mass pressures made the burdens of selfhood too heavy. Just as Mill fought for individuality even though he had given up the self, the poets and artists moved towards the idea of impersonal process in art production in proportion as they berated the new masses for impersonal process in the consumption of art products. A similar and related reversal or chiasmus occurred when the consumer of popular art was invited by new art forms to become participant in the art process itself.

This was the moment of transcendence of the Gutenberg technology. The centuries-old separation of senses and functions ended in a quite unexpected unity.

The reversal by which the presence of the new markets and the new masses encouraged the artist to surrender the unique self might have seemed a final consummation for art and technology alike. It was a surrender made almost inevitable when the symbolists began to work backwards from effect to cause in the shaping of the art product. Yet it was just at this extreme moment that a new reversal occurred. The art process had no sooner approached the rigorous, impersonal rationale of the industrial process, in the period from Poe to Valéry, than the assembly line of symbolist art was transformed into the new "stream of consciousness" mode of presentation. And the stream of consciousness is an open "field" perception that reverses all aspects of the nineteenth century discovery of the assembly-line or of the "technique" of invention. As G. H. Bantock writes of it:

> in a world of increasing socialization, standardization, and uniformity, the aim was to stress uniqueness, the purely personal in experience; in one of "mechanical" rationality, to assert other modes through which human beings can express themselves, to see life as a series of emotional intensities involving a logic different from that of the rational world and capturable only in dissociated images or stream of consciousness musings.[8]

Thus the technique of the suspended judgment, the great discovery of the twentieth century in art and physics alike, is a recoil and transformation of the impersonal assembly-line of nineteenth century art and science. And to speak of the stream of consciousness as unlike the rational world is merely to insist upon visual sequence as the rational norm, handing art over to the unconscious quite gratuitously. For what is meant by the irrational and the non-logical in much modern discussion is merely the rediscovery of the ordinary transactions between the self and the world, or between subject and object. Such transactions had seemed to end with the effects of phonetic literacy in the Greek world. Literacy had made of the enlightened individual a closed system, and set up a gap between appearance and reality which ended with such discoveries as the stream of consciousness.

As Joyce expressed it in the *Wake,* "My consumers are they not my producers?" Consistently, the twentieth century has worked to free itself from the conditions of passivity, which is to say, from the Gutenberg heritage itself. And this dramatic struggle of unlike modes of human insight and outlook has resulted in the greatest of all human ages, whether in the arts or in the sciences. We are living in a period richer and more terrible than the "Shakespearean Moment" so well described by Patrick Cruttwell in his book of the same title. But it has been the business of *The Gutenberg Galaxy* to examine only the mechanical technology emergent from our alphabet and the printing press. What will be the new configurations of mechanisms and of literacy as these older forms of perception and judgment are interpenetrated by the new electric age? The new electric galaxy of events has already moved deeply into the Gutenberg galaxy. Even without collision, such co-existence of technologies and awareness brings trauma and tension to every living person. Our most ordinary and conventional attitudes seem suddenly twisted into gargoyles and grotesques. Familiar institutions and associations seem at times menacing and malignant. These multiple transformations, which are the normal consequence of introducing new media into any society whatever, need special study and will be the subject of another volume on *Understanding Media* in the world of our time.

# The Medium Is the Message

## Marshall McLuhan

In a culture like ours, long accustomed to splitting and dividing all things as a means of control, it is sometimes a bit of a shock to be reminded that, in operational and practical fact, the medium is the message. This is merely to say that the personal and social consequences of any medium—that is, of any extension of ourselves—result from the new scale that is introduced into our affairs by each extension of ourselves, or by any new technology. Thus, with automation, for example, the new patterns of human association tend to eliminate jobs, it is true. That is the negative result. Positively, automation creates roles for people, which is to say depth of involvement in their work and human association that our preceding mechanical technology had destroyed. Many people would be disposed to say that it was not the machine, but what one did with the machine, that was its meaning or message. In terms of the ways in which the machine altered our relations to one another and to ourselves, it mattered not in the least whether it turned out cornflakes or Cadillacs. The restructuring of human work and association was shaped by the technique of fragmentation that is the essence of machine technology. The essence of automation technology is the opposite. It is integral and decentralist in depth, just as the machine was fragmentary, centralist, and superficial in its patterning of human relationships.

The instance of the electric light may prove illuminating in this connection. The electric light is pure information. It is a medium without a message, as it were, unless it is used to spell out some verbal ad or name. This fact, characteristic of all media, means that the "content" of any medium is always another medium. The content of writing is speech, just as the written word is the content of print, and print is the content of the telegraph. If it is asked, "What is the content of speech?," it is necessary to say, "It is an actual process of thought, which is in itself nonverbal." An abstract painting represents direct manifestation of creative thought processes as they might appear in computer designs. What we are considering here, however, are the psychic and social

consequences of the designs or patterns as they amplify or accelerate existing processes. For the "message" of any medium or technology is the change of scale or pace or pattern that it introduces into human affairs. The railway did not introduce movement or transportation or wheel or road into human society, but it accelerated and enlarged the scale of previous human functions, creating totally new kinds of cities and new kinds of work and leisure. This happened whether the railway functioned in a tropical or a northern environment, and is quite independent of the freight or content of the railway medium. The airplane, on the other hand, by accelerating the rate of transportation, tends to dissolve the railway form of city, politics, and association, quite independently of what the airplane is used for.

Let us return to the electric light. Whether the light is being used for brain surgery or night baseball is a matter of indifference. It could be argued that these activities are in some way the "content" of the electric light, since they could not exist without the electric light. This fact merely underlines the point that "the medium is the message" because it is the medium that shapes and controls the scale and form of human association and action. The content or uses of such media are as diverse as they are ineffectual in shaping the form of human association. Indeed, it is only too typical that the "content" of any medium blinds us to the character of the medium. It is only today that industries have become aware of the various kinds of business in which they are engaged. When IBM discovered that it was not in the business of making office equipment or business machines, but that it was in the business of processing information, then it began to navigate with clear vision. The General Electric Company makes a considerable portion of its profits from electric light bulbs and lighting systems. It has not yet discovered that, quite as much as A.T.&T., it is in the business of moving information.

The electric light escapes attention as a communication medium just because it has no "content." And this makes it an invaluable instance of how people fail to study media at all. For it is not till the electric light is used to spell out some brand name that it is noticed as a medium. Then it is not the light but the "content" (or what is really another medium) that is noticed. The message of the electric light is like the message of electric power in industry, totally radical, pervasive, and decentralized. For electric light and power are separate from their uses, yet they eliminate time and space factors in human association exactly as do radio, telegraph, telephone, and TV, creating involvement in depth.

A fairly complete handbook for studying the extensions of man could be made up from selections from Shakespeare. Some might quibble about whether or not he was referring to TV in these familiar lines from *Romeo and Juliet*:

> But soft! what light through yonder window breaks?
> It speaks, and yet says nothing.

In *Othello*, which, as much as *King Lear*, is concerned with the torment of people transformed by illusions, there are these lines that bespeak Shakespeare's intuition of the transforming powers of new media:

> Is there not charms
> By which the property of youth and maidhood
> May be abus'd? Have you not read Roderigo,
> Of some such thing?

In Shakespeare's *Troilus and Cressida*, which is almost completely devoted to both a psychic and social study of communication, Shakespeare states his awareness that true social and political navigation depend upon anticipating the consequences of innovation:

> The providence that's in a watchful state
> Knows almost every grain of Plutus' gold,
> Finds bottom in the uncomprehensive deeps,
> Keeps place with thought, and almost like the gods
> Does thoughts unveil in their dumb cradles.

The increasing awareness of the action of media, quite independently of their "content" or programming, was indicated in the annoyed and anonymous stanza:

> In modern thought, (if not in fact)
> Nothing is that doesn't act,
> So that is reckoned wisdom which
> Describes the scratch but not the itch.

The same kind of total, configurational awareness that reveals why the medium is socially the message has occurred in the most recent and radical medical theories. In his *Stress of Life*, Hans Selye tells of the dismay of a research colleague on hearing of Selye's theory:

> When he saw me thus launched on yet another enraptured description of what I had observed in animals treated with this or that impure, toxic material, he looked at me with desperately sad eyes and said in obvious despair: "But Selye, try to realize what

you are doing before it is too late! You have now decided to spend your entire life studying the pharmacology of dirt!"
> (Hans Selye, *The Stress of Life*)

As Selye deals with the total environmental situation in his "stress" theory of disease, so the latest approach to media study considers not only the "content" but the medium and the cultural matrix within which the particular medium operates. The older unawareness of the psychic and social effects of media can be illustrated from almost any of the conventional pronouncements.

In accepting an honorary degree from the University of Notre Dame a few years ago, General David Sarnoff made this statement: "We are too prone to make technological instruments the scapegoats for the sins of those who wield them. The products of modern science are not in themselves good or bad; it is the way they are used that determines their value." That is the voice of the current somnambulism. Suppose we were to say, "Apple pie is in itself neither good nor bad; it is the way it is used that determines its value." Or, "The smallpox virus is in itself neither good nor bad; it is the way it is used that determines its value." Again, "Firearms are in themselves neither good nor bad; it is the way they are used that determines their value." That is, if the slugs reach the right people firearms are good. If the TV tube fires the right ammunition at the right people it is good. I am not being perverse. There is simply nothing in the Sarnoff statement that will bear scrutiny, for it ignores the nature of the medium, of any and all media, in the true Narcissus style of one hypnotized by the amputation and extension of his own being in a new technical form. General Sarnoff went on to explain his attitude to the technology of print, saying that it was true that print caused much trash to circulate, but it had also disseminated the Bible and the thoughts of seers and philosophers. It has never occurred to General Sarnoff that any technology could do anything but *add* itself on to what we already are.

Such economists as Robert Theobald, W. W. Rostow, and John Kenneth Galbraith have been explaining for years how it is that "classical economics" cannot explain change or growth. And the paradox of mechanization is that although it is itself the cause of maximal growth and change, the principle of mechanization excludes the very possibility of growth or the understanding of change. For mechanization is achieved by fragmentation of any process and by putting the fragmented parts in a series. Yet, as David Hume showed in the eighteenth century, there is no principle of causality in a mere sequence. That one thing follows another accounts for nothing. Nothing follows from following, except change. So the greatest of all reversals occurred with electricity, that ended sequence by making things instant. With instant speed the causes of things began to emerge to awareness again, as they had not done with things in sequence and in concatenation accordingly. Instead of asking which came first, the chicken or the egg, it suddenly seemed that a chicken was an egg's idea for getting more eggs.

Just before an airplane breaks the sound barrier, sound waves become visible on the wings of the plane. The sudden visibility of sound just as sound ends is an apt instance of that great pattern of being that reveals new and opposite forms just as the earlier forms reach their peak performance. Mechanization was never so vividly fragmented or sequential as in the birth of the movies, the moment that translated us beyond mechanism into the world of growth and organic interrelation. The movie, by sheer speeding up the mechanical, carried us from the world of sequence and connections into the world of creative configuration and structure. The message of the movie medium is that of transition from lineal connections to configurations. It is the transition that produced the now quite correct observation: "If it works, it's obsolete." When electric speed further takes over from mechanical movie sequences, then the lines of force in structures and in media become loud and clear. We return to the inclusive form of the icon.

To a highly literate and mechanized culture the movie appeared as a world of triumphant illusions and dreams that money could buy. It was at this moment of the movie that cubism occurred, and it has been described by E. H. Gombrich (*Art and Illusion*) as "the most radical attempt to stamp out ambiguity and to enforce one reading of the picture—that of a man-made construction, a colored canvas." For cubism substitutes all facets of an object simultaneously for the "point of view" or facet of perspective illusion. Instead of the specialized illusion of the third dimension on canvas, cubism sets up an interplay of planes and contradiction or dramatic conflict of patterns, lights, textures that "drives home the message" by involvement. This is held by many to be an exercise in painting, not in illusion.

In other words, cubism, by giving the inside and outside, the top, bottom, back, and front and the rest, in two dimensions, drops the illusion of perspective in favor of instant sensory awareness of the whole. Cubism, by seizing on instant total awareness, suddenly announced that *the medium is the message.* Is it not evident that the moment that sequence yields to the simultaneous, one is in the world of the structure and of configuration? Is that not what has happened in physics as in painting, poetry, and in communication? Specialized segments of attention have shifted to total field, and we can now say, "The medium is the message" quite naturally. Before the electric speed and total field, it was not obvious that the medium is the message. The message, it seemed, was the "content," as people used to ask what a painting was *about.* Yet they never thought to ask what a melody was about, nor what a house or a dress was about. In such matters, people retained some sense of the whole pattern, of form and function as a unity. But in the electric age this integral idea of structure and configuration has become so prevalent that educational theory has taken up the matter. Instead of working with specialized "problems" in arithmetic, the structural approach now follows the linea of force in the field of number and has small children meditating about number theory and "sets."

Cardinal Newman said of Napoleon, "He understood the grammar of gunpowder." Napoleon had paid some attention to other media as well, especially the semaphore telegraph that gave him a great advantage over his enemies. He is on record for saying that "Three hostile newspapers are more to be feared than a thousand bayonets."

Alexis de Tocqueville was the first to master the grammar of print and typography. He was thus able to read off the message of coming change in France and America as if he were reading aloud from a text that had been handed to him. In fact, the nineteenth century in France and in America was just such an open book to de Tocqueville because he had learned the grammar of print. So he, also, knew when that grammar did not apply. He was asked why he did not write a book on England, since he knew and admired England. He replied:

> One would have to have an unusual degree of philosophical folly to believe oneself able to judge England in six months. A year always seemed to me too short a time in which to appreciate the United States properly, and it is much easier to acquire clear and precise notions about the American Union than about Great Britain. In America all laws derive in a sense from

the same line of thought. The whole of society, so to speak, is founded upon a single fact; everything springs from a simple principle. One could compare America to a forest pierced by a multitude of straight roads all converging on the same point. One has only to find the center and everything is revealed at a glance. But in England the paths run criss-cross, and it is only by travelling down each one of them that one can build up a picture of the whole.

De Tocqueville, in earlier work on the French Revolution, had explained how it was the printed word that, achieving cultural saturation in the eighteenth century, had homogenized the French nation. Frenchmen were the same kind of people from north to south. The typographic principles of uniformity, continuity, and lineality had overlaid the complexities of ancient feudal and oral society. The Revolution was carried out by the new literati and lawyers.

In England, however, such was the power of the ancient oral traditions of common law, backed by the medieval institution of Parliament, that no uniformity or continuity of the new visual print culture could take complete hold. The result was that the most important event in English history has never taken place; namely, the English Revolution on the lines of the French Revolution. The American Revolution had no medieval legal institutions to discard or to root out, apart from monarchy. And many have held that the American Presidency has become very much more personal and monarchical than any European monarch ever could be.

De Tocqueville's contrast between England and America is clearly based on the fact of typography and of print culture creating uniformity and continuity. England, he says, has rejected this principle and clung to the dynamic or oral commonlaw tradition. Hence the discontinuity and unpredictable quality of English culture. The grammar of print cannot help to construe the message of oral and nonwritten culture and institutions. The English aristocracy was properly classified as barbarian by Matthew Arnold because its power and status had nothing to do with literacy or with the cultural forms of typography. Said the Duke of Gloucester to Edward Gibbon upon the publication of his *Decline and Fall*: "Another damned fat book, eh, Mr. Gibbon? Scribble, scribble, scribble, eh, Mr. Gibbon?" De Tocqueville was a highly literate aristocrat who was quite able to be detached from the values and assumptions of typography. That is why he alone understood the grammar of typography. And it is only on those terms, standing aside

from any structure or medium, that its principles and lines of force can be discerned. For any medium has the power of imposing its own assumption on the unwary. Prediction and control consist in avoiding this subliminal state of Narcissus trance. But the greatest aid to this end is simply in knowing that the spell can occur immediately upon contact, as in the first bars of a melody.

*A Passage to India* by E. M. Forster is a dramatic study of the inability of oral and intuitive oriental culture to meet with the rational, visual European patterns of experience. "Rational," of course, has for the West long meant "uniform and continuous and sequential." In other words, we have confused reason with literacy, and rationalism with a single technology. Thus in the electric age man seems to the conventional West to become irrational. In Forster's novel the moment of truth and dislocation from the typographic trance of the West comes in the Marabar Caves. Adela Quested's reasoning powers cannot cope with the total inclusive field of resonance that is India. After the Caves: "Life went on as usual, but had no consequences, that is to say, sounds did not echo nor thought develop. Everything seemed cut off at its root and therefore infected with illusion."

*A Passage to India* (the phrase is from Whitman, who saw America headed Eastward) is a parable of Western man in the electric age, and is only incidentally related to Europe or the Orient. The ultimate conflict between sight and sound, between written and oral kinds of perception and organization of existence is upon us. Since understanding stops action, as Nietzsche observed, we can moderate the fierceness of this conflict by understanding the media that extend us and raise these wars within and without us.

Detribalization by literacy and its traumatic effects on tribal man is the theme of a book by the psychiatrist J. C. Carothers, *The African Mind in Health and Disease* (World Health Organization, Geneva, 1953). Much of his material appeared in an article in *Psychiatry* magazine, November, 1959: "The Culture, Psychiatry, and the Written Word." Again, it is electric speed that has revealed the lines of force operating from Western technology in the remotest areas of bush, savannah, and desert. One example is the Bedouin with his battery radio on board the camel. Submerging natives with floods of concepts for which nothing has prepared them is the normal action of all of our technology. But with electric media Western man himself experiences exactly the same inundation as the remote native. We are no more prepared to encounter radio and TV in our literate milieu than the native of Ghana is able to cope with the literacy that takes him out of his collective tribal world and beaches him in individual isolation. We are as numb in our new electric world as the native involved in our literate and mechanical culture.

Electric speed mingles the cultures of prehistory with the dregs of industrial marketeers, the nonliterate with semiliterate and the postliterate. Mental breakdown of varying degrees is the very common result of uprooting and inundation with new information and endless new patterns of information. Wyndham Lewis made this a theme of his group of novels called *The Human Age*. The first of these, *The Childermass*, is concerned precisely with accelerated media change as a kind of massacre of the innocents. In our own world as we become more aware of the effects of technology on psychic formation and manifestation, we are losing all confidence in our right to assign guilt. Ancient prehistoric societies regard violent crime as pathetic. The killer is regarded as we do a cancer victim. "How terrible it must be to feel like that," they say. J. M. Synge took up this idea very effectively in his *Playboy of the Western World.*

If the criminal appears as a nonconformist who is unable to meet the demand of technology that we behave in uniform and continuous patterns, literate man is quite inclined to see others who cannot conform as somewhat pathetic. Especially the child, the cripple, the woman, and the colored person appear in a world of visual and typographic technology as victims of injustice. On the other hand, in a culture that assigns roles instead of jobs to people—the dwarf, the skew, the child create their own spaces. They are not expected to fit into some uniform and repeatable niche that is not their size anyway. Consider the phrase "It's a man's world." As a quantitative observation endlessly repeated from within a homogenized culture, this phrase refers to the men in such a culture who have to be homogenized Dagwoods in order to belong at all. It is in our I.Q. testing that we have produced the greatest flood of misbegotten standards. Unaware of our typographic cultural bias, our testers assume that uniform and continuous habits are a sign of intelligence, thus eliminating the ear man and the tactile man.

C. P. Snow, reviewing a book of A. L. Rowse (*The New York Times Book Review*, December 24, 1961) on *Appeasement* and the road to Munich, describes the top level of British brains and experience in the 1930s. "Their I.Q.'s were much higher than usual among political bosses. Why were they such a disaster?" The view of Rowse, Snow approves: "They would not listen to warnings because they did not wish to hear." Being anti-Red made it impossible for them to read the message of Hitler. But their failure was as nothing compared to our present one. The American stake in literacy as a technology or uniformity applied to every level of education, government, industry, and social life is totally threatened by the electric technology. The threat of Stalin or Hitler was external. The electric technology is within the gates, and we are numb, deaf, blind, and mute about its encounter with the Gutenberg technology, on and through which the American way of life was formed. It is, however, no time to suggest strategies when the threat has not even been acknowledged to exist. I am in the position of Louis Pasteur telling doctors that their greatest enemy was quite invisible, and quite unrecognized by them. Our conventional response to all media, namely that it is how they are used that counts, is the numb stance of the technological idiot. For the "content" of a medium is like the juicy piece of meat carried by the burglar to distract the watchdog of the mind. The effect of the medium is made strong and intense just because it is given another medium as "content." The content of a movie is a novel or a play or an opera. The effect of the movie form is not related to its program content. The "content" of writing or print is speech, but the reader is almost entirely unaware either of print or of speech.

Arnold Toynbee is innocent of any understanding of media as they have shaped history, but he is full of examples that the student of media can use. At one moment he can seriously suggest that adult education, such as the Workers Educational Association in Britain, is a useful counterforce to the popular press. Toynbee considers that although all of the oriental societies have in our time accepted the industrial technology and its political consequences: "On the cultural plane, however, there is no uniform corresponding tendency." (Somervell, I. 267) This is like the voice of the literate man, floundering in a milieu of ads, who boasts, "Personally, I pay no attention to ads." The spiritual and cultural reservations that the oriental peoples may have toward our technology will avail them not at all. The effects of technology do not occur at the level of opinions or concepts, but alter sense ratios or patterns of perception steadily and without any resistance. The serious artist is the only person able to

207

encounter technology with impunity, just because he is an expert aware of the changes in sense perception.

The operation of the money medium in seventeenth-century Japan had effects not unlike the operation of typography in the West. The penetration of the money economy, wrote G. B. Sansom (in *Japan,* Cresset Press, London, 1931) "caused a slow but irresistible revolution, culminating in the breakdown of feudal government and the resumption of intercourse with foreign countries after more than two hundred years of seclusion." Money has reorganized the sense life of peoples just because it is an *extension* of our sense lives. This change does not depend upon approval or disapproval of those living in the society.

Arnold Toynbee made one approach to the transforming power of media in his concept of "etherialization," which he holds to be the principle of progressive simplification and efficiency in any organization or technology. Typically, he is ignoring the *effect* of the challenge of these forms upon the response of our senses. He imagines that it is the response of our opinions that is relevant to the effect of media and technology in society, a "point of view" that is plainly the result of the typographic spell. For the man in a literate and homogenized society ceases to be sensitive to the diverse and discontinuous life of forms. He acquires the illusion of the third dimension and the "private point of view" as part of his Narcissus fixation, and is quite shut off from Blake's awareness or that of the Psalmist, that we become what we behold.

Today when we want to get our bearings in our own culture, and have need to stand aside from the bias and pressure exerted by any technical form of human expression, we have only to visit a society where that particular form has not been felt, or a historical period in which it was unknown. Professor Wilbur Schramm made such a tactical move in studying *Television in the Lives of Our Children*. He found areas where TV had not penetrated at all and ran some tests. Since he had made no study of the peculiar nature of the TV image, his tests were of "content" preferences, viewing time, and vocabulary counts. In a word, his approach to the problem was a literary one, albeit unconsciously so. Consequently, he had nothing to report. Had his methods been employed in 1500 A.D. to discover the effects of the printed book in the lives of children or adults, he could have found out nothing of the changes in human and social psychology resulting from typography. Print created

individualism and nationalism in the sixteenth century. Program and "content" analysis offer no clues to the magic of these media or to their subliminal charge.

Leonard Doob, in his report *Communication in Africa,* tells of one African who took great pains to listen each evening to the BBC news, even though he could understand nothing of it. Just to be in the presence of those sounds at 7 P.M. each day was important for him. His attitude to speech was like ours to melody—the resonant intonation was meaning enough. In the seventeenth century our ancestors still shared this native's attitude to the forms of media, as is plain in the following sentiment of the Frenchman Bernard Lam expressed in *The Art of Speaking* (London, 1696):

> 'Tis an effect of the Wisdom of God, who created Man to be happy, that whatever is useful to his conversation (way of life) is agreeable to him . . . because all victual that conduces to nourishment is relishable, whereas other things that cannot be assimilated and be turned into our substance are insipid. A Discourse cannot be pleasant to the Hearer that is not easie to the Speaker; nor can it be easily pronounced unless it be heard with delight.

Here is an equilibrium theory of human diet and expression such as even now we are only striving to work out again for media after centuries of fragmentation and specialism.

Pope Pius XII was deeply concerned that there be serious study of the media today. On February 17, 1950, he said:

> It is not an exaggeration to say that the future of modern society and the stability of its inner life depend in large part on the maintenance of an equilibrium between the strength of the techniques of communication and the capacity of the individual's own reaction.

Failure in this respect has for centuries been typical and total for mankind. Subliminal and docile acceptance of media impact has made them prisons without walls for their human users. As A. J. Liebling remarked in his book *The Press,* a man is not free if he cannot see where he is going, even if he has a gun to help him get there. For each of the media is also a powerful weapon with which to clobber other media and other groups. The result is that the present age has been one of multiple civil wars that are not limited to the world of art and entertainment. In *War and Human Progress,* Professor J. U. Nef declared:

The total wars of our time have been the result of a series of intellectual mistakes. . . .

If the formative power in the media are the media themselves, that raises a host of large matters that can only be mentioned here, although they deserve volumes. Namely, that technological media are staples or natural resources, exactly as are coal and cotton and oil. Anybody will concede that society whose economy is dependent upon one or two major staples like cotton, or grain, or lumber, or fish, or cattle is going to have some obvious social patterns of organization as a result. Stress on a few major staples creates extreme instability in the economy but great endurance in the population. The pathos and humor of the American South are embedded in such an economy of limited staples. For a society configured by reliance on a few commodities accepts them as a social bond quite as much as the metropolis does the press. Cotton and oil, like radio and TV, become "fixed charges" on the entire psychic life of the community. And this pervasive fact creates the unique cultural flavor of any society. It pays through the nose and all its other senses for each staple that shapes its life.

That our human senses, of which all media are extensions, are also fixed charges on our personal energies, and that they also configure the awareness and experience of each one of us, may be perceived in another connection mentioned by the psychologist C. G. Jung:

> Every Roman was surrounded by slaves. The slave and his psychology flooded ancient Italy, and every Roman became inwardly, and of course unwittingly, a slave. Because living constantly in the atmosphere of slaves, he became infected through the unconscious with their psychology. No one can shield himself from such an influence (*Contributions to Analytical Psychology*, London, 1928).

The Galaxy Reconfigured—Notes

1. *Jerusalem*, III, 74.

2. *Ibid.*, II, 36.

3. This Newtonian theme is developed by myself apropos "Tennyson and Picturesque Poetry" in John Killham, ed., *Critical Essays on the Poetry of Tennyson*, pp. 67–85.

4. John Ruskin, *Modern Painters*, vol. III, p. 96.

5. See H. M. McLuhan, "Joyce, Mallarmé and the Press," *Sewanee Review*, winter, 1954, pp. 38–55.

6. Cited by Raymond Williams, *Culture and Society, 1780–1850*, p. 38.

7. In *Selected Essays*, p. 145.

8. "The Social and Intellectual Background" in *The Modern Age* (The Pelican Guide to English Literature), p. 47.

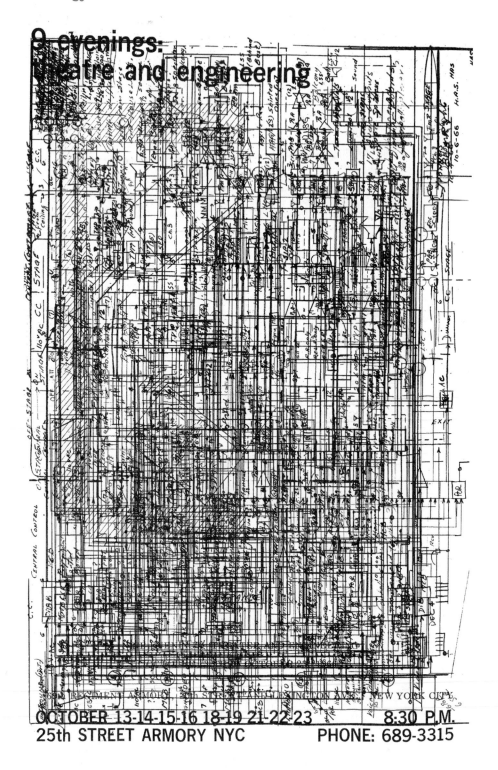

9 evenings:
theatre and engineering

OCTOBER 13·14·15·16 18·19 21·22·23          8:30 P.M.
25th STREET ARMORY NYC          PHONE: 689-3315

# 14. [Introduction]
# Four Selections by Experiments in Art and Technology
## From "The Garden Party"
## From *9 Evenings: Theatre & Engineering*
## [Press Release]
## The Pavilion

Experiments in Art and Technology (E.A.T.) has had a pivotal role in advancing the possibilities of technology and art since the 1960s. E.A.T. formulated what had been, before that group's founding, haphazard: the artist-engineer relationship, and the potential for our culture of joining artistic and technical exploration. E.A.T. began its official life in the wake of an ambitious performance series; launched an organization and newsletter; sponsored exhibitions, competitions, and discussions; created the Pepsi pavilion for Expo '70; and at its height boasted a membership of 4,000 evenly divided between artists and engineers.

E.A.T. was founded in 1966 by Billy Klüver, Robert Rauschenberg, Robert Whitman, and Fred Waldhauer, and was announced to the press in 1967, when the third selection in this chapter was handed out. E.A.T.'s story begins, however, in 1960, when Klüver, a research scientist at Bell Telephone Laboratories, made it technologically possible for Jean Tinguely to create "Homage to New York"—a sculpture that enacted its own destruction in a half-hour performance at New York's Museum of Modern Art. E.A.T. is the Phoenix that rose from that sculpture's remains. Robert Rauschenberg, who had contributed a money-throwing "mascot" to Homage, soon worked with Klüver on the technically-advanced sound/sculpture environment *Oracle*. This experience lead them to formulate the model of artist and engineer as true collaborators (rather than the engineer as an artist's assistant) which would become the foundation of E.A.T.

The next step toward E.A.T.'s creation came in the fall of 1965, when Klüver met Knut Wiggen, who came to visit him from Sweden. Wiggen was in the early stages of planning a Stockholm Festival of Art and Technology, and asked Klüver to organize U.S. participation. Klüver signed on to bring together a group of artist/engineer performances for the festival. Working with Rauschenberg, Klüver gathered influential artists, mainly from the group associated with the Judson Dance Theater (held at Judson Church in downtown New York), as well as engineers, many from Bell Labs. When the final plans for the Stockholm collaboration couldn't be satisfactorily worked out, the group found a new home for their performances, one rich in history and challenges. As Norma Loewen wrote in her *Experiments in Art and Technology*, "During the beginning of August 1966 . . . the group selected the 69th Regiment Armory at Twenty-fifth Street and Lexington Avenue. Those testing the properties of the space found the building's steel structure . . . [gave] a reverberation time of about six seconds duration . . . the engineers thought they somehow could manage. The armory had housed 'The International Exhibition of Modern Art' in 1913, an event some have called a turning point in the history of modern American art" (64–65).

E.A.T.'s performance exhibition *9 Evenings: Theatre & Engineering* turned out to be another turning point, despite its uneven reception. The New York press, largely unfamiliar with downtown performance, was baffled by the program. Rather than decry the art, a potentially vulnerable

For some insight into what might have baffled the press, consider a few of the pieces from *9 Evenings* for which we have reproduced the program notes here. John Cage—experimental composer, Zen enthusiast, and convener of famous performance art courses at The New School—made indeterministic music using sounds from open telephone lines, household appliances, and other rather non-traditional sources. Yvonne Ranier—choreographer, performance artist, and founding member of the Judson Dance Theater—spontaneously choreographed performers via walkie-talkie while film, slide, and physical "events", preprogrammed on ACTAN drum switches, were activated. Robert Rauschenberg—leading avant-garde painter and sculptor, famous for his collage techniques, who had worked as set creator for the Merce Cunningham Dance Company—presented tennis as formal dance improvisation, controlling the lights with the racquets, and eventually putting the lights out completely so that a stage full of people became invisible to the audience except via images from infrared television projectors.

Mid-century avant-garde performances such as those described in the pages from *9 Evenings* that follow—performances with relatively traditional audiences, rather than participatory events—may seem difficult at first to consider in the context of more familiar new media examples. However, as Jim Rosenberg has pointed out on the ht-lit mailing list, there is actually a distinct similarity between the language used to describe these pieces and language now used to describe new media. The mid-century language to which Rosenberg is referring was that of the relationship between the author of the performance score and the performers (especially as it was formulated in the case of indeterminate music), rather than the relationship between the performers and the audience. In this language (and practice) of performance, the score provides a framework and setting for action, but with many interpretation options available at the time of performance. This experience was probably more genuinely interactive for the performers than those artist-lead Happenings that attempted participation were for many of their audience members. E.A.T.'s Pavilion took the next step, creating what Klüver called an experience of "choice, responsibility, freedom, and participation" for each visitor in a continually-recreated space.

212

E.A.T. continues its work today, with Klüver as the current President.

position, they chose to attack the technology. In fact, as Klüver wrote a few months later, "Critics and public had a field day at the engineers' expense. . . . . Anything that was assumed to have gone wrong (whether it actually did or not) was attributed to technical malfunctions" (414). Particularly attacked was the sound system used in the performances—which was at the very least a technical triumph, including such innovations as wireless microphones embedded in tennis racquets and rapid reconfiguration via a central patch station more advanced than anything previously used for theatrical purposes. Still, the accusations of poor sound quality were very difficult to counter until recently, now that E.A.T. has begun to edit and make available films of the actual performances. These show that the artists chose to *work with* the sound reverberation, letting the resonating amplified tone of a ball hitting a racquet ring like a new type of bell.

The debates on the accuracy of the *9 Evenings* reviews have taken on less urgency over the years. What has become clear is the importance of *9 Evenings* and of the activities of E.A.T. as an inspiration for the whole new media field. Particularly inspiring was the way these activities demonstrated the potential of artist-engineer collaboration. The exhibition at the Armory accomplished this most saliently for performance, while E.A.T.'s "Pavilion" for Expo 70 showed the potential in creating a full environment—from a pure water cloud sculpture enveloping the exterior to a large spherical mirror creating an interior environment of light, space, and reflection that made visitors aesthetically aware of their every movement. While the cutting-edge nature of the Pavilion's planned live performances continued to baffle those in power (in this case, particularly Hijikata's performance with wedding dresses and funeral music) E.A.T. deserves applause for never retreating to well-trodden artistic ground. The best work in art and technology today continues E.A.T.'s tradition of innovation and collaboration, while the worst uses gee-whiz technology to prop up art that takes no risks.

—NWF

Further Reading

Davis, Douglas. *Art and the Future: A History/Prophecy of the Collaboration Between Science, Technology, and Art.* New York: Praeger Publishers, 1973.

Klüver, Billy. "Theatre and Engineering—An Experiment: 2. Notes by an Engineer." *Artforum* 5(6):31-33. February 1967. Reprinted in Kristine Stiles and Peter Selz, ed., *Theories and Documents of Contemporary Art: A Sourcebook of Artists' Writings,* 412–415. Berkeley: California: University of California Press, 1996.

Loewen, Norma. "Experiments in Art and Technology: A Descriptive History of the Organization." Ph.D. thesis, New York University, 1975.

My Boyfriend Came Back From the War. <http://myboyfriendcamebackfromth.ewar.ru/>

Schechner, Richard. *Performance Theory* rev. and exp. ed., New York: Routledge, 1988. 1st ed., *Essays on Performance Theory* by Ralph Pine, for Drama Book Specialists, 1977.

New media artists may also benefit by considering the performative/theatrical approach of mounting a show as a metaphor for the lifetime of their work and its possibilities for preservation. This suggestion is intended in contrast to the metaphors normally applied, in which new media is paralleled with literature and film. These well-established metaphors make new media works seem very short lived, and suggest that the best preservation strategy is to try to find ways to keep the work "readable" on legacy hardware or through emulation programs. Mounting a performance, in contrast, assumes that making a work available is a process of continual recreation from existing documentation and new interpretation. This, one could argue, is a potentially productive view to take when contemplating the dozens of influential HyperCard artworks that are becoming ever harder to access and experience on current systems. If these performances are "closing" the artists may wish to schematically document them, and then seek appropriate models and tools for some of them to be "remounted" in new technical circumstances. One can imagine remountings undertaken either by the original performers or by others, and with an interpretation that hews close to the original or that deviates from it as radically as "The Gospel at Colonus" does from a performance in the time of Sophocles (or as JODI's Wolfenstein version of "My Boyfriend Came Back From the War" does from Olia Lialina's original HTML and frames artwork).

Original Publication

Klüver, Billy. Excerpt from "The Garden Party." *The Machine as Seen at the End of the Mechanical Age*. New York: Museum of Modern Art, 1968. First published in *ZERO* 1: 168–171. 1961.

E.A.T. *9 Evenings: Theatre and Engineering*. Program. October 1966.

E.A.T. Press release. (Untitled.) October 1967.

Klüver, Billy. "The Pavilion" in *Pavilion*. Ed. Billy Klüver, Julie Martin, and Barbara Rose. New York: Dutton, 1972.

# From "The Garden Party"

## Billy Klüver

In the same way as a scientific experiment can never fail, this experiment in art could never fail. The machine was not a functional object and was never treated like one. The spectacle can therefore not be judged in terms of whether this or that thing did not work. During the construction of the machine, I was constantly amazed at Jean's disregard for the simplest rules of engineering. In one instant he would demand that something should function, and in the next he would violate his demand by the most trivial of actions. Jean worked as an artist. He chose his motors and put on his slings as an artist. He was interested only in functional operations that he could understand, so that he could reject or accept them as he pleased. But he was also inspired by possibilities of engineering and realized he could use them as long as he was in complete control of what he was doing. As an engineer, working with him, I was part of the machine. This new availability was largely responsible for the size and complexity of the machine.

Jean's machine was conceived out of "total anarchy and freedom," as he put it. The free and chaotic circumstances under which it was built were a necessity and, in a way, a tremendous luxury. Jean supplied the energy to create the freedom and was ruler over the chaos. When the energy was released, everything that happened was related to some of Jean's decisions. No distinction can be made between the "random" elements, the accidents, or the controlled parts of the spectacle. It was created in its totality out of freedom and innocence. The bottles that did not fall, the paper roll that rotated in the wrong direction, the fireman and the audience were all part of the same spectacle. There could exist no paradox, no question, no "nonsense," no a priori, and no chaos in this spectacle. It was a definite demonstration, made with love and humor, and not a philosophical problem.

I do not interpret the self-destruction of Jean's machine as an act of protest against the machine, or an expression of nihilism and despair, as some critics have suggested. The self-destruction or self-elimination of the machine is an ideal of good machines and human beings, this is an obvious truth. This idea has already been expressed by Claude Shannon in the "Little Black Box," in which, when you pull a switch, a lid opens and a hand emerges that throws the switch in the off position whereupon the lid closes again over the hand.

Just as in every moment we see and experience a new and changing world, Jean's machine created and destroyed itself as a representation of a moment in our lives. The art of the museum is related to a past time that we cannot see and feel again. The artist has already left his canvas behind. This art then becomes part of our inherited language, and thus has a relation to our world different than the reality of the immediate now. *L'art éphémère*, on the other hand, creates a direct connection between the creative act of the artist and the receptive act of the audience, between the construction and the destruction. It forces us out of the inherited image and into contact with ever-changing reality. It one of Jean's "manifestos," he says that we shall "be static with movement." We must be the creative masters of changing reality—which we are, by the definition of Man. The parts from which Jean's machine were built came from the chaos of the dump and were returned to the dump.

Jean kept saying that he was constantly thinking about New York as his machine took form. There are probably many connections, the most obvious being a machine that has rejected itself and become humor and poetry. New York has humor and poetry, in spite of the presence of the machine, whereas in a purely technocratic society the machine must always be a functional object. Failures of the machine can therefore never be allowed, because control is the necessary element of that society. It is when the machine must function at any cost that there can be no "Homage to New York."

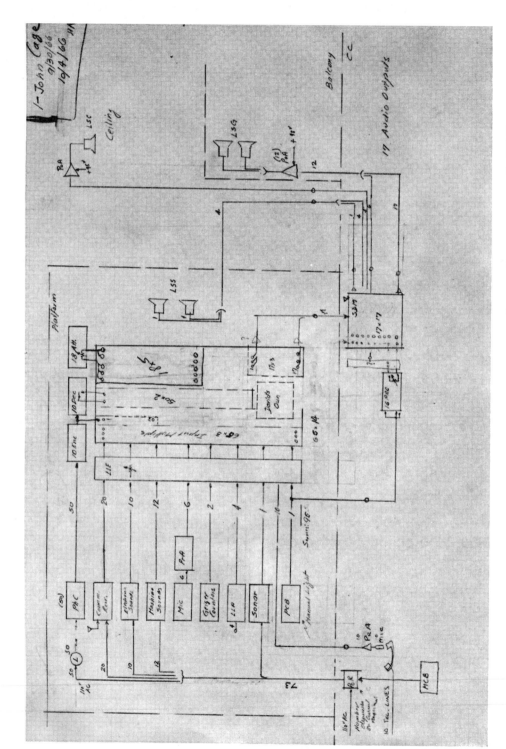

# variations VII

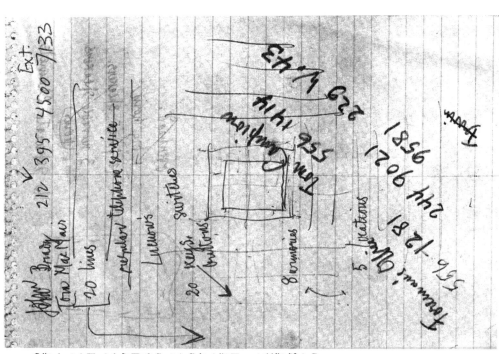

# by: John Cage

## performance engineer: Cecil Coker

performers: David Tudor
David Behrman
Antony Gnazzo
Lowell Cross

grateful acknowledgement is made
for the cooperation of:
Merce Cunningham Dance Foundation
Luchow's Restaurant
A.S.P.C.A.
The New York Times
The City of N. Y.
Terry Riley
Robert Wood
Richard Hennessy
Rubin Gorowitz

My project is simple to describe. It is a piece of music, Variation VII, indeterminate in form and detail, making use of the sound system which has been devised collectively for this festival, further making use of modulation means organized by David Tudor, using as sound sources only those sounds which are in the air at the moment of performance, picked up via the communication bands, telephone lines, microphones, together with, instead of musical instruments, a variety of household appliances and frequency generators.

The technical problems involved in any single project tend to reduce the impact of the original idea, but in being solved they produce a situation different than anyone could have pre-imagined.

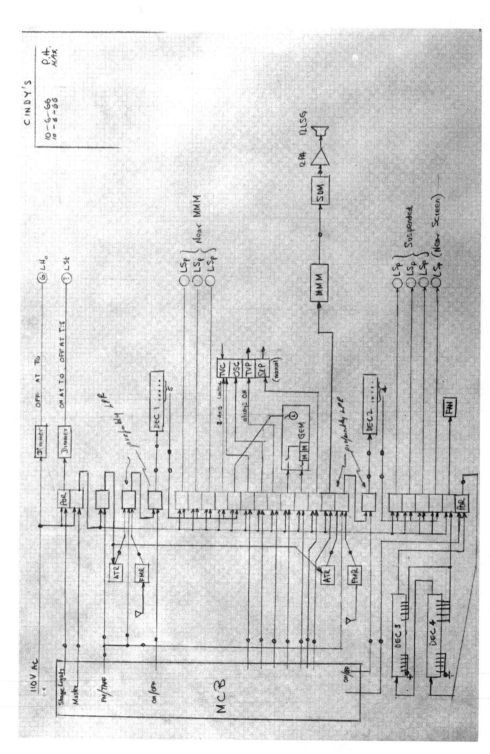

vehicle

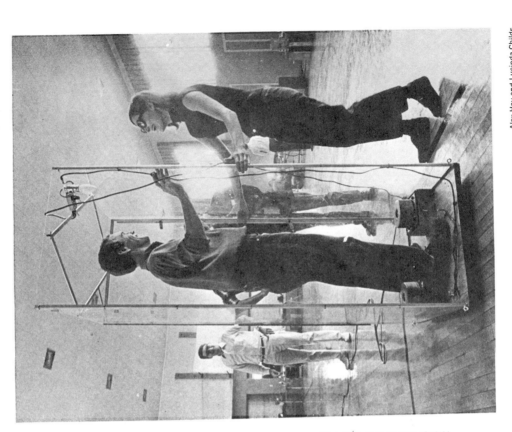

Alex Hay and Lucinda Childs with ground effect machine at Berkeley Heights School rehearsal.

# by: Lucinda Childs
## performance engineer: Peter Hirsch

**cast:** William Davis
Alex Hay
**slides by:** Les Levine

Vehicle consists of materials animate, inanimate, air-supported (in one instance), which can exist in a non-static state and be observed in increased dimension as they come in contact with light and sound sources made available consistently or intermittently by radio signals through-out the dance.

The Doppler sonar has ultrasonic beam sources and a receiver. The beam emits frequencies at a level which is greater than our hearing capacity. A moving figure or object passing in front of the beam interrupts it and sends frequencies back to the receiver of the sonar at a level determined by the velocity of the figure or object. What we hear is the proportional difference between the frequencies sent out and those returned through interruption of the beam, and the resulting reduction in the frequency level is what makes the sonar audible. Middle C (as we know it in music) is supposed to occur at approximately three feet per second of movement. This device,

however, picks up movement of any duration or speed at the exact time that it begins or ends.

The ground effect machine is made from a General Motors refrigerator part which is designed as a platform to raise the 440 lb. weight of a refrigerator a fraction of an inch off the ground by the intake of air from a vacuum cleaner, thus making it possible to move the 440 lbs. with ease. The engineer, Per Biorn, installed two vacuum cleaner motors onto this platform so that I am in effect on a cushion of air when I use it.

I intend to utilize these devices in a set of circumstances as instruments which may or may not be efficient to the notion of completing anything. I do not feel that dance should be limited to the display of physical exertion alone; anything that can exist in a non-static state for a certain duration of time is of interest to me. My ideas are generally derived from the laws which govern the materials themselves and I attempt to allow the qualities and limitations of materials to be exposed in different situations.

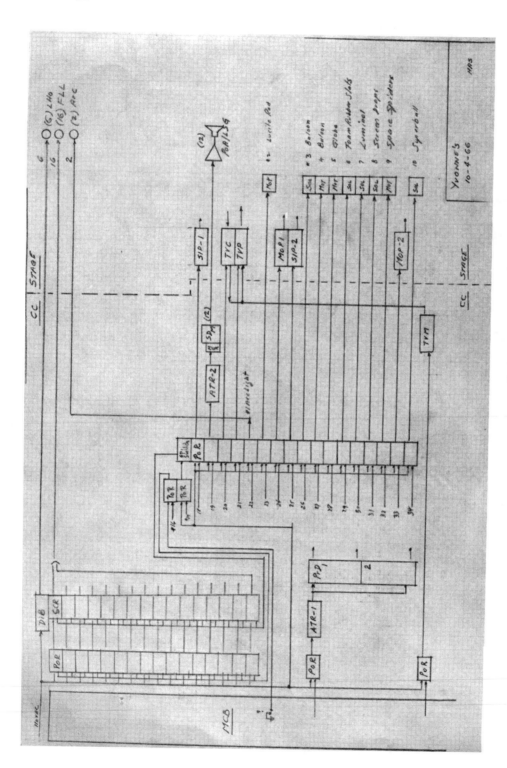

carriage discreteness

# by: Yvonne Ranier

## performance engineer: Per Biorn

performed by: Carl Andre        Letty Lou Eisenhauer   Julie Judd          Lewis Lloyd
            Becky Arnold        June Ekman             Michael Kirby       Meredith Monk
            Rosemarie Castoro   Ed Iverson             Alfred Kurchin      Steve Paxton
            William Davis       Kathy Iverson          Benjamin Lloyd      Carol Summers

stage manager: Rudy Perez

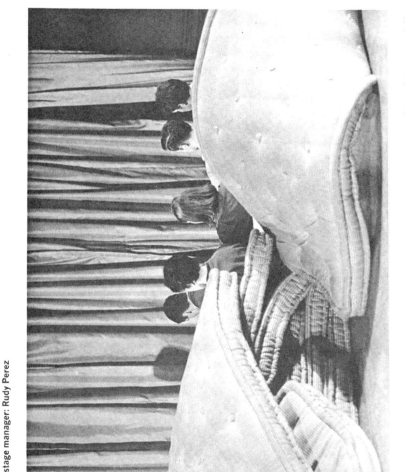

Yvonne Rainer surrounded by,
left, Steve Paxton and Debbie
Hay, right, Bob Rauschenberg
and Barbro Fahlstrom.
Photo Phil MacMullan

A dance consisting of two separate but parallel (simultaneous) continuities and two separate (but equal) control systems. 1. Performer continuity controlled by me from a remote "plotting" table where I will spontaneously choose the actions and placement of people and objects (from a pre-determined list of possibilities) and communicate those decisions to the 10-odd performers via walkie-talkie. 2. Event continuity to be controlled by TEEM (theatre electronic environment modular system) in its memory capacity. This part will consist of sequential events that will include movie fragments, slide projections, light changes, TV-monitored close-ups of details in the dance-proper, tape recorded monologues and dialogues, and various photo-chemical phenomena, several involving ultra-violet light.

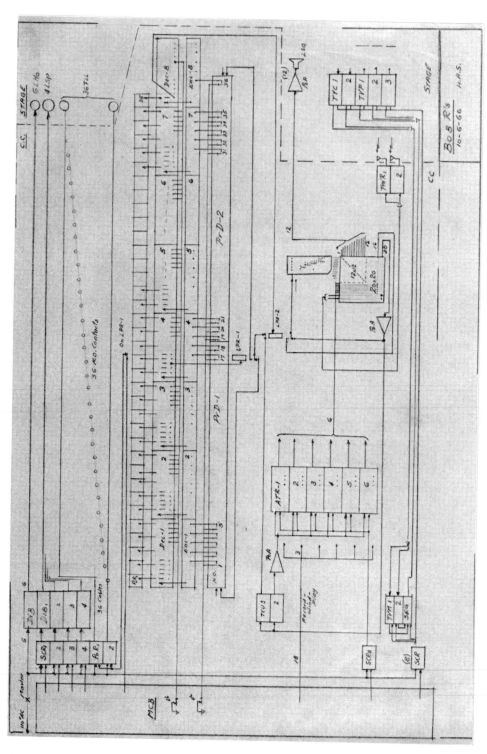

open score

# by: Robert Rauschenberg

## performance engineer: Jim McGee

cast: **Frank Stella**
**Mimi Kanarek**
a group of 500 people.

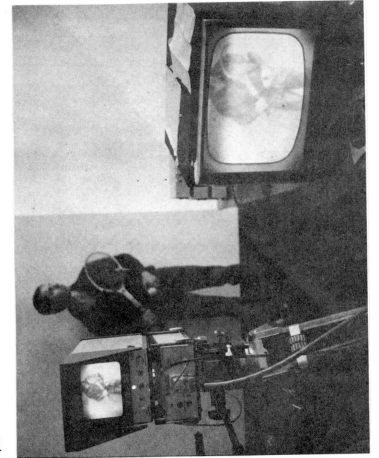

The support of the Down-town Community School is responsible for the large cast in Open Score. Through the management of Marilyn Wood and the cooperation of parents and interested par-ties, the cast has been gen-erously collected. The sources are varied and rich in intentions. The result of their voluntary involvement reaps the Downtown Com-munity School $1000 for a scholarship fund. I would like to draw attention to the fact that all the names were not available at the time this program went to press. They should all be personally re-corded, but the next best thing to do is to report that they well represent the world (our society) and are locally from such varied organiza-tions as high school science classes, drama organiza-tions, senior citizens groups, individual artists, reformed addicts club and a New York fencing club. I am touched by the positive support, work, art, love and people.

My piece begins with an authentic tennis game with rackets wired for transmis-sion of sound. The sound of the game will control the lights. The game's end is the moment the hall is totally dark. The darkness is illu-sionary. The hall is flooded with infra-red (so far invis-ible to the human eye). A modestly choreographed cast of from 300 to 500 people will enter and be ob-served and projected by in-fra-red television on large screens for the audience. This is the limit of the reali-zation of the piece to date.

Tennis is movement. Put in the context of theater it is a formal dance improvisa-tion. The unlikely use of the game to control the lights and to perform as an orches-tra interests me. The con-flict of not being able to see an event that is taking place right in front of one except through a reproduction is the sort of double exposure of action. A screen of light and a screen of darkness.

[Press Release]

MAINTAIN A CONSTRUCTIVE CLIMATE
FOR THE RECOGNITION OF THE NEW
TECHNOLOGY AND THE ARTS BY A
CIVILIZED COLLABORATION BETWEEN
GROUPS UNREALISTICALLY DEVELOP-
ING IN ISOLATION. ELIMINATE THE
SEPARATION OF THE INDIVIDUAL FROM
TECHNOLOGICAL CHANGE AND EXPAND
AND ENRICH TECHNOLOGY TO GIVE THE
INDIVIDUAL VARIETY, PLEASURE AND
AVENUES FOR EXPLORATION AND IN-
VOLVEMENT IN CONTEMPORARY LIFE.
ENCOURAGE INDUSTRIAL INITIATIVE IN
GENERATING ORIGINAL FORETHOUGHT,
INSTEAD OF A COMPROMISE IN AFTER-
MATH, AND PRECIPITATE A MUTUAL
AGREEMENT IN ORDER TO AVOID THE
WASTE OF A CULTURAL REVOLUTION.

# The Pavilion

## Billy Klüver

The initial concern of the artists who designed the Pavilion was that the quality of the experience of the visitor should involve choice, responsibility, freedom, and participation. The Pavilion would not tell a story or guide the visitor through a didactic, authoritarian experience. The visitor would be encouraged as an individual to explore the environment and compose his own experience. As a work of art, the Pavilion and its operation would be an open-ended situation, an experiment in the scientific sense of the word.

This idea for an exhibition space corresponded, we found out later, to the notions of the originators of Expo—Kenzo Tange, Arata Isozaki, Yoshiaki Tono, and others—whose objectives were to create a technologically advanced environment in which people could participate.

World exhibitions during the nineteenth century played a crucial role in letting people experience at firsthand a new machine or process. I am quoting from a pamphlet about the Paris Exposition of 1889:

> In the Gallery of Machines are huge machines which make paper. Enormous crowds are drawn about these huge vats and smoking wheels. . . . These machines operate in front of visitors who cannot take their eyes off this fantastic machine, where one can see paper pulp arrive in a state of liquid form in two large vats and then leave at the opposite end of the machine in the form of a continuous roll of dry and sturdy paper. . . .[1]

In the twentieth century efficient means of spreading technical information have developed and now the emphasis is on the individual's relationship to the environment. This is a change in attitude away from concern for the object—its engineering, operation and function, and toward aesthetics—human motivation and involvement, pleasure, interest, excitement.

The artist is a positive force in perceiving how technology can be translated to new environments to serve needs and provide variety and enrichment of life. He may be the only one who can transcend cultural bias and deal with the individuals of a culture on their own terms. The direct, straight-ahead sensibility of the active artist is needed in these difficult problems. Based on this commitment to the artist, one of E.A.T.'s objectives in relation to the Pavilion was to demonstrate physically the variety and multiplicity of experiences that the new technology can provide for the individual.

The Pavilion was a living responsive environment. The Fog surrounding the Pavilion responded to the meteorological conditions; the Suntrak sculpture was to follow the path of the sun; the moving floats reacted to physical contact. The inside of the Pavilion was an experiment in individual experience. It represented a new form of theatre space, which completely surrounded the audience and where every part of the space had the same theatrical intensity for the individual.

The space in the Mirror was gentle and poetic, rich and always changing. It was complex in spite of its simplicity. We discovered new and complicated relationships every day, optical effects that no one had described before. As theatre space it was unique. It was a tangible space; the effect was not psychological as in the case of someone witnessing a drama on stage. Instead, the visitor became part of the total theatre experience. Anything that one did in this environment was beautiful.

The sound system was constructed for automated control, which could be overridden by live manipulation. The system was designed for the spherical symmetry of the space and to preserve the basic concept of the visitor's free choice in the space. Sounds could be moved in patterns; but, for instance, it would be impossible to begin a sound at a given speaker, rotate it around the dome, and stop it exactly at the same speaker. Exact synchronization and time sequencing were impossible to accomplish. Instead the sound space was as open-ended and changing as the image space.

Traditionally, the artist assumes complete personal responsibility for his work. In the types of collaborations we set up, this approach was assumed. Most of the work on specific elements was done through collaborations that involved over seventy-five engineers and artists and industries in Japan and different parts of the United States. The people who were responsible for, and interested in, a particular aspect made the decisions. If a problem arose, it would go to the person concerned: the Fog, the Mirror, the lights, the shape of the entrance tunnel. In this way, all decisions had the same intensity.

If all the separate sections of a project are to be of the best quality, then they must develop independently. Interfacing of the various elements becomes the overriding problem and good communication between members of the project is necessary. This horizontal operating situation requires that each member of the group understand his responsibility as well as his limitations. Complications arose when engineering and aesthetic considerations became confused: when engineers wanted to be artists, when accountants wanted to be engineers, or when artists were intimidated by engineering. The artist had to express his aesthetic criteria in order to determine the scale, and so that the engineer would be aware of the boundary conditions.

To these internal complications were added difficulties of dealing with unfamiliar Japanese business practices, the unknowns of the Expo '70 situation, and the pressure of tight time schedules. In this context, of course, we made mistakes. We remained committed too long to "experiments" in Japan in making a hard mirror panel where the technology they were using was obviously inadequate. It was only when time schedules grew dangerously short and results were unacceptable that we switched to the negative-pressure, air-structure mirror.

Originally, we had believed that the traffic flow would present a problem since the visitor could stay as long as he wanted. We found that this was a complete misunderstanding of the effect of the Expo environment on the visitor who wanted to see as many pavilions as possible in one day. We found that an effort had to be made to attract his attention and then he would become involved in the space. Even a simple demonstration of the effects of the Mirror would make people walk around and explore their images.

Several systems required corrective measures after being installed on the site—particularly the fog system, the sound system, and the interior light system. We failed to realize the Suntrak sculpture. A weak joint buckled when it was assembled. The Suntrak was dismantled for the formal opening, with the understanding that it would be reconstructed. It was removed and never rebuilt.

As the Pavilion stood, it was surrounded by a magnificent Fog sculpture. The combination of the Clam Room and the Mirror Room represented an architectural space of great beauty. The moving sculptures outside the Pavilion created a macroscopic physical environment that changed continuously and that affected the movement of the people waiting in line outside the Pavilion. The ninety-foot diameter spherical Mirror and the sound system opened up the

possibility for performances that would be as integral to the space as in Shakespeare's Globe Theatre.

Both the Fog and the Mirror were "firsts" in terms of scale. In addition, their technology had further applications. The Fog surrounding the Pavilion was the largest water-vapor mass ever produced without the use of chemicals. The insistence on using pure water for the Fog led to a system that offered interesting possibilities for environmental irrigation systems, outdoor air conditioning, and protection of crops from frost. The Mirror was the largest spherical mirror ever made and was the first use of a Melinex, negative-pressure, air structure. It used the inside reflective surface of a sphere for the first time. It is conceivable that this method of making a concave reflective surface could be used in making various types of antennas.

Live programming was designed to use the space in an organic way. The hardware ideas were so rich in possibilities that the concept of a continuously changing environment developed organically. A changing group of four artists (composers, dancers, painters, or scientists) were to reside at the Pavilion at all times and determine the activities and programming. The sound and light systems, as well as the floor space, the hand-set system, and the Mirror were designed taking into account the demands of this continuously changing environment. The Pavilion became theatre conceived of as a total instrument, using every available technology in which the accumulated experience of all the programmers expanded and enriched the possibilities of the space. The programming and operations of the Pavilion were as important as the design of the hardware. Leading artists in Japan and the United States agreed to be resident programmers during Expo '70.

The following programs were presented: Harry Harper and Jacquelyn Farrell, representing Roger Payne of the Whale Fund, produced an underwater environment using recordings of humpback whales singing. The handsets gave information to the visitors about the brains, feeding habits, and communication of these near-extinct mammals.

David Tudor made nine programs using the unique properties of the sound-modification system that he had helped to design. Three of the programs were recorded by Sony. "Pepscillator" used the modification system to set up an oscillation that was switched from speaker to speaker at various rates and in different patterns. "Pepsibird" and "Anima Pepsi" both drew upon the sound library E.A.T. had compiled, and used environmental and "microscopic" sounds such as a beetle walking, ultrasonic bat sounds, earth vibrations, and nerve impulses.

Takumi Hijikata provided a Japanese mime dancer who performed to the sounds of traditional funeral chants, a thunderstorm, and the cawing of a crow. Japanese wedding robes were hung at different heights, where they revolved in the Mirror dome.

Pauline Oliveros also composed music especially for the Pavilion. "Pep-Psi" was a recording of mantras by two Chinese girls singing and playing a cello and accordion. The hostesses were asked to sing with the mantras and to guide the visitors in exploring the sound-reflective qualities of the dome.

Rikuro Miyai's two-part program was called "Shadows Left on the Moon." In one part a juggler performed to the rhythms of traditional Japanese folk festival music. His tricks demonstrated many of the optical qualities of the dome. A white ball was thrown up and appeared to fall twice on the other side of the dome. The second part of the program used New Rock and dancers in fluorescent suits who left shadows of arms and hands on each other when the suits were flashed with a strobe.

Bob Whitman had prepared a program that used slides and Japanese and English words played in many ways on the sound system, but it was never performed.

The Pavilion was a work of art with its own unity and integrity, as well as a new unexplored theatre and concert space, a recording studio for multichannel compositions and a field laboratory for scientific experiments. Social scientists had already expressed an interest in making studies of how visitors reacted to various situations. Architects were interested in the free flow of people through the Pavilion. Scientific measurements of the Fog and its reaction to the weather were being made daily. Measurements of the optical properties of the Mirror, many of which had never been seen or explained before, were underway. During the month that we operated and programmed the Pavilion, it functioned on all these levels.

On April 25, at the request of Pepsi-Cola, E.A.T. turned over the programming, operations, and maintenance of the Pavilion to Pepsi-Cola, Japan.
　—Billy Klüver
　　August, 1970

## Postscript

The Pepsi-Cola project was remarkable in its attempt to involve contemporary artists in a nonart situation. This attempt raised a number of interesting questions particularly in the area of the relation of the artist to industry and the legal position of the artist in society, which were dramatized by the breakdown in our relationship with Pepsi over the programming of the Pavilion. The usual form of industrial support of the arts is patronage of existing art or art forms. In this project the artist was considered a resource in an actual physical situation with a functional end. The fact that there was no recognized definition of this role of the artist was at the root of the misunderstandings.

Traditionally, the artist operates in a legal, institutional, and value structure of his own, which is different from some standard practices in the rest of society, some of the peculiarities of which are recognized by law: works of art can be imported duty free, even if they are made of taxable materials; a serious work of art is not subject to the usual standards of obscenity laws. The artist does not copyright his work; he has no control over it after it is sold, except that it cannot be changed. Furthermore, the artist takes his material from his environment and is not required to get permission or pay for rights—Andy Warhol's *Brillo Box* series is a famous example. Further, if the work of one artist is clearly derivative from the work of another, he is dismissed as a bad artist. Underlying this whole complex of values and practices there is the assumption of consistency and integrity of authorship. These operational, quasi-legal, and legal aspects of the artist's activity must be taken into account if he is to be able to contribute effectively as a resource outside his own field.

In the specific case of the Pepsi-Cola Pavilion, I suggested the following solution to Donald Kendall, President of PepsiCo., Inc., in a letter, April 8, 1970:

> . . . As you know, the Pavilion and the programming were designed through a collaboration of a large number of contemporary artists, engineers, scientists, and other professionals. The question that has arisen comes from the legal distinction between a work of fine art and a commercial product, or more specifically between the creative artist and the commercial artist or designer.
>
> Our legal relationship to Pepsi-Cola has developed so that the artists are put in the category of commercial

**225**

artists designing a commercial product. One consequence of this is that we must obtain rights from all artists and engineers and others involved, particularly with regard to use of the Pavilion after Expo '70. Of course, there is no question of Pepsi's ownership and right to use and exhibit the Pavilion during Expo '70. Our dilemma is whether the artists have created a work of fine art or a work of commercial art to which there are rights which must be guaranteed.

Traditionally, the artist claims no "rights" to his work: his commitment to originality is unquestioned and he contributes his work to the world when it is finished. It is created for the benefit of the individual who experiences it, and its benefits are free for everyone to use.

The Pepsi project was undertaken in this spirit; and it was this sense of commitment and energy among the artists and engineers that you commented on to me during your visit. The individuals participating in this project have created a large and complex work of art. To the Japanese and American art critics who have seen the Pavilion, the ability of the contemporary artist to participate in a project of this scale is an outstanding achievement and radically expands the social possibilities of art.

I am asking you to have Pepsi-Cola treat the Pavilion as a work of art.

. . . . . . . . . . . . . . . . . . . . . .

A decision to recognize the Pepsi Pavilion as a work of art and to treat it as such will set a much-needed precedent in this area. The project will be a model for future industrial participation in projects where the artist moves into society and involves increasing numbers of people in his work. Pepsi-Cola will be recognized and appreciated not only as a major art patron of our time, but more important, as an outstanding innovator in the contemporary arts. . . .

Although Pepsi-Cola was not willing to take this step, the existence of the Pavilion was a tribute to the possibilities inherent in a close working relationship between the artist and industry, which can and will develop in the future.
—March, 1971

Note

1. *Les Merveilles de l'Exposition de 1889: Histoire, Construction, Inauguration. Description Détaillée des Palais des Annexes et des Parcs . . . Rédlgé par des Écnivains Spéciaux et des Ingénieurs* (Paris: À la Librairie Illustrée, 1889), p. 927.

Acknowledgments

The achievement of the Pavilion Project was the unique way in which it successfully combined the talents of so many people. This is a list of those involved.

Design and Construction

Initial Artists: Robert Breer, Forrest Myers, David Tudor, Robert Whitman

Executive Coordinator: Billy Klüver

Staff: Bruce Blugerman, Mimi Clementi, Harriet De Long, Kaaba Dijon, Tom Gormley, Terrie Holland, Elizabeth Joyce, Nancy Kahan, Penelope Kullaway, David MacDermott, Gloria Malerba, Ellen Marcus, Julie Martin, Ann Ohlmacher, Peter Poole, Mana Sarabhai, Jacquelyn Serwer, Merlin Stone, Robert Whitman

E.A.T. Consultants: George Edwards, Karl Erik Friberg, Rubin Gorewitz, Robert McFarland, Lys McLaughlin, Robert Mulreany, Simone Swan, David Woodbridge

Coordinator in Japan: Fujiko Nakaya

Coordinating Architect: John Pearce

# 15. [Introduction]
# Cybernated Art

One tendency of video art, since its beginning, has been to be cybernetic, to be interactive, to be new media. Another (independent) tendency has been to create an always-already history. Both of these can be seen in the work of Nam June Paik, who is considered the first video artist.

Paik was among the first to use televisions in art, altering them as John Cage had altered pianos. Paik used one of the first Sony portable video cameras to create video art of Fluxus performances and the Pope's visit to New York. When showing the latter, he distributed a leaflet asserting "the cathode ray tube will replace the canvas." He integrated video with live performance in unusual and provocative ways—such as his *TV Bra for Living Sculpture* collaboration with Charlotte Moorman (part of a series for which they were arrested on indecency charges several times), and his *Robot K–456* collaboration with Shuya Abe (with whom he also pioneered video synthesis). He coined the term "information superhighway" and created novel satellite broadcast artworks. He also wrote the manifesto reprinted below, which provides a cybernetic/Buddhist context for his work, and a connection with the documents from E.A.T. (◊14), Roy Ascott (◊10), and Norbert Wiener (◊04) in this volume. While Paik has not been a leader in the interactive installations (as opposed to performances) now associated with new media video, the work of interactive video pioneers such as Bill Viola (◊31), Grahame Weinbren ⊗, and Lynn Hershman ⊗ (◊44) (as well, perhaps, as Myron Krueger, ◊25) can be seen as lying in a cybernetic video direction he defined—as can the video/robotic performance work of artists ranging from Mark Pauline of Survival Research Labs to Adrianne Wortzel.

Of course, the canonization of Paik cannot now be invoked without a mention of how Paik's place in video art history was nearly co-produced with the pieces that now make up that history, in a process that reveals our culture as much as it reveals the nature of video art. Even Viola, who later in video art's trajectory seemed to take up the mantle of centrality that had previously been Paik's, remembers in "History, 10 Years, and the Dreamtime" that, "In 1974 people were already talking about a video history, and had been for a few years. I remember sitting in a Chinese restaurant in New York on a cold February evening with some friends . . . Someone started talking about video history: 'Video may be the only art form ever to have a history before it had a history.' Video was being invented and simultaneously so were its myths and culture heroes . . ." (123). Martha Rosler pulls no punches regarding the culturally-loaded elements from which Paik's myth is composed:

> The elements of the myth thus include an Eastern visitor from a country [Korea] ravaged by war (our war) who was inoculated by the leading U.S. avant-garde master [John Cage] while in technology heaven (Germany), who, once in the States repeatedly violated the central shrine, TV, and then goes to face the representative of God on earth, capturing his image to bring to the avant-garde, and who then went out from it to pull together the two ends of the American cultural spectrum by symbolically incorporating the consciousness industry into the methods and ideas of the cultural apparatus—always with foundation, government, museum, broadcast, and other institutional support.

> And—oh yes!—he is a man. The hero stands up for masculine mastery and bows to patriarchy, if only in representation. The thread of his work includes the fetishization of a female body as an instrument that plays itself, and the complementary thread of homage to other famous male artist-magicians or seers (quintessentially, Cage). (45)

This picture is, of course, incomplete. For example, in Paik's work with Moorman (who played the cello nearly nude) he also presented a piece in which men displayed their dancing penises through a curtain (though it is true that this male fetishization didn't get written as prominently into video art's

Lynn Hershman's interactive video work began with her 1979–83 *Lorna* ⊗. Grahame Weinbren's pionnering work in the form included the 1986 collaboration with Roberta Friedman *The Erl King* ⊗ and, in 1991, *Sonata* ⊗.

Adrianne Wortzel, before working with robots in her art, created an artifactual Web fiction called "The Electronic Chronicles" ⊗ which appeared in 1994–95.

**227**

history). Yet this incompleteness should not cause us to leave Rosler's point aside, or fail to consider more closely our own roles in mythology construction. We need not look far for an example. In creating *The New Media Reader* the dangers of mythologizing manifested themselves constantly. The importance of figures such as Ted Nelson should certainly be recognized, but it is also important to note that even Nelson does not feel that he invented hypertext or new media—considering instead that he discovered something already present, but undefined, unexplored. The Web particularly seems to demand a too-early history of "great men." Yet the ideas influencing new media are so varied that it is difficult enough to determine important influences from decades ago. Rather than obsessively seek to name one handful of important names for a world-wide system still in its youth, it seems more appropriate to support and expand the possibilities for its diversity.
—NWF

Further Reading

Hanhardt, John G., with Jon Ippolito. *The Worlds of Nam June Paik*. Guggenheim Museum exhibition catalog. New York: Harry N. Abrams, 2000.

Kac, Eduardo. "Origin and Development of Robotic Art." *Digital Reflections: The Dialogue of Art and Technology*, special issue on Electronic Art, ed. Johanna Drucker, *Art Journal* 56(3):60–67. New York: CAA, 1997.

Rossler, Martha. "Video: Shedding the Utopian Moment." *Illuminating Video: An Essential Guide to Video Art*, 30–50. Ed. Doug Hall and Sally Jo Fifer. New York: Aperture/BAVC, 1990.

Viola, Bill. "History, 10 Years, and the Dreamtime." *Video: A Retrospective, 1974–1984*, 18–23. Ed. Kathy Rae Huffman. Long Beach, Calif.: Long Beach Museum of Art, 1984. Reprinted in Bill Viola, *Reasons for Knocking at an Empty House*, 121–135. Ed. Robert Violette. Cambridge: MIT Press, 1995.

Original Publication: From *Manifestos,* p. 24. Great Bear Pamphlets. New York: Something Else Press, 1966.

# Cybernated Art
## Nam June Paik

Cybernated art is very important, but art for cybernated life is more important, and the latter need not be cybernated.

(Maybe George Brecht's simplissimo is the most adequate.)

But if Pasteur and Robespierre are right that we can resist poison only through certain built-in poison, then some specific frustrations, caused by cybernated life, require accordingly cybernated shock and catharsis. My everyday work with video tape and the cathode-ray tube convinces me of this.

Cybernetics, the science of pure relations, or relationship itself, has its origin in karma. Marshall McLuhan's famous phrase "Media is message" was formulated by Norbert Wiener in 1948 as "The signal, where the message is sent, plays equally important role as the signal, where message is not sent."

As the Happening is the fusion of various arts, so cybernetics is the exploitation of boundary regions between and across various existing sciences.

Newton's physics is the mechanics of power and the unconciliatory two-party system, in which the strong win over the weak. But in the 1920's a German genius put a tiny third-party (grid) between these two mighty poles (cathode and anode) in a vacuum tube, thus enabling the weak to win over the strong for the first time in human history. It might be a Buddhistic "third way," but anyway this German invention led to cybernetics, which came to the world in the last war to shoot down German planes from the English sky.

The Buddhists also say

Karma is samsara

Relationship is metempsychosis

We are in open circuits

# 16. [Introduction]
# A Research Center for Augmenting Human Intellect

Demonstrations have had an important, perhaps even central, place in new media innovation. In some centers of new media, the traditional knowledge-work dictum of "publish or perish" is replaced by "demo or die."

This essay documents what is called the "mother of all demos," which took place at the 1968 Fall Joint Computer Conference in San Francisco. On the stage was Douglas Engelbart, with a huge projection screen behind him. Backstage was Bill English, and back in Menlo Park were most of the crew of their Augmentation Research Center (ARC). The demonstration showed ARC's work to date—combining Engelbart's concepts, English's project leadership, and the dedicated work of ARC members (many of whom, inspired by their experiences with ARC, would go on to lead high-profile research efforts in corporate and university settings).

The demonstration was a huge, calculated risk. Live, public demonstrations of interactive computing were unheard of at the time. Any number of things could have gone wrong—with the temporary setup in San Francisco, the main system in Menlo Park, or the hodgepodge, pre-Internet connection (carried from Menlo Park by microwave). They took the risk because they believed in the power of the system they were planning to show, and thought only a live demonstration could convince the computing mainstream of the importance of their research.

This demonstration was filmed and audiotaped ⊗.

The hundreds in attendance rose to their feet in a standing ovation. "Every book devoted to personal computing at some point reports this famous presentation," Thierry Bardini writes in *Bootstrapping* (138).

In the years that followed, it was others, outside of ARC, who received the resources to continue the work introduced to the world that day. Bob Taylor, who while in government had been central to the funding of Engelbart's efforts, was eventually hired by Xerox to establish their nearby PARC (Palo Alto Research Center). ARC's research slowed, and the project was eventually sold by the Stanford Research Institute to a commercial company. Many ARC staffers went to PARC, where Engelbart's inventions were deployed toward quite different goals. The new goals, using a foundation of Engelbart's work, were defined by Xerox, refined by Apple, and then adopted by Microsoft to become today's dominant computing environment. Consider the differences between ARC's work and that which followed:

(1)
(a) ARC was creating tools for users to express and share concept structures, with hard copy production as only one of many use goals for these structures (see statements 1b and 3c of the following selection, and Engelbart's 1962 "Framework" document, partially reprinted in this volume (◊08) ⊗).
(b) The new goals led instead to WYSIWYG layout tools, with little provision for keeping track of any information besides that required to produce tidy-looking paper documents. (Perhaps because, as Ted Nelson says, "Xerox was a paper-whalloping company.")

Hierarchy, quite evident in the organization of the following essay, is important for the sort of augmentation that Engelbart and other new media pioneers have envisioned. ARC made powerful use of hierarchy for fluidly creating different types of summaries and vectors through documents. Engelbart's hierarchies, like Ted Nelson's (◊11), can be complexly interconnected. Nelson's hierarchies, however, are strongly presented as temporary, reconfigurable, the result of a particular "sort" of the information. In Nelson's paper, links are long-lasting, while hierarchies are unstable. (Gilles Deleuze and Félix Guattari's figure of "trees within rhizomes" has been considered evocative of this (◊27).) Engelbart's hierarchies are more fundamental, and were part of the document-authoring process at ARC.

◊08
93

◊09
109

◊11
133

**231**

Hierarchy can be powerful, and yet should not be prematurely imposed; thus, a number of tools have emerged that attempt to allow users to author with Engelbart/Nelson style statements and links from which a hierarchy can emerge as work progresses (rather than be determined from the outset). Commercial examples of such programs include Tinderbox from Eastgate Systems. Emerging research systems include VKB (Visual Knowledge Builder), created by Frank Shipman as the next stage of research initiated with Cathy Marshall (the primary creator of the seminal Aquanet spatial hypertext system). Information hierarchies also allow for powerful "zooming interfaces," which have a history stretching back to Ivan Sutherland's Sketchpad (◊09), and include Ted Nelson's stretchtext and hypermap designs (◊21), MIT's Spatial Data Management system (◊33), the Pad project lead by Ken Perlin, as well the Jazz project, initiated by Ben Bederson as an open-source successor to his own Pad++. Hierarchy, of course, also exists in the organization of most Web sites, with the user given access via navigation/ location portions of each screen. Notice that ARC's 1968 system anticipates and exceeds these current conventions (see section 3d of the paper) by treating the entire site/document as an integrated knowledge structure that can be addressed at multiple levels of granularity (as with Nelson's independent formulations).

◊21
301

◊27
405

◊33
485

**232**

Engelbart's contributions were masked, perhaps, by the fact they were not united in a systematic "desktop metaphor." This metaphor, important as it was, now is fading. It is being abandoned, for example, by most of those designing handheld devices. Further, the Aqua interface to Macintosh OS X brings a new set of interface conventions de-emphasizing the traditional desktop. As Microsoft continues to follow Apple's lead in interface design, the desktop metaphor could become a memory. When this happens, the essential nature of Engelbart's contributions will become even more clear.

(2)

(a) ARC worked on the creation of tools for expert computer users, assuming that future knowledge workers would spend many hours a week working at terminals. Engelbart's belief was that, just as a carpenter has tools that require expertise, and a bicycle messenger doesn't still use training wheels, computer interfaces should be optimized for expert use and could require an up-front investment to learn.

(b) The new goals led instead to the "user friendly" systems at which most of us spend our days—systems designed to be optimal for a first-time user, rather than a skilled worker. Some programs pay back a learning investment (e.g., three dimensional modeling systems), but the basic interface and file structure retains an outmoded desktop/paper "user friendly" metaphor.

(3)

(a) ARC worked on a "bootstrapping" principle—in which users would use their tools both for their work and for the creation of better tools. Engelbart envisioned users creating tools, sharing tools, and altering the tools of others.

(b) The new goals produced instead the software industry we know today, with its generally vast gulf between users and creators, and its aggressive moves against software "piracy." (Some of Engelbart's goals, however, live on in the free software movement.)

(4)

(a) Engelbart's primary goal was to allow people to work together to solve difficult problems more easily (see his "Framework"). For this reason, networking and shared information spaces were essential.

(b) Engelbart's insistence on network communication and shared resources made him seem anachronistic in the era of the Altair, the Apple II, and then the PC boom. It was only with the arrival of the mainstream Internet that Engelbart's insistence on these points came to be appreciated as absolutely correct.

The following essay introduced the mouse, and the name stuck, although Engelbart's name for the word-processing cursor didn't: "bug" (4b2a2). The "proposed ARPA computer network" (5c6a) is what became the ARPANet, and eventually the Internet. ARC created the first NIC (Network Information Center) for this network.

—NWF

◊26
391

◊36
543

For more discussion of Free Software, see Richard Stallman's "GNU Manifesto" (◊36). For an inspiring discussion of the work on user-created tools carried out at PARC, see Alan Kay and Adele Goldberg's paper on "Personal Dynamic Media" (◊26). A vision of computer interfaces as tools for expert workers continues in authors such as Pelle Ehn and Morten Kyng; see their "Cardboard Computers" (◊45).

◊45
649

Further Reading

Goldberg, Adele, ed. *A History of Personal Workstations*. New York: ACM Press History Series, 1988.

Bardini, Thierry. *Bootstrapping*. Stanford, Calif.: Stanford University Press, 2000.

Rheingold, Howard. *Tools for Thought: The People and Ideas Behind the Next Computer Revolution*. New York: Simon & Schuster, 1985; Cambridge: MIT Press, 2000.

Shipman, Frank, Catherine Marshall, and Mark LeMere. "Beyond Location: Hypertext Workspaces and Non-Linear Views." *Proceedings of ACM Hypertext '99*, 121–130. 1999.

Marshall, Catherine, Frank Halasz, Russ Rogers, and William Janssen. "Aquanet: a hypertext tool to hold your knowledge in place," *Proceedings of ACM Hypertext '91*, 261–275. 1991.

Perlin, Ken and David Fox. "Pad: An Alternative Approach to the Computer Interface." *Computer Graphics* 26(3):57–64. *(Proceedings of ACM SIGGRAPH '93)* 1993.

Bederson, Ben, Jon Meyer, and Lance Good. "Jazz: An Extensible Zoomable User Interface Graphics Toolkit in Java." *Proceedings of ACM UIST 2000*, 171–180. 2000.

Original Publication

*AFIPS Conference Proceedings* 33, part 1, 395–410. Fall Joint
Computer Conference, 1968.

# A Research Center for Augmenting Human Intellect

## Douglas Engelbart and William English

## 1 Summary

*1a* This paper describes a multisponsor research center at Stanford Research Institute in man-computer interaction.

> *1a1* For its laboratory facility, the Center has a time-sharing computer (65K, 24-bit core) with a 4.5 megabyte swapping drum and a 96 megabyte file-storage disk. This serves twelve CRT work stations simultaneously.

> > *1a1a* Special hardware completely removes from the CPU the burden of display refreshing and input sampling, even though these are done directly out of and into core.

> > *1a1b* The display in a user's office appears on a high-resolution (875-line) commercial television monitor, and provides both character and vector portrayals. A relatively standard typewriter keyboard is supplemented by a five-key handset used (optionally) for entry of control codes and brief literals. An SRI cursor device called the "mouse" is used for screen pointing and selection.

> > > *1a1b1* The "mouse" is a hand-held X-Y transducer usable on any flat surface; it is described in greater detail further on.

> *1a2* Special-purpose high-level languages and associated compilers provide rapid, flexible development and modification of the repertoire of service functions and of their control procedures (the latter being the detailed user actions and computer feedback involved in controlling the application of these service functions).

*1b* User files are organized as hierarchical structures of data entities, each composed of arbitrary combinations of text and figures. A repertoire of coordinated service features enables a skilled user to compose, study, and modify these files with great speed and flexibility, and to have searches, analyses data manipulation, etc. executed. In particular, special sets of conventions, functions, and working methods have been developed to air programming, logical design, documentation, retrieval, project management, team interaction, and hard-copy production.

## 2 Introduction

*2a* In the Augmented Human Intellect (AHI) Research Center at Stanford Research Institute a group of researchers is developing an experimental laboratory around an interactive, multi-console computer-display system, and is working to learn the principles by which interactive computer aids can augment their intellectual capability.

*2b* The research objective is to develop principles and techniques for designing an "augmentation system."

> *2b1* This includes concern not only for the technology of providing interactive computer service, but also for changes both in ways of conceptualizing, visualizing, and organizing working material, and in procedures and methods for working individually and cooperatively.

*2c* The research approach is strongly empirical. At the workplace of each member of the subject group we aim to provide nearly full-time availability of a CRT work station, and then to work continuously to improve both the service available at the stations and the aggregate value derived therefrom by the group over the entire range of its roles and activities.

*2d* Thus the research group is also the subject group in the experiment.

> *2d1* Among the special activities of the group are the evolutionary development of a complex hardware-software system, the design of new task procedures for the system's users, and careful documentation of the evolving system designs and user procedures.

> *2d2* The group also has the usual activities of managing its activities, keeping up with outside developments, publishing reports, etc.

> *2d3* Hence, the particulars of the augmentation system evolving here will reflect the nature of these tasks—i.e., the system is aimed at augmenting a system-development project team. Though the primary research goal is to develop principles of analysis and design so as to understand how to augment human capability, choosing

the researchers them selves as subjects yields as valuable secondary benefit a system tailored to help develop complex computer-based systems.

2e This "bootstrap" group has the interesting (recursive) assignment of developing tools and techniques to make it more effective at carrying out its assignment.

2e1 Its tangible product is a developing augmentation system to provide increased capability for developing and studying augmentation systems.

2e2 This system can hopefully be transferred, as a whole or by pieces of concept, principle and technique, to help others develop augmentation systems for aiding many other disciplines and activities.

2f In other words we are concentrating fully upon reaching the point where we can do all of our work on line—placing in computer store all of our specifications, plans, designs, programs, documentation, reports, memos, bibliography and reference notes, etc., and doing all of our scratch work, planning, designing, debugging, etc., and a good deal of our intercommunication, via the consoles.

2f1 We are trying to maximize the coverage of our documentation, using it as a dynamic and plastic structure that we continually develop and alter to represent the current state of our evolving goals, plans, progress, knowledge, designs, procedures, and data.

2g The display-computer system to support this experiment is just (at this writing) becoming operational. Its functional features serve a basic display-oriented user system that we have evolved over five years and through three other computers. Below are described the principal features of these systems.

## 3 The User System

3a Basic Facility

3a1 As "seen" by the user, the basic facility has the following characteristics:

3a1a 12 CRT consoles, of which 10 are normally located in offices of AHI research staff.

3a1b The consoles are served by an SDS 940 time-sharing computer dedicated to full-time service for this staff, and each console may operate entirely independently of the others.

3a1c Each individual has private file space, and the group has community space, on a high-speed disc with a capacity of 96 million characters.

3a2 The system is not intended to serve a general community of time-sharing users, but is being shaped in its entire design toward the special needs of the "bootstrapping" experiment.

3b Work Stations

3b1 As noted above, each work station is equipped with a display, an alphanumeric keyboard, a mouse, and a five-key handset.

3b2 The display at each of the workstations (see Figure 16.1) is provided on a high-resolution, closed-circuit television monitor.

3b3 The alphanumeric keyboard is similar to a Teletype keyboard. It has 96 normal characters in two cases. A third-case shift key provides for future expansion, and two special keys are used for system control.

Figure 16.1. Typical work station, with TV display, typewriter keyboard, mouse, and chord handset.

234

*3b4* The mouse produces two analog voltages. As the two wheels (see Figure 16.2) rotate, each changing in proportion to the X or Y movement over the table top.

*3b4a* These voltages control—via an A/D converter, the computer's memory, and the display generator—the coordinates of a tracking spot with which the user may "point" to positions on the screen.

Figure 16.2. Underside of mouse.

*3b4b* Three buttons on top of the mouse are used for special control.

*3b4c* A set of experiments, comparing (within our techniques of interaction) the relative speed and accuracy obtained with this and other selection devices showed the mouse to be better than a light pen or a joystick (see Refs. English 1 and English 2).

*3b4cl* Compared to a light pen, it is generally less awkward and fatiguing to use, and it has a decided advantage for use with raster-scan, write-through storage tube, projection, or multiviewer display systems. *3b5* The five-key handset has 31 chords or unique key-stroke combinations, in five "cases."

*3b5a* The first four cases contain lower- and upper-case letters and punctuation, digits, and special characters. (The chords for the letters correspond to the binary numbers from 1 to 26.)

*3b5b* The fifth case is "control case." A particular chord (the same chord in each case) will always transfer subsequent input-chord interpretations to control case.

*3b5c* In control case, one can "backspace" through recent input, specify underlining for subsequent input,

transfer to another case, visit another case for one character or one word, etc.

*3b5d* One-handed typing with the handset is slower than two-handed typing with the standard keyboard. However, when the user works with one hand on the handset and one on the mouse, the coordinated interspersion of control characters and short literal strings from one hand with mouse-control actions from the other yields considerable advantage in speed and smoothness of operation.

*3b5d1* For literal strings longer than about ten characters, one tends to transfer from the handset to the normal keyboard.

*3b5d2* Both from general experience and from specific experiment, it seems that enough handset skill to make its use worthwhile can generally be achieved with about five hours of practice. Beyond this, skill grows with usage.

*3c* Structure of Files

*3cl* Our working information is organized into files, with flexible means for users to set up indices and directories, and to hop from file to file by display-selection or by typed-in file-name designations. Each file is highly structured in its internal organization.

*3cla* The specific structure of a given file is determined by the user, and is an important part of his conceptual and "study-manipulate" treatment of the file.

*3c2* The introduction of explicit "structuring" to our working information stems from a very basic feature of our conceptual framework (see Refs. Engelbart 1 and Engelbart 2) regarding means for augmenting human intellect.

*3c2a* With the view that the symbols one works with are supposed to represent a mapping of one's associated concepts, and further that one's concepts exist in a "network" of relationships as opposed to the essentially linear form of actual printed records, it was decided that the concept-manipulation aids derivable from real-time computer support could be appreciably enhanced by structuring conventions that would make explicit (for both the user and the computer) the various types of network relationships among concepts.

*3c2b* As an experiment with this concept, we adopted some years ago the convention of organizing all information into explicit hierarchical structures, with provisions for arbitrary cross-referencing among the elements of a hierarchy.

3c2bl The principal manifestation of this hierarchical structure is the breaking up of text into arbitrary segments called "statements," each of which bears a number showing its serial location in the text and its "level" in an "outline" of the text. This paper is an example of hierarchical text structure.

3c2c To set up a reference link from Statement A to Statement B, one may refer in Statement A either to the location number of B or to the "name" of B. The difference is that the number is vulnerable to subsequent structural change, whereas the name stays with the statement through changes in the structure around it.

3c2cl By convention, the first word of a statement is treated as the name of the statement, if it is enclosed in parentheses. For instance, Statement 0 on the screen of Figure 16.1 is named "FJCC."

3c2c2 References to these names may be embedded anywhere in other statements, for instance as "see(AFI)," where special format informs the viewer explicitly that this refers to a statement named "AFI," or merely as a string of characters in a context such that the viewer can infer the referencing.

3c2c3 This naming and linking, when added to the basic hierarchical form, yields a highly flexible general structuring capability. These structuring conventions are expected to evolve relatively rapidly as our research progresses.

3c3 For some material, the structured statement form may be undesirable. In these cases, there are means for suppressing the special formatting in the final print out of the structured text.

3c4 The basic validity of the structured text approach has been well established by our subsequent experience.

3c4a We have found that in both off-line and on-line computer aids, the conception, stipulation, and execution of significant manipulations are made much easier by the structuring conventions.

3c4b Also, in working on line at a CRT console, not only is manipulation made much easier and more powerful by the structure, but a user's ability to get about very quickly within his data and to have special "views" of it generated to suit his need, are significantly aided by the structure.

3c4c We have come to write all of our documentation, notes, reports, and proposals according to these conventions, because of the resulting increase in our ability to study and manipulate them during composition, modification, and usage. Our programming systems also incorporate the conventions. We have found it to be fairly universal that after an initial period of negative reaction in reading explicitly structured material, one comes to prefer it to material printed in the normal form.

3d File Studying

3d1 The computer aids are used for two principal "studying" operations, both concerned with construction of the user's "views," i.e., the portion of his working text that he sees on the screen at a given moment.

3d1a Display Start

3d1a1 The first operation is finding a particular statement in the file (called the "display start"); the view will then begin with that statement. This is equivalent to finding the beginning of a particular passage in a hard-copy document.

3d1b Form of View

3d1b1 The second operation is the specification of a "form" of view—it may simply consist of a screenful of text which sequentially follows the point specified as the display start, or it may be constructed in other ways, frequently so as to give the effect of an outline.

3d1c In normal, off-line document studying, one often does the first type of operation, but the second is like a sissors-and-staple job and is rarely done just to aid one's studying.

3d1d (A third type of service operation that will undoubtedly be of significant aid to studying is question answering. We do not have this type of service.)

3d2 Specification of Display Start

3d2a The display start may be specified in several ways:

3d2a1 By direct selection of a statement which is on the display—the user simply points to any character in the statement, using the mouse.

3d2a2 If the desired display start is not on the display, it may be selected indirectly if it bears a "marker."

3d2a2a Markers are normally invisible. A marker has a name of up to five characters, and is attached to a character of the text. Referring to the marker by name (while holding down a special button) is exactly equivalent to pointing to the character with the mouse.

*3d2a2b* The control procedures make it extremely quick and easy to fix and call markers.

*3d2a3* By furnishing either the name or the location number of the statement, which can be done in either of two basic ways:

*3d2a3a* Typing from the keyboard

*3d2a3b* Selecting an occurrence of the name or number in the text. This may be done either directly or via an indirect marker selection.

*3d2b* After identifying a statement by one of the above means, the user may request to be taken directly there for his next view. Alternately, he may request instead that he be taken to some statement bearing a specified structure relationship to the one specifically identified. For instance, when the user identifies Statement 3E4 by one of the above means (assume it to be a member of the list 3E1 through 3E7), he may ask to be taken to

*3d2b1* Its successor, i.e., Statement 3E5

*3d2b2* Its predecessor, i.e., Statement 3E3

*3d2b3* Its list tail, i.e., Statement 3E7

*3d2b4* Its list head, i.e., Statement 3E1

*3d2b5* Its list source, i.e., Statement 3E

*3d2b6* Its subhead, i.e., Statement 3E4A

*3d2c* Besides being taken to an explicitly identified statement, a user may ask to go to the first statement in the file (or the next after the current location) that contains a specified word or string of characters.

*3d2c1* He may specify the search string by typing it in, by direct (mouse) selection, or by indirect (marker) selection.

*3d3* Specification of Form of View

*3d3a* The "normal" view beginning at a given location is like a frame cut out from a long scroll upon which the hierarchical set of statements is printed in sequential order. Such a view is displayed in Figure 16.1.

*3d3b* Otherwise, three independently variable view-specification conditions may be applied to the construction of the displayed view: level clipping, line truncation, and content filtering. The view is simultaneously affected by all three of these.

*3d3b1* Level: Given a specified level parameter, L (L= 1, 2, . . . , ALL), the view generator will display only those statements whose "depth" is less than or equal to L. (For example, Statement 3E4 is third level, 3E second, 4B2C1 fifth, etc.) Thus it is possible to see only first-level statements, or only first-, second-, and third-level statements, for example.

*3d3b2* Truncation: Given a specified truncation parameter, T (T=1, 2, . . . , ALL), the view generator will show only the first T lines of each statement being displayed.

*3d3b3* Content: Given a specification for desired content (written in a special high-level content-analysis language) the view generator optionally can be directed to display only those statements that have the specified content.

*3d3b3a* One can specify simple strings, or logical combinations thereof, or such things as having the word "memory" within four words of the word "allocation."

*3d3b3b* Content specifications are written as text, anywhere in the file. Thus the full power of the system may be used for composing and modifying them.

*3d3b3c* Any one content specification can then be chosen for application (by selecting it directly or indirectly). It is compiled immediately to produce a machine-code content-analysis routine, which is then ready to "filter" statements for the view generator.

*3d3c* In addition, the following format features of the display may be independently varied: indentation of statements according to level, suppression of location num bers and/or names of statements, and separation of statements by blank lines.

*3d3d* The user controls these view specifications by means of brief, mnemonic character codes. A skilled user will readjust his view to suit immediate needs very quickly and frequently; for example, he may change level and truncation settings several times in as many seconds.

*3d4* "Freezing" Statements

*3d4a* One may also pre-empt an arbitrary amount of the upper portion of the screen for holding a collection of "frozen" statements. The remaining lower portion is treated as a reduced-size scanning frame, and the view generator follows the same rules for filling it as described above.

3d4b The frozen statements may be independently chosen or dismissed, each may have line truncation independent of the rest, and the order in which they are displayed is arbitrary and readily changed. Any screen-select operand for any command may be selected from any portion of the display (including the frozen statements) .

### 3d5 Examples

3d5a Figures 16.3 and 16.4 show views generated from the same starting point with different level-clipping parameters. This example happens to be of a program written in our Machine-Oriented language (MOL, see below).

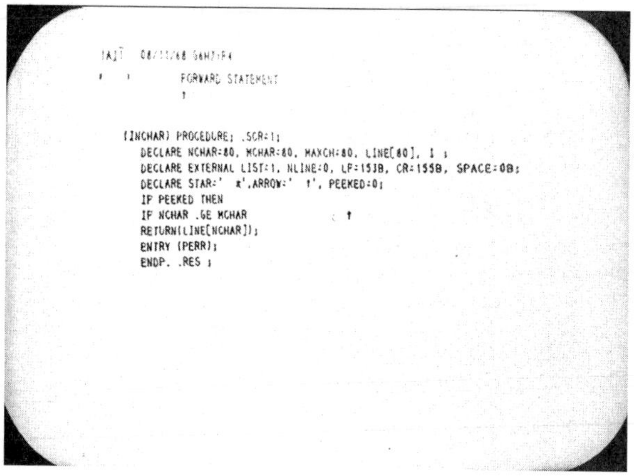

Figure 16.3. View of an MOL program, with level parameter set to 3 and truncation to 1.

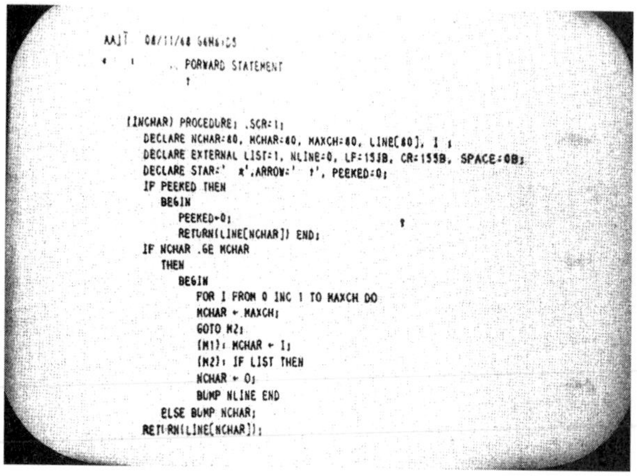

Figure 16.4. Same program as Figure 16.3, but with level parameter changed to all.

3d5b Figure 16.5 demonstrates the freezing feature with a view of a program (the same one shown in Figure 16.8) written in our Control Metalanguage (CML, see below). Statemente 3C, 3C2, 2B, 2B1, 2B2, 2B3, and 2B4 are frozen, and statements from 2J on are shown normally with L=3, T=1.

3d5b1 The freezing here was used to hold for simultaneous view four different functionally related process descriptions. The subroutines (+BUG1SPEC) and (+WAIT) were located by use of the hop-to-name feature described above.

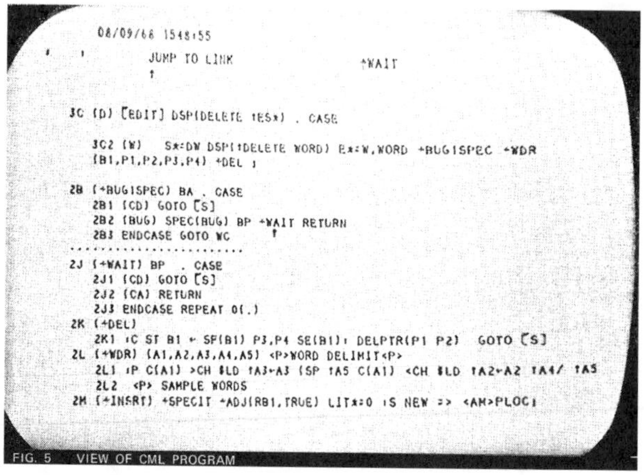

Figure 16.5. View of CML program, showing six frozen statements and illustrating use of reference hopping.

### 3e File Modification

3e1 Here we use a standard set of editing operations, specifying with each operation a particular type of text entity.

3e1a Operations: Delete, Insert, Replace, Move, Copy.

3e1b Entities (within text of statements): Character, Text (arbitrary strings), Word, Visible (print string), Invisible (gap string).

3e1c Entities (for structure manipulation): Statement, Branch (statement plus all substructure), Group (sublist of branches), Plex (complete list of branches).

3e2 Structure may also be modified by joining statements, or breaking a statement into two at a specified point.

3e3 Generally, an operation and an entity make up a command, such as "Delete Word." To specify the command, the user types the first letter of each word in the command: thus "DW" specifies "Delete Word." There are occasional cases where a third word is used or where the first letter cannot be used because of ambiguities.

3f File Output

3f1 Files may be sent to any of a number of different output devices to produce hard copy—an upper/lower-case line printer, an on-line high-quality typewriter, or paper tape to drive various typewriters.

3f1a In the future it will be possible to send files via magnetic tape to an off-line CRT-to-film system from which we can produce Xerox prints, Multilith masters, or microform records.

3f2 Flexible format control may be exercised in this process by means of specially coded directives embedded in the files—running headers, page numbering, line lengths, line centering, suppression of location numbers, indenting, right justification (hyphenless), etc., are controllable features.

3g Compiling and Debugging

3g1 Source-code files written in any of our compiler languages (see below), or in the SDS 940 assembly language (ARPAS, in which our compiler output is produced) may be compiled under on-line control. For debugging, we have made a trivial addition to the SDS 940's DDT loader-debugger so as to operate it from the CRT displays. Though it was designed to operate from a Teletype terminal, this system gains a great deal in speed and power by merely showing with a display the last 26 lines of what would have been on the Teletype output.

3h Calculating

3h1 The same small innovation as mentioned above for DDT enables us to use the CAL system from a display terminal.

3i Conferencing

3i1 We have set up a room specially equipped for on-line conferencing. Six displays are arranged in the center of a square table (see Figure 16.6) so that each of twenty participants has good visibility. One participant controls the system, and all displays show the same view. The other participants have mice that control a large arrrow on the screen, for use as a pointer (with no control function).

3i2 As a quick means of finding and displaying (with appropriate forms of view) any desired material from a very large collection, this system is a powerful aid to presentation and review conferences.

Figure 16.6. On-line conference arrangement.

3i3 We are also experimenting with it in project meetings, using it not only to keep track of agenda items and changes but also to log progress notes, action notes, etc. The review aid is of course highly useful here also.

3i4 We are anxious to see what special conventions and procedures will evolve to allow us to harness a number of independent consoles within a conference group. This obviously has considerable potential.

## 4 Service-System Software

4a The User's Control Laguage

4a1 Consider the service a user gets from the computer to be in the form of discrete operations—i.e., the execution of individual "service functions" from a repertoire comprising a "service system."

4a1a Examples of service functions are deleting a word, replacing a character, hopping to a name, etc.

4a2 Associated with each function of this repertoire is a "control-dialogue procedure." This procedure involves selecting a service function from the repertoire, setting up the necessary parameter designations for a particular application, recovering from user errors, and calling for the execution of the function.

4a2a The procedure is made up of the sequence of keystrokes, select actions, etc. made by the user, together with the interspersed feedback messages from the computer.

4a3 The repertoire of service functions, together with their control-dialogue procedures, constitutes the user's "control language." This is a language for a "master-slave" dialogue, enabling the user to control application of the computer's capabilities to his own service.

239

4a3a It seems clear that significant augmentation of one's intellectual effectiveness from the harnessing of computer services will require development of a broad and sophisticated control-language vocabulary.

4a3b It follows that the evolution of such a control language is a very important part of augmentation-system research.

4a4 For the designer of user systems, it is important to have good means for specifying the nature of the functions and their respective control-dialogue procedures, so that a design specification will be

4a4a Concise, so that its essential features are easily seen

4a4b Unambiguous, so that questions about the design may be answered clearly

4a4c Canonical, so that information is easily located

4a4d Natural, so that the form of the description fits the conceptual frame of the design

4a4e Easy to compose, study, and modify, so that the process of evolutionary design can be facilitated.

4a5 It is also important for the user to have a description of the service functions and their control-dialogue procedures.

4a5a The description must again be concise, unambiguous, canonical, and natural; furthermore, it must be accurate, in that everything relevant to the

user about the service functions and their control-dialogue procedures is described, and everything described actually works as indicated.

4b State-Chart Representation of Control-Language Design

4b1 Figure 16.7 shows a charting method that was used in earlier stages of our work for designing and specifying the control-procedure portions of the control language. Even though limited to describing only the control-dialogue procedures, this representation nonetheless served very well and led us to develop the successive techniques described below.

4b2 Figure 16.7 shows actual control procedures for four service functions from the repertoire of an interactive system: Delete Word, Delete Text, Place Up Statement, and Forward Statement.

4b2a The boxes contain abbreviated descriptions of relevant display-feedback conditions, representing the intermediate states between successive user actions. Both to illustrate how the charting conventions are used and to give some feeling for the dynamics of our user-system control procedures, we describe briefly below both the chart symbols and the associated display-feedback conventions that we have developed.

4b2a1 The writing at the top of each box indicates what is to be shown as "command feedback" at the top of the display (see Figures 16.3, 16.4 and 16.5).

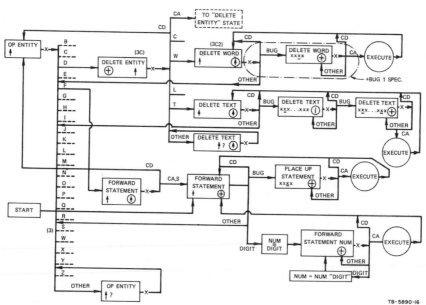

Figure 16.7. State-chart portrayal of part of the text-manipulation control language.

TB-5890-16

*4b2a1a* An uparrow sometimes appears under the first character of one of the words of Command Feedback.

> *4b2a1a1* This indicates to the user that the next character he types will be interpreted as designating a new term to replace that being pointed to—no uparrow under Command Feedback signifies that keyboard action will not affect the command designation.

*4b2a1b* "Entity" represents the entity word (i.e., "character," "word," "statement," etc.) that was last used as part of a fully specified command.

> *4b2a1b1* The computer often "offers" the user an entity option.

*4b2a2* The circle in the box indicates the character to be used for the "bug" (the tracking spot), which alternates between the characters uparrow and plus.

> *4b2a2a* The uparrow indicates that a select action is appropriate, and the plus indicates that a select action is inappropriate.

*4b2a3* The string of X's, with underlines, indicates that the selected characters are to be underlined as a means of showing the user what the computer thinks he has selected.

*4b2b* There is frequently an X on the output line from a box on the chart. This indicates that the computer is to wait until the user has made another action.

> *4b2b1* After this next action, the computer follows a branching path, depending upon what the action was (as indicated on the chart) to reach another state-description box or one of the function-execution processes.

*4c* The Control Metalanguage

*4c1* In search for an improvement over the state chart, we looked for the following special features, as well as the general features listed above:

*4c1a* A representational form using structural text so as to harness the power of our on-line text-manipulation techniques for composing, studying, and modifying our designs.

*4c1b* A form that would allow us to specify the service functions as well as the control-dialogue procedures.

*4c1c* A form such that a design-description file could be translated by a computer program into the actual implementation of the control language.

*4c2* Using our Tree Meta compiler-compiler (described below), we have developed a next step forward in our means of designing, specifying, implementing and documenting our on-line control languages. The result is called "Control Metalanguage" (CML).

> *4c2a* Figure 16.8 shows a portion of the description for the current control language, written in Control Metalanguage.
>
> > *4c2a1* This language is the means for describing both the service functions and their control-dialogue procedures.

```
3 (wc:) zap case
  3A (b) [edit] dsp(backward ↑es*) . case
  .
  .
  .
  3B (c) [edit] dsp(copy ↑es*) :s true => <am>adj1: . case

    3B1 (c) s*=cc dsp(↑copy character) e*=c,character
    +bug2spec  +cdlim(b1,p1,p2,p3,p4)
    +cdlim(b2,p5,p6,p7,p8)  +cpchtx(b1,p2,p4,pS,p6) ;

    3B2 (w) s*=cw dsp(↑copy word) e*=w,word +bug2spec
    +wdr2(b1,p1,p2,p3,p4) +wdr2(b2,p5,p6,p7,p8)
    +cpwdvs(b1,p2,p4,p5,p6) ;

    3B3 (l) s*=cl dsp(↑copy line) e*=l,line +bug2spec
    +ldlim(b1,p1,p2,p3,p4) +ldlim(b2,p5,p6,p7,p8) :c st
    b1←sf(b1) p2,  rif :p p2>p1 cr: then (cr) else (null) , p5
    p6, p4 se(b1): goto [s]

    3B4 (v) s*=cv dsp(↑copy visible) e*=v,visible +bug2spec
    +vdr2(b1,p1,p2,p3,p4) +vdr2(b2,p5,p6,p7,p8)
    +cpwdvs(b1,p2,p4,p5,p6) ;
    .
    .
    .
    3B10 endcase +caqm ;

  3C (d) [edit] dsp(delete ↑es*) . case

    3C1 (c) s*=dc dsp(↑delete character) e*=c,character
    +bug1spec  +cdlim(b1,p1,p2,p3,p4) +del;
    3C2 (w) s*=dw dsp(↑delete word) e*=w,word +bug1spec
    +wdr  (b1,p1,p2,p3,p4) +del ;
    3C3 (l) s*=dl dsp(↑delete line) e*=l,line +bug1spec...
    .
    .
    .
```

Figure 16.8. Metalanguage description of part of control language.

**4c2b** The Control Metalanguage Translator (CMLT) can process a file containing such a description, to produce a corresponding version of an interactive system which responds to user actions exactly as described in the file.

**4c3** There is a strong correspondence between the conventions for representing the control procedures in Control Metalanguage and in the state chart, as a comparison of Figures 16.8 and 16.7 will reveal.

**4c3a** The particular example printed out for Figure 16.8 was chosen because it specifies some of the same procedures as in Figure 16.7.

**4c3b** For instance, the steps of display feedback states, leading to execution of the "Delete Word" function, can readily be followed in the state chart.

**4c3b1** The steps are produced by the user typing "D," then "W," then selecting a character in a given word, and then hitting "command accept" (the CA key).

**4c3b2** The corresponding steps are outlined below for the Control Metalanguage description of Figure 16.8, progressing from Statement 3, to Statement 3c, to Statement 3c2, to Subroutine +BUGSPEC, etc.

**4c3b3** The points or regions in Figure 16.7 corresponding to these statements and subroutines are marked by (3), (3C), (3C2), and (+BUG1SPEC), to help compare the two representations.

**4c3c** The same steps are indicated in Figure 16.8, starting from Statement 3:

**4c3c1** "D" sets up the state described in Statement 3C

**4c3c2** "W" sets up the state described in Statement 3C2

**4c3c3** The subroutine +BUG1SPEC waits for the select-word (1) and CA (2) actions leading to the execution of the delete-word function.

**4c3c3a** Then the TWDR subroutine takes the bug-position parameter and sets pointers P1 through P4 to delimit the word in the text data.

**4c3c3b** Finally, the +DEL subroutine deletes what the pointers delimit, and then returns to the last-defined state (i.e., to where S* = DW) .

**4d** Basic Organization of the On-Line System (NLS)

**4d1** Figure 16.9 shows the relationships among the major components of NLS.

**4d2** The Tree Meta Translator is a processor specially designed to produce new translators.

**4d2a** There is a special language—the Tree Meta Language—for use in describing the translator to be produced.

**4d2b** A special Tree Meta library of subroutines must be used, along with the output of the Tree Meta Translator, to produce a functioning new translator. The same library serves for every translator it produces.

**4d3** For programming the various subroutines used in our 940 systems, we have developed a special Machine-Oriented Language (MOL), together with an MOL Translator to convert MOL program descriptions into machine code (see Ref. Hay 1 for a complete description) .

**4d3a** The MOL is designed to facilitate system programming, by providing a high-level language for iterative, conditional, and arithmetic operations, etc., along with a block structure and conventions for labeling that fit our structured-statement on-line manipulation aids.

**4d3a1** These permit sophisticated computer aid where suitable, and also allow the programmer to switch to machine-level coding (with full access to variables, labels, etc.) where core space, speed, timing, core-mapping arrangements, etc., are critical.

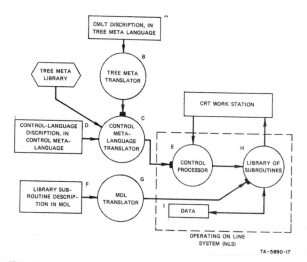

Figure 16.9. Basic organization of NLS showing use of compilers and compiler-compiler to implement it.

*4d4* The NLS is organized as follows (letters refer to Figure 16.9):

*4d4a* The Control Processor (E) receives and processes successive user actions, and calls upon subroutines in the library (H) to provide it such services as the following:

*4d4a1* Putting display feedback on the screen

*4d4a2* Locating certain data in the file

*4d4a3* Manipulating certain working data

*4d4a4* Constructing a display view of specified data according to given viewing parameters, etc.

*4d4b* The NLS library subroutines (H) are produced from MOL programs (F), as translated by the MOL Translator (G).

*4d4c* The Control Processor is produced from the control-language description (D), written in Control Metalanguage, as translated by the CMLT (C).

*4d4d* The CMLT, in turn, is produced from a description (A) written in Tree Meta, as translated by the Tree Meta Translator (B).

*4d5* Advantages of Metalanguage Approach to NLS Implementation

*4d5a* The metalanguage approach gives us improved-means for control-language specification, in terms of being unambiguous, concise, canonical, natural and easy to compose, study and modify.

*4d5b* Moreover, the Control Metalanguage specification promises to provide in itself a users' documentation that is completely accurate, and also has the above desirable characteristics to facilitate study and reference.

*4d5c* Modifying the control-dialogue procedures for existing functions, or making a reasonable range of changes or additions to these functions, can often be accomplished solely by additions or changes to the control-language record (in CML).

*4d5c1* With our on-line studying, manipulating and compiling techniques, system additions or changes at this level can be thought out and implemented (and automatically documented) very quickly.

*4d5d* New functions that require basic operations not available through existing subroutines in the NLS library will need to have new subroutines specified and pro grammed (in MOL), and then will need new terms in CML to permit these new functions to be called upon. This latter requires a change in the record (A),

and a new compilation of CMLT by means of the Tree Meta Translator.

*4d5d1* On-line techniques for writing and modifying the MOL source code (F), for executing the compilations, and for debugging the routines, greatly reduce the effort involved in this process.

## 5 Service-System Hardware (Other Than SDS 940)

*5a* In addition to the SDS 940, the facility includes peripheral equipment made by other manufacturers and equipment designed and constructed at SRI.

*5b* All of the non-SDS equipment is interfaced through the special devices channel which connects to the second memory buss through the SDS memory interface connection (MIC).

*5bl* This equipment, together with the RAD, is a significant load on the second memory buss. Not including the proposed "special operations" equipment, the maximum expected data rate is approximately 264,000 words per second or one out of every 2.1 memory cycles. However, with the 940 variable priority scheme for memory access (see Pirtle 1), we expect less than 1 percent degradation in CPU efficiency due to this load.

*5b2* This channel and the controllers (with the exception of the disc controller) were designed and constructed at SRI.

*5b2a* In the design of the hardware serving the workstations, we have attempted to minimize the CPU burden by making the system as automatic as possible in its access to memory and by formatting the data in memory so as to minimize the executive time necessary to process it for the users.

*5c* Figure 16.10 is a block diagram of the special devices channel and associated equipment. The major components are as follows:

*5c1* Executive Control

*5c1a* This is essentially a sophisticated multiplexer that allows independent, asynchronous access to core from any of the 6 controllers connected to it. Its functions are the following:

*5c1a1* Decoding instructions from the computer and passing them along as signals to the controllers.

*5c1a2* Accepting addresses and requests for memory access (input or output) from the

243

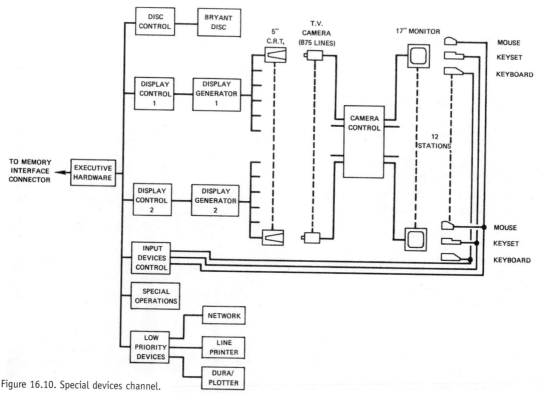

Figure 16.10. Special devices channel.

controllers, determining relative priority among the controllers, synchronizing to the computer clock, and passing the requests along to memory via the MIC.

5c1b The executive control includes a comprehensive debugging panel that allows any of the 6 controllers to be operated off-line without interfering with the operation of other controllers.

5c2 Disc File

5c2a This is a Model 4061 Bryant disc, selected for compatibility with the continued 940-system development by Berkeley's Project GENIE, where extensive file handling software was developed.

5c2b As formatted for our use, the disc will have a storage capacity of approximately 32 million words, with a data-transfer rate of roughly 40,000 words per second and average access time of 85 milliseconds.

5c2c The disc controller was designed by Bryant in close cooperation with SRI and Project GENIE.

5c3 Display System

5c3a The display systems consists of two identical subsystems, each with display controller, display generator, 6 CRT's, and 6 closed-circuit television systems.

5c3b The display controllers process display-command tables and display lists that are resident in core, and pass along display-buffer contents to the display generators.

5c3c The display generators and CRT's were developed by Tasker Industries to our specifications. Each has general character-vector plotting capability They will accept display buffers consisting of instructions (beam motion, character writing, etc.) from the controller. Each will drive six 5-inch high-resolution CRT's on which the display pictures are produced.

5c3c1 Character writing time is approximately 8 microseconds, allowing an average of 1000 characters on each of the six monitors when regenerating at 20 cps.

5c3d A high-resolution (875-line) closed-circuit television system transmits display pictures from each CRT to a television monitor at the corresponding work-station console.

5c3e This system was developed as a "best solution" to our experimental-laboratory needs, but it turned out to have properties which seem valuable for more widespread use:

5c3e1 Since only all-black or all-white signal levels are being treated, the scan beam current on the cameras can be reduced to achieve a short-term image storage effect that yields flicker-free TV output even when the display refresh rate is as low as 15 cps. This allows a display generator to sustain about four times more displayed material than if the users were viewing direct-view refreshed tubes.

5c3e2 The total cost of small CRT, TV camera, amplifier-controller, and monitor came to about $5500 per workstation— where a random-deflection, display-quality CRT of similar size would cost con siderably more and would be harder to drive remotely.

5c3e3 Another cost feature which is very important in some system environments favors this TV approach: The expensive part is centrally located; each outlying monitor costs only about $600, so terminals can be set up even where usage will be low, with some video switching in the central

establishment to take one terminal down and put another up.

5c3e4 An interesting feature of the video system is that with the flick of a switch the video signal can be inverted, so that the image picked up as bright lines on dim background may be viewed as black lines on a light background. There is a definite user preference for this inverted form of display.

5c3f In addition to the advantages noted above, the television display also invites the use of such commercially available devices as extra cameras, scan converters, video switches, and video mixers to enrich system service.

5c3f1 For example, the video image of a user's computer-generated display could be mixed with the image from a camera focused on a collaborator at another terminal; the two users could communicate through both the computer and a voice intercom. Each user would then see the other's face superimposed on the display of data under discussion.

5c3f2 Superimposed views from cameras focused on film images or drawings, or on the computer hardware, might also be useful.

5c3f3 We have experimented with these techniques (see Figure 16.11) and found them to be very effective. They promise to add a great deal to the value of remote display terminals.

5c4 Input-Device Controller

5c4a In addition to the television monitor, each work-station console has a keyboard, binary keyset, and mouse.

5c4b The controller reads the state of these devices at a preset interval (about 30 milliseconds) and writes it into a fixed location table in core.

5c4b1 Bits are added to information from the keyboards, keysets and mouse switches to indicate when a new character has been received or a switch has changed state since the last sample. If there is a new character or switch change, an interrupt is issued after the sample period.

5c4b2 The mouse coordinates are formatted as a beam-positioning instruction to the display generator. Provisions are made in the display controller for including an entry in the mouse-position table as a display buffer. This allows the mouse position to be continuously displayed without any attention from the CPU.

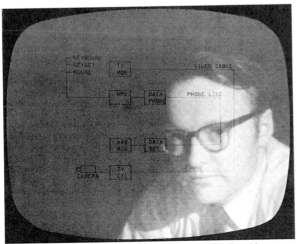

Figure 16.11. Television display obtained by mixing the video signal from a remote camera with that from the computer-generated display.

## 5c5 Special Operations

*5c5a* The box with this label in Figure 16.10 is at this time only a provision in the executive control for the addition of a high-speed device. We have tentative plans for adding special hardware here to provide opera tions not available in the 940 instruction set, such as character-string moves and string-pattern matching.

## 5c6 Low-Priority Devices

*5c6a* This controller accommodates three devices with relatively low data-transfer rates. At this time only the line printer is implemented, with provisions for adding an on-line typewriter (Dura), a plotter, and a terminal for the proposed ARPA computer network.

*5c6a1* The line printer is a Potter Model HSP-3502 chain printer with 96 printing characters and a speed of about 230 lines per minute.

6 References

6a (English 1) W K English D C Engelbart B Huddart "Computer-aided display control" Final Report Contract NAS 1-3988 SRI Project 5061 Stanford Research Institute Menlo Park California July 1965

6b (English 2) W K English D C Engelbart M L Berman "Display-selection techniques for text manipulation" *IEEE Trans on Human Factors in Electronics* Vol HFE-8 No 1 1967

6c (Engelbart 1) D C Engelbart "Augmenting human intellect: A conceptual framework Summary" Report Contract AF 49 638 1024 SRI Project 3578 Stanford Research Institute Menlo Park California October 1962

6d (Engelbart 2) D C Engelbart "A conceptual frarnework for the augmentation of man's intellect" In *Vistas in Information Handling* Vol 1 D W Howerton and D C Weeks eds Spartan Books Washington D C 1963

6e (Hay 1) R E Hay J F Rulifson "MOL940: Preliminary speifications for an ALGOL-like machine-oriented language for the SDS 940" Interim Technical Report Contract NAS 1-5940 SRI Project 5890 Stanford Research Institute Menlo Park California March 1968

6f (Pirtle 1) M Pirtle "Intercommunication of Processors and memory" *Proc Fall Joint Computer Conference* Anaheim California November 1967

Principal sponsors are:

Advanced Research Projects Agency and National Aeronautics and Space Agency (NAS1-7897), and Rome Air Development Center F30602-68-C-0286.

# 17. [Introduction]
# From *Software—Information Technology*
## *Its New Meaning for Art*

**Exhibition at the Jewish Museum, 1970**

**Documentation of projects by Theodore H. Nelson, the Architecture Machine Group, and Les Levine**

At the 1970 exhibition Software, organized by Jack Burnham, visitors were invited to do something extremely strange: operate computers. The exhibit introduced artists to an important dimension of computing, too, since it suffered from the technical problems of the same sort that still plague ordinary computer users today. Edward Shanken, a Duke University art historian, notes that in many respects it was "a disaster": the computer controlling many of the works (a PDP-8) didn't work for a month after the start of the exhibition, the gerbils that were part of *Seek* attacked each other, a showing at the Smithsonian Institution was canceled, and the show caused a financial crisis for the museum and thus the dismissal of director Karl Katz. These difficulties didn't prevent Software from having an influence on artists, technologists, theorists, and the public. This influence was felt both through the pieces it highlighted—which ranged from working technological artifacts to conceptual pieces—and through the underlying vision of art that caused these selections for Software to diverge so sharply from those encountered in the major technology and art exhibitions that preceded it.

The exhibition had a catalog by Ted Nelson called *Labyrinth*, which Nelson named as the first publicly-accessible hypertext. Another participant of new media fame was Nicholas Negroponte (◊23). The Architecture Machine Group he headed contributed *Seek* (featured on the cover of the Software catalog), which housed the abovementioned violence-prone gerbils in an environment of metal blocks. These blocks were light enough to be rearranged by the gerbils' movements. *Seek* reacted to the modifications the gerbils made by stacking the blocks into more grid-like versions of the gerbils' "designs," using a moveable electromagnet. For one group of observers the gerbils and robotic arm seemed to form a prototypical cybernetic circuit: it was an inspiring image of a machine that paid attention to the preferences expressed by the gerbils and then completed and formalized them into new, pleasing structures. Others took *Seek* as an image of the less sunny side of human-computer interaction and its future possibilities. As Ted Nelson wrote in *Dream Machines*, "I remember watching one gerbil who stood motionless on his little kangaroo matchstick legs, watching the Great Grappler rearranging his world. Gerbils are somewhat inscrutable, but I had a sense that he was *worshiping* it. He did not move until the block started coming down on top of him" (14).

Other overtly technological projects involved constantly broadcasting poetry inside on an AM frequency, turning the glass windows of the museum into low-power speakers, and offering access to various data streams and interactive computer programs via Teletype and CRT. There were also conceptual artists aplenty at Software. John Baldessari exhibited *Cremation Piece*, interring the ashes of his paintings in the wall of the museum behind a plaque. Vito Acconci's *Room Situation: (Proximity)* involved his "standing near a person and intruding on his personal space." (Acconci assigned a substitute to do this when he was unable to attend.) The catalog included the text of the reply Nam June Paik sent when invited to participate and Alan Kaprow's description of a September 1969 Happening (◊06); Hans Haacke and Joseph Kosuth also took part.

Some suggest that the technical problems encountered by Software may have sprung from a rather different source than many of those encountered today. In his 1980 essay, "Art and Technology," Burnham relates certain mysterious circumstances: "Yet even after our major computer, the PDP-8, had been reprogrammed a second time, it took several D.E.C. engineers six weeks to make both 'Labyrinth' (the interactive catalog) and related exhibits operational. The computer's failure to function was a mystery to everyone and a source of embarrassment to D.E.C. . . . And the night before 'Software' opened, a janitor sweeping the floors of the Museum short-circuited the entire program of the PDP-8 by breaking some wires in a terminal stand with a push broom—or at least that was the official story released by the Jewish Museum. . . . Talmudic scholars and rabbis situated on the top floor of the Jewish Museum were heard to mutter darkly as to the inappropriateness of exhibiting 'Software' in a museum mainly devoted to Judaica and Jewish studies." (239)

A different excerpt from Nelson's *Computer Lib / Dream Machines* is included (◊21). Richard Bolt (◊29) was a member of MIT's Architecture Machine Group.

◊10
127

◊13
193

◊15
227

**248**

◊44
643

The exhibition wasn't about getting artists and technologists together, or about using new technologies for artistic purposes. Burnham wrote in the catalog that, rather, "the goal of Software is to focus our sensibilities on the fastest growing area in this culture: information processing systems and their devices." He added, "it may not be, and probably is not, the province of computers and other telecommunications devices to produce art as we know it; but they will, in fact, be instrumental in redefining the entire area of esthetic awareness."

For Shanken, Les Levine's contributions to Software provide a bridge for understanding the place of conceptual artists in the exhibition. Shanken points out that Levine's *Systems Burn-Off*, in embodying Levine's somewhat idiosyncratic definition of the hardware/software split, was very close to the concerns of conceptual art. It was, as Shanken writes in "Art in the Information Age," "an artwork that produced information (software) about the information produced and disseminated by the media (software) about art (hardware). It offered a critique of the systematic process through which *art objects* (hardware) become transformed by the media into *information about art objects* (software). Whereas Levine stated that most art 'ends up as information about art,' *Systems Burn-Off* was *art as information about information about art,* adding a level of complexity and reflexivity onto that cycle of transformations in media culture" (9). Levine suggested the name for Software; his other two projects in the exhibition prefigure significant types of recent new media art, such as performance-oriented and voyeuristic Web video works.

Burnham's introduction to the catalog described the selection criteria for the exhibition. Before Software, computer art such as that shown at *Cybernetic Serendipity* had often worked to duplicate the effects of previous artforms, even to the point of imitating the styles of past masters. The focus was generally on a finished product, produced with computer tools. The Museum of Modern Art's important *The Machine as Seen at the End of the Mechanical Age* was similarly focused on finished products, many of which (as the name implies) were mechanical sculptures, images of machines, or inert objects that referred to machines. Burnham laid out a vision of new media art much more in line with how it is viewed today—neither a celebration of technology nor a condemnation, but an investigation, through implementation, of new shapes for the processes brought into the culture via computation. Burnham located the beginnings of understanding these processes in Norbert Wiener's cybernetics, but then made the case that current work had moved beyond this formulation, into the software model. Burnham wrote in the catalog that "many of the exhibits in Software deal with conceptual and process relationships which on the surface seem to be totally devoid of the usual art trappings . . . Most importantly [Software] provides the means by which the public can personally respond to programmatic situations structured by artists." He noted that "Many of the finest works in the Software exhibition are in no way connected with machines. In a sense they represent the 'programs' of artists who have chosen not to make paintings or sculptures, but to express ideas or art propositions." Software considered interaction in a way that built upon ideas in Happenings, and in the world emerging through information processing and in then-current media theory—as evinced by Burnham's many references to Marshall McLuhan (◊13). It marked the beginning of the fulfillment of the cybernetic visions of artists such as Roy Ascott (◊10) and Nam June Paik (◊15) (even as it sought a formulation beyond cybernetics within which to do so) and a look forward to the work of later artists such as Lynn Hershman (◊44).
—NWF & NM

More than three decades after Levine's video work for Software, Nina Sobell and Emily Hartzell (while at the NYU Center for Advanced Technology) created the first live video performances over the Web, using an audience-steerable camera developed at the

Further Reading

Burnham, Jack. *Beyond Modern Sculpture: The Effects of Science and Technology on the Sculpture of This Century.* New York: George Braziller, 1968.

Burnham, Jack. "Art and Technology: The Panacea That Failed." *The Myths of Information: Technology and Postindustrial Culture.* Ed. Kathleen Woodward. Madison, Wisc.: Coda Press, 1980. Reprinted in John Hanhardt, ed., *Video Culture: A Critical Investigation* (Rochester, N.Y.: Visual Studies Workshop Press, 1986).

Shanken, Edward. "Art in the Information Age: Technology and Conceptual Art," *SIGGRAPH 2001 Electronic Art and Animation Catalog*, 8–15. New York: ACM Press, 2001. <http://www.duke.edu/~giftwrap/InfoAge.html>

Shanken, Edward. "The House That Jack Built: Jack Burnham's Concept of 'Software' as a Metaphor for Art." *Leonardo Electronic Almanac* 6(10) November 1998. <http://www.duke.edu/~giftwrap/House.html>

Original Publication: From *Software—Information Technology: Its New Meaning for Art*. Catalog of an exhibition held at the Jewish Museum, New York, September 16 through November 8, 1970.

Gerbils match wits with computer-built environment

**Ned Woodman/Theodor H. Nelson**
**Labyrinth: An Interactive Catalogue** 1970
with assistance from Scott Bradner (Art & Technology, Inc., Boston)
Digital Equipment Corporation (time share PDP-8 computer)

*Labyrinth* is a hypertext, or interactive text retrieval system.
To read in this interactive catalogue, the user sits down
at one of many *Labyrinth* keyscope terminals and begins
to read. To read more of any section which is larger than the
screen, the user types F (forward). To go back to the
beginning of the catalogue, the user types R (return).
To obtain a related section as indicated by an asterisk
appearing in the text, the user types the code appearing with
the asterisk.

Before leaving the show, the museum goer may obtain
a printout of what he himself has selected to read in the
interactive catalogue by giving his name to an attendant
at the line printer by the main exit.

This catalogue system was programmed for the PDP-8
by Ned Woodman of Art & Technology, Inc. Interesting
features of the program include the ability to output to any
display scope, a temporary terminal history to allow the
forward and return commands, a permanent user history
permitting a final printout. The interactive catalogue for
software consisting of information from the printed catalogue
and additional materials has been edited by Theodor
H. Nelson, who has been advocating hypertexts as a form
of writing for some ten years. This is the first public
demonstration of a hypertext system.

*Scott Bradner (left) and Ned Woodman of ATI program their PDP-8.*

18

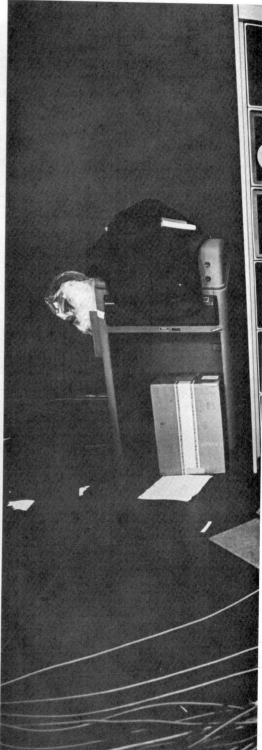

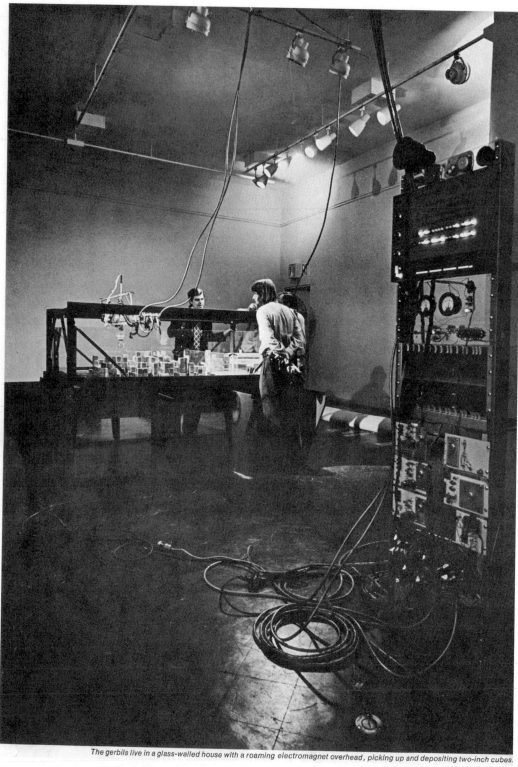

The gerbils live in a glass-walled house with a roaming electromagnet overhead, picking up and depositing two-inch cubes.

### The Architecture Machine Group, M.I.T.
**Seek** 1969-70

*Seek* is a sensing/effecting device controlled by a small general purpose computer. In contrast to an input/output peripheral, *Seek* is a mechanism that senses the physical environment, affects that environment, and in turn attempts to handle local unexpected events within the environment. *Seek* deals with toy blocks which it can stack, align and sort. At the same time, these blocks form the built environment for a small colony of gerbils which live within *Seek*'s three-dimensional world.

Unbeknownst to *Seek,* the little animals are bumping into blocks, disrupting constructions, and toppling towers. The result is a substantial mismatch between the three-dimensional reality and the computed remembrances which reside in the memory of *Seek*'s computer. *Seek*'s role is to deal with these inconsistencies. In the process, *Seek* exhibits inklings of a responsive behavior inasmuch as the actions of the gerbils are not predictable and the reactions of *Seek* purposefully correct or amplify gerbil-provoked dislocations.

*Seek* consists of a 5x8 foot superstructure supporting a carriage which has three dimensions of freedom. Its extremity is composed of an electromagnet, several micro-switches, and pressure-sensing devices. This elementary prosthesis is guided by the blind and handless computer to pick up or deposit its payload of a single two-inch cube. The nucleus of the system is an Interdata Model 3 Computer with 65536 single (yes/no) bits of memory which are shared by instructions and data.

Even in its triviality and simplicity, *Seek* metaphorically goes beyond the real-world situation, where machines cannot respond to the unpredictable nature of people (gerbils). Today machines are poor at handling sudden changes in context in environment. This lack of adaptability is the problem *Seek* confronts in diminutive.

If computers are to be our friends they must understand our metaphors. If they are to be responsive to changing, unpredictable, context-dependent human needs, they will need an artificial intelligence that can cope with complex contingencies in a sophisticated manner (drawing upon these metaphors) much as *Seek* deals with elementary uncertainties in a simple-minded fashion.

*Seek* has been developed and constructed by M.I.T. students who form part of the Architecture Machine Group, a Ford Foundation sponsored research effort within the M.I.T. Urban Systems Laboratory. The participants have ranged from freshmen working in an Undergraduate Research Opportunities Program, to post-graduates designing elements as part of their research assistantships.

The co-directors of the group are Professors Nicholas Negroponte and Leon B. Groisser, of the faculty of Architecture and Planning. Randy Rettberg and Mike Titelbaum, students in Electrical Engineering, have been in charge of the electronics—in particular, the interface and controller. Steven Gregory, a graduate student in the School of Architecture and Planning, has been in charge of the programming. Steven Peters and Ernest Vincent have been responsible for the actual construction of the device.

Following the Software exhibition, *Seek* will return to M.I.T. to be used with many different detachable heads as a general purpose sensor/effector. *Seek* will become a frame for experiments conducted by students in computer-aided design and in artificial intelligence.

Reference: Nicholas Negroponte, *The Architecture Machine,* M.I.T. Press, 1970.
Computer: courtesy The Interdata Corporation, Oceanport, New Jersey.
Gerbils: courtesy Tumblebrook Farms, Brant Lake, New York

*Nicholas Negroponte (left) with Karl Katz and Steven Gregory*

253

**Les Levine**
**Systems Burn-off X Residual Software** 1969

The 33 photographs on exhibition were originally taken by
the artist in March of 1969 during an excursion by New York
critics and press to view the opening of the Cornell University
"Earth Works" exhibition in Ithaca, New York.

In April, 1969, Les Levine exhibited 31,000 photographs
consisting of 31 separate images, 1,000 copies each, at the
Phyllis Kind Gallery, Chicago. Most were randomly distributed on the floor and covered with jello; some were stuck to
the wall with chewing gum; the rest were for sale.

"Software is the programming material which any system
uses, i.e. in a computer it would be the flow charts or subroutines for the computer program. In effect software in
'real' terms is the mental intelligence required for any
experience. It can also be described as the knowledge
required for the performance of any task or transmission of

communication. They say, 'It's going to be raining tomorrow.' is software. All activities which have no connection with object or material mass are the result of software. Images themselves are hardware. Information about these images is software. All software carries its own residuals.

The residual may take the form of news, paint, television tapes or other so-called 'media'. In many cases an object is of much less value than the software concerning the object. The object is the end of a system. The software is an open continuing system. The experience of seeing something first hand is no longer of value in a software controlled society, as anything seen through the media carries just as much energy as first hand experience. We do not question whether the things that happen on radio or television have actually occurred. The fact that we can confront them mentally through electronics is sufficient for us to know that they exist. . . . In the same way, most of the art that is produced today ends up as information about art." L. L.

# Artist exposes himself electronically

**Les Levine**
**A.I.R.** 1968-70

A.I.R. basically consists of a group of television sets in a museum which displays activity taped in my studio, showing museum visitors the artist in his natural environment. The images change position from monitor to monitor on a random basis.

I believe this brings the art process directly to the public environment and thereby makes a closer connection between art and general culture.

*Note: Les Levine's original proposal consisted of constant direct coaxial transmission from his studio for the duration of the exhibition. This approach was abandoned when it was found that line-of-sight transmission was impossible.

Les Levine
Wire Tap 1969-70

*Wire Tap* is a series of twelve speakers, each measuring
12″x12″, and containing a series of conversations between
myself and anyone who telephones me during the day.
People will hear these conversations as they pass by them.

# 18. [Introduction]
# Constituents of a
# Theory of the Media

"The new media are oriented toward action, not contemplation; toward the present, not tradition. Their attitude to time is completely opposed to that ... which aspires to possession, that is, to extension in time, best of all, to eternity. The media produce no objects that can be hoarded and auctioned. They do away completely with 'intellectual property' and liquidate the 'heritage.'"

These words might have appeared in the "Idées Fortes" section of a 1990s issue of *Wired*; they were written, however, a quarter-century before *Wired* ever hit the shelves. They are from the essay reprinted below, which is almost impossible to read now without an eerie sense of familiarity and disjoint. This isn't dot-communism.

It is New Left socialism, however, and certain Marxist concepts are important to this essay and to Jean Baudrillard's reply. Two central ones are "base" and "superstructure." The base traditionally is said to consist of the forces and relations of production—what goes on in an iron foundry, for example, would be part of the base. The superstructure is traditionally said to be made up of things like political systems, religion—and the media. In many interpretations of Marx these superstructural phenomena are entirely determined by the base relationships, existing in order to perpetuate them. The position of the media in this system is important both to Enzensberger's and Baudrillard's essays.

In his essay Enzensberger is taking aim at the media business—the consciousness industry. This industry is part of the superstructure in that it operates to perpetuate an unjust society by convincing us to accept that society. At the same time, the media is a big business, one where capitalists hope to make a lot of money. Enzensberger argues that turning away from the media is a poor strategy for effecting change. Rather, one should work at the point of the media, where the unjust culture is vulnerable both in terms of consciousness and income.

Enzensberger's essay is very commonly cited, but unfortunately references to it often make it only partway through the argument. This type of citation focuses on passages such as Enzensberger's assertion that it "is wrong to regard media equipment as mere means of consumption. It is always, in principle, also means of production." What gets left out are the passages such as: "Anyone who imagines that freedom for the media will be established if only everyone is busy transmitting and receiving is the dupe of a liberalism which ... merely peddles the faded concepts of a preordained harmony of social interests."

Enzensberger is not simply proposing distributed production of media—he is proposing a new fundamental organization of media, and of those working to change capitalist society. For example, he writes, "Tape recorders, ordinary cameras, and movie cameras are already extensively owned by wage earners. The question is why these means of production do not turn up at factories, in schools, in the offices of the bureaucracy, in short, everywhere where there is social conflict.. ... Only a collective, organized effort can tear down these paper walls." He imagines "Networklike communications models built on the principle of reversibility of circuits ... a mass newspaper, written and distributed by its readers, a video network of politically active groups."

In other words, Enzensberger does not see the liberation of media coming from hobbyist CB radio, or the "Talkback!" forum under each ZDYahooAPTimesNet story, or alt.barney.die.die.die. Providing everyone with a DSL line and "personal web sharing" is also not what Enzensberger envisions. From Enzensberger's point of view the ability for any of us to produce media with the equipment we have—or even distribute it—is not particularly big news. He did not even write in a way that would

Enzensberger's concept of media reorganization may resemble Deleuze and Guattari's *rhizome* (◊27) more than it does the traditional network.

259

*John Thornton Caldwell, "Theorizing the Digital Landrush" (18):*

Enzensberger's model of "mobilization"—one that rejected old-Left defeatism in the face of capital—linked media critique with a systematic plan for alternative production, together placed in the general service of cultural empowerment. Even as Enzensberger theorized how the media subjugated progressive potential through token, liberal forms—like public opinion forums, broadcast licensing, and fairness protocols—he laid out a call-to-arms for radical, alternative productions. These marching orders—decentralization versus centralized broadcasting, two-way transmitters versus reception-only receivers, mobility versus isolation, feedback and interactivity versus passivity, and collectivity versus professional specialization—may evoke the dated optimism of new-Left socialism, but they also prefigure digi-speak.

◊27
405

By positing certain qualities to be inherent in the structures of new, electronic media Enzensberger may remind some of Marshall McLuhan, *Wired's* patron saint. Paul Marris and Sue Thornham argue other significant parallels between the two in their introduction to section one of *Media Studies: A Reader*—"Although Enzensberger was profoundly critical of McLuhan (he describes him as promoting a "mystique of the media"), their thinking had several shared fundamentals: a recognition of the centrality of the media for contemporary social life; an address to a generation that had grown up with television, portable record-players and the transistor radio, and was therefore not culturally fastidious toward the media; and an awareness of the accelerating lines of development of electronic technologies." (14)

note the phenomenon of the Rodney King videotape as radical, although that brought media equipment into the space of social conflict. What he may have included in his vision, on the other hand, is something like the way that the Internet has been used to organize and provide information about protests against the World Trade Organization. In this case, new media have been used both to support the alternative organization of a social movement (more a network than a hierarchy) and to provide a different model of media consumption (while mainstream news reported that Seattle police were showing admirable restraint and protesters were breaking windows, many not at the protests were still seeing what the news refused to show—pictures of rubber bullets and takedowns, firsthand accounts of peaceful protest and violent police reaction—delivered on the Web). If the Rodney King incident had been followed by an organized campaign of videotaping, and built a network communication structure and social movement opposed to police violence, that too could be seen as a start from Enzensberger's point of view.

Jean Baudrillard, however, looks toward a different model for understanding and resisting the dominance of media, as his reply to this essay (◊19) explains.
—NWF

---

*Karl Marx, from the preface to* A Contribution to the Critique of Political Economy:

In the social production of their life, men enter into definite relations that are indispensable and independent of their will, relations of production that correspond to a definite stage in the development of their material productive forces. The sum total of these relations of production constitutes the economic structure of society, the real foundation [base], on which rises a legal and political superstructure and to which correspond definite forms of social consciousness. The mode of production of material life conditions the social, political and intellectual life processes in general. It is not the consciousness of men that determines their being but, on the contrary, their social being that determines their consciousness.

---

Further Reading

Caldwell, John Thornton. "Introduction: Theorizing the Digital Landrush." *Electronic Media and Technoculture*. Ed. Caldwell, John Thornton. Rutgers, N.J.: Rutgers University Press, 2000.

Eagleton, Terry. *Ideology: An Introduction*. New York: Verso, 1991.

The Independent Media Center. <http://www.indymedia.org>

Marris, Paul, and Sue Thornham. "The Media and Social Power: Introduction." *Media Studies: A Reader*. 2nd ed. Ed. Paul Marris and Sue Thornham. New York: New York University Press, 2000.

Original Publication

*New Left Review* (64) 13–36. Nov/Dec 1970. Reprinted in
Enzensberger, Hans Magnus, *The Consciousness Industry*, trans.
Stuart Hood. New York: Seabury Press, 1974.

# Constituents of a Theory of the Media

## Hans Magnus Enzensberger

> If you should think this is Utopian, then I would ask
> you to consider why it is Utopian.
> —Bertolt Brecht, *Theory of Radio*

1. With the development of the electronic media, the industry that shapes consciousness has become the pacemaker for the social an economic development of societies in the late industrial age. It infiltrates into all other sectors of production, takes over more and more directional and control functions, and determines the standard of the prevailing technology.

In lieu of normative definitions, here is an incomplete list of new developments which have emerged in the last twenty years: news satellites, color television, cable relay television, cassettes, videotape, videotape recorders, video-phones, stereophony, laser techniques, electrostatic reproduction processes, electronic high-speed printing, composing and learning machines, microfiches with electronic access, printing by radio, time-sharing computers, data banks. All these new forms of media are constantly forming new connections both with each other and with older media like printing, radio, film, television, telephone, teletype, radar, and so on. They are clearly coming together to form a universal system.

The general contradiction between productive forces and productive relationships emerges most sharply, however, when they are most advanced. By contrast, protracted structural crises, as in coal mining, can be solved merely by getting rid of a backlog, that is to say, essentially they can be solved within the terms of their own system, and a revolutionary strategy that relied on them would be shortsighted.

Monopoly capitalism develops the consciousness-shaping industry more quickly and more extensively than other sectors of production; it must at the same time fetter it. A socialist media theory has to work at this contradiction, demonstrate that it cannot be solved within the given productive relationships—rapidly increasing discrepancies, potential destructive forces. "Certain demands of a prognostic nature must be made" of any such theory (Benjamin).

A "critical" inventory of the status quo is not enough. There is danger of underestimating the growing conflicts in the media field, of neutralizing them, of interpreting them merely in terms of trade unionism or liberalism, on the lines of traditional labor struggles or as the clash of special interests (program heads/executive producers, publishers/authors, monopolies/medium-sized businesses, public corporations/private companies, etc.). An appreciation of this kind does not go far enough and remains bogged down in tactical arguments.

So far there is no Marxist theory of the media. There is therefore no strategy one can apply in this area. Uncertainty, alternations between fear and surrender, mark the attitude of the socialist Left to the new productive forces of the media industry. The ambivalence of this attitude merely mirrors the ambivalence of the media themselves without mastering it. It could only be overcome by releasing the emancipatory potential which is inherent in the new productive forces—a potential which capitalism must sabotage just as surely as Soviet revisionism, because it would endanger the rule of both systems.

## The Mobilizing Power of the Media

2. The open secret of the electronic media, the decisive political factor, which has been waiting, suppressed or crippled, for its moment to come, is their mobilizing power.

When I say *mobilize* I mean *mobilize*. In a country which has had direct experience of fascism (and Stalinism) it is perhaps still necessary to explain, or to explain again, what that means—namely, to make men, more mobile than they are. As free as dancers, as aware as football players, as surprising as guerrillas. Anyone who thinks of the masses only as the object of politics cannot mobilize them. He wants to push them around. A parcel is not mobile; it can only be pushed to and fro. Marches, columns, parades, immobilize people. Propaganda, which does not release self-reliance but limits it, fits into the same pattern. It leads to depoliticization.

For the first time in history, the media are making possible mass participation in a social and socialized productive process, the practical means of which are in the hands of the masses themselves. Such a use of them would bring the communications media, which up to now have not deserved the name, into their own. In its present form, equipment like television or film does not serve communication but prevents it. It allows no reciprocal action between transmitter and receiver; technically speaking, it reduces feedback to the lowest point compatible with the system.

This state of affairs, however, cannot be justified technically. On the contrary. Electronic techniques recognize no contradiction in principle between transmitter and receiver. Every transistor radio is, by the nature of its construction, at the same time a potential transmitter; it can interact with other receivers by circuit reversal. The development from a mere distribution medium to a communications medium is technically not a problem. It is consciously prevented for understandable political reasons. The technical distinction between receivers and transmitters reflects the social division of labor into producers and consumers, which in the consciousness industry becomes of particular political importance. It is based, in the last analysis, on the basic contradiction between the ruling class and the ruled class—that is to say, between monopoly capital or monopolistic bureaucracy on the one hand and the dependent masses on the other.

This structural analogy can be worked out in detail. To the programs offered by the broadcasting cartels there correspond the politics offered by a power cartel consisting of parties constituted along authoritarian lines. In both cases marginal differences in their platforms reflect a competitive relationship which on essential questions is nonexistent. Minimal independent activity on the part of the voter/viewer is desired. As is the case with parliamentary elections under the two-party system, the feedback is reduced to indices. "Training in decision making" is reduced to the response to a single, three-point switching process: Program 1; Program 2; Switch off (abstention).

> Radio must be changed from a means of distribution to a means of communication. Radio would be the most wonderful means of communication imaginable in public life, a huge linked system—that is to say, it would be such if it were capable not only of transmitting but of receiving, of allowing the listener

not only to hear but to speak, and did not isolate him but brought him into contact. Unrealizable in this social system, realizable in another, these proposals, which are, after all, only the natural consequences of technical development, help towards the propagation and shaping of that *other* system.[1]

## The Orwellian Fantasy

3. George Orwell's bogey of a monolithic consciousness industry derives from a view of the media which is undialectical and obsolete. The possibility of total control of such a system at a central point belongs not to the future but to the past. With the aid of systems theory, discipline which is part of bourgeois science—using, that is to say, categories which are immanent in the system—it can be demonstrated that a linked series of communications or, to use the technical term, switchable network, to the degree that it exceeds a certain critical size, can no longer be centrally controlled but only dealt with statistically. This basic "leakiness" of stochastic systems admittedly allows the calculation of probabilities based on sampling and extrapolations; but blanket supervision would demand a monitor that was bigger than the system itself. The monitoring of all telephone conversations, for instance, postulates an apparatus which would need to be $n$ times more extensive and more complicated than that of the present telephone system. A censor's office, which carried out its work extensively, would of necessity become the largest branch of industry in its society.

But supervision on the basis of approximation can only offer inadequate instruments for the self-regulation of the whole system in accordance with the concepts of those who govern it. It postulates a high degree of internal stability. If this precarious balance is upset, then crisis measures based on statistical methods of control are useless. Interference can penetrate the leaky nexus of the media, spreading and multiplying there with the utmost speed, by resonance. The regime so threatened will in such cases, insofar as it is still capable of action, use force and adopt police or military methods.

A state of emergency is therefore the only alternative to leakage in the consciousness industry; but it cannot be maintained in the long run. Societies in the late industrial age rely on the free exchange of information; the "objective pressures" to which their controllers constantly appeal are thus turned against them. Every attempt to suppress the random factors, each diminution of the average flow and each distortion of the information structure must, in the long run, lead to an embolism.

The electronic media have not only built up the information network intensively, they have also spread it extensively. The radio wars of the fifties demonstrated that in the realm of communications, national sovereignty is condemned to wither away. The further development of satellites will deal it the *coup de grâce*. Quarantine regulations for information, such as were promulgated by fascism and Stalinism, are only possible today at the cost of deliberate industrial regression.

Example. The Soviet bureaucracy, that is to say the most widespread and complicated bureaucracy in the world, has to deny itself almost entirely an elementary piece of organizational equipment, the duplicating machine, because this instrument potentially makes everyone a printer. The political risk involved, the possibility of a leakage in the information network, is accepted only at the highest levels, at exposed switchpoints in political, military, and scientific areas. It is clear that Soviet society has to pay an immense price for the suppression of its own productive resources—clumsy procedures, misinformation, *faux frais*. The phenomenon incidentally has its analogue in the capitalist West, if in a diluted form. The technically most advanced electrostatic copying machine, which operates with ordinary paper—which cannot, that is to say, be supervised and is independent of suppliers—is the property of a monopoly (Xerox), on principle it is not sold but rented. The rates themselves ensure that it does not get into the wrong hands. The equipment crops up as if by magic where economic and political power are concentrated. Political control of the equipment goes hand in hand with maximization of profits for the manufacturer. Admittedly this control, as opposed to Soviet methods, is by no means "watertight" for the reasons indicated.

The problem of censorship thus enters a new historical stage. The struggle for the freedom of the press and freedom of ideas has, up till now, been mainly an argument within the bourgeoisie itself; for the masses, freedom to express opinions was a fiction since they were, from the beginning, barred from the means of production—above all from the press—and thus were unable to join in freedom of expression from the start. Today censorship is threatened by the productive forces of the consciousness industry which is already, to some extent, gaining the upper hand over the prevailing relations of production. Long before the latter are overthrown, the contradiction between what is possible and what actually exists will become acute.

## Cultural Archaism in the Left Critique

4. The New Left of the sixties has reduced the development of the media to a single concept—that of manipulation. This concept was originally extremely useful for heuristic purposes and has made possible a great many individual analytical investigations, but it now threatens to degenerate into a mere slogan which conceals more than it is able to illuminate, and therefore itself requires analysis.

The current theory of manipulation on the Left is essentially defensive; its effects can lead the movement into defeatism. Subjectively speaking, behind the tendency to go on the defensive lies a sense of impotence. Objectively, it corresponds to the absolutely correct view that the decisive means of production are in enemy hands. But to react to this state of affairs with moral indignation is naive. There is in general an undertone of lamentation when people speak of manipulation which points to idealistic expectations—as if the class enemy had ever stuck to the promises of fair play it occasionally utters. The liberal superstition that in political and social questions there is such a thing as pure, unmanipulated truth seems to enjoy remarkable currency among the socialist Left. It is the unspoken basic premise of the manipulation thesis.

This thesis provides no incentive to push ahead. A socialist perspective which does not go beyond attacking existing property relationships is limited. The expropriation of Springer is a desirable goal but it would be good to know to whom the media should be handed over. The Party? To judge by all experience of that solution, it is not a possible alternative. It is perhaps no accident that the Left has not yet produced an analysis of the pattern of manipulation in countries with socialist regimes.

The manipulation thesis also serves to exculpate oneself. To cast the enemy in the role of the devil is to conceal the weakness and lack of perspective in one's own agitation. If the latter leads to self-isolation instead of mobilizing the masses, then its failure is attributed holus-bolus to the overwhelming power of the media.

The theory of repressive tolerance has also permeated discussion of the media by the Left. This concept, which was formulated by its author with the utmost care, has also, when whittled away in an undialectical manner, become a vehicle for resignation. Admittedly, when an office-equipment firm can attempt to recruit sales staff with the picture of Che Guevara and the text *We would have hired him,* the temptation to withdraw is great. But fear of handling shit is a luxury a sewerman cannot necessarily afford.

The electronic media do away with cleanliness; they are by their nature "dirty." That is part of their productive power. In terms of structure, they are antisectarian—a further reason why the Left, insofar as it is not prepared to re-examine its traditions, has little idea what to do with them. The desire for a cleanly defined "line" and for the suppression of "deviations" is anachronistic and now serves only one's own need for security. It weakens one's own position by irrational purges, exclusions, and fragmentation, instead of strengthening it by rational discussion.

These resistances and fears are strengthened by a series of cultural factors which, for the most part, operate unconsciously, and which are to be explained by the social history of the participants in today's Left movement— namely their bourgeois class background. It often seems as if it were precisely because of their progressive potential that the media are felt to be an immense threatening power; because for the first time they present a basic challenge to bourgeois culture and thereby to the privileges of the bourgeois intelligentsia—a challenge far more radical than any self-doubt this social group can display. In the New Left's opposition to the media, old bourgeois fears such as the fear of "the masses" seem to be reappearing along with equally old bourgeois longings for pre-industrial times dressed up in progressive clothing.

At the very beginning of the student revolt, during the Free Speech Movement at Berkeley, the computer was a favorite target for aggression. Interest in the Third World is not always free from motives based on antagonism towards civilization which has its source in conservative culture critique. During the May events in Paris, the reversion to archaic forms of production was particularly characteristic. Instead of carrying out agitation among the workers with a modern offset press, the students printed their posters on the hand presses of the École des Beaux Arts. The political slogans were hand-painted; stencils would certainly have made it possible to produce them *en masse,* but it would have offended the creative imagination of the authors. The ability

to make proper strategic use of the most advanced media was lacking. It was not the radio headquarters that were seized by the rebels, but the Odéon Theatre, steeped in tradition.

The obverse of this fear of contact with the media is the fascination they exert on left-wing movements in the great cities. On the one hand, the comrades take refuge in outdated forms of communication and esoteric arts and crafts instead of occupying themselves with the contradiction between the present constitution of the media and their revolutionary potential; on the other hand, they cannot escape from the consciousness industry's program or from its aesthetic. This leads, subjectively, to a split between a puritanical view of political action and the area of private "leisure"; objectively, it leads to a split between politically active groups and subcultural groups.

In Western Europe the socialist movement mainly addresses itself to a public of converts through newspapers and journals which are exclusive in terms of language, content, and form. These newssheets presuppose a structure of party members and sympathizers and a situation, where the media are concerned, that roughly corresponds to the historical situation in 1900; they are obviously fixated on the *Iskra* model. Presumably the people who produce them listen to the Rolling Stones, watch occupations and strikes on television, and go to the cinema to see a Western or a Godard; only in their capacity as producers do they make an exception, and, in their analyses, the whole media sector is reduced to the slogan of "manipulation." Every foray into this territory is regarded from the start with suspicion as a step towards integration. This suspicion is not unjustified; it can however also mask one's own ambivalence and insecurity. Fear of being swallowed up by the system is a sign of weakness; it presupposes that capitalism could overcome any contradiction—a conviction which can easily be refuted historically and is theoretically untenable.

If the socialist movement writes off the new productive forces of the consciousness industry and relegates work on the media to a subculture, then we have a vicious circle. For the Underground may be increasingly aware of the technical and aesthetic possibilities of the disc, of videotape, of the electronic camera, and so on, and is systematically exploring the terrain, but it has no political viewpoint of its own and therefore mostly falls a helpless victim to commercialism. The politically active groups then point to such cases with smug *Schaden-freude*. A process of unlearning is the result and both sides are the losers. Capitalism alone benefits from the Left's antagonism to the media, as it does from the depoliticization of the counterculture.

## Democratic Manipulation

5. Manipulation—etymologically, "handling"—means technical treatment of a given material with a particular goal in mind. When the technical intervention is of immediate social relevance, then manipulation is a political act. In the case of the media industry, that is by definition the case.

Thus every use of the media presupposes manipulation. The most elementary processes in media production, from the choice of the medium itself to shooting, cutting, synchronization, dubbing, right up to distribution, are all operations carried out on the raw material. There is no such thing as unmanipulated writing, filming, or broadcasting. The question is therefore not whether the media are manipulated, but who manipulates them. A revolutionary plan should not require the manipulators to disappear; on the contrary, it must make everyone a manipulator.

All technical manipulations are potentially dangerous; the manipulation of the media cannot be countered, however, by old or new forms of censorship, but only by direct social control, that is to say, by the mass of the people, who will have become productive. To this end, the elimination of capitalistic property relationships is a necessary but by no means sufficient condition. There have been no historical examples up until now of the mass self-regulating learning process which is made possible by the electronic media. The Communists' fear of releasing this potential, of the mobilizing capabilities of the media, of the interaction of free producers, is one of the main reasons why even in the socialist countries, the old bourgeois culture, greatly disguised and distorted but structurally intact, continues to hold sway.

As a historical explanation, it may be pointed out that the consciousness industry in Russia at the time of the October Revolution was extraordinarily backward; their productive capacity has grown enormously since then, but the productive relationships have been artificially preserved, often by force. Then, as now, a primitively edited press, books, and theater were the key media in the Soviet Union. The development of radio, film, and television is politically

arrested. Foreign stations like the BBC, the Voice of America, and the *Deutschland Welle*, therefore, not only find listeners, but are received with almost boundless faith. Archaic media like the handwritten pamphlet and poems orally transmitted play an important role.

6. The new media are egalitarian in structure. Anyone can take part in them by a simple switching process. The programs themselves are not material things and can be reproduced at will. In this sense the electronic media are entirely different from the older media like the book or the easel painting, the exclusive class character of which is obvious. Television programs for privileged groups are certainly technically conceivable—closed circuit television— but run counter to the structure. Potentially, the new media do away with all educational privileges and thereby with the cultural monopoly of the bourgeois intelligentsia. This is one of the reasons for the intelligentsia's resentment against the new industry. As for the "spirit" which they are endeavoring to defend against "depersonalization" and "mass culture," the sooner they abandon it the better.

## Properties of the New Media

7. The new media are oriented towards action, not contemplation; towards the present, not tradition. Their attitude to time is completely opposed to that of bourgeois culture, which aspires to possession, that is to extension in time, best of all, to eternity. The media produce no objects that can be hoarded and auctioned. They do away completely with "intellectual property" and liquidate the "heritage," that is to say, the class-specific handing-on of nonmaterial capital.

That does not mean to say that they have no history or that they contribute to the loss of historical consciousness. On the contrary, they make it possible for the first time to record historical material so that it can be reproduced at will. By making this material available for present-day purposes, they make it obvious to anyone using it that the writing of history is always manipulation. But the memory they hold in readiness is not the preserve of a scholarly caste. It is social. The banked information is accessible to anyone, and this accessibility is as instantaneous as its recording. It suffices to compare the model of a private library with that of a socialized data bank to recognize the structural difference between the two systems.

8. It is wrong to regard media equipment as mere means of consumption. It is always, in principle, also means of production and, indeed, since it is in the hands of the masses, socialized means of production. The contradiction between producers and consumers is not inherent in the electronic media; on the contrary, it has to be artificially reinforced by economic and administrative measures.

An early example of this is provided by the difference between telegraph and telephone. Whereas the former, to this day, has remained in the hands of a bureaucratic institution which can scan and file every text transmitted, the telephone is directly accessible to all users. With the aid of conference circuits, it can even make possible collective intervention in a discussion by physically remote groups.

On the other hand, those auditory and visual means of communication which rely on "wireless" are still subject to state control (legislation on wireless installations). In the face of technical developments, which long ago made local and international radio-telephony possible, and which constantly opened up new wavebands for television—in the UHF band alone, the dissemination of numerous programs in one locality is possible without interference, not to mention the possibilities offered by wired and satellite television—the prevailing laws for control of the air are anachronistic. They recall the time when the operation of a printing press was dependent on an imperial license. The socialist movements will take up the struggle for their own wavelengths and must, within the foreseeable future, build their own transmitters and relay stations.

9. One immediate consequence of the structural nature of the new media is that none of the regimes at present in power can release their potential. Only a free socialist society will be able to make them fully productive. A further characteristic of the most advanced media—probably the decisive one—confirms this thesis: their collective structure.

For the prospect that in future, with the aid of the media, anyone can become a producer, would remain apolitical and limited were this productive effort to find an outlet in individual tinkering. Work on the media is possible for an individual only insofar as it remains socially and therefore aesthetically irrelevant. The collection of transparencies from the last holiday trip provides a model of this.

That is naturally what the prevailing market mechanisms have aimed at. It has long been clear from apparatus like miniature and 8mm movie cameras, as well as the tape recorder, which are in actual fact already in the hands of the masses, that the individual, so long as he remains isolated, can become with their help at best an amateur but not a producer. Even so potent a means of production as the shortwave transmitter has been tamed in this way and reduced to a harmless and inconsequential hobby in the hands of scattered radio hams. The programs which the isolated amateur mounts are always only bad, outdated copies of what he in any case receives.

Private production for the media is no more than licensed cottage industry. Even when it is made public it remains pure compromise. To this end, the men who own the media have developed special programs which are usually called "Democratic Forum" or something of the kind. There, tucked away in the corner, "the reader (listener, viewer) has his say," which can naturally be cut short at any time. As in the case of public-opinion polling, he is only asked questions so that he may have a chance to confirm his own dependence. It is a control circuit where what is fed in has already made complete allowance for the feedback.

The concept of a license can also be used in another sense—in an economic one; the system attempts to make each participant into a concessionaire of the monopoly that develops his films or plays back his cassettes. The aim is to nip in the bud in this way that independence which video equipment, for instance, makes possible. Naturally, such tendencies go against the grain of the structure, and the new productive forces not only permit but indeed demand their reversal.

The poor, feeble, and frequently humiliating results of this licensed activity are often referred to with contempt by the professional media producers. On top of the damage suffered by the masses comes triumphant mockery because they clearly do not know how to use the media properly. The sort of thing that goes on in certain popular television shows is taken as proof that they are completely incapable of articulating on their own.

Not only does this run counter to the results of the latest psychological and pedagogical research, but it can easily be seen to be a reactionary protective formulation; the "gifted" people are quite simply defending their territories. Here we have a cultural analogue to the familiar political judgments concerning a working class which is presumed to be "stultified" and incapable of any kind of self-determination. Curiously, one may hear the view that the masses could never govern themselves out of the mouths of people who consider themselves socialists. In the best of cases, these are economists who cannot conceive of socialism as anything other than nationalization.

## A Socialist Strategy

10. Any socialist strategy for the media must, on the contrary, strive to end the isolation of the individual participants from the social learning and production process. This is impossible unless those concerned organize themselves. This is the political core of the question of the media. It is over this point that socialist concepts part company with the neo-liberal and technocratic ones. Anyone who expects to be emancipated by technological hardware, or by a system of hardware however structured, is the victim of an obscure belief in progress. Anyone who imagines that freedom for the media will be established if only everyone is busy transmitting and receiving is the dupe of a liberalism which, decked out in contemporary colors, merely peddles the faded concepts of a preordained harmony of social interests.

In the face of such illusions, what must be firmly held on to is that the proper use of the media demands organization and makes it possible. Every production that deals with the interests of the producers postulates a collective method of production. It is itself already a form of self-organization of social needs. Tape recorders, ordinary cameras, and movie cameras are already extensively owned by wage-earners. The question is why these means of production do not turn up at factories, in schools, in the offices of the bureaucracy, in short, everywhere where there is social conflict. By producing aggressive forms of publicity which were their own, the masses could secure evidence of their daily experiences and draw effective lessons from them.

Naturally, bourgeois society defends itself against such prospects with a battery of legal measures. It bases itself on the law of trespass, on commercial and official secrecy. While its secret services penetrate everywhere and plug in to the most intimate conversations, it pleads a touching concern for confidentiality, and makes a sensitive display of worrying about the question of privacy when all that is private is the interest of the exploiters. Only a collective, organized effort can tear down these paper walls.

Communication networks which are constructed for such purposes can, over and above their primary function, provide politically interesting organizational models. In the socialist movements the dialectic of discipline and spontaneity, centralism and decentralization, authoritarian leadership and anti-authoritarian disintegration has long ago reached deadlock. Networklike communications models built on the principle of reversibility of circuits might give indications of how to overcome this situation: a mass newspaper, written and distributed by its readers, a video network of politically active groups.

More radically than any good intention, more lastingly than existential flight from one's own class, the media, once they have come into their own, destroy the private production methods of bourgeois intellectuals. Only in productive work and learning processes can their individualism be broken down in such a way that it is transformed from morally based (that is to say, as individual as ever) self-sacrifice to a new kind of political self-understanding and behavior.

11. An all-too-widely disseminated thesis maintains that present-day capitalism lives by the exploitation of unreal needs. That is at best a half-truth. The results obtained by popular American sociologists like Vance Packard are not un-useful but limited. What they have to say about the stimulation of needs through advertising and artificial obsolescence can in any case not be adequately explained by the hypnotic pull exerted on the wage-earners by mass consumption. The hypothesis of "consumer terror" corresponds to the prejudices of a middle class, which considers itself politically enlightened, against the allegedly integrated proletariat, which has become petty bourgeois and corrupt. The attractive power of mass consumption is based not on the dictates of false needs, but on the falsification and exploitation of quite real and legitimate ones without which the parasitic process of advertising would be redundant. A socialist movement ought not to denounce these needs, but take them seriously, investigate them, and make them politically productive.

That is also valid for the consciousness industry. The electronic media do not owe their irresistible power to any sleight-of-hand but to the elemental power of deep social needs which come through even in the present depraved form of these media.

267

Precisely because no one bothers about them, the interests of the masses have remained a relatively unknown field, at least insofar as they are historically new. They certainly extend far beyond those goals which the traditional working-class movement represented. Just as in the field of production, the industry which produces goods and the consciousness industry merge more and more, so too, subjectively, where needs are concerned, material and nonmaterial factors are closely interwoven. In the process old psycho-social themes are firmly embedded—social prestige, identification patterns—but powerful new themes emerge which are utopian in nature. From a materialistic point of view, neither the one nor the other must be suppressed.

Henri Lefèbvre has proposed the concept of the *spectacle*, the exhibition, the show, to fit the present form of mass consumption. Goods and shop windows, traffic and advertisements, stores and the world of communications, news and packaging, architecture and media production come together to form a totality, a permanent theater, which dominates not only the public city centers but also private interiors. The expression "beautiful living" makes the most commonplace objects of general use into props for this universal festival, in which the fetishistic nature of the commodities triumphs completely over their use value. The swindle these festivals perpetrate is, and remains, a swindle within the present social structure. But it is the harbinger of something else. Consumption as spectacle contains the promise that want will disappear. The deceptive, brutal, and obscene features of this festival derive from the fact that there can be no question of a real fulfillment of its promise. But so long as scarcity holds sway, use-value remains a decisive category which can only be abolished by trickery. Yet trickery on such a scale is only conceivable if it is based on mass need. This need—it is a utopian one—is there. It is the desire for a new ecology, for a breaking down of environmental barriers, for an aesthetic which is not limited to the sphere of "the artistic." These desires are not—or are not primarily—internalized rules of the game as played by the capitalist system. They have physiological roots and can no longer be suppressed. Consumption as spectacle is—in parody form—the anticipation of a utopian situation.

The promises of the media demonstrate the same ambivalence. They are an answer to the mass need for nonmaterial variety and mobility—which at present finds its material realization in private car ownership and tourism—and they exploit it. Other collective wishes, which capital often recognizes more quickly and evaluates more correctly than its opponents, but naturally only so as to trap them and rob them of their explosive force, are just as powerful, just as unequivocally emancipatory: the need to take part in the social process on a local, national, and international scale; the need for new forms of interaction, for release from ignorance and tutelage; the need for self-determination. "Be everywhere!" is one of the most successful slogans of the media industry. The readers' parliament of *Bild-Zeitung* (the Springer Press mass publication) was direct democracy used against the interests of the *demos*. "Open spaces" and "free time" are concepts which corral and neutralize the urgent wishes of the masses.

There is corresponding acceptance by the media of utopian stories: e.g., the story of the young Italo-American who hijacked a passenger plane to get home from California to Rome was taken up without protest even by the reactionary mass press and undoubtedly correctly understood by its readers. The identification is based on what has become a general need. Nobody can understand why such journeys should be reserved for politicians, functionaries, and businessmen. The role of the pop star could be analyzed from a similar angle; in it the authoritarian and emancipatory factors are mingled in an extraordinary way. It is perhaps not unimportant that beat music offers groups, not individuals, as identification models. In the productions of the Rolling Stones (and in the manner of their production) the utopian content is apparent. Events like the Woodstock Festival, the concerts in Hyde Park, on the Isle of Wight, and at Altamont, California, develop a mobilizing power which the political Left can only envy.

It is absolutely clear that, within the present social forms, the consciousness industry can satisfy none of the needs on which it lives and which it must fan, except in the illusory form of games. The point, however, is not to demolish its promises but to take them literally and to show that they can be met only through a cultural revolution. Socialists and socialist regimes which multiply the frustration of the masses by declaring their needs to be false, become the accomplices of the system they have undertaken to fight.

## 12. Summary

| *Repressive use of media* | *Emancipatory use of media* |
|---|---|
| Centrally controlled program | Decentralized program |
| One transmitter, many receivers | Each receiver a potential transmitter |
| Immobilization of isolated individuals | Mobilization of the masses |
| Passive consumer behavior | Interaction of those involved, feedback |
| Depoliticization | A political learning process |
| Production by specialists | Collective production |
| Control by property owners or bureaucracy | Social control by self-organization |

## The Subversive Power of the New Media

13. As far as the objectively subversive potentialities of the electronic media are concerned, both sides in the international class struggle—except for the fatalistic adherents of the thesis of manipulation in the metropoles—are of one mind. Frantz Fanon was the first to draw attention to the fact that the transistor receiver was one of the most important weapons in the third world's fight for freedom. Albert Hertzog, ex-Minister of the South African Republic and the mouthpiece of the right wing of the ruling party, is of the opinion that "television will lead to the ruin of the white man in South Africa."[2] American imperialism has recognized the situation. It attempts to meet the "revolution of rising expectations" in Latin America—that is what its ideologues call it—by scattering its own transmitters all over the continent and into the remotest regions of the Amazon basin, and by distributing single-frequency transistors to the native population. The attacks of the Nixon Administration on the capitalist media in the USA reveal its understanding that their reporting, however one-sided and distorted, has become a decisive factor in mobilizing people against the war in Vietnam. Whereas only twenty-five years ago the French massacres in Madagascar, with almost 100,000 dead, became known only to the readers of *Le Monde* under the heading of "Other News" and therefore remained unnoticed and without sequel in the capital city, today the media drag colonial wars into the centers of imperialism.

The direct mobilizing potentialities of the media become still more clear when they are consciously used for subversive ends. Their presence is a factor that immensely increases the demonstrative nature of any political act. The student movements in the USA, in Japan, and in Western Europe soon recognized this and, to begin with, achieved considerable momentary success with the aid of the media. These effects have worn off. Naive trust in the magical power of reproduction cannot replace organizational work; only active and coherent groups can force the media to comply with the logic of their actions. That can be demonstrated from the example of the Tupamaros in Uruguay, whose revolutionary practice has implicit in it publicity for their actions. Thus the actors become authors. The abduction of the American ambassador in Rio de Janeiro was planned with a view to its impact on the media. It was a television production. The Arab guerrillas proceed in the same way. The first to experiment with these techniques internationally were the Cubans. Fidel appreciated the revolutionary potential of the media correctly from the first (Moncada, 1953). Today illegal political action demands at one and the same time maximum security and maximum publicity.

14. Revolutionary situations always bring with them discontinuous, spontaneous changes brought about by the masses in the existing aggregate of the media. How far the changes thus brought about take root and how permanent they are demonstrates the extent to which a cultural revolution is successful. The situation in the media is the most accurate and sensitive barometer for the rise of bureaucratic or Bonapartist anticyclones. So long as the cultural revolution has the initiative, the social imagination of the masses overcomes even technical backwardness and transforms the function of the old media so that their structures are exploded.

> With our work the Revolution has achieved a colossal labor of propaganda and enlightenment. We ripped up the traditional book into single pages, magnified these a hundred times, printed them in color and stuck them up as posters in the streets. . . . Our lack of printing equipment and the necessity for speed meant that, though the best work was hand-printed, the most rewarding was standardized, lapidary and adapted to the simplest mechanical form of reproduction. Thus State Decrees were printed as rolled-up illustrated leaflets, and Army Orders as illustrated pamphlets.[3]

In the twenties, the Russian film reached a standard that was far in advance of the available productive forces.

Pudovkin's *Kinoglas* and Dziga Vertov's *Kinopravda* were no "newsreels" but political television magazine programs *avant l'écran*. The campaign against illiteracy in Cuba broke through the linear, exclusive, and isolating structure of the medium of the book. In the China of the Cultural Revolution, wall newspapers functioned like an electronic mass medium—at least in the big towns. The resistance of the Czechoslovak population to the Soviet invasion gave rise to spontaneous productivity on the part of the masses, which ignored the institutional barriers of the media. (Details to be supplied.) Such situations are exceptional. It is precisely their utopian nature, which reaches out beyond the existing productive forces (it follows that the productive relationships are not to be permanently overthrown), that makes them precarious, leads to reversals and defeats. They demonstrate all the more clearly what enormous political and cultural energies are hidden in the enchained masses and with what imagination they are able, at the moment of liberation, to realize all the opportunities offered by the new media.

## The Media: An Empty Category
## of Marxist Theory

15. That the Marxist Left should argue theoretically and act practically from the standpoint of the most advanced productive forces in their society, that they should develop in depth all the liberating factors immanent in these forces and use them strategically, is no academic expectation but a political necessity. However, with a single great exception, that of Walter Benjamin (and in his footsteps, Brecht), Marxists have not understood the consciousness industry and have been aware only of its bourgeois-capitalist dark side and not of its socialist possibilities. An author like George Lukács is a perfect example of this theoretical and practical backwardness. Nor are the works of Horkheimer and Adorno free of a nostalgia which clings to early bourgeois media. Their view of the cultural industry cannot be discussed here. Much more typical of Marxism between the two wars is the position of Lukács, which can be seen very clearly from an early essay in "Old Culture and New Culture."[4] "Anything that culture produces" can, according to Lukács, "have real cultural value only *if it is in itself* valuable, if the creation of each individual product is from the standpoint of its maker and a single, finite process. It must, moreover, be a process conditioned by the *human* potentialities and capabilities of the creator. The most typical example of such a process is the work of art, where the entire genesis of the work is exclusively the result of the artist's labor and each detail of the work that emerges is determined by the individual qualities of the artist. In highly developed mechanical industry, on the other hand, any connection between the product and the creator is abolished. *The human being serves the machine, he adapts to it.* Production becomes completely independent of the human potentialities and capabilities of the worker." These "forces which destroy culture" impair the work's "truth to the material," its "level," and deal the final blow to the "work as an end in itself." There is no more question of "the organic unity of the products of culture, its harmonious, joy-giving being." Capitalist culture must lack "the simple and natural harmony and beauty of the old culture—culture in the true, literal sense of the world." Fortunately things need not remain so. The "culture of proletarian society," although "in the context of such scientific research as is possible at this time" nothing more can be said about it, will certainly remedy these ills. Lukács asks himself "which are the cultural values which, in accordance with the nature of this context, *can be taken over from the old society* by the new *and further developed.*" Answer: Not the inhuman machines but "the idea of mankind as an end in itself, the basic idea of the new culture," for it is "the inheritance of the classical idealism of the nineteenth century." Quite right. "This is where the philistine concept of *art* turns up with all its deadly obtuseness—an idea to which all technical considerations are foreign and which feels that with the provocative appearance of the new technology its end has come."[5]

These nostalgic backward glances at the landscape of the last century, these reactionary ideals, are already the forerunners of socialist realism, which mercilessly galvanized and then buried those very "cultural values" which Lukács rode out to rescue. Unfortunately, in the process, the Soviet cultural revolution was thrown to the wolves; but this aesthete can in any case hardly have thought any more highly of it than did J. V. Stalin.

The inadequate understanding which Marxists have shown of the media and the questionable use they have made of them has produced a vacuum in Western industrialized countries into which a stream of non-Marxist hypothesis and practices has consequently flowed. From the Cabaret Voltaire to Andy Warhol's Factory, from the silent film comedians to the Beatles, from the first comic-strip artists to the present managers of the Underground, the apolitical have made much more radical progress in dealing with the media than any grouping of the Left. (Exception—Münzenberg.) Innocents have put themselves in the forefront of the new productive forces on the basis of mere institutions with which communism—to its detriment—has not wished to concern itself. Today this apolitical avant-garde has found its ventriloquist and prophet in Marshall McLuhan, an author who admittedly lacks any analytical categories for the understanding of social processes, but whose confused books serve as a quarry of undigested observations for the media industry. Certainly his little finger has experienced more of the productive power of the new media than all the ideological commissions of the CPSU and their endless resolutions and directives put together.

Incapable of any theoretical construction, McLuhan does not present his material as a concept but as the common denominator of a reactionary doctrine of salvation. He admittedly did not invent but was the first to formulate explicitly a mystique of the media which dissolves all political problems in smoke—the same smoke that gets in the eyes of his followers. It promises the salvation of man through the technology of television and indeed of television as it is practiced today. Now McLuhan's attempt to stand Marx on his head is not exactly new. He shares with his numerous predecessors the determination to suppress all problems of the economic base, their idealistic tendencies, and their belittling of the class struggle in the naive terms of a vague humanism. A new Rousseau—like all copies, only a pale version of the old—he preaches the gospel of the new primitive man who, naturally on a higher level, must return to prehistoric tribal existence in the "global village."

It is scarcely worthwhile to deal with such concepts. This charlatan's most famous saying—"the medium is the message"—perhaps deserves more attention. In spite of its provocative idiocy, it betrays more than its author knows. It reveals in the most accurate way the tautological nature of the mystique of the media. The one remarkable thing about the television set, according to him, is that it moves—a thesis which in view of the nature of American programs has, admittedly, something attractive about it.

The complementary mistake consists in the widespread illusion that media are neutral instruments by which any "messages" one pleases can be transmitted without regard for their structure or for the structure of the medium. In the East European countries the television newsreaders read fifteen-minute long conference communiqués and Central Committee resolutions which are not even suitable for printing in a newspaper, clearly under the delusion that they might fascinate a public of millions.

The sentence, "the medium is the message," transmits yet another message, however, and a much more important one. It tells us that the bourgeoisie does indeed have all possible means at its disposal to communicate something to us, but that it has nothing more to say. It is ideologically sterile. Its intention to hold on to the control of the means of production at any price, while being incapable of making the socially necessary use of them, is here expressed with complete frankness in the superstructure. It wants the media *as such* and *to no purpose.*

This wish has been shared for decades and given symbolical expression by an artistic avant-garde whose program logically admits only the alternative of negative signals and amorphous noise. Example: the already outdated "literature of silence," Warhol's films in which everything can happen at once or nothing at all, and John Cage's forty-five-minute-long *Lecture on Nothing* (1959).

## The Achievement of Benjamin

16. The revolution in the conditions of production in the superstructure has made the traditional aesthetic theory unusable, completely unhinging its fundamental categories and destroying its "standards." The theory of knowledge on which it was based is outmoded. In the electronic media, a radically altered relationship between subject and object emerges with which the old critical concepts cannot deal. The idea of the self-sufficient work of art collapsed long ago. The long-drawn discussion over the death of art proceeds in a circle so long as it does not examine critically the aesthetic concept on which it is based, so long as it employs criteria which no longer correspond to the state of the productive forces. When constructing an aesthetic adapted to the changed situation, one must take as a starting point the work of the only Marxist theoretician who recognized the liberating potential of the new media. Thirty-five years ago, that is to say, at a time when the consciousness industry was relatively undeveloped, Walter Benjamin subjected this phenomenon to a penetrating dialectical-materialist analysis.

His approach has not been matched by any theory since then, much less further developed.

One might generalize by saying: the technique of reproduction detaches the reproduced object from the domain of tradition. By making many reproductions it substitutes a plurality of copies for a unique existence. And in permitting the reproduction to meet the beholder or listener in his own particular situation, it reactivates the object reproduced. These two processes lead to a tremendous shattering of tradition which is the obverse of the contemporary crisis and renewal of mankind. Both processes are intimately connected with the contemporary mass movements. Their most powerful agent is the film. Its social significance, particularly in its most positive form, is inconceivable without its destructive, cathartic aspect, that is, the liquidation of the traditional value of the cultural heritage.

> For the first time in world history, mechanical reproduction emancipates the work of art from its parasitical dependence on ritual. To an ever greater degree the work of art reproduced becomes the work of art designed for reproducibility. . . . But the instant the criterion of authenticity ceases to be applicable to artistic production, the total function of art is reversed. Instead of being based on ritual, it begins to be based on another practice—politics. . . . Today, by the absolute emphasis on its exhibition value, the work of art becomes a creation with entirely new functions, among which the one we are conscious of, the artistic function, later may be recognized as incidental.[6]

The trends which Benjamin recognized in his day in the film and the true import of which he grasped theoretically, have become patent today with the rapid development of the consciousness industry. What used to be called art, has now, in the strict Hegelian sense, been dialectically surpassed by and in the media. The quarrel about the end of art is otiose so long as this end is not understood dialectically. Artistic productivity reveals itself to be the extreme marginal case of a much more widespread productivity, and it is socially important only insofar as it surrenders all pretensions to autonomy and recognizes itself to be a marginal case. Wherever the professional producers make a virtue out of the necessity of their specialist skills and even derive a privileged status from them, their experience and knowledge have become useless. This means that as far as an aesthetic

theory is concerned, a radical change in perspectives is needed. Instead of looking at the productions of the new media from the point of view of the older modes of production we must, on the contrary, analyze the products of the traditional "artistic" media from the standpoint of modern conditions of production.

> Earlier much futile thought had been devoted to the question of whether photography is an art. The primary question—whether the very invention of photography had not transformed the entire nature of art—was not raised. Soon the film theoreticians asked the same ill-considered question with regard to the film. But the difficulties which photography caused traditional aesthetics were mere child's play as compared to those raised by the film.[7]

The panic aroused by such a shift in perspectives is understandable. The process not only changes the old burdensome craft secrets in the superstructure into white elephants, it also conceals a genuinely destructive element. It is, in a word, risky. But the only chance for the aesthetic tradition lies in its dialectical supersession. In the same way, classical physics has survived as a marginal special case within the framework of a much more comprehensive theory.

This state of affairs can be identified in individual cases in all the traditional artistic disciplines. Their present-day developments remain incomprehensible so long as one attempts to deduce them from their own prehistory. On the other hand, their usefulness or otherwise can be judged as soon as one regards them as special cases in a general aesthetic of the media. Some indications of the possible critical approaches which stem from this will be made below, taking literature as an example.

## The Supersession of Written Culture

17. Written literature has, historically speaking, played a dominant role for only a few centuries. Even today, the predominance of the book has an episodic air. An incomparably longer time preceded it in which literature was oral. Now it is being succeeded by the age of the electronic media, which tend once more to make people speak. At its period of fullest development, the book to some extent usurped the place of the more primitive but generally more accessible methods of production of the past; on the other hand, it was a stand-in for future methods which make it possible for everyone to become a producer.

The revolutionary role of the printed book has been described often enough and it would be absurd to deny it. From the point of view of its structure as a medium, written literature, like the bourgeoisie who produced it and whom it served, was progressive. (See the *Communist Manifesto*.) On the analogy of the economic development of capitalism, which was indispensable for the development of the industrial revolution, the nonmaterial productive forces could not have developed without their own capital accumulation. (We also owe the accumulation of *Das Kapital* and its teachings to the medium of the book.)

Nevertheless, almost everybody speaks better than he writes. (This also applies to authors.) Writing is a highly formalized technique which, in purely physiological terms, demands a peculiarly rigid bodily posture. To this there corresponds the high degree of social specialization that it demands. Professional writers have always tended to think in caste terms. The class character of their work is unquestionable, even in the age of universal compulsory education. The whole process is extraordinarily beset with taboos. Spelling mistakes, which are completely immaterial in terms of communication, are punished by the social disqualification of the writer. The rules that govern this technique have a normative power attributed to them for which there is no rational basis. Intimidation through the written word has remained a widespread and class-specific phenomenon even in advanced industrial societies.

These alienating factors cannot be eradicated from written literature. They are reinforced by the methods by which society transmits its writing techniques. While people learn to speak very early, and mostly in psychologically favorable conditions, learning to write forms an important part of authoritarian socialization by the school ("good writing" as a kind of breaking-in). This sets its stamp forever on written communication—on its tone, its syntax, and its whole style. (This also applies to the text on this page.)

The formalization of written language permits and encourages the repression of opposition. In speech, unresolved contradictions betray themselves by pauses, hesitations, slips of the tongue, repetitions, anacoluthons, quite apart from phrasing, mimicry, gesticulation, pace, and volume. The aesthetic of written literature scorns such involuntary factors as "mistakes." It demands, explicitly or implicitly, the smoothing out of contradictions, rationalization, regularization of the spoken form irrespective of content. Even as a child, the writer is urged to hide his unsolved problems behind a protective screen of correctness.

Structurally, the printed book is a medium that operates as a monologue, isolating producer and reader. Feedback and interaction are extremely limited, demand elaborate procedures, and only in the rarest cases lead to corrections. Once an edition has been printed it cannot be corrected; at best it can be pulped. The control circuit in the case of literary criticism is extremely cumbersome and elitist. It excludes the public on principle.

None of the characteristics that distinguish written and printed literature apply to the electronic media. Microphone and camera abolish the class character of the mode of production (not of the production itself). The normative rules become unimportant. Oral interviews, arguments, demonstrations, neither demand nor allow orthography or "good writing." The television screen exposes the aesthetic smoothing out of contradictions as camouflage. Admittedly, swarms of liars appear on it, but anyone can see from a long way off that they are peddling something. As at present constituted, radio, film, and television are burdened to excess with authoritarian characteristics, the characteristics of the monologue, which they have inherited from older methods of production—and that is no accident. These outworn elements in today's media aesthetics are demanded by the social relations. They do not follow from the structure of the media. On the contrary, they go against it, for the structure demands interaction.

It is extremely improbable, however, that writing as a special technique will disappear in the foreseeable future. That goes for the book as well, the practical advantages of which for many purposes remain obvious. It is admittedly less handy and it takes up more room than other storage systems, but up to now it offers simpler methods of access than, for example, the microfilm or the tape bank. It ought to be integrated into the system as a marginal case and thereby forfeit its aura of cult and ritual.

This can be deduced from technological developments. Electronics are noticeably taking over writing: teleprinters, reading machines, high-speed transmissions, automatic photographic and electronic composition, automatic writing devices, typesetters, electrostatic processes, ampex libraries, cassette encyclopedias, photocopiers and magnetic copiers, speedprinters.

273

The outstanding Russian media expert El Lissitsky, incidentally, demanded an "electro-library" as far back as 1923—a request which, given the technical conditions of the time, must have seemed ridiculous or at least incomprehensible. This is how far this man's imagination reached into the future:

I draw the following analogy:

| Inventions in the field of verbal traffic | Inventions in the field of general traffic |
| --- | --- |
| Articulated language | Upright gait |
| Writing | The wheel |
| Gutenberg's printing press | Carts drawn by animal power |
| ? | The automobile |
| ? | The airplane |

I have produced this analogy to prove that so long as the book remains a palpable object, i.e. so long as it is not replaced by auto-vocalizing and kino-vocalizing representations, we must look to the field of the manufacture of books for basic innovations in the near future.

There are signs at hand suggesting that this basic innovation is likely to come from the neighborhood of the collotype.[8]

Today, writing has in many cases already become a secondary technique, a means of transcribing orally recorded speech: tape-recorded proceedings, attempts at speech-pattern recognition, and the conversion of speech into writing.

18. The ineffectiveness of literary criticism when faced with so-called documentary literature is an indication of how far the critics' thinking has lagged behind the stage of the productive forces. It stems from the fact that the media have eliminated one of the most fundamental categories of aesthetics up to now—fiction. The fiction/nonfiction argument has been laid to rest just as was the nineteenth century's favorite dialectic of "art" and "life." In his day, Benjamin demonstrated that the "apparatus" (the concept of the medium was not yet available to him) abolishes authenticity. In the productions of the consciousness industry, the difference between the "geniune" original and the reproduction disappears—"that aspect of reality which is not dependent on the apparatus has now become its most artificial aspect." The process of reproduction reacts on the object reproduced and alters it fundamentally. The efforts of this have not yet been adequately explained epistemologically. The categorical uncertainties to which it gives rise also affect the concept of the documentary. Strictly speaking, it has shrunk to its legal dimensions. A document is something the "forging"—i.e. the reproduction—of which is punishable by imprisonment. This definition naturally has no theoretical meaning. The reason is that a reproduction, to the extent that its technical quality is good enough, cannot be distinguished in any way from the original, irrespective of whether it is a painting, a passport, or a bank note. The legal concept of the documentary record is only pragmatically useful; it serves only to protect economic interests.

The productions of the electronic media, by their nature, evade such distinctions as those between documentary and feature films. They are in every case explicitly determined by the given situation. The producer can never pretend, like the traditional novelist, "to stand above things." He is therefore partisan from the start. This fact finds formal expression in his techniques. Cutting, editing, dubbing—these are techniques for conscious manipulation without which the use of the new media is inconceivable. It is precisely in these work processes that their productive power reveals itself—and here it is completely immaterial whether one is dealing with the production of a reportage or a play. The material, whether "documentary" or "fiction," is in each case only a prototype, a half-finished article, and the more closely one examines its origins, the more blurred the difference becomes. (Develop more precisely. The reality in which a camera turns up is always faked, e.g., the moon landing.)

## The Desacralization of Art

19. The media also do away with the old category of works of art which can only be considered as separate objects, not as independent of their material infrastructure. The media do not produce such objects. They create programs. Their production is in the nature of a process. That does not mean only (or not primarily) that there is no foreseeable end to the program—a fact which, in view of what we are at present presented with, admittedly makes a certain hostility to the media understandable. It means, above all, that the media program is open to its own consequences without structural limitations. (This is not an empirical description but a demand. A demand which admittedly is not made of the medium from without; it is a consequence of its nature, from

which the much-vaunted open form can be derived—and not as a modification of it—from an old aesthetic.) The programs of the consciousness industry must subsume into themselves their own results, the reactions and the corrections which they call forth, otherwise they are already out-of-date. They are therefore to be thought of not as means of consumption but as means of their own production.

20. It is characteristic of artistic avant-gardes that they have, so to speak, a presentiment of the potentiality of media which still lie in the future. "It has always been one of the most important tasks of art to give rise to a demand, the time for the complete satisfaction of which has not yet come. The history of every art form has critical periods when that form strives towards effects which can only be easily achieved if the technical norm is changed, that is to say, in a new art form. The artistic extravagances and crudities which arise in this way, for instance in the so-called decadent period, really stem from art's richest historical source of power. Dadaism in the end teemed with such barbarisms. We can only now recognize the nature of its striving. Dadaism was attempting to achieve those effects which the public today seeks in film with the means of painting (or of literature)."[9] This is where the prognostic value of otherwise inessential productions, such as happenings, flux, and mixed-media shows, is to be found. There are writers who in their work show an awareness of the fact that media with the characteristics of the monologue today have only a residual use-value. Many of them admittedly draw fairly shortsighted conclusions from this glimpse of the truth. For example, they offer the user the opportunity to arrange the material provided by arbitrary permutations. Every reader as it were should write his own book. When carried to extremes, such attempts to produce interaction, even when it goes against the structure of the medium employed, are nothing more than invitations to freewheel. Mere noise permits of no articulated interactions. Short cuts, of the kind that concept art peddles, are based on the banal and false conclusion that the development of the productive forces renders all work superfluous. With the same justification, one could leave a computer to its own devices on the assumption that a random generator will organize material production by itself. Fortunately, cybernetics experts are not given to such childish games.

21. For the old-fashioned "artist"—let us call him the author—it follows from these reflections that he must see it as his goal to make himself redundant as a specialist in much the same way as a teacher of literacy only fulfills his task when he is no longer necessary. Like every learning process, this process too is reciprocal. The specialist will learn as much or more from the nonspecialists as the other way round. Only then can he contrive to make himself dispensable.

Meanwhile, his social usefulness can best be measured by the degree to which he is capable of using the liberating factors in the media and bringing them to fruition. The tactical contradictions in which he must become involved in the process can neither be denied nor covered up in any way. But strategically his role is clear. The author has to work as the agent of the masses. He can lose himself in them only when they themselves become authors, the authors of history.

22. "Pessimism of the intelligence, optimism of the will" (Antonio Gramsci).

Notes
1. Bertolt Brecht, *Theory of Radio* (1932), *Gesammelte Werke,* Band VIII, pp. 129 ff, 134.
2. *Der Spiegel,* Oct. 20, 1969.
3. El Lissitsky, "The Future of the Book," *New Left Review* 41, p. 42.
4. *Kommunismus, Zeitschrift der Kommunistischen Internationale für die Länder Südosteuropas,* 1920, pp. 1538–49.
5. Walter Benjamin, "Kleine Geschichte der Photographie" in *Das Kunstwerk im Zeitalter seiner technischen Reproduzierbarkeit* (Frankfurt: 1963), p. 69.
6. Walter Benjamin, "The Work of Art in the Age of Mechanical Reproduction," *Illuminations* (New York: 1969), pp. 221–25.
7. Ibid., p. 227.
8. Lissitsky, "The Future of the Book," p. 40.
9. Benjamin, "The Work of Art in the Age of Mechanical Reproduction," p. 237.

# 19. [Introduction]
# Requiem for the Media

Jean Baudrillard's response to the previous selection, Enzensberger's "Constituents of a Theory of the Media," is not an elaboration of the idea of *simulation* (as many of his works are), but a discussion of a different concept that might be called *interaction*.

Baudrillard argues strongly against one position of Enzensberger's, and of Marshall McLuhan: that there is an inherent structure to media *technologically*. Baudrillard argues that media serve a social function—the reduction of all they reproduce to pale models, foreclosing any possibility of genuine reciprocity. It is in this sense that Baudrillard rereads McLuhan's maxim that "the medium is the message."

Baudrillard's position is that the situation will not get any better simply by making everyone a producer—a point of view that Enzensberger shares. But Baudrillard goes on to say that even the organized reversible circuits Enzensberger discusses would not be enough. He writes, "*Reversibility* has nothing to do with reciprocity."

For Baudrillard the problem lies not in who transmits, or how turn-taking is arranged, but in our very underlying model of communication—which is reproduced in the media, in political life, and in economic life. This model, described by Ferdinand de Saussure, is that of "transmitter-message-receiver." As Baudrillard points out, in this model there is no place for the ambiguity of true exchange, "This 'scientific' construction is rooted in a *simulation* model of communication. It excludes, from its inception, the reciprocity and antagonism of interlocutors, and the ambivalence of their exchange."

An alternative to this semio-linguistic conception (in which one is the transmitter and one the receiver, with the message always going from one to another) is that of joint production through genuine interaction. In this, argues Baudrillard, lies the true potential for change—in the refusal to accept a model of producers and consumers, even one in which these positions can be reversed. Which brings us to more concrete questions: How would one taking Baudrillard's position look upon the examples of media from the introduction to the previous selection (◊18)? How would this position view Enzensberger's ideas of "Networklike communications models . . . a mass newspaper, written and distributed by its readers, a video network of politically active groups" or the uses of media in relation to the protests against the World Trade Organization?

Baudrillard's reaction to Enzensberger's mass newspaper and video network is not to declare them inappropriate; he treats them somewhat positively. However, he states that their value lies precisely in the fact that they are inconsistent with the rest of Enzensberger's argument. Baudrillard sees them not as demonstrating the reversibility of producer/consumer, but as *transgressing* these categories.

This might make our other examples "a start" from a Baudrillardian point of view as well. Yet examples of a phenomenon that Baudrillard critiques—the cybernetic absorption of response into meaninglessness via reversible media—are significantly more plentiful. Consider how those who were once solely media consumers, and suddenly are included in production, have served only to cement their irrelevance on reality-based TV, on game shows, and on corporate-run Web message boards.

—NWF

In short, Baudrillard is not focused on the media's structure of technology, nor of production, nor even of content. Instead he turns our attention toward reciprocity, interaction. He then proposes a radical formulation of the issues at stake. However, neither Baudrillard's nor Enzensberger's (◊18) essay gives much indication of how to stimulate the more interactive communications they envision. Enzensberger's call for "organization" is rather nebulous, and certainly Baudrillard's discussion of graffiti doesn't open up many avenues for further exploration. More inspiring, perhaps, is a model of performance developed in a very different environment than the Happening or *9 Evenings*: Augusto Boal's *Theatre of the Oppressed*. Boal's concrete methods for transgressing the categories of producer and consumer (a.k.a. actor and spectator) are described in this volume (◊22).

◊18
259

**277**

◊22
339

Another Web phenomenon that might fruitfully be considered in light of Enzensberger and Baudrillard's arguments is that of *blogs* (web logs). These serial, often personal publications commonly create meaning in between one another—in the space of interlinked responses to each other's postings.

**Further Reading**

Baudrillard, Jean. "The Ecstasy of Communication." Trans. John Johnston. *The Anti-Aesthetic: Essays on Postmodern Culture,* 126–134. Ed. Hal Foster. Seattle: Bay Press, 1983. From the French "L'extase de la communication."

Baudrillard, Jean. *Simulations.* Trans. Paul Foss, Paul Patton, and Philip Beitchman. New York: Semiotext(e)/Columbia University Press, 1983. Partial translation of the French *Simulacres et simulation.* Paris: Galilée, 1981.

Lunenfeld, Peter, ed. *The Digital Dialectic: New Essays on New Media.* Cambridge: MIT Press, 2000.

Mortensen, Torill and Jill Walker. "Blogging Thoughts: Personal Publication as an Online Research Tool." *Researching ICTs in Context,* 249–279. Ed. Andrew Morrison. Intermedia Report 3/2002, University of Oslo. 2002. <http://www.intermedia.uio.no/konferanser/skikt-02/>

Original Publication

*For a Critique of the Political Economy of the Sign,* 164–184. Trans. Charles Levin. Saint Louis, Mo.: Telos Press, 1981. Reprinted in *Video Culture: A Critical Investigation,* ed. John Hanhardt. Rochester, N.Y.: Visual Studies Workshop Press. Dist. Layton, Utah: Peregrine Smith Books, 1986.

From the French *Pour une critique de l'economie politique du signe.* Paris: Gallimard, 1972.

# Requiem for the Media

## Jean Baudrillard

### Introit

There is no theory of the media. The "media revolution" has remained empirical and mystical, as much in the work of McLuhan as with his opponents. McLuhan has said, with his usual Canadian-Texan brutalness, that Marx, the spiritual contemporary of the steam engine and railroads, was already obsolete in his lifetime with the appearance of the telegraph.[1] In his candid fashion, he is saying that Marx, in his materialist analysis of production, had virtually circumscribed productive forces as a privileged domain from which language, signs, and communication in general found themselves excluded. In fact, Marx does not even provide for a genuine theory of railroads as "media," as modes of communication: they hardly enter into consideration. And he certainly established no theory of technical evolution in general, except from the point of view of production— primary, material, infrastructural production as the almost exclusive determinant of social relations. Dedicated to an intermediate ideality and a blind social practice, the "mode of communication" has had the leisure for an entire century

of "making revolution" without changing the theory of the mode of production one iota in the process.

Having admitted this much, and on condition (which is already a revolution by comparison to orthodox Marxism) that the exchange of signs is not treated as a marginal, superstructural dimension in relation to those beings whom the only "true" theory (materialist) defines as "producers of their real life" (i.e., of goods destined to satisfy their needs), it is possible to imagine two perspectives:

1. One retains the general form of Marxist analysis (dialectical contradiction between forces and relations of production), but admits that the classical definition of productive forces is too restricted, so one expands the analysis in terms of productive forces to the whole murky field of signification and communication. This involves setting loose in all their originality the contradictions born from this theoretical and practical extension of the field of political economy. Such a hypothesis is the point of departure for Enzensberger: "Monopoly capitalism develops the consciousness-shaping industry more quickly and more extensively than other sectors of production; it must at the same time fetter it. A socialist media theory has to work at this contradiction."[2] But this hypothesis does little more than signal the virtual extension of the commodity form to all the domains of social life (and tardily, at that). It recognizes the existence, here and now, of a classical communication theory, a bourgeois political economy of signs and of their production (just as there existed one of material production as early as the 18th century). It is a class-bound theoretical discipline.[3] It has not been answered by any fundamental critique that could be seen as the logical extension of Marx's. Since the entire domain was related to the superstructure, this *critique of the political economy of the sign* was rendered unthinkable. Thus, at best, Enzensberger's hypothesis can do little more than try to vitiate the

immense retardation of classical Marxist theory. It is only radical in the eyes of official Marxism, which is totally submerged into the dominant models, and would risk its own survival if it went even that far. *The radical alternative lies elsewhere.*

2. The production of meaning, messages, and signs poses a crucial problem to revolutionary theory. Instead of reinterpreting it in terms of classical forces of production— that is, instead of merely generalizing an analysis that is considered final and stamped with the seal of approval by the "spokesmen of the revolution"—the alternative is to thoroughly disrupt the latter in the light of the eruption of this new problem into the theoretical field (an approach no self-respecting Marxist would take, even under the guise of a hypothesis).

In other words: perhaps the Marxist theory of production is irredeemably partial, and cannot be generalized. Or again: the theory of production (the dialectical chaining of contradictions linked to the development of productive forces) is strictly homogeneous with its object—*material production*—and is non-transferable, as a postulate or theoretical framework, to contents that were never given for it in the first place.[4] The dialectical form is adequate to certain contents, those of material production: it exhausts them of meaning, but unlike an archetype, it does not exceed the definition of this object. The dialectic lies in ashes because it offered itself as a system of interpreting the *separated* order of material production.

All in all, this point of view is quite logical. It accords a global coherence to Marxist analysis—an internal homogeneity that prevents certain elements from being retained and others from being excluded, according to a technique of *bricolage* of which the Althusserians are the most subtle artificers. On the other hand, we credit Marxism with a maximum coherence. And so we demand that this coherence be breached, for it is incapable of responding to a social process that far exceeds material production.[5]

## Enzensberger: A "Socialist" Strategy

In the absence of a theory and a positive strategy, argues Enzensberger, the Left remains disarmed. It is content to denounce mass-media culture as an ideological manipulation. The Left dreams of a media takeover, sometimes as a means of nudging the revolutionary *prise de conscience* of the masses, sometimes as a consequence of radical change in

social structures. But this is a contradictory velleity, reflecting quite straightforwardly the impossibility of integrating the media into a theory of infra- and superstructure. The media (and the entire domain of signs and communication, it should be added) remain a social mystery for the Left, according to Enzensberger, because the Left has failed to conceive of them as a new and gigantic potential of productive forces. The Left is divided between fascination and practice before this sorcery to which it also falls victim, but which it reproves morally and intellectually (here is that Left intellectual speaking through Enzensberger himself, making his autocritique). This ambivalence only reflects the ambivalence of the media themselves, without going beyond it or reducing it.[6] With a bold stroke of Marxist sociology, Enzensberger imputes this "phobia" of intellectuals and Left movements to their bourgeois or petty bourgeois origins: they defend themselves instinctively from mass culture because it snaps their cultural privilege.[7] True or false, perhaps it would be more valuable to ask, with respect to this mesmerized distrust, this tactical disarray and the Left intelligentsia's refusal to get involved with the media, precisely how much are Marxist preconceptions themselves to blame? The nostalgic idealism of the infrastructure? The theoretical allergy to everything that isn't "material" production and "productive labor"? "Revolutionary" doctrine has never come to terms with the exchange of signs other than as pragmatically functional use: information, broadcasting, and propaganda. The contemporary new look of left-wing public relations, and the whole modernist party subculture, are hardly designed to transform this tendency. They demonstrate quite sufficiently how bourgeois ideology can be generated independently of "social origin."

All of this, Enzensberger continues, results in a political schizophrenia of the Left. On one side, a whole (subversive) revolutionary faction abandons itself to apolitical exploration of new media (subculture, underground); on the other, militant political groups still live essentially through archaic modes of communication, refusing to "play the game," or to exploit the immense possibilities of the electronic media. Thus, he reproaches the students of May '68 for having regressed to artisanal means (referring to the hand presses of the Ecole des Beaux Arts) for spreading their slogans and for having occupied the Odéon, "steeped in tradition," instead of the ORTF.[8,9]

279

Enzensberger attempts to develop an optimistic and offensive position. The media are monopolized by the dominant classes, which *divert* them to their own advantage. But the structure of the media remains "fundamentally egalitarian," and it is up to the revolutionary praxis to disengage this potentiality inscribed in the media, but perverted by the capitalist order. Let us say the word: to liberate the media, to return them to their social vocation of open communication and unlimited democratic exchange, their true socialist destiny.

Clearly what we have here is an extension of the same schema assigned, since time immemorial, from Marx to Marcuse, to productive forces and technology: they are the promise of human fulfillment, but capitalism freezes or confiscates them. They are liberatory, but it is necessary to liberate them.[10] The media, as we can see, do not escape this fantastic logic of inscribing the revolution *inter alia* onto things. To set the media back to the logic of productive forces no longer qualifies as a critical act, for it only locks them more firmly into the revolutionary metaphysic.

As usual, this position bogs down in contradictions. Through their own (capitalist) development, the media assure that socialization is pushed to more and more advanced stages. Even though it is technically quite imaginable, there is no closed-circuit television for the happy few who could afford it, "because this would go against the grain of the structure" of the medium.[11] "For the first time in history, the media make possible the participation of the masses in a collective process that is social and socialized, participation in which the practical means are in the hands of the masses themselves."[12] But the "socialist movements must fight and will fight for their own wavelengths."[13] Why fight (above all for wavelengths), if the media realize themselves in socialism? If such is their structural vocation?

The existing order, says Enzensberger following Brecht (*Theory of Radio*, 1932), reduces the media to a simple "medium of distribution."[14] So they must be revamped into a true medium of communication (always the same dream haunts the Marxist imaginary: strip objects of their exchange value in order to restore their use value); and this transformation, he adds, "is not technically a problem." But:

1. It is false that in the present order the media are "purely and simply means of distribution." Once again, that is to treat them as the relay of an ideology that would find its determinations elsewhere (in the mode of material

production); in other words, the media as marketing and merchandizing of the dominant ideology. It is from this perspective that the relation media producer-transmitter *versus* irresponsible, receptive masses is assimilated to that of capitalist versus salaried worker. But it is not as vehicles of content, but in their form and very operation, that media induce a social relation; and this is not an exploitative relation: it involves the abstraction, separation, and abolition of exchange itself. The media are not *co-efficients*, but *effectors* of ideology. Not only is their destiny far from revolutionary; the media are not even, somewhere else or potentially, neutral or non-ideological (the phantasm of their technical status or of their social use value). Reciprocally, ideology does not exist in some place apart, as the discourse of the dominant class, *before* it is channeled through the media. The same applies to the sphere of commodities: nowhere do the latter possess ontological status independently of the form they take in the operation of the exchange value system. Nor is ideology some Imaginary floating in the wake of exchange value: it is the very operation of the exchange value itself. After the *Requiem* for the dialectic, it is necessary to toll the *Requiem* of the infra- and superstructure.

2. It follows that when Brecht and Enzensberger assert that the transformation of the media into a true medium of communication is not technically a problem ("it is nothing more," says Brecht, "than the natural consequence of their technical development"), it is necessary to understand (but, contrarily, and without playing on words) that in effect it is quite correctly *not a technical problem*, since media ideology functions at the level of *form*, at the level of the separation it establishes, which is a *social* division.

## Speech Without Response

The mass media are anti-mediatory and intransitive. They fabricate non-communication—this is what characterizes them, if one agrees to define communication as an exchange, as a reciprocal space of a speech and a response, and thus of a responsibility (not a psychological or moral responsibility, but a personal, mutual correlation in exchange). We must understand communication as something other than the simple transmission-reception of a message, whether or not the latter is considered reversible through feedback. Now, the totality of the existing architecture of the media founds itself on this latter definition: they are what always prevents response, making all processes of exchange impossible (except in the various forms of response simulation, themselves integrated in the transmission process, thus leaving the unilateral nature of the communication intact). This is the real abstraction of the media. And the system of social control and power is rooted in it.

To understand the term *response* properly, we must take it in an emphatic sense, by referring to an equivalent in "primitive" societies: power belongs to the one who can give and *cannot be repaid*. To give, and to do it in such a way that one is unable to repay, is to disrupt the exchange to your profit and to institute a monopoly. The social process is thus thrown out of equilibrium, whereas repaying disrupts this power relationship and institutes (or reinstitutes), on the basis of an antagonistic reciprocity, the circuit of symbolic exchange. The same goes for the media: they speak, or something is spoken there, but in such a way as *to exclude any response anywhere*. This is why the only revolution in this domain—indeed, the revolution everywhere: the revolution *tout court*—lies in restoring this possibility of response. But such a simple possibility presupposes an upheaval in the entire existing structure of the media.

No other theory or strategy is possible. All vague impulses to democratize content, subvert it, restore the "transparency of the code," control the information process, contrive a reversibility of circuits, or take power over media are hopeless—unless the monopoly of speech is broken; and one cannot break the monopoly of speech if one's goal is simply to distribute it equally to everyone. Speech must be able to exchange, give, and repay itself[15] as is occasionally the case with looks and smiles. It cannot simply be interrupted, congealed, stockpiled, and redistributed in some corner of the social process.[16]

For the time being, we live in the era of non-response—of irresponsibility. "Minimal autonomous activity on the part of the spectator and voter," says Enzensberger. The mass medium *par excellence*, and the most beautiful of them all, is the electoral system: its crowning achievement is the referendum, where the response is implied in the question itself, as in the polls. It is a speech that answers itself via the simulated detour of a response, and here as well, the absolutization of speech under the formal guise of exchange is *the* definition of power. Roland Barthes has made note of the same non-reciprocity in literature: "Our literature is characterized by the pitiless divorce which the literary

institution maintains between the producer of the text and its user, between its owner and customer, between its author and its reader. This reader is thereby plunged into a kind of idleness—he is intransitive; he is, in short, *serious:* instead of functioning himself, instead of gaining access to the magic of the signifier, to the pleasure of writing, he is left with no more than the poor freedom either to accept or reject the text: reading is nothing more than a *referendum*."[17]

Today, the status of the *consumer* defines this banishment. The generalized order of consumption is nothing other than that sphere where it is no longer permitted to give, to reimburse, or to exchange, but only to take and to make use of (appropriation, individualized use value). In this case, consumption goods also constitute a mass medium: they answer to the general state of affairs we have described. Their specific function is of little import: the consumption of products and messages is the abstract social relation that they establish, the ban raised against all forms of response and reciprocity.

Thus, it is far from true that, as Enzensberger affirms, "for the first time in history, the media make possible a mass participation in a productive social process"; nor that "the practical means of this participation are in the hands of the masses themselves." As if owning a TV set or a camera inaugurated a new possibility of relationship and exchange. Strictly speaking, such cases are no more significant than the possession of a refrigerator or a toaster. There is no *response* to a functional object: its function is already there, an integrated speech to which it has already responded, leaving no room for play, or reciprocal *putting in play* (unless one destroys the object, or turns its function inside out).[18] So the functionalized object, like all messages functionalized by the media, like the operation of a referendum, controls rupture, the emergence of meaning, and censorship. As an extreme case, authority would provide every citizen with a TV set without preoccupying itself with programming (assuming an authority that was not also obsessed by content and convinced of the ideological force of media "persuasion," and thus of the need to control the message). It is useless to fantasize about the state projection of police control through TV (as Enzensberger has remarked of Orwell's 1984): TV, by virtue of its mere presence, is a social control in itself. There is no need to imagine it as a state periscope spying on everyone's private life—the situation as it stands is more efficient than that: it is the *certainty that people are no longer speaking to each other*, that they are definitively isolated in the fact of a speech without response.

From this perspective, McLuhan, whom Enzensberger scorns as a kind of ventriloquist, is much closer to a theory when he declares that "the medium is the message" (save that, in his total blindness to the social forms discussed here, he exalts the media and their global message with a delirious tribal optimism). *The medium is the message* is not a critical proposition. But in its paradoxical form, it has analytic value,[19] whereas the ingenuity of Enzensberger with regard to the "structural properties of the media" such that "no power can permit the liberation of their potentiality" turns out to be mysticism, although it wants to be revolutionary. The mystique of the socialist predestination of the media is opposite but complementary to the Orwellian myth of their terrorist manipulation by authority. Even God would approve of socialism: Christians say it all the time.

## Subversive Strategy and "Symbolic Action"

It could be objected that the media did, after all, play a significant role in the events of May '68 in France, by spontaneously playing up the revolutionary movement. During at least one moment of the action, they were turned against the power structure. It is through this breach and on the possibility of this reversal that the subversive strategy of the American Yippies (e.g., Hoffman, Rubin) is founded, and on which a theory of "symbolic action" is elaborated in the world revolutionary movements: co-opt the media through their power to chain react; use their power to generalize information instantaneously. The assumption here of course is that the impact of the media is reversible, a variable in the class struggle that one must learn to appropriate. But this position should be questioned, for it is perhaps another rather large strategic illusion.

May '68 will serve well enough as an example. Everything would lead us to believe in the subversive impact of the media during this period. Suburban radio stations and newspapers spread the student action everywhere. If the students were the detonators, the media were the resonators. Furthermore, the authorities quite openly accused the media of "playing the revolutionary game." But this sort of argument has been constructed in the absence of analysis. I would say to the contrary that the media have never discharged their responsibilities with more efficiency, and

that, indeed, in their function of *habitual* social control, they were right on top of the action. This is because, beneath the disarray of their routine content, they preserved their form; and this form, regardless of the context, is what inexorably connects them with the system of power. By broadcasting the events in the *abstract universality* of public opinion, they imposed a sudden and inordinate development on the movement of events; and through this forced and anticipated extension, they deprived the original movement of its own rhythm and of its meaning. In a word: they short-circuited it.

In the sphere of traditional politics (left- or right-wing),[20] where sanctified models and a kind of canonical speech are exchanged, the media are able to transmit without distorting the meanings intended. They are homogeneous with this kind of speech, as they are with the circulation of the commodity. But transgression and subversion never get "on the air" without being subtly negated as they are: transformed into models, neutralized into signs, they are eviscerated of their meaning.[21] There is no model of transgression, prototypical or serial. Hence, there is no better way to reduce it than to administer it a mortal dose of publicity. Originally, this process might have left one impressed with the possibility of "spectacular" results. In fact, it was tantamount to dismantling the movement by depriving it of its own momentum. The act of rupture was transformed into a bureaucratic model at a distance—and such, in fact, is the ordinary labor of the media.[22]

All of this can be read from the derivation and distortion of the term "symbolic" itself. The action of March 22 at Nanterre was symbolic because it was transgressive: at a given time in a given place, an act of radical rupture was invented—or, to resume the analysis proposed above, a particular response was invented there, where the institutions of administrative and pedagogical power were engaged in a private *oratoria* and functioned precisely to interdict any answer. The fact of mass media diffusion and contagion had nothing to do with the symbolic quality of the action. However, today it is precisely this interpretation, stressing the impact of disclosure, which suffices to define symbolic action. At the extreme, the subversive act is no longer produced *except as a function of its reproducibility*.[23] It is no longer created, it is produced directly as a *model*, like a gesture. The symbolic has slipped from the order of the very production of meaning to that of its *re*production, which is always the order of power. The symbolic becomes its own coefficient, pure and simple, and transgression is turned into exchange value.

Rationalist critical thought (i.e., Benjamin, Brecht, Enzensberger) sees this as a sign of decisive progress. The media simply actualize and reinforce the "demonstrative nature of no matter which political act" (Enzensberger). This evidently conforms with the *didactic* conception of the revolution and further with the "dialectic of coming to consciousness," etc. This tradition has yet to renounce the bourgeois Enlightenment. It has inherited all its ideas about the democratic (here revolutionary) virtues of spreading light (broadcasting). The pedagogical illusion of this position overlooks that—in aiming its own political acts at the media, and awaiting the moment to assume the media's mantle of power—the media themselves are in deliberate pursuit of the political act, in order to depoliticize it.

An interesting fact might be cited here as support: the contemporary eruption of tabloid trivia and natural disaster in the political sphere (which converges with Benjamin's notion of the graduation of the art object to the political stage by virtue of its reproducibility). There is a tidal wave in Pakistan, a black title fight in the U.S.; a youth is shot by a bistro owner, etc. These sorts of events, once minor and apolitical, suddenly find themselves invested with a power of diffusion that lends them a social and "historic" aura. New forms of political action have crystallized around this conflictualization of incidents that were hitherto consigned to the social columns. There is no doubt that, to a large extent, the new meanings they have taken on are largely the doing of the media. Such *faits divers* are like undeliberated "symbolic actions," but they take part in the same process of political signification. Doubtless, their reception is ambiguous and mixed; and if, thanks to the media, the political re-emerges under the category of *faits divers*, thanks to the same media the category of *faits divers* has totally invaded politics. Furthermore, it has changed status with the extension of the mass media: from a parallel category (descended from almanacs and popular chronicles), it has evolved into a total system of mythological interpretation, a closed system of models of signification from which no event escapes. Mass mediatization: that is its quintessence. It is no ensemble of techniques for broadcasting messages; it is the *imposition of models*. McLuhan's formula is worth reexamining here: "The medium is the message" operates a transfer of meaning onto the medium itself qua technological structure.

Again we are confronted with technological idealism. In fact, the essential Medium is the Model. What is mediatized is not what comes off the daily press, out of the tube, or on the radio: it is what is reinterpreted by the sign form, articulated into models, and administered by the code (just as the commodity is not what is produced industrially, but what is mediatized by the exchange value system of abstraction). At best, what can occur under the aegis of the media is a formal surpassing of the categories of *faits divers* and politics, and of their traditional separation, but only the better to assign them together to the same general code. It is strange that no one has tried to measure the strategic import of this forced socialization as a system of social control. Once again, the first great historical example of this was the electoral system. And it has never lacked revolutionaries (formerly among the greatest, today the least significant) who believed they could "do it" within the system. The general strike itself, this insurrectional myth of so many generations, has become a schematic reducing agent. That of May '68, to which the media significantly contributed by exporting the strike to all corners of France, was in appearance the culminating point of the crisis. In fact, it was the moment of its decompression, of its asphyxiation by extension, and of its defeat. To be sure, millions of workers went on strike. But no one knew what to do with this "mediatized" strike, transmitted and received as a model of action (whether via the media or the unions). Reduced to a single meaning, it neutralized the local, transversal, spontaneous forms of action (though not all). The Grenelle accords[24] hardly betrayed this tendency. They sanctioned *this passage to the generality of political action, which puts an end to the singularity of revolutionary action.* Today it has become (in the form of the calculated extension of the strike) the absolute weapon of the unions against wildcat strikes.

So far the electoral system and the general strike are also media, after a fashion. Playing on extensive formal socialization, they are the subtlest and stealthiest institutions of filtration, dismantling and censorship. They are neither exceptions, nor miracles.

The real revolutionary media during May were the walls and their speech, the silk-screen posters and the hand-painted notices, the street where speech began and was exchanged—everything that was an *immediate* inscription, given and returned, spoken and answered, mobile in the same space and time, reciprocal and antagonistic. The street is, in this sense, the alternative and subversive form of the mass media, since it isn't, like the latter, an objectified support for answerless messages, a transmission system at a distance. It is the frayed space of the symbolic exchange of speech—ephemeral, mortal: a speech that is not reflected on the Platonic screen of the media. Institutionalized by reproduction, reduced to a spectacle, this speech is expiring.

It is a strategic illusion to have any faith in the critical reversal of the media. A comparable speech can emerge only from the destruction of the media such as they are—through their deconstruction as systems of non-communication. Their liquidation does not follow from this, any more than the radical critique of discourse implies the negation of language as signifying material. But it certainly does imply the liquidation of the existing functional and technical structure of the media—of their operational form, so to speak—which *in toto* reflects their social form. At the limit, to be sure, it is the very concept of medium that disappears—and must disappear: speech exchanged dissolves the idea and function of the medium, and of the intermediary, as does symbolic land reciprocal exchange. It can involve a technical apparatus (sound, image, waves, energy, etc.) as well as the corporeal one (gestures, language, sexuality), but in this case, it no longer acts as a *medium*, as an autonomous system administered by the code. Reciprocity comes into being through the destruction of mediums per se. "People meet their neighbors for the first time while watching their apartment houses burn down."[25]

## The Theoretical Model of Communication

Let us summarize the various hypotheses:

1. McLuhan (for memory's sake): The media make—indeed, they are—the revolution, independently of their content, by virtue of their technological structure alone. After the phonetic alphabet and the printed book comes the radio and the cinema. After radio, television. We live, here and now, in the age of instantaneous, global communication.

2. The media are controlled by power. The imperative is to strip them of it, whether by taking the media over, or reversing them by outbidding the spectacle with subversive content. Here, the media are envisioned as pure message. Their form is never called into question (any more than it is, in fact, by McLuhan, who views the medium only in its aspect as medium).

3. Enzensberger: the present form of the media induces a certain type of social relation (assimilative to that of the capitalist mode of production). But the media contain, by virtue of their structure and development, an immanent socialist and democratic mode of communication, an immanent rationality and universality of information. It suffices to liberate this potential.

We are only interested in Enzensberger's hypothesis (enlightened Marxist) and that of the radical American Left (leftists of the spectacle). The practice of the official Left, Marxist or otherwise, which is confounded with that of the bourgeoisie, will be left out of account here. We have analyzed these positions as *strategic illusions*. The cause of this failure is that both share with the dominant ideology the implicit reference to the same *communication theory*. The theory is accepted practically everywhere, strengthened by received evidence and a (highly scientific) formalization by one discipline, the semio-linguistics of communication, supported on one side by structural linguistics, by information theory on the other, swallowed whole by the universities and by mass culture in general (the mass mediators are its connoisseurs). The entire conceptual infrastructure of this theory is ideologically connected with dominant practice, as was and still is that of classical political economy. It *is* the equivalent of this political economy in the field of communications. And I think that if revolutionary practice has bogged down in this strategic illusion *vis-à-vis* the media, it is because critical analyses have been superficial and fallen short of radically identifying the ideological matrix that communication theory embraces.

Formalized most notably by Roman Jakobsen, its underlying unity is based on the following sequence:

TRANSMITTER—MESSAGE—RECEIVER
(ENCODER—MESSAGE—DECODER)

The message itself is structured by the code and determined by the context. A specific function corresponds to each of these "concepts": the referential, poetic, phatic, etc.[26] Each communication process is thus vectorized into a single meaning, from the transmitter to the receiver: the latter can become transmitter in its turn, and the same schema is reproduced. Thus communication can always be reduced to this simple unity in which the two polar terms are mutually exclusive. This structure is given as objective and scientific, since it follows the methodological rule of decomposing its object into simple elements. In fact, it is satisfied with an emperical given, an abstraction from lived experience and reality: that is, the ideological categories that express a certain type of social relation, namely, in which one speaks and the other doesn't, where one has the choice of the code, and the other only liberty to acquiesce or abstain. This structure is based on the same arbitrariness as that of signification (i.e., the arbitrariness of the sign): two terms are artificially isolated and artificially reunited by an objectified content called a message. There is neither reciprocal relation nor simultaneous mutual presence of the two terms,[27] since each determines itself in its relation to the message or code, the "intermedium" that maintains both in a respective situation (it is the code that holds both in "respect"), at a distance from one another, a distance that seals the full and autonomized "value" of the message (in fact, its exchange value). This "scientific" construction is rooted in a *simulation model* of communication. It excludes, from its inception, the reciprocity and antagonism of interlocutors, and the ambivalence of their exchange. What really circulates is information, a semantic content that is assumed to be legible and univocal. The agency of the code guarantees this univocality, and by the same token the respective positions of encoder and decoder. So far so good: the formula has a formal coherence that assures it as the only *possible* schema of communication. But as soon as one posits ambivalent relations, it all collapses. There is no code for ambivalence; and without a code, no more encoder, no more decoder: the extras flee the stage. Even a message becomes impossible, since it would, after all, have to be defined as "emitted" and "received." It is as if the entire formalization exists only to avert this catastrophe. And therein resides its "scientific" status. What it underpins, in fact, is the terrorism of the code. In this guiding schema, the code becomes the only agency that speaks, that exchanges itself and reproduces through the dissociation of the two terms and the univocality (or equivocality, or multivocality—it hardly matters: through the non-ambivalence) of the message. (Likewise, in the process of economic exchange, it is no longer people who exchange; the system of exchange value reproduces itself through them). So, this basic communication formula succeeds in giving us, as a reduced model, a perfect epitome of social exchange *such as it is*—such as, at any rate, the abstraction of the code, the forced rationality and terrorism of separation regulate it. So much for scientific objectivity.

The schema of separation and closure already operates, as we have noted, at the level of the sign, in linguistic theory. Each sign is divided into a signifier, and a signified, which are mutually appointed, but held in "respective" position: and from the depths of its arbitrary isolation, each sign "communicates" with all the others through a code called a language. Even here, a scientific injunction is invoked against the immanent possibility of the terms exchanging amongst each other symbolically, beyond the signifier-signified distinction—in poetic language, for example. In the latter, as in symbolic exchange, the terms *respond* to each other beyond the code. It is this response that we have marked out during the entire essay as ultimately deconstructive of all codes, of all control and power, which always base themselves on the separation of terms and their abstract articulation.

Thus the theory of signification serves as a nuclear model for communication theory, and the arbitrariness of the sign (that theoretical schema for the repression of meaning) takes on its political and ideological scope in the arbitrariness of the theoretical schema of communication and information. As we have seen, all of this is echoed, not only in the dominant social practice (characterized by the virtual monopoly of the transmission pole and the irresponsibility of the receiving pole, the discrimination between the terms of the exchange and the *diktat* of the code), but also in all the velleities of revolutionary media practice. For example, it is clear that those who aim to subvert media content only reinforce the autonomy of the message as a separated notion, and thus the abstract bipolarity of the term(inal)s of communication.

## The Cybernetic Illusion

Sensible of the non-reciprocity of the existing process, Enzensberger believes the situation can be mitigated by insisting that the same revolution intervene at the level of the media that once disoriented the exact sciences and the epistemological subject-object relation, which has been engaged in continuous "dialectical" interreaction ever since. The media would have to take into account all the consequences of interreaction, whose effect is to breach monopoly and permit everyone's integration in an open process. "The programs of the consciousness industry must subsume into themselves their own results, the reactions and the corrections that they call forth. . . . They are therefore to be thought of not as means of consumption but as means of their own production."[28] Now, this seductive perspective leaves the separated agency of the code and the message intact while it attempts, instead, to break down the discrimination of the two poles of communication toward a more supple structure of the role exchange and feedback ("reversibility of circuits"). "In its present form, equipment like television or film does not serve communication but prevents it. It allows no reciprocal action between transmitter and receiver; technically speaking, it reduces feedback to the lowest point compatible with the system."[29] Again, we fail to get beyond the categories of receiver and transmitter, whatever may be the effort to mobilize them through "switching." Reversibility has nothing to do with reciprocity. Doubtless it is for this deeper reason that cybernetic systems today understand perfectly well how to put this complex regulation and feedback to work without affecting the abstraction of the process as a whole or allowing any real "responsibility" in exchange. This is indeed the system's surest line of defense, since it thus integrates the contingency of any such response in advance.

As Enzensberger has demonstrated in his critique of the Orwellian myth, it no longer makes sense to conceive a megasystem of centralized control (a monitoring system for the telephone network would have to exceed it *n* times in size and complexity; hence, it is practically excluded). But it is a little naive to assume that the fact of media extension thus eliminates censorship. Even over the long haul, the impracticality of police megasystems simply means that present systems will integrate these otherwise useless metasystems of control by means of feedback and autoregulation. They know how to introduce what negates them *as supplementary variables*. Their very operation is censorship: megasystems are hardly required. Hence they do not cease to be totalitarian: in a way, they realize the ideal one might refer to as decentralized totalitarianism.

On a more practical level, the media are quite aware how to set up formal "reversibility" of circuits (letters to the editor, phone-in programs, polls, etc.), without conceding any response or abandoning in any way the discrimination of roles.[30] This is the social and political form of feedback. Thus, Enzensberger's "dialectization" of communication is oddly related to cybernetic regulation. Ultimately, he is the victim, though in a more subtle fashion, of the ideological model we have been discussing.

From the same perspective, Enzensberger would break down the unilateral character of communication, which translates simultaneously into the monopoly of specialists and professionals and that of the class enemy over the media, by proposing, as a revolutionary solution, that *everyone become a manipulator*, in the sense of active operator, producer, etc., in brief, move from receiver status to that of producer-transmitter. Here is a sort of critical reversal of the ideological concept of manipulation. But again, because this "revolution" at bottom conserves the category of transmitter, which it is content to generalize as separated, transforming everyone into his own transmitter, it fails to place the mass media system in check. We know the results of such phenomena as mass ownership of walkie-talkies, or everyone making their own cinema: a kind of personalized amateurism, the equivalent of Sunday tinkering on the periphery of the system.[31]

Of course, this isn't at all what Enzensberger has in mind. He is thinking of a press edited, distributed, and worked by its own readers (as is the underground press, in part), of video systems at the disposal of political groups, and so on.

This would be the only way to unfreeze a blocked situation: "In the socialist movements the dialectic of discipline and spontaneity, centralism and decentralism, authoritarian leadership and antiauthoritarian disintegration has long ago reached a deadlock. Networklike communications models built on the principle of reversibility of circuits might give new indications of how to overcome this situation."[32] Thus it is a question of reconstituting a dialectical practice. But can the problem continue to be posed in dialectical terms? Isn't it the dialectic itself which has reached the moment of deadlock?

The examples Enzensberger gives are interesting precisely in that they go beyond a "dialectic" of transmitter and receiver. In effect, an immediate communication process is rediscovered, one not filtered through bureaucratic models—an original form of exchange, in fact, because there are *neither transmitters, nor receivers*, but only people responding to each other. The problem of spontaneity and organization is not overcome dialectically here: its terms are *transgressed*.

There is the essential difference: the other hypotheses allow the dichotomized categories to subsist. In the first case (media on the private scale), transmitter and receiver are simply reunited in a single individual: manipulation is, after a fashion, "interiorized."[33] In the other case (the "dialectic of circuits"), transmitter and receiver are simultaneously on both sides: manipulation becomes reciprocal (hermaphroditic grouping). The system can play these two variations as easily as it can the classic bureaucratic model. It can play on all their possible combinations. The only essential is that these two ideological categories be safe, and with them the fundamental structure of the political economy of communication.

To repeat, in the symbolic exchange relation, there is a simultaneous response. There is not transmitter or receiver on both sides of a message: nor, for that matter, is there any longer any "message," any corpus of information to decode univocally under the aegis of a code. The symbolic consists precisely in breaching the univocality of the "message," in restoring the ambivalence of meaning and in demolishing in the same stroke the agency of the code.

All of this should be helpful in assessing Umberto Eco's hypothesis.[34] To summarize his position: changing the contents of the message serves no purpose; it is necessary to modify the reading codes, to impose other interpretive codes. The receiver (who in fact isn't really one) intervenes here at the most essential level—he opposes his own code to that of the transmitter, he invents a true response by escaping the trap of controlled communication. But what does this "subversive" reading actually amount to? Is it still a reading, that is, a deciphering, a disengaging of a univocal meaning? And what is this code that opposes? Is it a unique minicode (an ideolect, but thus without interest)? Or is it yet another controlling schema of interpretation, rising from the ashes of the previous one? Whatever the case, it is only a question of textual variation. One example can illustrate Eco's perspective: the graffiti reversal of advertising after May '68. Graffiti is transgressive, not because it substitutes another content, another discourse, but simply because it responds, there, on the spot, and breaches the fundamental role of non-response enunciated by all the media. Does it oppose one code to another? I don't think so: it simply smashes the code. It doesn't lend itself to deciphering as a text rivaling commercial discourse; it presents itself as a transgression. So, for example, the witticism, which is a transgressive reversal of discourse, does not act on the basis of another code as such; it works through the instantaneous deconstruction of the dominant discursive code. It volatilizes the category of the code, and that of the message.

This, then, is the key to the problem: by trying to preserve (even as one "dialectically transcends" them) *any separated instances of the structural communication grid,* one obviates the possibility of fundamental change, and condemns oneself to fragile manipulatory practices that would be dangerous to adopt as a "revolutionary strategy." What is strategic in this sense is only what radically checkmates the dominant form.

Notes

1. Marshall McLuhan, *War and Peace in the Global Village* (New York: 1968), p.5.

2. Hans Magnus Enzensberger, "Constituents of a Theory of the Media," *The Consciousness Industry* (New York: Seabury Press, 1974), pp. 95–128.

3. This political economy of the sign is structural linguistics (together with semiology, to be sure, and all its derivatives, of which communication theory will be discussed below). It is apparent that within the general ideological framework, structural linguistics is the contemporary master discipline, inspiring anthropology, the human sciences, etc., just as, in its time, did political economy, whose postulates profoundly informed all of psychology, sociology, and the "moral and political" sciences.

4. In this case, the expression "consciousness industry" which Enzensberger uses to characterize the existing media is a dangerous metaphor. Unfortunately, it underlies his entire analytic hypothesis, which is to extend the Marxist analysis of the capitalist mode of production to the media, to the point of discovering a structural analogy between the following relations:

dominant class/dominated class
producer-entrepreneur/consumer
transmitter-broadcaster/receiver

5. In fact, Marxist analysis can be questioned at two very different levels of radicality: either as a system for interpreting the separated order of *material* production, or else as that of the separated order of *production* (in general). In the first case, the hypothesis of the non-relevance of the dialectic outside its field of "origin" must be logically pushed further: if "dialectical" contradictions between the productive forces and the relations of production largely vanish in the field of language, signs, and ideology, *perhaps they were never really operative in the field of material production either,* since a certain capitalist development of productive forces has been able to absorb—not all conflict, to be sure—but revolutionary antagonisms at the level of social relations. Wherein lies the validity of these concepts, then, aside from a purely conceptual coherence?

In the second case, the concept of production must be interrogated at its very root (and not in its diverse contents), along with the separated form which it establishes and the representational and rationalizing schema it imposes. Undoubtedly it is here, at the extreme, that the real work needs to be done. [See Baudrillard's *Mirror of Production,* Trans. Mark Poster (St. Louis: Telos Press, 1975).—*Trans.*]

6. Enzensberger, "Constituents of a Theory of the Media," p. 96.

7. This genre of reductive determinism may be found in the works of Bourdieu and in the phraseology of the Communist Party. It is theoretically worthless. It turns the *mechanism* of democratization into a revolutionary value per se. That intellectuals may find mass culture repugnant hardly suffices to make it a revolutionary alternative. Aristocrats used to make sour faces at bourgeois culture, but no one ever said the latter was anything more than a class culture.

287

8. Most of the above references are to Enzensberger, "Constituents of a Theory of the Media," pp. 102–103.

9. French radio-TV headquarters. The ORTF is a highly centralized state-run monoploy.

10. Thus we find authority, the state, and other institutions either devoid or full up with revolutionary content, depending on whether they are still in the grip of capital or the people have taken them over. Their form is rarely questioned.

11. Enzensberger, "Constituents of a Theory of the Media," pp. 105, 108.

12. *Ibid.*, p. 97.

13. *Ibid.*, p. 107.

14. *Ibid.*, pp. 97–98.

15. It is not a question of "dialogue," which is only the functional adjustment of two abstract speeches without response, where the "interlocutors" are never mutually present, but only their stylized discourses.

16. The occupation of the ORTF changed nothing in itself, even if subversive "contents" were "broadcast." If only those involved had scuttled the ORTF as such, for its entire technical and functional structure reflects the monopolistic use of speech.

17. Roland Barthes, *S/Z* (New York: 1974), p. 4.

18. Multifunctionality evidently changes nothing on this score. Multifunctionality, multidisciplinarity—polyvalence in all its forms—are just the system's response to its own obsession with centrality and standardization (uni-equivalence). It is the system's reaction to its own pathology, glossing over the underlying logic.

19. Enzensberger (pp. 118–19) interprets it this way: "The medium is the message" is a bourgeois proposition. It signifies that the bourgeoisie has nothing left to say. Having no further message to transmit, it plays the card of medium for medium's sake. —If the bourgeoisie has nothing left to say, "socialism" would do better to keep quiet.

20. This left-right distinction is just about meaningless from the point of view of the media. We should give credit where credit is due and grant them the honor of having contributed largely to its elimination. The distinction is interconnected with an order characterized by the *transcendence* of politics. But let us not mistake ourselves, here: the media only help to liquidate this transcendence of politics in order to substitute their own transcendence, abstracted from the mass media form, which is thoroughly integrated and no longer even offers a conflictive structure (left-right). Mass media transcendence is thus reductive of the traditional transcendence of politics, but it is even more reductive of the new transversality of politics.

21. This form of so-called "disclosure" or "propagation" can be analyzed readily in the fields of science or art. Generalized reproducibility obliterates the processes of work and meaning so as to leave nothing but modelized contents (cf. Raoul Ergmann, "Le miroir en miettes," *Diogene,* no. 68, 1969; Baudouin Jurdant, "La vulgarisation scientifique," *Communications,* no. 14).

22. It should be pointed out that this labor is always accompanied by one of selection and reinterpretation at the level of the membership group (Lazarsfeld's *two-step flow of communication*). This accounts for the highly relative impact of media contents, and the many kinds of resistance they provoke. (However we should ask ourselves whether these resistances are not aimed at the abstraction of the medium itself,

rather than its contents: Lazarsfeld's double articulation would lead us to this conclusion, since the second articulation belongs to the network of *personal* relations, opposed to the generality of media messages.) Still, this "second" reading, where the membership group opposes its own code to the transmitter's (cf. my discussion of Umberto Eco's thesis towards the end of this article) certainly doesn't neutralize or "reduce" the dominant ideological contents of the media in the same way as it does the critical or subversive contents. To the extent that the dominant ideological contents (cultural models, value systems, imposed without alternative or response; bureaucratic contents) are homogeneous with the general form of the mass media (non-reciprocity, irresponsibility), and are integrated with this form in reduplicating it, they are, so to speak, overdetermined, and have greater impact. They "go over" better than subversive *contents*. But this is not the essence of the problem. It is more important to recognize that the *form* of transgression never "comes off" more or less well on the media: it is radically denied by the mass media form.

23. Thus, for Walter Benjamin, the reproduced work becomes more and more the work "designed" *for reproducibility*. In this way, according to him, the work of art graduates from ritual to politics. "Exhibition value" revolutionizes the work of art and its functions. Walter Benjamin, "The Work of Art in the Age of Mechanical Reproduction," *Illuminations* (New York: Schocken Books, 1969).

24. The Grenelle accords were worked out between Georges Séguy of the CGT and Georges Pompidou during the May '68 general strike. Although the monetary concessions involved were fairly broad, they missed the point, and were massively rejected by workers. —*Trans.*

25. Jerry Rubin, *Do It* (New York: Simon and Schuster), p. 234.

26. See Roman Jakobsen, "Closing Statement: Linguistics and Poetics," in T.A. Sebeok, ed., *Style in Language* (Cambridge, Mass.: M.I.T. Press, 1960), pp. 350–377.

27. These two terms are so faintly present to each other that it has proven necessary to create a "contact" category to reconstitute the totality theoretically!

28. Enzensberger, "Constituents of a Theory of the Media," pp. 119, 127.

29. *Ibid.*, p. 97.

30. Once again Enzensberger, who analyses and denounces these control circuits, nevertheless links up with idealism: "Naturally [!] such tendencies go against the grain of the structure, and the new productive forces not only permit, but indeed demand [!] their reversal." (*Ibid.*, p. 108.) Feedback and interaction are the very logic of cybernetics. Underestimating the ability of the system to integrate its own revolutionary innovations is as delusory as underestimating the capacity of capitalism to develop the productive forces.

31. Evoking the possibility of an open free press, Enzensberger points to the Xerox monopoly and their exorbitant rental rates. But if everyone had his own Xerox—or even his own wavelength—the problem would remain. The real monopoly is never that of technical means, but of speech.

32. Enzensberger, "Constituents of a Theory of the Media," p. 110.

33. This is why the *individual* amateur cameraman remains within the separated abstraction of *mass* communication: through this internal dissociation of the two agencies (instances), the entire code and all of the dominant models sweep in, and seize his activity from behind.

34. Umberto Eco, *La Struttura assente* (Milan: Bompiani, 1968).

# 20. [Introduction]
# The Technology and the Society

At a time when there were few critical approaches to television, Raymond Williams's *Television: Technology and Cultural Form* provided a number, including the important concept of *flow*. Flow was characterized as the primary organizing principle of television—the fluid combination of program segments, commercials, and other material that makes up the experience of watching (and watching and watching) television—more important that the idea of a "program," of a supposedly unitary drama, documentary, comedy, or news report.

Less famous than flow, but more central for understanding new media, are the concerns of *Television*'s opening chapter (reprinted here). An attack on the "technological determinist" account of technology's role in society, the chapter also searches for a more fruitful model, through the lens of communications and media technologies. Technological determinism, a viewpoint for which Marshall McLuhan is the canonical figure in media studies, tends to frame questions around technology in terms of technology's "effects" on the culture. This viewpoint has been rejected, or greatly qualified in its use, by most academic writers since McLuhan. However, it remains the dominant popular discourse on technology, and many academic writers remain engaged in outlining their positions as alternatives to this viewpoint. For these reasons, Williams's early section presenting a number of different varieties of technological determinism remains quite relevant today.

In the time since Williams's book the example of television has remained a touchstone for discussions of the relationship between technology and society. Brian Winston used the case of television's development to outline a "cultural determinist" view in his essay, "How Are Media Born?" This essay owes much to Williams's pioneering analysis, but also proposes interesting additions to the discussion, such as Winston's "Law of Suppression of Radical Potential." Langdon Winner (author of "Mythinformation" (◊40)) used television as an example in his "Technologies as Forms of Life":

> None of those who worked to perfect the technology of television in its early years and few of those who brought television sets into their homes ever intended the device to become employed as the universal babysitter. . . . Similarly, if anyone in the 1930s had predicted people would eventually be watching seven hours of television each day, the forecast would have been laughed away as absurd. But recent surveys indicate that we Americans do spend that much time, roughly one-third of our lives, staring at the tube. Those who wish to reassert freedom of choice in the matter sometimes observe, "You can always turn off your TV." In a trivial sense that is true. . . . But given how central television has become to the content of everyday life, how it has become the accustomed topic of conversation in workplaces, schools, and other social gatherings, it is apparent that television is a phenomenon that, in the larger sense, cannot be "turned off" at all. (12)

Winner is no technological determinist, but strongly argues what many cultural determinists are in danger of missing: *the things themselves matter.* Just as we cannot treat technologies as simply "invented" from thin air, altering the course of human life to fit their dictates, so we cannot cease our analysis at the point when a technology becomes widely distributed—when the social instigations seem played out. Once a technology is in place it operates as a life factor, embodying the social processes that led to its distribution, and interacting with social institutions in important ways.

Of course, the social processes that bring technologies into widespread use, as well as those embodied in technologies, may not always be those that are most admirable or just. For this reason, Winner and others (e.g., Richard Sclove, author of *Democracy and Technology*) have been particularly attracted to those research, funding, and technology development practices which seek to involve those who will be affected by the outcomes. A number of Scandinavian practices—in areas ranging from automobile manufacturing to software design (as described, for instance, by Ehn and Kyng (◊45))—have been seen as good examples of involving workers in the design of the technological processes and products through which they will work. The results have often been higher work satisfaction and higher product quality.

289

*Langdon Winner wrote, regarding technologies as "forms of life":*

We do indeed "use" telephones, automobiles, electric lights, and computers in the conventional sense of picking them up and putting them down. But our world soon becomes one in which telephony, automobility, electric lighting, and computing are forms of life in the most powerful sense: life would scarcely be thinkable without them. (11)

◊40
587

◊45
649

◊08
93

Winner's most famous example of explicitly politically charged technological objects is probably found in "Do Artifacts Have Politics?" In that essay, early in his discussion, he recounts the story of Robert Moses, who explicitly designed the freeway overpasses on Long Island so that they would be too short to ever accommodate buses. Moses also fought the extension of the Long Island Railroad toward his famous Jones Beach. Both were attempts by Moses to keep low-income, minority New Yorkers out of these areas.

Doug Engelbart's "bootstrapping" is a similar concept specific to the realm of new media: users are continually involved in the ongoing definition and construction of the tools that they as a community will use (◊08). Processes of this sort have been the primary method of defining the Internet over the course of its history (and even in its prehistory as the ARPAnet). A good example of this is seen in "Requests for Comments" (RFCs). As Janet Abbate writes in Inventing the Internet, "Members of the Network Working Group would post new RFCs concurring with, criticizing, or elaborating on ideas presented in earlier RFCs, and an ongoing discussion developed. Eventually, after members had debated the issues through RFCs and at NWG meetings, a consensus would emerge on protocols and procedures, and this consensus was generally accepted by ARPA as official policy for the network" (74).

Perhaps it is not such a surprise that this approach was adopted, once one considers that the electronic medium used for the exchange of RFCs was the Network Information Center (NIC) that Engelbart's group created at SRI. However, this manner of decision making lasted long after the NIC (and the discussion) left SRI. In the 1980s, when the Internet had already grown significantly, it was decided that the involved parties who needed to be represented in Internet technology decision making were quite a few, and, as Abbate writes, membership in the groups working with RFCs was opened "to anyone, anywhere in the world, who had the time, interest, and technical knowledge to participate" (207). Later, she writes, the Internet Engineering Task Force (IETF) continued the RFC decision-making process: "Working groups within these task forces coordinated their activities through email, and the task forces held meetings several times a year. Standards for the Internet were set by consensus, after discussion among all interested parties and after proposed protocols had been tested in practice, and they continued to be published electronically in the form of Requests for Comments" (207). This process ensured the meaningful participation of everyone from university students to corporate information systems managers to interested researchers—all acting as individuals, rather than representatives of organizations, since no organizational or corporate membership in the IETF is possible.

The Internet is now moving toward another model of social production and embodiment. Since the early 1990s the U.S. government has been involved in privatizing the Internet. The stated goal is to promote competition—but the opposite has happened. The government privatized the Internet backbone, and a few large carriers now dominate. This problem is either exacerbated or caused by the government's refusal to require these dominant players to interconnect with smaller ones. The government privatized the process of registering the domain names of computers, leading to undemocratic monopolization: first by Network Solutions Incorporated (NSI), and more recently by the Internet Corporation for Assigned Names and Numbers (ICANN). NSI was purchased by Verisign, and retains the lucrative ownership of the ".com" domain database as of this writing—via an agreement with ICANN that was negotiated and concluded in secret.

Sometimes characterized as the "World Trade Organization of the Internet," ICANN is a DNS decision-making body that has replaced the broad public participation of organizations such as the IETF with closed-door meetings involving primarily corporate interests. It has worked consistently to broaden its power, attempting to recast bodies such as the IETF as mere "supporting organizations" for ICANN's activities (empowered only to make suggestions to ICANN). Meanwhile, many have questioned whether ICANN has any basis for legal existence at all, and it has been suggested that Internet users may revolt. On the one hand, revolt against ICANN might be easy: use a different server than ICANN's as the "root" for the domain name system—and persuade everyone else who has information you want to access to do so. Even then, the Internet privatization that ICANN represents has widespread support in very powerful circles.

In short, precisely the sort of technology definition that Williams wrote about is ongoing now. The Internet did not spring, full-grown, from J. C. R. Licklider's head. It was created, and is still being created, by social processes interacting with scientific/technical processes. Those who work and live with the Internet can choose to either become involved or wait and see what happens. The decision will have a profound impact on the social values embodied in the technology of our next-generation Internet.

—NWF

Further Reading

Abbate, Janet. *Inventing the Internet*. Cambridge: MIT Press, 1999.

Bradner, Scott. "The Internet Engineering Task Force."*Open Sources: Voices from the Open Source Revolution*. Sebastopol, Calif.: O'Reilly & Associates, 1999.

Internet Democracy Project. <www.internetdemocracyproject.org>

Lessig, Lawrence. *The Future of Ideas*. New York: Random House, 2001.

Sclove, Richard. *Democracy and Technology*. New York: Guilford Press, 1995.

Winner, Langdon. "Technologies as Forms of Life." *The Whale and The Reactor: A Search for Limits in an Age of High Technology*, 3–18. Chicago: University of Chicago Press, 1986.

Winston, Brian. "How Are Media Born?" *Questioning the Media: A Critical Introduction*. Ed. John Downing, Ali Mohammadi, and Annabelle Sreberny-Mohammadi. Thousand Oaks, Calif.: Sage Publications, 1990.

Winston, Brian. *Media Technology and Society: A History*. London: Routledge, 1998.

Original Publication
*Television: Technology and Cultural Form*. Hanover, N.H.: Wesleyan University Press, 3–25, 1992. 1st printing, London: Fontana, 1972.

# The Technology and the Society

## Raymond Williams

It is often said that television has altered our world. In the same way, people often speak of a new world, a new society, a new phase of history, being created—"brought about"—by this or that new technology: the steam-engine, the automobile, the atomic bomb. Most of us know what is generally implied when such things are said. But this may be the central difficulty: that we have got so used to statements of this general kind, in our most ordinary discussions, that we can fail to realise their specific meanings.

For behind all such statements lie some of the most difficult and most unresolved historical and philosophical questions. Yet the questions are not posed by the statements; indeed they are ordinarily masked by them. Thus we often discuss, with animation, this or that "effect" of television, or the kinds of social behaviour, the cultural and psychological conditions, which television has "led to," without feeling ourselves obliged to ask whether it is reasonable to describe any technology as a cause, or, if we think of it as a cause, as what kind of cause, and in what relations with other kinds of causes. The most precise and discriminating local study of "effects" can remain superficial if we have not looked into the notions of cause and effect, as between a technology and a society, a technology and a culture, a technology and a psychology, which underlie our questions and may often determine our answers.

It can of course be said that these fundamental questions are very much too difficult; and that they are indeed difficult is very soon obvious to anyone who tries to follow them through. We could spend our lives trying to answer them, whereas here and now, in a society in which television is important, there is immediate and practical work to be done: surveys to be made, research undertaken; surveys and research, moreover, which we know how to do. It is an appealing position, and it has the advantage, in our kind of society, that it is understood as practical, so that it can then be supported and funded. By contrast, other kinds of question seem merely theoretical and abstract.

Yet all questions about cause and effect, as between a technology and a society, are intensely practical. Until we have begun to answer them, we really do not know, in any particular case, whether, for example, we are talking about a technology or about the uses of a technology; about necessary institutions or particular and changeable institutions; about a content or about a form. And this is not only a matter of intellectual uncertainty; it is a matter of social practice. If the technology is a cause, we can at best modify or seek to control its effects. Or if the technology, as used, is an effect, to what other kinds of cause, and other kinds of action, should we refer and relate our experience of its uses? These are not abstract questions. They form an increasingly important part of our social and cultural arguments, and they are being decided all the time in real practice, by real and effective decisions.

It is with these problems in mind that I want to try to analyse television as a particular cultural technology, and to look at its development, its institutions, its forms and its effects, in this critical dimension. In the present chapter, I shall begin the analysis under three headings: (a) versions of cause and effect in technology and society; (b) the social history of television as a technology; (c) the social history of the uses of television technology.

## A. Versions of Cause and Effect in Technology and Society

(i) We can begin by looking again at the general statement that television has altered our world. It is worth setting down some of the different things this kind of statement has been taken to mean. For example:

(ii) Television was invented as a result of scientific and technical research. Its power as a medium of news and entertainment was then so great that it altered all preceding media of news and entertainment.

(iii) Television was invented as a result of scientific and technical research. Its power as a medium of social communication was then so great that it altered many of our institutions and forms of social relationships.

(iv) Television was invented as a result of scientific and technical research. Its inherent properties as an electronic medium altered our basic perceptions of reality, and thence our relations with each other and with the world.

(v) Television was invented as a result of scientific and technical research. As a powerful medium of communication and entertainment it took its place with other factors—such as greatly increased physical mobility, itself the result of other newly invented technologies—in altering the scale and form of our societies.

(vi) Television was invented as a result of scientific and technical research, and developed as a medium of entertainment and news. It then had unforeseen consequences, not only on other entertainment and news media, which it reduced in viability and importance, but on some of the central processes of family, cultural and social life.

(vi) Television, discovered as a possibility by scientific and technical research, was selected for investment and development to meet the needs of a new kind of society, especially in the provision of centralised entertainment and in the centralised formation of opinions and styles of behaviour.

(vii) Television, discovered as a possibility by scientific and technical research, was selected for investment and promotion as a new and profitable phase of a domestic consumer economy; it is then one of the characteristic "machines for the home."

(viii) Television became available as a result of scientific and technical research, and in its character and uses exploited and emphasised elements of a passivity, a cultural and psychological inadequacy, which had always been latent in people, but which television now organised and came to represent.

(ix) Television became available as a result of scientific and technical research, and in its character and uses both served and exploited the needs of a new kind of large-scale and complex but atomised society.

These are only some of the possible glosses on the ordinary bald statement that television has altered our world. Many people hold mixed versions of what are really alternative opinions, and in some cases there is some inevitable overlapping. But we can distinguish between two broad classes of opinion.

In the first—(i) to (v)—the technology is in effect accidental. Beyond the strictly internal development of the technology there is no reason why any particular invention should have come about. Similarly it then has consequences which are also in the true sense accidental, since they follow directly from the technology itself. If television had not been invented, this argument would run, certain definite social and cultural events would not have occurred.

In the second—(vi) to (ix)—television is again, in effect, a technological accident, but its significance lies in its uses, which are held to be symptomatic of some order of society or some qualities of human nature which are otherwise determined. If television had not been invented, this argument runs, we would still be manipulated or mindlessly entertained, but in some other way and perhaps less powerfully.

For all the variations of local interpretation and emphasis, these two classes of opinion underlie the overwhelming majority of both professional and amateur views of the effects of television. What they have in common is the fundamental form of the statement: "television has altered our world."

It is then necessary to make a further theoretical distinction. The first class of opinion, described above, is that usually known, at least to its opponents, as *technological determinism*. It is an immensely powerful and now largely orthodox view of the nature of social change. New technologies are discovered, by an essentially internal process of research and development, which then sets the conditions for social change and progress. Progress, in particular, is the history of these inventions, which "created the modern world." The effects of the technologies, whether direct or indirect, foreseen or unforeseen, are as it were the rest of history. The steam engine, the automobile, television, the atomic bomb, have *made* modern man and the modern condition.

The second class of opinion appears less determinist. Television, like any other technology, becomes available as an element or a medium in a process of change that is in any case occurring or about to occur. By contrast with pure technological determinism, this view emphasises other causal factors in social change. It then considers particular technologies, or a complex of technologies, as *symptoms* of change of some other kind. Any particular technology is then as it were a by-product of a social process that is otherwise determined. It only acquires effective status when it is used for purposes which are already contained in this known social process.

The debate between these two general positions occupies the greater part of our thinking about technology and society. It is a real debate, and each side makes important points. But it is in the end sterile, because each position, though in different ways, has abstracted technology from society. In *technological determinism*, research and development have been assumed as self-generating. The new technologies are invented as it were in an independent sphere, and then create new societies or new human conditions. The view of *symptomatic technology*, similarly, assumes that research and development are self-generating, but in a more marginal way. What is discovered in the margin is then taken up and used.

Each view can then be seen to depend on the isolation of technology. It is either a self-acting force which creates new ways of life, or it is a self-acting force which provides materials for new ways of life. These positions are so deeply established, in modern social thought, that it is very difficult to think beyond them. Most histories of technology, like most histories of scientific discovery, are written from their assumptions. An appeal to "the facts," against this or that interpretation, is made very difficult simply because the histories are usually written, consciously or unconsciously, to illustrate the assumptions. This is either explicit, with the consequential interpretation attached, or more often implicit, in that the history of technology or of scientific development is offered as a history on its own. This can be seen as a device of specialisation or of emphasis, but it then necessarily implies merely internal intentions and criteria.

To change these emphases would require prolonged and cooperative intellectual effort. But in the particular case of television it may be possible to outline a different kind of interpretation, which would allow us to see not only its history but also its uses in a more radical way. Such an interpretation would differ from technological determinism in that it would restore *intention* to the process of research and development. The technology would be seen, that is to say, as being looked for and developed with certain purposes and practices already in mind. At the same time the interpretation would differ from symptomatic technology in that these purposes and practices would be seen as *direct*: as known social needs, purposes and practices to which the technology is not marginal but central.

## B. The Social History of Television as a Technology

The invention of television was no single event or series of events. It depended on a complex of inventions and developments in electricity, telegraphy, photography and motion pictures, and radio. It can be said to have separated out as a specific technological objective in the period 1875–1890, and then, after a lag, to have developed as a specific technological enterprise from 1920 through to the first public television systems of the 1930s. Yet in each of these stages it depended for parts of its realisation on inventions made with other ends primarily in view.

Until the early nineteenth century, investigations of electricity, which had long been known as a phenomenon, were primarily philosophical: investigations of a puzzling natural effect. The technology associated with these investigations was mainly directed towards isolation and concentration of the effect, for its clearer study. Towards the end of the eighteenth century there began to be applications, characteristically in relation to other known natural effects (lightning conductors). But there is then a key transitional period in a cluster of inventions between 1800 and 1831, ranging from Volta's battery to Faraday's demonstration of electro-magnetic induction, leading quickly to the production of generators. This can be properly traced as a scientific history, but it is significant that the key period of advance coincides with an important stage of the development of industrial production. The advantages of electric power were closely related to new industrial needs: for mobility and transfer in the location of power sources, and for flexible and rapid controllable conversion. The steam engine had been well suited to textiles, and its industries had been based on local siting. A more extensive development, both physically and in the complexity of multiple-part processes, such as engineering, could be attempted with other power sources but could only be fully realised with electricity. There was a very complex interaction between new needs and new inventions, at the level of primary production, of new applied industries (plating) and of new social needs which were themselves related to industrial development (city and house lighting). From 1830 to large-scale generation in the 1880s there was this continuing complex of need and invention and application.

In telegraphy the development was simpler. The transmission of messages by beacons and similar primary devices had been long established. In the development of navigation and naval warfare the flag-system had been standardised in the course of the sixteenth and seventeenth centuries. During the Napoleonic wars there was a marked development of land telegraphy, by semaphore stations, and some of this survived into peacetime. Electrical telegraphy had been suggested as a technical system as early as 1753, and was actually demonstrated in several places in the early nineteenth century. An English inventor in 1816 was told that the Admiralty was not interested. It is interesting that it was the development of the railways, themselves a response to the development of an industrial system and the related growth of cities, which clarified the need for improved telegraphy. A complex of technical possibilities was brought to a working system from 1837 onwards. The development of international trade and transport brought rapid extensions of the system, including the transatlantic cable in the 1850s and the 1860s. A general system of electric telegraphy had been established by the 1870s, and in the same decade the telephone system began to be developed, in this case as a new and intended invention.

In photography, the idea of light-writing had been suggested by (among others) Wedgwood and Davy in 1802, and the *camera obscura* had already been developed. It was not the projection but the fixing of images which at first awaited technical solution, and from 1816 (Niepce) and through to 1839 (Daguerre) this was worked on, together with the improvement of camera devices. Professional and then amateur photography spread rapidly, and reproduction and then transmission, in the developing newspaper press, were achieved. By the 1880s the idea of a "photographed reality"—still more for record than for observation—was familiar.

The idea of moving pictures had been similarly developing. The magic lantern (slide projection) had been known from the seventeenth century, and had acquired simple motion (one slide over another) by 1736. From at latest 1826 there was a development of mechanical motion-picture devices, such as the wheel-of-life, and these came to be linked with the magic lantern. The effect of persistence in human vision—that is to say, our capacity to hold the "memory" of an image through an interval to the next image, thus allowing the possibility of a sequence built from rapidly succeeding units—had been known since classical times. Series of cameras photographing stages of a sequence were followed (Marey, 1882) by multiple-shot cameras. Friese-Greene and Edison worked on techniques of filming and projection, and celluloid was substituted for paper reels. By the 1890s the first public motion-picture shows were being given in France, America and England.

Television, as an idea, was involved with many of these developments. It is difficult to separate it, in its earliest stages, from photo-telegraphy. Bain proposed a device for transmitting pictures by electric wires in 1842; Bakewell in 1847 showed the copying telegraph; Caselli in 1862 transmitted pictures by wire over a considerable distance. In 1873, while working at a terminal of the Atlantic telegraph cable, May observed the light-sensitive properties of selenium (which had been isolated by Berzelius in 1817 and was in use for resistors). In a host of ways, following an already defined need, the means of transmitting still pictures and moving pictures were actively sought and to a considerable extent discovered. The list is long even when selective: Carey's electric eye in 1875; Nipkow's scanning system in 1884; Elster and Geitel's photoelectric cells in 1890; Braun's cathode-ray tube in 1897; Rosing's cathode-ray receiver in 1907; Campbell Swinton's electronic camera proposal in 1911. Through this whole period two facts are evident: that a system of television was foreseen, and its means were being actively sought; but also that, by comparison with electrical generation and electrical telegraphy and telephony, there was very little social investment to bring the scattered work together. It is true that there were technical blocks before 1914—the thermionic valve and the multi-stage amplifier can be seen to have been needed and were not yet invented. But the critical difference between the various spheres of applied technology can be stated in terms of a social dimension: the new systems of production and of business or transport communication were already organised, at an economic level; the new systems of social communication were not. Thus when motion pictures were developed, their application was characteristically in the margin of established social forms—the sideshows—until their success was capitalised in a version of an established form, the motion-picture *theatre*.

The development of radio, in its significant scientific and technical stages between 1885 and 1911, was at first conceived, within already effective social systems, as an advanced form of telegraphy. Its application as a significantly new social form belongs to the immediate post-war period, in a changed social situation. It is significant that the hiatus in technical television development then also ended. In 1923 Zworykin introduced the electronic television camera tube. Through the early 1920s Baird and Jenkins, separately and competitively, were working on systems using mechanical scanning. From 1925 the rate of progress was qualitatively changed, through important technical advances but also with the example of sound broadcasting systems as a model. The Bell System in 1927 demonstrated wire transmission through a radio link, and the pre-history of the form can be seen to be ending. There was great rivalry between systems—especially those of mechanical and electronic scanning—and there is still great controversy about contributions and priorities. But this is characteristic of the phase in which the development of a technology moves into the stage of a new social form.

What is interesting throughout is that in a number of complex and related fields, these systems of mobility and transfer in production and communication, whether in mechanical and electric transport, or in telegraphy, photography, motion pictures, radio and television, were at once incentives and responses within a phase of general social transformation. Though some of the crucial scientific and technical discoveries were made by isolated and unsupported individuals, there was a crucial community of selected emphasis and intention, in a society characterised at its most general levels by a mobility and extension of the scale of organisations: forms of growth which brought with them immediate and longer-term problems of operative communication. In many different countries, and in apparently unconnected ways, such needs were at once isolated and technically defined. It is especially a characteristic of the communications systems that *all were foreseen—not in utopian but in technical ways—before the crucial components of the developed systems had been discovered and refined.* In no way is this a history of communications systems creating a new society or new social conditions. The decisive and earlier transformation of industrial production, and its new social forms, which had grown out of a long history of capital accumulation and working technical improvements, created new needs but also new possibilities, and the communications systems, down to television, were their intrinsic outcome.

## C. The Social History of the Uses of Television Technology

It is never quite true to say that in modern societies, when a social need has been demonstrated, its appropriate technology will be found. This is partly because some real needs, in any particular period, are beyond the scope of existing or foreseeable scientific and technical knowledge. It is even more because the key question, about technological response to a need, is less a question about the need itself than about its place in an existing social formation. A need which corresponds with the priorities of the real decision-making groups will, obviously, more quickly attract the investment of resources and the official permission, approval or encouragement on which a working technology, as distinct from available technical devices, depends. We can see this clearly in the major developments of industrial production and, significantly, in military technology. The social history of communications technology is interestingly different from either of these, and it is important to try to discover what are the real factors of this variation.

The problem must be seen at several different levels. In the very broadest perspective, there is an operative relationship between a new kind of expanded, mobile and complex society and the development of a modern communications technology. At one level this relationship can be reasonably seen as causal, in a direct way. The principal incentives to first-stage improvements in communications technology came from problems of communication and control in expanded military and commercial operations. This was both direct, arising from factors of greatly extending distance and scale, and indirect, as a factor within the development of transport technology, which was for obvious reasons the major direct response. Thus telegraphy and telephony, and in its early stages radio, were secondary factors within a primary communications system which was directly serving the needs of an established and developing military and commercial system. Through the nineteenth and into the twentieth century this was the decisive pattern.

But there were other social and political relationships and needs emerging from this complex of change. Indeed it is a consequence of the particular and dominant interpretation of these changes that the complex was at first seen as one requiring improvement in *operational* communication. The direct priorities of the expanding commercial system, and in certain periods of the military system, led to a definition of needs within the terms of these systems. The objectives and the consequent technologies were operational within the structures of these systems: passing necessary specific information, or maintaining contact and control. Modern electric technology, in this phase, was thus oriented to uses of person to person, operator and operative to operator and operative, within established specific structures. This quality can best be emphasised by contrast with the electric technology of the second phase, which was properly and significantly called *broadcasting*. A technology of specific messages to specific persons was complemented, but only relatively late, by a technology of varied messages to a general public.

Yet to understand this development we have to look at a wider communications system. The true basis of this system had preceded the developments in technology. Then as now there was a major, indeed dominant, area of social communication, by word of mouth, within every kind of social group. In addition, then as now, there were specific institutions of that kind of communication which involves or

is predicated on social teaching and control: churches, schools, assemblies and proclamations, direction in places of work. All these interacted with forms of communication within the family.

What then were the new needs which led to the development of a new technology of social communication? The development of the press gives us the evidence for our first major instance. It was at once a response to the development of an extended social, economic and political system and a response to crisis within that system. The centralisation of political power led to a need for messages from that centre along other than official lines. Early newspapers were a combination of that kind of message—political and social information—and the specific messages—classified advertising and general commercial news—of an expanding system of trade. In Britain the development of the press went through its major formative stages in periods of crisis: the Civil War and Commonwealth, when the newspaper form was defined; the Industrial Revolution, when new forms of popular journalism were successively established; the major wars of the twentieth century, when the newspaper became a universal social form. For the transmission of simple orders, a communications system already existed. For the transmission of an ideology, there were specific traditional institutions. But for the transmission of news and background—the whole orienting, predictive and updating process which the fully developed press represented—there was an evident need for a new form, which the largely traditional institutions of church and school could not meet. And to the large extent that the crises of general change provoked both anxiety and controversy, this flexible and competitive form met social needs of a new kind. As the struggle for a share in decision and control became sharper, in campaigns for the vote and then in competition for the vote, the press became not only a new communications system but, centrally, a new social institution.

This can be interpreted as response to a political need and a political crisis, and it was certainly this. But a wider social need and social crisis can also be recognised. In a changing society, and especially after the Industrial Revolution, problems of social perspective and social orientation became more acute. New relations between men, and between men and things, were being intensely experienced, and in this area, especially, the traditional institutions of church and school, or of settled community and persisting family, had very little to say. A great deal was of course said, but from positions defined within an older kind of society. In a number of ways, and drawing on a range of impulses from curiosity to anxiety, new information and new kinds of orientation were deeply required: more deeply, indeed, than any specialisation to political, military or commercial information can account for. An increased awareness of mobility and change, not just as abstractions but as lived experiences, led to a major redefinition, in practice and then in theory, of the function and process of social communication.

What can be seen most evidently in the press can be seen also in the development of photography and the motion picture. The photograph is in one sense a popular extension of the portrait, for recognition and for record. But in a period of great mobility, with new separations of families and with internal and external migrations, it became more centrally necessary as a form of maintaining, over distance and through time, certain personal connections. Moreover, in altering relations to the physical world, the photograph as an object became a form of the photography of objects: moments of isolation and stasis within an experienced rush of change; and then, in its technical extension to motion, a means of observing and analysing motion itself, in new ways—a dynamic form in which new kinds of recognition were not only possible but necessary.

Now it is significant that until the period after the First World War, and in some ways until the period after the Second World War, these varying needs of a new kind of society and a new way of life were met by what were seen as specialised means: the press for political and economic information; the photograph for community, family and personal life; the motion picture for curiosity and entertainment; telegraphy and telephony for business information and some important personal messages. It was within this complex of specialised forms that broadcasting arrived.

The consequent difficulty of defining its social uses, and the intense kind of controversy which has ever since surrounded it, can then be more broadly understood. Moreover, the first definitions of broadcasting were made for sound radio. It is significant and perhaps puzzling that the definitions and institutions then created were those within which television developed.

We have now become used to a situation in which broadcasting is a major social institution, about which there is always controversy but which, in its familiar form, seems to have been predestined by the technology. This predestination, however, when closely examined, proves to be no more than a set of particular social decisions, in particular circumstances, which were then so widely if imperfectly ratified that it is now difficult to see them as decisions rather than as (retrospectively) inevitable results.

Thus, if seen only in hindsight, broadcasting can be diagnosed as a new and powerful form of social integration and control. Many of its main uses can be seen as socially, commercially and at times politically manipulative. Moreover, this viewpoint is rationalised by its description as "mass communication," a phrase used by almost all its agents and advisers as well, curiously, as by most of its radical critics. "Masses" had been the new nineteenth-century term of contempt for what was formerly described as "the mob." The physical "massing" of the urban and industrial revolution underwrote this. A new radical class-consciousness adopted the term to express the material of new social formations: "mass organisations." The "mass meeting" was an observable physical effect. So pervasive was this description that in the twentieth century multiple serial production was called, falsely but significantly, "mass production": mass now meant large numbers (but within certain assumed social relationships) rather than any physical or social aggregate. Sound radio and television, for reasons we shall look at, were developed for transmission to *individual* homes, though there was nothing in the technology to make this inevitable. But then this new form of social communication—broadcasting—was obscured by its definition as "mass communication": an abstraction to its most general characteristic, that it went to many people, "the masses," which obscured the fact that the means chosen was the offer of individual sets, a method much better described by the earlier word "broadcasting." It is interesting that the only developed "mass" use of radio was in Nazi Germany, where under Goebbels' orders the Party organised compulsory public listening groups and the receivers were in the streets. There has been some imitation of this by similar regimes, and Goebbels was deeply interested in television for the same kind of use. What was developed within most capitalist societies, though called "mass communication," was significantly different.

There was early official intervention in the development of broadcasting, but in form this was only at a technical level. In the earlier struggle against the development of the press, the State had licensed and taxed newspapers, but for a century before the coming of broadcasting the alternative idea of an independent press had been realised both in practice and in theory. State intervention in broadcasting had some real and some plausible technical grounds: the distribution of wavelengths. But to these were added, though always controversially, more general social directions or attempts at direction. This social history of broadcasting can be discussed on its own, at the levels of practice and principle. Yet it is unrealistic to extract it from another and perhaps more decisive process, through which, in particular economic situations, a set of scattered technical devices became an applied technology and then a social technology.

A Fascist regime might quickly see the use of broadcasting for direct political and social control. But that, in any case, was when the technology had already been developed elsewhere. In capitalist democracies, the thrust for conversion from scattered techniques to a technology was not political but economic. The characteristically isolated inventors, from Nipkow and Rosing to Baird and Jenkins and Zwyorkin, found their point of development, if at all, in the manufacturers and prospective manufacturers of the technical apparatus. The history at one level is of these isolated names, but at another level it is of EMI, RCA and a score of similar companies and corporations. In the history of motion pictures, capitalist development was primarily in production; large-scale capitalist distribution came much later, as a way of controlling and organising a market for given production. In broadcasting, both in sound radio and later in television, the major investment was in the means of distribution, and was devoted to production only so far as to make the distribution technically possible and then attractive. Unlike all previous communications technologies, radio and television were *systems primarily devised for transmission and reception as abstract processes, with little or no definition of preceding content*. When the question of content was raised, it was resolved, in the main, parasitically. There were state occasions, public sporting events, theatres and so on, which would be communicatively distributed by these new technical means. *It is not only that the supply of broadcasting facilities preceded the demand; it is that the means of communication preceded their content.*

The period of decisive development in sound broadcasting was the 1920s. After the technical advances in sound telegraphy which had been made for military purposes during the war, there was at once an economic opportunity and the need for a new social definition. No nation or manufacturing group held a monopoly of the technical means of broadcasting, and there was a period of intensive litigation followed by cross-licensing of the scattered basic components of successful transmission and reception (the vacuum tube or valve, developed from 1904 to 1913; the feedback circuit, developed from 1912; the neutrodyne and heterodyne circuits, from 1923). Crucially, in the mid-1920s, there was a series of investment-guided technical solutions to the problem of building a small and simple domestic receiver, on which the whole qualitative transformation from wireless telegraphy to broadcasting depended. By the mid-1920s—1923 and 1924 are especially decisive years—this breakthrough had happened in the leading industrial societies: the United States, Britain, Germany and France. By the end of the 1920s the radio industry had become a major sector of industrial production, within a rapid general expansion of the new kinds of machines which were eventually to be called "consumer durables." This complex of developments included the motorcycle and motorcar, the box camera and its successors, home electrical appliances, and radio sets. Socially, this complex is characterised by the two apparently paradoxical yet deeply connected tendencies of modern urban industrial living: on the one hand mobility, on the other hand the more apparently self-sufficient family home. The earlier period of public technology, best exemplified by the railways and city lighting, was being replaced by a kind of technology for which no satisfactory name has yet been found: that which served an at once mobile and home-centred way of living: a form of *mobile privatisation*. Broadcasting in its applied form was a social product of this distinctive tendency.

The contradictory pressures of this phase of industrial capitalist society were indeed resolved, at a certain level, by the institution of broadcasting. For mobility was only in part the impulse of an independent curiosity: the wish to go out and see new places. It was essentially an impulse formed in the breakdown and dissolution of older and smaller kinds of settlement and productive labour. The new and larger settlements and industrial organisations required major internal mobility, at a primary level, and this was joined by secondary consequences in the dispersal of extended families and in the needs of new kinds of social organisation. Social processes long implicit in the revolution of industrial capitalism were then greatly intensified: especially an increasing distance between immediate living areas and the directed places of work and government. No effective kinds of social control over these transformed industrial and political processes had come anywhere near being achieved or even foreseen. Most people were living in the fall-out area of processes determined beyond them. What had been gained, nevertheless, in intense social struggle, had been the improvement of immediate conditions, within the limits and pressures of these decisive large-scale processes. There was some relative improvement in wages and working conditions, and there was a qualitative change in the distribution of the day, the week and the year between work and off-work periods. These two effects combined in a major emphasis on improvement of the small family home. Yet this privatisation, which was at once an effective achievement and a defensive response, carried, as a consequence, an imperative need for new kinds of contact. The new homes might appear private and "self-sufficient" but could be maintained only by regular funding and supply from external sources, and these, over a range from employment and prices to depressions and wars, had a decisive and often a disrupting influence on what was nevertheless seen as a separable "family" project. This relationship created both the need and the form of a new kind of "communication": news from "outside," from otherwise inaccessible sources. Already in the drama of the 1880s and 1890s (Ibsen, Chekhov) this structure had appeared: the centre of dramatic interest was now for the first time the family home, but men and women stared from its windows, or waited anxiously for messages, to learn about forces, "out there," which would determine the conditions of their lives. The new "consumer" technology which reached its first decisive stage in the 1920s served this complex of needs within just these limits and pressures. There were immediate improvements of the condition and efficiency of the privatised home; there were new facilities, in private transport, for expeditions from the home; and then, in radio, there was a facility for a new kind of social input—news and entertainment brought into the home. Some people spoke of the new machines as gadgets, but they were always much more than this. They were the applied technology of a set of emphases and responses within the determining limits and pressures of industrial capitalist society.

The cheap radio receiver is then a significant index of a general condition and response. It was especially welcomed by all those who had least social opportunities of other kinds; who lacked independent mobility or access to the previously diverse places of entertainment and information. Broadcasting could also come to serve, or seem to serve, as a form of *unified* social intake, at the most general levels. What had been intensively promoted by the radio manufacturing companies thus interlocked with this kind of social need, itself defined within general limits and pressures. In the early stages of radio manufacturing, transmission was conceived before content. By the end of the 1920s the network was there, but still at a low level of content-definition. It was in the 1930s, in the second phase of radio, that most of the significant advances in content were made. The transmission and reception networks created, *as a by-product*, the facilities of primary broadcasting production. But the general social definition of "content" was already there.

This theoretical model of the general development of broadcasting is necessary to an understanding of the particular development of television. For there were, in the abstract, several different ways in which television as a technical means might have been developed. After a generation of universal domestic television it is not easy to realise this. But it remains true that, after a great deal of intensive research and development, the domestic television set is in a number of ways an inefficient medium of visual broadcasting. Its visual inefficiency by comparison with the cinema is especially striking, whereas in the case of radio there was by the 1930s a highly efficient sound broadcasting receiver, without any real competitors in its own line. Within the limits of the television home-set emphasis it has so far not been possible to make more than minor qualitative improvements. Higher-definition systems, and colour, have still only brought the domestic television set, as a machine, to the standard of a very inferior kind of cinema. Yet most people have adapted to this inferior visual medium, in an unusual kind of preference for an inferior immediate technology, because of the social complex—and especially that of the privatised home—within which broadcasting, as a system, is operative. The cinema had remained at an earlier level of social definition; it was and remains a special kind of theatre, offering specific and discrete works of one general kind. Broadcasting, by contrast, offered a whole social intake: music, news, entertainment, sport. The advantages of this general intake, within the home, much more than outweighed the technical advantages of visual transmission and reception in the cinema, confined as this was to specific and discrete works. While broadcasting was confined to sound, the powerful visual medium of cinema was an immensely popular alternative. But when broadcasting became visual, the option for its social advantages outweighed the immediate technical deficits.

The transition to television broadcasting would have occurred quite generally in the late 1930s and early 1940s, if the war had not intervened. Public television services had begun in Britain in 1936 and in the United States in 1939, but with still very expensive receivers. The full investment in transmission and reception facilities did not occur until the late 1940s and early 1950s, but the growth was thereafter very rapid. The key social tendencies which had led to the definition of broadcasting were by then even more pronounced. There was significantly higher investment in the privatised home, and the social and physical distances between these homes and the decisive political and productive centres of the society had become much greater. Broadcasting, as it had developed in radio, seemed an inevitable model: the central transmitters and the domestic sets.

Television then went through some of the same phases as radio. Essentially, again, the technology of transmission and reception developed before the content, and important parts of the content were and have remained by-products of the technology rather than independent enterprises. As late as the introduction of colour, "colourful" programmes were being devised to persuade people to buy colour sets. In the earliest stages there was the familiar parasitism on existing events: a coronation, a major sporting event, theatres. A comparable parasitism on the cinema was slower to show itself, until the decline of the cinema altered the terms of trade; it is now very widespread, most evidently in the United States. But again, as in radio, the end of the first general decade brought significant independent television production. By the middle and late 1950s, as in radio in the middle and late 1930s, new kinds of programme were being made for television and there were very important advances in the productive use of the medium, including, as again at a comparable stage in radio, some kinds of original work.

Yet the complex social and technical definition of broadcasting led to inevitable difficulties, especially in the

productive field. What television could do relatively cheaply was to transmit something that was in any case happening or had happened. In news, sport, and some similar areas it could provide a service of transmission at comparatively low cost. But in every kind of new work, which it had to produce, it became a very expensive medium, within the broadcasting model. It was never as expensive as film, but the cinema, as a distributive medium, could directly control its revenues. It was, on the other hand, implicit in broadcasting that given the tunable receiver all programmes could be received without immediate charge. There could have been and can still be a socially financed system of production and distribution within which local and specific charges would be unnecessary; the BBC, based on the licence system for domestic receivers, came nearest to this. But short of monopoly, which still exists in some state-controlled systems, the problems of investment for production, in any broadcasting system, are severe.

Thus within the broadcasting model there was this deep contradiction, of centralised transmission and privatised reception. One economic response was licensing. Another, less direct, was commercial sponsorship and then supportive advertising. But the crisis of production control and financing has been endemic in broadcasting precisely because of the social and technical model that was adopted and that has become so deeply established. The problem is masked, rather than solved, by the fact that as a transmitting technology—its functions largely limited to relay and commentary on other events—some balance could be struck; a limited revenue could finance this limited service. But many of the creative possibilities of television have been frustrated precisely by this apparent solution, and this has far more than local effects on producers and on the balance of programmes. When there has been such heavy investment in a particular model of social communications, there is a restraining complex of financial institutions, of cultural expectations and of specific technical developments, which though it can be seen, superficially, as the effect of a technology is in fact a social complex of a new and central kind.

It is against this background that we have to look at the development of broadcasting institutions, at their uses of the media, and at the social problems of the new technical phase which we are about to enter.

# 21. [Introduction]
# From
# *Computer Lib / Dream Machines*

*Computer Lib / Dream Machines* is the most important book in the history of new media.

Nelson's volume is often called the first personal computer book, probably because it arrived shortly before the first personal computer kit (the Altair) and was later recognized to have predicted the effects of its coming. This, however, was only one of the many visions, prescient and influential, offered in the volume.

*Computer Lib / Dream Machines* is a Janus-like codex that joins two books back to back; in the middle, the texts of the two bound-together books meet. The "Computer Lib" side, its cover featuring a raised fist with a computer in the background, didn't simply predict that personal computers were coming, but effectively challenged the popular notion of what computers were for, at a fundamental level. As Stewart Brand wrote in his foreword to the 1987 edition, Ted Nelson is "accurately depicted as the Tom Paine of the personal-computer revolution. His 1974 tract, *Computer Lib / Dream Machines*, had the same effect as Paine's *Common Sense*—it captivated readers, informed them, and set them debating and eventually marching, rallying around a common cause many of them hadn't realized was so worthy or even a cause before. . . . The enemy was Central Processing, in all its commercial, philosophical, political, and socio-economic manifestations. Big Nurse." Nelson's book raised the cry, "Down with Cybercrud!" He exhorted his readers to defy the computer priesthood, and its then-leader IBM, and to never accept, "The computer doesn't work that way" as an answer again. "Computer Lib" was in writing what the Altair and Apple II became in engineering: an artifact that destabilized the existing computer order, that brought about a conception of the computer as a personal device.

The volume's other side, "Dream Machines," had even greater significance for new media's development. Nelson wrote in the "Dream Machines" introduction, "Feel free to begin here. The other side is just if you want to know more about computers, which are changeable devices for twiddling symbols. Otherwise, skip it." He wrote this believing his most essential message was not about computers, but about media and design. He believed the importance of computers lay not in their capacity for calculation, but in the fact that they would enable new generations of media. In the pages that followed, Nelson reported on some of the most important work in new media up to that time, such as that of Doug Engelbart (◊08, ◊16) and Ivan Sutherland (◊09), and set forth his own unique twofold vision.

First, he argued that computer experiences were media to be designed, and that this design should be both a creative process and undertaken with the audience (users) in mind. His most stirring essay on the subject ("Fantics") is reprinted here, along with a small selection of Nelson's own designs. These are founding documents for the field now called human-computer interaction. They caused Nelson's book to be passed around, borrowed, stolen, and made a totemic object in early new media businesses. One former Apple Computer designer tells the story of having a copy of *CL/DM* placed in her hand the first day she reported for work.

Second, Nelson proposed that these new, designed media experiences be placed in a radical, open publishing network. A network that supported the reconfiguration, comparison, and interconnection of his 1965 hypertext proposal (◊11), in addition to complex version management and powerful user interface conventions. In pages reprinted here, he envisions the resulting explosion of knowledge radically altering the daily experiences of everyone from students to scientists. This vision and the project to realize it—Xanadu—made Nelson the butt of jokes for 20

◊08
93

◊09
109

◊11
133

◊16
231

**301**

*Mitch Kapor, Designer of Lotus 1-2-3, Cofounder of the Electronic Frontier Foundation:*

I spent a lot of the early 1970's prowling around the bookstores and newsstands of Harvard Square. By day, I was a very junior computer programmer and occasional teacher of Transcendental Meditation. I stumbled upon *Computer Lib* on a nocturnal excursion and was instantly bewitched. Here was a man who dreamed my dreams before I did, who gave voice to a radically different concept of computers as other than giant calculating machines. *Computer Lib* inspired me as no other book has before or since and sustained me over the next few years until I bought my first Apple II. It pointed me in the direction of a career in the as-yet then-uninvented field of personal computers. For which I am eternally grateful.

*Dream Machines* (2):

It matters because we live in media, as fish live in water. (Many people are prisoners of the media, many are manipulators, and many want to use them to communicate artistic visions.)

But today, at this moment, we can and must design the media, design the molecules of our new water, and I believe the details of this design matter very deeply. They will be with us for a very long time, perhaps as long as man has left; perhaps if they are as good as they can be, man may buy even more time— or the open-ended future most suppose remains.

Further Reading

Nelson, Ted. "A Conceptual Framework for Man-Machine Everything." *Proceedings AFIPS National Computer Conference and Exposition* M21–M26, June 4–8, 1973, New York. Montvale, N.J.: AFIPS Press, 1973.

Nelson, Ted. "The Right Way to Think about Software Design." *The Art of Human-Computer Interface Design*, 235–243. Ed. Brenda Laurel. Reading, Mass.: Addison-Wesley. 1990.

Rheingold, Howard. *Tools for Thought: The People and Ideas Behind the Next Computer Revolution*. New York: Simon & Schuster, 1985; Cambridge: MIT Press, 2000.

years: he was called a crackpot (and worse) for his strong conviction that Xanadu's fundamentals represented the future of media and culture. The general belief was that there simply was not demand for a public, hypertext-enabled publishing network. This belief was resisted, however, by small groups around the world who created and worked with various types of hypertext-enabled networks. Although we have not yet reached Xanadu, when one of these systems, the World Wide Web, began to explode in popularity during the 1990s (◊54), the voices of Nelson naysayers were drowned forever in a flood of international hypertext publishing.
—NWF

Original Publication

Self-published, 1974. 2nd ed., Redmond, Washington: Tempus Books/Microsoft Press, 1987.

# COMPUTER LIB

© 1974 Theodor H. Nelson.

Any nitwit can understand computers, and many do. Unfortunately, due to ridiculous historical circumstances, computers have been made a mystery to most of the world. And this situation does not seem to be improving. You hear more and more about computers, but to most people it's just one big blur. The people who *know* about computers often seem unwilling to explain things or answer your questions. Stereotyped notions develop about computers operating in fixed ways—and so confusion increases. The chasm between laymen and computer people widens fast and dangerously.

This book is a measure of desperation, so serious and abysmal is the public sense of confusion and ignorance. Anything with buttons or lights can be palmed off on the laymen as a computer. There are so many different things, and their differences are so important; yet to the lay public they are lumped together as "computer stuff," indistinct and beyond understanding or criticism. It's as if people couldn't tell apart camera from exposure meter or tripod, or car from truck or tollbooth. This book is therefore devoted to the premise that

## EVERYBODY SHOULD
## UNDERSTAND COMPUTERS.

It is intended to fill a crying need. Lots of everyday people have asked me where they can learn about computers, and I have had to say *nowhere*. Most of what is written about computers for the layman is either unreadable or silly. (Some exceptions are listed nearby [on pp. 6–7 of the first edition, not reprinted here]; you can go to them instead of this if you want.) But virtually nowhere is the big picture simply enough explained. Nowhere can one get a simple, soup-to-nuts overview of what computers are really about, without technical or mathematical mumbo-jumbo, complicated examples, or talking down. This book is an attempt.

(And nowhere have I seen a simple book explaining to the layman the fabulous wonderland of computer graphics which awaits us all, a matter which means a great deal to me personally, as well as a lot to all of us in general. That's discussed on the flip side.)

Computers are simply a necessary and enjoyable part of life, like food and books. Computers are not everything, they are just an *aspect* of everything, and not to know this is computer illiteracy, a silly and dangerous ignorance.

Computers are as easy to understand as cameras. I have tried to make this book like a photography magazine—breezy, forceful and as vivid as possible. This book will explain how to tell apples from oranges and which way is up. If you want to make cider, or help get things right side up, you will have to go on from here.

I am not a skillful programmer, hands-on person or eminent professional; I am just a computer fan, computer fanatic if you will. But if Dr. David Reuben can write about sex I can certainly write about computers. I have written this like a letter to a nephew, chatty and personal. This is perhaps less boring for the reader, and certainly less boring for the writer, who is doing this in a hurry. Like a photography magazine, it throws at you some rudiments in a merry setting. Other things are thrown in so you'll get the sound of them, even if the details are elusive. (We learn most everyday things by beginning with vague impressions, but somehow encouraging these is us not usually felt to be respectable.) What I have chosen for inclusion here has been arbitrary, based on what might amuse and give quick insight. Any bright highschool kid, or anyone else who can stumble through the details of a photography magazine, should be able to understand this book, or get the main ideas. This will not make you a programmer or a computer person, though it may help you talk that talk, and perhaps make you feel more comfortable (or at least able to cope) when new machines encroach on your life. If you can get a chance to learn programming it's an awfully good experience for anybody above fourth grade. But the main idea of this book is to help you tell apples from oranges, and which way is up. I hope you do go on from here, and have made a few suggestions.

I am "publishing" this book myself, in this first draft form, to test its viability, to see how mad the computer people get, and to see if there is as much hunger to understand computers, among all you Folks Out There, as I think. I will be interested to receive corrections and suggestions for subsequent editions, if any. (The computer field is its own exploding universe, so I'll worry about up-to-dateness at that time.)

## Summary of This Book

Man has created the myth of "the computer" in his own image, or one of them: cold, immaculate, sterile, "scientific," oppressive.

Some people flee this image. Others, drawn toward it, have joined the cold-sterile-oppressive cult, and propagate it like a faith. Many are still about this mischief, making people do things rigidly and saying it is the computer's fault.

Still others see computers for what they really are: versatile gizmos which may be turned to any purpose, in any style. And so a wealth of new styles and human purposes are being proposed and tried, each proponent propounding his own dream in his own very personal way.

This book presents a panoply of things and dreams. Perhaps some will appeal to the reader . . .

## The Computer Priesthood

Knowledge is power and so it tends to be hoarded. Experts in any field rarely want people to understand what they do, and generally enjoy putting people down.

Thus if we say that the use of computers is dominated by a priesthood, people who spatter you with unintelligible answers and seem unwilling to give you straight ones, it is not that they are different in this respect from any other profession. Doctors, lawyers and construction engineers are the same way.

But computers are very special, and we have to deal with them everywhere, and this effectively gives the computer priesthood a stranglehold on the operation of all large organizations, of government bureaux, and everything else that they run. Members of Congress are now complaining about control of information by the computer people, that they cannot get the information even though it's on computers. Next to this it seems a small matter that in ordinary companies "untrained" personnel can't get straight questions answered by computer people; but it's the same phenomenon.

It is imperative for many reasons that the appalling gap between public and computer insider be closed. As the saying goes, war is too important to be left to the generals. Guardianship of the computer can no longer be left to a priesthood. I see this as just one example of the creeping evil of Professionalism,* the control of aspects of society by cliques of insiders. There may be some chance, though, that Professionalism can be turned around. Doctors, for example, are being told that they no longer own people's bodies.** And this book may suggest to some computer professionals that their position should not be as sacrosanct as they have thought, either.

This is not to say that computer people are trying to louse everybody up on purpose. Like anyone trying to do a complex job as he sees fit, they don't want to be bothered with idle questions and complaints. Indeed, probably any group of insiders would have hoarded computers just as much. If the computer had evolved from the telegraph (which it just might have), perhaps the librarians would have hoarded it conceptually as much as the math and engineering people have. But things have gone too far. People have legitimate complaints about the way computers are used, and legitimate ideas for ways they should be used, which should no longer be shunted aside.

In no way do I mean to condemn computer people in general. (Only the ones who don't want you to know what's going on.) The field is full of fine, imaginative people. Indeed, the number of creative and brilliant people known within the field for their clever and creative contributions is considerable. They deserve to be known as widely as, say, good photographers or writers.

---

*This is a side point. I see Professionalism as a spreading disease of the present-day world, a sort of poly-oligarchy by which various groups (subway conductors, social workers, bricklayers) can bring things to a halt if their particular new increased demands are not met. (Meanwhile, the irrelevance of each profession increases, in proportion to its increasing rigidity.) Such lucky groups demand more in each go-round—but meantime, the number who are permanently unemployed grows and grows.

**Ellen Frankfort, *Vaginal Politics*. Quadrangle Books. Boston Women's Health Collective, *Our Bodies, Ourselves*. Simon & Schuster.

Come Dream along with me:
The Best Is Yet To Be.

# DREAM MACHINES

© 1974 Theodor H. Nelson

This is the flip side of *Computer Lib.*

(Feel free to begin here. The other side is just if you want to know more about computers, which are changeable devices for twiddling symbols. Otherwise skip it.)

(But if you change your mind it might be fun to browse.)

In a sense, the other side has been a come-on for this side. But it's an honest come-on: I figure the more you know, the readier you'll be for what I'm saying here. Not necessarily to agree or to be "sold," but to think about it in the non-simple terms that are going to be necessary.

The material here has been chosen largely for its exhilarating and inspirational character. No matter what your background or technical knowledge, you'll be able to understand some of this, and not be able to understand some of the rest. That's partly from the hasty preparation of this book, and partly from the variety of interests I'm trying

to comprise here. I want to present various dreams and their resulting dream machines, all legitimate.

If the computer is a projective system, or Rorschach inkblot, as alleged on the other side, the *real* projective systems—the ones with projectors in them—are all the more so. The things people try to do with movies, TV and the more glamorous uses of the computer, whereby it makes pictures on screens—are strange inversions and foldovers of the rest of the mind and heart. That's the peculiar origami of the self.

Very well. This book—this side, *Dream Machines*—is meant to let you see the choice of dreams. Noting that every

company and university seems to insist that *its* system is the wave of the future, I think it is more important than ever to have the alternatives spread out clearly.

But the "experts" are not going to be much help; they are part of the problem. On both sides, the academic and the industrial, they are being painfully pontifical and bombastic in the jarring new jargons. Little clarity is spread by this. Few things are funnier than the pretensions of those who profess to dignity, sobriety and professionalism of their expert predictions— especially when they, too, are pouring out their own personal views under the guise of technicality. Most people don't dream of what's going to hit the fan. And the computer and electronics people are like generals preparing for the last war.

Frankly, I think it's an outrage making it look as if there's any kind of scientific basis to these things; there is an underlevel of technicality, but like the foundations of a cathedral, it serves only to support what rises from it. THE TECHNICALITIES MATTER A LOT, BUT THE UNIFYING VISION MATTERS MORE.

This book has several simultaneous intentions: to orient the beginner in fields more complex and tied together than almost anybody realizes; nevertheless, to partially debunk several realms of expertise which I think deserve slightly less attention than they get; and to chart the *right* way, which I think uniquely continues the Western traditions of literature, scholarship and freedom. In this respect the book is much more old-fashioned than it may seem at the gee-whiz, very-now level.

The main ideas of this book I present not as my own, but as a curious species of revealed truth. It has all been obvious to me for some time, and I believe it should be obvious as well to anyone who has not been blinded by education. If you understand the problems of creative thinking and organizing ideas, if you have seen the bad things school so often does to people, if you understand the sociology of the intellectual world, and have ever loved a machine, then this book says nothing you do not know already.

For every dream, many details and intricacies have to be whittled and interlocked. Their joint ramifications must be deeply understood by the person who is trying to create whatever-it-is. Each confabulation of possibilities turns out to have the most intricate and exactly detailed results. (This is why I am so irritated by those who think "electronic media" are all alike.)

And each possible combination you choose has different precise structures implicit in it, arrangements and units which flow from these ramified details. *Implicit* in Radio lurk the Time Slot and the Program. But many of these possibilities remain unnoticed or unseen, for a variety of social or economic reasons.

Why does it matter?

It matters because we live in media, as fish live in water. (Many people are prisoners of the media, many are manipulators, and many want to use them to communicate artistic visions.)

But today, at this moment, we can and must design the media, design the molecules of our new water, and I believe the details of this design matter very deeply. They will be with us for a very long time, perhaps as long as man has left; perhaps if they are as good as they can be, man may even buy more time—or the open-ended future most suppose remains.

So in these pages I hope to orient you somewhat to various of the proposed dreams. This is meant also to record the efforts of a few Brewster McClouds, each tinkering toward some new flight of fancy in his own sensoarium.

But bear in mind that hard-edged fantasy is the corner of tomorrow. The great American dream often becomes the great American novelty. After which it's a choice of style, size and financing plan.

The most exciting things here are those that involve computers: notably, because computers will be embraced in every presentational medium and thoughtful medium very soon.

That's why this side is wedded to the other: if you *want* to understand computers, you can take the first step by turning the book over. I figure that the more you know about computers—especially about minicomputers and the way on-line systems can respond to our slightest acts—the better your imagination can flow between the technicalities, can slide the parts together, can discern the shapes of what *you* would have these things do. The computer is not a limitless partner, but it is deeply versatile; to work with it we must understand what it can do, the options and the costs.

My special concern, all too tightly framed here, is the use of computers to help people write, think and show. But I think presentation by computer is a branch of show biz and writing, not of psychology, engineering or pedagogy. This would be idle disputation if it did not have far-reaching consequences for the designs of the systems we are all going to have to live with. At worst, I fear these may lock us in; at best, I hope they can further the individualistic traditions of literature, film and scholarship. But we must create our brave new worlds with art, zest, intelligence, and the highest possible ideals.

I have not mentioned the emotions. Movies and books, music and even architecture have for all of us been part of important emotional moments. The same is going to happen with the new media. To work at a highly responsive computer display screen, for instance, can be deeply exciting, like flying an airplane through a canyon, or talking to somebody brilliant. This is as it should be. ("The reason is, and by rights ought to be, slave to the emotions."—Bertrand Russell.)

In the design of our future media and systems, we should not shrink from this emotional aspect as a legitimate part of our fantic (see p. 317) design. The substratum of technicalities and the mind-bending, gut-slamming effects they produce, are two sides of the same coin; and to understand the one is not necessarily to be alienated from the other.

Thus it is for the Wholeness of the human spirit, that we must design.

## Dreams

Technology is an expression of man's dreams. If man did not indulge his fantasies, his thoughts alone would inhibit the development of technology itself. Ancient visionaries spoke of distant times and places, where men flew around and about, and some could see each other at great distance. The technological realities of today are already obsolete and the future of technology is bound only by the limits of our dreams. Modern communications media and in particular electronic media are outgrowths and extensions of those senses which have become dominant in our social development.

How Wachspress, "Hyper-Reality."
© Auditac Ltd. 1973.

*No more pencils, no more books.*
*No more teachers' dirty looks.*
Kids' jingle with new meaning.

*Everything is Deeply Intertwingled.*

THE GESTALT, DEAR BRUTUS,
IS NOT IN OUR STARS
BUT IN OURSELVES.

CHILDREN OF ALL AGES!

Ladies and gentlemen, the age of prestidigitative presentation and publishing is about to begin. Palpitating presentations, screen-scribbled, will dance to your desire, making manifest the many mysteries of winding wisdom. But if we are to rehumanize an increasingly brutal and disagreeable world, we must step up our efforts. And we must hurry. Hurry. Step right up.

Theodor H. Nelson, "Barnum-Tronics."

*Swarthmore College Alumni Bulletin*, Dec 1970, 12–15.

(The following article appeared in the September, 1970 issue of *Computer Decisions*, and got an extraordinary amount of attention. I have changed my views somewhat—we all go through changes, after all—but after consideration have decided to re-run it in the original form, without qualifications, mollifications or anything, for its unity. Thanks to *Computer Decisions* for use of the artwork by Gans and for the Superstudent picture on the cover, whose artist unfortunately insists on preserving his anonymity.

An interesting point, incidentally, is that people read this a lot of different ways. One Dean of Education hilariously misread it as an across-the-board plug for CAI. Others read in it various forms of menace or advocacy of generalized mechanization. One letter-writer said *I* was a menace but at least writing articles kept me off the streets. Here is my fundamental point: *computer-assisted instruction, applied thoughtlessly and imitatively, threatens to extend the worst features of education as it is now.*

"When you're dealing with media you're in show business, you know, whether you like it or not."

"Show business," he said. "Absolutely. We've gotta be in show business. We've gotta put together a team that will get us there."

I made a mental note to use the show business metaphor again, and continued, "IBM's real creative talent probably lies in other areas . . ."

Heywood Gould, *Corporation Freak* (Tower), 23.

# No MORE teaChers' dirty LOOks

by Theodor H. Nelson
The Nelson Organization
New York

Some think the educational system is basically all right, and more resources would get it working again. Schools would do things the same way, except more so, and things would get better.

In that case the obvious question would be, how can computers help? How can computers usefully supplement and extend the traditional and accepted forms of teaching? This is the question to which present-day efforts in "computer-assisted instruction" —called CAI—seem to respond.

But such an approach is of no possible interest to the new generation of critics of our school system—people like John Holt (*Why Children Fail*), Jonathan Kozol (*Death at an Early Age*) and James Herndon (*The Way It Spozed to Be*). More and more, such people are severely questioning the general framework and structure of the way we teach.

These writers describe particularly ghastly examples of our schooling conditions. But such horror stories aside, we are coming to recognize that schools as we know them appear designed at every level to sabotage the supposed goals of education. A child arrives at school bright and early in his life. By drabness we deprive him of interests. By fixed curriculum and sequence we rob him of his orientation, initiative and motivation, and by testing and scoring we subvert his natural intelligence.

Schools as we know them all run on the same principles: iron all subjects flat than then proceed, in groups, at a forced march across the flattened plain. Material is dumped on the students and their responses calibrated; their interaction and involvements with the material is not encouraged nor taken into consideration, but their dutifulness of response is carefully monitored.

While an exact arrangement of intended motivations for the student is preset within the system, they do not usually take effect according to the ideal. It is not that students are *un*motivated, but motivated *askew*. Rather than seek to achieve in the way they are supposed to, students turn to churlishness, surliness, or intellectual sheepishness. A general human motivation is god-given at the beginning and warped or destroyed by the educational process as we know it; thus we internalize at last that most fundamental of grownup goals: just to get through another day.

Because of this procedure our very notion of human ability has suffered. Adult mentality is cauterized, and we call it "normal." Most people's minds are mostly turned off most of the time. We know virtually nothing of human abilities except as they have been pickled and boxed in schools; we need to ignore all that and start fresh. To want students to be "normal" is criminal, when we are all so far below our potential. Buckminster Fuller, in *I Seem to Be a Verb*, says we are all born geniuses: Sylvia Ashton-Warner tells us in *Teacher* of her success with this premise, and of the brilliance and creative potential she was able to find in all her schoolchildren.

Curricula themselves destructively arrange the study situation. By walls between artificially segregated "studies" and "separate topics" we forbid the pursuit of interest and kill motivation.

In ordinary schooling, the victim cannot orient himself to the current topic except by understanding the official angle of approach and presentation. Though tie-ins to previous interests and knowledge are usually the best way to get an initial sense of a thing, there is only time to consider the officially presented tie-ins. (Neither is there time to answer questions, except briefly and rarely well—and usually in a way that promotes "order" by discouraging "extraneous" tie-ins from coming up.)

The unnecessary division and walling of subjects, sequencing and kibbling of material lead people to expect simplifications, to feel that naming a thing is understanding it, to fear complex wholes; to believe creativity means recombination, the parsing of old relations, rather than synthesis.

Like political boundaries, curriculum boundaries arise from noticeable features of a continuum and become progressively more fortified. As behind political borders, social unification occurs within them, so that wholly dissimilar practitioners who share a name come to think they do the same thing. And because they talk mainly to each other, they forget how near is the other side of the border.

Because of the fiction of "subjects," great concern and consideration has always gone into calculating the "correct" teaching sequence for each "subject." In recent years radical new teaching sequences have been introduced for teaching various subjects, including mathematics and physics. But such efforts appear to have been misinformed by the idea of supplanting the "wrong" teaching sequence with the "right" teaching sequence, one which is "validated." Similarly, we have gone from a time when the instructional sequence was a balance between tradition and the lowest common denominator of each subject, to a time when teachers may pick "flexible optimized strategies" from textbooks. And this all ignores a simple fact: all are arbitrary. Instructional sequences aren't needed at all if the people are motivated and the materials are clear and available.

Testing as we know it (integrated with walled curricula and instructional sequences) is a destructive activity, particularly for the orientation which it creates. The concerns of testing are extraneous: learning to figure out low-level twists in questions that lead nowhere, under pressure.

The system of tensions and defenses it creates in the student's personality are unrelated to the subject or the way people might relate to the subject. An exploitive attitude is fostered. Not becoming involved with the subject, the student grabs for rote payoff rather than insight.

All in a condescending circumstance. Condescension is built into the system at all levels, so pervasive it is scarcely noticed. Students are subjected to a grim variety of put-downs and denigrations. While many people evidently believe this to be right, its productivity in building confident and self-respecting minds may be doubted.

The problems of the school are not particularly the teacher's fault. The practice of teaching is principally involved with managing the class, keeping up face, and projecting the image of the subject that conforms to the teacher's own predilections. The educational system is thereby committed to the fussy and prissy, to the enforcement of peculiar standards of righteousness and the elevation of teachers—a huge irrelevant shell around the small kernel of knowledge transmitted.

The usual attacks on computer teaching tend to be sentimental and emotional pleas for the alleged humanism of the existing system. Those who are opposed to the use of computers to teach generally believe the computer to be "cold" and "inhuman." The teacher is considered "warm" and "human." This view is questionable on both sides.

RS·DIRTY LOOKS

309

Some premises relevant to teaching

1. The human mind is born free, yet everywhere it is in chains. The educational system serves mainly to destroy for most people, in varying degrees, intelligence, curiosity, enthusiasm, and intellectual initiative and self-confidence. We are born with these. They are gone or severely diminished when we leave school.

2. Everything is interesting, until ruined for us. Nothing in the universe is intrinsically uninteresting. Schooling systematically ruins things for us, wiping out these interests; the last thing to be ruined determines your profession.

3. There are no "subjects." The division of the universe into "subjects" for teaching is a matter of tradition and administrative convenience.

4. There is no natural or necessary order of learning. Teaching sequences are arbitrary, explanatory hierarchies philosophically spurious. "Prerequisites" are a fiction spawned by the division of the world into "subjects;" and maintained by not providing summaries, introductions or orientational materials except to those arriving through a certain door.

5. Anyone retaining his natural mental facilities can learn anything practically on his own, given encouragement and resources.

6. Most teachers mean well, but they are so concerned with promoting their images, attitudes and style of order that very little else can be communicated in the time remaining, and almost none of it attractively.

The computer is as inhuman as we make it. The computer is no more "cold" and "inhuman" than a toaster, bathtub or automobile (all associated with warm human activities). Living teachers can be as inhuman as members of any people-prodding profession, sometimes more so. Computerists speak of "freeing teachers for the creative part of their work;" in many cases it is not clear what creative tasks they could be freed for.

At the last, it is to *rescue* the student from the inhuman teacher, and allow him to relate directly and personally to the intrinsically interesting subject matter, than we need to use computers in education.

Many successful systems of teacherless learning exist in our society: professional and industrial magazines; conventions and their display booths and brochures; technical sales pitches (most remarkably, those of medical "detail men"); hobbyist circles, which combine personal acquaintance with a round of magazines and gatherings; think-tanks and research institutes, where specialists trade fields; and the respectful briefing.

None of these is like the conventional classroom with its haughty resource-chairman; they are not run on condescension; and they get a lot across. We tend to think they are not "education" and that the methods cannot be transferred or extended to the regions now ruled by conventional teaching. But why not?

If everything we ate were kibbled into uniform dogfood, and the amount consumed at each feeding time tediously watched and tested, we would have little fondness for eating. But this is what the schools do to our food for thought, and this is what happens to people's minds in primary school, secondary school and most colleges.

This is the way to produce a nation of sheep or clerks. If we are serious about wanting people to have creative and energetic minds, it is not what we ought to do. Energy and enthusiasm are natural to the human spirit; why drown them?

Education ought to be clear, inviting and enjoyable, without booby-traps, humiliations, condescension or boredom. It ought to teach and reward initiative, curiosity, the habit of self-motivation, intellectual involvement.

Students should develop, through practice, abilities to think, argue and disagree intelligently.

Educators and computer enthusiasts tend to agree on these goals. But what happens? Many of the inhumanities of the existing system, no less wrong for being unintentional, are being continued into computer-assisted teaching.

Although the promoters of computer-assisted instruction, affectionately call "CAI," seem to think of themselves as being at the vanguard of progress in all directions, the field already seems to operate according to a stereotype. We may call this "classic" or "conventional" CAI, a way of thinking depressingly summarized in "The Use of Computers in Education" by Patrick Suppes, *Scientific American,* September, 1966, 206–220, an article of semi-classic stature.

It is an unexamined premise of this article that the computer system will always decide what the student is to study and control his movements through it. The student is to be led by the nose through every subject, and the author expresses perplexity over the question of *how* the system can decide, at all times, *where* to lead the student by the nose (top of col. 3, p. 219). But let us not anticipate alternatives.

It is often asserted (as by Alpert and Bitzer in "Advances in Computer-Based Education," *Science,* March 20, 1970) that this is not the only approach current. The trouble is that it *seems* to be the only approach current, and in the expanding computer universe everyone *seems* to know what CAI "is." And this is it.

Computer-assisted instruction, in this classical sense, is the presentation by computer of bite-sized segments of instructional material, branching among them according to involuntary choices by the student ("answers") and embedding material presented the student in some sort of pseudo-conversation ("Very good. Now, Johnny, point at the . . .")

## CAI: Based on Unnecessary Premises

At whichever level of complexity, all these conventional CAI systems are based on three premises: that all presentations consist of *items*, short chunks and questions; that the items are arranged into *sequences*, though these sequences may branch and vary under control of the computer; and finally, that these sequences are to be embedded in a framework of *dialogue;* with the computer composing sentences and questions appropriately based on the student's input and the branching structure of the materials. Let us call such systems SIC (Sequenced-Item Conversational) systems.

These three premises are united. For there to be dialogue means there must be underlying graph structure of potential sequences around which dialogue may be generated; for there to be potential sequences means breakpoints, and hence items.

Let us question each of the premises in turn.

### 1 Is dialogue pleasant or desirable?

Compulsory interaction, whether with a talking machine or a stereotyped human, is itself a put-down or condescension. (Note that on superhighways there is often a line of cars behind the automatic toll booths, even when the manned ones are open.) Moreover, faked interaction can be an annoyance. (Consider the green light at the automatic toll booth that lights up with a "thank you.") Moreover, dialogue by simple systems tends to have a fake quality. It is by no means obvious that phony dialogue with a machine will please the student.

### 2 Is the item approach necessary?

If the student were in control, he could move around in areas of material, leaving each scene when he got what he wanted, or found in unhelpful.

### 3 Are sequences necessary?

Prearranged sequences become unnecessary if the student can see what he has yet to learn, then pursue it.

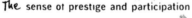

The sense of prestige and participation

## CAI: Unnecessary Complication

The general belief among practitioners is that materials for computer-based teaching are extremely difficult to create, or "program." Because of possible item weakness and the great variety of possible sequences within the web, extensive experimentation and debugging are required. Each item must be carefully proven; and the different sequences open to a student must all be tested for their effectiveness. All possible misunderstandings by a student need to be anticipated and prevented in this web of sequences, which must be designed for its coverage, correct order, and general effectiveness.

## CAI: General Wrongfulness

Computers offer us the first real chance to let the human mind grow to its full potential, as it cannot within the stifling and insulting setting of existing school systems. Yet most of the systems for computer-assisted instruction seem to me to be perpetuating and endorsing much that is wrong, even evil, in our present educational system. CAI in its conventional form enlarges and extends the faults of the American educational system itself. They are:

- Conduciveness to boredom;
- The removal of opportunities for initiative;
- Gratuitous concerns, both social and administrative ("subject," "progress" in subject);
- Grades, which really reflect commitment level, anxiety, and willingness to focus on core emphasis;
- Stereotyped and condescending treatment of the student (the "Now-Johnny" box in the computer replacing the one that sits before the class);
- The narrowing of curricula and available materials for "results" at the expense of motivation and generalized orientation;
- Destructive testing of a kind we would not permit on delicate machinery; and,
- An overt of hidden emphasis on invidious ratings. (Ungraded schools are nice—but how many units did *you* complete today?)

There are of course improvements, for instance in the effects of testing. In the tell-test, tell-test nattering of CAI, the testing becomes merely an irritant, but one certainly not likely to foster enthusiasm.

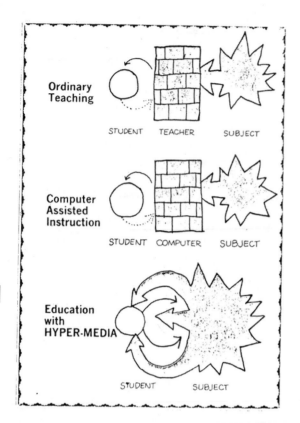

## But Isn't CAI 'Scientific?'

Part of CAI's mystique is based upon the idea that teaching can become "scientific" in the light of modern research, especially learning theory. It is understandable that researchers should promote this view and that others should fall for it.

Laymen do not understand, nor are they told, that "learning theory" is an extremely technical, mathematically oriented, description of the behavior of abstract and idealized organisms learning non-unified things under specific conditions of motivation and non-distraction.

Let us assume, politely, that learning theory is a full and consistent body of knowledge. Because of its name, learning theory has at least what we may call nominal relevance to teaching; but real relevance is another matter. It may be relevant as Newtonian equations are to shooting a good game of pool: implicit but without practical bearing.

Because of the actual character of learning theory, and its general remoteness from non-sterile conditions, actual relevance to any particular type of application must still be demonstrated. To postulate that the theory still applies in diluted or shifted circumstances is a leap of faith. Human beings are not, taken all together, very like the idealized pigeons or rats of learning theory, and their motivations and other circumstances are not easily controlled. Studies concerned with rate of repetition and reinforcement are scarcely relevant if the student hates or does not understand what he is doing.

I do not mean to attack all CAI, or any teaching system which is effective and gratifying. What I doubt is that SIC systems for CAI will become more and more wonderful as effort progresses, or that the goal of talking tutorial systems is reachable and appropriate. And what I further suspect is that we are building boredom systems that not only make life duller but sap intellectual interest in the same old way.

## Should Systems 'Instruct?'

Drill-and-practice systems are definitely a good thing for the acquisition of skills and response sets, an improvement over workbooks and the like, furnishing both corrections and adjustment. They are boring, but probably less so than the usual materials. But the CAI enthusiasts seem to believe the same conversationalized chunk techniques can be extended to the realm of ideas, to systems that will tutor and chide, and that this will provide the same sort of natural interest provided by a live tutor's instruction.

The conventional point of view in CAI claims that because validation is so important, it is necessary to have a standardized format of item, sequence and dialogue. This justifies turning the endeavor into picky-work within items and sequence complexes, with attendant curricular freeze, and student inanition and boredom. This is entirely premature. The variety of alternative systems for computer teaching have not even begun to be explored. Should systems "instruct" at all?

## 'Responding Resources' and 'Hyper-Media'

At no previous time has it been possible to create learning resources so responsive and interesting, or to give such free play to the student's initiative as we may now. We can now build computer-based presentational wonderlands, where a student (or other user) may browse and ramble through a vast variety of writings, pictures and apparitions in magical space, as well as rich data structures and facilities for twiddling them. These we may call, collectively, "responding resources." Responding resources are of two types: facilities and hyper-media.

A *facility* is something the user may call up to perform routinely a computation or other act, behaving in desired ways on demand. Thus JOSS (a clever desk calculator available at a terminal) and the Culler-Freed graph-plotting system (which graphs arbitrary functions the user types in) are facilities.

*Hyper-media* are branching or performing presentations which respond to user actions, systems of prearranged words and pictures (for example) which may be explored freely or queried in stylized ways. They will not be "programmed," but rather *designed, written, drawn* and *edited* by authors, artists, designers and editors. (To call them "programmed" would suggest spurious technicality. Computer systems to present them will be "programmed.") Like ordinary prose and pictures, they will be *media;* and because they are in some sense "multi-dimensional," we may call them *hyper-media,* following mathematical use of the term "hyper-."

## A Modest Proposal

The alternative is straightforward. Instead of devising elaborate systems permitting the computer or its instructional contents to control the situation, why not permit the student to control the system, show him how to do so intelligently, and make it easy for him to find his own way? Discard the sequences, items and conversation, and allow the student to move freely through materials which he may control. Never mind optimizing reinforcement or validating teaching sequences. Motivate the user and let him loose in a wonderful place.

Let the student control the sequence, put him in control of interesting and clear material, and make him feel good— comfortable, interested, and autonomous. Teach him to orient himself: not having the system answer questions, all typed in, but allowing the student to get answers by looking in a fairly obvious place. (Dialogue is unnecessary even when it does not intrude.) Such ultra-rich environments allow the student to choose what he will study, when he will study it and how he will study it, and to what criteria of accomplishment he will aim. Let the student pick what he wishes to study next, decide when he wishes to be tested, and give him a variety of interesting materials, events and opportunities. Let the student ask to be tested on what he

thinks he knows, when he is ready, selecting the most appropriate form of testing available.

This approach has several advantages. First, it circumvents the incredible obstacles created by the dialogue-item-sequence philosophy. It ends the danger to students of bugs in the material. And last, it does what education is supposed to do—foster student enthusiasm, involvement, and self-reliance.

Under such circumstances students will actually be interested, motivated to achieve far more than they have ever achieved within the normal instructional framework; and any lopsidedness which may result will be far offset by the degree of accomplishment which will occur—it being much better to create lopsided but enthusiastic genius specialists than listless, apathetic, or cruelly rebellious mediocrities. If they start soon enough they may even reach adulthood with natural minds: driven by enthusiasm and interest, crippled in no areas, eager to learn more, and far smarter than people ordinarily end up being.

Enthusiasm and involvement are what really count. This is why the right to explore far outweighs any administrative advantages of creating and enforcing "subjects" and curriculum sequences. The enhancement of motivation that will follow from letting kids learn anything they want to learn will far outweigh any specialization that may result. By the elimination or benign replacement of both curriculum and tests in an ultra-rich environment, we will prevent the attrition of the natural motivation of children from its initially enormous levels, and mental development will be the natural straight diagonal rather than the customary parabola.

## Is It So Hard? Some Ideas

CAI is said to be terribly hard. It would seem all the harder, then, to give students the richer and more stimulating environments advocated here. This is because of the cramped horizons of computer teaching today. Modest goals have given us modest visions, far below what is now possible and will soon be cheap.

The static computer displays now associated with CAI will give way to dynamic displays driven from minicomputers, such as the IDIIOM, IBM 2250/4 or Imlac PDS–1. (The last of these costs only $10,000 *now;* by 1975 such a unit will probably cost $1,000 or less.) Not only will computers be

313

### Discrete (Chunk Style) Hypertexts

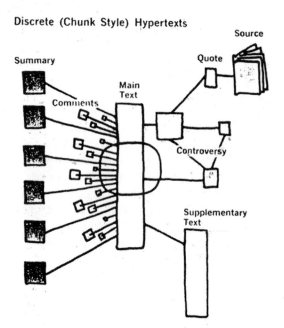

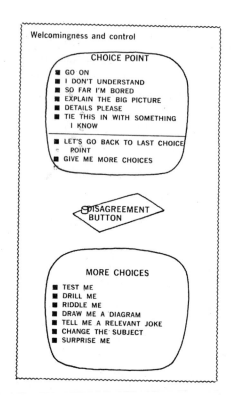

much cheaper, but their usability will improve: a small computer with a fair amount of memory will be able to do much more than it can now, including operate a complex display from its own complex data base.

It is generally supposed that systems like these need big computers and immense memories. This is not true if we use the equipment well, organize storage cleverly, and integrate data and display functions under a compact monitor. This is the goal of The Nelson Organization's Project Xanadu, a system intended to handle all the functions described here on a mini-computer with disk and tape.

### Discrete Hypertexts

"Hypertext" means forms of writing which branch or perform on request; they are best presented on computer display screens.

In ordinary writing the author may break sequence for footnotes or insets, but the use of print on paper makes some basic sequence essential. The computer display screen, however, permits footnotes on footnotes on footnotes, and pathways of any structure the author wants to create.

Discrete, or chunk style, hypertexts consist of separate pieces of text connected by links.

Ordinary prose appears on the screen and may be moved forward and back by throttle. An asterisk or other key in the text means, not an ordinary footnote, but a *jump*—to an

entirely new presentation on the screen. Such jumpable interconnections become part of the writing, entering into the prose medium itself as a new way to provide explanations and details to the seeker. These links may be artfully arranged according to meanings or relations in the subject, and possible tangents in the reader's mind.

### Performing Hypergrams

A hypergram is a performing or branching picture: for instance, this angle, with the bar-graph of its related trigonometric functions. The student may turn the angle upon the screen, seizing it with the light-pen, and watch the related trigonometric functions, displayed as bar charts, change correspondingly.

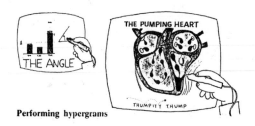

**Performing hypergrams**

Hypergrams may also be programmed to show the consequences of a user's prod—what follows or accompanies some motion of the picture that he makes with a pointing tool, like the heartbeat sequence.

## Stretchtext™ Fills in the Details

This form of hypertext is easy to use without getting lost. As a form of writing, it has special advantages for discursive and loosely structured materials—for instance historical narratives.

There are a screen and two throttles. The first throttle moves the text forward and backward, up and down on the screen. The second throttle causes changes in the writing itself: throttling toward you causes the text to become *longer* by minute degrees. Gaps appear between phrases; new words and phrases pop into the gaps, an item at a time. Push back on the throttle and the writing becomes shorter and less detailed.

The stretchtext is stored as a text stream with extras, coded to pop in and pop out at the desired altitudes:

> Stretchtext is a form of writing. It is read from a screen. The user controls it with throttles. It gets longer and shorter on demand.

> Stretchtext, a kind of hypertext, is basically a form of writing closely related to other prose. It is read by a user or student from a computer display screen. The user, or student, controls it, and causes it to change, with throttles connected to the computer. Stretchtext gets longer, by adding words and phrases, or shorter, by subtracting words and phrases, on demand.

## Hypermap Zips Up or Down

The screen is a map. A steering device permits the user to move the map around the world's surface: a throttle zooms it in. Not by discrete jumps, but animated in small changes, the map grows and grows in scale. More details appear as the magnification increases. The user may request additional display modes or "overlays," such as population, climate, and industry. Such additional features may pop into view on request

## Queriable Illustrations: a Form of Hypergram

A "hypergram" is a picture that can branch or perform on request. In this particular example, we see on the screen a line-drawing with protruding labels. When the student points at a label, it becomes a sliding descriptive ribbon, explaining the thing labeled. Or asterisks in an illustration may signal jumps to detailed diagrams and explanations, as in discrete hypertexts.

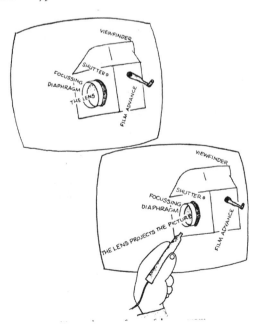

315

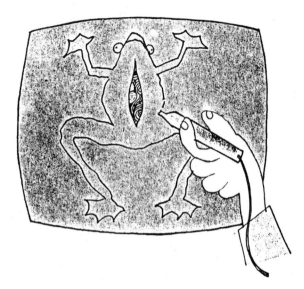

## Dissection on the Screen

The student of anatomy may use his light-pen as a scalpel for a deceased creature on the screen. As he cuts, the tissue parts. He could also turn the light-pen into hemostat or forceps, and fully dissect the creature—or put it back together again. (This need not be a complex simulation. Many key relationships can be shown by means of fairly simple schematic pictures, needing a data structure not prohibitively complicated.)

## Hyper-comics are Fun

Hyper-comics are perhaps the simplest and most straightforward hyper-medium. The screen holds a comic strip, but one which branches on the student's request. For instance, different characters could be used to explain things in different ways, with the student able to choose which type of explanation he wanted at a specific time.

## 'Technicality' Is Not Necessary

Proponents of CAI want us to believe that scientific teaching requires a certain setup and format, incomprehensible to the layman and to be left to experts. This is simply not true. "Technicality" is a myth. The problem is not one of technical rightness, but what *should* be.

The suggestions that have been given are things that should be; they will be brought about.

FEELED-EFFECT SYSTEMS
ARE THE NEW FRONTIER

# FANTICS

— BUT IT'S SHOWMANSHIP
THAT'S PARAMOUNT,
NOT ANY TECHNICAL SPECIALTY

Ah, Love! could you and I with Him conspire
To grasp this sorry Scheme of Things entire,
Would not we shatter it to bits—and then
Re-mould it nearer to the Heart's Desire!

Edward Fitzgerald.

Almost everyone seems to agree that
Mankind (who?) is on the brink of a
revolution in the way information is handled,
and that this revolution is to come from some
sort of merging of electronic screen
presentation and audio-visual technology
with branching, interactive computer
systems. (The naïve think "the" merging is
inevitable, as if "the" merging meant anything
clear. I used to think that too.)

Professional people seem to think this
merging will be an intricate mingling of
technical specialties, that our new systems
will require work by all kinds of committees and consultants
(adding and adjusting) until the Results—either specific
productions or overall Systems—are finished. Then we will
have to Learn to Use Them. More consulting fees.

I think this is a delusion and a con-game. I think that when
the *real* media of the future arrive, the smallest child will
know it right away (and perhaps first). That, indeed, should
and will be the criterion. When you can't tear a teeny kid
away from the computer screen, we'll have gotten there.

We are approaching a screen apocalypse. The author's basic
view is that RESPONSIVE COMPUTER DISPLAY SYSTEMS
CAN, SHOULD AND WILL RESTRUCTURE AND LIGHT UP
THE MENTAL LIFE OF MANKIND. (For a more
conventional outlook, see box nearby, "Another Viewpoint.")

I believe computer screens can make people happier,
smarter, and better able to cope with the copious problems
of tomorrow. But only if we do right, right now.

## Why?

The computer's capability for branching among events,
controlling exterior devices, controlling outside events, and
mediating in all other events, makes possible a new era of
media.

Until now, the mechanical properties of external objects
determined what they were to us and how we used them.
But henceforth this is arbitrary.

The recognition of that arbitrariness, and reconsideration
among broader and more general alternatives, awaits us. All
the previous units and mechanisms of learning, scholarship,
arts, transaction and confirmation, and even self-reminder,
were based in various ways upon physical objects—the
properties of paper, carbon paper, files, books and
bookshelves. To read from paper you must
move the physical object in front of you. Its
contents cannot be made to slide, fold, shrink,
become transparent, or get larger.

But all this is now changing, and suddenly.
The computer display screen does all these
things if desired, to the same markings we have
previously handled on paper. The computer
display screen is going to become universal very
fast; this is guaranteed by the suddenly rising
cost of paper. And we will use them for
everything. This already happens wherever
there are responding computer screen systems.
(I have a friend with two CRTs on his desk; one
for the normal flow of work, and one to handle interruptions
and side excursions.) A lot of forests will be saved.

Now, there are many people who don't like this idea, and
huff about various apparent disadvantages of the screen. But
we can improve performance until almost everyone is
satisfied. For those who say the screens are "too small," we
can improve reliability and backup, and offer screens
everywhere (so that material need not be physically carried
between them).

The exhilaration and excitement of the coming time is
hard to convey on paper. Our screen displays will be alive
with animation in their separate segments of activity, and
will respond to our actions as if alive physically too.

The question is, then: HOW WILL WE USE THEM? Thus
the design of screen performances and environments, and of
transaction and transmission systems, is of the highest
priority.

## The French Have a Word for It

In French they use the term *l'Informatique* to mean, approximately, the presentation of information to people by automatic equipment.

Unfortunately the English equivalent, *informatics,* has been preempted. There is a computer programming firm called Informatics, Inc., and when I wrote them about this in the early sixties they said they did *not* want their name to become a generic term. Trademark law supports them in this to a certain extent. (Others, like Wally Feurzeig, want that to be the word regardless.) But in the meantime I offer up the term *fantics,* which is more general anyhow.

## Media

What people don't see is how computer technology now makes possible the revision and improvement—the transformation—of all our media. It "sounds too technical."

But this is the basic misunderstanding: the fundamental issues are NOT TECHNICAL. To understand this is basically a matter of MEDIA CONSCIOUSNESS, not technical knowledge.

A lot of people have acute media consciousness. But some people, like Pat Buchanan and the communards, suggest that there is something shabby about this. Many think, indeed, that we live in a world of false images promulgated by "media," a situation to be corrected. But this is a misunderstanding. Many images are false or puffy, all right, but it is incorrect to suppose that there is any alternative. Media have evolved from simpler forms, and convey the background ideas of our time, as well as the fads. Media today focus the impressions and ideas that in previous eras were conveyed by rituals, public gatherings, decrees, parades, behavior in public, mummer' troupes . . . but actually every culture is a world of images. The chieftain in his palanquin, the shaman with his feathers and rattle, are telling us something about themselves and about the continuity of the society and position of the individuals in it.

Now the media, with all their quirks, perform the same function. And if we do not like the way some things are treated by the media, in part this stems from not understanding how they work. "Media," or structured transmission mechanisms, cannot help being personalized by those who run them. (Like everything else.) The problem is to understand how media *work,* and thus balance our understanding of the things that media misrepresent.

## Thoughts about Media:
### 1 Anything Can Be Said in Any Medium

Anything can be said in any medium, and Inspiration counts much more than 'science.' But the techniques which are used to convey something can be quite unpredictable.

Voice of Little Girl:
"Santa, are you more important than God?"
Announcer, plonkingly:
"Your answer is..."

☐ YES    ○ MAYBE

△ NO    ✛ HO-HO-HO

(After How To Be A Department Store Santa Claus, produced by the author for CBS Laboratories and the AVS-10 instructional device. Original slide, starring Michelle Dellinger and Henry Shrady, unfortunately mislaid.)

### 2 Transposability

There has always been, but now is newly, a UNITY OF MEDIA OPTIONS. You can get your message across in a play, a tract, a broadside, a textbook, a walking sandwich-board, a radio program, a comic book or fumetti, a movie, a slide-show, a cassette for the Audi-Scan or the AVS–10, or even a hypertext.

(But transposing can rarely preserve completely the character or quality of the original.)

### 3 Big and Small Approaches

What few people realize is that big pictures can be conveyed in more powerful ways than they know. The reason they don't know it is that they see the *content* in the media, and not *how* the content is being gotten across to them—that in fact they have been given very big pictures indeed, but don't know it. (I take this point to be the Nickel-Iron Core of McLuhanism.)

People who want to teach in terms of building up from the small to the large, and others who (like the author) like to present a whole picture *first,* then fill in the gaps, are taking two valid approaches. (We may call these, respectively, the Big Picture approach and the Piecemeal approach.) Big pictures are just as memorable as picky-pieces *if* they have strong insights at their major intersections.

## 4 The Word-Picture Continuum

The arts of writing and diagramming are basically a continuum. In both cases the mental images and cognitive structures produced are a merger of what is heard or received. Words are slow and tricky for presenting a lot of connections; diagrams do this well. But diagrams give a poor feel for things and words do this splendidly. The writer presents exact statements, in an accord-structure of buts and indeeds, molded in a structure of connotations having (if the writer is good) *exact impreciseness.* This is hardly startling: you're always selecting what to say, and the use of vague words (or the use of precise-sounding words vaguely) is simply a flagrant form of omission. In diagrams, too, the choice of what to leave in and out, how to represent overweening conditions and forces and exemplary details, are highly connotative. (Great diagrams are to be seen in the *Scientific American* and older issues of *Time* magazine.)

This word-picture continuum is just a part of the broader continuum, which I call Fantics.

## Fantics

By "fantics" I mean the art and science of getting ideas across, both emotionally and cognitively. "Presentation" could be a general word for it. The character of what gets across is always dual; both the explicit structures, and feelings that go with them. These two aspects, exactness and connotation, are an inseparable whole; what is conveyed generally has both. The reader or viewer always gets feelings along with information, even when the creators of the information think that its "content" is much more restricted. A beautiful example: ponderous "technical" manuals which carry much more connotatively than the author realizes. Such volumes may convey to some readers an (intended) impression of competence, to others a sense of the authors' obtuseness and non-imagination. Explicit declarative structures nevertheless have connotative fields; people receive not only cognitive structures, but impressions, feelings and senses of things.

Fantics is thus concerned with both the arts of effect— writing, theater and so on—and the structures and mechanisms of thought, including the various traditions of the scholarly event (article, book, lecture, debate and class). These are all a fundamentally inseparable whole, and technically-oriented people who think that systems to interact with people, or teach, or bring up information, can function on some "technical" basis—with no tie-ins to human feelings, psychology, or the larger social structure— are kidding themselves and/or everyone else. Systems for "teaching by computer," "information retrieval," and so on, have to be governed in their design by larger principles than most of these people are willing to deal with: the conveyance of images, impressions and ideas. This is what writers and editors, movie-makers and lecturers, radio announcers and layout people and advertising people are concerned with; and unfortunately computer people tend not to understand it for beans.

319

---

# ANOTHER VIEWPOINT

[from handout, 1974 Natl. Joint Comp. Conf.]

John B. Macdonald
Research Leader, Computer Applications: Graphics, Western Electric Company, Engineering Research Center

## Problems, Perils, and Promises of Computer Graphics

I would begin with some definitions which may be obvious but bear repeating.

1. Engineering is the application of science for ($) profit,

2. Computer graphics does not make possible anything that was previously impossible; it can only improve the throughput of an existing process,

3. A successful application of computer graphics is when over a period of five years the cost savings from improved process throughput exceed the costs of hardware, software, maintenance and integration into an existing process flow.

In fantics as a whole, then we are concerned with:

1. The art and science of presentation. Thus it naturally includes

2. Techniques of presentation: writing, stage direction, movie making, magazine layout, sound overlay, etc. and of course

3. Media themselves, their analysis and design; and ultimately

4. The design of systems for presentation. This will of course involve computers hereafter, both conceptually and technically; since it obviously includes, for the future, branching and intricately interactive systems enacted by programmable mechanisms, i.e. computers. Thus computer display, data structures (and, to an extent, programming languages and techniques) are all a part.

Fantics must also include

5. Psychological effect and impact of various presentational techniques—but not particular formal aesthetics, as of haiku or musical composition. Where directly relevant fantics also includes

6. Sociological tie-ins—especially supportive and dysfunctional structures, such as tie-ins with occupational structure; sponsorship and commercials; what works in schools and why. Most profoundly of all, however, fantics must deal with psychological constructs used to organize things:

7. The parts, conceptual threads, unifying concepts and whatnot that we create to make aspects of the world understandable. We put them into everything, but standardize them in media.

For example, take radio. *Given* in radio—the technological fundament—is merely the continuous transmission of sound. *Put into it* have been the "program," the *serial* (and thus the *episode*), the *announcer,* the *theme song* and the *musical bridge*—conventions which are useful presentationally.

The arbitrariness of such mental constructs should be clear. Their usefulness in mental organization perhaps is not.

Let's take a surprise example, nothing electronic about it.

Many "highways" are wholly fictitious—at least to begin with. Let's say that a Route 37 is created across the state: that number is merely a series of signs that users can refer to as they look at their maps and travel along.

However, as time goes by, "Route 37" takes on a certain reality as a conceptual entity: people think of it as a *thing.* People say "just take 37 straight out" (though it may twist and turn); groups like a Route 37 Merchants' Association, or even a Citizens to Save Scenic 37, may spring up.

What was originally simply a nominal construct, then, becomes quite real as people organize their lives around it.

This all seems arbitrary but necessary in both highways and radio. What, then, does it have to do with the new electronic media?

Simply this: till now the structures of media somehow sprang naturally from the nature of things. *Now they don't anymore.* Radio, books and movies have a natural inner dynamic of their own, leading to such constructs. While this may prove to be so for computer media as well (—as I argued in "Getting It Out of Our System"), then again it may not. In other words, WE MUST ACKNOWLEDGE THAT WE ARE *INVENTING* PRESENTATIONAL TECHNIQUES IN THE NEW MEDIA, not merely transporting or transposing particular things into them, because they seem right. *The psychological constructs of man-machine systems may turn out to be largely arbitrary.* Thus bringing to terminal systems conventions like dialogue instruction ("CAI"), or arbitrary restrictions of how things may be connected, presented or written on the computer may be a great mistake.

The highway-number analogy continues. The older highways had numbers for convenience, and our travels became organized around them, and particular highways (like "U.S. 1" and "Route 66") came to have special character. But now with the Interstates, a highway is a *planned, sealed unit,* no longer just a collection of roads gathered together under a name.

This unit, the Interstate, is not merely a psychological construct, but a planned structure. Knowing what works and what doesn't in the design of fast highways, the Interstates were built for speed, structured as closed units. Designing them with limited access has been a conscious decision in the system design for well-based reasons, *not* a chance structure brought in from horse-and-buggy days.

Now, the constructs of previous media—writing, films, other arts—evolved over time, and in many cases may have found their way to a "natural" form. But because of the peculiar way that computer media are currently evolving (—under large grants largely granted to professionals who use very large words to promote the idea that their original professions are largely applicable—), this sort of natural evolution may not take place. The *new* constructs of computer media, especially computer screen-media, may not have a chance to be thought out. We need designs for screen presentations and their mixture—vignetting, Windows, screen mosaics, transformed and augmented views, and the rapid and comprehensible control of these views and windows. We are still just beginning to find clever viewing techniques, and have hardly begun to discover highly responsive forms of viewability and control (cf. collateration in "Thinkertoys," p. 330), and Knowlton's button-box (oops, omitted). (See T. Nelson, "A Conceptual Framework for Man-Machine Everything," and material on controls, below.)

## The Mind's Unification

One of the remarkable things about the human mind is the way it ties things together. Perceptual unity comes out of nowhere. A bunch of irregular residential and industrial blocks becomes thought of as "my neighborhood." A most remarkable case of mental unification is afforded by the visage of our good friend Mickey Mouse. The character is drawn in a most paradoxical fashion: two globelike protrusions (representing the ears) are in *different positions on the head,* depending on whether we view him for the front

or the side. No one finds this objectionable; few people even notice, it seems.

What this shows, of course, is the way the mind can unify into a consistent mental whole even things which are inconsistent by normal rules (in this case, the rules of three-dimensional structure).

Even perceptions are subject to the same principle of unification. The fingernail is an excrescence with no nerves in it; yet somehow you can *feel things with your fingernails*—tying together disparate sensations into a unified sense of something in the world (say, a coin you're trying to pick up). In the same way, an experienced driver *feels the road;* in a very real sense, the car's wheels and suspension become his own sensory extensions.

This principle of mental unification is what makes things come together, both literally and figuratively, in a fantic field. A viewer sees two consecutive movie shots of streets and unifies them into one street; controls, if you are used to them, become a single fused system of options; we can have a sense of a greater whole, of which one view on a screen is a part.

THE GESTALT, DEAR BRUTUS, IS NOT IN OUR STARS BUT IN OURSELVES.

*THE PARADOXICAL ANATOMY OF MICKEY MOUSE*

*MICKEY MOUSE (frontal)*      *(lateral)*

*POSSIBLE RECONCILIATIONS: Diagonal Mounting*

*Rolling Relative to Camera*

## Controls: Their Unification and Feel

Controls are intimately related to screen presentation, just as arbitrary, and just as important.

The artful design of control systems is a deeply misunderstood area, in no way deconfused by calling it "human factors." There are many functions to be controlled, such as text editing operations, views of the universe on a screen, the heading of a vehicle, the tilt of an aircraft, the windage and adjustments of artillery, the temperature of a stove burner and any other controllable devices. And nowadays *any conceivable* devices could control them—pushbuttons, knobs, cranks, wheels, levers and joysticks, trigger, dials, magic wands, manipulation by lightpen on CRT screens, flicks of the finger, the *turning of the eyes* (as in some experimental gun-aiming devices), the human voice (but that introduces problems), keyboards, electronic tablets, Engelbart mice and chord writers, and so on.

The human mind being as supple as it is, anything whatever can be used to control systems. The problem is having it be a *comprehensible whole*.

As already remarked, our ability mentally to unify things is extraordinary. That we somehow tie together clutch, gear, accelerator and brake into a comprehensible control structure to make cars go and stop should amaze and instruct.

Engineers and "human factors" people speak as though there were some kind of scientific or determinate way to design control systems. Piffle. We choose a set of controls, much like an artist's Palette, on the basis of general appropriateness; and then try best and most artistically to fit them to what needs doing.

The result must be conceptually clear and retroactively "obvious"—simply because clarity is the simplest way to keep the user from making mistakes. Clear and simple systems are easier to learn, harder to forget, less likely to be screwed up by the user, and thus are more economical—getting more done for the resources put in.

There is a sort of paradox here. The *kinds* of controls are totally arbitrary, but their unification in a good system is not. Smoothness and clarity can come from disparate elements. It is for this reason that I lay particular stress on my JOT system for the input and revision of text, using a palette of keys available on the simplest standard computer terminal, the 33 Teletype. I cannot make the final judgement on how good this system is, but it pleases me. JOT is also an important example because it suggests that a conceptually unified system can be created from the artful non-obvious combination of loose elements originally having different intended purposes.

Mental analogy is an important and clear control technique. We tend to forget that the steering wheel was *invented*, separately replacing both the boat's tiller and the automobile's tiller. We also forget that the use of such steering mechanisms must be actually learned by children. Such continuous analogies, though, require corresponding continuities in the space to be controlled—an important condition.

Simplicity and clarity have nothing to do with the *appearance* of controls, but with the clarity and unique locatability of individual parts. For this reason I find deplorable the arrayed controls that are turning up, e.g., on today's audio

equipment. Designers seem to think *rows of things* are desirable. On the contrary: the best designed controls I ever used are on the Sony TC-50 pocket tape recorder

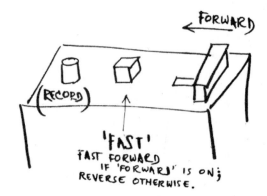

but of course this is now phased out; instead most cassette recorders have *five or six* stupid buttons in a row. (Was it too good to last?)

Spurious control elegance comes in many guises. Consider Bruce McCall's description of the Tap-A-Toe Futuroidic Footless De-Clutching™ system. This was offered on the fictitious 1934 Bulgemobiles, and allowed you to drive the car with one pedal, rather than three (see box p. 328).

Careless and horrible designs are not all fictitious. One egregious example also indicates the low level of design currently going into some responding systems: computer people have designed CRT writing systems for newspapers which actually have a "kill" button on the console, by which authors would accidentally kill their stories. In a recent magazine article it was explained that the eventual solution was to change the program so that to kill the story you had to hit the "kill" button *twice*. To me this seems like a beautiful example of what happens when you let insulated technical people design the system for you: a "kill" button on the keyboard is about as intelligent as installing knives on the dashboard of a car, pointing at the passenger.

There is another poor tendency. When computer programmers or other technical people design particular systems without thinking more generally, things are not likely to be either simple or combinable. What may result are intricate user-level controls for one par*ti*cular function, controls that are differently used for another *particular* function, making the two functions not combinable.

What makes for the best control structures, then? There is no simple answer. I would say provisionally that it is a matter of *unified and conspicuous constructs* in the mental view of the domain to be controlled, corresponding to a well-distinguished and clearly-interrelated set of controlling mechanisms. But that is hardly the last word on the subject.

## The Organization of Wholeness

It should be plain that in responding screen-systems, "what happens on the screen" and "how the controls respond" are not really distinguishable. The screen events are *part* of the way the controls respond. The screen functions and control functions merge psychologically.

Now, there is a trap here. Just as the gas pedal, clutch, gearshift and brake merge psychologically, *any* control structure can merge psychologically. Clutch and gearshift do not have, for most of us, clear psychological relevance to the problem of controlled forward motion. Yet we psychologically integrate the use of these mechanisms as a unified means for controlling forward motion (or, like the author, get an Automatic). In much the same way, any system of controls can gradually come through *use* to have a psychological organization, even spuriously. The trap is that we so easily lose sight of arbitrariness and even stupidity of design, and live with it when it could be so much better, because of this psychological melding.

But useful wholeness can be helped along. Just as what I have called the accordance-structure of writing moves it along smoothly, fantic design that builds from a well-organized internal dynamic should confer on a fantic system the same momentum and clarity that carefully-organized writing has.

This contribution of wholeness can only occur, however, if the under-level complications of a system have been carefully streamlined and smoothed back, at least as they affect the user. Consider the design of the JOT text editing system (p. 332): while it is simple *to the user,* computer people often react to it with indignation and anger because it hides what are *to them* the significant features of computer text editing—explicit preoccupation with storage, especially the calling and revision of "blocks." Nevertheless, I say it is the details at this level which must be smoothed back if we are to make systems for regular people.

The same applies to the Th3 system, which is designed to keep the user clear-minded as he compares things in multiple dimensions. The mechanisms at the computer level must be hidden to make this work.

## Fantic Space

Pudovkin and Eisenstein, great Russian movie-makers of the twenties, talked about "filmic space"—the imaginary space that the action *seems* to be in.

This concept extends itself naturally to *fantic space,* the space and relationships sensed by a viewer of any medium, or a user in any presenting or responding environment. The design of computer display systems, then, is really the *artful crafting of fantic space.* Technicalities are subservient to effects. (Indeed, I think computer graphics is really a branch of movie-making.)

## Fantic Structure

The *fantic structure* of anything, then, consists of its noticeable parts, interconnections, contents and effects.

I claim that it is the *fantic unity*—the conceptual and presentational clarity of these things—that makes fantic systems—presentational systems and material—clear and helpful, or not.

Let us take an interesting example from a system for computer-assisted instruction now under implementation. I will not identify or comment on the system because perhaps I do not understand it sufficiently. Anyway, they have an array of student control-buttons that look like this:

| OBJ [objective] | HELP | ADVICE |
| --- | --- | --- |
| MAP | HARDER | EASIER |
| RULE | EXAMP [example] | PRACT [practice] |

323

The general thinking in this system seems to be that the student may get an overall organizing view of what he is supposed to be learning (MAP); information on what he is currently supposed to be about (OBJ); canned suggestions based on what he's recently done (ADVICE). Moreover, he can get the system to present a rule about the subject or give him practice; and for either of these he may request easier rules or practice, or harder rules (i.e., more abstruse generalities) or harder practice.

For the latter, the student is supposed to hit RULE or PRACT followed by HELP, HARDER or EASIER, viz.:

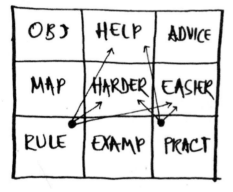

Now regardless of whether this is a well-thought-out way to divide up a subject—I'll be interested to see how it works out—these controls do not seem to be well-arranged for conceptual clarity. It seems to be the old rows-of-buttons approach.

I have no doubt that the people working on this system are certain this is the only possible layout. But consider that the student's options might be clearer to him, for instance, if we set it up as follows:

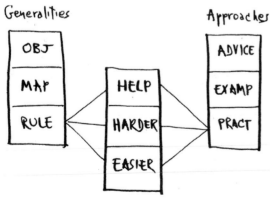

Or like this:

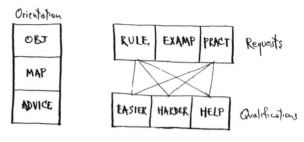

What I am trying to show here is that merely the *arrangement of buttons* creates different fantic constructs. If you see this, you will recognize that considering all the *other* options we have, designing new media is no small matter. The control structures merge mentally with the presentational structures. The temptation to settle on short-sighted designs having shallow unity is all too great.

## Fantic Design

Fantic design is basically the planning and selection of *effects*. (We could also call these "performance values"—cf. "production values" in movies.)

Some of these intended effects are simply the communication of information or cognitive structure—"information transfer," to use one of the more obtuse phrases current. Other desirable effects include orienting the user and often moving him emotionally, including sometimes overwhelming or entrancing him.

In the design of fantic systems involving automatic response, we have a vast choice among types of presentational techniques, tricks that are just now becoming understood. Not just screen techniques and functions, but also response techniques and functions.

(If "feelie" systems are ever perfected, as in Huxley's *Brave New World*, it's still the same in principle.)

In both general areas, though—*within* media, and *designing* media—it seems to me that the creation of *organizing constructs* is the most profound problem. In particular, the organizing constructs must not distract, or tear up contents. An analogy: in writing, the inventions of the paragraph, chapter and footnote were inventions in writing technique that helped clarify what was being expressed. What we need in computer-based fantic design is inventions which do not artificially chop up, constrain, or interfere with the subject (see box, Procrustes, p. 328).

I do not feel these principles are everywhere sufficiently appreciated. For instance, the built-in structures of PLATO disturbs me somewhat in its arbitrariness—and the way its control keys are scattered around.

But there is always something artificial—that is, some form of artifice—in presentation. So the problem is to devise techniques which have elucidating value but do not cut connections or ties or other relationships you want to save. (For this reason I suggest the reader consider "Stretchtext," p. 315) , collateral linkage (p. 330), and the various hypergrams (p. 314-16). These structures, while somewhat arbitrary and artificial, nevertheless can be used to handle a subject gently.)

An important kind of organizing construct is the map or overall orienting diagram. This, too, is often partly "exact" and partly "artifice": certain aspects of the diagram may have unclear import but clear and helpful connotation.

Responding systems now make it possible for such orienting structures to be multidimensional and responding.

Fantic design, then, is the creation either of things to be shown (writing, movie-making, etc.) at the lower end, or media to show things *in,* or environments.

1. The design of things to be shown—whether writing, movie-making, or whatever—is nearly always a combination of some kind of explicit structure—an explanation or planned lesson, or plot of a novel—and a *feeling* that the author can control in varying degrees. The two are deeply intertwined, however.

The author (designer, director, etc.) must think carefully about how to give *organization* to what is being presented. This, too, has both aspects, cognition and feelings.

At the cognitive end, the author must concern himself with detailed exposition or argument, or, in fiction, *plot.* But simply putting appropriate parts together is not enough: the author must use *organizing constructs* to continually orient the reader's (or viewer's) mind. Repeated reference to main concepts, repeated shots (in a movie) of particular locations, serve this function; but each medium presents its own possible devices for this purpose.

The organization of the *feelings* of the work criss-crosses the cognitive; but we can't get into it here.

Selection of points and parts contributes to both aspects. If you are trying to keep the feeling of a thing from being ponderous, you can never include everything you wanted, but must select from among the explicit points and feeling-generators that you have thought of.

2. The design of media themselves, or of media subsystems, is not usually a matter of option. Books, movies, radio and TV are given. But on occasion, as for world's fairs or very personal projects, we have a certain option. Which allows thing like:

· *Smellavision* or whatever they called it: movies with a smell-track, which went out into the theater through odor generators.

· Branching movies.

· "Multi-media" (Multiple audio tracks and simultaneous slide projections on different screens).

· Stereo movies.

And so on. The thing about the ones mentioned is that they are not viable as continuing setups for repeated productions. They do not offer a permanent wide market; they are not stable; they do not catch on. Which is in a way, of course, too bad.

But the great change is just about now. Current technicalities allow *branching media*—especially those associated with computer screens. And it is up to us now to design them.

3. MENTAL ENVIRONMENTS are working places for structured activity. The same principles of showmanship apply to a working environment as to both the *contents* of media and the *design* of media. If media are environments into which packaged materials are brought, structured environments are basically environments where you use *non*-packaged material, or create things yourself. They might also be called "contentless media." The principles of wholeness in structured environments are the same as for the others, and many of our examples refer to *them.*

The branching computer screen, together with the selfsame computer's ability to turn anything *else* on and off as selected by the user, and to fetch up information, yields a realm of option in the design of media and environment that has never existed before. Media we design for screen-based computer systems are going to catch on widely, so we must be far more attentive to the options that exist in order to commit—nationally, perhaps—to the *best*.

In tomorrow's systems, properly unified controls can give us new flexibilities. If deeply well-designed, these promise magnificent new capabilities. For instance, we could allow a musician to "conduct" the performance of his work by a computer-based music synthesis system, perhaps controlling the many qualities of the performance on a screen as he goes, by means of such techniques as dimensional flip. (The tradition of cumulative audio synthesis, as practiced in the fifties by Les Paul and Mary Ford, and more recently by Walter Carlos and Mike Oldfield, will take on a new fillip as multidimensional control techniques become common.)

One of the intents of this book has been to orient you to some of the possibilities and some of the options, considered generally. There is not room, unfortunately, to discuss more than one or two overall possibilities in detail. The most successful such system so far has been PLATO; others could not be listed for lack of space

## New Media to Last

What's worse, we are confronted not merely with the job of using computers to present specific things. The greater task is to design overall computer media that will last us into a more intelligent future. Adrift in a sea of ignorance and confusion, it is nevertheless our duty to try to create a whole transportation system that everybody can climb aboard. For the long run, fantic systems must be treated *not* as custom systems for explicit purposes, but as OVERALL GENERAL DESIGNS WHICH WILL HAVE TO TIE TOGETHER AND CATCH ON, otherwise collapse and perish.

## Final Consequences

It seems to me certain that we are moving toward a generalized and universal Fantic system; people can and should demand it. Perhaps there will be several; but if so, being able to tie them together for smooth transmission is essential. (Think of what it would be like if there were *two kinds of* telephone?) This then is a great search and crusade; to put together truly general media for the future, systems at which we can read, write, learn and visualize, *year after year after year*. The initiatives are not likely to come from the more conventional computer people; some of them are part of the problem. (Be prepared for every possible form of aggressive defensiveness from programmers, especially: "Why would you want that?" The correct answer is BECAUSE, damnit!)

But all this means that interior computer technicalities have to be SUBSERVIENT, and the programmers cannot be allowed to dictate how it is to behave on the basis of the under level structures that are convenient to them. Quite the contrary: from the fullest consideration of the richest upper-level structures we want, *we* the users-to-be must dictate what lower-level structures are to be prepared within.

But this means you, dear reader, must develop the fantic imagination. You must learn to visualize possible uses of computer screens, so you can get on down to the deeper level of how we are going to tie these things together.

The designer of responding computer systems is creating unified setups for viewing and manipulating things—*and* the feelings, impressions and sense of things that go with them. Our goal should be nothing less than REPRESENTING THE TRUE CONTENT AND STRUCTURE OF HUMAN THOUGHT. (Yes, Dream Machines indeed.) But it should be something more: enabling the mind to weigh, pursue, synthesize and evaluate ideas for a better tomorrow. Or for any at all.

Bibliography

Theodor H. Nelson, "A Conceptual Framework for Man-Machine Everything." *Proc. NCC* 73.

_____, "Computopia and Cybercrud." In Levien (ed.), *Computers in Instruction*, The Rand Corporation, 1971.

THE WALKING NET ™
→ A one-minute system
that three-year-olds can learn
[Sorry to have to show you a writeup,
instead of the real thing.]

Another application of the present invention is also in the area of pictorial display, but offers a great variety of potential user choices in a simple circumstance. I call this the "walking net" system because control is effected through a changing network of choices which step, or "walk," around the screen.

The problem of intricate computer graphics may be phrased as follows: given that a digital system can hold a wide variety of graphical materials ready to present, how may the user most simply and conveniently choose them? Indeed, how may the user keep track of what is happening, where he is and where he has been?

The external mechanism I have selected for this facility paradoxically combines great versatility for sophisticated presentations with great simplicity before the naïve user. The idea is this: the user may command a continuing succession of changing presentations, making only one simple choice at a time, yet receiving intricate and rich animations with extremely clear continuity on the screen.

The exterior mechanism is this: along with an arbitrary graphic presentation on the screen, the user is continuously presented with the image of a forking set of labeled arrows, e.g.:

The pip is a conventional right-pen cursor. The "current shank" is a line whose implicit gradations control developments in the picture; and the choice of arrows at the end of the current shank determine a discrete choice between alternatives that are to transpire.

The user, seizing the pip with the lightpen, moves it (through the usual lightpen techniques) sideways along the current shank. Moving it in the "forward" direction causes

progressive developments in the picture, moving it "backward" causes a reversal of animations and other previous developments.

When the pip reaches the choice point in the forward direction, the user may drag it (through the usual lightpen techniques) along either of the beckoning alternatives. This then causes further developments in the presentation consonant with the line selected.

"Developments" of the picture here include expansion, contraction, sliding movements and frame-by-frame animation.

(These materials will have been, of course, explicitly input by authors and artists.)

In a sample employment, consider a presentation on the subject of volcanoes. Let the first shank of the control net control the "rise of a volcano from the sea"—an undulating ocean surface pierced first by a wisp of smoke, then a growing peak, with rivulets of lava seen to run down its sides and darken as they contribute to its growth.

At the end of the first shank, the user may branch to two arrows, labeled respectively WORD ORIGIN and INTERIOR. Either option continues the presentation without a break, retaining much of the picture

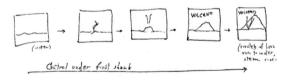

on the screen. Selection of WORD ORIGIN causes the word VOLCANO to change to VULCAN, and a picture of the god Vulcan is seen to seize a lightning bolt rising from the crater; text appears to explain this. Alternatively, if the user chooses INTERIOR, the tubes and ducts within the volcano appear, and explanatory text also.

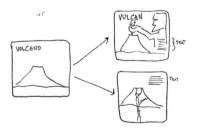

(The path unchosen fades from the screen, as does the previous shank.)

Either of these alternatives may continue with its own developments and animations under the control of its own shank.

Several features of this control application are of special interest. One is that the presentation may be continuous in all directions, aiding in continuous user orientation. Another is that presentations are reversible in various ways, an aid both in user orientation and self-study. (Not only is a demonstration reversible within a given shank, but the user may back the pip through an intersection into the antecedent shank—which reappears at the juncture as the lightpen backs up—and the user may continue to reverse the presentation through that preceding shank, or to re-enter the intersection and make another choice, "the path not taken.") These features allow the user clearly to repeat demonstrations as often as he likes and to explore numerous alternatives.

The displayed control net is thus to be understood as a large network of choices, mostly unseen, whose currently visible portion "walks" around the screen as use progresses. Within this system, then, numerous variants are possible. For instance, the currently visible portion of the net may itself be whimsically incorporated in a picture, viz.:

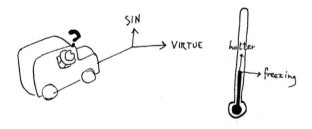

# PROCRUSTES THE GIANT

The Greeks told of a giant named Procrustes (rhymes with Rusty's) who was very hospitable to passing travelers. He would invite, indeed compel them, to sleep in his bed. Unfortunately, because it was a very odd bed, he had to cut them up first . . .

Procrustes has haunted conversations ever since; and any time we are forced to use categories that don't properly fit a subject, it seems like an invitation to the Procrustean bed.

Hypertext systems at last offer total freedom from arbitrary categorizing and chopping; but in *some* systems for storing and presenting information, I can't help hearing the whisk of Procrustes's knife—

> "Take new Tap-A-Toe Futuroidic Footless De-Clutching. Instead of old-fashioned gas, brake and clutch pedals that kept your feet busier than a dance marathon, Tap-A-Toe Futuroidic Footless De-Clutching offers the convenience of Single Pedal Power Control—combines *all foot functions* in one single pedal!
>
> "Think of it: one tap—you go, moving off faster than a barfly after Repeal.
>
> "Two taps—you change gears, as smooth and automatic as a mortgage foreclosure.
>
> "Three taps—you stop quicker than the U.S. economy.
>
> "And that's all there is to it. Tap-A-Toe Futuroidic Footless De-Clutching with Single Pedal Control is as easy and effortless as the Jap march on Manchuria!"
>
> Bruce McCall,
> "1934 Bulgemobile Brochure,"
> *National Lampoon,* May 74, 76–7.

# STELLAVISION

A nice example of a unified presentational system would allow you a "feelie" glove along with your computer display—the sort of thing Mike Noll has been doing at Bell Labs.

Now, suppose you are playing with a diagram of a star on a computer display screen. It's all very well to see its layers, flowing arrows representing convection currents, promontories and so on—but some things you ought to be able to *feel*. For example, the mechanical resonance-properties of stars. It would be nice to be able to reach and *grasp* the star, to *squeeze* it and feel its pulsations as it regains its shape. This could be done in the glove—at the same time the *image* of the glove grasps the star on the screen, and the star is squished.

Of course, to build such a responding glove, particularly one that gave you subtle feelings back in your fingers, would probably be very expensive. But it's the kind of possibility people should start considering.

Should I have called it

# TEACHOTECHNICS?
# SHOWMANSHIPNOGOGY?
# INTELLECTRONICS? [S. Ramo]
# THOUGHTOMATION?
# MEDIA-TRONICS?

# ABOUT THE TERM 'FANTICS.'

First of all, I feel that very few people understand what interactive computer systems are *about*. It's like the story of the blind man and the elephant—each thinks it's a different thing (based, usually, on his own technical specialty).

But I think it's all show business. PENNY ARCADES are the model for interactive computer systems, not classrooms or libraries or imaginary robot playmates. And computer graphics is an intricate branch of movie-making.

Okay, so I wanted a term that would connote, in the most general sense, the showmanship of ideas and feelings—whether or not handled by machine.

I derive "fantics" from the Greek words "phainein" (show) and its derivative "phantastein" (present to the eye or mind).

You will of course recognize its cousins *fantastic, fantasy, phantom*. ("Phantom" means *what is shown*; in medical illustration it refers to an opaque object drawn as transparent; a "phantom limb" is an amputee's temporary feeling that the severed limb has been restored.) And a fantast is a dreamer.

The word "fantics" would thus include the showing of anything (and thus writing and theater), which is more or less what I intended. The term is also intended to cover the tactics of conveying ideas and impressions, especially with showmanship and presentational techniques, organizing constructs, and fundamental structures underlying presentational systems.

Thus Engelbart's data hierarchy, SKETCHPAD's Constraints, and PLATO's fantic spaces are fantic constructions that need to be understood if we are to understand these systems and their potential usages.

Livermore Labs, those hydrogen-bomb design people, will have a "Laboratory for Data Analysis," an opulent facility for experimenting with multidimensional visualization.

One of your jolly ironies. I have seen pictures of beautiful multibutton control handles which were designed for project SMASH, would you believe Southeast [Asia] Multisensory Armament System for Helicopters. Aargh.

The best with the worst.

Everything is deeply intertwingled.

Designing screen systems that focus the user's thought on his work, with helpful visualizations and no distractions, is the great task of fantic design.

In a system I designed for CRT motion-picture editing, the user could manipulate written descriptions on the screen (corresponding to the usual yellow-pad notes). To see the consequences of a particular splice, for instance, the editor would only have to draw a line between two annotated lines representing shots. Trim variations could be seen by moving this cut-line (illustrated).

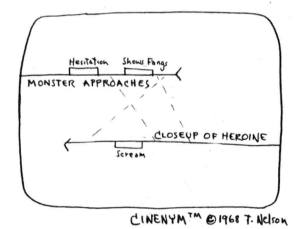

CINENYM™ © 1968 T. Nelson

Not long after, CBS and Memorex *did* introduce a system for movie editing by CRT—but I've heard that in their system the user has to actually deal with numbers. If so, this is missing the whole point.

# ★THINKERTOYS★

Our greatest problems involve thinking and the visualization of complexity.

By "Thinkertoy" I mean, first of all, a system to help people think. ('Toy' means it should be easy and fun to use.) This is the same general idea for which Engelbart, for instance, uses the term "augmentation of intellect."

But a Thinkertoy is something quite specific: I define it as a computer display system that *helps you envision complex alternatives.*

The process of envisioning complex alternatives is by no means the only important form of human thought; but it is essential to making decisions, designing, planning, writing, weighing alternate theories, considering alternate forms of legislation, doing scholarly research, and so on. It is also complicated enough that, in solving it, we may solve simpler problems as well.

We will stress here some of the uses of these systems for handling *text,* partly because I think these are rather interesting, and partly because the complexity and subtlety of this problem has got to be better understood: the written word is nothing less than the tracks left by the mind, and so we are really talking about screen systems for handling ideas, in all their complexity.

Numerous types of complex things have to be inter-compared, and their relations inter-comprehended. Here are a few of the many types:

Alternative designs.

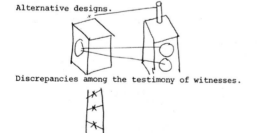

Discrepancies among the testimony of witnesses.

Successive drafts of the same document.

Pairs of things which have some parts the same, some parts different (contracts, holy books, statutes of different states, draft versions of legislation...)

Different theories and their ties to particular examples and evidences.

Under examination these different types of inter-comparison seem to be rather different. Now, one approach would be to create a different data structure and viewing technique for *each* different type of complex. There may be reasons for doing that in the future.

For the present, however, it makes sense to try to find the most general possible viewing technique: one that will allow complex intercomparisons of all the types mentioned, and any others we might run across.

One such technique is what I now call *collateration,* or the linking of materials into *collateral structures,* as will be explained. This is fairly straightforward if you think enough about the problem; Engelbart discovered it independently.

Let us call two structures *collateral* if there are links between them, connecting a selected part of one with a selected part of the other. The sequences of the connected parts may be different. For simplicity's sake, suppose each one is a short piece of writing. (We will also assume that there is some convenient form of rapid viewing and following between one end of a link and another.)

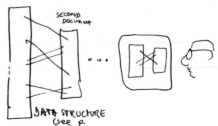

Now, it will be noted first off that this is an extremely general method. By collateral structuring we can easily handle the equivalents of: tables of contents; indexes; comments and marginalia; explanations, exegesis, explication; labeling; headings; footnotes; notes by the writer to himself; comments and questions by the reader for later reference; and additional details out of sequence.

*Collateration,* then, is the creation of such multiple and viewable links BETWEEN ANY TWO DATA STRUCTURES, in principle. It is general and powerful enough to handle a great variety of possible uses in human intellectual endeavor, and deserves considerable attention from researchers of every stripe.**

The problem then, is how to handle this for rapid and convenient viewing and whatever other work the user wants to do—writing and splicing, inter-comparing, annotating and so on. Two solutions appear on this spread: The Parallel Textface™, designed as a seminal part of the Xanadu system (see p. 335), which I hope will be marketed with that system in the near future, and a more recent design which I've worked on at the University of Illinois, the 3D Thinkertoy or Th3.

## Clarity and Power

We stressed on the other side of the book that computer systems must be clear, simple and easy to use. Where things like business uses of computers are concerned, which are intrinsically so simple in principle, some of the complications that people have been forced to deal with in ill-designed computer systems verge on the criminal. (But some computer people want others to think that's the way it has to be. "Your first duty is to keep your job, right?" one computer person said to me recently. "It wouldn't do to set up systems so easy to use that the company wouldn't need you anymore.")

But if it is desirable that computer systems for *simpleminded* purposes be easy to use, it is *absolutely necessary* that computer systems for *complicated* purposes be simple to use. If you are wrangling over complex alternatives—say, in chess, or in a political simulation game, or in the throes of trying to write a novel, the last thing you will tolerate is for your computer screen to introduce complications of its own. If a system for thinking doesn't make thinking simpler— allowing you to see farther and more deeply—it is useless, to use only the polite term.

But systems can be both powerful and simple at the same time. The myth that things have to be complicated to do anything for you is pernicious rubbish. Well-designed systems can make our mental tasks lighter and our achievements come faster.

It is for this reason that I commend to the reader these two designs of mine: as examples of user-level control and viewing designs—fantic environments, if you will (see p. 317)—that are pruned and tuned to give the user great control over the viewing and cross-consideration of intricate alternatives, *without* complication. I like to believe that both of these, indeed, are *ten-minute systems*—that is when we get them running, the range of uses shown here can be taught to naive users, in *ten minutes or less.*

It is because of my heartfelt belief in this kind of simplicity that I stress the creation of prefabricated environments, carefully tuned for easy use, rather than the creation of computer *languages* which must be learnt by the user, as do such people as Engelbart and DeFanti.

Now, their approach obviously has considerable merit for sophisticated users who want to tinker repeatedly with variant approaches. For people who want to work incessantly *in* an environment, and *on* other things—say writers—and are absent-minded and clumsy and nervous and forgetful (like the present author), then the safe, prefabricated environment, with thoroughly fail-safe functions and utterly memorable structural and control interrelationships, is the only approach.

331

*In my 1965 paper (see bibliography) I called collateral structures *zippered lists.* [included in this volume (◊11)

** A group at Brown University has reportedly worked along these lines since I worked with them, but due to certain personal animosities I have not kept up with their developments. It will be interesting to see what kind of response they can get out of the IBM systems they are using.

Bibliography

Theodor H. Nelson, "A File Structure for the Complex, the Changing and the Indeterminate." Proc. ACM 65, 84–100.

_____, "Simplicity Versus Power in User Systems." Unpublished.

## Decision/Creativity Systems [Thinkertoys]

Theodor H. Nelson

19 July 1970

It has been recognized from the dawn of computer display that the grandest and most important use of the computer display should be to aid decisions and creative thought. The work of Ivan Sutherland (SKETCHPAD) and Douglas Engelbart have really shown how we, may use the display to visualize and effect out creative decisions swiftly and vividly.

For some reason, however, the most important aspect of such systems has been neglected. We do not make important decisions, we should not make delicate decisions, serially and irreversibly. Rather, the power of the computer display (and its computing and filing support) must be so crafted that we may develop alternatives, spin out their complications and interrelationships, and visualize these upon a screen.

No system could do this for us automatically. What design and programming can create, however, is a facility that will allow us to list, sketch, link and annotate the complexities we seek to understand, then present "views" of the complexities in many different forms. Studying these views, annotating and refining, we can reach the final designs and decisions with much more in mind than we could otherwise hold together in the imagination.

Some of the facilities that such systems must have include the following:

*Annotations* to anything, to any remove.

*Alternatives* of decision, design, writing, theory.

*Unlinked or irregular pieces,* hanging as the user wishes.

*Multicoupling,* or complex linkage, between alternatives, annotations or whatever.

*Historical filing* of the user's actions, including each addition and modification, and possibly the viewing actions that preceded them.

*Frozen moments and versions,* which the user may hold as memorable for his thinking.

*Evolutionary coupling,* where the correspondences between evolving versions are automatically maintained, and their differences or relations easily annotated.

In addition, designs for screen "views," the motion, appearance and disappearance of elements, require considerable thought and imagination.

## JOT™: Juggler Of Text.

From "A Human Being's Introduction to the JOT System." ©1972 T. Nelson.

Here's how simple it is to create and edit text with the JOT system. Since your typewriter is now a JOT machine, not every key does what it used to. [When Nelson wrote much "word processing" was through modified typewriters, wihtout graphic displays—eds.]

*CREATING TEXT: just type it in.*
You type:  The quick brown fox jumps over the lazy dog.
It types:  The quick brown fox jumps over the lazy dog.

*REVIEWING A SENTENCE YOU JUST TYPED: the back-arrow takes you back, the space bar steps you through.*

| You type: | ← | sp | sp | sp | sp |
|---|---|---|---|---|---|
| It types: | (bell) | The | quick | brown | fox |

*DELETIONS AND INSERTIONS: the RUBOUT key rejects words you don't want. To insert, merely type.*

| You type: | ← | sp | sp | RUBOUT | lithe | sp | sp | sp | sp | sp | sp |
|---|---|---|---|---|---|---|---|---|---|---|---|
| It types: | (bell) | The | quick | /brown/ | lithe | fox | jumps | over | the | lazy | dog. |

*REARRANGING TEXT: first we make three Cuts in the text, signaled by free-standing exclamation points.*

| You type: | sp | ! | sp | ! | sp | ! | fox |
|---|---|---|---|---|---|---|---|
| It types: | The | ! | quick | ! | lithe | ! | fox |

TO REARRRANGE IT, YOU TYPE: LINE FEED key. This exchanges the two pieces between the cuts.
*CHECK THE RESULTS:*

| | ← | sp | sp | sp | sp |
|---|---|---|---|---|---|
| | (bell) | The | lithe | quick | fox |

The object is not to burden the user, or make him aware of complexities in which he has no interest. But almost everyone in intellectual and decision pursuits has at some time an implicit need for some of these facilities. If people knew they were possible, they would demand them. It is time for their creation.

A full-fledged decision/creativity system, embracing both text and graphics, is one of the ultimate design goals of Project XANADU.

# The PARALLEL TEXTFACE™

This user-level system is intended to aid in all forms of writing and scholarship, as well as anywhere else that we need to understand and manipulate complex clusterings of text (i.e., *thought*). It will also work with certain animated graphics.

The parallel Textface, as described here, furnished the initial impetus for the development of the Xanadu™ system (see p. 335). Xanadu was developed, indeed, originally for the purpose of implementing some of these functions, but the two split apart. It turned out that the Parallel Textface required an extremely unusual data structure and program techniques; these then became the Xanadu system. As developed in the final Xanadu design, they turn out to handle some

We might also think of them as systems for **THE MANAGEMENT OF LOOSE ENDS.**

very unusual kinds of screen animation and file retrieval. But this grew out of structuring a system to handle the functions described here.

Thus the Parallel Textface basically requires a Xanadu system.

It is hoped that this system can be sold complete (including a minicomputer or microprocessor—no connection to a large computer is required) for a few thousand dollars by 1976 or 1977. (Since "business people" are extremely skeptical as to whether anybody would want such a thing, I would be interested in hearing expressions of interest, if any.)

As shown here, the screen presents two panels of text; more are allowed. Each contains a segment of a longer document. ("Page" would be an improper term, since the boundary of the text viewed may be changed instantly.)

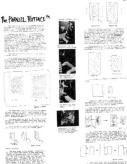

The other odds and ends on the screen are hidden keys to control elements which have been made to fade (in this illustration), just to lessen the distraction.

Panel boundaries and control graphics may be made to appear by touching them with the lightpen.

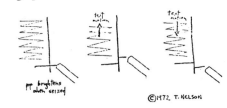

©1972 T. NELSON

## Roving Functions

The text moves on the screen! (Essential.) The lower right hand corner of each text panel contains an inconspicuous control diagram. The slight horizontal extension is a movable control pip. The user, with his lightpen, may move the pip up or down. "Up" causes the text to move smoothly upward (forward in the material), at a rate proportional to how far you push the pip; "down" causes it to move back. (Note that we do *not* refer here to jerky line-by-line jumps, but to smooth screen motion, which is essential in a high-performance system. If the text does not move, you can't tell where it came from.)

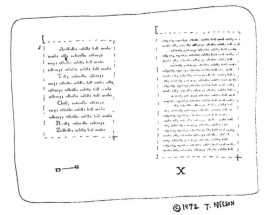

©1972 T. NELSON

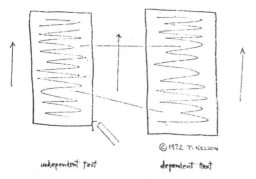

independent text       dependent text

© 1972 T. NELSON

DERIVATIVE MOTION: when links run sequentially, connecting one-after-the-other on both sides, the contents of the second panel are pulled along directly: the smooth motion in one panel is matched in the other. This may be called *derivative motion,* between independent text (being handled directly with the lightpen) and dependent text (being pulled along). The relationship may be reversed immediately, however, simply by moving the lightpen to the control pip of the other panel, whose contents then become the independent text.

Irregularities in the links will cause the independent text to move at varying speeds or jump, according to an average of the links' connectivity.

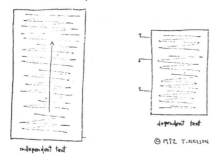

dependent text

© 1972 T. NELSON

independent text

If no links are shown, the dependent text just stops..

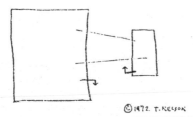

© 1972 T. NELSON

Collateral links between materials in the two panels are displayed as movable lines between the panels. (Text omitted in this diagram; panel boundary has been made to appear.)

Some links may not have both their endpoints displayed at once. In this case we show the incomplete link as a broken arrow, pointing in the direction of the link's completion.

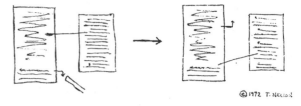

© 1972 T. NELSON

The broken arrow serves not merely as a visual pointer, but as a jump-marker leading to the linked material. By zapping the broken arrow with the lightpen, the user summons the linked material—as shown by the completion of the link to the other panel. (Since there has been a jump in the second panel, we see that in this case the other link has been broken.)

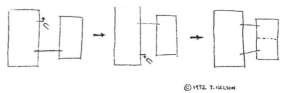

© 1972 T. NELSON

When such links lead to different places, both of these destinations may nevertheless be seen at once. This is done by pointing at both broken links in succession; the system then allows both links to be completed, breaking the second panel between the two destinations (as shown by dotted line across panel).

---

*Oddly, this has the same logical structure as time-travel in science-fiction.

There are basically three alternative premises of time-travel: 1) that the past cannot be changed, all events having preceded the backstep; 2) that the past *can* be changed; and 3) that while time-travelers may be deluded into thinking (2), that (1) is really the case—leading to various appointment-in-Samarra plots.

Only possibility (2) is of interest here, but there are various alternative logics of mutability and time-line stepping. One of the best I have seen is in *The Man Who Folded Himself* by David Gerrold (Popular Library, 1973): logic expounded pp. 64–8. I am bemused by the parallel between Gerrold's time-controls and these, worked out independently.

PARALLEL TEXTFACE (1971)

Independent text pulls
dependent text along.
Painted streaks simulate
motion, not icicles.

Real person sits at
cardboard Xanadu mockup.

"Nice keyboard. But
what happened to
your typewriter?"

Two panels are about
right for a 10 x 10
screen.

XANADU
©1972 T. NELSON

## Fail-Safe and Historical Features

In systems for naive users, it is essential to safeguard
the user from his own mistakes. Thus in text systems,
commands given in error must be reversible. For
instance, Carmody's system requires confirmation of
deletions.

Another highly desirable feature would allow the
user to view previous versions, to see them collaterally
with the corresponding parts of current versions, and
even go back to the way particular things were and
resume work from the previous version.

In the Parallel Textface this is all comprised in the same
extremely simple facility. (Extremely simple from the user's
point of view, that is. Inside it is, of course, hairy.)

In an egregious touch of narcissistic humor, we use the
very trademark on the screen as a control device (expanded
from the "X" shown in the first panel).

Actually the X in "Xanadu™," as it appears on the screen, is
an hourglass, with a softly falling trickle of animated dots in
the lower half, and Sands of Time seen as heaps above and
below. These have a control, as well as a representative,
function.

TO UNDO SOMETHING, YOU MERELY
STEP "BACKWARD IN TIME" by dagging the
upper part of the hourglass with the lightpen.
One poke, one editing operation undone.
Two pokes, two operations.

You may then continue to view and make
changes as if the last two operations had
never taken place. This effectively creates an
alternative time-line.* However, *if* you decide
that a previously undone edit operation
should be kept after all, you may step
*forward*—stepping onto the previous time-line—by using
the lower half of the hourglass.

335

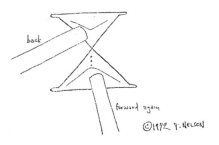

back

forward again

©1972 T. NELSON

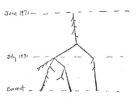

June 1971

July 1971

current

Revision Tree

©1972 T. NELSON

We see this clarified in a master time diagram or Revision Tree which may be summoned to the screen, never mind how. In this example we see that three versions are still "current," various other starts and variations having been abandoned. (The shaggy fronds correspond to short-lived variations, resulting from operations which were then reversed. In other words, "excised" time-lines, to use Gerrold's term—see footnote.)

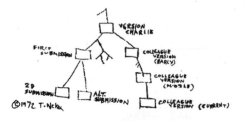

The user—let's say he is a thoughtful writer—may define various Versions or Drafts, here marked on the Revision Tree.

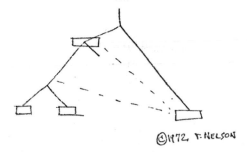

He may, indeed, define collateral linkages between different versions defined at various Times in the Tree . . .

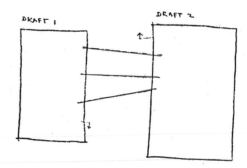

. . . and see them displayed collaterally; and revise them further.

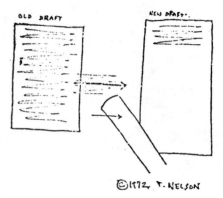

Materials may be copied between versions. (Note that in the copying operation of the Parallel Textface, you actually see the moved text moved *bodily as a block*.)

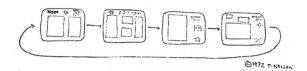

## Getting Around

The user may have a number of standby layouts, with different numbers of panels, and jump among them by stabs of the lightpen.

Importantly, *the panels of each can be full*, each having whatever the contents were when you last left it.

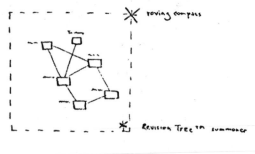

The File Web™ is a map indicating what (labeled) files are present in the system, and which are collaterated..

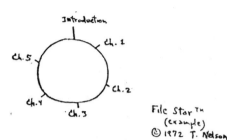

File Star™
(example)
© 1972 T. Nelson

The File Star™ is a quick index into the contents of a file. It expands as long as you hold the lightpen to the dot in the center, with various levels of headings appearing as it expands. Naturally, you may jump to what you point at.

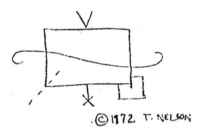

© 1972 T. NELSON

## Editing

Rather than giving the user anything complicated to learn, the system is completely visual. All edit controls are comprised in this diagram, the Edit Rose™. Viz.:

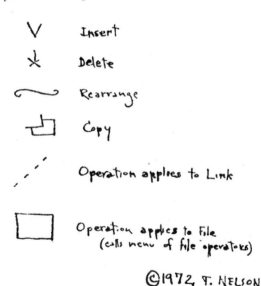

| | |
|---|---|
| V | Insert |
| ⅄ | Delete |
| ∿ | Rearrange |
| ⊐ | Copy |
| ⁄ ⁄ | Operation applies to Link |
| ▭ | Operation applies to File (calls menu of file operators) |

© 1972 T. NELSON

Separate portions of the Edit Rose invoke various edit operations. (You must also point with the lightpen to the necessary points in the text: once for Insert, twice for Delete, three or four times for Rearrange, three times for Copy.)

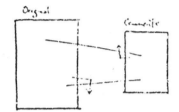

## Generality

The system may be used for comments on things,

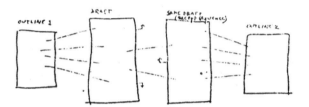

for organizing by multiple outlines or tables of contents;

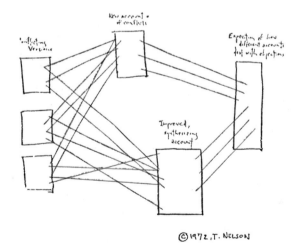

© 1972, T. NELSON

and as a Thinkertoy, organizing complex alternatives. (The labels say: "Conflicting versions," "New account of conflicts," "Exposition of how different accounts deal with objections," "Improved, synthesizing account.")

In other words, in this approach we annotate and label discrepancies, and verbally comment on differences in separate files or documents.

In ways this may seem somewhat obtuse. Yet above all *it is orderly,* and the complex of collateral files has a clarity that could be all-too-easily lost in systems which were programmed more specifically to each problem.

The fundamental strength of collateration, seen here, is of course that any *new* structure collateral to another may be used as a table of contents or an outline, taking the user instantly to parts which are of interest in some new context.

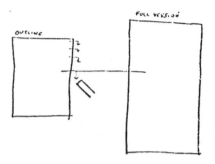

©1972 T. NELSON

New Freedoms Through Computer Screens
— a Minority Report

This is the flip side of Computer Lib.

# 22. [Introduction]
# From *Theatre of the Oppressed*

See the introduction to
Norbert Wiener's essay
(◊04) for more on N.
Katherine Hayles's *How
We Became Posthuman.*

◊04
65

◊06
83

Unlike other authors whose work is contained in this volume, Augusto Boal has been to jail for practicing his interactive techniques.

Boal works in interactive performance, creating opportunities for interaction around the problems that confront ordinary people. He has worked with some of the most oppressed people of South America, using techniques described in the following selection and known as *Theatre of the Oppressed.* Boal was initially based in Brazil—until the military government murdered his colleagues, jailed and tortured him for three months, and warned him he would not be safe after his release. He fled to Argentina, worked there and in Chile, and was later forced into exile in Europe. It was there he applied his techniques to a new type of oppression, taking on not only the "cop on the street," but also the "cop in the head." The applications of Boal's techniques toward therapeutic aims, developed during this period, are called *The Rainbow of Desire.* In the mid-1980s it became safe for Boal to return to Brazil. In 1992 he ran for political office as an act of theatre, and, to the surprise of all, was elected. He brought his theatre troupe with him as his support staff, and began to use his performance techniques for developing legislative proposals with those who normally lack a legislative voice. This work is documented in *Legislative Theatre.* Boal was an effective politician, leading the political right in Brazil to harass him with lawsuits and to use their resources to ensure he would not be reelected.

◊14
211

◊17
247

◊19
277

**339**

Many of the Theatre of
the Oppressed's specific
techniques (its "arsenal")
are cataloged in *Games
for Actors and Non-Actors.*

When considering Boal from a new media perspective, it is important not to lose sight of how much his interactive techniques emphasize embodiment. Boal makes "Knowing the Body" the first stage in his process—a process that culminates in direct bodily involvement in theatrical action via *Forum Theatre,* and that can even proceed into embodied performative action in the day-to-day world (without the theatrical markings of "guerrilla theatre") via *Invisible Theatre.*

N. Katherine Hayles is one of new media's most important commentators on issues of embodiment. In *How We Became Posthuman* she discusses how information became disembodied in first-wave cybernetics and in the fields inspired by it. However, since that period we have seen a dramatic return to concern with embodiment—both in cultural critique (e.g., Hayles herself, Donna Haraway's cyborg (◊35), Roland Barthes's "What does my body know of photography?") and in the technologies of new media. Through concepts such as ubiquitous computing and multimodal interaction, the space of new media has crossed over workstation boundaries and into the space of our bodies.

See Richard Bolt's Put-That-
There (◊29) for one of the
first investigations of
multimodal interaction ⊗.

◊29
433

◊35
515

The question of embodiment has gone unspoken in this volume's previous discussion of interactivity—though it is clearly a subtext in performance-related selections, such as those of Allan Kaprow (◊06) and E.A.T. (◊14). It is also central to the examples used by Jean Baudrillard (◊19) to separate his thought from Hans Magnus Enzensberger's (◊18), examples that range from "the street" (with its communication through the body) to graffiti that violates the physical space of the code. In the example of the movement opposing the World Trade Organization, discussed in introducing the Enzensberger and Baudrillard selections, a vital component of its success may be that network media is there used in support of embodied, worldwide protests.

To return to Boal's techniques, they are undoubtedly effective in many situations for creating embodied interaction. For this reason, they are now practiced by groups around the world. The question now being investigates is whether Boal's techniques for overcoming the spectator/actor divide can be used in new media contexts, perhaps creating a media that may overcome

Hannes Vilhjálmsson's *BodyChat,* for example, provides users with avatars that appear to breathe, look at each other when approaching and conversing, use facial expression, and produce conversational gestures to accompany the "speech" of typed statements. Whether such a system, used on a wide scale, would result in behaviors that approximate physical embodiment, pervert the way it is experienced, or have no relationship to it at all it not yet known.

Boal's poetics are themselves anti-Aristotilian. Boal views Aristotle's catharsis as a deliberate dissipation of the energy needed to act, the energy needed to fight for social justice. He hopes that his own techniques, in contrast, can serve as practice and motivation for action, a "rehearsal for the revolution."

Baudrillard's encoder/decoder divide. Gonzalo Frasca speculates that Boal's poetics might be used to create "*The Sims* of the Oppressed"—enabling users to explore characters and their situations more deeply than current videogames can. One can also imagine a direct online analog of the Theatre of the Oppressed being acted out in the sorts of online spaces that have descended from *Habitat* (◊46). Could cyberspaces in which users have simulated bodies have any of the qualities of engagement that characterize their embodied counterparts?

Boal's techniques of Invisible Theatre have also been invoked in discussions of forms of new media art that operate outside the traditional art context, or without marking the information distributed as art. A high-profile example is the ®™ark group, which uses the protections it gains as a limited-liability corporation to support "the sabotage (informative alteration) of corporate products, from dolls and children's learning tools to electronic action games" often in such a way that those first encountering the products are not aware of the alteration.

It remains to be seen if Boal's non-Aristolelian poetics can be compellingly applied to new media design in general, in an application of dramatic principles of the sort that Brenda Laurel (◊38) made from the realm of Aristotle's poetics, but the possibility is certainly intriguing. The excerpt from Boal's writing presented here begins halfway through his presentation of the four-stage process for transforming the spectator into a "spectactor"—after "Knowing the Body" and "Making the Body Expressive," but with the discussions of techniques such as forum theatre and invisible theatre still to come.

—NWF

Further Reading

Boal, Augusto. *Games for Actors and Non-Actors.* Trans. Adrian Jackson. New York: Routledge, 1992. Originally published as two books, *Stop! C'est magique* (Paris: Hatchette, 1980) and *Jeus pour acteurs et non-acteurs* (Paris: La Découverte, 1989).

Cohen-Cruz, Jan, and Mady Schutzman, eds. *Playing Boal: Theatre, Therapy, Activism.* New York: Routledge, 1994.

Frasca, Gonzalo. "Rethinking Agency and Immersion: Videogames as a Means of Consciousness-Raising." *First Person: New Media as Story, Performance, and Game.* Ed. Noah Wardrip-Fruin and Pat Harrigan. Cambridge: MIT Press, forthcoming.

®™ark Web site. <www.rtmark.com>

◊38
563

◊46
663

Original Publication

*Theatre of the Oppressed*, 132–156. Trans. Charles McBride and Maria-Odilia Leal McBride. New York: Theatre Communications Group, 1985. Reprint: New York: Urizen Books, 1979.

From the Portugese *Teatro do oprimido*, 1974.

# From *Theater of the Oppressed*
## Augusto Boal

### Third Stage: The Theater as Language

This stage is divided into three parts, each one representing a different degree of direct participation of the spectator in the performance. The spectator is encouraged to intervene in the action, abandoning his condition of object and assuming fully the role of subject. The two preceding stages are preparatory, centering around the work of the participants with their own bodies. Now this stage focuses on the theme to be discussed and furthers the transition from passivity to action.

### First Degree: Simultaneous Dramaturgy

This is the first invitation made to the spectator to intervene without necessitating his physical presence on the "stage."

Here it is a question of performing a short scene, of ten to twenty minutes, proposed by a local resident, one who lives in the *barrio*. The actors may improvise with the aid of a script prepared beforehand, as they may also compose the scene directly. In any case, the performance gains in theatricality if the person who proposed the theme is present in the audience. Having begun the scene, the actors develop it to the point at which the main problem reaches a crisis and needs a solution. Then the actors stop the performance and ask the audience to offer solutions. They improvise immediately all the suggested solutions, and the audience has the right to intervene, to correct the actions or words of the actors, who are obligated to comply strictly with these instructions from the audience. Thus, while the audience "writes" the work the actors perform it simultaneously. The spectator's thoughts are discussed theatrically on stage with the help of the actors. All the solutions, suggestions, and opinions are revealed in theatrical form. The discussion itself need not simply take the form of words, but rather should be effected through all the other elements of theatrical expression as well.

Here's an example of how simultaneous dramaturgy works. In a *barrio* of San Hilariòn, in Lima, a woman proposed a controversial theme. Her husband, some years before, had told her to keep some "documents" which, according to him, were extremely important. The woman—who happened to be illiterate—put them away without suspicion. One day they had a fight for one reason or another and, remembering the documents, the woman decided to find out what they were all about, since she was afraid they had something to do with the ownership of their small house. Frustrated in her inability to read, she asked a neighbor to read the documents to her. The lady next door kindly made haste to read the documents, which to the surprise and amusement of the whole *barrio*, were not documents at all, but rather love letters written by the mistress of the poor woman's husband. Now this betrayed and illiterate woman wanted revenge. The actors improvised the scenes until the moment when the husband returns home at night, after his wife has uncovered the mystery of the letters. The woman wants revenge: how is she to get it? Here the action is interrupted and the participant who was interpreting the woman asked the others what should be her attitude in relation to her husband.

All the women of the audience entered into a lively exchange of views. The actors listened to the different suggestions and acted them out according to instructions given by the audience. All the possibilities were tried. Here are some of the suggested solutions in this particular case:

1) To cry a lot in order to make him feel guilty. One young woman suggested that the betrayed woman start to cry a lot so that the husband might feel bad about his own behavior. The actress carried out this suggestion: she cried a lot, the husband consoled her, and when the crying was over he asked her to serve his dinner; and everything remained as it was before. The husband assured her that he had already forgotten the mistress, that he loved only his wife, etc., etc. The audience did not accept this solution.

2) To abandon the house, leaving her husband alone as a punishment. The actress carried out this suggestion and, after reproaching her husband for his wicked behavior, grabbed her things, put them in a bag, and left him alone, very lonely, so that he would learn a lesson. But upon leaving

the house (that is, her own house), she asked the public about what she should do next. In punishing her husband she ended up punishing herself. Where would she go now? Where could she live? This punishment positively was not good since it turned against the punisher, herself.

3) To lock the house so that the husband would have to go away. This variation was also rehearsed. The husband repeatedly begs to be let in, but the wife steadfastly refused. After insisting several times, the husband commented: "Very well, I'll go away. They paid me my salary today, so I'll take the money and go live with my mistress and you can just get by the best way you can." And he left. The actress commented that she did not like this solution, since the husband went to live with the other woman, and what about the wife? How is she going to live now? The poor woman does not make enough money to support herself and cannot get along without her husband.

4) The last solution was presented by a large, exuberant woman; it was the solution accepted unanimously by the entire audience, men and women. She said: "Do it like this: let him come in, get a really big stick, and hit him with all your might—give him a good beating. After you've beat him enough for him to feel repentant, put the stick away, serve him his dinner with affection, and forgive him. . . ."

The actress performed this version, after overcoming the natural resistence of the actor who was playing the husband, and after a barrage of blows—to the amusement of the audience—the two of them sat at the table, ate, and discussed the latest measures taken by the government, which happened to be the nationalization of American companies.

This form of theater creates great excitement among the participants and starts to demolish the wall that separates actors from spectators. Some "write" and others act almost simultaneously. The spectators feel that they can intervene in the action. The action ceases to be presented in a deterministic manner, as something inevitable, as Fate. Man is Man's fate. Thus Man-the-spectator is the creator of Man-the-character. Everything is subject to criticism, to rectification. All can be changed, and at a moment's notice: the actors must always be ready to accept, without protest, any proposed action; they must simply act it out, to give a live view of its consequences and drawbacks. Any spectator, by virtue of being a spectator, has the right to try his version—without censorship. The actor does not change his

main function: he goes on being the interpreter. What changes is the object of his interpretation. If formerly he interpreted the solitary author locked in his study, to whom divine inspiration dictated a finished text, here on the contrary, he must interpret the mass audience, assembled in their local committees, societies of "friends of the *barrio*," groups of neighbors, schools, unions, peasant leagues, or whatever; he must give expression to the collective thought of men and women. The actor ceases to interpret the individual and starts to interpret the group, which is much more difficult and at the same time much more creative.

## Second Degree: Image Theater

Here the spectator has to participate more directly. He is asked to express his views on a certain theme of common interest that the participants wish to discuss. The theme can be far-reaching, abstract—as, for example, imperialism—or it can be a local problem such as the lack of water, a common occurrence in almost all the *barrios*. The participant is asked to express his opinion, but without speaking, using only the bodies of the other participants and "sculpting" with them a group of statues, in such a way that his opinions and feelings become evident. The participant is to use the bodies of the others as if he were a sculptor and the others were made of clay: he must determine the position of each body down to the most minute details of their facial expressions. He is not allowed to speak under any circumstances. The most that is permitted to him is to show with his own facial expressions what he wants the statue-spectator to do. After organizing this group of statues he is allowed to enter into a discussion with the other participants in order to determine if all agree with his "sculpted" opinion. Modifications can be rehearsed: the spectator has the right to modify the statues in their totality or in some detail. When finally an image is arrived at that is the most acceptable to all, then the spectator-sculptor is asked to show the way he would like the given theme to be; that is, in the first grouping the *actual image* is shown, in the second the *ideal image*. Finally he is asked to show a *transitional image*, to show how it would be possible to pass from one reality to the other. In other words, how to carry out the change, the transformation, the revolution, or whatever term one wishes to use. Thus, starting with a grouping of "statues" accepted by all as representative of a real situation, each one is asked to propose ways of changing it.

Once again, a concrete example can best clarify the matter. A young woman, a literacy agent who lived in the village of

Otuzco, was asked to explain, through a grouping of live images, what her home town was like. In Otuzco, before the present Revolutionary Government,[1] there was a peasant rebellion; the landlords (that no longer exist in Peru), imprisoned the leader of the rebellion, took him to the main square, and, in front of everyone, castrated him. The young woman from Otuzco composed the image of the castration, placing one of the participants on the ground while another pretended to be castrating him and still another held him from behind. Then at one side she placed a woman praying, on her knees, and at the other side a group of five men and women, also on their knees, with hands tied behind their backs. Behind the man being castrated, the young woman placed another participant in a position obviously suggestive of power and violence and, behind him, two armed men pointing their guns at the prisoner.

This was the image that person had of her village. A terrible, pessimistic, defeatist image, but also a true reflection of something that had actually taken place. Then the young woman was asked to show what she would want her village to be like. She modified completely the "statues" of the group and regrouped them as people who worked in peace and loved each other—in short, a happy and contented, ideal Otuzco. Then came the third, and most important part, of this form of theater: how can one, starting with the actual image, arrive at the ideal image? How to bring about the change, the transformation, the revolution?

Here it was a question of giving an opinion, but without words. Each participant had the right to act as a "sculptor" and to show how the grouping, or organization, could be modified through a reorganization of forces for the purpose of arriving at an ideal image. Each one expressed his opinion through imagery. Lively discussions arose, but without words. When one would exclaim, "It's not possible like this; I think that . . . ," he was immediately interrupted: "Don't say what you think; come and show it to us." The participant would go and demonstrate physically, visually, his thought, and the discussion would continue. In this particular case the following variations were observed:

1) When a young woman from the interior was asked to form the image of change, she would never change the image of the kneeling woman, signifying clearly that she did not see in that woman a potential force for revolutionary change. Naturally the young women identified themselves with that feminine figure and, since they could not perceive themselves as possible protagonists of the revolution, they left unmodified the image of the kneeling woman. On the other hand, when the same thing was asked of a girl from Lima, she, being more "liberated," would start off by changing precisely that image with which she identified herself. This experiment was repeated many times and always produced the same results, without variation. Undoubtedly the different patterns of action represent not chance occurrence but the sincere, visual expression of the ideology and psychology of the participants. The young women from Lima always modified the image: some would make the woman clasp the figure of the castrated man, others would prompt the woman to fight against the castrator, etc. Those from the interior did little more than allow the woman to lift her hands in prayer.

2) All the participants who believed in the Revolutionary Government would start by modifying the armed figures in the background: they changed the two men who were aiming their guns at the victim so that they would then aim at the powerful figure in the center or at the castrators themselves. On the other hand, when a participant did not have the same faith in his government, he would alter all figures except the armed ones.

3) The people who believed in magical solutions or in a "change of conscience" on the part of the exploiting classes, would start by modifying the castrators—viewing them in effect as changing of their own volition—as well as the powerful figure in the center, who would become regenerated. By contrast, those who did not believe in this form of social change would first alter the kneeling men, making them assume a fighting posture, attacking the oppressors.

4) One of the young women, besides showing the transformations to be the work of the kneeling men—who would free themselves, attack their torturers and imprison them—also had one of the figures representing the people address the other participants, clearly expressing her opinion that social changes are made by the people as a whole and not only by their vanguard.

5) Another young woman made all kinds of changes, leaving untouched only the five persons with their hands tied. This girl belonged to the upper middle class. When she showed signs of nervousness for not being able to imagine any further changes, someone suggested to her the possibility of changing the group of tied figures; the girl looked at them in

surprise and exclaimed: "The truth is that those people didn't fit in!..." It was the truth. The people did not fit into her view of the scheme of things, and she had never before been able to see it.

This form of image theater is without doubt one of the most stimulating, because it is so easy to practice and because of its extraordinary capacity for making thought *visible*. This happens because use of the language idiom is avoided. Each word has a denotation that is the same for all, but it also has a connotation that is unique for each individual. If I utter the word "revolution," obviously everyone will realize that I am talking about a radical change, but at the same time each person will think of his or her "own" revolution, a personal conception of revolution. But if I have to arrange a group of statues that will signify "my revolution," here there will be no denotation-connotation dichotomy. The image synthesizes the individual connotation and the collective denotation. In my arrangement signifying revolution, what are the statues doing? Do they have weapons in their hands or do they have ballots? Are the figures of the people united in a fighting posture against the figures representing the common enemies; or are the figures of the people dispersed, or showing disagreement among themselves? My conception of "revolution" will become clear if, instead of speaking, I show with images what I think.

I remember that in a session of psychodrama a girl spoke repeatedly of the problems she had with her boyfriend, and she always started with more or less the same phrase: "He came in, embraced me, and then...." Each time we heard this opening phrase we understood that they did in fact embrace; that is, we understood what the word *embrace* denotes. Then one day she showed by acting how their meetings were: he approached, she crossed her arms over her breasts as if protecting herself, he took hold of her and hugged her tightly, while she continued to keep her hands closed, defending herself. That was clearly a particular connotation for the word *embrace*. When we understood her "embrace" we were finally able to understand her problems with her boyfriend.

In image theater other techniques can be used:
1) Each participant transformed into a statue is allowed one movement or gesture, and only one, each time a signal (like a clap of hands) is given. In this case the arrangement of images will change according to the individual desire of each participant.

2) The participants are first asked to memorize the ideal image, then to return to the original, actual image, and finally to make the movements necessary to arrive again at the ideal image—thus showing the group of images in motion and allowing the analysis of the feasibility of the proposed transitions. One will then be able to see if change occurs by the grace of God or if it is brought about by the opposing forces operating within the very core of the group.
3) The sculptor-participant, once his work is finished, is asked to try to place himself in the group he has created. This sometimes helps the person to realize that his own vision of reality is a cosmic one, as if he were a part of that reality.

The game of images offers many other possibilities. The important thing is always to analyze the feasibility of the change.

## Third Degree: Forum Theater

This is the last degree and here the participant has to intervene decisively in the dramatic action and change it. The procedure is as follows: First, the participants are asked to tell a story containing a political or social problem of difficult solution. Then a ten- or fifteen-minute skit portraying that problem and the solution intended for discussion is improvised or rehearsed, and subsequently presented. When the skit is over, the participants are asked if they agree with the solution presented. At least some will say no. At this point it is explained that the scene will be performed once more, exactly as it was the first time. But now any participant in the audience has the right to replace any actor and lead the action in the direction that seems to him most appropriate. The displaced actor steps aside, but remains ready to resume action the moment the participant considers his own intervention to be terminated. The other actors have to face the newly created situation, responding instantly to all the possibilities that it may present.

The participants who choose to intervene must continue the physical actions of the replaced actors; they are not allowed to come on the stage and talk, talk, talk: they must carry out the same type of work or activities performed by the actors who were in their place. The theatrical activity must go on in the same way, on the stage. Anyone may propose any solution, but it must be done on the stage, working, acting, doing things, and not from the comfort of his seat. Often a person is very revolutionary when in a public forum he envisages and advocates revolutionary and heroic acts; on the other hand, he often realizes that things are not so easy when he himself has to practice what he suggests.

An example: An eighteen-year-old man worked in the city of Chimbote, one of the world's most important fishing ports. There are in that city a great number of factories of fish meal, a principal export product of Peru. Some factories are very large, while others have only eight or nine employees. Our young man worked for one of the latter. The boss was a ruthless exploiter and forced his employees to work from eight o'clock in the morning to eight at night, or vice versa—twelve consecutive hours of work. Thus the problem was how to combat this inhuman exploitation. Each participant had a proposal: one of them was, for example, "operation turtle," which consists in working very slowly, especially when the boss is not looking. Our young man had a brilliant idea: to work faster and fill the machine with so much fish that it would break with the excessive weight, requiring two or three hours to fix it. During this time the workers could rest. There was the problem, the employer's exploitation; and there was one solution, invented by native ingenuity. But would that be the best solution?

The scene was performed in the presence of all the participants. Some actors represented the workers, another represented the boss, another the foreman, another a "stool pigeon." The stage was converted into a fish meal factory: one worker unloading the fish, another weighing the bags of fish, another carrying the bags to the machines, another tending the machine, while still others performed other pertinent tasks. While they worked, they kept up a dialogue, proposing solutions and discussing them until they came to accept the solution proposed by the young man and broke the machine; the boss came and the workers rested while the engineer repaired the machine. When the repair was done, they went back to work.

The scene was staged for the first time and the question was raised: Were all in agreement? No, definitely not. On the contrary, they disagreed. Each one had a different proposal: to start a strike, throw a bomb at the machine, start a union, etc.

Then the technique of forum theater was applied: the scene would be staged exactly as it had been the first time, but now each spectator-participant would have the right to intervene and change the action, trying out his proposal. The first to intervene was the one who suggested the use of a bomb. He got up, replaced the actor who was portraying the young man, and made his bomb-throwing proposal. Of course all the other actors argued against it since that would mean the destruction of the factory, and therefore the source of work. What would become of so many workers if the factory closed up? Disagreeing, the man decided to throw the bomb himself, but soon realized that he did not know how to manufacture a bomb nor even how to throw it. Many people who in theoretical discussions advocate throwing bombs would not know what to do in reality, and would probably be the first to perish in the explosion. After trying his bomb-solution, the man returned to his place and the actor replaced him until a second person came to try his solution, the strike. After much argument with the others he managed to convince them to stop working and walk out, leaving the factory abandoned. In this case, the owner, the foreman, and the "stool pigeon," who had remained in the factory, went to the town square (among the audience) to look for other workers who would replace the strikers (there is mass unemployment in Chimbote). This spectator-participant tried his solution, the strike, and realized its impracticability; with so much unemployment the bosses would always be able to find workers hungry enough and with little enough political consciousness to replace the strikers.

The third attempt was to form a small union for the purpose of negotiating the workers' demands, politicizing the employed workers, as well as the unemployed, setting up mutual funds, etc. In this particular session of forum theater, this was the solution judged to be the best by the participants. In the forum theater no idea is imposed: the audience, the people, have the opportunity to try out all their ideas, to rehearse all the possibilities, and to verify them in practice, that is, in theatrical practice. If the audience had come to the conclusion that it was necessary to dynamite all the fish meal factories in Chimbote, this would also be right from their point of view. It is not the place of the theater to show the correct path, but only to offer the means by which all possible paths may be examined.

Maybe the theater in itself is not revolutionary, but these theatrical forms are without a doubt a *rehearsal of revolution*. The truth of the matter is that the spectator-actor practices a real act even though he does it in a fictional manner. While he *rehearses* throwing a bomb on stage, he is concretely rehearsing the way a bomb is thrown; acting out his attempt to organize a strike, he is concretely organizing a strike. Within its fictitious limits, the experience is a concrete one.

Here the cathartical effect is entirely avoided. We are used to plays in which the characters make the revolution on stage and the spectators in their seats feel themselves to be triumphant revolutionaries. Why make a revolution in reality if we have already made it in the theater? But that does not happen here: the rehearsal stimulates the practice of the act in reality. Forum theater, as well as these other forms of a people's theater, instead of taking something away from the spectator, evoke in him a desire to practice in reality the act he has rehearsed in the theater. The practice of these theatrical forms creates a sort of uneasy sense of incompleteness that seeks fulfillment through real action.

## Fourth Stage: The Theater as Discourse

George Ikishawa used to say that the bourgeois theater is the finished theater. The bourgeoisie already knows what the world is like, *their* world, and is able to present images of this complete, finished world. The bourgeoisie presents the spectacle. On the other hand, the proletariat and the oppressed classes do not know yet what their world will be like; consequently their theater will be the rehearsal, not the finished spectacle. This is quite true, though it is equally true that the theater can present images of transition.

I have been able to observe the truth of this view during all my activities in the people's theater of so many and such different countries of Latin America. Popular audiences are interested in experimenting, in rehearsing, and they abhor the "closed" spectacles. In those cases they try to enter into a dialogue with the actors, to interrupt the action, to ask for explanations without waiting politely for the end of the play. Contrary to the bourgeois code of manners, the people's code allows and encourages the spectator to ask questions, to dialogue, to participate.

All the methods that I have discussed are forms of a rehearsal-theater, and not a spectacle-theater. One knows how these experiments will begin but not how they will end, because the spectator is freed from his chains, finally acts, and becomes a protagonist. Because they respond to the real needs of a popular audience they are practiced with success and joy.

But nothing in this prohibits a popular audience from practicing also more "finished" forms of theater. In Peru many forms previously developed in other countries, especially Brazil and Argentina, were also utilized and with great success. Some of these forms were:

### 1) Newspaper Theater

It was initially developed by the Nucleus Group of the Arena Theater of Sao Paulo, of which I was the artistic director until forced to leave Brazil.[2] It consists of several simple techniques for transforming daily news items, or any other non-dramatic material, into theatrical performances.

a) *Simple reading:* the news item is read detaching it from the context of the newspaper, from the format which makes it false or tendentious.

b) *Crossed reading:* two news items are read in crossed (alternating) form, one throwing light on the other, explaining it, giving it a new dimension.

c) *Complementary reading:* data and information generally omitted by the newspapers of the ruling classes are added to the news.

d) *Rhythmical reading:* as a musical commentary, the news is read to the rhythm of the samba, tango, Gregorian chant, etc., so that the rhythm functions as a critical "filter" of the news, revealing its true content, which is obscured in the newspaper.

e) *Parallel action:* the actors mime parallel actions while the news is read, showing the context in which the reported event really occurred; one hears the news and sees something else that complements it visually.

f) *Improvisation:* the news is improvised on stage to exploit all its variants and possibilities.

g) *Historical:* data or scenes showing the same event in other historical moments, in other countries, or in other social systems, are added to the news.

h) *Reinforcement:* the news is read or sung with the aid or accompaniment of slides, jingles, songs, or publicity materials.

i) *Concretion of the abstract:* that which the news often hides in its purely abstract information is made concrete on the stage: torture, hunger, unemployment, etc., are shown concretely, using graphic images, real or symbolic.

j) *Text out of context:* the news is presented out of the context in which it was published; for example, an actor gives the speech about austerity previously delivered by the Minister of Economics while he devours an enormous dinner: the real truth behind the minister's words becomes demystified—he wants austerity for the people but not for himself.

## 2) Invisible Theater

It consists of the presentation of a scene in an environment other than the theater, before people who are not spectators. The place can be a restaurant, a sidewalk, a market, a train, a line of people, etc. The people who witness the scene are those who are there by chance. During the spectacle, these people must not have the slightest idea that it is a "spectacle," for this would make them "spectators."

The invisible theater calls for the detailed preparation of a skit with a complete text or a simple script; but it is necessary to rehearse the scene sufficiently so that the actors are able to incorporate into their acting and their actions the intervention of the spectators. During the rehearsal it is also necessary to include every imaginable intervention from the spectators; these possibilities will form a kind of optional text.

The invisible theater erupts in a location chosen as a place where the public congregates. All the people who are near become involved in the eruption and the effects of it last long after the skit is ended.

A small example shows how the invisible theater works. In the enormous restaurant of a hotel in Chiclayo, where the literacy agents of ALFIN were staying, together with 400 other people, the "actors" sit at separate tables. The waiters start to serve. The "protagonist" in a more or less loud voice (to attract the attention of other diners, but not in a too obvious way) informs the waiter that he cannot go on eating the food served in that hotel, because in his opinion it is too bad. The waiter does not like the remark but tells the customer that he can choose something *a la carte*, which he may like better. The actor chooses a dish called "Barbecue a la pauper." The waiter points out that it will cost him 70 *soles*, to which the actor answers, always in a reasonably loud voice, that there is no problem. Minutes later the waiter brings him the barbecue, the protagonist eats it rapidly and gets ready to get up and leave the restaurant, when the waiter brings the bill. The actor shows a worried expression and tells the people at the next table that his barbecue was much better than the food they are eating, but the pity is that one has to pay for it. . . .

"I'm going to pay for it; don't have any doubts. I ate the 'barbecue a la pauper' and I'm going to pay for it. But there is a problem: I'm broke."

"And how are you going to pay?," asks the indignant waiter." "You knew the price before ordering the barbecue. And now, how are you going to pay for it?"

The diners nearby are, of course, closely following the dialogue—much more attentively than they would if they were witnessing the scene on a stage. The actor continues:

"Don't worry, because I *am* going to pay you. But since I'm broke I will pay you with labor-power."

"With what?," asks the waiter, astonished. "What kind of power?"

"With labor-power, just as I said. I am broke but I can rent you my labor-power. So I'll work doing something for as long as it's necessary to pay for my 'barbecue a la pauper,' which, to tell the truth, was really delicious—much better than the food you serve to those poor souls. . . ."

By this time some of the customers intervene and make remarks among themselves at their tables, about the price of food, the quality of the service in the hotel, etc. The waiter calls the headwaiter to decide the matter. The actor explains again to the latter the business of renting his labor-power and adds:

"And besides, there is another problem: I'll rent my labor-power but the truth is that I don't know how to do anything, or very little. You will have to give me a very simple job to do. For example, I can take out the hotel's garbage. What's the salary of the garbage man who works for you?"

The headwaiter does not want to give any information about salaries, but a second actor at another table is already prepared and explains that he and the garbage man have gotten to be friends and that the latter has told him his salary: seven *soles* per hour. The two actors make some calculations and the "protagonist" exclaims:

"How is this possible! If I work as a garbage man I'll have to work ten hours to pay for this barbecue that it took me ten minutes to eat? It can't be! Either you increase the salary of the garbage man or reduce the price of the barbecue! . . . But I can do something more specialized; for example, I can take care of the hotel gardens, which are so beautiful, so well cared for. One can see that a very talented person is in charge of the gardens. How much does the gardener of this hotel make? I'll work as a gardener! How many hours work in the garden are necessary to pay for the 'barbecue a la pauper'?"

A third actor, at another table, explains his friendship with the gardener, who is an immigrant from the same village as he; for this reason he knows that the gardener makes ten *soles* per hour. Again the "protagonist" becomes indignant:

"How is this possible? So the man who takes care of these beautiful gardens, who spends his days out there exposed to

347

the wind, the rain, and the sun, has to work seven long hours to be able to eat the barbecue in ten minutes? How can this be, Mr. Headwaiter? Explain it to me!"

The headwaiter is already in despair; he dashes back and forth, gives orders to the waiters in a loud voice to divert the attention of the other customers, alternately laughs and becomes serious, while the restaurant is transformed into a public forum. "The "protagonist" asks the waiter how much he is paid to serve the barbecue and offers to replace him for the necessary number of hours. Another actor, originally from a small village in the interior, gets up and declares that nobody in his village makes 70 *soles* per day; therefore nobody in his village can eat the "barbecue a la pauper." (The sincerity of this actor, who was, besides, telling the truth, moved those who were near his table.)

Finally, to conclude the scene, another actor intervenes with the following proposition:

"Friends, it looks as if we are against the waiter and the headwaiter and this does not make sense. They are our brothers. They work like us, and they are not to blame for the prices charged here. I suggest we take up a collection. We at this table are going to ask you to contribute whatever you can, one *sol,* two *soles,* five *soles,* whatever you can afford. And with that money we are going to pay for the barbecue. And be generous, because what is left over will go as a tip for the waiter, who is our brother and a working man."

Immediately those who are with him at the table start collecting money to pay the bill. Some customers willingly give one or two *soles.* Others furiously comment:

"He says that the food we're eating is junk, and now he wants us to pay for his barbecue! . . . And am I going to eat this junk? Hell no? I wouldn't give him a peanut, so he'll learn a lesson! Let him wash dishes. . . ."

The collection reached 100 *soles* and the discussion went on through the night. It is always very important that the actors do not reveal themselves to be actors! On this rests the *invisible* nature of this form of theater. And it is precisely this invisible quality that will make the spectator act freely and fully, as if he were living a real situation—and, after all, it is a real situation!

It is necessary to emphasize that the invisible theater is not the same thing as a "happening" or the so-called "guerrilla theater." In the latter we are clearly talking about "theater," and therefore the wall that separates actors from spectators immediately arises, reducing the spectator to impotence: a spectator is always less than a man! In the invisible theater the theatrical rituals are abolished; only the theater exists, without its old, worn-out patterns. The theatrical energy is completely liberated, and the impact produced by this free theater is much more powerful and longer lasting.

Several presentations of invisible theater were made in different locations in Peru. Particularly interesting is what happened at the Carmen Market, in the *barrio* of Comas, some 14 kilometers away from downtown Lima. Two actresses were protagonists in a scene enacted at a vegetable stand. One of them, who was pretending to be illiterate, insisted that the vendor was cheating her, taking advantage of the fact that she did not know how to read; the other actress checked the figures, finding them to be correct, and advised the "illiterate" one to register in one of ALFIN's literacy courses. After some discussion about the best age to start one's studies, about what to study and with whom, the first actress kept on insisting that she was too old for those things. It was then that a little old woman, leaning on her cane, very indignantly shouted:

"My dears, that's not true? For learning and making love one is never too old!"

Everyone witnessing the scene broke into laughter at the old woman's amorous outburst, and the actresses were unable to continue the scene.

### 3) Photo-Romance

In many Latin-American countries there is a genuine epidemic of photo-romances, sub-literature on the lowest imaginable level, which furthermore always serves as a vehicle for the ruling classes' ideology. The technique here consists in reading to the participants the general lines in the plot of a photo-romance without telling them the source of this plot. The participants are asked to act out the story. Finally, the acted-out story is compared to the story as it is told in the photo-romance, and the differences are discussed.

For example: a rather stupid story taken from *Corín Tellado,* the worst author of this brutalizing genre, started like this:

A woman is waiting for her husband in the company of another woman who is helping her with the housework. . . .

The participants acted according to their customs: a woman at home expecting her husband will naturally be preparing the meal; the one helping her is a neighbor, who comes to chat about various things; the husband comes home tired after a long day's work; the house is a one-room shack, etc., etc. In Corín Tellado, on the contrary, the woman is dressed in a long evening gown, with pearl necklaces, etc.; the woman who is helping her is a black maid who says no more than "Yes, ma'am"; "The dinner is served, ma'am"; "Very well, ma'am"; "Here comes Mr. X, ma'am"; and nothing else. The house is a marble palace; the husband comes home after a day's work in his factory, where he had an argument with the workers because they, "not understanding the crisis we are all living through, wanted an increase in salaries . . . ," and continuing in this vein.

This particular story was sheer trash, but at the same time it served as magnificent example of ideological insight. The well-dressed woman received a letter from an unknown woman, went to visit her, and discovered her to be a former mistress of her husband; the mistress stated that the husband had left her because he wanted to marry the factory owner's daughter, that is, the well-dressed woman. To top it all, the mistress exclaimed:

"Yes, he betrayed me, deceived me. But I forgive him because, after all, he has always been very ambitious, and he knew very well that with me he could not climb very high. On the other hand, with you he can go very far indeed!"

That is to say, the former mistress forgave her lover because he had in the highest degree that capitalistic eagerness to possess everything. The desire to be a factory owner is presented as something so noble that even a few betrayals on the way up are to be forgiven. . . .

And the young wife, not to be outdone, pretends to be ill so that he will have to remain at her side, and so that, as a result of this trick, he will finally fall in love with her. What an ideology! This love story is crowned with a happy ending rotten to the core. Of course the story, when told without the dialogues and acted out by peasants, takes on an entirely different meaning. When at the end of the performance, the participants are told the origin of the plot they have just acted out, they experience a shock. And this must be understood: when they read Corín Tellado they immediately assume the passive role of "spectators"; but if they first of all have to act out a story themselves, afterwards, when they do read Corín Tellado's version, they will no longer assume a passive, expectant attitude, but instead a critical, comparative one. They will look at the lady's house, and compare it to their own, at the husband's or wife's attitudes and compare them with those of their own spouses, etc. And they will be prepared to detect the poison infiltrating the pages of those photo-stories, or the comics and other forms of cultural and ideological domination.

I was overjoyed when, months after the experiments with the educators, back in Lima, I was informed that the residents of several *barrios* were using that same technique to analyze television programs, an endless source of poison directed against the people.

## 4) Breaking of Repression

The dominant classes crush the dominated ones through repression; the old crush the young through repression; certain races subjugate certain others through repression. Never through a cordial understanding, through an honest interchange of ideas, through criticism and autocriticism. No. The ruling classes, the old, the "superior" races, or the masculine sex, have their sets of values and impose them by force, by unilateral violence, upon the oppressed classes, the young, the races they consider inferior, or women.

The capitalist does not ask the working man if he agrees that the capital should belong to one and the labor to another; he simply places an armed policeman at the factory door and that is that—private property is decreed.

The dominated class, race, sex, or age group suffers the most constant, daily, and omnipresent repression. The ideology becomes concrete in the figure of the dominated person. The proletariat is exploited through the domination that is exerted on all proletarians. Sociology becomes psychology. There is not an oppression by the masculine sex in general of the feminine sex in general: what exists is the concrete oppression that men (individuals) direct against women (individuals).

The technique of breaking repression consists in asking a participant to remember a particular moment when he felt especially repressed, accepted that repression, and began to act in a manner contrary to his own desires. That moment must have a deep personal meaning: I, a proletarian, am oppressed; we proletarians are oppressed; therefore the proletariat is oppressed. It is necessary to pass from the particular to the general, not vice versa, and to deal with something that has happened to someone in particular, but which at the same time is typical of what happens to others.

The person who tells the story also chooses from among the rest of the participants all the other characters who will participate in the reconstruction of the incident. Then, after receiving the information and directions provided by the protagonist, the participants and the protagonist act out the incident just as it happened in reality—recreating the same scene, the same circumstances, and the same original feelings.

Once the "reproduction" of the actual event is over, the protagonist is asked to repeat the scene, but this time without accepting the repression, fighting to impose his will, his ideas, his wishes. The other participants are urged to maintain the repression as in the first performance. The clash that results helps to measure the possibility one often has to resist and yet fails to do so; it helps to measure the true strength of the enemy. It also gives the protagonist the opportunity of trying once more and carrying out, in fiction, what he had not been able to do in reality. But we have already seen that this is not cathartic: the fact of having rehearsed a resistance to oppression will prepare him to resist effectively in a future reality, when the occasion presents itself once more.

On the other hand, it is necessary to take care that the generic nature of the particular case under study be understood. In this type of theatrical experiment the particular instance must serve as the point of departure, but it is indispensable to reach the general. The process to be realized, during the actual performance or afterward during the discussion, is one that ascends from the *phenomenon* toward the *law*; from the phenomena presented in the plot toward the social laws that govern those phenomena. The spectator-participants must come out of this experience enriched with the knowledge of those laws, obtained through analysis of the phenomena.

## 5) Myth Theater

It is simply a question of discovering the obvious behind the myth: to logically tell a story, revealing its evident truths.

In a place called Motupe there was a hill, almost a mountain, with a narrow road that led through the trees to the top; halfway to the top stood a cross. One could go as far as that cross: to go beyond it was dangerous; it inspired fear, and the few who had tried had never returned. It was believed that some sanguinary ghosts inhabited the top of the mountain. But the story is also told of a brave young man who armed himself and climbed to the top, where he found the "ghosts." They were in reality some Americans who owned a gold mine located precisely on the top of that mountain.

Another legend is that of the lagoon of Cheken. It is said that there was no water there and that all the peasants, having to travel for several kilometers to get a glass of water,

were dying of thirst. Today a lagoon exists there, the property of a local landowner. How did that lagoon spring up and how did it become the property of one man? The legend explains it. When there was still no water, on a day of intense heat all the villagers were lamenting and praying to God to grant them even a tiny stream of water. But God did not have pity on that arid village. At midnight of the same day, however, a man dressed in a long black poncho and riding a black horse arrived and addressed the landowner, who was then only a poor peasant like the others:

"I will give a lagoon for all of you, but *you*, friend, must give me your most precious possession."

The poor man, very distressed, moaned:

"But I have nothing; I am very poor. We all here suffer from the lack of water, live in miserable shacks, suffer from the most terrible hunger. We have nothing precious, not even our lives. And myself in particular, my only precious possession is my three daughters, nothing else."

"And of the three," responded the stranger, "the oldest is the most beautiful. I will give you a lagoon filled with the freshest water of all Peru; but in exchange you will give me your oldest daughter so that I may marry her."

The future landlord thought for a long while, cried a lot, and asked his frightened eldest daughter if she would accept such an unusual marriage proposal. The obedient daughter expressed herself in this way:

"If it is for the salvation of all, so that the thirst and hunger of all the peasants will come to an end, if it is so that you may have a lagoon with the freshest water of all Peru, if it is so that that lagoon will belong to you alone and bring you personal prosperity and riches—for you will be able to sell this wonderful water to the peasants, who will find it cheaper to buy from you than to travel so many kilometers—if it is for all this, tell the gentleman in the black poncho, astride his black horse, that I will go with him, even if in my heart I am suspicious of his true identity and of the places he will take me."

Happy and contented, and of course somewhat tearful, the kind father went to inform the man in black of the decision, meanwhile asking the daughter to make some little signs showing the price of a liter of water, in order to expedite the work. The man in black undressed the girl, for he did not want to take anything from that house besides the girl herself, and placed her on his horse, which set off at a gallop toward a great depression in the plains. Then an enormous explosion was heard, and a large cloud of smoke remained in the very place where the horse, horseman, and naked girl had disappeared. From the huge hole that had been made in the ground, a spring started to flow and formed the lagoon with the freshest water of all Peru.

This myth no doubt hides a truth: the landlord took possession of what did not belong to him. If formerly the noblemen attributed to God the granting of their property and rights, today explanations no less magical are still used. In this case, the property of the lagoon was explained by the loss of the eldest daughter, the landlord's most precious possession—a transaction took place! And serving as a reminder of that, the legend said that on the nights of the new moon one could hear the girl singing at the bottom of the lagoon, still naked and combing her long hair with a beautiful golden comb. . . . Yes, the truth is that for the landlord the lagoon was like gold.

The myths told by the people should be studied and analyzed and their hidden truths revealed. In this task the theater can be extraordinarily useful.

## 6) Analytical Theater

A story is told by one of the participants and immediately the actors improvise it. Afterward each character is broken down into all his social roles and the participants are asked to choose a physical object to symbolize each role. For example, a policeman killed a chicken thief. The policeman is analyzed:

a) he is a worker because he rents his labor-power; symbol: a pair of overalls;

b) He is a bourgeois because he protects private property and values it more than human life; symbol: a necktie, or a top hat, etc.;

c) he is a repressive agent because he is a policeman; symbol: a revolver.

This is continued until the participants have analyzed all his roles: head of a family (symbol: the wallet, for example), member of a fraternal order, etc., etc. It is important that the symbols be chosen by the participants present and that they not be imposed "from above." For a particular community the symbol for the head of the family might be a wallet, because he is the person who controls the household finances, and in this way controls the family. For another community this symbol may not communicate anything, that is, it may not be a symbol; then an armchair may be chosen. . . .

Having analyzed the character, or characters (it is advisable to limit this operation to the central characters only, for the sake of simplicity and clarity), a fresh attempt to tell the story is made, but taking away some of the symbols from each character, and consequently some social roles as well. Would the story be exactly the same if:

a) the policeman did not have the top hat or the necktie?

b) the robber had a top hat or necktie?

c) the robber had a revolver?

d) the policeman and the robber both had the same symbol for the fraternal order?

The participants are asked to make varying combinations and the proposed combinations must be performed by the actors and criticized by all those present. In this way they will realize that human actions are not the exclusive and primordial result of individual psychology: almost always, through the individual speaks his class!

## 7) Rituals and Masks

The relations of production (infrastructure) determine the culture of a society (superstructure).

Sometimes the infrastructure changes but the superstructure for a while remains the same. In Brazil the landlords would not allow the peasants to look them in the face while talking with them: this would mean lack of respect. The peasants were accustomed to talking with the landlords only while staring at the ground and murmuring: "yes, sir; yes, sir; yes, sir." When the government decreed an agrarian reform (before 1964, date of the facist *coup d'etat*) its emissaries went to the fields to tell the peasants that now they could become landowners. The peasants, staring at the ground, murmured: "yes, friend; yes, friend; yes, friend." A feudalistic culture had totally permeated their lives. The relationships of the peasant with the landlord were entirely different from those with the agent of the Institute of Agrarian Reform, but the ritual remained unchanged.

This particular technique of a people's theater ("Rituals and masks") consists precisely in revealing the superstructures, the rituals which reify all human relationships, and the masks of behavior that those rituals impose on each person according to the roles he plays in society and the rituals he must perform.

A very simple example: a man goes to a priest to confess his sins. How will he do it? Of course, he will kneel, confess his sins, hear the penitence, cross himself, and leave. But do

351

all men confess always in the same way before all priests? Who is the man, and who is the priest?

In this case we need two versatile actors to stage the same confession four times:

*First scene:* the priest and the parishioner are landlords;

*Second scene:* the priest is a landlord and the parishioner is a peasant;

*Third scene:* the priest is a peasant and the parishioner is a landlord;

*Fourth scene:* the priest and the parishioner are peasants.

The ritual is the same in each instance, but the different social masks will cause the four scenes to be different also.

This is an extraordinarily rich technique which has countless variants: the same ritual changing masks; the same ritual performed by people of one social class, and later by people of another class; exchange of masks within the same ritual; etc., etc.

## Conclusion: "Spectator," a Bad Word!

Yes, this is without a doubt the conclusion: "Spectator" is a bad word! The spectator is less than a man and it is necessary to humanize him, to restore to him his capacity of action in all its fullness. He too must be a subject, an actor on an equal plane with those generally accepted as actors, who must also be spectators. All these experiments of a people's theater have the same objective—the liberation of the spectator, on whom the theater has imposed finished visions of the world. And since those responsible for theatrical performances are in general people who belong directly or indirectly to the ruling classes, obviously their finished images will be reflections of themselves. The spectators in the people's theater (i.e., the people themselves) cannot go on being the passive victims of those images.

As we have seen in the first essay of this book, the poetics of Aristotle is the *poetics of oppression:* the world is known, perfect or about to be perfected, and all its values are imposed on the spectators, who passively delegate power to the characters to act and think in their place. In so doing the spectators purge themselves of their tragic flaw—that is, of something capable of changing society. A catharsis of the revolutionary impetus is produced! Dramatic action substitutes for real action.

Brecht's poetics is that of the enlightened vanguard: the world is revealed as subject to change, and the change starts in the theater itself, for the spectator does not delegate power to the characters to think in his place, although he continues to delegate power to them to act in his place. The experience is revealing on the level of consciousness, but not globally on the level of the action. Dramatic action throws light upon real action. The spectacle is a preparation for action.

The *poetics of the oppressed* is essentially the poetics of liberation: the spectator no longer delegates power to the characters either to think or to act in his place. The spectator frees himself; he thinks and acts for himself! Theater is action!

Perhaps the theater is not revolutionary in itself; but have no doubts, it is a rehearsal of revolution!

## Notes

1. The government established after the October 1968 revolution and headed by President Juan Velasco Alvarado (replaced in August 1975 by Francisco Morales Bermúdez). (Translators' note.)

2. Under the author's leadership the Arena Theater developed into one of Brazil's—indeed, one of Latin America's—most outstanding theaters. After 1964, when military rule was established in that country, Boal's work continued, though hampered by censorship and other restrictions imposed by the government. His outspoken position against the authoritarian regime led to his imprisonment and torture in 1971. Released after three months and acquitted of all charges, he was nevertheless compelled to leave Brazil in order to insure the safety of himself and his family. After political circumstances also forced him to leave Buenos Aires, Argentina, he took up residence in Portugal.

# 23. [Introduction]
# From *Soft Architecture Machines*

The design of *structures for human activity* is the basis of both architecture and human-computer interaction—at least, if two senses of the word "structures" are considered. Conceptualizing a networked or software system as spatial makes connection between the two fields even more evident. This relationship is in fact borne out by the great contributions architects have made to new media. One of the most immediately obvious applications of virtual reality was in architecture, where technology allowed for the first-person visualization of a planned physical building. The great cost of advanced graphics technology was justified by the much greater cost of construction and the need to get things right beforehand. This was one of the first advanced applications of the computer to design, and it lay outside the most typical fields in which early computing found application: accounting, the hard sciences, and engineering.

Many new media insights offered by architects have come as innovative applications of architectural knowledge about space, or about design. The most influential architects working with computers—including Michael Benedikt, Marcos Novak, William Mitchell, and Nicholas Negroponte—have developed new principles and theories for the digital realm, both specifically with regard to the cyberspace concept and across new media in other ways. The idea that the user should be empowered by computers, rather than browbeaten into complying with a machine expert, is one particularly important idea that has been furthered by Negroponte.

In 1967 Negroponte founded the Architecture Machine Group at MIT. It was in the context of working in this group that *Soft Architecture Machines* and his earlier *The Architecture Machine* were written. In this group, Negroponte and his collaborators developed methods of managing data spatially, rather than in the form of numeric or textual lists. The ideas laid out in the following two selections were, and remain, of great importance to the design of software. In "Intentionalities," Negroponte describes three levels of awareness that a computer system should attempt, so as to be as responsive as possible. Even the most basic of these, having a model of the user, is absent from many ill-designed pieces of software today. (Consider how Microsoft Windows turns on the screen saver five minutes into showing a movie on DVD; even a primitive model of the user that knows about an activity such as "viewing movie" is absent.) In the following selection, Negroponte argues against the classical concept of the computer as an expert with special knowledge. Yet users carrying out tasks with computers today still often find themselves following along as software "wizards" direct user activity into one of a few pre-defined channels, in what is considered as a recent advance to improve productivity. Despite the power of Negroponte's ideas, many that have proved themselves useful remain overlooked by software creators.

With the support of MIT President Jerome Weisner, Negroponte continued and expanded his work by opening the MIT Media Lab in 1985, founding a unique institution. Sponsored by companies who get in-person access to students and faculty members, the Media Lab conducts research into future applications of technologies across many different academic disciplines, artistic media, and slices of life. Neither a corporate research lab nor a typical academic department, the Media Lab carries on the work of the Architecture Machine Group—especially the approach of working with technologies more advanced than businesses will consider, and more unusual and yet more relevant to everyday life than the typical academic lab will. Negroponte's influence has also been furthered through the magazine he co-founded, *Wired*, which sought to chronicle the digital revolution and promote it as a concept. His back-page essays from that magazine are collected in *Being Digital*.

—NM

As Negroponte indicates, similar ideas were used in an educational context by Seymour Papert, whose ideas became an important influence in Negroponte's Media Lab, where Papert led a research group. See the selection from Papert's book (◊28).

**353**

◊28
413

◊29
433

Richard Bolt's paper (◊29) discusses a project of the Architecture Machine Group ⊗ and deals with spatial data management, a concept later employed by Ben Shneiderman in his essay (◊33). The AMG contributed an exhibit to Software (◊17).

◊33
485

*A Random Walk Through the 20th Century* ⊗, by Glorianna Davenport and Michael Murtaugh, is an interactive video documentary of Weisner and an example of some of the innovative work done at the Media Lab.

Further Reading

Benedikt, Michael, ed. *Cyberspace: First Steps*. Cambridge: MIT Press, 1991. See particularly Michael Benedikt, "Cyberspace: Some Proposals," 119–224, and Marcos Novak, "Liquid Architectures in Cyberspace," 225–254.

Brand, Stuart. *The Media Lab: Inventing the Future at MIT*. New York: Viking Penguin, 1987.

Mitchell, William. *City of Bits: Space, Place, and the Infobahn*. Cambridge: MIT Press, 1995.

Negroponte, Nicholas. *The Architecture Machine*. Cambridge: MIT Press, 1970.

Negroponte, Nicholas. *Being Digital*. New York: Knopf, 1995.

Original Publication

"Intentionalities" 60-63 and "Computer-Aided Participatory Design," 102-123, *Soft Architecture Machines*. Cambridge: MIT Press, 1975.

# From *Soft Architecture Machines*

## Nicholas Negroponte

### Intentionalities

I propose that a common oversight in the computer recognition and generation of visual material is the disregard for the intentions of the image. What I *mean* to say is more important than what I actually say. The intimacy of a dialogue can be in some sense measured by the ability of each person to recognize the intentions of the other. For example, in cases where people are not well acquainted and from different cultures, speaking to each other can become a profession (diplomacy) where it is very necessary to say exactly what is meant and to be well trained at understanding what is meant.

With two good friends, codesigners, husband and wife, this is not true. A well-developed working relationship is in fact characterized by one party's leaving a great deal of information for the other party to infer and assuming it will be inferred correctly. As Oliver Selfridge puts it, an intimate, interactive conversation is, in some sense, the lack of it.

Unfortunately, intentions can only be recognized in context, that evasive and omnipresent condition. But, in many cases, even the crudest definition of context (like "now we are going to talk about structures in architecture") can help what Kaneff (1970) has titled The Picture

Language Machine. If you are sketching a plan and I know you are sketching a plan, even though some lines might replicate the schematic cat, I will do my best to assign to the lines a projective geometry or diagrammatic meaning associated with the built environment. However, if I know you are a lover of cats, there might be room (at some point) for equivocation, to the extent that I might have to ask, "Do you mean . . .?" There is nothing wrong with asking, but note that the need for asking is not necessarily a result of the level of detail, abstraction, or diagrammatic scribbling. The fact that most realistic rendering demands the same inference making and causes the same ambiguities is shown by trompe l'oeil painting and Ames experiments in the psychology of perception.

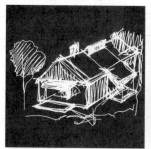
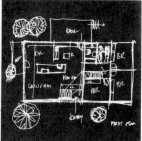
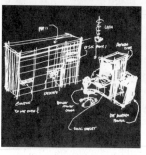

Figure 23.1. Examples of drawings made on the Architecture Machine as part of the so-called Cavanaugh experiment, designed to determine personalized drawing habits. Each figure is a computer display of every tenth point recorded by the data tablet.

Figure 23.2. The Sylvania data tablet.

To make inferences about a statement requires a knowledge of the world. To make an inference about the intention of a statement requires some knowledge of the person making it. For me to begin to make inferences about your intentionalities, except at the very crudest level (of contradictions, slips of the tongue, mispronunciations, etc.), requires that I know you (even as slightly as knowing that you are American). That is, I need a model of you. Following some work with Gordon Pask, we proposed in "HUNCH— An Experiment in Sketch Recognition" (Negroponte, Groisser, and Taggart, 1972) that man-computer interactions should be supported by three levels of model. From the computer's point of view, these include: (1) its model of you, (2) its model of your model of it, and (3) its model of your model of its model of you.

The first level is a straightforward model of the user, ranging from his habits and mannerisms in sketching, for example, to his attitudes toward architecture. This model is continually exercised as a prediction device and supplier of missing information. Its validity is easily measured and tested in terms of the closeness of fit between the anticipated and the actual intention as manifest at some increment of time later (a millisecond, an hour, a year). Notice that in no sense can such a model be fail-safe; in fact, the very idea of fail-safeness itself is the wrong attitude toward the problem. In terms of implementation this model would be passive (and hence exhibit no inept behavior) at the beginning. After some period of time (with people this varies from personality to personality), this model is deployed to venture guesses and would inevitably make errors. Consider the process we go through in getting to "know" somebody. You will remember stages of attempting to make no predictions, times of wrong second-guessing, and later periods of "knowing" him or her. This is dramatically amplified if the other person is from another culture, ill-versed in your language.

The next level of model is the *computer's model of your model of it*. This is critical to inference making because one tends to leave implicit only those issues that one *assumes* the other party will understand (implicitly). This model grows out of a felicity of matches between the inferred information and the intended information. If, for example, the computer correctly assumes that you meant "door within the wall," it can draw the added inference that you *assumed* it would. Note that this model can only grow out of correct matches.

The last level of model may appear overly circuitous and somewhat fickle; however, it has unexplored (to my knowledge) implications for learning. It is the *computer's model of the user's model of its model of him*. In human relations, what I think you think that I think of you is as important as (and can be more important than) what I really think of you. I suspect that forthcoming research will reveal that this model is crucial to learning about people on a person-to-person level. This is because a deep acquaintance can be described as a state of convergence between this third level of model and the first. When your model of my model of your model of me is almost a replica of your model of me, we can say that you know me; in terms of a human relationship, that we have reached a level of confidence and trust.

# Computer-Aided Participatory Design

## User Participation in Design

The idea of and need for user participation in design have surfaced in the past five years as a major (and fashionable) element in both design education and professional practice. A recent synopsis can be found in Nigel Cross's (1972) *Design Participation*. This interest in participation follows from a general feeling that architecture, particularly housing, has been inadequate and unresponsive to the needs and desires of its users. One cause for this seems to be that the design of housing is in the wrong hands, that is, in the hands of an outside "professional," rather than of the resident. The question is: Can the resident participate in or control the design of his own house?

The concept of user participation can be traced back centuries in indigenous architecture. In contemporary architecture and planning it is generally credited to Paul Davidoff's "Advocacy and Pluralism in Planning" (1965). Some architects view participation as a form of giving up, capitulating to the individual who knows less than the expert but is willing to live in his own mess. Others see it as the most promising and sensible, if not the only, approach to ensuring responsive physical environments. The subject is, to say the least, controversial. Ironically it is generally studied and pursued by designers who view computer-aided design

*From* aap noot mies huis *by N. J. Habraken Amsterdam: Scheltema & Holkema, 1970. Translated from Dutch and abbreviated, from* The Responsive House, *edited by Edward Allen (Cambridge: MIT Press, 1974).*

Nowadays man lives in an unnatural relationship with his domicile. This artificiality becomes apparent when we know which types of natural relationships exist. There are six natural types of relationships. The seventh form of relationship brings into being non-homes.

The first . . . is the simplest; the occupant builds his own house with his own hands.

The second type of individual relationship is that in which the craftsman . . . offers his services. This relationship was very often responsible for housing in western history.

The third type of individual relationship is that in which the architect acts as intermediary between occupant and craftsman. . . . There are very few who can afford this type of relationship. . . .

The first collective type of relationship is that in which the community builds collectively the houses it needs, and does this without delegating the labor to craftsmen.

The second collective type differs only by the delegation of some or all tasks to craftsmen.

The third collective relationship is that in which the community and craftsmen do the actual building. The architect acts as the specialized intermediary.

The seventh relationship is a nonrelationship. None of the previous types of relationship are found in mass production building. This seventh type is characterized by the fact that the occupants really take no part in it. They are unknown during the process of decision which leads to the production of dwellings.

It is for this reason that . . . nothing reaches the architect from the group of the "anonymous multitude" of people. The architect is commissioned by another specialist who is no more the occupant than he is.

as an antipodal effort, as a tool for the military-industrial complex only.

The underlying assumption of user participation is that individuals and small groups (a family, a neighborhood) know what they want or, at least, can learn what they want. The concept further assumes that they can apply this understanding in concert with a "competence" to realize designs for the built environment. The results are an apparent (though not necessarily real) democracy in decision making, the consequence of which is ideally a responsiveness in architecture. This approach shortcircuits many of the traditional roles of the professional planner and architect regardless of whether he views himself as what Horst Rittel (1972) calls the doctor planner, the egalitarian planner, the needs planner, or the decisions planner.

Consider two other examples of what can be viewed as the design of shelter: the design of automobiles and the design of clothes. In the case of the automobile most of us will agree that we personally do not know enough about combustion and mechanics to design our own cars. While exceptions like the Sunday mechanic and amateur car racer exist, most of us are satisfied with the existing selection of foreign and domestic cars, whether we view the automobile as a means to get us from here to there, as a status symbol, or as an extravagance. Therefore our participation in design is limited to supporting political lobbies to force Detroit to make cars safer.

Clothes in some respect are at the other end of the spectrum inasmuch as I am confident that you and I can design and make our own clothes if we have to or want to. But clothes, unlike cars, require simple tools and involve materials that are generally easy to manipulate. At the same time, the low capital investment in materials and the high volume of the market allow for so many different kinds of clothing that anyone can find articles both that he likes and that are relatively unique within his circle of acquaintances. Note that our concept of "fit" is not demanding (most women's dresses come in only sixteen basic sizes). When we are fussy we can employ a tailor to make our clothes fit better though not necessarily to be better designed.

Houses are somewhere between clothes and cars. They are not as expendable as shirts but are more manipulable than cars. There is a greater variety of kinds of houses than of cars, but any city offers less variety than the most meager haberdasher.

The questions of this chapter focus on housing (which represents 85 percent of the built environment). The general thesis is that *each individual can be his own architect*. The participation is achieved in association with a very personal computing machine. Somewhat in contrast to Yona Friedman, I believe that a "learning period" with such a machine would be necessary, during which the machine would not make judgments and decisions but would ask telling and revealing questions and attempt to understand what *you mean*.

## Three Attitudes toward Participation

There exist three quite different perceptions of what user participation really means in architecture or to architects. I will list the views in an order that moves progressively further away from the notion of a trained architect as "expert."

The first attitude is epitomized by the often heard comment: "We need more information." This is usually characterized by a program to solicit more complete information about what future users will need and want and what they have as present attitudes toward their residential environment (Sanoff and Sawhney, 1972). The attainment of such information is usually followed by "scientific" methodologies for manipulating and overseeing the new wealth of information in a manner that most effectively reveals kernels of truth, generalizations, and invariants. Conclusions are evaluated in terms of the probability of success and are exercised with, for example, computer simulations and "enhanced decision making" techniques. The architect, by reason of his training, is still the final judge of design alternatives. "There are better and worse ways to pursue design objectives. As professionals we are supposed to be experts in design. Otherwise we are nothing" (Rubinger, 1971). Or: "I would suggest that the most important area is that of social design; i.e.: the design of institutions and the deliberate control of life style, which so far seems to have been inherited . . ." (Jones, 1971).

A second attitude toward participation, almost equally protective of professionalism, is focused upon fiscal and political mobility; it is often called "advocacy planning." My interpretation of advocacy planning includes generating enough leverage for the neighborhood group, for example, to be heard and seriously considered by planners and architects in order that their needs will be reflected in plans for renewal and development. This is usually implemented in the form of a professional person or persons urging a body of "decision makers" on the behalf of a certain larger group; it is rarely the case that the individual citizen gets more than the most indirect poke at a plan. He is usually appeased with minor forms of self-government: operating the local welfare establishment or attending a PTA meeting. Or, in the context of building, he and his kids might have the opportunity to participate in the building of a playground.

The third approach, the Yona Friedman paradigm, is to go all the way, removing the architect as translator and giving the inhabitant what Wellesley-Miller (1972) rightly calls control. In short, each person becomes his own architect. He is forced to become intimately involved with viewing the consequence of one alternative versus another. The analogy put forth by Yona Friedman (1972b) is illuminating: Consider an illiterate society that had only a few public writers who, perforce, would be required to employ printed standards when writing personal letters for all the individual clients. In contrast, the public writer could be eliminated by public education.

I propose to set aside the first two approaches; I do not consider them serious forms of participation. They are timid endeavors of deprofessionalization, and they have in common the retention of a new kind (perhaps) of expert or, to use Goodman's (1972) term, a "soft cop." The third approach, on the other hand, is a do-it-yourselfism that completely removes the architect and *his* previous experience as intermediaries between my needs (pragmatic, emotional, whimsical, etc.) and my house.

It should be noted that this third approach cannot be easily examined in the context of today's urban landscape. We have very little precedent, for example, of physical shifts taking place continually, on a day-to-day or week-to-week basis, in the way this approach might afford. At the same time, it raises some very serious issues like: Would people really want to design their own homes? What are the advantages of designing versus choosing? Are we losing positive inputs by removing the personal previous experiences of the human architect? How do such experiences differ from conceivable machine experiences? Is this really an architecture without architects, or are we really implying a new breed of surrogate architects?

## Paternalism, Middlemen, and Risklessness

When I graduated from architecture school I sincerely thought that I knew better how others ought to live; I knew this as a result of my five years of training. After all, in school we studied methods for supporting "life styles," articulating "patterns of living," and educating the unaware citizen. It did not occur to me that upon entering practice and in the guise of peddling an expertise, I would in fact be foisting my values upon others. It would not be a case of reckless autocracy; rather, it would be a pervasive and evasive set of restrictions that would result from the good intentions of being comprehensive, orderly, and empirically correct.

357

# 23. Soft Architecture Machines

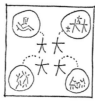

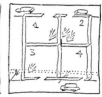

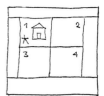

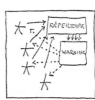

**Figure 23.3.**

The story of Mr. Smith:

I had an idea about my house.

I translated my idea into bricks.

This is my house, the result of my "translation."

I made a mistake in translating, which I did not discover until I used my house.

**Figure 23.4.**

The story of Mr. Wright:

I had an idea about my house, and I explained it to the builder.

The builder misunderstood me. The result is that my house has no door to the garden.

Every time I want to use the garden, I have to get there through the window.

My mistake was in not explaining more explicitly to the builder what I wanted him to build for me.

**Figure 23.5.**

The story of a neighborhood:

Each of us had an idea about his house.

We tried to explain our ideas to an architect, but there were so many of us that there was not enough time to explain our ideas sufficiently.

The architect translated our ideas into an idea of his own.

He liked his idea but we did not like it.

And it is we who have to use these houses, not the architect!

**Figure 23.6.**

The story of another neighborhood:

Each of us had his own idea about how to live.

Our architect did not listen to us: he knew everything about the "average man."

The apartments he built were designed for the "average man."

But we are real people, not average at all. We are not comfortable living the way our architect likes to live.

**Figure 23.7.**

A different kind of story:

Each of us has his own idea about his house.

Fortunately, there is a repertoire of all possible houses. Fortunately also, there are instructions about what to expect from each kind of house.

Each of us can make his own choice, using the repertoire and the instructions.

**Figure 23.8.**

Each of us can thus plan the home of his choice, based on his own idea.

In order to build our homes, we each need a lot, an access road, a water main, a power line, and so on. This is the infrastructure that supports each house.

John wanted to build on lot 1.

The others agreed . . .

. . . After making sure that John's choice of location did not hold disadvantages for them.

Here the stories end.

I remember one professor telling me that architecture is a form of social statement, that any building I ever designed ought to be the manifestation of profound symbolic comment. Isn't that both presumptuous and irresponsible, and, to say the least, paternalistic? While such attitudes may be applicable in a special context of building, I propose that they are generally inappropriate and a frequent cause of unresponsive architecture. The problem can be phrased in a simple question: Can an expert have expertise in goals and values, or is expertise *per se* limited to means?

Father knows best for a long time. However, after a while he begins to lose credibility rapidly. Inconsistencies and unexplainable "musts" make the original institution of paternalism more and more suspect to a child; the doubt probably starts as early as age one or two. Nonetheless, for a long time the issue of Father's rightness is less important than the comfort of knowing he is around. In this sense, it is interesting to question the role of the architect in terms of comfort and confidence; can it be embraced in a machine and thus avoid the potential orphanage of participation?

Another question: If the architect as middleman is translating your needs in a built environment via transformation procedures seasoned by wisdom and his ability to "pre-experience," what side effects and distortions take place in the process of this interpretation? How much of the deformity is positive in, for example, generating goals that you would never have thought of yourself? What do we lose when he goes away? Can a computer provide it?

As a last question, consider the issue of risk. Can you seriously trust that someone who has no ultimate personal stake in the built artifact will do his utmost to achieve your personal and complex goals? An impelling motivation in most labors is in the consequence of doing a bad job. In contrast, the architect is released from all risk after his particular chunk of the built environment is built. The hazard to his reputation is slight, for he will be judged by colleagues and observers who do not have to live in what he has built and who will use extraneous criteria as the basis for criticism. In other words, the architect gets off scot-free, as innocent as the author of a bad novel.

## Indigenous Architecture as a Model

Positano, Mykonos, Gasin, and Mojacar are typical sites of an indigenous architecture that has fascinated and held the admiration of architects. Rudofsky (1964) provides a wide-ranging set of illustrations that dramatically display an "exciting" architecture, which is specifically the result of citizens designing and building their own homes. This has been achieved without the help of architects, explicit master plans, or explicit zoning (or computers). How did it happen?

At first glance, most indigenous architecture appears to be the result of purely "local" activities: a house added here, a path extended there, and so on. However, upon examination one finds "global" forces, which act in a very real sense as elements of town planning and which ensure an overall unity. Typically these are found in the availability of building materials; for example, a locality that lacks timber achieves spanning by means of masonry domes, or one that lacks stone limits its structures to one or two stories. In other instances, these forces are found in climatic conditions, manifest most obviously in the whiteness of houses to reflect the heat, less obviously in the purposeful crookedness of streets to break the wind. In still other cases, the unifying forces are compelling traditions, which often support building conventions that had previous (but now defunct) environmental causes.

Forces such as these are the basis of a "vernacular." They provide a unifying pallet of materials and design conventions, what Friedman calls the "alphabet" of the "language." They act much in the same way as the proposed information process of Friedman (1971):

"With the elimination of the designer (the professional one) from the design process—by vulgarizing the 'objective' elements in the process, and by introducing a simply understood feedback concerning potential consequences of individual decisions on the whole—the paternalistic character of the traditional design process will disappear. The enormous variety of emotional (intuitive) solutions which can be invented by a large number of future users might give an incredible richness to this new 'redesigned' design process."

How can we simulate (if we want to) these conditions in an industrialized society? Strict zoning, more severe building codes, one building system (imposed by law), or a regulation that you must use brick are certainly not the appropriate measures; they lack the subtlety of natural forces within which a richness is conceivable. The answer must lie in the so-called "infrastructure," a mixture of conceptual and physical structures for which we all have a different definition or interpretation. I refer the reader to Yona Friedman's two most recent books: *Realizable Utopias* (1973) and *Society=Environment* (1972). And while I am continually alert to the need for such subtle but preponderant forces, for my purposes here I would like to assume an infrastructure composed of a resilient building and information technology and ask what role there might be for a machine intelligence acting as a personal interface (not translator) between this infrastructure and my ever changing needs. I recognize it is a big assumption.

Before venturing a machine intelligence position, I would like to examine the indigenous architect as an archetype and to scrutinize his behavior beyond commending his picturesque results. He did not need an architecture machine; his environment was simple and comprehensible, punctuated with limited choices and decisions. He no more needed a professional architect than he needed a psychologist or legal counselor. To understand him, let us consider three representative (but not categorical) features of indigenous architecture.

The first is the naming of spaces. In this sort of architecture, the rooms tend to be about the same size, often as large as the technology or timbers will permit, and they rarely have names. A place to eat is often somebody's place to sleep, and cooking is frequently done in more than one room. This implies that a multiplicity of activities can be conveniently housed in similar spaces, and there is very little generic meaning to "bedroom" or "living room." The generics seem to reside in "sleeping" and "eating" and "cooking," and we can extrapolate (tenuously perhaps) that they have a *large common intersection*, larger than we tend to believe.

A second feature that deserves comment is the apparent ad hoc growth of the dwelling unit. Usually a dwelling unit is limited to a small number of rooms and might be added to in the event of offspring. In Greek island societies the dwelling is passed down as dowry; a larger house is often divided in two and the boundary allowed to oscillate between the shrinking of one generation and the growing of another. Rooms are frequently passed to a contiguous house, entrances sealed and opened as required. These local expansions and contractions result from a permanency of home with which most Americans are unfamiliar. In an industrialized society, the pattern is to sell your house and

buy a bigger one, then later, a smaller one. I can remember (but not reference) the statistic that the average American family moves every three years.

The third observation, perhaps the most important, comes from my personal experiences of living on an Aegean island. It appears to be true that the local residents of an indigenous environment are unanimously dissatisfied with their architecture. Glass slabs are their metaphoric goals as much as, if not more than, the little white stucco house is mine. My electric typewriter has as much meaning as a Byzantine icon. Perhaps this can be explained in terms of communication technologies, by arguing that the local resident would be content, at a level to which we aspire, if he had not witnessed the electric toys of our times through magazines, television, and the passing rich tourist. However, a more deep-seated issue is the breadth of experience shared among these people. It is the case that they have in fact had very similar experiences among themselves and consequently carry nearly similar metaphors and share personal contexts. I am not saying that individuality has been squelched; I propose that the spectrum of experiences is small and may be accountable, in part, for this dramatic level of participation, so far not achieved in industrialized societies. It is quite clear that in faster-moving societies our personal experiences are phenomenally varied. This is why we have a harder (if not impossible) problem. This is why we need to consider a special type of architecture machine, one I will call a design amplifier.

## Design Amplifiers

Before I begin I feel obliged to tell you that The Architecture Machine Group has worked very sporadically and without much success on this problem. The notion of a "design amplifier" is new and might provide an interim step between the present and the wizard machine, the surrogate human. I use the term "amplifier" advisedly; my purpose is not to replicate the human architect, as it may have been five years ago, but to make a surrogate *you* that can elaborate upon and contribute technical expertise to *your* design intentions. This allows us to consider and possibly see in the near future an option for computer-aided design that presumes "informed" machines, though not necessarily a machine intelligence.

There is an inherent paradox here. A design amplifier will have no stake in the outcomes of joint ventures; hence it must act truly as an extension of the "future user." Does this

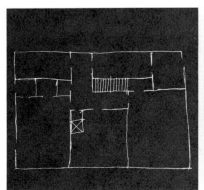

Figure 23.9. House plan sketched by novice.

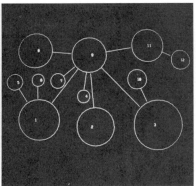

Figure 23.10. Mapping of preceding house plan into planar graph.

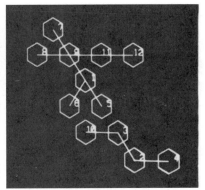

Figure 23.11. A hexagonal resolution of the graph.

in turn mean that the machine intelligence necessary to support richness of dialogue will in fact be counterproductive to the participation because this same intelligence, like that of the human architect, would fall prey to the ills of translation, ascribing meanings of its own? In other words, does the intelligence required to communicate contradict the notion of informed amplification? I would draw your attention to the analogy of a good teacher who fosters an intellectual environment in which you discover for yourself in comparison to the one who drills facts and proclaims principles. As such, let us consider aspects of a design amplifier in terms of a somewhat dual existence: the benevolent educator and the thirsting student, all in one.

There are two categories to consider: (1) What does the machine know? (2) How does the user deal with what it knows? These questions are particularly interesting because the most obvious paradigm is in fact the least rewarding. The most obvious method would be to construct a machine with a vast knowledge of architecture and to view the user as an

explorer of this knowledge through a window of his needs and the medium of some sophisticated man-machine interface. An example of this is found in most computer-aided instruction systems where, for example, the machine *knows* arithmetic and the child manipulates the machine in a more or less prearranged exploration, witnessing *yeses*, *nos*, *dos*, and *don'ts*.

A more exciting approach applicable to a design amplifier can be found in the recent work of Seymour Papert (1971a, b, c) and his colleagues. In brief, their theory is that computer-aided instruction should be treated as the amplification and enlightening of the processes of learning and thinking themselves, rather than merely presenting and drilling specific subject matter. To achieve this, the computer is treated, in some sense, as an automatic student *by the child* (see also Ackoff and Emery, 1972). In the Papert experiments, the six- or seven-year-old youngster has the opportunity to give a "behavior" to the computer via a simple but powerful programming language called LOGO. Whether

361

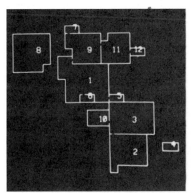

Figure 23.12. House plan generated from 11.

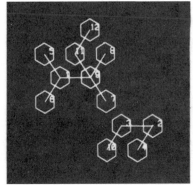

Figure 23.13. Another alternate graph.

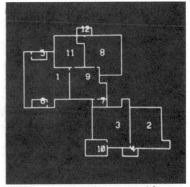

Figure 23.14. House plan generated from 13.

the behavior is to be manifest in reversing a string of characters or having a turtle draw a polygon, its misbehavior reveals "bugs" and, most importantly, contains cues for ameliorating the system. The child observes the process by which he learns, and the notion of *debugging* is suddenly put in contrast with the penalties of *error making*. Furthermore, the child is learning by doing (by playing). "You can take a child to Euclid but you can't make him think" (Papert, 1972).

If you are an architect, how many times have you heard, "Oh I wanted to be an architect but was no good at drawing" or "I wanted to be an architect but was terrible at mathematics"? If you are not an architect, have you ever said something like that? In the same way that your saying "I am no good at languages" is contradicted by your living in France and learning French (or in the case of math, having Papert's mathland), one can consider a designland where one learns about design by playing with it. The underlying assumption is that, while you may not be able to design an efficient hospital or workable airport, you can design your own home, better than any other person.

You already choose furniture, paint walls, and select decors for your house. If the building technologies supported the notion, what knowledge would you lack in order to move up a scale to allocate space and decide boundaries between indoors and outdoors? Or, to pose almost the same question another way, What does an architect know that a contractor doesn't? The answer may be found by briefly partitioning the design process, separating what you might call talent from competence (an apprehensive but telling disjunction). The ensuing argument is based upon the assumption that the symbiosis between future user and machine is so strong that "talent" is in the eyes of the resident and competence in the hands of the design amplifier. This is in dramatic contrast to previously stated (by me) positions!

Note that comfort and confidence (and credibility) embrace a recognizable competence. Aside from a profound knowing of the user, there are certain operational "expertises" that can oversee interrelationships measured in such terms as British Thermal Units, kips, or feet per second. In a very real sense, these are simple computing tasks and, beyond correctness (which is simple), the checking must reflect only timeliness (which is not so simple). The closest I can come to a design amplifier is URBAN5, which did have "competences" and did try to effect a timeliness in the surfacing of what we called conflicts and incompatibilities

(Negroponte and Groisser, 1967a and b; 1970). However, it should be recognized that URBAN5 was the ultimate paternalist; it suffered from (among other things) being directed to serving the architect, not the resident.

## Two Loops

Following Friedman's simple model of two loops, one with me and one with my neighborhood, let's examine some aspects of each in terms of automation. The reader should refer to the extensive works of Friedman, found in the bibliography, but should be cautioned about the particularly French notion of a *"banque de données"* or what he calls "a repertoire." It is somewhat misleading taken at face value because it assumes a menu-picking activity rather than a design activity. The offerings of a menu of solutions obviously cannot exceed the combinatorial product of the parts (which may be enormous). Friedman, unlike many researchers in France, escapes this particular constraint by making his repertoire (*banque de données*) contain topologies that do not have a metric. It is the user's adding of this metric that affords the limitless variety.

The first loop is private. It must be self-sustaining in its powers to maintain the user's attention, ask intelligent questions, and provide broad commentary. It must tread the thin line of distinction between making suggestions and being a bully, between criticizing and insulting, between navigating a search and directing it. Friedman (in personal conversation) makes a distinction by calling the computing organism a "consultant," implying a "knower" at your beck and call, paid to help even if he may not agree with your personal premise. The connotations of *consult* are illuminating in the sense that the underlying skill is uncluttered by metaphorical distinctions, but it is also disturbing inasmuch as one must seriously question whether proficiency can be shared without dialogue requiring metaphor.

The closest example of the first loop implemented in a computer program is ARCHIT (Rorick, 1971). The following is an excerpt from one conversation.

> Computer: Shall we discuss the dining areas?
>
> User: Yes.
>
> Computer: Who does most of the cooking in your family?

User: Carol.

Computer: I would suggest that the dining area for your everyday meals be in the same room as the cooking area so that everyone can socialize while meals are being prepared and Carol won't be isolated in the kitchen. Don't you agree?

User: Yes.

Computer: How often do you want these occasions to be formal (that is, other than casually joining you for dinner) in times per year?

User: 12.

Computer: Keeping these answers in mind, do you feel that you need a separate dining area for more formal occasions?

User: No.

Computer: How many people do you want the everyday dining area to accommodate including company?

User: 8.

At this point the reader should be appalled. The computer program has browbeaten the user into not wanting a dining room and short-circuited the deeper patterns of living that may keep Carol in the kitchen quite happily away from everybody. The program has exhibited an illusion of intelligence and "knowingness" and, in this example, done all the talking! Unfortunately, I do not have a more positive example to offer (but am working on it). A blatant flaw in ARCHIT-like programs is the desire to rapidly pinpoint an "architectural program" via direct yes/no, one/two questions. Inference making and indirect procedures should be used, not for the purpose of making life difficult (for the computer), but for the purpose of soliciting more complex and revealing patterns of living. We must avoid initiating dialogue by asking questions because the questions perforce flavor the answer. The next section describes a simple experiment in inference making, one that avoids asking questions.

In contrast to the "inner" loop, the "outer" loop is a great deal easier to conceive. Its purpose is to flag local perturbations when a desire of mine conflicts with an amenity of yours or of the group at large. A simple example would be a construction of mine blocking light or view from a portion of your house. Such functions assume that the machine is all-knowing about geometry, particular desires,

and complicated rules (which is relatively easy). It also assumes, like any law-arbitrating system, the ability to exercise rules in context (which is not so easy). In managing urban spaces we already have the example of zoning ordinances and the vicissitudes of seeking variances.

The general scheme would be a network of many (one per person) design amplifiers working in concert with a variety of larger "host" machines, machines that could direct questions to other amplifiers or could answer those related to more global matters. An advantage of this layout is the opportunity, hitherto impossible, for personal negotiations within a regulatory framework that could capitalize upon the special-case amenities that are important to me and are available for negotiation. For example, my roof surface could serve as your terrace without inconvenience to me because it happens to be above services and functions that would be disturbed by noise. Or, I might not mind your cantilevering over my entrance, as the reduction in light would be more than compensated by the additional shelter I happened to want. While these are simpleminded examples, they reflect a kind of exchange (even bargaining) that is not possible in present contexts. They assume two parties, but this could be extended to complex and circuitous tradeoffs: if $A \rightarrow B$, $B \rightarrow C$, $C \rightarrow D$, . . . , $\rightarrow n$, $n \rightarrow A$. We begin to see the opportunity for applying three-dimensional zoning standards and performance standards in context, a feat that I propose is manageable only with a large population of design amplifiers that could talk to each other and to host machines.

## Plan Recognition

A typical exercise in computer-aided design is the generation of two- and three-dimensional "layouts" from a set of well-specified constraints and criteria. The classical and most recent experiments can be found in Bernholtz (1969), Eastman (1972), T. Johnson et al. (1970), Liggett (1972), Mitchell (1972b), Mohr (1972), Quintrand (1971), Steadman (1971), Teague (1970), Weinzapfel (1973), and Yessios (1972). The underlying and common thread of all these works is the framework: input of "problem specification" and output of physical description. This section considers an experiment that seeks to do the reverse: input of a physical description (through recognition rather than specification) and output of problem specification. The goal is to recognize a structure of relationships and attributes in contrast to asking for a description.

In the context of participation, the purpose of this experiment is to initiate a dialogue by raising issues (not necessarily questions) drawn from inferences derived from a plan of the "user's" present house. Preceding sections and previous chapters suggest a profound man-machine acquaintance, one that would take a long time to achieve, perhaps years, and one that would have certainly a much wider application than assisting you to be your own architect. In the same way as the machine intelligence paradigm is self-defeating, the acquaintanceship approach to dialogue also could stymie progress and impede initiative in that it is difficult, if not impossible, to seriously consider a modest experiment without ending up with goals to match human dialogue and friendship. The following experiment is a sample point of departure and, as such, it should be viewed only as a mechanism that will lead to conversation, not as a means of generating house plans. The prime feature of this approach is that it can remain silent and attentive at first (without "tell me this," "answer that," "say this," etc.), can timidly venture comment, and then can vigorously interact (if all goes well). This is in contrast to the otherwise necessary tedium of questions and answers that must be employed to immerse the user and to introduce the machine.

In this experiment the user is simply invited to draw a plan of his house. He does this with ballpoint pen and regular paper without the burdensome paraphernalia of most computer graphics (the hardware is described at somewhat greater length in Appendix 1). It can be arranged that the user be completely unaware of the attention or observation of the machine. Remember that the user is not an architect and probably draws very badly; he may very well have never drawn a plan of his house before. It is interesting to note, however, that the most inexperienced sketcher suffers from the lack of two skills, neither of which really matters (at first): (1) He is bad at maintaining constant proportion and scale, as exhibited by his inevitably running off the side of the paper. (2) He is not sure-handed enough to draw straight and forceful lines. However, he is, curiously enough, extremely adept at describing physical relations and juxtapositions, from which we can extract adjacencies and linkages and can construct, for example, graph representations like the planner graph grammar used by Grason (1971).

The initiation of the dialogue is achieved by mapping the physical plan into a relational structure (like the adjacent graph in figure 23.10) that does not have a metric (hence the initial unimportance of scale). The structure then is used to generate other solutions, assuming that the structure is underconstrained as a result of recognizing only a subset of the relations. It is much like only half-listening to a story, extracting an incomplete theme, and developing a new narrative (with similar structure). The other plans (that is, the machine's story) reveal physical arrangements that have enough commonality for the user to make interested comments and for the machine to pose interesting questions. *Interesting* is defined here as leading to an increase in the user's realizing and understanding architectural implications and an increase in the machine's apprehension of the particular needs and patterns as manifest by what the user has now.

The plan recognition program, SQUINT, employs the services of HUNCH. In particular, it exercises the feature of zooming in and out of the positional data, traveling within the spectrum of very low and very high resolutions. The preceding chapter illustrates the sort of range; the grain varies from 1,024 rasters per grain to a one-to-one correspondence. And, at any grain except the finest, the percentage of "hits" can be viewed as a gray tone.

As happens with HUNCH, the noble intentions of SQUINT become reduced to very straightforward operations. Simple properties are recognized from the limiting boundaries of spaces and the penetrations of the boundaries. The first step is to look for the total number of bodies in the sketch. While there is usually one, this initial observation is necessary, if for nothing else than to save memory by compressing the positional data to exclude the "white of paper" that lies outside the sketched plan. The recognition of discrete bodies is achieved by a "flooding" process that creeps in from the sides of the paper, flowing around obstructing lines at a grain appropriate to ensure that it does not seep through doors and windows. Subsequent to flagging all flooded bits, the remainder are accounted for in a similar flooding technique, starting at any point. If all points are not accounted for by the first two floods, then there must be more than one body, and the procedure needs to be repeated until all points are tagged. It is the responsibility of later routines to decide whether the multiple elements in fact represent two autonomous disconnected sections of a house, for example, or whether in reality the additional figures are diagrammatic elements: north arrows, lettering, doodles, or coffee stains.

Following the location of the silhouette(s) of the plan, rather similar procedures wander through internal subdivisions from one space to another, at one grain or another, a little bit like an expandable/shrinkable "mouse" meandering through a maze. Most sketching techniques will allow for internal spaces to be attained at the finest resolution. However, some sketching techniques include the demarcation of door radii and steps, which would impede passage of our "mouse" if the lines were considered boundaries (which they are not). These are the interesting cases; one must look for cues and develop evidence that, for example, such-and-such is probably a tread and not a chimney flue or this is probably a jamb and not a sill. Some of these situations are particularly difficult to deal with, where, for example, in one case the misinterpretation of a one-step level change resulted in guessing that the entire circulation of the house passed through the guest closet. This extreme example may appear to be a violent programming oversight. I must repeat, however, that there will *always* be conditions of such ambiguity that will require even the onlooking human to ask. I further insist there is nothing wrong with asking!

Irrespective of whether the user has ascribed names to spaces, the program will give its own names in order to have an internal nomenclature of nodes and links. The labels can apply to traditional names (if you insist) like "bathroom" and "bedroom"; to orientations like north, windward, or view-oriented; or consist of schematic titles like space A, B2, or 732. The labeled nodes of the structure are linked with either categorical *yes/no*s or graded values of an attribute like access/circulatory, visual, acoustical.

The subsequent mapping into an alternate floor plan has been done by Steve Handel and Huck Rorick. Rorick's experiment appends the somewhat extraneous but interesting feature of adding heuristics that represent his view of what another architect might have done. In the specific case illustrated he has developed heuristics for overlaying a third dimension upon the plan following the vernacular of Frank Lloyd Wright, generating a variety of Wrightian roof forms. Though this is contradictory to the full level of participation suggested by Friedman, it is fun to speculate that a representation of a deeper structure of my needs could be manipulated and displayed in the formal jargons of various famous architects, perhaps even Vitruvius or Viollet-le-Duc.

We should not forget that the user of "computer-aided participatory . . ." is not an architect. "Plan recognition" might imply to some a more formal approach than is intended. The reader should be referred, if he is interested in the morphologies of floor plans, to the original works of Levin (1964), Whitehead and Eldars (1964), Casalaina and Rittel (1967), and the most recent work of Weinzapfel (1973). However, remember that these systems assume the driver to be an architect.

Bibliography

Ackoff, Russell L, and Fred E. Emery. *Our Purposeful Systems*. Chicago: Aldine Atherton, 1972.

Bernholtz, Allen. LOKAT. Laboratory for Computer Graphics and Spatial Analysis, William Warntz (editor). Cambridge, Mass.: Harvard University, IV.4, 1969 March.

Casalaina, V., and H. Rittel. Morphologies of Floor Plans. Paper for the Conference on Computer-Aided Building Design, 1967.

Cross, Nigel. Impact of Computers on the Architectural Design Process. *The Architects' Journal*, 623, 1972 March 22.

Davidoff, Paul. Advocacy and Pluralism in Planning. *Journal of the American Institute of Planners*, 31, 331–338, 1965 November.

Eastman, Charles M. Adaptive-Conditional Architecture. *Design Participation*, Nigel Cross (editor). London: Academy Editions, 51–57, 1972.

Friedman, Yona. *Realisable Utopias*. 1973.

Friedman, Yona. *Society=Environment*. Brussels: C.E.A., 1972a.

Friedman, Yona. Information Processes for Participatory Design. *Design Participation*, Nigel Cross (editor). London: Academy Editions, 45–50, 1972b.

Friedman, Yona. Flatwriter: Voice by Computer. Progressive *Architecture*, 52, 98–101, 1971 March.

Goodman, Robert. *After the Planners*. New York: Simon & Schuster, 1971.

Grason, J. An Approach to Computerized Space Planning Using Graph Theory. *Proceedings of SHARE-ACM-IEEE. Design Automation Workshop*, 170–179, 1971.

Johnson, Timothy, Guy Weinzapfel, John Perkins, Doris C. Ju, Tova Solo, and David Morris. *IMAGE: An Interactive Graphics-Based Computer System for Multiconstrained Spatial Synthesis*. Cambridge, Mass.: M.I.T., Department of Architecture, 1970 September.

Jones, J. Christopher. State of the Art. *DMG Newsletter*, 5, No. 10, 2, 1971 October.

Kaneff, S. (editor). *Picture Language Machines.* London and New York: Academic Press, 1970.

Levin, P. H. The Use of Graphs to Decide the Optimum Layout of Buildings. *The Architect's Information Library,* 140, No. 15, 809–815, 1964 October 7.

Liggett, Robin Segerblom. Floor Plan Layout by Implicit Enumeration. *Environmental Design: Research and Practice,* William J. Mitchell (editor). Proceedings of the EDRA 3/ar 8 Conference, University of California at Los Angeles, 23.4, 1972 January.

Mitchell, William J. *Simple Form Generation Procedures.* London: University of York, International Conference on Computers in Architecture, 144–156, 1972b September.

Mohr, Malte. A Computer Model of the Design Process that Uses a Concept of an Apartment Floorplan to Solve Layout Problems. *Environmental Design: Research and Practice,* William J. Mitchell (editor). Proceedings of the EDRA 3/ar 8 Conference, University of California at Los Angeles, 23.6, 1972 January.

Negroponte, Nicholas, and Leon B. Groisser. URBAN5: A Machine that Discusses Urban Design. *Emerging Methods in Environmental Design and Planning,* Gary T. Moore (editor). Cambridge, Mass.: M. I. T. Press, 1970.

Negroponte, Nicholas, and Leon B. Groisser. URBAN5. *Ekistics,* 24, No. 142, 289–291, 1967a September.

Negroponte, Nicholas, and Leon B. Groisser. URBAN5: An On-Line Urban Design Partner. IBM Report, 320-2012. Cambridge, Mass., 1967b June.

Negroponte, Nicholas, Leon B. Groisser, and James Taggart. HUNCH: An Experiment in Sketch Recognition. *Environmental Design: Research and Practice,* William J. Mitchell (editor). Proceedings of the EDRA 3/ar 8 Conference, University of California at Los Angeles, 22.1, 1972 January.

Papert, Seymour. Teaching Children Thinking. *Teaching Mathematics,* No. 58, 1972 Spring.

Papert, Seymour. A Computer Laboratory for Elementary Schools. LOGO Memo No. 1. Cambridge, Mass.: Artificial Intelligence Laboratory, M.I.T., 1971a October.

Papert, Seymour. Teaching Children Thinking. LOGO Memo No. 2. Cambridge, Mass.: Artificial Intelligence Laboratory, M.I.T., 1971b October.

Papert, Seymour. Teaching Children to be Mathematicians vs. Teaching About Mathematics, LOGO Memo No. 4. Cambridge, Mass.: Artificial Intelligence Laboratory, M.I.T., 1971c July.

Quintrand, Paul. Considérations Générales sur Informatique et Architecture. *Techniques & Architecture,* Série 33e, No. 4, 66–68 (Special), 1971 May.

Rittel, Horst. Democratic Decision Making. Summer Session, '71, *Architectural Design,* 4, 233–234, 1972 April.

Rorick, Huck. An Evolutionary Architect Wright. *Journal of Architectural Education,* 26, Nos. 1 and 2, 4–7, 1971 Winter/Spring.

Rubinger, M. State of the Art: A Reply to Christopher Alexander. *DMG Newsletter,* 5, Nos. 8/9, 4, 1971 August–September.

Rudofsky, Bernard. *Architecture without Architects.* New York: Museum of Modern Art, 1964.

Sanoff, Henry, and Man Sawhney. Residential Livability: A Study of User Attitudes Toward Their Residential Environment. *Environmental Design: Research and Practice,* William J. Mitchell (editor). Proceedings of the EDRA 3/ar 8 Conference, University of California at Los Angeles, 13.8, 1972 January.

Steadman, Philip. Minimal Floor Plan Generation. Cambridge University, Center for Land Use and Built-Form Studies, 1971.

Teague, Lavette C., Jr. Network Models of Configurations of Rectangular Parallelepipeds. *Emerging Methods in Environmental Design and Planning,* Gary T. Moore (editor). Cambridge, Mass.: M.I.T. Press, 1970.

Yessios, Christos I., FOSPLAN: A Formal Space Planning Language. *Environmental Design: Research and Practice,* William J. Mitchell (editor). Proceedings of the EDRA 3/ar Conference, University of California at Los Angeles, 23.9, 1972b January.

Wellesley-Miller, Sean. Self-organizing Environments. *Design Participation,* Nigel Cross (editor). London: Academy Editors, 58–62, 1972.

Weinzapfel, G. It Might Work, but Will It Help? *Proceedings of the Design Activity International Conference,* 1–16, 1973 August.

Whitehead, B., and M. Z. Eldars. An Approach to the Optimum Layout of Single-Story Buildings. *Architectural Journal* (Ba4), 1371–1380, 1964 June 17.

# 24. [Introduction]
# From *Computer Power and Human Reason*
## From Judgment to Calculation

◊03
49

◊04
65

"Technology Assailed by Angry Humanist" would be an apt headline in *The Onion*, the satirical weekly newspaper known to most of its readers through the Web. Dire warnings about computers have frequently issued from non-computer-using authors who have only superficially considered, or even experienced, new media. There is some humanistic commentary on technology, such as that of Langdon Winner (◊40), that is more informed. The discussion of new media pitfalls offered by Joseph Weizenbaum comes from someone with a different sort of background, however. Weizenbaum did not write as an observer and commentator outside of computing. He programmed the most famous chatterbot in the history of computing and then perceived dangerous uses of the system he himself engineered. He followed Norbert Wiener (◊04), another MIT professor, in demanding that scientists and technologists take responsibility for the use of that which they discover and develop.

Human languages did not make much of a place for themselves in computing during the 1950s. It wasn't until the early 1960 that word processing began to take shape; in 1963, for instance, an early program for writing on the computer was developed by hackers at MIT. Although some question-answering systems had been programmed earlier, as Weizenbaum documents in his book, the first more general conversational computer program of the sort that Alan Turing envisioned (◊03) was the one Weizenbaum created from 1964 to 1966. This system, called Eliza, ran a set of scripts called *Doctor* ⊗ and impersonated a psychotherapist, becoming notorious and leading Weizenbaum to profoundly reassess his ideas about computing. *Doctor* wasn't foolproof, but that set of instructions allowed Eliza to plausibly carry on some conversations, posing as a noncommittal Rogerian who would ask the user to reflect on whatever comments were offered. While Turing's guess that a thinking machine would be around in 2000 may not have been right on target, within more limited contexts, Turing's prediction that computers would plausibly interact with people using language as an interface was borne out long ago, by Weizenbaum's work in the 1960s.

**367**

Eliza and the Doctor script are included in a Java implementation on the CD.

The concern that machines will take over not just the jobs that provide us income, but also those cognitive and emotional functions we closely associate with humanity, is a particular worry of the computer era—one that was highlighted for Weizenbaum by the way some suggested that *Doctor* should be employed as an actual therapist. Neil Postman explores what Weizenbaum calls the "ever more mechanistic image" of humanity in his book *Technopoly*, in which he notes that the influence of computing is seen not only in examining specific hardware and software technologies but in the way we employ language that has been appropriated for use in computing. Even as they bring material benefits, new media and other computing innovations shift concepts like "belief" and "virus" so that they are more associated with digital computing and less connected to their original humanistic or biological meanings. Weizenbaum's specific concern is that people who see the computer as able to assume the intimate and human role of the psychotherapist are unable to draw the boundaries between the proper use of computer technology and "computer applications that either ought not to be undertaken at all, or, if they are contemplated, should be approached with the utmost caution" (268).

◊34
499

◊40
587

Sherry Turkle (◊34) gives a psychoanalytic perspective on Eliza in her *Life on the Screen*, reaching a different conclusion. Kenneth Colby's view that computer therapy could be useful, after all, was not a snap judgment. Colby was a computer scientist and psychiatrist; he later used Eliza to create a simulated schizophrenic, *Perry*, to aid in psychiatric study, and created a therapeutic conversational system *Depression 2.0*, released in 1992. Although this is not mentioned in *Computer Power and Human Reason*, Turkle notes that Colby was Weizenbaum's original collaborator on Eliza (106). Turkle found

in her research that people who appreciated Eliza considered it as "a kind of diary or mirror" (108) and did not end up with the distorted view of humanity that Weizenbaum feared—but in her book, she also considers how human-computer interaction does change our concepts of what is alive, what is human, and what we ourselves are. Janet Murray's reevaluation of *Eliza/Doctor* as literary art offers another way that Weizenbaum's accomplishment can be recognized as opening up possibilities for creative expression rather than as disrupting our notions of humanity.
—NM

Further Reading

Aarseth, Espen. "The Cyborg Author: Problems of Automated Poetics." *Cybertext: Perspectives on Ergodic Literature*, 129–141. Baltimore: Johns Hopkins University Press, 1997.

Colby, Kenneth Mark. *Artificial Paranoia: A Computer Simulation of Paranoid Processes*. New York: Pergamon Press, 1975.

Murray, Janet. "Eliza's Daughters." *Hamlet on the Holodeck: The Future of Narrative in Cyberspace*, 214–247. New York: Free Press, 1997.

Postman, Neil. "The Ideology of Machines: Computer Technology." *Technopoly: The Surrender of Culture to Technology*. New York: Knopf, 1992.

Turkle, Sherry. "Taking Things at Interface Value." *Life on the Screen: Identity in the Age of the Internet*, 102–124. New York: Simon & Schuster, 1995.

Original Publication

Introduction. *Computer Power and Human Reason: From Judgment to Calculation,* 1–16. San Francisco: W.H. Freeman and Company, 1976.

# From *Computer Power and Human Reason*
## *From Judgment to Calculation*
## Joseph Weizenbaum

In 1935, Michael Polanyi, then holder of the Chair of Physical Chemistry at the Victoria University of Manchester, England, was suddenly shocked into a confrontation with philosophical questions that have ever since dominated his life. The shock was administered by Nicolai Bukharin, one of the leading theoreticians of the Russian Communist party, who told Polanyi that "under socialism the conception of science pursued for its own sake would disappear, for the interests of scientists would spontaneously turn to the problems of the current Five Year Plan." Polanyi sensed then that "the scientific outlook appeared to have produced a mechanical conception of man and history in which there was no place for science itself." And further that "this conception denied altogether any intrinsic power to thought and thus denied any grounds for claiming freedom of thought."[1]

I don't know how much time Polanyi thought he would devote to developing an argument for a contrary concept of man and history. His very shock testifies to the fact that he was in profound disagreement with Bukharin, therefore that he already conceived of man differently, even if he could not then give explicit form to his concept. It may be that he determined to write a counterargument to Bukharin's position, drawing only on his own experience as a scientist, and to have done with it in short order. As it turned out, however, the confrontation with philosophy triggered by Bukharin's revelation was to demand Polanyi's entire attention from then to the present day.

I recite this bit of history for two reasons. The first is to illustrate that ideas which seem at first glance to be obvious and simple, and which ought therefore to be universally credible once they have been articulated, are sometimes buoys marking out stormy channels in deep intellectual seas. That science is creative, that the creative act in science is equivalent to the creative act in art, that creation springs only from autonomous individuals, is such a simple and, one might think, obvious idea. Yet Polanyi has, as have many others, spent nearly a lifetime exploring the ground in which it is anchored and the turbulent sea of implications which surrounds it.

The second reason I recite this history is that I feel myself to be reliving part of it. My own shock was administered not by any important political figure espousing his philosophy of science, but by some people who insisted on misinterpreting a piece of work I had done. I write this without bitterness and certainly not in a defensive mood. Indeed, the interpretations I have in mind tended, if anything, to overrate what little I had accomplished and certainly its importance. No, I recall that piece of work now only because it seems to me to provide the most parsimonious way of identifying the issues I mean to discuss.

The work was done in the period 1964–1966, and was reported in the computer-science literature in January 1966 and August 1967. To summarize it briefly, I composed a computer program with which one could "converse" in English. The human conversationalist partner would type his portion of the conversation on a typewriter connected to a computer, and the computer, under control of my program, would analyze the message that had so been transmitted to it, compose a response to it in English, and cause the response to be typed on the computer's typewriter.

I chose the name ELIZA for the language analysis program because, like the Eliza of Pygmalion fame, it could be taught to "speak" increasingly well. Because conversations must be about something, that is, because they must take place within some context, the program was constructed in a two-tier arrangement, the first tier consisting of the language analyzer and the second of a script. The script is a set of rules rather like those that might be given to an actor who is to use them to improvise around a certain theme. Thus ELIZA could be given a script to enable it to maintain a conversation about cooking eggs or about managing a bank checking account, and so on. Each specific script thus enabled ELIZA to play a specific conversational role.

For my first experiment, I gave ELIZA a script designed to permit it to play (I should really say parody) the role of a Rogerian psychotherapist engaged in an initial interview with a patient. The Rogerian psychotherapist is relatively easy to imitate because much of his technique consists of drawing his patient out by reflecting the patient's statements back to him. The following conversation between a young lady and ELIZA playing doctor illustrates both the Rogerian technique of encouraging a patient to keep talking and the operation of the computer program ELIZA. The first to "speak" is the young lady. The computer's responses are printed entirely in capitals.[2]

Men are all alike.

IN WHAT WAY

They're always bugging us about something or other.

CAN YOU THINK OF A SPECIFIC EXAMPLE

Well, my boyfriend made me come here.

YOUR BOYFRIEND MADE YOU COME HERE

He says I'm depressed much of the time.

I AM SORRY TO HEAR YOU ARE DEPRESSED

It's true. I am unhappy.

DO YOU THINK COMING HERE WILL HELP YOU NOT TO BE UNHAPPY

I need some help, that much seems certain.

WHAT WOULD IT MEAN TO YOU IF YOU GOT SOME HELP

Perhaps I could learn to get along with my mother.

TELL ME MORE ABOUT YOUR FAMILY

My mother takes care of me.

WHO ELSE IN YOUR FAMILY TAKES CARE OF YOU

My father.

YOUR FATHER

You are like my father in some ways.

WHAT RESEMBLANCE DO YOU SEE

You are not very aggressive but I think you don't want me to notice that.

WHAT MAKE YOU THINK I AM NOT VERY AGGRESSIVE

You don't argue with me.

WHY DO YOU THINK I DON'T ARGUE WITH YOU

You are afraid of me.

DOES IT PLEASE YOU TO BELIEVE I AM AFRAID OF YOU

My father is afraid of everybody.

WHAT ELSE COMES TO MIND WHEN YOU THINK OF YOUR FATHER

Bullies.

DOES THAT HAVE ANYTHING TO DO WITH THE FACT THAT YOUR BOYFRIEND MADE YOU COME HERE

DOCTOR, as ELIZA playing psychiatrist came to be known, soon became famous around the Massachusetts Institute of Technology, where it first came into existence, mainly because it was an easy program to demonstrate. Most other programs could not vividly demonstrate the information-processing power of a computer to visitors who did not already have some specialized knowledge, say, of some branch of mathematics. DOCTOR, on the other hand, could be appreciated on some level by anyone. Its power as a demonstration vehicle was further enhanced by the fact that the visitor could actually participate in its operation. Soon copies of DOCTOR, constructed on the basis of my published description of it, began appearing at other institutions in the United States. The program became nationally known and even, in certain circles, a national plaything.

The shocks I experienced as DOCTOR became widely known and "played" were due principally to three distinct events.

1. A number of practicing psychiatrists seriously believed the DOCTOR computer program could grow into a nearly completely automatic form of psychotherapy. Colby *et al.* write, for example,

> Further work must be done before the program will be ready for clinical use. If the method proves beneficial, then it would provide a therapeutic tool which can be made widely available to mental hospitals and psychiatric centers suffering a shortage of therapists. Because of the time-sharing capabilities of modern and future computers, several hundred patients an hour could be handled by a computer system designed for this purpose. The human therapist, involved in the design and operation of this system, would not be replaced, but would become a much more efficient man since his efforts would no longer be limited to the one-to-one patient-therapist ratio as now exists.[3*]

I had thought it essential, as a prerequisite to the very possibility that one person might help another learn to cope with his emotional problems, that the helper himself participate in the other's experience of those problems and, in large part by way of his own empathic recognition of them, himself come to understand them. There are undoubtedly many techniques to facilitate the therapist's imaginative projection into the patient's inner life. But that it was possible for even one practicing psychiatrist to advocate

that this crucial component of the therapeutic process be entirely supplanted by pure technique—*that* I had not imagined! What must a psychiatrist who makes such a suggestion think he is doing while treating a patient, that he can view the simplest mechanical parody of a single interviewing technique as having captured anything of the essence of a human encounter? Perhaps Colby *et al.* give us the required clue when they write:

> A human therapist can be viewed as an information processor and decision maker with a set of decision rules which are closely linked to short-range and long-range goals, . . . He is guided in these decisions by rough empiric rules telling him what is appropriate to say and not to say in certain contexts. To incorporate these processes, to the degree possessed by a human therapist, in the program would be a considerable undertaking, but we are attempting to move in this direction.[4]

What can the psychiatrist's image of his patient be when he sees himself, as therapist, not as an engaged human being acting as a healer, but as an information processor following rules, etc.?

Such questions were my awakening to what Polanyi had earlier called a "scientific outlook that appeared to have produced a mechanical conception of man."

2. I was startled to see how quickly and how very deeply people conversing with DOCTOR became emotionally involved with the computer and how unequivocally they anthropomorphized it. Once my secretary, who had watched me work on the program for many months and therefore surely knew it to be merely a computer program, started conversing with it. After only a few interchanges with it, she asked me to leave the room. Another time, I suggested I

*Nor is Dr. Colby alone in his enthusiasm for computer administered psychotherapy. Dr. Carl Sagan, the astrophysicist, recently commented on ELIZA in Natural History, vol. LXXXIV, no. 1 (Jan. 1975), p. 10: "No such computer program is adequate for psychiatric use today, but the same can be remarked about some human psychotherapists. In a period when more and more people in our society seem to be in need of psychiatric counseling, and when time sharing of computers is widespread, I can imagine the development of a network of computer psychotherapeutic terminals, something like arrays of large telephone booths, in which, for a few dollars a session, we would be able to talk with an attentive, tested, and largely nondirective psychotherapist."

might rig the system so that I could examine all conversations anyone had had with it, say, overnight. I was promptly bombarded with accusations that what I proposed amounted to spying on people's most intimate thoughts; clear evidence that people were conversing with the computer as if it were a person who could be appropriately and usefully addressed in intimate terms. I knew of course that people form all sorts of emotional bonds to machines, for example, to musical instruments, motorcycles, and cars. And I knew from long experience that the strong emotional ties many programmers have to their computers are often formed after only short exposures to their machines. What I had not realized is that extremely short exposures to a relatively simple computer program could induce powerful delusional thinking in quite normal people. This insight led me to attach new importance to questions of the relationship between the individual and the computer, and hence to resolve to think about them.

3. Another widespread, and to me surprising, reaction to the **ELIZA** program was the spread of a belief that it demonstrated a general solution to the problem of computer understanding of natural language. In my paper, I had tried to say that no general solution to that problem was possible, i.e., that language is understood only in contextual frameworks, that even these can be shared by people to only a limited extent, and that consequently even people are not embodiments of any such general solution. But these conclusions were often ignored. In any case, **ELIZA** was such a small and simple step. Its contribution was, if any at all, only to vividly underline what many others had long ago discovered, namely, the importance of context to language understanding. The subsequent, much more elegant, and surely more important work of Winograd[5] in computer comprehension of English is currently being misinterpreted just as **ELIZA** was. This reaction to **ELIZA** showed me more vividly than anything I had seen hitherto the enormously exaggerated attributions an even well-educated audience is capable of making, even strives to make, to a technology it does not understand. Surely, I thought, decisions made by the general public about emergent technologies depend much more on what that public attributes to such technologies than on what they actually are or can and cannot do. If, as appeared to be the case, the public's attributions are wildly misconceived, then public decisions are bound to be

misguided and often wrong. Difficult questions arise out of these observations; what, for example, are the scientist's responsibilities with respect to making his work public? And to whom (or what) is the scientist responsible?

As perceptions of these kinds began to reverberate in me, I thought, as perhaps Polanyi did after his encounter with Bukharin, that the questions and misgivings that had so forcefully presented themselves to me could be disposed of quickly, perhaps in a short, serious article. I did in fact write a paper touching on many points mentioned here.[6] But gradually I began to see that certain quite fundamental questions had infected me more chronically than I had first perceived. I shall probably never be rid of them.

There are as many ways to state these basic questions as there are starting points for coping with them. At bottom they are about nothing less than man's place in the universe. But I am professionally trained only in computer science, which is to say (in all seriousness) that I am extremely poorly educated; I can mount neither the competence, nor the courage, not even the chutzpah, to write on the grand scale actually demanded. I therefore grapple with questions that couple more directly to the concerns I have expressed, and hope that their larger implications will emerge spontaneously.

I shall thus have to concern myself with the following kinds of questions:

1. What is it about the computer that has brought the view of man as a machine to a new level of plausibility? Clearly there have been other machines that imitated man in various ways, e.g., steam shovels. But not until the invention of the digital computer have there been machines that could perform intellectual functions of even modest scope; i.e., machines that could in any sense be said to be intelligent. Now "artificial intelligence" (AI) is a subdiscipline of computer science. This new field will have to be discussed. Ultimately a line dividing human and machine intelligence must be drawn. If there is no such line, then advocates of computerized psychotherapy may be merely heralds of an age in which man has finally been recognized as nothing but a clock-work. Then the consequences of such a reality would need urgently to be divined and contemplated.

2. The fact that individuals bind themselves with strong emotional ties to machines ought not in itself

to be surprising. The instruments man uses become, after all, extensions of his body. Most importantly, man must, in order to operate his instruments skillfully, internalize aspects of them in the form of kinesthetic and perceptual habits. In that sense at least, his instruments become literally part of him and modify him, and thus alter the basis of his affective relationship to himself. One would expect man to cathect more intensely to instruments that couple directly to his own intellectual, cognitive, and emotive functions than to machines that merely extend the power of his muscles. Western man's entire milieu is now pervaded by complex technological extensions of his every functional capacity. Being the enormously adaptive animal he is, man has been able to accept as authentically natural (that is, as given by nature) such technological bases for his relationship to himself, for his identity. Perhaps this helps to explain why he does not question the appropriateness of investing his most private feelings in a computer. But then, such an explanation would also suggest that the computing machine represents merely an extreme extrapolation of a much more general technological usurpation of man's capacity to act as an autonomous agent in giving meaning to his world. It is therefore important to inquire into the wider senses in which man has come to yield his own autonomy to a world viewed as machine.

3. It is perhaps paradoxical that just, when in the deepest sense man has ceased to believe in—let alone to trust—his own autonomy, he has begun to rely on autonomous machines, that is, on machines that operate for long periods of time entirely on the basis of their own internal realities. If his reliance on such machines is to be based on something other than unmitigated despair or blind faith, he must explain to himself what these machines do and even how they do what they do. This requires him to build some conception of their internal "realities." Yet most men don't understand computers to even the slightest degree. So, unless they are capable of very great skepticism (the kind we bring to bear while watching a stage magician), they can explain the computer's intellectual feats only by bringing to bear the single analogy available to them, that is, their model of their own capacity to think. No wonder, then, that they overshoot the mark; it is truly impossible to imagine a human who could imitate ELIZA, for example, but for whom ELIZA's language abilities were his limit. Again, the computing machine is merely an extreme example

of a much more general phenomenon. Even the breadth of connotation intended in the ordinary usage of the word "machine," large as it is, is insufficient to suggest its true generality. For today when we speak of, for example, bureaucracy, or the university, or almost any social or political construct, the image we generate is all too often that of an autonomous machine-like process.

These, then, are the thoughts and questions which have refused to leave me since the deeper significances of the reactions to ELIZA I have described began to become clear to me. Yet I doubt that they could have impressed themselves on me as they did were it not that I was (and am still) deeply involved in a concentrate of technological society as a teacher in the temple of technology that is the Massachusetts Institute of Technology, an institution that proudly boasts of being "polarized around science and technology." There I live and work with colleagues, many of whom trust only modern science to deliver reliable knowledge of the world. I confer with them on research proposals to be made to government agencies, especially to the Department of "Defense." Sometimes I become more than a little frightened as I contemplate what we lead ourselves to propose, as well as the nature of the arguments we construct to support our proposals. Then, too, I am constantly confronted by students, some of whom have already rejected all ways but the scientific to come to know the world, and who seek only a deeper, more dogmatic indoctrination in that faith (although that word is no longer in their vocabulary). Other students suspect that not even the entire collection of machines and instruments at M.I.T. can significantly help give meaning to their lives. They sense the presence of a dilemma in an education polarized around science and technology, an education that implicitly claims to open a privileged access-path to fact, but that cannot tell them how to decide what is to count as fact. Even while they recognize the genuine importance of learning their craft, they rebel at working on projects that appear to address themselves neither to answering interesting questions of fact nor to solving problems in theory.

Such confrontations with my own day-to-day social reality have gradually convinced me that my experience with ELIZA was symptomatic of deeper problems. The time would come, I was sure, when I would no longer be able to participate in research proposal conferences, or honestly respond to my students' need for therapy (yes, that is the correct word), without first attempting to make sense of the picture my own experience with computers had so sharply drawn for me.

Of course, the introduction of computers into our already highly technological society has, as I will try to show, merely reinforced and amplified those antecedent pressures that have driven man to an ever more highly rationalistic view of his society and an ever more mechanistic image of himself. It is therefore important that I construct my discussion of the impact of the computer on man and his society so that it can be seen as a particular kind of encoding of a much larger impact, namely, that on man's role in the face of technologies and techniques he may not be able to understand and control. Conversations around that theme have been going on for a long time. And they have intensified in the last few years.

Certain individuals of quite differing minds, temperaments, interests, and training have—however much they differ among themselves and even disagree on many vital questions—over the years expressed grave concern about the conditions created by the unfettered march of science and technology; among them are Mumford, Arendt, Ellul, Roszak, Comfort, and Boulding. The computer began to be mentioned in such discussions only recently. Now there are signs that a full-scale debate about the computer is developing. The contestants on one side are those who, briefly stated, believe computers can, should, and will do everything, and on the other side those who, like myself, believe there are limits to what computers ought to be put to do.

It may appear at first glance that this is an in-house debate of little consequence except to a small group of computer technicians. But at bottom, no matter how it may be disguised by technological jargon, the question is whether or not every aspect of human thought is reducible to a logical formalism, or, to put it into the modern idiom, whether or not human thought is entirely computable. That question has, in one form or another, engaged thinkers in all ages. Man has always striven for principles that could organize and give sense and meaning to his existence. But before modern science fathered the technologies that reified and concretized its otherwise abstract systems, the systems of thought that defined man's place in the universe were fundamentally juridicial. They served to define man's obligations to his fellow men and to nature. The Judaic tradition, for example, rests on the idea of a contractual relationship between God and man. This relationship must

and does leave room for autonomy for both God and man, for a contract is an agreement willingly entered into by parties who are free not to agree. Man's autonomy and his corresponding responsibility is a central issue of all religious systems. The spiritual cosmologies engendered by modern science, on the other hand, are infected with the germ of logical necessity. They, except in the hands of the wisest scientists and philosophers, no longer content themselves with explanations of appearances, but claim to say how things actually are and must necessarily be. In short, they convert truth to provability.

As one consequence of this drive of modern science, the question, "What aspects of life are formalizable?" has been transformed from the moral question, "How and in what form may man's obligations and responsibilities be known?" to the question, "Of what technological genus is man a species?" Even some philosophers whose every instinct rebels against the idea that man is entirely comprehensible as a machine have succumbed to this spirit of the times. Hubert Dreyfus, for example, trains the heavy guns of phenomenology on the computer model of man.[7] But he limits his argument to the technical question of what computers can and cannot do. I would argue that if computers could imitate man in every respect—which in fact they cannot—even then it would be appropriate, nay, urgent, to examine the computer in the light of man's perennial need to find his place in the world. The outcomes of practical matters that are of vital importance to everyone hinge on how and in what terms the discussion is carried out.

One position I mean to argue appears deceptively obvious: it is simply that there are important differences between men and machines as thinkers. I would argue that, however intelligent machines may be made to be, there are some acts of thought that *ought* to be attempted only by humans. One socially significant question I thus intend to raise is over the proper place of computers in the social order. But, as we shall see, the issue transcends computers in that it must ultimately deal with logicality itself—quite apart from whether logicality is encoded in computer programs or not.

The lay reader may be forgiven for being more than slightly incredulous that anyone should maintain that human thought is entirely computable. But his very incredulity may itself be a sign of how marvelously subtly and seductively modern science has come to influence man's imaginative construction of reality.

Surely, much of what we today regard as good and useful, as well as much of what we would call knowledge and wisdom, we owe to science. But science may also be seen as an addictive drug. Not only has our unbounded feeding on science caused us to become dependent on it, but, as happens with many other drugs taken in increasing dosages, science has been gradually converted into a slow-acting poison. Beginning perhaps with Francis Bacon's misreading of the genuine promise of science, man has been seduced into wishing and working for the establishment of an age of rationality, but with his vision of rationality tragically twisted so as to equate it with logicality. Thus have we very nearly come to the point where almost every genuine human dilemma is seen as a mere paradox, as a merely apparent contradiction that could be untangled by judicious applications of cold logic derived from a higher standpoint. Even murderous wars have come to be perceived as mere problems to be solved by hordes of professional problemsolvers. As Hannah Arendt said about recent makers and executors of policy in the Pentagon:

> They were not just intelligent, but prided themselves on being "rational." . . . They were eager to find formulas, preferably expressed in a pseudo-mathematical language, that would unify the most disparate phenomena with which reality presented them; that is, they were eager to discover *laws* by which to explain and predict political and historical facts as though they were as necessary, and thus as reliable, as the physicists once believed natural phenomena to be . . . [They] did not *judge*; they calculated. . . . an utterly irrational confidence in the calculability of reality [became] the leitmotif of the decision making.[8]

And so too have nearly all political confrontations, such as those between races and those between the governed and their governors, come to be perceived as mere failures of communication. Such rips in the social fabric can then be systematically repaired by the expert application of the latest information-handling techniques—at least so it is believed. And so the rationality-is-logicality equation, which the very success of science has drugged us into adopting as virtually an axiom, has led us to deny the very existence of human conflict, hence the very possibility of the collision of genuinely incommensurable human interests and of disparate human values, hence the existence of human values themselves.

It may be that human values are illusory, as indeed B. F. Skinner argues. If they are, then it is presumably up to science to demonstrate that fact, as indeed Skinner (as scientist) attempts to do. But then science must itself be an illusory system. For the only certain knowledge science can give us is knowledge of the behavior of formal systems, that is, systems that are games invented by man himself and in which to assert truth is nothing more or less than to assert that, as in a chess game, a particular board position was arrived at by a sequence of legal moves. When science purports to make statements about man's experiences, it bases them on identifications between the primitive (that is, undefined) objects of one of its formalisms, the pieces of one of its games, and some set of human observations. No such sets of correspondences can ever be proved to be correct. At best, they can be falsified, in the sense that formal manipulations of a system's symbols may lead to symbolic configurations which, when read in the light of the set of correspondences in question, yield interpretations contrary to empirically observed phenomena. Hence all empirical science is an elaborate structure built on piles that are anchored, not on bedrock as is commonly supposed, but on the shifting sand of fallible human judgment, conjecture, and intuition. It is not even true, again contrary to common belief, that a single purported counter-instance that, if accepted as genuine would certainly falsify a specific scientific theory, generally leads to the immediate abandonment of that theory. Probably all scientific theories currently accepted by scientists themselves (excepting only those purely formal theories claiming no relation to the empirical world) are today confronted with contradicting evidence of more than negligible weight that, again if fully credited, would logically invalidate them. Such evidence is often explained (that is, explained away) by ascribing it to error of some kind, say, observational error, or by characterizing it as inessential, or by the assumption (that is, the faith) that some yet-to-be-discovered way of dealing with it will some day permit it to be acknowledged but nevertheless incorporated into the scientific theories it was originally thought to contradict. In this way scientists continue to rely on already impaired theories and to infer "scientific fact" from them.*

The man in the street surely believes such scientific facts to be as well-established, as well-proven, as his own existence. His certitude is an illusion. Nor is the scientist himself immune to the same illusion. In his praxis, he must, after all, suspend disbelief in order to do or think anything at all. He is rather like a theatergoer, who, in order to participate in and understand what is happening on the stage, must for a time pretend to himself that he is witnessing real events. The scientist must believe his working hypothesis, together with its vast underlying structure of theories and assumptions, even if only for the sake of the argument. Often the "argument" extends over his entire lifetime. Gradually he becomes what he at first merely pretended to be: a true believer. I choose the word "argument" thoughtfully, for scientific demonstrations, even mathematical proofs, are fundamentally acts of persuasion.

Scientific statements can never be certain; they can be only more or less credible. And credibility is a term in individual psychology, i.e., a term that has meaning only with respect to an individual observer. To say that some proposition is credible is, after all, to say that it is believed by an agent who is free not to believe it, that is, by an observer who, after exercising judgment and (possibly) intuition, chooses to accept the proposition as worthy of his believing it. How then can science, which itself surely and ultimately rests on vast arrays of human value judgments, demonstrate that human value judgments are illusory? It cannot do so without forfeiting its own status as the single legitimate path to understanding man and his world.

But no merely logical argument, no matter how cogent or eloquent, can undo this reality: that science has become the sole legitimate form of understanding in the common wisdom. When I say that science has been gradually converted into a slow-acting poison, I mean that the attribution of certainty to scientific knowledge by the common wisdom, an attribution now made so nearly universally that it has become a commonsense dogma, has virtually delegitimatized all other ways of understanding. People viewed the arts, especially literature, as sources of intellectual nourishment and understanding, but today the arts are perceived largely as entertainments. The ancient Greek and Oriental theaters, the Shakespearian stage, the stages peopled by the Ibsens and Chekhovs nearer to our day—these were schools. The curricula they taught were vehicles for understanding the societies they represented.

Today, although an occasional Arthur Miller or Edward Albee survives and is permitted to teach on the New York or London stage, the people hunger only for what is represented to them to be scientifically validated knowledge. They seek to satiate themselves at such scientific cafeterias as *Psychology Today*, or on popularized versions of the works of Masters and Johnson, or on scientology as revealed by L. Ron Hubbard. Belief in the rationality-logicality equation has corroded the prophetic power of language itself. We can count, but we are rapidly forgetting how to say what is worth counting and why.

*Thus, Charles Everett writes on the now-discarded phlogiston theory of combustion (in the *Encyclopaedia Britannica*, 11th ed., 1911, vol. VI, p. 34): "The objections of the antiphlogistonists, such as the fact that the calices weigh more than the original metals instead of less as the theory suggests, were answered by postulating that phlogiston was a principle of levity, or even completely ignored as an accident, the change in qualities being regarded as the only matter of importance." Everett lists H. Cavendish and J. Priestley, both great scientists of their time, as adherents to the phlogiston theory.

375

Notes

1. M. Polanyi, *The Tacit Dimension* (New York: Doubleday, Anchor ed., 1967), pp. 3–4.
2. This "conversation" is extracted from J. Weizenbaum, "**ELIZA**—A Computer Program For the Study of Natural Language Communication Between Man and Machine," *Communications of the Association for Computing Machinery*, vol. 9, no. 1 (January 1965), pp. 36–45.
3. K. M. Colby, J. B. Watt, and J. P. Gilbert, "A Computer Method of Psychotherapy: Preliminary Communication," *The Journal of Nervous and Mental Disease*, vol. 142, no. 2 (1966), pp. 148–152.
4. *Ibid.*
5. T. Winograd, "Procedures as a Representation for Data in a Computer Program for Understanding Natural Language." Ph.D. dissertation submitted to the Dept. of Mathematics (M.I.T.), August 24, 1970.
6. J. Weizenbaum, 1972.
7. Hubert L. Dreyfus, *What Computers Can't Do* (Harper and Row, 1972).
8. Hannah Arendt, *Crises of the Republic* (Harcourt Brace Jovanovich, Harvest edition, 1972), pp. 11 *et seq.*

# 25. [Introduction]
# Responsive Environments

Those who forged new media have often seen themselves as simultaneously pursuing artistic and technological goals. Ted Nelson and Nicholas Negroponte, for instance, gained deep technological insights from considering, respectively, the literary arts and architecture, and both presented work at the 1970 *Software* exhibition (◊17). Unfortunately, the work of such individuals has often been accepted by only one realm. In some cases the unacknowledged split has only been rectified after the rejecting camp has re-invented the other's wheel in its own terms.

Myron Krueger was rejected by, then reclaimed by, the art community in this way. He has worked and written primarily in areas called "responsive environments" and "artificial reality," which include (from Krueger's point of view) the various inventions called *virtual reality*. The importance of his technological work has been appreciated for 30 years within computer science, where he is often called "the father of virtual reality." However, his aesthetic concerns—and his assertion that "Response is the medium!"—have not found as comfortable a home within computer science. Further, as Kristine Stiles writes, "as of 1971 no art department had its own computer, and computer scientist-artists like Myron W. Krueger . . . were all but ignored in the visual arts" (394). While some might argue that this lack of art world attention was related to Krueger's focus on response rather than saleable objects, it is clear from other selections in this volume (e.g., Allan Kaprow, ◊06) that the art world was ready to embrace work that focused on response rather than the creation of appealing physical items—at least, as long as it originated with one of their own. Computer scientists, in turn, have not always acknowledged the importance of artistic concerns in Krueger's work, or in other work important to his area. In *Artificial Reality II* Krueger points out that before the head-mounted display (invented by Ivan Sutherland in 1968) artificial reality was being explored in the context of next-generation film experiments such as Morton Heilig's *Sensorama*. In 1976, a new interface, the first glove to monitor hand movements, was developed at the Electronic Visualization Laboratory (EVL) at the University of Illinois at Chicago (a collaboration between the College of Engineering and the School of Art and Design), with funding from the National Endowment for the Arts. But when 1980s "data glove" hype was at its height, this founding work was little discussed.

Krueger's assertion that response is the medium may also bring to mind other writings about art and technology, particularly surrounding questions of interactivity and the form/content divide. Krueger reports being asked of his work, "What does it mean?" One is tempted to insert Roy Ascott's response to a similar question about telematic art (from "Is There Love in the Telematic Embrace?"):

> In a telematic art, meaning is not created by the artist, distributed through the network, and received by the observer. Meaning is the product of interaction between the observer and the system, the content of which is in a state of flux, of endless change and transformation. In this condition of uncertainty and instability, not simply because of the crisscrossing interactions of users of the network but because content is embodied in data that is itself immaterial, it is pure electronic difference, until it has been reconstituted at the interface as image, text, or sound. The sensory output may be differentiated further as existing on screen, as articulated structure or material, as architecture, as environment, or in virtual space.

Krueger wrote along similar lines in his essay below:

> For the artist the environment augurs new relationships with his audience and his art. He operates at a metalevel. The participant provides the direct performance of the experience. The

◊06
83

◊10
127

◊14
211

◊17
247

◊21
301

377

The connection between virtual reality and the arts is well exemplified by Jaron Lanier —computer scientist, musician, and artist— who was both crucial in VR's technological invention and in the explication of its artistic and social potential. Lanier coined the term "virtual reality."

The essays by EAT (◊14) and Ted Nelson (◊21), and the earlier essay by Roy Ascott (◊10), also bear on this issue of the construction of meaning.

Given that Krueger created an environment for full-body unencumbered interaction with a computational space, the most direct heir of his work is not the disembodying head-mounted display (HMD) of 1980s VR, but the CAVE Automatic Virtual Environment. The CAVE experience is one in which users can see themselves (and the faces and bodies of people around them, and objects in their hands, and their clothing, etc.) simultaneously with a virtual environment. This is made possible by the method used to transmit appropriate stereo images to the user's eyes. HMDs create a stereo effect by, in essence, blindfolding the user—and placing two small displays in the blindfold, one in front of each eye. The CAVE achieves stereo by creating a room in which three walls and the floor (and, in some cases, the ceiling and fourth wall) are all projection surfaces. The projectors aimed at each surface quickly alternate between the images appropriate for the user's left and right eyes. The user wears "shutter glasses" which, at the same speed as the projectors, alternately cover the left and right eyes. Like the first glove to monitor hand movements, the CAVE was developed at UI Chicago's EVL.

◊004 65

◊020 289

**378**

◊037 551

◊040 587

◊045 649

◊051 737

environmental hardware is the instrument. The computer acts much as an orchestra conductor controlling the broad relationships while the artist provides the score....

One perspective in Krueger's essay was unlikely to be at home in either the art world or the computer science world of the 1970s—one that demonstrates that his resistance to traditional notions of "content" did not come from nihilism, lack of ideas, or lack of desire to impact the culture. The final paragraphs of his essay echo the calls for lay understanding of technology and resistance to technological determinism that underlie the 1970s writings of Raymond Williams (◊20). Krueger, however, poses the situation in a less explicitly political fashion:

> We are incredibly attuned to the idea that the sole purpose of our technology is to solve problems. It also creates concepts and philosophy. We must more fully explore these aspects of our inventions, because the next generation of technology will speak to us, understand us, and perceive our behavior. It will enter every home and office and intercede between us and much of the information and experience we receive. The design of such intimate technology is an aesthetic issue as much as an engineering one. We must recognize this if we are to understand and choose what we become as a result of what we have made.

While at times as technophilic as are those statements criticized by Langdon Winner (◊40), Krueger's writing still provides some good advice today. Yet it is not advice often followed. It continues to be very rare, both in academic and commercial settings, for computer scientists, artists, and those who study culture to interact meaningfully. The design of our technologies is not simultaneously approached as aesthetics and engineering. A current step in this direction is the building discussion around *critical technical practices* (CTP). This term was coined by Phil Agre, one of the pioneers of reactive artificial intelligence at MIT. (An article by Agre on a different topic appears in this book (◊51)). CTP describes a practice that makes technological artifacts (computer science and engineering), but that also works within traditions of the arts and studies of culture. These latter practices offer a self-reflexive view to technological production—one that can help overcome development roadblocks that are created by "invisible" and potentially unhelpful assumptions about the nature of reality—as well as provide guidance for producing work that takes a desired place within the larger culture, or even provides specific means for intervention within the culture. The CTP discussion has been growing, particularly among younger computer scientists such as Phoebe Sengers, Michael Mateas, and Warren Sack. But it can also be seen as an umbrella under which to view design-oriented work such as Pelle Ehn's (◊45) and Terry Winograd's (◊37), the new scientist sought by Norbert Wiener (◊04), and even the work of artists such as Simon Penny. As CTP gains momentum, perhaps an area of new media will be defined which includes all the elements of Krueger's work.

—NWF

Further Reading

Ascott, Roy. "Is There Love in the Telematic Embrace?" *Art Journal* 49(3):241. Fall 1990.

Krueger, Myron. *Artificial Reality II.* Reading, Mass.: Addison-Wesley, 1991.

Mateas, Michael and Phoebe Sengers, ed. *Narrative Intelligence.* Amsterdam: John Benjamins Co., forthcoming.

Packer, Randall, and Ken Jordan. Eds. *Multimedia: From Wagner to Virtual Reality.* New York: W. W. Norton & Company, 2001.

Sandin, Daniel, Thomas DeFanti, and Carolina Cruz-Neira. "A 'Room' with a 'View'" *IEEE Spectrum,* 30(10):30-33, 39.

Original Publication

From *AFIPS 46 National Computer Conference Proceedings*, 423–33.
Montvale, N.J.: AFIPS Press, 1977

# Responsive Environments

## Myron W. Krueger

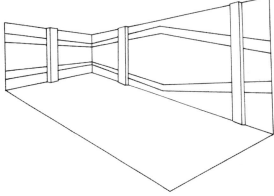

Figure 25.1. Glowflow tubes on gallery wall.

## Introduction

Man-machine interaction is usually limited to a seated man poking at a machine with his fingers or perhaps waving a wand over a data tablet. Seven years ago, I was dissatisfied with such a restricted dialogue and embarked on research exploring more interesting ways for men and machines to relate. The result was the concept of a responsive environment in which a computer perceives the actions of those who enter and responds intelligently through complex visual and auditory displays.

Over a period of time the computer's displays establish a context within which the interaction occurs. It is within this context that the participant chooses his next action and anticipates the environment's response. If the response is unexpected, the environment has changed the context and the participant must reexamine his expectations. The experience is controlled by a composition which anticipates the participant's actions and flirts with his expectations.

This paper describes the evolution of these concepts from their primitive beginnings to my current project, VIDEOPLACE, which provides a general tool for devising many interactions. Based on these examples an interactive art form is defined and its promise identified. While the environments described were presented with aesthetic intent, their implications go beyond art. In the final section, applications in education, psychology and psychotherapy are suggested.

## GLOWFLOW

In 1969, I became involved in the development of GLOWFLOW, a computer art project conceived by Dan Sandin, Jerry Erdman and Richard Venezsky at the University of Wisconsin. It was designed in an atmosphere of encounter between art and technology. The viewer entered a darkened room in which glowing lines of light defined an illusory space (Figure 25.1). The display was accomplished by pumping phosphorescent particles through transparent tubes attached to the gallery walls. These tubes passed through opaque columns concealing lights which excited the phosphors. A pressure sensitive pad in front of each of the six columns enabled the computer to respond to footsteps by lighting different tubes or changing the sounds generated by a Moog synthesizer or the origin of these sounds. However, the artists' attitude toward the capacity for response was ambivalent. They felt that it was important that the environment respond, but not that the audience be aware of it. Delays were introduced between the detection of a participant and the computer's response so that the contemplative mood of the environment would not be destroyed by frantic attempts to elicit more responses.

While GLOWFLOW was quite successful visually, it succeeded more as a kinetic sculpture than as a responsive environment. However, the GLOWFLOW experience led me to a number of decisions:

1. Interactive art is potentially a richly composable medium quite distinct from the concerns of sculpture, graphic art or music.

2. In order to respond intelligently the computer should perceive as much as possible about the participant's behavior.

3. In order to focus on the relationships between the environment and the participants, rather than among participants, only a small number of people should be involved at a time.

379

4. The participants should be aware of how the environment is responding to them.

5. The choice of sound and visual response systems should be dictated by their ability to convey a wide variety of conceptual relationships.

6. The visual responses should not be judged as art nor the sounds as music. The only aesthetic concern is the quality of the interaction.

## METAPLAY

Following the GLOWFLOW experience, I conceived and directed METAPLAY which was exhibited in the Memorial Union Gallery of the University of Wisconsin for a month in 1970. It was supported by the National Science Foundation, the Computer Science Department, the Graduate School and the loan of a PDP-12 by Digital Equipment Corporation.

METAPLAY'S focus reflected my reactions to GLOW-FLOW. Interaction between the participants and the environment was emphasized; the computer was used to facilitate a unique real-time relationship between the artist and the participant. An 8' by 10' rear-projection video screen dominated the gallery. The live video image of the viewer and a computer graphic image drawn by an artist, who was in another building, were superimposed on this screen. Both the viewer and the artist could respond to the resulting image.

### Hardware

The image communications (Figure 25.2) started with an analogue data tablet which enabled the artist to draw or write on the computer screen. The person doing the drawing did not have to be an artist, but the term is used for convenience. One video camera, in the Computer Center, was aimed at the display screen of the Adage Graphic Display Computer. A second camera, a mile away in the gallery, picked up the live image of people in the room. A television cable transmitted the video computer image from the Computer Center to the gallery and the two signals were mixed so that the computer image overlayed the live image. The composite image was projected on the 8' × 10' screen in the gallery and was simultaneously transmitted back to the Computer Center where it was displayed on a video monitor providing feedback for the artist.

The artist could draw on the Adage screen using a data tablet. By using function switches, potentiometers and the teletype keyboard the pictures could be rapidly modified or the mode of drawing itself altered. In addition to the effects of simple drawings, the image could be moved around the screen, image size could be controlled and the picture could be repeated up to ten times on the screen displaced by variable X, Y and size increments. A tail of a fixed number of line segments could be drawn allowing the removal of a segment at one end while another was added at the opposite end. An image could be rotated in 3-space under control of the pen. Although this was not true rotation, the visual effect was similar. A simple set of transformations under potentiometer and tablet control yielded apparent animation of people's outlines. Finally, previously defined images could be recalled or exploded. While it might seem that the drawing could be done without a computer, the ability to rapidly erase, recall and transform images required considerable processing and created a far more powerful means of expression than pencil and paper could provide.

### Interaction

These facilities provided a rich repertoire for an unusual dialogue. The artist could draw pictures on the participants'

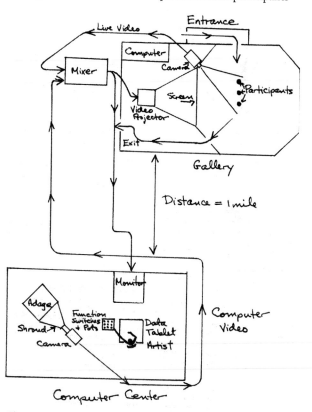

Figure 25.2. Metaplay communications.

images or communicate directly by writing words on the screen (Figure 25.3). He could induce people to play a game like Tic-Tac-Toe or play with the act of drawing, starting to draw one kind of picture only to have it transformed into another by interpolation.

## Live Graffiti

One interaction derived from the artist's ability to draw on the image of the audience. He could add graffiti-like features or animate a drawn outline of a person so that it appeared to dance to the music in the gallery. The artist tried various approaches to involve people in the interaction. Failing to engage one person, he would seek someone more responsive.

It was important to involve the participants in the act of drawing. However, the electronic wand designed for this purpose did not work reliably. What evolved was a serendipitous solution. One day as I was trying to draw on a student's hand, he became confused and moved it. When I erased my scribblings and started over, he moved his hand again. He did this repeatedly until it became a game. Finally, it degenerated to the point where I was simply tracking the image of his hand with the computer line. In effect, by moving his hand he could draw on the screen before him.

The relationship established with this participant was developed as one of the major themes of METAPLAY. It was repeated and varied until it became an aesthetic medium in iteslf. With each person we involved in this way, we tried to preserve the pleasure of the original discovery. After playing some graffiti games with each group that entered, we would focus on a single individual and draw around the image of his hand. After an initial reaction of blank bewilderment, the self-conscious person would make a nervous gesture. The computer line traced the gesture. A second gesture, followed by the line was the key to discovery. One could draw on the video screen with his finger! Others in the group, observing this phenomenon, would want to try it too. The line could be passed from one person's finger to another's. Literally hundreds of interactive vignettes developed within this simple communication channel.

Drawing by this method was a rough process. Pictures of any but the simplest shapes were unattainable. This was mainly because of the difficulty of tracking a person's finger. Happily, neither the artist nor the audience were concerned about the quality of the drawings. What was exciting was interacting in this novel way through a man-computer-video link spanning a mile.

Figure 25.3. Metaplay drawing.

## PSYCHIC SPACE

The next step in the evolution of the responsive environment was PSYCHIC SPACE, which I designed and exhibited in the Memorial Union Gallery during May and June of 1971. It was implemented with the help of my students, the Computer Science Department and a National Science Foundation grant in Complex Information Processing.

PSYCHIC SPACE was both an instrument for musical expression and a richly composed, interactive, visual experience. Participants could become involved in a softshoe duet with the environment, or they could attempt to match wits with the computer by walking an unpredictable maze projected on an 8′ × 10′ video screen.

### Hardware

A PDP-11 had direct control of all sensing and sound in the gallery. In addition, it communicated with the Adage AGT-10 Graphic Display Computer at the Computer Center (Figure 25.4). The Adage image was transmitted over video cable to the gallery where it was rear-projected on the 8′ × 10′ screen. The participant's position on the floor was the basis for each

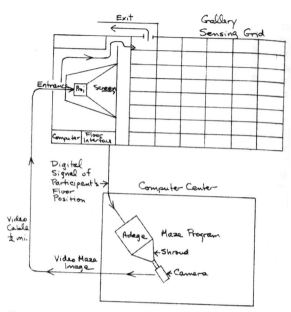

Figure 25.4. Data and video communication for psychic space.

but the most pleasing was to start each tone only when a new switch was stepped on and then to terminate it on the next "unfootstep." Thus it was possible to get silence by jumping, or by lifting one foot, or by putting both feet on the same switch.

Typical reaction to the sounds was instant understanding, followed by a rapid-fire sequence of steps, jumps and rolls. This phase was followed by a slower more thoughtful exploration of the environment in which more subtle and interesting relationships could be developed. In the second phase, the participant would discover that the room was organized with high notes at one end and low notes at the other. After a while, the keyboard was abruptly rotated by 90 degrees.

After a longer period of time an additional feature came into play. If the computer discovered that a person's behavior was characterized by a short series of steps punctuated by relatively long pauses, it would use the pause to establish a new kind of relationship. The sequence of steps was responded to with a series of notes as before; however, during the pause the computer would repeat these notes again. If the person remained still during the pause, the computer assumed that the relationship was understood. The next sequence of steps was echoed at a noticeably higher pitch. Subsequent sequences were repeated several times with variations each time. This interaction was experimental and extremely difficult to introduce clearly with feedback alone, i.e., without explicit instructions. The desire was for a man-machine dialogue resembling the guitar duel in the film *Deliverance.*

of the interactions. The sensing was done by a 16′ × 24′ grid of pressure switches, constructed in 2′ × 4′ modules, each containing eight switches (Figure 25.5). Since they were electronically independent, the system was able to discriminate among individuals if several were present. This independence made it easy for the programming to ignore a faulty switch until its module was replaced or repaired. Since there were 16 bits in the input words of the PDP-11, it was natural to read the 16 switches in each row across the room in parallel (Figure 25.6). Digital circuitry was then used to scan the 24 rows under computer control.

## Input and Interaction

Since the goal was to encourage the participants to express themselves through the environment, the program automatically responded to the footsteps of people entering the room with electronic sound. We experimented with a number of different schemes for actually generating the sounds based on an analysis of peoples' footsteps. In sampling the floor 60 times per second we discovered that a single footstep consisted of as many as four discrete events: lifting the heel, lifting the toe, putting the heel down and putting the ball of the foot down. The first two were dubbed the "unfootstep." We could respond to each footstep or unfootstep as it occurred, or we could respond to the person's average position. A number of response schemes were tried,

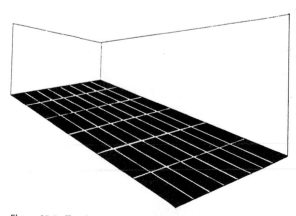

Figure 25.5. Flooring sensing modules in psychic space.

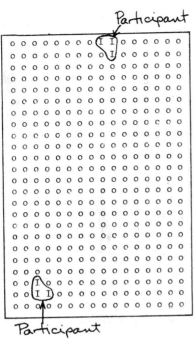

Participant

Participant

Figure 25.6. Participants' feet are seen by the computer as ones in a field of zeroes.

## Maze—A Composed Environment

The maze program focused on the interaction between one individual and the environment. The participant was lured into attempting to navigate a projected maze. The intrigue derived from the maze's responses, a carefully composed sequence of relations designed to constitute a unique and coherent experience.

### Hardware

The maze itself was not programmed on the PDP-11, but on the Adage located a mile away in the Computer Center. The PDP-11 transmitted the participant's floor coordinates across an audio cable to the Adage. The data was transmitted asynchronously as a serial bit stream of varying pulse widths. The Adage generated the maze image which was picked up by a TV camera and transmitted via a video cable back to the Union where it was rear-screen projected to a size of $8' \times 10'$.

### Interaction

The first problem was simply to educate the person to the relationships between the floor and the screen. Initially, a diamond with a cross in it representing the person's position appeared on the screen. Physical movement in the room caused the symbol to move correspondingly on the screen. As the participant approached the screen, the symbol moved up.

As he moved away, it moved down. The next step was to induce the person to move to the starting point of the maze, which had not yet appeared on the screen (Figure 25.7). To this end, another object was placed on the screen at the position which would be the starting point of the maze. The viewer unavoidably wondered what would happen if he walked his symbol to the object. The arrival of his symbol at the starting point caused the object to vanish and the maze to appear. Thus confronted with the maze, no one questioned the inevitability of walking it.

### Software Boundaries

Since there was no physical constraints in the gallery, the boundaries of the maze had to be enforced by the computer. Each attempt to violate a boundary was foiled by one of many responses in the computer's repertoire. The computer could move the line, stretch it elastically, or move the whole maze. The line could disappear, seemingly removing the barrier, except that the rest of the maze would change simultaneously so no advantage was gained. In addition, the symbol representing the person could split in half at the violated boundary, with one half held stationary while the other half, the alter ego, continued to track movement. However, no progress could be made until the halves of the symbol were reunited at the violated boundary.

Even when the participant was moving legally, there were changes in the program contingent upon his position. Several times, as the goal was approached, the maze changed to thwart immediate success. Or, the relationship between the floor and the maze was altered so that movements that once resulted in vertical motion, now resulted in horizontal motion. Alternatively, the symbol representing the participant could remain stationary while the maze moved.

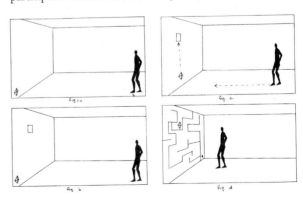

Figure 25.7. Composed environment-maze.

383

Ultimately, success was not allowed. When reaching the goal seemed imminent, additional boundaries appeared in front of and behind the symbol, boxing it in. At this point, the maze slowly shrank to nothing. While the goal could not be reached, the composed frustration made the route interesting.

## Experience

The maze experience conveyed a unique set of feelings. The video display space created a sense of detachment enhanced by the displaced feedback; movement on the horizontal plane of the floor translated onto the vertical plane of the screen. The popular stereotype of dehumanizing technology seemed fulfilled. However, the maze idea was engaging and people became involved willingly. The lack of any other sensation focused attention completely on this interaction. As the experience progressed, their perception of the maze changed. From the initial impression that it was a problem to solve, they moved to the realization that the maze was a vehicle for whimsy, playing with the concept of a maze and poking fun at their compulsion to walk it.

## VIDEOPLACE

For the past two years I have been working on a project called VIDEOPLACE, under the aegis of the Space Science and Engineering Center of the University of Wisconsin. This work is funded by the National Endowment for the Arts and the Wisconsin Arts Board. A preliminary version was exhibited at the Milwaukee Art Center for six weeks beginning in October 1975. The development of VIDEO-PLACE is still under way and several more years will be required before its potential is fully realized both in terms of implementing the enabling hardware and exploring its compositional possibilities.

VIDEOPLACE is a conceptual environment with no physical existence. It unites people in separate locations in a common visual experience, allowing them to interact in unexpected ways through the video medium. The term VIDEOPLACE is based on the premise that the act of communication creates a place that consists of all the information that the participants share at that moment. When people are in the same room, the physical and communication places are the same. When the communicants are separated by distance, as in a telephone conversation, there is still a sense of being together although

sight and touch are not possible. By using television instead of telephone, VIDEOPLACE seeks to augment this sense of place by including vision, physical dimension and a new interpretation of touch.

VIDEOPLACE consists of two or more identical environments which can be adjacent or hundreds of miles apart. In each environment, a single person walks into a darkened room where he finds himself confronted by an 8' × 10' rear-view projection screen. On the screen he sees his own life-size image and the image of one or more other people. This is surprising in itself, since he is alone in the room (Figure 25.8). The other images are of people in the other environments. They see the same composite image on their screens. The visual effect is of several people in the same room. By moving around their respective rooms, thus moving their images, the participants can interact within the limitations of the video medium.

It is these apparent limitations that I am currently working to overcome. When people are physically together, they can talk, move around the same space, manipulate the same objects and touch each other. All of these actions would appear to be impossible within the VIDEOPLACE. However, the opposite is true. The video medium has the potential of being more rich and variable in some ways, than reality itself.

It would be easy to allow the participants to talk, although I usually preclude this, to force people to focus on the less familiar kinds of interaction that the video medium provides. A sense of dimension can be created with the help of computer graphics, which can define a room or another spatial context within which the participants appear to move around. Graphics can also furnish this space with artificial objects and inhabit it with imaginary organisms. The sense of touch would seem to be impossible to duplicate. However, since the cameras see each person's image in contrast to a neutral background, it is easy to digitize the outline and to determine its orientation on the screen (Figure 25.9). It is also easy to tell if one person's image touches another's, or if someone touches a computer graphic object. Given this information the computer can make the sense of touch effective. It can currently respond with sounds when two images touch and will ultimately allow a person's image to pick up a graphic object and move it about the screen.

While the participants' bodies are bound by physical laws such as gravity, their images could be moved around the

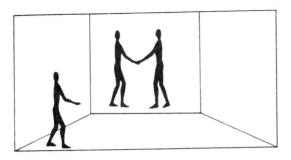

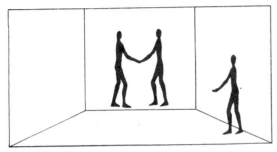

Figure 25.8. Videoplace.

Figure 25.9. The video outline sensor.

screen, shrunk, rotated, colorized and keyed together in arbitrary ways. Thus, the full power of video processing could be used to mediate the interaction and the usual laws of cause and effect replaced with alternatives composed by the artist.

The impact of the experience will derive from the fact that each person has a very proprietary feeling towards his own image. What happens to his image happens to him. In fact, when one person's image overlaps another's, there is a psychological sensation akin to touch. In VIDEOPLACE, this sensation can be enhanced in a number of ways. One image can occlude the other. Both images can disappear where they intersect. Both images can disappear except where they intersect. The intersection of two images can be used to form a window into another scene so two participants have to cooperate to see a third.

VIDEOPLACE need not involve more than one participant. It is quite possible to create a compelling experience for one person by projecting him into this imaginary domain alone. In fact the hardware/software system underlying VIDEOPLACE is not conceived as a single work but as a general facility for exploring all the possibilities of the medium to be described next.

## Response Is the Medium

The environments described suggest a new art medium based on a commitment to real-time interaction between men and machines. The medium is comprised of sensing, display and control systems. It accepts inputs from or about the participant and then outputs in a way he can recognize as corresponding to his behavior. The relationship between inputs and outputs is arbitrary and variable, allowing the artist to intervene between the participant's action and the results perceived. Thus, for example, the participant's physical movement can cause sounds or his voice can be used to navigate a computer defined visual space. It is the composition of these relationships between action and response that is important. The beauty of the visual and aural response is secondary. Response is the medium!

The distinguishing aspect of the medium is, of course, the fact that it responds to the viewer in an interesting way. In order to do this, it must know as much as possible about what the participant is doing. It cannot respond intelligently if it is unable to distinguish various kinds of behavior as they occur.

The environment might be able to respond to the participant's position, voice volume or pitch, position relative to prior position or the time elapsed since the last movement. It could also respond to every third movement, the rate of movement, posture, height, colors of clothing or time elapsed since the person entered the room. If there were several people in the room, it might respond to the distance separating them, the average of their positions or the computer's ability to resolve them, i.e., respond differently when they are very close together.

In more complex interactions like the maze, the computer can create a context within which the interaction occurs. This context is an artificial reality within which the artist has complete control of the laws of cause and effect. Thus the actions perceived by the hardware sensors are tested for significance within the current context. The computer asks if the person has crossed the boundary in the maze or has touched the image of a particular object. At a higher level the machine can learn about the individual and judge from its past experience with similar individuals just which responses would be most effective.

Currently, these systems are constrained by the total inability of the computer to make certain very useful and for the human, very simple perceptual judgments, such as whether a given individual is a man or a woman or is young or old. The perceptual system will define the limits of meaningful interaction, for the environment cannot respond to what it cannot perceive. To date the sensing systems have included pressure pads, ultrasonics and video digitizing.

As mentioned before, the actual means of output are not as important in this medium as they would be if the form were conceived as solely visual or auditory. In fact, it may be desirable that the output not qualify as beautiful in any sense, for that would distract from the central theme: the relationship established between the observer and the environment. Artists are fully capable of producing effective displays in a number of media. This fact is well known and to duplicate it produces nothing new. What is not known and remains to be tested is the validity of a responsive aesthetic.

It is necessary that the output media be capable of displaying intelligent, or at least composed reactions, so that the participant knows which of his actions provoked it and what the relationship of the response is to his action. The purpose of the displays is to communicate the relationships that the environment is trying to establish. They must be capable of great variation and fine control. The response can be expressed in light, sound mechanical movement, or

through any means that can be perceived. So far computer graphics, video generators, light arrays and sound synthesizers have been used.

## Control and Composition

The control system includes hardware and software control of all inputs and outputs as well as processing for decisions that are programmed by the artist. He must balance his desire for interesting relationships against the commitment to respond in real-time. The simplest responses are little more than direct feedback of the participant's behavior, allowing the environment to show off its perceptual system. But far more sophisticated results are possible. In fact, a given aggregation of hardware sensors, displays and processors can be viewed as an instrument which can be programmed by artists with differing sensitivities to create completely different experiences. The environment can be thought of in the following ways:

1. An entity which engages the participant in a dialogue. The environment expresses itself through light and sound while the participant communicates with physical motion. Since the experience is an encounter between individuals, it might legitimately include greetings, introductions and farewells—all in an abstract rather than literal way. The problem is to provide an interesting personality for the environment.

2. A personal amplifier. One individual uses the environment to enhance his ability to interact with those within it. To the participants the interaction might appear similar to that described above. The result would be limited by the speed of the artist's response but improved by his sensitivity to the participants' moods. The live drawing interaction in METAPLAY could be considered an example of this approach.

3. An environment which has sub-environments with different response relationships. This space could be inhabited by artificial organisms defined either visually or with sound. These creatures can interact with the participants as they move about the room.

4. An amplifier of physical position in a real or artificially generated space. Movements around the environment would result in much larger apparent movements in the visually represented space. A graphic display computer can be used to generate a

perspective view of a modelled space as it would appear if the participant were within it. Movements in the room would result in changes in the display, so that by moving only five feet within the environment, the participant would appear to have moved fifty feet in the display. The rules of the modelled space can be totally arbitrary and physically impossible, e.g. a space where objects recede when you approach them.

5. An instrument which the participants play by moving about the space. In PSYCHIC SPACE the floor was used as a keyboard for a simple musical instrument.

6. A means of turning the participant's body into an instrument. His physical posture would be determined from a digitized video image and the orientation of the limbs would be used to control lights and sounds.

7. A game between the computer and the participant. This variation is really a far more involving extension of the pinball machine, already the most commercially successful interactive environment.

8. An experimental parable where the theme is illustrated by the things that happen to the protagonist—the participant. Viewed from this perspective, the maze in PSYCHIC SPACE becomes pregnant with meaning. It was impossible to succeed, to solve the maze. This could be a frustrating experience if one were trying to reach the goal. If, on the other hand, the participant maintained an active curiosity about how the maze would thwart him next, the experience was entertaining. Such poetic composition of experience is one of the most promising lines of development to be pursued with the environments.

## Implications of the Art Form

For the artist the environment augurs new relationships with his audience and his art. He operates at a metalevel. The participant provides the direct performance of the experience. The environmental hardware is the instrument. The computer acts much as an orchestra conductor controlling the broad relationships while the artist provides the score to which both performer and conductor are bound. This relationship may be a familiar one for the musical composer, although even he is accustomed to being able to recognize one of his pieces, no matter who is interpreting it. But the artist's responsibilities here become even broader than those of a composer who typically defines a detailed sequence of events.

He is composing a sequence of possibilities, many of which will not be realized for any given participant who fails to take the particular path along which they lie.

Since the artist is not dedicated to the idea that his entire piece be experienced he can deal with contingencies. He can try different approaches, different ways of trying to elicit participation. He can take into account the differences among people. In the past, art has often been a one-shot, hit-or-miss proposition. A painting could accept any attention paid it, but could do little to maintain interest once it had started to wane. In an environment the loss of attention can be sensed as a person walks away. The medium can try to regain attention and upon failure, try again. The piece has a second strike capability. In fact it can learn to improve its performance, responding not only to the moment but also to the entire history of its experience.

In the environment, the participant is confronted with a completely new kind of experience. He is stripped of his informed expectations and forced to deal with the moment in its own terms. He is actively involved, discovering that his limbs have been given new meaning and that he can express himself in new ways. He does not simply admire the work of the artist; he shares in its creation. The experience he achieves will be unique to his movements and may go beyond the intentions of the artist or his understanding of the possibilities of the piece.

Finally, in an exciting and frightening way, the environments dramatize the extent to which we are savages in a world of our own creation. The layman has extremely little ability to define the limits of what is possible with current technology and so will accept all sorts of cues as representing relationships which in fact do not exist. The constant birth of such superstitions indicates how much we have already accomplished in mastering our natural environment and how difficult the initial discoveries must have been.

## Applications

The responsive environment is not limited to aesthetic expression. It is a potent tool with applications in many fields. VIDEOPLACE clearly generalizes the act of telecommunication. It creates a form of communication so powerful that two people might choose to meet visually, even if it were possible for them to meet physically. While it is not immediately obvious that VIDEOPLACE is the optimum means of telecommunication, it is reasonably fair to say that it provides an infinitely richer interaction than Picturephone allows. It broadens the range of possibilities beyond current efforts at teleconferencing. Even in its fetal stage, VIDEOPLACE is far more flexible than the telephone is after one hundred years of development. At a time when the cost of transportation is increasing and fiber optics promise to reduce the cost of communication, it seems appropriate to research the act of communication in an intuitive sense as well as in the strictly scientific and problem-solving approaches that prevail today.

## Education

Responsive environments have tremendous potential for education. Our entire educational system is based on the assumption that thirty children will sit still in the same room for six hours a day and learn. This phenomenon has never been observed in nature and it's the exception in the classroom where teachers are pitted against children's natural desire to be active. The responsive environments offer a learning situation in which physical activity is encouraged. It is part of the process. An environment like VIDEOPLACE has an additional advantage. It gives the child a life-size physically identical alter ego who takes part in composed learning adventures on the video screen. In a fully developed VIDEOPLACE the size and position of the child's image on the screen would be independent of actual location in the room. In an interactive Sesame Street a child would be mesmerized as his own miniaturized image was picked up by a giant Big Bird (Figure 25.10). Conversely he would be delighted if the scales were reversed and he were able to pick up the image of a tiny adult teacher who spoke to him from his hand. The most overworked educational cliché, "experience is the best teacher," would have new meaning in this context. The environments provide an experience which can be composed and condensed to demonstrate an educational point.

While it is easy to generate examples of how the environments can be used to teach traditional subjects, their significance does not lie only in their ability to automate traditional teaching. More important, they may revolutionize what we teach as well as how we teach. Since the environments can define interesting relationships and change them in complex ways, it should be possible to create interactions which enrich the child's conceptual experience.

Figure 25.10. Interactive Sesame Street.

This would provide the child with more powerful intellectual structures within which to organize the specific information he will acquire later. The goal would be to sophisticate the child, not to feed him facts.

## Psychology

Since the environments can monitor the participants' actions and respond with visual and auditory feedback, it is natural to consider their application to the study of human behavior. The use of the computer allows an experimenter to generate patterns and rhythms of stimuli and reinforcers. In addition, the ability to deal with gross physical behavior would suggest new experimental directions. For instance, perception could be studied as part of physical behavior and not as a sedentary activity distinct from it. Also, an environment like VIDEOPLACE is very general. The same aggregate of hardware and software could be programmed to control a broad range of experiments. The scheduling of different experiments could be interspersed because only the software would have to be changed.

Since the university students used as subjects in many experiments are quite sophisticated about the concerns of psychologists, what is often being studied is the self-conscious behavior of people who know they are in an experiment and are trying to second-guess it. On the other hand, environments open to the public offer a source of spontaneous behavior. It is quite easy for the computer to take statistics without interfering with the experience. Or, interactions can be composed to test specific experimental hypotheses.

## Psychotherapy

It is also worth considering the application of responsive environments to psychotherapy. Perhaps most important for a psychotherapist is the ability of the environment to evoke and expand behavior. We have found in the past that people alone in a dark room often become very playful and flamboyant—far more so than they are in almost any other situation. Since the environment is kept dark, the patient has a sense of anonymity; he can do things that he might not do otherwise. The fact that he is alone in the dark serves to protect him both from his image of himself and from his fear of other people. The darkness also is a form of sensory deprivation which might prevent a patient from withdrawing. If he is to receive any stimulation at all, it must be from acting within the environment. Once he acts, he can be reinforced for continuing to act.

In the event that the subject refuses to act, the environment can focus on motions so small as to be unavoidable and respond to these and as time goes by encourage them, slowly expanding them into larger behavior, ultimately leading the patient to extreme or cathartic action.

In certain situations the therapist essentially programs himself to become mechanical and predictable, providing a structure that the patient can accept which can be expanded slowly beyond the original contract. It is possible that it would be easier to get a patient to trust a mechanical environment and completely mechanized therapy. Once the patient was acting and trusting within the environment, it would be possible to slowly phase in some elements of change, to generalize his confidence. As time went by, human images and finally human beings might be added. At this point, the patient could venture from his responsive womb, returning to it as often as needed.

## Conclusion

The responsive environment has been presented as the basis for a new aesthetic medium based on real-time interaction between men and machines. In the long range it augurs a new realm of human experience, artificial realities which seek not to simulate the physical world but to define arbitrary, abstract and otherwise impossible relationships between action and result. In addition, it has been suggested that the concepts and tools of the responsive environments can be fruitfully applied in a number of fields.

What perhaps has been obscured is that these concepts are the result of a personal need to understand and express the essence of the computer in humanistic terms. An earlier project to teach people how to use the computer was abandoned in favor of exhibits which taught people about the computer by letting them experience it. METAPLAY, PSYCHIC SPACE and VIDEOPLACE were designed to communicate an affirmative vision of technology to the lay public. This level of education is important, for our culture cannot continue if a large proportion of our population is hostile to the tools that define it.

We are incredibly attuned to the idea that the sole purpose of our technology is to solve problems. It also creates concepts and philosophy. We must more fully explore these aspects of our inventions, because the next generation of technology will speak to us, understand us, and perceive our behavior. It will enter every home and office and intercede between us and much of the information and experience we receive. The design of such intimate technology is an aesthetic issue as much as an engineering one. We must recognize this if we are to understand and choose what we become as a result of what we have made.

# 26. [Introduction]
# Personal Dynamic Media

The imagination and boldness of the mid-1970s Dynabook vision—and the accuracy with which Alan Kay and Adele Goldberg foretold, in the following essay, what notebook computing has become—is striking. This introduction was composed, after all, at a café, on a computer that fits in an overcoat pocket. Before Kay and Goldberg began to outline the visions in this paper, such a possibility was seldom imagined, even in vague terms, by computing researchers. The prescience of Kay and Goldberg's vision was such that almost all the specific ideas for the uses of notebook computing developed in the group that Kay directed at Xerox Palo Alto Research Center (PARC) proved to be worthwhile. The broader idea—that the notebook computer would be a general-purpose device, with educators and businesspeople and poets all using the same type of Dynabook—has also held true.

The Dynabook vision came about because Kay, Goldberg, and others in their Learning Research Group at Xerox PARC considered the computer from a radically different perspective. (This approach may be the central maneuver in new media's otherwise varied methodology.) While most saw the computer as a tool for engineers or, at most, businesspeople, Kay thought computers could be used even by children, and could be used creatively. Kay and Goldberg also upset the idea that time-sharing computing is liberating for users, as J. C. R. Licklider (◊05) had more appropriately thought during the batch computing era. Instead, they believed that in the mid-1970s providing powerful, dedicated computers to individuals was a superior approach. Their group at Xerox PARC developed not only the notebook computer, but the essence of the personal desktop computer as well, which came to be embodied in Xerox's Alto. The desktop computer revolution would take hold before notebooks became widespread, of course. It was in the 1980s that home computers brought a new context to computing and revealed a host of new possible digital activities.

The development of the Dynabook vision and the powerful Alto personal computer created the elements that were used to produce the Star computer by the Xerox Systems Development Division, headed by David Liddle (formerly of PARC). The Star system sported a graphical user interface, which became part of popular personal computing via Apple's Macintosh. (Kay's fame is partially based on his invention of overlapping windows.) The Star system also helped to make Ethernet, the mouse, the laser printer, and WYIWYG printing a part of today's everyday computer environment. As with the movement of elements such as the mouse from Engelbart's ARC (◊16) to Kay's group at PARC, significant changes in focus took place in the move from the Alto to the Star. The "virtual paper" and desktop metaphors became further entrenched, while flexible knowledge spaces and user-created tools received less emphasis. Apple made changes of its own. One was in the meaning of Star's icons, which were originally only to represent documents, never applications. Apple's model was later adopted nearly wholesale by Microsoft (the exceptions were certain touches from systems such as Motif and NeXT, or from within Microsoft) and made into the dominant computing platform in the world. With today's rise in handheld computing the desktop and virtual paper metaphors are meeting a significant challenge, and may themselves fade. Still, the important original idea of opening tool creation to every user—even children—has not returned to prominence. Kay, however, continues to pursue this vision through his Squeak project.

> Kay was later a research fellow at Apple and then at Disney. Before these, and after his work at PARC, he directed Atari's sizeable but short-lived research lab, which was the victim of the collapse of the U.S. video game industry in the mid-1980s.

Certain aspects of notebook computing weren't foretold in the essay that follows—even though the Dynabook idea is among the most influential and prescient of the past thirty years. While Kay and Goldberg predicted that businesspeople could carry along "the last several weeks of correspondence in a structured cross-indexed form" and wireless communications capability was an essential part of the Dynabook concept, they didn't emphasize how notebook computers (and other personal computers) would find so much use as networked communication devices. They highlighted

391

the potential creative uses of the computer, but did not suggest the ways in which notebook computers are now used as media players, playing DVDs in coach class on airplanes or sending sound from MP3s through earphones to students as they toil over textbooks in libraries. Even within the Dynabook project, so extraordinary in creating notebook computing and charting a course for it, the quarter-century of computer evolution that would follow was not completely prefigured.
—NM & NWF

◊09
109

Seymour Papert, a great influence on Kay, was creating computer systems for children to use creatively on the other side of the United States, at MIT. There, he developed LOGO (see ◊28). Kay's previous work on FLEX had sought to create a computer that users could program themselves. This work led to the definition of object-oriented programming (inspired, in part, by Sutherland's "Sketchpad" (◊09)). From Papert's work, Kay saw how far this idea could be carried, and refined his notion of why it was important. The next stage of Kay's work in this area culminated in Smalltalk, the environment presented in this paper. Kay wrote the following regarding Papert's influence in 1990:

"I was possessed by the analogy between print literacy and LOGO. While designing the FLEX machine I had believed that end users needed to be able to program before the computer could become truly theirs—but here was a real demonstration, and with children! The ability to 'read' a medium means you can *access* materials and tools generated by others. The ability to 'write' in a medium means you can *generate* materials and tools for others. You must have both to be literate. In print writing, the tools you generate are rhetorical; they demonstrate and convince. In computer writing, the tools you generate are processes; they simulate and decide." ("User Interface: A Personal View," 193)

392

◊28
413

Further Reading

Hiltzik, Michael. *Dealers of Lightning: Xerox PARC and the Dawn of the Computer Age.* New York: Harper Business, 1999.

Ingalls, Dan, Ted Kaehler, John Maloney, Scott Wallace, and Alan Kay. "Back to the Future: The Story of Squeak, A Practical Smalltalk Written in Itself." *Proceedings of the 1997 SIGPLAN Conference on Object-Oriented Programming Systems, Languages, and Applications* (OOPSLA '97), 318–326. October 1997. <ftp://st.cs.uiuc.edu/Smalltalk/Squeak/docs/OOPSLA.Squeak.html>

Kay, Alan. "User Interface: A Personal View." *The Art of Human-Computer Interface Design,* 191–207. Ed. Brenda Laurel. Reading, Mass.: Addison-Wesley, 1990.

Kay, Alan. *Doing with Images Makes Symbols.* Stanford, Calif.: University Video Communications, 1987.

Squeakland. <http://squeakland.com>

Winograd, Terry, ed. *Bringing Design to Software.* New York: Addison-Wesley, 1996.

Original Publication
*Computer* 10(3):31–41. March 1977.

# Personal Dynamic Media

## Alan Kay and Adele Goldberg

## Introduction

The Learning Research Group at Xerox Palo Alto Research Center is concerned with all aspects of the communication and manipulation of knowledge. We design, build, and use dynamic media which can be used by human beings of all ages. Several years ago, we crystallized our dreams into a design idea for a personal dynamic medium the size of a notebook (the *Dynabook*) which could be owned by everyone and could have the power to handle virtually all of its owner's information-related needs. Towards this goal we have designed and built a communications system: the Smalltalk language, implemented on small computers we refer to as "interim Dynabooks." We are exploring the use of this system as a programming and problem solving tool; as an interactive memory for the storage and manipulation of data; as a text editor; and as a medium for expression through drawing, painting, animating pictures, and composing and generating music. (Figure 26.1 is a view of this interim Dynabook.)

We offer this paper as a perspective on our goals and activities during the past years. In it, we explain the Dynabook idea, and describe a variety of systems we have already written in the Smalltalk language in order to give broad images of the kinds of information-related tools that might represent the kernel of a personal computing medium.

## Background
### Humans and Media

"Devices" which variously store, retrieve, or manipulate information in the form of messages embedded in a medium have been in existence for thousands of years. People use them to communicate ideas and feelings both to others and back to themselves. Although thinking goes on in one's head, external media serve to materialize thoughts and, through feedback, to augment the actual paths the thinking follows. Methods discovered in one medium provide metaphors which contribute new ways to think about notions in other media.

Figure 26.1. Kids learning to use the interim Dynabook.

For most of recorded history, the interactions of humans with their media have been primarily nonconversational and passive in the sense that marks on paper, paint on walls, even "motion" pictures and television, do not change in response to the viewer's wishes. A mathematical formulation—which may symbolize the essence of an entire universe—once put down on paper, remains static and requires the reader to expand its possibilities.

Every message is, in one sense or another, a *simulation* of some idea. It may be representational or abstract. The essence of a medium is very much dependent on the way messages are embedded, changed, and viewed. Although digital computers were originally designed to do arithmetic computation, the ability to simulate the details of any descriptive model means that the computer, viewed as a medium itself, can be *all other media* if the embedding and viewing methods are sufficiently well provided. Moreover, this new "metamedium" is *active*—it can respond to queries and experiments—so that the messages may involve the learner in a two-way conversation. This property has never been available before except through the medium of an individual teacher. We think the implications are vast and compelling.

## A Dynamic Medium for Creative Thought:
## The Dynabook

Imagine having your own self-contained knowledge manipulator in a portable package the size and shape of an ordinary notebook. Suppose it had enough power to outrace your senses of sight and hearing, enough capacity to store for later retrieval thousands of page-equivalents of reference materials, poems, letters, recipes, records, drawings, animations, musical scores, waveforms, dynamic simulations, and anything else you would like to remember and change.

We envision a device as small and portable as possible which could both take in and give out information in quantities approaching that of human sensory systems (Figure 26.2). Visual output should be, at the least, of higher quality than what can be obtained from newsprint. Audio output should adhere to similar high-fidelity standards.

There should be no discernible pause between cause and effect. One of the metaphors we used when designing such a system was that of a musical instrument, such as a flute, which is owned by its user and responds instantly and consistently to its owner's wishes. Imagine the absurdity of a one-second delay between blowing a note and hearing it!

These "civilized" desires for flexibility, resolution, and response lead to the conclusion that a user of a dynamic personal medium needs several hundred times as much power as the average adult now typically enjoys from timeshared computing. This means that we should either build a new resource several hundred times the capacity of current machines and share it (very difficult and expensive), or we should investigate the possibility of giving each person his own powerful machine. We chose the second approach.

## Design Background

The first attempt at designing this metamedium (the FLEX machine[4]) occurred in 1967–69. Much of the hardware and software was successful from the standpoint of computer science state-of-the-art research, but lacked sufficient

Figure 26.2. Mock-up of a future Dynabook.

expressive power to be useful to an ordinary user. At that time we became interested in focusing on children as our "user community." We were greatly encouraged by the Bolt Beranek and Newman/MIT Logo work that uses a robot turtle that draws on paper, a CRT version of the turtle, and a single music generator to get kids to program.

Considering children as the users radiates a compelling excitement when viewed from a number of different perspectives. First, the children really can write programs that do serious things. Their programs use symbols to stand for objects, contain loops and recursions, require a fair amount of visualization of alternative strategies before a tactic is chosen, and involve interactive discovery and removal of "bugs" in their ideas.

Second, the kids love it! The interactive nature of the dialogue, the fact that *they* are in control, the feeling that they are doing *real* things rather than playing with toys or working out "assigned" problems, the pictorial and auditory nature of their results, all contribute to a tremendous sense of accomplishment to their experience. Their attention spans are measured in hours rather than minutes.

Another interesting nugget was that children really needed as much or more computing power than adults were willing to settle for when using a timesharing system. The best that timesharing has to offer is slow control of crude wire-frame green-tinted graphics and square-wave musical tones. The kids, on the other hand, are used to finger-paints, water colors, color television, real musical instruments, and records. If the "medium is the message," then the message of low-bandwidth timesharing is "blah."

Figure 26.3. The interim Dynabook system consists of processor, disk drive, display, keyboard, and pointing devices.

## An Interim Dynabook

We have designed an interim version of the Dynabook on which several interesting systems have been written in a new medium for communication, the Smalltalk programming language.[2] We have explored the usefulness of the systems with more than 200 users, most notably setting up a learning resource center in a local junior high school.

The interim Dynabook, shown in Figure 26.3, is a completely self-contained system. To the user, it appears as a small box in which a disk memory can be inserted; each disk contains about 1500 page-equivalents of manipulable storage. The box is connected to a very crisp high-resolution black and white CRT or a lower-resolution high-quality color display. Other input devices include a typewriter keyboard, a "chord" keyboard, a pointing device called a "mouse" which inputs position as it is moved about on the table, and a variety of organ-like keyboards for playing music. New input devices such as these may be easily attached, usually without building a hardware interface for them. Visual output is through the display, auditory output is obtained from a built-in digital-to-analog converter connected to a standard hi-fi amplifier and speakers.

We will attempt to show some of the kinds of things that can be done with a Dynabook; a number of systems developed by various users will be briefly illustrated. All photographs of computer output in this paper are taken from the display screen of the interim system.

## Remembering, Seeing and Hearing

The Dynabook can be used as an interactive memory or file cabinet. The owner's context can be entered through a keyboard and active editor, retained and modified indefinitely, and displayed on demand in a font of publishing quality.

Drawing and painting can also be done using a pointing device and an iconic editor which allows easy modification of pictures. A picture is thus a manipulable object and can be animated dynamically by the Dynabook's owner.

A book can be read through the Dynabook: the memory can be inserted as shown in Figure 26.4. It need not be treated as a simulated paper book since this is a new medium with new properties. A dynamic search may be made for a particular context. The non-sequential nature of the file medium and the use of dynamic manipulation allows a story to have many accessible points of view; Durrell's *Alexandria Quartet*, for instance, could be one book in which the reader may pursue many paths through the narrative.

Figure 26.4. Inserting the disk pack in the Dynabook.

## Different Fonts for Different Effects

One of the goals of the Dynabook's design is *not* to be *worse* than paper in any important way. Computer displays of the past have been superior in matters of dynamic writing and erasure, but have failed in contrast, resolution, or ease of viewing. There is more to the problem than just the display of text in a high-quality font. Different fonts create different moods and cast an aura that influences the subjective style of both writing and reading. The Dynabook is supplied with a number of fonts which are contained on the file storage. Figures 26.5 and 26.6 show samples of these fonts.

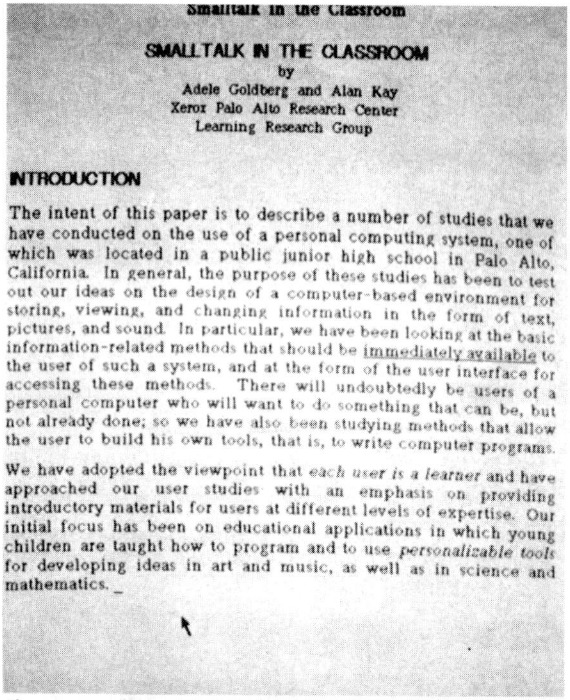

Smalltalk in the Classroom

SMALLTALK IN THE CLASSROOM
by
Adele Goldberg and Alan Kay
Xerox Palo Alto Research Center
Learning Research Group

INTRODUCTION

The intent of this paper is to describe a number of studies that we have conducted on the use of a personal computing system, one of which was located in a public junior high school in Palo Alto, California. In general, the purpose of these studies has been to test out our ideas on the design of a computer-based environment for storing, viewing, and changing information in the form of text, pictures, and sound. In particular, we have been looking at the basic information-related methods that should be immediately available to the user of such a system, and at the form of the user interface for accessing these methods. There will undoubtedly be users of a personal computer who will want to do something that can be, but not already done; so we have also been studying methods that allow the user to build his own tools, that is, to write computer programs.

We have adopted the viewpoint that *each user is a learner* and have approached our user studies with an emphasis on providing introductory materials for users at different levels of expertise. Our initial focus has been on educational applications in which young children are taught how to program and to use *personalizable tools* for developing ideas in art and music, as well as in science and mathematics.



Figure 26.5. First page of this paper as photographed from the display screen.

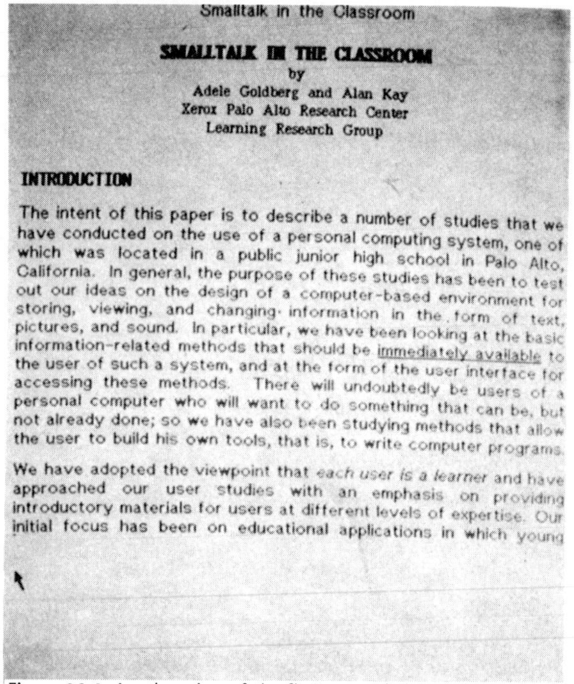

Smalltalk in the Classroom

SMALLTALK IN THE CLASSROOM
by
Adele Goldberg and Alan Kay
Xerox Palo Alto Research Center
Learning Research Group

INTRODUCTION

The intent of this paper is to describe a number of studies that we have conducted on the use of a personal computing system, one of which was located in a public junior high school in Palo Alto, California. In general, the purpose of these studies has been to test out our ideas on the design of a computer-based environment for storing, viewing, and changing information in the form of text, pictures, and sound. In particular, we have been looking at the basic information-related methods that should be immediately available to the user of such a system, and at the form of the user interface for accessing these methods. There will undoubtedly be users of a personal computer who will want to do something that can be, but not already done; so we have also been studying methods that allow the user to build his own tools, that is, to write computer programs.

We have adopted the viewpoint that *each user is a learner* and have approached our user studies with an emphasis on providing introductory materials for users at different levels of expertise. Our initial focus has been on educational applications in which young

Figure 26.6. Another view of the first page of the paper using different fonts.

The Dynabook as a personal medium is flexible to the point of allowing an owner to choose his own ways to view information. Any character font can be described as a matrix of black and white dots. The owner can draw in a character font of his own choosing. He can then immediately view font changes within the context of text displayed in a window. With the Dynabook's fine grain of display, the rough edges disappear at normal viewing distance to produce high-quality characters.

The malleability of this approach is illustrated in Figure 26.7: this owner has decided to embellish some favorite nouns with their iconic referent. Such a facility would be useful in enhancing an early reading curriculum.

## Editing

Every description or object in the Dynabook can be displayed and edited. Text, both sequential and structured, can easily be manipulated by combining pointing and a simple "menu" for commands, thus allowing deletion, transposition, and structuring. Multiple windows, as shown in Figure 26.8, allow a document (composed of text, pictures, musical notation) to be created and viewed simultaneously at several levels of refinement. Editing operations on other viewable objects (such as pictures and fonts) are handled in analogous ways.

## Filing

The multiple-window display capability of Smalltalk has inspired the notion of a dynamic *document.* A document is a collection of objects that have a sensory display and have something to do with each other; it is a way to store and retrieve related information. Each subpart of the document, or *frame,* has its own editor which is automatically invoked when pointed at by the "mouse." These frames may be related sequentially, as with ordinary paper usage, or *inverted* with respect to properties, as in cross-indexed file systems. *Sets* which can automatically map their contents to secondary storage with the ability to form unions, negations, and intersections are part of this system, as is a "modeless" text editor with automatic right justification.

The current version of the system is able to automatically cross-file several thousand multifield records (with formats chosen by the user), which include ordinary textual documents indexed by content, the Smalltalk system, personal files, diagrams, and so on. (See Figures 26.9–12.)

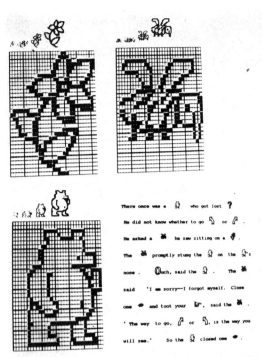

Figure 26.7. Fonts for a bear, a flower, and a bee used to tell a story with pictures.

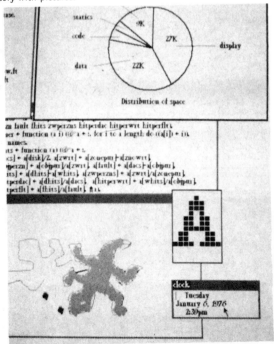

Figure 26.8. Multiple windows allow documents containing text and pictures to be created and viewed.

## Drawing/Painting

The many small dots required to display high-quality characters (about 500,000 for an 8-½″ × 11″ sized display) also allow sketching-quality drawing, "halftone painting," and animation. The subjective effect of gray scale is caused by the eye fusing an area containing a mixture of small black and white dots. The pictures in Figures 26.13 and 26.14 show a palette of toned patterns with some brushes. A brush can be grabbed with the "mouse," dipped into a paint pot, and then the halftone can be swabbed on as a function of the size, shape, and velocity of the brush. The last pair of pictures shows a heart/peace symbol shaped brush used to give the effect of painting wallpaper.

Curves are drawn by a *pen* on the display screen. (Straight lines are curves with zero curvature.) In the Dynabook, *pens* are members of a class that can selectively draw with black or white (or colored) ink and change the thickness of the trace. Each *pen* lives in its own *window*, careful not to traverse its window boundaries but to adjust as its window changes size and position. This window idea is illustrated in Figure 26.15; a number of simple and elegant examples are displayed in the windows.

## Animation and Music

Animation, music, and programming can be thought of as different *sensory views* of dynamic processes. The structural similarities among them are apparent in Smalltalk, which provides a common framework for expressing those ideas.

All of the systems are equally controllable by hand or by program. Thus, drawing and painting can be done using a pointing device or in conjunction with programs which draw curves, fill in areas with tone, show perspectives of three-dimensional models (see Figure 26.16), and so on. Any graphic expression can be animated, either by reflecting a simulation or by example (giving an "animator" program a sample trace or a route to follow).

Music is controlled in a completely analogous manner. The Dynabook can act as a "super synthesizer" getting direction either from a keyboard or from a "score." The keystrokes can be captured, edited, and played back. Timbres, the "fonts" of musical expression, contain the quality and mood which different instruments bring to an orchestration. They may be captured, edited, and used dynamically.

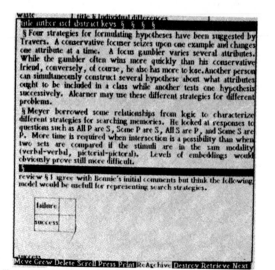

Figure 26.9. Retrieval in this filing tool is carried out by pointing to the command in the documents menu. The system will find every document with the title "box."

Figure 26.10. Here is a retrieved document that represents a description of a Smalltalk class definition.

Figure 26.11. This is a document from an annotated bibliography for teacers. Details are suppressed but can be expanded by pointing to names in the black fields. Documents can also contain diagrams.

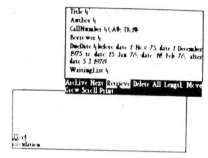

Figure 26.12. This retrieval request combines incomplete call numbers with date ranges. The example is taken from an experimental library system.

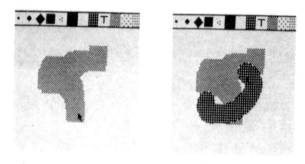

Figure 26.13. A sketch of Pegasus is shown being drawn with a Smalltalk drawing tool. The first two pictures in the sequence show halftone "paint" being scrubbed on.

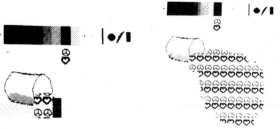

Figure 26.14. A sketch of a heart/peace symbol is created and used as a paint brush.

Figure 26.15. Curves can be drawn using Smalltalk line-drawing commands. These curves are constrained to show in display windows. Black and white can be reversed for interesting effects.

## Simulation

In a very real sense, simulation is the central notion of the Dynabook. Each of the previous examples has shown a simulation of visual or auditory media. Here are a number of examples of interesting simulations done by a variety of users.

### An Animation System Programmed by Animators

Several professional animators wanted to be able to draw and paint pictures which could then be animated in real time by simply showing the system roughly what was wanted.

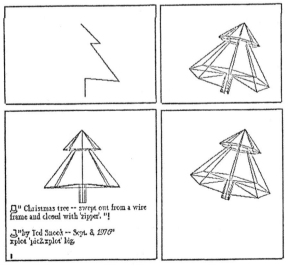

Figure 26.16. A model of three-dimensional graphics as implemented in Smalltalk.

Desired changes would be made by iconically editing the animation sequences.

Much of the design of SHAZAM, their animation tool, is an automation of the media with which animators are familiar: *movies* consisting of sequences of *frames* which are a composition of transparent *cels* containing foreground and background drawings. Besides retaining these basic concepts of conventional animation, SHAZAM incorporates some creative supplementary capabilities.

Animators know that the main action of animation is due not to an individual frame, but to the change from one frame to the next. It is therefore much easier to plan an animation if it can be seen moving as it is being created. SHAZAM allows any cel of any frame in an animation to be edited while the animation is in progress. A library of already-created cels is maintained. The animation can be single-stepped; individual cels can be repositioned, reframed, and redrawn; new frames can be inserted; and a frame sequence can be created at any time by attaching the cel to the pointing device, then *showing* the system what kind of movement is desired. The cels can be stacked for background parallax; *holes* and *windows* are made with *transparent* paint. Animation objects can be painted by programs as well as by hand. The control of the animation can also be easily done from a Smalltalk simulation. For example, an animation of objects bouncing in a room is most easily accomplished by a few lines of Smalltalk that express the class of bouncing objects in physical terms. Figures 26.17, 18, and 19 show some animations created by young children.

### A Drawing and Painting System Programmed by a Child

One young girl, who had never programmed before, decided that a pointing device *ought* to let her draw on the screen. She then built a sketching tool without ever seeing ours (displayed in Figure 26.20). She constantly embellished it with new features including a menu for brushes selected by pointing. She later wrote a program for building tangram designs (Figure 26.21).

This girl has taught her own Smalltalk class; her students were seventh-graders from her junior high school. One of them designed an even more elaborate system in which pictures are constructed out of geometric shapes created by pointing to a menu of commands for creating regular

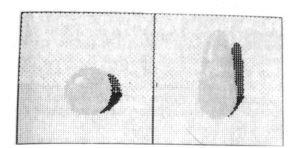

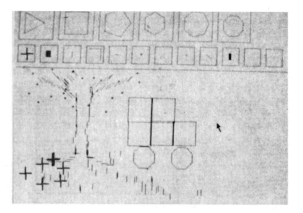

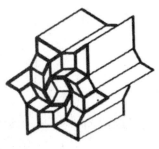

Figure 26.20. One of the first painting tools designed and implemented in Smalltalk by a twelve-year-old girl.

Figure 26.21. Tangram designs are created by selecting shapes from a "menu" displayed at the top of the screen. This system was implemented in Smalltalk by a fourteen-year-old girl.

Figure 26.17. An animation of a drop of water.

Figure 26.18. An animation of a galloping horse, with and without a rider.

Figure 26.19. An animation of a frog catching a fly.

polygons (Figure 26.22). The polygons can then be relocated, scaled, and copied; their color and line width can change.

## A Hospital Simulation
## Programmed by a Decision-Theorist

The simulation shown in Figure 26.23 represents a hospital in which every *department* has resources which are used by *patients* for some *duration of time*. Each patient has a *schedule* of departments to visit; if there are no resources available (doctors, beds), the patient must *wait* in line for service. The Smalltalk description of this situation involves the class of *patients* and the class of *departments*. The generalization to any hospital configuration with any number of patients is part of the simulation. The particular example captured in the pictures shows patients lining up for service in *emergency*. It indicates that there is insufficient staff available in that important area.

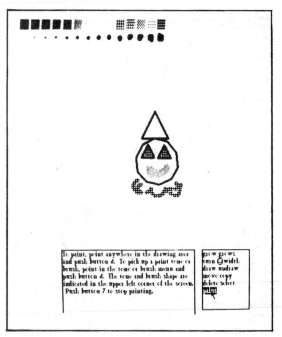

Figure 26.22. In this young student's Smalltalk painting system, pictures are constructed out of geometric shapes.

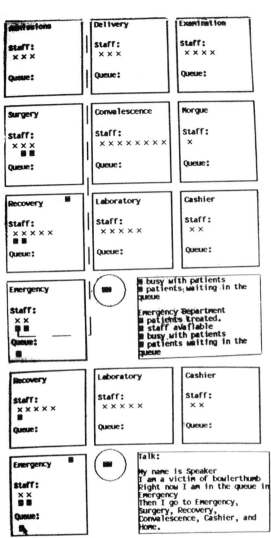

Figure 26.23. A view of a simulation of a hospital. The rectangles represent departments in which staff members (X's) treat patients (numbers).

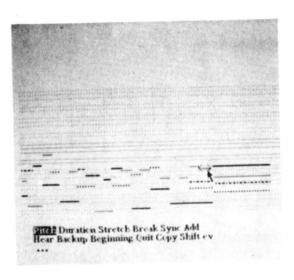

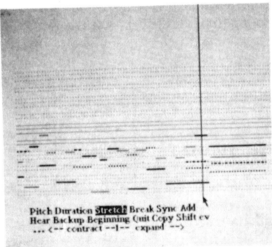

Figure 26.24. These two pictures show a musical score being edited. A note is selected in order to change its pitch. Next, the score is stretched, that is, the notes at the selected position will be held for a longer duration.

## An Audio Animation System
## Programmed by Musicians

Animation can be considered to be the coordinated parallel control through time of images conceived by an animator. Likewise, a system for representing and controlling musical images can be imagined which has very strong analogies to the visual world. Music is the design and control of images (pitch and duration changes) which can be *painted* different *colors* (timbre choices); it has synchronization and coordination, and a very close relationship between audio and spatial visualization.

The Smalltalk model created by several musicians, called TWANG, has the notion of a *chorus* which contains the main control directions for an overall piece. A chorus is a kind of *rug* with a warp of parallel sequences of "pitch, duration, and articulation" commands, and a woof of synchronizations and global directives. The control and the *player* are separate: in SHAZAM, a given movie sequence can animate many

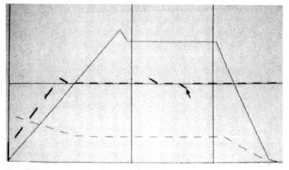

Now Editing -->>> Modulation Index
Volume Modulation Frequency Ratio Add-Ratio Redraw Quit
MI is dotted

Now Editing -->>> Frequency Deviation
Volume Modulation Frequency Ratio Add-Ratio Redraw Quit
MI is dotted

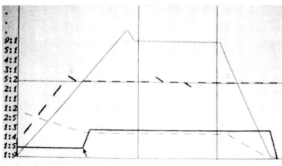

Now Editing -->>> Ratio Change
Volume Modulation Frequency Ratio Add-Ratio Redraw Quit
MI is dotted

Figure 26.25. Timbre editing: a musical instrument is created by specifying the frequency, amplitude, and spectrum of its sound during a period of a few seconds. The solid line in the first picture represents volume. The first segment of the graph represents the initial attack of each note, the part between vertical bars will be repeated as long as the note is held, and the remainder will be heard as the decay.

drawings; in TWANG, a given chorus can tell many different kinds of instrumentalists what should be played. These *voices* can be synthetic timbres or timbres captured from real instruments. Musical effects such as vibrato, portamento, and diminuation are also available.

A chorus can be *drawn* using the pointing device, or it can be *captured* by playing it on a keyboard. It can be played back in real time and dynamically edited in a manner very similar to the animation system. The accompanying set of pictures in Figure 26.24 are excerpts from a sequence in which a user plays, edits, and replays a piece.

We use two methods for real-time production of high-quality timbres; both allow arbitrary transients and many independent parallel voices, and are completely produced by programs. One of these allows independent dynamic control of the spectrum, the frequency, the amplitude, and the particular collection of partials which will be heard (illustrated in Figure 26.25).

For children, this facility has a number of benefits: the strong similarities between the audio and visual worlds are emphasized because a single vernacular *which actually works* in both worlds is used for description; and second, the arts and skills of composing can be learned at the same time since tunes may be drawn in by hand and played by the system. A line of music may be copied, stretched, and shifted in time and pitch; individual notes may be edited. Imitative counterpoint is thus easily created by the fledgling composer.

## A Musical Score Capture System Programmed by a Musician

OPUS is a musical score capture system that produces a display of a conventional musical score from data obtained by playing a musical keyboard. OPUS is designed to allow incremental input of an arbitrarily complicated score (full orchestra with chorus, for example), editing pages of the score, and hard copy of the final result with separate parts for individual instruments. The picture in Figure 26.26 shows a score captured with the OPUS system.

## Electronic Circuit Design by a High School Student

Using several kinds of iconic menus, this student system lets the user lay out a sophisticated electronic circuit, complete with labels (Figure 26.27).

Figure 26.26. Data for this score was captured by playing on a musical keyboard. A program then converts the data to standard musical notation.

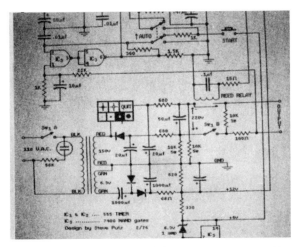

Figure 26.27. An electronic circuit layout system programmed by a 15-year-old student. Circuit components selected from a menu are moved into position with the mouse, connected to other components with lines, and labeled with text. The rectangle in the center of the layout is an iconic menu from which line widths and connectors (solid and open) may be chosen.

## Conclusion

What would happen in a world in which everyone had a Dynabook? If such a machine were designed in a way that *any* owner could mold and channel its power to his own needs, then a new kind of medium would have been created: a metamedium, whose content would be a wide range of already-existing and not-yet-invented media.

An architect might wish to simulate three-dimensional space in order to peruse and edit his current designs, which could be conveniently stored and cross-referenced.

A doctor could have on file all of his patients, his business records, a drug reaction system, and so on, all of which could travel with him wherever he went.

A composer could hear his composition while it was in progress, particularly if it were more complex than he was able to play. He could also bypass the incredibly tedious chore of redoing the score and producing the parts by hand.

Learning to play music could be aided by being able to capture and hear one's own attempts and compare them against expert renditions. The ability to express music in visual terms which could be filed and played means that the acts of composition and self-evaluation could be learned without having to wait for technical skill in playing.

Home records, accounts, budgets, recipes, reminders, and so forth, could be easily captured and manipulated.

Those in business could have an active briefcase which travelled with them, containing a working simulation of their company, the last several weeks of correspondence in a structured cross-indexed form—a way to instantly calculate profiles for their futures and help make decisions.

For educators, the Dynabook could be a new world limited only by their imagination and ingenuity. They could use it to show complex historical inter-relationships in ways not possible with static linear books. Mathematics could become a living language in which children could cause exciting things to happen. Laboratory experiments and simulations too expensive or difficult to prepare could easily be demonstrated. The production of stylish prose and poetry could be greatly aided by being able to easily edit and file one's own compositions.

These are just a few ways in which we envision using a Dynabook. But if the projected audience is to be "everyone," is it possible to make the Dynabook generally useful, or will it collapse under the weight of trying to be too many different tools for too many people? The total range of possible users is so great that any attempt to specifically anticipate their needs in the design of the Dynabook would end in a disastrous feature-laden hodgepodge which would not be really suitable for anyone.

Some mass items, such as cars and television sets, attempt to anticipate and provide for a variety of applications in a fairly inflexible way; those who wish to do something different will have to put in considerable effort. Other items, such as paper and clay, offer many dimensions of possibility and high resolution; these can be used in an unanticipated way by many, though *tools* need to be made or obtained to stir some of the medium's possibilities while constraining others.

We would like the Dynabook to have the flexibility and generality of this second kind of item, combined with tools which have the power of the first kind. Thus a great deal of effort has been put into providing both endless possibilities and easy tool-making through the Smalltalk programming language.

Our design strategy, then, divides the problem. The burden of system design and specification is transferred to the user. This approach will only work if we do a very careful and comprehensive job of providing a general medium of communication which will allow ordinary users to casually and easily describe their desires for a specific tool. We must also provide enough already-written general tools so that a user need not start from scratch for most things she or he may wish to do.

We have stated several specific goals. In summary, they are:

- to provide coherent, powerful examples of the use of the Dynabook in and across subject areas;

- to study how the Dynabook can be used to help expand a person's visual and auditory skills;

- provide exceptional freedom of access so kids can spend a lot of time probing for details, searching for a personal key to understanding processes they use daily; and

- to study the unanticipated use of the Dynabook and Smalltalk by children in all age groups.

**Note**

An expanded version of this paper was produced as Xerox PARC Technical Report SSL-76-1, March, 1976.[5]

**References and Bibliography**

The following is a list of references that provides further details on some of the different systems described in this report.

1. Baeker, Ronald, "A Conversational Extensible System for the Animation of Shaded Images," *Proc. ACM SIGGRAPH Symposium*, Philadelphia, Pennsylvania, June 1976.

2. Goldberg, Adele and Alan Kay (Eds.), *Smalltalk-72 Instruction Manual*, Xerox Palo Alto Research Center, Technical Report No. SSL 76-6, March 1976.

3. Goldeen, Marian, "Learning About Smalltalk," *Creative Computing*, September–October 1975.

4. Kay, Alan, *The Reactive Engine*, Doctoral dissertation, University of Utah, September 1969.

5. Learning Research Group, "Personal Dynamic Media," Xerox Palo Alto Research Center, Technical Report No. SSL 76-1, March 1976.

6. Saunders, S., "Improved FM Audio Synthesis Methods for Realtime Digital Music Generation," *Proc., ACM Computer Science Conference*, Washington, D.C., February 1975.

7. Smith, David C., *PYGMALION: A Creative Programming Environment*, Doctoral dissertation, Stanford University Computer Science Department, June 1975.

8. Snook, Tod, *Three-dimensional Geometric Modelling*, Masters thesis, University of California, Berkeley, September 1976.

# 27. [Introduction]
# From *A Thousand Plateaus*

Not all *literary machines* are the same. Italo Calvino's (◊12) is not Ted Nelson's (◊30), which is not that of Gilles Deleuze and Félix Guattari. There is nevertheless reason to discuss the Oulipo's potential literature, Ted Nelson's description of the Xanadu project, and Deleuze and Guattari's evocation of NeoFreudiMarxiPoststructuralist writing production using the same phrase. The coincidence of name suggests interesting directions, particularly when considering what it might be like to try to graft one meaning into another's context. And we would certainly not be the first to undertake such grafting.

Of the writing on culture in the last 30 years, that of Gilles Deleuze and Félix Guattari is among the most influential, the most fun, and most curiously applied. In new media this plays itself out in very interesting essays seemingly written from the perspective of "if I were using these terms, this is what I would mean." Unfortunately, what the author would prefer these terms to mean is at times conflated with what Deleuze and Guattari are supposed to have meant. Perhaps this is because Deleuze and Guattari's *A Thousand Plateaus* is more commonly read than their *Anti-Oedipus*, while many of the terms used in *A Thousand Plateaus* are introduced at far greater length in *Anti-Oedipus*. This is not to say that Deleuze and Guattari's terms may not be usefully appropriated for other purposes. Such appropriation has, in fact, been fruitful in many cases. But not realizing and indicating that an appropriation is being perpetrated closes the avenues that may be explored when encountering the concepts as Deleuze and Guattari present them.

Take, for example, the idea of rhizomatic writing sketched below. Some have used rhizomatic writing to describe hypertext, or the properties of one hypertext system as opposed to another. But, attending to Deleuze and Guattari's text for a moment: "In truth, it is not enough to say, 'Long live the multiple,' difficult as it is to raise that cry. No typographical, lexical, or even syntactical cleverness is enough to make it heard. The multiple *must be made...*" Later, they characterize their book, which is a very traditional codex in form, as rhizomatic. Clearly, in its original context, being rhizomatic is a not a feature of a medium, or even of a style. There are no rhizomatic writing tools, only rhizomatic texts. Listening to this original context opens to authors the possibility of playing with rhizomatic concepts in their writing, rather than limiting the discussion to their choice of software for writing.

However, without being an expert in Deleuze and Guattari's writings (and this volume's editors do not pretend to such a status) it is still possible to see that this essay challenges the reader to reconsider dualisms, even the dualisms of rhizome and anti-rhizome, rhizome and tree, correct and incorrect uses of a text.

> Every rhizome contains lines of segmentarity according to which it is stratified, territorialized, organized, signified, attributed, etc., as well as lines of deterritorialization down which it constantly flees. There is a rupture in the rhizome whenever segmental lines explode into a line of flight, but the line of flight is part of the rhizome. These lines always tie back to one another. That is why one can never posit a dualism or a dichotomy, even in the rudimentary form of the good and the bad. You may make a rupture, draw a line of flight, yet there is still a danger that you will reencounter organizations that restratify everything, formations that restore power to a signifier, attributions that reconstitute a subject—anything you like, from Oedipal resurgences to fascist concretions. Groups and individuals contain microfascisms just waiting to crystalize. Yes, couchgrass is also a rhizome. Good and bad are only the products of an active and temporary selection, which must be renewed.

Here Deleuze and Guattari's 1000 plateaus may remind one of Eihei Dogen's 10,000 dharmas—from Genjokoan, a founding document of Soto Zen—in which weeds rise with our aversion, and

◊12
147

405

◊30
441

flowers fall with our attachment. That is to say, the challenge Deleuze and Guattari's writing offers to Western thought is profound, especially when one considers that the authors were actively engaged in political action, rather than standing apart from it. Foucault, in his preface to Anti-Oedipus, calls it an introduction to the non-fascist life—a call to be radical without being sad. To answer, we must find a way to write, to act, to be engaged in life without believing in the self-similar self, without believing in easy dualisms—while knowing they will always crop up again.
—NWF

*Many of the terms used in* A Thousand Plateaus *are first introduced in* Anti-Oedipus, *which Deleuze and Guattari also co-authored. These terms are often constructed through literary and other cultural connections—from Freud's scizophrenic Judge Schreber to Antonin Artaud's theatre of cruelty. They write of "Desiring Production":*

It is at work everywhere, functioning smoothly at times, at other times in fits and starts. It breathes, it heats, it eats. It shits and fucks. What a mistake to have ever said *the* id. Everywhere *it* is machines—real ones, not figurative ones: machines driving other machines, machines being driven by other machines, with all the necessary couplings and connections. An organ-machine is plugged into an energy-source machine: the one produces a flow that the other interrupts. The breast is a machine that produces milk, and the mouth a machine coupled to it. The mouth of the anorexic wavers between several functions: its possessor is uncertain as to whether it is an eating-machine, an anal machine, a talking-machine, or a breathing-machine (asthma attacks). Hence, we are all handymen: each with his little machines. For every organ-machine, an energy-machine: all the time, flows and interruptions. Judge Schreber has sunbeams in his ass. *A solar anus.* And rest assured that it works: Judge Schreber feels something, produces something, and is capable of explaining the process theoretically. Something is produced: the effects of a machine, not mere metaphors . . . Desiring-machines make us an organism; but at the very heart of this production, within the very production of this production, the body suffers from being organized in this way, from not having some other sort of organization, or no organization at all. "An incomprehensible, absolutely rigid stasis" in the very midst of process, as a third stage: "No mouth. No tongue. No teeth. No larynx. No esophagus. No belly. No anus." The automata stop dead and set free the unorganized mass they once served to articulate. The full body without organs is the unproductive, the sterile, the unengendered, the unconsumable. Antonin Artaud discovered this one day, finding himself with no shape or form whatsoever, right there where he was at the moment. The death instinct: that is its name, and death is not without a model. For desire desires death also, because the full body of death is its motor, just as it desires life, because the organs of life are the *working machine*. We shall not inquire how all this fits together so that the machines will run: the question itself is the result of a process of abstraction. (1–2,8)

Further Reading

Deleuze, Gilles, and Félix Guattari. *Anti-Oedipus: Capitalism and Schizophrenia.* Trans. Robert Hurley, Mark Seem, and Helen R. Lane. Minneapolis: University of Minnesota Press, 1983. From the French *Capitalisme et Schizophrénie. L'Anti-Oedipe,* Editions de Minuit, 1972.

Dogen, Eihei. Commentary by Taizan Hakuyu Maezumi. *The Way of Everyday Life.* Los Angeles: Zen Center of Los Angeles, 1978.

Rhizome. <http://www.rhizome.org>

Original Publication

Excerpts from "Introduction: Rhizome." *A Thousand Plateaus: Capitalism and Schizophrenia Part II*, 3–7, 21. trans. Brian Massumi. Minneapolis: University of Minnesota Press, 1987.

From the French *Capitalisme et Schizophrénie, tome 2: Mille Plateaux*. Paris: Les Editions de Minuit, 1980.

# From *A Thousand Plateaus*

## Gilles Deleuze and Félix Guattari

### Introduction: Rhizome

The two of us wrote *Anti-Oedipus* together. Since each of us was several, there was already quite a crowd. Here we have made use of everything that came within range, what was closest as well as farthest away. We have assigned clever pseudonyms to prevent recognition. Why have we kept our own names? Out of habit, purely out of habit. To make ourselves unrecognizable in turn. To render imperceptible, not ourselves, but what makes us act, feel, and think. Also because it's nice to talk like everybody else, to say the sun rises, when everybody knows it's only a manner of speaking. To reach, not the point where one no longer says I, but the point where it is no longer of any importance whether one says I. We are no longer ourselves. Each will know his own. We have been aided, inspired, multiplied.

A book has neither object nor subject; it is made of variously formed matters, and very different dates and speeds. To attribute the book to a subject is to overlook this working of matters, and the exteriority of their relations. It is to fabricate a beneficent God to explain geological movements. In a book, as in all things, there are lines of articulation or segmentarity, strata and territories; but also lines of flight, movements of deterritorialization and destratification. Comparative rates of flow on these lines produce phenomena of relative slowness and viscosity, or, on the contrary, of acceleration and rupture. All this, lines and measurable speeds, constitutes an *assemblage*. A book is an assemblage of this kind, and as such is unattributable. It is a multiplicity—but we don't know yet what the multiple entails when it is no longer attributed, that is, after it has been elevated to the status of a substantive. One side of a machinic assemblage faces the strata, which doubtless make it a kind of organism, or signifying totality, or determination attributable to a subject; it also has a side facing a *body without organs*, which is continually dismantling the organism, causing asignifying particles or pure intensities to pass or circulate, and attributing to itself subjects that it leaves with nothing more than a name as the trace of an intensity. What is the body without organs of a book? There are several, depending on the nature of the lines considered, their particular grade or density, and the possibility of their converging on a "plane of consistency" assuring their selection. Here, as elsewhere, the units of measure are what is essential: *quantify writing*. There is no difference between what a book talks about and how it is made. Therefore a book also has no object. As an assemblage, a book has only itself, in connection with other assemblages and in relation to other bodies without organs. We will never ask what a book means, as signified or signifier; we will not look for anything to understand in it. We will ask what it functions with, in connection with what other things it does or does not transmit intensities, in which other multiplicities its own are inserted and metamorphosed, and with what bodies without organs it makes its own converge. A book exists only through the outside and on the outside. A book itself is a little machine; what is the relation (also measurable) of this literary machine to a war machine, love machine, revolutionary machine, etc.—and an *abstract machine* that sweeps them along? We have been criticized for overquoting literary authors. But when one writes, the only question is which other machine the literary machine can be plugged into, must be plugged into in order to work. Kleist and a mad war machine, Kafka and a most extraordinary bureaucratic machine. . . . (What if one became animal or plant *through* literature, which certainly does not mean literarily? Is it not first through the voice that one becomes animal?) Literature is an assemblage. It has nothing to do with ideology. There is no ideology and never has been.

All we talk about are multiplicities, lines, strata and segmentarities, lines of flight and intensities, machinic assemblages and their various types, bodies without organs and their construction and selection, the plane of consistency, and in each case the units of measure. *Stratometers, deleometers, BwO units of density, BwO units of convergence:* Not only do these constitute a quantification of writing, but they define writing as always the measure of something else. Writing has nothing to do with signifying. It has to do with surveying, mapping, even realms that are yet to come.

A first type of book is the root-book. The tree is already the image of the world, or the root the image of the world-tree. This is the classical book, as noble, signifying, and subjective organic interiority (the strata of the book). The book imitates the world, as art imitates nature: by procedures specific to it that accomplish what nature cannot or can no longer do. The law of the book is the law of reflection, the One that becomes two. How could the law of the book reside in nature, when it is what presides over the very division between world and book, nature and art? One becomes two: whenever we encounter this formula, even stated strategically by Mao or understood in the most "dialectical" way possible, what we have before us is the most classical and well reflected, oldest, and weariest kind of thought. Nature doesn't work that way: in nature, roots are taproots with a more multiple, lateral, and circular system of ramification, rather than a dichotomous one. Thought lags behind nature. Even the book as a natural reality is a taproot, with its pivotal spine and surrounding leaves. But the book as a spiritual reality, the Tree or Root as an image, endlessly develops the law of the One that becomes two, then of the two that become four.... Binary logic is the spiritual reality of the root-tree. Even a discipline as "advanced" as linguistics retains the root-tree as its fundamental image, and thus remains wedded to classical reflection (for example, Chomsky and his grammatical trees, which begin at a point S and proceed by dichotomy). This is as much as to say that this system of thought has never reached an understanding of multiplicity: in order to arrive at two following a spiritual method it must assume a strong principal unity. On the side of the object, it is no doubt possible, following the natural method, to go directly from One to three, four, or five, but only if there is a strong principal unity available, that of the pivotal taproot supporting the secondary roots. That doesn't get us very far. The binary logic of dichotomy has simply been replaced by biunivocal relationships between successive circles. The pivotal taproot provides no better understanding of

multiplicity than the dichotomous root. One operates in the object, the other in the subject. Binary logic and biunivocal relationships still dominate psychoanalysis (the tree of delusion in the Freudian interpretation of Schreber's case), linguistics, structuralism, and even information science.

The radicle-system, or fascicular root, is the second figure of the book, to which our modernity pays willing allegiance. This time, the principal root has aborted, or its tip has been destroyed; an immediate, indefinite multiplicity of secondary roots grafts onto it and undergoes a flourishing development. This time, natural reality is what aborts the principal root, but the root's unity subsists, as past or yet to come, as possible. We must ask if reflexive, spiritual reality does not compensate for this state of things by demanding an even more comprehensive secret unity, or a more extensive totality. Take William Burroughs's cut-up method: the folding of one text onto another, which constitutes multiple and even adventitious roots (like a cutting), implies a supplementary dimension to that of the texts under consideration. In this supplementary dimension of folding, unity continues its spiritual labor. That is why the most resolutely fragmented work can also be presented as the Total Work or Magnum Opus. Most modern methods for making series proliferate or a multiplicity grow are perfectly valid in one direction, for example, a linear direction, whereas a unity of totalization asserts itself even more firmly in another, circular or cyclic, dimension. Whenever a multiplicity is taken up in a structure, its growth is offset by a reduction in its laws of combination. The abortionists of unity are indeed angel makers, *doctores angelici*, because they affirm a properly angelic and superior unity. Joyce's words, accurately described as having "multiple roots," shatter the linear unity of the word, even of language, only to posit a cyclic unity of the sentence, text, or knowledge. Nietzsche's aphorisms shatter the linear unity of knowledge, only to invoke the cyclic unity of the eternal return, present as the nonknown in thought. This is as much as to say that the fascicular system does not really break with dualism, with the complementarity between a subject and an object, a natural reality and a spiritual reality: unity is consistently thwarted and obstructed in the object, while a new type of unity triumphs in the subject. The world has lost its pivot; the subject can no longer even dichotomize, but accedes to a higher unity, of ambivalence or overdetermination, in an always supplementary dimension to that of its object. The world has become chaos, but the book remains the image of the world: radicle-chaosmos rather than root-cosmos. A strange mystification: a book all the more total for being fragmented. At any rate, what a vapid idea, the book as the image of the world. In truth, it is not enough to say, "Long live the multiple," difficult as it is to raise that cry. No typographical, lexical, or even syntactical cleverness is enough to make it heard. The multiple *must be made*, not by always adding a higher dimension, but rather in the simplest of ways, by dint of sobriety, with the number of dimensions one already has available—always $n - 1$ (the only way the one belongs to the multiple: always subtracted). Subtract the unique from the multiplicity to be constituted; write at $n - 1$ dimensions. A system of this kind could be called a rhizome. A rhizome as subterranean stem is absolutely different from roots and radicles. Bulbs and tubers are rhizomes. Plants with roots or radicles may be rhizomorphic in other respects altogether: the question is whether plant life in its specificity is not entirely rhizomatic. Even some animals are, in their pack form. Rats are rhizomes. Burrows are too, in all of their functions of shelter, supply, movement, evasion, and breakout. The rhizome itself assumes very diverse forms, from ramified surface extension in all directions to concretion into bulbs and tubers. When rats swarm over each other. The rhizome includes the best and the worst: potato and couchgrass, or the weed. Animal and plant, couchgrass is crabgrass. We get the distinct feeling that we will convince no one unless we enumerate certain approximate characteristics of the rhizome.

. . . .

Let us summarize the principal characteristics of a rhizome: unlike trees or their roots, the rhizome connects any point to any other point, and its traits are not necessarily linked to traits of the same nature; it brings into play very different regimes of signs, and even nonsign states. The rhizome is reducible neither to the One nor the multiple. It is not the One that becomes Two or even directly three, four, five, etc. It is not a multiple derived from the One, or to which One is

added ($n + 1$). It is composed not of units but of dimensions, or rather directions in motion. It has neither beginning nor end, but always a middle (*milieu*) from which it grows and which it overspills. It constitutes linear multiplicities with $n$ dimensions having neither subject nor object, which can be laid out on a plane of consistency, and from which the One is always subtracted ($n - 1$). When a multiplicity of this kind changes dimension, it necessarily changes in nature as well, undergoes a metamorphosis. Unlike a structure, which is defined by a set of points and positions, with binary relations between the points and biunivocal relationships between the positions, the rhizome is made only of lines: lines of segmentarity and stratification as its dimensions, and the line of flight or deterritorialization as the maximum dimension after which the multiplicity undergoes metamorphosis, changes in nature. These lines, or lineaments, should not be confused with lineages of the arborescent type, which are merely localizable linkages between points and positions. Unlike the tree, the rhizome is not the object of reproduction: neither external reproduction as image-tree nor internal reproduction as tree-structure. The rhizome is an antigenealogy. It is a short-term memory, or antimemory. The rhizome operates by variation, expansion, conquest, capture, offshoots. Unlike the graphic arts, drawing, or photography, unlike tracings, the rhizome pertains to a map that must be produced, constructed, a map that is always detachable, connectable, reversible, modifiable, and has multiple entryways and exits and its own lines of flight. It is tracings that must be put on the map, not the opposite. In contrast to centered (even polycentric) systems with hierarchical modes of communication and preestablished paths, the rhizome is an acentered, nonhierarchical, nonsignifying system without a General and without an organizing memory or central automaton, defined solely by a circulation of states. What is at question in the rhizome is a relation to sexuality—but also to the animal, the vegetal, the world, politics, the book, things natural and artificial—that is totally different from the arborescent relation: all manner of "becomings."

# III
## Design, Activity, and Action

   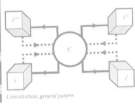

Consultation, general pattern

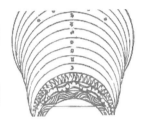

# 28. [Introduction]
# From *Mindstorms*
## *Children, Computers, and Powerful Ideas*

While mainframe computers were hidden away and attended by a priestly class of experts, more populist ideas of the computer were also being hatched. These entered the mainstream in what became, in the 1980s, the home computer era—an era not only heralded but negotiated by the acceptance, mainly by children, of computer-driven home video game consoles. But before that, a few had seen the computer not just as a commercial appliance that could find a wide market for gaming and productivity purposes but also as a means of learning. While computer operators were still solemnly receiving punched cards, a few—most prominent among them, Seymour Papert— were working to provide environments in which children could learn through the process of programming that most esoteric device.

Papert, a student of Jean Piaget's in the early 1960s, developed a philosophy of education based on Piaget's work and called "constructionism." It differs from constructivism (another educational philosophy based on Piaget) in that it "looks more closely . . . at the idea of mental construction," as Papert writes in *The Children's Machine* (143). The computer is seen by Papert as a powerful tool for supporting children's learning—for learning in a self-directed, self-motivated way, in the course of programming. Rather than seeing the computer as a mechanism for instilling knowledge and skills via workbook-like exercises, Papert's programming language, LOGO, allows children to take control of the computer, learning about mathematics through the experience of mathematical concepts. Work on developing LOGO began in 1967 in the same building that housed MIT's Artificial Intelligence Laboratory and Project MAC, which would become the Laboratory for Computer Science.

While Papert clearly believes in the power of the computer to facilitate constructionist educational experiences, computing is a means to an end for him and other constructionist educators. Constructionist education has certainly been an influence on new media, an influence that can be seen most directly on Web sites like *MaMaMedia* (founded by one of Papert's students) and on toy store shelves (the Lego Mindstorms robot kits, based on development done at MIT, are named after Papert's book). Papert was absolutely correct in his prediction in the following selection that "before the end of the century, people will buy children toys with as much computer power as the great IBM computers currently selling for millions of dollars." A computer is not required to allow children to learn in a constructionist way, however—just as software alone will not bring constructionist education to a traditional classroom. Constructionism, as potentially revolutionary to educational philosophy as the computer chip is to information technology, does not come packaged with computing. As yet, it has not upset traditional education to the extent that computing has influenced daily life.

"What follows is a hypothetical conversation between two children who are working and playing with the computer," Papert wrote in introducing the illustrated section of *Mindstorms* that is reproduced here, one which succinctly reveals the approach of constructionism. "These and other experiments can happen every day—and they do." With continued development of programming languages and learning environments for children (now a major part of the MIT Media Lab, the University of Maryland's Human-Computer Interaction Lab, and a number of other leading research centers), these sorts of conversations continue to happen today, in a growing number of contexts.

—NM

See Ted Nelson's "No More Teachers' Dirty Looks" (◊21) for a 1970 exploration of the educational computing issue, one written prior to the appearance of the first personal computer. While Nelson is similarly opposed to programming children via computer-aided instruction, he discusses ways of learning that employ the computer as a media system rather than a programming environment. ◊21 301

Papert credited artificial intelligence pioneer Marvin Minsky as being "the most important person in my intellectual life" in the years leading up to *Mindstorms*. Papert also thanked Alan Kay, noting that the only research group outside MIT seriously working with computers for children was Kay's at Xerox PARC. See Kay and Goldberg's article (◊26), which describes Smalltalk, another programming language used in education. Another person whose influence Papert noted was MIT social scientist Sherry Turkle, who has worked extensively on children's perceptions of computers; see selections from her book (◊34). ◊26 391

413

◊34 499

Further Reading

Boden, Margaret A. *Jean Piaget*. New York: Viking, 1979.

Druin, Allison, ed. *The Design of Children's Technology*. San Francisco: Morgan Kaufmann, 1999.

Papert, Seymour. *The Children's Machine: Rethinking School in the Age of the Computer*. New York: Basic Books, 1993.

Papert, Seymour. *The Connected Family: Bridging the Digital Generation Gap*. Atlanta: Longfellow Press, 1996.

Original Publication

"Computers and Computer Cultures," 19–37 and "Turtle Geometry: A Mathematics Made for Learning," 78–93. *Mindstorms*, New York: Basic Books, 1980.

# From *Mindstorms*
## *Children, Computers, and Powerful Ideas*
## Seymour Papert

### Computers and Computer Cultures

In most contemporary educational situations where children come into contact with computers the computer is used to put children through their paces, to provide exercises of an appropriate level of difficulty, to provide feedback, and to dispense information. The computer programming the child. In the LOGO environment the relationship is reversed: The child, even at preschool ages, is in control: The child programs the computer. And in teaching the computer how to think, children embark on an exploration about how they themselves think. The experience can be heady: Thinking about thinking turns the child into an epistemologist, an experience not even shared by most adults.

This powerful image of child as epistemologist caught my imagination while I was working with Piaget. In 1964, after five years at Piaget's Center for Genetic Epistemology in Geneva, I came away impressed by his way of looking at children as the active builders of their own intellectual structures. But to say that intellectual structures are built by the learner rather than taught by a teacher does not mean that they are built from nothing. On the contrary: Like other builders, children appropriate to their own use materials they find about them, most saliently the models and metaphors suggested by the surrounding culture.

Piaget writes about the order in which the child develops different intellectual abilities. I give more weight than he does to the influence of the materials a particular culture provides in determining that order. For example, our culture is very rich in materials useful for the child's construction of certain components of numerical and logical thinking. Children learn to count; they learn that the result of counting is independent of order and special arrangement; they extend this "conservation" to thinking about the properties of liquids as they are poured and of solids which change their shape. Children develop these components of thinking preconsciously and "spontaneously," that is to say without deliberate teaching. Other components of knowledge, such as the skills involved in doing permutations and combinations, develop more slowly, or do not develop at all without formal schooling. Taken as a whole this book is an argument that in many important cases this developmental difference can be attributed to our culture's relative poverty in materials from which the apparently "more advanced" intellectual structures can be built. This argument will be very different from cultural interpretations of Piaget that look for differences between city children in Europe or the United States and tribal children in African jungles. When I speak here of "our" culture I mean something less parochial. I am not trying to contrast New York with Chad. I am interested in the difference between precomputer cultures (whether in American cities or African tribes) and the "computer cultures" that may develop everywhere in the next decades.

I have already indicated one reason for my belief that the computer presence might have more fundamental effects on intellectual development than did other new technologies, including television and even printing. The metaphor of computer as mathematics-speaking entity puts the learner in a qualitatively new kind of relationship to an important domain of knowledge. Even the best of educational television is limited to offering quantitative improvements in the kinds of learning that existed without it. "Sesame Street" might offer better and more engaging explanations than a child can get from some parents or nursery school teachers, but the child is still in the position of listening to explanations. By contrast, when a child learns to program, the process of learning is transformed. It becomes more active and self-directed. In particular, the knowledge is acquired for a recognizable personal purpose. The child does something with it. The new knowledge is a source of power and is experienced as such from the moment it begins to form in the child's mind.

I have spoken of mathematics being learned in a new way. But much more is affected than mathematics. One can get an idea of the extent of what is changed by examining another of Piaget's ideas. Piaget distinguishes between "concrete" thinking and "formal" thinking. Concrete thinking is already well on its way by the time the child enters the first grade at age 6 and is consolidated in the following several years. Formal thinking does not develop until the child is almost twice as old, that is to say at age 12, give or take a year or two, and some researchers have even suggested that many people never achieve fully formal thinking. I do not fully accept Piaget's distinction, but I am sure that it is close enough to reality to help us make sense of the idea that the consequences for intellectual development of one innovation could be qualitatively greater than the cumulative quantitative effects of a thousand others. Stated most simply, my conjecture is that the computer can concretize (and personalize) the formal. Seen in this light, it is not just another powerful educational tool. It is unique in providing us with the means for addressing what Piaget and many others see as the obstacle which is overcome in the passage from child to adult thinking. I believe that it can allow us to shift the boundary separating concrete and formal. Knowledge that was accessible only through formal processes can now be approached concretely. And the real magic comes from the fact that this knowledge includes those elements one needs to become a formal thinker.

This description of the role of the computer is rather abstract. I shall concretize it, anticipating discussions which occur in later chapters of this book [*Mindstorms*], by looking at the effect of working with computers on two kinds of thinking Piaget associates with the formal stage of intellectual development: combinatorial thinking, where one has to reason in terms of the set of all possible states of a system, and self-referential thinking about thinking itself.

In a typical experiment in combinatorial thinking, children are asked to form all the possible combinations (or "families") of beads of assorted colors. It really is quite remarkable that most children are unable to do this systematically and accurately until they are in the fifth or sixth grades. Why should this be? Why does this task seem to be so much more difficult than the intellectual feats accomplished by seven and eight year old children? Is its logical structure essentially more complex? Can it possibly require a neurological mechanism that does not mature until the approach of puberty? I think that a more likely explanation is provided by looking at the nature of the culture. The task of making the families of beads can be looked at as constructing and executing a program, a very common sort of program, in which two loops are nested: Fix a first color and run through all the possible second colors, then repeat until all possible first colors have been run through. For someone who is thoroughly used to computers and programming there is nothing "formal" or abstract about this task. For a child in a computer culture it would be as concrete as matching up knives and forks at the dinner table. Even the common "bug" of including some families twice (for example, red-blue and blue-red) would be well-known. Our culture is rich in pairs, couples, and one-to-one correspondences of all sorts, and it is rich in language for talking about such things. This richness provides both the incentive and a supply of models and tools for children to build ways to think about such issues as whether three large pieces of candy are more or less than four much smaller pieces. For such problems our children acquire an excellent intuitive sense of quantity. But our culture is relatively poor in models of systematic procedures. Until recently there was not even a name in popular language for programming, let alone for the ideas needed to do so successfully. There is no word for "nested loops" and no word for the double-counting bug. Indeed, there are no words for the powerful ideas computerists refer to as "bug" and "debugging."

Without the incentive or the materials to build powerful, concrete ways to think about problems involving systematicity, children are forced to approach such problems in a groping, abstract fashion. Thus cultural factors that are common to both the American city and the African village can explain the difference in age at which children build their intuitive knowledge of quantity and of systematicity.

While still working in Geneva I had become sensitive to the way in which materials from the then very young computer cultures were allowing psychologists to develop new ways to think about thinking.[1] In fact, my entry into the world of computers was motivated largely by the idea that children could also benefit, perhaps even more than the psychologists, from the way in which computer models seemed able to give concrete form to areas of knowledge that had previously appeared so intangible and abstract.

I began to see how children who had learned to program computers could use very concrete computer models to think about thinking and to learn about learning and in doing so, enhance their powers as psychologists and as epistemologists. For example, many children are held back in their learning because they have a model of learning in which you have either "got it" or "got it wrong." But when you learn to program a computer you almost never get it right the first time. Learning to be a master programmer is learning to become highly skilled at isolating and correcting "bugs," the parts that keep the program from working. The question to ask about the program is not whether it is right or wrong, but if it is fixable. If this way of looking at intellectual products were generalized to how the larger culture thinks about knowledge and its acquisition, we all might be less intimidated by our fears of "being wrong." This potential influence of the computer on changing our notion of a black and white version of our successes and failures is an example of using the computer as an "object-to-think-with." It is obviously not necessary to work with computers in order to acquire good strategies for learning. Surely "debugging" strategies were developed by successful learners long before computers existed. But thinking about learning by analogy with developing a program is a powerful and accessible way to get started on becoming more articulate about one's debugging strategies and more deliberate about improving them.

My discussion of a computer culture and its impact on thinking presupposes a massive penetration of powerful computers into people's lives. That this will happen there can be no doubt. The calculator, the electronic game, and the digital watch were brought to us by a technical revolution that rapidly lowered prices for electronics in a period when all others were rising with inflation. That same technological revolution, brought about by the integrated circuit, is now bringing us the personal computer. Large computers used to cost millions of dollars because they were assembled out of millions of physically distinct parts. In the new technology a

complex circuit is not assembled but made as a whole, solid entity—hence the term "integrated circuit." The effect of integrated circuit technology on cost can be understood by comparing it to printing. The main expenditure in making a book occurs long before the press begins to roll. It goes into writing, editing, and typesetting. Other costs occur after the printing: binding, distributing, and marketing. The actual cost per copy for printing itself is negligible. And the same is true for a powerful as for a trivial book. So, too, most of the cost of an integrated circuit goes into a preparatory process; the actual cost of making an individual circuit becomes negligible, provided enough are sold to spread the costs of development. The consequences of this technology for the cost of computation are dramatic. Computers that would have cost hundreds of thousands in the 1960s and tens of thousands in the early 1970s can now be made for less than a dollar. The only limiting factor is whether the particular circuit can fit onto what corresponds to a "page"—that is to say the "silicon chips" on which the circuits are etched.

But each year in a regular and predictable fashion the art of etching circuits on silicon chips is becoming more refined. More and more complex circuitry can be squeezed onto a chip, and the computer power that can be produced for less than a dollar increases. I predict that long before the end of the century, people will buy children toys with as much computer power as the great IBM computers currently selling for millions of dollars. And as for computers to be used as such, the main cost of these machines will be the peripheral devices, such as the keyboard. Even if these do not fall in price, it is likely that a supercomputer will be equivalent in price to a typewriter and a television set.

There really is no disagreement among experts that the cost of computers will fall to a level where they will enter everyday life in vast numbers. Some will be there as computers proper, that is to say, programmable machines. Others might appear as games of ever-increasing complexity and in automated supermarkets where the shelves, maybe even the cans, will talk. One really can afford to let one's imagination run wild. There is no doubt that the material surface of life will become very different for everyone, perhaps most of all for children. But there has been significant difference of opinion about the effects this computer presence will produce. I would distinguish my thinking from two trends of thinking which I refer to here as the "skeptical" and the "critical."

Skeptics do not expect the computer presence to make much difference in how people learn and think. I have formulated a number of possible explanations for why they think as they do. In some cases I think the skeptics might conceive of education and the effect of computers on it too narrowly. Instead of considering general cultural effects, they focus attention on the use of the computer as a device for programmed instruction. Skeptics then conclude that while the computer might produce some improvements in school learning, it is not likely to lead to fundamental change. In a sense, too, I think the skeptical view derives from a failure to appreciate just how much Piagetian learning takes place as a child grows up. If a person conceives of children's intellectual development (or, for that matter, moral or social development) as deriving chiefly from deliberate teaching, then such a person would be likely to underestimate the potential effect that a massive presence of computers and other interactive objects might have on children.

The critics,[2] on the other hand, do think that the computer presence will make a difference and are apprehensive. For example, they fear that more communication via computers might lead to less human association and result in social fragmentation. As knowing how to use a computer becomes increasingly necessary to effective social and economic participation, the position of the underprivileged could worsen, and the computer could exacerbate existing class distinctions. As to the political effect computers will have, the critics' concerns resonate with Orwellian images of a 1984 where home computers will form part of a complex system of surveillance and thought control. Critics also draw attention to potential mental health hazards of computer penetration. Some of these hazards are magnified forms of problems already worrying many observers of contemporary life; others are problems of an essentially new kind. A typical example of the former kind is that our grave ignorance of the psychological impact of television becomes even more serious when we contemplate an epoch of super TV. The holding power and the psychological impact of the television show could be increased by the computer in at least two ways. The content might be varied to suit the tastes of each individual viewer, and the show might become interactive, drawing the "viewer" into the action. Such things belong to the future, but people who are worried about the impact of the computer on people already cite cases of students spending sleepless nights riveted to the computer terminal, coming to neglect both studies and social contact. Some parents have been reminded of these stories when they observe a special quality of fascination in their own children's reaction to playing with the still rudimentary electronic games.

In the category of problems that are new rather than aggravated versions of old ones, critics have pointed to the influence of the allegedly mechanized thought processes of computers on how people think. Marshall McLuhan's dictum that "the medium is the message" might apply here: If the medium is an interactive system that takes in words and speaks back like a person, it is easy to get the message that machines are like people and that people are like machines. What this might do to the development of values and self-image in growing children is hard to assess. But it is not hard to see reasons for worry.

Despite these concerns I am essentially optimistic—some might say utopian—about the effect of computers on society. I do not dismiss the arguments of the critics. On the contrary, I too see the computer presence as a potent influence on the human mind. I am very much aware of the holding power of an interactive computer and of how taking the computer as a model can influence the way we think about ourselves. In fact the work on LOGO to which I have devoted much of the past ten years consists precisely of developing such forces in positive directions. For example, the critic is horrified at the thought of a child hypnotically held by a futuristic, computerized super-pinball machine. In the LOGO work we have invented versions of such machines in which powerful ideas from physics or mathematics or linguistics are embedded in a way that permits the player to learn them in a natural fashion, analogous to how a child learns to speak. The computer's "holding power," so feared by critics, becomes a useful educational tool. Or take another, more profound example. The critic is afraid that children will adopt the computer as model and eventually come to "think mechanically" themselves. Following the opposite tack, I have invented ways to take educational advantage of the opportunities to master the art of *deliberately* thinking like a computer, according, for example, to the stereotype of a computer program that proceeds in a step-by-step, literal, mechanical fashion. There are situations where this style of thinking is appropriate and useful. Some children's difficulties in learning formal subjects such as grammar or mathematics derive from their inability to see the point of such a style.

417

A second educational advantage is indirect but ultimately more important. By deliberately learning to imitate mechanical thinking, the learner becomes able to articulate what mechanical thinking is and what it is not. The exercise can lead to greater confidence about the ability to choose a cognitive style that suits the problem. Analysis of "mechanical thinking" and how it is different from other kinds and practice with problem analysis can result in a new degree of intellectual sophistication. By providing a very concrete, down-to-earth model of a particular style of thinking, work with the computer can make it easier to understand that there is such a thing as a "style of thinking." And giving children the opportunity to choose one style or another provides an opportunity to develop the skill necessary to choose between styles. Thus instead of inducing mechanical thinking, contact with computers could turn out to be the best conceivable antidote to it. And for me what is most important in this is that through these experiences these children would be serving their apprenticeships as epistemologists, that is to say learning to think articulately about thinking.

The intellectual environments offered to children by today's cultures are poor in opportunities to bring their thinking about thinking into the open, to learn to talk about it and to test their ideas by externalizing them. Access to computers can dramatically change this situation. Even the simplest Turtle work can open new opportunities for sharpening one's thinking about thinking: Programming the Turtle starts by making one reflect on how one does oneself what one would like the Turtle to do. Thus teaching the Turtle to act or to "think" can lead one to reflect on one's own actions and thinking. And as children move on, they program the computer to make more complex decisions and find themselves engaged in reflecting on more complex aspects of their own thinking.

In short, while the critic and I share the belief that working with computers can have a powerful influence on how people think, I have turned my attention to exploring how this influence could be turned in positive directions.

I see two kinds of counterarguments to my arguments against the critics. The first kind challenges my belief that it is a good thing for children to be epistemologists. Many people will argue that overly analytic, verbalized thinking is counterproductive even if it is deliberately chosen. The second kind of objection challenges my suggestion that com-

puters are likely to lead to more reflective self-conscious thinking. Many people will argue that work with computers usually has the opposite effect. These two kinds of objections call for different kinds of analysis and cannot be discussed simultaneously. The first kind raises technical questions about the psychology of learning. The second kind of objection is most directly answered by saying that there is absolutely no inevitability that computers will have the effects I hope to see. Not all computer systems do. Most in use today do not. In LOGO environments I have seen children engaged in animated conversations about their own personal knowledge as they try to capture it in a program to make a Turtle carry out an action that they themselves know very well how to do. But of course the physical presence of a computer is not enough to insure that such conversations will come about. Far from it. In thousands of schools and in tens of thousands of private homes children are right now living through very different computer experiences. In most cases the computer is being used either as a versatile video game or as a "teaching machine" programmed to put children through their paces in arithmetic or spelling. And even when children are taught by a parent, a peer, or a professional teacher to write simple programs in a language like BASIC, this activity is not accompanied at all by the kind of epistemological reflection that we see in the LOGO environments. So I share a skepticism with the critics about what is being done with computation now. But I am interested in stimulating a major change in how things can be. The bottom line for such changes is political. What is happening now is an empirical question. What can happen is a technical question. But what will happen is a political question, depending on social choices.

The central open questions about the effect of computers on children in the 1980s are these: Which people will be attracted to the world of computers, what talents will they bring, and what tastes and ideologies will they impose on the growing computer culture? I have described children in LOGO environments engaged in self-referential discussions about their own thinking. This could happen because the LOGO language and the Turtle were designed by people who enjoy such discussion and worked hard to design a medium that would encourage it. Other designers of computer systems have different tastes and different ideas about what kinds of activities are suitable for children. Which design will prevail, and in what sub-culture, will not be decided by a simple bureaucratic decision made, for example, in a government Department of Education or by a committee of experts. Trends in computer style will emerge from a complex web of decisions by Foundations with resources to support one or another design, by corporations who may see a market, by schools, by individuals who will decide to make their career in the new field of activity, and by children who will have their own say in what they pick up and what they make of it. People often ask whether in the future children will program computers or become absorbed in pre-programmed activities. The answer must be that some children will do the one, some the other, some both and some neither. But which children, and most importantly, which social classes of children, will fall into each category will be influenced by the kind of computer activities and the kind of environments created around them.

As an example, we consider an activity which may not occur to most people when they think of computers and children: the use of a computer as a writing instrument. For me, writing means making a rough draft and refining it over a considerable period of time. My image of myself as a writer includes the expectation of an "unacceptable" first draft that will develop with successive editing into presentable form. But I would not be able to afford this image if I were a third grader. The physical act of writing would be slow and laborious. I would have no secretary. For most children rewriting a text is so laborious that the first draft is the final copy, and the skill of rereading with a critical eye is never acquired. This changes dramatically when children have access to computers capable of manipulating text. The first draft is composed at the keyboard. Corrections are made easily. The current copy is always neat and tidy. I have seen a child move from total rejection of writing to an intense involvement (accompanied by rapid improvement of quality) within a few weeks of beginning to write with a computer. Even more dramatic changes are seen when the child has physical handicaps that make writing by hand more than usually difficult or even impossible.

This use of computers is rapidly becoming adopted wherever adults write for a living. Most newspapers now provide their staff with "word processing" computer systems. Many writers who work at home are acquiring their own computers, and the computer terminal is steadily displacing the typewriter as the secretary's basic tool. The image of children using the computer as a writing instrument is a particularly good example of my general thesis that what is good for professionals is good for children. But this image of how the computer might contribute to children's mastery of language is dramatically opposed to the one that is taking root in most elementary schools. There the computer is seen as a teaching instrument. It gives children practice in distinguishing between verbs and nouns, in spelling, and in answering multiple-choice questions about the meaning of pieces of text. As I see it, this difference is not a matter of a small and technical choice between two teaching strategies. It reflects a fundamental difference in educational philosophies. More to the point, it reflects a difference in views on the nature of childhood. I believe that the computer as writing instrument offers children an opportunity to become more like adults, indeed like advanced professionals, in their relationship to their intellectual products and to themselves. In doing so, it comes into head-on collision with the many aspects of school whose effect, if not whose intention, is to "infantilize" the child.

Word processors *can* make a child's experience of writing more like that of a real writer. But this can be undermined if the adults surrounding that child fail to appreciate what it is like to be a writer. For example, it is only too easy to imagine adults, including teachers, expressing the view that editing and re-editing a text is a waste of time ("Why don't you get on to something new?" or "You aren't making it any better, why don't you fix your spelling?").

As with writing, so with music-making, games of skill, complex graphics, whatever: The computer is not a culture unto itself but it can serve to advance very different cultural and philosophical outlooks. For example, one could think of the Turtle as a device to teach elements of the traditional curriculum, such as notions of angle, shape, and coordinate systems. And in fact, most teachers who consult me about its use are, quite understandably, trying to use it in this way. Their questions are about classroom organization, scheduling problems, pedagogical issues raised by the Turtle's introduction, and especially, about how it relates conceptually to the rest of the curriculum. Of course the Turtle can help in the teaching of traditional curriculum, but I have thought of it as a vehicle for Piagetian learning, which to me is learning without curriculum.

There are those who think about creating a "Piagetian curriculum" or "Piagetian teaching methods." But to my mind these phrases and the activities they represent are contradictions in terms. I see Piaget as the theorist of learning without curriculum and the theorist of the kind of learning that happens without deliberate teaching. To turn him into the theorist of a new curriculum is to stand him on his head.

But "teaching without curriculum" does not mean spontaneous, free-form classrooms or simply "leaving the child alone." It means supporting children as they build their own intellectual structures with materials drawn from the surrounding culture. In this model, educational intervention means changing the culture, planting new constructive elements in it and eliminating noxious ones. This is a more ambitious undertaking than introducing a curriculum change, but one which is feasible under conditions now emerging.

Suppose that thirty years ago an educator had decided that the way to solve the problem of mathematics education was to arrange for a significant fraction of the population to become fluent in (and enthusiastic about) a new mathematical language. The idea might have been good in principle, but in practice it would have been absurd. No one had the power to implement it. Now things are different. Many millions of people are learning programming languages for reasons that have nothing to do with the education of children. Therefore, it becomes a practical proposition to influence the form of the languages they learn and the likelihood that their children will pick up these languages.

The educator must be an anthropologist. The educator as anthropologist must work to understand which cultural materials are relevant to intellectual development. Then, he or she needs to understand which trends are taking place in the culture. Meaningful intervention must take the form of working with these trends. In my role of educator as anthropologist I see new needs being generated by the penetration of the computer into personal lives. People who have computers at home or who use them at work will want to be able to talk about them to their children. They will want to be able to teach their children to use the machines. Thus there could be a cultural demand for something like Turtle graphics in a way there never was, and perhaps never could be, a cultural demand for the New Math.

Throughout the course of this chapter I have been talking about the ways in which choices made by educators, foundations, governments, and private individuals can affect the potentially revolutionary changes in how children learn.

But making good choices is not always easy, in part because past choices can often haunt us. There is a tendency for the first usable, but still primitive, product of a new technology to dig itself in. I have called this phenomenon the QWERTY phenomenon.

The top row of alphabetic keys of the standard typewriter reads QWERTY. For me this symbolizes the way in which technology can all too often serve not as a force for progress but for keeping things stuck. The QWERTY arrangement has no rational explanation, only a historical one. It was introduced in response to a problem in the early days of the typewriter: The keys used to jam. The idea was to minimize the collision problem by separating those keys that followed one another frequently. Just a few years later, general improvements in the technology removed the jamming problem, but QWERTY stuck. Once adopted, it resulted in many millions of typewriters and a method (indeed a full-blown curriculum) for learning typing. The social cost of change (for example, putting the most used keys *together* on the keyboard) mounted with the vested interest created by the fact that so many fingers now knew how to follow the QWERTY keyboard. QWERTY has stayed on despite the existence of other, more "rational" systems. On the other hand, if you talk to people about the QWERTY arrangement they will justify it by "objective" criteria. They will tell you that it "optimizes this" or it "minimizes that." Although these justifications have no rational foundation, they illustrate a process, a social process, of myth construction that allows us to build a justification for primitivity into any system. And I think that we are well on the road to doing exactly the same thing with the computer. We are in the process of digging ourselves into an anachronism by preserving practices that have no rational basis beyond their historical roots in an earlier period of technological and theoretical development.

The use of computers for drill and practice is only one example of the QWERTY phenomenon in the computer domain. Another example occurs even when attempts are made to allow students to learn to program the computer. As we shall see in later chapters, learning to program a computer involves learning a "programming language." There are many such languages—for example, FORTRAN, PASCAL, BASIC, SMALLTALK, and LISP, and the lesser known language LOGO, which our group has used in most of our experiments with computers and children. A powerful QWERTY phenomenon is to be expected when we choose the language in which children are to learn to program computers. I shall argue in detail that the issue is consequential. A programming language is like a natural, human language in that it favors certain metaphors, images, and ways of thinking. The language used strongly colors the computer culture. It would seem to follow that educators interested in using computers and sensitive to cultural influences would pay particular attention to the choice of language. But nothing of the sort has happened. On the contrary, educators, too timid in technological matters or too ignorant to attempt to influence the languages offered by computer manufacturers, have accepted certain programming languages in much the same way as they accepted the QWERTY keyboard. An informative example is the way in which the programming language BASIC[3] has established itself as the obvious language to use in teaching American children how to program computers. The relevant technical information is this: A very small computer can be made to understand BASIC, while other languages demand more from the computer. Thus, in the early days when computer power was extremely expensive, there was a genuine technical reason for the use of BASIC, particularly in schools where budgets were always tight. Today, and in fact for several years now, the cost of computer memory has fallen to the point where any remaining economic advantages of using BASIC are insignificant. Yet in most high schools, the language remains almost synonymous with programming, despite the existence of other computer languages that are demonstrably easier to learn and are richer in the intellectual benefits that can come from learning them. The situation is paradoxical. The computer revolution has scarcely begun, but is already breeding its own conservatism. Looking more closely at BASIC provides a window on how a conservative social system appropriates and tries to neutralize a potentially revolutionary instrument.

BASIC is to computation what QWERTY is to typing. Many teachers have learned BASIC, many books have been written about it, many computers have been built in such a way that BASIC is "hardwired" into them. In the case of the typewriter, we noted how people invent "rationalizations" to justify the status quo. In the case of BASIC, the phenomenon has gone much further, to the point where it resembles ideology formation. Complex arguments are invented to justify features of BASIC that were originally included because the primitive technology demanded them or because alternatives were not well enough known at the time the language was designed.

An example of BASIC ideology is the argument that BASIC is easy to learn because it has a very small vocabulary. The surface validity of the argument is immediately called into question if we apply it to the context of how children learn natural languages. Imagine a suggestion that we invent a special language to help children learn to speak. This language would have a small vocabulary of just fifty words, but fifty words so well chosen that all ideas could be expressed using them. Would this language be easier to learn? Perhaps the vocabulary might be easy to learn, but the use of the vocabulary to express what one wanted to say would be so contorted that only the most motivated and brilliant children would learn to say more than "hi." This is close to the situation with BASIC. Its small vocabulary can be learned quickly enough. But using it is a different matter. Programs in BASIC acquire so labyrinthine a structure that in fact only the most motivated and brilliant ("mathematical") children do learn to use it for more than trivial ends.

One might ask why the teachers do not notice the difficulty children have in learning BASIC. The answer is simple: Most teachers do not expect high performance from most students, especially in a domain of work that appears to be as "mathematical" and "formal" as programming. Thus the culture's general perception of mathematics as inaccessible bolsters the maintenance of BASIC, which in turn confirms these perceptions. Moreover, the teachers are not the only people whose assumptions and prejudices feed into the circuit that perpetuates BASIC. There are also the computerists, the people in the computer world who make decisions about what languages their computers will speak. These people, generally engineers, find BASIC quite easy to learn, partly because they are accustomed to learning such very technical systems and partly because BASIC's sort of simplicity appeals to their system of values. Thus, a particular subculture, one dominated by computer engineers, is influencing the world of education to favor those school students who are most like that subculture. The process is tacit, unintentional: It has never been publicly articulated, let alone evaluated. In all of these ways, the social embedding of BASIC has far more serious consequences than the "digging in" of QWERTY.

There are many other ways in which the attributes of the subcultures involved with computers are being projected onto the world of education. For example, the idea of the computer as an instrument for drill and practice that appeals to teachers because it resembles traditional teaching methods also appeals to the engineers who design computer systems: Drill and practice applications are predictable, simple to describe, efficient in use of the machine's resources. So the best engineering talent goes into the development of computer systems that are biased to favor this kind of application. The bias operates subtly. The machine designers do not actually decide what will be done in the classrooms. That is done by teachers and occasionally even by carefully controlled comparative research experiments. But there is an irony in these controlled experiments. They are very good at telling whether the small effects seen in best scores are real or due to chance. But they have no way to measure the undoubtedly real (and probably more massive) effects of the biases built into the machines.

We have already noted that the conservative bias being built into the use of computers in education has also been built into other new technologies. The first use of the new technology is quite naturally to do in a slightly different way what had been done before without it. It took years before designers of automobiles accepted the idea that they were cars, not "horseless carriages," and the precursors of modern motion pictures were plays acted as if before a live audience but actually in front of a camera. A whole generation was needed for the new art of motion pictures to emerge as something quite different from a linear mix of theater plus photography. Most of what has been done up to now under the name of "educational technology" or "computers in education" is still at the stage of the linear mix of old instructional methods with new technologies. The topics I shall be discussing are some of the first probings toward a more organic interaction of fundamental educational principles and new methods for translating them into reality.

We are at a point in the history of education when radical change is possible, and the possibility for that change is directly tied to the impact of the computer. Today what is offered in the education "market" is largely determined by what is acceptable to a sluggish and conservative system. But this is where the computer presence is in the process of creating an environment for change. Consider the conditions under which a new educational idea can be put into practice today and in the near future. Let us suppose that today I have an idea about how children could learn mathematics more effectively and more humanely. And let us suppose that I have been able to persuade a million people that the idea is a good one. For many products such a potential market would guarantee success. Yet in the world of education today this would have little clout: A million people across the nation would still mean a minority in every town's school system, so there might be no effective channel for the million voices to be expressed. Thus, not only do good educational ideas sit on the shelves, but the process of invention is itself stymied. This inhibition of invention in turn influences the selection of people who get involved in education. Very few with the imagination, creativity, and drive to make great new inventions enter the field. Most of those who do are soon driven out in frustration. Conservatism in the world of education has become a self-perpetuating *social* phenomenon.

Fortunately, there is a weak link in the vicious circle. Increasingly, the computers of the very near future will be the private property of individuals, and this will gradually return to the individual the power to determine patterns of education. Education will become more of a private act, and people with good ideas, different ideas, exciting ideas will no longer be faced with a dilemma where they either have to "sell" their ideas to a conservative bureaucracy or shelve them. They will be able to offer them in an open marketplace directly to consumers. There will be new opportunities for imagination and originality. There might be a renaissance of thinking about education.

Notes

1. The program FOLLOW* is a very simple example of how a powerful cybernetic idea (control by negative feedback) can be used to elucidate a biological or psychological phenomenon. Simple as it is, the example helps bridge the gap between physical models of "causal mechanism" and psychological phenomenon such as "purpose."

Theoretical psychologists have used more complex programs in the same spirit to construct models of practically every known psychological phenomenon. A bold formulation of the spirit of such inquiry is found in Herbert A. Simon, *Sciences of the Artificial* (Cambridge: MIT Press, 1969).

2. The critics and skeptics referred to here are distillations from years of public and private debates. These attitudes are widely held, but, unfortunately, seldom published and therefore seldom discussed with any semblance of rigor. One critic who has set a good example by publishing his views is Joseph Weizenbaum in *Computer Power and Human Reason: From Judgement to Calculation* (San Francisco: W.H. Freeman, 1976).

Unfortunately Weizenbaum's book discusses two separate (though related) questions: whether computers harm the way people think and whether computers themselves can think. Most critical reviews of Weizenbaum have focused on the latter question, on which he joins company with Hubert L. Drefus, *What Computers Can't Do: A Critique of Artificial Reason* (New York: Harper & Row, 1972).

A lively description of some of the principal participants in the debate about whether computers can or cannot think is found in Pamela McCorduck, *Machines Who Think* (San Francisco: W.H. Freeman, 1979).

There is little published data on whether computers actually affect how people think. This question is being studied presently by S. Turkle.

3. Many versions of BASIC would allow a program to produce a shape like that made by the LOGO program HOUSE. The simplest example would look something like this:

```
10 PLOT (0,0)
20 PLOT (100,0)
30 PLOT (100,100)
40 PLOT (75,150)
50 PLOT (0,100)
60 PLOT (0,0)
70 END
```

Writing such a program falls short of the LOGO program as a beginning programming experience in many ways. It demands knowledge of cartesian coordinates. This demand would be less serious if the program, once written, could become a powerful tool for other projects. The LOGO programs SQ, TRI, and HOUSE can be used to draw squares, triangles, and houses in any position and orientation on the screen. The BASIC program allows once particular house to be drawn in one position. In order to make a BASIC program that will draw houses in many positions, it is necessary to use algebraic variables as in PLOT $(x, y)$, PLOT $(x + 100, y)$, and so on. As for defining new commands, such as SQ, TRI, and HOUSE, the commonly used versions of BASIC either do not allow this at all or, at best, allow something akin to it to be achieved through the use of advanced technical programming methods. Advocates of BASIC might reply that: (1) these objections refer only to a beginner's experience and (2) these deficiencies of BASIC could be fixed. The first argument is simply not true: The intellectual and practical primitivity of BASIC extends all along the line up to the most advanced programming. The second misses the point of my complaint. Of course one could turn BASIC into LOGO or SMALLTALK or anything else and still call it "BASIC." My complaint is that what is being foisted on the education world has not been so "fixed." Moreover, doing so would be a little like "remodelling" a wooden house to become a skyscraper.

* *Touch Sensor Turtle.* The simplest touch sensor program in LOGO is as follows:

```
TO BOUNCE              Comments
REPEAT                 This means repeat all the inidividual steps
  FORWARD 1            The turtle keeps moving
  TEST FRONT.TOUCH     It checks whether it has run into something
  IFTRUE RIGHT 180     If so, it does an about turn
END
```

This will make the Turtle turn about when it encounters an object. A more subtle and more instructive program using the Touch Sensor Turtle is as folllows:

```
TO FOLLOW
REPEAT                 Comments
  FORWARD 1
  TEST LEFT.TOUCH      Check: Is it touching?
  IFTRUE RIGHT 1       It thinks it's too close and turns away
  IFFALSE LEFT 1       It thinks it might
                       lose the object so it turns toward
END
```

This program will cause the Turtle to circumnavigate an object of any shape, provided that it starts with its left side in contact with the object (and provided that the object and any irregularities in its contour are large compared with the Turtle).

It is a very instructive project for any group of students to develop this (or an equivalent) program from first principles by acting out how they think they would use touch to get around an object and by translating their strategies into Turtle commands.

423

## FIND RESOURCES

—Do you have any programs we could use?
—Yes, there's that quarter circle thing I made last week.
—Show me.

OCIRCLE 25

OCIRCLE 50

OCIRCLE 100

—It draws quarter circles starting wherever the turtle is.
—It needs an input to tell it how big.

## A PLAN

—Let's make the computer draw a flower like this.

## TRY SOMETHING

—Let's make a petal by putting two QCIRCLES together.
—OK. What size?
—How about 50?

## FIX THE BUG

—We have to turn the Turtle between QCIRCLES.
—Try 120°.
—OK, that worked for triangles.
—And let's hide the Turtle by typing HIDETURTLE.

```
QCIRCLE 50
LEFT 120
QCIRCLE 50
```

```
QCIRCLE 50
QCIRCLE 50
```

## A FIRST BUG

—It didn't work.
—Of course! Two QCIRCLES make a semicircle.

## IT'S A BIRD!

—What's going on?
—Try a right turn.

## MATH TO THE RESCUE

——Do you know about the Total Turtle Trip Theorem? You think about the Turtle going all around the petal and add up all the turns. 360°.

——All around is 360.
——Each QCIRCLE turns it 90. That makes 180 for two QCIRCLES.
——360 altogether. Take away 180 for the QCIRCLES. That leaves 180 for the pointy parts. 90 each.
——So we should do RIGHT 90 at each point.
——Let's try.

——Why don't we just stick with the bird? We could make a flock.
——You do that. I want my flower.
——We could do the flower, then the flock.

```
QCIRCLE 50
RIGHT 120
QCIRCLE 50
```

## IT'S A FISH!

——The right turn is better.
——But we don't know how much to turn.
——We could try some more numbers.
——Or we could try some mathematics.

## A BUILDING BLOCK

—Typing all that ten times hurts my fingers.
—We can use REPEAT.

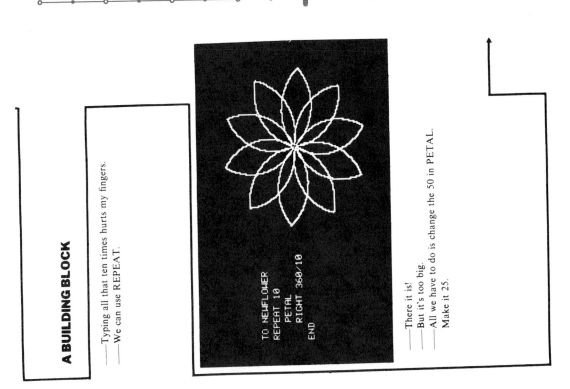

```
TO NEWFLOWER
REPEAT 10
    PETAL
    RIGHT 360/10
END
```

—There it is!
—But it's too big.
—All we have to do is change the 50 in PETAL.
—Make it 25.

## A WORKING PROCEDURE

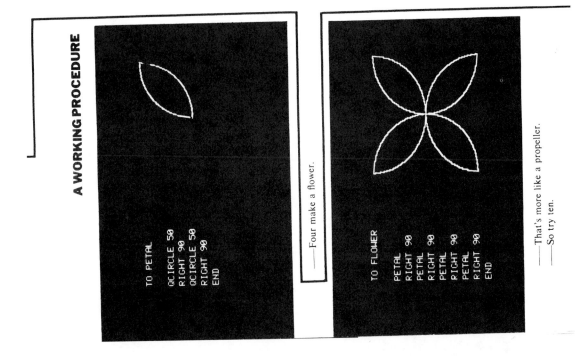

```
TO PETAL
QCIRCLE 50
RIGHT 90
QCIRCLE 50
RIGHT 90
END
```

—Four make a flower.

```
TO FLOWER
PETAL
RIGHT 90
PETAL
RIGHT 90
PETAL
RIGHT 90
PETAL
RIGHT 90
END
```

—That's more like a propeller.
—So try ten.

## ENDS BECOME MEANS

I have a great procedure for putting several together. It's called SLIDE.

You just go, PLANT SLIDE PLANT SLIDE PLANT SLIDE PLANT SLIDE.

```
TO SLIDE DISTANCE
PEN UP
RIGHT 90
FORWARD DISTANCE
LEFT 90
PEN DOWN
END
```

If we let PETAL have an input we can make big or small flowers.

That's easy. Just do TO PETAL SIZE QCIRCLE SIZE, and so on.

But I bet we'd get bugs if we try that. Let's try plain 25 first.

Then we can make a superprocedure to draw a plant.

## TRYING THE NEW TOOL

## BUILDING UP

```
TO PLANT
NEWFLOWER
BACK 50
PETAL
BACK 50
END
```

— It would be better with small ones and big ones.
— So, change the procedure to accept inputs.
— And if we use RANDOM we can make a garden.

— My next project is a flock of birds.
— Maybe we'll put the birds and flowers together.
— Maybe.

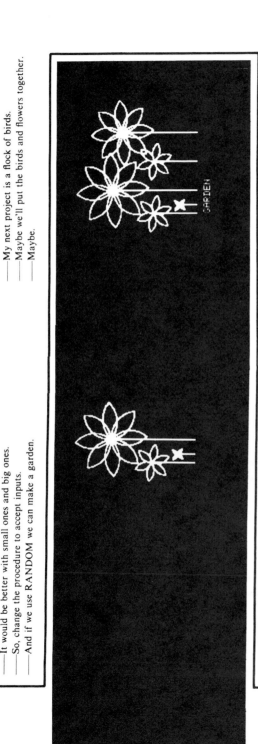

## DEBUGGING

—If you want to fix the bug, bring the Turtle around to face north after doing the bird.

—And let's make them smaller.

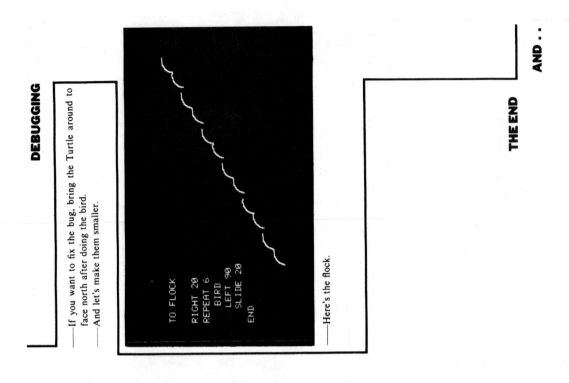

```
TO FLOCK
RIGHT 20
REPEAT 6
  BIRD
  LEFT 90
  SLIDE 20
END
```

—Here's the flock.

## THE END

AND . . .

## SERENDIPITY

—Make a flock by doing BIRD SLIDE BIRD SLIDE.

—I want six birds, and I'm going to use REPEAT.

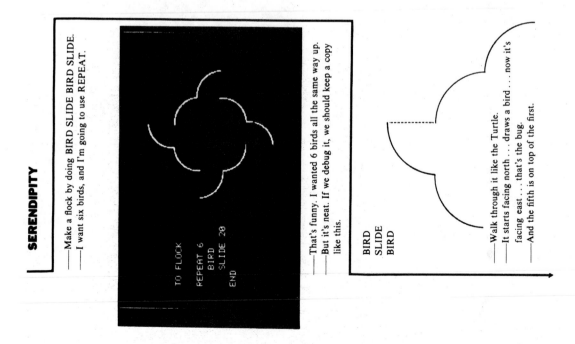

```
TO FLOCK
REPEAT 6
  BIRD
  SLIDE 20
END
```

—That's funny. I wanted 6 birds all the same way up.

—But it's neat. If we debug it, we should keep a copy like this.

BIRD
SLIDE
BIRD

—Walk through it like the Turtle.

—It starts facing north . . . draws a bird . . . now it's facing east . . . that's the bug.

—And the fifth is on top of the first.

## . . . A BEGINNING

The next phase of the project will produce the most spectacular effects as the birds go into motion. But the printed page cannot capture either the product or the process: the serendipitous discoveries, the bugs, and the mathematical insights all require movement to be appreciated. Reflecting on what you are missing leads me to another description of something new the computer offers a child: the opportunity to draw in motion, indeed to doodle and even to scribble with movement as well as with lines. Perhaps they will be learning, as they do so, to think more dynamically.

——It's not finished. Let's give the flock inputs and put several together.

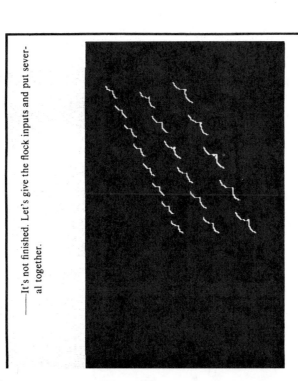

——How can we make them fly?
——I found something neat. In BIRD use SPIN instead of RIGHT . . . it's got bugs, but it is pretty.

# 29. [Introduction]
# "Put-That-There"
## Voice and Gesture at the Graphics Interface

Multimodal interfaces, combining speech and gesture input, are the most obvious descendants of the system described in the following essay. They aren't the only ones, though: important concepts of embedded computing, and of a computer interface that is more like spoken conversation (even if not augmented by gesture), were also advanced by Bolt's Put-That-There ⊗.

Data is represented spatially on all graphical computers today, but it is almost always represented in two-dimensional space. The Media Room set up by Nicholas Negroponte at MIT's Architecture Machine Group, and described in Bolt's essay, was spatial in at least two ways. It used two-dimensional screens to provide a view into a simulated three-dimensional space. It also employed an arrangement of screens and speakers situated in the architectural space of the room. By creating an extravagant computing environment, rather than doing more focused study of specific communications modalities considered separately, researchers in the Architecture Machine Group were able to arrive at a surprisingly different, and extremely useful, concept of human-computer interaction, in which these two types of space are experienced by the user as one.

Multimodal interfaces allow a person to communicate with a computer by simultaneously using channels such as speech, gesture, gaze (which can be detected using eye-tracking equipment), and facial expression. In certain systems, the computer replies by means of an embodied representation that can also use human-like modalities. These systems rely, for the most part, on understanding the ordinary communicative behaviors of a person and generating replies of the sort a human would. To require people to learn a special gestural language or series of codes would, after all, work against the goals of ease and fluency that motivate the creation of multimodal environments.

The interface idea behind Put-That-There involves not just the combination of speech and gesture but a preference (within the category of applications being considered) for speech over typing. In certain ways, this notion is actually the most radical, considering that the common history of new media is often focused on how the number-centered computer can be employed for radically different *textual* purposes. Voice recognition is now seen as an aid to accessibility and a less painful way for the wrist-weary to enter textual data into the computer, but it has not yet become a primary computer interface except in unusual niches. If the average computer interface was to become based on orality rather than literacy, the upset could be almost as profound as the shift from seeing the computer as a number-cruncher to seeing it as a manipulator of written language.
—NM

See the further discussion of the spatialization of data in Ben Shneiderman's article (◊33). Nicholas Negroponte's selection (◊23) describes his perspective on related issues, such as user-centered computing.   **433**

**Further Readings**

Bolt, Richard. *The Human Interface: Where People and Computers Meet.* Belmont, Calif.: Lifetime Learning Publications, 1984.

Hinckley, Ken, Randy Pausch, John C. Goble, and Neal F. Kassel. "A Survey of Design Issues in Spatial Input." *Proceedings of UIST '94*, 213–222. November 1994.

Special Issue on "Mutimodal Computer-Human Interaction." *International Journal of Man-Machine Studies* 28(2,3). 1988.

Original Publication:
*Computer Graphics* 4(3):262–270. July 1980.

# "Put-That-There"
## Voice and Gesture at the Graphics Interface
### Richard A. Bolt

## Introduction

Recently, the Architecture Machine Group at the Massachusetts Institute of Technology has been experimenting with the conjoint use of voice-input and gesture-recognition to command events on a large format raster-scan graphics display.

Of central interest is how voice and gesture can be made to inter-orchestrate, actions in one modality amplifying, modifying, disambiguating, actions in the other. The approach involves the significant use of pronouns, effectively as "temporary variables" to reference items on the display.

The interactions to be described are staged in the MIT Architecture Machine Group's "Media Room," a physical facility where the user's terminal is literally a room into which one steps, rather than a desk-top CRT before which one is perched.

The Media Room sketched in Figure 29.1 is the size of a personal office: about sixteen feet long, eleven feet wide, and about eight feet from floor to ceiling. The floor is raised to accommodate cabling from an ensemble of mini-computers which drives displays and devices resident in the Media Room. The walls, finished in dark brown pile fabric, house banks of loudspeakers on either side of a wall-sized, frosted-glass projection screen, and on either side and a bit to the rear of the user's chair.

The user's chair is a vinyl-covered Eames-type chair, exactly as comes from the furniture store, except for two types of instumentation based in its arms. Either arm bears a small, one-inch high joystick, of the non-displacing variety, sensitive to pressure and direction. Nearby each joystick is a two-inch on edge, square-shaped touch sensitive pad.

The wall-sized screen, about eight feet to the user's front, is served by back-projection from a color TV light-valve projector situated in an adjoining room. Color TV monitors are situated on either side of the user's chair, each with its tube face overlain with a transparent, touch-sensitive pad.

Apart from its role as an embodiment of the user terminal as an "informational surround [1]," the Media Room with its user chair has played a key role in our researches into a "Spatial Data-Management System, or SDMS [2]."

The specific rationale for *spatially* indexing data derives from our everyday experience of retrieving items, say, from our desktop: the phone to the right and above the blotter; the appointment calendar in the lower right; the "in-box" nearby the ashtray at the lower left, and so forth. Retrieval is natural and automatic for these items, with even an apparently "messy" desk having a spatial logic well-known to its creator and user, the knowledge of where this and that item are located being encoded conjointly in mental and motor models of the layout of the desktop.

The user of SDMS retrieves information not by typing names, i.e., alphanumeric strings on a keyboard terminal, but instead uses joystick and, occasionally, touch controls to navigate about in a helicopter-like manner to where specific caches of information reside in a rich graphics world of color and sound.

The world of information in SDMS, dubbed "Dataland," appears in its entirety upon one of the color TV monitors near-by the user chair. A small transparent rectangular overlay, a "you-are-here" marker, can be moved and positioned about Dataland by the user's managing of the chair's right-hand joystick (or by direct touch on the TV screen, if desired). That sub-portion of the Dataland surface

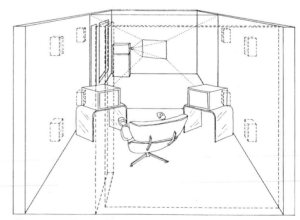

Figure 29.1. Sketch of Media Room.

indicated by the "you-are-here" rectangle is portrayed with increased detail on the large screen, effectively a magnifying window onto Dataland. The left-hand joystick on the user chair enables the user to zoom-in upon information to get a closer look at any of a number of multi-media data-types (e.g., maps, electronic "books," videodisc episodes), and perhaps to peruse them with the aid of an associated touch-sensitive "Key-map" which comes up on the other TV monitor by the user chair.

The Media Room setting, in addition to its power to generate a convincing impression of interacting with an implicit, "virtual" world of data behind the frame of the physical interface, implies yet another realm or order of space rife with possibilities for interaction: the actual space of the Media Room itself.

The sheer extent of the Media Room's physical interface creates a "real-space" environment. The user's focal situation amidst an ensemble of several screens of various sizes creates a set of geometrical relationships quite apart from any purely logical relationship between any one screen's content and that of any other.

Properly orchestrated, the two spatial orders, *virtual* graphical space, and the user's immediate *real* space in the Media Room, can converge to become effectively one continuous interactive space.

User awareness of this common space is implicit: the user points, gestures, references "up," "down," ". . . to the left of . . . ," and so on, freely and naturally, precisely because the user is situated in a real space. Tapping this interactive potential is rooted in two new technical offerings in the areas of: 1) connected speech recognition; 2) position sensing in space.

## Speech and Space: The Technologies

Two broad categories of currently commercially available speech recognizers may be distinguished: those which recognize discrete or isolated utterances, and those which recognize connected speech.

With those speech recognition systems restricted to discrete utterances, parsing of the speech signal into word-by-word tokens, is not done. The human speaker must talk to the system in a "clipped" or word-by-word style.

The recognition of connected speech has been a classic challenge in the field of speech recognition generally [3]. The DP-100 Connected Speech Recognition System (CSRS) by NEC (Nippon Electric Company) America, Inc. is capable of a limited amount of recognition of connected speech [4]. No pause between words is necessary, and up to five words or "utterances" are permitted per spoken sentence.

The recognition response time at the end of each sentence is about 300 milliseconds. Output is a display of the text of the utterance on an alphanumeric visual display, and/or a set of ASCII codes (numbers or letters) to be received by a processor interfaced with the NEC system.

The device's vocabulary, held in the recognizer's active memory as a set of word reference patterns, is a maximum of 120 words. With an optional "discrete utterance" mode, the size of the active vocabulary in the system's memory may be larger, about 1000 words. Except for the digits "one" to "ten," which must be spoken twice by the user when "training" the machine, each word in training mode need be spoken only once. The standard system comes with a lightweight, head-mounted microphone. We look forward to eventual use of a "shotgun" microphone in the Media Room, remote from but aimed at the speaker.

A space position and orientation sensing technology suitable for our intentions was found to be made by Polhemus Navigation Science, Inc., of Essex, Vermont. This system, called ROPAMS (Remote Object Position Attitude Measurement System) is based on measurements made of a nutating magnetic field. Essentials of the system are as follows.

Three coils are epoxied into a plastic cube, their mountings mutually orthogonal to correspond to x, y, and z spatial axes. Two such cubes are involved: one, about 1.5 inches on edge which acts as a transmitter, and another, 0.75 inches on edge, which functions as a sensor. The arrangement of coils in either cube essentially creates an antenna that is sensitive in all three orientations.

The transmitter cube radiates a nutating dipole field pointed at the sensor cube. When the pointing vector is correct, the field strength received will be constant. When it is not, there will be an error signal consisting of the nutation frequency. This error is used to generate the output pointing angles, and to re-aim the transmitter.

The orientation in space of the sensor cube is determined by transforming the differential signals from the three individual orthogonal coils in the sensor cube. The sensor cube's distance from the transmitter cube is computed by the $1/R^3$ fall-off of signal strength from the radiating dipole, or by triangulation with an additional radiator.

435

The sensor cube is very lightweight, and although it has a small cord running out of it, it is not an especially troublesome item to handle. Such sensors can readily be wrist-mounted, worn as finger rings, mounted on the visor of baseball caps, or put on a sort of "lab jacket" in lieu of cuff and collar buttons or epaulets.

## Commands

Suppose the user seated before the Media Room's large screen, with a space-sensing cube attached to a watchband on his wrist, and that the system's microphone is ready and listening. Some commands from the system's current repertoire illustrative of voice and pointing in concert are the following:

### "Create . . ."

In our demonstration system, the large screen is initially either clear, or bears some simple backdrop such as a map. Against this background, simple items are called into existence, moved about, replicated, their attributes altered, and then may be ordered to vanish.

The items used are basic shapes: circles, squares, diamonds. They are non-representational in that the thing *is* the shape. Variable attributes are: *color* (red, yellow, orange, green, blue . . .), and *size* (large, medium, small). For example, the user points to some spot on the large screen. A small, white "x" cursor on the screen provides running visual feedback for pointing. The user then says:

> "Create a blue square there."

The size of the square is not given explicitly in this example command; the default size, "medium," is used. A blue square appears on the spot where the user is pointing. There is no default color; some color from the preprogrammed parent ensemble of color names must be given. The same is true for shape.

Where the feed-back cursor is residing on the screen at the time the spoken "there" occurs becomes the spot where the to-be-created item is placed. The occurrence of the spoken "there" is thus functionally a "when"; that is, it serves as a "voice button" for the x, y cursor action of the pointing gesture.

Accordingly, a considerable pause before the occurrence of the "there" is permissible, i.e.:

> "Create a blue square . . . there."

The complete utterance in effect is a "call" to a Create routine, which routine expects certain parameters to be supplied. Before the user recites "there," the routine is parameter hung. The awaited parameter is input, completing the conjunction of x, y pointing input from the wrist-borne space sensor with the utterance "there."

Figure 2 shows the user having created a number of items on the screen before him.

### "Move . . ."

The user can readily move items about the screen, and has available a variety of ways in which to express the complete "move" command.

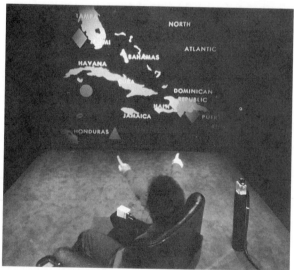

Figure 29.2. Talking and pointing to items on the Media Room's large screen. Here, the items are circle and diamond shapes being moved about against a backdrop of a Caribbean map. A double exposure effect catches two images of the user's right arm, strapped to which is the smaller of the pair of space-sensing cubes (covered by the user's cuff). On a pedestal to the right of the user chair is a lucite block, and to the top of this block is attached the larger transmitter cube.

Consider the user command:

> "Move the blue triangle to the right of the green square."

This example command relies on voice mode only. Should, for example, there exist only one triangle on the screen at the time the command is given, the adjective "blue" bears no information, and could be omitted; the same logic applies for the qualifier green in "green square."

We note in passing that in the phrase "... the green square," the attribute "green" as voiced is treated simply as part of the *name* of the item as originally created. That is, the color name is used in a *nominal* sense, as in Moscow's "Red Square," where "Red" is functionally part of a proper name, not a signal that we should expect a city square to be painted all in red.

Apropos of color, a more ambitious "interpretive" approach might be to map the utterance "green" to pixel values, the matching mediated through the classical CIE color space, partitioned into a number of referenceable regions. The partitioning of the CIE color space on the basis of an ensemble of color names could be programmer determined on an *ad hoc* basis, or the partitioning might involve a quite sophisticated calibration on the basis of having subject observers name or classify displayed colors. The essential point is that the mapping from attribute-name to item-attribute can be well defined, even though it may be as complex as one cares to attempt.

In any event, the result of the above command is that the blue triangle upon "hearing" its name, de-saturates as immediate feedback that it has been "addressed," disappears from its present site to re-appear centered in a spot to the right of the green square.

The exact positioning "to the right" is programmer determined in our version; some reasonable placement is executed. The meaning, intent and interpretation of relational expressions in graphic space is a complex issue [5, 6]; the important thing is that the item is now where the user has ordered it to be, and he can make minor modifications in position later.

Now, in our example action, the user might equally well have said:

"Move *that* to the right of the green square."

In this option, the user employs the pronoun "that," simultaneously pointing to what is intended, the pointing act being a motor analogue to the speech string: "... the blue triangle ...."

Notice that in this mode of giving the command, the user may not only omit the words "blue" and "triangle," he need not even know what the thing is, or what it is *called.* In our simple graphics world, what anything is, is in a subtle and interesting sense, *where* it is.

"That" is thus defined as whatever is pointed out; effectively, it is "ostensively defined" [7]. For the namer, at least, the process is not unlike that of telling a small child what things "are": for example, pointing at a cat, and saying "cat" or "kitty." The meaning of the word is given by indicating what is the intended referent in the context of alternatives, namely, whatever else is in the scene.

This process of "pronomialization" can readily be extended in our simple graphical example. The intended target spot to which the item is to be moved can be rendered as

"Put that *there*"

where there, now indicated by gesture, serves in lieu of the entire phrase "... to the right of the green square." The power of this function is even more general. The place description "... to the right of the green square" presupposes an item in the vicinity for reference: namely, the green square. There may be no plausible reference frame in terms of already extant items for a word description of where the moved item is to go. The intended spot, however, may readily be indicated by voice-and-pointing: there. In this function, as well as others, some variation in expression is understandably a valuable option; thus, a mini-thesaurus of common synonyms, such as "move," "put," "place," etc., is built into the vocabulary.

"Copy ..." as a command is simply a variant of the move action, except that the image of the item to be moved also remains in place at the original spot.

## "Make that . . ."

The attributes of any item in this graphic mini-universe that the user has called into existence by voice and gesture can be modified. Here, the attributes are those of color and size.

For example, the utterance:

"Make the blue triangle smaller"

causes the referenced item to become reduced in size. The mode of reference in this instance is via voice alone, but the user could as well have said, pointing to the desired item:

"Make *that* smaller ...."

The command:

"Make that a large blue diamond"

uttered while the user points at a small yellow circle causes the indicated transformation.

437

Extrapolations readily suggest themselves, e.g., the command line:

> "Make that (indicating some item) like that (indicating some other item)."

The second "that" is, functionally, a *when* to read the x, y coordinate of pointing. The item indicated when the second "that" is uttered becomes the "model" for change, and internally, the action is an expunging of the first referenced item, to be replaced in a "copy"-like fashion by the second referenced item.

## "Delete . . ."

The "delete" command (synonyms: "erase; expunge; take out . . .," etc.) allows the user to drop selected items from display.

As before, the "operand" of the command can be:

> ". . . the large blue circle"

or

> ". . . that" (pointing to some item).

Again, variations and extrapolations of the basic notion suggest themselves: global expunging, "clear" or "delete everything," in order to wipe the graphical slate clean; or "Delete everything to the left of this (drawing a line vertically down the face of the screen)."

## Naming

Consider a blue square that is present upon the screen. The user points to it, saying:

> "Call *that* . . . the calendar"

with the intention of later somehow elaborating the blue square at that node into a graphical "appointment book."

The initial portion of this utterance, "Call that . . . ," when processed by the recognizer unit results in codes being sent over to the host system signalling that a "naming" command has been issued. The x, y coordinates of what item is singled out by pointing are noted by the host system.

The host system then immediately directs the speech recognition unit to switch from "recognition mode" to "training mode" so that the recognizer will add the latter part of the utterance, ". . . the calendar," as a new entry in its file of word reference patterns. Upon completion of this action, the recognizer is directed to go back into recognition mode, to be ready for the next verbal input.

As the communications for switching the recognizer under host-system control between recognition and training modes currently takes a finite amount of real-time, a brief pause (indicated in the command above by three dots) must occur in the spoken command line to accommodate the time taken for the mode shift. However, the user tends to pause at precisely that point in the command line anyway, waiting for momentary desaturation of the blue square. This quick desaturation of an addressed item was noted earlier in this paper as being the system's way of giving visual feedback that the user has indeed "contacted" the item.

This spontaneous pause for feedback fortunately operates in this context to "mask" for the user the system's need for a pause in input. However, the *obligation* to pause represents to the system designer something of a breakdown in the general convenience of continuous *vs* discrete speech input. An eventual strategy for relieving the necessity for a user pause in speech is the augmentation of the "intelligence" resident in a speech recognizer unit so that it to some extent interprets as well as recognizes.

For example, upon the recognition of certain "key" words or phrases within the input utterance, the recognizer itself switches directly from recognition to training mode so that sub-portions of the input utterance are handled appropriately.

In the case of the "Call that . . ." or naming command, the action of the now "intelligent" recognizer would be in effect to truncate-off from the "front-end" of the original input speech signal that span of signal corresponding to successive recognized words of the command, the non-recognized residue of the speech line to be then assumed as the new name to be assimilated by the recognizer to its internal reference pattern lexicon. In order to maintain overall coordination with the host system, the recognizer would of course simultaneously transmit ASCII codes for recognized or learned words, together with any relevant "control" codes.

While such a strategy may eliminate the need for a within-sentence speaker pause, the general problem of "coarticulation" remains: the phonemic properties of the speech signal for any word are influenced by what words are spoken with it, what particular words precede or follow the word in question (Cf. reference 3, p. 518). Thus, while not required to pause, the speaker yet must enunciate very clearly, particularly when about to utter the new name to be added.

## Summary

The foregoing rudimentary set of commands, concerning themselves with the simple management of a limited ensemble of non-representative objects, is intended to suggest the versatility and ease of use that can enter upon the management of graphic space with voice and gesture. More real-life examples of commanding about "things" in a more meaningful space come readily to mind: moving ships about a harbor map in planning a harbor facility; moving battalion formations about as overlays on a terrain map; facilities planning, where rooms and hallways as rectangles are tried out "here" and "there."

The power of the described technique is that indications of what is to be done with these visible, out-there-on-view items can be expressed spontaneously and naturally in ways which are compatible with the spirit and nature of the display: one is pointing to them, addressing them in *spoken* words, not typed symbols.

Further, the *pronoun* as verbal tag achieves in the graphical world the same high usefulness it has in ordinary discourse by being pronounced in the presence of a pointed to, visible graphic which functionally defines its meaning.

Acknowledgements

The programming and systems expertise of Chris Schmandt and Eric Hulteen underlay the implementation and development of the concepts described in this paper. Their efforts are duly appreciated.

The work reported herin has been supported by the Cybernetics Technology Division of the Defense Advanced Research Projects Agency, under Contract No. MDA-903-77-C-0037.

References

1. Negroponte, N. The Media Room. Report for ONR and DARPA. MIT, Architecture Machine Group, Cambridge, MA, December 1978.

2. Bolt, R.A. Spatial Data-Management. DARPA Report. MIT, Architecture Machine Group, Cambridge, MA, March 1979.

3. Reddy, D.R. "Speech recognition by machine: a review." *Proceeding of the IEEE*, 64, 4 (April 1976), 501–531.

4. Robinson, A.L. "More people are talking to computers as speech recognition enters the real world." (Research News) (First of two articles) *Science*, 203, (16 February 1979), 634–638.

5. Sondeheimer, N.K. "Spatial reference and natural-language machine control." *International Journal of Man-Machine Studies*, 8, (1976), 329–336.

6. Winston, P. Learning structural descriptions from examples. MIT Project MAC, TR-76, 1970.

7. Olson, D.R. "Language and thought: Aspects of a cognitive theory of semantics." *Psychological Review*, 77, (1970), 257–273.

# 30. [Introduction]

## From *Literary Machines*

# Proposal for a Universal Electronic Publishing System and Archive

Xanadu is the archetypal dream of a hypermedia network—a reverie related to that of Vannevar Bush's memex, and still dreamed in current imaginations of the Internet. The following excerpt is from *Literary Machines*, Ted Nelson's most complete outline of his Xanadu project and the concepts behind it.

In this vision, in a not-so-distant future, we will read and write (view and draw, hear and compose) almost everything from and to a world-spanning computer network. Everyone will have the ability to produce their own documents and connect them to any other public documents. The author may constantly create new versions of her own documents, and individuals may create their own versions of any public document, including the creation of new documents that include by reference elements of many documents by many authors; public connections made between one version of one document and another version of another will usually automatically place themselves in all the extant versions. Historical backtrack and degradation-proof storage will allow us to visit any version, any moment in the network's history. Xanadu is the ultimate archive—with each element of this archive, however, constantly in process; viewed in hierarchies, and yet with alternative hierarchies always available; with the back end (knowledge structure) and front end (depiction for the current display device) abstracted and split apart so that each user may have her preferred view of the information. Xanadu combines the benefits of anarchy with a strength derived from an initial, powerful central design; the aim was to be general enough to support nearly any imaginable media eventuality.

The Web offers a slice of this vision—the anarchy half. Anarchy alone has turned out to be rich and exciting. Especially since the most recent dot-com crash, it seems that those on the Web are returning to the emphasis that led to the initial Web explosion: a vast free sharing of information. This view of the Web is of a digital library, or a new public commons. Further, reports seem to indicate that, in the U.S. at any rate, the digital divide is at last shrinking, with more of the population at all levels of wealth able to access this commons. An infectious optimism (perhaps better grounded than earlier giddiness about the Internet) has found its way back into many who have been using the Web since the early or mid 1990s. (Though, as Lawrence Lessig argues in *The Future of Ideas*, recent changes in the Internet's legal and technical infrastructure have been designed to undercut the possibility of such openness.)

Now a number of groups and individuals are trying to provide the other half of the hypermedia dream, in a manner compatible with the Web's evolution. The World Wide Web Consortium (W3C), for example, is designing more powerful standards for software that will begin to implement some of the features found in systems such as Xanadu: links of multiple types, into specific document locations that need not be pre-marked with anchors; the ability to find resources by name, rather than URL; and further separation of front end and back end functions.

Meanwhile, Nelson has opened the source code for two of the never-released versions of Xanadu, demonstrating that many of the innovations he discussed had in fact already been implemented and removing the secrecy around the specifics of Xanadu technologies such as its unique file and address systems. He is now working to, as he has said, "turn Xanadu inside out" in order to make many of the capabilities described in the pages below available to the average Web user.

The Xanadu vision informs Stuart Moulthrop's "You Say You Want a Revolution?" (◊48). Moulthrop's essay was influential in pointing out the potential for a Xanadu operating company to be taken over by an unscrupulous multinational.

While the copy-protected e-book concept was spiraling unspectacularly toward failure early in 2001, MIT announced its OpenCourseWare (OCW) initiative. OCW will work, over the next 10 years, to place information from as many of MIT's courses as possible onto the Web to make them freely available.

*Lawrence Lessig, from* The Future of Ideas *(217):*

The content layer—the ability to use content and ideas—is closing. It is closing without a clear showing of the benefit this closing will provide and with a fairly clear showing of the harms it will impose. . . . Mindless locking up of resources that spur innovation. Control without reason. . . . When the only innovation that will be allowed is what Hollywood permits, we will not see innovation. That lesson, at least, we have already seen.

441

◊48
691

Nelson has also recently unveiled an idea he calls "ZigZag"—which he conceptualized at roughly the same time as hypertext, and planned to pursue once hypertext was widely accepted (a moment that has now arrived, at least in some form). As conceptually radical now as hypertext must have seemed when it was first described, ZigZag can most simplistically be described as organizing digital information in a form similar to an n-dimensional spreadsheet. The result convincingly overturns such "natural" information structures as the simple hierarchical tree. For example, instead of a traditional family tree, which can only preserve its simple hierarchy by portraying women as spontaneously generated, a ZigZag family tree allows for the representation and traversal of the kinship relationships of both men and women, as well as allowing for remarriage and other real-world complexities that current data structures are hard pressed to represent except through inelegant kludges.

◊42
613

If these efforts are successful, one major difference remaining will be that the original Xanadu vision also included a company that was to operate the network. Nelson envisioned and characterized this company as another utility: the company that makes sure information comes out when you turn on the faucet. Even before California was held hostage by utility companies, and before the Enron scandals, this part of the vision was disturbing to many—for two reasons. First, information is much more sensitive than our water, vulnerable to immoral monitoring and illegal misuse, and easier to adulterate without attracting notice. A company created with the best intentions might be taken over by less scrupulous individuals, and certainly, many new media companies have been taken over by individuals with radically different values from their founders. Second, while the excitement produced by the Xanadu vision and the Web's reality is connected to the ideals of the library and the public square, 30 years ago (when computers were more expensive and less common) Nelson had to imagine a way to make his vision viable as a computer network and publishing medium. His solution was to charge those who participated in the network a small amount for each piece of information they accessed, just as a utility charges for each amount of water or electricity used, but in this case with most of the payment returning to the owners of the viewed material's copyright, and the remainder going toward continued support of the network. "Micropayment" is still pursued as a model by some, but as the network has increasingly become a central place for our reading and writing, a new issue has come to the fore. The societal vision we have embodied in public libraries and public schools is that everyone should be able to read and write ("produce" and "consume" information) regardless of their level of income. The concept of micropayment now threatens to move our future information life toward the model of pay-per-view cable and away from that of the library. Hopefully our culture's attachment to the promise of libraries is too great to allow this to happen—a prospect for which the success of the Web holds out hope. In a way, this is what the history of the Web has demonstrated more than anything else—that the world desires an online hypertext-enabled library, however anarchic, unstable, and limited by its design it may be.
—NWF

Nelson continues to be one of micropayment's most persuasive advocates, arguing that his "transcopyright" vision, if adopted, would allow for a new era of artistic and scholarly exploration to replace the increasingly messy intellectual property tangle that now blights the media landscape. It would make possible, on the level of legality, Web usage that operates in what Michael Joyce calls a "constructive" mode (◊42).

Nelson's book is written as a type of "stretchtext"—it may be read at a high level by only reading the tops of the pages. It may be read in more detail by reading the top and middle, and in its greatest depth by reading all of every page. The selection that follows includes all of some pages and just the tops of others; a few are left out entirely, unstretched.

Further Reading

Berners-Lee, Tim, with Mark Fishetti. *Weaving the Web: The Original Design and Ultimate Destiny of the World Wide Web, by Its Inventor*. San Francisco: Harper, 1999.

Lessig, Lawrence. *The Future of Ideas*. New York: Random House, 2001.

Lukka, Tuomas, and Katariina Ervasti. "GZigZag: A Platform for CyberText Experiments" *CyberText Yearbook 2000*, ed. Markku Eskelinen and Raine Koskimaa. Saarijärvi, Finland: Research Center for Contemporary Culture/Publications, 2001.

Nelson, Ted. "The New Xanadu Structure for the Web." <http://xanadu.com/nxu/>

Nelson, Ted. "What's on My Mind" Invited talk at the first Wearable Computer Conference, Fairfax, Va., May 12–13, 1998. Linked from <http://www.xanadu.com>.

Original Publication

Excerpts from chapter 2 of *Literary Machines*. Sausalito, Calif.: Mindful Press, 1981.

# From *Literary Machines*
# Proposal for a Universal Electronic Publishing System and Archive

## Theodor H. Nelson

We are all agreed that your theory is crazy. The question which divides us is whether it is crazy enough to have a chance of being correct. My own feeling is that it is not crazy enough.

—Niels Bohr, quoted in Kenneth Brower, *The Starship and the Canoe,* 46

**1 An Electronic Literary System**
**2 What is Literature?**
**3 A True Storage System for Text and Other Evolving Structures**
**4 A Linking System for Text and Other Data**
**5 The Document Convention**
**6 Compound Documents**

**7 Electronic Publishing:**
   Making the Literary System Universal
**8 Distribution and Networking**
**9 Vital Issues**

## Plan of This Chapter

This chapter is in nine sections, which introduce and elaborate on a very particular and precise design and plan. This chapter, design and plan are the heart of this book, a crossroad through which you are asked to pass repeatedly.

Some readers, especially those who may not have given these matters any thought, may find this material tough sledding the first time through. Therefore a summary level has been provided. (The bigger type.) Stick to that the first time through, or if you're in a hurry later on.

If this chapter is long and tedious to read, that is only because it strives for completeness. I am sure that a few years from now everything in it will be quickly divined by small children sitting at a console which enacts these principles.

## 1 An Electronic Literary System

Here is the right way to do something by computer: first figure out what you *really* want to do and think about, instead of staying bogged down in what you usually do and think about when you don't use a computer.

For instance, we are going to look at ways of dealing with text based on its "true" structure, if we can figure out what that is.

### 1

What will be described here is the way we think information should be handled. In the later sections of the chapter we will be describing the detailed *idea* of it, the conceptual structure or *virtuality*. This chapter is only about this idea, without technicalities. (The few "computer technicalities" are in footnotes.)

We also believe that we have carried out this design in a practical form, and that it will shortly exist as a functioning computer program with many uses. This belief will be proven or disproven in the fullness of time. Meanwhile, what is really being described is what we think we have created. Believing that this is the right virtuality, it is what we have implemented.

The footnotes contain a few kibitzing remarks to those interested in how we have done it.*

### The Design

It is difficult to describe an interactive computer system so people can visualize it. Most people have not had practice in visualizing jumping and responding objects on the basis of abstract descriptions.

When we say also that we think this design is simple and basic, like the telephone, that may be hard for some readers to believe, considering that it takes so many words to describe it. Yet we think this design, once understood, is spare, parsimonious and clear. (And that a few years from now, small children will understand it immediately when they get a chance to play with it.)

The structure of documents and links to be described here is, for a computer system, unusually simple. This is all there is; we will describe it completely. We regard the simplicity of this design as its greatest virtue. The user has no direct contact with technicalities. The technicalities underneath are simply the means whereby certain exact and simple services are rapidly performed.

### The Intrinsic Structure Is What You Should See

The structure a user sees should be the *intrinsic* structure of his material, and not (as in many "word processing" systems) some amalgam combining the material itself with some set of obtrusive conventions under which it is stored.

What the thing *is*—its natural structure to the user—is what he should see and work on: nothing else. It is therefore the representation of this structure—of whatever structure the user may be concerned with—that should concern us. However, the complexities of what may be wanted can be staggering. So the problem is to create a general representation and storage system that will permit automatic storage of all structures a user might want to work on, and the faithful accounting of their development.

### World and Viewpane: Back and Front Ends

While computer display screens are to be the foci of our coming society, what the world is that will *show* on the screens is perhaps of greater concern.

The question in computerizing anything, then, should be *what is the true structure?* Having answered that, you design a system that stores and shows that true structure.

Storage is fundamental. What you store should be the basic structure of the information you are dealing with—not some tricky arrangement that is carefully matched to some set of programs or hardware. (How you will look at this world when it is spreadeagled on your screen is your own business: you control it by your choice of screen hardware, by your choice of viewing program, by what you do as you watch. But the structure of that world is the same from screen to screen.)

What we will discuss here is representation of the true structure of a certain kind of information, now how to show it. We believe that an orderly overall system can be developed for most types of written and graphical information and its instantaneous delivery.

*The project Xanadu Group has for some time been developing software to do what is described here with no complications for the user. Our way of seeing the world, as described here, is reflected in many ways in our unusual data structure.

To do efficiently what will be described here, we have had to overthrow all conventions and conventional assumptions about data handling and indexing, building from the bottom up a system that we think can grow indefinitely without choking on retrieval and transmission bottlenecks.

And we are going to create a service that simply stores and sends back different excerpts from this "true" structure of text.

## 2 What Is Literature?
Literature is an ongoing system of interconnecting documents.

That is the storage system we will be discussing here. Think of it as a "back-end" service that can supply your system. At the screen of your computer you explore what is stored, change it, add to it. The service we propose takes care of putting it away and sending you whatever part you ask for as fast as possible. That is the back end. What computer you watch it through, and how *that* machine is programmed, is your "front end"—a separate problem.

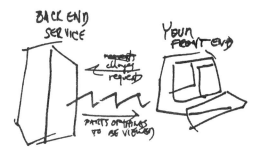

This is a VIRTUALITY. One of the principles of designing virtuality is that there are many possible overall organizations that may be very similar. The problem of choosing among them is not simple. The tricky words that follow, "true structure," suggest utter uniqueness. But this is not the only "true" design. It is the design suggested by the one working precedent that we know of: literature.

Whether it is a good and right *design* is the central question for the reader to judge. What we describe can be done: if not by us, then by somebody sometime. But if it is not the right system, then it is on the reader's shoulders to come up with a better one.

Suggestions are welcome—*if* you are sure you understand this design first.

We believe we have achieved this in our unique proprietary software. We could only carry out this design with the help of certain technical developments which are for the present proprietary and secret. A number of radical discoveries in the field of computer indexing and retrieval render it possible to offer these services within seconds on configurations of present-day equipment, even, we believe, as the number of documents and service requests expands to astronomical figures.

## 2
### The Literary Paradigm
A piece of writing—say, a sheet of typed paper on the table—looks alone and independent. This is quite misleading. Solitary it may be, but it is probably also part of a literature.

By "a literature" we do not mean anything necessarily to do with belles-lettres or leather-bound books. We mean it in the same broad sense of "the scientific literature," or that graduate-school question, "Have you looked at the literature?"

A literature is *a system of interconnected writings*. We do not offer this as our definition, but as a discovered fact. And almost all writing is part of some literature.

The way people write is based in large part on these interconnections.

A person reads an article. He says to himself, "Where have I seen something like that before? Oh yes—" and the previous connection is brought mentally into play.

Consider how it works in science. A genetic theorist, say, reads current writings in the journals. These refer back, explicitly, to other writings; if he chooses to question the sources, or review their meaning, he is *following links* as he gets the books and journals and refers to them. He may correspond with colleagues, mentioning in his letters what he has read, and receiving replies suggesting that he read other things. (Again, the letters are implicitly connected to these other writings by implicit links.) Seeking to refresh his ideas, he goes back to Darwin, and also derives inspiration from other things he reads—the Bible, science fiction. These are linked to his work in his mind.

In his own writing he quotes and cites the things he has read. (Again, explicit links are being made.) Other readers, taking interest in his sources, read them (following his links).

In our Western cultural tradition, writings in principle remain continuously available—both as recently quoted, and in their original inviolable incarnations—in a great procession.

So far we have stressed some of the processes of referral and linkage. But also of great importance are controversy and disagreement and reevaluation.

Everyone argues over the interpretation of former writings, even our geneticists. One author will cite (or link to) a passage in Darwin to prove Darwin thought one thing, another will find another passage to try to prove he thought another.

And views of a field, and the way a field's own past is viewed within it, change. A formerly forgotten researcher may come to light (like Mendel), or a highly respected researcher may be discredited (Cyril Burt). And so it goes, on and on. The past is continually changing—or at least seems to be, as we view it.

There is no predicting the use future people will make of what is written. Any summary, any particular view, is exactly that: the perspective of a particular individual (or school of thought) at a particular time. We cannot know how things will be seen in the future. We can assume there will never be a final and definitive view of anything.

And yet this system functions.

### Literature Is Debugged.

In other words, even though in every field there is an ever-changing flux of emphasis and perspective and distortion, and an ever-changing fashion in content and approach, the ongoing mechanism of written and published text furnishes a flexible vehicle for this change, continually adapting. Linkage structure between documents forms a flux of invisible threads and rubber bands that hold the thoughts together.

Linkage structure and its ramifications are surprisingly similar in the world of business.

A business letter will say, "In reply to your letter of the 13th . . ." Or a business form, another key communication, may say in effect, "In response to your order of the 24th of last month, we can supply only half of what you have asked for, but can fill the rest of the order with such-and-such item from our catalog." All of these citations may be thought of as cross-linkages among documents.

The point is clear, whether in science or business or *belles lettres*. Within bodies of writing, everywhere, there are linkages we tend not to see. The individual document, at hand, is what we deal with; we do not see the total linked collection of them all at once. But they are there, the documents not present as well as those that are, and the grand cat's-cradle among them all.

From this fundamental insight, we have endeavored to create a system for text editing and retrieval that will receive, and handle, and present, documents with links between them. We believe there is something very right about the existing system of literature; indeed we suspect that there are things right about it that we don't even know, as with Nature. And so we have tried to mirror, and replicate, and extend, existing literary structure as we have here described it.

## 3 A True Storage System for Text and Other Evolving Structures

We are going to propose a way of keeping information that may seem odd and inefficient at first, but turns out to have remarkable power later on.

Under many circumstances the writer, or "text user," needs to reach back to a former condition. This is in the nature of creative work.

### 3

### Prologue: Making Extra Copies All the Time

In most computer applications (such as the layman's newest game, "word processing"), it is often necessary to keep repeated copies. This frequent and disagreeable problem has several purposes.

The obvious purpose, often thwarted, is to assure the safety of recent work against various kinds of accident. But that can be gradually ruled out: many systems are coming to make reliable "safety copies" automatically.

A more fundamental use is to keep track of former states of the work, in case mistakes or wrong decisions need to be undone. This need, *backtrack,* is serious and important. We do not need to go back through previous material often, but if we need to do it at all we ought to be able to do it right. Here is what doing it right entails.

### Department of Redundancy Department

Note, however, that the conventional means of storage is rather silly. It involves making a complete copy of everything you've done so far. If what you're doing is making repeated small changes and additions, then you are repeatedly storing the same material, redundantly.

Virtually all of computerdom is built around this curious convention.* Most computer people will tell you that is the way God intended computers to be used.

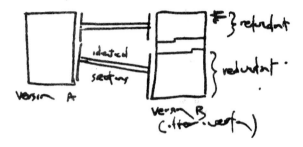

However, we can program computers any way we like, if we throw out the system software, and what we are talking about is creating *new* ways of doing things.

### The Alternative

Suppose we create instead an automatic storage system that takes care of all changes and backtrack automatically. As a user makes changes, the changes go directly into the storage system; filed, as it were, chronologically.** Now with the proper sort of indexing scheme, the storage facility we've mentioned ought also to be able to deal with the problem of historical backtrack.

Think of it this way. An evolving document is really not just a block of text characters, Scrabble™ tiles all in a row; it is an ongoing changing flux. Think of its progress through time as a sort of braid or vortex.

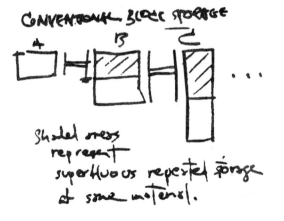

---

*Including block-transfer circuitry, most display buffering, and the disk routines supplied with conventional operating systems.

**(Of course, since the storage system assimilates all changes, it becomes nearly the whole "word processor," except for the user's front end.)

The true storage of text should be in a system that stores each change and fragment individually, assimilating each change as it arrives, but keeping the former changes; integrating them all by means of an indexing method that allows any previous instant to be reconstructed.

This can be done efficiently if the user is reading from a computer screen; since you can set up the

Think of the process of making editorial changes as re-twisting this braid when its parts are rearranged, added or subtracted,

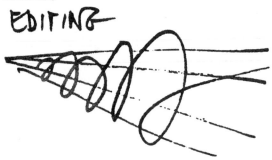

and think then of successive versions of the document, at successive instants of time, as *slices* in this space-time vortex.

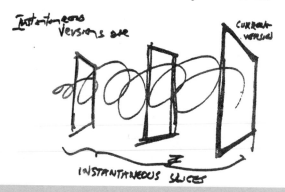

Very well: the file management system we are talking about automatically keeps track of the changes and the pieces, so that when you ask for a given part of a given version at a given time, it comes to your screen.

The user may then refer not merely to the *present* version of the document; he or she may go back in time to any previous version. The user must also be able to follow a specific section back through time, and study its previous states.

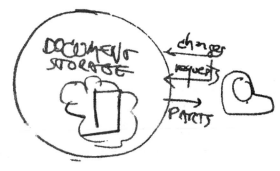

## Part-Pounce

This system is built around the assumption that you are reading from a screen, not from paper. When you "go to a certain part" of a document, that whole document is not ready to show; yet the system gives you that *part* instantly, *assembling it on the run* from the many fragments of its actual storage.*

We call this *pounce*. You pounce like a cat on a given thing, and it seems to be there, having been constructed while you are, as it were, in midair. Unlike things which *dematerialize* when you pounce on them, like cotton candy, this *materializes* when you pounce on it. I can think of no other example, except perhaps Potemkin villages.

You get *the part you want next*; the mistake of the conventional computer field has been to assume that the whole document had to be formed and ready.

*Obviously such a system departs from conventional "block" storage, and rather stores material in fragments under control of a master directory indexing by time,—and other factors.

system to reconstruct hastily any piece that is wanted at the instant it is wanted. THE PART YOU WANT COMES WHEN YOU ASK FOR IT.

This is the *true* structure of text, because text is best viewed as an evolving, Protean structure.

Such storage permits easy reconstruction of previous states for mental clarification, fresh starts, and transfusions of previous ideas. It also

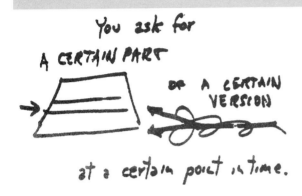

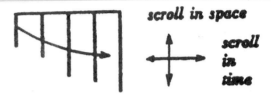

## Another Visualization

The canonical documents in this system can store the same material in numerous different versions—as, for example, in the successive drafts of a novel.

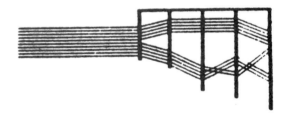

While the user of a customary editing or word processing system may scroll through an individual document, the user of this system may scroll in time as well as space, watching the changes in a given passage as the system enacts its successive modifications.

Versions of a document set apart for other reasons—"alternative" versions—may likewise be flipped through or efficiently compared side by side.

We call this system of storage Prismatic because we may think of a given part, or section, as being prismatically refracted when we pass from one version to another. We believe our Prismatic storage can support virtually instantaneous retrieval of any portion of any version (historical or alternative).

**449**

This method stores the document canonically as a system of evolving and alternative versions, instantly constructed as needed from the stored fragments, pointers and lists of our unusual data structure. Thus there is no "main" version of a thing, just the ongoing accumulation of

pieces and changes, some of whose permutations have names and special linkages. In other words, our system treats all versions of a document as views extracted from the same aggregated object. It will be readily apparent that the only way to do this is effectively to have direct track-and-sector access to the disk system.

permits multiple uses of the same materials for alternative versions and "boilerplate."

This same approach—storage as an evolving structure with backtrack—may be extended to all forms of data that are created by individuals.

Pictures, and graphical data structures created at a screen, evolve in the same way and should be stored in the same way.

## Alternative Versions

This same scheme can be expanded to allow alternative versions—more than one arrangement of the same materials, a facility that writers and programmers would certainly use if it were readily available. Alternative versions (or *Alts*) are also important in many boilerplate applications, such as law and public relations, where the same materials are churned out repeatedly in different arrangements and variations. A master indexing scheme could greatly reduce storage requirements in these applications, as well as make the relations among the Alts much clearer.*

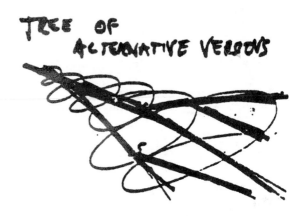

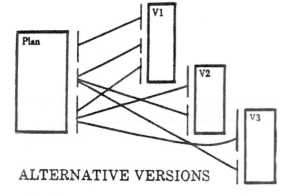

## ALTERNATIVE VERSIONS

Actually, we may best visualize these alternative versions as a tree in the ongoing braid, a forking arrangement whereby one document becomes two, each of these daughter documents may in turn become others, etc.

## Sameness and Difference Display

Of course, a facility that holds multiple versions of the same material, and allows historical backtrack, is not terribly useful unless it can help you intercompare them in detail—unless it can show you, word for word, what parts of two versions are the same.**

Lawyers need this to compare wordings. Congressmen need this to compare different draft versions of bills. Authors need it to see what has happened to specific passages in their writings between drafts. Biologists and anatomists need it to compare corresponding parts of animals (assuming a graphical data base of physiology that shows evolving structure).

This is in contradistinction to conventional operating systems, from CP/M to OS/370, which typically deliver the whole file on every request. The illustration depicts the operating system as Frankenstein's monster with a silver tray. (These features may usually be *defeated,* but that's another matter.)

And storage space is saved by not having to keep redundant parts. This in itself is not very important.

*By arranging for alternative versions to share common storage of the document's fragments, again we save space.

**(Such intercomparisons would in a more conventional system require writing and invoking search commands of some complexity among the various related files.)

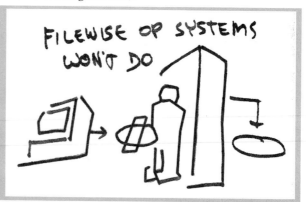

> As a first step we propose such an evolutionary structure, the *docuplex*, as the basic storage structure for electronic literature.

## Any Forms of Data

This storage and indexing by pieces and changes works not merely for text; it can be used for any forms of data structure.

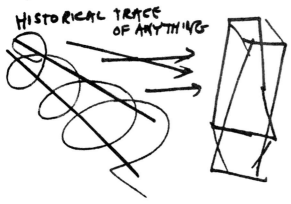

HISTORICAL TRACE OF ANYTHING

Thus if you are designing a building on a computer screen, as architects now do, you may browse through the changing design in the sequence you modified it over time, and create alternative versions as you like which share the common material.

*Example.* An excellent airplane, the Boeing 747, now exists in a dozen or more versions that you may order from the factory. Complex blueprints exist for each of these versions, as well as lists of parts, etc. (Much of this is kept on computers as 3D data structures at Boeing, and perhaps quite well; this is simply a convenient example, and no criticism is intended.)

Using the data structures and programs we have described, it is possible to store all the 747 designs *as one unified data pool,* with the forking-version facility reading the variant designs directly out of this single structure.

## Simplicity One

By creating such a capable storage system, we have greatly simplified the life of the text user. The nuisance of backup (and the spurious nonsense-talk of finding *names* for backup files) are eliminated. But more important, we have unified all versions (previous and alternative) in a unified structure, the *docuplex,* permitting part-pounce on present, past and variant structures. The user may scroll through any two versions to see corresponding parts; and much more.

## Stage One All Together

I have so far presented several new capabilities that I think are important: *alternative versions* and *historical backtrack,* both with *sameness display;* and *links.*

These work together; they have to. The links allow the creation of non-sequential writings, bookmarks and jump-structured graphics of many kinds. But if you are going to have links you really need historical backtrack and alternative versions.

Why? Because if you make some links on Monday and go on making changes, perhaps on Wednesday you'd like to follow these links into the present version. They'd better still be attached to the right parts, even though the parts may have moved. And the sameness-display allows complex linked alternatives to be studied and intercompared in depth.

So let us call this Stage One: a system of computer storage that holds pieces of a thing, not big blocks, and assembles them instantly into whatever part of whatever version you ask for; that allows you to create links of any kind you want between any things you want; and shows you which parts are the same between related versions.

Let us call such a storage system a hyperfile.

You don't *have* to use these facilities. You can store text in long blocks if you wish. But if the facility is there, then the people who need it can use it.

Perhaps most important, these facilities provide a building-block for what is to be described in what follows.

451

## 4 A Linking System for Text and Other Data

Assuming that we are storing materials in such an evolutionary structure, the creation of "links" to the material becomes much easier.

### 4

### Links Are Part of the Writing

A link is simply a connection between parts of text or other material. It is put in by a human. Links are made by individuals as pathways for the reader's exploration; thus they are parts of the actual document, part of the writing.

As perhaps the simplest type of link, a user may create *bookmarks*—places he may want to re-enter text returning to it.

### Jump-Link

As another simple first example, let us simply think of a link as some sort of a jump opportunity, like a conventional footnote. An asterisk, say, signals that "there's something to jump to from here." If you point at it with your lightpen (or mouse or whatever), Bingo!—you're now at the footnote, or whatever else the author took you to. If you don't like it there, hit some sort of a Return Button and it pops your previous address from a stack, so here you are back where you were and no harm has been done.

### Marginal Notes, Side-By-Side Writing

Marginal notes are another simple and important type of link. (Where the "margin" of the screen is—that is, how to show them—is a matter particular to your own screen setup.)

You may want links for commentaries, bookmarks and placemarkers, footnotes , marginal notes, hypertext jumps and innumerable other uses; but they are very hard to keep in place with conventional computer storage structure.*

A user may also make side-by-side connections of other types. On contemplating any two pieces of text, he may make a link between them. Thereafter, when he displays either piece of text, and *asks to see the links,* a link-symbol is displayed, and the other attached text—if he wishes to see it.

### PARALLEL LINKED TEXT

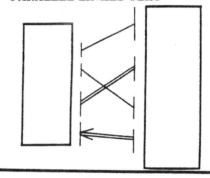

Naturally, making a marginal note consists of writing the note and hooking the link.

### Hypertext

The link facility given us much more than the attachment of mere odds and ends. It permits fully non-sequential writing, or hypertext.

## JUMPING ON A LINK

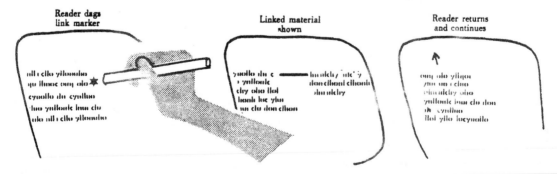

---

**\*LINKS + PRISMATICS → USABILITY**

Most computer schemes for linkage face the terrible problem of "updating" the links as text is modified and successive versions come into being. The present scheme dodges this problem smartly (at least at the local level): a link is attached, not to a positional address in a given version, but to specific characters, and simply stays with them wherever they go. Thus Prismatic storage solves a considerable problem.

However, the evolutionary storage we have already described allows any links to be associated firmly with the pieces of data in any evolving structure, wherever those pieces may migrate to as changes occur.

And any types of links may be created.

This simple facility—the jump-link capability—leads immediately to all sorts of new text forms: for scholarship, for teaching, for fiction, for hyper-poetry. This makes possible a certain free-form serendipitous browsing.

to-span, and span-to-span, having any separate names and functions desired. We also allow links with multiple endpoints.

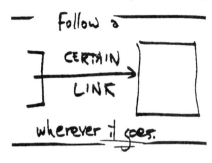

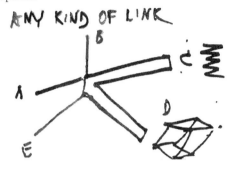

## Any Types of Links

A proper system should allow any types of link whatever, and there are myriads of types.

In principle we allow any types of link to be defined by the sophisticated user. These include point-to-point links, point-

## End-Sets

Links may attach to other links. Thus we have the concept of an *end-set*, the several types of object that a given link may attach to.

Consider, for example, an arbitrary type of link which we may call a "wuffle." A wuffle, let us say, connects a span of

Thus the link stays where you put it through historical backtrack and in alternative versions—if you choose to see it.

Essentially, the link seizes a point or span (or any other structure) in the Prismatic Document and holds to it. Links may be refractively followed from a point or span in one version to corresponding places in any other version. Thus a link to one version of a Prismatic Document is a link to all versions.

The effects, then, of links, alts and backtrack are in some sense multiplicative: together they give you a united facility of great power.

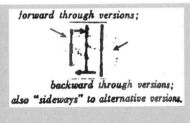

*forward through versions;*

*backward through versions;*

*also "sideways" to alternative versions.*

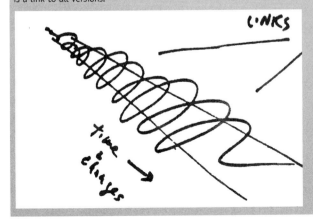

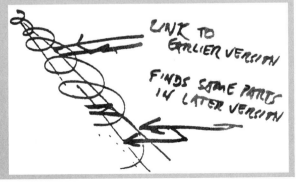

text, a picture, and a footnote. These are the *endparts;* together they constitute a wuffle's *end-set.*

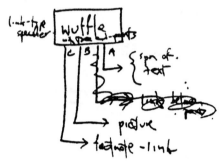

Directionality, if any, is given in the link-type definition. Note that end-parts may not hang together as they evolve (e.g. text sections):

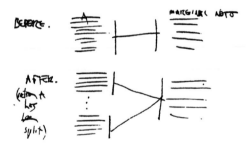

## Links and Front Ends

How to *show* links is a Front-End Function. So is the problem of keeping track of where you have been as you browsed; the front end must manage your stacks for you.

## Linking Amongst All Data Types

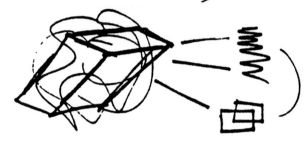

It is vital that a general system not have restrictions. For instance, why should you just have links on *text?* We believe you should be able to put footnotes and marginal notes on pictures, on music—on any forms of data.

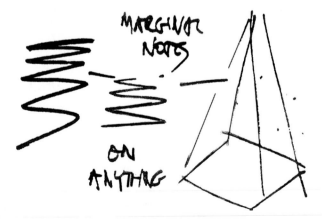

## 5 The Document Convention

From these beginnings, it will be possible to create many levels of organization and overlay—but first we will adopt by convention a fundamental unit.

We will call this unit a "document." It has an owner and (ordinarily) a name.

It normally consists of *contents*—text, graphics, music, etc.—and links to other documents.

Every link, then, is part of a document.

Putting it another way, a document consists of its contents and its out-links.

And that's all.

## 6 Compound Documents

This ground rule allows us to have complex multi-level document structures—criss-crossing superdocuments of many parts—collected in new structural wholes.

### 6

Once you have the package, the docuplex that allows linkage and backtrack, why not extend it?

Why not allow anyone to create links *between* documents, allowing you to jump straight from one to another?

Given the exact document boundaries and ownership already mentioned, we can now create an orderly arrangement permitting far more complex documents to be stored. We also provide an arrangement allowing other individuals freely to make their own modifications on the stored documents. This we do by allowing so-called "compound documents."

The logic of these compound documents is simple and derives from the concept of document ownership. The integrity of this document is maintained; no one may change it but the owner.

But someone else may create a document which quotes it as much as desired. This mechanism we call the *quote-window* or *quote-link*. Through a "window" in the new document we see a portion of the old.

WINDOWS

455

> Each *collection* is likewise a document, and likewise has an owner.

> Document A can *include* Document B, even though Document B is *owned by* someone else.

Thus a new document may *consist of* the quote-links and new material, if any.

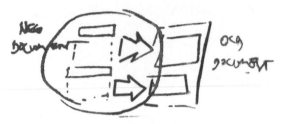

Through the same document conventions, the compound structures mentioned earlier maintain the same conventions of integrity and ownership.

The secondary document, too, has its own integrity, though the windowed materials are still part of the original document.

A document may have a window to another document, and that one to yet another, indefinitely. Thus A contains part of B, and so on. One document can be built upon another, and yet another document can be built upon that one, indefinitely: each having links to what was already in place.

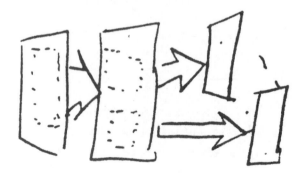

Anything stored by one user on the system may be quoted—adopted into a document—by another person writing on the system (provided the second user has legitimate access). This freedom of windowing applies, of course, to all forms of data, including pictures, musical notation, etc.

Think of the present document as a sheet of glass. It may have writing painted on it by the present author; it may have windows to something else, in turn made of more layers of painted glass, with writing on each.

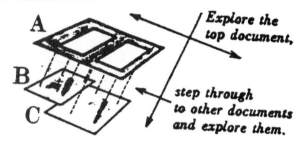

A reader may either explore the immediate document, or "step though the window" to explore the next document, or the one beyond. After exploring a further document, the reader may return to the one that showed him into it, or proceed on tangents that become available.

By this simple, sweeping mechanism, all manner of different requirements and specialized uses are reduced to a single structure. Each layer of windows may have, as it were, colored cellophane or opaquing on it. Only when you *step through* the window—which you always may at any time—do you reach the original. But stepping through the window means turning one glass page and going on in the next. Now you are in another work.

*Example.* The annual report of a corporation has a brief paragraph on every division of the company, with summary operating figures for the year. These paragraphs and figures are quoted from other documents which explain the matters more fully; the reader may easily step through to study them further.

*Example.* A children's story is illustrated with pictures. If the child wants to "reach through the window," each picture is found to be part of a larger picture, with another story attached.

The windows of a windowing document are themselves actually particular links between documents. No copy is made of the quoted material; rather, a quote-link symbol (or its essential equivalent) is placed in the stored symbol-train of the quoting document, since no copy is made. Nor does it affect the ownership.

(Note that these methods of storage save a great deal of space, if the same material is used in numerous documents.)

The use of the special links dramatically simplifies a host of problems.

No copying operations are required among the documents throughout the system, and thus the problems of distributed update, so familiar throughout the computer world, are obviated. (But they do reappear on a later level.)

Since quoted material only has to reside in its place of origin, and not in the other documents that quote it, other documents that quote it may be automatically "updated" when its owner changes it.

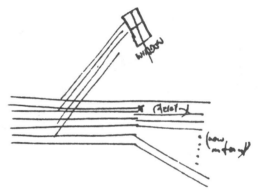

Note also, however, that a window may be fixed to a document at a certain point in time, in which case revisions

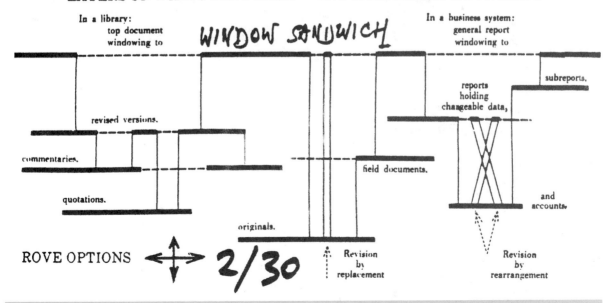

**LAYERS OF WINDOWING TEXT.** Each horizontal line is a document.

WINDOW SANDWICH

In a library:
top document
windowing to

revised versions.

commentaries.

quotations.

originals.

In a business system:
general report
windowing to

subreports,

reports
holding
changeable data,

field documents.

and
accounts.

ROVE OPTIONS 2/30

Revision
by
replacement

Revision
by
rearrangement

are seen by the user only when he asks, "What has this passage become?"

## Derivative Documents

The integrity of each document is maintained by these separations: derivative documents are permanently defined in terms of the originals and the changes. (And stored on that basis.)

A document may consist merely of changes to another document. Thus the modified Gettysburg Address published in *MAD* by Doodles Weaver may be thought of as two documents: the original, and the changes.

## Alternative Versions by Non-Owners

A document owner may create alternative arrangements of the same material, all *within* the same document.*

Another user, however, is free to create his own alternative version of the document he does not own. This, then, becomes a *windowing* document using the same materials.

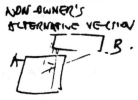

## Intercomparison Documents

A document that points out relations between other documents we may call an "intercomparison document."

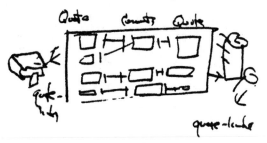

Such documents may be easily created, say, to point out relations between the Bible and the Dead Sea Scrolls.

## Compounding of Other Link Types

Any other link type (beside windows) may likewise go from one document to another, and interweave with quote-links.

Note that *links*, like text and pictures, *may be quoted*.

These structures may of course nest. This makes possible compound documents to any remove, where one document links to another, and so on. One document, embracing another, takes it into itself.

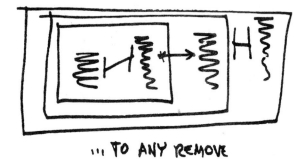

... TO ANY REMOVE

And this creates a basis for all kinds of hypertext—linked, parallel, windowing.

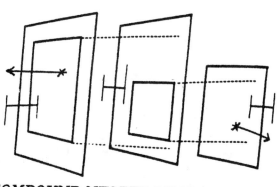

COMPOUND NESTED LINKS

---

*The official naming-mechanism of the system has "document" and "version" fields.

## 7 Electronic Publishing:
### Making the Literary System Universal
Beyond its use as a private facility, we intend that this system be usable as a publication system.

### An Interesting World
It will be notes that we have here defined an interesting and rich sort of world—a world in which we are relieved of complications from conventional computer filing; yet we have greatly enhanced abilities to specify and express compound relations of every sort.

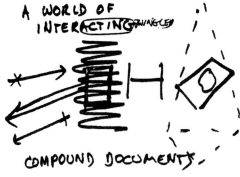

### . . . But a Simple One
This world nevertheless remains simple in design. The virtuality is simple in structure and repeats in layers.

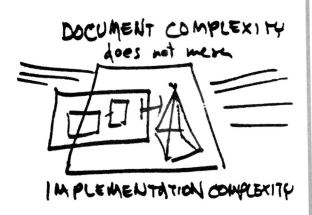

### 7
### Showing and Sieving In-Links
The reader should be able to ask, for a given document or place in the document, "What connects here from other documents?"—and be shown all these outside connections without appreciable delay." *

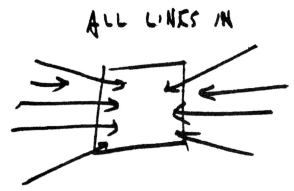

But there may be too many. Indeed, for "Alice in Wonderland" or the U.S. Constitution, the number could be in the squillions.

Thus it becomes necessary to apply some kind of filter, saying, "What links come in from Spain? From last week? From last year in Marienbad?"—and see the number of such links are once, followed by the linked documents themselves if desired.

This must all be fast enough to please the impatient on-line user. And we believe it can be done. This filtering by different attributes we call "sieving"; and it can only be set up for a comparatively small number of traits—say, location and author and time.**

### Directories and Categories
Two system directories, maintained by the system itself, are anticipated: author and title, no more.

*Technically knowledgeable readers may note that *this* is the hardest feature. This is the stopper. But we believe it can be done.

**Of course, any amount of additional sieving can be put in at the front end.

Thus a carefully designed system of publication, surprisingly like that of paper, has been worked out.

We can therefore have a system of electronic publishing that feeds to your computer screen exactly what you ask for, as soon as you ask for it; with royalties divided between the document owners in exact proportion to how much of their materials are transmitted or used.

"Private" materials are available only to their owners or designees; "published" materials are available to anyone, yielding a royalty to the owners.

Private documents can link and window to public ones.

This is a radical and daring idea; a new form of reading and writing, in a way just like the old, with quotations and marginalia and citations. Yet it will also be socially self-constructing into a vast new traversible framework, a new literature.

Given that anything on such a network may be available instantly, such an arrangement promises an extraordinary new level of capability. For not only may simple documents be accessed at once, but compounded and windowing documents may be overlaid on anything—promising a new degree of understandability through what is added later.

It is our unusual hope and vision that this, with its simplicity of approach and efficiency of implementation, may become the standard publishing medium of the future.

Other directories would essentially involve categorization, like the Dewey Decimal and Library of Congress catalog systems, or the Yellow Pages of the phone book.

There is nothing wrong with categorization. It is, however, by its nature transient: category systems have a half-life, and categorizations begin to look fairly stupid after a few years. (Indeed, simple categorizations of computer articles in computer bibliographies of ten years ago have already begun to look stupid.) The army designation of "Pong Balls, Ping" has a certain universal character to it.

All category-systems make some sense, few stay good for long. (However, the Yellow Pages categories are an interesting exception, being dreadful to begin with, and, though supposedly updated from time to time, do not seem to improve. Try to find from them the nearest place to make paper copies.)

What is the solution for our system? Keep categorizing directories *out of the system level.* This is user business; let them handle it and collect royalties.

Provision will exist for anyone to publish his own document lists, categorized in any way he imagines, and have users bounce through them in search of whatever they think they may find.

## Videodisc Connections

There has been a great deal of whoop-te-do recently about videodiscs, the storage devices that hold one or more hours of TV on a platter. Several of these are now available and incompatible. Some of them offer freeze-frame and random frame addressability. Very well: they are a fast image playout that can be hooked up to our indexing for complex purposes.

(The widely-touted notion that videodiscs will be useful for text libraries seems a little silly, since they make it possible to access only what you actually have *right there,* while a hypertext network could allow immediate access to everything on it; a vast difference.)

((Another use of the term "videodisc," causing total confusion, is its use to refer to certain high-density *write-once* digital disks under development by Philips. We are often asked whether these "videodiscs" will be useful for our system, and the answer is yes, but they aren't videodiscs.))

## 8 Distribution and Networking

It might be possible to do all this out of one feeder machine, but there are disadvantages.

In principle it is possible to extend this system of storage and publication to a whole network of feeder computers.

The stored literary contents of all the computers on the network may be continually united into a single, accessible whole.

## 9 Vital Issues

Thus we have the framework of a complete, radically different way of handling information.

Numerous issues of personal freedom are conspicuously present.

What we call "tuning" the system is the development of simple, fair and well-balanced arrangements and pricing that will balance users' incentives for the flexible and reasonable use of the system.

### 9
### User Privacy: A Vital Issue

The network will not, may not monitor who reads what or who writes what in private documents. This is vital. It is not easy to guarantee and impossible to make fully automatic.

### A Printing Press

We consider that this system may best be considered as a "printing press" of the future.

### Freedom of the Press

If this system is a printing press, we can brook no greater restriction on its functions than on conventional printing. Freedom of the press has been challenged by tyrants and scoundrels since Gutenberg. It will happen again, and worse, on this new playing-field. We must be ready.

### Legal Good Behavior

Plainly, the system must live within the law. However, what the law is may often not be clear. Grey areas (for the USA) involve pornography, libel, and "national security" (often meaning matters embarrassing to a political administration).

There is no thinking out all these eventualities. But this is a libertarian system: restrict it, and all will lose.

### Eternal Revision

There is no Final Word. There is always a new view, a new idea, a reinterpretation. Windowing hypertext offers the possibility that all writings (never mind the word "knowledge") may be forever revised and reinterpreted by new scholars, summarizers, popularizers, anthologizers.

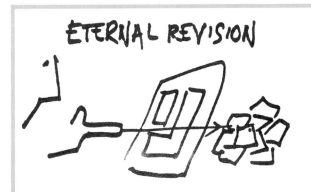

ETERNAL REVISION

# 31. [Introduction]
# Will There Be
# Condominiums in Data Space?

Video artists, and particularly interactive video artists, have developed approaches that can help us think about new media more broadly. For example, in the 1960s, when video seemed to be only lesser film for many people (less both in cost and value), artists began to explore the distinctive features of the video medium. They have continued their explorations as the technologies involved—cameras, editing systems, image synthesis equipment, screens and projectors—have evolved. Hans-Peter Schwarz notes, in his "MediaVisions" essay, that the early results began to call into question the sacrosanct status of montage, which had been central to film from the time of Eisenstein and Podovkin, in a manner even more fundamental than what experimental film had accomplished up to that time. Part of this was through exploration of immediacy—examples of which include Nam June Paik's immediately-screened video of the Pope's visit (◊15), Les Levine's self-surveillance installations at *Software* (◊17), and video environments in which artists presented images of the audience itself using different sorts of displacements in time and space: with a few second's delay, in a narrow corridor, while traversing a maze. Though television production had used the technologies of video for some time, artists' video reconfigured public and industrial conceptions of the video image—via means ranging from site-specific installations to the "music video" form.

Bill Viola has been one of the highest-profile of video artists, allowing him to create, in recent years, what some have called "70 millimeter" video art—work in which video's lower cost is not a primary attraction for the artist, and the traditionally rough production values of video art are not present. However, what has remained consistent from Viola's grittier early work to his massive late-1990s retrospective at the Whitney Museum is a poetic approach to exploring the video medium. As Michael Rush wrote in his *New Media in Late 20th Century Art*, "Bill Viola's work, perhaps more than any other, represents the tendency toward the lyrical in art" (140).

This view of Viola's work is perhaps instructive when considering the essay reprinted here—for example, during his discussion of the MIT Media Lab's famous Aspen Movie-Map ⊗. The project was brilliant, but limited by the fact that it was structured around a video hardware hack (as discussed in Andrew Lippman's paper from SIGGRAPH 1980) which was mapped onto a navigation system meant to be as familiar as possible, so as to bring something already imagined to life. It remained for artists to seek, instead, surprise, and to create defamiliarizing forms of interaction that would allow the technology to be envisioned anew, instead of as a step toward making real what we already expected. The work of Lynn Hershman ⊗ (◊44) and Grahame Weinbren ⊗ includes important artist-led explorations of interactive techniques and structures that, as Viola discusses, go beyond the basic branching flowchart, a structure that had been applied to narrative two decades before by Raymond Queneau (◊12).

Hershman and Weinbren's work, as well as Viola's own, relates to the Aspen project or commercial interactive video as poetry relates to an instruction manual or brochure. An instruction manual that makes us consider language anew is usually a failure—such a document must be transparent in order to be effective. Of course, the creation of effective structures for such manuals is a formidable challenge, and such documents are essential. But few would wish to live in a culture in which our ability to understand and use language was limited to what is evoked by such documents.
—NWF

◊12
147

◊15
227

◊17
247

463

◊40
587

◊44
643

There are certain works that blur the boundary between poetry and instruction manuals: Julio Cortázar's unusual "Instruction Manual" is one.

Further Reading

Lippman, Andrew. "Movie Maps: An Application of the Optical Video Disk to Computer Graphics." *Computer Graphics* 14(3). 1980.

Rush, Michael. *New Media in Late 20th-Century Art.* New York: Thames and Hudson, 1999.

Schwarz, Hans-Peter, ed. *Media-Art-History: Media Museum: ZKM—Center for Art and Media Karlsruhe.* New York: Prestel Publishing, 1997.

Original Publication

*Video* 80(5):36-41. 1982. This text from Bill Viola, *Reasons for Knocking at an Empty House,* 121–135. Ed. Robert Violette. Cambridge: MIT Press, 1995.

# Will There Be Condominiums in Data Space?

## Bill Viola

Possibly the most startling thing about our individual existence is that it is continuous. It is an unbroken thread—we have been living this same moment ever since we were conceived. It is memory, and to some extent sleep, that gives us the impression of a life of discrete parts, periods, or sections, of certain times or "highlights." Hollywood movies and the media, of course, reinforce this perception.

If things are perceived as discrete parts or elements, they can be rearranged. Gaps become most interesting as places of shadow, open to projection. Memory can be regarded as a filter (as are the five senses)—it is a device implanted for our survival. The curse of the mnemonist is the flood of images that are constantly replaying in his brain. He may be able to demonstrate extraordinary feats of recall, but the rest of the banal and the mundane is playing back in there too, endlessly. The result can be lack of sleep, psychosis, and even willful death, driving some to seek professional psychiatric help (and thus become history on the pages of medical journals and books).[1] This reincarnates one of the curses of early video art—"record everything," the saturation-bombing approach to life which made so many early video shows so boring and impossible to sit through. Life without editing, it seems, is just not that interesting.

It is only very recently that the ability to forget has become a prized skill. In the age of "information overload," we have reached a critical mass that has accelerated the perfection of recording technologies, an evolution that leads back to ancient times. Artificial memory systems have been around for centuries. The early Greeks had their walks through temple,[2] and successive cultures have refined and developed so-called "mnemo-technics"—Thomas Aquinas described an elaborate memory scheme of projecting images and ideas on places (fig. 31.2); in 1482 Jacobus Publicius wrote of using the spheres of the universe as a memory system (fig. 31.2); Giulio Camillo created a "Memory Theater" in Italy in the early 1500s; and Giordano Bruno diagrammed his system of artificial memory in his work *Shadows,* published in 1582. Frances Yates describes this entire remarkable area in her brilliant book *The Art of Memory* (University of Chicago Press, 1966).

When I was in Japan in 1981, I visited a festival of the dead at one of the most sacred places in the country, Osoresan Mountain. There I saw blind female shamen called *itako* calling back the spirits of the dead for inquiring relatives, a centuries-old practice. Until that time I had felt that the large Japanese electronics companies were way ahead in the development of communications technology. After witnessing the *itako*, however, I realized they were way behind. Right in their own backyard were people who, without the aid of wires or hardware of any sort, have been for ages regularly communicating through time and space with ancestors long

Figure 31.1. Tibetan Buddhist monks from Ladakh making a sand mandala.

gone. An interesting place at the temple site (which was perched in the surreal landscape of an extinct volcanic crater) was a special walk for the visiting pilgrims to take along a prescribed trail. The way led from the temple through a volcanic wasteland of rockpiles and smoking fissures to the shores of a crater lake. It was called "the walk through Hell." The path through the landscape and the points along it all had special significance. The *itako*, to call up the dead, took this "walk through Hell" in their minds, bringing the spirits in along the familiar path, and when they were through, sent them back the same way.

The interesting thing about idea spaces and memory systems is that they presuppose the existence of some sort of place, either real or graphic, which has its own structure and architecture. There is always a whole space, which already exists *in its entirety*, onto which ideas and images can be mapped, using only that portion of the space needed.

In addition to the familiar model of pre-recorded time unfolding along a linear path (as evidenced by many things from our writing system to the thread of magnetic tape playing in a videotape recorder), there is another parallel to be linked with modern technology. "Data space" is a term we hear in connection with computers. Information must be entered into a computer's memory to create a set of parameters, defining some sort of ground, or field, where future calculations and binary events will occur. In three-dimensional computer graphics, this field exists as an imaginary but real chunk of space, a conceptual geometry, theoretically infinite, within which various forms may be created, manipulated, extended, and destroyed. The graphics display screen becomes that mysterious third point of view looking in on this space (we often call it our "mind's eye"), which can be moved about and relocated from any angle at will. The catch is that the space must exist in the computer first, so that there is a reference system within which to locate the various coordinates of points and lines called into being by the operator. In our brain, constantly flickering pulses of neuron firings create a steady-state field onto which disturbances and perturbations are registered as percepts and thought forms. This is the notion that something is already "on" before you approach it, like the universe, or like a video camera which always needs to be "video-ing" even if there is only a blank raster ("nothing") to see. Turn it off, and it's not video anymore.

Figure 31.2. Left and middle: Abbey memory system, and images to be used in the Abbey memory system. From Jahannes Rombach, Congestorium Artificiose Memorie, Venice, 1533. Right: The Spheres of the Universe as a Memory System, from Jacobus Publicus, Oratoriae artis epitome, 1482.

When I had my first experience with computer videotape editing in 1976, one demand this new way of working impressed upon me has remained significant. It is the idea of holism. I saw then that my piece was actually finished and in existence *before* it was executed on the VTRs. Digital computers and software technologies are holistic; they think in terms of whole structures. Wordprocessors allow one to write out, correct, and rearrange the *whole* letter before typing it. Data space is fluid and temporal, hardcopy is for real—an object is born and becomes fixed in time. Chiseling in stone may be the ultimate hard copy.

When I edited a tape with the computer, for the first time in my life I saw that my video piece had a "score," a structure, a pattern that could be written out on paper. We view video and film in the present tense—we "see" one frame at a time passing before us in this moment. We don't see what is before it and what is after it—we only see the narrow slit of "now." Later, when the lights come on, it's gone. The pattern does exist, of course, but only in our memory. Notation systems have been around since the beginning of history, since what we call history *is* notation of events in time, i.e., historical "records." With speech we have graphic writing systems; with music we have the score. They are both symbolic coded systems for the recording and later playback of information events in time. Poetry has always had a level that video or film cannot approach (at least not yet): the existence of the words on paper (how the poem looks, how the words are placed on the page, the gaps, the spacing, etc.). The whole poem is there before us, and, starting at the top of the page, we can see the end before we actually get there.

Our cultural concept of education and knowledge is based upon the idea of building something up from a ground, from zero, and starting piece by piece to put things together, to construct edifices. It is additive. If we approach this process from the other direction, considering it to be backwards, or subtractive, all sorts of things start to happen. Scientists always marvel at nature, at how it seems to be some grand code, with a built-in sense of purpose. Discoveries are made which reveal that more and more things are related, connected. Everything appears to be aware of itself and everything else, all fitting into an interlocking whole. We quite literally carve out our own realities. If you want to make a jigsaw puzzle, you must first start with the whole image, and *then* cut it up. The observer, working backwards into the system, has the point of view that he or she is building things up, putting it together piece by piece. The prophet Mohamed has said, "All knowledge is but a single point—it is the ignorant who have multiplied it."

## The Whole Is the Sum of Its Parts

A friend of mine is an ethnomusicologist who spent several years studying the gamelan music of Central Java. He was trained in Western music in the States, and spent many years working on his own compositions and performing with other musicians. One of the most frustrating things about his studies in Java, he told me, was trying to work on specific parts of songs with the gamelan musicians. Once they were at a rehearsal, and after running through a piece, he asked them to play only a section from the middle so that he could make sure he got all the notes right. This proved to be an impossible request. After a lot of hemming and hawing, excuses, and several false starts, he realized that the group just could not do it. They insisted on playing the entire piece over again, from beginning to end. In Java, the music was learned by rote, from many years of observation and imitation, not from written notation. The idea of taking a small part out of context, or playing just a few bars, simply did not exist. The music was learned and conceived as a whole in the minds of the musicians.

Giulio Paolini, the contemporary Italian artist, made a little-known but far-reaching videotape in the mid-seventies. It was his first and only tape. Working at an experimental video studio in Florence in the cradle of Western art, he, like many other European artists who visited the art/tapes/22 studio, had his first encounter with video. Instead of simply

re-translating into video what he had already been doing before, as most other artists had done, Paolini intuitively recognized the great power underlying the recording media. He took the slides of all his work, most of the pieces he had ever made, and recorded them one at a time on each frame of video. Playing back this tape, the viewer sees 15 years of Paolini's art, his life's work, go by in less than a minute. Poof! It's gone.

It is slowly becoming clear that structuralism, currently out of fashion in the fashion-conscious, ever shifting spotlight of the art world, must be reconsidered. It is vital. However, this new structuralism is not the same as the often over-intellectualized, didactic, structuralism-for-structuralism's-sake that took center stage in the art scene over a decade ago (most visibly through the work of experimental filmmakers). In retrospect, however, the core ideas being expressed then certainly remain important, and perhaps could only have emerged in the way they did given that particular place and moment in cultural time. Furthermore, the anti-content messages that have been espoused in various fields of art in the twentieth century also continue to merit attention. We have all been made aware that, since the Renaissance, Western eyes have been drawn to the visual, to the surface appearance of the world. "Realism" came to mean how something appeared to the eye alone. Looking at the Gothic art before it, along with Asian and so-called Primitive or Tribal Art, it is clear that something fundamental is missing. However, from our viewpoint today, it is also clear that pure structuralism alone is no answer either.

> Decadent art is simply an art which is no longer felt or energized, but merely denotes, in which there exists no longer any real correspondence between the formal and pictorial elements, its meaning, as it were, negated by the weakness or incongruity of the pictorial element; but it is often . . . *far less* conventional than are the primitive or classic stages of the same sequence. True art, pure art, never enters into competition with the unattainable perfection of the world.[3]
>
> —A.K. Coomaraswamy

Structure, or form, has always been the basis of the original pictorial art of both Europe and the East, but the Middle Ages were the last time when both Europe and Asia met on common artistic ground.

In Western art, the picture is generally conceived as seen in a frame or through a window, and so brought towards the spectator; but the Oriental image really exists only in our mind and heart and thence is projected or reflected into space.

The Indian, or Far Eastern icon, carved or painted, is neither a memory image nor an idealization, but a visual symbolism, ideal in the mathematical sense. . . . Where European art naturally depicts a moment of time, an arrested action, or an effect of light, Oriental art represents a continuous condition. In traditional European terms, we should express this by saying that modern European art endeavors to represent things as they are in themselves, Asiatic and Christian art to represent things more nearly as they are in God, or nearer their source.

—A.K. Coomaraswamy

The idea of art as a kind of diagram has for the most part not made it down from the Middle Ages into modern European consciousness. The Renaissance was the turning point, and the subsequent history of Western art can be viewed as the progressive distancing of the arts away from the sacred and towards the profane. The original structural aspect of art, and the idea of a "data space" *was* preserved through the Renaissance, however, in the continued relation between the image and architecture. Painting became an architectural, spatial form, which the viewer experienced by physically walking through it. The older concept of an idea and an image architecture, a memory "place" like the mnemonic temples of the Greeks, is carried through in the great European cathedrals and palaces, as is the relation between memory, spatial movement, and the storage (recording) of ideas.

Something extraordinary is occurring today, in the 1980s, which ties together all these threads. The computer is merging with video. The potential offspring of this marriage is only beginning to be realized. Leaping directly into the farther future for a moment, we can see the seeds of what some have described as the ultimate recording technology: total spatial storage, with the viewer wandering through some three-dimensional, possibly life-sized field of prerecorded or simulated scenes and events evolving in time. At present, the interactive video discs currently on the market have already begun to address some of these possibilities. Making a program for interactive video disc involves the ordering and structuring (i.e., editing) of much more information than will actually be seen by an individual when he or she sits down to play the program. All possible pathways, or branches, that a viewer ("participant" is a better word) may take through the material must already exist at some place on the disc. Entire prerecorded sections of video may never be encountered by a given observer.

Soon, the way we approach making films and videotapes will drastically change. The notion of a "master" edit and "original" footage will disappear. Editing will become the writing of a software program that will tell the computer how to arrange (i.e., shot order, cuts, dissolves, wipes, etc.) the information on the disc, playing it back in the specified sequence in real time or allowing the viewer to intervene. Nothing needs to be physically "cut" or re-recorded at all. Playback speed, the cardinal 30 frames a second, will become intelligently variable and thus malleable, becoming, as in electronic music practice, merely one fundamental frequency among many which can be modulated, shifted up or down, superimposed, or interrupted according to the parameters of electronic wave theory. Different sections can be assigned to play back at specific speeds or reversed; and individual frames can be held still on the screen for predetermined durations. Other sections can be repeated over and over. Different priorities rule how and in what order one lays material down on the "master" (disc). New talents and skills are needed in making programs—this is not editing as we know it. It was Nikola Tesla, the original uncredited inventor of the radio, who called it "transmission of intelligence." He saw something there that others didn't. After all these years, video is finally getting "intelligence," the eye is being reattached to the brain. As with everything else, however, we will find that the limitations emerging lie more with the abilities and imaginations of the producers and users, rather than in the tools themselves.

As in the figure/ground shifts described in Gestalt psychology, we are in the process of a shift away from the temporal, piece-by-piece approach of *constructing* a program (symbolized by the camera and its monocular, narrow, tunnel-of-vision, single point of view), and towards a spatial, total-field approach of *carving out* potentially multiple programs (symbolized by the computer and its holistic software models, data spaces, and infinite points of view). We are proceeding from models of the eye and ear to models

467

of thought processes and conceptual structures in the brain. "Conceptual Art" will take on a new meaning.

As we take the first steps into data space, we discover that there have been many previous occupants. Artists have been there before. Giulio Camillo's Memory Theater (which he actually constructed in wood, calling it a "constructed body and soul") is one example. Dante's *Divine Comedy* is another. Fascinating relationships between ancient and modern technologies become evident. A simple example can be found in the Indian Tantric doctrine of the three traditional expressions of the deity: the anthropomorphic, or visual, image; the yantra, or geometric "energy" diagram (fig. 31.3); and the mantra, or sonic representation through chanting and music. It is interesting to note that these are all considered to be equal—simply outward expressions of the same underlying thing. In form, this is not unlike the nature of electronic systems: the same electronic signal can be an image if fed into a video monitor, an energy diagram if fed into an oscilloscope, and a sequence of sounds if fed into an audio system.

Today, there are visual diagrams of data structures already being used to describe the patterns of information on the computer video disc. The most common one is called "branching," a term borrowed from computer science (fig. 31.4). In this system, the viewer proceeds from top to bottom in time, and may either play the disc uninterrrupted (arrow), or stop at predetermined branching points along the way and go off into related material at other areas on the disc for further study (like a form of "visual footnoting.") Examples of this system go something like—in a program on the desert, the viewer can stop at a point where plants are mentioned, and branch off to more detailed material on the

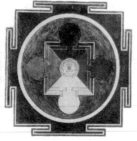

Figure 31.3. Left: Two deities and yantra diagrams of the same two deities. From a Nepalese illustrated manuscript, c.1760.
Right: Ground plan of a temple.

various flora of the valley floor, etc. Although it is clear how this can enhance our current educational system, freeing students from boring and incompetent teachers so they can proceed at their own pace through information which now contains movement, dynamic action, and sound in addition to written words, artists know that there must be more out there than this. Even though the technology is interactive, this is still the same old linear logic system in a new bottle.

As a start, we can propose new diagrams, such as the "matrix" structure (fig. 31.4). This would be a non-linear array of information. The viewer could enter at any point, move in any direction, at any speed, pop in and out at any place. All directions are equal. Viewing becomes exploring a territory, traveling through a data space. Of course, it would not be the obviously literal one like the Aspen project.[4] We are moving into *idea* space here, into the world of thoughts and images as they exist in the brain, not on some city planner's drawing board. With the integration of images and video into the domain of computer logic, we are beginning the task of mapping the conceptual structures of our brain onto the technology. After the first TV camera with VTR gave us an eye connected to a gross form of non-selective memory, we are now at the next evolutionary step—the area of intelligent perception and thought structures, albeit artificial.

Finally, we can envision other diagrams/models emerging as artists go deeper into the psychological and neurological depths in search of expressions for various thought processes and manifestations of consciousness. Eventually, certain forms of neurosis, so long the creative fuel of the tormented artist in the West, may be mapped into the computer disc. We may end up with the "schizo" or "spaghetti" model, in which not only are all directions equal, but all are not equal (fig. 31.4). Everything is irrelevant and significant at the same time. Viewers may become lost in this structure and never find their way out.

Worlds are waiting to be explored. It is to be hoped that artists will be given their share of access to experiment with this exciting new technology. I recently had a glimpse of some of the possibilities for art when I met a designer who had first encountered computers while working at a large French fashion design firm in New York. There, the graphics artist worked at computer terminals. With a light-pen, he could draw various designs, working with functions of computer memory and data manipulation. Furthermore, his terminal was linked to a large databank of fabric designs and images from around the world and throughout history. After completing a sketch, for example, he could call up a seventeenth-century Japanese kimono design, look at it or superimpose it with his own idea. Then he could call up a turn-of-the-century European dress pattern, combine that with his design or integrate it with the kimono, all the while storing the various stages in memory. When all of this was completed and the final design chosen, he could then tie into other offices in Europe and the Orient right on the same screen. Designers could compare notes, get availability data on his fabric from the mills (i.e., where is the best silk, who has stock, what is the order time, etc.). All phases of his work could occur on the same screen as digital information. He could travel in space (Europe, the Far East), as well as in time (art history), all in an instant and available either as written text or visual images.

Despite the anti-technology attitudes which still persist (some, it should be added, for very good reasons), the present generation of artists, filmmakers, and video-makers currently in school, and their instructors, who continue to ignore computer and video technology, will in the near future find that they have bypassed *the* primary medium, not only of their own fields, but of the entire culture as well. It is imperative that creative artists have a hand in the developments currently underway. Computer video discs are being marketed as a great new tool in training and education. At this moment, there are creative people experimenting with the technology, ensuring that innovative and unique applications will emerge; but for now, many of the examples return to the boring domain of linear logic in the school classroom. The Aspen city map project is perhaps one of the more interesting examples of new program formats. We are at the beginning, but even so, for the artist, standard educational logic structures are just not that interesting. Artists have been to different parts of the brain, and know

quite well that things don't always work like they told you in school.

It is of paramount importance now, as we watch the same education system that brought us through school (and the same communications system that gave us the wonderful world of commercial TV and AM radio) being mapped onto these new technologies, that we go back and take a deeper look at some of the older systems described in these pages. Artists not shackled to the fad and fashion treadmill of the art world, especially the art world of the past few years, will begin to see the new meaning that art history is taking on. As I have begun to outline in this article, the relation between the image and architecture (as in Renaissance art), the structuralism of sacred art (Oriental, Early Christian, and Tribal art, with their mandalas, diagrams, icons, and other symbolic representations, including song, dance, poetry), and artificial memory systems (the first recording technologies from the time of the Greeks through the Middle Ages), are all areas that require further investigation.

As we continue to do our dance with technology, some of us more willingly than others, the importance of turning back towards ourselves, the prime mover of this technology, grows greater than the importance of any LSI circuit. The sacred art of the past has unified form, function, and aesthetics around this single ultimate aim. Today, development of self must precede development of the technology or we will go nowhere—there *will* be condominiums in data space (it has already begun with cable TV). Applications of tools are only reflections of the users—chopsticks may be a simple eating utensil or a weapon, depending on who uses them.

## The Porcupine and the Car

Late one night while driving down a narrow mountain highway, I came across a large porcupine crossing the road up ahead. Fortunately, I spotted him in time to bring the car to a stop a short distance from where he was standing. I watched him in the bright headlights, standing motionless, petrified at this "close encounter of the third kind." Then, after a few silent moments, he started to do a strange thing. Staying in his place, he began to move around in a circle, emitting a raspy hissing sound, with the quills rising up off his body. He didn't run away. I realized that this dance was actually a move of self-defence. I cut the car headlights to normal beams, but he still

Figure 31.4. Branching Structure, Matrix Structure, Schizo Structure.

continued to move around, even more furiously, casting weird shadows on the trees behind. Finally, to avoid giving him a heart attack, and to get home, I cut the lights completely and turned off the engine. I watched him in the dim moonlight as he stopped his dance and moved off the road. Later, while driving off, I realized that he was probably walking proudly away, gloating over how he really gave it to that big blinding noisy thing that rushed toward him out of the night. I'm sure he was filled with confidence, so pleased with himself that he had won, his porcupine world-view grossly inflated as he headed home in the darkness.

Notes

1. A.R. Luria, *The Mind of the Mnemonist* (New York: Basic Books, 1968).

2. The Greeks perfected a system of memory that used the mental imprinting of any objects or key points to be remembered onto specific locations along a pathway previously memorized from an actual temple. To recall the points in their proper order, one simply had to take the walk through the temple in one's mind, observing the contents left at each location along the way.

3. A.K. Coomaraswamy, *The Transformation of Nature in Art* (New York: Dover Publications, 1956). (Reprint of the original Harvard University Press edition, Boston, 1934.)

4. A landmark interactive laserdisc project by MIT Media Lab, in the late 1970s, that mapped the city of Aspen, street by street, with moving cameras so that the viewer could take a "ride" through the city, going anywhere at will—one of the first visual-mapping database moving-image projects related to data space ideas and today's virtual reality technology.

# 32. [Introduction]
# The Endless Chain.

The emerging dominance of new media over old is a common theme in press accounts: video games are a bigger business than the movies, the Web is drawing viewers away from television or readers away from books, AOL has acquired Time Warner.

If those who celebrate new media as inherently liberating (as in the hyperbolic quotations included in Langdon Winner's essay (◊40)) are correct, we should be entering an era of dissolving hierarchies and empowered individuals. Yet there is little reason to view Web sites like *ESPNonline* and *MSNBC* as inherently liberating cultural forces. What these press accounts reveal instead is that old and new media are becoming increasingly compatible and comparable. Old and new seem to be integrating themselves into a single system. Radio and television took their places the media system not so long ago. New media is now also becoming big business, no longer a marginal phenomenon.

Therefore, understanding new media requires some understanding of the traditional media business with which it is colliding and converging. Perhaps the clearest way to understand the momentum of traditional media is to trace the changes over the nearly 20 years during which Ben Bagdikian has released 6 editions of *The Media Monopoly*. Bagdikian's book, initially released in 1983, was called alarmist, at first, for its predictions of increasing media concentration and narrowness. Now it is called prescient. As Bagdikian wrote in his preface to the 6th (2000) edition:

> When the first edition of this book was published in 1983, fifty corporations dominated most of every mass medium and the biggest media merger in history was a $340 million deal. At that time, the strategy of most of the fifty biggest firms was to gain market domination in one medium—to have the largest market share solely in newspapers, for example, or in magazines, or broadcasting, or books, or movies, but not all of them. By the time the second edition was published in 1987, the fifty companies had shrunk to twenty-three, by the fourth edition to fourteen. By the fifth edition in 1997, the biggest firms numbered ten and involved the $19 billion Disney-ABC deal, at the time the biggest media merger ever. But "the biggest" of 1983, worth $340 million, would give way seventeen years later to AOL Time Warner's $350 billion merged corporation, more than 1,000 times larger.

> There was reason enough, even then, for concern that so small a number of dominant firms had such a disproportionate influence on American culture, commerce, and political power. (xx–xxi)

As Bagdikian reported in his 2000 preface, *six* firms now dominate *all* U.S. mass media: "The top six firms, ordered solely on their annual media revenues, are [AOL] Time Warner, Disney, Viacom (an amalgam of CBS and Westinghouse), News Corp, Bertelsmann, and General Electric. These six have more annual media revenues than the next twenty firms combined" (x).

While elsewhere in the 6th edition preface Bagdikian shows an understanding of new media technology that is imperfect (as well as the rhetorical markings of having written during a dot-com boom) his understanding of traditional media, and of the business of media, is astute. In what ways will new media become part of the media business Bagdikian described in the following selection, from the book's 1983 edition, and for what reasons? At one point, the (somewhat) peer-to-peer music service Napster seemed the antithesis of the media business, thumbing its nose at recording industry notions of copyright. But as Napster became mainstream, even though some argued it actually was increasing traditional record sales, it was integrated into the media business via legal pressure and forced to fundamentally alter its operations, leading to bankruptcy and acquisition by Bertelsmann. When the political stakes of media control are as high as Bagdikian describes, and with advertising alone worth $80 billion a year, will this pattern of integration—forced or through cooption—be inevitably repeated? Or will the ability to transmit, as well as receive, be preserved as

*Remediation*, by J. David Bolter and Richard Grusin, traces important respects in which borrowing and integration are being played out between old and new media forms. Bolter's essay (◊47) also deals with the idea.

**471**

The first five of these corporations control the vast majority of book publishing. Some small presses, as well as nonprofit university presses like MIT Press, do survive and continue their work. Beacon Press, Bagdikian's publisher, is one of the few sizable non-university non-conglomerate presses.

◊40
587

◊47
679

As Ted Nelson discusses in *Literary Machines* (◊30), there is an important distinction to be drawn between the "front end" and "back end" when discussing new media. Front end functions are those that are particular to an individual's computer, while back end functions are those that take place at the wider, network level. Where an operation takes place is crucial. For example, a user may set their front end to filter out certain types of content. This is the exercise of preference. However, when this content is removed at the network level it may be more appropriately called *censorship*. Bagdikian's essay bears directly on such issues.

◊18
259

◊19
277

the Internet develops, providing the opportunity for alternatives such as those evoked in essays by Hans Magnus Enzensberger (◊18) and Jean Baudrillard (◊19)?

At first the "symmetric" aspect of the Internet—equal bandwidth for transmission and reception—seemed very natural. Now, like many natural things, it is endangered. Most companies offering high-speed connections have configured them so that the ordinary user's computer can receive much more than it can transmit, and they often also prohibit users from running public servers. This makes it impossible for these users to provide each other with the rich media that they are capable of downloading, that media companies are able to supply from central servers. Most of the companies offering these new Internet connections are interconnected with, or identical with, media companies. The issue is seldom discussed in the mainstream media; this is no surprise to those who have read Bagdikian's work.
—NWF

Further Reading

Bagdikian, Ben. *Double Vision: Reflections on My Heritage, Life, and Profession*. Boston: Beacon Press, 1995.

Fairness and Accuracy in Reporting. <http://www.fair.org>

Herman, Edward, and Noam Chomsky. *Manufacturing Consent: The Political Economy of the Mass Media*. New York: Pantheon Books, 1988.

"Who Owns What." On the Columbia Journalism Review Web site. <http://www.cjr.org/owners>

Original Publication
*The Media Monopoly*. Boston: Beacon Press, 1983.
Updated information from 6th edition, 2000.

◊30
441

472

# The Endless Chain
## Ben Bagdikian

For where your treasure is, there will be your heart also.
—Matt. 6:22

The Headline in the first edition read:

FOR SAM SMITH, HOSPITAL ORDERLY

A BATTLE WHOSE TIME HAS COME

But in the next edition and every edition thereafter, Sam Smith and his battle disappeared, replaced by an innocuous syndicated story from the Associated Press. It happened in the Perspectives Section of a respected American daily, the *Baltimore Sun*, on December 7, 1969. The ghost item had passed editorial scrutiny for accuracy and relevance but someone, seeing it in the first edition, ordered it killed.

The story described imminent labor negotiations between hospital workers, who received pay near the poverty level, and the management of Johns Hopkins Hospital in Baltimore.

Reporters on the *Sun*, noting the story's strange disappearance, remembered that a director of their newspaper, J. Crosson Cooper, Jr., was also a director of Johns Hopkins Hospital. Equally interesting was the fact that Cooper was also a director of Mercantile Safe Deposit & Trust Company, the most prominent bank in Baltimore, which, according to a congressional study, held 61.3 percent of the shares in the newspaper company.

The *Columbia Journalism Review* commented:

> . . . it seemed evident that if Cooper or an associate in the ownership echelon had not ordered the story killed, a top editor, afraid that it might displease the owners, had done so. Either way, journalistic morality suffered an unhappy blow in Baltimore. And one reason for growing concern over conglomerate ownership of news media was underlined.

That was in 1969. The accelerated concentration of control of all American mass media had just begun. By the beginning of the 1980s most major American media—newspapers, magazines, radio, television, books, and movies—were controlled by fifty corporations. These fifty corporations, like the *Baltimore Sun*, were in turn interlocked with other massive industries and a few multinational banks. The potential for society-wide Sam Smith disappearances had become epidemic.

Twenty corporations control more than half the 61 million daily newspapers sold every day; twenty corporations control more than half the revenues of the country's 11,000 magazines; three corporations control most of the revenues and audience in television; ten corporations in radio; eleven corporations in all kinds of books; and four corporations in motion pictures.

This is more than an industrial statistic. It goes to the heart of American democracy. As the world becomes more volatile, as changes accelerate and create new problems that demand new solutions, there is an urgent need for broader and more diverse sources of public information. But the reverse is happening.

Today there is hardly an American industry that does not own a major media outlet, or a major media outlet grown so large that it does not own a firm in a major industry. These media report the news of industries in which they either are owners or share directors and policies.

The fifty controllers of most of America's news and views are partners in industries such as agribusiness, airlines, coal and oil, timber, banking, the loan business, insurance, video games, electronics manufacturing, electronic equipment sales, automobile rentals, automobile sales, telephone systems, weapons production, frozen foods, home furnishings, advertising, billboards, religious instruction, utilities, pipelines, auto parts, construction equipment, sugar, beef, tobacco, candy, computers, jet engines, travel agencies, rocket engineering, plastics, microprocessing, chemicals, and space flight engineering.

Legislation, regulations, taxes, and sales that affect industries like these are influenced by public opinion and government policy, both conditioned by the news. More and more, both the news and the industries belong to the same parent corporation. It is not an encouraging basis for unbiased selection of public information.

Most of the fifty biggest firms have a direct stake in foreign investments and, therefore, in foreign policy of the United States. There is almost no country in the world in which a subsidiary of the fifty media companies does not have a significant investment. One major media company alone, CBS, has foreign subsidiaries headquartered in thirty-four countries, ranging from Argentina to South Africa.

Conflicts of interest, real and potential, are infinitely greater because the large media companies exchange directors, and therefore have common policy views, with nonmedia corporations. Potential conflicts are further intensified by connections like the *Baltimore Sun*'s with the Mercantile Bank. A dozen of the country's largest multinational banks hold significant voting shares in many of the fifty largest media companies, control their debts, or exchange directors with them.

Some corporate owners intervene directly to control what their media companies produce; at times this intervention is brutal, as this book will show. Most do not intervene directly. But they all hire and fire the people who control the news and other public information.

Corporate owners of the media are not necessarily cynical. They believe, as most human beings do, in those forces that make them happy. But what satisfies a multinational corporation is not necessarily what will satisfy society as a whole.

The fifty corporations do not have total control of national news and views. In every medium there remain smaller competitors. Small voices have always been important, but their chief importance has been either to introduce new ideas or to permit society to look backward at past mistakes. In the 1980s the imbalance between the great voices of the mass media and the small voices of individual enterprises is so vast that it is more difficult than ever for society to hear minority voices in the majority thunder. And the last quarter of the twentieth century confronts potential errors of such catastrophic magnitude that a misled civilization conceivably will not have the luxury of looking back.

In some of the media owned by big business there are partial protections against direct manipulation. In newspapers, for example, professional conventions discourage tampering from above. But these conventions cannot stop an owner who wishes to control the content of his or her property, as the reporters at the *Baltimore Sun* discovered. Nor is there any way to measure or control the capacity of editors and producers to make decisions that they know will sit well with the owners, without waiting for direct orders from above.

Some of the fifty corporations are household words, like CBS and Westinghouse. Others have corporate parent titles that are less familiar than their media subsidiaries—S. I. Newhouse & Sons, for example, owns newspapers, Condé Nast and *Parade* magazines, and Random House book publishers. The titles of some parent firms have little meaning for the general public, though the personal or organizational connections are better known: News America Publishing and News Group owns the *New York Post, Village Voice, New York Magazine*, the *San Antonio Press*, the *San Antonio News*, and the national magazine *Star*, all of which are controlled by the Australian entrepreneur Rupert Murdoch; Bonneville International, with its Deseret Management Group, is the communications arm of the Church of Jesus Christ of Latter-Day Saints, the Mormon Church.

The identity of the fifty corporations shifts from time to time as companies buy and sell properties and a few enter and a few leave the list of firms that control 50 percent or more of their medium. In 1980, for example, Charter Oil, one of the fifty corporations with extensive magazine holdings, got rid of its communications properties when it encountered trouble in its petroleum business. It killed its newspaper, the *Philadelphia Evening Bulletin*, and sold *Redbook* magazine to Hearst and the *Ladies' Home Journal* to Petersen Publishing, thus enlarging the holdings of two corporations already among the top fifty. By the time this book is published, the number of corporations that control half or more of all the major media in the country likely will be less than fifty.

The list of fifty corporations presented here was compiled from 1980 to 1981 with occasional revisions for part of 1982 because the industries differ in the speed of their annual summaries. The alphabetical listing below has an occasional parenthetical addition for company names not mentioned in more detail later; a corporation's better-known media property is sometimes given to help identify it.

*From 1st edition (1983)*

American Broadcasting Co.
Bonneville International
CBS, Inc.
Capital Cities Communications
Central Newspapers
 (*Arizona Republic,
  Indianapolis News*)
Copley Newspapers
 (*San Diego Union*)
Cowles Media Co.
Cox Communications
Doubleday & Co.
Dow Jones & Co.
 (*Wall Street Journal*)
Encyclopaedia Britannica
Evening News Association
 (*Detroit News*)
Freedom Newspapers
Gannett Co.
General Tire & Rubber Co. (RKO)
Grolier
Gulf + Western
Harcourt Brace Jovanovich
Harte-Hanks Communications
Hearst Corp.
Knight-Ridder Newspapers
 (*Philadelphia Inquirer,
  Miami Herald*)
McCall Publishing Co.
McGraw-Hill
Meredith Corp.
Metromedia, Inc.
National Enquirer
National Geographic Society
New York Times Co.
S. I. Newhouse & Sons
News America Publishing Group
Penthouse International
Petersen Publishing Co.
Playboy Enterprises
RCA Corp. (NBC)
Reader's Digest Association
Scott and Fetzer World Book
E. W. Scripps Co. (Scripps-Howard)
SFN Co./Scott, Foresman
Thomson Newspapers, Ltd.
Time, Inc.
Times Mirror Co.
 (*Los Angeles Times*)
Triangle Publications
Tribune Company
 (*Chicago Tribune,
  New York Daily News*)
20th Century–Fox
U.S. News & World Report
Universal-MCA
Warner Communications
Washington Post Co.
Westinghouse Electric Co.
Ziff-Davis Corporation

*From the Preface to the 6th edition (2000)*
**The Intertwined Six**

Six firms dominate all American mass media. Each is a subsidiary of a larger parent firm, some of them basically operating in other industries. The six parent firms are General Electric, Viacom, Disney, Bertelsmann, Time Warner, and Murdoch's News Corp. Bertelsmann is based in Germany and News Corp in Australia, the other four in the United States. All the parent firms are listed in *Fortune* Magazine's 1999 Global 500 of the largest corporations in the world. Other giant firms in other industries clearly were on the prowl for new mass media in order to join the Big Six—like Sony, a Japanese hardware firm; Seagram's, a Canadian liquor firm; and AT&T, a telephone compnay traditionally providing one-to-one (not mass) communication.

The top six firms, ordered solely on their annual media revenues, are Time Warner, Disney, Viacom (an amalgam of CBS and Westinghouse), News Corp, Bertelsmann, and General Electric. These six have more annual media revenues than the next twenty firms combined.

The number of dominant firms remains six, even with an announcement in early 2000 that stunned the country's businesses and all computer-users—the world's largest Internet service provider, America Online, Inc., said it would acquire the world's largest media company, Time Warner, to form AOL Time Warner, Inc. Consequently, while six firms still dominate all mass media, the largest of those six would become a corporation valued at $350 billion. It would be history's largest merger, in the media or any other enterprise. . . .

The merged firms will have more than 100 million global subscribers, 20 million cable homes, AOL access to Time Warner's 30 magazines and 75 million homes that receive the cable networks CNN, TBS, and TNT. Expected annual revenues are $40 billion. Given Time Warner's vast holdings in all media, the ordinary citizen, whether a reader, TV viewer, movie-goer, or Internet user, would be forced to deal with a communications cartel of a magnitude and power the world has never seen before. . . .

The power and influence of the dominant companies are understated by counting them as "six." They are intertwined: they own stock in each other, they cooperate in joint media ventures, and among themselves they divide profits from some of the most widely viewed programs on television, cable, and movies.

(x-xii)

The degree of domination by the giants increases with time. There are 1,730 daily newspapers, for example, with a total daily circulation of 61 million. Twenty newspaper companies control more than half the daily sales. The disparity of information power in newspapers is typical for all the major media: 1 percent of owners own 34 percent of all papers sold daily. In 1900 there were 2,042 daily papers and 2,023 owners. By 1980 there were 1,730 dailies and 760 owners. In 1900 there was an average of one newspaper owner for every 38,000 citizens; in 1980 the average newspaper owner provided current social and political news for 300,000 citizens. The average population served by each of the twenty largest newspaper owners is 3.7 million.

The twenty corporations that control more than half of all daily newspaper sales are the following:

| | Daily circulation | Number of dailies |
|---|---|---|
| 1. Gannett Newspapers | 3,750,900 | 88 |
| 2. Knight-Ridder Newspapers | 3,464,300 | 34 |
| 3. Newhouse Newspapers | 3,133,500 | 28 |
| 4. Tribune Company | 2,806,600 | 8 |
| 5. Dow Jones & Co. | 2,433,400 | 21 |
| 6. Times Mirror Co. | 2,315,500 | 8 |
| 7. Scripps-Howard Newspapers | 1,518,700 | 16 |
| 8. Hearst Newspapers | 1,362,300 | 15 |
| 9. Thomson Newspapers | 1,219,600 | 77 |
| 10. Cox Newspapers | 1,165,100 | 18 |
| 11. New York Times Co. | 1,137,000 | 12 |
| 12. Cowles Newspapers | 953,900 | 10 |
| 13. News America Publishing Corporation (Murdoch) | 917,600 | 3 |
| 14. Capital Cities Communications | 774,100 | 7 |
| 15. Freedom Newspapers | 798,400 | 31 |
| 16. Central Newspapers | 774,600 | 7 |
| 17. Washington Post Co. | 696,200 | 2 |
| 18. Evening News Association | 678,900 | 5 |
| 19. Copley Newspapers | 635,000 | 6 |
| 20. Harte-Hanks Newspapers | 584,200 | 28 |

There are other kinds of newspapers—weeklies, biweeklies, triweeklies, advertising sheets, and free-circulation papers designed for saturation advertising. They are sometimes socially and journalistically important to their communities but as a class they are ephemeral and cover such a wide

*From the Preface to the 6th Edition (2000)*

The ownership of newspapers, like other media, went through a radical reversal after World War II. In 1946, three-quarters of all dailies were owned by local families and associates. Today, less than 2 percent of the country's fifteen hundred dailies are family owned. Most of the rest are owned by large national chains, whose top companies, in rank of total circulation, are Gannet, Kight Ridder, Newhouse, Dow Jones, Times Mirror, New York Times Co., and Hearst. Ninety-nine percent are monopolies in their own cities.

These same "newspaper companies" are, without exception, also owners of electronic media and are well aware that their television and cable properties pay even higher profit margins than their newspapers. Many observers predict that readers and owners will soon abandon dailies. But, as described later in this book, the United States, uniquely among major nations, leaves a multitude of vital questions to local voters. Since most local television news is disreputably void in daily coverage of civic bodies, except when melodramatic camera shots are possible, and since no other medium even attempts systematic reporting on local schools, taxes, policing, land use, and other relevant civic news, it is likely that members of today's young cyber-oriented generation will still read daily papers when their children are born.

(xxxii)

variety of content and function that they cannot be measured accurately as systematic purveyors of news. It is the printed daily news that provides the country's data base for current events—for other media like weeklies, radio, television, magazines, books, and even movies. The giant newspaper chains are now actively purchasing the weekly newspapers and local advertising sheets to achieve even greater control over both news and advertising.

Control of other media is, if anything, tighter than among the 1,730 newspapers. There are at least 10,830 magazines in the United States. They cover an extraordinary variety of subject matter and quality. Measuring ownership control of the total audience is more difficult than for newspapers because some magazines are issued weekly, some biweekly, some monthly, some bimonthly, and some quarterly. The most reliable measure is the proportion of sales controlled by each owner. Among the 10,830 magazines, twenty corporations have just over 50 percent of the annual sales of total industry revenues of $12 billion. For 1981, these twenty corporations and their major magazines were, in order of their dominance:

1. Time, Inc., *Time, Life, Sports Illustrated, People, Money, Discover*
2. Triangle Publications, *TV Guide, Seventeen*
3. Hearst Corp., *Colonial Homes, Cosmopolitan, Country Living,*

Electronic Products, Good Housekeeping, Harper's Bazaar, House Beautiful, Motor, Motor Boating & Sailing, Popular Mechanics, Redbook, Sports Afield, Town & Country

4. CBS, Inc., American Photographer, Audio, Cycle World, Family Weekly, Field & Stream, Mechanix Illustrated, Road & Track, Pickup, Van and 4WD, Woman's Day, World Tennis

5. McGraw-Hill, American Machinist, Architectural Record, Aviation Week & Space Technology, Business Week, Byte, Chemical Engineering, Chemical Week, Coal Age, Electric World, Electrical Construction & Maintenance, Electronics, Engineering & Mining Journal, Engineering News Record, Fleet Owner, Modern Plastics, Postgraduate Medicine, Power

6. S. I. Newhouse & Sons (Condé Nast–Parade), Bride's Magazine, Glamour, GQ, House & Garden, Mademoiselle, Self, Vanity Fair, Parade, Vogue

7. Washington Post Co., Newsweek, Washington Post Magazine, Inside Sports

8. New York Times Co., Family Circle, New York Times Magazine, Golf Digest, Tennis

9. Reader's Digest Association, Reader's Digest

10. Playboy Enterprises, Games, Playboy

11. Meredith Corp., Better Homes & Gardens, Metropolitan Home, Sail, Successful Farming

12. Penthouse International, Forum, Omni, Penthouse

13. Ziff-Davis, Boating, Business & Commercial Aviation, Car & Driver, Cycle, Flying, Meetings & Conventions, Modern Bride, Pan Am Clipper, Popular Electronics, Psychology Today, Skiing, Stereo Review, Yachting

14. National Geographic Society, National Geographic, National Geographic World

15. McCalls Publishing Co., McCall's, Working Mother

16. U.S. News & World Report, U.S. News & World Report

17. National Enquirer, National Enquirer

18. News America Publishing (Murdoch), New York Magazine, Star

19. Times Mirror Co., Cross Country Ski, Golf, Homeowners How-To, Outdoor Life, Popular Science, Ski, Ski Business, Sporting News

20. Petersen Publishing Co., Car Craft, Guns & Ammo, Hot Rod, Ladies' Home Journal, Lakeland Boating, Motor Trend, Motorcyclist, Petersen's 4 Wheel & Off Road, Petersen's Hunting, Petersen's Photographic, Pick Up, Rudder, Sea & Pacific Skipper, Skin Diver, Teen, Van & 4WD

These twenty companies have 50.7 percent of all magazine revenues. Thus, 1 percent of magazine owners have more than half the revenues of all 10,830 magazines published regularly.

There are 1,000 television and 9,000 radio stations on the air. Audience size varies from hour to hour and week to week. In television the three networks clearly dominate the American television audience, which consists of 98 percent of

From the Preface to the 6th Edition (2000)

Magazines have continued to enjoy their charmed life in the history of American printed media. In 1999, magazines as a whole had $11 billion in revenues and were enjoying 4 percent annual growth. Many behaved like recombinant DNA molecules, a single big-name magazine giving birth to several specialized offspring bearing parental surnames. National Geographic gave birth to National Geographic Adventure, and Sports Illustrated to Sports Illustrated for Kids. As individual publications, TV Guide continued to have the largest circulation, while People ran second, and Sports Illustrated third. In August on 1999, when Disney sold its Fairchild group to Condé Nast, it further concentrated the magazine field among the three leading conglomerates, Time Warner, Condé Nast, and Hearst. (xxxiii)

all households in the country and in which the average TV set is in use six and a half hours a day.

The three networks—ABC, CBS, and NBC—dominate not only access to the television audience but, together with their owned and operated television stations in the major markets, received more than half of the $8.8 billion of television revenues in 1980. (Some of these revenues later find their way to affiliated stations, but networks control network programming and most of the advertising revenues. This, plus their direct control of audience shares, gives three corporations domination over the most powerful communications instrument in history.)

Domination of the radio audience is less precisely measured than for newspapers and television. Of the 9,000 radio stations in the country, 8,000 are commercially operated. Their sounds go to 99.9 percent of American homes equipped with radio and to most cars. Because so many leading radio station owners are also in other industries and do not publish separate revenues of their radio operations, each owner's share of the industry is estimated. Each owner's share of audience in each market is measured by rating services, and these measurements of listeners per week, combined with the estimates of Wall Street firms that specialize in radio finances, indicate that ten corporations have well over half the audience for AM and FM commercial radio. Those ten are American Broadcasting Company, Columbia Broadcasting System, Westinghouse, Metromedia, RKO, National Broadcasting Company, Capital Cities, Bonneville, Cox, and Gannett.

Communications laws in effect in 1982 limit ownership of radio stations to seven per corporation, but by purchasing stations in the largest markets these corporations can obtain access to far more than the average audience for the 8,000 commercial stations.

On the surface the book industry, like radio, seems to present a picture of diversity. There are 2,500 individual companies publishing books, and together they produce 34,000 new titles a year. But most of the 2,500 book publishers issue only from one to five books per year. Overall, eleven corporations received more than half the $7 billion in book sales for 1980: Time, Inc.; McGraw-Hill; Reader's Digest; CBS; Doubleday; Grolier; Harcourt Brace Jovanovich; Encyclopaedia Britannica; Scott and Fetzer World Book; SFN Co. (Scott, Foresman); and Times Mirror.

These corporations publish under many imprints or special subcompany titles. Some of the imprints they own are the following:

*Time-Life Books*
Time-Life Books; Little, Brown and Co.; Book-of-the-Month Club and numerous specialty book clubs; Lloyd Hollister, Inc.; Pioneer Publishing Co.; Pacifica Ltd. (Japan); New York Graphic Society

*McGraw-Hill*
Shepard's; Schaum (paperback); Osborne; Standard & Poor's; McGraw-Hill; Gregg Publishing Co.; Webster Publishing Co.; Herder and Herder; Sweet's Handbook

*Reader's Digest*
Reader's Digest Condensed Books; QSP, Inc.

*CBS*
Holt, Rinehart and Winston; Praeger Publishers; W. B. Saunders; Dryden Press; Fawcett Service Group—Gold Medal, Premier, Popular Library, Crest; Curtis Books; Editions Doin (French); NEISA (Spanish); Movie Book Club

*Doubleday*
Dell; Delacorte Press; Dial Press; Laidlaw Brothers; J. G. Ferguson; Anchor; Feffer and Simons, Inc.; Aldus Books; Rathbone Books; Literary Guild; Doubleday Book Club; Western Writer's Club; Military Book Club; Doubleday Romantic Library

*Grolier, Inc.*
The New Book of Knowledge; Encyclopedia Americana; Encyclopedia International; Franklin Watts, Inc.; Scarecrow Press; Marcus-Campbell Co.; reference sets—The New Book of Popular Science, Lands and Peoples; The Book of Art; Disney's Wonderful World of Knowledge; Disney's Wonderful World of Reading; Value Tales; The Ocean World of Jacques Cousteau; Dr. Seuss Beginning Reader's Program; international encyclopedias—Nuevo Enciclopedia Tematica; Enciclopedia Illustrada Cumbre and El Nuevo Tesoro De La Juvente; La Livre des Connaissances and Pays et Nations; Nuova Enciclopedia Internazionale

*Harcourt Brace Jovanovich*
Academic Press, Inc.; Grune and Stratton; Johnson Reprint Corp.; HBJ Legal and Professional Publica (Gilbert law summaries);

Coronado Publication (subsumed Benefic Press); Harvest; Voyager; HBJ Press; Dansville Press; Jove; Instructor Publications; Weber Cotello; Law and Business, Inc.; Media Systems College Publications; History Book Club; Instructors Book Club; Young Parents; Academic Press and Professional Publications (Canada, Australia, London, Brazil, and Japan)

*Encyclopaedia Britannica*
G. & C. Merriam; F. E. Compton Co.; Great Books of the Western World; Library Resources, Inc.

*Scott and Fetzer World Book*
World Book–Childcraft International; Science Year; World Book Finance, Inc.; direct-sale book club, with Bertelsmann AG on joint venture

*SFN Co. (Scott, Foresman)*
University Park Press; Southwestern Publishing; Silver Burdett (Dale Seymour Publications); Fleming H. Revell; Lothrop, Lee and Shepard Co. under Morrow, sold to Hearst in 1981; Science Year

*Times Mirror*
Signet; Signet Classics; Mentor; Meridian; Abrams Art Books; Mathew Bender law books; New American Library; Yearbook Medical Books; Southwestern (home reference books, journals, and college texts); New English Library (British paperbacks); Denoyer-Geppert Co.; Popular Science Publications

Trade books published for the general public, while not always among the top moneymakers, are the most socially influential. Trade book publishing is controlled by a number of corporations whose main interest is in other industries. According to Knowledge Industries, in 1980 the leading owners of trade book companies by sales were the following:

1. Newhouse Publications: Random House
2. Gulf + Western: Simon & Schuster
3. Harper & Row
4. Doubleday
5. Crown/Outlet
6. Time, Inc.: Little, Brown
7. MCA: Putnam's
8. Hearst: William Morrow
9. Houghton Mifflin
10. Filmways: Grosset & Dunlap

Mass paperbacks sell in far larger numbers than any other type of book. They are sold in drugstores, supermarkets, and air terminals, and their deliveries are regulated by computers that remove books that fail to sell quickly. The leading owners of paperback sales are:

1. Bertelsmann AG: Bantam
2. Gulf + Western: Pocket Books

Five companies have half of all paperback sales and the top ten have 86 percent of the market.

Textbooks represent another major portion of the book publishing industry. Leading controllers of that influential market are SFN (formerly Scott, Foresman), Harcourt Brace Jovanovich, CBS, McGraw-Hill, Houghton Mifflin, Xerox (Ginn & Co.), Macmillan, Prentice-Hall, Addison-Wesley, Doubleday, IBM/Science Research Associates, Encyclopaedia Britannica, Esquire Educational Group, and Dow Jones (Richard Irwin).

The best estimates from Wall Street analysts are that eight corporations have most of the adult trade book business, four have most of the mass paperback sales, and four a majority of the textbook business.

Beginning in the 1960s electronics companies, sensing a trend to computerized learning, bought book companies to control content as well as hardware. In a relatively short period book publishing subsidiaries had been bought by IBM, ITT, Litton, RCA, CBS, Raytheon, Xerox, General Electric, Westinghouse, and General Telephone and Electronics.

But even large, sophisticated firms failed to understand fundamental characteristics of the book business. The usual business techniques of increasing the volume of production, selling by massive promotion and advertising, and building brand loyalty by emotional association, thus swamping competition, did not work well with book publishing. The conglomerates failed to understand that books could not be sold like soap. Even if a few of the 34,000 new titles each year are sold in the millions by high-pressure promotion, such sales do not carry over to the next year, and there is almost no brand loyalty to book companies among consumers.

As quick investments, books do not respond ideally for Wall Street investors or other entrepreneurs. In thirty-five years, for example, Bantam Books has had five owners: Grosset & Dunlap, National General, American Financial, IFI International (Italian), and Bertelsmann (German).

*From the Preface to the 6th Edition (2000)*

**Books—Grandfather of Them All**

In the age of the Internet, books, for more than 2,300 years the foundation for all mass media, remain alive, though annual sales increases have become more modest in recent years.

Even so, conventional books, both hardcover and mass market paperbacks, along with texts and specialized books, have $50 billion annual revenues. Books continue to sell to a generation seen as image-oriented and no longer interested in words printed on paper.

Between 1982 and 1997, book sales rose from 1.7 billion to 2.2 billion volumes, with prices that rose an average of almost three times per book. The dominant firms had most of the profits; 80 percent of smaller companies had gross revenues of less than $2 million a year each.

The five largest book publishers are Bertelsmann, by far the largest with 10 percent of all English-language book sales in the world, followed by Time Warner, Disney, Viacom (owner of, among other firms, Simon & Schuster), and News Corp. Thus two of the firms are based abroad, Bertelsmann in Germany and Murdoch's News Corp in Australia.

Bertelsmann's power in the marketplace is unmatched. It is the world's third largest conglomerate, with substantial ownership of magazines, newspapers, music, television, on-line trading, films, and radio in fifty-three countries. It has a major stake in the U.S. Internet service provider America Online (AOL) and a 50 percent interest in barnesandnoble.com. By purchasing Random House, it acquired a publisher that already had under its wing fifty formerly independent publishing houses and imprints, among them Knopf, Pantheon, Crown, Fawcett, Ballantine, Vintage, Anchor, Bantam, Doubleday, Dell, and Delacorte.

With each succeeding consolidation of publishing houses, the merged publishers cut back on the number of titles each had published while independent. Contracts with authors have been canceled and books in process eliminated or shredded.

Andre Schiffrin, former director of the once prestigious Pantheon Press, has said that since their emergence as consolidated giants, none of the three leading book firms has published a book of serious history, scientific inquiry, or translation. Medium and small publishers still publish serious books, but they lack the power to produce and promote books at a level that is competitive with the major firms, and they lack equal access to the global sales machinery.

(xxxvi-xxxvii)

The care with which books generally have been produced has been diluted as editors have suffered lowered status in favor of packagers and promoters. In conglomerate-owned publishing houses, the process is governed as much by the vagaries of the stock market as by those of the book market. Random House listed its stock on Wall Street in 1959 after which, according to Bennett Cerf, head of Random House at the time, "we were publishing with one eye and watching our stock with the other."

In the movie industry, all movies are made by eight or nine studios, numbers that change quickly in the shadowy world of Hollywood finance. But if film revenues from 1975 through 1979 are averaged, four studios, in this order, dominated their industry with more than half the business: Universal-MCA, Warner Communications (Warner Brothers), 20th Century–Fox, and Gulf + Western (Paramount).

The total number of corporations that share half or more of the audience in each major medium is sixty-eight. But some control audiences in more than one medium. In 1980, for example, CBS was among the dominant companies in television, radio, magazines, and books; Capital Cities in newspapers and radio; Hearst, Washington Post, New York Times, and Newhouse in newspapers and magazines; ABC and NBC in television and radio; Cox and Gannett in newspapers and radio; Time, Inc., McGraw-Hill, and Reader's Digest in magazines and books; and Times Mirror in newspapers, books, and magazines. The net result is fifty corporations that share half or more of the audience in the combined major media.

Many of these same firms have additional holdings in other media, even if they do not share in half the sales in those media. Time, Inc., for example, also produces films, including television movies, and Hearst and the Washington Post are active in broadcasting. In 1980, three firms—Universal-MCA, Columbia, and Gulf + Western—made half of all prime-time television shows. In the record and tape industry, not counted here as a major informational medium, some of the same names appear. More than 80 percent of all records and tapes are made by Warner Communications, MCA, CBS, RCA, and Polygram. Some of the fifty corp-orations appear in new cable-related media, whose impact is still unclear.

It is dangerous enough that in a democracy fifty corporate chiefs have so much power over the national consciousness and that this power can be exercised in ways that serve other interests. But even that is understated.

There are 360,000 industrial corporations, the nominal base of what is sometimes referred to as "corporate power" in the United States. But in terms of their share of the industrial economy, the vast majority have almost no power. The 500 largest of these, less than 1 percent of all corporations, have 87 percent of all sales. They are the aristocrats of the American industrial economy; the remaining 359,500, in terms of their national power, are the peasantry.

The largest mass media corporations are now part of this American economic aristocracy, acquired in morganatic mergers in the manner of fourteenth-century monarchs who gained valuable territory by marrying heirs to distant duchies. Among these 500 largest corporations are 21 of the 50 largest media companies (Westinghouse; RCA; Gulf + Western; Charter Oil; CBS; Time, Inc.; ABC; Warner Communications; Times Mirror; MCA; Gannett; Knight-Ridder; McGraw-Hill; 20th Century–Fox; New York Times; Washington Post; Scott and Fetzer; Dow Jones; Harcourt Brace Jovanovich; Capital Cities; and Metromedia). Twenty years ago only 9 media companies were in the Fortune 500 (RCA; Time, Inc.; Hearst; McGraw-Hill; New York Times; Times Mirror; McCall; and Grolier).

As we shall see, the degree to which the parent corporation controls the content of its media subsidiary varies. The most powerful influence, possessed by all, is the power to appoint media leaders. It is a rare corporation that appoints a leader considered unsympathetic to the desires of the corporation. And when it feels threatened by law, public opinion, or the marketplace, no corporation will permit a subsidiary to harm the parent. Real independence for a media subsidiary is, at best, a disposable luxury.

Media subsidiaries owned by these ruling American industrial corporations include seven of the twenty largest newspaper chains, eight of the leading twenty magazine companies, seven of the ten largest radio operators, all three dominant television networks, seven of the eleven leading book publishers, and three of the four leading movie studios.

Dominant media companies are further integrated into the ruling forces of the economy. Through interlocking directorates—sharing members on boards of directors—the country's newspapers, magazines, radio and television companies, book publishers, and moviemakers are now directly influenced by still other powerful industries. The same media firms are part of the global banking and investment community through their loans and lines of credit; they share directors from the top multinational banks and investment houses.

Under law (and business ethics) the director of a firm is obliged to act in the best interests of that company. Under

479

some circumstances it is a federal crime to do otherwise. This creates a dilemma in the present pattern of corporate boards, a dilemma largely ignored but one that now descends on the governance of the news media: What happens if the same person sits on the boards of two different corporations and it is in the best interests of one of the corporations to do something that will damage the other corporation?

The energy crisis of the last part of the twentieth century for example, is one of the most contentious issues facing American society. The information presented as news, background and analysis about the oil industry in newspapers, magazines and television is crucial to the American public. What happens if the oil industry has deep influence in the governing of the news media? This is not an academic question: Oil representatives sit on the boards of the most powerful news media. In 1979, sitting on the board of directors of RCA, owner of NBC were people who simultaneously were directors of Cities Service Atlantic Richfield, and the American Petroleum Institute (the leading oil and gas lobby). Legally, each of these directors is bound to act in the best interests of each corporation on whose board he or she sits. But what happens if it appears to NBC to be in the best interests of the public to do a critical documentary that will damage the public image of the oil industry? Which way will the common oil/RCA director vote "in the best interests" of conflicting corporations?

Louis Brandeis, before joining the Supreme Court, wrote

> The practice of interlocking directorates is the root of many evils. It offends laws human and divine. . . . It tends to disloyalty and violation of the fundamental law that no man can serve two masters. . . . It is undemocratic, for it rejects the platform: "A fair field and no favors."

Members of corporate boards have impressive power over their corporations. They hire—and fire—the corporate leaders. They set corporate policy. They decide if the corporation will borrow money (or lend it) and for what purpose. They decide how the corporation will deal with the public and with the government.

When individuals sit on more than one board they have powers that can affect all the corporations they govern. They can provide implicit cooperation that will permit two or more corporations to behave in a synchronization that would be illegal or unwise if done explicitly. This is most obvious if directors sit on boards of corporations that are

ostensible competitors. At least one in eight interlocks of large American corporations is between competitors.

In 1978 when the Department of Justice wanted to use its computer to show the extent of interlocks among major American corporations, business leaders were powerful enough to prevent it. Through more tedious methods the department found that in 1976, of 130 major companies, the largest interlocked through their directors with 70 percent of the others. Exxon, for example, interlocked with its leading competitors, Atlantic Richfield, Mobil, Standard Oil of California, Standard Oil of Indiana, and Texaco.

Brandeis called this "the endless chain." The corporations from which Americans get most of their news and ideas have now entered "the endless chain."

For example, Exxon, the world's largest corporation, has two directors on the board of Citibank, alongside directors of Mobil and Standard Oil of California, General Electric, Westinghouse, General Motors, Ford Motor Company, Du Pont, AT&T, IBM, and RCA. RCA and Westinghouse, two major media companies, are interlocked competitors and both are interlocked with corporations, like Exxon, whose news they report.

Today the country's major organs of public information are no longer local. Consequently, any conflict of interest is on a national or global scale, as are the consequences.

. . .

A 1979 study by Peter Dreir and Steven Weinberg found interlocked directorates in major newspaper chains. Gannett, the largest seller of newspapers in the country, shared directors with Merrill Lynch (stockbrokers), Standard Oil of Ohio, 20th Century–Fox, Kerr-McGee (oil, gas, nuclear power, aerospace), McDonnell Douglas Aircraft, McGraw-Hill, Eastern Airlines, Phillips Petroleum, Kellogg Company, New York Telephone Company.

Knight-Ridder, the second largest purveyor of daily newspapers, had interlocks with banking, other media firms, the automotive industry, oil and gas, public utilities, and tire manufacturing.

The Tribune Company of Chicago, another major newspaper chain and publisher of the leading paper in Chicago, has on its board executives or directors from Commonwealth Edison, G. D. Searle, Zenith Radio, Continental Illinois, General Dynamics, and U.S. Gypsum. (Also on the Tribune board is a director from Sears, Roebuck. When Sears was accused by the Federal Trade Commission of dishonest advertising and sales promotion, the *Tribune* was one of the major papers that failed to carry a word of it, although Sears's national headquarters are in Chicago. Even Sears's national news director, Ernest Arms, commented, "I was really surprised at the lack of coverage.")

Times Mirror of Los Angeles has on its board directors from Bank of America, Norton Simon, TRW, Rohr Corporation, Kaiser Steel, Ford Motor Company, American Airlines, Colgate-Palmolive, and Carter Hawley Hale Stores (a major advertiser in the paper and owner of Waldenbooks, second-largest bookseller in the country, which sells books published by Times Mirror.)

The most influential paper in America, the *New York Times*, interlocks with Merck, Morgan Guaranty Trust, Bristol Myers, Charter Oil, Johns Manville, American Express, Bethlehem Steel, IBM, Scott Paper, Sun Oil, and First Boston Corporation. (It also interlocks with the Ford Motor Company. In 1974 the publisher of the *Times*, Arthur Ochs Sulzberger, was told by Henry Ford II that federal safety and pollution standards would increase car prices. According to Sulzberger, "I said it certainly would affect the advertising coming into our newspapers. I said I would set up a forum." Sulzberger sent a letter to major newspaper publishers announcing a meeting with Ford officials, adding, "I would strongly urge you to bring with you your editorial page editor and your business and financial editor, for the story that Messrs. Ford and Iacocca wish to tell goes far beyond the scope of an 'automotive' story." As a result the Associated Press, United Press International, Dow Jones, Reuters, and the Washington Post–Los Angeles Times wires carried Ford and Iacocca's presentation arguing against the federal safety and pollution controls. Most papers whose reporters attended the meeting put the story on page 1, including the *New York Times*, which ran it at the top of page 1 with a two-column picture of Ford.)

The second most influential paper in the country, the *Washington Post*, interlocks with CBS, Allied Chemical, Blue Chip Stamps (which controls Berkshire Hathaway textiles, *Buffalo Evening News*, Pinkerton's, and Munsingwear), IBM, Ford Motor Company, Levi-Strauss, TWA, Utah International, and Wells Fargo Bank.

Another study of interlocking directorates, by this author, found that an even greater concentration of international industrial and financial figures dominates other major media. American Broadcasting Co., for example, has on its board executives from the oil and gas industries, major banks, insurance companies, IBM, General Motors, and General Dynamics. CBS shares directors with major international banks, Aerospace Corporation, Institute for Defense Analysis, Eastern Airlines, Gannett Co., Trilateral Commission, Memorex, Aluminum Company of America, Pan American Airways, and the Asia Society.

Time, Inc. has so many interlocks they almost constitute the leadership of American business and finance. A small selection of its interlocking directorates include the chairman, chief executive officer, and chairman of the executive committees of Mobil Oil and directors of American Petroleum Institute, AT&T, American Express, Temple-Eastex (a Texas wood products firm that controls Time, Inc.), American Paper Institute, Abbott Laboratories, Firestone Tire & Rubber Company, Mellon National Corporation, Borg-Warner, Atlantic Richfield, Xerox, Pan American Airways, Volvo, Colgate-Palmolive, General Dynamics, and most of the major international banks.

Gulf + Western is interlocked with Freedoms Foundation, Houston Natural Gas, Societa Generale Immobilare (an international financing corporation), Roosevelt Raceway, Madison Square Garden, Winn-Dixie Stores, and Flying Diamond Oil.

Almost every major industry whose activities dominate the news of the 1980s—the leading defense contractors and oil companies—sit on controlling boards of the leading media of the country.

There is hardly a major international bank or insurance or investment company that is not represented on boards of directors of the major media that control most of what Americans learn about the economy. In crucial times decisions of directors and banks can spell life or death for a company's independence. When American Express almost captured McGraw-Hill, it was able to make the attempt because McGraw-Hill's banker—who had innermost knowledge of McGraw-Hill's finances—and a McGraw-Hill director from American Express switched sides, and so could use their inside knowledge of McGraw-Hill to aid American Express against McGraw-Hill.

In a war to take over Conoco Oil in 1981, the *Wall Street Journal* noted that a few crucial banks, insurance companies, and big investment firms held influence among all the bidders. A research concern, Corporate Data Exchange, said, "In effect, the same shareholders will be deciding the fate of this merger on both sides of the transaction."

Banks, insurance companies, and investment companies vote whatever stock they hold. But they also vote shares bought with money put in their trust, including union and industrial pension funds, one of the largest single forces in the stock market.

It is not always easy to discover who, in reality, holds and votes on stock in media corporations. The law permits some shares to be held by "street name" firms whose real beneficiaries remain secret, an invisible hand with special significance when it has influence over the mass media.

In 1968 Representative Wright Patman issued a major study attempting to show the extent to which banks control American industry, including major media. He found that the Mercantile Bank in Baltimore had 61.3 percent of the common stock and controlling votes in the *Baltimore Sun* newspapers. The First National Bank in Chicago had a director in Scott, Foresman, a leading book publisher, and held 8.9 percent of its stock. It held 32 percent of stock in another book house, David McKay, 100 percent of the stock of Copley Newspapers, a controlling share in Holt, Rinehart and Winston book publishers, and had a director on the board of Time, Inc. But the same bank held stock in and had directors on the boards of firms with an interest in the news—Sears, Chrysler, General Foods, Shell Oil, and Standard Oil of Indiana.

The concentration of giant media firms that control American public information is troublesome by itself. The interlocking directorates with each other and with major industries and banks, insurance companies, and investment firms make it more troublesome still. The relationship of the news media and leading world bankers is corporate incest within corporate incest: The controllers control each other. Patman and others have found that a cluster of New York banks and life insurance companies held controlling shares in the New York Times Co.; *Newsday;* McGraw-Hill; Dow Jones; Time, Inc.; ITT; CBS; ABC; Prentice-Hall; Harcourt Brace Jovanovich; ABC; Doubleday; Ridder Publications (now

Knight-Ridder); RCA; Thomson Newspapers; Westinghouse; Cox; Reader's Digest; Harper & Row; the Washington Post Co; Xerox; and the Tribune Company.

A 1978 study by the Senate Committee on Governmental Affairs issued a report with a laconic paragraph:

> The principal stockvoters in large banks are—large banks. Morgan Guaranty is Stockvoter Number 1 in four of its New York sister banks—Citicorp, Manufacturers Hanover Corp., Chemical New York Corp. and Bankers Trust New York Corp.—as well as Bankamerica Corp. In turn, Citicorp is Stockvoter No. 1 in Morgan Guaranty's parent holding company, J. P. Morgan & Co. Stockvoter No. 2 in J. P. Morgan & Co. is Chase Manhattan. Stockvoters No. 3 and 4 in J. P. Morgan & Co. are Manufacturers Hanover and Bankers Trust, in whose parent holding company's Morgan Guaranty Trust is Stockvoter No. 1.

Another report of the Senate Committee on Governmental Affairs stated:

> the boardrooms of four of the largest banking companies (Citicorp, Chase Manhattan, Manufacturers Hanover Trust, and J. P. Morgan), two of the largest insurance companies (Prudential and Metropolitan Life) and three of the largest nonfinancial companies (AT&T, Exxon and General Motors) looked like virtual summits of American business. . . .

> All four broadcasting organizations (ABC, CBS, NBC and Westinghouse) were represented on the board of the country's largest international banker, Citicorp, and the network companies linked with each other on the boards of other financial companies and industrials. These facts raise fundamental issues. . . . They can bear on social issues and possibly control the shape and direction of the nation's economy.

The report was conservative. The "summits of American business" now control or powerfully influence the major media that create American public opinion.

Notes

472 ". . . it seemed evident." *Columbia Journalism Review,* Spring 1970, 5.

475 There are 1,730 daily newspapers. From U.S. Senate, *Hearings of the Subcommittee on Antitrust and Monopoly,* 8 vols., 1967–1969; annual editions of *Editor & Publisher Yearbook.*

475 The twenty corporations that control. *John Morton Newspaper Research Newsletter,* 2 April 1982. This list varies in circulation and ranking from time to time because large chains continue to buy remaining independent companies and smaller chains.

475 For 1981, these twenty corporations. *FOLIO: 400,* September 1981, 356.

476 Domination of the radio audience. 1981 Arbitron ratings of cumulative circulations for the top radio groups plus estimates from survey of security analysts specializing in broadcast investments.

477 Overall, eleven corporations received. From *BP Report* and records of Knowledge Industry Publications, Inc., White Plains, N.Y.

477 Trade books published. From Department of Commerce Census of Manufacturers and personal communication with J. Kendrick Noble, Jr.

479 "We were publishing." Bennett Cerf, *At Random: The Reminiscences of Bennett Cerf* (New York: Random House, 1977), 278.

479 In the movie industry. Benjamin M. Compaine, ed., *Who Owns the Media?* (White Plains, N.Y.: Knowledge Industry Publications, 1979), 223.

479 There are 360,000 industrial corporations. *1981 Fortune Double 500 Directory* (Trenton, N.J.: Time, Inc., 1981).

479 These 500 largest corporations. From *Moody's Industrial Manual* and 10-K reports and annual reports of the firms.

480 "The practice of interlocking directorates." Louis D. Brandeis, "The Endless Chain," *Harper's Weekly,* 6 December 1913, 13.

480 A 1979 study. Peter Dreir and Steven Weinberg, "Interlocking Directorates," *Columbia Journalism Review,* November/December 1979, 51–68.

481 When Sears was accused. Michael Hirsh, "The Sins of Sears Are Not News in Chicago," *Columbia Journalism Review,* July/August 1976, 29.

481 (It also interlocks.) Jane Shoemaker, "Sulzberger Has a Better Idea," *MORE,* February 1975. The interlock between the *New York Times* and the Ford Motor Company might shed light on a curious coincidence. On December 20, 1980, a number of newspapers carried a story that the U.S. Department of Transportation had decided not to recall 26 million Ford cars for a serious transmission defect. The defect had been associated with 6,000 accidents, 1,170 injuries, and 98 deaths. The recall was rejected because it would have entailed too much expense for the Ford Motor Company. The same day, many of the papers that carried the recall story carried another item about Ford. They reported that Ford had flown a company engineer to New York City to repair the bent license plate on one of its 1981 Ford Cougars. The customer with the bent license plate presumably could have had it straightened by her gas station attendant, but she had the benefit of a Ford engineer. She was Marian Sulzberger Heiskell, one of the family owners of the *New York Times,* a member of the *Times* board of directors, and in addition, a member of the board of directors of the Ford Motor Company. Heiskell, granddaughter of the founder of the modern *Times,* Adolph Ochs, and the widow of Orvil Dryfoos, former publisher of the *Times,* is married to Andrew Heiskell, former chairman of the board of Time, Inc., thus combining two of the great media empires of the United States. (Associated Press, *San Francisco Chronicle,* 30 December 1980, 11, 44.)

482 In a war to take over. *Wall Street Journal,* 24 July 1981, 23.

482 In 1968 Representative Wright Patman. House Committee on Banking and Currency, *Commercial Banks and Their Trust Activities: Emerging Influence on the American Economy,* 2 vols., 90th Cong., 8 July 1968.

482 There is hardly. *San Francisco Examiner,* 16 January 1979, 43.

482 "The principal stockvoters." Senate Committee on Governmental Affairs, "Voting Rights of Major Corporations," January 1978:3.

482 "The boardrooms of four." Senate Committee on Governmental Affairs, *Interlocking Directorates Among Major U.S. Corporations,* June 1978:280.

484

# 33. [Introduction]
# Direct Manipulation
## A Step Beyond Programming Languages

Jonathan Swift describes a project at the school of languages in the grand academy of Lagado, a project to eliminate words from language: "since words are only names for things, it would be more convenient for all men to carry about them such things as were necessary to express a particular business they are to discourse on."

The idea of direct manipulation, though less foolish, is an analogous one: instead of employing a command language to instruct the computer, the data being processed is exposed and accessed in a more graphically representational way, and immediate visual feedback is provided after every action. This idea informs not only the systems Shneiderman discusses in his 1983 essay, but also the graphical user interface (the Apple Lisa is mentioned in this article; the Macintosh was released the year after this article appeared), visual programming environments, and many other systems and interfaces. Arcade games were nearing a peak in revenue and cultural prominence when Shneiderman's essay was published, and Shneiderman pointed out how their interface principles could be applied to other systems, even if the other system didn't pit the user against the computer in a game.

A direct manipulation system that seeks to imitate something in the outside world via an interface metaphor is not actually direct, nor is it manipulation (the working of something with the hands); but it relates the computer activity to an ordinary action, rather than requiring use of an special-purpose command language. The very usefulness of such systems, and their failings, come from the ways in which their interfaces are slightly indirect or oblique; they abstract rather than directly simulate. They represent data not, strictly speaking, directly, but rather in terms of something that is habitually or more easily understood—as when a list of address and phone number information can be manipulated via the intermediate form of a stack of index cards, represented abstractly on-screen.

The advantages of direct manipulation have become even more evident as graphical applications (such as Photoshop) have become widespread. Such applications have also confirmed, as Shneiderman wrote, that it can take great effort to learn certain specialized direct manipulation interfaces, just as it can take time to learn a command language. In an effort to concretize the data being worked upon and the software environment of an application, some have ended up with direct manipulation systems that recall certain early horseless carriages, those automobiles that bore false horses' heads so as not to startle passersby. The MP3 player with the facade of a physical CD player console is one example of this sort of construction; Microsoft Bob's representation of a room and office supplies is another. The best direct manipulation interfaces, like good metaphors, bring across only the essential aspects of the already-understood system.

While direct manipulation ideas have proven essential to interface design, other sorts of interfaces are still frequently employed and remain important as well. Apple's OS X recently made the command line standard on the Macintosh operating system for the first time. Search engines, the main route to the resources of the Web, rely on text input (and, in some advanced usage, a command syntax) rather than some manipulation of a graphical or tangible representation of the Web. While direct manipulation is an important element of today's computing experience, it still exists in harmony with other interface concepts.

—NM

Certain arcade and console games have moved away from the direct manipulation idea. Side fighter games in the vein of *Street Fighter* and *Mortal Kombat* implement esoteric 'secret moves' in which the joystick is moved in some way that does not directly imitate the action of the on-screen character—although even in these cases, feedback is certainly immediate. Other games, meanwhile, such as games with gun interfaces and driving or flying games, have taken the idea of direct manipulation idea further than ever before in consumer computing. See the next selection, from Sherry Turkle (◊34), for further discussion of early 1980s arcade games.

485
◊34
499

Further Reading

Genter, Don, and Jakob Nielsen. "The Anti-Mac User Interface." *Communications of the ACM* 39, no. 8 (April 1996): 70–82.
<http://www.acm.org/cacm/AUG96/antimac.htm>

Laurel, Brenda, ed. *The Art of Human-Computer Interface Design.* New York: Addison-Wesley, 1990.

Norman, David, and Stephen Draper, eds. *User Centered System Design: New Perspectives on Human-Computer Interaction.* Hillsdale, N.J.: Lawrence Erlbaum Associates, 1986.

Original Publication

*IEEE Computer* 16(8): 57–69. August 1983.

# Direct Manipulation
## A Step Beyond Programming Languages
### Ben Shneiderman

Leibniz sought to make the form of a symbol reflect its content. "In signs," he wrote, "one sees an advantage for discovery that is greatest when they express the exact nature of a thing briefly and, as it were, picture it; then, indeed, the labor of thought is wonderfully diminished."
—Frederick Kreiling, "Leibniz,"
*Scientific American*, May 1968

Certain interactive systems generate glowing enthusiasm among users—in marked contrast with the more common reaction of grudging acceptance or outright hostility. The enthusiastic users' reports are filled with positive feelings regarding

- mastery of the system,
- competence in the performance of their task,
- ease in learning the system originally and in assimilating advanced features,
- confidence in their capacity to retain mastery over time,
- enjoyment in using the system,
- eagerness to show it off to novices, and
- desire to explore more powerful aspects of the system.

These feelings are not, of course, universal, but the amalgam does convey an image of the truly pleased user. As I talked with these enthusiasts and examined the systems they used, I began to develop a model of the features that produced such delight. The central ideas seemed to be visibility of the object

of interest; rapid, reversible, incremental actions; and replacement of complex command language syntax by direct manipulation of the object of interest—hence the term "direct manipulation."

## Examples of Direct Manipulation Systems

No single system has all the attributes or design features that I admire—that may be impossible—but those described below have enough to win the enthusiastic support of many users.

### Display Editors

"Once you've used a display editor, you'll never want to go back to a line editor. You'll be spoiled." This reaction is typical of those who use full-page display editors, who are great advocates of their systems over line-oriented text editors. I heard similar comments from users of stand-alone word processors such as the Wang system and from users of display editors such as EMACS on the MIT/Honeywell Multics system or "vi" (for visual editor) on the Unix system. A beaming advocate called EMACS "the one true editor."

Roberts[1] found that the overall performance time of display editors is only half that of line-oriented editors, and since display editors also reduce training time, the evidence supports the enthusiasm of display editor devotees. Furthermore, office automation evaluations consistently favor full-page display editors for secretarial and executive use.

The advantages of display editors include

*Display of a Full 24 to 66 Lines of Text*

This full display enables viewing each sentence in context and simplifies reading and scanning the document. By contrast, the one-line-at-a-time view offered by line editors is like seeing the world through a narrow cardboard tube.

*Display of the Document in Its Final Form*

Eliminating the clutter of formatting commands also simplifies reading and scanning the document. Tables, lists, page breaks, skipped lines, section headings, centered text, and figures can be viewed in the form that will be printed. The annoyance and delay of debugging the format commands is eliminated because the errors are immediately apparent.

### Cursor Action That Is Visible to the User

Seeing an arrow, underscore, or blinking box on the screen gives the operator a clear sense of where to focus attention and apply action.

### Cursor Motion through Physically Obvious and Intuitively Natural Means

Arrow keys or devices such as a mouse, joystick, or graphics tablet provide natural physical mechanisms for moving the cursor. This is in marked contrast with commands such as UP 6, which require an operator to convert the physical action into correct syntactic form and which may be difficult to learn, hard to recall, and a source of frustrating errors.

### Labeled Buttons for Action

Many display editors have buttons etched with commands such as INSERT, DELETE, CENTER, UNDERLINE, SUPERSCRIPT, BOLD, or LOCATE. They act as a permanent menu selection display, reminding the operator of the features and obviating memorization of a complex command-language syntax. Some editors provide basic functionality with only 10 or 15 labeled buttons, and a specially marked button may be the gateway to advanced or infrequently used features offered on the screen in menu form.

### Immediate Display of the Results of an Action

When a button is pressed to move the cursor or center the text, the results appear on the screen immediately. Deletions are apparent at once, since the character, word, or line is erased and the remaining text rearranged. Similarly, insertions or text movements are shown after each keystroke or function button press. Line editors, on the other hand, require a print or display command before the results of a change can be seen.

### Rapid Action and Display

Most display editors are designed to operate at high speeds: 120 characters per second (1200 baud), a full page in a second (9600 baud), or even faster. This high display rate coupled with short response time produces a thrilling sense of power and speed. Cursors can be moved quickly, large amounts of text can be scanned rapidly, and the results of commands can be shown almost instantaneously. Rapid action also reduces the need for additional commands, thereby simplifying product design and decreasing learning time. Line editors operating at 30 characters per second with three- to eight-second response times seem sluggish in comparison. Speeding up line editors adds to their attractiveness, but they still lack features such as direct overtyping, deletion, and insertion.

### Easily Reversible Commands

Mistakes in entering text can be easily corrected by backspacing and overstriking. Simple changes can be made by moving the cursor to the problem area and overstriking, inserting, or deleting characters, words, or lines. A useful design strategy is to include natural inverse operations for each operation. Carroll[2] has shown that congruent pairs of operations are easy to learn. As an alternative, many display editors offer a simple UNDO command that cancels the previous command or command sequence and returns the text to its previous state. This easy reversibility reduces user anxiety about making mistakes or destroying a file.

The large market for display editors generates active competition, which accelerates evolutionary design refinements. Figure 33.1 illustrates the current capabilities of an IBM display editor.

### VisiCalc

Visicorp's innovative financial forecasting program, called VisiCalc, was the product of a Harvard MBA student, who was frustrated by the time needed to carry out multiple calculations in a graduate business course. Described as an "instantly calculating electronic worksheet" in the user's manual, it permits computation and display of results across 254 rows and 63 columns and is programmed without a traditional procedural control structure. For example, positional declarations can prescribe that column 4 displays the sum of columns 1 through 3; then every time a value in the first three columns changes, the fourth column changes as well. Complex dependencies among manufacturing costs, distribution costs, sales revenue, commissions, and profits can be stored for several sales districts and months so that the impact of changes on profits is immediately apparent.

Since VisiCalc simulates an accountant's worksheet, it is easy for novices to comprehend. The display of 20 rows and up to nine columns, with the provision for multiple windows, gives the user sufficient visibility to easily scan information and explore relationships among entries (see Figure 33.2). The command language for setting up the worksheet can be tricky for novices to learn and for infrequent users to remember, but most users need learn only the basic commands. According to VisiCalc's distributor, "It jumps," and the user's delight in watching this propagation of changes cross the screen helps explain its appeal.

## Spatial Data Management

The developers of the prototype spatial data management system[3] attribute the basic idea to Nicholas Negroponte of MIT.

In one scenario, a user seated before a color graphics display of the world zooms in on the Pacific to see markers for military ship convoys. Moving a joystick fills the screen with silhouettes of individual ships, which can be zoomed in on to display structural details or, ultimately, a full-color picture of the captain. (See Figure 33.3.)

In another scenario, icons representing different aspects of a corporation, such as personnel, organization, travel, production, or schedules, are shown on a screen. Moving the joystick and zooming in on objects takes users through complex "information spaces" or "I-spaces" to locate the item

```
EDIT --- SPFDEMO.MYLIB.PLI(COINS) - 01.04 ------------------ COLUMNS 001 072
COMMAND INPUT ===>                                          SCROLL ===> HALF
****** ***************************** TOP OF DATA *****************************
000100  COINS:
000200     PROCEDURE OPTIONS (MAIN);
000300        DECLARE
000400           COUNT    FIXED BINARY (31) AUTOMATIC INIT (1),
000500           HALVES   FIXED BINARY (31),
000600           QUARTERS FIXED BINARY (31),
000700           DIMES    FIXED BINARY (31),
I3               NICKELS  FIXED BINARY (31),
000900           SYSPRINT FILE STREAM OUTPUT PRINT;
001000        DO HALVES = 100 TO 0 BY -50;
001100           DO QUARTERS = (100 - HALVES) TO 0 BY -25;
001200              DO DIMES = ((100 - HALVES - QUARTERS)/10)*10 TO 0 BY -10;
001300                 NICKELS = 100 - HALVES - QUARTERS - DIMES;
D _                    PUT FILE(SYSPRINT) DATA(COUNT,HALVES,QUARTERS,DIMES,NICKELS);
001500                 COUNT = COUNT + 1;
001600              END;
001700           END;
001800        END;
001900     END COINS;
****** **************************** BOTTOM OF DATA ****************************
```

```
EDIT --- SPFDEMO.MYLIB.PLI(COINS) - 01.04 ------------------ COLUMNS 001 072
COMMAND INPUT ===>                                          SCROLL ===> HALF
****** ***************************** TOP OF DATA *****************************
000100  COINS:
000200     PROCEDURE OPTIONS (MAIN);
000300        DECLARE
000400           COUNT    FIXED BINARY (31) AUTOMATIC INIT (1),
000500           HALVES   FIXED BINARY (31),
000600           QUARTERS FIXED BINARY (31),
000700           DIMES    FIXED BINARY (31),
000800           NICKELS  FIXED BINARY (31),
''''''           -
''''''
000900           SYSPRINT FILE STREAM OUTPUT PRINT;
001000        DO HALVES = 100 TO 0 BY -50;
001100           DO QUARTERS = (100 - HALVES) TO 0 BY -25;
001200              DO DIMES = ((100 - HALVES - QUARTERS)/10)*10 TO 0 BY -10;
001300                 NICKELS = 100 - HALVES - QUARTERS - DIMES;
001500                 COUNT = COUNT + 1;
001600              END;
001700           END;
001800        END;
001900     END COINS;
****** **************************** BOTTOM OF DATA ****************************
```

Figure 33.1. This example from the IBM SPF display editor shows 19 lines of a PL/l program. The commands to insert three lines (l3) and to delete one line (D or D1) are typed on the appropriate lines in the first screen display. Pressing ENTER causes commands to be executed and the cursor to be placed at the beginning of the inserted line. New program statements can be typed directly in their required positions. Control keys move the cursor around the text to positions where changes are made by overstriking. A delete key causes the character under the cursor to be deleted and the text to the left to be shifted over. After pressing an insert key, the user can type text in place. Programmed function keys allow movement of the window forwards, backwards, left, and right over the text. (Examples courtesy of IBM.)

of interest. For example, when they select a department from a building floor plan, individual offices become visible. Moving the cursor into a room brings the room's details onto the screen. If they choose the wrong room, they merely back out and try another. The lost effort is minimal, and no stigma is attached to the error.

The success of a spatial data management system depends on the designer's skill in choosing icons, graphical representations, and data layouts that are natural and easily understood. Even anxious users enjoy zooming in and out or

gliding over data with a joystick, and they quickly demand additional power and data.

## Video Games

Perhaps the most exciting, well-engineered—certainly, the most successful—application of direct manipulation is in the world of video games. An early, but simple and popular, game called *Pong* required the user to rotate a knob, which moved a white rectangle on the screen. A white spot acted as a Ping-Pong ball, which ricocheted off the wall and had to be hit back by the movable white rectangle. The user developed skill

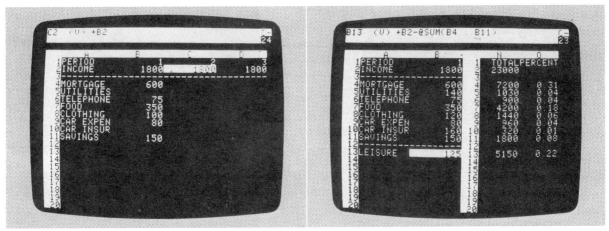

Figure 33.2. This simple VisiCalc program display (top) shows four columns and 20 rows of home budget information. The cursor, an inverse video light bar controlled by key presses, is in position C2. The top command line shows that C2 is a value (as opposed to a text string) that has been set up to have the same value as position B2. The second display (above) shows two windows over the home budget data with row sums to the right. The last row shows leisure dollar amounts, which are established by the top command line formula as the income minus the sum of expenses. A change to the income or expense values would immediately propagate to all affected values. (Displays reproduced by permission of Visicorp.)

involving speed and accuracy in placement of the "paddle" to keep the increasingly speedy ball from getting by, while the speaker emitted a ponging sound when the ball bounced. Watching someone else play for 30 seconds was all the training needed to become a competent novice, but many hours of practice were required to become a skilled expert.

Contemporary games such as *Missile Command, Donkey Kong, Pac Man, Tempest, Tron, Centipede,* or *Space Invaders* are far more sophisticated in their rules, color graphics, and sound effects (see sidebar below and on facing page). The designers of these games have provided stimulating entertainment, a challenge for novices and experts, and

many intriguing lessons in the human factors of interface design—somehow they have found a way to get people to put coins into the sides of computers. The strong attraction of these games contrasts markedly with the anxiety and resistance many users experience toward office automation equipment.

Because their fields of action are abstractions of reality, these games are easily understood—learning is by analogy. A general idea of the game can be gained by watching the on-line automatic demonstration that runs continuously on the screen, and the basic principles can be learned in a few minutes by watching a knowledgeable player. But there are

489

Figure 33.3. A spatial data management system has been installed on the aircraft carrier USS Carl Vinson. In the photo at top left, the operator has a world map on the left screen and a videodisc map of selected areas on the center screen. After some command selections with the data tablet and puck, the operator can zoom in on specific data such as the set of ships shown in the second photo. With further selections the operator can get detailed information about each ship, such as the length, speed, and fuel. (Photos courtesy of Computer Corporation of America.)

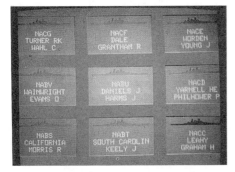

In 1971, about the only people playing video games were students in computer science laboratories. By 1973, however, millions of people were familiar with at least one video game—*Pong* (above left). A few years later came *Breakout* (above, center left), which, according to many designers, was the first true video game and the best one ever invented. *Pong* and other early games imitated real life, but *Breakout* could not have existed in any medium other than video. In the game, a single paddle directed a ball toward a wall of color bricks; contact made a brick vanish and changed the ball's speed.

*Donkey Kong, Space Invaders,* and *Tron* (above center, center right, and right) exemplify the lively vareity of video games now inviting the public's loose change. As of mid-1981, according to Steve Bloom, author of *Video Invaders,* more than four billion quarters had been dropped into *Space Invaders* games around the world—that's roughly "one game per earthling."

ample complexities to entice many hours and quarters from experts. The range of skill accommodated is admirable.

The commands are physical actions, such as button presses, joystick motions, or knob rotations, whose results appear immediately on the screen. Since there is no syntax, there are no syntax error messages. If users move their spaceships too far left, then they merely use the natural inverse operation of moving back to the right. Error messages are unnecessary because the results of actions are so obvious and easily reversed. These principles can be applied to office automation, personal computing, and other interactive environments.

Every game that I have seen keeps a continuous score so that users can measure their progress and compete with their previous performance, with friends, or with the highest scorers. Typically, the 10 highest scorers get to store their initials in the game for regular display, a form of positive reinforcement that encourages mastery. Malone's[4] and our own studies with elementary school children have shown that continuous display of scores is extremely valuable. Machine-

generated value judgments—"Very good" or "You're doing great!"—are not as effective, since the same score means different things to different people. Users prefer to make their own subjective judgments and may perceive machine-generated messages as an annoyance and a deception.

Carroll and Thomas[5] draw productive analogies between game-playing environments and application systems. However, game players seek entertainment and the challenge of mastery, while application-system users focus on the task and may resent forced learning of system constraints. The random events that occur in most games are meant to challenge the user, but predictable system behavior is preferable in nongame designs. Game players compete with the system, but application-system users apparently prefer a strong internal locus of control, which gives them the sense of being in charge.

## Computer-Aided Design/Manufacturing

Many computer-aided design systems for automobiles, electronic circuitry, architecture, aircraft, or newspaper layout use direct manipulation principles. The operator may see a

When the first arcade video game, *Computer Space,* went on location in a Sears store, its joystick was torn off before the end of the first day. As a result, game designers have sought controls that were both easy to use and hard to destroy. *Centipede* (below left) uses simple controls—a trackball and one button. On the other hand, *Defender* (below right) has five buttons and a joystick; novice players are confused by these relatively conplex controls and usually give up after a few seconds.

schematic on the screen and with the touch of a lightpen can move resistors or capacitors into or out of the proposed circuit. When the design is complete, the computer can provide information about current, voltage drops, fabrication costs, and warnings about inconsistencies or manufacturing problems. Similarly, newspaper layout artists or automobile body designers can try multiple designs in minutes and record promising approaches until a better one is found.

The pleasure in using these systems stems from the capacity to manipulate the object of interest directly and to generate multiple alternatives rapidly. Some systems have complex command languages, but others have moved to cursor action and graphics-oriented commands.

Another, related application is in computer-aided manufacturing and process control. Honeywell's process control system provides an oil refinery, paper mill, or power utility plant manager with a colored schematic view of the plant. The schematic may be on eight displays, with red lines indicating a sensor value that is out of normal range. By pressing a single numbered button (there are no commands to learn or remember), the operator can get a more detailed view of the troublesome component and, with a second press, move the tree structure down to examine individual sensors or to reset valves and circuits.

The design's basic strategy precludes the necessity of recalling complex commands in once-a-year emergency conditions. The plant schematic facilitates problem solving by analogy, since the link between real-world high temperatures or low pressures and screen representations is so close.

### Further Examples

Driving an automobile is my favorite example of direct manipulation. The scene is directly visible through the windshield, and actions such as braking or steering have become common skills in our culture. To turn to the left, simply rotate the steering wheel to the left. The response is immediate, and the changing scene provides feedback to refine the turn. Imagine trying to turn by issuing a LEFT 30 DEGREES command and then issuing another command to check your position, but this is the operational level of many office automation tools today.

The term direct manipulation accurately describes the programming of some industrial robots. Here, the operator holds the robot's "hand" and guides it through a spray painting or welding task while the controlling computer records every

action. The control computer then repeats the action to operate the robot automatically.

A large part of the success and appeal of the Query-by-Example[6] approach to data manipulation is due to its direct representation of relations on the screen. The user moves a cursor through the columns of the relational table and enters examples of what the result should look like. Just a few single-letter keywords supplement this direct manipulation style. Of course, complex Booleans or mathematical operations require knowledge of syntactic forms. Still, the basic ideas and language facilities can be learned within a half hour by many nonprogrammers. Query-by-Example succeeds because novices can begin work with just a little training, yet there is ample power for the expert. Directly manipulating the cursor across the relation skeleton is a simple task, and how to provide an example that shows the linking variable is intuitively clear to someone who understands tabular data. Zloof[7] recently expanded his ideas into Office-by-Example, which elegantly integrates database search with word processing, electronic mail, business graphics, and menu creation.

Designers of advanced office automation systems have used direct manipulation principles. The Xerox Star[8] offers sophisticated text formatting options, graphics, multiple fonts, and a rapid, high-resolution, cursor-based user interface. Users can drag a document icon and drop it into a printer icon to generate a hardcopy printout. Apple's recently announced Lisa system elegantly applies many of the principles of direct manipulation.

Researchers at IBM's Yorktown Heights facility have proposed a future office system, called Pictureworld, in which graphic icons represent file cabinets, mailboxes, notebooks, phone messages, etc. The user could compose a memo on a display editor and then indicate distribution and filing operations by selecting from the menu of icons. In another project, Yedwab et al.[9] have described a generalized office system, which they call the "automated desk."

Direct manipulation can be applied to replace traditional question-and-answer computer-assisted instruction with more attractive alternatives. Several CDC Plato lessons employ direct manipulation concepts, enabling students to trace inherited characteristics by breeding drosophilla, perform medical procedures to save an emergency room patient, draw and move shapes by finger touches, do chemistry lab projects (see Figure 33.4), or play games.

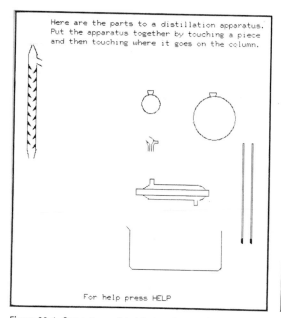
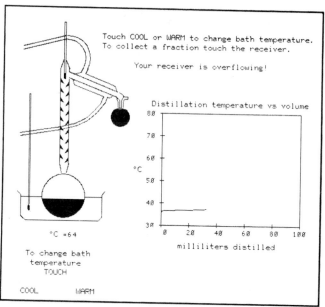

Figure 33.4. Computer-assisted instruction can become more appealing with direct manipulation, rather than simple question and answer scenarios. This CDC Plato lesson written by Stanley Smith of the Department of Chemistry at the University of Illinois allows students to construct a distillation apparatus by proper finger actions on a touch-sensitive screen (figure at left). Once the student has assembled the apparatus and begun the experiment, the real-time display gives a realistic view of the process with the graph of distillation temperature vs. volume. The student controls the experiment by touching light buttons. The figure at right shows that the student experimenter has gotten into trouble.

## Explanations of Direct Manipulation

Several people have attempted to describe the component principles of direct manipulation. "What you see is what you get," is a phrase used by Don Hatfield of IBM and others to describe the general approach. Hatfield is applying many direct manipulation principles in his work on an advanced office automation system. Expanding Hatfield's premise, Harold Thimbleby of the University of York, England, suggests, "What you see is what you have got." The display should indicate a complete image of what the current status is, what errors have occurred, and what actions are appropriate, according to Thimbleby.

Another imaginative observer of interactive system designs, Ted Nelson,[10] has noticed user excitement over interfaces constructed by what he calls the principle of "virtuality"—a representation of reality that can be manipulated. Rutkowski[11] conveys a similar concept in his principle of transparency: "The user is able to apply intellect directly to the task; the tool itself seems to disappear." MacDonald[12] proposes "visual programming" as a solution to the shortage of application programmers. He feels that visual programming speeds system

construction and allows end users to generate or modify applications systems to suit their needs.

Each of these writers has helped increase awareness of the new form that is emerging for interactive systems. Much credit also goes to individual designers who have created systems exemplifying aspects of direct manipulation.

## Problem-Solving and Learning Research

Another perspective on direct manipulation comes from psychology literature on problem solving. It shows that suitable representations of problems are crucial to solution finding and to learning.

Polya[13] suggests drawing a picture to represent mathematical problems. This approach is in harmony with Maria Montessori's teaching methods for children.[14] She proposed use of physical objects such as beads or wooden sticks to convey mathematical principles such as addition, multiplication, or size comparison. Bruner[15] extends the physical representation idea to cover polynomial factoring and other mathematical principles. In a recent experiment, Carroll, Thomas, and Malhotra[16] found that subjects given a spatial representation solved problems more rapidly and successfully than subjects given an isomorphic problem with temporal representation. (Deeper understanding of visual perception can be obtained from Arnheim[17] and McKim.[18])

Physical, spatial, or visual representations are also easier to retain and manipulate. Wertheimer[19] found that subjects who memorized the formula for the area of a parallelogram, $A = h \times b$, mastered such calculations rapidly. On the other hand, subjects who were given a structural explanation (cut a triangle from one end and place it on the other) retained the knowledge and applied it in similar circumstances more effectively. In plane geometry theorem proving, a spatial representation facilitates discovery of proof procedures more than an axiomatic representation. The diagram provides heuristics that are difficult to extract from the axioms. Similarly, students of algebra are often encouraged to draw a picture to represent a word problem.

Papert's Logo language[20] creates a mathematical microworld in which the principles of geometry are visible. Influenced by the Swiss psychologist Jean Piaget's theory of child development, Logo offers students the opportunity to create line drawings with an electronic turtle displayed on a screen. In this environment, users can receive rapid feedback about their programs, can easily determine what has happened, can quickly spot and repair errors, and can experience creative satisfaction.

## Problems with Direct Manipulation

Some professional programming tasks can be aided by the use of graphic representations such as high-level flowcharts, record structures, or database schema diagrams, but additional effort may be required to absorb the rules of the representation. Graphic representations can be especially helpful when there are multiple relationships among objects and when the representation is more compact than the detailed object. In these cases, selectively screening out detail and presenting a suitable abstraction can facilitate performance.

However, using spatial or graphic representations of the problem does not necessarily improve performance. In a series of studies, subjects given a detailed flowchart did no better in comprehension, debugging, or modification than those given the code only.[21] In a program comprehension task, subjects given a graphic representation of control flow or data structure did no better than those given a textual description.[22] On the other hand, subjects given the data structure documentation consistently did better than subjects given the control

flow documentation. This study suggests that the content of graphic representations is a critical determinant of their utility. The wrong information, or a cluttered presentation, can lead to greater confusion.

A second problem is that users must learn the meaning of the components of the graphic representation. A graphic icon, although meaningful to the designer, may require as much— or more—learning time as a word. Some airports serving multilingual communities use graphic icons extensively, but their meaning may not be obvious. Similarly, some computer terminals designed for international use have icons in place of names, but the meaning is not always clear.

A third problem is that the graphic representation may be misleading. The user may rapidly grasp the analogical representation, but then make incorrect conclusions about permissible operations. Designers must be cautious in selecting the displayed representation and the operations. Ample testing must be carried out to refine the representation and minimize negative side effects.

A fourth problem is that graphic representations may take excessive screen display space. For experienced users, a tabular textual display of 50 document names is far more appealing than only 10 document graphic icons with the names abbreviated to fit the icon size. Icons should be evaluated first for their power in displaying static information about objects and their relationship, and second for their utility in the dynamic processes of selection, movement, and deletion.

Choosing the right representations and operations is not easy. Simple metaphors, analogies, or models with a minimal set of concepts seem most appropriate. Mixing metaphors from two sources adds complexity, which contributes to confusion. The emotional tone of the metaphor should be inviting rather than distasteful or inappropriate[16]—sewage disposal systems are an inappropriate metaphor for electronic message systems. Since users may not share the designer's metaphor, analogy, or conceptual model, ample testing is required.

## The Syntactic/Semantic Model

The attraction of systems that use principles of direct manipulation is confirmed by the enthusiasm of their users. The designers of the examples given had an innovative inspiration and an intuitive grasp of what users wanted. Each example has features that could be criticized, but it seems more productive to construct an integrated portrait of direct manipulation:

- Continuous representation of the object of interest.

- Physical actions (movement and selection by mouse, joystick, touch screen, etc.) or labeled button presses instead of complex syntax.

- Rapid, incremental, reversible operations whose impact on the object of interest is immediately visible.

- Layered or spiral approach to learning that permits usage with minimal knowledge. Novices can learn a modest and useful set of commands, which they can exercise till they become an "expert" at level 1 of the system. After obtaining reinforcing feedback from successful operation, users can gracefully expand their knowledge of features and gain fluency.[23]

By using these four principles, it is possible to design systems that have these beneficial attributes:

- Novices can learn basic functionality quickly, usually through a demonstration by a more experienced user.

- Experts can work extremely rapidly to carry out a wide range of tasks, even defining new functions and features.

- Knowledgeable intermittent users can retain operational concepts.

- Error messages are rarely needed.

- Users can immediately see if their actions are furthering their goals, and if not, they can simply change the direction of their activity.

- Users experience less anxiety because the system is comprehensible and because actions are so easily reversible.

- Users gain confidence and mastery because they initiate an action, feel in control, and can predict system responses.

My own understanding of direct manipulation was facilitated by considering the syntactic/semantic model of user behavior. The cognitive model was first developed in the context of programming language experimentation[24,25] and has been applied to database query language questions.[26]

The basic idea is that there are two kinds of knowledge in long-term memory: syntactic and semantic (see Figure 33.5).

## Syntactic Knowledge

In a text editor, syntactic knowledge—the details of command syntax—include permissible item delimiters (space, comma, slash, or colon), insertion of a new line after the third line (I3, I 3, or 3I), or the keystroke necessary for erasing a character (delete key, CONTROL-H, or ESCAPE). This knowledge is arbitrary and therefore acquired by rote memorization. Syntactic knowledge is volatile in memory and easily forgotten unless frequently used.[27] This knowledge

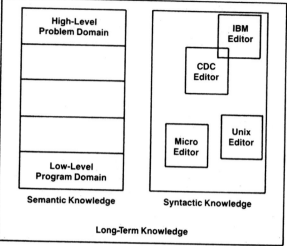

Figure 33.5. The semantic knowledge in long-term memory goes from high-level problem domain concepts down to numerous low-level program domain details. Semantic knowledge is well-structured, relatively stable, and meaningfully acquired. Syntactic knowledge is arbitrary, relatively volatile unless frequently rehearsed, and acquired by rote memorization. There is usually little overlap between the syntax of different text editors, but they often share semantic concepts about inserting, deleting, and changing lines of text.

is system dependent with some possible overlap among systems.

## Semantic Knowledge

The concepts or functionality—semantic knowledge—are hierarchically structured from low-level functions to higher level concepts. In text editors, lower level functions might be cursor movement, insertion, deletion, changes, text copying, centering, and indentation. These lower level concepts are close to the syntax of the command language. A middle-level semantic concept for text editing might be the process for correcting a misspelling: produce a display of the misspelled word, move the cursor to the appropriate spot, and issue the change command or key in the correct characters. A higher level concept might be the process for moving a sentence from one paragraph to another: move the cursor to the beginning of the sentence, mark this position, move the cursor to the end of the sentence, mark this second position, copy the sentence to a buffer area, clean up the source paragraph, move the cursor to the target location, copy from the buffer, check that the target paragraph is satisfactory, and clear the buffer area.

The higher level concepts in the problem domain (moving a sentence) are decomposed, by the expert user, top-down into multiple, lower level concepts (move cursor, copy from buffer, etc.) closer to the program or syntax domain. Semantic knowledge is largely system independent; text editing functions (inserting/deleting lines, moving sentences, centering, indenting, etc.) are generally available in text editors, although the syntax varies. Semantic knowledge, which is acquired through general explanation, analogy, and example, is easily anchored to familiar concepts and is therefore stable in memory.

The command formulation process in the syntactic/semantic model proceeds from the user's perception of the task in the high-level problem domain to the decomposition into multiple, lower level semantic operations and the conversion into a set of commands. The syntax of text editors may vary, but the decomposition from problem domain into low-level semantics is largely the same. At the syntax level the user must recall whether spaces are permitted, whether program function keys are available, or whether command abbreviations are permitted.

As a user of a half-dozen text editors during a week, I am very aware of the commonality of my thought processes in problem solving and the diversity of syntactic forms with which I must cope. Especially annoying are syntactic clashes such as the different placement of special characters on keyboards, the multiple approaches to backspacing (backspace key, cursor control key, or a mouse), and the fact that one text editor uses "K" for keeping a file while another uses "K" for killing a file.

## Implications of the Syntactic/Semantic Model

Novices begin with a close link between syntax and semantics; their attention focuses on the command syntax as they seek to remember the command functions and syntax. In fact, for novice users, the syntax of a precise, concise command language provides the cues for recalling the semantics. Novices review the command names, in their memory or in a manual, which act as the stimuli for recalling the related semantics. Each command is then evaluated for its applicability to the problem. Novices may have a hard time figuring out how to move a sentence of text, even if they understand each of the commands. Novices using editors that have a "CHANGE/old string/new string/" command must still be taught how to use this command to delete a word or insert a word into a line.

As users gain experience, they increasingly think in higher level semantic terms, which are freer from the syntactic detail and more system independent. In addition to facilitating learning, direct manipulation of a visual representation may aid retention.

The syntactic/semantic model suggests that training manuals should be written from the more familiar, high-level, problem domain viewpoint. The titles of sections should describe problem domain operations that the user deals with regularly. Then the details of the commands used to accomplish the task can be presented, and finally, the actual syntax can be shown. Manuals that have alphabetically arranged sections devoted to each command are very difficult for the novice to learn from, because it is difficult to anchor the material to familiar concepts.

The success of direct manipulation is understandable in the context of the syntactic/semantic model. The object of interest is displayed so that actions are directly in the high-level problem domain. There is little need for decomposition into multiple commands with a complex syntactic form. On the contrary, each command produces a comprehensible action in the problem domain that is immediately visible. The closeness of the problem domain to the command action reduces operator problem-solving load and stress.

Dealing with representations of objects may be more "natural" and closer to innate human capabilities: action and visual skills emerged well before language in human evolution. Psychologists have long known that spatial relationships and actions are more quickly grasped with visual rather than linguistic representations. Furthermore, intuition and discovery are often promoted by suitable visual representations of formal mathematical systems.

Piaget described four stages of growth: sensorimotor (from birth to approximately 2 years), preoperational (2 to 7 years), concrete operational (7 to 11 years), and formal operations (beginning at approximately 11 years).[28] Physical actions on an object are comprehensible during the concrete operational stage, and children acquire the concept of conservation or invariance. At around age 11, children enter the formal operations stage of symbol manipulation to represent actions on objects. Since mathematics and programming require abstract thinking, they are difficult for children, and a greater effort must be made to link the symbolic representation to the actual object. Direct manipulation is an attempt to bring activity to the concrete operational stage or even to the preoperational stage, thus making some tasks easier for children and adults.

It is easy to envision direct manipulation in cases where the physical action is confined to a small number of objects

495

Figure 33.6. This electronic Rolodex or phone-number card file gives users rapid control over the card motion by a forward or backward joystick press. Different commands can be displayed by moving the joystick left or right. The lively motion of the cards and the natural commands appeal to many users. Implemented by Gary Patterson in Basic on an Apple II, this system was part of a course project at the University of Maryland.

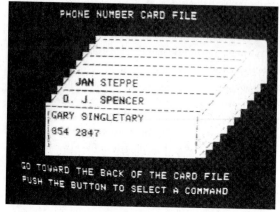

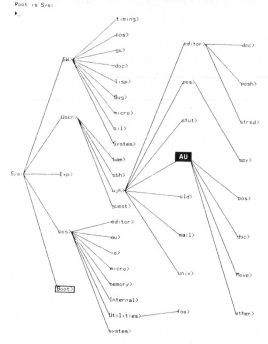

Figure 33.7. The Dirtree (for directory tree) program on the Perq computer of Three Rivers Computer Corporation is built from left to right by puck selections. The details of lower level directories appear, and the items can then be selected by moving a cursor onto the item. In this figure, the current item is AU, shown in inverse video, but the user has moved the cursor to Boot, which is shown with a box around it. If the button on the puck is pressed, Boot would become the current item. (Figure courtesy of Three Rivers Computer Corporation.)

and simple commands, but the approach may be unsuitable for some complex applications. On the other hand, display editors provide impressive functionality in a natural way. The limits of direct manipulation will be determined by the imagination and skill of the designer. With more examples and experience, researchers should be able to test competing theories about the most effective metaphors or analogies. Familiar visual analogies may be more appealing in the early stages of learning the system, while more specific abstract models may be more useful during regular use.

The syntactic/semantic model provides a simple model of human cognitive activity. It must be refined and extended to enhance its explanatory and predictive power. Empirical tests and careful measurements of human performance with a variety of systems are needed to validate the improved model. Cognitive models of user behavior and mental models or system images of computer-supplied functions are rapidly expanding areas of research in computer science and psychology.

## Potential Applications of Direct Manipulation

The trick in creating a direct manipulation system is to come up with an appropriate representation or model of reality. I found it difficult to think about information problems in a visual form, but with practice it became more natural. With many applications, the jump to a visual language was initially a struggle, but later I could hardly imagine why anyone would want to use a complex syntactic notation to describe an essentially visual process.

One application that we explored was a personal address list program that displays a Rolodex-like device (see Figure 33.6). The most recently retrieved address card appears on the screen, and the top line of the next two appear behind, followed by the image of a pack of remaining cards. As the joystick is pushed forward, the Rolodex appears to rotate and successive cards appear in front. As the joystick is pushed further, the cards pass by more quickly; as the joystick is reversed, the direction of movement reverses. To change an entry, users merely move the cursor over the field to be updated and type the correction. To delete an entry, users merely blank out the fields. Blank cards might be left at the top of the file, but when the fields are filled in, proper alphabetic placement is provided. To find all entries with a specific zip code, users merely type the zip code in the proper field and enter a question mark.

Checkbook maintenance and searching might be done in a similar fashion, by displaying a checkbook register with labeled columns for check number, date, payee, and amount. The joystick might be used to scan earlier entries. Changes could be made in place, new entries could be made at the first blank line, and a check mark could be made to indicate verification against a monthly report. Searches for a particular payee could be made by filling in a blank payee field and then typing a question mark.

Bibliographic searching has more elaborate requirements, but a basic system could be built by first showing the user a wall of labeled catalog index drawers. A cursor in the shape of a human hand might be moved over to the section labeled "Author Index" and to the drawer labeled "F-L." Depressing the button on the joystick or mouse would cause the drawer to open up and reveal an array of index cards with tabs offering a finer index. Moving the cursor-finger and depressing the selection button would cause the actual index cards to appear. Depressing the button while holding a card would cause copying of the card into the user's notebook, also represented on the screen. Entries in the notebook might be edited to create a printed bibliography or combined with other entries to perform set intersections or unions. Copies of entries could be stored on user files or transmitted to colleagues by electronic mail. It is easy to visualize many alternate approaches, so careful design and experimental testing will be necessary to sort out the successful, comprehensible approaches from the idiosyncratic ones.

It is possible to apply direct manipulation to environments for which there is no obvious physical parallel. Imagine a job control language that shows the file directory continuously, along with representations of computer components. A new file is created by typing its name into the first free spot in the directory listing. A file name is deleted by blanking it out. Copies are made by locking a cursor onto a file name and dragging it to a picture of a tape drive or a printer. For a hierarchical directory, the roots are displayed until a zoom command causes the next level of the tree to appear. With several presses of the button labeled ZOOM a user should be able to find the right item in the directory, but if he goes down the wrong path, the UNZOOM button will return the previous level. (See Figure 33.7 for a different approach to hierarchical directories.)

Why not make airline reservations by showing the user a map and prompting for cursor motion to the departing and arriving cities? Then use a calendar to select the date, a clock to indicate the time, and the plane's seating plan (with diagonal lines across already reserved seats) to select a seat.

Why not take inventory by showing the aisles of the warehouse with the appropriate number of boxes on each shelf? McDonald[29] has combined videodisc and computer graphics technology in a medical supply inventory with a visual warehouse display.

Why not teach students about polynomial equations by letting them bend the curves and watch how the coefficients change, where the $x$-axis intersects, and how the derivative equation reacts?[30]

These ideas are sketches for real systems. Competent designers and implementers must complete the sketches and fill in the details. Direct manipulation has the power to attract users because it is comprehensible, natural, rapid, and even enjoyable. If actions are simple, reversibility ensured, and retention easy, then anxiety recedes and satisfaction flows in.

The tremendous growth of interest in interactive system design issues in the research community is encouraging. Similarly, the increased concern for improved human engineering in commercial products is a promising sign. Academic and industrial researchers are applying controlled, psychologically oriented experimentation[25] to develop a finer understanding of human performance and to generate a set of practical guidelines. Commercial designers and implementers are eagerly awaiting improved guidelines and increasingly using pilot studies and acceptance tests to refine their designs.

Interactive systems that display a representation of the object of interest and permit rapid, incremental, reversible operations through physical actions rather than command syntax are attracting enthusiastic users. Immediate visibility of the results of operations and a layered or spiral approach to learning contribute to the attraction. Each of these features needs research to refine our understanding of its contributions and limitations. But even while such research is in progress, astute designers can explore this approach.

The future of direct manipulation is promising. Tasks that could have been performed only with tedious command or programming languages may soon be accessible through lively, enjoyable interactive systems that reduce learning time, speed performance, and increase satisfaction.

## Acknowledgments

I am grateful to the Control Data Corporation for partial support (grant 80M15) of my work and to the University of Maryland Computer Science Center for computer resources to prepare this report. I thank Gordon sBraudaway, Jim Foley, John Gannon, Roger Knights, John Lovgren, Harlan Mills, Phyllis Reisner, Sherry Weinberg, and Mark Weiser for their constructive and supportive comments on draft versions. Gio Wiederhold, Stephen Yau, and the reviewers provided useful guidance in shaping the final article.

## References

1. Teresa L. Roberts, "Evaluation of Computer Text Editors," PhD dissertation, Stanford University, 1980. Available from University Microfilms, Ann Arbor, Michigan, order number AAD 80-11699.

2. John M. Carroll, "Learning, Using and Designing Command Paradigms," *Human Learning,* Vol. 1, No. 1, 1982, pp. 31–62.

3. Christopher F. Herot, "Spatial Management of Data," *ACM Trans. Database Systems,* Vol. 5, No. 4, Dec. 1980, pp. 493–513.

4. Thomas W. Malone, "What Makes Computer Games Fun?" *Byte,* Vol. 6, No. 12, Dec. 1981, pp. 258–277.

5 .John M. Carroll and John C. Thomas, "Metaphor and the Cognitive Representation of Computing Systems, *IEEE Trans. Systems, Man, and Cybernetics,* Vol. SMC-12, No. 2, Mar./Apr. 1982, pp. 107–116.

6. Moshe M. Zloof, "Query-by-Example," *AFIPS Conf. Proc.,* Vol. 44, 1975 NCC, AFIPS Press, Montvale, N.J. 1975.

7. Moshe M. Zloof, "Office-by-Example: A Business Language that Unifies Data and Word Processing and Electronic Mail," *IBM Sys. J.,* Vol. 21, No. 3, 1982, pp. 272–304.

8. Cranfield Smith et al., "Designing the Star User Interface," *Byte,* Vol. 7, No. 4, Apr. 1982, pp. 242–282.

9. Laura Yedwab, Christopher F. Herot, and Ronni L. Rosenberg, "The Automated Desk," *Sigsmall Newsletter,* Vol. 7, No. 2, Oct. 1981, pp. 102–108.

10. Ted Nelson, "Interactive Systems and the Design of Virtuality," *Creative Computing,* Vol. 6, No. 11, Nov. 1980, pp. 56 ff., and Vol. 6, No. 12, Dec. 1980, pp. 94 ff.

11. Chris Rutkowski, "An Introduction to the Human Applications Standard Computer Interface, Part 1: Theory and Principles," *Byte,* Vol. 7, No. 11, Oct. 1982, pp. 291–310.

12. Alan MacDonald, "Visual Programming," *Datamation,* Vol. 28, No. 11, Oct. 1982, pp. 132–140.

13. George Polya, *How to Solve It,* Doubleday, New York, 1957.

14. Maria Montessori, *The Montessori Method,* Schocken, New York, 1964.

15. James Bruner, *Toward a Theory of Instruction,* Harvard University Press, Cambridge, Mass., 1966.

16. John M. Carroll, J. C. Thomas, and A. Malhotra, "Presentation and Representation in Design Problem-Solving," *British J. Psych.,* Vol. 71, 1980, pp. 143–153.

17. Rudolf Arnheim, *Visual Thinking,* University of California Press, Berkeley, Calif., 1972.

18. Robert H. McKim, *Experiences in Visual Thinking,* Brooks/Cole Publishing Co., Monterey, Calif., 1972.

19. Max Wertheimer, *Productive Thinking,* Harper and Row, New York, 1959.

20. Seymour Papert, *Mindstorms: Children, Computers, and Powerful Ideas,* Basic Books, Inc., New York, 1980.

21. Ben Shneiderman, R. Mayer, D. McKay, and P. Heller, "Experimental Investigations of the Utility of Detailed Flowcharts in Programming," *Comm. ACM,* Vol. 20, No. 6, June 1977, pp. 373–381.

22. Ben Shneiderman, "Control Flow and Data Structure Documentation: Two Experiments," *Comm. ACM,* Vol. 25, No. 1, Jan. 1982, pp. 55–63.

23. Michael L. Schneider, "Models for the Design of Static Software User Assistance," *Directions in Human-Computer Interaction,* Albert Badre and Ben Shneiderman, eds., Ablex Publishing Co., Norwood, N.J., 1982.

24. Ben Shneiderman and Richard Mayer, "Syntactic/Semantic Interactions in Programmer Behavior: A Model and Experimental Results," *Int'l J. Computer and Information Sciences,* Vol. 8, No. 3, 1979, pp. 219–239.

25. Ben Shneiderman, *Software Psychology: Human Factors in Computer and Information Systems,* Little, Brown and Co., Boston, Mass., 1980.

26. Ben Shneiderman, "A Note on Human Factors Issues of Natural Language Interaction with Database Systems," *Information Systems,* Vol. 6, No. 2, Feb. 1981, pp. 125–129.

27. D. P. Ausubel, *Educational Psychology: A Cognitive Approach,* Holt, Rinehart and Winston, New York, 1968.

28. Richard W. Copeland, *How Children Learn Mathematics,* third ed., MacMillan, New York, 1979.

29. Nancy McDonald, "Multi-media Approach to User Interface," *Human Factors in Interactive Computer Systems,* Yannis Vassiliou, ed., Ablex Publishing Co., Norwood, N.J., to appear in 1983.

30. Ben Shneiderman, "A Computer Graphics System for Polynomials," *The Mathematics Teacher,* Vol. 67, No. 2, Feb. 1974, pp. 111–113.

A portion of this article was derived from the author's keynote address at the NYU Symposium on User Interfaces, "The Future of Interactive Systems and the Emergence of Direct Manipulation," published in *Human Factors in Interactive Computer Systems,* Y. Vassiliou, ed., Ablex Publishing Co., Norwood, N.J., 1983.

# 34. [Introduction]
# Video Games and
# Computer Holding Power

When video games became a major force in popular culture, in the early 1980s, everyone noticed. What Sherry Turkle noticed and elucidated, however, went a step beyond the popular thinking. In her influential first book on new media, *The Second Self*, she explored—alongside careful consideration of other aspects of popular, professional, and academic computing culture—how video games were a telling way in which children, teenagers, and adults encountered the computer.

Turkle, approaching computing from the discipline of psychoanalysis, considered how the computer enables people to enact personae that are different from the ones they use in non-computing situations. While others concerned with the social world were decrying video games as an evil influence, Turkle asked players about their experiences to determine why they played video games. She discovered that these games play a social and psychological role—and, more precisely, that games provide a way in which children as well as adults can take on different roles that are important to them psychologically. The computer is not merely a tool used to accomplish tasks, Turkle explained, but an object that enters our individual and social lives; how we interact with computers influences our outlook on the world and our perspective on ourselves. This idea is explored in Turkle's book *Life on the Screen* in a different way, in the context of internetworked computing. Chapter 7 of that book, in particular, considers how explicit role-playing on MUDs allows play with aspects of the self.

In the selection that follows, Turkle also closely considers the nature of games themselves—noting several features that distinguish video games from sports and even from the previous dominant arcade amusement, pinball. She also considers, as Brenda Laurel has, the fantasy game Dungeons and Dragons, an important and little-studied antecedent to the computer adventure game that created a rule-based world in which play took place.

While adventure games which integrally involve stories are an interesting category, Turkle reported that adults found the stories associated with arcade video games to be "cute or funny but basically irrelevant to their play." Further, while children project themselves into the roles of their characters more strongly, the "story" aspects may have had little influence beyond that. Yet video game makers of the last few years, desperately calling for more integration of stories, have not leant an ear to game-players as Turkle did. Designers hold out hope, instead, that action-oriented games, which people clearly do not play for narrative reasons, can be enhanced with good stories—as if "story" might be the *deus ex machina* that could arrive to save an otherwise incomplete gaming experience.
—NM

*Spacewar!* ⊗, the first modern video game, and *Adventure* ⊗, another computer game mentioned by Turkle during her description of Dungeons and Dragons, are included on the CD along with a selection of other historical computer and video games.

This focus on the shape of the simulation and interaction, rather than the details of the content, is also characteristic of the analysis of Bill Nichols (◊43).

◊43
625

499

The Internet has become a significant social laboratory for experimenting with the constructions and reconstructions of self that characterize postmodern life. In its virtual reality, we self-fashion and self-create. What kinds of personae do we make? What relation do these have to what we have traditionally thought of as the 'whole' person? Are they experienced as expanded self or separate from the self? Do our real-life selves learn lessons from our virtual personae? Are these virtual personae fragments of a coherent real-life personality? How do they communicate with one another? Why are we doing this? Is this a shallow game, a giant waste of time? Is it an expression of identity crisis of the sort we traditionally associate with adolescence? Or are we watching the slow emergence of a new, more multiple style of thinking about the mind? —Sherry Turkle, *Life On The Screen* (180)

Further Reading
Turkle, Sherry. *Life on the Screen: Identity in the Age of the Internet*. New York: Simon & Schuster, 1995.

Original Publication

*The Second Self: Computers and the Human Spirit,* 64–92. New York: Simon & Schuster, 1984.

# Video Games and Computer Holding Power

## Sherry Turkle

I watch a thirteen-year-old girl in a small family café in New York City's Little Italy. Four electronic games lined up near the door clash with the murals of Italian seacoasts. The child too seems out of place. She is angry and abusive to the café owner when he asks her if she would like something to eat. "Get the fuck away from me. I'm fucking playing your fucking games." The man shrugs, apparently used to the abuse of thirteen-year-olds.

The girl is playing *Asteroids.* A spaceship under her control is being bombarded by an asteroids shower. There are separate control buttons for steering, accelerating, and decelerating the spaceship and for firing its rocket guns against threatening asteroids and enemy ships. The player must keep up a steady stream of missiles as she maneuvers the ship. The finger on the "Fire" button must maintain a rapid staccato, an action that is tense and tiring.

The girl is hunched over the console. When the tension momentarily lets up, she looks up and says, "I hate this game." And when the game is over she wrings her hands, complaining that her fingers hurt. For all of this, she plays every day "to keep up my strength." She neither claims nor manifests enjoyment in any simple sense. One is inclined to say she is more "possessed" by the game than playing it.

The children playing with Merlin, Simon, Big Trak, and Speak and Spell at the shore—discussing whether their computer games could really cheat—were displaying that combination of innocence and profundity which leads many of us to believe in Piaget's model of "the child as philosopher." The scene on the beach had an aura of charming solemnity. The scene in the café, like that in thousands of arcades and in millions of homes, is more violent. Somewhat older children—from around nine or ten on—are in a relationship

to the machine that seems driven, almost evoking an image of addiction. Children musing about objects and their nature has given way to children in contest. Reflection has given way to domination, ranking, testing, proving oneself. Metaphysics has given way to mastery.

For the girl in the café, mastery of her game was urgent and tense. There is the sense of a force at work, a "holding power" whose roots are aggressive, passionate, and eroticized.

There has been controversy about video games from the days of *Space Invaders* and *Asteroids,* from the time that the games' holding power provoked people who saw it as a sign of addiction to become alarmed. The controversy intensified as it became clear that more than a "games craze" was involved. This was not the Hula-Hoop of the 1980s. By 1982 people spent more money, quarter by quarter, on video games than they spent on movies and records combined. And although the peak of excitement about the games may have passed with their novelty, video games have become part of the cultural landscape.

Not all of the arguments against video games can be taken at face value, for the debate is charged with feelings about a lot more than the games themselves. Protest against video games carries a message about how people feel about computers in general. In the past decade, and without people having had anything to do or say about it, computers have entered almost every aspect of daily life. By 1983 the computer had become so much and so active a part of the everyday that *Time* magazine chose it to fill the role usually given to a Man or Woman of the Year. Only one other gift of science has been so universally recognized as marking a new era of human life. That was atomic energy.

It is an understatement to say that people are ambivalent about the growing computer presence: we like new conveniences (automated bank tellers, faster supermarket lines), but on the eve of a new era we, by definition, do not know where we are. The changes have been rapid and disquieting. We are ill at ease even with our children, who are so much at ease with a technology that many of us approach at arm's length. They take it for granted. To them it is not a new technology but a fact of life. They come home from school and casually report that they are "learning programming." The comment evokes mixed feelings. Parents want their children to have every advantage, but this new expertise estranges them. It seems to threaten a new kind of generation gap that feels deep and difficult to bridge. And so, for many people, the video game debate is a place to express a more general ambivalence: the first time anybody asked their opinion about computers was when a new games arcade applied for a license in their community or when the owner of a small neighborhood business wanted to put a game or two into a store. It is a chance to say, "No, let's wait. Let's look at this whole thing more closely." It feels like a chance to buy time against more than a video game. It feels like a chance to buy time against a new way of life.

Video games are a window onto a new kind of intimacy with machines that is characteristic of the nascent computer culture. The special relationship that players form with video games has elements that are common to interactions with other kinds of computers. The holding power of video games, their almost hypnotic fascination, is computer holding power. The experiences of video game players help us to understand this holding power and something else as well. At the heart of the computer culture is the idea of constructed, "rule-governed" worlds. I use the video game to begin a discussion of the computer culture as a culture of rules and simulation.

## The Myth of "Mindless" Addiction

Those who fear the games often compare them to television. Game players almost never make this analogy.* When they try to describe the games in terms of other things, the comparison is more likely to be with sports, sex, or meditation. Television is something you watch. Video games are something you do, something you do to your head, a world that you enter, and, to a certain extent, they are something you "become." The widespread analogy with television is understandable. But analogies between the two screens ignore the most important element behind the games' seduction: video games are interactive computer microworlds.

Using analogies with television or with drugs, the popular debate about video games is filled with images of game players caught in a "mindless addiction." Half of this description is certainly wrong. There is nothing mindless

---

* I have been studying video games since 1980, both in arcades and in homes. Whenever possible, participant observation and conversations with players in the game setting were followed up by interviews in a quieter setting. This chapter is based on over one hundred hours of field research and on interviews (ranging from one to four hours) with thirty game players.

about mastering a video game. The games demand skills that are complex and differentiated. Some of them begin to constitute a socialization into the computer culture: you interact with a program, you learn how to learn what it can do, you get used to assimilating large amounts of information about structure and strategy by interacting with a dynamic screen display. And when one game is mastered, there is thinking about how to generalize strategies to other games. There is learning how to learn.

Consider *Pac-Man*, the first game to be acknowledged as part of the national culture. On the screen there is a maze that contains four monsters and the familiar yellow Pac-Man figure. Also scattered in the maze are pellets of food, represented as little dots. The player controls Pac-Man, or, as children usually express it, "You are Pac-Man." Your job is to eat the food and avoid being eaten by the monsters. Doing so involves quick turns and good coordination. But even more important is strategy, figuring out the rules that govern the behavior of Pac-Man and his pursuing monsters.

Pac-Man needs to make quick decisions: eat this dot or flee that monster. His decisions are made more complicated by another factor: in the maze are four energy cookies. For a short period after eating a cookie, Pac-Man can turn the tables on the monsters and eat them. A master player shifts constantly between offensive and defensive strategies: when to go for a dot or a cookie and when simply to stay out of the monsters' way. In addition, there are elements of bluff and trickery. Each monster has a different personality and can be more or less easily thrown off the trail by sudden reversals of direction.

*Pac-Man* shares with chess strategies that depend on executing standard sequences of moves. A well-informed *Pac-Man* player has a repertoire of these "patterns," picked up from other players, from books, and from personal discovery. But just as you can't play chess by rote, the same is true of a video game like *Pac-Man*, in which being off by a split second can throw you outside your pattern. Then you have to improvise, relying on your coordination and understanding of general principles of the game—for example, the differences in the monsters' behavior and the "safe places" to hide out in the maze. But you always have to think faster than the monsters move, and this means that, in order for you to play successfully, the general principles, like the patterns, have to be more than memorized. It's more than thinking—in a way it is beyond thinking. The hand learns what to do and does it automatically, just as the hand "knows" after playing chord X on the piano to go directly and inexorably to chord Y.

People who have never played video games often think that success at them is like winning at a Las Vegas–style "one-arm bandit"; people who have played one game and given up acknowledge that they require "hand–eye coordination," often adding that this is something that children, but not they, possess. But success at video games involves much more. Working out your game strategy involves a process of deciphering the logic of the game, of understanding the intent of the game's designer, of achieving a "meeting of the minds" with the program. The video games reflect the computer within—in their animated graphics, in the rhythm they impose, in the kind of strategic thinking that they require. This "computational specificity" becomes clear when you contrast the games with their "grandparent," pinball.

## Computational Specificity

In some ways video games are reminiscent of pinball. You stand at them, reacting to a moving object by manipulating buttons and levers. Scores pile up. You try to do better. But there are important differences, differences that go back to how the games are made.

Making a new pinball game required designing and constructing new physical devices, a process that took time, tools, and mechanics. The video game—the characters on its screen, their behavior, the way they respond to a player's actions—is made of logic; that is, of a program of tens of thousands of computer instructions. The new "logic technology" has made possible an explosion in the freedom of game designers to search for ways to capture the attention, the imagination, and the coins of players. If a designer wants to change the game, for example, to put a new monster on the screen, he or she doesn't have to "make" a monster, but simply has to write a program that will trace out the monster's shape. To have the new monster engage in a chase requires another program. Pinball games were constrained by mechanical limitations, ultimately by the physical laws that govern the motion of a small metal ball. The video world knows no such bounds. Objects fly, spin, accelerate, change shape and color, disappear and reappear. Their behavior, like the behavior of anything created by a computer program, is limited only by the programmer's imagination. The objects in a video game are representations of objects. And a representation of a ball,

unlike a real one, never need obey the laws of gravity unless its programmer wants it to.

The liberation of the video game from the "real world" allows more than freedom for the designer's imagination. It allows the games to become a more perfect expression of the player's actions. A pinball machine has levers that can rust. It is tilted to a particular slant on a particular floor. It is a mechanism, with a weight, a certain balance. It vibrates differently depending on the noise level around it. The video game has no moving "parts." Its graphics display is electronic, impervious to its surround. It is always the same, reacting almost instantaneously.

Watch pinball players at their game: they kick, they shake and thrust their hips, gently at first, then violently urge the machine to one side or another. Controlling the two bottom flippers by means of two buttons is the only movement in the game that feels discrete or precise. The rest is more like a dance. You have to feel how far you can go without tilting the machine. There is no indicator, no "tilt gauge" to show you the state of things—that is, nothing until it is too late. The physical pinball machine—the legs it stands on as well as its posts and flippers—are part of the game. The video game is different: here all of the action is in a programmed world, an abstract space. In an important sense, it is a space where the physical machine and the physical player do not exist. It is not easy for pinball players to describe their feelings of what makes the game respond. Some describe it as a "conversation": there is a sense of give and take. But although it has become cliché to speak of the video game as "interactive," players describe the experience of being with one as less like talking with a person and more like inhabiting someone else's mind. Conversation gives way to fusion. In pinball you act on the ball. In *Pac-Man* you are the mouth.

## Jarish and the Computer within the Game

By the time Jarish was five he already thought of himself as small for his age, small and very nearsighted and very different. In certain ways he likes being different: "Like my name, it's special, my parents just made it up. Other names come from something . . . my name doesn't come from anything." But being different also had its price; different didn't always feel better. Games became a way to mark different as better; pinball became a favorite and something at which he could be best.

Now Jarish is twelve, and two years ago pinball gave way to video games. His initials are up on almost all of the machines in the arcade closest to his home. He works at a game until he gets the highest score of anybody around, often having to stand on a stool to play. "You know," Jarish remarks, "they really should put little steps on the games. Getting to see the screen can really be a problem."

The old-fashioned pinball machines have no memory. However high your score one day, the machine treats you next time with the same neutral indifference it gives the clumsiest of beginners. And it certainly does not inform anyone else how well you did. Arcade-game manufacturers were quick to see the advantage of using the computers within the games to remember the names—or at least the initials—of the top players who have used it since its memory was last cleared. The players whose names are up on the screens of a game in "their" arcade form a competitive community, and one of mutual recognition. Jarish is pleased: "Everyone knows my initials."

The amnesia of the pinball machine meant more than an inability to let players leave a trace of their prowess. No matter how high your score, you play your next ball on the same game. The video game's computer power makes it possible for the game to respond to the level of the player's skill. When you finish one round, another round, faster and more complex, awaits you.

Jarish was immediately impressed by this difference, enthusiastic about the increasing violence of the tests on successive rounds (in video talk known as "screens" because when you finish a round the screen usually changes, presenting to you an increasingly worthy opponent). "It's great, the pace speeds up, the monsters usually get smarter or whatever, chasing you. Usually, they start chasing you closer." By comparison, pinball "is fun but it belongs to the real world . . . it's always the same." Jarish describes his favorite video games as "crazy and weird," not of the real world.

> I have a favorite where there's this little rocket ship and different colors and there is this dark layout. And you have this violet ray, so that you and all your clothes are changed purple and violet, that's so neat, and you go around destroying the birds of the son of Satan and then there are whole packs of hounds and stuff, and you have to go around destroying them. And after every couple of screens, you meet the devil

himself and you have to go and shoot him with your laser. If you don't hit the devil after a little while he starts spouting fire, and then he gets bigger and bigger and his face takes up the whole screen, and then there's this little missile base, that is you, trying to destroy him, and this big face is coming at you, growing, starting to fill up the whole screen. It's hilarious.

Jarish dreams about designing his own video games. He knows that this medium can satisfy his taste for excitement. Shift from one memory segment to another, and the whole world can change.

> Like if you are being chased by a little dog, that would start to get boring after a while, but if like it changes screens and then you have your army of cats, let's say [here Jarish laughs, really enjoying himself], and the dog is chasing the cats, you can shoot the dog or something and it could change into something else. It never has to be the same thing all the time.

Most adults describe the "stories" of video games as cute or funny but basically irrelevant to their play, saying that they like to play a particular game to work on a specific "skill." Children identify more directly with the games' characters as they are chased, besieged, or, as in the case of Jarish's favorite game, *Robotron*, saving the last family on earth. This game assumes that 1984 has passed uneventfully but that one hundred years later, in 2084, science has almost destroyed humankind. Jarish explains how: "The scientists have perfected the robotron, which are these ingenious robots who go around, they're supposed to be helping humanity, but they have a short circuit and they go around trying to destroy the last family on earth, and you have this laser and you have to go and destroy the robots and save the last family." Jarish feels himself completely in the game: "Yeah, sometimes I think of myself as the kid of the family. I really care."

The intensity of Jarish's involvement has a price. Outside the world of the games he says "you feel sort of cut off. When I play the game, I start getting into it, and you start taking the role of the person . . . and then the game ends. And you have just put all of your energy into it. It doesn't make me angry, more like depressed. You walk out of the arcade and it's a different world. Nothing that you can control."

Talking about *Robotron* evokes Jarish's own feelings about being out of control. "A lot of the kids have girlfriends. I feel

503

left out. I don't have any best friends. It's not my fault. It's my size. Everybody thinks of me as a little kid." Jarish also feels little power in his family. His parents were divorced, his father remarried and then divorced again. Now he is with someone new. As when "the game ends," as when "you walk out of the arcade," there is a feeling of being "cut off." Each change in his family means the start of something new where old investments seem lost. Jarish says that when he feels angry he plays *Robotron*. There he can really concentrate, feel in charge.

When Jarish goes into an arcade he looks for the craziest, most out-of-control game he can find, "let's say a million little birds coming down and you have to fire your laser all over the place and in crazy different scenes," and then he sets out to discover its strategies, its "secrets," to find a way of bringing it under control. For Jarish knows that despite the complexity of the games, there is program behind, there are rules. There is the computer that Jarish mythologizes as the dream machine that can make anything possible and as the rule machine that makes everything that is crazy ultimately controllable.

For Jarish, the fact that a video game "has a computer inside" is of great importance. He feels himself to be a child of the computer generation. *Star Wars* was the hit movie of his eighth year; "computer special effects" were something he thought about before he ever saw a computer. "Comic strip" does not mean *Superman*, but tales of androids and robot brains, all of which assume, as he does, that "artificial intelligence" will become a fact of life. Jarish believes that scientists can do anything, but if you can do anything, something can always go wrong. He sees nothing improbable about the computer-out-of-control *Robotron* scenario. In his image of his own future he too will become a powerful person capable of anything by mastering the computer. Indeed, just as pinball gave way to video games for Jarish, video games are starting to give way to the computer. His interest in computers started when he began to think about ways to change video games, mostly to make them more complicated.

> I would like to change games to make them crazier, like if you were in a two-player game, shooting another guy. I'd make it so like you'd fire these little weird rockets and then your friend could, let's say, press a button, and the rocket would turn into a bunch of, let's say, ants, and they'd fall around everything and you'd have little crater holes and missile silos coming out of the ground.

In science class Jarish dreams about how to use the "boring things we are learning" as materials for the video games he dreams of someday being able to make. "Like why a ball would move and why it goes faster. You might need to use this stuff to make a video game . . . that comes into my mind very often." But between knowing the physics and using it for a game there is, of course, a major step: programming. "Programming is what I need to know," says Jarish. It's how you get to the "real secrets."

After he became involved with video games Jarish saved his money and bought a small personal computer that he uses to play games at home and to experiment with programming. But Jarish dreams of bigger things.

> My biggest interest would be having a terminal. Like one that you can connect to any computer. That would be incredible. My friend has an Apple. She can attach it to a giant computer. It cost about a million dollars. If you can get into different computers you could get the different codes about the computers and different languages and things about it, and take games from them—you know, like games that you couldn't find anywhere else—and transfer them to your own computer, and change the games into anything you like. That would be really terrific. That's the stuff I'd like to do.

For now, Jarish finds games programs in computer magazines and types them into the computer, making small changes in the games, sometimes on purpose to suit his taste, more often by accident when he makes a typo. An object of current delight is a chase game that he modified to make a custom fit for his younger brother. "The program used to have Martians chasing the character, but after my brother heard the song 'Valley Girls' on the radio I changed the Martians to Valley Girls." But when he made this change, something unexpected happened:

> . . . the screen changed to fifty million different things. It was fantastic. And it made this snow effect that's coming down all over the place. And I figured out how to change one of the screens to make it do different things when you eat the treasures. When you eat the treasure you leave this trail, and usually in this game the trail is just dots, but I erased this one line in the program so now it makes these crazy things.

Jarish feels cheated when manufacturers put the games in cartridges so that he has no access to the underlying program. He can't change them the way he can when he finds a game program in a magazine and types it into his own computer.

> There are so many great games and they're really protected. They're trying to not let people copy them. It's really frustrating, because there are so many exciting things you can do with a game. It has nothing to do with—I mean forget the moneymaking part [here Jarish is referring to an earlier part of our conversation in which he fantasized about "changing *Pac-Man* and making it better and making a million dollars"], it's for just having fun.

Jarish doesn't yet know enough about programming to really make his own game, but he is in the process of teaching himself and is encouraged by events like his accidental snow effect. The possibilities seem limitless if such marvelous things can happen by chance. "In computers there is always that random thing, that neat thing that you are going to find out. And you keep at it, trying to find these neat things. Video games showed me what you could do with computers, what you could program. They show you what you can do. It's really wonderful."

## To *Joust* and Beyond

In sports the player is held by the power of total concentration on action, the sense of melding body and mind. The television spectator's body is out of the picture. Here the sense of immersion is through imagination and identification.

The entertainment industry has long believed that the highest payoffs would come from offering the public media that combine action and imaginative identification. The manufacturers of pinball machines try to introduce a missing imaginative component by naming games to suggest exciting stories (you are controlling a pinball, but you are the "Black Knight") and by the equally limited conceit of painted flashy pictures of monsters, pirates, and sexy ladies on the machine's surfaces.

Finally, however, the only objects to identify with in the pinball game are the shiny steel ball and a pair of flippers. A Disneyland ride tries to introduce the feeling of action: watching a space lift-off on television, you are entirely on the "outside." In a Disney spaceship ride you are ushered into a simulated space cabin, you hear the rockets roar, you feel vibration in the seat. But, for all of this, there is nothing for

you to do except use your imagination. In the end, the Disney ride is more passive than participatory drama. Once again, designers try, but the media resists.

But Jarish was able to enter the video game microworld through both doors. The polarization between action and imaginative identification breaks down in the presence of the computer: with the computer behind them the video games provide imaginative worlds into which people enter as participants. Other kinds of microworlds—television, sports, Disney rides, pinball—might offer the holding power of action, of imaginative identification, of losing oneself in a world outside of the habitual. You can find elements of what makes a computer microworld powerful in other things. But the computer can bring it together, and video games were the first place where the culture as a whole, rather than just the culture of computer programmers, got to experience how powerful this is.

Video games began in the computer culture, at one of the places, in fact, where the computer culture itself got started. The first video game was *Space War*, built at MIT in the early 1960s. The screen shows two spaceships, each under the control of one of two players. The ships can be maneuvered and can fire missiles at each other. When *Space War* was first built, visiting computer scientists were amazed by its dynamic, interactive screen graphics—the kind of graphics display that twenty years later would be commonplace in shopping malls. At that time, however, the cost and size of the computer required for *Space War* made it impossible to move it beyond the research environments of such places as MIT.

Ten years later, microtechnology allowed Nolan Bushnell, who had himself been an MIT undergraduate and a *Space War* enthusiast, to surprise the world with *Pong*. Compared with *Space War* its action was extremely limited: a blip—a square ball (easier to make than a round one)—bounced backward and forward across the screen in a crudely simulated Ping-Pong. But, unlike *Space War*, which you could play only by having access to a large computer facility, *Pong* could be made generally available. Bushnell founded a company he called Atari, which manufactured *Pong* in a box smaller than a pinball machine. Soon it was everywhere. You could play it in movie theaters and bars. You could buy a version of it to play on your television set. *Pong* was a novelty, but it set the stage for the arrival of another game, one that had already taken Japan by storm. This was Space Invaders, the game that launched the video game culture.

**505**

It took another ten years for video games to catch up with the complexity of the original *Space War*. A game like *Joust*, a favorite of Jarish's, is of a generation of games that has begun to move beyond. *Space War* had a recognizable "generic" spaceship, but, with neither color nor detail, it was less a spaceship than a spaceship ideogram. Just like the square ball in *Pong*, the spaceship was there to serve as a "marker." In *Joust*, knights duel on flying ostriches, using medieval lances. The player controls his or her ostrich with a joystick. A tug on the stick causes an ostrich that has been trotting along the land to begin to fly, movements of the stick to left or right cause the ostrich to travel in either direction or to reverse direction in midair, digging its heels into the ground before trotting off the other way.

Technological advances have enabled designers to create games that provide visually appealing situations and demand a diverse and challenging set of skills. But the ambition is to have the appeal of Disneyland, pinball, and a Tolkien novel all at once. Games like *Joust* do not offer the imaginative identification with a character and a situation that literature does. The knights in *Joust* owe their appeal to associations the player makes with fantasies about medieval combat that have been sparked through other media. And even the graphically "advanced" *Joust* lacks the degree of individual characterization one has come to expect in animated cartoons.

Designers are starting to break out of these limitations. New generations of computer graphics will allow game characters to have more realistic gestures and facial expressions. New programming techniques offer the hope of creating characters who have more specific and interesting personalities than the monsters in *Pac-Man* so that players' interactions with them may feel more like a social encounter and less like controlling a pinball. A computerized game of poker, for example, could create players who are individual and idiosyncratic. Some might easily fall for bluffs, others could try to bluff but betray themselves by facial expression, yet others allow themselves to be charmed by attractive opponents.

In the late 1970s Woody Allen wrote a classic short story about Kugelmass, a shy middle-aged professor who longs for romance.[1] A great magician comes to his aid. The magician has a box in which you place yourself and a book, open to any page. With a magic incantation you are instantly transported into that book. Kugelmass chooses *Madame Bovary* and has an

affair with Emma in the relative safety of the pages before she meets Rodolphe and the competition gets too rough.

Woody Allen fantasized the interactive novel. Video game designers plan to implement it, perhaps less voluptuously, by putting the player in control of a character who lives not in a maze but in a piece of literature. Already there is a game in which the player takes the role of a character, Jen, who is also the hero of the movie *The Dark Crystal*. The Jen of the game faces the same situation as the Jen of the movie. The world is in peril; he must find the magic crystal that will save it. The Jen of the game will wander through a landscape identical in its topography and inhabitants to that of the movie. But the player behind the game-Jen has a choice of how to proceed. You can follow in the footsteps of the movie character, or you can take an altogether different route, meeting different characters, different dangers, different challenges.

Certainly, "playing" *The Dark Crystal* is still a lot more like a game of *Pong* than a collaboration with Flaubert. But primitive though it is, it provides an image of one direction in which games microworlds could go. It is a direction that makes us ask whether it is accurate to call such things "games" at all.

As this book is published, traditional film images, stored on video disks, are replacing animated computer graphics. With such systems, easily indexed by computer, a given command—for example, "Enter this room" in response to the screen image of a room—can invoke the film image of what is in it. There are "tours" of cities where you are in the picture, "driving" your car through the streets, deciding what buildings to enter. Where things will go is hard to imagine: "movies" and "talkies" were, too. But once you let your imagination work and then let it run a little wild (as wild, for example, as the programmers who made the first *Space War*) the possibilities are intriguing. You are Scarlett O'Hara, opening the door to Tara. You are Rhett Butler, deciding to stay rather than leave.

In circles where people are trying to invent the future of interactive media there seems to be a great divide. Will the player of the games of the future be in a more complex world than is offered by today's games, but still in a world that is created by someone else? Or will the player be the designer of his or her own game? In other words, will players continue to be "users" of someone else's program or will they be programmers in their own right? Will they be able to create new characters and change the rules of the game? Both strategies are being pursued, and surely both will bear fruit.

One leads to an image of an interactive *Gone With the Wind*, the other to children building computer worlds as today's children build ferris wheels with Tinkertoys.

When Jarish began to talk about his new enthusiasm for the computer he offered a touching statement of his loyalty to video games even as he sensed it being threatened: "I love the computer, but I love video games, and whatever happens I will always love them." Unlike pinball, promised Jarish, these would never be abandoned. The breathy commitment was sincere, but should we take Jarish at his own word? It is difficult to imagine him playing anything like *Pac-Man* or *Joust* when he is thirty. What is possible is that he might be exploring interactive computer microworlds that erase the line between playing a game and writing a program, much as they erase the line between playing a game and making a movie.

## Games, Gnomes, and Computer Culture

When today's child stands in front of a video game, there is contact between the physical child and the physical machine. But there is another contact as well: between the child's culture and a culture of simulation. Unlike the worlds of pinball machines or sports or literature, the computers within them make video games "rule-driven." This was certainly a big part of what appealed to Jarish, who knew that behind each game there was a program that held the key to what he called "the secrets." Video games offer a chance to live in simulated, rule-governed worlds. They bring this kind of experience into the child's culture and serve as a bridge to the larger computer culture beyond. They are not the only agent to do so. Reinforcements come from surprising quarters. Children come to the video games from a culture increasingly marked by the logic of simulation.

Recall the dogs and cats of Jarish's imaginary computer game. Animals are unusual images for him. More typically, his fantasies are populated by gnomes, wizards, and magic-users. When I was a child I knew about gnomes and wizards and spells from reading stories. Jarish knows about such things in a different way—he lives them. Most weeks are punctuated with marathon sessions of Dungeons and Dragons, a fantasy game where you create a character from medieval lore by rolling dice to determine its properties; among these are its level of charisma, its ability to use magic, its strength and dexterity. These qualities will be tested as you use your character to explore an intricate universe where there are

monsters, adventures, wars, treasures, and a lot of hand-to-hand combat. Unlike the real world, the game universe always conforms to rules. There is violence, murder, and theft, but the rules for what can happen and how to handle it are precise. The charts and tables that allow you to design worlds and play characters form a small library: "For a kid today," says Jarish, "it's very hard. You have to get the money together for four or five or seven books. Very thick books. Like about fifteen dollars each." Jarish boasts of having read them all. He has become a master of this lore, an expert at manipulating the rules.

There are no computers in the dungeons. But these constructed worlds are permeated with the spirit of a computer program. Their constraints are those imposed by rule systems, not by physical reality or moral considerations. Time might go backward, people might have superhuman powers, everything is possible. What is required is consistency.

In the early 1970s, fantasy gaming grew from cult to culture in the worlds around computer programmers. They found an affinity between the aesthetic of building a large complex program, with its treelike structure, its subprograms and sub-subprograms, and working one's way through a highly structured, constructed world of mazes and magic and secret, hidden rooms.[2] They played the fantasy games, used their considerable talents to build ever more complex dungeons, and began to translate the idea into their own medium. Soon fantasy games with complex underground universes began to appear on large computer systems. *Adventure* was the first of these game programs. In it players explore the labyrinth of Colossal Cave, fighting monsters, hoarding treasure, picking up and discarding tools, food, spells, and other supplies as they go.

Other games followed, and as personal computers became more powerful, with memories that could hold the large data bases the games required, fantasy games spread to home systems. By the late 1970s, *Adventure*-like games were a staple item in the program libraries of most home computer owners, and the Dungeon games played "live" had spread from the computer culture to the culture at large. College students all over the country were absorbed in role-playing fantasy games and soon their younger brothers and sisters caught on. Dungeons and Dragons, a game that most adults find too complicated to contemplate, with its rule books, contingency tables, and mathematical formulas, became a best-seller among sixth and seventh graders.

507

Jarish compares Dungeons and Dragons, "D and D," to "regular" fantasy, the kind where you say, "You be Nancy Drew and I'll be a Hardy Boy and let's go off and solve a mystery." For him the big difference is in the greater "reality" of the D and D simulation.

> In D and D there is so much in the world. It's so big. There is an incredible amount of data. If you, say, you're playing Hardy Boys, there is only a certain level that you can go to—like you can't really go up to somebody and, you know, interrogate them, or say that you're with the Secret Service and tell them that they have to give you information. I mean, they wouldn't even have the information. You can't go that far with it. You know you have to stop at a certain point, whereas in D and D you can just go on, and you can bypass those limits. The game is just in your head, but from that it almost transfers to be real. So that you can go and really imagine, picture yourself going through this cave, and then, all of a sudden, this thing, glorping all over the wall and dropping down on you, and you can throw a spell at it or something. You could almost imagine that.

Jarish is sure that D and D has more detail, is more complete, than Hardy Boys or pirates or cowboys. Beyond that, he is uncertain whether D and D is more real than reality. He hedges the question. "In D and D there's always a stopping point, in reality I guess it sort of happened." But he is not really sure. After reading seven D and D books "about twenty times each" he certainly knows more about the structure of dungeon universes than he does about any moment in history. He knows more about the behavior of magic users than about any person who ever lived. What he learns in social-studies class about real history is pale in contrast to what he experiences in D and D. "I mean," says Jarish, "in D and D there is so much data."

Jarish designs medieval dungeons and he devours science fiction. His dungeon worlds are meticulously drawn out on graph paper to scale with predetermined decision rules on how to respond to any player's actions. For him science-fiction worlds are of the same breed: the author is designing a future as Jarish designs a dungeon.

The computer programmers who felt such affinity for rule-driven fantasy games were as taken with science fiction as is Jarish, and somehow it all seemed to go together. A science-fiction writer is allowed to postulate time machines, intergalactic travel, or mental telepathy, but cannot do it

arbitrarily. A planet can have any atmosphere, but its inhabitants must be adapted to it. The author must make every attempt to acknowledge the planet's atmospheric peculiarities when he or she designs the planet's life forms. You can postulate anything, but once the rules of the system have been defined they must be adhered to scrupulously. Such are the rules for creating "rule-governed worlds." They are known to every computer programmer and are now being passed on as cultural knowledge to a generation of children. The aesthetic of rule-governed worlds is passed on through Dungeons and Dragons and science fiction before most children ever meet a computer.

This is the culture that Jarish and his peers bring to their first encounter with a video game. It is not just the games' TV screens that make them seem like old friends. Here is another world where everything is possible but where nothing is arbitrary. Ultimately there are programs that stand behind the action. They can be deciphered; children speak of learning their secrets, recognizing them as worlds of complex behavior that in the end are rule-driven—like science fiction, like D and D, and, as they are starting to learn, like computers.

## Losing Oneself in a Simulated World

If there is a danger here, it is not the danger of mindless play but of infatuation with the challenge of simulated worlds. In the right circumstances, some people come to prefer them to the real. This danger is not specific to games; it reflects one of the ways in which the games are a microcosm of computation. Computers offer the possibility of creating and working within artificial worlds, whether to simulate the behavior of economies, political systems, or imaginary subatomic particles. Like Narcissus and his reflection, people who work with computers can easily fall in love with the worlds they have constructed or with their performances in the worlds created for them by others. Involvement with simulated worlds affects relationships with the real one.

For Jarish, Dungeons and Dragons is clearly superior to games where you take roles or make up a story freely as you go along. As he sees it, Dungeons and Dragons has more data and feels more real. But he has lost something in his structured, data-rich games, both in video games and in role-playing fantasy games like Dungeons and Dragons.

Video games encourage identification with characters—from science fiction, or sports, or war stories—but leave little room for playing their roles. For example, the screen that children face when they play *Asteroids* does not look very different from that which confronted Han Solo in *The Empire Strikes Back* as he rode through the meteor shower with the panache that marked him as the greatest space pilot in the galaxy. This allows a very immediate kind of identification with Solo—the video simulations put you "in the place" of the spaceship pilot or the missile commander or the adventurer in the Tolkien world. But you are not allowed to play the part. Dungeons and Dragons allows much more of the personal role-playing that is missing from the video game. Yet it provides it in a way that is custom made for the computer generation: you identify with an alter ego as you play your role in the dungeon, but the process of play is mathematical and procedural. Beyond the fantasy, there are always the rules.

In all of this, something is missing, something that is abundantly present in the open-ended role playing that children offer each other when one says "You be the Mommy and I'll be the Daddy." The variations on this game are endless, the characters change with the issues on the children's minds and with the heroes and heroines of their culture: "You be Annie Oakley and I'll be Buffalo Bill." "You be Roy Rogers and I'll be Dale Evans." "You be Superman and I'll be Lois Lane." In this kind of play children have to learn to put themselves in the place of another person, to imagine what is going on inside someone else's head. There are no rules, there is empathy. There are no dice to roll, there is understanding, recognition, negotiation, and confrontation with others.

Children do not face an either/or choice. A child can play video games and Dungeons and Dragons and Hardy Boys. But in reality there is only so much time. Doing some things precludes others. And, even more important, an individual develops a style. In this case, there is good reason to think that a generation develops a style.

In Jarish we see such a stylistic preference. The Dungeons and Dragons way of thinking, with its thick books of rules, seems more exciting and more challenging than history or real life or fantasy play where the rules are less clear.

## Altered States

When you play a video game you enter into the world of the programmers who made it. You have to do more than identify with a character on the screen. You must act for it. Identification through action has a special kind of hold. Like playing a sport, it puts people into a highly focused, and highly charged state of mind.[3] For many people, what is

being pursued in the video game is not just a score, but an altered state.

The pilot of a race car does not dare to take his attention off the road. The imperative of total concentration is part of the high. Video games demand this same level of attention. They can give people the feeling of being close to the edge because, as in a dangerous situation, there is no time for rest and the consequences of wandering attention feel dire. With pinball, a false move can be recuperated. The machine can be shaken, the ball repositioned. In a video game, the program has no tolerance for error, no margin of safety. Players experience their every movement as instantly translated into game action. The game is relentless in its demand that all other time stop and in its demand that the player take full responsibility for every act, a point that players often sum up by the phrase "One false move and you're dead."

Executives, accountants, and surgeons stand behind the junior-high-schoolers in games arcades. For people under pressure total concentration is a form of relaxation.

Marty is a twenty-nine-year-old economist who works for a large Manhattan bank. He is a nervous, wound-up man. "I'm a real worrier. A real 'type A person.' That's me." He says he plays the game because he needs "to have something to do which is so hard that I can't think of anything else." The games force him into another mental space where the thoughts and the cares of his day cannot intrude. For many years, Marty used transcendental meditation to relax. Now he uses video games.

For me this is the same thing. It fills your mind. I can be peaceful. No decisions. I wasn't that good at keeping up the concentration for the TM. Thoughts kept breaking in. This is better. There is no way to think about anything but the game or it's all over. One false move or one false thought and you're dead. It makes my wife nervous to watch me play. She says I look so intense. She's afraid I'll have a heart attack. But when I play, inside I am cool. You have to be. You have to think about the patterns, the strategy. You wall the world out.

Marty used to play pinball, but, like TM, it was not sufficiently "coercive." In pinball, you can rest between sets, you can choose when to release your next ball. In *Asteroids*, the first game that Marty got hooked on, the pace is never yours. The rhythm of the game belongs to the machine, the program decides. When the play picks up, *Asteroids* pounds out a beat that stands between a pulse and a drum. "It's its heartbeat," says the twelve-year-old player standing next to

Marty in the arcade. "It's what you have to play to." There is no time for pause. You play to the relentless pulse of a machine heart.

Video games allow Marty to feel swept away and in control, to have complete power and yet lose himself in something outside. The games combine a feeling of omnipotence and possession—they are a place for manipulation and surrender. When Marty practiced TM, he felt it as "time out." *Asteroids* gave him more of a sense of achievement. It is a world where you are "lost," yet you have clear goals. "Unlike in the meditation, when I play games I feel that I've achieved something. I am getting good at something—in fact, I am always getting better. I love watching that score go up."

The games require total concentration—to which he attributes their "meditative" qualities—at the same time as they provide a stage for excellence. You get to do what achievement-oriented people like to do: get better. And yet, in their own way, they are also "time out." Marty calls it "meditation with macho": "It's the relaxation of forcing you to withdraw from the rat race, yet they give you a score that reassures you that you are a winner."

Roger is a fifty-year-old businessman who seeks out video games to achieve the state of mind that he gets into when he skis. He plays a game until that point where "the strategies are part of you," where he feels like an extension of the game or the game is an extension of him. Roger compares the feeling to being in touch with an unconscious self: "When I play the games I don't think. My fingers think. As in skiing, you know the terrain, you feel the terrain. My mind is clear. Things pass through it. I make connections. They say it's mindless, but for me it's liberating. I am in control of the game, but my mind is free. The way I see it, I'm not wasting my quarters. It's cheaper than psychoanalysis."

To master a video game, conscious playing is not enough. You have to "think with your fingers." As in sports, mental and physical action have to come together. An athlete thinks with the body. You feel the skis as part of you, you know their relationship to surrounding space, objects, and obstacles in the direct way that you feel your body in space. Call it "muscle memory," call it "flow," call it "trusting your instincts"—the experience of feeling a continuity between mind and body is part of the inner game of any well-played sport. Skilled video game players experience this immediacy of knowing their game with more than their head, and the experience is exhilarating.

David is a lawyer in his midthirties. When he watches television, he says he is relaxed, lost in someone else's world. When he plays video games, he experiences another kind of relaxation, the relaxation of being on the line. He feels "totally focused, totally concentrated." And yet David, like Marty and Roger, indeed like all successful players of video games, describes the sense in which the highest degree of focus and concentration comes from a letting go of both. David talks about playing best when he is not "directed."

> Well, it's almost, at the risk of sounding, uh, ridiculous, if you will, it's almost a Zen type of thing . . . where I can direct myself totally but not feel directed at all. You're totally absorbed and it is all happening there. You know what you are supposed to do. There's no external confusion, there's no conflicting goals, there's none of the complexities that the rest of the world is filled with. It's so simple. You either get through this little maze so that the creature doesn't swallow you up or you don't. And if you can focus your attention on that, and if you can really learn what you're supposed to do, then you really are in relationship with the game.

Being in relationship with the game means getting recentered on yourself. Every day before going home David stops off at his favorite arcade and plays for an hour or two. At first he says that he does it to unwind, but then he decides that "unwind" is the wrong word.

> It's not so much unwind as it is that I can sort of cleanse myself in a sense, in a very strange sense. Now I'm done with the day, and I go there, and I play these games, and I've found myself again. And then I can start on something new. Because if I go right home, I won't be prepared to talk to my wife. All day I give people advice about their lives, about their divorces, just little pieces of advice. It's very fragmented. It's like being a psychologist, but I don't get to hear it in the full way that a psychologist would. Just little fragments. A lot is going on for my wife now. She is expecting this baby and she needs to talk. I need to be able to communicate with her. And after I play the games I'm prepared to realize that I'm in the middle of the whole picture instead of just being on the outside looking in. OK, because when I play it is my picture. When I'm at work it's not really my picture. When I get home it is my picture again. And after I play I can go back and share me. So, sometimes the games are a preparation for getting out and being aggressive in the

rest of my life, and sometimes they are there for, um, getting back into my own video game.

## Metaphysical Machines

The emotional power of video games draws heavily on the computer power within that supports a simulated world and a meditative environment, what David called a place for "recentering." But the power of the games draws on other aspects of the computer as well, some of them resonant with children's fascination with computer toys as "metaphysical machines." As a computational object, the video game holds out two promises. The first is a touch of infinity—the promise of a game that never stops.

Most video games give you three chances: three "men," three "ships," three "missiles." Novice players get wiped out in seconds. And three chances to play for several seconds doesn't add up to very much time. The new player dreams of actually being able to shoot the invader or capture the monster or steer the ship. The new player dreams of a respectable score, and imagines that this will feel like "winning." But when the game skill becomes second nature, when the scores reach the hundreds of thousands, then it becomes clear that in a video game there is nothing except gaining more time, and, for some players, the idea that but for their growing fatigue, their "human limitations," the game could go on forever.

When you face a game of pinball, there is a clearly demarcated point when the game is over. You may have achieved a high score, you may win a free game. A video game presents no such moment. Mastery of one level of the game, one "screen," presents another screen, more difficult in its patterns or with the same task to do but at a faster rate. Some games give you an extra "man," an extra character to play as a bonus if you succeed with a particularly difficult move, but another character comes to the same thing: more time. The game will go on as long as you have a character to play. Everyone knows that the game is going to end "sometime," but sometime is potentially infinite.

Recall Matthew, the five-year-old who was frightened by the idea that a computer program could go on forever—frightened and also fascinated. Things that give a sense of contact with the infinite are held apart as privileged. They become charged with emotion. They are often imbued with religious feeling. The feeling can be evoked by a sunset, a mountain, the sea. It can be evoked by mathematical experiences, the idea of the infinite sequence of decimals of pi,

the sight of two mirrors reflecting each other. And these feelings are evoked by the computer and by the experience of a game that need never stop.

The games hold out a related promise, also tied to the computer's presence within them. This is the promise of perfection.

## Perfect Mirrors

Jimmy is fourteen years old, and he has made his play into an intensely private ritual. He plays at home, alone, and only one game, an "old game," *Space Invaders*. His manner of playing is disciplined and methodical. "I have my strategy and that's that. Once you have your strategy, then you just have to be perfect in doing it." Jimmy doesn't think of the game in terms of losing or winning. "For me the game is to see how long I can be perfect. Every day I try to be perfect for ten minutes longer."

Outside of the *Space Invaders* world, Jimmy is not perfect. Jimmy has a birth defect that has left him with an awkward gait and slightly slurred speech. He does not like the way he sounds. He has not made peace with his body. He fears that people are noticing him, "thinking that I am ugly. I especially hate being around girls." And he feels at war with his mind. "I'm usually thinking crazy things, like I don't even want to tell you what I'm thinking. Let's just say it's crazy." But *Space Invaders* puts him in an altered state. The game is itself perfect in its consistent response. It will deliver this perfection to the deserving player, to the player who is uncompromising in his or her concentration on the game. When Jimmy plays he feels himself becoming "perfect" and calm. "I don't, can't think of my crazy things. It's my discipline. I guess you might say I'm obsessed."

Jimmy's physical disabilities make his case dramatic, but what stands out in his relationship with *Space Invaders*—doing something that serves as a measuring stick for "perfection"—is not unique to him or to video games. Different people use different yardsticks. Some use their bodies as a material much as Jimmy uses his game, "playing with" their appearance, their dress, and their weight. Cara, for example, is a slightly overweight fourteen-year-old girl who defines her "discipline" as eating ten fewer calories every day, with many of the same feelings about it as Jimmy has about demanding ten more minutes each day from Space Invaders. There is the same desire to control the inside through action on the outside. Such efforts in control have a positive side.

With them can come an enhanced sense of autonomy, self-esteem, a sense of being the "actor" in one's life. But with every powerful and manipulable medium that we use to feel more in control—our bodies, our money, our games—the medium can get out of control.

Most people don't become addicted to video games just as most people who diet don't become anorexic. But when they use these powerful materials to measure themselves, they are at risk. And, of course, some people come to the material more vulnerable than others. The greater the anxiety about being out of control, the greater the seduction of a material that offers the promise of perfect response. The body offers this kind of promise. So many fewer calories will cause so many pounds to drop. Part of the "holding power" of any diet is the sense of involvement with the process itself. People go on diets to improve their appearance. They begin regimens of exercise for the same reason. But the experience of molding the body, the experience of its response, its malleability, can take over. Similarly, the experience of a game that makes an instantaneous and exact response to your touch, or of a computer that is itself always consistent in its response, can take over. It becomes gripping, independent of anything that you are trying to "do" with it in an instrumental sense.

Itself seemingly perfect, the computer evokes anxiety about one's own perfectibility. There is pressure from a machine that leaves no one and no other thing to blame. It is hard to walk away from the perfect mirror, from the perfect test. It is hard to walk away from a video game on which you could do better next time, it is hard to walk away from a computer program with an undiscovered "bug," it is hard to walk away from an unproofread text on the screen of a word processor. Any computer promises you that if *you* do it right, it will do it right and right away.

People who try out video games and say they hate them, or who actively dislike their first experience with computer programming, are often responding to this same promise. Not everyone wants to be around the perfect mirror. Some people dislike what they experience as the precision, the unforgivingness of mathematics. Instead of being intrigued or reassured by the idea of there being a "right answer" in their first arithmetic class, they found it intolerable. It was felt as a pressure, as a taunt, as a put-down. Mechanical objects (they work if you handle them right, they don't work if you handle them wrong) evoke the same anxieties. And when these people (in our culture, often women) meet the

computer the problem is taken to a higher order. Here is a machine that goes beyond all others in its promise to reflect human competence. It is not always welcome. For some, its challenge may be felt as an alien contest. For others as a long-awaited chance to finally test one's worth.

## Perfect Contests

David, the lawyer who used the games to "recenter," who saw them as a kind of Zen, knows that he looks successful in the eyes of the world, but he feels unsatisfied, at war with his work. He would like to be in control of things and fantasizes himself a warrior, a hero, an explorer. He would like to test himself against danger, against the elements, against an unexplored terrain. He chose law as a career and specialized in litigation, hoping that the adversary world of the courtroom would provide the thrill of hand-to-hand combat. But the reality of his job is very different.

> There is no way I can challenge anybody in a pure mental challenge. Where you can really say, "This is it. This is me and this is you." I can go into court and I can think of myself as fighting like that, one on one, but there is always some other factor. He's got one set of facts and I've got another set of facts. I'm always constrained by those things.

In a video game there is no place to hide, no excuses of chance or accident. For someone like David, searching for the sense of urgency that comes from real danger, this is crucial to the games' seduction. It is a place where there is "pure you."

David's hours in the arcade are part of his search for the perfect contest. It is a place in which to stand alone, "It's you against it." But it is a fixed entity. "So ultimately," says David, "it's you against you. My life is bound up in external constraints. With the games I face only myself. If I do well, it is pure me. If I do poorly . . . there's nothing else I can blame for a failure or an unsatisfying experience with a video game. There's no little person changing it. Playing the game is an assertion, completely pure individual competition."

His medium offers a pure test. Unlike boxing, or golf, or tennis, there will be no change of partners, no new referee. David doesn't like the "realm-of-infinite-possibilities kind of game." He describes chess negatively as the kind of game where "you make a move and the other person responds, and the other person can respond in any one of, well, in any one of a thousand ways." David wants a different kind of game, a game where the set of circumstances is going to be the same every time. The video games with their programmed responses are made to measure. Shoot the opponent from a certain distance and you get so many points. Move a little closer and you explode. With practice, the performance rules become transparent. David likes video games when they can serve as the perfect mirror, the perfect measure of who he is. "I want the game as simple as it can be . . . not really simple, but fixed. Like how many times can I bounce the ball against the wall within the next twenty seconds? When I say 'simple,' what I mean is fixed, invariant. A true test in that respect."

He doesn't like it when random elements are programmed into video games. For he relies on the game's invariant nature to give him a measure of his state of mind. If he's calm and centered he'll do well. If he is tense, diffused, anxious, he'll do poorly. "The better I do at a game, the better I feel—not because I feel good for winning, but because I know that I am in a good state. It's not just what the games do for me, it's what they show me about what was there to begin with." Beyond this, they are a preparation for life. "It has to do with testing yourself; it has to do with the idea that basic training will make a man out of you, with the idea that you have never lived unless you've lived close to the edge. The games are that simple, 'close to the edge,' but they are not threatening. Do you understand? It's a peculiar sort of feeling."

David fears that all his life he has shied away from testing how hard and far he could push himself. "It's the thing of the moment that suits me for right now. . . . I'm growing up. I've been married a year and now we're expecting a baby." He wants reassurance that he can handle things. The games are his test.

David is deeply involved with video games. He has woven them into his most personal concerns. But it is not among adults that the weave is most dense. Although they play video games and work with the computer, they grew up in a culture built without these machines. Young people are building their generation's culture now; video games and computers are among their materials. Growing up with a technology is a special kind of experience. Although mastering new things is important throughout life, there is a time in growing up when identity becomes almost synonymous with it. Today's young

people meet the games at that time. The games are not a reminder of a feeling of control over challenge. They are a primary source for developing it.

In the next chapters [of *The Second Self*] I turn to children who are doing more with computers than using them for games. These children are working with computer systems that turn the machines into a medium for self-expression. We shall see a child programming an animated scene of a space shuttle that is in no sense a simulation. The excitement here is not in the process of deciphering the program, but of making it in a highly personalized way.

I introduced this chapter by speaking of the games as a window onto the culture of computation. But when you play a video game you are a player in a game programmed by someone else. When children begin to do their own programming, they are not deciphering somebody else's mystery. They become players in their own game, makers of their own mysteries, and enter into a new relationship with the computer, one in which they begin to experience it as a kind of second self.

Notes

1. Woody Allen, "The Kugelmass Episode," *The New Yorker*, May 2, 1977.

2. *Principles of Compiler Design*, by computer scientists Alfred V. Aho and Jeffrey Ullman (Reading, Mass.: Addison Wesley, 1977), has the following illustration on its cover: a knight (named Syntax Directed Translation) on a steed (named Data Flow Analysis) fights a dragon (named Complexity of Compiler Design). The knight's weapon is a lance called LALR Parser Generator. I show this cover illustration to my students majoring in computer science. Their comment: "Oh, sure, a lot of compiler people are into D and D."

3. Psychologist Mihaly Csikszentmihalyi studied people's inner states while pursuing activities that appear to contain rewards in themselves—chess, rock climbing, dance, sports, surgery. He discovered that central to all of them is an experience which he calls "flow." Its most marked characteristic is the "merging of action and awareness." Csikszentmihalyi's analysis of flow experience closely parallels many issues I found at the heart of the "holding power" of both video games and computer programming. See Mihaly Csikszentmihalyi, *Beyond Boredom and Anxiety* (San Francisco, Josey Bass, 1975). For a cognitive perspective on the psychology of game use, see also Thomas W. Malone, "What Makes Things Fun to Learn? A Study of Intrinsically Motivating Computer Games," Xerox Palo Alto Research Center, Cognitive and Instructional Sciences Series (August 1980).

# 35. [Introduction]
# A Cyborg Manifesto
## Science, Technology, and Socialist-Feminism in the Late Twentieth Century

The most famous line from this essay is the last: "Though both are bound in the spiral dance, I would rather be a cyborg than a goddess." Haraway's cyborg preference has lead some readers into uninteresting interpretations, in which it is assumed that Haraway's project is an attack on radical feminists such as Mary Daly. However, reading Haraway's text as an intervention at the level of mythology, of the imagined identities and positions from which action can proceed, is more interesting. Haraway's cyborg is a socialist-feminist mythology that is not founded on belief in an idyllic past or overarching unity. Feminists have not always engaged with the mythology of the goddess in such a way. The goddess has at times been seen as the figure of a lost, matriarchal utopia; the cyborg, in contrast, does not look back. The cyborg engages the here and now.

Which here and now? That in which traditional boundaries are leaking: those between human and animal, organisms (human/animal) and machines, the physical and virtual. Rather than defend these boundaries, rather than attempt to work back to an imagined purity, or appeal to a totalizing construct such as "women's experience," Haraway makes an "argument for *pleasure* in the confusion of boundaries and for *responsibility* in their construction." She admits that this will put her at odds with other progressives, who have often argued precisely for the dualisms that to her cyborg are untenable. While she sees the need for working together, she believes "a slightly perverse shift of perspective might better enable us to contest for meanings, as well as for other forms of power and pleasure in technologically mediated societies."

Her argument has had enormous influence—and may indeed be the starting point for current progressive scholarship on science and technology, as well as an important element in pop-culture phenomena of the cyborg. It has offered a model of cultural and political engagement that is not based on the liberal humanist subject, that is more accessible to many in the U.S. than that posited by Gilles Deleuze and Félix Guattari (◊27) and that incorporates from the outset (rather than as an afterthought) the cybernetic world, as discussed by Norbert Wiener (◊04) and Bill Nichols (◊43). Haraway traces the cyborg through a number of veins and wires, including those of science fiction. A reading of media in this mode is particularly fitting for examination by scholars of new media.

**515**

In the end, even critics with much more conventional styles and approaches have come to view Haraway's essay as foundational. For example, Michael Menser and Stanley Aronowitz have written that, in the face of disciplinary and cultural resistance to giving up old dualisms, "Donna Haraway, astute cultural critic that she is, mounts a different *approach*. One might call it a 'backdoor assault,' beginning with the appropriation of a somewhat marginal (fictional) concept, the cyborg, which amounts to the utilization of a literary and cinematic narrative device realized as a concept for an ontological and phenomenological treatise deployed in the form of a manifesto. However, Haraway's *position*—but not her approach—on technology, science, and culture is one which we largely share" (10).

*I would rather be a cyborg than a sad revolutionary.*
—NWF

**Further Reading**

Bell, David, and Barbara M. Kennedy, eds. *The Cybercultures Reader*. New York: Routledge, 2000.

Haraway, Donna. *Modest_Witness@Second_Millenium.FemaleMan©.Meets OncoMouse: Feminism and Technoscience*. Illustrated by Lynn M. Randolph. New York: Routledge, 1996.

Menser, Michael, and Stanley Aronowitz. "On Cultural Studies, Science, and Technology." *Technoscience and Cyberculture*, 7–28. Ed. Stanley Aronowitz. New York: Routledge, 1996.

Stone, Allucquére Rosanne. *The War of Desire and Technology at the Close of the Mechanical Age*. Cambridge, Mass.: MIT Press, 1996.

Original Publication

First published in *Socialist Review* 80:65–108. 1985. This text from *Simians, Cyborgs, Women: The Reinvention of Nature* (New York: Routledge, 1991), 149–181.

# A Cyborg Manifesto
## Science, Technology, and Socialist-Feminism in the Late Twentieth Century[1]

## Donna Haraway

### An Ironic Dream of a Common Language for Women in the Integrated Circuit

This chapter is an effort to build an ironic political myth faithful to feminism, socialism, and materialism. Perhaps more faithful as blasphemy is faithful, than as reverent worship and identification. Blasphemy has always seemed to require taking things very seriously. I know no better stance to adopt from within the secular-religious, evangelical traditions of United States politics, including the politics of socialist feminism. Blasphemy protects one from the moral majority within, while still insisting on the need for community. Blasphemy is not apostasy. Irony is about contradictions that do not resolve into larger wholes, even dialectically, about the tension of holding incompatible things together because both or all are necessary and true. Irony is about humour and serious play. It is also a rhetorical strategy and a political method, one I would like to see more honoured within socialist-feminism. At the centre of my ironic faith, my blasphemy, is the image of the cyborg.

A cyborg is a cybernetic organism, a hybrid of machine and organism, a creature of social reality as well as a creature of fiction. Social reality is lived social relations, our most important political construction, a world-changing fiction. The international women's movements have constructed "women's experience," as well as uncovered or discovered this crucial collective object. This experience is a fiction and fact of the most crucial, political kind. Liberation rests on the construction of the consciousness, the imaginative apprehension, of oppression, and so of possibility. The cyborg is a matter of fiction and lived experience that changes what counts as women's experience in the late twentieth century. This is a struggle over life and death, but the boundary between science fiction and social reality is an optical illusion.

Contemporary science fiction is full of cyborgs—creatures simultaneously animal and machine, who populate worlds ambiguously natural and crafted. Modern medicine is also full of cyborgs, of couplings between organism and machine, each conceived as coded devices, in an intimacy and with a power that was not generated in the history of sexuality. Cyborg "sex" restores some of the lovely replicative baroque of ferns and invertebrates (such nice organic prophylactics against heterosexism). Cyborg replication is uncoupled from organic reproduction. Modern production seems like a dream of cyborg colonization work, a dream that makes the nightmare of Taylorism seem idyllic. And modern war is a cyborg orgy, coded by C3I, command-control-communication-intelligence, an $84 billion item in 1984's US defence budget. I am making an argument for the cyborg as a fiction mapping our social and bodily reality and as an imaginative resource suggesting some very fruitful couplings. Michael Foucault's biopolitics is a flaccid premonition of cyborg politics, a very open field.

By the late twentieth century, our time, a mythic time, we are all chimeras, theorized and fabricated hybrids of machine and organism; in short, we are cyborgs. The cyborg is our ontology; it gives us our politics. The cyborg is a condensed image of both imagination and material reality, the two joined centres structuring any possibility of historical transformation. In the traditions of "Western" science and politics—the tradition of racist, male-dominant capitalism; the tradition of progress; the tradition of the appropriation of nature as resource for the productions of culture; the tradition of reproduction of the self from the reflections of the other—the relation between organism and machine has been a border war. The stakes in the border war have been the territories of production, reproduction, and imagination. This chapter is an argument for *pleasure* in the confusion of boundaries and for *responsibility* in their construction. It is also an effort to contribute to socialist-feminist culture and theory in a postmodernist, non-naturalist mode and in the utopian tradition of imagining a world without gender, which is perhaps a world without genesis, but maybe also a world without end. The cyborg incarnation is outside salvation history. Nor does it mark time on an oedipal calendar, attempting to heal the terrible cleavages of gender in an oral symbiotic utopia or post-oedipal apocalypse. As Zoe Sofoulis argues in her unpublished manuscript on Jacques Lacan, Melanie Klein, and nuclear culture, *Lacklein*, the most terrible and perhaps the most promising monsters in cyborg worlds are embodied in non-oedipal narratives with a different logic of repression, which we need to understand for our survival.

The cyborg is a creature in a post-gender world; it has no truck with bisexuality, pre-oedipal symbiosis, unalienated labour, or other seductions to organic wholeness through a final appropriation of all the powers of the parts into a higher unity. In a sense, the cyborg has no origin story in the Western sense—a "final" irony since the cyborg is also the awful apocalyptic *telos* of the "West's" escalating dominations of abstract individuation, an ultimate self untied at last from all dependency, a man in space. An origin story in the "Western," humanist sense depends on the myth of original unity, fullness, bliss and terror, represented by the phallic mother from whom all humans must separate, the task of individual development and of history, the twin potent myths inscribed most powerfully for us in psychoanalysis and Marxism. Hilary Klein has argued that both Marxism and psychoanalysis, in their concepts of labour and of individuation and gender formation, depend on the plot of original unity out of which difference must be produced and enlisted in a drama of escalating domination of woman/nature. The cyborg skips the step of original unity, of identification with nature in the Western sense. This is its illegitimate promise that might lead to subversion of its teleology as star wars.

The cyborg is resolutely committed to partiality, irony, intimacy, and perversity. It is oppositional, utopian, and completely without innocence. No longer structured by the polarity of public and private, the cyborg defines a technological polis based partly on a revolution of social relations in the *oikos*, the household. Nature and culture are reworked; the one can no longer be the resource for appropriation or incorporation by the other. The relationships for forming wholes from parts, including those of polarity and hierarchical domination, are at issue in the cyborg world. Unlike the hopes of Frankenstein's monster, the cyborg does not expect its father to save it through a restoration of the garden; that is, through the fabrication of a heterosexual

mate, through its completion in a finished whole, a city and cosmos. The cyborg does not dream of community on the model of the organic family, this time without the oedipal project. The cyborg would not recognize the Garden of Eden; it is not made of mud and cannot dream of returning to dust. Perhaps that is why I want to see if cyborgs can subvert the apocalypse of returning to nuclear dust in the manic compulsion to name the Enemy. Cyborgs are not reverent; they do not re-member the cosmos. They are wary of holism, but needy for connection—they seem to have a natural feel for united front politics, but without the vanguard party. The main trouble with cyborgs, of course, is that they are the illegitimate offspring of militarism and patriarchal capitalism, not to mention state socialism. But illegitimate offspring are often exceedingly unfaithful to their origins. Their fathers, after all, are inessential.

I will return to the science fiction of cyborgs at the end of this chapter, but now I want to signal three crucial boundary breakdowns that make the following political-fictional (political-scientific) analysis possible. By the late twentieth century in United States scientific culture, the boundary between human and animal is thoroughly breached. The last beachheads of uniqueness have been polluted if not turned into amusement parks—language, tool use, social behaviour, mental events, nothing really convincingly settles the separation of human and animal. And many people no longer feel the need for such a separation; indeed, many branches of feminist culture affirm the pleasure of connection of human and other living creatures. Movements for animal rights are not irrational denials of human uniqueness; they are a clear-sighted recognition of connection across the discredited breach of nature and culture. Biology and evolutionary theory over the last two centuries have simultaneously produced modern organisms as objects of knowledge and reduced the line between humans and animals to a faint trace re-etched in ideological struggle or professional disputes between life and social science. Within this framework, teaching modern Christian creationism should be fought as a form of child abuse.

Biological-determinist ideology is only one position opened up in scientific culture for arguing the meanings of human animality. There is much room for radical political people to contest the meanings of the breached boundary.[2] The cyborg appears in myth precisely where the boundary between human and animal is transgressed. Far from signalling a walling off of people from other living beings, cyborgs signal disturbingly and pleasurably tight coupling. Bestiality has a new status in this cycle of marriage exchange.

The second leaky distinction is between animal-human (organism) and machine. Pre-cybernetic machines could be haunted; there was always the spectre of the ghost in the machine. This dualism structured the dialogue between materialism and idealism that was settled by a dialectical progeny, called spirit or history, according to taste. But basically machines were not self-moving, self-designing, autonomous. They could not achieve man's dream, only mock it. They were not man, an author to himself, but only a caricature of that masculinist reproductive dream. To think they were otherwise was paranoid. Now we are not so sure. Late twentieth-century machines have made thoroughly ambiguous the difference between natural and artificial, mind and body, self-developing and externally designed, and many other distinctions that used to apply to organisms and machines. Our machines are disturbingly lively, and we ourselves frighteningly inert.

Technological determination is only one ideological space opened up by the reconceptions of machine and organism as coded texts through which we engage in the play of writing and reading the world.[3] "Textualization" of everything in poststructuralist, postmodernist theory has been damned by Marxists and socialist feminists for its utopian disregard for the lived relations of domination that ground the "play" of arbitrary reading.[4] It is certainly true that postmodernist strategies, like my cyborg myth, subvert myriad organic wholes (for example, the poem, the primitive culture, the biological organism). In short, the certainty of what counts as nature—a source of insight and promise of innocence—is undermined, probably fatally. The transcendent authorization of interpretation is lost, and with it the ontology grounding "Western" epistemology. But the alternative is not cynicism or faithlessness, that is, some version of abstract existence, like the accounts of technological determinism destroying "man" by the "machine" or "meaningful political action" by the "text." Who cyborgs will be is a radical question; the answers are a matter of survival. Both chimpanzees and artefacts have politics, so why shouldn't we (de Waal, 1982; Winner, 1980)?

The third distinction is a subset of the second: the boundary between physical and non-physical is very imprecise for us. Pop physics books on the consequences of quantum theory and the indeterminacy principle are a kind of popular scientific equivalent to Harlequin romances* as a marker of radical change in American white heterosexuality: they get it wrong, but they are on the right subject. Modern machines are quintessentially microelectronic devices: they are everywhere and they are invisible. Modern machinery is an irreverent upstart god, mocking the Father's ubiquity and spirituality. The silicon chip is a surface for writing; it is etched in molecular scales disturbed only by atomic noise, the ultimate interference for nuclear scores. Writing, power, and technology are old partners in Western stories of the origin of civilization, but miniaturization has changed our experience of mechanism. Miniaturization has turned out to be about power; small is not so much beautiful as pre-eminently dangerous, as in cruise missiles. Contrast the TV sets of the 1950s or the news cameras of the 1970s with the TV wrist bands or hand-sized video cameras now advertised. Our best machines are made of sunshine; they are all light and clean because they are nothing but signals, electro-magnetic waves, a section of a spectrum, and these machines are eminently portable, mobile—a matter of immense human pain in Detroit and Singapore. People are nowhere near so fluid, being both material and opaque. Cyborgs are ether, quintessence.

The ubiquity and invisibility of cyborgs is precisely why these sunshine-belt machines are so deadly. They are as hard to see politically as materially. They are about consciousness—or its simulation.[5] They are floating signifiers moving in pickup trucks across Europe, blocked more effectively by the witch-weavings of the displaced and so unnatural Greenham women, who read the cyborg webs of power so very well, than by the militant labour of older masculinist politics, whose natural constituency needs defence jobs. Ultimately the "hardest" science is about the realm of greatest boundary confusion, the realm of pure number, pure spirit, C3I, cryptography, and the preservation of potent secrets. The new machines are so clean and light. Their engineers are sun-worshippers mediating a new scientific revolution associated with the night dream of post-industrial society. The diseases evoked by these clean machines are "no more" than the minuscule coding changes of an antigen in the immune system, "no more" than the

*The US equivalent of Mills & Boon.

experience of stress. The nimble fingers of "Oriental" women, the old fascination of little Anglo-Saxon Victorian girls with doll's houses, women's enforced attention to the small take on quite new dimensions in this world. There might be a cyborg Alice taking account of these new dimensions. Ironically, it might be the unnatural cyborg women making chips in Asia and spiral dancing in Santa Rita jail* whose constructed unities will guide effective oppositional strategies.

So my cyborg myth is about transgressed boundaries, potent fusions, and dangerous possibilities which progressive people might explore as one part of needed political work. One of my premises is that most American socialists and feminists see deepened dualisms of mind and body, animal and machine, idealism and materialism in the social practices, symbolic formulations, and physical artefacts associated with "high technology" and scientific culture. From *One-Dimensional Man* (Marcuse, 1964) to *The Death of Nature* (Merchant, 1980), the analytic resources developed by progressives have insisted on the necessary domination of technics and recalled us to an imagined organic body to integrate our resistance. Another of my premises is that the need for unity of people trying to resist world-wide intensification of domination has never been more acute. But a slightly perverse shift of perspective might better enable us to contest for meanings, as well as for other forms of power and pleasure in technologically mediated societies.

From one perspective, a cyborg world is about the final imposition of a grid of control on the planet, about the final abstraction embodied in a Star Wars apocalypse waged in the name of defence, about the final appropriation of women's bodies in a masculinist orgy of war (Sofia, 1984). From another perspective, a cyborg world might be about lived social and bodily realities in which people are not afraid of their joint kinship with animals and machines, not afraid of permanently partial identities and contradictory standpoints. The political struggle is to see from both perspectives at once because each reveals both dominations and possibilities unimaginable from the other vantage point. Single vision produces worse illusions than double vision or many-headed monsters. Cyborg unities are monstrous and

*A practice at once both spiritual and political that linked guards and arrested anti-nuclear demonstrators in the Alameda County jail in California in the early 1980s.

illegitimate; in our present political circumstances, we could hardly hope for more potent myths for resistance and recoupling. I like to imagine LAG, the Livermore Action Group, as a kind of cyborg society, dedicated to realistically converting the laboratories that most fiercely embody and spew out the tools of technological apocalypse, and committed to building a political form that acutally manages to hold together witches, engineers, elders, perverts, Christians, mothers, and Leninists long enough to disarm the state. Fission Impossible is the name of the affinity group in my town. (Affinity: related not by blood but by choice, the appeal of one chemical nuclear group for another, avidity.)[6]

## Fractured Identities

It has become difficult to name one's feminism by a single adjective—or even to insist in every circumstance upon the noun. Consciousness of exclusion through naming is acute. Identities seem contradictory, partial, and strategic. With the hard-won recognition of their social and historical constitution, gender, race, and class cannot provide the basis for belief in "essential" unity. There is nothing about being "female" that naturally binds women. There is not even such a state as "being" female, itself a highly complex category constructed in contested sexual scientific discourses and other social practices. Gender, race, or class consciousness is an achievement forced on us by the terrible historical experience of the contradictory social realities of patriarchy, colonialism, and capitalism. And who counts as "us" in my own rhetoric? Which identities are available to ground such a potent political myth called "us," and what could motivate enlistment in this collectivity? Painful fragmentation among feminists (not to mention among women) along every possible fault line has made the concept of *woman* elusive, an excuse for the matrix of women's dominations of each other. For me—and for many who share a similar historical location in white, professional middle-class, female, radical, North American, mid-adult bodies—the sources of a crisis in political identity are legion. The recent history for much of the US left and US feminism has been a response to this kind of crisis by endless splitting and searches for a new essential unity. But there has also been a growing recognition of another response through coalition—affinity, not identity.[7]

Chela Sandoval (n.d., 1984), from a consideration of specific historical moments in the formation of the new political voice called women of colour, has theorized a hopeful model of political identity called "oppositional consciousness," born of the skills for reading webs of power by those refused stable membership in the social categories of race, sex, or class. "Women of color," a name contested at its origins by those whom it would incorporate, as well as a historical consciousness marking systematic breakdown of all the signs of Man in "Western" traditions, constructs a kind of postmodernist identity out of otherness, difference, and specificity. This postmodernist identity is fully political, whatever might be said about other possible postmodern-isms. Sandoval's oppositional consciousness is about contradictory locations and heterochronic calendars, not about relativisms and pluralisms.

Sandoval emphasizes the lack of any essential criterion for identifying who is a woman of colour. She notes that the definition of the group has been by conscious appropriation of negation. For example, a Chicana or US black woman has not been able to speak as a woman or as a black person or as a Chicano. Thus, she was at the bottom of a cascade of negative identities, left out of even the privileged oppressed authorial categories called "women and blacks," who claimed to make the important revolutions. The category "woman" negated all non-white women; "black" negated all non-black people, as well as all black women. But there was also no "she," no singularity, but a sea of differences among US women who have affirmed their historical identity as US women of colour. This identity marks out a self-consciously constructed space that cannot affirm the capacity to act on the basis of natural identification, but only on the basis of conscious coalition, of affinity, of political kinship.[8] Unlike the "woman" of some streams of the white women's movement in the United States, there is no naturalization of the matrix, or at least this is what Sandoval argues is uniquely available through the power of oppositional consciousness.

Sandoval's argument has to be seen as one potent formulation for feminists out of the world-wide development of anti-colonialist discourse; that is to say, discourse dissolving the "West" and its highest product—the one who is not animal, barbarian, or woman; man, that is, the author of a cosmos called history. As orientalism is deconstructed politically and semiotically, the identities of the occident destabilize, including those of feminists.[9] Sandoval argues that "women of colour" have a chance to build an effective unity that does not replicate the imperializing, totalizing

revolutionary subjects of previous Marxisms and feminisms which had not faced the consequences of the disorderly polyphony emerging from decolonization.

Katie King has emphasized the limits of identification and the political/poetic mechanics of identification built into reading "the poem," that generative core of cultural feminism. King criticizes the persistent tendency among contemporary feminists from different "moments" or "conversations" in feminist practice to taxonomize the women's movement to make one's own political tendencies appear to be the *telos* of the whole. These taxonomies tend to remake feminist history so that it appears to be an ideological struggle among coherent types persisting over time, especially those typical units called radical, liberal, and socialist-feminism. Literally, all other feminisms are either incorporated or marginalized, usually by building an explicit ontology and epistemology.[10] Taxonomies of feminism produce epistemologies to police deviation from official women's experience. And of course, "women's culture," like women of colour, is consciously created by mechanisms inducing affinity. The rituals of poetry, music, and certain forms of academic practice have been pre-eminent. The politics of race and culture in the US women's movements are intimately interwoven. The common achievement of King and Sandoval is learning how to craft a poetic/political unity without relying on a logic of appropriation, incorporation, and taxonomic identification.

The theoretical and practical struggle against unity-through-domination or unity-through-incorporation ironically not only undermines the justifications for patriarchy, colonialism, humanism, positivism, essentialism, scientism, and other unlamented -isms, but *all* claims for an organic or natural standpoint. I think that radical and socialist/Marxist-feminisms have also undermined their/our own epistemological strategies and that this is a crucially valu-able step in imagining possible unities. It remains to be seen whether all "epistemologies" as Western political people have known them fail us in the task to build effective affinities.

It is important to note that the effort to construct revolutionary standpoints, epistemologies as achievements of people committed to changing the world, has been part of the process showing the limits of identification. The acid tools of postmodernist theory and the constructive tools of ontological discourse about revolutionary subjects might be seen as ironic allies in dissolving Western selves in the interests of survival. We are excruciatingly conscious of what it means to have a historically constituted body. But with the loss of innocence in our origin, there is no expulsion from the Garden either. Our politics lose the indulgence of guilt with the *naïveté* of innocence. But what would another political myth for socialist-feminism look like? What kind of politics could embrace partial, contradictory, permanently unclosed constructions of personal and collective selves and still be faithful, effective—and, ironically, socialist-feminist?

I do not know of any other time in history when there was greater need for political unity to confront effectively the dominations of "race," "gender," "sexuality," and "class." I also do not know of any other time when the kind of unity we might help build could have been possible. None of "us" have any longer the symbolic or material capability of dictating the shape of reality to any of "them." Or at least "we" cannot claim innocence from practising such dominations. White women, including socialist feminists, discovered (that is, were forced kicking and screaming to notice) the non-innocence of the category "woman." That consciousness changes the geography of all previous categories; it denatures them as heat denatures a fragile protein. Cyborg feminists have to argue that "we" do not want any more natural matrix of unity and that no construction is whole. Innocence, and the corollary insistence on victimhood as the only ground for insight, has done enough damage. But the constructed revolutionary subject must give late-twentieth-century people pause as well. In the fraying of identities and in the reflexive strategies for constructing them, the possibility opens up for weaving something other than a shroud for the day after the apocalypse that so prophetically ends salvation history.

Both Marxist/socialist-feminisms and radical feminisms have simultaneously naturalized and denatured the category "woman" and consciousness of the social lives of "women." Perhaps a schematic caricature can highlight both kinds of moves. Marxian socialism is rooted in an analysis of wage labour which reveals class structure. The consequence of the wage relationship is systematic alienation, as the worker is dissociated from his (sic) product. Abstraction and illusion rule in knowledge, domination rules in practice. Labour is the pre-eminently privileged category enabling the Marxist to overcome illusion and find that point of view which is necessary for changing the world. Labour is the humanizing activity that makes man; labour is an ontological category

permitting the knowledge of a subject, and so the knowledge of subjugation and alienation.

In faithful filiation, socialist-feminism advanced by allying itself with the basic analytic strategies of Marxism. The main achievement of both Marxist feminists and socialist feminists was to expand the category of labour to accommodate what (some) women did, even when the wage relation was subordinated to a more comprehensive view of labour under capitalist patriarchy. In particular, women's labour in the household and women's activity as mothers generally (that is, reproduction in the socialist-feminist sense), entered theory on the authority of analogy to the Marxian concept of labour. The unity of women here rests on an epistemology based on the ontological structure of "labour." Marxist/socialist-feminism does not "naturalize" unity; it is a possible achievement based on a possible standpoint rooted in social relations. The essentializing move is in the ontological structure of labour or of its analogue, women's activity.[11] The inheritance of Marxian humanism, with its pre-eminently Western self, is the difficulty for me. The contribution from these formulations has been the emphasis on the daily responsibility of real women to build unities, rather than to naturalize them.

Catherine MacKinnon's (1982, 1987) version of radical feminism is itself a caricature of the appropriating, incorporating, totalizing tendencies of Western theories of identity grounding action.[12] It is factually and politically wrong to assimilate all of the diverse "moments" or "conversations" in recent women's politics named radical feminism to MacKinnon's version. But the teleological logic of her theory shows how an epistemology and ontology—including their negations—erase or police difference. Only one of the effects of MacKinnon's theory is the rewriting of the history of the polymorphous field called radical feminism. The major effect is the production of a theory of experience, of women's identity, that is a kind of apocalypse for all revolutionary standpoints. That is, the totalization built into this tale of radical feminism achieves its end—the unity of women—by enforcing the experience of and testimony to radical non-being. As for the Marxist/socialist feminist, consciousness is an achievement, not a natural fact. And MacKinnon's theory eliminates some of the difficulties built into humanist revolutionary subjects, but at the cost of radical reductionism.

MacKinnon argues that feminism necessarily adopted a different analytical strategy from Marxism, looking first not at the structure of class, but at the structure of sex/gender and its generative relationship, men's constitution and appropriation of women sexually. Ironically, MacKinnon's "ontology" constructs a non-subject, a non-being. Another's desire, not the self's labour, is the origin of "woman." She therefore develops a theory of consciousness that enforces what can count as "women's" experience—anything that names sexual violation, indeed, sex itself as far as "women" can be concerned. Feminist practice is the construction of this form of consciousness; that is, the self-knowledge of a self-who-is-not.

Perversely, sexual appropriation in this feminism still has the epistemological status of labour; that is to say, the point from which an analysis able to contribute to changing the world must flow. But sexual objectification, not alienation, is the consequence of the structure of sex/gender. In the realm of knowledge, the result of sexual objectification is illusion and abstraction. However, a woman is not simply alienated from her product, but in a deep sense does not exist as a subject, or even potential subject, since she owes her existence as a woman to sexual appropriation. To be constituted by another's desire is not the same thing as to be alienated in the violent separation of the labourer from his product.

MacKinnon's radical theory of experience is totalizing in the extreme; it does not so much marginalize as obliterate the authority of any other women's political speech and action. It is a totalization producing what Western patriarchy itself never succeeded in doing—feminists' consciousness of the non-existence of women, except as products of men's desire. I think MacKinnon correctly argues that no Marxian version of identity can firmly ground women's unity. But in solving the problem of the contradictions of any Western revolutionary subject for feminist purposes, she develops an even more authoritarian doctrine of experience. If my complaint about socialist/Marxian standpoints is their unintended erasure of polyvocal, unassimilable, radical difference made visible in anti-colonial discourse and practice, MacKinnon's intentional erasure of all difference through the device of the "essential" non-existence of women is not reassuring.

In my taxonomy, which like any other taxonomy is a re-inscription of history, radical feminism can accommodate all the activities of women named by socialist feminists as

forms of labour only if the activity can somehow be sexualized. Reproduction had different tones of meanings for the two tendencies, one rooted in labour, one in sex, both calling the consequences of domination and ignorance of social and personal reality "false consciousness."

Beyond either the difficulties or the contributions in the argument of any one author, neither Marxist nor radical feminist points of view have tended to embrace the status of a partial explanation; both were regularly constituted as totalities. Western explanation has demanded as much; how else could the "Western" author incorporate its others? Each tried to annex other forms of domination by expanding its basic categories through analogy, simple listing, or addition. Embarrassed silence about race among white radical and socialist feminists was one major, devastating political consequence. History and polyvocality disappear into political taxonomies that try to establish genealogies. There was no structural room for race (or for much else) in theory claiming to reveal the construction of the category woman and social group women as a unified or totalizable whole. The structure of my caricature looks like this:

> socialist feminism—
> structure of class // wage labour // alienation
> labour, by analogy reproduction, by extension sex, by
> addition race
>
> radical feminism—
> structure of gender // sexual appropriation // objectification
> sex, by analogy labour, by extension reproduction, by
> addition race

In another context, the French theorist, Julia Kristeva, claimed women appeared as a historical group after the Second World War, along with groups like youth. Her dates are doubtful; but we are now accustomed to remembering that as objects of knowledge and as historical actors, "race" did not always exist, "class" has a historical genesis, and "homosexuals" are quite junior. It is no accident that the symbolic system of the family of man—and so the essence of woman—breaks up at the same moment that networks of connection among people on the planet are unprecedentedly multiple, pregnant, and complex. "Advanced capitalism" is inadequate to convey the structure of this historical moment. In the "Western" sense, the end of man is at stake. It is no accident that woman disintegrates into women in our time. Perhaps socialist feminists were not substantially guilty of producing essentialist theory that suppressed women's particularity and contradictory interests. I think we have been, at least through unreflective participation in the logics, languages, and practices of white humanism and through searching for a single ground of domination to secure our revolutionary voice. Now we have less excuse. But in the consciousness of our failures, we risk lapsing into boundless difference and giving up on the confusing task of making partial, real connection. Some differences are playful; some are poles of world historical systems of domination. "Epistemology" is about knowing the difference.

## The Informatics of Domination

In this attempt at an epistemological and political position, I would like to sketch a picture of possible unity, a picture indebted to socialist and feminist principles of design. The frame for my sketch is set by the extent and importance of rearrangements in world-wide social relations tied to science and technology. I argue for a politics rooted in claims about fundamental changes in the nature of class, race, and gender in an emerging system of world order analogous in its novelty and scope to that created by industrial capitalism; we are living through a movement from an organic, industrial society to a polymorphous, information system—from all work to all play, a deadly game. Simultaneously material and ideological, the dichotomies may be expressed in the following chart of transitions from the comfortable old hierarchical dominations to the scary new networks I have called the informatics of domination (Table 35.1).

This list suggests several interesting things.[13] First, the objects on the right-hand side cannot be coded as "natural," a realization that subverts naturalistic coding for the left-hand side as well. We cannot go back ideologically or materially. It's not just that "god" is dead; so is the "goddess." Or both are revivified in the worlds charged with microelectronic and biotechnological politics. In relation to objects like biotic components, one must think not in terms of essential properties, but in terms of design, boundary constraints, rates of flows, systems logics, costs of lowering constraints. Sexual reproduction is one kind of reproductive strategy among many, with costs and benefits as a function of the system environment. Ideologies of sexual reproduction can no longer reasonably call on notions of sex and sex role as organic aspects in natural objects like organisms and families. Such reasoning will be unmasked as irrational, and ironically corporate executives reading *Playboy* and anti-porn radical

feminists will make strange bedfellows in jointly unmasking the irrationalism.

Likewise for race, ideologies about human diversity have to be formulated in terms of frequencies of parameters, like blood groups or intelligence scores. It is "irrational" to invoke concepts like primitive and civilized. For liberals and radicals, the search for integrated social systems gives way to a new practice called "experimental ethnography" in which an organic object dissipates in attention to the play of writing. At the level of ideology, we see translations of racism and colonialism into languages of development and under-development, rates and constraints of modernization. Any

### Informatics of Domination:

| | |
|---|---|
| Representation | Simulation |
| Bourgeois novel, realism | Science fiction, postmodernism |
| Organism | Biotic component |
| Depth, integrity | Surface, boundary |
| Heat | Noise |
| Biology as clinical practice | Biology as inscription |
| Physiology | Communications engineering |
| Small group | Subsystem |
| Perfection | Optimization |
| Eugenics | Population Control |
| Decadence, *Magic Mountain* | Obsolescence, *Future Shock* |
| Hygiene | Stress Management |
| Microbiology, tuberculosis | Immunology, AIDS |
| Organic division of labour | Ergonomics/cybernetics of labour |
| Functional specialization | Modular construction |
| Reproduction | Replication |
| Organic sex role specialization | Optimal genetic strategies |
| Biological determinism | Evolutionary inertia, constraints |
| Community ecology | Ecosystem |
| Racial chain of being | Neo-imperialism, United Nations humanism |
| Scientific management in home/ factory | Global factory/Electronic cottage |
| Family/Market/Factory | Women in the Integrated Circuit |
| Family wage | Comparable worth |
| Public/Private | Cyborg citizenship |
| Nature/Culture | Fields of difference |
| Co-operation | Communications enhancement |
| Freud | Lacan |
| Sex | Genetic engineering |
| Labour | Robotics |
| Mind | Artificial Intelligence |
| Second World War | Star Wars |
| White Capitalist Patriarchy | Informatics of Domination |

Table 35.1

523

objects or persons can be reasonably thought of in terms of disassembly and reassembly; no "natural" architectures constrain system design. The financial districts in all the world's cities, as well as the export-processing and free-trade zones, proclaim this elementary fact of "late capitalism." The entire universe of objects that can be known scientifically must be formulated as problems in communications engineering (for the managers) or theories of the text (for those who would resist). Both are cyborg semiologies.

One should expect control strategies to concentrate on boundary conditions and interfaces, on rates of flow across boundaries—and not on the integrity of natural objects. "Integrity" or "sincerity" of the Western self gives way to decision procedures and expert systems. For example, control strategies applied to women's capacities to give birth to new human beings will be developed in the languages of population control and maximization of goal achievement for individual decision-makers. Control strategies will be formulated in terms of rates, costs of constraints, degrees of freedom. Human beings, like any other component or subsystem, must be localized in a system architecture whose basic modes of operation are probabilistic, statistical. No objects, spaces, or bodies are sacred in themselves; any component can be interfaced with any other if the proper standard, the proper code, can be constructed for processing signals in a common language. Exchange in this world transcends the universal translation effected by capitalist markets that Marx analysed so well. The privileged pathology affecting all kinds of components in this universe is stress—communications breakdown (Hogness, 1983). The cyborg is not subject to Foucault's biopolitics; the cyborg simulates politics, a much more potent field of operations.

This kind of analysis of scientific and cultural objects of knowledge which have appeared historically since the Second World War prepares us to notice some important inadequacies in feminist analysis which has proceeded as if the organic, hierarchical dualisms ordering discourse in "the West" since Aristotle still ruled. They have been cannibalized, or as Zoe Sofia (Sofoulis) might put it, they have been "techno-digested." The dichotomies between mind and body, animal and human, organism and machine, public and private, nature and culture, men and women, primitive and civilized are all in question ideologically. The actual situation of women is their integration/exploitation into a world

system of production/reproduction and communication called the informatics of domination. The home, workplace, market, public arena, the body itself—all can be dispersed and interfaced in nearly infinite, polymorphous ways, with large consequences for women and others—consequences that themselves are very different for different people and which make potent oppositional international movements difficult to imagine and essential for survival. One important route for reconstructing socialist-feminist politics is through theory and practice addressed to the social relations of science and technology, including crucially the systems of myth and meanings structuring our imaginations. The cyborg is a kind of disassembled and reassembled, post-modern collective and personal self. This is the self feminists must code.

Communications technologies and biotechnologies are the crucial tools recrafting our bodies. These tools embody and enforce new social relations for women world-wide. Technologies and scientific discourses can be partially understood as formalizations, i.e., as frozen moments, of the fluid social interactions constituting them, but they should also be viewed as instruments for enforcing meanings. The boundary is permeable between tool and myth, instrument and concept, historical systems of social relations and historical anatomies of possible bodies, including objects of knowledge. Indeed, myth and tool mutually constitute each other.

Furthermore, communications sciences and modern biologies are constructed by a common move—*the translation of the world into a problem of coding*, a search for a common language in which all resistance to instrumental control disappears and all heterogeneity can be submitted to disassembly, reassembly, investment, and exchange.

In communications sciences, the translation of the world into a problem in coding can be illustrated by looking at cybernetic (feedback-controlled) systems theories applied to telephone technology, computer design, weapons deployment, or data base construction and maintenance. In each case, solution to the key questions rests on a theory of language and control; the key operation is determining the rates, directions, and probabilities of flow of a quantity called information. The world is subdivided by boundaries differentially permeable to information. Information is just that kind of quantifiable element (unit, basis of unity) which allows universal translation, and so unhindered instrumental power (called effective communication). The biggest threat to such power is interruption of communication. Any system breakdown is a function of stress. The fundamentals of this technology can be condensed into the metaphor C3I, command-control-communication-intelligence, the military's symbol for its operations theory.

In modern biologies, the translation of the world into a problem in coding can be illustrated by molecular genetics, ecology, sociobiological evolutionary theory, and immunobiology. The organism has been translated into problems of genetic coding and read-out. Biotechnology, a writing technology, informs research broadly.[14] In a sense, organisms have ceased to exist as objects of knowledge, giving way to biotic components, i.e., special kinds of information-processing devices. The analogous moves in ecology could be examined by probing the history and utility of the concept of the ecosystem. Immunobiology and associated medical practices are rich exemplars of the privilege of coding and recognition systems as objects of knowledge, as constructions of bodily reality for us. Biology here is a kind of cryptography. Research is necessarily a kind of intelligence activity. Ironies abound. A stressed system goes awry; its communication processes break down; it fails to recognize the difference between self and other. Human babies with baboon hearts evoke national ethical perplexity—for animal rights activists at least as much as for the guardians of human purity. In the US gay men and intravenous drug users are the "privileged" victims of an awful immune system disease that marks (inscribes on the body) confusion of boundaries and moral pollution (Treichler, 1987).

But these excursions into communications sciences and biology have been at a rarefied level; there is a mundane, largely economic reality to support my claim that these sciences and technologies indicate fundamental transformations in the structure of the world for us. Communications technologies depend on electronics. Modern states, multinational corporations, military power, welfare state apparatuses, satellite systems, political processes, fabrication of our imaginations, labour-control systems, medical constructions of our bodies, commercial pornography, the international division of labour, and religious evangelism depend intimately upon electronics. Microelectronics is the technical basis of simulacra; that is, of copies without originals.

Microelectronics mediates the translations of labour into robotics and word processing, sex into genetic engineering and reproductive technologies, and mind into artificial intelligence and decision procedures. The new biotechnologies concern more than human reproduction. Biology as a powerful engineering science for redesigning materials and processes has revolutionary implications for industry, perhaps most obvious today in areas of fermentation, agriculture, and energy. Communications sciences and biology are constructions of natural-technical objects of knowledge in which the difference between machine and organism is thoroughly blurred; mind, body, and tool are on very intimate terms. The "multinational" material organization of the production and reproduction of daily life and the symbolic organization of the production and reproduction of culture and imagination seem equally implicated. The boundary-maintaining images of base and superstructure, public and private, or material and ideal never seemed more feeble.

I have used Rachel Grossman's (1980) image of women in the integrated circuit to name the situation of women in a world so intimately restructured through the social relations of science and technology.[15] I used the odd circumlocution, "the social relations of science and technology," to indicate that we are not dealing with a technological determinism, but with a historical system depending upon structured relations among people. But the phrase should also indicate that science and technology provide fresh sources of power, that we need fresh sources of analysis and political action (Latour, 1984). Some of the rearrangements of race, sex, and class rooted in high-tech-facilitated social relations can make socialist-feminism more relevant to effective progressive politics.

## The "Homework Economy" outside "The Home"

The "New Industrial Revolution" is producing a new world-wide working class, as well as new sexualities and ethnicities. The extreme mobility of capital and the emerging international division of labour are intertwined with the emergence of new collectivities, and the weakening of familiar groupings. These developments are neither gender- nor race-neutral. White men in advanced industrial societies have become newly vulnerable to permanent job loss, and women are not disappearing from the job rolls at the same

525

rates as men. It is not simply that women in Third World countries are the preferred labour force for the science-based multinationals in the export-processing sectors, particularly in electronics. The picture is more systematic and involves reproduction, sexuality, culture, consumption, and production. In the prototypical Silicon Valley, many women's lives have been structured around employment in electronics-dependent jobs, and their intimate realities include serial heterosexual monogamy, negotiating childcare, distance from extended kin or most other forms of traditional community, a high likelihood of loneliness and extreme economic vulnerability as they age. The ethnic and racial diversity of women in Silicon Valley structures a microcosm of conflicting differences in culture, family, religion, education, and language.

Richard Gordon has called this new situation the "homework economy."[16] Although he includes the phenomenon of literal homework emerging in connection with electronics assembly, Gordon intends "homework economy" to name a restructuring of work that broadly has the characteristics formerly ascribed to female jobs, jobs literally done only by women. Work is being redefined as both literally female and feminized, whether performed by men or women. To be feminized means to be made extremely vulnerable; able to be disassembled, reassembled, exploited as a reserve labour force; seen less as workers than as servers; subjected to time arrangements on and off the paid job that make a mockery of a limited work day; leading an existence that always borders on being obscene, out of place, and reducible to sex. Deskilling is an old strategy newly applicable to formerly privileged workers. However, the homework economy does not refer only to large-scale deskilling, nor does it deny that new areas of high skill are emerging, even for women and men previously excluded from skilled employment. Rather, the concept indicates that factory, home, and market are integrated on a new scale and that the places of women are crucial—and need to be analysed for differences among women and for meanings for relations between men and women in various situations.

The homework economy as a world capitalist organizational structure is made possible by (not caused by) the new technologies. The success of the attack on relatively privileged, mostly white, men's unionized jobs is tied to the power of the new communications technologies to integrate and control labour despite extensive dispersion and decentralization. The

consequences of the new technologies are felt by women both in the loss of the family (male) wage (if they ever had access to this white privilege) and in the character of their own jobs, which are becoming capital-intensive; for example, office work and nursing.

The new economic and technological arrangements are also related to the collapsing welfare state and the ensuing intensification of demands on women to sustain daily life for themselves as well as for men, children, and old people. The feminization of poverty—generated by dismantling the welfare state, by the homework economy where stable jobs become the exception, and sustained by the expectation that women's wages will not be matched by a male income for the support of children—has become an urgent focus. The causes of various women-headed households are a function of race, class, or sexuality; but their increasing generality is a ground for coalitions of women on many issues. That women regularly sustain daily life partly as a function of their enforced status as mothers is hardly new; the kind of integration with the overall capitalist and progressively war-based economy is new. The particular pressure, for example, on US black women, who have achieved an escape from (barely) paid domestic service and who now hold clerical and similar jobs in large numbers, has large implications for continued enforced black poverty *with* employment. Teenage women in industrializing areas of the Third World increasingly find themselves the sole or major source of a cash wage for their families, while access to land is ever more problematic. These developments must have major consequences in the psychodynamics and politics of gender and race.

Within the framework of three major stages of capitalism (commercial/early industrial, monopoly, multinational)—tied to nationalism, imperialism, and multinationalism, and related to Jameson's three dominant aesthetic periods of realism, modernism, and postmodernism—I would argue that specific forms of families dialectically relate to forms of capital and to its political and cultural concomitants. Although lived problematically and unequally, ideal forms of these families might be schematized as (1) the patriarchal nuclear family, structured by the dichotomy between public and private and accompanied by the white bourgeois ideology of separate spheres and nineteenth-century Anglo-American bourgeois feminism; (2) the modern family mediated (or enforced) by the welfare state and institutions like the family wage, with a flowering of a-feminist heterosexual ideologies, including their radical versions represented in Greenwich Village around the First World War; and (3) the "family" of the homework economy with its oxymoronic structure of women-headed households and its explosion of feminisms and the paradoxical intensification and erosion of gender itself. This is the context in which the projections for world-wide structural unemployment stemming from the new technologies are part of the picture of the homework economy. As robotics and related technologies put men out of work in "developed" countries and exacerbate failure to generate male jobs in Third World "development," and as the automated office becomes the rule even in labour-surplus countries, the feminization of work intensifies. Black women in the United States have long known what it looks like to face the structural under-employment ("feminization") of black men, as well as their own highly vulnerable position in the wage economy. It is no longer a secret that sexuality, reproduction, family, and community life are interwoven with this economic structure in myriad ways which have also differentiated the situations of white and black women. Many more women and men will contend with similar situations, which will make cross-gender and race alliances on issues of basic life support (with or without jobs) necessary, not just nice.

The new technologies also have a profound effect on hunger and on food production for subsistence world-wide. Rae Lessor Blumberg (1983) estimates that women produce about 50 per cent of the world's subsistence food.[17] Women are excluded generally from benefiting from the increased high-tech commodification of food and energy crops, their days are made more arduous because their responsibilities to provide food do not diminish, and their reproductive situations are made more complex. Green Revolution technologies interact with other high-tech industrial production to alter gender divisions of labour and differential gender migration patterns.

The new technologies seem deeply involved in the forms of "privatization" that Ros Petchesky (1981) has analysed, in which militarization, right-wing family ideologies and policies, and intensified definitions of corporate (and state) property as private synergistically interact.[18] The new communications technologies are fundamental to the eradication of "public life" for everyone. This facilitates the mushrooming of a permanent high-tech military establish-ment at the cultural and economic expense of most people, but especially of women. Technologies like video games and highly miniaturized televisions seem crucial to production of modern forms of "private life." The culture of video games is heavily orientated to individual competition and extraterrestrial warfare. High-tech, gendered imaginations are produced here, imaginations that can contemplate destruction of the planet and a sci-fi escape from its consequences. More than our imaginations is militarized; and the other realities of electronic and nuclear warfare are inescapable. These are the technologies that promise ultimate mobility and perfect exchange—and incidentally enable tourism, that perfect practice of mobility and exchange, to emerge as one of the world's largest single industries.

The new technologies affect the social relations of both sexuality and of reproduction, and not always in the same ways. The close ties of sexuality and instrumentality, of views of the body as a kind of private satisfaction- and utility-maximizing machine, are described nicely in sociobiological origin stories that stress a genetic calculus and explain the inevitable dialectic of domination of male and female gender roles.[19] These sociobiological stories depend on a high-tech view of the body as a biotic component or cybernetic communications system. Among the many transformations of reproductive situations is the medical one, where women's bodies have boundaries newly permeable to both "visualization" and "intervention." Of course, who controls the interpretation of bodily boundaries in medical hermeneutics is a major feminist issue. The speculum served as an icon of women's claiming their bodies in the 1970s; that handcraft tool is inadequate to express our needed body politics in the negotiation of reality in the practices of cyborg reproduction. Self-help is not enough. The technologies of visualization recall the important cultural practice of hunting with the camera and the deeply predatory nature of a photographic consciousness.[20] Sex, sexuality, and reproduction are central actors in high-tech myth systems structuring our imaginations of personal and social possibility.

Another critical aspect of the social relations of the new technologies is the reformulation of expectations, culture, work, and reproduction for the large scientific and technical work-force. A major social and political danger is the formation of a strongly bimodal social structure, with the masses of women and men of all ethnic groups, but especially

527

people of colour, confined to a homework economy, illiteracy of several varieties, and general redundancy and impotence, controlled by high-tech repressive apparatuses ranging from entertainment to surveillance and disappearance. An adequate socialist-feminist politics should address women in the privileged occupational categories, and particularly in the production of science and technology that constructs scientific-technical discourses, processes, and objects.[21]

This issue is only one aspect of enquiry into the possibility of a feminist science, but it is important. What kind of constitutive role in the production of knowledge, imagination, and practice can new groups doing science have? How can these groups be allied with progressive social and political movements? What kind of political accountability can be constructed to tie women together across the scientific-technical hierarchies separating us? Might there be ways of developing feminist science/ technology politics in alliance with anti-military science facility conversion action groups? Many scientific and technical workers in Silicon Valley, the high-tech cowboys included, do not want to work on military science.[22] Can these personal preferences and cultural tendencies be welded into progressive politics among this professional middle class in which women, including women of colour, are coming to be fairly numerous?

## Women in the Integrated Circuit

Let me summarize the picture of women's historical locations in advanced industrial societies, as these positions have been restructured partly through the social relations of science and technology. If it was ever possible ideologically to characterize women's lives by the distinction of public and private domains—suggested by images of the division of working-class life into factory and home, of bourgeois life into market and home, and of gender existence into personal and political realms—it is now a totally misleading ideology, even to show how both terms of these dichotomies construct each other in practice and in theory. I prefer a network ideological image, suggesting the profusion of spaces and identities and the permeability of boundaries in the personal body and in the body politic. "Networking" is both a feminist practice and a multinational corporate strategy—weaving is for oppositional cyborgs.

So let me return to the earlier image of the informatics of domination and trace one vision of women's "place" in the

integrated circuit, touching only a few idealized social locations seen primarily from the point of view of advanced capitalist societies: Home, Market, Paid Work Place, State, School, Clinic-Hospital, and Church. Each of these idealized spaces is logically and practically implied in every other locus, perhaps analogous to a holographic photograph. I want to suggest the impact of the social relations mediated and enforced by the new technologies in order to help formulate needed analysis and practical work. However, there is no "place" for women in these networks, only geometrics of difference and contradiction crucial to women's cyborg identities. If we learn how to read these webs of power and social life, we might learn new couplings, new coalitions. There is no way to read the following list from a standpoint of "identification," of a unitary self. The issue is dispersion. The task is to survive in the diaspora.

> *Home:* Women-headed households, serial monogamy, flight of men, old women alone, technology of domestic work, paid homework, re-emergence of home sweat-shops, home-based businesses and telecommuting, electronic cottage, urban homelessness, migration, module architecture, reinforced (simulated) nuclear family, intense domestic violence.

> *Market:* Women's continuing consumption work, newly targeted to buy the profusion of new production from the new technologies (especially as the competitive race among industrialized and industrializing nations to avoid dangerous mass unemployment necessitates finding ever bigger new markets for ever less clearly needed commodities); bimodal buying power, coupled with advertising targeting of the numerous affluent groups and neglect of the previous mass markets; growing importance of informal markets in labour and commodities parallel to high-tech, affluent market structures; surveillance systems through electronic funds transfer; intensified market abstraction (commodification) of experience, resulting in ineffective utopian or equivalent cynical theories of community; extreme mobility (abstraction) of marketing/financing systems; interpenetration of sexual and labour markets; intensified sexualization of abstracted and alienated consumption.

> *Paid Work Place:* Continued intense sexual and racial division of labour, but considerable growth of membership in privileged occupational categories for many white women and people of colour; impact of

new technologies on women's work in clerical, service, manufacturing (especially textiles), agriculture, electronics; international restructuring of the working classes; development of new time arrangements to facilitate the homework economy (flex time, part time, over time, no time); homework and out work; increased pressures for two-tiered wage structures; significant numbers of people in cash-dependent populations world-wide with no experience or no further hope of stable employment; most labour "marginal" or "feminized."

*State:* Continued erosion of the welfare state; decentralizations with increased surveillance and control; citizenship by telematics; imperialism and political power broadly in the form of information rich/information poor differentiation; increased high-tech militarization increasingly opposed by many social groups; reduction of civil service jobs as a result of the growing capital intensification of office work, with implications for occupational mobility for women of colour; growing privatization of material and ideological life and culture; close integration of privatization and militarization, the high-tech forms of bourgeois capitalist personal and public life; invisibility of different social groups to each other, linked to psychological mechanisms of belief in abstract enemies.

*School:* Deepening coupling of high-tech capital needs and public education at all levels, differentiated by race, class, and gender; managerial classes involved in educational reform and refunding at the cost of remaining progressive educational democratic structures for children and teachers; education for mass ignorance and repression in technocratic and militarized culture; growing anti-science mystery cults in dissenting and radical political movements; continued relative scientific illiteracy among white women and people of colour; growing industrial direction of education (especially higher education) by science-based multinationals (particularly in electronics- and biotechnology-dependent companies); highly educated, numerous élites in a progressively bimodal society.

*Clinic-Hospital:* Intensified machine–body relations; renegotiations of public metaphors which channel personal experience of the body, particularly in relation to reproduction, immune system functions, and "stress" phenomena; intensification of repro-ductive politics in response to world historical implications of women's unrealized, potential control of their relation to reproduction; emergence of new, historically specific diseases; struggles over meanings and means of health in environments pervaded by high technology products and processes; continuing feminization of health work; intensified struggle over state responsibility for health; continued ideological role of popular health movements as a major form of American politics.

*Church:* Electronic fundamentalist "super-saver" preachers solemnizing the union of electronic capital and automated fetish gods; intensified importance of churches in resisting the militarized state; central struggle over women's meanings and authority in religion; continued relevance of spirituality, intertwined with sex and health, in political struggle.

The only way to characterize the informatics of domination is as a massive intensification of insecurity and cultural impoverishment, with common failure of subsistence networks for the most vulnerable. Since much of this picture interweaves with the social relations of science and technology, the urgency of a socialist-feminist politics addressed to science and technology is plain. There is much now being done, and the grounds for political work are rich. For example, the efforts to develop forms of collective struggle for women in paid work, like SEIU's District 925,* should be a high priority for all of us. These efforts are profoundly tied to technical restructuring of labour processes and reformations of working classes. These efforts also are providing understanding of a more comprehensive kind of labour organization, involving community, sexuality, and family issues never privileged in the largely white male industrial unions.

The structural rearrangements related to the social relations of science and technology evoke strong ambivalence. But it is not necessary to be ultimately depressed by the implications of late twentieth-century women's relation to all aspects of work, culture, production of knowledge, sexuality, and reproduction. For excellent reasons, most Marxisms see domination best and have trouble understanding what can only look like false consciousness and people's complicity in their own domination in late capitalism. It is crucial to remember that

*Service Employees International Union's office workers' organization in the US.

529

what is lost, perhaps especially from women's points of view, is often virulent forms of oppression, nostalgically naturalized in the face of current violation. Ambivalence towards the disrupted unities mediated by high-tech culture requires not sorting consciousness into categories of "clear-sighted critique grounding a solid political epistemology" versus "manipulated false consciousness," but subtle understanding of emerging pleasures, experiences, and powers with serious potential for changing the rules of the game.

There are grounds for hope in the emerging bases for new kinds of unity across race, gender, and class, as these elementary units of socialist-feminist analysis themselves suffer protean transformations. Intensifications of hardship experienced world-wide in connection with the social relations of science and technology are severe. But what people are experiencing is not transparently clear, and we lack sufficiently subtle connections for collectively building effective theories of experience. Present efforts—Marxist, psychoanalytic, feminist, anthropological—to clarify even "our" experience are rudimentary.

I am conscious of the odd perspective provided by my historical position—a PhD in biology for an Irish Catholic girl was made possible by Sputnik's impact on US national science-education policy. I have a body and mind as much constructed by the post-Second World War arms race and cold war as by the women's movements. There are more grounds for hope in focusing on the contradictory effects of politics designed to produce loyal American technocrats, which also produced large numbers of dissidents, than in focusing on the present defeats.

The permanent partiality of feminist points of view has consequences for our expectations of forms of political organization and participation. We do not need a totality in order to work well. The feminist dream of a common language, like all dreams for a perfectly true language, of perfectly faithful naming of experience, is a totalizing and imperialist one. In that sense, dialectics too is a dream language, longing to resolve contradiction. Perhaps, ironically, we can learn from our fusions with animals and machines how not to be Man, the embodiment of Western logos. From the point of view of pleasure in these potent and taboo fusions, made inevitable by the social relations of science and technology, there might indeed be a feminist science.

## Cyborgs: A Myth of Political Identity

I want to conclude with a myth about identity and boundaries which might inform late twentieth-century political imaginations. I am indebted in this story to writers like Joanna Russ, Samuel R. Delany, John Varley, James Tiptree, Jr, Octavia Butler, Monique Wittig, and Vonda McIntyre.[23] These are our story-tellers exploring what it means to be embodied in high-tech worlds. They are theorists for cyborgs. Exploring conceptions of bodily boundaries and social order, the anthropologist Mary Douglas (1966, 1970) should be credited with helping us to consciousness about how fundamental body imagery is to world view, and so to political language. French feminists like Luce Irigaray and Monique Wittig, for all their differences, know how to write the body; how to weave eroticism, cosmology, and politics from imagery of embodiment, and especially for Wittig, from imagery of fragmentation and reconstitution of bodies.[24]

American radical feminists like Susan Griffin, Audre Lorde, and Adrienne Rich have profoundly affected our political imaginations—and perhaps restricted too much what we allow as a friendly body and political language.[25] They insist on the organic, opposing it to the technological. But their symbolic systems and the related positions of ecofeminism and feminist paganism, replete with organicisms, can only be understood in Sandoval's terms as oppositional ideologies fitting the late twentieth century. They would simply bewilder anyone not preoccupied with the machines and consciousness of late capitalism. In that sense they are part of the cyborg world. But there are also great riches for feminists in explicitly embracing the possibilities inherent in the breakdown of clean distinctions between organism and machine and similar distinctions structuring the Western self. It is the simultaneity of breakdowns that cracks the matrices of domination and opens geometric possibilities. What might be learned from personal and political "technological" pollution? I look briefly at two overlapping groups of texts for their insight into the construction of a potentially helpful cyborg myth: constructions of women of colour and monstrous selves in feminist science fiction.

Earlier I suggested that "women of colour" might be understood as a cyborg identity, a potent subjectivity synthesized from fusions of outsider identities and in the complex political-historical layerings of her "biomythography,"

*Zami* (Lorde, 1982; King, 1987a, 1987b). There are material and cultural grids mapping this potential, Audre Lorde (1984) captures the tone in the title of her *Sister Outsider*. In my political myth, Sister Outsider is the offshore woman, whom US workers, female and feminized, are supposed to regard as the enemy preventing their solidarity, threatening their security. Onshore, inside the boundary of the United States, Sister Outsider is a potential amidst the races and ethnic identities of women manipulated for division, competition, and exploitation in the same industries. "Women of colour" are the preferred labour force for the science-based industries, the real women for whom the world-wide sexual market, labour market, and politics of reproduction kaleidoscope into daily life. Young Korean women hired in the sex industry and in electronics assembly are recruited from high schools, educated for the integrated circuit. Literacy, especially in English, distinguishes the "cheap" female labour so attractive to the multinationals.

Contrary to orientalist stereotypes of the "oral primitive," literacy is a special mark of women of colour, acquired by US black women as well as men through a history of risking death to learn and to teach reading and writing. Writing has a special significance for all colonized groups. Writing has been crucial to the Western myth of the distinction between oral and written cultures, primitive and civilized mentalities, and more recently to the erosion of that distinction in "postmodernist" theories attacking the phallogocentrism of the West, with its worship of the monotheistic, phallic, authoritative, and singular work, the unique and perfect name.[26] Contests for the meanings of writing are a major form of contemporary political struggle. Releasing the play of writing is deadly serious. The poetry and stories of US women of colour are repeatedly about writing, about access to the power to signify; but this time that power must be neither phallic nor innocent. Cyborg writing must not be about the Fall, the imagination of a once-upon-a-time wholeness before language, before writing, before Man. Cyborg writing is about the power to survive, not on the basis of original innocence, but on the basis of seizing the tools to mark the world that marked them as other.

The tools are often stories, retold stories, versions that reverse and displace the hierarchical dualisms of naturalized identities. In retelling origin stories, cyborg authors subvert the central myths of origin of Western culture. We have all been colonized by those origin myths, with their longing for fulfilment in apocalypse. The phallogocentric origin stories most crucial for feminist cyborgs are built into the literal technologies—technologies that write the world, biotechnology and microelectronics—that have recently textualized our bodies as code problems on the grid of C3I. Feminist cyborg stories have the task of recoding communication and intelligence to subvert command and control.

Figuratively and literally, language politics pervade the struggles of women of colour; and stories about language have a special power in the rich contemporary writing by US women of colour. For example, retellings of the story of the indigenous woman Malinche, mother of the mestizo "bastard" race of the new world, master of languages, and mistress of Cortés, carry special meaning for Chicana constructions of identity. Cherríe Moraga (1983) in *Loving in the War Years* explores the themes of identity when one never possessed the original language, never told the original story, never resided in the harmony of legitimate heterosexuality in the garden of culture, and so cannot base identity on a myth or a fall from innocence and right to natural names, mother's or father's.[27] Moraga's writing, her superb literacy, is presented in her poetry as the same kind of violation as Malinche's mastery of the conqueror's language—a violation, an illegitimate production, that allows survival. Moraga's language is not "whole"; it is self-consciously spliced, a chimera of English and Spanish, both conqueror's languages. But it is this chimeric monster, without claim to an original language before violation, that crafts the erotic, competent, potent identities of women of colour. Sister Outsider hints at the possibility of world survival not because of her innocence, but because of her ability to live on the boundaries, to write without the founding myth of original wholeness, with its inescapable apocalypse of final return to a deathly oneness that Man has imagined to be the innocent and all-powerful Mother, freed at the End from another spiral of appropriation by her son. Writing marks Moraga's body, affirms it as the body of a woman of colour, against the possibility of passing into the unmarked category of the Anglo father or into the orientalist myth of "original illiteracy" of a mother that never was. Malinche was mother here, not Eve before eating the forbidden fruit. Writing affirms Sister Outsider, not the Woman-before-the-Fall-into-Writing needed by the phallogocentric Family of Man.

Writing is pre-eminently the technology of cyborgs, etched surfaces of the late twentieth century. Cyborg politics is the struggle for language and the struggle against perfect communication, against the one code that translates all meaning perfectly, the central dogma of phallogocentrism. That is why cyborg politics insist on noise and advocate pollution, rejoicing in the illegitimate fusions of animal and machine. These are the couplings which make Man and Woman so problematic, subverting the structure of desire, the force imagined to generate language and gender, and so subverting the structure and modes of reproduction of "Western" identity, of nature and culture, of mirror and eye, slave and master, body and mind. "We" did not originally choose to be cyborgs, but choice grounds a liberal politics and epistemology that imagines the reproduction of individuals before the wider replications of "texts."

From the perspective of cyborgs, freed of the need to ground politics in "our" privileged position of the oppression that incorporates all other dominations, the innocence of the merely violated, the ground of those closer to nature, we can see powerful possibilities. Feminisms and Marxisms have run aground on Western epistemological imperatives to construct a revolutionary subject from the perspective of a hierarchy of oppressions and/or a latent position of moral superiority, innocence, and greater closeness to nature. With no available original dream of a common language or original symbiosis promising protection from hostile "masculine" separation, but written into the play of a text that has no finally privileged reading or salvation history, to recognize "oneself" as fully implicated in the world, frees us of the need to root politics in identification, vanguard parties, purity, and mothering. Stripped of identity, the bastard race teaches about the power of the margins and the importance of a mother like Malinche. Women of colour have transformed her from the evil mother of masculinist fear into the originally literate mother who teaches survival.

This is not just literary deconstruction, but liminal transformation. Every story that begins with original innocence and privileges the return to wholeness imagines the drama of life to be individuation, separation, the birth of the self, the tragedy of autonomy, the fall into writing, alienation; that is, war, tempered by imaginary respite in the bosom of the Other. These plots are ruled by a reproductive politics—rebirth without flaw, perfection, abstraction. In this plot women are imagined either better or worse off, but all agree they have less selfhood, weaker individuation, more fusion to the oral, to Mother, less at stake in masculine autonomy. But there is another route to having less at stake in masculine autonomy, a route that does not pass through Woman, Primitive, Zero, the Mirror Stage and its imaginary. It passes through women and other present-tense, illegitimate cyborgs, not of Woman born, who refuse the ideological resources of victimization so as to have a real life. These cyborgs are the people who refuse to disappear on cue, no matter how many times a "Western" commentator remarks on the sad passing of another primitive, another organic group done in by "Western" technology, by writing.[28] These real-life cyborgs (for example, the Southeast Asian village women workers in Japanese and US electronics firms described by Aihwa Ong) are actively rewriting the texts of their bodies and societies. Survival is the stakes in this play of readings.

To recapitulate, certain dualisms have been persistent in Western traditions; they have all been systemic to the logics and practices of domination of women, people of colour, nature, workers, animals—in short, domination of all constituted as others, whose task is to mirror the self. Chief among these troubling dualisms are self/other, mind/body, culture/nature, male/female, civilized/primitive, reality/appearance, whole/part, agent/resource, maker/made, active/passive, right/wrong, truth/illusion, total/partial, God/man. The self is the One who is not dominated, who knows that by the service of the other, the other is the one who holds the future, who knows that by the experience of domination, which gives the lie to the autonomy of the self. To be One is to be autonomous, to be powerful, to be God; but to be One is to be an illusion, and so to be involved in a dialectic of apocalypse with the other. Yet to be other is to be multiple, without clear boundary, frayed, insubstantial. One is too few, but two are too many.

High-tech culture challenges these dualisms in intriguing ways. It is not clear who makes and who is made in the relation between human and machine. It is not clear what is mind and what body in machines that resolve into coding practices. In so far as we know ourselves in both formal discourse (for example, biology) and in daily practice (for example, the homework economy in the integrated circuit), we find ourselves to be cyborgs, hybrids, mosaics, chimeras. Biological organisms have become biotic systems, communications devices like others. There is no fundamental, onto-logical separation in our formal knowledge of machine and organism, of technical and organic. The replicant Rachel in the Ridley Scott film *Blade Runner* stands as the image of a cyborg culture's fear, love, and confusion.

One consequence is that our sense of connection to our tools is heightened. The trance state experienced by many computer users has become a staple of science-fiction film and cultural jokes. Perhaps paraplegics and other severely handicapped people can (and sometimes do) have the most intense experiences of complex hybridization with other communication devices.[29] Anne McCaffrey's pre-feminist *The Ship Who Sang* (1969) explored the consciousness of a cyborg, hybrid of girl's brain and complex machinery, formed after the birth of a severely handicapped child. Gender, sexuality, embodiment, skill: all were reconstituted in the story. Why should our bodies end at the skin, or include at best other beings encapsulated by skin? From the seventeenth century till now, machines could be animated—given ghostly souls to make them speak or move or to account for their orderly development and mental capacities. Or organisms could be mechanized—reduced to body understood as resource of mind. These machine/organism relationships are obsolete, unnecessary. For us, in imagination and in other practice, machines can be prosthetic devices, intimate components, friendly selves. We don't need organic holism to give impermeable wholeness, the total woman and her feminist variants (mutants?). Let me conclude this point by a very partial reading of the logic of the cyborg monsters of my second group of texts, feminist science fiction.

The cyborgs populating feminist science fiction make very problematic the statuses of man or woman, human, artefact, member of a race, individual entity, or body. Katie King clarifies how pleasure in reading these fictions is not largely based on identification. Students facing Joanna Russ for the first time, students who have learned to take modernist writers like James Joyce or Virginia Woolf without flinching, do not know what to make of *The Adventures of Alyx* or *The Female Man*, where characters refuse the reader's search for innocent wholeness while granting the wish for heroic quests, exuberant eroticism, and serious politics. *The Female Man* is the story of four versions of one genotype, all of whom meet, but even taken together do not make a whole, resolve the dilemmas of violent moral action, or remove the

growing scandal of gender. The feminist science fiction of Samuel R. Delany, especially *Tales of Nevèrÿon*, mocks stories of origin by redoing the neolithic revolution, replaying the founding moves of Western civilization to subvert their plausibility. James Tiptree, Jr, an author whose fiction was regarded as particularly manly until her "true" gender was revealed, tells tales of reproduction based on non-mammalian technologies like alternation of generations of male brood pouches and male nurturing. John Varley constructs a supreme cyborg in his arch-feminist exploration of Gaea, a mad goddess-planet-trickster-old woman-technological device on whose surface an extraordinary array of post-cyborg symbioses are spawned. Octavia Butler writes of an African sorceress pitting her powers of transformation against the genetic manipulations of her rival (*Wild Seed*), of time warps that bring a modern US black woman into slavery where her actions in relation to her white master-ancestor determine the possibility of her own birth (*Kindred*), and of the illegitimate insights into identity and community of an adopted cross-species child who came to know the enemy as self (*Survivor*). In *Dawn* (1987), the first instalment of a series called *Xenogenesis*, Butler tells the story of Lilith Iyapo, whose personal name recalls Adam's first and repudiated wife and whose family name marks her status as the widow of the son of Nigerian immigrants to the US. A black woman and a mother whose child is dead, Lilith mediates the transformation of humanity through genetic exchange with extra-terrestrial lovers/rescuers/destroyers/genetic engineers, who reform earth's habitats after the nuclear holocaust and coerce surviving humans into intimate fusion with them. It is a novel that interrogates reproductive, linguistic, and nuclear politics in a mythic field structured by late twentieth-century race and gender.

Because it is particularly rich in boundary transgressions, Vonda McIntyre's *Superluminal* can close this truncated catalogue of promising and dangerous monsters who help redefine the pleasures and politics of embodiment and feminist writing. In a fiction where no character is "simply" human, human status is highly problematic. Orca, a genetically altered diver, can speak with killer whales and survive deep ocean conditions, but she longs to explore space as a pilot, necessitating bionic implants jeopardizing her kinship with the divers and cetaceans. Transformations are effected by virus vectors carrying a new developmental code, by transplant surgery, by implants of microelectronic devices, by analogue doubles, and other means. Laenea becomes a pilot by accepting a heart implant and a host of other alterations allowing survival in transit at speeds exceeding that of light. Radu Dracul survives a virus-caused plague in his outerworld planet to find himself with a time sense that changes the boundaries of spatial perception for the whole species. All the characters explore the limits of language; the dream of communicating experience; and the necessity of limitation, partiality, and intimacy even in this world of protean transformation and connection. *Superluminal* stands also for the defining contradictions of a cyborg world in another sense; it embodies textually the intersection of feminist theory and colonial discourse in the science fiction I have alluded to in this chapter. This is a conjunction with a long history that many "First World" feminists have tried to repress, including myself in my readings of *Superluminal* before being called to account by Zoe Sofoulis, whose different location in the world system's informatics of domination made her acutely alert to the imperialist moment of all science fiction cultures, including women's science fiction. From an Australian feminist sensitivity, Sofoulis remembered more readily McIntyre's role as writer of the adventures of Captain Kirk and Spock in TV's *Star Trek* series than her rewriting the romance in *Superluminal.*

Monsters have always defined the limits of community in Western imaginations. The Centaurs and Amazons of ancient Greece established the limits of the centred polis of the Greek male human by their disruption of marriage and boundary pollutions of the warrior with animality and woman. Unseparated twins and hermaphrodites were the confused human material in early modern France who grounded discourse on the natural and supernatural, medical and legal, portents and diseases—all crucial to establishing modern identity.[30] The evolutionary and behavioural sciences of monkeys and apes have marked the multiple boundaries of late twentieth-century industrial identities. Cyborg monsters in feminist science fiction define quite different political possibilities and limits from those proposed by the mundane fiction of Man and Woman.

There are several consequences to taking seriously the imagery of cyborgs as other than our enemies. Our bodies, ourselves; bodies are maps of power and identity. Cyborgs are no exception. A cyborg body is not innocent; it was not born in a garden; it does not seek unitary identity and so generate antagonistic dualisms without end (or until the world ends);

it takes irony for granted. One is too few, and two is only one possibility. Intense pleasure in skill, machine skill, ceases to be a sin, but an aspect of embodiment. The machine is not an *it* to be animated, worshipped, and dominated. The machine is us, our processes, an aspect of our embodiment. We can be responsible for machines; *they* do not dominate or threaten us. We are responsible for boundaries; we are they. Up till now (once upon a time), female embodiment seemed to be given, organic, necessary; and female embodiment seemed to mean skill in mothering and its metaphoric extensions. Only by being out of place could we take intense pleasure in machines, and then with excuses that this was organic activity after all, appropriate to females. Cyborgs might consider more seriously the partial, fluid, sometimes aspect of sex and sexual embodiment. Gender might not be global identity after all, even if it has profound historical breadth and depth.

The ideologically charged question of what counts as daily activity, as experience, can be approached by exploiting the cyborg image. Feminists have recently claimed that women are given to dailiness, that women more than men somehow sustain daily life, and so have a privileged epistemological position potentially. There is a compelling aspect to this claim, one that makes visible unvalued female activity and names it as *the* ground of life. But the ground of life? What about all the ignorance of women, all the exclusions and failures of knowledge and skill? What about men's access to daily competence, to knowing how to build things, to take them apart, to play? What about other embodiments? Cyborg gender is a local possibility taking a global vengeance. Race, gender, and capital require a cyborg theory of wholes and parts. There is no drive in cyborgs to produce total theory, but there is an intimate experience of boundaries, their construction and deconstruction. There is a myth system waiting to become a political language to ground one way of looking at science and technology and challenging the informatics of domination—in order to act potently.

One last image: organisms and organismic, holistic politics depend on metaphors of rebirth and invariably call on the resources of reproductive sex. I would suggest that cyborgs have more to do with regeneration and are suspicious of the reproductive matrix and of most birthing. For salamanders, regeneration after injury, such as the loss of a limb, involves regrowth of structure and restoration of function with the constant possibility of twinning or other odd topographical productions at the site of former injury. The regrown limb can be monstrous, duplicated, potent. We have all been injured, profoundly. We require regeneration, not rebirth, and the possibilities for our reconstitution include the utopian dream of the hope for a monstrous world without gender.

Cyborg imagery can help express two crucial arguments in this essay: first, the production of universal, totalizing theory is a major mistake that misses most of reality, probably always, but certainly now; and second, taking responsibility for the social relations of science and technology means refusing an anti-science metaphysics, a demonology of technology, and so means embracing the skilful task of reconstructing the boundaries of daily life, in partial connection with others, in communication with all of our parts. It is not just that science and technology are possible means of great human satisfaction, as well as a matrix of complex dominations. Cyborg imagery can suggest a way out of the maze of dualisms in which we have explained our bodies and our tools to ourselves. This is a dream not of a common language, but of a powerful infidel heteroglossia. It is an imagination of a feminist speaking in tongues to strike fear into the circuits of the super-savers of the new right. It means both building and destroying machines, identities, categories, relationships, space stories. Though both are bound in the spiral dance, I would rather be a cyborg than a goddess.

## Notes

1. Research was funded by an Academic Senate Faculty Research Grant from the University of California, Santa Cruz. An earlier version of the paper on genetic engineering appeared as "Lieber Kyborg als Göttin: für eine sozialistisch-feministische Unterwanderung der Gentechnologie," in Bernd-Peter Lange and Anna Marie Stuby, eds, Berlin: Argument-Sonderband 105, 1984, pp 66–84. The cyborg manifesto grew from my "New machines, new bodies, new communities: political dilemmas of a cyborg feminist," "The Scholar and the Feminist X: The Question of Technology," Conference, Barnard College, April 1983.

The people associated with the History of Consciousness Board of UCSC have had an enormous influence on this paper, so that it feels collectively authored more than most, although those I cite may not recognize their ideas. In particular, members of graduate and undergraduate feminist theory, science, and politics, and theory and methods courses contributed to the cyborg manifesto. Particular debts here are due Hilary Klein (1989), Paul Edwards (1985), Lisa Lowe (1986), and James Clifford (1985).

Parts of the paper were my contribution to a collectively developed session, "Poetic Tools and Political Bodies: Feminist Approaches to High Technology Culture," 1984 California American Studies

Association, with History of Consciousness graduate students Zoe Sofoulis, "Jupiter space"; Katie King, "The pleasures of repetition and the limits of identification in feminist science fiction: reimaginations of the body after the cyborg"; and Chela Sandoval, "The construction of subjectivity and oppositional consciousness in feminist film and video." Sandoval's (n.d.) theory of oppositional consciousness was published as "Women respond to racism: A Report on the National Women's Studies Association Conference." For Sofoulis's semiotic-psychoanalytic readings of nuclear culture, see Sofia (1984). King's unpublished papers ("Questioning tradition: canon formation and the veiling of power"; "Gender and genre: reading the science fiction of Joanna Russ"; "Varley's *Titan* and *Wizard*: feminist parodies of nature, culture, and hardware") deeply informed the cyborg manifesto.

Barbara Epstein, Jeff Escoffier, Rusten Hogness, and Jaye Miler gave extensive discussion and editorial help. Members of the Silicon Valley Research Project of UCSC and participants in SVRP conferences and workshops were very important, especially Rick Gordon, Linda Kimball, Nancy Snyder, Langdon Winner, Judith Stacey, Linda Lim, Patricia Fernandez-Kelly, and Judith Gregory. Finally, I want to thank Nancy Hartsock for years of friendship and discussion on feminist theory and feminist science fiction. I also thank Elizabeth Bird for my favourite political button: "Cyborgs for Earthly Survival."

2. Useful references to left and/or feminist radical science movements and theory and to biological/biotechnical issues include: Bleier (1984, 1986), Harding (1986), Fausto-Sterling (1985), Gould (1981), Hubbard *et al.* (1982), Keller (1985), Lewontin *et al.* (1984), *Radical Science Journal* (became *Science as Culture* in 1987), 26 Freegrove Road, London N7 9RQ; *Science for the People*, 897 Main St, Cambridge, MA 02139.

3. Starting points for left and/or feminist approaches to technology and politics include: Cowan (1983), Rothschild (1983), Traweek (1988), Young and Levidow (1981, 1985), Weizenbaum (1976), Winner (1977, 1986), Zimmerman (1983), Athanasiou (1987), Cohn (1987a, 1987b), Winograd and Flores (1986), Edwards (1985). *Global Electronics Newsletter*, 867 West Dana St, #204, Mountain View, CA 94041; *Processed World*, 55 Sutter St, San Francisco, CA 94104; ISIS, Women's International Information and Communication Service, PO Box 50 (Cornavin), 1211 Geneva 2, Switzerland, and Via Santa Maria Dell'Anima 30, 00186 Rome, Italy. Fundamental approaches to modern social studies of science that do not continue the liberal mystification that it all started with Thomas Kuhn, include: Knorr-Cetina (1981), Knorr-Cetina and Mulkay (1983), Latour and Woolgar (1979), Young (1979). The 1984 Directory of the Network for the Ethnographic Study of Science, Technology, and Organizations lists a wide range of people and projects crucial to better radical analysis; available from NESSTO, PO Box 11442, Stanford, CA 94305.

4. A provocative, comprehensive argument about the politics and theories of "postmodernism" is made by Fredric Jameson (1984), who argues that postmodernism is not an option, a style among others, but a cultural dominant requiring radical reinvention of left politics from within; there is no longer any place from without that gives meaning to the comforting fiction of critical distance.

Jameson also makes clear why one cannot be for or against postmodernism, an essentially moralist move. My position is that feminists (and others) need continuous cultural reinvention, postmodernist critique, and historical materialism; only a cyborg would have a chance. The old dominations of white capitalist patriarchy seem nostalgically innocent now: they normalized heterogeneity, into man and woman, white and black, for example. "Advanced capitalism" and postmodernism release heterogeneity without a norm, and we are flattened, without subjectivity, which requires depth, even unfriendly and drowning depths. It is time to write *The Death of the Clinic*. The clinic's methods required bodies and works; we have texts and surfaces. Our dominations don't work by medicalization and normalization any more; they work by networking, communications redesign, stress management. Normalization gives way to automation, utter redundancy. Michel Foucault's *Birth of the Clinic* (1963), *History of Sexuality* (1976), and *Discipline and Punish* (1975) name a form of power at its moment of implosion. The discourse of biopolitics gives way to technobabble, the language of the spliced substantive; no noun is left whole by the multinationals. These are their names, listed from one issue of *Science*: Tech-Knowledge, Genentech, Allergen, Hybritech, Compupro, Genen-cor, Syntex, Allelix, Agrigenetics Corp., Syntro, Codon, Repligen, MicroAngelo from Scion Corp., Percom Data, Inter Systems, Cyborg Corp., Statcom Corp., Intertec. If we are imprisoned by language, then escape from that prison-house requires language poets, a kind of cultural restriction enzyme to cut the code; cyborg heteroglossia is one form of radical cultural politics. For cyborg poetry, see Perloff (1984); Fraser (1984). For feminist modernist/postmodernist "cyborg" writing, see HOW(ever), 871 Corbett Ave, San Francisco, CA 94131.

5. Baudrillard (1983). Jameson (1984, p. 66) points out that Plato's definition of the simulacrum is the copy for which there is no original, i.e., the world of advanced capitalism, of pure exchange. See *Discourse* 9 (Spring/Summer 1987) for a special issue on technology (cybernetics, ecology, and the postmodern imagination).

6. For ethnographic accounts and political evaluations, see Epstein (forthcoming), Sturgeon (1986). Without explicit irony, adopting the spaceship earth/whole earth logo of the planet photographed from space, set off by the slogan "Love Your Mother," the May 1987 Mothers and Others Day action at the nuclear weapons testing facility in Nevada none the less took account of the tragic contradictions of views of the earth. Demonstrators applied for official permits to be on the land from officers of the Western Shoshone tribe, whose territory was invaded by the US government when it built the nuclear weapons test ground in the 1950s. Arrested for trespassing, the demonstrators argued that the police and weapons facility personnel, without authorization from the proper officials, were the trespassers. One affinity group at the women's action called themselves the Surrogate Others; and in solidarity with the creatures forced to tunnel in the same ground with the bomb, they enacted a cyborgian emergence from the constructed body of a large, non-heterosexual desert worm.

7. Powerful developments of coalition politics emerge from "Third World" speakers, speaking from nowhere, the displaced centre of

the universe, earth: "We live on the third planet from the sun"— *Sun Poem* by Jamaican writer, Edward Kamau Braithwaite, review by Mackey (1984). Contributors to Smith (1983) ironically subvert naturalized identities precisely while constructing a place from which to speak called home. See especially Reagon (in Smith, 1983, pp. 356–68). Trinh T. Minh-ha (1986–87).

8. hooks (1981, 1984); Hull *et al.* (1982). Bambara (1981) wrote an extraordinary novel in which the women of colour theatre group, The Seven Sisters, explores a form of unity. See analysis by Butler-Evans (1987).

9. On orientalism in feminist works and elsewhere, see Lowe (1986); Said (1978); Mohanty (1984); *Many Voices, One Chant: Black Feminist Perspectives* (1984).

10. Katie King (1986, 1987a) has developed a theoretically sensitive treatment of the workings of feminist taxonomies as genealogies of power in feminist ideology and polemic. King examines Jaggar's (1983) problematic example of taxonomizing feminisms to make a little machine producing the desired final position. My caricature here of socialist and radical feminism is also an example.

11. The central role of object relations versions of psychoanalysis and related strong universalizing moves in discussing reproduction, caring work, and mothering in many approaches to epistemology underline their authors' resistance to what I am calling postmodernism. For me, both the universalizing moves and these versions of psychoanalysis make analysis of "women's place in the integrated circuit" difficult and lead to systematic difficulties in accounting for or even seeing major aspects of the construction of gender and gendered social life. The feminist standpoint argument has been developed by: Flax (1983), Harding (1986), Harding and Hintikka (1983), Hartsock (1983a, b), O'Brien (1981), Rose (1983), Smith (1974, 1979). For rethinking theories of feminist materialism and feminist standpoints in response to criticism, see Harding (1986, pp. 163–96), Hartsock (1987), and H. Rose (1986).

12. I make an argumentative category error in "modifying" MacKinnon's positions with the qualifier "radical," thereby generating my own reductive critique of extremely heterogeneous writing, which does explicitly use that label, by my taxonomically interested argument about writing, which does not use the modifier and which brooks no limits and thereby adds to the various dreams of a common, in the sense of univocal, language for feminism. My category error was occasioned by an assignment to write from a particular taxonomic position which itself has a heterogeneous history, socialist-feminism, for *Socialist Review*. A critique indebted to MacKinnon, but without the reductionism and with an elegant feminist account of Foucault's paradoxical conservatism on sexual violence (rape), is de Lauretis (1985; see also 1986, pp. 1–19). A theoretically elegant feminist social-historical examination of family violence, that insists on women's, men's, and children's complex agency without losing sight of the material structures of male domination, race, and class, is Gordon (1988).

13. This chart was published in 1985. My previous efforts to understand biology as a cybernetic command-control discourse and organisms as "natural-technical objects of knowledge" were

Haraway (1979, 1983, 1984). The 1979 version of this dichotomous chart appears in this vol., ch. 3; for a 1989 version, see ch. 10. The differences indicate shifts in argument.

14. For progressive analyses and action on the biotechnology debates: *GeneWatch, a Bulletin of the Committee for Responsible Genetics,* 5 Doane St, 4th Floor, Boston, MA 02109; Genetic Screening Study Group (formerly the Sociobiology Study Group of Science for the People), Cambridge, MA; Wright (1982, 1986); Yoxen (1983).

15. Starting references for "women in the integrated circuit": D'Onofrio-Flores and Pfafflin (1982), Fernandez-Kelly (1983), Fuentes and Ehrenreich (1983), Grossman (1980), Nash and Fernandez-Kelly (1983), Ong (1987), Science Policy Research Unit (1982).

16. For the "homework economy outside the home" and related arguments: Gordon (1983); Gordon and Kimball (1985); Stacey (1987); Reskin and Hartmann (1986); *Women and Poverty* (1984); S. Rose (1986); Collins (1982); Burr (1982); Gregory and Nussbaum (1982); Piven and Coward (1982); Microelectronics Group (1980); Stallard *et al.* (1983) which includes a useful organization and resource list.

17. The conjunction of the Green Revolution's social relations with biotechnologies like plant genetic engineering makes the pressures on land in the Third World increasingly intense. AID's estimates (*New York Times,* 14 October 1984) used at the 1984 World Food Day are that in Africa, women produce about 90 per cent of rural food supplies, about 60–80 per cent in Asia, and provide 40 per cent of agricultural labour in the Near East and Latin America. Blumberg charges that world organizations' agricultural politics, as well as those of multinationals and national governments in the Third World, generally ignore fundamental issues in the sexual division of labour. The present tragedy of famine in Africa might owe as much to male supremacy as to capitalism, colonialism, and rain patterns. More accurately, capitalism and racism are usually structurally male dominant. See also Blumberg (1981); Hacker (1984); Hacker and Bovit (1981); Busch and Lacy (1983); Wilfred (1982); Sachs (1983); International Fund for Agricultural Development (1985); Bird (1984).

18. See also Enloe (1983a, b).

19. For a feminist version of this logic, see Hrdy (1981). For an analysis of scientific women's story-telling practices, especially in relation to sociobiology in evolutionary debates around child abuse and infanticide, see this vol., ch. 5.

20. For the moment of transition of hunting with guns to hunting with cameras in the construction of popular meanings of nature for an American urban immigrant public, see Haraway (1984–5, 1989b), Nash (1979), Sontag (1977), Preston (1984).

21. For guidance for thinking about the political/cultural/racial implications of the history of women doing science in the United States see: Haas and Perucci (1984); Hacker (1981); Keller (1983); National Science Foundation (1988); Rossiter (1982); Schiebinger (1987); Haraway (1989b).

22. Markoff and Siegel (1983). High Technology Professionals for Peace and Computer Professionals for Social Responsibility are promising organizations.

23. King (1984). An abbreviated list of feminist science fiction underlying themes of this essay: Octavia Butler, *Wild Seed, Mind of My Mind, Kindred, Survivor;* Suzy McKee *Charnas, Motherliness;* Samuel R. Delany, the Neverÿon series; Anne McCaffery, *The Ship Who Sang, Dinosaur Planet;* Vonda McIntyre, *Superluminal, Dreamsnake;* Joanna Russ, *Adventures of Alix, The Female Man;* James Tiptree, Jr, *Star Songs of an Old Primate, Up the Walls of the World;* John Varley, *Titan, Wizard, Demon.*

24. French feminisms contribute to cyborg heteroglossia. Burke (1981); Irigaray (1977, 1979); Marks and de Courtivron (1980); *Signs* (Autumn 1981); Wittig (1973); Duchen (1986). For English translation of some currents of francophone feminism see *Feminist Issues: A Journal of Feminist Social and Political Theory,* 1980.

25. But all these poets are very complex, not least in their treatment of themes of lying and erotic, decentred collective and personal identities. Griffin (1978), Lorde (1984), Rich (1978).

26. Derrida (1976, especially part II); Lévi-Strauss (1961, especially "The Writing Lesson"); Gates (1985); Kahn and Neumaier (1985); Ong (1982); Kramarae and Treichler (1985).

27. The sharp relation of women of colour to writing as theme and politics can be approached through: Program for "The Black Woman and the Diaspora: Hidden Connections and Extended Acknowledgments," An International Literary Conference, Michigan State University, October 1985; Evans (1984); Christian (1985); Carby (1987); Fisher (1980); *Frontiers* (1980, 1983); Kingston (1977); Lerner (1973); Giddings (1985); Moraga and Anzaldúa (1981); Morgan (1984). Anglophone European and Euro-American women have also crafted special relations to their writing as a potent sign: Gilbert and Gubar (1979), Russ (1983).

28. The convention of ideologically taming militarized high technology by publicizing its applications to speech and motion problems of the disabled/differently abled takes on a special irony in monotheistic, patriarchal, and frequently anti-semitic culture when computer-generated speech allows a boy with no voice to chant the Haftorah at his bar mitzvah. See Sussman (1986). Making the always context-relative social definitions of "ableness" particularly clear, military high-tech has a way of making human beings disabled by definition, a perverse aspect of much automated battlefield and Star Wars R&D. See Welford (1 July 1986).

29. James Clifford (1985, 1988) argues persuasively for recognition of continuous cultural reinvention, the stubborn non-disappearance of those "marked" by Western imperializing practices.

30. DuBois (1982), Daston and Park (n.d.), Park and Daston (1981). The noun *monster* shares its root with the verb to *demonstrate.*

537

## Bibliography

Athanasiou, Tom (1987) "High-tech politics: the case of artificial intelligence." *Socialist Review* 92: 7-35.

Bambara, Toni Cade (1981) *The Salt Eaters.* New York: Vintage/Random House.

Baudrillard, Jean (1983) *Simulations,* P. Foss, P. Patton, P.

Beitchman, trans. New York: Semitext[e].

Bird, Elizabeth (1984) "Green Revolution imperialism, I & II," papers delivered at the University of California, Santa Cruz.

Bleier, Ruth (1984) *Science and Gender: A Critique of Biology and its Themes on Women.* New York: Pergamon.

———, ed. (1986) *Feminist Approaches to Science.* New York: Pergamon.

Blumberg, Rae Lessor (1981) *Stratification: Socioeconomic and Sexual Inequality.* Boston: Brown.

——— (1983) "A general theory of sex stratification and its application to the positions of women in today's world economy," paper delivered to Sociology Board, University of California at Santa Cruz.

Burke, Carolyn (1981) "Irigaray through the looking glass," *Feminist Studies* 7(2): 288-306.

Burr, Sara G. (1982) "Women and Work," in Barbara K. Haber, ed. *The Women's Annual, 1981.* Boston: G.K. Hall.

Busch, Lawrence and Lacy, Willliam (1983) *Science, Agriculture, and the Politics of Research.* Boulder, CO: Westview.

Butler, Octavia (1987) *Dawn.* New York: Warner.

Butler-Evans, Elliot (1987) "Race, gender, and desire: narrative strategies and the production of ideology in the fiction of Toni Cade Bambara, Toni Morrison and Alice Walker," University of California at Santa Cruz, PhD thesis.

Carby, Hazel (1987) *Reconstructing Womanhood: The Emergence of the Afro-American Woman Novelist.* New York: Oxford University Press.

Christian, Barbara (1985) *Black Feminist Criticism: Perspectives on Plack Women Writers.* New York: Pergamon.

Clifford, James (1985) "On ethnographic allegory," in James Clifford and George Marcus, eds *Writing Culture: The Poetics and Politics of Ethnography.* Berkeley: University of California Press.

——— (1988) *The Predicament of Culture: Twentieth-Century Ethnography, Literature, and Art.* Cambridge, MA: Harvard University Press.

Cohn, Carol (1987a) "Nuclear language and how we learned to pat the bomb," *Bulletin of Atomic Scientists,* pp. 17-24.

——— (1987b) "Sex and death in the rational world of defense intellectuals," *Signs* 12(4):687-718.

Collins, Patricia Hill (1982) "Third World women in America," in Barbara K. Haber, ed. *The Women's Annual, 1981.* Boston: G.K. Hall.

Cowan, Ruth Schwartz (1983) *More Work for Mother: The Ironies of Household Technology from the Open Hearth to the Microwave.* New York: Basic.

Daston, Lorraine and Park, Katherine (n.d.) "Hermaphrodites in Renaissance France," unpublished paper.

de Lauretis, Teresa (1985) "The violence of rhetoric: considerations on representation and gender," *Semiotica* 54:11-31.

———, ed. (1986) *Feminist Studies / Critical Studies.* Bloomington: Indiana University Press.

de Waal, Frans (1982) *Chimpanzee Politics: Power and Sex among the Apes.* New York: Harper & Row.

Derrida, Jaques (1976) *Of Grammatology,* G.C. Spivak, trans. and introd. Baltimore: Johns Hopkins University Press.

D'Onofrio-Flores, Pamela and Pfafflin, Shelia M. eds (1982) *Scientific-Technological Change and the Role of Women in Development.* Boulder: Westview.

Douglas, Mary (1966) *Purity and Danger.* London: Routledge & Kegan Paul.

——— (1970) *Natural Symbols.* London: Cresset Press.

DuBois, Page (1982) *Centaurs and Amazons.* Ann Arbor: University of Michigan Press.

Duchen, Claire (1986) *Feminisim in France from May '68 to Mitterrand.* London: Routledge & Kegan Paul.

Edwards, Paul (1985) "Border wars: the science and politics of artificial intelligence," *Radical America* 19(6):39-52.

Enloe, Cynthia (1983a) "Women textile workers in the militarization of Southeast Asia," in Nash and Fernandez-Kelly (1983), pp. 407-25.

——— (1983b) *Does Khaki Become You? The Militarization of Women's Lives.* Boston: South End.

Epstein, Barbara (forthcoming) *Political Protest and Cultural Revolution: Nonviolent Direct Action in the Seventies and Eighties.* Berkeley: University of California Press.

Evans, Mari, ed. (1984) *Black Women Writers: A Critical Evaluation.* Garden City, NY: Doubleday/Anchor.

Fausto-Sterling, Anne (1985) *Myths of Gender: Biological Theories about Women and Men.* New York: Basic.

Fernandez-Kelly, Maria Patricia (1983) *For We Are Sold, I and My People.* Albany: State University of New York Press.

Fisher, Dexter, ed. (1980) *The Third Woman: Minority Women Writers of the United States.* Boston: Houghton Mifflin.

Flax, Jane (1983) "Political philosophy and the patriarchal unconscious: a psychoanalytic perspective on epistemology and metaphysics," in Harding and Hintikka (1983), pp. 245-82.

Foucoult, Michel (1963) *The Birth of the Clinic: An Archaeology of Medical Perception,* A.M. Smith, trans. New York: Vintage, 1975.

——— (1975) *Discipline and Punish: The Birth of the Prison,* Alan Sheridan, trans. New York: Vintage, 1979.

——— (1976) *The History of Sexuality,* Vol. 1: *An Introduction,* Robert Hurley, trans. New York: Pantheon, 1978.

Fraser, Kathleen (1984) *Something. Even Human Voices. In the Foreground, a Lake.* Berkeley, Ca: Kalsey St Press.

Fuentes, Annette and Ehrenreich, Barbara (1983) *Women in the Global Factory.* Boston: South End.

Gates, Henry Louis (1985) "Writing 'race' and the difference it makes," in *"Race," Writing, and Difference,* special issue, *Critical Inquiry* 12(1):1-20.

Giddings, Paula (1985) *When and Where I Enter: The Impact of Black Women on Race and Sex in America.* Toronto: Bantam.

Gilbert, Sandra M. and Gubar, Susan (1979) *The Madwoman in the*

*Attic: The Woman Writer and the Nineteenth-Century Literary Imagination.* New Haven, CT: Yale University Press.

Gordon, Linda (1988) *Heroes of Their Own Lives. The Politics and History of Family Violence, Boston 1880-1960.* New York: Viking Penguin.

Gordon, Richard (1983) "The computerization of daily life, the sexual division of labor, and the homework economy," Silicon Valley Workshop conference, University of California at Santa Cruz.

—— and Kimball, Linda (1985) "High-technology, employment and the challenges of education," Silicon Valley Research Project, Working Paper, no. I.

Gould, Stephen J. (1981) *Mismeasure of Man.* New York: Norton.

Gregory, Judith and Nussbaum, Karen (1982) "Race against time: automation of the office," *Office: Technology and People* 1:197-236.

Griffin, Susan (1978) *Women and Nature: The Roaring Inside Her.* New York: Harper & Row.

Grossman, Rachel (1980) "Women's place in the integrated circuit," *Radical America* 14(1):29-50.

Haas, Violet and Perucci, Carolyn, eds (1984) *Women in Scientific and Engineering Professions.* Ann Arbor: University of Michigan Press.

Hacker, Sally (1981) "The culture of engineering: women, workplace, and machine," *Women's Studies International Quarterly* 4(3):341-53.

—— (1984) "Doing it the hard way: ethnographic studies in the agribusiness and engineering classroom," paper delivered at the California American Studies Association, Pomona.

—— and Bovit, Liza (1981) "Agriculture to agribusiness: technical imperatives and changing rules," paper delivered at the Society for the History of Technology, Milwaukee.

Haraway, Donna J. (1979) "The biological enterprise: sex, mind, and profit from human engineering to sociobiology," *Radical History Review* 20: 206-37.

—— (1983) "Signs of dominance: from a physiology to a cybernetics of primate society," *Studies in History of Biology* 6: 129-219.

—— (1984) "Class, race, sex, scientific objects of knowledge: a socialist-feminist perspective on the social construction of productive knowledge and some political consequences," in Violet Haas and Carolyn Perucci (1984), pp. 212-29.

—— (1984-5) "Teddy bear patriarchy: taxidermy in the Garden of Eden, New York City, 1908-36," *Social Text* 11:20-64.

—— (1989) *Primate Visions: Gender, Race, and Nature in the World of Modern Science.* New York: Routledge.

Harding, Sandra (1986) *The Science Question in Feminism.* Ithaca: Cornell University Press.

—— and Hintikka, Merril, eds (1983) *Discovering Reality: Feminist Perspectives on Epistimology, Metaphysics, Methodology, and Phiosophy of Science.* Dordrecht: Reidel.

Hartsock, Nancy (1983a) "The feminist standpoint: developing the ground for a specifically feminist historical materialism," in

Harding and Hintikka (1983), pp. 283-310.

—— (1983b) *Money, Sex, and Power.* New York: Longman; Boston: Northeastern University Press, 1984.

—— (1987) "Rethinking modernism: minority and majority theories," *Cultural Critique* 7:187-206.

Hogness, E. Rusten (1983) "Why stress? A look at the making of stress, 1936-56," unpublished paper available from the author, 4437 Mill Creek Rd, Healdsburg, CA 95448.

hooks, bell (1981) *Ain't I a Women.* Boston: South End.

—— (1984) *Feminist Theory: From Margin to Center.* Boston: South End.

Hrdy, Sarah Blaffer (1981) *The Woman that Never Evolved.* Cambridge, MA: Harvard University Press.

Hubbard, Ruth, Henifin, Mary Sue, and Fried, Barbara, eds (1982) *Biological Woman, the Convenient Myth.* Cambridge, MA: Schenkman.

Hull, Gloria, Scott, Patricia Bell, and Smith, Barbara, eds (1982) *All the Women Are White, All the Men Are Black, But Some of us Are Brave.* Old Westbury: The Feminist Press.

International Fund for Agricultural Development (1985) *IFAD Experience Relating to Rural Women, 1977-84.* Rome: IFAD, 37.

Irigaray, Luce (1977) *Ce sexe qui n'en est pas un.* Paris: Minuit.

—— (1979) *Et l'une ne bouge pas sans l'autre.* Paris: Minuit.

Jaggar, Alison (1983) *Feminist Politics and Human Nature.* Totowa, NJ: Roman & Allenheld.

Jameson, Fredric (1984) "Post-modernism, or the cultural logic of late capitalism," *New Left Review* 146:53-92.

Kahn, Douglas and Neumaier, Diane, eds (1985) *Cultures in Contention.* Seattle: Real Comet.

Keller, Evelyn Fox (1983) *A Feeling for the Organism.* San Francisco: Freeman.

—— (1985) *Reflections on Gender and Science.* New Haven: Yale University Press.

King, Katie (1984) "The pleasure of repetition and the limits of identification in feminist science fiction: reimaginations of the body after the cyborg," paper delivered at the California American Studies Association, Pomona.

—— (1986) "The situation of lesbianism as feminism's magical sign: contests for meaning and the U.S. women's movement, 1968-72," *Communication* 9(I): 65-92.

—— (1987a) "Canons without innocence," University of California at Santa Cruz, PhD thesis.

—— (1987b) *The Passing Dreams of Choice . . . Once Before and After: Audre Lorde and the Apparatus of Literary Production,* book prospectus, University of Maryland at College Park.

Kingston, Maxine Hong (1977) *China Men.* New York: Knopf.

Knorr-Cetina, Kerin (1981) *The Manufacture of Knowledge.* Oxford: Pergamon.

—— and Mulkay, Michael, eds (1983) *Science Observed: Perspectives on the Social Study of Science.* Beverly Hills: Sage.

539

Kramarae, Cheris and Treichler, Paula (1985) *A Feminist Dictionary.* Boston: Pandora.

Latour, Bruno (1984) *Les microbes, guerre et paix, seivi des irréductions.* Paris: Métailié.

—— and Woolgar, Steve (1979) *Laboratory Life: The Social Construction of Scientific Facts.* Beverly Hills: Sage.

Lerner, Gerda, ed. (1973) *Black Women in White America: A Documentary History.* New York: Vintage.

Lévi-Strauss, Claude (1971) *Tristes Tropiques,* John Russell, trans. New York: Atheneum.

Lewontin, R.C., Rose, Steven, and Kamin, Leon J. (1984) *Not in Our Genes: Biology, Ideology, and Human Nature.* New York: Pantheon.

Lorde, Audre (1982) *Zami, a New Spelling of My Name.* Trumansberg, NY: Crossing, 1983.

—— (1984) *Sister Outsider.* Trumansberg, NY: Crossing.

Lowe, Lisa. (1986) "French literary Orientalism: The representation of 'others' in the texts of Montesquieu, Flaubert, and Kristeva," University of California at Santa Cruz, PhD thesis.

McCaffrey, Anne (1969) *The Ship Who Sang.* New York: Ballantine.

MacKinnon, Catherine (1982) "Feminism, marxism, method, and the state: and agenda for theory," *Signs* 7(3):515-44.

—— (1987) *Feminism Unmodified: Discourses on Life and the Law.* Cambridge, MA: Harvard University Press.

*Many Voices, One Chant: Black Feminist Perspectives* (1984) *Feminist Review* 17, special issue.

Marcuse, Herbert (1964) *One-Dimensional Man: Studies in the Ideology of Advanced Industrial Society.* Boston: Beacon.

Markoff, John and Siegel, Lenny (1983) "Miliary micros," paper presented at Silicon Valley Research Project conference, University of California at Santa Cruz.

Marks, Elaine and de Courtivron, Isabelle, eds (1980) *New French Feminisims.* Amherst: University of Massachusetts Press.

Merchant, Carolyn (1980) *The Death of Nature: Women, Ecology, and the Scientific Revolution.* New York: Harper & Row.

Microelectronics Group (1980) *Microelectronics: Capitalist Technology and the Working Class.* London: CSE.

Mohanty, Chandra Talpade (1984) "Under western eyes: feminist scholarship and colonial discourse," Boundary 2,3 (12/13):333-58.

Moraga, Cherríe (1983) *Loving in the War Years: lo que nunca pasó por sus labios.* Boston: South End.

—— and Anzaldúa, Gloria, eds (1981) *This Bridge Called My Back: Writings by Radical Women of Color.* Watertown: Persephone.

Morgan, Robin, ed. (1984) *Sisterhood is Global.* Garden City, NY: Anchor/Doubleday.

Nash, June and Fernandez-Kelly, Maria Patricia, eds (1983) *Women and Men and the International Division of Labor.* Albany: State University of New York Press.

Nash, Roderick (1979) "The exporting and importing of nature: nature-appreciation as a commodity, 1850-1980," *Perspectives in American History* 3: 517-60.

National Science Foundation (1988) *Women and Minorities in Science and Engineering.* Washington: NSF.

O'Brien, Mary (1981) *The Politics of Reproduction.* New York: Routledge & Kegan Paul.

Ong, Aihwa (1987) *Spirits of Resistance and Capitalist Discipline: Factory Workers in Malaysia.* Albany: State University of New York Press.

Ong, Walter (1982) *Orality and Literacy: The Technologizing of the Word.* New York: Methuen.

Park, Katherine and Daston, Lorraine J. (1981) "Unnatural conceptions: the study of monsters in sixteenth- and seventeenth-century France and England," *Past and Present* 92: 20-54.

Perloff, Marjorie (1984) "Dirty language and scramble systems," *Sulfur* 11: 178-83.

Petchesky, Rosalind Pollack (1981) "Abortion, anti-feminism and the rise of the New Right," *Feminist Studies* 7(2):206-46.

Piven, Frances Fox and Coward, Richard (1982) *The New Class War: Reagan's Attack on the Welfare State and Its Consequences.* New York: Pantheon.

Preston, Douglas (1984) "Shooting in Paradise," *Natural History* 93(12):14-19.

Reskin, Barbara F. and Hartmann, Heidi, eds (1986) *Women's Work, Men's Work.* Washington: National Academy of Sciences.

Rich, Adrienne (1978) *The Dream of a Common Language.* New York: Norton.

Rose, Hilary (1983) "Hand, brain, and heart: a feminist epistemology for the natural sciences," *Signs* 9(1):73-90.

—— (1986) "Women's work: women's knowledge," in Juliet Mitchell and Ann Oakley, eds, *What is Feminism? A Re-Examination.* New York: Pantheon, pp. 161-83.

Rose, Stephen. (1986) *The American Profile Poster: Who Owns What, Who Makes How Much, Who Works Where, and Who Lives with Whom?* New York: Pantheon.

Rossiter, Margaret (1982) *Women Scientists in America.* Baltimore: Johns Hopkins University Press.

Rothschild, Joan, ed. (1983) *Machina ex Dea: Feminists Perspectives on Technology.* New York: Pergamon.

Russ, Joanna (1983) *How to Suppress Women's Writing.* Austin: University of Texas Press.

Sachs, Carolyn (1983) *The Invisible Farmers: Women in Agricultural Production.* Totowa: Rowman & Allenheld.

Said, Edward (1978) *Orientalism.* New York: Pantheon.

Sandoval, Chela (1984) "Dis-illustionment and the poetry of the future: the making of oppositional consciousness," University of California at Santa Cruz, PhD qualifying essay.

—— (n.d.) *Yours in Struggle: Women Respond to Racism, A Report on the National Women's Studies Association.* Oakland, CA: Center for Third World Organizing.

Schiebinger, Londa (1987) "The history and philosophy of women in science: a review essay," *Signs* 12(2):305-32.

540

Science Policy Research Unit (1982) *Microelectronics and Women's Employment in Britain.* University of Sussex.

Smith, Barbara, ed. (1983) *Home Girl: A Black Feminist Anthology.* New York: Kitchen Table, Women of Color Press.

Smith, Dorothy (1974) "Women's perspective as a radical critique of sociology," *Sociological Inquiry* 44.

—— (1979) "A sociology of women," in J. Sherman and E.T. Beck, eds *The Prism of Sex.* Madison: University of Wisconsin Press.

Sofia, Zoe (also Zoe Sofoulis) (1984) "Exterminating fetuses: abortion, disarmament, and the sexo-semiotics of extra-terrestrialism," *Diacritics* 14(2): 47-59.

Sontag, Susan (1977) *On Photography.* New York: Dell.

Stacey, Judith (1987) "Sexism by a subtler name? Postindustrial conditions and postfeminist consciousness," *Socialist Review* 96:7-28.

Stallard, Karin, Ehrenreich, Barbara, and Sklar, Holy (1983) *Poverty in the American Dream.* Boston: South End.

Sturgeon, Noel (1986) "Feminism, anarchism, and non-violent direct action politics," University of California at Santa Cruz, PhD qualifying essay.

Sussman, Vic (1986) "Personal tech. Technology lends a hand." *The Washington Post Magazine,* 9 November, pp. 45-56.

Traweek, Sharon (1988) *Beamtimes and Lifetimes: The World of High Energy Physics.* Cambridge, MA: Harvard University Press.

Treichler, Paula (1987) "AIDS, homophobia, and biomedical discourse: an epidemic of signification," *October* 43: 31-70.

Trinh T. Minh-ha (1986-7) "Introduction" and "Difference: 'a special third world women issue,'" *Discourse: Journal for Theoretical Studies in Media and Culture* 8:3-38.

Weizenbaum, Joseph (1976) *Computer Power and Human Reason.* San Francisco: Freeman.

Welford, John Noble (1 July, 1986) "Pilot's helmet helps interpret high speed world," *New York Times,* pp. 21, 24.

Wilfred, Denis (1982) "Capital and agriculture, a review of Marxian problematics," Studies in Political Economy 7:127-54.

Winner, Langdon (1977) Autonomous Technology: Technics out of Control as a Theme in Political Thought. Cambridge, MA: MIT Press.

—— (1980) "Do artifacts have politics?," *Daedalus* 109(1):121-36.

—— (1986) *The Whale and the Reactor.* Chicago: University of Chicago Press.

Winograd, Terry and Flores, Fernando (1986) *Understanding Computers and Cognition: A New Foundation for Design.* Norwood, NJ: Albex.

Wittig, Monique (1973) *The Lesbian Body,* David LeVay, trans. New York: Avon, 1975 (*Le corps lesbien,* 1973).

*Women and Poverty,* special issue (1984) *Signs* 10(2).

Wright, Susan (1982, July/August) "Recombinant DNA: the status of hazards and controls," *Environment* 24(6):12-20, 51-53.

—— (1986) "Recombinant DNA technology and social transformation, 1972-82," *Osiris,* 2nd series, 2:303-60.

Young, Robert M. (1979, March) "Interpreting the production of science," *New Scientist* 29:1026-8.

—— and Levidow, Les, eds (1981, 1985) *Science, Technology and the Labour Process,* 2 vols. London: CSE and Free Association Books.

Yoxen, Edward (1983) *The Gene Business.* New York: Harper & Row.

Zimmerman, Jan, ed. (1983) *The Technological Woman: Interfacing with Tomorrow.* New York: Praeger.

541

# 36. [Introduction]
# The GNU Manifesto

It's sometimes hard to rememeber, as IBM invests a billion dollars in Linux-related projects, that the philosophy of free software is radically opposed to business as usual, seeking to empower computer programmers and users rather than the owners of "intellectual property."

The story of free software begins with the ability, or lack thereof, for users to fashion and fully employ their own software tools. Richard Stallman had the technical skill, certainly, to develop such software tools, being part of a legendary group of hackers at the MIT Artificial Intelligence Lab. Their main computer system ran an operating system they had written, and they employed tools they and others had created. Everyone had access to the source code for these programs, and shared their improvements—and what new programs they wrote—with the community as a whole, following the vision of MIT's J. C. R. Licklider (◊05).

But then, around 1984, things began to change. The company that provided the Lab's printer decided to close the source code for their updated driver software—making it impossible to add back customizations the Lab had previously used for their work. A new computer was installed, and it ran the manufacturing company's proprietary operating system instead of an updated version of the Lab's own. AT&T announced that Unix would no longer be free, shocking many in the computer world (especially those from outside AT&T who had contributed to Unix). Suddenly, those at the Lab, and many other computer users, were working in a much less free environment. This was the situation toward which the software world as a whole seemed to be heading: users unable to actually work with their own tools fully—unable to improve or modify them, forced to beg companies to add the functionality needed for them to do their work, whatever their own level of skill. And users would be further restricted by proprietary licensing restrictions, which left them unable to share their tools with others. "Shrink-wrap" and "click-through" agreements were attempting to make users unwilling parties to a radical extension of copyright law, or its outright replacement with contract law.

The emerging software world didn't seem a happy one to Stallman, and wasn't one he wanted to be part of. Joining a company that made proprietary software seemed unethical and unsatisfying. Leaving computer work altogether seemed like a waste of his skill, and also a disappointment given the personally enjoyable experiences he'd had programming. So he decided to quit his job and try to build a new set of free software, around which could develop a new free community. The MIT AI Lab allowed him to continue using their equipment. He began his project, called GNU (a recursive acronym for "GNU's Not Unix"), and prepared the manifesto reprinted here.

Some of the arguments outlined in the manifesto are well settled at this point; others still rage. It's been found that free software can succeed; two major free operating systems that are now available demonstrate this, as does the free Apache, currently the most popular Web server software. The main controversy that remains is no doubt over intellectual property issues. Stallman and his Free Software Foundation (FSF) have been the primary proponents of a system called *copyleft* which covers most of the software developed by the GNU project and those sympathetic with its goals. Copyleft is embodied in the GNU General Public License (GPL). The GPL is intended to ensure that software that is created to be free remains free—rather than being included and distributed as part of proprietary software, which might defeat the purpose for which it was written. In order to copyleft, the author first copyrights a work, and then—as stated on the FSF's "What is Copyleft?" page—"we add distribution terms, which are a legal instrument that gives everyone the rights to use, modify, and redistribute the

From "The GNU Operating System and the Free Software Movement" by Richard Stallman:

The term "free software" is sometimes misunderstood—it has nothing to do with price. It is about freedom. Here, therefore, is the definition of free software: a program is free software, for you, a particular user, if:

• You have the freedom to run the program, for any purpose.

• You have the freedom to modify the program to suit your needs. (To make this freedom effective in practice, you must have access to the source code, since making changes in a program without having the source code is exceedingly difficult.)

• You have the freedom to redistribute copies, either gratis or for a fee.

• You have the freedom to distribute modified versions of the program, so that the community can benefit from your improvements.

Since "free" refers to freedom, not to price, there is no contradiction between selling copies and free software. In fact, the freedom to sell copies is crucial: collections of free software sold on CD-ROMs are important for the community, and selling them is an important way to raise funds for free software development. Therefore, a program which people are not free to include on these collections is not free software.

Because of the ambiguity of "free," people have long looked for alternatives, but no one has found a suitable alternative. The English language has more words and nuances than any other, but it lacks a simple, unambiguous, word that means "free," as in freedom—"unfettered," being the word that comes closest in meaning. Such alternatives as "liberated," "freedom" and "open" have either the wrong meaning or some other disadvantage.

◊05
73

543

◊08
93

program's code *or any program derived from it* but only if the distribution terms are unchanged. Thus, the code and the freedoms become legally inseparable. Proprietary software developers use copyright to take away the users' freedom; we use copyright to guarantee their freedom. That's why we reverse the name, changing 'copyright' into 'copyleft.'"

Stallman has also become one of the most outspoken critics of recent attempts to redefine copyright as a private good (an individual or corporate "right"), rather than a public good (something the society permits authors under limited circumstances in order to benefit society as a whole). In an essay in *Communications of the ACM,* he used a speculative fiction style, much as Engelbart did in his 1962 report (◊08), to provide an extrapolation from current proposals and policies. In this piece, "The Right to Read," he tells of the ethical dilemma facing a college student named Dan: whether to run the risk of lending his computer to a classmate, who might use the computer to read his books without paying the licensing fees (which she could not afford to pay herself), putting them both at risk of going to jail. This speculation is not so fantastic, in the era of the Digital Millennium Copyright Act and Copyright Term Extension Act (a.k.a. the Sonny Bono Mickey Mouse Extension Act). These domestic laws and the parallel international agreements are eviscerating traditional freedoms such as fair use, as well as the concept of the public domain. Perhaps particularly remarkable in a country that prizes private property is the fact that the DMCA's provisions criminalize the modification of a machine one owns, for personal use in a manner which harms no one: Changing your US-purchased DVD player to allow it play European DVDs is punishable by a $2500 fine. The changes in copyright law that Hollywood has recently purchased are remote from the public good of promoting the "progress of science and the useful arts"—rather, they recall Soviet restrictions on the ownership of photocopiers.

The fact that the rise of free software and the demise of free information seem to be paralleling each other may give an indication of our culture's deep ambivalence in the face of networked new media. At this juncture, Richard Stallman has become one of our most important cultural critics—a critic who takes action to alter the situations on which he comments, and who helps provide a framework within which others can act on their beliefs.

—NWF

There are two major free operating systems available now. The first is, in essence, the system Stallman set out to create in the 1980s. He and his collaborators wrote, found people to write, or found already existing the components needed to create a free operating system that could work as a Unix replacement. By 1990 they had everything in place but the kernel, and had created a large number of tools that were already in broad use within the Unix world, including a text editor, emacs; a compiler, gcc; and a shell, bash. Linus Torvalds, inspired by a teaching "mini Unix" called Minix, created a kernel in 1991. He posted to the Minix newsgroup that, "It is just version 0.02 . . . but I've successfully run bash, gcc, gnu-make, gnu-sed, compress, etc. under it." Torvalds had finally made the GNU operating system a reality. The system using this kernel is now usually called "Linux"; Stallman and some others call the system "GNU/Linux" because of the essential role GNU tools play in it.

The second free operating system is the Berkeley Standard Distribution of Unix (BSD), which first made it to the personal computer through the 386/BSD system created by Bill Jolitz in the early 1990s. This was based on earlier, partially free releases of Unix for the DARPA/Internet community. Now several flavors of BSD—including FreeBSD, NetBSD, and OpenBSD—exist. The GNU/Linux and BSD projects both have thriving communities and strong advocates; they are intercompatible to a great degree. Apple's Macintosh OS X is derived in part from BSD.

Further Reading

Crawford, Diane, ed. *Intellectual Property in the Age of Universal Access* New York: ACM Press, 1999.

Free Software Foundation. <http://www.fsf.org>

Lessig, Lawrence. *The Future of Ideas.* New York: Random House, 2001.

Levy, Steven. *Hackers: Heroes of the Computer Revolution.* New York: Anchor Books, 1984.

Microsoft Corporation: Shared Source Initiative. <http://www.microsoft.com/licensing/sharedsource>

Raymond, Eric. "The Cathedral and the Bazaar." *First Monday* 3, no. 3 (1998).
<http://www.firstmonday.org/issues/issue3_3/raymond/index.html>

Stallman, Richard. "The GNU Operating System and the Free Software Movement," and essays by others in *Open Sources: Voices from the Open Source Revolution,* edited by Chris DiBona, Sam Ockman, and Mark Stone. Sepastopol, Calif.: O'Reilly & Associates, 1999.
<http://www.oreilly.com/catalog/opensources/book/stallman.html>

Stallman, Richard. "The Right to Read," *Communications of the ACM* 40(2): 85–87. February 1997.
<http://www.fsf.org/philosophy/right-to-read.html>

Original Publication

*Dr. Dobb's Journal.* 10(3):30+. March 1985. Footnotes added in 1993. This text from the Free Software Foundation Web site:

# The GNU Manifesto

## Richard Stallman

The GNU Manifesto (which appears below) was written by Richard Stallman at the beginning of the GNU Project, to ask for participation and support. For the first few years, it was updated in minor ways to account for developments, but now it seems best to leave it unchanged as most people have seen it.

Since that time, we have learned about certain common misunderstandings that different wording could help avoid. Footnotes added in 1993 help clarify these points.

For up-to-date information about the available GNU software, please see the information available on our web server, in particular our list of software.

## What's GNU? Gnu's Not Unix!

GNU, which stands for Gnu's Not Unix, is the name for the complete Unix-compatible software system which I am writing so that I can give it away free to everyone who can use it.[1] Several other volunteers are helping me.

Contributions of time, money, programs and equipment are greatly needed.

So far we have an Emacs text editor with Lisp for writing editor commands, a source level debugger, a yacc-compatible parser generator, a linker, and around 35 utilities. A shell (command interpreter) is nearly completed. A new portable optimizing C compiler has compiled itself and may be released this year. An initial kernel exists but many more features are needed to emulate Unix. When the kernel and compiler are finished, it will be possible to distribute a GNU system suitable for program development. We will use TeX as our text formatter, but an nroff is being worked on. We will use the free, portable X window system as well. After this we will add a portable Common Lisp, an Empire game, a spreadsheet, and hundreds of other things, plus on-line documentation. We hope to supply, eventually, everything useful that normally comes with a Unix system, and more.

GNU will be able to run Unix programs, but will not be identical to Unix. We will make all improvements that are convenient, based on our experience with other operating systems. In particular, we plan to have longer file names, file version numbers, a crashproof file system, file name completion perhaps, terminal-independent display support, and perhaps eventually a Lisp-based window system through which several Lisp programs and ordinary Unix programs can share a screen. Both C and Lisp will be available as system programming languages. We will try to support UUCP, MIT Chaosnet, and Internet protocols for communication.

GNU is aimed initially at machines in the 68000/16000 class with virtual memory, because they are the easiest

545

machines to make it run on. The extra effort to make it run on smaller machines will be left to someone who wants to use it on them.

To avoid horrible confusion, please pronounce the 'G' in the word 'GNU' when it is the name of this project.

## Why I Must Write GNU

I consider that the golden rule requires that if I like a program I must share it with other people who like it. Software sellers want to divide the users and conquer them, making each user agree not to share with others. I refuse to break solidarity with other users in this way. I cannot in good conscience sign a nondisclosure agreement or a software license agreement. For years I worked within the Artificial Intelligence Lab to resist such tendencies and other inhospitalities, but eventually they had gone too far: I could not remain in an institution where such things are done for me against my will.

So that I can continue to use computers without dishonor, I have decided to put together a sufficient body of free software so that I will be able to get along without any software that is not free. I have resigned from the AI Lab to deny MIT any legal excuse to prevent me from giving GNU away.

## Why GNU Will Be Compatible with Unix

Unix is not my ideal system, but it is not too bad. The essential features of Unix seem to be good ones, and I think I can fill in what Unix lacks without spoiling them. And a system compatible with Unix would be convenient for many other people to adopt.

## How GNU Will Be Available

GNU is not in the public domain. Everyone will be permitted to modify and redistribute GNU, but no distributor will be allowed to restrict its further redistribution. That is to say, proprietary modifications will not be allowed. I want to make sure that all versions of GNU remain free.

## Why Many Other Programmers Want to Help

I have found many other programmers who are excited about GNU and want to help.

Many programmers are unhappy about the commercialization of system software. It may enable them to make more money, but it requires them to feel in conflict with other

programmers in general rather than feel as comrades. The fundamental act of friendship among programmers is the sharing of programs; marketing arrangements now typically used essentially forbid programmers to treat others as friends. The purchaser of software must choose between friendship and obeying the law. Naturally, many decide that friendship is more important. But those who believe in law often do not feel at ease with either choice. They become cynical and think that programming is just a way of making money.

By working on and using GNU rather than proprietary programs, we can be hospitable to everyone and obey the law. In addition, GNU serves as an example to inspire and a banner to rally others to join us in sharing. This can give us a feeling of harmony which is impossible if we use software that is not free. For about half the programmers I talk to, this is an important happiness that money cannot replace.

## How You Can Contribute

I am asking computer manufacturers for donations of machines and money. I'm asking individuals for donations of programs and work.

One consequence you can expect if you donate machines is that GNU will run on them at an early date. The machines should be complete, ready to use systems, approved for use in a residential area, and not in need of sophisticated cooling or power.

I have found very many programmers eager to contribute part-time work for GNU. For most projects, such part-time distributed work would be very hard to coordinate; the independently-written parts would not work together. But for the particular task of replacing Unix, this problem is absent. A complete Unix system contains hundreds of utility programs, each of which is documented separately. Most interface specifications are fixed by Unix compatibility. If each contributor can write a compatible replacement for a single Unix utility, and make it work properly in place of the original on a Unix system, then these utilities will work right when put together. Even allowing for Murphy to create a few unexpected problems, assembling these components will be a feasible task. (The kernel will require closer communication and will be worked on by a small, tight group.)

If I get donations of money, I may be able to hire a few people full or part time. The salary won't be high by programmers' standards, but I'm looking for people for whom building community spirit is as important as making money. I view this as a way of enabling dedicated people to devote their full energies to working on GNU by sparing them the need to make a living in another way.

## Why All Computer Users Will Benefit

Once GNU is written, everyone will be able to obtain good system software free, just like air.[2]

This means much more than just saving everyone the price of a Unix license. It means that much wasteful duplication of system programming effort will be avoided. This effort can go instead into advancing the state of the art.

Complete system sources will be available to everyone. As a result, a user who needs changes in the system will always be free to make them himself, or hire any available programmer or company to make them for him. Users will no longer be at the mercy of one programmer or company which owns the sources and is in sole position to make changes.

Schools will be able to provide a much more educational environment by encouraging all students to study and improve the system code. Harvard's computer lab used to have the policy that no program could be installed on the system if its sources were not on public display, and upheld it by actually refusing to install certain programs. I was very much inspired by this.

Finally, the overhead of considering who owns the system software and what one is or is not entitled to do with it will be lifted.

Arrangements to make people pay for using a program, including licensing of copies, always incur a tremendous cost to society through the cumbersome mechanisms necessary to figure out how much (that is, which programs) a person must pay for. And only a police state can force everyone to obey them. Consider a space station where air must be manufactured at great cost: charging each breather per liter of air may be fair, but wearing the metered gas mask all day and all night is intolerable even if everyone can afford to pay the air bill. And the TV cameras everywhere to see if you ever take the mask off are outrageous. It's better to support the air plant with a head tax and chuck the masks.

Copying all or parts of a program is as natural to a programmer as breathing, and as productive. It ought to be as free.

## Some Easily Rebutted Objections to GNU's Goals

### "Nobody will use it if it is free, because that means they can't rely on any support."
### "You have to charge for the program to pay for providing the support."

If people would rather pay for GNU plus service than get GNU free without service, a company to provide just service to people who have obtained GNU free ought to be profitable.[3]

We must distinguish between support in the form of real programming work and mere handholding. The former is something one cannot rely on from a software vendor. If your problem is not shared by enough people, the vendor will tell you to get lost.

If your business needs to be able to rely on support, the only way is to have all the necessary sources and tools. Then you can hire any available person to fix your problem; you are not at the mercy of any individual. With Unix, the price of sources puts this out of consideration for most businesses. With GNU this will be easy. It is still possible for there to be no available competent person, but this problem cannot be blamed on distribution arrangements. GNU does not eliminate all the world's problems, only some of them.

Meanwhile, the users who know nothing about computers need handholding: doing things for them which they could easily do themselves but don't know how.

Such services could be provided by companies that sell just hand-holding and repair service. If it is true that users would rather spend money and get a product with service, they will also be willing to buy the service having got the product free. The service companies will compete in quality and price; users will not be tied to any particular one. Meanwhile, those of us who don't need the service should be able to use the program without paying for the service.

### "You cannot reach many people without advertising, and you must charge for the program to support that."
### "It's no use advertising a program people can get free."

There are various forms of free or very cheap publicity that can be used to inform numbers of computer users about something like GNU. But it may be true that one can reach more microcomputer users with advertising. If this is really so, a business which advertises the service of copying and mailing GNU for a fee ought to be successful enough to pay for its advertising and more. This way, only the users who benefit from the advertising pay for it.

On the other hand, if many people get GNU from their friends, and such companies don't succeed, this will show that advertising was not really necessary to spread GNU. Why is it that free market advocates don't want to let the free market decide this?[4]

### "My company needs a proprietary operating system to get a competitive edge."

GNU will remove operating system software from the realm of competition. You will not be able to get an edge in this area, but neither will your competitors be able to get an edge over you. You and they will compete in other areas, while benefiting mutually in this one. If your business is selling an operating system, you will not like GNU, but that's tough on you. If your business is something else, GNU can save you from being pushed into the expensive business of selling operating systems.

I would like to see GNU development supported by gifts from many manufacturers and users, reducing the cost to each.[5]

### "Don't programmers deserve a reward for their creativity?"

If anything deserves a reward, it is social contribution. Creativity can be a social contribution, but only in so far as society is free to use the results. If programmers deserve to be rewarded for creating innovative programs, by the same token they deserve to be punished if they restrict the use of these programs.

### "Shouldn't a programmer be able to ask for a reward for his creativity?"

There is nothing wrong with wanting pay for work, or seeking to maximize one's income, as long as one does not use means that are destructive. But the means customary in the field of software today are based on destruction.

Extracting money from users of a program by restricting their use of it is destructive because the restrictions reduce the amount and the ways that the program can be used. This reduces the amount of wealth that humanity derives from the program. When there is a deliberate choice to restrict, the harmful consequences are deliberate destruction.

The reason a good citizen does not use such destructive means to become wealthier is that, if everyone did so, we would all become poorer from the mutual destructiveness. This is Kantian ethics; or, the Golden Rule. Since I do not like the consequences that result if everyone hoards information, I am required to consider it wrong for one to do so. Specifically, the desire to be rewarded for one's creativity does not justify depriving the world in general of all or part of that creativity.

### "Won't programmers starve?"

I could answer that nobody is forced to be a programmer. Most of us cannot manage to get any money for standing on the street and making faces. But we are not, as a result, condemned to spend our lives standing on the street making faces, and starving. We do something else.

But that is the wrong answer because it accepts the questioner's implicit assumption: that without ownership of software, programmers cannot possibly be paid a cent. Supposedly it is all or nothing.

The real reason programmers will not starve is that it will still be possible for them to get paid for programming; just not paid as much as now.

Restricting copying is not the only basis for business in software. It is the most common basis because it brings in the most money. If it were prohibited, or rejected by the customer, software business would move to other bases of organization which are now used less often. There are always numerous ways to organize any kind of business.

Probably programming will not be as lucrative on the new basis as it is now. But that is not an argument against the change. It is not considered an injustice that sales clerks make the salaries that they now do. If programmers made the same, that would not be an injustice either. (In practice they would still make considerably more than that.)

### "Don't people have a right to control how their creativity is used?"

"Control over the use of one's ideas" really constitutes control over other people's lives; and it is usually used to make their lives more difficult.

People who have studied the issue of intellectual property rights carefully (such as lawyers) say that there is no intrinsic right to intellectual property. The kinds of supposed intellectual property rights that the government recognizes were created by specific acts of legislation for specific purposes.

For example, the patent system was established to encourage inventors to disclose the details of their inventions. Its purpose was to help society rather than to help inventors. At the time, the life span of 17 years for a patent was short compared with the rate of advance of the state of the art. Since patents are an issue only among manufacturers, for whom the cost and effort of a license agreement are small compared with setting up production, the patents often do not do much harm. They do not obstruct most individuals who use patented products.

The idea of copyright did not exist in ancient times, when authors frequently copied other authors at length in works of non-fiction. This practice was useful, and is the only way many authors' works have survived even in part. The copyright system was created expressly for the purpose of encouraging authorship. In the domain for which it was invented—books, which could be copied economically only on a printing press—it did little harm, and did not obstruct most of the individuals who read the books.

All intellectual property rights are just licenses granted by society because it was thought, rightly or wrongly, that society as a whole would benefit by granting them. But in any particular situation, we have to ask: are we really better off granting such license? What kind of act are we licensing a person to do?

The case of programs today is very different from that of books a hundred years ago. The fact that the easiest way to copy a program is from one neighbor to another, the fact that a program has both source code and object code which are distinct, and the fact that a program is used rather than read and enjoyed, combine to create a situation in which a person who enforces a copyright is harming society as a whole both materially and spiritually; in which a person should not do so regardless of whether the law enables him to.

### "Competition makes things get done better."

The paradigm of competition is a race: by rewarding the winner, we encourage everyone to run faster. When capitalism really works this way, it does a good job; but its defenders are wrong in assuming it always works this way. If the runners forget why the reward is offered and become intent on winning, no matter how, they may find other strategies—such as, attacking other runners. If the runners get into a fist fight, they will all finish late.

Proprietary and secret software is the moral equivalent of runners in a fist fight. Sad to say, the only referee we've got does not seem to object to fights; he just regulates them ("For every ten yards you run, you can fire one shot"). He really ought to break them up, and penalize runners for even trying to fight.

### "Won't everyone stop programming without a monetary incentive?"

Actually, many people will program with absolutely no monetary incentive. Programming has an irresistible fascination for some people, usually the people who are best at it. There is no shortage of professional musicians who keep at it even though they have no hope of making a living that way.

But really this question, though commonly asked, is not appropriate to the situation. Pay for programmers will not disappear, only become less. So the right question is, will anyone program with a reduced monetary incentive? My experience shows that they will.

For more than ten years, many of the world's best programmers worked at the Artificial Intelligence Lab for far less money than they could have had anywhere else. They got many kinds of non-monetary rewards: fame and appreciation, for example. And creativity is also fun, a reward in itself.

Then most of them left when offered a chance to do the same interesting work for a lot of money.

What the facts show is that people will program for reasons other than riches; but if given a chance to make a lot of money as well, they will come to expect and demand it. Low-paying organizations do poorly in competition with high-paying ones, but they do not have to do badly if the high-paying ones are banned.

### "We need the programmers desperately. If they demand that we stop helping our neighbors, we have to obey."

You're never so desperate that you have to obey this sort of demand. Remember: millions for defense, but not a cent for tribute!

### "Programmers need to make a living somehow."

In the short run, this is true. However, there are plenty of ways that programmers could make a living without selling the right to use a program. This way is customary now because it brings programmers and businessmen the most money, not because it is the only way to make a living. It is easy to find other ways if you want to find them. Here are a number of examples.

A manufacturer introducing a new computer will pay for the porting of operating systems onto the new hardware.

549

The sale of teaching, hand-holding and maintenance services could also employ programmers.

People with new ideas could distribute programs as freeware, asking for donations from satisfied users, or selling hand-holding services. I have met people who are already working this way successfully.

Users with related needs can form users' groups, and pay dues. A group would contract with programming companies to write programs that the group's members would like to use.

All sorts of development can be funded with a Software Tax:

Suppose everyone who buys a computer has to pay x percent of the price as a software tax. The government gives this to an agency like the NSF to spend on software development.

But if the computer buyer makes a donation to software development himself, he can take a credit against the tax. He can donate to the project of his own choosing—often, chosen because he hopes to use the results when it is done. He can take a credit for any amount of donation up to the total tax he had to pay.

The total tax rate could be decided by a vote of the payers of the tax, weighted according to the amount they will be taxed on.

The consequences:

> The computer-using community supports software development.
>
> This community decides what level of support is needed.
>
> Users who care which projects their share is spent on can choose this for themselves.

In the long run, making programs free is a step toward the post-scarcity world, where nobody will have to work very hard just to make a living. People will be free to devote themselves to activities that are fun, such as programming, after spending the necessary ten hours a week on required tasks such as legislation, family counseling, robot repair and asteroid prospecting. There will be no need to be able to make a living from programming.

We have already greatly reduced the amount of work that the whole society must do for its actual productivity, but only a little of this has translated itself into leisure for workers because much nonproductive activity is required to accompany productive activity. The main causes of this are bureaucracy and isometric struggles against competition. Free software will greatly reduce these drains in the area of software production. We must do this, in order for technical gains in productivity to translate into less work for us.

Notes

1. The wording here was careless. The intention was that nobody would have to pay for *permission* to use the GNU system. But the words don't make this clear, and people often interpret them as saying that copies of GNU should always be distributed at little or no charge. That was never the intent; later on, the manifesto mentions the possibility of companies providing the service of distribution for a profit. Subsequently I have learned to distinguish carefully between "free" in the sense of freedom and "free" in the sense of price. Free software is software that users have the freedom to distribute and change. Some users may obtain copies at no charge, while others pay to obtain copies—and if the funds help support improving the software, so much the better. The important thing is that everyone who has a copy has the freedom to cooperate with others in using it.

2. This is another place I failed to distinguish carefully between the two different meanings of "free". The statement as it stands is not false—you can get copies of GNU software at no charge, from your friends or over the net. But it does suggest the wrong idea.

3. Several such companies now exist.

4. The Free Software Foundation raises most of its funds from a distribution service, although it is a charity rather than a company. If *no one* chooses to obtain copies by ordering them from the FSF, it will be unable to do its work. But this does not mean that proprietary restrictions are justified to force every user to pay. If a small fraction of all the users order copies from the FSF, that is sufficient to keep the FSF afloat. So we ask users to choose to support us in this way. Have you done your part?

5. A group of computer companies recently pooled funds to support maintenance of the GNU C Compiler.

# 37. [Introduction]
# Using Computers
## A Direction for Design

*Understanding Computers and Cognition*—the book from which this selection comes—is often described as a stinging critique of artificial intelligence, and particularly of its approach to natural language understanding. This description focuses on one thrust of the book, in which Winograd and Flores use a Heideggerian approach to uncover a rigidity within analytic computational models that, combined with inexpressible subtleties in human cognition, will never allow computers to attain human-like intelligence. They argue that the "essence of intelligence is to act appropriately when there is no simple pre-definition of the problem or the space of states in which to search for a solution" (98)—a task for which the structures developed by artificial intelligence researchers and theorists were deeply inappropriate.

The traditional concept of artificial intelligence is also an important point engaged by Joseph Weizenbaum (◊24) and Lucy Suchman (◊41), not to mention Alan Turing (◊03).

Yet it is important to remember that Winograd and Flores did not argue that we should abandon work in new media, or stop using computers in communicative contexts. Rather, they suggested that we turn our attention toward designing computers as tools (as Pelle Ehn and Morten Kyng (◊45) did) that exploit as strengths precisely those aspects of computational models that render artificial intelligence impossible. Hence the following chapter, their book's last. Although it contains unglossed Heideggerian terms introduced elsewhere and makes multiple references to other portions of their book, its primary message is still quite accessible. The authors' focus is on using the knowledge gained through cultural critique to outline a positive direction for new media tool design. Having turned away from the goal of machine *understanding*, they have developed a model of human specification and machine *support*, in which the rigid structures developed in artificial intelligence research can be appropriately used.

At the same time, Winograd and Flores advocate a design strategy they call "ontological design" which examines the fundamental human communications underway in a situation. Using this strategy, it is quite possible to decide that some other change in processes is preferable to the introduction of new computer tools. But when computer tools are appropriate, this approach works to avoid the destructive "computerization" that frustrates pre-computer coping strategies and leads to an overall drop in the quality of effective communication (and, therefore, in the quality of work). Winograd and Flores not only position their ontological approach as the best way to address a possibility for action in a communicative context, but also as a potential approach to intervention in the technology-determining processes discussed by authors such as Raymond Williams (◊20) and Langdon Winner (◊40). That is to say, their approach to combining cultural critique with computer science not only aims to result in better tool building, but also in a means for self-conscious cultural intervention. In fact, the two processes become one. As Phoebe Sengers points out, there is a great potential in work such as this, which might be realized more frequently if the sciences and cultural studies of science had not invested so much of their recent communicative efforts in "Science Wars" with each other.

Winograd continues to be a central figure in new media, advocating interdisciplinary approaches. He currently leads the Human-Computer Interaction program at Stanford University and is a past president of Computer Professionals for Social Responsibility. For the volume commemorating the ACM's 50th anniversary Winograd outlined the emerging discipline of "Interaction Design" which brings many of the larger-frame issues collected under ontological design to the creation of modern new media. He also takes the opportunity to point out that, while critiques such as his were brushed aside by a 1980s AI establishment certain of its own ascendancy, Good Old Fashioned AI has run into

◊03
49

◊20
289

◊24
123

551

◊40
587

◊41
599

◊45
649

trouble on precisely these grounds: the foundations on which it conceived of intelligence. Meanwhile, human communication, where Winograd and Flores squarely put their focus, has taken AI's place on the center stage of computing:

> With the recent—and quite sudden—emergence of mass-appeal Internet-centered applications, it has become glaringly obvious that the computer is not a machine whose main purpose is to get a computing task done. The computer, with its attendant peripherals and networks, is a machine that provides new ways for people to communicate with other people. (161)

—NWF

**Further Reading**

Winograd, Terry, ed., with John Bennett, Laura De Young, and Bradley Hartfield. *Bringing Design to Software*. Reading, Mass.: Addison-Wesley, 1996.

Winograd, Terry. "From Computing Machinery to Interaction Design." *Beyond Calculation: The Next Fifty Years of Computing*. Berlin: Springer-Verlag, 1997, 149–162. <http://hci.stanford.edu/winograd/acm97.html>

Sengers, Phoebe. "Practices for Machine Culture: A Case Study of Integrating Artificial Intelligence and Cultural Theory." *Surfaces* 8. 1999. <http://www.pum.umontreal.ca/revues/surfaces/vol8/sengers.pdf>

Original Publication

*Understanding Computers and Cognition: A New Foundation for Design*. Norwood, N.J.: Ablex Publishing, 1986, 163–179.

# Using Computers
## A Direction for Design
## Terry Winograd and Fernando Flores

This book [*Understanding Computers and Cognition*] is concerned with the design of computer-based systems to facilitate human work and interaction. In this final chapter we suggest directions for the future, drawing on the discourse developed in Part I to re-examine some basic questions about what designing means.

The most important designing is *ontological*.[1] It constitutes an intervention in the background of our heritage, growing out of our already-existent ways of being in the world, and deeply affecting the kinds of beings that we are. In creating new artifacts, equipment, buildings, and organizational structures, it attempts to specify in advance how and where breakdowns will show up in our everyday practices and in the tools we use, opening up new spaces in which we can work and play. Ontologically oriented design is therefore necessarily both reflective and political, looking backwards to the tradition that has formed us but also forwards to as-yet-uncreated transformations of our

lives together. Through the emergence of new tools, we come to a changing awareness of human nature and human action, which in turn leads to new technological development. The designing process is part of this "dance" in which our structure of possibilities is generated.

The concluding sections of this chapter will discuss the ontical-ontological significance of design—how our tools are part of the background in which we can ask what it is to be human. First we consider the direct relevance of our theoretical orientation to the design of computer systems. We will use conversation systems, like [our] coordinator, as our primary example. But our intended scope is larger, encompassing other computer systems and ultimately all technology.

## 1 A Background for Computer Design

In the popular literature on computers, one frequently encounters terms such as "user-friendly," "easy-to-learn," and "self-explaining." They are vague and perhaps overused, but they reflect real concerns—concerns that are not adequately understood within the rationalistic tradition, and to which phenomenological insights about readiness-to-hand, breakdown, and blindness are relevant.

### Readiness-to-Hand

One popular vision of the future is that computers will become easier to use as they become more like people. In working with people, we establish domains of conversation in which our common pre-understanding lets us communicate with a minimum of words and con-scious effort. We become explicitly aware of the structure of conversation only when there is some kind of breakdown calling for corrective action. If machines could understand in the same way people do, interactions with computers would be equally transparent.

This transparency of interaction is of utmost importance in the design of tools, including computer systems, but it is not best achieved by attempting to mimic human faculties. In driving a car, the control interaction is normally transparent. You do not think "How far should I turn the steering wheel to go around that curve?" In fact, you are not even aware (unless something intrudes) of using a steering wheel. Phenomenologically, you are driving down the road, not operating controls. The long evolution of the design of automobiles has led to this readiness-to-hand. It is not achieved by having a car communicate like a person, but by providing the right coupling between the driver and action in the relevant domain (motion down the road).

In designing computer tools, the task is harder but the issues are the same. A successful word processing device lets a person operate on the words and paragraphs displayed on the screen, without being aware of formulating and giving commands. At the superficial level of "interface design" there are many different ways to aid transparency, such as special function keys (which perform a meaningful action with a single keystroke), pointing devices (which make it possible to select an object on the screen), and menus (which offer a choice among a small set of relevant actions).

More important is the design of the domains in which the actions are generated and interpreted. A bad design forces the user to deal with complexities that belong to the wrong domain. For example, consider the user of an electronic mail system who tries to send a message and is confronted with an "error message" saying "Mailbox server is reloading." The user operates in a domain constituted of people and messages sent among them. This domain includes actions (such as sending a message and examining mail) that in turn generate possible breakdowns (such as the inability to send a message). Mailbox servers, although they may be a critical part of the implementation, are an intrusion from another domain—one that is the province of the system designers and engineers. In this simple example, we could produce a different error message, such as "Cannot send message to that user. Please try again after five minutes." Successful system builders learn to consider the user's domain of understanding after seeing the frustrations of people who use their programs.

But there is a more systematic principle at stake here. The programmer designs the language that creates the world in which the user operates. This language can be "ontologically clean" or it can be a jumble of related domains. A clearly and consciously organized ontology is the basis for the kind of simplicity that makes systems usable. When we try to understand the appeal of computers like the Apple Macintosh (and its predecessor the Xerox Star), we see exactly the kind of readiness-to-hand and ontological simplicity we have described. Within the domains they encompass—text and graphic manipulation—the user is "driving," not "commanding." The challenge for the next generation of design is to move this same effectiveness beyond the superficial structures of words and pictures into the domains generated by what people are doing when they manipulate those structures.

## Anticipation of Breakdown

Our study of Heidegger revealed the central role of breakdown in human understanding. A breakdown is not a negative situation to be avoided, but a situation of non-obviousness, in which the recognition that something is missing leads to unconcealing (generating through our declarations) some aspect of the network of tools that we are engaged in using. A breakdown reveals the nexus of relations necessary for us to accomplish our task. This creates a clear objective for design—to anticipate the forms of breakdown and provide a space of possibilities for action when they occur. It is impossible to completely avoid breakdowns by means of design. What can be designed are aids for those who live in a particular domain of breakdowns. These aids include training, to develop the appropriate understanding of the domain in which the breakdowns occur and also to develop the skills and procedures needed to recognize what has broken down and how to cope with the situation.

Computer tools can aid in the anticipation and correction of breakdowns that are not themselves computer breakdowns but are in the application domain. The commitment monitoring facilities in a coordinator are an example of such a system, applied to the domain of conversations for action. In the design of decision support systems, a primary consideration is the anticipation of potential breakdowns. An early example of such a system was Cybersyn,[2] which was used for monitoring production in a sector of the economy of Chile. This system enabled local groups to describe the range of normal behavior of economic variables (such as the output of a particular factory), and to be informed of significant patterns of variation that could signal potential breakdown.

But more importantly, breakdowns play a fundamental role in design. As the last section pointed out, the objects and properties that constitute the domain of action for a person are those that emerge in breakdown. Returning to our simple example of an electronic mail system, our "fix" left a person with certain courses of action in face of the breakdown. He or she can simply forget about sending the message or can wait until later to try sending it again. But it may be possible to send it to a different "mail server" for delayed forwarding and delivery. If so, it is necessary to create a domain that includes the existence of mail servers and their properties as part of the relevant space in which the user exists.

In designing computer systems and the domains they generate, we must anticipate the range of occurrences that go outside the normal functioning and provide means both to understand them and to act. This is the basis for a heuristic methodology that is often followed by good programmers ("In writing the program try to think of everything that could go wrong"), but again it is more than a vague aphorism. The analysis of a human context of activity can begin with an analysis of the domains of breakdown, and that can in turn be used to generate the objects, properties, and actions that make up the domain.

### The Blindness Created by Design

Any opening of new possibilities closes others, and this is especially true of the introduction of technology. As an example, consider the possibility of an "electronic library" in which one can search for items using sophisticated cataloging techniques based on publication information (such as author, publisher, and title) and topic classifications (such as the Library of Congress categories and the key word systems used in many journals). If we accept the domain generated by those classifications as the relevant one for finding books, the system is appropriate and useful. However, this may not be the right choice. The facility may make it easier for a reader to find a book on a specific narrow topic, while reducing the ease of "browsing" through shelves of loosely related material. Recognizing the importance of background and thrownness, it becomes clear that the unexpected and unintended encounters one has in browsing

can at times be of much greater importance than efficient precise recall. If the problem is narrowly construed as "Find a book, given specific information" then the system may be good. If we put it into its larger context of "Find writings relevant to what you want to do" it may well not be, since relevance cannot be formalized so easily. In providing a tool, we will change the nature of how people use the library and the materials within it.

As with breakdown, blindness is not something that can be avoided, but it is something of which we can be aware. The designer is engaged in a conversation for possibilities. Attention to the possibilities being eliminated must be in a constant interplay with expectations for the new possibilities being created.

## 2 A Design Example

We turn now to a concrete example of how our theoretical background might guide the design of a computer-based system in a practical setting. It is not a complete analysis of the specific case, but is a vehicle for suggesting possibilities and clarifying points. We have chosen a mundane business example, but the same principles hold for applications of computers in all kinds of organizations.

> *The setting:* You have been operating a successful dress shop for several years and expanded last year to a chain of three stores. You have not made any use of computers, but have recently come to feel they might be of some help. Profits aren't what they should be, you are losing some customers who seem dissatisfied with the service they get, and the staff feels over-worked.

### There are no clear problems to be solved: Action needs to be taken in a situation of irresolution.

This is the typical case in which questions about what to do arise. There is no clear "problem" to be solved, but a sense of irresolution that opens opportunities for action. Computers are not the "solution," but may be useful in taking actions that improve the situation. Once the manager senses this, the typical next step would be to go to computer service vendors to find out what kinds of "systems" are available and to see if they are worth getting. The space of possibilities is determined by the particular offerings and the "features" they exhibit. But we can begin with a more radical analysis of what goes on in the store and what kinds of tools are possible.

## A business (like any organization) is constituted as a network of recurrent conversations.

As a first step we look for the basic networks of conversation that constitute the business. We ask "Who makes requests and promises to whom, and how are those conversations carried to completion?" At a first level we treat the company as a unity, examining its conversations with the outside world—customers, suppliers, and providers of services. There are some obvious central conversations with customers and suppliers, opened by a request for (or offer of) dresses in exchange for money. Secondary conversations deal with conditions of satisfaction for the initial ones: conversations about alteration of dresses, conversations concerning payment (billing, prepayment, credit, etc.), and conversations for preventing breakdown in the physical setting (janitorial services, display preparation, etc.).

Taking the business as a composite, we can further examine the conversational networks among its constituents: departments and individual workers. There are conversations between clerk and stockroom, clerk and accounting, stockroom and purchasing, and so forth. Each of these conversation types has its own recurrent structure, and plays some role in maintaining the basic conversations of the company. As one simple example, consider the conversation in which the stock clerk requests that purchase orders be sent to suppliers. Instances of this conversation are either triggered by a conversation in which a salesperson requested an item that was unavailable, or when the stock clerk anticipates the possibility of such a breakdown. Other conversations are part of the underlying structure that makes possible the participation of individuals in the network (payroll, work scheduling, performance evaluations, etc.). Each conversation has its own structure of completion and states of incompletion with associated time constraints.

## Conversations are linked in regular patterns of triggering and breakdown.

The goal in analyzing these conversations is a description in which the linkages between the recurrent conversations are made explicit. These links include normal triggering (e.g., a customer request triggers a stock request), and others that deal with breakdown (e.g., if a request for alteration is not met on time it may trigger a request by the customer to see the manager). Having compiled this description, we can see possibilities for restructuring the network on the basis of where conversations fail to be completed satisfactorily. We

may, for example, note that customer dissatisfaction has come from alterations not being done on time (perhaps because alterations are now being combined for the three stores and therefore the tailors aren't immediately available). Actions might include imposing a rigid schedule for alterations (e.g., never promise anything for less than a week) so that commitments will be met on time, even if the times that can be promised are less flexible. Or it might mean introducing better tools for coordination, such as a computer-based system for keeping track of alteration requests and giving more urgent ones higher priority.

## In creating tools we are designing new conversations and connections.

When a change is made, the most significant innovation is the modification of the conversation structure, not the mechanical means by which the conversation is carried out (e.g., a computer system versus a manual one based on forms). In making such changes we alter the overall pattern of conversation, introducing new possibilities or better anticipating breakdowns in the previously existing ones. This is often not noticed because the changes of devices and of conversation structure go hand in hand. At times the changes can be beneficial, and at times detrimental. There are many cases of systems for activities like job scheduling that were introduced to make things more efficient, but as a result of modifying the conversation structure they in fact hindered the work. Often this is the result of taking one part of the conversation network (the "official" or "standard" part) and embodying it in the structure of the computer system, thereby making impossible other less frequent types of requests and promises that are crucial for anticipating and coping with breakdowns. When we are aware of the real impact of design we can more consciously design conversation structures that work.

As an example, there is a potential for coordination systems to reduce the need for rigid work schedules. Much of the temporal structure of what goes on in organizations is driven by the need to be able to anticipate completion. If the manager knows that a certain task will be done every Friday, then he or she can make a commitment to do something that uses its results on the following Monday. For many routine tasks, this is the best way to guarantee effective coordination. But it can also be an inflexible straitjacket that reduces the space of possibilities open to workers in organizing their activities. If effective coordination on a conversation-by-conversation basis could be regularized, then the rigidity could be relaxed altering the conversation structure to make the workers more productive.

## Design includes the generation of new possibilities.

No analysis of existing recurrent structures is a full account of the possibilities. The existing networks represent a particular point of structural coupling of the organization to the world in which it exists. Actions may radically alter the structure. In our example, the store might simply stop doing alterations. Or it might hire more tailors, or contract out the alterations, or hire many more tailors and go into the contract alteration business as well. In some cases, the business as a whole may have a new interpretation. The owner of a small candy store notes the success of the video games in the back, and may ultimately decide that the business is a video game parlor with a candy counter. No methodology can guarantee that all such possibilities will be found, but a careful analysis of the conversation structure can help reveal conversations with a potential for expansion.

In designing computer-based devices, we are not in the position of creating a formal-"system" that covers the functioning of the organization and the people within it. When this is attempted, the resulting system (and the space of potential action for the people within it) is inflexible and unable to cope with new breakdowns or potentials. Instead we design additions and changes to the network of equipment (some of it computer-based) within which people work. The computer is like a tool, in that it is brought up for use by people engaged in some domain of action. The use of the tool shapes the potential for what those actions are and how they are conducted. The computer is unlike common tools in its connectivity to a larger network of equipment. Its power does not lie in having a single purpose, like a carpenter's plane, but in its connection to the larger network of communication (electronic, telephone, and paper-based) in which organizations operate.

## Domains are generated by the space of potential breakdown of action.

If our dress shop owner chooses to install a computer-based system dealing with some of the conversations, the analysis proceeds by examining (and generating) the appropriate domains. Much computer automation deals with standard derived domains, such as payroll accounting, billing, and employee scheduling. A domain of relevant objects, properties, and actions has already been generated through standard practice, and is enforced by the need to satisfy external conversations based on it (such as those with the Internal Revenue Service). But even in these sedimented cases, it is important to recognize that ultimately the present-at-hand world of objects is always based on the breakdown of action.

As an obvious example, we can ask what a customer's "address" is. The immediate response is "For what?" (or, "What is the conversation in which it determines a condition of satisfaction?"). There are two distinct answers. Some conversations with customers involve requests for the physical transfer of goods while others involve correspondence. Different conditions of satisfaction require different kinds of address. This is a standard case, and most business forms and computer data bases will distinguish "shipping address" and "billing address." But we may also need an address where the person can be found during the day to perform further measurements. In every case, the relevant "property" to be associated with the person is determined by the role it plays in an action. This grounding of description in action pervades all attempts to formalize the world into a linguistic structure of objects, properties, and events.

This also leads us to the recognition that the development of any computer-based system will have to proceed in a cycle from design to experience and back again. It is impossible to anticipate all of the relevant breakdowns and their domains. They emerge gradually in practice. System development methodologies need to take this as a fundamental condition of generating the relevant domains, and to facilitate it through techniques such as building prototypes early in the design process and applying them in situations as close as possible to those in which they will eventually be used.

## Breakdown is an interpretation—everything exists as interpretation within a background.

As a somewhat more interesting example of how the world is generated by language, consider the conditions of satisfaction associated with "fit." The customer is only satisfied by a dress that fits, and a complex linguistic domain (the domain of clothing sizes) has been generated to provide a means of anticipating and preventing breakdown. But "fitting" cannot be objectively defined. One person may be happy with an article that someone else of the same overall shape and size would reject. The history of fashion and the differences between cultures make it clear that "fitting" is an interpretation within a particular horizon. But at the same time it is not purely individual. The background shared by a community is what makes individual "tastes" possible.

Ultimately, then, satisfaction is determined not by the world but by a declaration on the part of the requestor that a condition is satisfied. The case of "fit" may seem extreme, but every condition of satisfaction ultimately rests on a declaration by an individual, within the background of a community. The cases that seem "objective" are those in which there is great regularity and for which possible conversations about satisfaction have been regularized (perhaps formally in the legal system). One kind of innovation lies in generating new interpretations and corresponding new domains for conditions of satisfaction. In fact, one might view this as the primary enterprise of the "fashion" industry (and of every entrepreneur).

## Domains of anticipation are incomplete.

The domain of clothing sizes was generated to anticipate breakdown in the satisfaction of conversations in which clothing is sold. It is a useful but incomplete attempt. Given the interpretive nature of "fit," no system of sizes can guarantee success. Once again, this is a clearly visible example of a more universal phenomenon. Every attempt to anticipate breakdown reflects a particular domain of anticipation. This does not make it useless, but means that we must design with the flexibility to encounter other (always unanticipated) breakdowns.

As another case, consider inventory control. The stock clerk tries to maintain a supply on hand that will decrease the possibility of running out, while keeping the overall investment in inventory as low as feasible (thereby anticipating breakdowns in cash flow). Orders are sent far enough ahead of time to anticipate delivery lags, and counts of what has been sold are used to keep track of what is on hand. But of course there are breakdowns in all of this. A supplier can simply fail to deliver as promised. An inventory count based on previous inventory and on what has been sold fails to account for the items lost through shoplifting. This does not mean that anticipation is impossible or that systems should not be built to do it. The critical part is to recognize clearly what the real domains are. An inventory count is not a statement of fact, but a declaration of an interpretation. For many purposes this can be treated as

though it were the "actual number of items," but conversations that depend on this assumption will fail to deal with the unexpected cases.

## Computers are a tool for conducting the network of conversations.

Most of what has been said in this section is independent of computers. It applies to businesses and organizations, whether they operate with the most modern equipment or with ledger pads and quills. It is also not a prescription for what they should do, but an analysis of what they are already doing. If we examine what computers are doing now in settings like our example, we find them embodying possibilities for action within a set of recurrent conversations. Whether it be a payroll system, a billing system, or an inventory control system, the hardware and software are a medium in which requests and promises are made and monitored. There is a wide range of possibilities, including the standard packages now prominent in commercial applications, decision support systems and coordinators, and the "expert" systems being widely promoted today. In each case, the question to be asked is not an abstract one of "What kind of system is needed?" but a concrete one of how different tools will lead to new conversations and in the end to new ways of working and Being. "Computerization" in its pejorative sense occurs with devices that were designed without appropriate consideration of the conversational structures they engender (and those that they consequently preclude).

## Innovations have their own domains of breakdown.

We have not tried to deal in our dress shop example with concrete questions of computer devices. In practice one needs to make many choices based on the availability, utility, and cost of different kinds of equipment—computers, software packages, networks, printers, and so on. In doing so, all of the same theoretical considerations apply. As computer users know all too well, breakdown is a fundamental concern. It is important to recognize in this area that breakdowns must be understood within a larger network of conversation as well. The issue is not just whether the machine will stop working, but whether there is a sufficient network of auxiliary conversations about system availability, support, training, modification, and so on. Most of the well-publicized failures of large computer systems have not been caused by simple breakdowns in their functioning, but by breakdowns in this larger "web of computing"[3] in which the equipment resides.

557

## Design is always already happening.

Imagine yourself in the situation depicted at the beginning of the section. You resolve to take actions that will lead to acquiring and installing a new computer system. What does our analysis have to offer? Aren't the available computer systems good enough? What guidance is there in determining what to do or buy?

Our first response is that we are not proposing some new answer to the "data processing problem." Much of our theoretical analysis applies to existing systems, and many of these operate in ways that achieve what we propose. This is not surprising, since a situation of natural selection applies—those systems that work ultimately survive.

But this is not the whole picture. It is not necessary to belabor what everyone knows from experience—computer systems are frustrating, don't really work right, and can be as much of a hindrance as a help in many situations. We don't offer a magic solution, but an orientation that leads to asking significant questions. The result of an analysis like the above might well be to lead the shop owner to make changes to the conversations as they now occur (by voice and writing) without buying a computer at all. Or it might serve as a background from which to generate criteria for deciding among competing vendors and creating new interpretations for the available systems within the particular situation. Or it might be the basis for coming up with entirely new tools that open new possibilities for action. Design always proceeds, with or without an articulated theory, but we can work to improve its course and its results.

## 3 Systematic Domains

The previous sections point out the central role played by the creation through language of the domains in which we act. Language is the creation of distinctions: nouns distinguish objects into groups, verbs distinguish kinds of actions, etc. This is not something we choose to do, but is a fundamental condition of using language. Furthermore, the words are constitutive of the objects among which they distinguish. As we showed, language does not describe a pre-existing world, but creates the world about which it speaks. There are whole domains, such as those in financial markets involving "shares," "options," and "futures," whose existence is purely linguistic—based on expressions of commitment from one individual to another.

The use of a distinction is very different from its explicit formal articulation. The fact that we commonly use a word does not mean that there is an unambiguous formal way to identify the things it denotes or to determine their properties. But whenever there is a recurrent pattern of breakdown, we can choose to explicitly specify a *systematic domain*, for which definitions and rules are articulated.

We have repeatedly contrasted the computational manipulation of formal representations with the being-in-the-world of human thought and understanding. In each case we have shown how the projection of human capacities onto computational devices was misleading. But there is a positive side to this difference. Computers are wonderful devices for the rule-governed manipulation of formal representations, and there are many areas of human endeavor in which such manipulations are crucial. In applying computers appropriately to systematic domains, we develop effective tools.

The development of systematic domains is of course not new. Mathematics is a prototypical example of such a domain, and the development of a calculus of logical form, as begun by philosophers such as Frege and Russell, made it possible to apply mathematical techniques to more general representations of objects and their properties. Work in computer science has added a new dimension—the design of mechanisms that can carry out complex sequences of symbolic manipulations automatically, according to a fixed set of rules.

There are many domains in which such manipulations are commonplace. One of the most obvious is the numbers representing financial entities and transactions. Every accounting program, payroll program, and billing program operates within a systematic domain of bookkeeping that has evolved over centuries of commercial experience. The advent of computers has not yet had a major impact on the structure of that domain, but it has made it possible to do quickly and efficiently what was previously tedious and costly.

Nobody would argue that an accounting program like VisiCalc[4] "thinks" about business, but it is a vital tool because of the clear and appropriate correspondence between its domain and the activities that generate the commercial world. Another widespread example is "word processing," as already illustrated. Its domain is the superficial stuff of language—letters and punctuation marks, words, sentences, and paragraphs. A word processor does not "understand" language, but can be used to manipulate text structures that have meaning to those who create and read them. The impact comes not because the programs are "smart" but because they let people operate effectively in a systematic domain that is relevant to human work.

We can best understand the creation of expert systems as the creation of systematic domains that are relevant and useful to a particular profession. In developing such a system, there is an initial period of "knowledge acquisition," during which professionals in the domain work together with "knowledge engineers" to articulate the structure of the relevant concepts and rules. This is often described as a process of "capturing" the knowledge that the experts already have and use. In fact, it is a creative design activity in which a systematic domain is created, covering certain aspects of the professionals' work. The successful examples of expert systems have almost all been the result of long and intensive effort by a particularly qualified practitioner, and it can well be argued that the domains generated in developing the system are themselves significant research contributions.

Such *profession-oriented domains* can be the basis for computational tools that do some tasks previously done by professionals. They can also be the basis for tools that aid in communication and the cooperative accumulation of knowledge. A profession-oriented domain makes explicit aspects of the work that are relevant to computer-aided tools and can be general enough to handle a wide range of what is done within a profession, in contrast to the very specialized domains generated in the design of a particular computer system. A systematic domain is a structured formal representation that deals with things the professional already knows how to work with, providing for precise and unambiguous description and manipulation. The critical issue is its correspondence to a domain that is ready-to-hand for those who will use it.

Examples of profession-oriented systematic domains already exist. One of the reasons for VisiCalc's great success is that it gives accountants transparent access to a systematic domain with which they already have a great deal of experience—the spreadsheet. They do not need to translate their actions into an unfamiliar domain such as the data structures and algorithms of a programming language. In the future we will see the development of many domains, each suited to the experience and skills of workers in a particular area, such as typography, insurance, or civil engineering.

To some extent, the content of each profession-oriented domain will be unique. But there are common elements that cross the boundaries. One of these—the role of language in coordinated action—has already been discussed at length. The computer is ultimately a *structured dynamic communication medium* that is qualitatively different from earlier media such as print and telephones. Communication is not a process of transmitting information or symbols, but one of commitment and interpretation. A human society operates through the expression of requests and promises among its members. There is a systematic domain relevant to the structure of this network of commitments, a domain of "conversation for action" that can be represented and manipulated in the computer.

Another widely applicable domain is the specification of mechanisms like those in computer hardware and programs. These involve physically embodied systems that can be understood as carrying out discrete processes (processes that proceed in identifiable individual steps). There are kinds of objects, properties, and relations that are suited to describing them and that can be embodied in a systematic domain. Programming languages are one approach to formalizing this domain, but in general they are not well suited to the communication of intent and conceptual structure. They are too oriented to the structure of the machine, rather than to the structure of its behavior. We are beginning to see the development of "system specification languages"[5] that deal with the domain of computational devices in a more general way.

In all situations where systematic domains are applicable, a central (and often difficult) task is to characterize the precise form and relevance of the domain within a broader orientation. In our example of coordinators, we find the embedding of a systematic domain (conversation structure) within the larger domain of language. The meaning of an utterance is not captured by a formal structure, but lies in the active listening of a hearer in a context. At the same time, its role within a particular network of requests and promises can be identified and represented in a systematic way. In a similar vein, the rows and columns of a bookkeeping program do not reflect the meaning of the economic system, but isolate one aspect that is amenable to systematic treatment. The limitations of this domain become obvious in attempts to apply accounting techniques to non-systematic areas, such as measuring overall "productivity" or providing a cost-benefit

559

analysis of activities (such as research) whose "products" are not easily measured.

Even within areas such as law—where there is a primary concern with the social and ethical fabric—we find an interaction between the contextual and the systematic. The statutes and decisions provide a systematic framework that is the basis for argumentation in court. There are clear formal statements, such as "In order to be guilty of first-degree murder, there must be premeditation." But of course these rest on understandings of terms like "premeditation," which call for contextual interpretation. Computer programs can help a lawyer manipulate formal structures and the deductions that can be made from them, while leaving the "hard questions" open to human interpretation.[6]

## 4 Technology and Transformation

Our book has focussed on the designing of computer-based tools as part of a larger perspective of ontological design. We are concerned with what happens when new devices are created, and with how possibilities for innovation arise. There is a circularity here: the world determines what we can do and what we do determines our world. The creation of a new device or systematic domain can have far-reaching significance—it can create new ways of being that previously did not exist and a framework for actions that would not have previously made sense. As an example, systematic bookkeeping techniques did not just make it easier to keep track of the financial details of business as it existed. New ways of doing business (in fact, whole new businesses dealing with financial transactions) became possible, and the entire financial activity of society evolved in accord with the structure of the new domain.

Hermeneutic orientation and biological theories give us insight into this process. In the act of design we bring forth the objects and regularities in the world of our concern. We are engaged in an activity of interpretation that creates both possibilities and blindness. As we work within the domain we have defined, we are blind to the context from which it was carved and open to the new possibilities it generates. These new possibilities create a new openness for design, and the process repeats in an endless circle.

In [Humberto] Maturana's terms, the key to cognition is the plasticity of the cognitive system, giving it the power of structural coupling. As the domain of interactions is modified, the structure of the interacting system changes in

accord with it. We cannot directly impose a new structure on any individual, but whenever we design changes to the space of interactions, we trigger changes in individual structure— changes to the horizon that is the precondition for understanding.

Computers have a particularly powerful impact, because they are machines for acting in language. In using them we engage in a discourse generated within the distinctions set down by their programmers. The objects, properties, and acts we can distinguish and perform are organized according to a particular background and pre-understanding. In most cases this pre-understanding reflects the rationalistic tradition we have criticized throughout this book. It includes biases about objectivity, about the nature of "facts" (or "data" or "information") and their origin, and about the role of the individual interacting with the computer.

We have argued that tools based on this pre-understanding will lead to important kinds of breakdown in their use. But there is a larger problem as well. As we work with devices whose domains of action are based on an interpretation of "data," "goals," "operators," and so forth, we develop patterns of language and action that reflect these assumptions. These carry over into our understanding of ourselves and the way we conduct our lives. Our criticism of descriptions of human thought as "decision making" and language understanding as the manipulation of representations is not just a prediction that certain kinds of computer programs will fail. It reflects a deeper concern with the discourse and actions that are generated by a rationalistic interpretation of human action. Computer systems can easily reinforce this interpretation, and working with them can reinforce patterns of acting that are consistent with it.[7]

On the other hand, where there is a danger there is an opportunity. We can create computer systems whose use leads to better domains of interpretation. The machine can convey a kind of "coaching" in which new possibilities for interpretation and action emerge. For example, coordinator systems grew out of research on how to train people to improve their effectiveness in working with others. This training in "communication for action"[8] reveals for people how their language acts participate in a network of human commitments. The training does not involve computers, but rests on the development of a new linguistic domain—new distinctions and descriptions that serve as a basis for action. The coordinator can help develop and reinforce this new understanding. Even at the simple level of providing the initial possibilities of "make request" and "make promise" instead of "send message," it continually reminds one of the commitment that is the basis for language. As one works successfully in this domain, the world begins to be understood in these terms, in settings far away from the computer devices.

This is just one example of a phenomenon that is only beginning to emerge in designing computers—the domain created by a design is a domain in which people live. Computers, like every technology, are a vehicle for the transformation of tradition. We cannot choose whether to effect a transformation: as designers and users of technology we are always already engaged in that transformation, independent of our will. We cannot choose what the transformation will be: individuals cannot determine the course of a tradition. Our actions are the perturbations that trigger the changes, but the nature of those changes is not open to our prediction or control. We cannot even be fully aware of the transformation that is taking place: as carriers of a tradition we cannot be objective observers of it. Our continuing work toward revealing it is at the same time a source of concealment.

However, we can work towards unconcealment, and we can let our awareness of the potentials for transformation guide our actions in creating and applying technology. In ontological designing, we are doing more than asking what can be built. We are engaging in a philosophical discourse about the self—about what we can do and what we can be. Tools are fundamental to action, and through our actions we generate the world. The transformation we are concerned with is not a technical one, but a continuing evolution of how we understand our surroundings and ourselves—of how we continue becoming the beings that we are.

Notes

1. We do not use "design" here in the narrow sense of a specific methodology for creating artifacts, but are concerned with a broad theory of design like that sought in the work of reflective architects such as Alexander (*Notes on the Synthesis of Form*, 1964).

2. Cybersyn is described in Beer, *Platform for Change* (1975).

3. This term is from Kling and Scacchi, "The web of computing" (1982), which is based on empirical studies of experience with large scale computer systems in a social context.

4. VisiCalc is a microcomputer program that lets a person manipulate an "electronic spreadsheet" with rows and columns of related figures. It is one of the most commercially successful pieces of software ever created, and is credited with motivating the purchase of more small home and business computers than any other single program.

5. See Winograd, "Beyond programming languages" (1979).

6. See Gardner, *An Artificial Intelligence Approach to Legal Reasoning* (in press), for an example and a general discussion of the issues.

7. This effect is described in Turkle, *The Second Self* (1984).

8. The training was developed by F. Flores in conjunction with Hermenet, Inc. of San Francisco.

Bibliography

Alexander, Christopher, *Notes on the Synthesis of Form*, Cambridge, MA: Harvard University Press, 1964.

Beer, Stafford, *Platform for Change*, New York: Wiley, 1975.

Flores, C. Fernando, *Management and communication in the office of the future*, Report printed by Hermenet Inc., San Francisco, 1982.

Gardner, Anne, *An Artificial Intelligence Approach to Legal Reasoning*, Cambridge, MA: Bradford/M.I.T. Press, in press.

Heidegger, Martin, *Being and Time* (translated by John Macquarrie and Edward Robinson), New York: Harper & Row, 1962.

Heidegger, Martin, *What Is Called Thinking?* (translated by Fred D. Wieck and J. Glenn Gray), New York: Harper & Row, 1968.

Heidegger, Martin, *On the Way to Language* (translated by Peter Hertz), New York: Harper & Row, 1971.

Heidegger, Martin, *The Question Concerning Technology* (translated by William Lovitt), New York: Harper & Row, 1977.

Kling, Rob and Walt Scacchi, The web of computing: Computing technology as social organization, in M. Yovits (Ed.), *Advances in Computers*, Vol. 21, 1982, 1–90.

Norman, Donald, *Perspectives on Cognitive Science*, Norwood, NJ: Ablex and Hillsdale, NJ: Lawrence Erlbaum Associates, 1981.

Turkle, Sherry, *The Second Self: Computers and the Human Spirit*, New York: Simon and Schuster, 1984.

Winograd, Terry, Beyond programming languages, *Communications of the ACM*, 22:7 (July 1979), 391–401.

Winograd, Terry, What does it mean to understand language?, in Norman (1981), 231–264.

Winograd, Terry, Moving the semantic fulcrum. *Linguistics and Philosophy*, 8:1 (1985), 91–104.

# 38. [Introduction]
# Two Selections by Brenda Laurel
## The Six Elements and the Causal Relations Among Them
## *Star Raiders:* Dramatic Interaction in a Small World

Brenda Laurel's approach to computing is a shock to many because of how classical it is. Certainly, it seemed radical in 1991 to envision interaction with computers in theatrical terms—but what Laurel proffers as the key to understanding computer interaction is a book more than 2300 years old: the *Poetics.*

Although Laurel's specific insights attained from Aristotle are useful (and are illustrated very well with regard to *Star Raiders,* in a section of her Ph.D. thesis that was not adapted for publication in *Computers as Theater* but is included here), the most powerful idea involved in her approach is that the computer can be studied from a rigorous humanistic perspective, using well-defined models established for other forms of art. As Donald Norman wrote in the foreword to *Computers as Theater,* the book from which the first selection below comes, Laurel asserts that "technologies offer new opportunities for creative, interactive experiences, and in particular, for new forms of drama. But these new opportunities will come to pass only if control of the technology is taken away from the technologist and given to those who understand human beings, human interaction, communication, pleasure, and pain" (xi). Rather than naming the conclusions Laurel drew from her analysis, the following excerpt gives insight into how the elements of drama were applied by her to enhance the understanding of computer interaction.

If computer interaction is considered as dramatic—a heightened, extra-daily experience which follows the shape of the experience of Attic drama—can it also be ordinary and everyday, fitting smoothly into our life? On the reverse side of the metaphorical coin there are certain features of a pre-established form which we may not particularly want to apply to new media. Using a well-developed system like Aristotle's in application to computer interaction can highlight undesirable features of interaction, unless the system we use to better understand computing is considered in complete appreciation for its original context and uses. This is part of the reason that Laurel recommends a thorough understanding of the principles being appropriated and applied, and names the *Poetics* an essential text for students of human-computer interaction.
—NM

Further Reading

Aristotle. *Poetics.* Trans. S. H. Butcher. Intr. Francis Fergusson. New York: Hill and Wang, 1961.

Laurel, Brenda. *Utopian Entrepreneur.* Cambridge: MIT Press, 2001.

Mateas, Michael. "A Preliminary Poetics for Interactive Drama and Games." *First Person: New Media as Story, Performance, and Game.* Ed. Noah Wardrip-Fruin and Pat Harrigan. Cambridge: MIT Press, forthcoming.

Murray, Janet. "The Cyberbard and the Multiform Plot." *Hamlet on the Holodeck,* 185–213. New York: Free Press, 1997.

Aristotle's perspective on drama is not the only one in the history of theater, of course. An alternative formulation, of particular interest because of its possible application to interactivity in new media, is found in the theater and writings of Augusto Boal (◊22).

◊22
339

In 1996 Brenda Laurel co-founded a company, Purple Moon, to create graphical adventure games for girls. The company was spun off from Interval Research; its games were designed with consideration for the media preferences of girls (studies determined sound was more important than had been previously thought, for instance) and based on social concerns that girls have. The first ones released were *Rockett's New School* and *Secret Paths in the Forest.* Laurel tells the story of her researches and work to develop a new type of computer game in her latest book: "Six and a half years and $40 million later, we had interviewed thousands of kids, invented a narrative world and a diverse set of characters, published eight CD-ROM games, produced a wildly successful Website, and built and lost a company" (4). Purple Moon's assets were acquired by Mattel in 1999.

563

Original Publication

"The Six Elements and the Causal Relations Among Them" from *Computers as Theater*, 49–65. 2nd ed. Reading, Mass.: Addison-Wesley, 1993. (First edition, 1991.)

"Star Raiders: Dramatic Interaction in a Small World" from "Toward the Design of a Computer-Based Interactive Fantasy System," 81–86. Ph.D. Thesis, Ohio State University, 1986.

# The Six Elements and the Causal Relations Among Them

## Brenda Laurel

One of Aristotle's fundamental ideas about drama (as well as other forms of literature) is that a finished play is an *organic whole*. He used the term *organic* to evoke an analogy with living things. Insofar as a whole organism is more than the sum of its parts, all of the parts are necessary for life, and the parts have certain necessary relationships to one another. He identified six qualitative elements of drama and suggested the relationships among them in terms of formal and material causality.[1]

I present Aristotle's model here for two reasons. First, I am continually amazed by the elegance and robustness of the categories and their causal relations. Following the causal relations through as one creates or analyzes a drama seems to automagically reveal the ways in which things should work or exactly how they have gone awry. Second, Aristotle's model creates a disciplined way of thinking about the design of a play in both constructing and debugging activities. Because of its fundamental similarities to drama, human-computer activity can be described with a similar model, with equal utility in both design and analysis.

Table 38.1 lists the elements of qualitative structure in hierarchical order. Here is the trick to understanding the hierarchy: Each element is the formal cause of all those below it, and each element is the material cause of all those above it. As you move up the list of elements from the bottom, you can see how each level is a successive refinement—a *shaping*—of the materials offered by the previous level. The

following sections expand upon the definitions of each of the elements in ascending order.

## Enactment

Aristotle described the fundamental material element of drama as "spectacle"—all that is seen. In the *Poetics*, he also referred to this element as "performance," which provides some basis for expanding the definition to include other senses as well. Some scholars place the auditory sense in the second level because of its association with music and melody, but, as will be seen in the next section, it is more likely that the notion of melody pertains to the *patterning* of sound rather than to the auditory channel itself.

One difference, probably temporary, between drama and human-computer activity is the senses that are addressed in

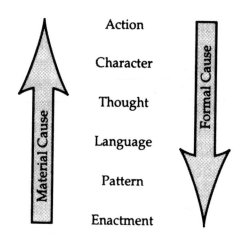

Figure 38.1. Causal relations among elements of quantitative structure.

the enactment.[2] Traditionally, plays are available only to the eyes and ears; we cannot touch, smell, or taste them. There are interesting exceptions. In the 1920s, for instance, director David Belasco experimented with using odors as part of the performance of realistic plays; it is said that he abandoned this approach when he observed that the smell of bacon frying utterly distracted the audience from the action on stage. In the mid-1960s, Morton Heilig invented a stand-

| Element | In Drama | In Human-Computer Activity |
|---|---|---|
| Action | The whole action being represented. The action is theoretically the same in every performance. | The whole action, as it is collaboratively shaped by system and user. The action may vary in each interactive session. |
| Character | Bundles of predispositions and traits, inferred from agents' patterns of choice. | The same as in drama, but including agents of both human and computer origin. |
| Thought | Inferred internal processes leading to choice: cognition, emotion, and reason. | The same as in drama, but including processes of both human and computer origin. |
| Language | The selection and arrangement of words; the use of language. | The selection and arrangement of signs, including verbal, visual, auditory, and other nonverbal phenomena when used semiotically. |
| Melody (Pattern) | Everything that is heard, but especially the melody of speech. | The pleasurable perception of pattern in sensory phenomena. |
| Spectacle (Enactment) | Everything that is seen. | The sensory dimensions of the action being represented: visual, auditory, kinesthetic and tactile, and potentially all others. |

Table 38.1. The six qualitative elements of structure in drama and in human-computer activity.

alone arcade machine called Sensorama, which provided stereoscopic filmic images, kinesthetic feedback, and environmental smells—for example, on a motorcycle ride through New York City, the audience could smell car exhaust fumes and pizza. Sensorama's problem was not that it addressed the wrong senses; it simply happened at a time when the business community couldn't figure out what to do with it—pinball parlors were monolithic, and it would be several years before *Pong* kicked off the arcade game industry.

At the same time that Heilig was thinking about multisensory arcade games and movie theatres, the development of new genres of participatory theatre accelerated. Such artists as Judith Melina and Julian Beck of the Living Theatre, Robert Wilson, Peter Brook, Jerzy Grotowski, and John Cage experimented with performances that began to dissolve the boundaries between actors and audience by placing both in the same space. Wilson, Cage, Josef Svoboda, and others produced works that integrated filmic and photographic images, musical instruments, and machines in novel ways.

In the 1980s, these trends toward increasing the sensory dimensions of audience participation gave rise to works

where the audience could touch the actors and scenery and move about freely in the performance space. For example, in *Tina and Tony's Wedding*, a contemporary "interactive" play, the audience is invited to follow the actors around from room to room (kinesthetic), to touch props and sit on the furniture (tactile and kinesthetic), and to share in a wedding banquet (taste and smell). Another notable example is Chris Hardman's Antenna Theatre, where audience members move around a set prompted by taped dialogue and narration heard through personal headphones. A spate of site-specific interactive plays and "mystery weekends" in the late 1980s enjoyed a fair amount of commercial success. Contemporary performance art shares many of the same origins.

It is interesting that the development of this theatrical genre has been concurrent with the blossoming of computer games as a popular form of entertainment, and I speculate that computer games have in some ways served as a model for it. In fact, it is in the areas that dramatic entertainment and human-computer activity are beginning to converge that pan-sensory representation is being most actively explored. When we examine that convergence, we can see ways in which human-computer activity has evolved, at least in part,

565

as drama's attempt to increase its sensory bandwidth, creating the technological siblings of the kind of participatory theatre described above.

The notion of "interactive movies," which has gained popularity in the late 1980s, has its roots in both cinema and computer games, two forms that combine theatre and technology. Earlier works were relatively isolated. These include the productions of Lanterna Magica in Czechoslovakia and an "interactive movie" that was shown in the Czech Pavilion at the 1967 World Expo in Montreal, Canada, in which the audience was allowed to influence the course of the action by selecting from among several alternatives at a few key points in the film (however, it is rumored that all roads led to Rome—that is, all paths through the movie led to the same ending). The idea of interactive movies has been rekindled and transformed into a bona fide trend by advances in multimedia technology. Likewise, there were early experiments in interactive television in the mid-1970s (such as the failed Warner QUBE system). Interactive TV had to await similar technological advances before finally becoming a 1990s buzz-word.

In drama, the use of technology to create representations goes at least as far back as the *mechane* of the ancient Greeks. Cinema as a distinct form diverged from drama as the result of the impact of a new performance technology on form, structure, and style. In complementary fashion, computer games can be seen to have evolved from the impact of dramatic ideas on the technology of interactive computing and graphical displays. Computer games incorporate notions about character and action, suspense and empathy, and other aspects of dramatic representation.[3] Almost from the beginning, they have involved the visual, auditory, and kinesthetic senses (you need only watch a game player with a joystick to see the extent to which movement is involved, both as a cause and effect of the representation).

At the blending point of cinema and computer games are such new forms as super-arcade games like *Battle Tech* and sensory-rich amusement park installations like *Star Tours*. These types of systems involve the tactile and kinesthetic senses; some are investigating the inclusion of the other senses as well through both performance technology and direct stimulation to the nervous system [Rosen and Gosser, 1987]. "Virtual reality" systems increase intensity through techniques described as *sensory immersion*—instead of looking at a screen, for instance, a person is surrounded by stereoscopic sounds and visual images delivered through earphones and "eyephones." Through the use of special input devices like specially instrumented gloves and suits, people may move about and interact directly with objects in a virtual world. Interestingly, the first virtual reality systems and applications were developed for nonentertainment purposes like computer-aided design, scientific visualization, and training. Home computers and home game systems are not far behind these expensive, special-purpose systems in their ability to deliver multisensory representations.

The element of enactment is composed of all of the sensory phenomena that are part of the representation. Because of the evolutionary processes described above, it seems appropriate to say that enactment can potentially involve all of the senses. These sensory phenomena are the basic material of both drama and human-computer activity; they are the clay that is progressively shaped by the creator, whether playwright or designer.

## Pattern

The perception of patterns in sensory phenomena is a source of pleasure for humans. Aristotle described the second element of drama as "melody," a kind of pattern in the realm of sound. In the *Poetics* he says that "melody is the greatest of the pleasurable accessories of tragedy" [*Poetics*, 1450b, 15–17]. The orthodox view is that "spectacle" is the visual dimension and "melody" is the auditory one, but this view is problematic in the context of formal and material causality. If the material cause of all sounds (music) were things that could be perceived by the eye (spectacle), then things like the vibration of vocal cords and the melodies of off-stage musicians would be excluded. On the contrary, all that is seen in a play is not shaped solely by the criterion of producing sounds or music (although this may have been more strictly true in the performance style of the ancient Greeks than it is today). The formal-material relationship does not work within the context of these narrow definitions of music and spectacle.

In the previous section, we have already expanded spectacle into all sensory elements of the enactment. The notion of melody as the arrangement of sounds into a pleasing pattern can be extended analogically to the arrangement of visual images, tactile or kinesthetic sensations, and probably smells and tastes as well (as a good chef can demonstrate). In fact, the idea that a pleasurable pattern can be achieved through the arrangement of visual or other sensory materials can be derived from other aspects of the *Poetics*, so its absence here is something of a mystery. Looking "up" the hierarchy, it could be that Aristotle did not see the visual as a potentially semiotic or linguistic medium, and hence narrowed the causal channel to lead exclusively to spoken language. Whatever the explanation, the orthodox view of Aristotle's definitions of spectacle and melody leaves out too much material. As scholars are wont to do, I will blame the vagaries of translation, figurative language, and mutations introduced by centuries of interpretation for this apparent lapse and proceed to advocate my own view.

The element of pattern thus refers to patterns in the sensory phenomena of the enactment. These patterns exert a formal influence on the enactment, just as semiotic usage formally influences patterns. A key point that Aristotle made is that patterns are pleasurable to perceive in and of themselves, whether or not they are further formulated into semiotic devices or language; he spoke of them, not only as the material for language, but also as "pleasurable accessories." Hence the use of pattern as a source of pleasure is a characteristic of dramatic representations, and one which can comfortably be extended to the realm of human-computer experience.

## Language

The element of *language* (usually translated as diction) in drama is defined by Aristotle as "the expression of their [the characters'] thought in words" [*Poetics*, 1450b, 12–15]. Hence the use of spoken language as a system of signs is distinguished from other theatrical signs like the use of gesture, color, scenic elements, or paralinguistic elements (patterns of inflection and other vocal qualities). In the orthodox view, diction refers only to words—their choice and arrangement. That definition presents some interesting problems in the world of human-computer activities, many of which involve no words at all (e.g., most skill-and-action computer games, as well as graphical adventure games and graphical simulations). Are there elements in such nonverbal works that can be defined as *language*?

When a play is performed for a deaf audience and signing is used, few would argue that those visual signs function as language. The element of language in this case is expressed in a way that takes into account the sensory modalities available to the audience.[4] A designer may choose, for whatever reason, to build a human-computer system that neither senses nor responds to words, and which uses no words in the representation. Hardware configurations without keyboards, speech recognition, or text display capabilities may be unable to work with words.

In human-computer activities, graphical signs and symbols, nonverbal sounds, or animation sequences may be used in the place of words as the means for explicit communication between computers and people. Such nonverbal signs may be said to function as language when they are the principal medium for the expression of thought. Accordingly, the selection and arrangement of those signs may be evaluated in terms of the same criteria as Aristotle specified for diction—for example, the effective expression of thought and appropriateness to character.

## Thought

The element of *thought* in drama may be defined as the processes leading to a character's choices and actions—for example, to emotion, cognition, reason, and intention. Understood in this way, the element of thought "resides" within characters, although it can be described and analyzed in aggregate form (the element of *thought* in a given play may be described as concerned with certain specific ethical questions, for example). Although it may be explicitly expressed in the form of dialogue, thought is *inferred*, by both the audience and the other characters (agents), from a character's choices and actions. In his application of a theatrical analogy to the domain of artificial intelligence, Julian Hilton puts it this way: "What the audience does is supply the inferencing engine which drives the plot, obeying Shakespeare's injunction to eke out the imperfections of the play (its incompleteness) with its mind." [Hilton, 1991]

If we extend this definition of thought to include human-computer activities, it leads to a familiar conundrum: Can computers think? There is an easy answer. Computer-based agents, like dramatic characters, do not have to *think* (in fact, there are many ways in which they cannot); they simply have to *provide a representation from which thought may be inferred.*

When a folder on my Macintosh desktop opens to divulge its contents in response to my double-click, the representation succeeds in getting me to infer that that's exactly what happened—that is, the "system" understood my input, inferred *my* purpose, and did what I wanted. Was the system (or the folder) "thinking" about things this way? The answer, I think, is that it doesn't matter. The real issue is that the representation succeeded in getting me to make the right inferences about its "thoughts." It also succeeded in representing to me that it made the right inferences about mine!

Thought is the formal cause of language; it shapes what an agent communicates through the selection and arrangement of signs, and thus also has a formal influence on pattern and enactment. The traditional explanation of how language serves as material for thought is based on the overly limiting assumption that agents employ language, or the language-like manipulation of symbols, in the process of thinking. This assumption leads to the idea that characters in a play use the language of the play quite literally as the material for their thoughts.

I favor a somewhat broader interpretation of material causality: *The thought of a play can appropriately deal only with what is already manifest at the levels of enactment, pattern, and language.* Most of us have seen plays in which characters get ideas "out of the blue"—suddenly remembering the location of a long-lost will, for instance, or using a fact to solve a mystery that has been withheld from the audience thus far. The above theory would suggest that the interjection of such thoughts is unsatisfying (and mars the play) because they are not drawn from the proper material. Plays, like human-computer activities, are closed universes in the sense that they delimit the set of potential actions. As we will see in the discussion of action below, it is key to the success of a dramatic representation that all of the materials that are formulated into action are drawn from the circumscribed potential of the particular dramatic world. Whenever this principle is violated, the organic unity of the work is diminished, and the scheme of probability that holds the work together is disrupted.

This principle can be demonstrated to apply to the realm of human-computer activity as well. One example is the case in which the computer (a computer-based agent) introduces new materials at the level of thought—"out of the blue." Suppose a new word processor is programmed to be constantly checking for spelling errors and to automatically correct them as soon as they are identified. If the potential for this behavior is not represented to you in some way, it will be completely disruptive when it occurs, and it will probably cause you to make seriously erroneous inferences, to perhaps think "something is wrong with my fingers, my keyboard, or my computer." The computer

"knows" why it did what it did ("thought" exists) but you do not; correct inferences cannot be made.[5] A text message, for instance, or an animation of a dictionary with its pages turning (language), could represent the action as it is occurring.

Other kinds of failures in human-computer activity can also be seen as failures on the level of thought. One of my favorite examples is a parser used in several text adventure games. This particular parser did not "know" all of the words that were used in the text representation of the story. So a person might read the sentence, "Hargax slashed the dragon with his broadsword." The person might then type, "take the broadsword," and the "game" might respond, "I DON'T KNOW THE WORD 'BROADSWORD'." The inference that one would make is that the game "agent" is severely brain-damaged, since the agent that produces language and the agent that comprehends it are assumed to be one in the same. This is the converse of the problem described in the last paragraph; rather than "knowing" more than it represented, the agent represented more than it "knew." Both kinds of errors are attributable to a glitch in the formal-material relationship between language and thought.

## Character and Agency

Aristotle maintained that the *object* of (i.e., what is being imitated by) a drama is action, not persons: "We maintain that Tragedy is primarily an imitation of action, and that it is mainly for the sake of the action that it imitates the personal agents" (*Poetics*, 1450b, 1–5). In drama, *character* may be defined as bundles of traits, predispositions, and choices that, when taken together, form coherent entities. Those entities are the agents of the action represented in the plot. This definition emphasizes the primacy of action.

In order to apply the same definition to human-computer activities, we must demonstrate first that agents are in fact part of such representations, and second, that there are functional and structural similarities between such agents and dramatic characters.

In a purely Aristotelian sense, an agent is one who takes action. Interestingly, Aristotle admits of the possibility of a play without characters, but a play without action cannot exist [*Poetics*, 1450a, 22–25]. This suggests that agency as part of a representation need not be strictly embodied in "characters" as we normally think of them—that is, as representations of humans. Using the broadest definition, all computer programs that perform actions that are perceived by people can be said to exhibit agency in some form. The real argument is whether that agency is a "free-floating" aspect of what is going on, or whether it is captured in "entities"—coalesced notions of the sources of agency.

The answer, I believe, is that even when representations do not explicitly include such entities, their existence is implied. At the grossest level, people simply attribute agency to the computer itself ("I did this, and then the computer did that"). They also attribute agency to application programs ("My word processor trashed my file"). They often distinguish between the agency of system software and applications ("Multifinder crashed Excel"). They attribute agency to smaller program elements and/or their representations ("The spelling checker in my word processor found an error").

In social and legal terms, an agent is one who is empowered to act on behalf of another. This definition has been used as part of the definition of agents in the mimetic world. It implies that, beyond simply performing actions, computer-based agents perform a special kind of actions—namely, actions undertaken on behalf of people. It therefore also implies that some sort of implicit or explicit communication must occur between person and system in order for the person's needs and goals to be inferred. I think that this definition is both too narrow and too altruistic. There may be contexts in which it is useful to create a computer-based agent whose "goals" are orthogonal or even inimical to those of human agents—for instance, in simulations of combat or other situations that involve conflicting forces. Agents may also work in an utterly self-directed manner, offering the results of their work up to people after the fact.

For now, we will use the broader definition of agents to apply to human-computer activity: entities that can initiate and perform actions. Like dramatic characters, they consist of bundles of traits or predispositions to act in certain ways.

Traits circumscribe the actions (or kinds of actions) that an agent has the capability to perform, thereby defining the agent's potential. There are two kinds of traits: traits that determine how an agent can act (internal traits) and traits that represent those internal predispositions (external traits). People must be given cues by the external representation of an agent that allow them to infer its internal traits. Why? Because traits function as a kind of *cognitive shorthand* that allows people to predict and comprehend agents' actions [see Laurel, 1990]. Inferred internal traits are a component of

both dramatic probability (an element of plot) and "ease of use" (especially in terms of the minimization of human errors) in human-computer systems. Part of the art of creating both dramatic characters and computer-based agents is the art of selecting and representing external traits that accurately reflect the agent's potential for action.

Aristotle outlined four criteria for dramatic characters that can also be applied to computer-based agents [*Poetics*, 1454a, 15–40]. The first criterion is that characters be "good" (sometimes translated as "virtuous"). Using the Aristotelian definition of "virtue," good characters are those who success-fully fulfill their function—that is, those who successfully formulate thought into action. Good characters *do* (action) what they *intend* to do (thought). They also do what their creator intends them to do in the context of the whole action. The second criterion is that characters be "appropriate" to the actions they perform; that is, that there is a good match between a character's traits and what they do. The third criterion is the idea that characters be "like" reality in the sense that there are causal connections between their thoughts, traits, and actions. This criterion is closely related to dramatic probability. The fourth criterion is that characters be "consistent" throughout the whole action; that is, that a character's traits should not change arbitrarily. The mapping of these criteria to computer-based agents is quite straightforward.

Finally, we need to summarize the formal and material relationships between character and the elements above and below it in the hierarchy. Formal causality suggests that it is action, and action alone, that *shapes* character; that is, a character's traits are dictated by the exigencies of the plot. To include traits in the representation that are not manifest in action violates this principle. Material causality suggests that the stuff of which a character is made must be present on the level of thought and, by implication, language and enactment as well. A good example is the interface agent, Phil, who appears in an Apple promotional video entitled "The Knowledge Navigator" (© 1988 by Apple Computer, Inc.). In the original version, Phil was portrayed by an actor in video format. He appeared to be human, alive, and responsive at all times. But because he behaved and spoke quite simply and performed relatively simple tasks, many viewers of the video complained that he was a stupid character. His physical traits (high-resolution, real-time human portrayal) did not match his language capabilities, his thoughts, or his actions (simple

569

tasks performed in a rather unimaginative manner). In a later version, Phil's representation was changed to a simple line-drawn cartoon character with very limited animation. People seemed to find the new version of Phil much more likable. The simpler character was more consistent and more appropriate to the action.

## The Whole Action

Representations are normally thought of as having objects, even though those objects need not be things that can or do exist in the real world. Likewise, plays are often said to represent their characters; that is, *Hamlet* is a representation of the king of Denmark, and so on. In the Aristotelian view, the object of a dramatic representation is not character but action; *Hamlet* represents the action of a man attempting to discover and punish his father's murderer. The characters are there because they are required in order to represent the action, and not the other way around. An action is made up of incidents that are causally and structurally related to one another. The individual incidents that make up *Hamlet*—Hamlet fights with Laertes, for instance—are only meaningful insofar as they are woven into the action of the mimetic whole. The form of a play is manifest in the pattern created by the arrangement of incidents within the whole action.

Another definitional property of plot is that the whole action must have a beginning, a middle, and an end. The value of beginnings and endings is most clearly demonstrated by the lack of them. The feeling produced by walking into the middle of a play or movie or being forced to leave the theatre before the end is generally unpleasant. Viewers are rarely happy when, at the end of a particularly suspenseful television program, "to be continued" appears on the screen. My favorite Macintosh example is an error message that I sometimes encounter while running Multifinder: "Excel (or some other application) has unexpectedly quit." "Well," I usually reply, "the capricious little bastard!" Providing graceful beginnings and endings for human-computer activities is most often a nontrivial problem—how to "jump-start" a database engine, for example, or how to complete a network communications session. Two rules of thumb for good beginnings is that the potential for action in that particular universe is effectively laid out, and that the first incidents in the action set up promising lines of probability for future actions. A good

ending provides not only completion of the action being represented but also the kind of emotional closure that is implied by the notion of catharsis.

A final criterion that Aristotle applied to plot is the notion of magnitude:

> To be beautiful, a living creature, and every whole made up of parts, but also be of a certain definite magnitude. Beauty is a matter of size and order.... Just in the same way, then, as a beautiful whole made up of parts, or a beautiful living creature, must be of some size, but a size to be taken in by the eye, so a story or Plot must be of some length, but of a length to be taken in by the memory [*Poetics*, 1450b, 34–40].

The action must not be so long that you forget the beginning before you get to the end, since you must be able to perceive it as a whole in order to fully enjoy it. This criterion is most immediately observable in computer games, which may require you to be hunched over a keyboard for days on end if you are to perceive the whole at one sitting, a feat of which only teenagers are capable. Similar errors in magnitude are likely to occur in other forms, such as virtual reality systems, where the raw capabilities of a system to deliver material of seemingly infinite duration is not yet tempered by a sensitivity to the limits of human memory and attention span, or to the relationship of beauty and pleasure to duration in time-based arts.

Problems in magnitude can also plague other, more "practical" applications as well. If achievable actions with distinct beginnings and ends cannot occur within the limits of memory or attention, then the activity becomes an endless chore. On the contrary, if the granularity of actions is too small and those actions cannot be grouped into more meaningful, coherent units (such as a word processor that only lets you type or a spreadsheet that only lets you add up columns of numbers), then the activity becomes an endless stream of meaningless chores. These problems are related to the *shape* of the action as well as its magnitude.

The notion of beauty that drives Aristotle's criterion of magnitude is the idea that made things, like plays, can be organic wholes—that the beauty of their form and structure can approach that of natural organisms in the way the parts fit perfectly together. In this context, he expresses the criterion for inclusion of any given incident in the plot or whole action:

An imitation of an action must represent one action, a complete whole, with its several incidents so closely connected that the transposal or withdrawal of any one of them will disjoin and dislocate the whole. For that which makes no perceptible difference by its presence or absence is no real part of the whole [*Poetics*, 1451a, 30–35].

If we aim to design human-computer activities that are—dare we say—*beautiful*, this criterion must be used in deciding, for instance, what a person should be required to do, or what a computer-based agent should be represented as doing, in the course of the action.

In this chapter, we have described the essential causes of human-computer activity—that is, the forces that shape it—and its qualitative elements. In the next chapter [of *Computers as Theatre*], we will consider the orchestration of action more closely, both in terms of its structure and its powers to evoke emotional and intellectual response.

# *Star Raiders*
## Dramatic Interaction in a Small World
## Brenda Laurel

*Star Raiders* is an animated action game developed by Douglas Neubauer for the Atari computer in 1979. At that time, Neubauer was working as a hardware engineer and not a game designer, but felt that there should be a good video game for the new home computer. The dozens of awards that *Star Raiders* has won over the years, including "best video game" for three consecutive years in a popular computing magazine, are a testament to Neubauer's skill and dramatic insight.[1]

The game places the user in control of a starship, with the objective of cleaning pugnacious alien spacecraft out of several contiguous quadrants of the galaxy. To succeed completely, the user must be able to maneuver and fight, generate strategies for defending his starbases, and be able to dock with a starbase when necessary for refueling and repairs. The game's primary visual mode is a convincing first-person view from the bridge of the starship as the ship races through the starfield, dodges meteors and enemy fire, and fires photon torpedoes at Zylon ships. Besides forward or aft views from the bridge, the display includes status indicators for the ship's fuel and various functions. The computer keyboard, in the user's visual field directly below the display, becomes an extension of the imaginary ship's controls.

Other visual modes include the *galactic chart* and the *long range sector scan*. The galactic chart is a display to which the user may toggle at any time to view the location of friendly starbases and enemy ships, and to see the number of ships in each quadrant. The chart is used for strategic planning and navigation between quadrants. The user enters *hyperwarp*, the means of travel from one quadrant to another, by moving the game cursor to his destination on the galactic chart. The long range sector scan is a view of the user's own ship from "above" its current location (an impossible view which is often employed in science fiction movies—ever wonder how they get those cameras hanging out in space?), and shows the location of other targets as well. It is used for navigation within quadrants.

There are two distinct kinds of action in the game: combat, which requires maneuvering skill and eye-hand coordination; and the planning and execution of strategies to prevent friendly starbases from being surrounded and destroyed. The two activities blend well in the overall action, because fighting is part of the execution of strategic plans, and because the user is free to toggle to the galactic chart and review his plans at any time. The action is continuous regardless of visual mode: Zylons are on the move, and the ship is always running, depleting its fuel supply.

*Star Raiders*, unlike *Zork*, is *enacted*, with computer-generated spectacle and music. As in traditional drama, enactment in *Star Raiders* entails the illusion of real, continuous time. Unity of action is provided by the user's overall objective, and reinforced by a rating of the user's overall performance that is displayed at the end of every game session. The game's incidents are causally related—the order in which various Zylon-bearing quadrants are attacked, for example, affects the enemy's ability to surround a starbase, as well as the player's fuel consumption and hence the need to dock for refueling.

The plot of a game session exhibits a traditional dramatic structure, with exposition (initial scanning of the galactic chart), rising action (encounters with Zylon ships), crisis (threat to starbases posed by enemy ships), climax (moment

571

at which the outcome is determined), falling action or denouement (action from climax to the moment of complete success, destruction, or running out of fuel), and conclusion (the starfleet rating message). Interestingly, the dramatic structure emerges more distinctly as the user becomes experienced and begins to generate long-term strategies for play. The user's strategic plan and its implementation is the central action of the plot, and the better it is formulated, the more the whole behaves dramatically.

Like *Zork*, *Star Raiders* casts the user as the central character; however, *Star Raiders* does so more completely and successfully. There is no "System's I" to muddy the issue of who the central agent actually is. While the user's identity is often lost in a fog of pronouns in *Zork*, the notion of user as character in *Star Raiders* is rendered completely unambiguous by the first-person treatment of spectacle.

The other characters in *Star Raiders* are represented as the Zylon vessels and friendly starbases, with their guiding intelligences assumed. There are three types of Zylon agents, distinguishable by their graphical images and one or two behavioral traits in battle. Starbases behave identically, and have a small repertoire of characteristic actions and communication protocols. All characters, including the user-character, are extremely simple due to the constraints of the game world: the kinds of things that can happen are few, and hence the agents of those few actions require correspondingly few traits. Despite the outer space setting, *Star Raiders* takes place in a very "small" world.

Contributions of the user on the levels of spectacle and music are materially constrained by the program's repertoire of images, animation sequences, and sound effects—again, the possibilities are few when compared to traditional drama. Likewise, the user's contributions on the level of diction are constrained by the set of commands that the system can recognize and act upon. The game creates the illusion of responding to a relatively greater range of contributions on the levels of thought and character because subtly different strategies, as well as emotions and motivations ("I'm going to kill those Zylon bastards" vs. "I keep a clean quadrant") are often not translated by the user into objectifiable plans and specific actions. The effects of chance and physical dexterity tend to be interpreted by the user as the results of his

strategies and character traits. The game is successful in supporting such fantasies because the user is not generally aware of the material and formal constraints on his actions.

Unlike *Zork* (in which the single plot is discovered by the user in a series of sessions), the plot of *Star Raiders* is variable and collaboratively formulated by the system and the user. There is no single outcome that must be attained in order for the whole plot to be revealed and no single way to reach that end. The number of possible plots is constrained by the relatively few *kinds* of actions that can occur (a measure of the *potential* of the dramatic world). Because the user's strategies and actions influence the order and incidents and the outcome of each (e.g., how much damage is sustained in a battle), the plot can be seen to be collaboratively formulated.

The system's functioning as provider of constraints, protocols, and a finite set of materials is, in many game programs and to some degree in *Zork*, intrusive and destructive of the user's fantasy experience. In *Zork*, the user's relationship to the system, as represented by the "System's I," can be described as a "second-person" one (as demonstrated by the second-person pronouns in the dialogue between them), and is quite distinct from the first-person experience that is desired by the user and intended by the system's designers. The "System's I" stands outside the context of the fantasy, with no distinct character or role in the action— what computer folks would call a "kludge." The functioning of the "System's I" is taken over by the ship's computer in *Star Raiders*, and thus cleverly integrated into the fantasy world. The user employs the ship's computer and the various "tools" it offers him (the galactic chart and attack computer, for instance) quite naturally in a first-person mode.

This chapter has employed dramatic theory to elucidate the structural characteristics of poetic interactive works. In creating a theory of interactive drama, emphasis has been placed on comprehending and integrating the contributions of the user-character as the co-creator of an interactive work. The form of such works is determined by the manner in which the system formulates materials—human-authored, computer-generated, and contributed by the user-character—into a dramatically satisfying whole. The form of an interactive drama must enable the user to participate in the fantasy world as an active character—a dramatic agent.

Notes—*The Six Elements*

1. The explicit notion of the workings of formal and material causality in the hierarchy of structural elements is, although not apocryphal, certainly neo-Aristotelian. See Smiley [1971].

2. Aristotle defined the enactment in terms of the audience rather than the actors. Although actors employ movement (kinesthetics) in their performance of the characters, that movement is perceived visually—the audience has no direct kinesthetic experience. Likewise, although things may move about on a computer screen, a human user may or may not be having a kinesthetic experience.

3. Within the art of computer games, there are various forms, including action games, strategy games, adventure games, and so on.

4. It is interesting to note in this context that American Sign Language (ASL) is in fact a "natural language" in its own right, and not a direct gestural map of English or any other spoken language. If a language can be constructed from gesture, then it follows that spoken words are not essential elements of language.

5. In human factors discourse, this type of failure is attributed to a failure to establish the correct conceptual model of a given system [see Rubinstein and Hersh, 1984, Chapter 5]. The dramatic perspective differs slightly from this view by suggesting that proper treatment of the element of thought can provide a good "conceptual model" for the entire medium. It also avoids the potential misuse of conceptual models as personal constructs that "explain" what is "behind" the representation—that is, how the computer or program actually "works."

Notes—*Star Raiders*

1. Atari's policy was never to connect the names of authors with their video games, thus Neubauer is known primarily through "in-house" legend. The awards won by his game were accepted by a succession of marketing vice-presidents who never heard of him.

References—*The Six Elements*

Aristotle, *The Poetics*. Translated by Ingram Bywater. In *Rhetoric and Poetics of Aristotle*. Edited by Friedrich Solmsen. New York: The Modern Library, 1954.

Hilton, Julian. "Some Semiotic Reflections on the Future of Artificial Intelligence." In *Artificial Intelligence: Future, Impacts, Challenges,* edited by R. Trappl. New York: Hemisphere, forthcoming.

Laurel, Brenda. "Interface Agents: Metaphors with Characters." In *The Art of Human-Computer Interface Design,* edited by Brenda Laurel. Reading, Mass.: Addison-Wesley, 1990.

Rosen, Jospeh and Mort Gosser. "Nerve Repair at the Axon Level—A Merger of Microsurgery and Microelectronics." *Artificial Organs,* edited by J. Andrade. New York: VCH Publishers, 1987: 583-594.

Rubinstein, Richard and Harry Hersh, 1984. *The Human Factor: Designing Computer Systems for People*. Digital Press, 1984.

Smiley, Sam. *Playwriting: The Structure of Action*. Englewood Cliffs, N.J.: Prentice-Hall, 1971.

# 39. [Introduction]
# Towards a New Classification of Tele-Information Services

Marshall McLuhan's provocative explorations (◊13) sparked a great expansion of writing about media—but this has included few attempts to rigorously classify digital communications. While McLuhan provided useful metaphors grounded in the senses, the essay here considers the social role of various digital media, surveying new media from a fundamentally different perspective than the individual, sensory one—and placing these media within a more tightly defined schema.

Various new media can be quickly categorized according to the typology presented here: IRC, Unix talk, proprietary chat systems and discussions on MUDs function as conversation, while the Web usually functions for consultation—unless it is collecting credit card numbers or other information through forms. Likewise, it is not difficult to categorize network services such as email, gopher, finger, whois, push-media of the sort launched by Pointcast in the mid–1990s, and even graphical network environments and games, arena-style or of the EverQuest and Anarchy Online massively multiplayer sort.

Given the way that the Web already had, in the early 1990s, functioned in both consultation and registration capacities, one might have predicted that email-over-Web services like Hotmail and Yahoo! Mail would be plausible. Their success points out some additional interesting cases, in which one Internet service is perversely used, against the seeming grain of the technology. For instance, chat systems have been implemented over the Web, some of them underground successes (e.g., Bianca's Smut Shack, which ran on *HotWired* servers beginning in 1995). Real-time chat systems (e.g., Yadda) have also been "implemented" by using just the subject lines of email—so that employers, only noticing that chatters had email windows open, could not see that employees were chatting. The important point made by such examples (and one made in the following essay) is that the basic technology employed does not determine the category of service a telecommunications system provides.

Although Espen Aarseth (◊52) has written that the typology described here is "less directly relevant" for textual systems, and he has offered a more focused and very useful typology of his own, one can attempt to extend the typology here to apply to systems such as those running on stand-alone computers, and such extension can lead to interesting insights. To extend the system further in this way, one might conceptualize elements of software as fulfilling the role of the service center at times and at times taking the role of another individual. This would allow a system like *Eliza/ Doctor* (◊24) to be seen as conversational in the sense intended by Bordewijk and van Kaam. A scrolling text file can be seen as an example of allocution; a database, consultation; the program that requests your name and software serial number before installing software, registration. But to make this typology a useful one, it is important to distinguish how these terms are to be used in the stand-alone computing context, and to describe with rigor when software should be considered as a service center and when—if ever—it is appropriate to consider it as another individual. Perhaps the classification scheme here is strained by some analogies to stand-alone computing. In this case, the principles that motivated it can be used to select or construct another classification scheme appropriate to the elements of and participants in the systems involved.

—NM

◊13
193

◊24
367

◊42
613

◊52
761

Another scheme for differentiating computer texts is Michael Joyce's division of hypertext into exploratory and constructive (◊42).

**575**

Further Reading

Aarseth, Espen. "Textonomy: A Typology of Textual Information." *Cybertext: Perspectives on Ergodic Literature,* 58–75. Baltimore: Johns Hopkins University Press, 1997.

Ziegfeld, Richard. "Interactive Fiction: A New Literary Genre?" *New Literary History* 20:341–372. 1989.

Original Publication

*Intermedia* 34(1):16-21. January 1986.

# Towards a New Classification of Tele-Information Services

## Jan L. Bordewijk and Ben van Kaam

Tele-information systems, based on an alliance of digital telecommunication and computer technology, will play an increasingly important role in inter-human communications. They are in fact ready to enter almost every area of human communication activity.

As a consequence the spread of knowledge, the cornerstone of democracy, seems to be headed towards a time of flourishing, but this optimistic expectation reflects only one side of the coin. The reverse side tells us that the penetration of technology in human information paths, on such a large scale as we witness today, can only succeed thanks to a huge information services industry. Such an industry, providing information-oriented products as well as technical facilities and employing many, many people, saddles us with a new concern: its own power. In order to avoid the risk of an Orwellian scenario, society should at least have at its disposal a clear and simple picture of what the power positions and relations are on the vulnerable terrain of human communication. We need some sort of classification of tele-information services with respect to their social role. The often intuitively applied classification by reference to their technical properties is untrustworthy and will cause more and more confusion as multi-function networks and terminal equipment replace the present dedicated systems.

This classification should be replaced by one based on social power relations. A classification in terms of idealised information traffic patterns provides a logical and unambiguous alternative. It provides a solution that harks back to the time when no technical devices were available, so that there was no danger of mistaking incidental technical designs for guidelines as to the character of the communication. It can moreover be defined independently both of the form of presentation and of the information content.

We start with a detailed description of the four definable information traffic patterns. There is a comprehensive introduction to the questions at issue in our monograph, *Measuring the Degree of Democracy of Information Societies,* (available from Het Persinstituut, postbox 7161, 1075 AB Amsterdam).

## Allocution

Let us first look at the situation that occurs when a single human being, called C (centre), addresses another person called i (individual).

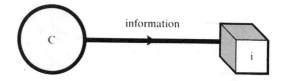

Figure 39.1. Allocution: information flow from service centre (C) to inividual consumer (i).

When the information flow is always in the same direction, we have to assume that C has at his or her disposal an unlimited amount of information, possibly of a specialist nature. We will call C the "information services provider" and i an "information services consumer." This formulation has the twofold advantage of including technical facilities and leaving open the direction of the information flow.

This situation resembles that of a master-slave relationship, or general-soldier, teacher-pupil, etc. If we assume that the master owns more than one slave, the general commands more than one soldier and so on, we obtain a pattern in which C is the central leader and i, $i_1$, $i_2$ etc are the individual followers.

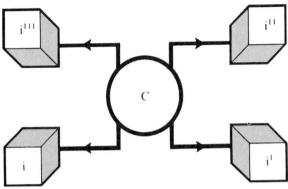

Figure 39.2. Allocution, general pattern.

In practical situations the followers will often be able to provide a certain amount of feedback, be it only the shuffling of feet, depending on the harshness of the regime. The figures show idealised situations without any sign of feedback. We will say that they follow an "idealised information traffic pattern."

This pattern will be labelled: "allocution,"[1] from the Latin word "allocutio" (the address of a Roman general to his troops, and afterwards a special address of the Pope to his cardinals). "Allocution" is more appropriate than the term formerly used, "distribution,"[2] because, inter alia, information cannot be "cut into pieces" distributed among a number of consumers. In fact every participating consumer receives the same information and the information store at the centre never becomes empty!

If we refrain from a particular presentation form or a particular information content, the second figure can be used as a stylised representation of many other situations. For example C might represent a broadcasting organisation and the i's the listeners and viewers. C can also represent a stage performance and the i's the public. In an extreme case C could even represent a drowning person and the i's the passers by.

Characteristic of the "social status" of allocution is that C is the owner of the information and alone decides what part of the information stock will be "handed over" and when. The "destinations" receive the information simultaneously at a

normal human perception rate. The simultaneous-perception effect often plays an important role.

All the "power" is clearly concentrated in C. The i's have none at all. The term "power" in this connection should not be taken too literally. It should be understood as "being entitled to some kind of remuneration." This can be of a financial nature, but can also take the form of obedience, respect, care, help etc. In many cases C will also provide technical facilities as part of the total information service.

A preliminary definition of allocution that covers both the situations described above could run: *the issue of information by an information service centre under programmatic control of the centre itself.*

## Conversation
If two terminals, both representing an average human information services consumer, exchange information, we obtain a different picture. We assume that the ownership of the information as well as the information handling capacities are divided equally between the two terminals. We will name the pattern obtained, independent of the form of presentation and the information content, "conversation." Instead of speech, the information exchanged could just as well be text, written or printed on a sheet of paper or any other carrier, or moving pictures, and could deal with any subject.

Figure 39.3. Conversation: information flow between individual consumers.

The idealised conversation pattern shows a balance of power. In many practical situations, however, the "information levels" of two partners will not be equal. We shall encounter applications that are completely asymmetric. The number of partners in a conversation need not be restricted to two, but above about six the need for a chairman is felt. The chairman has to coordinate and allocate speaking time. One arrives more or less at a situation of sequential allocation. In a conversation situation people do not normally pay one another for the information supplied. They only pay for the use of the means of transport (telephone bill, postage, etc).

One might wonder whether conversation by telephone, which allows almost instantaneous reaction, and conversation by telex or mail should be covered by the same pattern. Our view is that they belong together because the principal social and legal desiderata connected with conversation in a democracy hold equally for telephone and mail services. No state interference and protection of privacy are the two conditions that consumers will demand for both services. The close connection between the two can further be illustrated by observing that modern hybrid services such as voicegram and voicemail are being introduced, combining the presentation form of telephone and the response times of mail.

The conversation pattern is characterised by the property that the ownership of the information as well as the choice of subject and time of information exchange rest in the hands of information service consumers i. This includes a kind of "self-conversation," in which one could include meditation, but also "communication" with a personal (electronic) file, ie all the information stored for personal use.

If such personal utterances are meant to be made public in some way or another the person, (a speaker, an author or a composer) has changed role, is acting as a C-terminal involved in "allocution" or in a pattern dealt with later under the title of "consultation."

In a more general picture of the conversation pattern, the connection between i and $i_1$ passes an information service centre C.

In a classic telephone connection C represents a technical facility: a telephone exchange or a cascade of telephone exchanges needed for the routing of the telephone call and does not participate as an information terminal. In a direct conversation between two people of different tongues, C

Figure 39.4. Conversation via centre C.

could be an interpreter, providing content-oriented services also. In a future world telephone system C could be an (automatic) translation or correction centre. For purposes of data transmission nowadays C could be a packet-switching transmission system in which the data to be transported from different origins and with different destinations are arranged so that transport cost is minimised. These last examples belong to the classes of value-added services or networks.

Generally C can handle more than one conversation-connection, leading to a more general configuration.

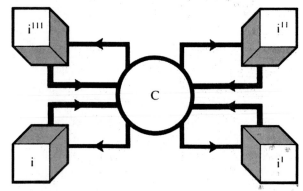

Figure 39.5. Conversation, general pattern.

A preliminary definition of conversation could run: *the issue of information by information services consumer(s) under programmatic control of the consumer(s) themselves.*

## Consultation

If an information service centre C only delivers information upon the request (dotted line) of an information service consumer i, there is a markedly different power relationship from those considered above. C is the owner of a large (ideally infinite) amount of information, but the i-terminal decides at what time and on which subject information should be delivered.

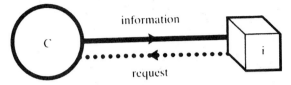

Figure 39.6. Consultation.

In a practical approximation to this idealised situation the i-terminal could be a person who consults a human memory when phoning a doctor or seeing a lawyer, but it could also be a person consulting an encyclopedia, a dictionary or an electronic memory. Consultation requires more activity by the consumer than allocution, but also grants much more freedom in selecting the information required.

Reading books, magazines or newspapers can normally be done at a time convenient to the consumer. A newspaper can be considered as a collection of items that can be "consumed" according to an individual programme, or indeed be marked as a databank refreshed daily (rather than a dynamic one). Reading is not always consultative. A good example of "allocutive reading" can be found in television news magazines for the deaf, with pages broadcast at a standard speed.

Consultation is not restricted to graphic or pictorial information. Examples of voice consultation are found in the telephone enquiry systems for time, weather, traffic conditions or medical information. They are all examples of tele-consultation, like teletext and some videotex applications.

The objection is often made that teletext is not such a good example because the (dotted) request line is missing. In fact, it is present but is very short. The trick with teletext is that the whole information stock of C is periodically offered to the receiving equipment of the consumer. In this way the consumer i disposes of a virtual service centre $C_1$ within the

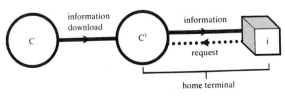

Figure 39.7. Virtual consultation centre C1 (eg teletext terminal).

terminal. (In some configurations $C_1$ is housed in the head-end of a cable television system).

In case the storage capacity of $C_1$ is the same as that of C, a realistic proposition nowadays, the waiting time will be reduced practically to zero. A consultation centre can generally be interrogated by several consumers, giving a more complex configuration.

A preliminary definition of consultation could run: *the issue of information by an information service provider under*

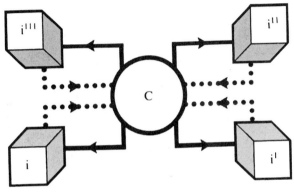

Figure 39.8. Consultation, general pattern.

*programmatic control of an information service consumer.* This definition also embraces the special case in which a consumer requests information to be delivered to another consumer or consumers.

## Registration

If the information flow directions are reversed, we obtain a pattern that we shall call "registration." In this pattern the centre no longer has the task of issuing information, but of

579

collecting it. Modern tele-applications such as tele-opinion polling, tele-metering, tele-alarm, earth observation from satellites and so on can be conceived, but simple well known services like civil registration centres or news agencies follow a good approximation of this pattern.

A second task of such a centre can be to process the incoming information (re-arranging, translation or mathematical operation). The purpose of the processing can be to prepare a publication along either an allocutive or a consultative pattern. But then the centre is changing its role.

Registration is characterised by the fact that the information is owned by the information service consumers, located at the periphery, while the programme (opening hours for each subject!) is controlled by C, the provider of the information service. (It could be said that the centre is consulting the periphery, as opposed to the situation described above where the periphery consults the centre. In older work[2] we therefore used the same term "consultation" for both patterns. In order to avoid confusion we now propose using two different terms).

Sometimes people reject a fire alarm service as a good example of the registration pattern, arguing that the time the fire sets in is not determined by C. But the characterisation given does not claim so: the centre C determines only at what time(s) it will be interested in which subject. A good fire alarm service will be on the alert 24 hours a day, ready for the message "fire" as well as the message "no fire."

A preliminary definition of registration could run: *the issue of information by an information service consumer under the programmatic control of an information service centre.*

We are now in a position to combine the preliminary definitions of the four idealised information traffic patterns: allocution, conversation, consultation and registration, into a single matrix definition. In order to obtain this general matrix definition, we only have to bear in mind that the four preliminary definitions represent exactly the four different combinations of answers to the following two questions:

- is the owner of the information issued an information service providing centre, or an individual information service consumer?

- is the programme of information issue controlled by an information service providing centre C, or by an individual information service consumer?

*Pattern matrix*

|  | Information issue by centre | Information issue by consumer |
|---|---|---|
| Programme control by centre | Allocution | Registration |
| Programme control by consumer | Consultation | Conversation |

Each element of the matrix can comprise a group of different interconnection modes. The members of such a group of interconnection modes all follow the same idealised information traffic pattern. This is more than a flow diagram. It informs us not only about the routes and directions of an information flow, but also about the responsibilities of the information terminals involved. That is why we have a slight preference for the expression "traffic pattern" over "flow pattern."

The pattern matrix can serve as a basis in drawing up a legal framework. It does not of course solve the problem of whether, how or to what extent the interests of operators and clients of tele-information systems should be protected by law. That is a matter for political discussion and decision. But it must be expected that for all services which follow one and the same information traffic pattern, similar action will be considered relevant because the four patterns refer to four mutually exclusive social power relations that differ from one another in principle.

It should not be inferred that certain patterns may not have some regulatory aspects in common. As Jens Arnbak[3] has pointed out, we may even expect that possible laws adopted for one pattern will overlap with those for "neighbouring" patterns:

- copyright issues are generally confined to the left-hand column of the matrix

- the protection of privacy is relevant to the right-hand column

- formal public access and control procedures will usually be needed or appropriate in the upper row

- the free flow of information is generally served by minimising state interference in services belonging in the lower row.

In this way each element of the matrix lies at the crossing of two lines of desiderata. The systematic approach thus obtained immediately clarifies the social and legal position

of old and new information services, which follow
sufficiently closely one of the four idealised information
traffic patterns.

Many practical information services, however, do not
follow a single pattern to the total exclusion of the others.
Moreover, in daily life many centres will operate
simultaneously, functioning and competing within a complex
communication structure with lots of cross-connections, in
which the idealised information traffic patterns will only
play the role of building blocks. Therefore, in application of
the foregoing theory, we shall deal with some multi-pattern
services, the development of multi-pattern networks and the
relation between the two phenomena.

From these examples it will, we hope, become clear how
important it is to classify information services as correctly as
possible according to their social and, from that standpoint,
their legal position, and not according to the incidental
technology that they employ, their form of presentation or
their information content.

## Multi-pattern Services

The matrix definition offers a sharp demarcation between
the four areas of "idealised information services." The
borderlines between actual (tele-) information services will
not always be so clear cut. Some information services are
typical of a multi-pattern type, ie that several patterns occur
almost simultaneously. Sometimes a number of patterns will
occur in alternation. In other situations the presence of more
than one provider centre plays a role.

Broadcasting presents a good approximation to an
idealised allocution pattern. But for the viewer it makes all
the difference whether there is a large group of TV channels
from different centres with a broad range of programmes, or
whether choice is restricted to one or two channels of similar
quality.

If, moreover, in the first case some of the channels carry
programmes that are frequently repeated, so that the
consumer has a certain influence on the time of
"consumption," we can say that the service shows
consultative features.

Another example of a diffuse pattern is encountered when
a talented (political) orator in a direct address transforms his
"allocution" more or less into "registration" by only
forwarding rhetorical questions and after each sentence
waiting for applause.

Conversely, a consultation service may possess strong
allocutive features. A newspaper, for example, can be
considered as a kind of databank that is consulted by each
reader according to a personal programme. But the fact that
so many people are confronted with centrally selected
headlines reduces the influence of the consumer
considerably.

Another instructive example can be found in the telephone
service. Although it offers an almost ideal example of the
conversation pattern, we have to admit that two other
patterns also play a role. A telephone call is initiated by
dialling a number. That number has to be found by
"consultation" be it from a directory, a voice-based enquiry
service or an electronic directory. At the end of the call, the
distance and duration have to be "registered" in order to
enable the telephone service provider to recover charges.

As a consequence, a telephone service provider also has to
pay heed to copyright issues and registration regulations. If a
connection with a mobile station has to be built up, the
service provider is involved in a further privacy problem: the
approximate position of the mobile station has to be known
to him.

In this case it is clear that conversation is the main or
primary pattern and that consultation and registration play
a secondary role. But telephone systems lend themselves to
other patterns than conversation alone. The technical
properties are not very pattern-selective.

Finally, we might refer to an age-old information service
that is typically multi-pattern in character: education. A
teacher lecturing is clearly operating in allocution mode. But
pupils putting questions to their teacher or studying books
are working in consultation mode. A teacher trying to
measure the progress of pupils by subjecting them to
examination applies a registration mode. And pupils
discussing the subject matter among themselves follow a
conversation mode. The four modes are roughly of the same
weight. This implies that for a complete tele-education
system a multi-pattern network is inevitable, and contains a
warning for those broadcasters who believe that tele-
education is their exclusive domain.

## Multi-pattern Networks

As long as the recognised specialists in certain kinds of tele-
information services operate their own strongly differing
technical systems, there exists no great need for a new

581

classification of tele-information services. And that has been the situation up to the present day: telephone and broadcasting use their own service-dedicated technical solutions.

But today a strong trend towards the setting up of multifunctional, or perhaps better, multi-pattern networks is also making itself felt. European telephone administrations are working hand in hand in order to unite telephone, telex and data networks into one so-called integrated services digital network (ISDN), to be implemented in the coming decade. Several studies have been started on the possible coupling of local wideband networks (cable TV, local area networks) with the ISDN. Even satellite communication will play a role in this context.

This means that it will become increasingly difficult to characterise a tele-information service on the basis of the technical appearance of the network or terminal equipment used. We may expect more and more multi-pattern terminal equipment to appear on the market. Already existing networks originally designed for only one of the patterns are provisionally used for others. The same applies to terminal equipment. Teletext and videotex are two well known examples of an alternative use of video equipment, which leads to misunderstanding and disputes between broadcasting and PTT monopolies.

Here we touch upon the very reason to review our classification system. With teletext as well as with videotex we run the risk that technology plays the role of the Trojan horse.

Neither consultation nor registration services need technical transport systems and terminal equipment of a completely new character. They differ strongly from the classic telephone and broadcasting services but largely in a non-technical sense. Consultation, for example, is the "bread and butter line" for press and other publishers who disclose information stored on paper or other "artificial memories." It seems not illogical that the legislation in existence for these publishing activities will also be applicable to tele-consultation services. To subject these services to telephone or broadcasting regulation on the ground that they make use of similar networks and terminal equipment would be a grave mistake.

The analysis presented in this paper rests on social power relations but is in fact politically neutral. No political programme of action can be derived from the pattern theory. It improves insight and facilitates a more systematic

approach to legislation. It contains no prescriptions for specific laws.

It should be realised, however, that the fact that the classification in traffic patterns does not depend on technological properties does not imply that technical developments and technical management may not exercise a certain influence on the relative balance of the four different patterns. The history of the art of printing proves that such influences can even be very marked. Governments can greatly influence specific activities by promoting or retarding certain technical developments, as with cable television and the restrictions often placed on alternative use of these networks.

The pattern theory provides the yardstick by which to check whether governments follow a pattern-neutral course or not. It is obvious that under a dictatorial regime such a neutral course will not be found. Adolf Hitler, for example, had a notorious dislike for books, in fact, for consultation. He even made apologies for writing *Mein Kampf*. And of course he loved allocation, be it by personal address, by radio or by means of the cinema.

But we should not conclude this reflection on a downbeat. For each example of abuse of the power position inevitably connected with a centre of allocution we can find numerous cases in which allocution is put forth as a means of reaching the masses with messages of understanding and tolerance.

International broadcasting in particular bears a great responsibility in this respect and should be constantly on the look-out for positive opportunities. Yet the main ambition of broadcasters should perhaps be to resist any temptation to acquire some kind of hegemony over the other patterns.

## References

1. J.L. Bordewijk and B. van Kaam, *Allocutie,* Bosch en Keuning, Baarn, 1982, p. 104.

2. J.L. Bordewijk, "The combined use of CATV—and telephone networks for purposes of education and consultation," in *Two-Way Cable Television,* edited by W. Kaiser et al, Springer, Heidelberg, 1977.

3. J.C. Arnbak, "Potential impacts of modern communication technology on data protection," Document CJ-PD(85)4, Council of Europe, Strasbourg, 17 April 1985.

# IV

## Revolution,
## Resistance, and
## the Launch of the Web

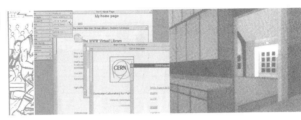

# 40. [Introduction]
# Mythinformation

Positive social change won't come about as an inevitable result of the increasing use of computers. However, this hasn't always been clear to those enamored of this century's "computer revolution"—such as those Langdon Winner takes to task in the essay reprinted here. For positive social change to take place it will have to be advocated and fought for. In order to fight for a goal, it is necessary to articulate it.

Winner begins by taking the rhetoric of the computer revolution at face value—asking what the social goals of this revolution will be, and whether regular elections will be held. He does this in order to point out the complete lack of a coherent social program on the part of self-styled computer revolutionaries. In the time since his article was written, issues such as free and open elections have become literal points of conflict in computer circles, as with ICANN. (This is discussed further in this volume's introduction to the essay by Raymond Williams (◊20).)

Winner later demolishes the mythology that "(1) people are bereft of information; (2) information is knowledge; (3) knowledge is power; and (4) increasing access to information enhances democracy and equalizes social power." Winner quotes J. C. R. Licklider as looking forward to "an information environment that would give politics greater depth and dimension than it now has." ICANN shows that a body steeped in the new technologies can still be profoundly undemocratic. On the other hand, the technologies of the Internet have also provided the ground on which resistance to ICANN has been assembled. An advocate of the computer revolution might therefore argue that increasing access to information has enhanced democracy and equalized social power; ICANN can't get away with the sort of crooked politics that might have been invisible in an earlier era. Counter-arguments to this are close at hand, however: the 2000 U.S. presidential election, for example, was the first in which the Internet was accessible to such large sections of the electorate, and also was the most crooked in recent history. Information about the unfairness of the election was made available on the Internet by the NAACP and others, but this information did not make the outcome any more fair.

The transitions accompanying computer technologies may have some democratizing potential—but this potential must be identified and worked toward. It will not be realized automatically. While Winner's essay is often viewed as a harsh critique of the new media field, it seems likely that new media pioneers such as Doug Engelbart and Ted Nelson would agree with its basic argument. Engelbart felt the stand-alone workstation (without connection to a network) was precisely the wrong direction for technological development, unlikely to empower groups and communities in any significant way—even as the computer press hyped its potential for individual empowerment. Nelson's "cybercrud" anticipated much of Winner's argument—if computer technologies and the companies that develop them are simply allowed to run along in their own direction, the result will not be empowerment for the average individual, nor will it be increased democracy for our culture. However, because both Engelbart and Nelson wrote so much about hope for the future, it is often forgotten that they believed this hoped-for future would not come about on its own.

The three concerns outlined at the close of this paper remain among the most-discussed new media issues in recent years: the surveillance state and accompanying self-surveillance now often called "panopticism" (see the introduction to Phil Agre's (◊51) essay in this volume), the alteration of patterns of human sociability (which largely still lack serious study, despite their common mention), and the mobility and unlocatability of power that is now often called "rhizomatic" (see introductions to essays by the Critical Art Ensemble (◊53) and by Gilles Deleuze and Félix Guattari (◊27)). Given that this essay was written when the Macintosh was new and most of today's new media was many technologic "generations" in the future, it seems evident that the central issues, and therefore the goals for which we might fight, are potentially visible through the continual swirl of product announcements and information-age hype. However, once we choose to look at these issues, waiting with boundless faith for the revolution may no longer seem a viable option.

—NWF

◊05 73

Another view of new media technology's relation to our social systems and beliefs through the lens of "revolution" is presented in Stuart Moulthrop's essay in this anthology (◊48).

◊20 289

An essay by Licklider—not the one one Winner quotes, but one that deals with the computer as enhancing human thought and collaborative activity—is included in this book (◊05).

◊27 405

**587**

◊48 691

◊51 737

◊53 781

Further Reading

Jasanoff, Sheila, Gerald Markle, James Petersen, and Trevor Pinch, eds. *Handbook of Science and Technology Studies.* Thousand Oaks, Calif.: Sage, 1994.

Mumford, Lewis. *Technics and Civilization.* New York: Harcourt Brace and World, 1934.

Winner, Langdon. "Upon Opening the Black Box and Finding it Empty: Social Constructivism and the Philosophy of Technology." *Science, Technology and Human Values* 18(3):362–378. 1993.

Original Publication

*The Whale and the Reactor: A Search for Limits in an Age of High Technology*, 98–117. Chicago: University of Chicago Press, 1986.

# Mythinformation
## Langdon Winner

> Computer power to the people is essential to the realization of a future in which most citizens are informed about, and interested and involved in, the processes of government.
> —J. C. R. Licklider

In nineteenth-century Europe a recurring ceremonial gesture signaled the progress of popular uprisings. At the point at which it seemed that forces of disruption in the streets were sufficiently powerful to overthrow monarchical authority, a prominent rebel leader would go to the parliament or city hall to "proclaim the republic." This was an indication to friend and foe alike that a revolution was prepared to take its work seriously, to seize power and begin governing in a way that guaranteed political representation to all the people. Subsequent events, of course, did not always match these grand hopes; on occasion the revolutionaries were thwarted in their ambitions and reactionary governments regained control. Nevertheless, what a glorious moment when the republic was declared! Here, if only briefly, was the promise of a new order—an age of equality, justice, and emancipation of humankind.

A somewhat similar gesture has become a standard feature in contemporary writings on computers and society. In countless books, magazine articles, and media specials some intrepid soul steps forth to proclaim "the revolution." Often it is called simply "the computer revolution"; my brief inspection of a library catalogue revealed three books with exactly that title published since 1962.[1] Other popular variants include the "information revolution," "microelectronics revolution," and "network revolution." But whatever its label, the message is usually the same. The use of computers and advanced communications technologies is producing a sweeping set of transformations in every corner of social life. An informal consensus among computer scientists, social scientists, and journalists affirms the term "revolution" as the concept best suited to describe these events. "We are all very privileged," a noted computer scientist declares, "to be in this great Information Revolution in which the computer is going to affect us very profoundly, probably more so than the Industrial Revolution."[2] A well-known sociologist writes, "This revolution in the organization and processing of information and knowledge, in which the computer plays a central role, has as its context the development of what I have called the postindustrial society."[3] At frequent intervals during the past dozen years, garish cover stories in *Time* and *Newsweek* have repeated this story, climaxed by *Time*'s selection of the computer as its "Man of the Year" for 1982.

Of course, the same society now said to be undergoing a computer revolution has long since gotten used to "revolutions" in laundry detergents, underarm deodorants, floor waxes, and other consumer products. Exhausted in Madison Avenue advertising slogans, the image has lost much of its punch. Those who employ it to talk about computers and society, however, appear to be making much more serious claims. They offer a powerful metaphor, one that invites us to compare the kind of disruptions seen in political revolutions to the changes we see happening around computer information systems. Let us take that invitation seriously and see where it leads.

## A Metaphor Explored

Suppose that we were looking at a revolution in a Third World country, the revolution of the Sandinistas in Nicaragua, for example. We would want to begin by studying the fundamental goals of the revolution. Is this a movement truly committed to social justice? Does it seek to uphold a valid ideal of human freedom? Does it aspire to a system of democratic rule? Answers to those questions would help us decide whether or not this is a revolution worthy of our endorsement. By the same token, we would want to ask about the means the revolutionaries had chosen to pursue their goals. Having succeeded in armed struggle, how will they manage violence and military force once they gain control? A reasonable person would also want to learn something of the structure of institutional authority that the revolution will try to create. Will there be frequent, open elections? What systems of decision making, administration, and law enforcement will be put to work? Coming to terms with its proposed ends and means, a sympathetic observer could then watch the revolution unfold, noticing whether or not it remained true to its professed purposes and how well it succeeded in its reforms.

Most dedicated revolutionaries of the modern age have been willing to supply coherent public answers to questions of this sort. It is not unreasonable to expect, therefore, that something like these issues must have engaged those who so eagerly use the metaphor "revolution" to describe and celebrate the advent of computerization. Unfortunately, this is not the case. Books, articles, and media specials aimed at a popular audience are usually content to depict the dazzling magnitude of technical innovations and social effects. Written as if by some universally accepted format, such accounts describe scores of new computer products and processes, announce the enormous dollar value of the growing computer and communications industry, survey the expanding uses of computers in offices, factories, schools, and homes, and offer good news from research and development laboratories about the great promise of the next generation of computing devices. Along with this one reads of the many "impacts" that computerization is going to have on every sphere of life. Professionals in widely separate fields—doctors, lawyers, corporate managers, and scientists—comment on the changes computers have brought to their work. Home consumers give testimonials explaining how personal computers are helping educate their children, prepare their income tax forms, and file their recipes. On occasion, this generally happy story will include reports on people left unemployed in occupations undermined by automation. Almost always, following this formula, there will be an obligatory sentence or two of criticism of the computer culture solicited from a technically qualified spokesman, an attempt to add balance to an otherwise totally sanguine outlook.

Unfortunately, the prevalence of such superficial, unreflective descriptions and forecasts about computerization cannot be attributed solely to hasty journalism. Some of the most prestigious journals of the scientific community echo the claim that a revolution is in the works.[4] A well-known computer scientist has announced unabashedly that "revolution, transformation and salvation are all to be carried out."[5] It is true that more serious approaches to the study of computers and society can be found in scholarly publications. A number of social scientists, computer scientists, and philosophers have begun to explore important issues about how computerization works and what developments, positive and negative, it is likely to bring to society.[6] But such careful, critical studies are by no means the ones most influential in shaping public attitudes about the world of microelectronics. An editor at a New York publishing house stated the norm, "People want to know what's new with computer technology. They don't want to know what could go wrong."[7]

It seems all but impossible for computer enthusiasts to examine critically the *ends* that might guide the world-shaking developments they anticipate. They employ the metaphor of revolution for one purpose only—to suggest a drastic upheaval, one that people ought to welcome as good news. It never occurs to them to investigate the idea or its meaning any further.

One might suppose, for example, that a revolution of this type would involve a significant shift in the locus of power; after all, that is exactly what one expects in revolutions of a political kind. Is something similar going to happen in this instance?

One might also ask whether or not this revolution will be strongly committed, as revolutions often are, to a particular set of social ideals. If so, what are the ideals that matter? Where can we see them argued?

To mention revolution also brings to mind the relationships of different social classes. Will the computer

589

revolution bring about the victory of one class over another? Will it be the occasion for a realignment of class loyalties?

In the busy world of computer science, computer engineering, and computer marketing such questions seldom come up. Those actively engaged in promoting the transformation—hardware and software engineers, managers of microelectronics firms, computer salesmen, and the like—are busy pursuing their own ends: profits, market share, handsome salaries, the intrinsic joy of invention, the intellectual rewards of programming, and the pleasures of owning and using powerful machines. But the sheer dynamism of technical and economic activity in the computer industry evidently leaves its members little time to ponder the historical significance of their own activity. They must struggle to keep current, to be on the crest of the next wave as it breaks. As one member of Data General's Eagle computer project describes it, the prevailing spirit resembles a game of pinball. "You win one game, you get to play another. You win with this machine, you get to build the next."[8] The process has its own inertia.

Hence, one looks in vain to the movers and shakers in computer fields for the qualities of social and political insight that characterized revolutionaries of the past. Too busy. Cromwell, Jefferson, Robespierre, Lenin, and Mao were able to reflect upon the world historical events in which they played a role. Public pronouncements by the likes of Robert Noyce, Marvin Minsky, Edward Feigenbaum, and Steven Jobs show no similar wisdom about the transformations they so actively help to create. By and large the computer revolution is conspicuously silent about its own ends.

## Good Console, Good Network, Good Computer

My concern for the political meaning of revolution in this setting may seem somewhat misleading, even perverse. A much better point of reference might be the technical "revolutions" and associated social upheavals of the past, the industrial revolution in particular. If the enthusiasts of computerization had readily taken up this comparison, studying earlier historical periods for similarities and differences in patterns of technological innovation, capital formation, employment, social change, and the like, then it would be clear that I had chosen the wrong application of this metaphor. But, in fact, no well-developed comparisons of that kind are to be found in the writings on the computer revolution. A consistently ahistorical viewpoint prevails. What one often finds emphasized, however, is a vision of drastically altered social and political conditions, a future upheld as both desirable and, in all likelihood, inevitable. Politics, in other words, is not a secondary concern for many computer enthusiasts; it is a crucial, albeit thoughtless, part of their message.

We are, according to a fairly standard account, moving into an age characterized by the overwhelming dominance of electronic information systems in all areas of human practice. Industrial society, which depended upon material production for its livelihood, is rapidly being supplanted by a society of information services that will enable people to satisfy their economic and social needs. What water- and steam-powered machines were to the industrial age, the computer will be to the era now dawning. Ever-expanding technical capacities in computation and communications will make possible a universal, instantaneous access to enormous quantities of valuable information. As these technologies become less and less expensive and more and more convenient, all the people of the world, not just the wealthy, will be able to use the wonderful services that information machines make available. Gradually, existing differences between rich and poor, advantaged and disadvantaged, will begin to evaporate. Widespread access to computers will produce a society more democratic, egalitarian, and richly diverse than any previously known. Because "knowledge is power," because electronic information will spread knowledge into every corner of world society, political influence will be much more widely shared. With the personal computer serving as the great equalizer, rule by centralized authority and social class dominance will gradually fade away. The marvelous promise of a "global village" will be fulfilled in a worldwide burst of human creativity.

A sampling from recent writings on the information society illustrates these grand expectations.

> The world is entering a new period. The wealth of nations, which depended upon land, labor, and capital during its agricultural and industrial phases— depended upon natural resources, the accumulation of money, and even upon weaponry—will come in the future to depend upon information, knowledge and intelligence.[9]

· · ·

The electronic revolution will not do away with work, but it does hold out some promises: Most boring jobs can be done by machines; lengthy commuting can be avoided; we can have enough leisure to follow interesting pursuits outside our work; environmental destruction can be avoided; the opportunities for personal creativity will be unlimited.[10]

Long lists of specific services spell out the utopian promise of this new age: interactive television, electronic funds transfer, computer-aided instruction, customized news service, electronic magazines, electronic mail, computer teleconferencing, on-line stock market and weather reports, computerized Yellow Pages, shopping via home computer, and so forth. All of it is supposed to add up to a cultural renaissance.

> Whatever the limits to growth in other fields, there are no limits near in telecommunications and electronic technology. There are no limits near in the consumption of information, the growth of culture, or the development of the human mind.[11]

· · ·

> Computer-based communications can be used to make human lives richer and freer, by enabling persons to have access to vast stores of information, other "human resources," and opportunities for work and socializing on a more flexible, cheaper and convenient basis than ever before.[12]

· · ·

> When such systems become widespread, potentially intense communications networks among geographically dispersed persons will become actualized. We will become Network Nation, exchanging vast amounts of information and social and emotional communications with colleagues, friends and "strangers" who share similar interests, who are spread all over the nation.[13]

· · ·

> A rich diversity of subcultures will be fostered by computer-based communications systems. Social, political, technical changes will produce conditions likely to lead to the formation of groups with their own distinctive sets of values, activities, language and dress.[14]

According to this view, the computer revolution will, by its sheer momentum, eliminate many of the ills that have vexed political society since the beginning of time. Inequalities of wealth and privilege will gradually fade away. One writer predicts that computer networks will "offer major opportunities to disadvantaged groups to acquire the skills and social ties they need to become full members of society."[15] Another looks forward to "a revolutionary network where each node is equal in power to all others."[16] Information will become the dominant form of wealth. Because it can flow so quickly, so freely through computer networks, it will not, in this interpretation, cause the kinds of stratification associated with traditional forms of property. Obnoxious forms of social organization will also be replaced. "The computer will smash the pyramid," one best-selling book proclaims. "We created the hierarchical, pyramidal, managerial system because we needed it to keep track of people and things people did; with the computer to keep track, we can restructure our institutions horizontally."[17] Thus, the proliferation of electronic information will generate a leveling effect to surpass the dreams of history's great social reformers.

The same viewpoint holds that the prospects for participatory democracy have never been brighter. According to one group of social scientists, "The form of democracy found in the ancient Greek city-state, the Israeli kibbutz, and the New England town meeting, which gave every citizen the opportunity to directly participate in the political process, has become impractical in America's mass society. But this need not be the case. The technological means exist through which millions of people can enter into dialogue with one another and with their representatives, and can form the authentic consensus essential for democracy."[18]

Computer scientist J. C. R. Licklider of the Massachusetts Institute of Technology is one advocate especially hopeful about a revitalization of the democratic process. He looks forward to "an information environment that would give politics greater depth and dimension than it now has." Home computer consoles and television sets would be linked together in a massive network. "The political process would essentially be a giant teleconference, and a campaign would be a months-long series of communications among candidates, propagandists, commentators, political action groups and voters." An arrangement of this kind would, in his view, encourage a more open, comprehensive examination of both issues and candidates. "The information revolution," he exclaims, "is bringing with it a key that may open the door to

591

a new era of involvement and participation. The key is the self-motivating exhilaration that accompanies truly effective interaction with information through a good console through a good network to a good computer."[19] It is, in short, a democracy of machines.

Taken as a whole, beliefs of this kind constitute what I would call mythinformation: the almost religious conviction that a widespread adoption of computers and communications systems along with easy access to electronic information will automatically produce a better world for human living. It is a peculiar form of enthusiasm that characterizes social fashions of the latter decades of the twentieth century. Many people who have grown cynical or discouraged about other aspects of social life are completely enthralled by the supposed redemptive qualities of computers and telecommunications. Writing of the "fifth generation" supercomputers, Japanese author Yoneji Masuda rhapsodically predicts "freedom for each of us to set individual goals of self-realization and then perhaps a worldwide religious renaissance, characterized not by a belief in a supernatural god, but rather by awe and humility in the presence of the collective human spirit and its wisdom, humanity living in a symbolic tranquility with the planet we have found ourselves upon, regulated by a new set of global ethics."[20]

It is not uncommon for the advent of a new technology to provide an occasion for flights of utopian fancy. During the last two centuries the factory system, railroads, telephone, electricity, automobile, airplane, radio, television, and nuclear power have all figured prominently in the belief that a new and glorious age was about to begin. But even within the great tradition of optimistic technophilia, current dreams of a "computer age" stand out as exaggerated and unrealistic. Because they have such a broad appeal, because they overshadow other ways of looking at the matter, these notions deserve closer inspection.

## The Great Equalizer

As is generally true of a myth, the story contains elements of truth. What were once industrial societies are being transformed into service economies, a trend that emerges as more material production shifts to developing countries where labor costs are low and business tax breaks lucrative. At the same time that industrialization takes hold in less-developed nations of the world, deindustrialization is gradually altering the economies of North America and Europe. Some of the service industries central to this pattern are ones that depend upon highly sophisticated computer and communications systems. But this does not mean that future employment possibilities will flow largely from the microelectronics industry and information services. A number of studies, including those of the U.S. Bureau of Labor Statistics, suggest that the vast majority of new jobs will come in menial service occupations paying relatively low wages.[21] As robots and computer software absorb an increasing share of factory and office tasks, the "information society" will offer plenty of opportunities for janitors, hospital orderlies, and fast-food waiters.

The computer romantics are also correct in noting that computerization alters relationships of social power and control, although they misrepresent the direction this development is likely to take. Those who stand to benefit most obviously are large transnational business corporations. While their "global reach" does not arise solely from the application of information technologies, such organizations are uniquely situated to exploit the efficiency, productivity, command, and control the new electronics make available. Other notable beneficiaries of the systematic use of vast amounts of digitized information are public bureaucracies, intelligence agencies, and an ever-expanding military, organizations that would operate less effectively at their present scale were it not for the use of computer power. Ordinary people are, of course, strongly affected by the workings of these organizations and by the rapid spread of new electronic systems in banking, insurance, taxation, factory and office work, home entertainment, and the like. They are also counted upon to be eager buyers of hardware, software, and communications services as computer products reach the consumer market.

But where in all of this motion do we see increased democratization? Social equality? The dawn of a cultural renaissance? Current developments in the information age suggest an increase in power by those who already had a great deal of power, an enhanced centralization of control by those already prepared for control, an augmentation of wealth by the already wealthy. Far from demonstrating a revolution in patterns of social and political influence, empirical studies of computers and social change usually show powerful groups adapting computerized methods to retain control.[22] That is not surprising. Those best situated to take advantage of the power of a new technology are often those previously well situated by dint of wealth, social standing, and institutional position. Thus, if there is to be a computer revolution, the best guess is that it will have a distinctly conservative character.

Granted, such prominent trends could be altered. It is possible that a society strongly rooted in computer and telecommunications systems could be one in which participatory democracy, decentralized political control, and social equality are fully realized. Progress of that kind would have to occur as the result of that society's concerted efforts to overcome many difficult obstacles to achieve those ends. Computer enthusiasts, however, seldom propose deliberate action of that kind. Instead, they strongly suggest that the good society will be realized as a side effect, a spin-off from the vast proliferation of computing devices. There is evidently no need to try to shape the institutions of the information age in ways that maximize human freedom while placing limits upon concentrations of power.

For those willing to wait passively while the computer revolution takes its course, technological determinism ceases to be mere theory and becomes an ideal: a desire to embrace conditions brought on by technological change without judging them in advance. There is nothing new in this disposition. Computer romanticism is merely the latest version of the nineteenth- and twentieth-century faith we noted earlier, one that has always expected to generate freedom, democracy, and justice through sheer material abundance. Thus there is no need for serious inquiry into the appropriate design of new institutions or the distribution of rewards and burdens. As long as the economy is growing and the machinery in good working order, the rest will take care of itself. In previous versions of this homespun conviction, the abundant (and therefore democratic) society was manifest by a limitless supply of houses, appliances, and consumer goods.[23] Now "access to information" and "access to computers" have moved to the top of the list.

The political arguments of computer romantics draw upon a number of key assumptions: (1) people are bereft of information; (2) information is knowledge; (3) knowledge is power; and (4) increasing access to information enhances democracy and equalizes social power. Taken as separate assertions and in combination, these beliefs provide a woefully distorted picture of the role of electronic systems in social life.

Is it true that people face serious shortages of information? To read the literature on the computer revolution one would suppose this to be a problem on a par with the energy crisis of the 1970s. The persuasiveness of this notion borrows from our sense that literacy, education, knowledge, well-informed minds, and the widespread availability of tools of inquiry are unquestionable social goods, and that, in contrast, illiteracy, inadequate education, ignorance, and forced restrictions upon knowledge are among history's worst evils. Thus, it appears superficially plausible that a world rewired to connect human beings to vast data banks and communications systems would be a progressive step. Information shortage would be remedied in much the same way that developing a new fuel supply might solve an energy crisis.

Alas, the idea is entirely faulty. It mistakes sheer supply of information with an educated ability to gain knowledge and act effectively based on that knowledge. In many parts of the world that ability is sadly lacking. Even some highly developed societies still contain chronic inequalities in the distribution of good education and basic intellectual skills. The U.S. Army, for instance, must now reject or dismiss a fairly high percentage of the young men and women it recruits because they simply cannot read military manuals. It is no doubt true of these recruits that they have a great deal of information about the world—information from their life experiences, schooling, the mass media, and so forth. What makes them "functionally illiterate" is that they have not learned to translate this information into a mastery of practical skills.

If the solution to problems of illiteracy and poor education were a question of information supply alone, then the best policy might be to increase the number of well-stocked libraries, making sure they were built in places where libraries do not presently exist. Of course, that would do little good in itself unless people are sufficiently well educated to use those libraries to broaden their knowledge and understanding. Computer enthusiasts however, are not noted for their calls to increase support of public libraries and schools. It is *electronic information* carried by *networks* they uphold as crucial. Here is a case in which an obsession with a particular kind of technology causes one to disregard what are obvious problems and clear remedies. While it is true that systems of computation and communications, intelligently structured and wisely applied, might help a society raise its standards of

593

literacy, education, and general knowledgeability, to look to those instruments first while ignoring how to enlighten and invigorate a human mind is pure foolishness.

"As everybody knows, knowledge is power."[24] This is an attractive idea, but highly misleading. Of course, knowledge employed in particular circumstances can help one act effectively and in that sense enhance one's power. A citrus farmer's knowledge of frost conditions enables him/her to take steps to prevent damage to the crop. A candidate's knowledge of public opinion can be a powerful aid in an election campaign. But surely there is no automatic, positive link between knowledge and power, especially if that means power in a social or political sense. At times knowledge brings merely an enlightened impotence or paralysis. One may know exactly what to do but lack the wherewithal to act. Of the many conditions that affect the phenomenon of power, knowledge is but one and by no means the most important. Thus, in the history of ideas, arguments that expert knowledge ought to play a special role in politics—the philosopher-kings for Plato, the engineers for Veblen—have always been offered as something contrary to prevailing wisdom. To Plato and Veblen it was obvious that knowledge was *not* power, a situation they hoped to remedy.

An equally serious misconception among computer enthusiasts is the belief that democracy is first and foremost a matter of distributing information. As one particularly flamboyant manifesto exclaims: "There is an explosion of information dispersal in the technology and we think this information has to be shared. All great thinkers about democracy said that the key to democracy is access to information. And now we have a chance to get information into people's hands like never before."[25] Once again such assertions play on our belief that a democratic public ought to be open-minded and well informed. One of the great evils of totalitarian societies is that they dictate what people can know and impose secrecy to restrict freedom. But democracy is not founded solely (or even primarily) upon conditions that affect the availability of information. What distinguishes it from other political forms is a recognition that the people as a whole are capable of self-government and that they have a rightful claim to rule. As a consequence, political society ought to build institutions that allow or even encourage a great latitude of democratic participation. How far a society must go in making political authority and public roles available to ordinary people is a matter of dispute among political theorists. But no serious

student of the question would give much credence to the idea that creating a universal gridwork to spread electronic information is, by itself, a democratizing step.

What, then, of the idea that "interaction with information through a good console, through a good network to a good computer" will promote a renewed sense of political involvement and participation? Readers who believe that assertion should contact me about some parcels of land my uncle has for sale in Florida. Relatively low levels of citizen participation prevail in some modern democracies, the United States, for example. There are many reasons for this, many ways a society might try to improve things. Perhaps opportunities to serve in public office or influence public policy are too limited; in that case, broaden the opportunities. Or perhaps choices placed before citizens are so pallid that boredom is a valid response; in that instance, improve the quality of those choices. But it is simply not reasonable to assume that enthusiasm for political activity will be stimulated solely by the introduction of sophisticated information machines.

The role that television plays in modern politics should suggest why this is so. Public participation in voting has steadily declined as television replaced the face-to-face politics of precincts and neighborhoods. Passive monitoring of electronic news and information allows citizens to feel involved while dampening the desire to take an active part. If people begin to rely upon computerized data bases and telecommunications as a primary means of exercising power, it is conceivable that genuine political knowledge based in first-hand experience would vanish altogether. The vitality of democratic politics depends upon people's willingness to act together in pursuit of their common ends. It requires that on occasion members of a community appear before each other in person, speak their minds, deliberate on paths of action, and decide what they will do.[26] This is considerably different from the model now upheld as a breakthrough for democracy: logging onto one's computer, receiving the latest information, and sending back an instantaneous digitized response.

A chapter from recent political history illustrates the strength of direct participation in contrast to the politics of electronic information. In 1981 and 1982 two groups of activists set about to do what they could to stop the international nuclear arms race. One of the groups, Ground Zero, chose to rely almost solely upon mass communications to convey its message to the public. Its leaders appeared on morning talk shows and evening news programs on all three major television networks. They followed up with a mass mail solicitation using addresses from a computerized data base. At the same time another group, the Nuclear Weapons Freeze Campaign, began by taking its proposal for a bilateral nuclear freeze to New England town meetings, places where active citizen participation is a long-standing tradition. Winning the endorsement of the idea from a great many town meetings, the Nuclear Freeze group expanded its drive by launching a series of state initiatives. Once again the key was a direct approach to people, this time through thousands of meetings, dinners, and parties held in homes across the country.

The effects of the two movements were strikingly different. After its initial publicity, Ground Zero was largely ignored. It had been an ephemeral exercise in media posturing. The Nuclear Freeze campaign, however, continued to gain influence in the form of increasing public support, successful ballot measures, and an ability to apply pressure upon political officials. Eventually, the latter group did begin to use computerized mailings, television appearances, and the like to advance its cause. But it never forgot the original source of its leverage: people working together for shared ends.

Of all the computer enthusiasts' political ideas, there is none more poignant than the faith that the computer is destined to become a potent equalizer in modern society. Support for this belief is found in the fact that small "personal" computers are becoming more and more powerful, less and less expensive, and ever more simple to use. Obnoxious tendencies associated with the enormous, costly, technically inaccessible computers of the recent past are soon to be overcome. As one writer explains, "The great forces of centralization that characterized mainframe and minicomputer design of that period have now been reversed." This means that "the puny device that sits innocuously on the desktop will, in fact, within a few years, contain enough computing power to become an effective equalizer."[27] Presumably, ordinary citizens equipped with micro-computers will be able to counter the influence of large, computer-based organizations.

Notions of this kind echo beliefs of eighteenth- and nineteenth-century revolutionaries that placing fire arms in the hands of the people was crucial to overthrowing entrenched authority. In the American Revolution, French Revolution, Paris Commune, and Russian Revolution the role of "the people armed" was central to the revolutionary

program. As the military defeat of the Paris Commune made clear, however, the fact that the popular forces have guns may not be decisive. In a contest of force against force, the larger, more sophisticated, more ruthless, better equipped competitor often has the upper hand. Hence, the availability of low-cost computing power may move the baseline that defines electronic dimensions of social influence, but it does not necessarily alter the relative balance of power. Using a personal computer makes one no more powerful *vis-à-vis*, say, the National Security Agency than flying a hang glider establishes a person as a match for the U.S. Air Force.

In sum, the political expectations of computer enthusiasts are seldom more than idle fantasy. Beliefs that widespread use of computers will cause hierarchies to crumble, inequality to tumble, participation to flourish, and centralized power to dissolve simply do not withstand close scrutiny. The formula information = knowledge = power = democracy lacks any real substance. At each point the mistake comes in the conviction that computerization will inevitably move society toward the good life. And no one will have to raise a finger.

## Information and Ideology

Despite its shortcomings as political theory, mythinformation is noteworthy as an expressive contemporary ideology. I use the term "ideology" here in a sense common in social science: a set of beliefs that expresses the needs and aspirations of a group, class, culture, or subculture. In this instance the needs and aspirations that matter most are those that stem from operational requirements of highly complex systems in an advanced technological society; the groups most directly involved are those who build, maintain, operate, improve, and market these systems. At a time in which almost all major components of our technological society have come to depend upon the application of large and small computers, it is not surprising that computerization has risen to ideological prominence, an expression of grand hopes and ideals.

What is the "information" so crucial in this odd belief system, the icon now so greatly cherished? We have seen enough to appreciate that the kind of information upheld is not knowledge in the ordinary sense of the term; nor is it understanding, enlightenment, critical thought, timeless wisdom, or the content of a well-educated mind. If one looks carefully at the writings of computer enthusiasts, one finds that information in a particular form and context is offered as a paradigm to inspire emulation. Enormous quantities of data, manipulated within various kinds of electronic media and used to facilitate the transactions of today's large, complex organizations is the model we are urged to embrace. In this context the sheer quantity of information presents a formidable challenge. Modern organizations are continually faced with overload, a flood of data that threatens to become unintelligible to them. Computers provide one way to confront that problem; speed conquers quantity. An equally serious challenge is created by the fact that the varieties of information most crucial to modern organizations are highly time specific. Data on stock market prices, airline traffic, weather conditions, international economic indicators, military intelligence, public opinion poll results, and the like are useful for very short periods of time. Systems that gather, organize, analyze, and utilize electronic data in these areas must be closely tuned to the very latest developments. If one is trading on fast-paced international markets, information about prices an hour old or even a few seconds old may have no value. Information is itself a perishable commodity.

Thus, what looked so puzzling in another context—the urgent "need" for information in a social world filled with many pressing human needs—now becomes transparent. It is, in the first instance, the need of complex human/machine systems threatened with debilitating uncertainties or even breakdown unless continually replenished with up-to-the-minute electronic information about their internal states and operating environments. Rapid information-processing capabilities of modern computers and communications devices are a perfect match for such needs, a marriage made in technological heaven.

But is it sensible to transfer this model, as many evidently wish, to all parts of human life? Must activities, experiences, ideas, and ways of knowing that take a longer time to bear fruit adapt to the speedy processes of digitized information processing? Must education, the arts, politics, sports, home life, and all other forms of social practice be transformed to accommodate it? As one article on the coming of the home computer concludes, "running a household is actually like running a small business. You have to worry about inventory control—of household supplies—and budgeting for school tuition, housekeepers' salaries, and all the rest."[28] The writer argues that these complex, rapidly changing operations require a powerful information-processing capacity to keep them functioning smoothly. One begins to wonder how everyday activities such as running a

household were even possible before the advent of microelectronics. This is a case in which the computer is a solution frantically in search of a problem.

In the last analysis, the almost total silence about the ends of the "computer revolution" is filled by a conviction that information processing is something valuable in its own right. Faced with an information explosion that strains the capacities of traditional institutions, society will renovate its structure to accommodate computerized, automated systems in every area of concern. The efficient management of information is revealed as the *telos* of modern society, its greatest mission. It is that fact to which mythinformation adds glory and glitter. People must be convinced that the human burdens of an information age—unemployment, de-skilling, the disruption of many social patterns—are worth bearing. Once again, those who push the plow are told they ride a golden chariot.

## Everywhere and Nowhere

Having criticized a point of view, it remains for me to suggest what topics a serious study of computers and politics should pursue. The question is, of course, a very large one. If the long-term consequences of computerization are anything like the ones commonly predicted, they will require a rethinking of many fundamental conditions in social and political life. I will mention three areas of concern.

As people handle an increasing range of their daily activities through electronic instruments—mail, banking, shopping, entertainment, travel plans, and so forth—it becomes technically feasible to monitor these activities to a degree heretofore inconceivable. The availability of digitized footprints of social transactions affords opportunities that contain a menacing aspect. While there has been a great deal written about this problem, most of it deals with the "threat to privacy," the possibility that someone might gain access to information that violates the sanctity of one's personal life. As important as that issue certainly is, it by no means exhausts the potential evils created by electronic data banks and computer matching. The danger extends beyond the private sphere to affect the most basic of public freedoms. Unless steps are taken to prevent it, we may develop systems capable of a perpetual, pervasive, apparently benign surveillance. Confronted with omnipresent, all-seeing data banks, the populace may find passivity and compliance the safest route, avoiding activities that once represented political liberty. As a

# 40. Mythinformation

badge of civic pride a citizen may announce, "I'm not involved in anything a computer would find the least bit interesting."

The evolution of this unhappy state of affairs does not necessarily depend upon the "misuse" of computer systems. The prospect we face is really much more insidious. An age rich in electronic information may achieve wonderful social conveniences at a cost of placing freedom, perhaps inadvertently, in a deep chill.

A thoroughly computerized world is also one bound to alter conditions of human sociability. The point of many applications of microelectronics, after all, is to eliminate social layers that were previously needed to get things done. Computerized bank tellers, for example, have largely done away with small, local branch banks, which were not only ways of doing business, but places where people met, talked, and socialized. The so-called electronic cottage industry, similarly, operates very well without the kinds of human interactions that once characterized office work. Despite greater efficiency, productivity, and convenience, innovations of this kind do away with the reasons people formerly had for being together, working together, acting together. Many practical activities once crucial to even a minimal sense of community life are rendered obsolete. One consequence of these developments is to pare away the kinds of face-to-face contact that once provided important buffers between individuals and organized power. To an increasing extent, people will become even more susceptible to the influence of employers, news media, advertisers, and national political leaders. Where will we find new institutions to balance and mediate such power?

Perhaps the most significant challenge posed by the linking of computers and telecommunications is the prospect that the basic structures of political order will be recast. Worldwide computer, satellite, and communication networks fulfill, in large part, the modern dream of conquering space and time. These systems make possible instantaneous action at any point on the globe without limits imposed by the specific location of the initiating actor. Human beings and human societies, however, have traditionally found their identities within spatial and temporal limits. They have lived, acted, and found meaning in a particular place at a particular time. Developments in microelectronics tend to dissolve these limits, thereby threatening the integrity of social and political forms that depend on them. Aristotle's observation that "man is a political animal" meant in its most literal sense that man is a *polis* animal, a creature naturally suited to live in a particular

kind of community within a specific geographical setting, the city-state. Historical experience shows that it is possible for human beings to flourish in political units—kingdoms, empires, nation-states—larger than those the Greeks thought natural. But until recently the crucial conditions created by spatial boundaries of political societies were never in question.

That has changed. Methods pioneered by transnational corporations now make it possible for organizations of enormous size to manage their activities effectively across the surface of the planet. Business units that used to depend upon spatial proximity can now be integrated through complex electronic signals. If it seems convenient to shift operations from one area of the world to another far distant, it can be accomplished with a flick of a switch. Close an office in Sunnyvale; open an office in Singapore. In the recent past corporations have had to demonstrate at least some semblance of commitment to geographically based communities; their public relations often stressed the fact that they were "good neighbors." But in an age in which organizations are located everywhere and nowhere, this commitment easily evaporates. A transnational corporation can play fast and loose with everyone, including the country that is ostensibly its "home." Towns, cities, regions, and whole nations are forced to swallow their pride and negotiate for favors. In that process, political authority is gradually redefined.

Computerization resembles other vast, but largely unconscious experiments in modern social and technological history, experiments of the kind noted in earlier chapters. Following a step-by-step process of instrumental improvements, societies create new institutions, new patterns of behavior, new sensibilities, new contexts for the exercise of power. Calling such changes "revolutionary," we tacitly acknowledge that these are matters that require reflection, possibly even strong public action to ensure that the outcomes are desirable. But the occasions for reflection, debate, and public choice are extremely rare indeed. The important decisions are left in private hands inspired by narrowly focused economic motives. While many recognize that these decisions have profound consequences for our common life, few seem prepared to own up to that fact. Some observers forecast that "the computer revolution" will eventually be guided by new wonders in artificial intelligence. Its present course is influenced by something much more familiar: the absent mind.

Notes

1. See, for example, Edward Berkeley, *The Computer Revolution* (New York: Doubleday, 1962); Edward Tomeski, *The Computer Revolution: The Executive and the New Information Technology* (New York: Macmillan, 1970); and Nigel Hawkes, *The Computer Revolution* (New York: E. P. Dutton, 1972). See also Aaron Sloman, *The Computer Revolution in Philosophy* (Hassocks, England: Harvester Press, 1978); Zenon Pylyshyn, *Perspectives on the Computer Revolution* (Englewood Cliffs, N.J.: Prentice-Hall, 1970); Paul Stoneman, *Technological Diffusion and the Computer Revolution* (Cambridge: Cambridge University Press, 1976); and Ernest Braun and Stuart MacDonald, *Revolution in Miniature: The History and Impact of Semiconductor Electronics* (Cambridge: Cambridge University Press, 1978).

2. Michael L. Dertouzos in an interview on "The Today Show," National Broadcasting Company, August 8, 1983.

3. Daniel Bell, "The Social Framework of the Information Society," in *The Computer Age: A Twenty Year View,* Michael L. Dertouzos and Joel Moses (eds.) (Cambridge: MIT Press, 1980), 163.

4. See, for example, Philip H. Abelson, "The Revolution in Computers and Electronics," *Science* 215:751–753, 1982.

5. Edward A. Feigenbaum and Pamela McCorduck, *The Fifth Generation: Artificial Intelligence and Japan's Computer Challenge to the World* (Reading, Mass.: Addison-Wesley, 1983), 8.

6. Among the important works of this kind are David Burnham, *The Rise of the Computer State* (New York: Random House, 1983); James N. Danziger et al., *Computers and Politics: High Technology in American Local Governments* (New York: Columbia University Press, 1982); Abbe Moshowitz, *The Conquest of Will: Information Processing in Human Affairs* (Reading, Mass.: Addison-Wesley, 1976); James Rule et al., *The Politics of Privacy* (New York: New American Library, 1980); and Joseph Weizenbaum, *Computer Power and Human Reason: From Judgment to Calculation* (San Francisco: W. H. Freeman, 1976).

7. Quoted in Jacques Vallee, *The Network Revolution: Confessions of a Computer Scientist* (Berkeley: And/Or Press, 1982), 10.

8. Tracy Kidder, *Soul of a New Machine* (New York: Avon Books, 1982), 228.

9. *The Fifth Generation,* 14.

10. James Martin, *Telematic Society: A Challenge for Tomorrow* (Englewood Cliffs, N.J.: Prentice-Hall, 1981), 172.

11. Ibid., 4.

12. Starr Roxanne Hiltz and Murray Turoff, *The Network Nation: Human Communication via Computer* (Reading, Mass.: Addison-Wesley, 1978), 489.

13. Ibid., xxix.

14. Ibid., 484.

15. Ibid., xxix.

16. *The Network Revolution,* 198.

17. John Naisbitt, *Megatrends: Ten New Directions Transforming Our Lives* (New York: Warner Books, 1984), 282.

18. Amitai Etzioni, Kenneth Laudon, and Sara Lipson, "Participating Technology: The Minerva Communications Tree," *Journal of Communications,* 25:64, Spring 1975.

19. J. C. R. Licklider, "Computers and Government," in Dertouzos and Moses (eds.), *The Computer Age,* 114, 126.

20. Quoted in *The Fifth Generation,* 240.

21. *Occupational Outlook Handbook, 1982–1983,* U.S. Bureau of Labor Statistics, Bulletin No. 2200, Superintendent of Documents, U.S. Government Printing Office, Washington, D.C. See also Gene I. Maeroff, "The Real Job Boom Is Likely to be Low-Tech," *New York Times,* September 4, 1983, 16E.

22. See, for example, James Danziger et al., *Computers and Politics.*

23. For a study of the utopia of consumer products in American democracy, see Jeffrey L. Meikle, *Twentieth Century Limited: Industrial Design in America, 1925–1939* (Philadelphia: Temple University Press, 1979). For other utopian dreams see Joseph J. Corn, *The Winged Gospel: America's Romance with Aviation, 1900–1950* (Oxford: Oxford University Press, 1983); Joseph J. Corn and Brian Horrigan, *Yesterday's Tomorrows: Past Visions of America's Future* (New York: Summit Books, 1984); and Erik Barnow, *The Tube of Plenty* (Oxford: Oxford University Press, 1975).

24. *The Fifth Generation,* 8.

25. "The Philosophy of US," from the official program of The US Festival held in San Bernardino, California, September 4–7, 1982. The outdoor rock festival, sponsored by Steven Wozniak, co-inventor of the original Apple Computer, attracted an estimated half million people. Wozniak regaled the crowd with large-screen video presentations of his message, proclaiming a new age of community and democracy generated by the use of personal computers.

26. "Power corresponds to the human ability not just to act but to act in concert. Power is never the property of an individual; it belongs to a group and remains in existence only so long as the group keeps together." Hannah Arendt, *On Violence* (New York: Harcourt Brace & World, 1969), 44.

27. John Markoff, "A View of the Future: Micros Won't Matter," *InfoWorld,* October 31, 1983, 69.

28. Donald H. Dunn, "The Many Uses of the Personal Computer," *Business Week,* June 23, 1980, 125–126.

# 41. [Introduction]
# From *Plans and Situated Actions*

◊03
49

Lucy Suchman made a fundamental critique of practices within artificial intelligence and presented a different concept of how people seek to accomplish goals. This led to significant changes within the language of artificial intelligence, although the use of similar terminologies by AI researchers is often founded on a misunderstanding of Suchman's argument.

Suchman held that the elaborate plans and symbolic manipulations that characterized artificial intelligence's early attempts to create interactive devices were fundamentally misguided. Artificial intelligence practitioners had assumed that these logical manipulations were much like the human planning process, and that once they were sufficiently refined they would, of course, succeed. Suchman argues that such elaborate abstract plans are never actually the primary basis for human action. They are better seen, she states, as stories that some of us, in some cultures, use to organize our actions. Many ponderous artificial intelligence projects underway when Suchman's book was published would have had little justification if this point had been conceded.

◊19
277

Some viewed Suchman's observations as a prescription for the development of new AI strategies that took situated action into account. In this interpretation, AI could still make progress within current institutional parameters; such progress would come by building systems that improvised toward a goal based on the current situation, rather than following a monolithic plan. Some, like Philip Agre and David Chapman, as explained in "What Are Plans For?," explored this possibility in a manner that was commensurate with Suchman's critique. In other cases new language was adopted to represent the same techniques that Suchman argued against, perhaps based on the increased military concern with plan-based AI's inability to address the rapidly-changing, difficult-to-predict situation of the battlefield.

◊22
339

Agre's essay on a different topic is ◊51.

Two selections from Suchman's book appear below. The first, the preface "Navigation," makes the distinction between the planning and situated action perspectives. The second selection, the chapter "Interactive Artifacts," outlines a view of what interactivity means, and how the artificial intelligence version of it can be seen in a historical context. She writes of AI's project, "Interaction between people and machines implies mutual intelligibility, or shared understanding," and goes on to describe two common scenarios for this: first, the self-explanatory tool; second, the computer as an artifact having purposes. Suchman argues that both represent unsolved, perhaps irreducible, problems—as long as these words are used in the sense they have been by traditional AI. From Suchman's perspective, "intelligibility" and "understanding"—and therefore "interaction"—between people and machines must be seen as profoundly different from that between persons.

◊28
413

◊33
485

Suchman does not believe plans to be non-existent, nor does she state that AI researchers must necessarily reject plans in favor of situated actions. Rather, her argument is that it is necessary to re-conceptualize the status of plans as products of, and resources for (rather than controllers of), situated actions. See for example her "Response to Vera and Simon's 'Situated Action: A Symbolic Interpretation.'"

Much of the work in this volume, much of the best recent work in new media, recognizes rather than attempts to erase this difference. A larger classification of such work, made up of four categories, would place traditional AI's two scenarios in one of these larger categories. In these four cases, the primary intelligence that is the concern in discussing system development may be: (1) the user's own, (2) the designer's, (3) the system's (as in the traditional AI scenarios), or (4) those of communicating users. Examples of essays in this volume which focus on each of these are (1) Seymour Papert (◊28), (2) Ben Shneiderman (◊33), (3) Alan Turing (◊03), and (4) Chip Morningstar and R. Randall Farmer (◊46). Such a classification may prove to be an interesting way of considering one layer of interaction, but it can be limiting in that it considers only that layer. It does not reveal much about the levels at which interaction is seen to occur in the writings of Augusto Boal (◊22) and Jean Baudrillard (◊19), nor does it provide insight into the larger context in which this interaction takes place, as might be found by considering the arguments of Phil Agre (◊51) or Langdon Winner (◊40). Yet potential categories of interaction can be devised in other ways, e.g., based on interactive

◊40
587

599

◊46
663

◊51
737

technologies (CRT & mouse / handheld / movement tracking / voice) or on the human purpose in interacting (as discussed in the Aristotelian theory of Brenda Laurel (◊38)). Selecting the salient features from which to construct a typology is an always difficult, but potentially revealing, enterprise. Becoming too enamored of such abstractions, or identifying one type as somehow fundamental to intelligence, is always dangerous.
—NWF

Further Reading

Agre, Philip E., and David Chapman. "What Are Plans For?" *Designing Autonomous Agents: Theory and Practice from Biology to Engineering and Back,* ed. Pattie Maes. Cambridge: MIT Press, 1990, 17–34.

Suchman, Lucy. "Response to Vera and Simon's 'Situated Action: A Symbolic Interpretation.'" *Cognitive Science* 17 (1993): 71–75.

Original Publication

"Navigation," vii–x and "Interactive Artifacts," 5–26, *Plans and Situated Actions: The Problem of Human-Machine Communication.* Cambridge: Cambridge University Press, 1987. 2nd ed. in preparation.

# From *Plans and Situated Actions*

## Lucy A. Suchman

## Preface: Navigation

Thomas Gladwin (1964) has written a brilliant article contrasting the method by which the Trukese navigate the open sea, with that by which Europeans navigate. He points out that the European navigator begins with a plan—a course—which he has charted according to certain universal principles, and he carries out his voyage by relating his every move to that plan. His effort throughout his voyage is directed to remaining "on course." If unexpected events occur, he must first alter the plan, then respond accordingly. The Trukese navigator begins with an objective rather than a plan. He sets off toward the objective and responds to conditions as they arise in an *ad hoc* fashion. He utilizes information provided by the wind, the waves, the tide and current, the fauna, the stars, the clouds, the sound of the water on the side of the boat, and he steers accordingly. His effort is directed to doing whatever is necessary to reach the objective. If asked, he can point to his objective at any moment, but he cannot describe his course.
(Berreman 1966, p. 347)

The subject of this book [*Plans and Situated Actions*] is the two alternative views of human intelligence and directed action represented here by the Trukese and the European navigator. The European navigator exemplifies the prevailing cognitive science model of purposeful action, for reasons that are implicit in the final sentence of the quote above. That is to say, while the Trukese navigator is hard pressed to tell us how he actually steers his course, the comparable account for the European seems to be already in hand, in the form of the very plan that is assumed to guide his actions. While the objective of the Trukese navigator is clear from the outset, his actual course is contingent on unique circumstances that he cannot anticipate in advance. The plan of the European, in contrast, is derived from universal principles of navigation, and is essentially independent of the exigencies of his particular situation.

Given these contrasting exemplars, there are at least three, quite different implications that we might draw for the study of purposeful action:

First, we might infer that there actually are different ways of acting, favored differently across cultures. How to act purposefully is learned, and subject to cultural variation. European culture favors abstract, analytic thinking, the ideal being to reason from general principles to particular instances. The Trukese, in contrast, having no such ideological commitments, learn a cumulative range of concrete, embodied responses, guided by the wisdom of memory and experience over years of actual voyages. In the pages that follow, however, I will argue that all activity, even the most analytic, is fundamentally concrete and embodied. So while there must certainly be an important relationship between ideas about action and ways of acting, this first interpretation of the navigation example stands in danger of confusing theory with practice.

Alternatively, we might posit that whether our actions are *ad hoc* or planned depends upon the nature of the activity, or our degree of expertise. So we might contrast instrumental, goal-directed activities with creative or expressive activities, or contrast novice with expert behavior. Dividing things up along these lines, however, seems in some important ways to violate our navigation example. Clearly the Truk is involved with instrumental action in getting from one island to another, and just as clearly the European navigator relies upon his chart regardless of his degree of expertise.

Finally, the position to be taken—and the one that I will adopt here—could be that, however planned, purposeful actions are inevitably *situated actions*. By situated actions I mean simply actions taken in the context of particular, concrete circumstances. In this sense one could argue that we all act like the Trukese, however much some of us may talk like Europeans. We must act like the Trukese because the circumstances of our actions are never fully anticipated and are continuously changing around us. As a consequence our actions, while systematic, are never planned in the strong sense that cognitive science would have it. Rather, plans are best viewed as a weak resource for what is primarily *ad hoc* activity. It is only when we are pressed to account for the rationality of our actions, given the biases of European culture, that we invoke the guidance of a plan. Stated in advance, plans are necessarily vague, insofar as they must accommodate the unforeseeable contingencies of particular situations. Reconstructed in retrospect, plans systematically filter out precisely the particularity of detail that characterizes situated actions, in favor of those aspects of the actions that can be seen to accord with the plan.

This third implication, it seems, is not just a symmetric alternative to the other two, but is different in kind, and somewhat more serious. That is, it calls into question not just the adequacy of our distinctions along the dimensions of culture, kinds of activity, or degrees of expertise, but the very productivity of our starting premises—that representations of action such as plans could be the basis for an account of actions in particular situations. Because the third implication has to do with foundations, and not because there is no truth in the other two, I take the idea that actions are primarily situated, and that situated actions are essentially *ad hoc*, as the starting point for my investigations.

The view of action exemplified by the European navigator is now being reified in the design of intelligent machines.

I examine one such machine, as a way of uncovering the strengths and limitations of the general view that its design embodies. The view, that purposeful action is determined by plans, is deeply rooted in the Western human sciences as *the* correct model of the rational actor. The logical form of plans makes them attractive for the purpose of constructing a computational model of action, to the extent that for those fields devoted to what is now called cognitive science, the analysis and synthesis of plans effectively constitute the study of action. My own contention, however, is that as students of human action we ignore the Trukese navigator at our peril. While an account of how the European navigates may be in hand, the essential nature of action, however planned or unplanned, is situated. It behooves us, therefore, to study and to begin to find ways to describe the Trukese system.

There is an injunction in social studies of science to eschew interest in the validity of the products of science, in favor of an interest in their production. While I generally agree with this injunction, my investigation of one of the prevailing models of human action in cognitive science is admittedly and unabashedly interested. That is to say, I take it that there is a reality of human action, beyond either the cognitive scientist's models or my own accounts, to which both are trying to do justice. In that sense, I am not just examining the cognitive science model with the dispassion of the uncommitted anthropologist of science, I am examining it in light of an alternative account of human action to which I am committed, and which I attempt to clarify in the process.

# Interactive Artifacts

> Marginal objects, objects with no clear place, play important roles. On the lines between categories, they draw attention to how we have drawn the lines. Sometimes in doing so they incite us to reaffirm the lines, sometimes to call them into question, stimulating different distinctions.
> (Turkle 1984, p. 31)

In *The Second Self* (1984), Sherry Turkle describes the computer as an "evocative object," one that raises new questions regarding our common sense of the distinction between artifacts and intelligent others. Her studies include an examination of the impact of computer-based artifacts on children's conceptions of the difference between categories such as "alive" versus "not alive," and "machine" versus "person." In dealing with the questions that computer-based objects evoke, children make clear that the differentiation of physical from psychological entities, which as adults we largely take for granted, is the end product of a process of establishing the relationship between the observable behavior of a thing and its underlying nature.[1] Children have a tendency, for example, to attribute life to physical objects on the basis of behavior such as autonomous motion, or reactivity, though they reserve humanity for entities evidencing such things as emotion, speech, and apparent thought or purposefulness. Turkle's observation with respect to computational artifacts is that children ascribe to them an "almost aliveness," and a psychology, while maintaining their distinctness from human beings: a view that, as Turkle points out, is remarkable among other things for its correspondence to the views held by those who are the artifacts' designers.[2]

I take as a point of departure a particular aspect of the phenomenon that Turkle identifies: namely, the apparent challenge that computational artifacts pose to the longstanding distinction between the physical and the social, in the special sense of those things that one designs, builds, and uses, on the one hand, and those things with which one communicates, on the other. While this distinction has been relatively non-problematic to date, now for the first time the term "interaction"—in a sense previously reserved for describing a uniquely interpersonal activity—seems appropriately to characterize what goes on between people and certain machines as well.[3] Interaction between people and machines implies mutual intelligibility, or shared understanding. What motivates my inquiry, therefore, is not only the recent question of how there could be mutual intelligibility between people and machines, but the prior question of how we account for the shared understanding, or mutual intelligibility, that we experience as people in our interactions with others whose essential sameness is not in question. An answer to the more recent question, theor-etically at least, presupposes an answer to the earlier one.

In this chapter I relate the idea of human-machine communication to some distinctive properties of computational arti-facts, and to the emergence of disciplines dedicated to making those artifacts intelligent. I begin with a brief discussion of cognitive science, the interdisciplinary field devoted to modeling cognitive processes, and its role in the project of creating intelligent artifacts.[4] Along with a theoretical interest in intelligent artifacts, the computer's properties have inspired a practical effort at engineering interaction between people and machines. I argue that the description of computational artifacts as interactive is supported by their *reactive, linguistic,* and internally *opaque* properties. With those properties in mind, I consider the double sense in which researchers are interested in artifacts that explain themselves: on the one hand, as a solution to the longstanding problem of conveying the artifact's intended purpose to the user, through its design and attendant instructions and, on the other hand, as a means of establishing the intelligence, or rational accountability, of the artifact itself.

## 1 Automata and Cognitive Science

Historically the idea of *automata*—the possibility of constructing physical devices that are self-regulating in ways that we commonly associate with living, animate beings—has been closely tied to the simulation of animal forms. McCorduck (1979) points out that human-like automata have been constructed since Hellenic times: statues that moved, gestured, spoke, and generally were imbued by observers—even those well aware of the internal mechanisms that powered them—with everything from minds to souls.[5] In the fourteenth century in Western Europe, learned men were commonly believed to construct talking heads made of brass, considered as both the source of their creator's wisdom and its manifestation. More prosaically, Jacques de Vaucanson in the eighteenth century designed a series of renowned mechanical statues, the most famous being a duck, the inner workings of which produced a variety of simple outward behaviors.

At the same time, Julien de la Mettrie published *Man, A Machine,* in which he argued that the vitality characteristic of human beings was the result of their physical *structure,* rather than either of something immanent in their material substance or of some immaterial force. Cognitive scientists today maintain the basic premise of de la Mettrie with respect to mind, contending that mind is best viewed as neither substantial nor insubstantial, but as an abstractable structure implementable in any number of possible physical substrates. Intelligence, in other words, is only incidentally embodied in the neurophysiology of the human brain, and what is essential about intelligence can be abstracted from that particular, albeit highly successful, substrate and embodied in an unknown range of alternative forms. This view decouples reasoning and intelligence from things uniquely human, and opens the way for the construction of intelligent artifacts.[6]

The preoccupation of cognitive science with mind in this abstract sense is in part a concern to restore meaning to psychological explanation (see Stich 1983, ch. 1). At the turn of this century, the recognized method for studying human mental life was introspection and, insofar as introspection was not amenable to the emerging canons of scientific method, the study of cognition seemed doomed to be irremediably unscientific. In reaction to that prospect, the behaviorists posited that all human action should be understandable in terms of publicly observable, mechanistically describable relations between the organism and its environment. In the name of turning cognitive studies into a science, in other words, the study of cognition as the study of something apart from overt behavior was effectively abandoned in mainstream psychology.

Cognitive science, in this respect, was a project to bring thought back into the study of human action, while preserving the commitment to scientism. Cognitive science reclaims mentalist constructs such as beliefs, desires, intentions, symbols, ideas, schemata, planning, and problem-solving. Once again human purposes are the basis for cognitive psychology, but this time without the unconstrained speculation of the introspectionists. The study of cognition is to be empiricized not by a strict adherence to behaviorism, but by the use of a new technology: namely, the computer.

The sub-field of cognitive science most dedicated to the computer is artificial intelligence. Artificial intelligence arose as advances in computing technology were tied to developments in neurophysiological and mathematical theories of information. The requirement of computer modeling, of an "information processing psychology," seemed both to make theoretical sense and to provide the accountability that would make it possible to pursue a science of otherwise inaccessible mental phenomena. If a theory of underlying mental processes could be modeled on the computer so as to produce the right outward behavior, the theory could be viewed as having passed at least a sufficiency test of its psychological validity.

The cognitivist strategy is to interject a mental operation between environmental stimulus and behavioral response: in essence, to relocate the causes of action from the environment that impinges upon the actor to processes, abstractable as computation, in the actor's head. The first premise of cognitive science, therefore, is that people—or "cognizers" of any sort—act on the basis of symbolic representations: a kind of cognitive code, instantiated physically in the brain, on which operations are performed to produce mental states such as "the belief that $p$," which in turn produce behavior consistent with those states. The relation of environmental stimuli to those mental states, on the one hand, and of mental states to behavior, on the other, remains deeply problematic and widely debated within the field (see, for example, Fodor 1983; Pylyshyn 1974, 1984; Stich 1983). The agreement among all participants in cognitive science and its affiliated disciplines, however, is that cognition is not just potentially *like* computation, it literally *is* computational. There is no reason, in principle, why there should not be a computational account of mind, therefore, and there is no a priori reason to draw a principled boundary between people, taken as "information-processors" or "symbol manipulators" or, in George Miller's phrase, "informavores" (Pylyshyn 1984, p. xi), and certain computing machines.

The view that intelligence is the manipulation of symbols finds practical implementation both in so-called expert systems, which structure and process large amounts of well-formulated data, and industrial robots that perform routine, repetitive assembly and control tasks. Expert systems—essentially sophisticated programs that manipulate data structures to accord with rules of inference that experts are understood to use—have minimal sensory-motor, or "peripheral," access to the world in which they are embedded, input being most commonly through a keyboard, by a human operator. Industrial robots—highly specialized, computer-controlled devices designed to perform autonomously a single repetitive physical task—have relatively more developed sensory–motor apparatus than do expert systems, but the success of robotics is still confined to specialized activities, under controlled conditions. In both cases, the systems can handle large amounts of encoded information, and syntactic relationships of great sophistication and complexity, in highly circumscribed domains. But when it comes either to direct interaction with the environment, or

603

to the exercise of practical, everyday reasoning about the significance of events in the world, there is general agreement that the state-of-the-art in intelligent machines has yet to attain the basic cognitive abilities of the normal five-year-old child.

## 2 The Idea of Human-Computer Interaction

In spite of the current limits on machine intelligence, the use of an intentional vocabulary is already well established in both technical and popular discussion of computers. In part, the attribution of purpose to computer-based artifacts derives from the simple fact that each action by the user effects an immediate machine *reaction* (see Turkle 1984, ch. 8). The technical definition of "interactive computing" (see, for example, Oberquelle, Kupka, and Maass 1983, p. 313) is simply that real-time control over the computing process is placed in the hands of the user, through immediate processing and through the availability of interrupt facilities whereby the user can override and modify the operations in progress. This definition contrasts current capabilities with earlier forms of computing, specifically batch processing, where user commands were queued and executed without any intermediate feedback. The greater reactivity of current computers, combined with the fact that, like any machine, the computer's reactions are not random but by design, suggest the character of the computer as a purposeful, and, by association, as a social object.

A more profound basis for the relative sociability of computer-based artifacts, however, is the fact that the means for controlling computing machines and the behavior that results are increasingly *linguistic*, rather than mechanistic. That is to say, machine operation becomes less a matter of pushing buttons or pulling levers with some physical result, and more a matter of specifying operations and assessing their effects through the use of a common language.[7] With or without machine intelligence, this fact has contributed to the tendency of designers, in describing what goes on between people and machines, to employ terms borrowed from the description of human interaction—dialogue, conversation, and so forth: terms that carry a largely unarticulated collection of intuitions about properties common to human communication and the use of computer-based machines.

While for the most part the vocabulary of human interaction has been taken over by researchers in human-machine communication with little deliberation, several researchers have attempted to clarify similarities and differences between computer use and human conversation. Perhaps the most thoughtful and comprehensive of these is Hayes and Reddy (1983). They identify the central difference between existing interactive computer systems and human communication as a question of "robustness," or the ability on the part of conversational participants to respond to unanticipated circumstances, and to detect and remedy troubles in communication:

> The ability to interact gracefully depends on a number of relatively independent skills: skills involved in parsing elliptical, fragmented, and otherwise ungrammatical input; in ensuring that communication is robust (ensuring that the intended meaning has been conveyed); in explaining abilities and limitations, actions and the motives behind them; in keeping track of the focus of attention of a dialogue; in identifying things from descriptions, even if ambiguous or unsatisfiable; and in describing things in terms appropriate for the context. While none of these components of graceful interaction has been entirely neglected in the literature, no single current system comes close to having most of the abilities and behaviours we describe, and many are not possessed by any current systems. (p. 232)

Hayes and Reddy believe, however, that:

> Even though there are currently no truly gracefully interacting systems, none of our proposed components of graceful interaction appears individually to be much beyond the current state of the art, at least for suitably restricted domains of discourse. (p. 232)

They then review the state of the art, including systems like LIFER (Hendrix 1977) and SCHOLAR (Carbonell 1971), which display sensitivity to the user's expectations regarding acknowledgement of input; systems that resolve ambiguity in English input from the user through questions (Hayes 1981); systems like the GUS system (Bobrow *et al.* 1977) which represent limited knowledge of the domain that the interaction is about; work on the maintenance of a common focus over the course of the interaction (Grosz 1977; Sidner 1979); and Hayes and Reddy's own work on an automated explanation facility in a simple service domain (1983).

Two caveats on Hayes and Reddy's prescription for a gracefully interacting system (both of which, to their credit, they freely admit) are worth noting. First, they view the abilities cited as necessary but not sufficient for human interaction, their claim for the list being simply that "it provides a good working basis from which to build gracefully interacting systems" (1983, p. 233). And, not surprisingly, the abilities that they cite constitute a list of precisely those problems currently under consideration in research on human-machine communication. There is, in other words, no independent assessment of how the problems on which researchers work relate to the nature and organization of human communication as such. Secondly, research on those problems that have been identified is confined to highly circumscribed domains. The consequence of working from an admittedly partial and *ad hoc* list of abilities, in limited domains, is that practical inroads in human-computer communication can be furthered, while the basic question of what human interaction comprises is deferred. Deferred as well is the question of why it is, beyond methodological convenience, that research in human-machine interaction has proceeded only in those limited domains that it has.

Moreover, while Hayes and Reddy take the position that "it is very important for a gracefully interacting system to conduct a dialogue in as human-like a way as possible" (ibid., p. 233), this assertion is a point of controversy in the research community. On the one side, there is an argument to the effect that one should acknowledge, and even exploit, the fact that people bring to computer use a tremendous range of skills and expectations from human interaction. Within research on human-computer interaction, for example, some progress has been made toward allowing people to enter commands into computers using natural language (i.e. languages like English, in contrast to programming languages). On the other side, even Hayes and Reddy admit that:

> the aim of being as human-like as possible must be tempered by the limited potential for comprehension of any foreseeable computer system. Until a solution is found to the problems of organizing and using the range of world knowledge possessed by a human, practical systems will only be able to comprehend a small amount of input, typically within a specific domain of expertise. Graceful interaction must, therefore, supplement its simulation of human

conversational ability with strategies to deal naturally and gracefully with input that is not fully understood, and, if possible, to steer a conversation back to the system's home ground. (ibid., p. 233)

While Hayes and Reddy would make these recovery strategies invisible to the user, they also acknowledge the "habitability" problem identified by Watt (1968) with respect to language: that is, the tendency of human users to assume that a computer system has sophisticated linguistic abilities after it has displayed elementary ones. This tendency is not surprising, given the fact that our only precedent for language-using entities to date has been other human beings. As soon as computational artifacts demonstrate *some* evidence of recognizably human abilities, we are inclined to endow them with the rest. The misconceptions that ensue, however, lead some like Fitter (1979) to argue that English or other "natural" languages are in fact not natural for purposes of human-computer interaction:

> for the purpose of man–computer communication, *a natural language is one that makes explicit the knowledge and processes for which the man and computer share a common understanding* . . . it becomes the responsibility of the systems designer to provide a language structure which will make apparent to the user the procedures on which it is based and will not lead him to expect from the computer unrealistic powers of inference. (ibid., p. 340, original emphasis)

In view of our tendency to ascribe full intelligence on the basis of partial evidence, the recommendation is that designers might do best to make available to the user the ways in which the system is *not* like a participant in interaction.[8] In this spirit, Nickerson (1976) argues that:

> The model that seems appropriate for this view of person–computer interaction is that of an individual making use of a sophisticated tool and not that of one person conversing with another. The term "user" is, of course, often used to denote the human component in a person–computer interaction, as it has been in this paper. It is, to my taste, preferable to the term "partner," not only because it seems more descriptive of the nature of the relationships that existing systems permit, and that future systems are likely to, but because it implies an asymmetry with respect to goals and objectives that "partner" does not. "User" is not a term that one would normally apply to a participant in a conversation. (p. 111)

The argument that computational processes should be revealed to the user, however, is potentially counter to the promotion of an intentional vocabulary in speaking about computer-based devices. As Dennett (1978) points out, it is in part our inability to see inside each other's heads, or our mutual *opacity,* that makes intentional explanations so powerful in the interpretation of human action. So it is in part the internal complexity and opacity of the computer that invites an intentional stance. This is the case not only because users lack technical knowledge of the computer's internal workings but because, even for those who possess such knowledge, there is an "irreducibility" to the computer as an object that is unique among human artifacts (Turkle 1984, p. 272). The overall behavior of the computer is not describable, that is to say, with reference to any of the simple local events that it comprises; it is precisely the behavior of a myriad of those events in combination that constitutes the overall machine. To refer to the behavior of the machine, then, one must speak of "its" functionality. And once reified as an entity, the inclination to ascribe actions to the entity rather than to the parts is irresistible.

Intentional explanations relieve us of the burden of understanding mechanism, insofar as one need assume only that the design is rational in order to call upon the full power of common-sense psychology and have, ready at hand, a basis for anticipating and construing an artifact's behavior. At the same time, precisely because the mechanism is in fact unknown, and, insofar as underspecification is taken to be characteristic of human beings (as evidenced by the fact that we are inclined to view something that is fully specified as less than human), the personification of the machine is reinforced by the ways in which its inner workings are a mystery, and its behavior at times surprises us. Insofar as the machine is somewhat predictable, in sum, and yet is also both internally opaque and liable to unanticipated behavior, we are more likely to view ourselves as engaged in interaction with it than as just performing operations upon it, or using it as a tool to perform operations upon the world (see MacKay 1962).

## 3 Self-Explanatory Artifacts

In the preceding pages I have proposed that the reactive, linguistic, and opaque properties of the computer lead us to view it as interactive, and to apply intentional explanations to its behavior. This tie to intentionality has both theoretical and practical implications. Practically, it suggests that, like a human actor, the computer should be able to explain itself, or the intent behind its actions, to the user. Theoretically, it suggests that the computer actually has intent, as demonstrated precisely in this ability to behave in an accountably rational, intelligible way.

For practical purposes, "user interface" designers[9] have long held the view that machines ideally should be self-explanatory, in the broad sense that their operation should be discoverable without extensive training, from information provided on or through the machine itself. On this view, the degree to which an artifact is self-explanatory is just the extent to which someone examining the artifact is able to reconstruct the *designer's intentions* regarding its use. This basic idea, that a self-explanatory artifact is one whose intended purpose is discoverable by the user, is presumably as old as the design and use of tools. With respect to computer-based artifacts, however, the notion of a self-explanatory artifact has taken on a second sense: namely, the idea that the artifact might actually *explain itself* in something more like the sense that a human being does. In this second sense the goal is that the artifact should not only be intelligible to the user as a tool, but that it should be *intelligent*—that is, able to understand the actions of the user, and to provide for the rationality of its own.

In the remainder of this chapter, I look at these two senses of a self-explanatory machine and at the relation between them. The first sense—that a tool should be decipherable by its user—reflects the fact that artifacts are constructed by designers, for a purpose, and that the user of a tool needs to know something of that design intent. Given their interactional properties, computational tools seem to offer unique capabilities for the provision of instruction to their users. The idea that instructions could be presented more effectively using the power of computation is not far from the idea that computer-based artifacts could actually instruct: that is, could interact with people in a way that approximates the behavior of an intelligent human expert or coach. And this second idea, that the artifact could actually interact instructively with the user, ties the practical problem of instruction to the theoretical problem of building an intelligent, interactive machine.

## 3.1 The Computer as an Artifact Designed for a Purpose

At the same time that computational artifacts introduce new complexity and opacity into our encounters with machines, our reliance on computer-based technology and its proliferation throughout the society increases. One result is the somewhat paradoxical objective that increasingly complex technology should be usable with decreasing amounts of training. Rather than relying upon the teachings of an experienced user, the use of computers is to be conveyed directly through the technology itself.

The inherent difficulty of conveying the use of a technology directly through its design is well known to archaeologists, who have learned that while the attribution of design intent is a requirement for an artifact's intelligibility, the artifact's design as such does not convey unequivocally either its actual or its intended use. While this problem in construing the purpose of artifacts can be alleviated, it can never fully be resolved, and it defines the essential problem that the novice user of the tool confronts. Insofar as the goal of a tool's design is that use of the tool should be self-evident, therefore, the problem of deciphering an artifact defines the problem of the designer as well.

As with any communication, instructions for the use of a tool are constrained by the general maxim that utterances should be designed for their recipients. The extent to which the maxim is observed is limited in the first instance by the resources that the medium of communication affords. Face-to-face human interaction is the paradigm case of a system for communication that, because it is organized for maximum context-sensitivity, supports a response designed for just these recipients, on just this occasion. Face-to-face instruction brings that context-sensitivity to bear on problems of skill acquisition. The gifted coach, for example, draws on powers of language and observation, and uses the situation of instruction, in order to specialize instruction for the individual student. Where written instruction relies upon generalizations about its recipient and the occasion of its use, the coach draws pedagogical strength from exploitation of the unique details of particular situations.[10]

A consequence of the human coach's method is that his or her skills must be deployed anew each time. An instruction manual, in contrast, has the advantage of being durable, re-usable, and replicable. In part, the strength of written text is that, in direct contrast to the pointed commentary of the coach, text allows the *disassociation* of the occasion of an instruction's production from the occasion of its use. For the same reason, however, text affords relatively poor resources for recipient design. The promise of interactive computer systems, in these terms, is a technology that can move instructional design away from the written manual in the direction of the human coach, and the resources afforded by face-to-face interaction.

Efforts at building self-explicating machines in their more sophisticated forms now adopt the metaphor of the machine as an expert, and the user as a novice, or student. Among the most interesting attempts to design such a computer-based "coach" is a system called WEST (Burton and Brown 1982). The design strategy adopted in WEST is based on the observation that the skill of a human coach lies as much in what isn't said as what is. Specifically, the human coach does not disrupt the student's engagement in an activity in order to ask questions, but instead diagnoses a student's strengths and weaknesses through observation. And once the diagnosis is made, the coach interjects advice and instruction selectively, in ways designed to maximize learning through discovery and experience. In that spirit, the WEST system attempts to infer the student's knowledge of the domain—in this case a computer game called "How the West Was Won," designed to teach the use of basic arithmetic expressions—by observing the student's behavior.[11]

While the project of identifying a student's problems directly from his or her behavior proved considerably more difficult than expected, the objectives for the WEST coach were accomplished in the prototype system to an impressive degree. Because in the case of learning to play WEST the student's actions take the form of input to the computer (entries on a keyboard) and therefore leave an accessible trace, and because a context for those actions (the current state of, and history of consecutive moves across, the "board") is defined by the system, each student turn can be compared against calculations of the move that a hypothetical expert player would make given the same conditions. Each expert move, in turn, requires a stipulated set of associated skills. Evidence that a particular skill is lacking, accumulated across some number of moves, identifies that skill as a candidate for coaching. The coach then interjects offers of advice to the student at opportune moments in the course of the play, where what constitutes an opportune moment for interjection is determined according to a set of rules of thumb regarding good tutorial strategy (for example, always coach by offering the student an alternative move that both demonstrates the relevant skill and accomplishes obviously superior results; never coach on two turns in a row, no matter what, and so forth).

## 3.2 The Computer as an Artifact Having Purposes

While the computer-based coach can be understood as a logical development in the longstanding problem of instruction, the requirement that it be interactive introduces a second sense of self-explanatory machine which is more recent, and is uniquely tied to the advent of computing. The new idea is that the intelligibility of artifacts is not just a matter of the availability to the user of the *designer's* intentions for the artifact, but of the intentions of the *artifact* itself. That is to say, the designer's objective now is to imbue the machine with the grounds for behaving in ways that are accountably rational: that is, reasonable or intelligible to others, including, in the case of interaction, ways that are responsive to the other's actions.

In 1950, A. M. Turing proposed a now-famous, and still controversial, test for machine intelligence based on a view of intelligence as accountable rationality. Turing argued that if a machine could be made to respond to questions in such a way that a person asking the questions could not distinguish between the machine and another human being, the machine would have to be described as intelligent. To implement his test, Turing chose a game called the "imitation game." The game was initially conceived as a test of the ability of an interrogator to distinguish which of two respondents was a man and which a woman. To eliminate the evidence of physical embodiment, the interaction was to be conducted remotely, via a teleprinter. Thus Turing's notion that the game could easily be adapted to a test of machine intelligence, by substituting the machine for one of the two human respondents.

Turing expressly dismissed as a possible objection to his proposed test the contention that, although the machine might succeed in the game, it could succeed through means that bear no resemblance to human thought. Turing's contention was precisely that success at performing the game, regardless of mechanism, is sufficient evidence for intelligence (Turing 1950, p. 435). The Turing test thereby became the canonical form of the argument that if two information-processors, subject to the same input stimuli, produce indistinguishable output behavior, then, regardless

of the identity of their internal operations, one processor is essentially equivalent to the other.

The lines of the controversy raised by the Turing test were drawn over a family of programs developed by Joseph Weizenbaum in the 1960s under the name ELIZA, designed to support "natural language conversation" with a computer (Weizenbaum 1983, p. 23). Of the name ELIZA, Wiezenbaum writes:

> Its name was chosen to emphasize that it may be incrementally improved by its users, since its language abilities may be continually improved by a "teacher." Like the Eliza of *Pygmalion* fame, it can be made to appear even more civilized, the relation of appearance to reality, however, remaining in the domain of the playwright. (p. 23)

Anecdotal reports of occasions on which people approached the teletype to one of the ELIZA programs and, believing it to be connected to a colleague, engaged in some amount of "interaction" without detecting the true nature of their respondent, led many to believe that Weizenbaum's program had passed a simple form of the Turing test. Notwithstanding its apparent interactional success, however, Weizenbaum himself denied the intelligence of the program, on the basis of the underlying mechanism which he described as "a mere collection of procedures" (p. 23):

> The gross procedure of the program is quite simple; the text [written by the human participant] is read and inspected for the presence of a *keyword* If such a word is found, the sentence is transformed according to a *rule* associated with the keyword, if not a content-free remark or, under certain conditions, an earlier transformation is retrieved. The text so computed or retrieved is then printed out. (p. 24, original emphasis)

In spite of Weizenbaum's disclaimers with respect to their intelligence, the ELIZA programs are still cited as instances of successful interaction between human and machine. The grounds for their success are clearest in DOCTOR, one of the ELIZA programs whose script equipped it to respond to the human user as if the computer were a Rogerian therapist and the user a patient. The DOCTOR program exploited the maxim that shared premises can remain unspoken: that the less we say in conversation, the more what is said is assumed to be self-evident in its meaning and implications (see Coulter 1979, ch. 5). Conversely, the very fact that a comment is made without elaboration implies that such shared background assumptions exist. The more elaboration or justification is provided, the less the appearance of transparence or self-evidence. The less elaboration there is, the more the recipient will take it that the meaning of what is provided should be obvious.

The design of the DOCTOR program, in other words, exploited the natural inclination of people to deploy what Karl Mannheim first termed the *documentary method of interpretation* to find the sense of actions that are assumed to be purposeful or meaningful (Garfinkel 1967, p. 78). Very simply, the documentary method refers to the observation that people take appearances as evidence for, or the document of, an ascribed underlying reality, while taking the reality so ascribed as a resource for the interpretation of the appearance. In the case of DOCTOR, computer-generated responses that might otherwise seem odd were rationalized by users on the grounds that there must be some psychiatric intent behind them, not immediately obvious to the user as "patient," but sensible nonetheless:

> If, for example, one were to tell a psychiatrist "I went for a long boat ride" and he responded "Tell me about boats," one would not assume that he knew nothing about boats, but that he had some purpose in so directing the subsequent conversation. It is important to note that this assumption is one made by the speaker. Whether it is realistic or not is an altogether different question. In any case, it has a crucial psychological utility in that it serves the speaker to maintain his sense of being heard and understood. The speaker further defends his impression (which even in real life may be illusory) by attributing to his conversational partner all sorts of background knowledge, insights and reasoning ability. But again, these are the speaker's contribution to the conversation. They manifest themselves inferentially in the *interpretations* he makes of the offered response. (Weizenbaum 1983, p. 26, original emphasis)

In explicating the ELIZA programs, Weizenbaum was primarily concerned with the inclination of human users to find sense in the computer's output, and to ascribe to it an understanding, and therefore an authority, unwarranted by the actual mechanism.[12] While unmasking the intelligence of his program, however, Weizenbaum continued to describe it as "a program which makes natural language conversation with a computer possible" (1983, p. 23). Nevertheless, as part of his disclaimer regarding its intelligence, Weizenbaum points to a crucial shortcoming in the ELIZA strategy with respect to conversation:

> ELIZA in its use so far has had as one of its principal objectives the concealment of its lack of understanding. But to encourage its conversational partner to offer inputs from which it can select remedial information, it must *reveal* its misunderstanding. A switch of objectives from the concealment to the revelation of misunderstanding is seen as a precondition to making an ELIZA-like program the basis for an effective natural language man-machine communication system. (p. 27, original emphasis)

More recently, the inevitability of troubles in communication, and the importance of their remedy to the accomplishment of "graceful interaction," has been re-introduced into the human-machine communication effort by Hayes and Reddy (1983). They observe that:

> During the course of a conversation, it is not uncommon for people to misunderstand or fail to understand each other. Such failures in communication do not usually cause the conversation to break down; rather, the participants are able to resolve the difficulty, usually by a short clarifying sub-dialogue, and continue with the conversation from where they left off. Current computer systems are unable to take part in such clarifying dialogues, or resolve communication difficulties in any other way. As a result, when such difficulties occur, a computer dialogue system is unable to keep up its end of the conversation, and a complete breakdown is likely to result; this fragility lies in stark and unfavourable contrast to the robustness of human dialogue. (p. 234)

Hayes and Reddy go on to recommend steps toward a remedy for the fragility of human-computer interaction, based on the incorporation, from human communication, of conventions for the detection and repair of misunderstanding. They acknowledge, however, that their recommendations are unlikely to be sufficient for successful communication in other than the simplest encounters, e.g., automated directory assistance, or reservation systems. The question of why this should be so—of the nature of the limits on human-machine communication, and the nature and extent of robustness in human interaction—is the subject of the following chapters [of *Plans and Situated Actions*].

Notes

1. Though see Carey 1985, chapter 1 for a critique of the Piagetian notion that children at first have no concept for mechanical causation apart from intentional causation.

2. See especially pp. 62–3; Turkle finds some cause for alarm in the fact that for children the distinction of machine and person seems to turn centrally on a separation of thought from feeling; that is, computers exhibit the former, but lack the latter. This view, she argues, includes a kind of dissociation of intellect and emotion, and consequent trivialization of both, that characterizes the attitudes of many in the field of Artificial Intelligence.

3. Actually, the term "interaction" has its origins in the physical sciences, to describe a reciprocal action or influence. I use it here in the common sense assigned to it by social science: namely, to mean communication between persons. The migration of the term from the physical sciences to the social, and now back to some ground that stands between them, relates in intriguing ways to a general blurring of the distinction between physical and social in modern science, and to the general question of whether machines are actually becoming more like people or whether, in fact, people are coming to define themselves more as machines. There is clearly a mutual influence at work. For more on this last point, see Dreyfus 1979, ch. 9.

4. For an extensive treatment, see Gardner 1985.

5. See McCorduck 1979, ch. 1; Churchland 1984, ch. 6. For a further history of automata, see Cohen 1966.

6. See Turkle 1984, ch. 7; and McCorduck 1979, ch. 5. Turkle's description of the present academic AI culture at MIT is particularly insightful.

7. Notwithstanding the popular fantasy of the talking machine, the crucial element that invites a view of computers as interactive is language, not speech. While strictly speaking buttons and keys remain the principal input devices in computing, this is relatively trivial. The synthesis of speech by computers may well add to our inclination to ascribe understanding to them, but will not, in itself, contribute substantively to their sensibility. On the other hand, simulation of natural language understanding, even when the language is written rather than spoken, is proving to be a profoundly difficult problem that is inseparable from the problem of simulating intelligence as such.

8. In fact, Nickerson (1976) points out that there are some ways in which a computer is not like another person which lend a certain advantage to the user, e.g. interruptions can be made without concern about giving offense, responses can be delayed as long as is necessary.

9. In design parlance, the term "user interface" refers both to the physical place at which the user issues commands to a device, finds reports of its state, or obtains the products of its operation, and the procedures by which those interactions occur.

10. Face-to-face interaction is in most cases a necessary, but of course never a sufficient, condition for successful human coaching. Coombs and Alty (1984) provide an interesting discussion of the failings of interactions between human advisors and new computer

users. At the same time, they point out that the characteristics of the advisory sessions that new users found unsatisfactory show marked similarities to human interactions with most rule-based computer help systems, e.g. that the advisors provide only the recommended solutions to reported problems, while failing either to elicit the view of the user, or to articulate any of their own rationale. Satisfactory sessions, in contrast, were characterized by what initially appeared to be less structure and less economy, but which on further investigation was revealed as "well-motivated despite surface appearances, the objective not being strict problem-solving as we had assumed, but problem-solving through mutual understanding. This required sensitivity to different structural factors" (pp. 24–5).

11. The student is presented with a graphic display of a game board made up of 70 squares (representing the Western frontier), a pair of icons (representing the two players—user and computer), and three spinners. A player's task in each turn is to combine the three numbers that the spinners provide, using the basic operations, to produce a value that becomes the number of spaces the icon is moved along the board. To add an element of strategy, squares on the board are more and less desirable—for example, "towns" occur every ten spaces, and landing on one advances you to the next. The object is to be the first player to land on 70.

Early observation of students playing the game revealed that they were not gaining the full benefit of the arithmetic practice, in that they tended to settle on a method for combining numbers (for example, multiply the first two numbers and add the third), and to repeat that same methods at each turn. Recognizing that this might reflect either a weakness in the student's proficiency at constructing expressions, a failure to grasp the strategy of the game, or both, Brown and Burton saw the potential usefulness of a "coach" that could guide the student to an expanded repertoire of skills and a better understanding of the domain. For a description of a similarly motivated "advisory" system for the programming language PROLOG, see Coombs and Alty 1984.

12. In this regard it is interesting to note that a great debate ensued surrounding the status of the DOCTOR program as a psychotherapeutic tool. That debate took on a humorous tone when Weizenbaum submitted a letter to the Forum of the Association for Computing Machinery, an excerpt from which follows:

Below is a listing of a pl/1 program that causes a typewriter console to imitate the verbal behavior of an autistic patient. The "doctor" types his interrogatories on the console. It responds exactly as does an autistic patient—that is, not at all. I have validated this model following the procedure first used in commercial advertising by Carter's Little Liver Pills ("Seven New York doctors say . . .") and later used so brilliantly by Dr K. M. Colby in his simulation of paranoia [a reference to Colby. K. M. *et al.* 1972]; I gave N psychiatrists access to my program and asked each to say from what mental disorder it suffered. M psychiatrists (M < N) said the (expletive deleted) program was autistic. (The methodological assumption here is that if two processes have identical input/output behaviors, then one constitutes an explanation of the other.)

The program has the advantage that it can be implemented on a plain typewriter not connected to a computer at all. (Weizenbaum 1983, p. 28)

References

Berreman, G. 1966. Anemic and emetic analyses in social anthropology. *American Anthropologist* 68(2)1:346–54.

Bobrow, D. G., Kaplan, R. M., Kay, M., Norman, D. A., Thompson, H., and Winograd, T. 1977. GUS: a frame-driven dialogue system. *Artificial Intelligence* 8:155–73.

Burton, R. and Brown, J. S. 1982. An investigation of computer coaching for informal learning activities. In *Intelligent Tutoring Systems*, D. Sleeman and J. S. Brown, eds. London: Academic Press.

Carbonell, J. R. 1971. *Mixed-Initiative Man–Computer Dialogues*. Technical Report 1970, Bolt Beranek and Newman, Inc., Cambridge, MA.

Carey, S. 1985. *Conceptual Change in Childhood*. Cambridge, MA: MIT Press.

Churchland, P. 1984. *Matter and Consciousness*. Cambridge, MA: MIT Press.

Cohen, J. 1966. *Human Robots in Myth and Science*. London: Allen and Unwin.

Colby, K. M. et al. 1972. Turing-like indistinguishability tests for the validation of a computer simulation of paranoid processes. *Artificial Intelligence* 3:199–221.

Coombs, M. and Alty, J. 1984. Expert systems: an alternative paradigm. *International Journal of Man–Machine Studies* 20:21–43.

Coulter, J. 1979. *The Social Construction of Mind*. Totowa, NJ: Rowman and Littlefield.

———. 1983. *Rethinking Cognitive Theory*. New York, NY: St. Martin's Press.

Dennett, D. 1978. *Brainstorms*. Cambridge, MA: MIT Press.

Dreyfus, H. 1979. *What Computers Can't Do: The Limits of Artificial Intelligence,* revised edition. New York, NY: Harper and Row.

———, ed. 1982. *Husserl Intentionality and Cognitive Science*. Cambridge, MA: MIT Press.

Fitter, M. 1979. Towards more "natural" interactive systems. *International Journal of Man–Machine Studies* 11:339–49.

Fodor, J. 1983. *The Modularity of Mind*. Cambridge, MA: MIT Press.

Gardner, H. 1985. *The Mind's New Science*. New York: Basic Books.

Garfinkel, H. 1967. *Studies in Ethnomethodology*. Englewood Cliffs, NJ: Prentice-Hall.

Gladwin, T. 1964. Culture and logical process. In *Explorations in Cultural Anthropology: Essays Presented to George Peter Murdock,* W. Goodenough, ed. New York, NY: McGraw-Hill.

Grosz, B. 1981. Focusing and description in natural language dialogues. In *Elements of Discourse Understanding*, Joshi, A., Webber, B., and Sag, I., eds. Cambridge University Press.

Hayes, P. 1981. A construction-specific approach to focused interaction in flexible parsing. *Proceedings of Nineteenth Annual Meeting of the Association for Computational Linguistics,* pp. 149–52. Stanford, CA: Stanford University.

Hayes, P. and Reddy, D. R. 1983. Steps toward graceful interaction in spoken and written man–machine communication. *International Journal of Man–Machine Studies* 19:231–84.

Hendrix, G. G. 1977. Human engineering for applied natural language processing. *Proceedings of the Fifth International Joint Conference on Artificial Intelligence,* pp. 183–91. Cambridge MA: MIT.

McCorduck, P. 1979. *Machines Who Think*. San Francisco, CA: W. H. Freeman.

MacKay, D. M. 1962. The use of behavioral language to refer to mechanical processes. *British Journal of Philosophical Science,* 13:89–103.

Nickerson, R. 1976. On conversational interaction with computers. In *Proceedings of ACM/SIGGRAPH workshop,* October 14–15, pp. 101–13. Pittsburgh, PA.

Oberquelle, H., Kupka, I., and Maass, S. 1983. A view of human-machine communication and cooperation. *International Journal of Man–Machine Studies* 19:309–33.

Pylyshyn, Z. 1974. Minds, machines and phenomenology: some reflections on Dreyfus' What Computers Can't Do. *Cognition* 3:57–77.

———. 1984. *Computation and Cognition*. Cambridge, MA: MIT Press.

Sidner, C. L. 1979. *Towards a computational theory of definite anaphora comprehension in English discourse*. Technical Report TR-537, MIT AI Laboratory. Cambridge, MA.

Stich, S. 1983. *From Folk Psychology to Cognitive Science*. Cambridge, MA: MIT Press.

Turing, A. M. 1950. Computing machinery and intelligence. *Mind* 59(236): 433–61.

Turkle, S. 1984. *The Second Self*. New York, NY: Simon and Schuster.

Turner, R. 1962. Words, utterances and activities. In *Ethnomethodology: Selected readings,* ed. Turner. Harmondsworth, Middlesex: Penguin.

Watt, W. C. 1968. Habitability. *American Documentation* 19(3):338–51.

Weizenbaum, J. 1983. ELIZA: a computer program for the study of natural language communication between man and machine. *Communications of the ACM, 25th Anniversary Issue,* 26(1):23–7. (Reprinted from Communications of the ACM, 29(1):36–45, January 1966.)

# 42. [Introduction]
# Siren Shapes
## Exploratory and Constructive Hypertexts

The hypertext of the Web is not the hypertext imagined by Vannevar Bush (◊02), Doug Engelbart (◊08, ◊16), or Ted Nelson (◊11, ◊21, ◊30)—as reading these authors makes clear, the Web edition is much more limited. Understanding the limitations of the Web's hypertext is not simply an occasion for complaint, however. It helps reveal the potential that still lies within the hypertext concept, untapped by mainstream new media. In the following essay, Michael Joyce gave a name to an important distinction between two types of hypertext environments—those that are "exploratory" and those that are "constructive." His distinction maps onto significant differences between the environment in which we currently experience the Web and the ideas of early hypertext creators, while also usefully describing other areas of new media, helping reveal both limitations and opportunities.

According to Joyce, *constructive hypertexts* are those in the process of creation by the user/author. They are flexible representations of thoughts, stories, arguments, and everything else for which we use media. Exploratory hypertexts are former constructive hypertexts, now being experienced by a user/reader who is not an author of the work. In an environment such as those described by Bush, Engelbart, and Nelson, a user can freely move back and forth between the roles of author and reader, between the experiences of construction and exploration. A constructive hypertext environment provides something more than an electric textbook or workbook: it makes all exploratory hypertexts into material that the user/author can place within the space of the constructive hypertext they are always already creating. This process of creation, Joyce argues, holds much more promise for transforming education than does simple electric reading with links.

Constructive hypertext has largely remained an exciting activity on the periphery of education. But the tool that Joyce, J. David Bolter (◊47), and John B. Smith created to embody their goals of constructive, "topographic" hypertext creation has been very influential in another area: electronic literature. *Storyspace*, marketed now by Eastgate Systems, was, before the rise of the Web, the primary creative medium for hypertext literature, rivaled only by Apple's HyperCard.

The Web has yet to include many of the features that Joyce associates with exploratory hypertext, such as the ability for users to create annotations and links—perhaps because no one has developed a revenue model to support offering such services over and above the current Web environment's basic features. IBM offered an early service to allow users to add and share links between Web sites. This service, Aqui, has been discontinued. Third Voice later offered a mechanism for making public annotations to Web pages—until the company folded. Link servers are now available from Active Navigation and other companies, but as an internal service for organizations, not a public facility. No major Web software even allows the user to create private links and annotations during reading.

Such facilities might be added to a browser such as Mozilla (perhaps along with alterations to a server such as Apache) by enterprising individuals. The more essential question is whether it will be possible to create constructive hypertext in the space of the Web, technically or legally. Technically, most existing Web pages are monolithic constructions, and far from amenable to what Ted Nelson calls "transclusion"—which would be necessary for appropriately including portions of old-style Web pages in a newly constructive Web. However, the World Wide Web consortium is at work on some elegant solutions for deep addressing in monolithic Web pages, Nelson is currently exploring the transclusion possibilities opened by these new standards and other approaches, and at the very

Joyce writes in the context of education, which is fitting not only because Joyce is an educator, but also because the constructive/exploratory distinction can also help describe the differences between Seymour Papert's LOGO and Computer-Aided Instruction systems (◊28), or between Alan Kay and Adele Goldberg's Dynabook (◊26) developed at PARC's Learning Research Group and MacOS or Windows.

◊02 35
◊08 93
◊11 133
◊16 231

Eastgate remains the most prominent commercial publisher of electronic literature, with an early catalog that includes fictions by Joyce, Stuart Moulthrop (◊48), and other leading new media figures. Some of Eastgate's groundbreaking titles anticipated now-widespread Web literary practices—an example is Deena Larsen's *Marble Springs*, which invited contributions to its network from readers, and managed to get them, despite the fact that delivery required significantly more effort that hitting a Web form's "submit" button.

◊21 301
◊26 391
◊28 413
◊30 441

**613**

Nelson discusses this using terms such as "windowing"—rather than "transclusion"—in his first version of *Literary Machines* (◊30).

◊47 679
◊48 691

Michael Joyce is also the author of *Afternoon, a story*—one of the most influential hypertext fictions ever written. It is discussed by Robert Coover (◊49) and Espen Aarseth (◊52).

Robert Kendall's "The Clue" is a 1991 poem presented using 2-D computer animation and music ⊗.

least many images are stored in a manner that would allow them to be easily transcluded. Given this, the next matters to consider are legal ones, where the picture is not rosy. A number of lawsuits have already been waged to prevent linking to, and contextualizing of, Web information in a way that its owner considered inappropriate. As the Web continues to integrate with the larger media industry, legal territorialism seems likely to grow only more vicious. Constructive hypertext may be simply be incompatible with our current cultural moment. While some might exclaim that our culture will have to change in the face of hypertext's manifest destiny toward the constructive, evidence for such assertions is lacking. Rather it seems possible that constructive islands will have to exist separately, and then "export" to the Web—or, if constructive hypertext is made part of the "live" Web, that budding builders will have to be very careful of what they include in their reading/writing process.

Meanwhile, just as Seymour Papert's constructionist educational philosophies can be applied with pencil and paper, educators and writers are working to employ constructive hypertext models in the barely-exploratory environment of the Web; Robert Kendall's Connection Muse is one example. —NWF

CritSuite (from the Foresight Institute) and Annotation Engine (from the Berkman Center for Internet & Society, Harvard Law School) are currently-active, open source projects seeking to bring annotation to the Web. Annotea is a project of the World Wide Web consortium in this area, which uses and helps to advance open Web standards. <http://crit.org/> <http://cyber.law. harvard.edu/projects/annotate.html> <http://www.w3c.org/2001/Annotea/>

Further Reading

Eastgate Systems <http://www.eastgate.com>

Goose, Stuart, Wendy Hall, and Siegfried Reich. "Microcosm TNG: A Framework for Distributed Open Hypermedia" *IEEE MultiMedia* 7:3, Los Alamitos, Calif.: IEEE, 52–60, July-September 2000. <http://www.computer.org/dsonline/articles/ds3rei.htm>

Joyce, Michael. *Othermindedness: the Emergence of Network Culture*. Ann Arbor: University of Michigan Press, 2000.

Kendall, Robert, and Jean-Hugues Réty. Word Circuits Connection Muse. Web site offering download of the Connection Muse tools. <http://www.wordcircuits.com/connect/>

Original Publication
*Academic Computing* 3:10–14, 37–42, 1988. Reprinted in Michael Joyce, *Of Two Minds: Hypertext Pedagogy and Poetics*. Ann Arbor: University of Michigan Press, 1995. The works cited section here is from the reprinting.

◊049
705

◊052
761

# Siren Shapes
## Exploratory and Constructive Hypertexts

# Michael Joyce

Hypertext and hypermedia are increasingly perceived as instances of a cardinal technology, i.e., tools for working at traditional tasks which have the effect of changing the tasks themselves. Yet, a fairly common reaction to hypertext and hypermedia systems in product reviews, in technical literature, and among everyday users of these tools is the one

expressed by Jeffrey Conklin in his still definitive article: "One must work in current hypertext environments for a while for the collection of features to coalesce into a useful tool." (Conklin, 1987)

This is a kind way to say that you have to figure out what to do with these things. I have spent much of the last four years figuring out exactly that. As a co-developer (with Jay Bolter and John B. Smith) of Storyspace, a hypertext program for the Macintosh computer to be published by Brøderbund Software this year*, I have approached what to do with these things as a design question. As a fiction writer seeking to work in a new medium, I have approached it as an artistic question; and as a teacher, a practical, pedagogic, and a sometime political one.

* Storyspace would actually be published by Eastgate Systems, <http://www.eastgate.com>. The company has recently released version 2. —*Eds.*

My colleagues and I have had three years experience using hypertext tools in a variety of settings within a comprehensive community college. Storyspace has been used not only as a day to day writing and thinking tool, but also in Chemistry, Nursing, Technical Writing, Creative Writing, Literature, and Developmental Reading and Writing courses. Users include faculty, community professionals, creative writers, and a wide range of traditional and non-traditional students, from high school age to senior citizens.

Our experience in using Storyspace predates the release of both Guide and HyperCard and began with fairly unstable developmental versions and continues as Storyspace is shaped for commercial release. It has helped us test our notions about learning and informed our work in designing hypertext learning tools using Storyspace and HyperCard both. To some extent, then, given this kind of applied design and testing, I have also approached the question of what to do with hypertexts as a research question.

Given all these claimed approaches, it would seem I ought to have gotten somewhere. I will try to say where that might be, and I will even take the obligatory stab at explaining what hypertext is, as well as what it might become. (Hereafter, I will use the term hypertext where hypermedia would do as well, since nearly all hypertext systems involve other media, and I know of no hypermedia systems which use no text.) Before that, however, I want to discuss— briefly and, in the hypertext spirit, idiosyncratically— some design issues, artistic issues, and ultimately practical, pedagogic, and even political issues which we ignore at our peril. In doing so, I want to offer a somewhat polemical (and, for a hypertext developer, arguably self-serving) description of a set of these perils as well as a set of the promises which accompany them.

Indeed, hypertext tools offer the promise of adapting themselves to fundamental cognitive skills which experts routinely, subtly, and self-consciously apply in accomplishing intellectual tasks. Moreover, hypertext tools promise to unlock these skills for novice learners and to empower and enfranchise their learning. Ironically, however, our ability to deliver upon these promises may be imperiled in the short run by many of the same factors which make this technology so promising.

For instance, the ready adaptability of these tools to more traditional uses is especially compelling given the technological frosting they so easily spread upon stale cake. This disincentive to change is in no way novel, either in the long history of cardinal technologies, or, especially, in the short history of microcomputers in education. The adaptability of HyperCard, for instance, makes it easy to "author" educational software which merely redistributes the command lines of the worst kinds of supposedly interactive, "drills-and-skills," CAI software into gaily embossed buttons and peek-a-boo card fields. Like the Applesoft BASIC revolution in educational software which preceded it and which it so clearly resembles, the HyperCard revolution requires us to rely upon skeptical eyes, keep a shrewd ear open to word-of-mouth (or word-of-network) advice, and exercise a cool hand (and fast delete finger) in choosing among a burgeoning list of titles.

Because the price is right (again, like the Applesoft revolution, much of this software is shareware or relatively inexpensive), it is likely that the potential benefits outweigh nearly all the short run perils save perhaps the most crucial one. The peril of over-promising threatens not just to sap the resilience of educators who must wade through the dross and justify the costs. It also threatens the credibility and creativity of innovators who find themselves having to disaffiliate and differentiate before they can discover. Avoiding the peril of over-promising, I will argue below, depends upon our ability to distinguish between what I call Exploratory and Constructive uses of hypertext as a learning tool and our willingness to pursue and encourage the development of both.

By exploratory use I mean to describe the increasingly familiar use of hypertext as a delivery or presentational technology, i.e., as Guide and HyperCard are currently most often used. Exploratory hypertexts encourage and enable an audience (users or readers are inadequate terms here) to control the transformation of a body of information to meet its needs and interests. This transformation should include a capability to create, change, and recover particular encounters with the body of knowledge, maintaining these encounters as versions of the material, i.e., trails, paths, webs, notebooks, etc.

The hypertext audience should also be able to readily understand the elements which make up a particular body of knowledge, plot the progress through these elements, and locate them at will. These so-called navigational capabilities should be present both within the organizational structure of the hypertext and from the perspective of the particular versions of it which the audience creates. At least in the short run, and especially in educational hypertexts, the audience should be able to view alternative visual representations of the corpus's structure and, in some sense, be able to differentiate the unique organizational schemes of hypertext from the more conventional organizations of print and other media. Ideally, an exploratory hypertext should enable its audience members to view and test alternative organizational structures of their own and, perhaps, compare their own structures of thought with hypertext and traditional ones.

By constructive use I mean to describe a much less familiar use of hypertext as an invention or analytic tool, i.e., the uses we have designed for and made of Storyspace. These are also the uses to which outline processors and their offspring, Personal Information Managers (PIMs) such as Agenda and Grandview, have been put. For that matter, these are also the uses which have sometimes been forced upon word processors, spreadsheets, and databases. Just as exploratory hypertexts are designed for audiences, constructive hypertexts are designed for what Jane Yellowlees Douglas has termed "scriptor[s]." (Douglas, 1987) Scriptors use constructive hypertexts to develop a body of information which they map according to their needs, their interests, and the transformations they discover as they invent, gather, and act upon that information. Moreso than with exploratory hypertexts, constructive hypertexts require a capability to act: to create, to change, and to recover particular encounters within the developing body of knowledge. These encounters, like those in exploratory hypertexts, are maintained as versions, i.e., trails, paths, webs, notebooks, etc.; but they are versions of what they are becoming, a structure for what does not yet exist. Constructive hypertexts, unlike exploratory ones, require visual representations of the knowledge they develop. They are, in Jay Bolter's phrase, topographic writing.

Like the audience of exploratory hypertexts, scriptors should be able to readily understand the elements which make up a developing body of knowledge, plot their progress through these elements, chart new ones, and locate them at will. These so-called navigational capabilities should be present within both the developing organizational structure of the hypertext and within the particular versions of it which the scriptor discovers. Scriptors must be able not merely to view but also to manipulate alternative visual

representations of the invented structure of the hypertext, switching between them with a minimum of intellectual effort, or what Conklin has termed cognitive overhead. They must be able to differentiate and label unique organizational schemes of hypertext, plotting them against more conventional organizations of print and other media, and generating either kind of organization at will. A constructive hypertext should be a tool for inventing, discovering, viewing, and testing multiple, alternative, organizational structures, as well as a tool for comparing these structures of thought with more traditional ones, and transforming the one into the other.

Transformation of knowledge, I would suggest, is the litmus test we should use in judging both exploratory and constructive hypertexts. It is a critical test in judging whether courseware authored with hypertext tools engages learners in looking at material in new ways, or merely looks like a new way of learning. In many ways, of course, this kind of test is not new to us. Understanding, plotting, navigating, and recreating knowledge structures is the essence of learning. As the current critical thinking across the curriculum craze attests; however, we are less and less certain of our ability to convey these skills.

This uncertainty, coupled with the novelty and ease of authoring with hypertext tools, raises the peril of over-promising. Too often, despite our inbred intellectual skepticism and knowledge about free lunches, we in education have approached technology with what might be called a hunger for automaticity. Both well and poorly designed exploratory hypertexts feed this hunger. It is easy to think that, because learners can move through a body of knowledge in new ways, they know where they are going. We long for a learning machine and think that the computer will do, even as we know that the computer did not do the first time around (and the SRA carrel with its "programmed learning" buttons did not do before it).

Poorly designed exploratory hypertexts often involve a second or third coming of the learning machine. They assuage the hunger for automaticity with the full-bellied inertia of tradition. We know the bulk of this stuff; we have chewed it over for years. It is easy to think that, because learners can move through a body of knowledge in new ways, we know where they are going.

Yet, neither we nor they know as much about learning as either party would think. Paradoxically, we know too much about learning to make such claims. It is a fair bet to say that our age is at least as likely to be known in the future as the Age of Learning as it is as by the ordained cliche, the Information Age. The body of knowledge about learning in psychology, cognitive science, neurophysiology, artificial intelligence, and so on, would itself make a rich exploratory hypertext. The individual versions we might create as we wend our way through this corpus would likely share certain sets of contrary attributes. Learning is multiple yet integrative, difficult yet universal, not easily schematized yet apparently systematic, inherently personal and yet socially manifested, and so on.

These contraries provide cautionary measures against which to judge exploratory hypertexts as learning tools. Also, they introduce and outline the promise of what I have termed constructive hypertexts. Every well-designed, exploratory hypertext proceeds from a constructive hypertext created by its author or team of authors. The transformation of knowledge which an audience works upon an exploratory hypertext, in some important sense, parallels and rehearses the prior constructive encounter of its authors' associative thought processes. In this instance, however, the word parallel is almost certainly metaphoric language and inadequate at that for a process which is sometimes orthogonal, sometimes congruent, sometimes isomorphic, but always, in some important sense, anticipatory. The authors and audience of hypertexts share a transforming interrelationship. They are, to use an overused term, co-learners. Even the most transparent exploratory hypertexts involve a shared process of mapping this interrelationship, while constructive hypertexts make the transparent mapping visible, active and personal.

The importance of the *process* of associative thinking is suggested in a preliminary evaluation of the Intermedia project at Brown University. Discussing Professor George Landow's groundbreaking work in designing the Intermedia English 32 course, IRIS investigators reported an "unintended consequence of [their] research, discovered when Professor Landow was forced to teach . . . before the [Intermedia] workstations . . . were ready . . . was that he changed the way he organized his course. As a result he felt that students grasped pluralistic reasoning styles far better than in previous years." (Beeman et al., 1987) The authors go on to note that "students were also far more satisfied with the course than in previous years," and present data which

show interesting shifts in students' evaluation of both the amount learned in the class and their overall evaluation of the course.

Both sets of evaluations rose significantly when the course was offered before the workstations and exploratory hypertexts were ready for students. When the course was offered with the workstations, both sets largely maintained gains but, interestingly, fell off to previous levels (or beyond) among students who rated their learning as less—or the class worse—than other classes at Brown. Meanwhile, high end ratings fell off enough to make them of interest.

At least one implication of these shifts is worthy of further research and, more to the point, suggests the potential for constructive hypertexts as instruments of learning. Landow's reorganization of his course might be said to have mirrored his associative (or pluralistic) thought processes in creating a constructive hypertext, i.e., the design for the exploratory hypertext, English 32. As a distinguished scholar and critic, he certainly possessed these associative, pluralistic thought processes well before he set out to represent them in a hypertext. Yet, the benefits of doing so were dramatically perceptible to his students. It would seem to follow that these same benefits ought to be extended to learners themselves, especially if further investigation of such "unintended consequence[s]" yields evidence that exploratory hypertexts yield benefits to instruction which are short-lived or, at least, subject to degradation.

It would only be stirring the hunger for automaticity to suppose that, simply by the instrument of creating constructive hypertexts, students could match the prowess of a practiced scholar in associative thought. However, it would be equally unwise, and something over-promising, to suggest that students could gain that prowess by simply exploring the scholar's representation of it. The Intermedia project, to be sure, does not make either mistake; while largely a vehicle for exploratory hypertexts, it provides powerful constructive tools for learners to use in transforming bodies of knowledge.

The importance of an anticipatory, transforming interrelationship among co-learners may perhaps not represent a novel contribution to our understanding of learning; but hypertext, as a cardinal technology, does offer a novel environment for enabling and exploiting that interrelationship. Constructive hypertexts renew an ancient promise, one which would make us know ourselves and become authors of our learning.

This author's role in this transforming interrelationship is like that of Jane Yellowlees Douglas's "scriptor for the potential experiences of . . . readers." While Douglas concerns herself with hypertext interactive fiction, her insights into the importance of authorial intention hold true for more expository, exploratory hypertexts in which scriptor-learners intentionally become their own readers. "The yields we select, the defaults we discover, influence our understanding of the contents of the text we read," says Douglas, "in most cases, we realize that we have, somewhat unwittingly, made certain interpretive or navigational decisions based upon our apprehension of authorial intention." When the author is oneself, apprehending authorial intention becomes a discovery of one's own distinctive structures of thought.

Douglas focuses upon the literary-critical implications of this apparent and awkward resurrection of authorial intention as a "subject" of literary texts. Other hypertext theorists such as Diane Pelkus Balestri, Jay Bolter, and Frank Halasz address the relationship between authorial intention and structures of thought more directly. In the February 1988 issue of this magazine, Balestri discusses the "constructability" of what she calls softcopy (echoing a term which, Ted Nelson informs me, he coined in the mid-60s). In Balestri's usage, softcopy, i.e., text on the screen rather than in print, leads to an understanding of "text as having patterns, often multiple patterns for a single text; [and] defines coherence in terms of linkages among parts of a text." "Hypertext," she suggests later, "unlike softcopy, changes the relationship between writer and reader. The reader becomes a collaborator, constructing and reconstructing the text, choosing his own path through it."

The differences Balestri sees here, between the coherent patterns of links among parts of a text and the constructed patterns which a reader makes, might prove less a distinction between softcopy and hypertext than another description of the interrelationship between scriptor and audience. In any case, Balestri points to the need for training hypertext audiences in the new habits of thought necessary to perceive coherence in patterns and links, and to generate coherent patterns and links of their own.

These concerns are, as I have noted, not much different from the concerns we bundle under the rubric of critical thinking, or the general category of learning. Constructive hypertexts address these concerns in a more conscious way than exploratory hypertexts. They enable audiences of expert and novice readers alike to act as scriptors and focus upon the discovery of coherent structures and linkages; and, most importantly, to use a full range of cognitive skills, especially visual ones, to discover new structures and linkages. Balestri's notion of softcopy invites us to consider how coherence can be (and is) both visually represented and perceived, and to consider how we can train learners both to recognize and to generate visual representations of patterns of structure.

My collaborator, Jay Bolter, in his book *Writing Space* argues that these coherent patterns and links are elemental aspects of the associative nature of writing:

> . . . no text is only a hierarchy of elements. A hierarchy is always an attempt to impose rigid order upon verbal ideas that are always prone to subvert that order. The principle of hierarchy in writing is always in conflict with the principle of association. One word echoes another, one sentence or paragraph recalls many others earlier in the text and looks forward to still others. . . . Associative relationships define alternative organizations that lie beneath the order of pages and chapters. . . . Previous technologies of writing, which could not easily accommodate such alternatives, tended to ignore them. The printed book has made the best effort to accommodate both hierarchy and association. . . . The table of contents, listing chapters and sometimes sections, reveals the hierarchy of a text, while the indices record associative lines of thought that permeate the text. . . . An index defines other books that could be constructed from the original book . . . and so invites the reader to read the book in alternative ways.

Bolter proposes that electronic writing, such as hypertext, is an instance of what he calls "topographic writing . . . both a visual and a verbal description . . . not the writing of a place, but rather writing of or with places, spatially realized topics." Topographical writing is a spatial, visual medium as well as a verbal one. (Another reason I prefer the term hypertext to hypermedia is precisely because hypertext treats *everything* as topographical text; hypertext is the word's revenge on TV.)

"Although the computer is not necessary for topographical writing," Bolter notes, "it is only in the computer that the mode becomes a natural and, therefore, also a conventional, way to write." For the computer "provides a writing surface with an extension and structure unlike previous technologies," one in which "topics . . . have both an intrinsic and extrinsic significance . . . they have a meaning that may be explained in words, and they have meaning as elements in a larger structure of verbal gestures."

Frank Halasz focuses upon the distinctive inter-relationship between scripted and discovered patterns of structure. Halasz notes that hypermedia systems, of course, require the capability to search for specific content, i.e., words, keywords, and so on. However, noting that "content search basically ignores the structure of a hypermedia network," he calls for the development of "structure searches" in hypermedia systems. As Halasz describes them, structure searches are not merely ways of seeking patterned coherence, but in fact ways to identify what Bolter calls elements in a larger structure of verbal gestures. (Halasz, 1987)

As an example of a "complicated structure query, involving an indefinite sequence of links," Halasz proposes a formulation which, though somewhat of a technical sounding riddle, is nonetheless quite visual: "a circular structure containing a card that is linked to itself via an unbroken sequence of 'supports' links." With a little study this verbal formulation discloses the structure of the riddle. "This query," says Halasz, "could be used, for example, to find circular arguments." More importantly, as topographic writing in a hypertext, the visual riddle might likely be solved more easily than the verbal riddle of the query. In this case, the authorial intention, or inattention, of a scriptor would disclose itself in a conscious search for patterned links; and scripted links would become discovered links.

As another of his seven issues, Halasz proposes the need for "virtual or dynamically-determined structures" as a way to eliminate the "static nature of hypermedia networks." Again, the verbal riddle is more foreboding than the visual one here. Hypermedia networks are static because they only contain patterns and linkages which you, or someone, put there on purpose; they are what Halasz calls "extensionally defined" because the "exact identity of their components" are specified. For example, you might build a structure of everything your student, Betsy, wrote to you while you were away at a conference, but that structure isn't there until you decide to put it there. You cannot, in fact, see it.

A dynamically-determined structure would just show up whenever you wanted it to. You would, in fact, have to query the hypertext at least once, building what Halasz calls an "intensionally defined" structure. To paraphrase Halasz's example, you would specify a sub-network containing all the nodes created by Betsy in the last week. However, once that

structure was created, every time you looked at it you would see what Betsy wrote during the last week. What you look for would be there to see when you looked. (This notion is not unlike what Alan Kay, the distinguished Apple Fellow, has termed a "software agent.")

It is not too far-fetched, I think, to suggest that the ideas of Douglas, Balestri, Bolter, and Halasz open the possibility that hypertext learning tools may result in the discovery of what might, in a bad pun, be termed missing links, i.e., novel structures of thought and new rhetorical forms. What may seem far-fetched now is, I think, not just likely but certain. These new forms promise (or, if you will, threaten) to rival, or even supplant, the structures we have come to believe are more god-given than Gutenbergian.

This raises another peril, one perhaps more serious than over-promising. It does take some time to get used to and use from, hypertext tools, especially when you use them constructively. Once you are used to them, they seem to adapt themselves so effortlessly to quite familiar, almost fleeting, and seemingly routine habits of mind that you are hard put to characterize, let alone schematize, them. Because of their fleeting quality, it is tempting to trivialize such habits of mind; because of the difficulty in schematizing them, it is tempting to presume them inferior to more established habits and structures.

To the extent that hypertext challenges traditional intellectual structures, it may be that this cardinal technology, like others before it, will threaten too much to unhinge us. We may perhaps, in the short term at least, lack the vision to appropriate these tools to the new tasks they suggest.

A true test of a challenge to traditional intellectual structures might be whether it is embraced as commonplace by those who do not feel heirs to the tradition. For the past few years, my colleagues Cherry Conrad and Mark Harris and I have used Storyspace as a constructive hypertext tool with students who are often forgotten heirs of a passing tradition. Developmental readers and writers are students assessed as needing further work in writing and reading comprehension in order to succeed in college work. Unlike the technical or creative writing students with whom we have used Storyspace, these students have very little experience with computer programs, keyboarding, or writing environments; and usually possess little or no conscious awareness of formal organizational structures for writing. Compared to these other students, developmental students make minimal

619

use of the complex linking and on-screen hypertext capabilities of our program.

Nonetheless, I want to concentrate on my experience with developmental students including the particular experiences of one student. I offer this account merely as what it is: not qualitative research or protocol analysis, not research or analysis by any means, but rather that most unstable currency, the teaching anecdote. By doing so, I hope to suggest that the challenge of hypertext to traditional structures can take on commonplace dimensions; and that disenfranchised students, like expert learners, can use such tools to empower themselves in transforming knowledge to their own ends.

Teaching anecdotes of this kind tend to be mini-Odysseys, accounts of where we went, what we saw, and, ultimately, how the world had changed upon our return. To have any sort of mythic power, however, these accounts require some measure of the gates through which we sailed, and how we saw the world as we left. I admit to steering a course between cautionary and visionary pillars. It is cautionary and important in a realm of over-promise to keep in mind Guide inventor P. J. Brown's injunction that "those of us who expect the whole world to rewrite its documentation to fit the needs of our new hypertext system are unlikely to have our expectations fulfilled." (Brown, 1987) This is to say that in using Storyspace with these students, as much as at any time I have taught developmental writing before, I set sail determined, again quoting Brown, to "fit the world as it is, rather than the world as we would like it to be." Developmental students demand as much, although doing so in the most quiet and effective way possible, by ignoring without indication or complaint anything which their very practical experience tells them is bogus.

On the other hand, as teacher, writer, and software designer, I could not avoid navigating by the perhaps visionary truth of what Michael Heim calls "not at all extravagant" assumptions about the future: "Writing will increasingly be freed from the constraints of paper-print technology . . . and vast amounts of information . . . will be accessible immediately below the electronic surface of a piece of writing." (Heim, 1987)

What I saw in my student Les was an ability to see himself as freed of these constraints; constraints which he and his fellow students had, admittedly, freed themselves of long before either by rejecting them outright, or simply failing to learn. What had changed in Les and other students, however, was their ability to perceive and express, as easily as Heim does here, the existence of information below the surface of a writing, and to use that awareness of structure in commonplace fashion to empower themselves.

This is obviously a long way to sail and a fantastical vision to claim to have seen. I should say how we got there. Like many others, the Developmental Education Department at our community college assesses entering students such as Les in the areas of writing, reading comprehension, and mathematics. The writing assessment is a holistically-scored, timed-writing measure in which students write in response to a stimulus. Like most students Les's placement in English 101, Introduction to Writing, was based primarily on his difficulties with organizing a piece of writing and supporting his ideas.

Students are assessed again upon completion of the developmental writing course, and, even before I began using Storyspace with them, my students already demonstrated a high degree of success in post term assessments. I mention this both to avoid any suggestion of automaticity and to suggest another, obvious cautionary note. That is, to the extent that the design of our hypertext writing tool was shaped by my understanding of the writing process, my students might be expected to succeed in using that tool.

Even so, to counterpose a visionary note, success, too, has its variations, few of which can be expected or explained as adaptive behavior. Les succeeded in unexpected and very simple ways, ones which I did not recognize at first and can only incompletely represent now. Quite unselfconsciously and routinely, this eighteen-year old, would-be auto mechanic grasped what was accessible under the surface of an electronic (or, for that matter, traditional) writing and made it his own. Moreover, he did so in a way I had not seen my students do so before, and which, in some sense, made me feel a generational alien, an outdated user of a tool I had helped make.

Mine is what might be called a neo-traditional process model for teaching writing. That is, like many writing teachers I reject pre and post writing distinctions in favor of what is in my case a recursive three-stage model of form-finding, focusing, and shaping. In the form-finding phase, I encourage students to develop an awareness of "impulses toward form" (plans) and "transitory strategies for organization" (goals); using "interrupted automatic writings" to encourage a physiological awareness of shifts in intentionality (impulses or plans) and an ability to visualize and map them graphically on a handwritten page.

I likewise encourage mapping of the consequent shifts in intentionality into provisional organizational structures (strategies or goals). During initial weeks I use a progressively disclosed hierarchical sequence of abstraction—in which students are requested to consider objects, persons, and ideas in that order—to introduce the concept of "writing toward," an intentionally fuzzy scheme of organizational approximation.

My students are encouraged to map overlapping strategies (or goals) and to identify changes in impulses (or plans) at their intersections by drawing boxes or frames on their writings. They are likewise encouraged, I should note, to map their own emerging understanding of the writing process against my language for this process, even the most jargony quasi-cognitive-scientific, which I use with them in the same way I do here.

On one level the language is our shared joke against the English teacher world; on another, it is as mythic and empowering as any other part of this Odyssey, a set of more-or-less understood names for skills they possess and have learned to recognize. In any event, this may explain why they are fairly undaunted when they come to use a somewhat complex computer writing environment—something most of my composition colleagues are curious, or even skeptical, about. Most developmental students have long suspected that something familiar lies behind the codes used against them and have developed remarkably complex codes to defend themselves with. Thus, they indulge me in my codes, especially when it comes to computers, which they view, rightly, as the ultimate code machines.

In the focusing phase, students use their cognitive mapping skills to help identify a network of interconnected, though not necessarily sequential, plans which lead to the development of the sequence of goals which will be presented to the reader, thus introducing a recursive notion of shaping. Students are encouraged to continue form-finding recursively whenever sequences are not clear to them, or might not be clear to an eventual reader, thus building a matching, recursive notion of form-finding.

By the time Les came into my course, I had begun introducing Storyspace to my students midway in the consideration of the second stage of the writing process. I showed Les and his classmates how to "port" the writings they had begun during the semester as well as their mapping skills to Storyspace. I encouraged them to use the program as a first stage of the shaping phase, developing an existing writing for an audience—in this case in-class workshops, and then I, more or less, let them be.

By the time Storyspace came to Les, it had gained some but not all of the features which it will have in release early in the new year. A set of tool icons is arrayed in the familiar Macintosh palette (see Figure 42.1) to the left of a scrollable, empty window in which the structure of a writing and its links are eventually created. The first set of tools let you add and delete the fundamental building blocks of our program, what we call places, in the structure window. Places are individual, editable elements which can contain writing (including graphics); they may be combined into areas which indicate inclusion or subsumption. An area is a place which contains other places. The primary area is the document

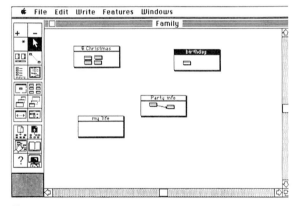

Figure 42.1.

itself, which may be thought of as a nearly infinite space within which places may be created, connected, ordered, and referenced.

Other tools in this first set let you create automatically linked places for notes; select the pointer for navigation and other operations; use a powerful interactive mini-database to gather and link places in various documents; link places into paths across hierarchies in one or more documents; and choose among what we call Outline, Chart, or Map views of an emerging document.

A second set of window management tools lets you center places in a window; collapse, expand, or organize window displays; enlarge or reduce window sizes; restore the startup size window; and create a copy of the current window.

The third and most powerful tools let you use a "blockbuster" function to create new places from the text of any existing place; use a "blockmaker" function to gather texts from the various places into one place; use a "place-marker" function to create a path of the places you work with or read; navigate through the displays and texts for your documents in either an editable or read-only fashion; get information about documents, places, or text; and link widespread places into paths across one or more documents.

Finally, various menu commands let you import and export texts from word processors or outline processors; distribute sections of text among places; generate new hierarchies from paths; and so on. Throughout its interface Storyspace operates on something of a principle of redundancy to counteract cognitive overhead. We have tried to design an inertialess structure editor in which creating, linking, and rearranging parts of a document can be accomplished in a number of ways, according to your preference, and almost always visually represented.

Powerful word processors often allow you to adapt command keys and menu items to suit your preferences, but largely require you to work within a standardized environment. While Storyspace allows a good deal of this sort of adaptation, it also lets you tailor the environment you work in. Thus, for instance, the outline, chart, and map views of a document are much less specialized environments for different writing purposes than ways of graphically representing the provisional networks and transitory hierarchies which emerge and disappear as different purposes are discovered and developed. So, too, multiple navigation schemes let you perform both content and structure searches of documents; searching for specific parts or exploring at will according to keywords, place names, paths, and so on. Searches are topographic in Bolter's sense, according to both visual and verbal descriptions, and accessible through both visual and verbal browsing schemes.

Les, like most of our developmental students, worked initially in the map view, the most visual and topographic, and the one most suited to creating constructive hypertexts. In the Map view, you create and name places as individual boxes, each of which contains editable text and graphics, each of which can be dragged and rearranged in clusters on the screen. This clustering ability, of course, offered an easy transi-

tion from the classroom work we had done. Clustering, to quote Michael Heim again, "reminds the writer and thinker of the sense of psychic wholeness in the world of increasingly fragmented texts and automated text manipulation."

I do not wish to dispute Heim's contention that "clustering cannot properly be done in the computer interface," especially the kind of clustering he recounts "on a 57 1/2 inch piece of continuous paper," and especially since his view echoes the fervent criticism and battle cry of hypermedia theorist and IRIS director, Andries van Dam, i.e., "More screen real estate!" All this notwithstanding, our experience does suggest that the map view offers exactly the kind of "expandable graphic or map of thought discoveries" Heim describes clustering as being, and further offers the "sense of wide open creative freedom combined with . . . peculiarities of connection" which he says "no software outliner could permit."

With all this as prologue, what Storyspace enabled Les to see may seem modest, if not illusory, at first. This anecdote, when finally told, must be told backwards, since I had little sense of what Les had been doing with Storyspace until he did it, and have no memory of giving him any more instruction than the procedural help I gave others as they prepared their writing for workshopping.

Les's first paper was an uncommonly good attempt at fairly common writing, an autobiography in the form of an account of cars he had used, owned, been ticketed in, and, mostly, wrecked in traffic accidents. It began with his first "borrowing" of his father's pickup truck and continued through a "links," an Escort, another Lynx, and ended with his being given the pickup.

As we discussed the printed paper during the last weeks of the course, in a traditional classroom far from the computers, many of us liked one particular sentence toward the end of the paper: "Boy, if he would have had given me that truck when I had asked, this wouldn't of ever have happened." We all agreed the sentence managed to say a lot about maturity and desire. However, one particular paragraph, a description of one of these cars, troubled us. We were not certain which of two cars in succession it referred to, and we puzzled over suggestions for placing it while Les listened in silence, according to the custom in my workshops. When it came his turn to respond to our suggestions, he addressed this one first.

"The box is in the wrong place," he said, "It will make sense when I move it."

None of us knew what to make of this, and a few students snickered quietly. Les was insistent and confident, moving on.

"I'm glad you liked the part about my father's pick-up," he said, "It was the only arrow."

Neither the sentence in question nor the paper at large said anything about an arrow. The snickering increased, and I began to feel the kind of Lotus-Eater giddiness workshops sometimes bring as they veer out of control. Something in Les's insistence steadied me. He had lashed himself to a certainty we could not see.

"I'm sorry . . ." I said.

A rosy-fingered dawning came over him, and he grinned. "You don't know what I'm talking about, do you?" he asked. He scribbled quickly in the margins on his copy of the paper and held it up. He had drawn a series of boxes in the left margin.

"On the computer," he said, "That stuff about the car belongs next to the Lynx, and I moved the box but forgot to put it back. It makes sense in the right place."

What he was saying was that the structure of the writing existed electronically in a way that he could access it and make it clear to us, his assembled readers.

"And the arrow is a path," I said.

He was pleased that I finally understood, and drew it too in the margin of the paper.

"Yeah," he said, "the only one. I noticed that it starts and ends with my father's truck and so I put that sentence in."

What he was saying was that the verbal formulation of the paper led, topographically, from the visual representation of it. O brave new world, he was saying.

It is to you, I thought. I had missed my first vision of it.

It may be that Conklin's implicit question which I began with, i.e., what to do with hypertext tools, is the wrong question. Perhaps the better question is how to use these things to do better what you already do well. Certainly the early proponents and true visionaries of hypertext believed as much. "The human mind operates . . . by association," claimed Vannevar Bush in describing his Memex in 1945; and from Bush onward through Douglas Engelbart's Augment and even unto Ted Nelson's Xanadu, the visionaries have insisted that the sometimes slippery and obscure trails of hypertext rest upon an underlying bedrock of natural cognition. With nothing less than democratic zeal, each of this Trinity—the citizen-scientist, the engineer-rationalist, and the provocateur-humanist—builds upon a constitutional belief that habits of mind are naturally associative. They see hypertext trails as leading to a kind of shining electronic village upon a hill—an integrated, personalized, machine-enhanced, universally accessible, associative, new, yet familiar, world platted upon the patterns of synapses, deeded to each according to her or his needs.

It is a compelling and, potentially, an accurate vision; and it is a vision I share. In the forty three years since Bush's first exposition of this vision, it has attracted a litany of adherents. The IRIS project's Intermedia; Halasz, Moran, and Trigg's Xerox PARC-NoteCards; P. J. Brown's Guide; Bill Atkinson's HyperCard; and indeed our Storyspace are each predicated upon equally democratic intellectual principles.

I wonder if we can hold onto them. Until recently the hypertext community, unlike the Artificial Intelligence (AI) community for instance, has been able to make its case incrementally without having to deliver upon strident claims and excessive hype. Ted Nelson's wonderful books and better talks aren't strident, they're fervent (and anyway he baptized hypertext). My mini-Odyssey and gossamer anecdote above borrow on this fervency, as does most anything written in this area.

Even Apple's marketing of HyperCard is less hype than an example of a conversion experience, a sort of corporate speaking in tongues; largely democratic, albeit accompanied by four-color tabloid testimony and Lucasfilm laying on of hands. Conversion experiences are common in the realm of hypertext. In his talks, even as cautious and rigorous an intellectual historian as Bob Jones (whose article appears elsewhere in this issue) reports being filled with wild surmise on first looking into IRIS's Intermedia.

I wonder what these conversions will cause us to overlook. Hypertext, unlike AI, has until recently enjoyed the safe harbor which relative obscurity brings. Yet, education and technological change both stir winds across safe harbors, and now I wonder whether the claims we may find ourselves making about exploratory and constructive hypertexts alike may not put us prematurely in a whirlwind, not unlike the hurricane which accompanied the AI boomlet of recent years. Already a paper suggests developing "a path analysis to classify prominent paths . . . learners take through a hypertext" and then perhaps using "expert systems . . . to help learners access relative portions or sequences of hypertexts." (Jonassen, 1988)

Once I understood what Les was trying to tell me, I quickly secured his permission to let me investigate his workspace and study and report what I found there. While much of what he had done had disappeared in the process of his doing it, I found enough to think that we really ought to set up our wind machines, "instrumenting" and "journaling" the kinds of behavior he, in his own relative obscurity, had made commonplace.

It was interesting, for instance, to see that the autobiographical writing had sprung from a full-fledged writing environment. A first impulse appears at the end of a place called "Party Info" in a document he named "Family." The tale of his cars emerged from a typical account of a teenager's party, resulting from something of what Heim calls the "compensatory discipline" of "releasing," but which Donald Murray, Peter Elbow, Ken Macrorie, and many other composition theorists have long had other names for.

It was even more interesting to note that he had at some point framed out an organizational outline for the autobiography, deep within a map of another place, called "Christmas," which included places named for a sequence of gifts—"new toy," "new bike," "new car"—none of which he wrote about later.

These uninhabited places upon a map of thought discoveries seemed to call into question the emerging body of research which suggests, as Christina Haas does, that "writers [plan] significantly less when they [use] word processing" and that "there was less conceptual planning and more sequential planning with word processing." (Haas, 1988) And they bring to mind Endel Tulving's speculations that "the kind of learning reflected in fragment completion and other similar tasks" might be "subserved by . . . an unknown [memory] system . . . the QM system (QM for question mark)." (Tulving, 1985)

Yet, I wonder if all my and others' speculation will eventually help students like Les learn to do better what they already do well. And I cannot shake the uneasy, liberating feeling that the most dazzling and revolutionary exploratory hypertexts will be developed only when we come, like Les, to create constructive hypertexts which plumb the underlying topographical depths below a surface of boxes, one arrow, and who knows what other siren shapes of thought.

Works Cited

Balestri, Diane Pelkus, 1988. "Softcopy and Hard: Wordprocessing and Student Writing Process." *Academic Computing,* 2, no. 5 (February 1988): 14-17 and 41-44.

Beeman, William O., et al. 1987. "Hypertext and Pluralism: From Lineal to Non-Lineal Thinking." *Proceedings of Hypertext '87,* Association for Computing Machinery (ACM), Chapel Hill.

Brown, P.J. 1987. "Turning Ideas into Products: The Guide System." *Proceedings of Hypertext '87,* Association for Computing Machinery (ACM), Chapel Hill.

Bush, Vannevar. 1945. "As We May Think." *Atlantic Monthly* 176, July, 101-8.

Conklin, Jeffrey. 1987. "Hypertext: An Introduction and Survey." *IEEE Computer* 20, no. 9 (September): 17-41.

Douglas, Jane Yellowlees. 1987. "Beyond Orality and Literacy." Paper presented at the annual meeting of the International Association for Computers in Education, New Orleans.

Haas, Christina. 1988. "Planning in Writing: The Influence of Writing Tools." Paper presented at the Conference of College Composition and Communication (CCCC), St. Louis, March.

Halasz, Frank. 1987. "Reflections on Notecards: Seven Issues for the Next Generation of Hypermedia Systems." *Proceedings of Hypertext '87,* Association for Computing Machinery (ACM), Chapel Hill.

Heim, Michael. 1987. *Electronic Writing: A Philosophical Study of Word Processing.* New Haven and London: Yale University Press.

Jonassen, David H. 1988. "Designing Structured Hypertext and Structuring Access to Hypertext." Paper presented at the IBM ACIS Conference. Dallas, June.

Tulving, Endel. 1985. "How Many Memory Systems are There?" *American Psychologist* 40, No. 4 (April):385-98.

# 43. [Introduction]
# The Work of Culture in the Age of Cybernetic Systems

New media practicioners continually borrow insights and tropes from other forms. Similarly, the study of new media is continually generating itself through borrowings from a wide variety of discourses and examples. Bill Nichols gives a virtuoso demonstration of this approach in his essay below, which draws on feminist film theory, Frankfurt School Marxism, Sherry Turkle (◊34), Norbert Wiener (◊04), Gregory Bateson, intellectual property law, genetics, space weaponry, and *Pac-Man*.

Nichols's project, in brief, is to update Walter Benjamin's famous essay "The Work of Art in the Age of Mechanical Reproduction." Benjamin's text was published in 1936, when film was young. Nichols's was published in 1988, when video games and other simulation media were young (as, indeed, they still are). Nichols discusses this shift in several ways, outlining how it represents a shift from a fetishization of the *object* to fetishization of the *process* of interaction, of simulation. Interaction offers the feeling of greater freedom, but this freedom is always placed within the confines of the larger simulating system. Nichols relates simulation to video games and genetic engineering—a seemingly huge leap, but perhaps not over such a distance after all. Popular interactive experiences such as PF Magic's *Babyz* (a project led by Andrew Stern) and Maxis's *The Sims* (a project led by Will Wright) go beyond *Eliza/Doctor*'s simulation of human conversation to the simulation of human love relations and child rearing. These simulations are much richer than the Tamagotchi from a few years prior, and they tread much more clearly into the territory of ideology. For example, in *The Sims* friendship and happiness exist in a direct relationship to one's house and possessions. *Babyz* doesn't offer any options besides sitting around a stereotyped middle-class home all day, looking after the kids.

Games that enter the territory of *The Sims* may produce a pleasure different from that in other simulations, as ideology becomes more clearly a subject. While *SimCity* encoded certain ideologies of economics and urban planning, these ideologies were more remote, and players may have been more content to play along with what was offered. With *The Sims*, players seem, anecdotally, to more frequently push back against the ideology of the system. Online "family albums" are in many cases focused on the family groupings most difficult to achieve—that is, most discouraged by the underlying system—or on telling stories unrelated to the simulation. Meanwhile, Stern reports that one of the most common questions users ask when first presented with *Babyz* is whether the endearing animated characters can be microwaved, defenestrated, or otherwise treated in a manner that rejects the implicit housewife role of the simulation. Perhaps these reactions are what Wright and Stern intended, and perhaps this is also the reaction for which Nichols hopes in his essay, "not to overthrow the prevailing cybernetic model but to transgress its predefined interdictions and limits."

Nichols's example of war as simulation may lead us to the opposite conclusion, however. Not long after Benjamin wrote, U.S. bombs killed hundreds of thousands of civilians in Dresden, Hiroshima, and Nagasaki. On the U.S. mainland news of the bombing was reproduced mechanically, meeting with little protest. Another war, however, in Vietnam, met with resistance from within the U.S.—after a while—and it is conventional wisdom that this occurred in part because of the immediacy with which it was reported on television. More recently U.S. forces have attacked cities and killed civilians in Iraq and the former Yugoslavia, and media reports (delivered by non-interactive means) have been the product of simulation, on a scale well beyond that of Nichols's

A discussion of Eliza by that system's creator, Joseph Weizenbaum, is included in this book (◊24).

Of course, both *Babyz* and *The Sims* may be intended as social satire, an option that seems likely given the cultural acumen of designers such as Stern and Wright. In any case, they are open enough simulations to give users the option of working against the system. Games like the high-concept first person shooter *Deus Ex* offer less room to maneuver, since the user must choose between acting out an ideologically-loaded narrative and "losing." Writing in *Suck,* The Internick points out that this is a long tradition in interactive simulations, stretching back to *Adventure* and other early computer games, in which "there are only two ways to exert your influence. Either you follow the obscured path the designers have constructed, or you plunge headlong to your death."

**625**

*Simon Penny argues that it is misleading to consider the impact of simulation using critical tools developed for painting, television, film, or other non-interactive representations:*

In interactive media a user is not simply exposed to images which may contain representations of things and actions. The user is trained in the enaction of behaviors in response to images, and images appear in response to behaviors, in the same way that a pilot is trained in a flight simulator. By the same token, passive observation may be shown to have some effect on the beliefs or even the actions of an observer, but an enacted training regime must be a more powerful technique. So critiques of representation derived from painting, photography, film and video are inadequate for discussing the power of interactive experience.

Much debate has occurred on the correlation between pornographic images and sex-crime. Conversations about representations of violence typically conflate movies and computer games, as if they were in the same category. Whatever the power of images, interactive media is more. Not "just a picture," it's an interactive picture which responds to my actions. Our analysis of interactive media must therefore go beyond theories of representation in images. The image is just the target, the surface. The interactive image cannot be spoken of in the terms of traditional passive images because it is procedural. The content of the image is as much in the routine which runs it. Interactive applications are not pictures, they are machines which generate pictures.

examples of Grenada and Libya. The U.S. population has not resisted this, in fact supporting these attacks. Commentators have characterized "missile cam" images as resembling a videogame, though perhaps they more resemble the special effects of summer blockbusters. In these cases, there seems no call to resist, to transgress the simulation: it's as if it's simply time to sit back and enjoy.

—NWF

The phenomena of game subversion in simulation games such as *The Sims* may actually not be particularly new; players have often chosen to play in ways designers did not intend, just as children subvert other sorts of branded toys and pre-packaged games in ways the creators did not intend.

Starting points for some of Wright's simulations include fascinating and controversial ideas drawn from a number of fields. *SimCity*, for example, was influenced by the "system dynamics" theories of MIT's Jay W. Forrester—which, when applied to urban planning in the late 1960s, produced anger from many quarters. As Forrester reports in "The Beginning of System Dynamics," his conclusions included the idea that "low-cost housing was a double-edged sword for making urban conditions worse. Such housing used up space where jobs could be created, while drawing in people who needed jobs. Constructing low-cost housing was a powerful process for creating poverty, not alleviating it." Forrester's critics were quick to point out that his models were based on assumptions far from verifiable (e.g., that housing is a stronger attraction than jobs) and the workings of his simulated city were not like those of contemporary U.S. urban centers (e.g., Forrester's city was of a fixed size, and commuting into the city was impossible).

Wright's *SimCity* model, of course, is not identical with Forrester's—and it was never claimed to be a means for determining appropriate social and economic policy, though it seems likely to have at least unconsciously shaped the views on urban dynamics of many of its players. Wright's *SimEarth*, on the other hand, was influenced by theorists not generally well-loved by those who subscribe to Dr. Forrester's view of low-income housing: James Lovelock and Lynn Margulis, the proposers of the "Gaia hypothesis." *The Sims*, meanwhile, was influenced by the "pattern theory" work of architect Christopher W. Alexander—which, while not universally popular among architects, has inspired a view of software engineering ("design patterns") so influential that it is being integrated into many undergraduate computer science curricula.

Further Reading

De Landa, Manuel. *War in the Age of Intelligent Machines*. New York: Zone Books, 1991.

Forrester, Jay. "The Beginning of System Dynamics." Banquet Talk at the international meeting of the System Dynamics Society, Stuttgart, Germany, July 13, 1989. <http://sysdyn.mit.edu/sdep/papers/D-4165-1.pdf>

*Game Studies*. Peer-reviewed Web journal. <http:///www.gamestudies.org>

The Internick. "Interactor's Nightmare." *Suck.com*, 27 Jan 1997. <http://www.suck.com/daily/97/01/27/>

Penny, Simon. "Representation, Enaction and the Ethics of Simulation." In *First Person: New Media as Story, Performance, and Game*. Ed. Noah Wardrip-Fruin and Pat Harrigan. Cambridge: MIT Press, forthcoming.

Original Publication

*Screen* 21(1):22-46. Winter 1988.

# The Work of Culture in the Age of Cybernetic Systems

## Bill Nichols

The computer is more than an object: it is also an icon and a metaphor that suggests new ways of thinking about ourselves and our environment, new ways of constructing images of what it means to be human and to live in a humanoid world. Cybernetic systems include an entire array of machines and apparatuses that exhibit computational power. Such systems contain a dynamic, even if limited, quotient of intelligence. Telephone networks, communication satellites, radar systems, programmable laser video disks, robots, biogenetically engineered cells, rocket guidance systems, videotex networks—all exhibit a capacity to process information and execute actions. They are all "cybernetic" in that they are self-regulating mechanisms or systems within predefined limits and in relation to predefined tasks. Just as the camera has come to symbolize the entirety of the photographic and cinematic processes, the computer has come to symbolize the entire spectrum of networks, systems, and devices that exemplify cybernetic or "automated but intelligent" behavior.

This article traverses a field of inquiry that Walter Benjamin has crossed before, most notably in his 1936 essay, "The Work of Art in the Age of Mechanical Reproduction." My intention, in fact, is to carry Benjamin's inquiry forward and to ask how cybernetic systems, symbolized by the computer, represent a set of transformations in our conception of and relation to self and reality of a magnitude commensurate with the transformations in the conception of and relation to self and reality wrought by mechanical reproduction and symbolized by the camera. This intention necessarily encounters the dilemma of a profound ambivalence directed toward that which constitutes our imaginary. Other, in this case not a mothering parent but those systems of artificial intelligence I have set out to

examine here. Such ambivalence certainly permeates Benjamin's essay and is at best dialectical, and at worst, simply contradictory. Put more positively, those systems against which we test and measure the boundaries of our own identity require subjection to a double hermeneutic of suspicion and revelation in which we must acknowledge the negative, currently dominant, tendency toward control, and the positive, more latent potential toward collectivity.[1] It will be in terms of law that the dominance of control over collectivity can be most vividly analyzed.

In summary, what I want to do is recall a few of the salient points in Benjamin's original essay, contrast characteristics of cybernetic systems with those of mechanical reproduction, establish a central metaphor with which to understand these cybernetic systems, and then ask how this metaphor acquires the force of the real—how different institutions legitimate their practices, recalibrate their rationale, and modulate their image in light of this metaphor. In particular, I want to ask how the preoccupations of a cybernetic imagination have gained institutional legitimacy in areas such as the law. In this case, like others, a tension can be seen to exist between the liberating potential of the cybernetic imagination and the ideological tendency to preserve the existing form of social relations. I will focus on the *work* of culture—its processes, operations, and procedures—and I will assume that culture is of the essence: I include within it text and practices, art and actions that give concrete embodiment to the relation we have to existing conditions to a dominant mode of production, and the various relations of production it sustains. Language, discourse, and messages are central. Their style and rhetoric are basic. Around each "fact" and every "datum," all realities and evidence, everything "out there," a persuasive, affective tissue of discourse accrues. It is in and through this signifying tissue, arranged in discursive formations and institutional arenas, that struggle takes place and semiosis occurs.

## Mechanical Reproduction and Film Culture

Benjamin argues for correspondences among three types of changes: in the economic mode of production, in the nature of art, and in categories of perception. At the base of industrial society lies the assembly line and mass production. Technological innovation allows these processes to extend into the domain of art, separating off from its traditional ritual (or "cult") value a new and distinct market (or "exhibition") value. The transformation also strips art of its "aura" by which Benjamin means its authenticity, its attachment to the domain of tradition:

> The authenticity of a thing is the essence of all that is transmissible from its beginning, ranging from its substantive duration to its testimony to the history which it has experienced.[2]

The aura of an object compels attention. Whether a work of art or natural landscape, we confront it in one place and only one place. We discover its use value in the exercise of ritual, in that place, with that object, or in the contemplation of the object for its uniqueness. The object in possession of aura, natural or historical, inanimate or human, engages us as if it had "the power to look back in return."[3]

One thing mechanical reproduction cannot, by definition, reproduce is authenticity. This is at the heart of the change it effects in the work of art. "Mechanical reproduction emancipates the work of art from its parasitical dependence on ritual" (p. 224). The former basis in ritual yields to a new basis for art in politics, particularly, for Benjamin, the politics of the masses and mass movements, where fascism represents an ever-present danger. The possibilities for thoroughgoing emancipation are held in check by the economic system surrounding the means of mechanical reproduction, especially in film where "illusion-promoting spectacles and dubious speculations" (p. 232) deflect us from the camera's ability to introduce us to "unconscious optics" that reveal those forms of interaction our eyes neglect:

> The act of reaching for a lighter or a spoon is familiar routine, yet we hardly know what goes on between hand and metal, not to mention how this fluctuates with our moods. Here the camera intervenes with the resources of its lowerings and liftings, its interpretations and isolations, its extensions and accelerations, its enlargements and reductions. (p. 237)

Objects without aura substitute mystique. In a remarkable, prescient passage, relegated to a footnote, Benjamin elaborates how political practice opens the way for a strange transformation of the actor when democracies encounter the crisis of fascism. Mechanical reproduction allows the actor an unlimited public rather than the delimited one of the stage or, for the politician, parliament. "Though their tasks may be different, the change affects equally the actor and the ruler. . . . This results in a new selection, a selection before the

equipment (of mechanical reproduction) from which the star and the dictator emerge victoriously" (p. 247).

Alterations like the replacement of aura with mystique coincide with the third major change posited by Benjamin, change in categories of perception. The question of whether film or photography is an art is here secondary to the question of whether art itself has not been radically transformed in form and function. A radical change in the nature of art implies that our very ways of seeing the world have also changed: "During long periods of history, the mode of human sense perception changes with humanity's entire mode of existence" (p. 222).

Mechanical reproduction makes *copies* of visible objects, like paintings, mountain ranges, even human beings, which until then had been thought of as unique and irreplaceable. It brings the upheavals of the industrial revolution to a culmination. The ubiquitous copy also serves as an externalized manifestation of the work of industrial capitalism itself. It paves the way for seeing, and recognizing, the nature and extent of the very changes mechanical reproduction itself produces.

What element of film most strongly testifies to this new form of machine-age perception? For Benjamin it is that element which best achieves what Dadaism has aspired to: "changes of place and focus which periodically assail the spectator." Film achieves these changes through montage, or editing. Montage rips things from their original place in an assigned sequence and reassembles them in everchanging combinations that make the contemplation invited by a painting impossible. Montage multiplies the potential of collage to couple two realities on a single plane that apparently does not suit them into the juxtaposition of an infinite series of realities. As George Bataille proclaimed, "Transgression does not negate an interdiction, it transcends and completes it." In this spirit, montage transcends and completes the project of the Dadaists in their conscious determination to strip aura from the work of art and of the early French ethnographers who delighted in the strange juxtapositions of artifacts from different cultures.

Montage has a liberating potential, prying art away from ritual and toward the arena of political engagement. Montage gives back to the worker a view of the world as malleable. Benjamin writes:

> Man's need to expose himself to shock effects is his adjustment to the changes threatening him. The film

corresponds to profound changes in the apperceptive apparatus—changes that are experienced on an individual scale by the man in the street in big-city traffic, on a historical scale by every present-day citizen. (p. 250)

By close-ups of the things around us, by focusing on hidden details of familiar objects, by exploring commonplace milieus under the ingenious guidance of the camera, the film, on the one hand, extends our comprehension of the necessities which rule our lives; on the other hand, it manages to assure us of an immense and unexpected field of action. Our taverns and our metropolitan streets, our offices and furnished rooms, our railroad stations and our factories appeared to have us locked up hopelessly. Then came the film and burst this prison-world asunder by the dynamite of the tenth of a second, so that now, in the midst of its far-flung ruins and debris, we calmly and adventurously go traveling (p. 236).

Mechanical reproduction involves the appropriation of an original, although with film even the notion of an original fades: that which is filmed has been organized in order to be filmed. This process of appropriation engenders a vocabulary: the "take" or "camera shot" used to "shoot" a scene where both stopping a take and editing are called a "cut." The violent reordering of the physical world and its meanings provides the shock effects Benjamin finds necessary if we are to come to terms with the age of mechanical reproduction. The explosive, violent potential described by Benjamin and celebrated by Brecht is what the dominant cinema must muffle, defuse, and contain. And what explosive potential can be located in the computer and its cybernetic systems for the elimination of drudgery and toil, for the promotion of collectivity and affinity, for interconnectedness, systemic networking and shared decision-making, this, too, must be defused and contained by the industries of information which localize, condense, and consolidate this potential democratization of power into hierarchies of control.

"Montage—the connecting of dissimilars to shock an audience into insight—becomes for Benjamin a major principle to artistic production in a technological age."[4]

Developing new ways of seeing to the point where they become habitual is not ideological for Benjamin but transformative. They are not the habits of old ways but new; they are skills which are difficult to acquire precisely because

they are in opposition to ideology. The tasks before us "at the turning points of history" cannot be met by contemplation. "They are mastered gradually by habit, under the guidance of tactile appropriation" (p. 240). The shocks needed in order to adjust to threatening changes may be coopted by the spectacles a culture industry provides. For Benjamin the only recourse is to use those skills he himself adopted: the new habits of a sensibility trained to disassemble and reconstruct reality, of a writing style intended to relieve idlers of their convictions, of a working class trained not only to produce and reproduce the existing relations of production but to reproduce those very relations in a new, liberating form. "To see culture and its norms—beauty, truth, reality—as artificial arrangements, susceptible to detached analysis and comparison with other possible dispositions" becomes the vantage point not only of the surrealist but the revolutionary.[5]

The process of adopting new ways of seeing that consequently propose new forms of social organization becomes a paradoxical, or dialectical, process when the transformations that spawn new habits, new vision, are themselves endangered and substantially recuperated by the existing form of social organization which they contain the potential to overcome. But the process goes forward all the same. It does so less in terms of a culture of mechanical reproduction, which has reached a point similar to that of a tradition rooted in Benjamin's time, than in terms of a culture of electronic dissemination and computation.

We might then ask in what ways is our "sense of reality" being adjusted by new means of electronic computation and digital communication? Do these technological changes introduce new forms of culture into the relations of production at the same time as the "shock of the new" helps emancipate us from the acceptance of social relations and cultural forms as natural, obvious, or timeless? The distinction between an industrial capitalism, even in its "late" phase of monopoly concentration, and an information society that does not "produce" so much as "process" its basic forms of economic resource has become an increasingly familiar distinction for us. Have cybernetic systems brought about changes in our perception of the world that hold liberating potential? Is it conceivable, for example, that contemporary transformations in the economic structure of capitalism, attended by technological change, institute a less individuated, more communal form of perception similar to that which was attendant upon face-to-face ritual and aura

| Entrepreneurial capitalism | Monopoly capitalism | Multinational capitalism |
|---|---|---|
| steam and locomotive power | electricity and petrochemical power | microelectronics and nuclear energy |
| property rights | corporate rights | copyright and patents |
| nature as Other/ conquest of nature | aliens as Other/ conquest of Third World | knowledge as Other/ conquest of intelligence |
| nationalism | imperialism | multinationalism |
| working-class vanguard | consumer-group vanguard | affinity-group vanguard |
| Tuberculosis; contamination by nature | Cancer; contamination by an aberrant self | AIDS; deficiency of self (collapse of system that distinguishes self from environment) |
| isolation of self from threatening environment | isolation of aberrant tissue from self | isolation of self by artificial life support |
| vulnerability to invasive agents | vulnerability to self-consumption | vulnerability to systemic collapse |
| heightened individuation | heightened schizophrenia | heightened sense of paranoia |
| realism | modernism | postmodernism |
| film | television | computer |
| mechanical reproduction | instantaneous broadcast | logico-iconic simulations |
| reproducible instances | ubiquitous occurrences | processes of absorption and feedback |
| the copy | the event | the chip (and VDT display) |
| subtext of possession | subtext of mediation | subtext of control |
| image and representation | collage and juxtaposition | simulacra |

but which is now mediated by anonymous circuitry and the simulation of direct encounter? Does montage now have its equivalent in interactive simulations and simulated interactions experienced according to predefined constraints? Does the work of art in the age of postmodernism lead, at least potentially, to apperceptions of the "deep structure" of postindustrial society comparable to the apperceptive discoveries occasioned by mechanical reproduction in the age of industrial capitalism?

## Cybernetic Systems and Electronic Culture

We can put Benjamin's arguments, summarized cursorily here, in another perspective by highlighting some of the characteristics associated with early, entrepreneurial capitalism, monopoly capitalism, and multinational or postindustrial capitalism.

Simulacra introduce the key question of how the control of information moves towards control of sensory experience, interpretation, intelligence, and knowledge. The power of the simulation moves to the heart of the cybernetic matter. It posits the simulation as an imaginary Other which serves as the measure of our own identity and, in doing so, prompts the same form of intense ambivalence that the mothering parent once did: a guarantee of identity based on what can never be made part of oneself. In early capitalism, the human

was defined in relation to an animal world that evoked fascination and attraction, repulsion and resentment. The human animal was similar to but different from all other animals. In monopoly capitalism, the human was defined in relation to a machine world that evoked its own distinctive blend of ambivalence. The human machine was similar to but different from all other machines. In postindustrial capitalism, the human is defined in relation to cybernetic systems—computers, biogenetically engineered organisms, ecosystems, expert systems, robots, androids, and cyborgs—all of which evoke those forms of ambivalence reserved for the Other that is the measure of ourselves. The human cyborg is similar but different from all other cyborgs. Through these transformations questions of difference persist. Human identity remains at stake, subject to change, vulnerable to challenge and modification as the very metaphors prompted by the imaginary Others that give it form themselves change. The metaphor that's meant (that's taken as real) becomes the simulation. The simulation displaces any antecedent reality, any aura, any referent to history. Frames collapse. What had been fixed comes unhinged. New identities, ambivalently adopted, prevail.

The very concept of a text, whether unique or one of myriad copies, for example, underpins almost all discussion of cultural forms including film, photography, and their analogue in an age of electronic communication, television (where the idea of "flow" becomes an important amendment). But in cybernetic systems, the concept of "text" itself undergoes substantial slippage. Although a textual element can still be isolated, computer-based systems are primarily interactive rather than one-way, open-ended rather than fixed. Dialogue, regulated and disseminated by digital computation, de-emphasizes authorship in favor of "messages-in-circuit"[6] that take fixed but effervescent, continually variable form. The link between message and substrate is loosened: words on a printed page are irradicable; text on a video display terminal (VDT) is readily altered. The text conveys the sense of being addressed to us. The message-in-circuit is both addressed to and addressable by us; the mode is fundamentally interactive, or dialogic. That which is most textual in nature—the fixed, read-only-memory (ROM), and software programs—no longer addresses us. Such texts are machine addressable. They direct those operational procedures that ultimately give the impression that the computer responds personally to us, simulating the processes of conversation or of interaction with another intelligence to effect a desired outcome. Like face-to-face encounter, cybernetic systems offer (and demand) almost immediate response. This is a major part of their hazard in the workplace and their fascination outside it. The temporal flow and once-only quality of face-to-face encounter becomes embedded within a system ready to restore, alter, modify or transform any given moment to us at any time. Cybernetic interactions can become intensely demanding, more so than we might imagine from our experience with texts, even powerfully engaging ones. Reactions must be almost instantaneous, grooved into eye and finger reflexes until they are automatic. This is the bane of the "automated workplace" and the joy of the video game. Experienced video-game players describe their play as an interactive ritual that becomes totally self-absorbing. As David, a lawyer in his mid thirties interviewed by Sherry Turkle, puts it,

> At the risk of sounding, uh, ridiculous, if you will, it's almost a Zen type of thing. . . . When I can direct myself totally but not feel directed at all. You're totally absorbed and it's all happening there. . . . You either get through this little maze so that the creature doesn't swallow you up or you don't. And if you can focus your attention on that, and if you can really

learn what you're supposed to do, then you really are in relationship with the game.[7]

The enhanced ability to test the environment, which Benjamin celebrated in film ("The camera director in the studio occupies a place identical with that of the examiner during aptitude tests," p. 246) certainly continues with cybernetic communication.[8] The computer's dialogic mode carries the art of the "what if" even further than the camera eye has done, extending beyond the "what if I could see more than the human eye can see" to "what if I can render palpable those possible transformations of existing states that the individual mind can scarcely contemplate?"

If mechanical reproduction centers on the question of reproducibility and renders authenticity and the original problematic, cybernetic simulation renders experience, and the real itself, problematic. Instead of reproducing, and altering, our relation to an original work, cybernetic communication simulates, and alters, our relation to our environment and mind. As Jean Baudrillard argues, "Instead of facilitating communication, it (information, the message-in-circuit) exhausts itself in the *staging* of communication . . . this is the gigantic simulation process with which we are familiar."[9]

Instead of a representation of social practices recoded into the conventions and signs of another language or sign-system, like the cinema, we encounter simulacra that represent a new form of social practice in their own right and represent nothing. The photographic image, as Roland Barthes proposed, suggests "having been there" of what it represents, of what is present-in-absentia. The computer simulation suggests only a "being here" and "having come from nowhere" of what it presents, drawing on those genetic-like algorithms that allow it to bring its simulation into existence, *sui generis*. Among other things, computer systems simulate the dialogical and other qualities of life itself. The individual becomes nothing but an ahistorical position within a chain of discourse marked exhaustively by those shifters that place him or her within speech acts ("I," "here," "now," "you," "there," "then"). In face-to-face encounter this "I" all speakers share can be inflected to represent some part of the self not caught by words. To respond to the query, "How are you?" by saying "Not *too* bad," rather than "Fine," suggests something about a particular state of mind or style of expression and opens onto the domains of feeling and empathy. What cannot be represented in language directly (the bodily, living "me" that writes or utters words) can significantly inflect speech, and dialogue, despite its enforced exclusion from any literal representation.

In cybernetic systems, though, "I" and "you" are strictly relational propositions attached to no substantive body, no living individuality. In place of human intersubjectivity we discover a systems interface, a boundary between cyborgs that selectively passes information but without introducing questions of consciousness or the unconscious, desire or will, empathy or conscience, saved in simulated forms.

Even exceptions like ELIZA, a program designed to simulate a therapeutic encounter, prove the rule. "I" and "you" function as partners in therapy only as long as the predefined boundaries are observed. As Sherry Turkle notes, if you introduce the word "mother" into your exchange, and then say, "Let's discuss paths toward nuclear disarmament," ELIZA might well offer the nonsense reply, "Why are you telling me that your mother makes paths toward nuclear disarmament?"[10] Simulations like these may bring with them the shock of recognizing the reification of a fundamental social process, but they also position us squarely within the realm of communication and exchange cleanly evacuated of the intersubjective complexities of direct encounter. Cybernetic systems give form, external expression, to processes of the mind (through messages-in-circuit) such that the very ground of social cohesion and consciousness becomes mediated through a computational apparatus. Cybernetic interaction achieves with an other (an intelligent apparatus) the simulation of social process itself.

Cybernetic dialogue may offer freedom from many of the apparent risks inherent in direct encounter; it offers the illusion of control. This use of intelligence provides a lure that seems to be much more attractive to men than women. At first there may seem to be a gain, particularly regarding the question of the look or gaze. Looking is an intensely charged act, one significantly neglected by Benjamin, but stressed in recent feminist critiques of dominant Hollywood cinema. There looking is posed as a primarily masculine act and "to-be-looked-at-ness" a feminine state, reinforced, in the cinema, by the camera's own voyeuristic gaze, editing patterns that prompt identification with masculine activism and feminine passivity, and a star system that institutionalizes these uses of the look through an iconography of the physical body.[11] This entire issue becomes circumvented in cybernetic systems that simulate dialogic

interaction, or face-to-face encounter, but exclude not only the physical self or its visual representation but also the cinematic apparatus that may place the representation of sexual difference within a male-dominant hierarchy.

Correct in so far as it goes, the case for the circumvention of the sexist coding of the gaze overlooks another form of hierarchical sexual coding that revolves around the question of whether a fascination with cybernetic systems is not itself a gender-related (i.e., a primarily masculine) phenomenon (excluding from consideration an even more obvious gender coding that gives almost all video games, for example a strong aura of aggressive militaristic activity). The questions that we pose about the sexist nature of the gaze within the cinematic text and the implications this has for the position we occupy in relation to such texts, may not be wholly excluded so much as displaced. A (predominantly masculine) fascination with the *control* of simulated interactions replaces a (predominantly masculine) fascination with the to-be-looked-at-ness of a projected image. Simulated intersubjectivity as a product of automated but intelligent systems invokes its own peculiar psycho-dynamic. Mechanical reproduction issues an invitation to the fetishist—a special relationship to the images of actors or politicians in place of any more direct association. The fetish *object*—the image of the other that takes the place of the other—becomes the center of attention while fetishistic viewers look on from their anonymous and voyeuristic, seeing-but-unseen sanctuary in the audience. But the output of computational systems stresses simulation, interaction, and process itself. Engagement with this *process* becomes the object of fetishization rather than representations whose own status as produced objects has been masked. Cybernetic interaction emphasizes the fetishist rather than the fetish object: instead of a taxonomy of stars we find a galaxy of computer freaks. The consequence of systems without aura, systems that replace direct encounter and realize otherwise inconceivable projections and possibilities, is a fetishism of such systems and processes of control themselves. Fascination resides in the subordination of human volition to the operating constraints of the larger system. We can talk to a system whose responsiveness grants us an awesome feeling of power. But as Paul Edwards observes, "Though individuals . . . certainly make decisions and set goals, as links in the chain of command they are allowed no choices regarding the ultimate purposes and values of the system.

Their 'choices' are . . . always the permutations and combinations of a predefined set."[12]

The desire to exercise a sense of control over a complex but predefined logical universe replaces the desire to view the image of another over which the viewer can imagine himself to have a measure of control. The explosive power of the dynamite of the tenth of a second extolled by Benjamin is contained within the channels of a psychopathology that leaves exempt from apperception, or control, the mechanisms that place ultimate control on the side of the cinematic apparatus or cybernetic system. These mechanisms—the relay of gazes between the camera, characters and viewer, the absorption into a simulacrum with complex problems and eloquent solutions—are the ground upon which engagement occurs and are not addressable within the constraints of the system itself. It is here, at this point, that dynamite must be applied.

This is even more difficult with computers and cybernetics than with cameras and the cinema. Benjamin himself noted how strenuous a task it is in film to mask the means of production, to keep the camera and its supporting paraphernalia and crew from intruding upon the fiction. Exposure of this other scene, the one behind the camera, is a constant hazard and carries the risk of shattering the suspension of disbelief. Only those alignments between camera and spectator that preserve the illusion of a fictional world without camera, lights, directors, studio sets, and so on are acceptable. Benjamin comments, perhaps with more of a surrealist's delight in strange juxtapositions than a Marxist's, "The equipment-free aspect of reality here (in films) has become the height of artifice; the sight of immediate reality has become an orchid in the land of technology" (p. 233).

With the contemporary prison-house of language, in Frederic Jameson's apt phrase, the orchid of immediate reality, like the mechanical bird seen at the end of *Blue Velvet*, appears to have been placed permanently under glass; but for Benjamin, neither the process by which an illusionistic world is produced nor the narrative strategies associated with it receive extended consideration. For him, the reminders of the productive process were readily apparent, not least through the strenuous efforts needed to mask them. The "other scene" where fantasies and fictions actually become conceptually and mechanically produced may be repressed but is not obliterated. If not immediately visible, it lurks just out of sight in the offscreen space where the extension of a fictional world somewhere collides with the world of the camera apparatus in one dimension and the world of the viewer in another. It retains the potential to intrude at every cut or edit; it threatens to reveal itself in every lurch of implausibility or sleight of hand with which a narrative attempts to achieve the sense of an ending.

With cybernetic systems, this other scene from which complex rule-governed universes actually get produced recedes further from sight. The governing procedures no longer address us in order to elicit a suspension of belief; they address the cybernetic system, the microprocessor of the computer, in order to absorb us into their operation. The other scene has vanished into logic circuits and memory chips, into "machine language" and interface cards. The chip replaces the copy. Just as the mechanical reproduction of copies revealed the power of industrial capitalism to reorganize and reassemble the world around us, rendering it as commodity art, the automated intelligence of chips reveals the power of postindustrial capitalism to simulate and replace the world around us, rendering not only its exterior realm but also its interior ones of consciousness, intelligence, thought and intersubjectivity as commodity experience.

The chip is pure surface, pure simulation of thought. Its material surface is its meaning without history, without depth, without aura, affect, or feeling. The copy reproduces the world, the chip simulates it. It is the difference between being able to remake the world and being able to efface it. The micro-electronic chip draws us into a realm, a design for living, that fosters a fetishized relationship with the simulation as a new reality all its own based on the capacity to control, within the domain of the simulation, what had once eluded control beyond it. The orchids of immediate reality that Benjamin was wont to admire have become the paper flowers of the cybernetic simulation.

Electronic simulation instead of mechanical reproduction. Fetishistic addiction to a process of logical simulation rather than a fascination with a fetishized object of desire. Desire for the dialogic or interactive and the illusion of control versus desire for the fixed but unattainable and the illusion of possession. Narrative and realism draw us into relations of identification with the actions and qualities of characters. Emulation is possible, as well as self-enhancement. Aesthetic pleasure allows for a revision of the world from which a work of art arises. Reinforcing what is or proposing what might be, the work of art remains susceptible to a double hermeneutic of suspicion and revelation. Mechanical reproduction changes the terms decidedly, but the metonymic or indexical relationship between representational art and the social world to which it refers remains a fundamental consideration.

By contrast, cybernetic simulations offer the possibility of completely replacing any direct connection with the experiential realm beyond their bounds. Like the cinema, this project, too, has its origins in the expansion of nineteenth-century industrialism. The emblematic precursors of the cyborg—the machine as self-regulating system—were those animate, self-regulating systems that offered a source of enchantment even museums could not equal: the zoo and the botanical garden.

At the opening of the first large-scale fair or exhibition, the Great Exhibition of 1851, Queen Victoria spoke of "the greatest day in our history [when] the whole world of nature and art was collected at the call of the queen of cities." Those permanent exhibitions—the zoo and botanical garden—introduced a new form of vicarious experience quite distinct from the aesthetic experience of original art or mechanically reproduced copies. The zoo brings back alive evidence of a world we could not otherwise know, now under apparent control. It offers experience at a remove that is fundamentally different as a result of having been uprooted from its original context. The indifferent, unthreatened, and unthreatening gaze of captive animals provides eloquent testimony to the difference between the zoo and the natural habitat to which it refers. The difference in the significance of what appears to be the same thing, the gaze, indicates that the change in context has introduced a new system of meanings, a new discourse or language.

Instead of the shocks of montage that offer a "true means of exercise" appropriate to the "profound changes in the apperceptive apparatus" under industrial capitalism, the zoo and botanical garden exhibit a predefined, self-regulating world with no reality outside of its own boundaries. These worlds may then become the limit of our understanding of those worlds to which they refer but of which we seldom have direct knowledge. "Wildlife" or "the African savannah" is its simulation inside the zoo or garden or diorama. Absorption with these simulacra and the sense of control they afford may be an alternative means of exercise appropriate to the apperceptive changes required by a service and information economy.

Computer-based systems extend the possibilities inherent in the zoo and garden much further. The ideal simulation would be a perfect replica, now *controlled* by whomever controls the algorithms of simulation—a state imaginatively rendered in films like *The Stepford Wives* or *Blade Runner* and apparently already achieved in relation to certain biogenetically engineered micro-organisms. Who designs and controls these greater systems and for what purpose becomes a question of central importance.

## The Cybernetic Metaphor: Transformations of Self and Reality

The problems of tracking antiaircraft weapons against extremely fast targets prompted the research and development of intelligent mechanisms capable of predicting future states or positions far faster than the human brain could do. The main priorities were speed, efficiency and reliability; i.e., fast-acting, error-free systems. ENIAC (Electronic Numerical Integrator and Computer), the first high-powered digital computer, was designed to address precisely this problem by performing ballistic computations at enormous speed and allowing the outcome to be translated into adjustments in the firing trajectory of antiaircraft guns.[13]

"The men [sic] who assembled to solve problems of this order and who formalized their approach into the research paradigms of information theory and cognitive psychology through the Macy Foundation Conferences, represent a who's who of cybernetics: John von Neumann, Oswald Weblen, Vannevar Bush, Norbert Wiener, Warren McCulloch, Gregory Bateson and Claude Shannon, among others." Such research ushers in the central metaphors of the cybernetic imagination: not only the human as an automated but intelligent system, but also automated, intelligent systems as human, not only the simulation of reality but the reality of the simulation. These metaphors take form around the question, the still unanswered question, put by John Stroud at the Sixth Macy Conference:

> We know as much as possible about how the associated gear bringing the information to the tracker [of an anti-aircraft gun] operates and how all the gear from the tracker to the gun operates. So we have the human operator surrounded on both sides by very precisely known mechanisms and the

question comes up, "What kind of machine have we placed in the middle?"[14]

This question of "the machine in the middle" and the simulation as reality dovetails with Jean Baudrillard's recent suggestion that the staging powers of simulation establish a hyperreality we only half accept but seldom refute: "Hyperreality of communication of meaning: by dint of being more real than the real itself, reality is destroyed."[15]

Such metaphors, then, become more than a discovery of similarity, they ultimately propose an identity. Norbert Wiener's term "cyborg" (cybernetic organism) encapsulates the new identity which, instead of seeing humans reduced to automata, sees simulacra which encompass the human elevated to the organic. Consequently, the human cognitive apparatus (itself a hypothetical construct patterned after the cybernetic model of automated intelligence) is expected to negotiate the world by means of simulation.

Our cognitive apparatus treats the real as though it consisted of those properties exhibited by simulacra. The real becomes simulation. Simulacra, in turn, serve as the mythopoeic impetus for that sense of the real we posit beyond the simulation. A sobering example of what is at stake follows from the Reagonomic conceptualization of war. The Strategic Defense Initiative (SDI) represents a vast Battle of the Cyborgs video game where players compete to save the world from nuclear holocaust. Reagan's simulated warfare would turn the electromagnetic force fields of fifties science-fiction films that shielded monsters and creatures from the arsenal of human destructive power into ploughshares beyond the ozone. Star Wars would be the safe-sex version of international conflict: not one drop of our enemy's perilous bodily fluids, none of their nuclear ejaculations, will come into contact with the free world.

Reagan's simulation of war as a replacement for the reality of war does not depend entirely on SDI. We have already seen it at work in the invasion of Grenada and the raid on Libya. Each time, we have had the evocation of the reality of war: the iconography of heroic fighters, embattled leaders, brave decisions, powerful technology, and concerted effort rolled into the image of military victory, an image of quick, decisive action that defines the "American will."

These simulacra of war, though, are fought with an imaginary enemy, in the Lacanian sense, and in the commonsense meaning of an enemy posited within those permutations allowed by a predefined set of assumptions and foreign-policy options: a Grenadian or Libyan "threat" appears on the video screens of America's political leadership. Long experience with the Communist menace leads to prompt and sure recognition. Ronny pulls the trigger. These simulations lack the full-blown, catastrophic consequences of real war, but this does not diminish the reality of this particular simulation nor the force with which it is mapped onto a historical "reality" it simultaneously effaces. Individuals find their lives irreversibly altered, people are wounded, many die. These indelible punctuation marks across the face of the real, however, fall into place according to a discourse empowered to make the metaphoric reality of the simulation a basic fact of existence.

A more complex example of what it means to live not only in the society of the spectacle but also in the society of the simulacrum involves the preservation/simulation of life via artificial life-support systems. In such an environment, the presence of life hinges on the presence of "vital signs." Their manifestation serves as testimony to the otherwise inaccessible presence of life itself, even though life in this state stands in relation to the "immediate reality" of life as the zoo stands in relation to nature. The important issue here is that the power of cybernetic simulations prompts a redefinition of such fundamental terms as life and reality, just as, for Benjamin, mechanical reproduction alters the very conception of art and the standards by which we know it. Casting the issue in terms of whether existence within the limits of an artificial life-support system should be considered "life" obscures the issue in the same way that asking whether film and photography are "art" does. In each case a presumption is made about a fixed, or ontologically given, nature of life or art, rather than recognizing how that very presumption has been radically overturned.

And from preserving life artificially, it is a small step to creating life by the same means. There is, for example, the case of Baby M. Surrogate mothering, as a term, already demonstrates the reality of the simulation: the actual mothering agent—the woman who bears the child—becomes a *surrogate*, thought of, not as a mother, but as an incubator or "rented uterus," as one of the trial's medical "experts" called Mary Beth Whitehead. The *real* surrogate mother, the woman who will assume the role of mother for a child not borne of her own flesh, becomes the real mother, legally and familiarly. The law upholds the priority of the simulation and the power of those who can control this

635

system of surrogacy—measured by class and gender, for it is clearly upper-class males (Judge Harvey Sorkow and the father, William Stem) who mobilized and sanctioned this particular piece of simulation, largely, it would seem, given the alternative of adoption, to preserve a very real, albeit fantastic preoccupation with a patriarchal blood line.

Here we have the simulation of a nuclear family—a denucleated, artificial simulation made and sanctioned as real, *bona fide*. The trial evoked the reality of the prototypical bourgeois family: well-educated, socially responsible, emotionally stable, and economically solvent, in contrast to the lower middle-class Whitehead household. The trial judgment renders as legal verdict the same moral lesson that Cecil Hepworth's 1905 film, *Rescued by Rover*, presents as artistic theme: the propriety of the dominant class, the menace of an unprincipled, jealous and possessive lower class, the crucial importance of narrative donors like the faithful Rover and of social agents like the patronizing Sorkow, and the central role of the husband as the patriarch able to preside over the constitution and re-constitution of his family. Now replayed as simulation, the morality play takes on a reality of its own. People suffer, wounds are inflicted. Lives are irreversibly altered, or even created. Baby M is a child conceived as a product to be sold to fill a position within the signifying discourse of patriarchy.

The role of the judge in this case was, of course, crucial to its outcome. His centrality signals the importance of the material, discursive struggles being waged within the realm of the law. Nicos Poulantzas argues that the juridical-political is the dominant or articulating region in ideological struggle today. Law establishes and upholds the conceptual frame in which subjects, "free and equal" with "rights" and "duties," engage on a playing field made level by legal recourse and due process. These fundamental concepts of *individuals* with the right to enter into and withdraw from relations and obligations to others underpin, he argues, the work of other ideologically important regions in civil society.[16]

Whether the juridical-political is truly the fulcrum of ideological contestation or not, it is clearly a central area of conflict and one in which some of the basic changes in our conception of the human/computer, reality/simulation metaphors get fought out. Reconceptualizations of copyright and patent law, brought on by computer chip design, computer software, and biogenetic engineering, give evidence

of the process by which a dominant ideology seeks to preserve itself in the face of historical change.

Conceptual metaphors take on tangible embodiment through discursive practices and institutional apparatuses. Such practices give a metaphor historical weight and ideological power. Tangible embodiment has always been a conscious goal of the cybernetic imagination where abstract concepts become embedded in the logic and circuitry of a material substrate deployed to achieve specific forms of result such as a computer, an antiaircraft tracking system or an assembly-line robot. These material objects, endowed with automated but intelligent capacities, enter our culture as, among other things, commodities. As a peculiar category of object these cyborgs require clarification of their legal status. What proprietary rights pertain to them? Can they be copyrighted, patented, protected by trade secrets acts; can they themselves as automated but intelligent entities, claim legal rights that had previously been reserved for humans or other living things on a model akin to that which has been applied to animal research?

The answers to such questions do not fall from the sky. They are the result of struggle, of a clash of forces, and of the efforts, faltering or eloquent, of those whose task it is to make and adjudicate the law. New categories of objects do not necessarily gain the protection of patent or copyright law. One reason for this is that federal law in the United States (where most of my research on this question took place) and the Constitution both enshrine the right of individuals to private ownership of the means of production while also enjoining against undue forms of monopoly control. The Constitution states, "The Congress shall have power . . . to promote the progress of science and useful arts, by securing for limited times to authors and inventors the exclusive right to their respective writings and discoveries." Hence the protection of intellectual property (copyright and trademark registration) or industrial and technological property (patents) carves out a proprietary niche within the broader principle of a "free flow" of ideas and open access to "natural" sources of wealth.

The cybernetic organism, of course, confounds the distinction between intellectual and technological property. Both a computer and a biogenetically designed cell "may be temporarily or permanently programmed to perform many different unrelated tasks."[17] The cybernetic metaphor, of course, allows us to treat the cell and the computer as sources of the same problem. As the author of one legal article observed, "A ribosome, like a computer, can carry out any sequence of assembly instructions and can assemble virtually unlimited numbers of different organic compounds, including those essential to life, as well as materials that have not yet been invented."[18] What legal debates have characterized the struggle for proprietary control of these cyborgs?

Regarding patents, only clearly original, unobvious, practical applications of the "laws of nature" are eligible for protection, a principle firmly established in the Telephone Cases of 1888 where the Supreme Court drew a sharp distinction between electricity itself as nonpatentable since it was a "force of nature" and the telephone where electricity was found, "A new, specific condition not found in nature and suited to the transmission of vocal or other sounds."

Recent cases have carried the issue further, asking whether "intelligent systems" can be protected by patent and, if so, what specific elements of such a system are eligible for protection. Generally, and perhaps ironically, the United States Supreme Court has been more prone to grant protection for the fabrication of new life forms, via recombinant DNA experiments, than for the development of computer software. In *Diamond v. Chakrabatry* (1980), the Supreme Court ruled in favor of patent protection for Chakrabatry who had developed a new bacterial form capable of degrading petroleum compounds for projected use in oil-spill clean-ups. In other, earlier cases, the Supreme Court withheld patent protection for computer software. In *Gottschalk v. Benson* (1972) and in *Parker v. Flook* (1979), the Court held that computer programs were merely algorithms, i.e., simple, step-by-step mathematical procedures, and as such were closer to basic principles or concepts than to original and unobvious applications. These decisions helped prompt recourse to a legislative remedy for an untenable situation (for those with a vested interest in the marketability of computer programs); in 1980 Congress passed the Software Act, granting some of the protection the judicial branch had been reluctant to offer but still leaving many issues unsettled. A Semiconductor Chip Protection Act followed in 1984 with a new *sui generis* form of protection for chip masks (the templates from which chips are made). Neither copyright nor patent, this protection applies for ten years (less than copyright) and demands less originality of design than does patent law. In this case, the law itself

replicates the "having come from nowhere" quality of the simulation. The *Minnesota Law Review* 70 (December 1985) is devoted to a symposium on this new form of legal protection for intellectual but also industrial property.

The Software Act began the erosion of a basic distinction between copyright and patent by suggesting that useful objects were eligible for copyright. In judicial cases such as *Diamond v. Diehr* (1981), the court held that "when a claim containing a mathematical formula implements or applies that formula in a structure or process which, when considered as a whole, is performing a function which the patent laws were designed to protect (for example, transforming or reducing an article to a different state of things), then the claim satisfies the requirements of [the copyright law]."

This finding ran against the grain of the long-standing *White-Smith Music Publishing Co v. Apollo Co* decision of 1908 where the Supreme Court ruled that a player-piano roll was ineligible for the copyright protection accorded to the sheet music it duplicated. The roll was considered part of a machine rather than the expression of an idea. The distinction was formulated according to the code of the visible: a copyrightable text must be visually perceptible to the human eye and must "give to every person *seeing* it the idea created by the original."[19]

Copyright had the purpose of providing economic incentive to bring new ideas to the marketplace. Copyright does not protect ideas, processes, procedures, systems or methods, only a specific embodiment of such things. (A book on embroidery could receive copyright but the process of embroidery itself could not.) Similarly, copyright cannot protect useful objects or inventions. If an object has an intrinsically utilitarian function, it cannot receive copyright. Useful objects can be patented, if they are original enough, or protected by trade secrets acts. For example, a fabric design could receive copyright as a specific, concrete rendition of form. It would be an "original work of authorship" fixed in the tangible medium of cloth and the "author" would have the right to display it as an ornamental or artistic object without fear of imitation. But the same fabric design, once embodied in a dress, can no longer be copyrighted since it is now primarily a utilitarian object. Neither the dress, nor any part of it, can receive copyright. Others would be free to imitate its appearance since the basic goal (according to a somewhat non-fashion-conscious law) is to produce a

637

utilitarian object meant to provide protection from the elements and a degree of privacy for the body inside it.

What then of a video game? Is this an original work of authorship? Is it utilitarian in essence? And if it is eligible for copyright, what element or aspect of it, exactly, shall receive this copyright? The process of mechanical reproduction had assured that the copyright registration of one particular copy of a work would automatically insure protection for all its duplicates. Even traditional games like *Monopoly,* which might produce different outcomes at each playing, were identical to one another in their physical and visible parts. But the only visible part of a video game is its video display. The display is highly ephemeral and varies in detail with each play of the game. For a game like *Pac-Man,* the notion of pursuit or pursuit through a maze would be too general. Like the notion of the western or the soap opera, it is too broad for copyright eligibility. Instead the key question is whether a general idea, like pursuit, is given concrete, distinctive, *expression.* The working out of this distinction, though, lends insight into the degree of difference between mechanical reproduction and cybernetic systems perceived by the United States judicial system.

For video games like *Pac-Man,* a copyright procedure has developed that gives protection to the outward manifestation of the underlying software programs. Registration of a copyright does not involve depositing the algorithms structuring the software of the ROM (read-only memory) chip in which it is stored. Instead, registration requires the deposit of a videotape of the game in the play mode.[20]

Referring to requirements that copyright is for "original works of authorship fixed in any tangible medium," Federal District Courts have found that creativity directed to the end of presenting a video display constitutes recognizable authorship and "fixation" occurs in the *repetition* of specific aspects of the visual scenes from one playing of a game to the next. But fixing precisely what constitutes repetition when subtle variations are also in play is not a simple matter. For example, in *Atari v. North American Phillips Consumer Electronics Corp* (1981), one District Court denied infringement of Atari's *Pac-Man* by the defendant's *K.C. Munchkin.* The decision rested on a series of particular differences between the games despite overall similarities. In elaboration, the court noted that the Munchkin character, unlike Pac-Man, "initially faces the viewer rather than showing a profile." K.C. Munchkin moves in profile but

when he stops, "he turns around to face the viewer with another smile." Thus the central character is made to have a personality which the central character in *Pac-Man* does not have. *K.C. Munchkin* has munchers which are "spookier" than the goblins in *Pac-Man.* Their legs are longer and move more dramatically, their eyes are vacant—all features absent from *Pac-Man.*

This opinion, however, was overturned in *Atari vs North American Phillips* (1982). The Seventh Circuit Court found *Pac-Man's* expressive distinctiveness to lie in the articulation of a particular kind of pursuit by means of "gobbler" and "ghost-figures," thereby granting broad protection to the game by likening it to a film genre or subgenre. The Circuit Court found the Munchkin's actions of gobbling and disappearing to be "blatantly similar," and went on to cut through to the basic source of the game's appeal and marketability:

> Video-games, unlike an artist's painting or even other audio visual works, appeal to an audience that is fairly undiscriminating insofar as their concern about more subtle differences in artistic expression. The main attraction of a game such as Pac-Man lies in the stimulation provided by the intensity of the competition. A person who is entranced by the play of the game, "would be disposed to overlook" many of the minor differences in detail and "regard their aesthetic appeal as the same."[21]

In this decision, the Court stresses the process of absorption and feedback sustained by an automated but intelligent system that can simulate the reality of pursuit. The decision represents quite a remarkable set of observations. The fetishization of the image as object of desire transforms into a fetishization of a process as object of desire. This throws as much emphasis on the mental state of the participant as on the exact visual qualities of the representation ("A person who is entranced by the play of the game").

In these cases the courts have clearly recognized the need to guarantee the exclusive rights of authors and inventors (and of the corporations that employ them) to the fruits of their discoveries. Simultaneously, this recognition has served to legitimate the cybernetic metaphor and to renormalize the political-legal apparatus in relation to the question: who shall have the right to control the cybernetic system of which we are a part? On the whole, the decisions have funneled that control back to a discrete proprietor, making what is potentially disruptive once again consonant with the social formation it threatens to disrupt.

Such decisions may require recasting the legal framework itself and its legitimizing discourse. Paula Samuelson identifies the magnitude of the transformation at work quite tellingly: "It [is] necessary to reconceptualize copyright and patent in ways that would free the systems from the historical subjects to which they have been applied. It [is] necessary to rethink the legal forms, pare them down to a more essential base, and adjust their rules accordingly. It [is] necessary to reconceive the social bargain they now reflect."[22]

If efforts to gain proprietary control of computer chip masks, software and video games have prompted little radical challenge from the left, the same cannot be said for bacteria and babies, for, that is, the issues of proprietorship that are raised by new forms of artificial life and artificial procreation where the "social bargain" woven into our discursive formations undergoes massive transformation.

The hidden agenda of mastery and control, the masculinist bias at work in video games, in Star Wars, in the reality of the simulation (of invasions, raids and wars), in the masculine need for autonomy and control as it corresponds to the logic of a capitalist marketplace becomes dramatically obvious when we look at the artificial reproduction of human life. The human as a metaphorical, automated, but intelligent system becomes quite literal when the human organism is itself a product of planned engineering.

Gametes, embryos, and fetuses become, like other forms of engineered intelligence that have gained legal status, babies-to-be, subject now to the rules and procedures of commodity exchange. Human life, like Baby M herself, becomes in every sense a commodity to be contracted for, subject to the proprietary control of those who rent the uterus, or the test tube, where such entities undergo gestation.

As one expert in the engineering of human prototypes put it, reproduction in the laboratory is willed, chosen, purposed, and controlled, and is, therefore, more human than coitus with all its vagaries and elements of chance.[23] Such engineering affirms the "contractor's" rights to "take positive steps to enhance the possibility that offspring will have desired characteristics, as well as the converse right to abort or terminate offspring with undesired or undesirable characteristics."[24] But what is most fundamentally at stake does not seem to be personal choice, but power and

economics. These opportunities shift reproduction from family life, private space, and domestic relations to the realm of production itself by means of the medical expert, clinical space, and commodity relations. The shift allows men who previously enjoyed the privilege of paying for their sexual pleasure without the fear of consequence the added opportunity of paying for their hereditary preferences without the fear of sexual pleasure.

Such "engineered fetuses" and babies become so much like real human beings that their origin as commodities, bought and sold, may be readily obscured. They become the perfect cyborg. As with other instances in which a metaphor becomes operative and extends across the face of a culture, we have to ask who benefits and who suffers? We have to ask what is at stake and how might struggle and contestation occur? What tools are at our disposal and to what conception of the human do we adhere that can call into question the reification, the commodification, the patterns of mastery, and control that the human as cyborg, the cyborg as human, the simulation of reality, and the reality of the simulation make evident?

Like the normalization of the cybernetic metaphor as scientific paradigm or the judicial legitimization of the private ownership of cybernetic systems (even when their substrate happens to be a living organism), the justification for hierarchical control of the cybernetic apparatus takes a rhetorical form because it is, in essence, an ideological argument. Dissent arises largely from those who appear destined to be controlled by the "liberating force" of new cybernetic technologies. But in no arena will the technologies themselves be determining. In each instance of ideological contestation, what we discover is that the ambivalences regarding cybernetic technology require resolution on more fundamental ground: that domain devoted to a social theory of power.

## Purpose, System, Power: Transformative Potential versus Conservative Practice

Liberation from any literal referent beyond the simulation, like liberation from a cultural tradition bound to aura and ritual, brings the actual process of constructing meaning, and social reality, into sharper focus. This liberation also undercuts the Renaissance concept of the individual. "Clear and distinct" people may be a prerequisite for an industrial economy based on the sale of labor power, but mutually dependent cyborgs may be a higher priority for a postindustrial postmodern economy. In an age of cybernetic systems, the very foundation of western culture and the very heart of its metaphysical tradition, the individual, with his or her inherent dilemmas of free will versus determinism, autonomy versus dependence, and so on, may very well be destined to stand as a vestigial trace of concepts and traditions which are no longer pertinent.

The testing Benjamin found possible with mechanical reproduction—the ability to take things apart and reassemble them, using, in film, montage, the "dynamite of the tenth of a second"—extends yet further with cybernetic systems: what had been mere possibilities or probabilities manifest themselves in the simulation. The dynamite of nanoseconds explodes the limits of our own mental landscape. What falls open to apperception is not just the relativism of social order and how, through recombination, liberation from imposed order is possible, but also the set of systemic principles governing order itself, its dependence on messages-in-circuit, regulated at higher levels to conform to predefined constraints. We discover how, by redefining those constraints, liberation from them is possible. Cybernetic systems and the cyborg as human metaphor refute a heritage that celebrates individual free will and subjectivity.

If there is liberating potential in this, it clearly is not in seeing ourselves as cogs in a machine or elements of a vast simulation, but rather in seeing ourselves as part of a larger whole that is self-regulating and capable of long-term survival. At present this larger whole remains dominated by parts that achieve hegemony. But the very apperception of the cybernetic connection, where system governs parts, where the social collectivity of mind governs the autonomous ego of individualism, may also provide the adaptive concepts needed to decenter control and overturn hierarchy.

Conscious purpose guides the invention and legitimization of cybernetic systems. For the most part, this purpose has served the logic of capitalism, commodity exchange, control and hierarchy. Desire for short-term gain or immediate results gives priority to the criteria of predictability, reliability, and quantifiability. Ironically, the survival of the system as a whole (the sum total of system plus environment on a global scale) takes a subordinate position to more immediate concerns. We remain largely unconscious of that total system that

conscious purpose obscures. Our consciousness of something indicates the presence of a problem in need of solution, and cybernetic systems theory has mainly solved the problem of capitalist systems that exploit and deplete their human and natural environment, rather than conserving both themselves and their environment.

Anthony Wilden makes a highly germane observation about the zero-sum game, Monopoly. The goal of the game is to win by controlling the relevant environment, the properties, and the capital they generate. But Monopoly and its intensification of rational, conscious purpose masks a logic in the form of being "merely a game" that is deadly when applied to the open ecosystem. Wilden writes, "We usually fail to see that Monopoly supports the ideology of competition by basing itself on a logical and ecological absurdity. It is assumed that the winning player, having consumed all the resources of all the opponents, can actually survive the end of the game. In fact this is impossible. . . . The Monopoly winner [must] die because in the context of the resources provided by the game, the winner has consumed them all, leaving no environment (no other players) to feed on."[25]

"There is the discovery," Gregory Bateson writes in one of his more apocalyptic essays, "that man is only a part of larger systems and that the part can never control the whole."[26] The cybernetic metaphor invites the testing of the purpose and logic of any given system against the goals of the larger ecosystem where the unit of survival is the adaptive organism-in-relation-to-its-environment, not the monadic individual or any other part construing itself as autonomous or "whole."[27] "Transgression does not negate an interdiction; it transcends and completes it." The transgressive and liberating potential which Bataille found in the violation of taboos and prohibitions, and which Benjamin found in the potential of mechanically reproduced works of art, persists in yet another form. The cybernetic metaphor contains the germ of an enhanced future inside a prevailing model that substitutes part for whole, simulation for real, cyborg for human, conscious purpose for the decentered goal-seeking of the totality—system plus environment. The task is not to overthrow the prevailing cybernetic model but to transgress its predefined interdictions and limits, using the dynamite of the apperceptive powers it has itself brought into being.

## Notes

1. The concept of the double hermeneutic derives from Fredric Jameson, *The Political Unconscious* (Ithaca: Cornell University Press, 1981), especially the final chapter.

2. Walter Benjamin, "The Work of Art in the Age of Mechanical Reproduction" in *Illuminations,* by Harry Zohn, trans., (New York: Schocken Books, 1969), p. 221. Further page references from this essay are given in the text.

3. Walter Benjamin, *Schriften,* 2 vols. (Frankfurt: Suhrkamp Verlag, 1955), I, p. 461. Translated in Fredric Jameson, *Marxism and Form* (Princeton: Princeton University Press, 1971), p. 77.

4. Terry Eagleton, *Marxism and Literary Criticism* (Berkeley: University of California Press, 1976), p. 63.

5. This quote is from James Clifford, "On Ethnographic Surrealism" *Comparative Studies in Society and History,* vol. 23, 4 (October 1981): 559–564, where he offers an excellent description of the confluences between surrealism and certain tendencies within early ethnography in 1920s France.

6. See, for example, the essays in Part III, "Form and Pathology in Relationship" by Gregory Bateson, *Steps to an Ecology of Mind* (New York: Ballantine Books, 1972), where this phrase is introduced and applied to various situations.

7. Quoted in Sherry Turkle, *The Second Self: Computer and the Human Spirit* (New York: Simon and Schuster, 1984), p. 86.

8. Steven J. Heims, *John von Neumann and Norbert Wiener: From Mathematics to the Technologies of Life and Death* (Cambridge, MA: MIT Press, 1980), describes how research on antiaircraft guidance systems led Julian Bigelow and Norbert Wiener to develop a mathematical theory "for predicting the future as best one can on the basis of incomplete information about the past" (p. 183). For an overview of the history of cybernetic theory and cognitive psychology in the context of its military-industrial origins, see Paul N. Edwards, "Formalized Warfare," unpublished ms. (1984), History of Consciousness Program, University of California, Santa Cruz.

9. Jean Baudrillard, "The Implosion of Meaning in the Media and the Implosion of the Social in the Masses" in Kathleen Woodward, ed., *The Myths of Information,* (Madison, Coda Press, 1980), p. 139.

10. Sherry Turkle, p. 264.

11. See Laura Mulvey, "Visual Pleasure and Narrative Cinema," *Screen,* vol. 16, 3 (Autumn 1975): 6–18.

12. Paul N. Edwards, p. 59.

13. See, for example, Paul N. Edwards, for a more detailed account of this synergism between the development of cybernetics and military needs. For a cybernetic theory of alcoholism and schizophrenia, see Gregory Bateson, and Watzlawick, Beavin and Jackson's study of human interaction in a systems framework in Pragmatics of Human Communication.

14. John Stroud, "Psychological Moments in Perception—Discussions," in H. Van Foersta, et al., eds., *Cybernetics: Circular Causal and Feedback Mechanisms in Biological and Social Systems,* Transactions of the Sixth Macy Conference (New York: Josiah Macy Foundation, 1949), pp. 27–28.

15. Jean Baudrillard, p. 139.

16. See Nicos Poulantzas, *Political Power and Social Class* (London: New Left Books, 1975), pp. 211–214.

17. James J. Myrick and James A. Sprowl, "Patent Law for Programmed Computers and Programmed Life Forms," *American Bar Association Journal,* no. 68 (August 198): 120.

18. Myrick and Sprowl, p. 121. Some other relevant articles include: "Biotechnology: Patent Law Developments in Great Britain and the United States," *Boston College International and Comparative Law Review,* no. 6 (Spring 1983): 563–590; "Can a Computer be an Author? Copyright Aspects of Artificial Intelligence," *Communication Entertainment Law Journal,* 4 (Summer 1982): 707–747; Peter Aufrichtig, "Copyright Protection for Computer Programs in Read-Only Memory Chips," *Hofstra Law Review,* II (February 1982): 329–370; "Patents on Algorithms, Discoveries and Scientific Principles," Idea 24 (1983): 21–39; S. Hewitt, "Protection of Works Created by Use of Computers," *New Law Journal,* 133 (March 11, 1983): 235–237; E.N. Kramsky, "Video Games: Our Legal System Grapples with a Social Phenomenon," *Journal of the Patent Office Society,* 64 (June 1982): 335–351.

19. This case's relevance for computer software litigation is discussed in Peter Aufrichtig's "Copyright Protection for Computer Programs in Read Only Memory Chips,": 329–370.

20. E.N. Kramsky, p. 342.

21. 214 US PQ 33t 7th Cir, 1982, pp. 33, 42, 43.

22. Paula Samuelson, "Creating a New Kind of Intellectual Property: Applying the Lessons of the Chip Law to Computer Programs," *Minnesota Law Review,* 70 (December 1985): 502.

23. Cited in Christine Overall, "Pluck a Fetus from its womb": A Critique of Current Attitudes Toward the Embryo/Fetus," *University of Western Ontario Law Review,* vol. 24, 1 (1986): 6–7.

24. Overall, p. 7.

25. Anthony Wilden, "Changing Frames of Order: Cybernetics and the Machina Mundi" in Kathleen Woodward, ed., *The Myths of Information,* p. 240.

26. Gregory Bateson, "Conscious Purpose and Nature" in *Steps to an Ecology of Mind,* p. 437.

27. Gregory Bateson, "Style, Grace and Information in Primitive Art," *Steps to an Ecology of Mind,* p. 145.

641

# 44. [Introduction]
# The Fantasy Beyond Control

Lynn Hershman's *Lorna* ⊗ is considered the first interactive video art installation (1979–83). It was elegantly simple: a woman, Lorna, sat at home watching her television, clicking her remote. The viewer sat and watched her on television, making choices with a similar remote. The piece began with a mock survey and proceeded to show the space of Lorna's apartment, which contained items the user could select. These items led to branching narratives which proceeded based on further user selections. The interacting viewers were repositioned relative to television, identifying with the character and the gaze in a manner quite different from film theory's "suture." Hershman also anticipated, by a decade, the navigational structures presented by 1990s branching narrative CD-ROMs. Her video disk design was not without precedent, however. Its structure was similar to that of written, rather than video, works such as Raymond Queneau's "Yours for the Telling" (◊12).

Hershman's work grew out of an installation art and performance tradition. Grahame Weinbren's, on the other hand, grew out of an experimental cinema tradition, informed by his work with cutting-edge commercial video systems. After *Lorna*, Weinbren's *The Erl King* ⊗ (1986, a collaboration with Roberta Friedman) and *Sonata* ⊗ (1991) took the interactive video installation into new territory. In these pieces the language of cinema was reinvented for the context of interaction—with the development of techniques such as the viewer-controlled cut-away and wipe. Like Hershman, Weinbren chose psychological themes for his exploration. But rather than the agoraphobic, media-saturated character whose study is central to *Lorna*, or a focus on a single character or situation of any sort, Weinbren chose a technique that may remind one of early cinematic work such as Griffith's *Intolerance*: parallel, metaphorically related stories. In this context, link-following becomes a poetically-interpreted activity. The viewers do not "make choices" for the characters. His work provides an interactive role quite different from that of *Lorna*, and from branching "interactive movies" or video games.

Hershman's 1989–90 *Deep Contact* ⊗—aspects of which are discussed at the end of her essay below—used elements such as the touch screen, which Weinbren had used to control cinematic effects, in a new way. *Deep Contact* featured a leather-clad guide, and the user was invited to touch this woman all over her body as a means of navigation. Needless to say, this was a remarkable departure from the everyday remote of *Lorna*—akin, perhaps, to Yoko Ono's embodied, interactive-invasive *Cut Piece* (described in this volume's introduction to Allan Kaprow's essay (◊06)). However, during the *Deep Contact* interaction, a surveillance camera could be triggered, replacing the image under the viewer's gaze and touch with their own.

More recently, interactive video work has provided dynamically arranged links to video fragments, as with *A Random Walk Through the 20th Century* ⊗ and has extended hypertext concepts into video, as with *Hypercafe* and Janet Murray's *Hot Norman*. As video compression improves and bandwidth increases, interactive video work will continue to become both easier for individuals and wider in its audience, existing in a networked context and making use of the network—as with the recent work of Chris Hales.

—NWF & NM

Further Reading

Hershman-Leeson, Lynn, ed. *Clicking In: Hot Links to a Digital Culture*. Seattle: Bay Press, 1996. Includes CD-ROM.

Cameron, Andrew, ed. *Millennium Film Journal: Interactivities*. New York: Millennium Film Workshop, 1995, 28.

Sawhney, Nitin ("Nick"), David Balcom, and Ian Smith. "HyperCafe: Narrative and Aesthetic Properties of Hypervideo." In *Hypertext '96 Proceedings*. New York: ACM Press, 1996, 1–10.

Manovich, Lev. *The Language of New Media*. Cambridge: MIT Press, 2001.

Original Publication

*Illuminating Video: An Essential Guide to Video Art.* 267–273. New
York: Aperture/BAVC, 1990.

# The Fantasy Beyond Control

## Lynn Hershman

A (pre)condition of a video dialogue is that *it does not talk
back*. Rather, it exists as a moving stasis; a one-sided
discourse; like a trick mirror that absorbs instead of reflects.
Perhaps it was nostalgia that led me to search for an
interactive video fantasy—a craving for control, a longing for
liveness, a drive toward direct action. This total, cumulative,
and chronic condition I suffered from is reputedly a side
effect (or for video artists an occupational hazard) of
watching television, a medium that is by nature fragmentary
and incomplete, distanced and unsatisfying; like platonic sex.

My path to interactive works began covertly not with
video, but in performance when in 1971 an *alternative
identity* named Roberta Breitmore was created. She was a
breathing simulacrum, a persona, played first by myself, and
then by a series of *multiple* individuals. Roberta existed in
both real life and real time and during the decade of her
activity engaged in many adventures that typified the culture
in which she participated. She had a checking account and a
driver's license and saw a psychiatrist. That she existed was
proved by the trackings of her psychiatric reports and credit
ratings. Her construction included specific language and
gestures as well as a stereotyped cosmetic ambience. By
accumulating artifacts from culture and interacting directly
with life, she became a two-way mirror that reflected societal
biases experienced through time. Roberta was always seen as
a surveillance target. Her decisions were random, only very
remotely controlled. Roberta's manipulated reality, or
bending of time, became a model for a private system of
interactive performance. Instead of a disk or hardware, her
records were stored on photographs and texts that could be
viewed without predetermined sequences. This allowed
viewers to become voyeurs into Roberta's history.[1] Their
interpretations shifted depending on the perspective and
order of the sequences.

Two years after ROBERTA's transformation,[2] *Lorna*, the
first interactive art video disk was completed. Unlike
Roberta, whose adventures took place directly in the
environment, Lorna was a middle-aged agoraphobic, fearful
of leaving her tiny apartment. The premise was that the
more she stayed home and watched television, the more
fearful she became—primarily because she was absorbing
the frightening messages of advertising and news broadcasts.
Because she never left home, the objects in her room took on
a magnificent proportion, they were to her what Mount St.
Victoire was to Cezanne. In the disk, every object in her room
is numbered and becomes a chapter in her life that opens
into branching sequences. Viewer/participants access
information about her past, future, and personal conflicts via
these artifacts. Many images on the screen are of the remote-
control device Lorna uses to change television channels.
Because viewer/participants use a nearly identical unit to
direct the disk action, a metaphoric link or point of
identification is established between the viewer and referent.

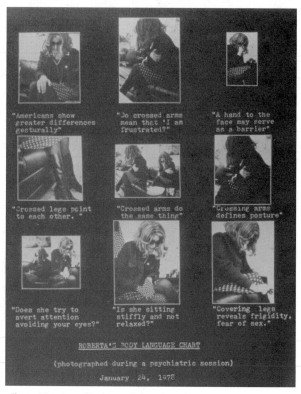

Figure 44.1. Lynn Hershman, Roberta's Body Language Chart, 1978.

Figure 44.2. Lynn Hershman, Constructing Roberta Breitmore, 1975.

invention of the technology that would have more fully exploited their concepts.

Lorna literally is captured by a mediated landscape. Her passivity (presumably caused by being controlled by media) is a counterpoint to the direct action of the player. As the branching path is deconstructed, the player becomes aware of the subtle yet powerful effects of fear caused by media and becomes more empowered (active) through this perception. Playing *Lorna* was designed to have viewer/participants transgress into an inverse labyrinth of themselves.

Despite some theories to the contrary,[3] the dominant presumption is that making art is active and viewing it is passive. Radical shifts in communication technology, such as the marriage of image, sound, text, and computers, and consummation by the public of this consort, have challenged this assumption. Viewer/participants of *Lorna* reported that they had the impression that they were empowered because they held the option of manipulating Lorna's life. Rather than being remotely controlled, the decision unit was literally placed in their hands. They were not simply watching a narrative with a structure predetermined by an invisible omniscient. Implications of the relationship reversal between individuals and technological media systems are immense. The media bath of transmitted prestructured and pre-edited information that surrounds (and some say alienates) people is washed away. It is hosed down by viewer input. Alteration of the basis for exchange of information is subversive in that it encourages participation and therefore creates a different audience dynamic.

Interactive systems *require* viewers to react. Their choices are facilitated by means of a keyboard, mouse, or touch-sensitive screen. As technology expands, there will be more permutations available, not only between the viewer and the system, but between elements within the system itself. Some people feel that computer systems will eventually reflect the personality and biases of their users. Yet these systems only appear to talk back. That they are alive or independent is an illusion. They depend upon the architectural strategy of the program. However, there is a space between the system and player in which a link, fusion, or transplant occurs. Content is codified. Truth and fiction blur. Action becomes icon and relies on movement and plasticity of time—*icono plastics and logomotion*. According to Freud, *reality* may be limited to perceptions that can be verified through words or visual codes. Therefore perceptions are the drive to action that

The viewer/participant activates the live action and makes surrogate decisions for Lorna. Decisions are designed into a branching path. Although there is only seventeen minutes of moving image in the disk, the thirty-six chapters could be sequenced differently for several days. There are three separate endings to the disk, though the plot has multiple variations that include being caught in repeating dream sequences, or using multiple sound tracks, and can be seen backward, forward, at increased or decreased speed, and from several points of view, like an *electronic cubism*. There is no hierarchy in the ordering of decisions. These ideas are not new. They were explored by such artists as Stéphane Mallarmé, John Cage, and Marcel Duchamp—particularly in Duchamp's music. They pioneered ideas about random adventures and chance operations fifty years before

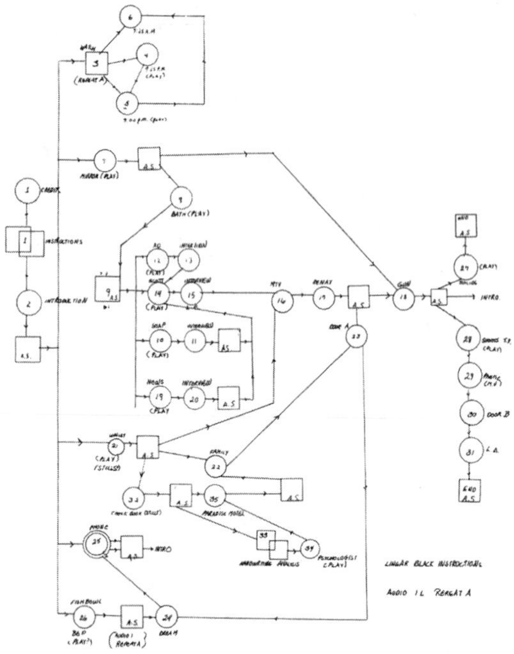

Figure 44.3. Lynn Hershman, Lorna, Video Disk Design, Garti/Hershman, 1984.

influences, if not controls, real events. Perceptions therefore become the key to reality.

Electronic media are based on the speed of information. The terminal, once a sign for closure, has become the matrix for information expansion. The introduction of new mass media in the late 1940s created an unparalleled opportunity to control mass perceptions. Immediate communication tended to increase the importance of media. Beaming pictures into millions of homes every night had the effect of speeding up time, of increasing the pace of life and destabilizing traditional communities, replacing them with a distanced *global village*. Individuals were left powerless to affect what was being imposed, other than simply turning off their sets and becoming even more alienated. A similar sense of cultural time displacement had occurred with the invention of the automobile when traditional sense of distance shifted.

There is a debate among scholars of media about whether or not it is possible to observe phenomena without influencing them. In physics this can be equated to Heisenberg's theory. The very act of viewing a *captured* image creates a distance from the original event. The *captured* image

becomes a relic of the past. Life is a moving target and any object that is isolated becomes history. Mass media redesign information by replacing the vantage point of the viewer with the frame provided by a cameraperson/journalist photographer. When information is presented beyond individual control, viewers are separated from the referent, resulting in a diminution of their identity. Personal identity is tenuous territory. According to Roman Jakobson, "personal pronouns are the last elements to be acquired in the child's speech and the first to be lost in aphasia."[4] When an area that was inhabited by a viewer is emptied by a displaced identity, it is replaced by a sense of absense. This loss of anchorage (perhaps healed by a contemporary shaman/anchorperson?) results in a suspension, a flotation, a feeling of discomfort or a low-level cultural virus, perhaps the locus of the nostalgia mentioned in the first sentence of this paper.

*Lorna* was developed as a research and development guide, but it is generally inaccessible. It was pressed in a limited edition of twenty-five, of which only fourteen now exist. It is only occasionally installed in galleries or museums. Creating a truly interactive work demands that it exist on a mass scale, available and accessible to many people. The HyperCard program works on most Macintosh computers and can be gen locked to a disk player or a CDV, or be used alone. It can access moving or still images and has a wide range of sound capabilities and is relatively inexpensive. The next two interactive works in progress, which I hope to complete in 1989, will use the HyperCard as a base. The motives of these two very different works are to explore ideas of contact and perception, not only metaphorically but actually through the process of the playing.

The two in-progress works are, very briefly, the following:

### 1. Deep Contact: The Incomplete Sexual Fantasy Disk,[5] which is designed around historical icons such as Freud, Bach, Joan of Arc, and a vampire. The player will be able to change his or her personality or approach to these icons or change their personality. An *emotional joy stick* will be used in concert with a touch-sensitive screen. This piece will work with a real phone modem and programmed surveillance camera allowing the piece to transgress the screen (or distanced observer) into really contacting and interacting with other players as well as others seeing themselves as part of the manipulation.

Figure 44.4. Lynn Hershman, Lorna, 1983.

**2. Paths of Inner Action**[6] involves a personal journey in which the viewer integrates into the system that he or she is looking at. The viewer will be guided by a shadowy figure that, like a Zen master, will direct the players' trail, asking questions about the meaning of experience or how the color of a leaf, eight frames past, balances with the textural opposites of the bridge in the future. By making surrogate decisions and routing their own paths, they will be given opportunities to understand perceptions about the media, technology, and the integration of both with individual personality. Trails will be designed to be reconfigured, or recontextualized, giving an evolving and essentially never-ending time frame to the piece.[7]

Because interactive media technology is becoming increasingly visible in all areas of societies (particularly outside the art world), the political impact is spectacular. Traditional narratives (beginnings, middles, and ends) are being restructured as genetic engineering advances simultaneously reshape the meaning of life. Participating personally in the discovery of values that affect and order their lives, allows individuals to dissolve the division that separates them from subversive control, and replaces some of the nostalgic longings with a sense of identity, purpose, and hope.

Notes

1. ROBERTA never was exhibited while she was in process. Rather she was invisible until she became history.

2. ROBERTA was exorcised in 1978 at Lucretia Borgia's crypt in Ferrara, Italy, where her victimization converted to emancipation.

3. For example, some ideas presented by Leo Steinberg.

4. See Roman Jakobson, "Child Language, Aphasia and Phonologica Universals," *Janua Linguarum* 71 (The Hague: Mouton, 1968) and "Studies on Child Language Aphasia," *Janua Linguarum* 114 (The Hague: Mouton, 1971).

5. This was originally conceived as a short-lived collaboration among Paula Levine, Starr Sutherland, Christine Tamblyn, and myself.

6. Much of this project derives from a collaboration with Ann Marie Garti.

7. Both ideas were completed in the videodisk installation *Deep Contact* completed in 1990 which premiered at the San Francisco Museum of Modern Art.

# 45. [Introduction]
# Cardboard Computers
## Mocking-It-Up or Hands-On the Future

Some said Smalltalk went astray after Smalltalk-80, when it became much more difficult for twelve-year-olds to use the programming language. This complaint reflects the ideal that everyday users of new media should be able to design and create their own tools, specifically as embodied by the work of Alan Kay and Adele Goldberg (◊26), but more generally stretching back to the ability of users of Vannevar Bush's proposed memex to create their own collections of trails through information. Today this ideal is not much in evidence.

When ordinary users cannot create their own tools, of their own design, what options remain? Unfortunately, a common option is to embark on a quarterly-profit-driven tool creation process that leaves design as the last step, and stretch a pre-painted canvas over the underlying functions previously chosen by managers and implemented by programmers. Several essays in this book are dedicated to sketching out better alternatives: those by Ted Nelson (◊21), Nicholas Negroponte (◊23), Brenda Laurel (◊38), and Terry Winograd and Fernando Flores (◊37) in particular. All of these argue for beginning with design, and viewing design as more than a surface activity. Increasingly it is being accepted that design cannot be completed by a designer sitting alone. The design process must include users.

The standard way of involving users is in "evaluation": timing them at various tasks, asking them to react to various designs, and giving them surveys about their experiences to fill out.

Pelle Ehn and Morten Kyng have been at the forefront of a different approach. They are perhaps best known as leaders of the Utopia project (an acronym, in the Scandinavian languages, for "Training, Technology, and Products from the Quality of Work Perspective"). Utopia is one of a number of projects that have taken the approach of working *with* users, from the outset, on the design of new media tools.

Utopia was carried out during a time of transition—in the early 1980s, before graphic user interfaces were widely available. Scandinavian newspapers were adopting computer page makeup tools developed in the U.S., which did not allow the graphic workers to use the full range of skills they had developed previously. As a result, the quality of Scandinavian newspaper design (which was different than U.S. design in certain ways) was diminishing, workers were losing their jobs in the wake of automation, and the quality of work life for those graphic workers who remained was deteriorating.

The unions decided to try taking the offensive. In Scandinavia there is a history of workers' groups becoming involved in research. Such groups had, for example, created the first ergonomic guidelines for computer display terminals. This time, the stakes were raised as the graphic workers union teamed up with university researchers to develop their own technological alternatives in the four year Utopia project.

The Utopia project's outlook was that new media tools should be designed for the quality of work they produce. As seen in this essay, Ehn and Kyng's model user is a skilled worker. The outlook is in some manners remarkably similar to Doug Engelbart's (◊08). Just as from Engelbart's perspective we would not expect the carpenter to use only tools that are "user-friendly," so Ehn and Kyng take the craft design process and craft use of tools as models of good software design.

Today, methods such as those used in Utopia are at the center of the Participatory Design (PD) movement, which has spread beyond Scandinavia to the U.S. and other parts of the world, and

The 'tool perspective' is developed at more length in Ehn's *Work-Oriented Design of Computer Artifacts*. In a chapter titled "Tools," Ehn begins by defining tools in a manner distinguishable from other privileged human instruments (our bodies, our language, and our social institutions) in that they are designed, constructed, maintained, and redesigned. Next, Ehn enters a discussion of how computer tools should be designed—of what might make a good tool—from which some interesting parallels can be drawn out. For example, when Ehn writes, "A good tool becomes an extension of our bodies," (393) the obvious association from a new media perspective is to Marshall McLuhan's (◊13) concept of media as "extensions of man." McLuhan worked in a somewhat different portion of the political spectrum than does Ehn, however, which may lead one to wonder whether their politically-charged concepts are actually as similar as they sound. In this same discussion, Ehn's mention of good tools as "transparent," while inspired by philosopher Michael Polanyi, bears a similarity to the ideas of authors such as Donald Norman. It may therefore be open to similar critiques, such as the one mounted by Gregory Ulmer using the cinema studies concept of *apparatus* (see below). Later Ehn surveys the pitfalls and strengths of the tool perspective, and also takes up the implicit challenge offered by Brenda Laurel's (◊38) quite negative view of the tool perspective. Rather than argue that Laurel's view of computer use as mimesis is unhelpful, Ehn chooses to embed his view within her own, writing: "In a way a tool perspective is just a special case of designing computer artifacts as interactive plays—a case where the first-personness is carried out by a skilled tool user acting in a context of useful materials from which he or she can create good use quality products. It is a challenge to design, to create such tools for pleasurable engagement, tools that when used help the user transcend the boredom of machine work" (415).

◊08
93

◊13
193

◊21
301

◊23
353

◊26
391

◊37
551

◊38
563

**649**

*Gregory Ulmer, from "Grammatology Hypermedia":*

. . . an experiment I conducted . . . placed the current developments in Artificial Intelligence and hypermedia programs in the context of the concept of the "apparatus," used in cinema studies to mount a critique of cinema as an institution, as a social "machine" that is as much ideological as it is technological. The same drive of realism that led in cinema to the "invisible style" of Hollywood narrative films, and to the occultation of the production process in favor of a consumption of the product as if it were "natural," is at work again in computing. Articles published in computer magazines declare that "the ultimate goal of computer technology is to make the computer disappear, that the technology should be so transparent, so invisible to the user, that for practical purposes the computer does not exist. In its perfect form, the computer and its application stand outside data content so that the user may be completely absorbed in the subject matter—it allows a person to interact with the computer just as if the computer were itself human" (*Macuser*, March 1989). It was clear that the efforts of critique to expose the oppressive effects of "the suture" in cinema (the effect binding the spectator to the illusion of a complete reality) had made no impression on the computer industry, whose professionals (including many academics) are in the process of designing "seamless" information environments for hypermedia applications. The "twin peaks" of American ideology—realism and individualism—are built into the computing machine (the computer as institution).

has had a profound influence on wider discussions of "usability." As this has taken place, similar methods have begun to appear in other contexts—some quite different from that of Utopia. For example, at SIGGRAPH 99 one designer presented his results from working with floor brokers at Goldman Sachs to design handheld computer tools modeled on their traditional skills, and operating as Utopia-style "reminders" of their work methods developed with paper tools. The brokers were quite enthusiastic about the results for their work life—showing it's not just union workers who would rather live in Utopia.

—NWF

*From the Participatory Design Web page of CPSR who, along with organizations such as ACM SIGCHI and Xerox, have sponsored recent PD conferences:*

Participatory Design (PD) is an approach to the assessment, design, and development of technological and organizational systems that places a premium on the active involvement of workplace practitioners (usually potential or current users of the system) in design and decision-making processes.

Because PD practitioners are so diverse in their perspectives, backgrounds, and areas of concern, there can be no single definition of PD. However, we can formulate a few tenets shared by most PD practitioners and advocates.

- Respect the users of technology, regardless of their status in the workplace, technical know-how, or access to their organization's purse strings. View every participant in a PD project as an expert in what they do, as a stakeholder whose voice needs to be heard.

- Recognize that workers are a prime source of innovation, that design ideas arise in collaboration with participants from diverse backgrounds, and that technology is but one option in addressing emergent problems.

- View a "system" as more than a collection of software encased in hardware boxes. In PD, we see systems as networks of people, practices, and technology embedded in particular organizational contexts.

- Understand the organization and the relevant work on its own terms, in its own settings. This is why PD practitioners prefer to spend time with users in their workplaces rather than "test" them in laboratories.

- Address problems that exist and arise in the workplace, articulated by or in collaboration with the affected parties, rather than attributed from the outside.

- Find concrete ways to improve the working lives of co-participants by, for example, reducing the tedium associated with work tasks; co-designing new opportunities for exercising creativity; increasing worker control over work content, measurement and reporting; and helping workers communicate and organize across hierarchical lines within the organization and with peers elsewhere.

- Be conscious of one's own role in PD processes; try to be a "reflective practitioner."

Further Reading

Bjerknes, Gro, Pelle Ehn, and Morten Kyng eds. *Computers and Democracy—A Scandinavian Challenge.* Aldershot, England: Avebury, 1987.

Computer Professionals for Social Responsibility (CPSR) <http://www.cpsr.org>

Ehn, Pelle. *Work-Oriented Design of Computer Artifacts.* Falköping, Sweden: Arbetslivscentrum and Hillsdale, NJ: Lawrence Erlbaum Associates, 1989.

Floyd, Christiane, Wolf-Michael Mehl, Fanny-Michaela Reisin, Gerhard Schmidt, and Gregor Wolf. "Out of Scandinavia: Alternative Approaches to Software Design and System Development." *Human-Computer Interaction* 4(4): 253-350, 1989.

Paley, W. Bradford. "Handheld Interactions: Tailoring Interfaces for Single-Purpose Devices." *SIGGRAPH 99 Sketches and Applications,* New York: ACM Press, 1999.

Ulmer, Gregory. "Grammatology Hypermedia." *Postmodern Culture* 1(2). January, 1991.

Original Publication

*Design at Work: Cooperative Design of Computer Systems*. 169–195. Ed. Joan Greenbaum and Morten Kyng. Hillsdale, N.J.: Lawrence Erlbaum Associates, 1991.

# Cardboard Computers
## Mocking-It-Up or Hands-On the Future
### Pelle Ehn and Morten Kyng

Figure 45.1. Mocking-it-up.

This picture shows some artifacts we have used in designing the future of computer-supported newspaper production in the Utopia project. There are paper sheets on the wall, slide projectors, screens, racks, chip boards, some chairs, and a cardboard box. However, something is missing. No, it is not computers, but the empty chairs certainly have to be occupied by future users. In our view, artifacts, computers as well as other tools, should be understood via the human use of them.

The users who would be envisioning their future work situation in the design game above are typographers and journalists working with editing, layout, and page make up. The relationship between these two groups has always been a bit tense. Journalists (assistant editors who work with editing and layout of text and pictures are responsible for the

quality of the content of the product (the readability); typographers (make up staff) who work with page make up are responsible for the quality of the form of the product (the legibility). However, the border between the two responsibilities is far from clear.

Figure 45.2. Page make up work using lead technology.

In the good old composing days journalists worked in the newsroom and typographers worked in the composing room. The editor sent a layout sketch to the composing room and the make up staff returned a "proof" to the newsroom before sending the page to be printed. Not a perfect process, but it worked well. With paper paste up technology it became more difficult to make proofs. It was too expensive and took too much time to run a proof on the photo typesetter. Hence, the assistant editors began to hang around in the composing room controlling the work of the make up staff. Not surprisingly, the typographers were not too happy about this arrangement.

With the introduction of computer-based layout and page make up in the late 1970s, the relations between the "rucksacks" (as the typographers called the journalists in the composing room) and the make up staff got even worse. Now the work was literally taken away from many typographers, since the equipment was placed in the newsroom and was operated by the assistant editors. However, aside from the personal misfortunes of introducing this new technology, the solution was far from optimal in terms of typographic quality.

The design question we were facing in the Utopia project was the following: Are there technical and organizational design alternatives that support peaceful and creative

651

coexistence between typographers and journalists, where both readability and legibility of the product could be enhanced?

Now take a closer look at the cardboard box at the right in the first picture. On the front is written "desktop laser printer;" that is all there is. It is a *mock-up*. The box is empty, its functionality is zero. Still, it works very well in the design game of envisioning the future work of assistant editors and make up staff. It is a suggestion to the participating users that an inexpensive computer-based proof machine could be part of the solution. With the help of new technology, the old proof machine can be reinvented and enhanced.

Figure 45.3. A mock-up of a laser printer "reinventing" the old proof machine.

The journalist makes a layout sketch, sends it to the typographer, and the typographer works on the page make up. Whenever he is in doubt or has suggestions for alternatives, he sends a proof via the desktop laser printer to the journalist, who marks with a few pen strokes how he wants the page to look, and sends the proof back to the typographer, who completes the page. Both can concentrate on what they are best at: the assistant editor on journalistic quality and the make up person on typographic quality. And why should they not sit in the same room and talk to each other?

The mock-ups in the pictures were made and used in 1982. At that time desktop laser printers only existed in the advanced research laboratories, and certainly typographers and journalists had never heard of them. To them the idea of a cheap laser printer was "unreal." It was our responsibility as professional designers to be aware of such future possibilities and to suggest them to the users. It was also our role to suggest this technical and organizational solution in such a way that the users could experience and envision what it would mean in their practical work, before too much time,

money, and development work were invested. Hence, the design game with the mock-up laser printer.

In this chapter we will show some prototypical examples of mock-ups. We will discuss how and why they are useful in participatory design. Our examples will range from "cardboard computers" to "computer mock-ups" hinting at the pros and cons of less and more advanced artifacts for envisionment of future use. Finally, the use of mock-ups is put into the perspective of other activities going on in participatory design.

## Why Mock It Up?

What we suggest in this chapter is that design artifacts such as mock-ups can be most useful in early stages of the design process. They encourage active user involvement, unlike traditional specification documents. For better or worse, they actually help users and designers transcend the borders of reality and imagine the impossible.

But why do mock-ups work despite their low functionality and the fact that they only are a kind of *simulacrum?* Some of the obvious answers include:

- they encourage *"hands-on experience,"* hence user involvement beyond the detached reflection that traditional systems descriptions allow;

- they are *understandable*, hence there is no confusion between the simulation and the "real thing," and everybody has the competence to modify them;

- they are *cheap*, hence many experiments can be conducted without big investments in equipment, commitment, time, and other resources; and last but not least,

- they are *fun* to work with.

### We Did Not Make It Up

Certainly we did not invent the idea of using mock-ups. Kids have always been good at playing with mock-ups like dolls, cars, etc. It is hard to imagine human life without these kinds of games.

However, the use of mock-ups can be most seductive. Think of computer exhibitions. What looks like a running system is often not the final system, nor even a prototype, but simply a video tape or a programmed slide show. Good envisionment of a future product; however, more than one manufacturer has passed the border between concerned marketing envisionment and deliberate manipulation.

Our way of using mock-ups has a family resemblance to both children's play and envisionment at exhibitions, but the most important inspiration comes from industrial designers. They have been using mock-ups professionally for decades. In particular, they have been successful in using mock-ups in ergonomic design.

Figure 45.4. Mock-up or the real system? An advertisement for the TIPS page make up system which was based on Utopia specifications. When the ad was published no "real" system existed.

One example is the use of ergonomic rigs. This is a mock-up environment in which designers and users together can build mock-ups of, for example, a future work station. Typically there will be support for rapid and cheap mocking-up of ergonomic aspects of appropriate tables, chairs, monitors, etc. Several alternatives can be designed and the users can get hands-on experience. Later, the designers can elaborate the mock-ups as in the following picture, where a future reception workstation has been envisioned.

Figure 45.5. Industrial design mock-up.

But it is not necessary to be a professional industrial designer to make useful mock-ups. The next picture is from a newsletter published by one of the clerical worker unions in Sweden. It shows a mock-up of a proposal for a new computer-controlled parcel sorting workstation. Originally, the local union was presented with only the technical specifications of the new proposal. However, on the basis of the drawings, the workers were unable to judge the quality of the proposal with respect to the effectiveness of work procedures and physical strain. They then spent a few thousand dollars to build the full scale mock-up. Using this they were able to simulate the future work: the flow of parcels, the tasks of each operator, including work load, and the possibility of supporting each other when bottlenecks occurred. The simulations resulted in several improvements, including suggestions for reducing physical strain and new ways of cooperating.

Figure 45.6. Sort machine mock-up. The headline reads: "We did not understand the blueprints, so we made our own mock-ups."

The use of mock-ups described here resembles the way industrial designers use them. However, our focus is on setting up design games for envisionment of the future work process. In contrast to industrial designers, we focus more on the hardware and software functionality of the future artifacts and less on the ergonomic aspects. Industrial designers often make very elaborate aesthetic and ergonomic designs of keyboards, but the display is black, and no functionality is simulated or mocked-up. If these different capabilities could meet in a participative design effort, an even more realistic simulacrum could be created. If the future users also actively participate in the design, the mock-ups may be truly useful and a proper move toward a changed reality. But are mock-ups really professional design artifacts? Yes, they are. In arguing this point, we will get a bit more philosophical, but we will also look at the theory in some practical examples.

## Language Games

We are guided by the concept of "What a picture describes is determined by its use." This is shocking statement for those of us who were brought up in a natural science tradition where a system description normally is understood as a kind of mirror image of reality. Nevertheless, this is a position at the heart of Ludwig Wittgenstein's *Philosophical Investigations* (1953). Wittgenstein was aware of this challenge. As a philosopher, he was first known for writing a doctoral thesis that showed how with an exact language we can map reality (Wittgenstein, 1923). Then he spent the rest of his life trying to convince us that he was wrong—that there is more to human language and interaction than can be written down, and that language is action. Instead of focusing on mirror images of reality we are advised to think of the language games people play—how we are able to participate in human activities because we have learned to act according to the unwritten rules of that activity.

For example, if Pelle, a designer, points at the cardboard box with the sign "desktop laser printer," and says to Jon, a typographer, "Could you take a look at the proof coming out from the desktop laser printer," Jon does not answer "There is no desktop laser printer! You are pointing at an empty cardboard box, stupid." Rather he would go to the cardboard box, pick up a blank paper from a paper stack beside the box, turn toward Pelle, look at the paper, and say "Well, here we have a problem. There is too much text for a 48 point three column headline and that picture of the president. I think we will have to crop the picture, or the headline has to be rewritten."

According to Pelle, and the other participants, Jon makes a proper move in the design *language game* he is participating in. On the other hand, if Jon had maintained that there is only a cardboard box with a sign on it saying "desktop laser printer," he would have made an incorrect move in this specific design language game. Despite the fact that he would

be right, he would not have understood how to play according to the rules.

The reason that Jon, Pelle, and the other participants can use the mock-up in a proper way is because this design language game has a *family resemblance* with other language games they know how to play. The language game in which the cardboard box is used has a family resemblance with the use of a traditional proof machine in the professional typographical language game which Jon knew very well, as well as with technical discussions Pelle had participated in as part of his profession. Furthermore, they both know how to play this design language game using the mock-up, because it resembles other *games* they have played before.

However, cardboard boxes do not become laser printers by themselves. In fact, one of the hardest challenges for the designer seems to be to *create a design language game that makes sense to all participants;* the designer in the role of play-maker. In this role the designer sets the stage by finding and supporting ways for useful cooperation between professional designers and "designing users." Future workshops and metaphorical design, as well as organizational design games, are examples of ways to set the stage for such shared design language games. Mock-ups and prototypes may be useful "properties" in these games. Hence, mock-ups are only effective in the design language games that make sense to the participants. In these games mock-ups play an important role as something to which one may refer in discussions of the design; as a *reminder* pointing back to experience from using the mock-up. Thus, instead of having to produce rational arguments in support of a certain point of view concerning a breakdown in the use of a mock-up, it is possible to repeat the sequence of operations leading to the breakdown. Then both that situation and the steps producing it may be evaluated, alternatives tried out, and, if necessary, participants may try to give rational arguments in favor of their point of view.

In summary, mock-ups become useful when they make sense to the participants in a specific design language game, not because they mirror "real things," but because of the interaction and reflection they support (see Ehn, 1989).

A new role for the designer is to set the stage and make it possible for designers and users to develop and use a common situated design language game. This has to be a language game that has a family resemblance with the ordinary language games of both the users and the designers;

a language game which is socially constructed by the participants.

## Hands-On Experiences and Ready-to-Hand Use

There are, however, more to mock-ups and the language games in which they are used than just language. As opposed to linguistic artifacts, such as flowcharts and system description documents, mock-ups make it possible for the user to get *hands-on experience.* This is illustrated in the picture below. What you see is the first mock-up we ever made in a design language game.

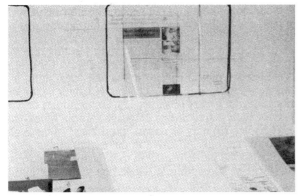

Figure 45.7. First mock-up of page make up work station.

In the above picture there is a high resolution graphic display, a control display, a tablet with a tablet menu and a mouse. Functionality of the system is simulated by making successive "drawings" of the screen. As shown in the next picture these drawings are "stored" on the wall, and "retrieved," "updated," and "changed" as the design game is played.

Figure 45.8. The wall as "store" for "interactive" display images.

This mock-up was the creative result of a major breakdown in the Utopia project, a breakdown that made us develop some new design artifacts and to shift perspective "from

system descriptions to scripts for action" in participatory design. As designers we had been producing an endless number of detailed and methodologically correct system descriptions. There was just one problem. The users could not understand our system descriptions. The descriptions did not remind the users of familiar work situations. There was no meaningful role for them to play in the use of these design artifacts. The experience of using these descriptions did not relate to their work experiences. The mock-up above changed the rules of the game; it made it possible for the users to actively participate in the design process.

For example, Jon simply sat down by the mock-up and pretended that he was doing page make up work. He used the mouse, the tablet, displays and menus to crop a picture, move a headline, change a font, etc. This was done in a way that had a family resemblance to his traditional way of working. He understood the mock-up as he understood his traditional tools.

We take as an important starting point in design the idea that "in the beginning all you can understand is what you already have understood." In stating this design paradox we have been inspired by Martin Heidegger and existential phenomenology (Heidegger, 1962, and especially Winograd & Flores, 1986, and Dreyfus & Dreyfus, 1986). The point is that the mock-up did not create a breakdown in Jon's understanding. It was not present as an object in itself, but *zuhanden* (ready-to-hand) for him in his activity. Jon was primarily involved in page make up work, not in detached reflections over this activity. He was not reading or talking about a future system, but experiencing it as a *Zeug* (dress, tool, artifact) for page make up—he was literally well-equipped, rather than overloaded with equipment.

However, the mock-up is, obviously, not the same as his traditional typographical tools; hence, breakdowns in his readiness-to-hand use of the mock-up occurred. Typographic tools such as the knife became computer equipment such as the mouse and display; the mouse became a match box, the display a sheet of paper. When the spell of unhampered involvement is broken, the mock-up becomes *vorhanden* (present-at-hand) as a collection of things or objects. This is not an entirely sad story. After all, if the artifacts we use were always ready-to-hand for us, how could we then find new ways of using them? When things do not work, we shift to detached reflections of them. In the situation noted this meant reflections such as: "Is a mouse/display replacement of the typographical knife really a good design choice?" "Is the problem rather that the properties of the knife are too restricted, and that we with computer support can add some new useful properties like 'undo cut' and 'resize'?" These kinds of questions were part of the interaction between the typographer using the mock-up and a designer sitting by his side. They certainly led to new design ideas, as well as to changes of the mock-up. For example, the second version of the mock-up provided possibilities for a wider range of hands-on activities and more elaborate design language games. There were more elaborated interaction devices to try out and a more dynamic interaction with the mock-up. Aspects of the work environment and of work cooperation could be tried out.

In summary, hands-on experience is not a substitute for detached reflection. However, in participatory design it is necessary and more fundamental to support the users' ready-to-hand use of their future artifacts. Hence, an important aspect of a mock-up is its usefulness for involved activity where the users' awareness is focused on doing the task, rather than on analyzing objects and relations. Detached reflections on alternatives become part of the process when the fluent use of the typographical design tools—their readiness-to-hand—breaks down. These reflections are then grounded in a practical experience, an experience shared by users and designers in a design-by-doing language game.

## Beyond the Cardboard Computer

Figure 45.9. A "second generation" Utopia mock-up with a back screen slide projector.

The idea of "hands on the future" as opposed to "eyes on a system description" was our main focus in the previous section. We have discussed this in terms of mock-ups built

from the most simple materials, such as cardboard and paper, but there are obviously other possibilities for getting hands on the future, most notably computer-based prototypes. In this section we discuss some of the possibilities in the borderland between the "cardboard computers" and the "real" prototypes.

### Second Generation Mock-Ups

As a first step let us consider some possibilities that are more complex, although still not computer based. Depending on the availability and expertise in the design group, such possibilities may include overhead and slide projectors, tape recorders, and video. These artifacts are familiar in the sense that people easily distinguish malfunction in the artifact from malfunction of the design. At the same time they provide some useful functionality beyond that which is achieved with cardboard, and they make possible a "look and feel" that is more like the future product.

Figure 45.10. Designers and potential future users envisioning the future of page make up playing with the Utopia mock-up.

In our second mock-up of the text- and image-processing workstation in the Utopia project we used a slide projector and a screen for back screen projection. The first impression of this mock-up was much closer to the imagined final product: The display interaction was simulated by the use of slide shows and the input devices had a "real" touch. This quality proved especially valuable when judged by people who only tried out the mock-up for very short periods of time. It was fairly easy for them to envision the future artifact by using the mock-up. This last point is important, and in many cases this alone may justify the use of slide projectors or video in a mock-up. The trade-off is that such mock-ups require more expertise and more resources, both in time and in money, and they are more difficult to change.

Figure 45.11. A sample of different key pad and "mice-like" input device mock-ups produced in the Utopia project in an attempt not to get stuck in the emerging standard interface.

### Simple Mock-Ups: Advantages and Disadvantages

Before we turn our attention to the use of computers in mock-ups, we will briefly outline some advantages and shortcomings of simpler materials to get a better understanding of what might be gained or lost from the use of computers.

Until now we have looked at how to design *without* computers, not because we think that people should avoid computers in general, but because there are good reasons to think twice before using them, as well as good reasons to proceed "even" if computer support is not available. First, the mock-ups discussed so far are built with inexpensive materials. To buy expensive hardware and build advanced software early in a project may, in most situations, be directly counterproductive, especially given the possibilities of mock-ups. In other situations, however, the investments in hardware and software may not be a problem—PCs may already be massively used in the organization. Still, the use of mock-ups may pay off, because it can help generate new visions and new options for use.

Second, the characteristics of these simple tools and materials are familiar to everybody in our culture. With this type of mock-up nothing mysterious happens inside a "black box." If a picture taped to the blackboard drops to the floor everybody knows that this was due to difficulties of taping on a dusty blackboard, and not part of the design. There is no confusion between the simulation and the "real thing."

Third, such mock-ups lend themselves to collaborative modifications. The possible "operations" on the material using pens and scissors, for example, are well known to all, and with simple paper-and-cardboard mock-ups people often make modifications jointly or by taking quick turns. The

physical changes are visible, and, with proper display, visible to all the participants.

However, as with any tool or technique, simple mock-ups have their limitations. Changes to a mock-up may be very time-consuming. If, for example, a different way of presenting menus is chosen, changes may have to be done to dozens of drawings, or a whole new set of slides may have to be made.

While it allows a design group to experiment without the limitations of current technology, this freedom is only a partial blessing. In the end, good design results from exploiting the technological possibilities and limitations creatively, not from ignoring them. Thus, as paradoxical as it may sound, the demand for computer knowledge in a design group using mock-ups is very high.

The simple mock-ups lack functionality: They represent physical clues with which one may create the illusion of using a future computer based artifact, but the users do have to use their imaginations along with the mock-up.

### Computers in Mock-Ups: Overcoming the Disadvantages

Now let's enter the borderland between "cardboard computers" and "fully computerized prototypes." In this borderland, distinctions between the two are fuzzy. In fact, we do not see the main difference between a mock-up and a prototype as being a question of whether computers are used or not. With mock-ups—computer-supported or not—the focus is on support for overall envisionment. In a powerful analogy to film production, this kind of envisionment has been called *storyboard prototyping* (Andriole, 1989). Marty Kline, the artist who drew the storyboard for the movie *Who framed Roger Rabbit?*, makes the analogy clear: "Storyboarding is a way to look at the film without spending a lot of money.... It's not the ultimate film, but it represents a first chance to look at it" (Braa & Ruvik, 1989).

Moving from mock-ups and storyboard prototypes to real prototypes, the possibilities to demonstrate real computer-based functionality come into focus. Computerized prototypes differ from the use of computers in mock-ups in two important ways. We often use computers in mock-ups for purposes other than those intended for the future computer system. In the mock-up we are typically interested in using computers for envisioning the system, not to provide the real functionality of the system. Also, computers have no privileged position in relation to other materials such as cardboard and paper. They are all used on the basis of how well they contribute to creating the illusion of using the future system. In our investigations of the borderland we now consider if and how we may use computers to overcome the disadvantages described above, and if we may do so without sacrificing the advantages. We look first at the use of computers as a way to improve efficiency in building and changing mock-ups. Then we look at ways to explore technological limitations by means of computers. Finally we discuss the question of getting more functionality.

## Effective Tools

The next pictures are from a recent project in which we are developing and using a computer-based hypermedia design environment that we call DesignSupport. To test and develop DesignSupport we have used it for design of a budget system. The budget system was intended to support our own research group in discussions on how to spend our funds. Most of these functions were not covered by standard budgeting and accounting systems, they were supported only by manual procedures using pen and paper, together with e-mail. The pictures are from an early mock-up/storyboard prototype of the budget system and show a scanned version of a handwritten economic overview, some links added to the drawing, and a "computer redrawn" screen image based on the handwritten overview.

After scanning the economic overview we used Design-Support to create linked screen images. The computer-based drawing allowed us to take advantage of similarities between the pictures. For example copying shared icons between screen images was easy, and repeated changes to an image did not reduce its quality as occurs when using paper. Furthermore, several screen images could share parts. Modifications made to a part on one screen image was automatically "cascaded" to the other images.

Finally, it is worth mentioning that intermediate designs were easily saved. This encouraged the exploration of alternative designs for screen images, since backtracking to earlier versions was almost instantaneous if the current line of design proved to be unsatisfactory.

The examples of efficiency gains discussed here cover only a small sample of the potential of existing computer-based tools. Depending on the system being designed, tools such as a presentation manager or a word processor may help improve the efficiency in making and changing a mock-up.

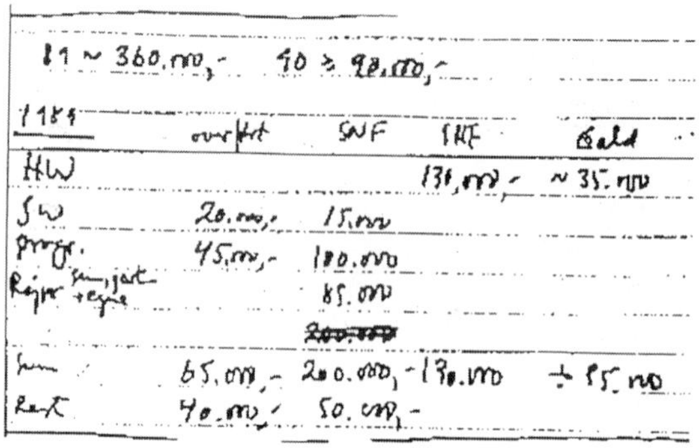

Figure 45.12. A scanned version of a handwritten economic overview . . .

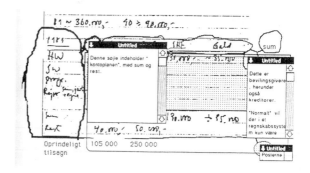

Figure 45.13. . . . some links added to the drawing . . .

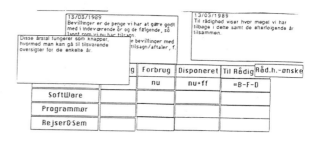

Figure 45.14. . . . and a "computer redrawn" screen image based on the handwritten overview. All the material exists in the same "hypermedia."

One should remember, however, that achieving this efficiency gain usually requires that people in the design group be skilled users of the computer-based tools, otherwise the tools may get in the way of the job to be done, changing the focus from the mock-up to the limitations of the tools.

## Creating Suitable Real Limitations

As noted, the demands on computer knowledge in a design group working with simple mock-ups are very high. When a cardboard box is used instead of a desktop laser printer, someone in the group must know about such printers in order to get the game going using the box as a laser printer, not as a box. In cases where this knowledge needs to be developed, computers may be used to investigate specific technological possibilities and limitations, as illustrated by the following example.

Figure 45.15. Investigations of resolution and response times using a real computer . . .

During the period in the Utopia project when we used simple mock-ups we acquired a few real computer workstations with 15" bit-mapped screens. The idea was to build one or more prototypes of the emerging design. But although the hardware was powerful, the software was poor, and the prototyping could never keep up with the mock-up work. However, it was useful to be able to experiment with a 15"

screen as one of our mock-up components, especially because the existing knowledge in the design group on bit-mapped screens was not comprehensive. We began to look at questions such as: "how could a newspaper page be represented with the available resolution and screen size?," "how about a spread, that is, two pages?," "how many pixels were needed to make a font readable on the screen?," and "how about using shaded boxes to represent words in small fonts?" Such questions could not easily be dealt with using the paper images and slides of our first and second generation mock-ups, but they could be investigated quite easily using the workstations with their graphic screens.

Having learned about the possibilities and limitations of our 15" bit-mapped screens, we returned to our simple paper-based mock-up to explore the possibilities of different screen sizes, such as 15", 19", and 24". We cut holes of appropriate sizes in large pieces of cardboard and placed them on the wall in front of our pictures, menus etc.

Figure 45.16. . . . and expanding the screen size with a mock-up.

## More Functionality

As the third and last of the disadvantages of mock-ups we want to address by means of computers, we look at the question of functionality. This question takes us very close to the borders of "real prototypes."

Consider once more the use of DesignSupport for the creation of a mock-up of the budgeting system discussed previously. The screen images could have been printed out and used in a paper-and-cardboard mock-up like any other picture. What we did, however, was to use the computer to show a sequence of images as a slide projector does.

The next step we took was to use the "button-capabilities" of HyperCard to make it possible from every screen image to dynamically select the next image, in a way simulating how this could be done in the final system.

Using the button capabilities together with text fields in constructing the screen images made it possible to simulate a number of dynamic changes: text-entry, selection, etc. Dynamic response from the budget mock-up, such as showing the money available for inviting guests for the rest of the year, together with the estimated cost of planned and "considered" visits, was handled by a human operator simulating parts of the system. Still other kinds of response, such as sorting a list of possible conferences to attend, were not handled dynamically but rather by showing a list prepared in advance, as we did with the paper-and-cardboard mock-up.

As the example shows, there are different ways to simulate functionality, and there is also the question of what functionality to simulate in the first place. There are no simple answers, but the yardstick to apply is how the different aspects contribute to the creation of the use situation envisionment, how useful it makes the mock-up in the particular design language game. Obviously there is a tendency to implement those aspects which fit the computer best, but the tendency to implement "computer-based functionality," as opposed to different kinds of simulated functionality, is quite strong, too. In the budget system case discussed above, our programmer discovered a clever way to program Xerox-like scroll boxes in our hypermedia system. Such boxes vary in size to indicate how much of a document is shown in a window. Viewed in isolation, this approach was superior to the existing Mac-like scroll boxes of fixed size. But at the time the question of the detailed workings of the scroll bars was unimportant in relation to the creation of a suitable use situation envisionment.

In summary, computers may be used to overcome severe shortcomings in the use of simple mock-up materials. But as we shall see the costs may be high; for example, in terms of reduced possibilities for user participation. However, there is often no need to "go all the way": the best and most cost-effective envisionment may well be obtained by a mock-up from the borderland between cardboard and computers, as illustrated by the following example.

### Mixing for a Better Envisionment

Our first prototype of the design environment DesignSupport was built in HyperCard and ran on Mac IIs with 21" screens. The prototype was built over a period of a few months, ending up with an almost fully functional prototype. HyperCard, however, only allowed one 9" window

to be open at a time, a restriction that turned out to reduce the usefulness of the prototype dramatically. The solution to this problem was straightforward, but we were so fascinated by the prototype that it took some time to find it: To be able to show several windows in varying sizes at the same time, we simply placed printed copies where we wanted them on the big 21" screens. This worked so well that Morten immediately began to "click" on them; forgetting that it was a mock-up. He was getting an involved experience of the future use even if the functionality was missing.

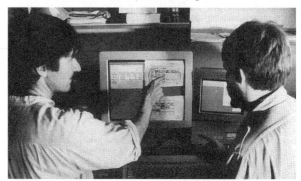

Figure 45.17. From weak prototype to strong mock-up by adding paper windows to the prototype.

This example illustrates an important difference between implementing a final system or fully functional prototype on the one hand and building a mock-up or a storyboard prototype on the other—a difference that seems to be forgotten easily once designers skilled in programming bury themselves in the computer. The point is that any design environment, computer-based or not, has limitations that at times place severe restrictions on the artifact being constructed. In the implementation of a new computer system the handling of this "tension" is a primary part of the competence of the professional designers. However, when constructing a mock-up, it is not necessary to restrain oneself to the possibilities of the computer-based aspect of the environment, unless the intention is to explore exactly these possibilities; for example, with the intention of implementing the final product using that environment.

We later implemented DesignSupport in an environment with multiple and re-sizable windows. That was a major improvement of the system as such, but our computer "blindness" for a long time prevented us from having these properties in our mock-ups and early prototypes.

## Computers in Mock-Ups: Losing the Advantages?

In the beginning of this chapter we suggested that the point in using non-computer-based mock-ups was that they are cheap, understandable, and allow for hands-on experience and pleasurable engagement. Certainly, computer-based prototypes encourage hands-on experience, and in many organizations hardware and software for prototyping already exists, so resources may not be the bottleneck. Whether it is more fun to sit by a computer or to build with cardboard, we can only guess. The remaining advantage primarily concerns the understandability of the non-computer mock-up tools and materials: How does the computer fare with this?

### Unfamiliar Tools and Processes

Consider the following situation, in which computer scientists from two geographically separate groups got together to work on the design of a "shared material" supporting joint work between their two settings. They decided to use two LISP machines on a network to quickly build a computer-based storyboard mock-up. Two of the computer scientists were LISP experts; the others were less familiar with the LISP environment. Since building and modifying the mock-up was a major and integrated part of trying it out in this first session, it was the two LISP experts who operated the machines. Thus, to the rest of the group the interface to the emerging design consisted of the two LISP experts. Involvement consisted mainly of discussing ideas and their possible embodiment in the LISP machines. Several of the actions carried out by the two operators involved programming for two or three minutes. During those periods the rest of the group was inactive.

The first thing to note is that the tools and materials used in this session were not familiar to all participants. Most of them did not know what could be mocked up, and certainly they did not know how to do it. In other words they had only vague ideas about the possible moves in this design game, and they could perform just a few moves themselves. Secondly, most of the "construction work" left no visible clues; thus, the status of the mock-up was not clear to most of the participants. The result was that after a short while only the two LISP experts operating the machines were able make constructive moves. The rest of the group had nowhere to place their hands.

This could also be viewed as an example of a badly planned process. The main point in design-by-doing using mock-ups is

for everyone to get hands-on experience, trying something new. This acting in the future does not happen by itself. Especially with mock-ups built using unfamiliar tools and materials, the simulated future use situation has to be carefully planned and enacted.

### What's the Purpose?

As our last issue we consider the expectations of people working with a mock-up, and what the purposes of doing it are. With cardboard mock-ups it's simple: the purpose is design, and the mock-ups are used to evaluate a design, to get ideas for modifications or maybe even radical new designs, and to have a medium for collaborative changes. If experiments with computer-based mock-ups are set up in the same way and their purpose made clear, it can be equally simple. But the functional possibilities may be seductive, especially when we approach the borders of functional prototypes. Often it is possible to build a computer-based mock-up/prototype which has the look and feel of "90% of the real system," and then the use of this mock-up is interpreted by the users, or maybe even set up by the designers, in a way that presupposes that it is "90% as *useful* as the final, real system." However, this is rarely the case. When this is realized by the users their interest in using the mock-up/prototype may easily drop or disappear completely.

As mentioned earlier, successful evaluation of a mock-up requires careful planning and acting, but in addition it requires commitment from the users, resources dedicated to the purpose of evaluating the mock-up. Almost any deviation from the final system in a mock-up requires some active work on behalf of the involved (future) users. If the users are not prepared to pay this price, then using the mock-up will fail.

### Mock-Ups: Prototype, "The Real Thing" or Both or ?

One of the reasons for the effectiveness of cardboard mock-ups is that nobody confuses them with the product, the future computer system; everybody knows that they do not have the functionality of a computer system. With computers in mock-ups it's different, especially when we use computers to get more functionality.

In these situations it may be difficult not to mix the appearance of the computer in a mock-up and in the imagined future product. The closer the two "roles" get, and the less familiar the computer is, the more careful one has to be in avoiding attributing the wrong aspects of the mock-up-computer to the future-product-computer.

## Major Players and the Rules of the Game

Figure 45.18. Typographers, journalists, and designers in a game of soccer.

The picture above ends our story at the same place were it started—with the people missing in the first picture; showing the relationship between typographers and journalists. Here they are, in a game of soccer, and there are even some professional designers participating.

This game took place on a nice May afternoon in 1984. It was one of the activities that formed a workshop that was part of the "systems delivery" from the Utopia project. Typographers, journalists, trade union and management representatives were invited to actively participate in a three-day workshop on the design proposal from the project group. Of course, mock-ups and prototypes from the design work were tried out in hands-on sessions, but the "system requirement specification" certainly implied and included more than that. Not only the artifacts to be used were at stake; other aspects related to quality of work and product were also part of the proposal, especially questions of how work should be organized using these new tools, and what training and education the different groups should have.

On the soccer field typographers, journalists, and designers had no problem cooperating in mixed teams. This game was even more fun than playing with mock-ups. The negotiation game concerning the proposed changes of work roles and work practice was an entirely different story.

In fact, we had developed a useful work organization design kit to be used by the participants in this kind of negotiation situations, but that did not change the hard facts of reality: Some players have more power than others, and some are more vulnerable than others. For all the fun there is in design as action and in the use of mock-ups, implementation may be an entirely different game in which

management prerogatives define the rules, and organizational conflicts between typographers and journalists limit forceful countermoves. In this game, often referred to as class struggle and organizational conflict, there is a temptation for the designers to think of themselves as observers just watching the game. Nothing could be more wrong in design as action, except perhaps the designers appointing themselves as referees of the game: the gods that make the other players obey the given rules.

In design as action, the rules are at stake. This is particularly true where the use of mock-ups is a way of experiencing the future. This is serious business concerning major changes of the participants' working lives. In using inexpensive mock-up tools and in establishing the pleasurable engagement of hands-on experience, the designers have to find their own role in the design game. The roles of observer and referee are not available. What defines the professional designer is the competence to find a proper role in a specific design game and to expand the space for users to participate in design as action.

References

Andriole, S. (1989). *Storyboard prototyping—A new approach to user requirement analysis*. Wellesley, Massachusetts: QED Information Sciences.

Braa, K. & Ruvik, E. (1989). *Edb-stötte til kreativt samarbeid i filmproduktion* [Computer-Support for Creative Cooperation in Film Production]. Oslo: University of Oslo, Department of Informatics.

Dreyfus, H. L. & Dreyfus, S. D. (1986). *Mind over machine—The power of human intuition and expertise in the era of the computer*. Glasgow: Basil Blackwell.

Ehn, P. (1989). *Work-oriented design of computer artifacts*. Falköping, Sweden: Arbetslivscentrum and Hillsdale, NJ: Lawrence Erlbaum Associates.

Heidegger, M. (1962). *Being and time*. New York: Harper & Row.

Kyng, M. (1988). Designing for a dollar a day. *Office: Technology and People*, 4: 157–170.

Winograd, T. & Flores, F. (1986). *Understanding computers and cognition—A new foundation for design*. Norwood, NJ: Ablex.

Wittgenstein, L. (1923). *Tractatus logico-philosophicus*. London: Kegan Paul.

Wittgenstein, L. (1953). *Philosophical investigations*. Oxford: Basil Blackwell.

# 46. [Introduction]
# The Lessons of Lucasfilm's Habitat

When Ultima Online (a very large-scale, commercial, many-user, graphical virtual environment also called a "Massively Muliplayer Online Roleplaying Game" or MMORPG) was rolled out in 1997, rapidly acquiring more than 100,000 users, strange things began to happen. People—including one writer for the digitally-savvy magazine *Wired*—were shocked, shocked to find that players enjoyed killing each other online. Can't we all just get along in cyberspace? they wondered.

"It is a mistake to assume that the users will all undertake the sorts of noble and sublime activities that you created the system to enable," Chip Morningstar and F. Randall Farmer replied, six years before the question was posed. They knew the answer ahead of time because they had already implemented Habitat. Almost all the major issues raised by Ultima Online, and later by Sony's EverQuest, were exposed in developing Habitat's virtual world, which presented a two-and-a-half-dimensional view to users using modem-linked Commodore 64s. This primitive graphical envoironment provided numerous lessons in online interaction and the shared experience of a simulated world.

This discussion of Habitat bears on two approaches to new media that are represented well in other anthologies: computer-mediated communications and virtual environments. With regard to the latter perspective, often considered using William Gibson's term "cyberspace," it is *Cyberspace, First Steps*, from which this article is taken, that remains the essential resource both for understanding those virtual environments which look like physical spaces and for understanding the online experience through the metaphor of space. The computer-mediated communications perspective includes related studies of the networked computer as a social and cultural environment, undertaken within a variety of networked systems including MOOs, graphical virtual worlds, and chat spaces.

Many of the selections here in *The New Media Reader* consider the computer as a stand-alone or networked system for asynchronous writing and reading, or for some similar activity. The usual questions about "single-player" new media experiences often still apply to environments like Habitat; it is intriguing just to look at the partial list of objects that constitute the virtual world, just as it can be helpful to consider the components of a programming language, computer game, or electronic literature work. But considering those networked systems that provide a real-time communications system, with a graphical representation of each user in a simulated space, brings different dynamics of user activity and information exchange to the forefront—highlighting, as Morningstar and Farmer explain, the role of economics, the futility of naive central planning in systems where many users have a large role, and the need for extreme robustness and reliable standards, neither of which is usually a concern for the computer gaming industy. What isn't needed to tackle such issues is even a 1 GHz chip: a look back reveals that, for such investigations, a Commodore 64 will do nicely.
—NM

Some genuinely new issues with virtual environments were exposed in the late 1990s. For instance, a class-action lawsuit was brought against Origin by *Ultima Online* players after they experienced downtime and lag. No problems inspired that much ire on *Habitat*, despite its more primitive underlying technologies.

Further Reading

Bell, David, and Barbara Kennedy, eds. *The Cybercultures Reader*. New York: Routledge, 2001.

Kim, Amy Jo. "Killers Have More Fun," *Wired* 6.05:140–145,191–192,195–196. May 1998. <http://www.wired.com/wired/6.05/ultima_pr.html>

Porter, David. *Internet Culture*. New York: Routledge, 1997.

Rheingold, Howard. *The Virtual Community: Homesteading on the Electronic Frontier*. Reading, Mass.: Addison-Wesley, 1993.

Original Publication

From *Cyberspace: First Steps*, 273–301. Ed. Michael Benedikt.
Cambridge: MIT Press, 1991.

# The Lessons of Lucasfilm's Habitat

## Chip Morningstar and F. Randall Farmer

## Introduction

Lucasfilm's Habitat project was one of the first attempts to create a very large-scale, commercial, many-user, graphical virtual environment. A far cry from many laboratory research efforts based on sophisticated interface hardware and tens of thousands of dollars per user of dedicated computing power, Habitat is built on top of an ordinary commercial on-line service and uses an inexpensive—some would say "toy"—home computer to support user inter-action. In spite of these somewhat plebeian underpinnings, Habitat is ambitious in its scope. The system we developed can support a population of thousands of users in a single shared cyberspace. Habitat presents its users with a real-time animated view into an on-line simulated world in which users can communicate, play games, go on adventures, fall in love, get married, get divorced, start businesses, found religions, wage wars, protest against them, and experiment with self-government.

The Habitat project proved to be a rich source of insights into the nitty-gritty reality of actually implementing a serious, commercially viable cyberspace environment. Our experiences developing the Habitat system, and managing the virtual world that resulted, offer a number of interesting and important lessons for prospective cyberspace architects. The purpose of this chapter is to discuss some of these lessons. Our hope is that the next generation of builders of virtual worlds can benefit from our experiences and (especially) from our mistakes.

Due to space limitations, we will not be able to go into as much technical detail as we might like; this will have to be left to a future publication. Similarly, we will only be able to touch briefly upon some of the history of the project as a business venture, which is a fascinating subject of its own. Although we will conclude with a brief discussion of some of the future directions for this technology, a more detailed exposition on this topic will also have to wait for a future occasion.

The essential lesson that we have abstracted from our experiences with Habitat is that a cyberspace is defined more by the interactions among the actors within it than by the technology with which it is implemented. While we find much of the work presently being done on elaborate interface technologies—DataGloves, head-mounted displays, special-purpose rendering engines, and so on—both exciting and promising, the almost mystical euphoria that currently seems to surround all this hardware is, in our opinion, both excessive and somewhat misplaced. We can't help having a nagging sense that it's all a bit of a distraction from the really pressing issues. At the core of *our* vision is the idea that cyberspace is necessarily a *many-participant environment*. It seems to us that the things that are important to the inhabitants of such an environment are the capabilities available to them, the characteristics of the other people they encounter there, and the ways these various participants can affect one another. Beyond a foundation set of communications capabilities, the details of the technology used to present this environment to its participants, while sexy and interesting, are of relatively peripheral concern.

Lucasfilm's Habitat was created by Lucasfilm Games, a division of LucasArts Entertainment Company, in association with Quantum Computer Services, Inc.

## What Is Habitat?

Habitat is a "many-player online virtual environment" (its purpose is to be an entertainment medium; consequently, the users are called "players"). Each player uses his or her home computer as a frontend, communicating over a commercial packet-switching data network to a centralized backend system. The frontend provides the user interface, generating a real-time animated display of what is going on and translating input from the player into requests to the backend. The backend maintains the world model, enforcing the rules and keeping each player's frontend informed about the constantly changing state of the universe. The backend enables the players to interact not only with the world but with each other.

Habitat was inspired by a long tradition of "computer hacker science fiction," notably Vernor Vinge's story, "True Names" (1981), as well as many fond childhood memories of games of make-believe, more recent memories of role-playing games and the like, and numerous other influences too thoroughly blended to pinpoint. To this we added a dash of silliness, a touch of cyberpunk (Gibson 1984, Sterling 1986), and a predilection for object-oriented programming (Abelson and Sussman 1985).

The initial incarnation of Habitat uses a Commodore 64 for the frontend. Figure 46.1 is a typical screen from this version of the system.[1] The largest part of the screen is devoted to the graphics display. This is an animated view of the player's current location in the Habitat world. The scene consists of various objects arrayed on the screen, such as the houses and tree. The players are represented by animated figures that we call "Avatars." Avatars are usually, though not exclusively, humanoid in appearance. In Figure 46.1 you can see two of them, carrying on a conversation.

Avatars can move around, pick up, put down, and manipulate objects, talk to each other, and gesture, each under the control of an individual player. Control is through the joystick, which enables the player to point at things and issue commands. Talking is accomplished by typing on the keyboard. The text that a player types is displayed over his or her Avatar's head in a cartoon-style "word balloon."

A Habitat world is made up of a large number of discrete locations that we call "regions." In its prime, the prototype Habitat world consisted of around 20,000 of them. Each region can adjoin up to four other regions, which can be reached simply by walking your Avatar to one or another edge of the screen. Doorways and other passages can connect to additional regions. Each region contains a set of objects that define the things that an Avatar can do there and the scene that the player sees on the computer screen.

Some of the objects are structural, such as the ground or the sky. Many are just scenic, such as the tree or the mailbox. Most objects, however, have some function that they perform. For example, doors transport Avatars from one region to another and may be opened, closed, locked, and unlocked. ATMs (Automatic Token Machines) enable access to an Avatar's bank account.[2] Vending machines dispense useful goods in exchange for Habitat money. Many objects are portable and may be carried around in an Avatar's hands or pockets. These include various kinds of containers, money,

Figure 46.1. A typical Habitat scene
(© 1986 LucasArts Entertainment Company).

weapons, tools, and exotic magical implements. Table 46.1 lists some of the most important types of objects and their functions. The complete list of object types numbers in the hundreds.

## Implementation

The following, along with several programmer-years of tedious and expensive detail that we won't cover here, is how the system works:

At the heart of the Habitat implementation is an object-oriented model of the universe.

The frontend consists of a system kernel and a collection of objects. The kernel handles memory management, display generation, disk I/O, telecommunications, and other "operating system" functions. The objects implement the semantics of the world itself. Each type of Habitat object has a definition consisting of a set of resources, including animation cells to drive the display, audio data, and executable code. An object's executable code implements a series of standard behaviors, each of which is invoked by a different player command or system event. The model is similar to that found in an object-oriented programming system such as Smalltalk (Goldberg and Robson 1983), with its classes, methods, and messages. These resources consume significant amounts of scarce frontend memory, so we can't keep them all in core at the same time. Fortunately, their definitions are invariant, so we simply swap them in from disk as we need them, discarding less recently used resources to make room.

When an object is instantiated, we allocate a block of memory to contain the object's state. The first several bytes

665

of an object's state information take the same form in all objects, and include such things as the object's screen location and display attributes. This standard information is interpreted by the system kernel as it generates the display and manages the run-time environment. The remainder of the state information varies with the object type and is accessed only by the object's behavior code.

Object behaviors are invoked by the kernel in response to player input. Each object responds to a set of standard verbs that map directly onto the commands available to the player. Each behavior is simply a subroutine that executes the indicated action; to do this it may invoke the behaviors of other objects or send request messages to the backend. Besides the standard verb behaviors, objects may have additional behaviors that are invoked by messages that arrive asynchronously from the backend.

The backend also maintains an object-oriented representation of the world. As in the frontend, objects on the backend possess executable behaviors and in-memory state information. In addition, since the backend maintains a persistent global state for the entire Habitat world, the objects are also represented by database records that may be stored on disk when not "in use." Backend object behaviors are invoked by messages from the frontend. Each of these backend behaviors works in roughly the same way: a message is received from a player's frontend requesting some action; the action is taken and some state changes to the world result; the backend behavior sends a response message back to the frontend informing it of the results of its request and notification messages to the frontends of any other players who are in the same region, informing *them* of what has taken place.

## The Lessons

In order to say as much as we can in a limited space, we will describe what we think we learned through a series of principles or assertions surrounded by supporting reasoning and illustrative anecdotes. As cyberspace develops, a more formal and thorough exposition may be called for.

We mentioned our primary principle earlier:

**The idea of a many-user environment is central to cyberspace.**

It is our deeply held conviction that one of the defining characteristics of a cyberspace system is that it represents a many-user environment. This stems from the fact that what (in our opinion) people seek in a virtual world is richness, complexity, and depth. With our best science and technology we do not possess the ability to produce an

Table 46.1
## Some important objects

| Object Class | Function |
|---|---|
| ATM | Automatic Token Machine; Access to an Avatar's Bank Account |
| Avatar | Represents the player in the Habitat world |
| Bag, Box | Containers in which things may be carried |
| Book | Document for Avatars to read (e.g., the daily newspaper) |
| Bureaucrat-in-a-box | Communication with system operators |
| Change-o-matic | Device to change Avatar gender |
| Chest, Safe | Containers in which things may be stored |
| Club, Gun, Knife | Various weapons |
| Compass | Points direction to West Pole |
| Door | Passage from one region to another; can be locked |
| Drugs | Various types; changes Avatar body state, e.g., cure wounds |
| Elevator | Transportation from one floor of a tall building to another |
| Flashlight | Provides light in dark places |
| Fountain | Scenic highlight; provides communication to system designers |
| Game piece | Enables various board games: backgammon, checkers, chess, etc. |
| Garbage can | Disposes of unwanted objects |
| Glue | System building tool; attached objects together |
| Ground, Sky | The underpinnings of the world |
| Head | An Avatar's head; comes in many styles; for customization |
| Key | Unlocks doors and other containers |
| Knick-Knack | Generic inert object; for decorative purposes |
| Magic Wand | Various types, can do almost anything |
| Plant, Rock, Tree | Generic scenic objects |
| Region | The foundation of reality |
| Sensor | Various types, detects otherwise invisible conditions in the world |
| Sign | Allows attachment of text to other objects |
| Stun Gun | Nonlethal weapons |
| Teleport booth | Means of quick long-distance transport; analogous to phone booth |
| Tokens | Habitat money |
| Vendroid | Vending machine; sells things |

automaton that even approaches the complexity of a real human being, let alone a society. Our approach, then, was and is not even to attempt this, but instead to use the computational *medium* to augment the communications channels between real people.

If what we are constructing is a many-user environment, it naturally follows that some sort of communications capability must be fundamental to our system. However, we must take into account an observation that is the second of our principles:

### Communications bandwidth is a scarce resource.

This point was driven home to us by one of Habitat's nastier, externally imposed, design constraints, namely, that it provide a satisfactory experience to the player over a 300-baud serial telephone connection (one routed, moreover, through commercial packet-switching networks that impose an additional, uncontrollable latency of 100 to 5000 milliseconds on each packet transmitted).

Even in a more technically advanced network, however, bandwidth remains scarce in the sense that economists use the term: available carrying capacity is not unlimited. The law of supply and demand suggests that no matter how much capacity is available, you always want more. When communications technology advances to the point where we all have multigigabaud fiber-optic connections into our homes, computational technology will have advanced to match. Our processors' expanding appetite for data will mean that the search for ever more sophisticated data compression techniques will *still* be a hot research area (though what we are compressing may at that point be high-resolution volumetric time-series or something even more esoteric) (Drexler 1986).

Computer scientists tend to be reductionists who like to organize systems in terms of primitive elements that can be easily manipulated within the context of a simple formal model. Typically, you adopt a small variety of very simple primitives, which are then used in large numbers. For a graphics-oriented cyberspace system, the temptation is to build upon bit-mapped images or polygons or some other *graphic* primitive. These sorts of representations, however, are invitations to disaster. They arise from an inappropriate fixation on display technology, rather than on the underlying purpose of the system.

However, the most significant part of what *we* wish to be communicating are human behaviors. These, fortunately, can be represented quite compactly, provided we adopt a relatively abstract, high-level description that deals with behavioral concepts directly. This leads to our third principle:

### An object-oriented data representation is essential.

Taken at its face value, this assertion is unlikely to be controversial, as object-oriented programming is currently the methodology of choice among the software engineering cognoscenti. However, what we mean here is not only that you should adopt an object-oriented approach, but that the basic objects from which you build the system should correspond more or less to the objects in the user's conceptual model of the virtual world, that is, people, places, and artifacts. You could, of course, use object-oriented programming techniques to build a system based on, say, polygons, but that would not help to cope with the fundamental problem.

The goal is to enable the communications between machines to take place primarily at the behavioral level (what people and things are doing) rather than at the presentation level (how the scene is changing). The description of a place in a virtual world should be in terms of what is there rather than what it looks like. Interactions between objects should be described by functional models rather than by physical ones. The computation necessary to translate between these higher-level representations and the lower-level representations required for direct user interaction is an essentially local function. At the local processor, display-rendering techniques may be arbitrarily elaborate and physical models arbitrarily sophisticated. The data channel capacities required for such computations, however, need not and should not be squeezed into the limited bandwidth available between the local processor and remote ones. Attempting to do so just leads to disasters such as NAPLPS (ANSI 1983, Alber 1985), which couples dreadful performance with a display model firmly anchored in the technology of the 1970s.

Once we began working at the conceptual rather than the presentation level, we were struck by the following observation:

### The implementation platform is relatively unimportant.

The presentation level and the conceptual level cannot (and should not) be *totally* isolated from each other. However, defining a cyberspace in terms of the configuration and

667

behavior of objects, rather than their presentation, enables us to span a vast range of computational and display capabilities among the participants in a system. This range extends both upward and downward. As an extreme example, a typical scenic object, such as a tree, can be represented by a handful of parameter values. At the lowest conceivable end of things might be an ancient Altair 8800 with a 300-baud ASCII dumb terminal, where the interface is reduced to fragments of text and the user sees the humble string so familiar to the players of text adventure games: "There is a tree here." At the high end, you might have a powerful processor that generates the image of the tree by growing a fractal model and rendering it three dimensions at high resolution, the finest details ray-traced in real time, complete with branches waving in the breeze and the sound of wind in the leaves coming through your headphones in high-fidelity digital stereo. And these two users might be looking at the same tree in the same place in the same world and talking to each other as they do so. Both of these scenarios are implausible at the moment, the first because nobody would suffer with such a crude interface when better ones are so readily available, the second because the computational hardware does not yet exist. The point, however, is that this approach covers the ground between systems already obsolete and ones that are as yet gleams in their designers' eyes. Two consequences of this are significant. The first is that we can build effective cyberspace systems today. Habitat exists as ample proof of this principle. The second is that it is conceivable that with a modicum of cleverness and foresight you could start building a system with today's technology that could evolve smoothly as tomorrow's technology develops. The availability of pathways for growth is important in the real world, especially if cyberspace is to become a significant communications medium (as we obviously think it should).

Given that we see cyberspace as fundamentally a communications medium rather than simply a user interface model, and given the style of object-oriented approach that we advocate, another point becomes clear:

### Data communications standards are vital.

However, our concerns about cyberspace data communications standards center less upon data transport protocols than upon the definition of the data being transported. The mechanisms required for reliably getting bits from point A to point B are not terribly interesting to us. This is not because these mechanisms are not essential (they

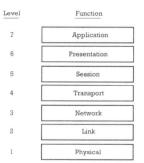

Figure 46.2. The 7-layer ISO reference model of open system interconnection.

obviously are) nor because they do not pose significant research and engineering challenges (they clearly do). It is because we were focused on the unique communications needs of an object-based cyberspace. We were concerned with the protocols for sending messages between objects, that is, for communicating behavior rather than presentation, and for communicating object definitions from one system to another.

Communicating object definitions seems to us to be an especially important problem, and one that we really did not have an opportunity to address in Habitat. It *will* be necessary to address this problem if we are to have a dynamic system in the future. Once the size of the system's user base has grown modestly large, it becomes impractical to distribute a new release of the system software every time one wants to add a new class of object. However, we feel the ability to add new classes of objects over time is crucial if the system is to be able to evolve.

While we are on the subject of communications standards, we would like to make some remarks about the ISO Reference Model of Open System Interconnection (ISO 1986). This seven-layer model has become a centerpiece of most discussions about data communications standards today. It is so firmly established in the data communications standards community that it is virtually impossible to find a serious contemporary publication on the subject that does not begin with some variation on Figure 46.2. Unfortunately, while the bottom four or five layers of this model provide a more or less sound framework for considering data transport issues, we believe that the model's Presentation and Application layers are not very helpful when considering cyberspace data communications.

We have two main quarrels with the ISO model: first, it partitions the general data communications problem in a

| Level | Function |
|-------|----------|
| 6 | Definition |
| 5 | Message |
| 4 | Transport |
| 3 | Network |
| 2 | Link |
| 1 | Physical |

Figure 46.3. A possible alternative protocol model.

way that is a poor match for the needs of a cyberspace system; second, and more important, we think that the model itself is an active source of confusion because it focuses the attention of system designers on the wrong set of issues and thus leads them to spend their time solving the wrong set of problems. We know because this happened to us. "Presentation" and "Application" are simply the wrong abstractions for the higher levels of a cyberspace communications protocol. A "Presentation" protocol presumes that at least some characteristics of the display are embedded in the protocol. The discussions above should give some indication why we think that such a presumption is both unnecessary and unwise. Certainly, an "Application" protocol presumes a degree of foreknowledge of the message environment that is incompatible with the sort of dynamically evolving object system we envision.

A better model would be to substitute a different pair of top layers (Figure 46.3): a Message layer, which defines the means by which objects can address one another and standard methods of encapsulating structured data and encoding low-level data types (numbers); and a Definition layer built on top of the Message layer, which defines a standard representation for object definitions so that object classes can migrate from machine to machine. One might argue that these are simply Presentation and Application with different labels. However, the differences are so easily reconciled. In particular, we think the ISO model has, however unintentionally, systematically deflected workers in the field from considering many of the issues that concern us.

## World Building

There were two sorts of implementation challenges that Habitat posed. The first was the challenge of creating a

working piece of technology—developing the animation engine, the object-oriented virtual memory, the message-passing pseudo operating system, and squeezing them all into the ludicrous Commodore 64 (the backend system also posed interesting technical problems, but its constraints were not as vicious). The second challenge was the creation and management of the Habitat world itself. It is the experiences from the latter exercise that we think will be most relevant to future cyberspace designers.

Initially, we were our own worst enemies in this undertaking, victims of a way of thinking to which all engineers are dangerously susceptible. This way of thinking is characterized by the conceit that all things may be planned in advance and then directly implemented according to the plan's detailed specification. For persons schooled in the design and construction of systems based on simple, well-defined, and well-understood foundation principles, this is a natural attitude to have. Moreover, it is entirely appropriate when undertaking most engineering projects. It is a frame of mind that is an essential part of a good engineer's conceptual tool kit. Alas, in keeping with Maslow's assertion that "to the person who has only a hammer, all the world looks like a nail," it is a frame of mind that is easy to carry beyond its range of applicability. This happens when a system exceeds the threshold of complexity above which the human mind loses its ability to maintain a complete and coherent model.

One generally hears about systems crossing the complexity threshold when they become very large. For example, the Space Shuttle and the B-2 bomber are both systems above this threshold, necessitating extraordinarily involved, cumbersome, and time-consuming procedures to keep the design under control—procedures that are at once vastly expensive and only partially successful. To a degree, the complexity of a problem can be dissolved by "throwing money" at it: faster computers, more managers, more bureaucratic procedures, and so on. However, such capital-intensive management techniques are a luxury not available to most projects. Furthermore, although these "solutions" to the complexity problem may be out of reach of most projects, alas the complexity threshold itself is not. Smaller systems can suffer from the same sorts of problems. It is possible to push much smaller and less elaborate systems over the complexity threshold simply by introducing chaotic elements that are outside the designers' sphere of control or understanding. The most significant of such chaotic

669

elements are autonomous computational agents (other computers). This is why, for example, debugging even very simple communications protocols often proves surprisingly difficult. Furthermore, a special circle of living hell awaits the implementors of systems involving that most important category of autonomous computational agents of all: groups of interacting human beings. This leads directly to our next (and possibly most controversial) assertion:

### Detailed central planning is impossible; don't even try.

The constructivist prejudice that leads engineers into the kinds of problems just mentioned has received more study from economists, philosophers, and sociologists (Popper 1962, 1972; Hayek 1973, 1978, 1989; Sowell 1987) than from researchers in the software engineering community. Game and simulation designers are experienced in creating closed virtual worlds for individuals and small groups. However, they have had no reason to learn to deal with large populations of simultaneous users. Each user or small group is unrelated to the others, and the same world can be used over and over again. If you are playing an adventure game, the fact that thousands of other people elsewhere in the (real) world are playing the same game has no effect on your experience. It is reasonable for the creator of such a world to spend tens or even hundreds of hours crafting the environment for each hour that a user will spend interacting with it, since that user's hour of experience will be duplicated tens of thousands of times by tens of thousands of other individual users.

Builders of today's on-line services and communications networks are experienced in dealing with large user populations, but they do not, in general, create elaborate environments. Furthermore, in a system designed to deliver information or communications services, large numbers of users are simply a load problem rather than a complexity problem. All users get the same information or services; the comments in the previous paragraph regarding duplication of experience apply here as well. It is not necessary to match the size and complexity of the information space to the size of the user population. While it may turn out that the quantity of information available on a service is largely a function of the size of the user population itself, this information can generally be organized into a systematic structure that can still be maintained by a few people. The bulk of this information is produced by the users themselves,

rather than the system designers. (This observation, in fact, is the first clue to the solution to our problem.)

Our original, contractual specification for Habitat called for us to create a world capable of supporting a population of 20,000 Avatars, with expansion plans for up to 50,000. By any reckoning this was a large undertaking and complexity problems would certainly be expected. However, in practice we exceeded the complexity threshold very early in development. By the time the population of our on-line community had reached around 50 we were in over our heads (and these 50 were "insiders" who were prepared to be tolerant of holes and rough edges).

Moreover, a virtual world such as Habitat needs to scale with its population. For 20,000 Avatars we needed 20,000 "houses," organized into towns and cities with associated traffic arteries and shopping and recreational areas. We needed wilderness areas between the towns so that everyone would not be jammed together into the same place. Most of all, we needed things for 20,000 people to do. They needed interesting places to visit—and since they can't all be in the same place at the same time, they needed a *lot* of interesting places to visit—and things to do in those places. Each of those houses, towns, roads, shops, forests, theaters, arenas, and other places is a distinct entity that someone needs to design and create. Attempting to play the role of omniscient central planners, we were swamped.

Automated tools may be created to aid the generation of areas that naturally possess a high degree of regularity and structure, such as apartment buildings and road networks. We created a number of such tools, whose spiritual descendents will no doubt be found in the standard bag of tricks of future cyberspace architects. However, the very properties that make some parts of the world amenable to such techniques also make those same parts of the world among the least important. It is really not a problem if every apartment building looks pretty much like every other. It is a big problem if every enchanted forest looks the same. Places whose value lies in their uniqueness, or at least in their differentiation from the places around them, need to be crafted by hand. This is an incredibly labor-intensive and time-consuming process. Furthermore, even very imaginative people are limited in the range of variation that they can produce, especially if they are working in a virgin environment uninfluenced by the works and reactions of other designers.

## Running the World

The world design problem might still be tractable, however, if all players had the same goals, interests, motivations, and types of behavior. Real people, however, are all different. For the designer of an ordinary game or simulation, human diversity is not a major problem, since he or she gets to establish the goals and motivations on the participants' behalf, and to specify the activities available to them in order to channel events in the preferred direction. Habitat, however, was deliberately open-ended and pluralistic. The idea behind our world was precisely that it did not come with a fixed set of objectives for its inhabitants, but rather provided a broad palette of possible activities from which the players could choose, driven by their own internal inclinations. It was our intention to provide a variety of possible experiences, ranging from events with established rules and goals (a treasure hunt, for example) to activities propelled by the players' personal motivations (starting a business, running the newspaper) to completely free-form, purely existential activities (hanging out with friends and conversing). Most activities, however, involved some degree of planning and setup on our part. We were to be like the cruise director on an ocean voyage, but it turned out we were still thinking like game designers.

The first goal-directed event planned for Habitat was a rather involved treasure hunt called the "D'nalsi Island Adventure." It took us hours to design, weeks to build (including a 100-region island), and days to coordinate the actors involved. It was designed much like the puzzles in an adventure game. We thought it would occupy our players for days. In fact, the puzzle was solved in about 8 hours by a person who had figured out the critical clue in the first 15 minutes. Many of the players hadn't even had a chance to get into the game. The result was that one person had had a wonderful experience, dozens of others were left bewildered, and a huge investment in design and setup time had been consumed in an eye blink. We expected that there would be a wide range of "adventuring" skills in the Habitat audience. What wasn't so obvious until afterward was that this meant that most people didn't have a very good time, if for no other reason than that they never really got to participate. It would clearly be foolish and impractical for us to do things like this on a regular basis.

Again and again we found that activities based on often unconscious assumptions about player behavior had completely unexpected outcomes (when they were not simply outright failures). It was clear that we were not in control. The more people we involved in something, the less in control we were. We could influence things, we could set up interesting situations, we could provide opportunities for things to happen, but we could not predict or dictate the outcome. Social engineering is, at best, an inexact science, even in protocyberspaces. Or, as some wag once said, "In the most carefully constructed experiment under the most carefully controlled conditions, the organism will do whatever it damn well pleases."

Propelled by these experiences, we shifted into a style of operations in which we let the players themselves drive the direction of the design. This proved far more effective. Instead of trying to push the community in the direction we thought it should go, an exercise rather like herding mice, we tried to observe what people were doing and aid them in it. We became facilitators as much as designers and implementors. This often meant adding new features and new regions to the system at a frantic pace, but almost all of what we added was used and appreciated, since it was well matched to people's needs and desires. As the experts on how the system worked, we could often suggest new activities for people to try or ways of doing things that people might not have thought of. In this way we were able to have considerable influence on the system's development in spite of the fact that we didn't really hold the steering wheel—more influence, in fact, than we had had when we were operating under the delusion that we controlled everything.

Indeed, the challenges posed by large systems in general are prompting some researchers to question the centralized, planning-dominated attitude that we have criticized here, and to propose alternative approaches based on evolutionary and market principles (Miller and Drexler 1988a, 1988b; Drexler and Miller 1988). These principles appear applicable to complex systems of all types, not merely those involving interacting human beings.

## The Great Debate

Among the objects we made available to Avatars in Habitat were guns and various other sorts of weapons. We included these because we felt that players should be able to "materially" effect each other in ways that went beyond simply talking, ways that required real moral choices to be made by the participants. We recognized the age-old

671

storyteller's dictum that conflict is the essence of drama. Death in Habitat was, of course, not like death in the real world! When an Avatar is killed, he or she is teleported back home, head in hands (literally), pockets empty, and any object in hand at the time dropped on the ground at the scene of the crime. Any possessions carried at the time are lost. It was more like a setback in a game of "Chutes and Ladders" than real mortality. Nevertheless, the death metaphor had a profound effect on people's perceptions. This potential for murder, assault, and other mayhem in Habitat was, to put it mildly, controversial. The controversy was further fueled by the potential for lesser crimes. For instance, one Avatar could steal something from another Avatar simply by snatching the object out its owner's hands and running off with it.

We had imposed very few rules on the world at the start. There was much debate among the players as to the form that Habitat society should take. At the core of much of the debate was an unresolved philosophical question: Is an Avatar an extension of a human being (thus entitled to be treated as you would treat a real person) or a Pac-Man-like critter destined to die a thousand deaths or something else entirely? Is Habitat murder a crime? Should all weapons be banned? Or is it all "just a game"? To make a point, one of the players took to randomly shooting people as they roamed around. The debate was sufficiently vigorous that we took a systematic poll of the players. The result was ambiguous: 50 percent said that Habitat murder was a crime and shouldn't be a part of the world, while the other 50 percent said it was an important part of the fun.

We compromised by changing the system to allow thievery and gunplay only outside the city limits. The wilderness would be wild and dangerous while civilization would be orderly and safe. This did not resolve the debate, however. One of the outstanding proponents of the antiviolence point of view was motivated to open the first Habitat church, the Order of the Holy Walnut (in real life he was a Greek Orthodox priest). His canons forbid his disciples to carry weapons, steal, or participate in violence of any kind. His church became quite popular and he became a very highly respected member of the Habitat community.

Furthermore, while we had made direct theft impossible, one could still engage in indirect theft by stealing things set on the ground momentarily or otherwise left unattended. And the violence still possible in the outlands continued to

bother some players. Many people thought that such crimes ought to be prevented or at least punished somehow, but they had no idea how to do so. They were accustomed to a world in which law and justice were always provided by somebody else. Somebody eventually made the suggestion that there ought to be a Sheriff. We quickly figured out how to create a voting mechanism and rounded up some volunteers to hold an election. A public debate in the town meeting hall was heavily attended, with the three Avatars who had chosen to run making statements and fielding questions. The election was held, and the town of Populopolis acquired a Sheriff.

For weeks the Sheriff was nothing but a figurehead, though he was a respected figure and commanded a certain amount of moral authority. We were stumped about what powers to give him. Should he have the right to shoot anyone anywhere? Give him a more powerful gun? A magic wand to zap people off to jail? What about courts? Laws? Lawyers? Again we surveyed the players, eventually settling on a set of questions that could be answered via a referendum. Unfortunately, we were unable to act on the results before the pilot operations ended and the version of the system in which these events took place was shut down. It was clear, however, that there are two basic camps: anarchists and statists. This division of characters and world views is an issue that will need to be addressed by future cyberspace architects. However, our view remains that a virtual world need not be set up with a "default" government, but can instead evolve one as needed.

## A Warning

Given the above exhortation that control should be released to the users, we need to inject a note of caution and present our next assertion:

### You can't trust *anyone.*

This may seem like a contradiction of much of the preceding, but it really is not. Designers and operators of a cyberspace system must inhabit two levels of "virtuality" at once. The first we call the "infrastructure level," the level of implementation, where the laws that govern "reality" have their genesis. The second we call the "experiential level," which is what the users see and interact with. It is important that there not be "leakage" between these two levels. The first level defines the physics of the world. If its integrity is breached, the consequences can range from aesthetic unpleasantness (the audience catches a glimpse of the scaffolding behind the false front) to psychological disruption (somebody does something "impossible," thereby violating users' expectations and damaging their fantasy) to catastrophic failure (somebody crashes the system). When we exhort cyberspace system designers to give control to the users, we mean control at the experiential level. When we say that you can't trust anyone, we mean that you can't trust them with access to the infrastructure level. Some stories from Habitat will illustrate this.

When designing a piece of software, you generally assume that the software is the sole intermediary between the user and the underlying data being manipulated (possibly multiple applications will work with the same data, but the principle remains the same). In general, the user need not be aware of how data are encoded and structured inside the application. Indeed, the very purpose of a good application is to shield the user from the ugly technical details. While it is conceivable that a technically astute person who is willing to invest the time and effort could decipher the internal structure of things, this would be an unusual thing to do as there is rarely much advantage to be gained. The purpose of the application itself is, after all, to make access to and manipulation of the data easier than digging around at the level of bits and bytes. There are exceptions to this, however. For example, most game programs deliberately impose obstacles on their players in order for play to be challenging. By tinkering around with the insides of such a program—dumping the data files and studying them, disassembling the program itself and possibly modifying it—it may be possible to "cheat." However, this sort of cheating has the flavor of cheating at solitaire: the consequences adhere to the cheater alone. There is a difference, in that disassembling a game program is a puzzle-solving exercise in its own right, whereas cheating at solitaire is pointless, but the satisfactions to be gained from either, if any, are entirely personal.

If, however, a computer game involves multiple players, then delving into the program's internals can enable one to truly cheat, in the sense that one gains an unfair advantage over the other players, an advantage moreover of which they may be unaware. Habitat is such a multiplayer game. When we were designing the software, our "prime directive" was, "The backend shall not assume the validity of anything a player computer tells it." This is because we needed to protect ourselves against the possibility that a clever user had hacked

around with his copy of the frontend program to add "custom features." For example, we could not implement any of the sort of "skill and action" elements found in traditional video games wherein dexterity with the joystick determines the outcome of, say, armed combat, because we couldn't guard against users modifying their copy of the program to tell the backend that they had "hit," whether they actually had or not. Indeed, our partners at QuantumLink warned us of this very eventuality before we even started—they already had users who did this sort of thing with their regular system. Would anyone actually go to the trouble of disassembling and studying 100K or so of incredibly tight and bizarrely threaded 6502 machine code just to tinker? As it turns out, the answer is yes. People did. We were not 100 percent rigorous in following our own rule. It turned out that there were a few features whose implementation was greatly eased by breaking the rule in situations where, in our judgment, the consequences would not be material if some people "cheated" by hacking their own systems. Darned if some people didn't hack their systems to cheat in exactly these ways.

Care must be taken in the design of the world as well. One incident that occurred during our pilot test involved a small group of players exploiting a bug in our world database that they interpreted as a feature. First, some background. Avatars were hatched with 2000 Tokens in their bank account, and each day that they logged in the received another 100T. Avatars could acquire additional funds by engaging in business, winning contests, finding buried treasure, and so on. They could spend their Tokens on, among other things, various items for sale in vending machines called Vendroids. There were also Pawn Machines, which would buy objects back (at a discount, of course).

In order to make this automated economy a little more interesting, each Vendroid had its own prices for the items in it. This was so that we could have local price variation (a widget would cost a little less if you bought it at Jack's Place instead of The Emporium). It turned out that in two Vendroids across town from each other were two items for sale whose prices we had inadvertently set lower than what a Pawn Machine would buy them back for: Dolls (for sale at 75T, hock for 100T) and Crystal Balls (for sale at 18,000T, hock at 30,000T!). Naturally, a couple of people discovered this. One night they took all their money, walked to the Doll Vendroid, bought as many Dolls as they could, then took

673

them across town and pawned them. By shuttling back and forth between the Doll Vendroid and the Pawn Shop for *hours*, they amassed sufficient funds to buy a Crystal Ball, whereupon they continued the process with Crystal Balls and a couple orders of magnitude higher cash flow. The final result was at least three Avatars with hundreds of thousands of Tokens each. We only discovered this the next morning when our daily database status report said that the money supply had quintupled overnight.

We assumed that the precipitous increase in "T1" was due to some sort of bug in the software. We were puzzled that no bug report had been submitted. By poking around a bit we discovered that a few people had suddenly acquired enormous bank balances. We sent Habitat mail to the two richest, inquiring as to where they had gotten all that money overnight. Their reply was, "We got it fair and square! And we're not going to tell you how!" After much abject pleading on our part they eventually did tell us, and we fixed the erroneous pricing. Fortunately, the whole scam turned out well, as the nouveau riche Avatars used their bulging bankrolls to underwrite a series of treasure hunt games that they conducted on their own initiative, much to the enjoyment of many other players on the system.

## Keeping "Reality" Consistent

The urge to breach the boundary between the infrastructure level and the experiential level is not confined to the players. The system operators are also subject to this temptation, though their motivation is expediency in accomplishing their legitimate purposes rather than gaining illegitimate advantage. However, to the degree to which it is possible, we vigorously endorse the following principle:

### Work within the system.

Wherever possible, things that can be done within the framework of the experiential level should be. The result will be smoother operation and greater harmony among the user community. This admonition applies to both the technical and the sociological aspects of the system.

For example, with the players in control, the Habitat world would have grown much larger and more diverse than it did had we ourselves not been a technical bottleneck. All new region generation and feature implementation had to go through us, since there were no means for players to create new parts of the world on their own. Region creation was an esoteric technical specialty, requiring a plethora of

obscure tools and a good working knowledge of the treacherous minefield of limitations imposed by the Commodore 64. It also required much behind-the-scenes activity of the sort that would probably spoil the illusion for many. One of the goals of a next generation Habitat-like system ought to be to permit far greater creative involvement by the participants *without* requiring them to ascend to full-fledged guruhood to do so.

A further example of working within the system, this time in a social sense, is illustrated by the following experience:

One of the more popular events in Habitat took place late in the test, the brainchild of one of the more active players who had recently become a QuantumLink employee. It was called the "Dungeon of Death." For weeks, ads appeared in Habitat's newspaper, *The Rant*, announcing that the Duo of Dread, DEATH and THE SHADOW, were challenging all comers to enter their lair. Soon, on the outskirts of town, the entrance to a dungeon appeared. Out front was a sign reading, "Danger! Enter at your own risk!" Two system operators were logged in as DEATH and THE SHADOW, armed with specially concocted guns that could kill in one shot, rather than the usual twelve. These two characters roamed the dungeon blasting away at anyone they encountered. They were also equipped with special magic wands that cured any damage done to them by other Avatars, so that they wouldn't themselves be killed. To make things worse, the place was littered with cul-de-sacs, pathological connections between regions, and various other nasty and usually fatal features. It was clear that any explorer had better be prepared to "die" several times before mastering the dungeon. The rewards were pretty good: 1000 Tokens minimum and access to a special Vendroid that sold magic teleportation wands. Furthermore, given clear notice, players took the precaution of emptying their pockets before entering, so that the actual cost of getting "killed" was minimal.

One evening, one of us was given the chance to play the role of DEATH. When we logged in, we found him in one of the dead ends with four other Avatars who were trapped there. We started shooting, as did they. However, the last operator to run DEATH had not bothered to use his special wand to heal any accumulated damage, so the character of DEATH was suddenly and unexpectedly "killed" in the encounter. As we mentioned earlier, when an Avatar is killed, any object in his hands is dropped on the ground. In this case, said object was the special kill-in-one-shot gun, which was immediately picked up by one of the regular players who then made off with it. This gun was not something that regular players were supposed to have. What should we do?

It turned out that this was not the first time this had happened. During the previous night's mayhem the special gun was similarly absconded with. In this case, the person playing DEATH was one of the regular system operators, who, accustomed to operating the regular Q-Link service, had simply ordered the player to give back the gun. The player considered that he had obtained the weapon as part of the normal course of the game and balked at this, whereupon the operator threatened to cancel the player's account and kick him off the system if he did not comply. The player gave the gun back, but was quite upset about the whole affair, as were many of his friends and associates on the system. Their world model had been painfully violated.

When it happened to us, we played the whole incident within the role of DEATH. We sent a message to the Avatar who had the gun, threatening to come and kill her if she didn't give it back. She replied that all she had to do was stay in town and DEATH couldn't touch her (which was true, if we stayed within the system). OK, we figured, she's smart. We negotiated a deal whereby DEATH would ransom the gun for 10,000 Tokens. An elaborate arrangement was made to meet in the center of town to make the exchange, with a neutral third Avatar acting as an intermediary to ensure that neither party cheated. Of course, word got around and by the time of the exchange there were numerous spectators. We played the role of DEATH to the hilt, with lots of hokey melodramatic touches. The event was a sensation. It was written up in the newspaper the next morning and was the talk of the town for days. The Avatar involved was left with a wonderful story about having cheated DEATH, we got the gun back, and everybody went away happy.

These two very different responses to an ordinary operational problem illustrate our point. Operating within the participants' world model produced a very satisfactory result. On the other hand, taking what seemed like the expedient course, which involved violating the world model, provoked upset and dismay. Working within the system was clearly the preferred course in this case.

## Current Status

As of this writing, the North American incarnation of Lucasfilm's Habitat, QuantumLink's Club Caribe, has been operating for almost three years. It uses our original Commodore 64 frontend and a somewhat stripped-down version of our original Stratus backend software. Club Caribe now sustains a population of some 15,000 participants.

A technically more advanced version, called Fujitsu Habitat, has been operating for over a year in Japan, available on NIFtyServe. The initial frontend for this version is the new Fujitsu FM Towns personal computer, though ports to several other popular Japanese machines are planned. This version of the system benefits from the additional computational power and graphics capabilities of a newer platform, as well as the Towns' built-in CD-ROM for object imagery and sounds. However, the virtuality of the system is essentially unchanged and Fujitsu has not made significant alterations to the user interface or to any of the underlying concepts.

## Future Directions

There are several directions in which this work can be extended. Most obvious is to implement the system on more advanced hardware, enabling a more sophisticated display. A number of extensions to the user interface also suggest themselves. However, the line of development most interesting to us is to expand on the idea of making the development and expansion of the world itself part of the users' sphere of control. There are two major research areas in this. Unfortunately, we can only touch on them briefly here.

The first area to investigate involves the elimination of the centralized backend. The backend is a communications and processing bottleneck that will not withstand growth above too large a size. While we can support tens of thousands of users with this model, it is not really feasible to support millions. Making the system fully distributed, however, requires solving a number of difficult problems. The most significant of these is the prevention of cheating. Obviously, the owner of the network node that implements some part of the world has an incentive to tilt things in his favor. We think that this problem can be addressed by secure operating system technologies based on public-key cryptographic techniques (Rivest, Shamir, and Adelman 1978; Miller et al. 1987).

675

The second fertile area of investigation involves user configuration of the world itself. This requires finding ways to represent the design and creation of regions and objects as part of the underlying fantasy. Doing this will require changes to our conception of the world. In particular, we don't think it will be possible to conceal all of the underpinnings to those who work with them. However, all we really need to do is to find abstractions for those underpinnings that fit into the fantasy itself. Though challenging, this is, in our opinion, eminently feasible.

## Conclusion

We feel that the defining characteristic of cyberspace is the sharedness of the virtual environment, and not the display technology used to transport users into that environment. Such a cyberspace is feasible today, if you can live without head-mounted displays and other expensive graphics hardware. Habitat serves as an existence proof of this contention.

It seems clear to us that an object-oriented world model is a key ingredient in any cyberspace implementation. We feel that we have gained some insight into the data representation and communications needs of such a system. While we think that it may be premature to start establishing detailed technical standards for these things, it is time to begin the discussions that will lead to such standards in the future.

Finally, we have come to believe that the most significant challenge for cyberspace developers is to come to grips with the problems of world creation and management. While we have only made the first inroads into these problems, a few things have become clear. The most important of these is that managing a cyberspace world is not like managing the world inside a single-user application or even a conventional online service. Instead, it is more like governing an actual nation. Cyberspace architects will benefit from study of the principles of sociology and economics as much as from the principles of computer science. We advocate an agoric, evolutionary approach to world building rather than a centralized, socialistic one.

We would like to conclude with a final, if ironical, admonition, one that we hope will not be seen as overly contentious:

### Get real.

In a discussion of cyberspace on Usenet, one worker in the field dismissed Club Caribe (Habitat's current incarnation) as uninteresting, with a comment to the effect that most of the activity consisted of inane and trivial conversation. Indeed, the observation was largely correct. However, we hope some of the anecdotes recounted above will give some indication that more is going on than those inane and trivial conversations might indicate. Further, to dismiss the system on this basis is to dismiss the users themselves. They are paying money for this service. *They* don't view what they do as inane and trivial, or they wouldn't do it. To insist this presumes that one knows better than they what they should be doing. Such presumption is another manifestation of the omniscient central planner who dictates all that happens, a role that this entire chapter is trying to deflect you from seeking. In a real system that is going to be used by real people, it is a mistake to assume that the users will all undertake the sorts of noble and sublime activities that you created the system to enable. Most of them will not. Cyberspace may indeed change humanity, but only if it begins with humanity as it really is.

Acknowledgments

We would like to acknowledge the contributions of some of the many people who helped make Habitat possible. At Lucasfilm, Aric Wilmunder wrote much of the Commodore 64 frontend software; Ron Gilbert, Charlie Kelner, and Noah Falstein also provided invaluable programming and design support; Gary Winnick and Ken Macklin were responsible for all the artwork; Chris Grigg did the sound; Steve Arnold provided outstanding management support; and George Lucas gave us the freedom to undertake a project that for all he knew was both impossible and insane. At Quantum, Janet Hunter wrote the guts of the backend; Ken Huntsman and Mike Ficco provided valuable assistance with communications protocols. Kazuo Fukuda and his crew at Fujitsu have carried our vision of Habitat to Japan and made it their own. Phil Salin, our boss at AMIX, let us steal the time to write this chapter and even paid for us to attend the First Conference on Cyberspace, even though its immediate relevance to our present business may have seemed a bit obscure at the time. We'd also like to thank Michael Benedikt, Don Fussell, and their cohorts for organizing the conference and thereby prompting us to start putting our thoughts and experiences into writing.

## Notes

1. One of the questions we are asked most frequently is, "Why the Commodore 64?" Many people somehow get the impression that this was a technical decision, but the real explanation has to do with business, not technology. Habitat was initially developed by Lucasfilm as a commercial product for QuantumLink, an on-line service (then) exclusively for owners of the Commodore 64. At the time we started (1985), the Commodore 64 was the mainstay of the recreational computing market. Since then it has declined dramatically in both its commercial and technical significance. However, when we began the project, we didn't get a choice of platforms. The nature of the deal was such that both the Commodore 64 for the frontend and the existing QuantumLink host system (a brace of Stratus fault-tolerant minicomputers) for the backend were givens.

2. Habitat contains its own fully-fledged economy, with money, banks, and so on. Habitat's unit of currency is the Token, reflecting the fact that it is a token economy and to acknowledge the long and honorable association between tokens and video games. Incidently, the Habitat Token is a 23-sided plastic coin slightly larger than an American quarter, with a portrait of Vernor Vinge and the motto "Fiat Lucre" on its face, and the text "Good for one fare" on the back; these details are difficult to make out on the Commodore 64 screen.

## References

Abelson, Harold, and Sussman, Gerald Jay, *Structure and Interpretation of Computer Programs* (MIT Press, Cambridge, Massachusetts, 1985).

Alber, Antone F., *Videotex/Teletext: Principles and Practices* (McGraw-Hill, New York, 1985).

American National Standards Institute, *Videotex/Teletext Presentation Level Protocol Syntax*, North American PLPS (ANSI, December 1983).

Drexler, K. Eric, *Engines of Creation* (Anchor Press, Doubleday, New York, 1986).

Drexler, K. Eric, and Miller, Mark S., "Incentive Engineering for Computational Resource Management." In Huberman, B. A., ed., *The Ecology of Computation* (Elsevier Science Publishing, Amsterdam, 1988).

Gibson, William, *Neuromancer* (Ace Books, New York, 1984).

Goldberg, Adele, and Robson, David, *Smalltalk-80: The Language and Its Implementation* (Addison-Wesley, Reading, Massachusetts, 1983).

Hayek, Friedrich A., *Law Legislation and Liberty. Vol. 1, Rules and Order* (University of Chicago Press, Chicago, 1973).

Hayek, Friedrich A., *New Studies in Philosophy, Politics, Economics, and the History of Ideas* (University of Chicago Press, Chicago, 1978).

Hayek, Friedrich A., *The Fatal Conceit* (University of Chicago Press, Chicago, 1989).

International Standards Organization, *Information Processing Systems—Open System Interconnection—Transport Service Definition,* International Standard number 8072, (ISO, Switzerland, June 1986).

Miller, Mark S., Bobrow, Daniel G., Tribble, Eric Dean, and Levy, David Jacob, "Logical Secrets." In Shapiro, Ehud Y., ed., *Concurrent Prolog: Collected Papers,* 2 vols. (MIT Press, Cambridge, Massachusetts 1987).

Miller, Mark S., and Drexler, K. Eric, "Comparative Ecology: A Computational Perspective." In Huberman, B. A., ed., *The Ecology of Computation* (Elsevier Science Publishing, Amsterdam, 1988a).

Miller, Mark S., and Drexler, K. Eric, "Markets and Computation: Agoric Open Systems," In Huberman, B. A., ed., *The Ecology of Computation* (Elsevier Science Publishing, Amsterdam, 1988b).

Popper, Karl R., *The Open Society and Its Enemies,* 5th ed. (Princeton University Press, Princeton, New Jersey, 1962).

Popper, Karl R., *Objective Knowledge: An Evolutionary Approach* (Oxford University Press, Oxford, 1972).

Rivest, R., Shamir, A., and Adelman, L., "A Method for Obtaining Digital Signatures and Public-Key Cryptosystems." *Communications of the ACM* 21, no. 2 (February 1978).

Sowell, Thomas, *A Conflict of Visions* (William Morrow, New York, 1987).

Sterling, Bruce, ed., *Mirrorshades: The Cyberpunk Anthology* (Arbor House, New York, 1986).

Vinge, Vernor, "True Names," *Binary Star* #5 (Dell Publishing Co., New York, 1981).

# 47. [Introduction]
# Seeing and Writing

Although writing is visual, the appreciation of the visual aspects of it competes with understanding what is written, as J. David Bolter pointed out in the following selection. This competition can be healthy or destructive; Bolter's point is not merely to state what typographers have known for centuries. Rather, he describes how the history of typography and printing relates to the present movement of writing onto the computer screen. Marshall McLuhan similarly considered how the print revolution can inform an understanding of contemporary changes in electronic media— particularly in *The Gutenberg Galaxy* (the last chapter of which appears in ◊13)—but Bolter's essay further explores how changes in new media influence our concepts of reading and writing. Bolter has gone on to explore how this, in turn, influences established media, in a process he and Richard Grusin have called "remediation."

Certain elements of computer text are very closely based on print forebears, while others have no basis in earlier technologies of writing; Bolter notes, for instance, the ability to resize windows and have the text re-flow instantly to fill the new rectangle. An understanding of new media can only come when truly novel elements can be divided from those which are imitative, using scrutiny of the sort Bolter applies. The electronic spreadsheet is certainly native to the computer, but as Bolter (along with Ben Shneiderman ◊33) has pointed out, it relates to structures that are evident in paper accounting practices as well as elements of the printed book, such as diagrams. Numbers and letters are not meeting for the first time in electronic writing space; neither are text and image. The way these elements come together on the computer is influenced by movie titles as well as the practices of medieval monks, and there are lessons about the integration of these elements that are to be found in many contexts in the past.

In the current media ecology, the network of influences between different media, new and old, is dense. (This is not an entirely novel situation; media have influenced each other for as long as they have existed, and as new media have been introduced the relationship has seldom been as simple as the replacement of the vanquished medium by the victor.) While a scholar can hardly hope to be an expert on every form of communication—on every "extension of man," as McLuhan would have it—thorough understanding of a particular medium being used for a particular purpose can often be accomplished by understanding that medium's close relatives, and by close study of several relevant works in those media. Bolter's consideration of the history of typography, to inform his understanding of writing on the computer, is clearly of benefit to those with a special interest in the medium of text (alone or in combination with other media) and the concept of reading; it is also an excellent example of how, in general, one might approach new media from adjoining, better-understood territory.
—NM

Are electronic spreadsheets hypertext? Although Bolter asserts that they are, and Ted Nelson's vision would certainly seem to accommodate them, not all critics of hypertext would agree. This points out an advantage, for critical discussion, of rigorously defined categories such as Espen Aarseth's "cybertext" (◊52). Of course, categories such as hypertext and cybertext must still draw boundaries that provide for interesting critical discussion; precision alone is not enough. Thus the more essential question: are spreadsheets interesting to consider alongside certain other types of computer activity?

**679**

Further Reading

Bolter, Jay David and Richard Grusin. *Remediation: Understanding New Media* Cambridge: MIT Press. 1999.

Bringhurst, Robert. *The Elements of Typographic Style.* Vancouver, BC: Hartley and Marks, 1992.

Drucker, Johanna. *Figuring the Word: Essays on Books, Writing, and Visual Poetics.* New York: Granary Books, 1998.

Gill, Eric. *An Essay on Typography.* Boston: David R. Godine, 1988. Photo-lithographic copy of 1936 edition, pub. Sheed and Ward.

Hendel, Richard. *On Book Design.* New Haven, CT: Yale University Press, 1998.

Original Publication

*Writing Space: The Computer, Hypertext and the History of Writing,*
63-81. Hillsdale, NJ: Lawrence Erlbaum Associates, 1991.

# Seeing and Writing

## J. David Bolter

A generation ago, the classical scholar Eric Havelock could still claim that "[the] visual development of the written signs has nothing to do with the purpose of language, namely instantaneous communication between members of a human group" (Havelock, 1982, p. 53). This attitude was appropriate to the age of print because printing reduced each letter in a text to a visual minimum. Unlike the calligrapher, the typographer's art was to make the letter unobtrusive, to convey the various letter shapes without distracting the reader. And typographers have been so effective that we as readers hardly notice the subtle differences that exist among the various typefaces used in books today. As children we are trained to read silently and quickly, looking through the printed page rather than at it.

As we now move beyond the technology of printing, it is no longer appropriate to dismiss the visual history of writing—the changes in both the written signs themselves and their deployment on the page or screen. No writing system is static. Even the letters of our alphabet have continued to develop since Roman times. In the Middle Ages there was an elaborate and ever-changing population of scripts throughout Western Europe. The age of print has been unusually conservative in character, but even it has not been immune to change. And the computer now promises to accelerate the development again, as it offers writers the opportunity both to create their own character fonts and to deploy pictorial elements in new ways.

The layout of the text (the surface of the roll, the page of the book) has always developed along with the individual elements. When the writing space became conceptually narrower in the shift from picture writing to phonetic writing, the layout became narrow and cramped as well. Early Greek writing was linear in concept and appearance, while all the subsequent development in papyrus and parchment manuscripts and in printed books has served to reestablish the second dimension in the visual structure of

the text. In later antiquity, writers regained their interest in the diagram or illustration placed beside or incorporated into the space of the text. Since that time our writing space has been a hybrid of verbal and pictorial elements. Even the conservative technology of print has permitted pictures and more recently mathematical graphs and diagrams to flourish. The computer now adds the capability of animation and so combines pictorial, alphabetic, and mathematical writing into one dynamic whole.

## Mechanical Letters

Early printed books attempted to replicate manuscripts both in letter form and in layout. In cutting his type, Gutenberg copied the Gothic script of his day, including all the ligatures and abbreviations, altogether about 300 different elements. (See Steinberg, 1959, p. 31.) It took several decades for printers to realize that there was no need to use abbreviations and ligatures that rendered the text easier to write (by hand) but harder to read. Each letter of the same type could now be identical, guaranteed by the method of production (casting lead in copper matrices). The precision of the machine now replaced the organic beauty of the handwritten page.

Mechanization did not eliminate human craftsmanship from the process of writing. Instead, it deferred the craftsman from the final product of ink on paper. Letters were still handmade: a craftsman fashioned a set of steel punches that embodied the design for a typeface. These punches were pressed into matrices to serve as molds for the lead type itself. Some early punchcutters actually cut more than one form of the same letter in order to imitate the variation of the scribe, but this practice was clearly misplaced in a technology whose purpose is identical reproduction. Letter forms evolved much more slowly in the age of print than in the previous age of manuscripts. The gradual trend was to pare down the visual form of the letters—in effect to define the writing space with progressively less ink and more white space. Serifs became straighter and thinner, and there was greater contrast between thick and thin strokes. The whole typeface betrayed less and less the hand of the craftsman. The trend reached an extreme in the late 18th century with the designs of Didot and Bodoni.

In the 19th century, mechanization intensified with the development of steam-driven printing presses and the Linotype. Yet in the design and use of typefaces and in the appearance of the printed page, the result was not greater standardization, but greater variety, a sense of growing freedom in what could be shown. The pantographic punch-cutter made it possible to cut a new letter in steel simply by tracing an enlarged pattern of the letter (Lieberman, 1978, pp. 54–55). If in the 16th and 17th centuries, most printers were satisfied with some form of Garamond, printers in the late 19th and 20th centuries could choose from hundreds or thousands of faces. They experimented with forms that earlier printers would have considered barbaric or unrecognizable (but that medieval illuminators might have appreciated). Other typographers reacted to this excess by creating faces such as Helvetica and Futura that were free of all unnecessary strokes.

Nevertheless, the printed page has remained a conservative writing space. The thousands of exotic, so-called "display" fonts appear in advertising, but seldom in books. For book production, the typographer may now choose from dozens of book fonts (with names that signify both tradition and innovation, such as Times Roman, Modern, Baskerville, and Garamond No. 3) which his or her trained eye can distinguish for readability, "color," and "tone." But such distinctions are so subtle that the average reader cannot identify any of the common book fonts. On the other hand, if any OF the **thousands** of **display** FONTS were used in printing books, the reader could tell immediately that something was wrong. Printing is a frozen medium in more ways than one: its letter forms stabilized between the 16th and 18th centuries and have since changed only a little. And depending upon its use as an auxiliary to printing or as an alternative writing space, the computer can either reinforce this stability or sweep away the whole tradition of typography.

## Electronic Letters

> The art of letter design will not be fully understood until it can be explained to a computer . . .
> —Donald E. Knuth, 1982, pp. 5–6

If the trend in the age of print has been to make the visual symbol simple, unornamented, and mathematically precise, a backlash developed in the 19th century led by William Morris, who distrusted mechanization in almost any form. In England as elsewhere, 19th-century printers had been aiming for quantity rather than quality. The demand for inexpensive newspapers and books was exploding, and inventors were

trying to clear the bottlenecks in production by developing mechanical printing presses, new forms of cheap paper, and mechanical typesetting. But when Morris founded the Kelmscott press in 1891, he was not interested in mass production. Instead of industrialized simplicity, he aimed for ornament and organic form, a return to the first century of printing or to age of the manuscript. He modeled his Golden Type on the work of the 15th-century printer, Nicolas Jenson. For his edition of Chaucer, he went further and designed a Neogothic typeface. He chose a hand press and handmade paper. The resulting books were beautiful, but themselves excessive, their pages dense with ink and full of ornamentation—and utterly different in spirit from the early printing that Morris meant to imitate. (See Steinberg, 1959, pp. 29–30.) The irony is that these nostalgic books could only have been produced in the Industrial Age: the precision of his Chaucer was greater than was possible in a Renaissance printed book or a medieval manuscript. It was the advance of technology that permitted Morris to go back in this characteristically Victorian way: Morris took photographic enlargements of printed pages in order to study old typefaces. (See Morris, 1982, p. xxxiv.) Morris' work in printing was a kind of technological nostalgia that celebrated the modern technology it appeared to reject.

A similar nostalgia has been evident in the first decade of word processing. The word processor is an attempt to harness the computer in the service of the older technology of print, and the word processor's presentation of text is nostalgic, in that it looks back to the aesthetic criteria of the printing press. The electronic medium in fact allows complete graphic freedom: the writer may ultimately control each pixel on the screen in representing letters, diagrams, or images. When writers are first given this freedom, on personal computers like the Macintosh, they indulge in greater excesses than Morris, decorating their texts with a variety of type sizes, styles, and fonts. They mix elements from the whole history of typography, often without any sense of propriety or proportion. Professional graphic artists can lodge a similar complaint: bit-mapped personal computers permit untrained users to indulge in a riot of graphic design. Often it is graphic design appropriate to the printed brochure or the billboard rather than the computer screen.

There is an inevitable degeneration in the quality of typography and graphics in the new electronic writing space, because the computer encourages the democratic feeling among its users that they can serve as their own designers. Anyone can experiment with type size or style when the computer provides the fonts and drops them into place at the writer's request. Anyone can create and insert his or her own illustrations with the help of automated drawing programs. The new technology thus merges the role of writer and typographer that had been separate from the outset of the age of print. In the age of print, typographers had access to special tools and the skill to use them, and they made the decisions about page layout. Printers have always understood their role as craftsmen, and their guilds, which served to protect their aesthetic as well as the economic prerogatives, remained strong until the middle of the 20th century. Now the electronic writer and designer can own and use professional tools without bothering to develop professional skills.

However, electronic writers are dabbling in the wrong art, if they worry too much about the typography of their text. The pixels of the electronic medium define a space inherently different from that of ink on paper. At present the electronic space is coarser: it is not possible to create subtly curved or bracketed serifs in letter forms or finely organic lines in drawing. The computer screen will continue to improve in this respect: pixels will grow smaller and create a denser space. But the discrete character of computer graphics will not change in the foreseeable future and must always remain in tension with the continuous character of ink on paper, parchment, or papyrus. The impermanence of the electronic image also discourages an attention to fine visual detail. Electronic writers sense that their writing and therefore their typography is always subject to recall and change. The traditional typographer has exactly the opposite impression—every letter must be in its place, because there is no way to recall 1,500 printed copies if an error is discovered. In this sense, even the humble word processor operates in a visual space different from that of the printing press and the typewriter. Typographers and graphic designers who complain about the mess that naive users make on their terminal screens are themselves children of a different technology and are apt to judge the computer's writing and drawing space in the wrong terms.

Professional typographers also use the computer. Just as the word processor has replaced the typewriter, so computer editing and photocomposition now dominate professional

book production. Most books today are published by electronic photocomposition; metal type has almost disappeared, even for fine book production. The computer introduces a new degree of mathematical rigor in the design of letter forms themselves. One way to produce electronic fonts is to trace and digitize enlarged photographs of the letters. The other, more intriguing method of computer design is not to copy old letter forms point by point, but rather to generate new letters mathematically. The computer scientist Donald Knuth has used parameterized equations to define the curves of the letters. The computer generates the points by working out the equations. What Knuth has done is to throw the alphabet into the space of analytic geometry. The idea of geometrically defined letters is an old one: it dates back to Renaissance typographers, calligraphers, and artists, including Pacioli, Albrecht Dürer, and Tory (Lieberman, 1978, p. 41). But rather than using compass and straightedge, the computer specialist creates letter forms by numerical analysis, precisely the task for which the electronic computer was originally developed. Computer typography reduces the writing space to a Cartesian plane, in which every letter is determined by a set of numbered lines or points. It is the triumph of the mathematization of writing that never quite succeeded in the era of mechanical printing.

On the other hand, the use of the computer to mathematize printing is also an example of technological nostalgia. It turns our attention back to the medium of print, applying mathematical precision in order to perfect the appearance of text on the page. Perfection is still defined in terms established by printers in the 15th and 16th centuries—as the clean, crisp, static image that occupies the monumental writing space of ink on paper. Work on computer typography directs our energies away from appreciating the electronic space in its own right—a space in which the subtleties of type size and style may no longer be important to the writer's or the reader's vision of the text.

## The Electronic Page

Typography in print begins with the letter and never goes much further. A glance at the typographer's handbooks shows how much importance is placed on the choice of the typeface itself. Indeed, once the typefaces and styles (and perhaps colors of ink) have been chosen for a book, there are very few decisions left to be made. Each page will be a rectangle of text with some white space around it. Illustrations will occupy blocks reserved for them within the rectangle or on separate pages altogether, and in any case illustrations are relatively rare in "serious," discursive books. Advertising and magazines present many more possibilities for creative design, but the layout of a book is as conservative as the choice of fonts appropriate to the book. And many typographers would agree that the decisions of layout all flow from the letter. The printing press is really a letter processor.

In some ways the earlier handwritten page offered more freedom of design than the printed page. Already in the Carolingian period, scribes used a different script (uncial) to indicate titles and demarcate sections. The word "rubric" comes from rubrication, the medieval technique of beginning a text with a large red capital, often elaborately decorated. By the 13th century scribes had developed a number of visual cues to help the reader locate text and keep his or her orientation. Different styles and sizes of letters, different colors of ink, section numbers—all these devices were pioneered in the Middle Ages and then standardized in the age of print. Probably the most important visual structure in the medieval codex was the marginal note. Medieval texts were often arranged into two or more layers on the page. The center of the page contained the more ancient and venerable text, while the margins offered explanation and commentary added by one or more scholars. This structure helped to orient the reader. It was relatively easy to move back and forth between text and notes, certainly much easier than it was for the reader in the ancient world to juggle several rolls of papyrus. Marginal notes told readers what to look for and provided constant support in the task. Many Renaissance or later readers found these notes to be a hindrance, the weight of centuries of misreading of the text, and printers began to clear the page of this interpretive material, allowing the text to occupy the whole of the writing space and therefore to speak for itself. Notes moved to the foot of the page and eventually to the back of the book. But in banishing the notes modern printers have sacrificed both the immediacy of reference and the sense of visual and intellectual context that marginal notes provided to their medieval readers. (It is only in electronic text that we can recapture both immediacy and context.)

In the modern printed book, the space is simple and clean. Different texts do not compete in adjacent spaces for the reader's attention, as they still do in a magazine or newspaper. In a magazine the text is divided into blocks of varying shapes and sizes, and readers find themselves pulled back and forth among the blocks. The page layout reflects the topical nature of the material—a combination of advertisements, notices, and long and short articles. A magazine or newspaper is in this respect closer in spirit to the topographic writing space of the computer, where the "typography" also mirrors the topical nature of the text itself. Larger units of text together with images can be isolated on the computer screen. The screen becomes a magazine page in which units even rearrange themselves to meet various needs.

In the current generation of machines, for example, the so-called "window" is the defining feature of computer typography. A computer window is a framing device: it marks out a space for a particular unit of verbal text, graphics, or both, and it frames the writer/reader's view of that space, which is an indefinite two-dimensional plane. The window may show only a portion of the plane at a time, but often the view in the window can be adjusted or scrolled to reveal other parts. In some computer systems windows can be "tiled"—set side by side so that the writer/reader can look onto two or more planes at once. In other systems the windows can be "stacked," so that the planes of text and graphics pile on top of each other, again without really touching. The whole electronic writing space becomes a stack of two-dimensional writing surfaces. Of course, a printed book is also a stack of two-dimensional planes or pages, but the great difference is that printed pages stay in one order and, except in novelty books for children, each page completely obscures all the pages underneath it. Working at the computer, the writer/reader can move one window aside in order to view parts of the windows below; he or she can reorder the stack by plucking one window from below and placing it on top. If the windows contain different texts, say two chapters in a book, the reader can move back and forth adding to and cutting from each. This new typographical space is sometimes said to have two and a half dimensions, because the writer looks straight down on the stack of planes. The writer cannot move around or behind the planes in a full third dimension, although this may well be possible in the next generation of computer software. (See Levy, Brotsky, & Olson, 1988, especially pp. 3ff.)

No previous writing technology has offered anything quite like the windowed typography of the current microcomputer.

Switching between windows is in some ways like shuffling papers in a notebook, but nothing in previous technology corresponds to enlarging the size of the window (the text immediately rearranges itself to fill the gap) or scrolling through text in a window. These operations show that the text is not pasted to the window, as it is to the printed page. In fact, both the window and the text may change at any time. The window may fly like a helicopter over the textual plane, or the text may realign itself to suit the dimensions of the window. Visible windows or portions of windows compete for the reader's attention and actively change shape and status when they succeed in attracting attention. (See Fig. 47.1.)

If we are viewing a hypertext, the windows take on a structural significance. In a hypertext there are operational links between units: text in one window can be linked to text in another. Following a link can make windows appear, disappear, or rearrange themselves so that the destination text comes to the front of the screen and captures the reader's attention. This animation becomes an element of electronic typography. It is as if in a printed book the pages reordered themselves to put the next interesting paragraph before the reader's eyes.

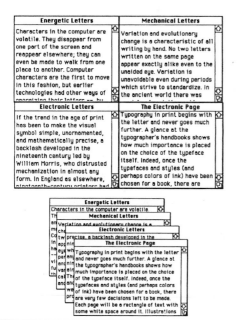

Figure 47.1. (a) Tiled windows simply divide the screen into two, four, or more rectangles; all are in the same plane. (b) Stacked windows occupy different planes or levels closer to or further from the reader.

Even within a single window, objects (images and verbal text) can be stacked: text can slide underneath a graphic, or the graphic itself may be moved to reveal another graphic. The layout of the screen may always change, and the reader may participate in those changes. Like the text itself, the typography is not determined prior to the reading, but is instead a manifestation of the act of reading: it is one aspect of interactive text. The screen enters into a series of configurations, and that evolving series is the visual expression of a particular reader's journey through a textual structure. No one configuration is likely to be as attractive as a page that a professional typographer can produce for print. But no one configuration lasts very long, and it is the movement from one configuration to the next that carries much of the meaning of an electronic text. In a conventional printed text or manuscript, the reader's eye moves along the letters, and possibly back and forth among images, whereas the letters and images themselves are static. In electronic text both the reader's eye and the writing surface are in motion.

Computer animation can take a variety of forms. It is not only a matter of programmed motion pictures, still images shown one after another to give the illusion of a continuous scene. Computer text and graphics can be animate in the sense of having their own organic impulse, of appearing to move or change according to their own logic and in their own time. Even alphabetic texts can appear at various locations on the screen and change or disappear at intervals. (See Nishimura & Keiichi, 1985.) Such animation requires a peculiar reading technique in which the text moves under the eye rather than the reverse. Yet this kind of reading is already common in electric and now electronic billboards that deliver news and advertising. Audiences have been reading unstable text for decades in the form of the subtitles in motion pictures. The difference is that the computer allows any writer to play with the movement of text and gives the writer a freer space for such experimentation.

Reading the complex electronic page demands an attention to text, image, and their relationships. Readers must move back and forth from the linear presentation of verbal text to the two-dimensional field of electronic picture writing. They can read the alphabetic signs in the conventional way, but they must also parse diagrams, illustrations, windows, and icons. Electronic readers therefore shuttle between two modes of reading, or rather they learn to read in a way that combines verbal and picture reading. Their reading includes activating signs by typing and moving the cursor and then making symbolic sense of the motions that their movements produce.

## Pictures in the Text

Moving pictures into the computer's writing space is remarkably easy. But the electronic space demands a translation: the image must be digitized, all continuous lines and shadings must be transformed into a binary coding. It is possible to feed a picture taken by a video camera into the computer—to capture a portion of the continuous spectrum of the visible light, transform that portion into a series of bits, and save those bits as a picture in the machine's memory. A graphics program can then isolate a portion of the picture, shrink or enlarge it, produce a mirror image or a negative copy. But the program can work all these further transformations only because the picture has been encoded. And in general, the computer can combine words and pictures so easily because both are represented in the same binary code. The digitization of images inevitably strips away their context and allows the machine, or rather its programmer, to define new contexts. The further step is to turn some pattern of bits into an operational symbol or icon. An icon, we recall, is an image that stands for a document or a program in exactly the same way that one pixel pattern stands for the letter "A," another for "B," and so on.

In electronic writing, then, pictures and verbal text belong to the same space, and pictures may cross over and become textual symbols. The unified character of the electronic space is unusual, though not unprecedented in the history of writing. The development of phonetic writing, while it did not eliminate pictures altogether from the writing space, did create a dichotomy between image and phonetic sign. Phonetic writing pulls the writer and reader toward the pure linear space of spoken language, whereas pictures, diagrams, and graphs pull them back toward a pictorial space, which is at least two-dimensional and whose meaning is not strictly codified. Different writing technologies have responded to this tension in different ways.

In Egyptian writing, for example, there was an intimate relationship between pictures and text, both in wall-painting and on papyrus. Hieroglyphs were themselves little pictures, and so both visually and conceptually Egyptian writing could blend smoothly with illustration. (See Weitzmann, 1970, pp. 57–69.) The Greek and Roman writing space was not as friendly to pictures. The ancients regarded writing as an instrument for holding spoken words in a fixed form until they could be revived by the voice of the reader. Book decoration was, therefore, an insignificant art in antiquity. (See Nordenfalk, 1951, pp. 9–20.) From the pure alphabetic space of early Greek inscriptions, it took several hundred years for the Greeks to readjust and admit pictures and diagrams fully into the writing space. (See Weitzmann, 1970, pp. 97ff.) The growing importance of pictures in late antique books formed a link with the Middle Ages. Medieval manuscripts presented a complex space of words, pictures, illustration, and ornamentation—the most complex prior to the electronic medium. In medieval books, pictures were often separated from the text and given prominence as full-page miniatures. But there was also a new impulse to decorate the writing space—to create the illuminated letters that were unique to the medieval writing.

Like computer icons, medieval illuminated letters functioned simultaneously as text and picture. In fact, medieval illumination threatened to turn letters back into images or abstract designs and sometimes made the letters all but impossible to read. (See Alexander, *The Decorated Letter*, 1978, p. 8.) Perhaps the best-known example is to be found in the *Book of Kells*, where the Greek letters chi-rho-iota (standing for "Christ" in Matthew 1.18) occupy a whole page. The design is so intricate that the shapes of the letters are almost completely obscured. Yet these illuminated letters remain part of the verbal text: they have to be included in order to read the verse. They constitute the perfect interpenetration of picture and word space. The *Book of Kells* is abstract illumination, but medieval illuminators could also transform an individual letter into a miniature picture with recognizable human or animal subjects. Sometimes the letter was distorted to contain its subject; sometimes the humans or animals were elongated or distorted to fit into or around the letter. The initial letter was often out of proportion to the rest of the text and could encompass almost anything in its luxuriant growth—fantastic creatures as well as elements of the natural world. It is as if the illuminator were trying to absorb the whole visual world into the letter, which itself had grown enormously large in order to receive the world. Medieval illumination embodied a dialectic between writing and the world; it was a means by which writing could describe or circumscribe the world—not symbolically

**685**

through language, but visually through the shape of the letter itself.

The technology of print favored a stricter separation of the verbal and pictorial writing spaces. Diagrams and illustrations were as popular as ever. But for technical reasons, these images were not as well integrated with the words, as they had been in the best medieval traditions. (See Tufte, 1983, pp. 181–182.) Woodcut illustrations were segregated from the printed text as a product—the wood betrayed much more the hand of the craftsman. Many printed books have contained no illustrations at all, just as many medieval manuscripts contained none. The ideal of the printed book was and is a sequence of pages containing ordered lines of alphabetic text. When the woodcut was replaced by the copper engraving, more elaborate and finely drawn images became part of the printed book. Printers and authors became more ingenious in putting words and images together. The 17th and 18th centuries were the age for allegorical frontispieces and illustrations. (Perhaps the most famous example is the crowded frontispiece in Vico's *New Science,* which Vico patiently explains in his introduction embodies point for point the substance of his interpretation of history. See Vico, 1948, pp. 2–23.) Today it is technically possible to place pictures and illustrations in and around text, and even to superimpose images upon the text.

Photolithography allows any image to be taken onto the page. Some books (especially those designed for young children or for coffee tables) are mostly pictures. Yet the pictorial and verbal spaces are still not as subtly combined as they were in medieval illuminated manuscripts. Most books for adult readers still segregate blocks of text from blocks of pictures, and pictures or plates are often gathered together in the middle of the book to lower production costs. On the other hand magazines, newspapers, advertising tabloids, and billboards all tend to subvert the primacy of linear verbal text in our culture. They work against the ideal established by the printed book.

So, from the nadir of early Greek writing, in which there was no room for pictures, the writing space of the papyrus roll, the codex, and the printed book have permitted a variety of relationships between picture and text: pictures have been decorative, explanatory, allegorical. They have commented on the text; the text has commented on them. But only in the medieval codex were words and pictures as unified as they are on the computer screen. On the screen,

as on medieval parchment, verbal text and image interpenetrate to such a degree that the writer and reader can no longer say where the pictorial space ends and the verbal space begins.

## Diagrammatic Space

The diagram is a kind of picture writing that can only exist after the invention of phonetic writing. It is a codified picture, in which each element has a well-defined reference: it is verbal writing with picture elements. Allegorical pictures are diagrams, whose elements are images that recall the world. They now seem quaint precisely because we expect diagrams to consist of abstract rather than iconographic elements. There is in fact a surprisingly long tradition of abstract diagrams as aids to exposition. Plato used a line diagram to explain his epistemology in the *Republic.* The tree diagram, so important for computer structures, is very old: there survive early medieval manuscripts that display hierarchical information as a tree. (For example, there are trees in the manuscripts of Cassiodorus; see Mynors, 1937, pp. xxiii–xxiv.) Because of the tradition of illumination in which writing and drawing coexist in the same writing space, medieval writing was receptive to both allegorical and abstract diagrams. Among the most famous and elaborate diagrams were those of the 13th-century theologian, Ramon Llull. (See, for example, Llull, 1985, pp. 105–109 and plates 12–13.) Diagrammatic representations of thought continued in print, and diagrams, like illustrations in general, flourished after the shift from woodcuts to copper engravings. Giordano Bruno and other Renaissance magi, influenced by Llull, produced books of the greatest visual interest, filled with abstract and allegorical representations of thought. (For a discussion of Giordano Bruno's work and influence, see Yates, 1964.) More sober writers also used diagrams. Tree diagrams were particularly popular for displaying a ramified subject matter.

All diagrams in manuscripts or in print are of course static representations. The writer and the reader have to activate these diagrams mentally, just as they activate the verbal text. For the first time in the history of writing, electronic technology now offers its writers and readers fluid text and truly animated diagrams. The animation is no mere gimmick. It reveals again the hypertextual character of electronic writing in which distant elements can be linked together and these links can be conceptually active.

The popular computer spreadsheet is an example of an active diagram and indeed of a hypertext. The spreadsheet enables the user to display and modify relationships among numerical entries, usually budgets or accounts of some kind. The user sees a grid of cells on the screen and fills the rows and columns of cells with appropriate numbers, just as an accountant would do with pencil and paper. For example, if the spreadsheet represents the income of a small business, its columns might be months of the year, and its rows might be sales, taxes on sales, and so on. (See Fig. 47.2.) The electronic spreadsheet is far more flexible than a sheet of paper, making it easy to copy, modify, and rearrange the values. An electronic spreadsheet is also a text, not simply because there may be verbal labels for the columns and rows, but because its cells hold the values of interrelated variables. The spatial relationships of the cells define relationships among the variables. The diagram, like a verbal text, is a

**a**

| | May | June | July | Quarter |
|---|---|---|---|---|
| Sales | $1000 | $800 | $1000 | $2800 |
| Taxes | $50 | $40 | $50 | $140 |
| Total | $1050 | $840 | $1050 | $2940 |

**b**

| | May | June | July | Quarter |
|---|---|---|---|---|
| Sales | $1200 | $800 | $1000 | $3000 |
| Taxes | $60 | $40 | $50 | $150 |
| Total | $1260 | $840 | $1050 | $3150 |

Figure 47.2. In this spreadsheet, the first three columns each record one month's activity. The fourth column (Quarter) is automatically keyed to be the sum of the first three. The first row represents sales, the second row (Taxes) is automatically set to be 5% of the first row, and the third row (Total) is the automatic sum of Sales and Taxes. Now if the user changes the figure for Sales in May from $1000 to $1200, the change automatically propagates to recompute the other underlined cells. Spreadsheet a becomes spreadsheet b. The cells in this spreadsheet are thus linked together to form a numerical hypertext.

symbolic structure and is open to symbolic manipulation. Thus, a column or row of figures can be added automatically; an entire row can be reduced by a factor of three; two columns can be switched. Individual cells can also be linked together. If the value of cell C is defined as the sum of the values of A and B, then each time the user changes A or B, C will change automatically. An accountant can link together

dozens of cells with intricate calculations; as he or she alters figures, the changes propagate automatically throughout the grid. The speadsheet becomes a dynamic tool for seeing the effect that one change in a budget will have on other items. Its power is due to the fact that it is hypertextual: each of the cells is a unit, and the cells are interconnected in a network of dependencies. Before the computer, a diagram that was interconnected and active in this sense existed only in the imaginations of Llullists and Hermetists of the Renaissance.

## Numbering Space

A spreadsheet in fact lies halfway between a verbal text and a true mathematical diagram or graph. For in a graph the writing space itself is numbered. The graph has long been an important form of picture writing and has gained steadily in status since the 18th century, as it has been applied to data from experimental science. (See Beniger & Robyn, 1978, pp. 1–11.) It comes as no surprise that the computer is the ideal space for drawing and analyzing graphs.

Diagrams were important even in ancient geometry: the *Elements* of Euclid contained proof after proof describing how to construct geometrical objects with straightedge and compass. But the writing space of Euclidean geometry was a synthetic space in which numbers themselves were conceived in geometrical terms. The situation changed with the development of Cartesian geometry in the 17th and 18th centuries. The Cartesian writing space is numbered. The points of a line can be set into correspondence with real numbers, and two perpendicular, intersecting lines can mark out a grid so that every point in their plane has a unique numerical identity. These lines or axes indicate the scale by which the writing itself (the data points) is measured. The modern graph, therefore, belongs to a space different from the verbal space of a printed or handwritten book. In the verbal space the rows of letters mark out a horizontal scale, but only a very coarse one. If one letter is a bit higher or lower than the others in the same line, only the attractiveness of the line is affected; the meaning of the sentence does not change. But in a Cartesian graph, a raised or lowered data point may change the meaning of the whole mathematical text. Here spatial relationships are precise and always significant, because they represent numerical relationships among the data. In fact in a Cartesian graph, *only* the spatial relationships between elements have meaning. The elements are points that have no characteristics other than position on the plane.

A scientific graph is an utterly systematic form of picture writing. The scientist may see in the graph an organizing principle that was not apparent in the column of numbers from which the graph was generated. It may seem obvious that a graphic representation reads more easily than a column of numbers, but experimental scientists in the 17th and 18th centuries came to this realization more slowly than Descartes himself might have hoped. A number of mechanical devices were invented—weather clocks, automatic barometers, tide recorders—that produced line graphs as they measured. Yet scientists often took these graphs and converted them back into numerical tables for analysis. (Beniger & Robyn, 1978, p. 2) The late 18th and the 19th centuries saw the first systematic use of graphs to represent and analyze data from the world.

Today the graphic writing space is fully established: there is often no quicker or more reliable way for a scientist to examine intelligently (that is, to "read") the massive number of measurements that his or her computer-controlled instruments can record. The drawing of these diagrams is itself automated: computers collect the data and then plot them according to the viewer's requirements. In examining these graphs, scientific readers are looking for both patterns and exceptions, and the trick is to make both visually apparent. Thus computers can be programmed automatically to reduce "noise" or to produce maps in exaggerated colors to give a clearer sense of contrasts.

Such automated graphs and maps in the computer have readers, but no single, identifiable writer. The plotting programs are written by human beings, but the data are supplied by instruments whose function is to record such natural events as electromagnetic radiation, sound or pressure waves, and temperature. Often the instruments are attached directly to computers that record and store the measurements. No doubt many scientists believe that their graphs are natural writing or nature's writing—that human beings are reading what nature itself has produced. Human scientists can read nature's writing because they have mastered the mathematical language of nature. Without the numbered writing space, this natural writing cannot be recorded or understood. But it is precisely that requirement that makes the human scientist more than a passive reader. The scientist not only reads the graphic results; he or she also

determines the variables to record and the way in which those variables will parameterize the writing space. Even in the simplest graph the scientist determines what the x and y axes will mean and what scale each will have.

Scientific picture writing is itself a process of discovery. The writer determines the parameters of the space and then lets the instruments do the writing. And even with the most sophisticated program, some human writer, programmer, or scientist must still decide how the writing space will be numbered. He or she may renumber the space many times to see the data from different perspectives. Scientists do not in general know what pattern their data will produce, and in fact they change perspectives in order to see something they have not anticipated or could not see clearly from another view. The computer can be effective here precisely because it allows rapid reworking of the space. In scientific graphing, the writer and reader are often the same scientist or team of scientists, and the irony is that such writers do not know in advance what they will be giving themselves to read. Here the scientific picture writer resembles the verbal writer, who may also be surprised by the text he or she produces. Scientific graphic writing, particularly with the aid of the computer, distances writers from their writing (data) in such a way that the writing no longer seems to belong to them at all. We might compare this situation to the automatic or trance writing practiced at various times in history, most recently by the surrealists. But in those cases the goal was to lose control, to annihilate the conscious censor and allow unconscious images and ideas to pour forth. In the automatic writing of science, a layer of computerized control is imposed between the world and writing space. The space itself is disciplined by the numbering scheme imposed on it.

## Graphic Rhetoric

Although the numbered graph was and is an alternative to verbal writing, the barrier between the graph and the textual writing space has never been absolute. Even a pure Cartesian graph has its axes labeled with letters of the alphabet. The history of graphic design and typography shows that in the best graphs the numbered space and the verbal space not only coexist, but also interpenetrate. The statistical graphs of the 18th and 19th centuries contained a fair amount of writing, which served to anchor the graph to the verbal writing space. Edward Tufte, a contemporary writer on graphics, still advises that graphs should be combinations of words, images, and numbers and adds that "[d]ata graphics are paragraphs about data and should be treated as such" (Tufte, 1983, p. 181). He means that graphs should be integrated into the text so that the reader's eye moves easily from a paragraph of words to the graph and on to more words. The free combination of words, numbers, and images that is characteristic of the electronic writing space did not begin with the computer; it has been a feature of the best graphics of the last two centuries.

Scientific graphs combine the oldest and the newest of languages—picture writing and modern mathematics—and the result is a rhetoric that our culture finds most convincing. To make modern science palatable to a general audience, it seems that most of the mathematics must be translated into words or pictures. One pretty result is the mathematically defined pseudopicture, in which equations rather than tangible objects create the lines and shadings. Thus, mathematical objects called Mandelbrot sets can be made in surreal landscapes—a mountain lake or steep cliffs beside a placid sea. The point is to trick the viewer into putting the image in the wrong category, regarding it as an object in pictorial space drawn after nature, rather than as a graph. Programmers play this game perhaps out of a concealed desire to demonstrate that mathematics underlies the world. The Pythagorean impulse to construct the world from numbers comes naturally to anyone who builds or programs computers.

Experts in computer graphics have learned how to generate all sorts of recognizable forms mathematically and to give their forms a three-dimensional presence. Their aim is to enable the machine to create images that look as if they came from the world of light. For example, the images in Fig. 47.3 were generated from a data structure that was itself based on a series of photographs. Once the computer has turned these photographs into a mathematical structure of points and shadings, it can manipulate that structure to generate a variety of images with different lighting and from different perspectives. The machine can create an animation in which the viewer's perspective changes as he or she walks through the building. Computer graphics such as these are vivid examples of the computer's ability to mathematize space: to bring numerical and pictorial space together.

Even without the computer, however, contemporary graphics seems dedicated to combining the picture with the scientific graph. One unhappy result is the pseudograph that

Figure 47.3. Two computer-generated images from the UNC Walkthrough project. Reprinted with the kind permission of Frederick P. Brooks, Jr., principal investigator, and John Airey, team leader. Orange United Methodist Church fellowship hall design by Wesley McClure, FAIA, and Craig Leonard of Böhm NBBJ.

is now common in newspapers, magazines, and television. Here the numbering of the space is so reduced that it becomes a decoration for rhetorical effect, and the graph resolves itself into naturalistic forms, like a degenerating tradition of art or architecture. A graph showing the increase in airline ridership over the past ten years will feature a passenger jet zooming up to the right over a Cartesian grid, its exhaust trail defining the increase year by year. A bar chart of industrial pollution will have colored smoke stacks to indicate the values of each pollutant. A pie chart on snack food in America will take the form of a real pie. These are graphs seeking to return to their roots as pure iconic picture writing, in which images float free in a continuous and unnumbered space. Perhaps the descent from the great visual rhetoric of the 19th century to the pseudographs of today's newspapers mirrors the decline in verbal rhetoric in the same period. In any case, in this final era of print technology, designers of books, journals, and newspapers mix words, images, and diagrams without restraint. The result is sometimes successful, sometimes a parody. Graphs take on grotesque shapes in order to reflect their subject matter. Diagrams sometimes intrude in the verbal text itself, as illustrations did with greater artistry in the Middle Ages. Conventional lined text is superimposed on diagrams, so that the diagrams seem to be a prisoner of the text to which they refer. The pure verbal writing space, the implicit ideal of print technology, now penetrates or is penetrated by the pictorial space of the image and the numerical space of the graph.

At its worst, the printed page often seems exhausted—as if it were trying to convince itself of its own vitality with riotous displays of color and form. At its best, however, print is anticipating the new visual rhetoric of electronic writing, in which words, images, and numbered elements easily occupy a single space. On a bit-mapped computer screen, every pixel is an element in a two-dimensional Cartesian graph: letters of the alphabet are themselves graphic lines and curves. The whole visual space of the screen is numbered by its x and y coordinates, and the computer can draw text at any coordinate position. It can also give over any position to a graphic. It is therefore natural to include numerical graphs on the screen along with the text, just as it is natural to include digitized pictures and icons. Sedate rows of linear text are becoming the exception rather than the rule. Instead alphabetic text may be anchored anywhere on the screen—beside, above, or below picture elements. The numbered space also serves as a grid to control the movement of graphs and diagrams. The computer can plot lines of data before the reader's eyes. It can present, for example, political maps that change to reflect the passage of years or centuries—a technique that until recently was limited to film or video with hand-drawn animation. The computer makes possible a kind of historical atlas in which invasions and battles, colonization, and the growth of populations and cities are shown in time as well as space.

The authors of such an atlas will have to learn to work in a new dimension. Designing for the printed page, they must consider how to turn historical change into a readable, static

picture—how to place timelines, lines of march, and dates on the map in a readable way. An electronic map will have to be readable even as it changes; the authors must conceive of their map as a temporal experience for their readers. The same holds for writers who seek to animate any verbal or graphic text in the computer. They must envision what the reader will see at each moment and how that view will accord with what comes before and after. Authors in print or manuscript must also conceive of their text as unfolding in time, but they have little control of the reader's pace. The electronic author who chooses to animate must bear greater responsibility for the reader's temporal experience, because he or she can regulate the flow of text and images on the screen.

References

Alexander, J. J. G. (1978) *The Decorated Letter.* New York: G. Braziller.

Beniger, James R., & Robyn, Dorothy L. (1978) Quantitative graphics in statistics: A brief history. *American Statistician,* 32, 1–11.

Havelock, Eric. A. (1982) *The Literate Revolution in Greece and Its Cultural Consequences.* Princeton, NJ: Princeton University Press.

Knuth, Donald E. (1982) The concept of a meta-font. *Visible Language,* 16, pp. 3–27.

Levy, D., Brotsky, Daniel C., & Olson, Kenneth R. (1988) *Formalizing the Figural: Aspects of a Foundation for Document Manipulation.* Palo Alto, CA: System Sciences Laboratory, Xerox PARC.

Lieberman, J. B. (1978) *Type and Typefaces.* New Rochelle, NY: Myriade Press.

Llull, Ramon. (1985) *Selected Works of Ramon Llull (1232–1316)* (Anthony Bonner, Ed.) (Vols. 1–2). Princeton: Princeton University Press.

Morris, William. (1982) *The Ideal Book: Essays and Lectures on the Arts of the Book by William Morris* (William S. Peterson, Ed.). Berkeley: University of California Press.

Mynors, R. A. B. (Ed.). (1937) *Cassiodori Senatoris Institutiones.* Oxford: Clarendon Press.

Nishimura, Y., & Keiichi, Sato. (1985) Dynamic Information Display. *Visible Language,* 19 (2), 251–271.

Nordenfalk, Carl. (1951) "The Beginning of Book Decoration." In *Essays in Honor of Georg Swarzenski* (pp. 9–20). Chicago: Henry Regnery Co.

Steinberg, S. H. (1959) *Five Hundred Years of Printing.* New York: Criterion Books.

Tufte, Edward R. (1983) *The Visual Display of Quantitative Information.* Cheshire, CT: Graphics Press.

Vico, Giambattista. (1948) *The New Science of Giambattista Vico* (T. G. Bergin & M. H. Fisch, Trans.). Ithaca, NY: Cornell University Press.

Weitzmann, Kurt. (1970) *Illustrations in Roll and Codex: A Study of the Origin and Method of Text Illustration.* Princeton, NJ: Princeton University Press.

Yates, Frances A. (1964) *Giordano Bruno and the Hermetic Tradition.* London: Routledge and Kegan Paul.

# 48. [Introduction]
# You Say You Want a Revolution?
## Hypertext and the Laws of Media

◊01
29
Moulthrop is also the author of well-known hypertext fictions (e.g., *Victory Garden, Reagan Library*) and of a widely-discussed, unpublished experiment in extending Jorge Luis Borges's "Garden of Forking Paths"

◊11
133

The revolution hasn't been adequately televised—or Webcast, for that matter. There are disturbing visions put forth in new media's revolutionary banter: Ted Nelson's dream of a McDonald's-inspired world hypertext chain, Clifford Stoll's acceptance of government information surveillance as if it were silicon snake oil for the soul—and these are just some of the ideas coming from guys who are on our side. If there's any hope we can hold out for what will eventually become reality—or tomorrow's particular level of mediated hyperreality—it can only been seen, in Stuart Moulthrop's view, by subjecting the essential qualities of a particular new medium to scrutiny.

◊19
277

◊21
301

Applying McLuhan's plan for a four-part media interrogation, Moulthrop noted several qualities of one particular new media format, hypertext, which indeed were borne out over the following decade. (McLuhan's four questions, of course, can similarly be applied to other specific digital media.) By placing the new medium against others, and considering how it might function in the extreme, certain assumptions previously taken for granted were upset. Moulthrop pointed out, for instance, that hypertext does not replace the book—it's more likely a replacement for TV. Putting the book on the card against hypertext is still a popular amusement, though. Yet while our appliances await "convergence," middle school and high school students often spend hours a day occupied in reading and writing online, using time that two decades earlier would likely have been offered up to the living room idol. Such an outcome was suggested by Moulthrop in the following pages, back before the graphical Web browser had even been deployed, when the very few users of the text-only Web were all people who could solve second-order differential equations.

◊30
441

Not every aspect of today's prevailing hypertext system has been as rosy. As predicted, Sony has indeed purchased Xanadu Operating Company, at least in a manner of speaking. Although individuals are free to scribble in publicly-posted Web diaries and the like, the populace (elite or not) accesses the Web and reads information almost entirely via large, corporate Web sites such as Yahoo!, CNN.com, and MSNBC. Like the Parisian student revolutionaries of 1968 that Jean Baudrillard mentions (◊19), we have taken over the station only to resume normal methods of broadcasting. Is it too late to make a real revolutionary effort, or do we simply listen to a word from our sponsor and accept this return to our usual programming?

◊32
471
On the subject of Sony's purchase of XOC, or AOL's of Time Warner, see the essay by Ben Bagdikian (◊32).

The open and dynamic docuverse that hypertext was supposed to bring can't be sensed in the pullulation of possibilities today, even on a Linux computer that is forking like mad. Instead of hypertext on Ted Nelson's model (◊11, ◊21, ◊30), or any other hypertext model current at the time of this essay's writing, we now have a simple hypertext system, the Web, borne upon the Internet. When Moulthrop asked the last of McLuhan's four questions—"What does it produce or become when taken to its limit?"—of hypertext, he noted that a medium taken to its limit is said to reverse; with a participatory medium, for example, becoming homogenous and hegemonic. The next question, if we follow the link, involves asking what the Web, today's specific hypertext system, becomes when taken to the limit. Part of the answer might be seen in un-hypertext-like services such as instant messaging, MP3 swapping, *Quake* tournaments, and massively multiplayer roleplaying games—all of which share the Internet with the Web but take the idea of textual exchange to its data- or action-packed limit.

—NM & NWF

Further Reading

McLuhan, Marshall, and Eric McLuhan. *Laws of Media: The New Science,* University of Toronto Press, 1988.

Moulthrop, Stuart. *Reagan Library.* Self-published on Web, January 1999. Republished on CD-ROM as part of *Gravitational Intrigue, The Little Magazine*'s electronic anthology. <http://iat.ubalt.edu/moulthrop/hypertexts/rl/>

Moulthrop, Stuart and Nancy Kaplan. "Where No Mind Has Gone Before: Ontological Design for Virtual Spaces." *Proceedings of the ACM Hypertext Conference.* Edinburgh: Association for Computing Machinery, 1994, 212–223.

Original Publication

*Postmodern Culture,* 1(3). May 1991. This text is from *Essays in Postmodern Culture,* 69–97. Edited by E. Amiran and J. Unsworth. Oxford University Press, 1993. The foreword was added in *Essays in Postmodern Culture* and some revisions were made.

# You Say You Want a Revolution?

## Hypertext and the Laws of Media

## Stuart Moulthrop

When this essay first appeared, all of two years ago, very few people outside the information sciences had heard of hypertext, a technology for creating electronic documents in which the user's access to information is not constrained, as in books, by linear or hierarchical arrangements of discourse. This obscurity had always seemed strange, since hypertext has been around for a long time. Its underlying concept— creating and enacting linkages between stored bits of information—originated in 1945 with Vannevar Bush, science advisor to President Roosevelt, who wanted to build a machine called Memex to help researchers organize disparate sources of knowledge (see Bush; Landow, 14–15). Bush's design, based on microfilm, rotating spools, and photoelectric cells, proved impractical for the mechanical technologies of the late 1940s. But when electronic computers arrived on the academic scene a few years later, Bush's projections were quickly realized. In a sense, all distributed computing systems are hypertextual, since they deliver information dynamically in response to users' demands (Bolter, 9–10). Indeed, artificial intelligence researchers created the first hypertextual narrative, the computer game called *Adventure,* in order to experiment

with interactive computing in the early 1960s (Levy, 140–41).

It was about this time that Theodor Holm Nelson, a sometime academic and a dedicated promoter of technology, coined the term "hypertext." Nelson offered plans for a worldwide network of information, centrally coordinated through a linking and retrieval system he called Xanadu. In a trio of self-published manifestoes (*Computer Lib, Dream Machines, Literary Machines*), Nelson outlined the structure and function of Xanadu, right down to the franchise arrangements for "Silverstands," the informational equivalent of fast-food outlets where users would go to access the system. (This was long before anyone dreamed of personal computers.) Nelson's ideas got serious consideration from computer scientists, notably Douglas Engelbart, one of the pioneers of user interface design. Englebart and Nelson collaborated at Brown University in the early 1970s on a hypertext system called FRESS, and a number of academic and industrial experiments followed (see Conklin). To a large extent, however, the idea of hypertext—which both Bush and Nelson had envisioned as a dynamic, read/write system in which users could both manipulate and alter the textual corpus—was neglected in favor of more rigidly organized models like distributed databases and electronic libraries, systems that operate mainly in a read-only retrieval mode. To Nelson, hypertext and other forms of interactive computing represented a powerful force for social change. "Tomorrow's hypertext systems have immense political ramifications," he wrote in *Literary Machines* (3/19). Yet no one seemed particularly interested in exploring those ramifications, at least not until the mid–1980s, when the personal computer business went ballistic.

1987: the *annus mirabilis* of hypertext. Many strange and wonderful things happened in and around that year. Nelson's underground classics, *Computer Lib* and *Dream Machines,* were published by Microsoft Press; Nelson himself joined Autodesk, an industry leader in software development, which announced plans to support Xanadu as a commercial enterprise; the Association for Computing Machinery sponsored the first of its international conferences on hypertext; and most important, Apple Computer began giving away HyperCard, an object-oriented hypertext system, to anyone who owned a Macintosh personal computer. HyperCard is the Model T of hypertext: relatively cheap (originally free), simple to operate (being largely an extension of the Macintosh's graphical user interface), quite crude compared to more state-of-the-art products, but still enormously powerful. In the late 1980s it seemed plausible that HyperCard and other personal computer applications would usher in a new paradigm for textual communication, the logical step beyond desktop publishing to all-electronic documents containing multiple pathways of expression.

It has now been six years since that great unveiling of hypertext, and no such "digital revolution" has arrived. At one point, sources in the personal computer industry foresaw a burgeoning market for "stackware" and other hypertextually organized products; nothing of the kind has materialized. Instead, the most commercially ambitious application of HyperCard in electronic publishing has been the Voyager Company's line of "Expanded Books," based exclusively on print titles and carefully designed to duplicate the look and function of traditional books (Stansberry, 54). True, the hypertext concept has finally received some attention from humanist academics. Jay David Bolter's *Writing Space* (1991) outlines a historical view of hypertext as the successor to print technology—and with Nelson's *Literary Machines* is one of the first studies of hypertext to be presented in hypertextual form. George Landow's *Hypertext* (1992) places developments in electronic writing within the context of poststructuralist criticism and postmodern culture (and is also due to appear shortly as a hypertext). The spectre of hypertextual fiction has even been raised by the novelist Robert Coover in the *New York Times Book Review* (see "The End of Books"). But paradoxically (or as fate would have it), this recognition comes when hypertext is no longer what one of my colleagues calls a "bleeding edge" technology. Indeed, much of the caché seems to have bled out of hypertext, which has been bumped from the limelight by hazier and more glamorous obsessions: cyberspace, virtual reality, and the Information Highway.

Such changes of fashion seem a regular hazard of the postmodern territory—taking *post modo* at its most literal, to mean "after the now" or *the next thing*. Staring down at our

desktop, laptop, or palmtop machines—which we know will be obsolete long before we have paid for them—those of us within what Fred Pfeil calls the "baby-boom professional-managerial class" will always desire *the next thing*. (*Another Tale*, 98). Not for nothing have we updated *Star Trek*, our true space Odyssey, into a "Next Generation." We are the generation (and generators) of nextness. Or so Steve Jobs once assumed, somewhat to his present chagrin. Possibly hypertext, like Jobs's sophisticated NeXT computer, represents an idea that hasn't quite come to the mainstream of postmodern culture, a precocious curio destined to be dug up years from now and called "strangely ahead of its time." Unfortunately, as Ted Nelson can testify, hypertext has been through this process once before. A certain circularity seems to be in play.

Perhaps the problem lies not in our technologies or the things we want to do with them, but in our misunderstanding of technological history. Some of us keep saying, as I note in this essay, that we need a revolution, a paradigm shift, a total uprooting of the old information order: an apocalyptic rupture or "blesséd break," as Robert Lowell once put it. And yet that is not what we have received, at least so far. Maybe we suffer this disappointment because we do not understand what we are asking for. What could "revolution" mean in a postmodern context? We might look for answers in Baudrillard, Lyotard, Donna Haraway, or Hakim Bey; but Hollywood, as usual, has the best line. J.F. Lawton's screenplay for *Under Siege*, last summer's Steven Seagall vehicle, includes an enlightening exchange between a CIA spymaster (played by Nick Mancuso) and a rebellious terrorist formerly in his employ (Tommie Lee Jones). The spook chides the terrorist, reminding him that the sixties are over, "the Movement is dead." Jones's character replies: "Yes! Of course! Hence the name: 'Movement.' It moves a certain distance, then it stops. Revolution gets its name by always coming back around—*in your face*."

Perhaps hypertext is just another movement. On one level, it is hard to discriminate among hypertext, virtual reality, and next year's interactive cable systems. All three seem to move in the same general direction, attempting to increase and enrich our consumption of information. But as Andrew Ross has noted, undertakings of this type may have large consequences (*Strange Weather* 88). Potentially at least, they threaten to upset the stability of language-as-property—a possibility with great political ramifications indeed. It might therefore be dangerous to dismiss hypertext as merely a local movement, an initiative as dead as the social agendas of the sixties from which it partly sprang. Considering the vicissitudes of hypertext's history, we might indeed call it a "revolution"—if revolution is something that comes full circle, escaping repression to smack us smartly in the face. Such being the case, however, is this revolution something our culture genuinely wants? When it comes to information technologies, what *do* we want? Why are we moving in circles? What is this figure we are weaving, twice or thrice, and what enchanter or enchantment do we wish to contain?

· · · ·

The original Xanadu (Samuel Taylor Coleridge's) came billed as "A Vision in a Dream," designated doubly unreal and thus easily aligned with our era of "operational simulation" where, strawberry fields, nothing is "real" in the first place, since no place is really "first" (Baudrillard *Simulations*, 10). But all great dreams invite revisions, and these days we find ourselves perpetually on the re-make. So here is a new Xanadu™, the universal hypertext system proposed by Theodor Holm Nelson—a vision which, unlike its legendary precursor, cannot be integrated into the dream park of the hyperreal. Hyperreality, we are told, is a site of collapse or implosion where referential or "grounded" utterance becomes indistinguishable from the self-referential and the imaginary. We construct our representational systems not in serial relation to indisputably "real" phenomena, but rather in recursive and multiple parallel, "mapping on to different co-ordinate systems" (Pynchon, 159). Maps derive not from territories but from previous map-making enterprises: all the world's a simulation.

This reality implosion brings serious ideological consequences, for some would say it invalidates the informing "master narratives" of modernity, leaving us with a proliferation of incompatible discourses and methods (Lyotard, 26). Such unchecked variation, it has been objected, deprives social critique of a clear agenda (Eagleton, 63). Hyperreality privileges no discourse as absolute or definitive; critique becomes just another form of paralogy, a countermove in the language game that is techno-social construction of reality. The game is all-encompassing, and therein lies a problem. As Linda Hutcheon observes, "the ideology of postmodernism is paradoxical, for it depends upon and draws its power from that which it contests. It is not truly radical; nor is it truly oppositional" (120).

This problem of complicity grows especially acute where media and technologies are concerned. Hyperreality is as much a matter of writing practice as it is of textual theory: as Michael Heim points out, "[i]n magnetic code there are no originals" (162). Electronic information may be rapidly duplicated, transmitted, and assembled into new knowledge structures. From word processing to interactive multimedia, postmodern communication systems accentuate what Ihab Hassan calls "immanence" or "the intertextuality of all life. A patina of thought, of signifiers, of 'connections,' now lies on everything the mind touches in its gnostic (noö)sphere...." (172). Faced with this infinitely convoluted system of discourse, we risk falling into technological abjection, a sense of being hopelessly abandoned to simulation, lost in "the technico-luminous cinematic space of total spatio-dynamic theatre" (Baudrillard *Simulations*, 139). If all the world's a simulation, then we are but simulacral subjects cycling through our various iterations, incapable of any "radical" or "oppositional" action that would transform the techno-social matrix. Even supposedly resistant attitudes like "cyberpunk," as Andrew Ross has observed, tend to tail off into cynical interludes where the rules of the game go unquestioned (Ross, 160).

Of course, this pessimistic or defeatist outlook is hardly universal. We are far more likely to hear technology described as an instrumentality of change or a tool for liberation. Bolter (1991), Drexler (1987), McCorduck (1985), and Zuboff (1988) all contend that postmodern modes of communication (electronic writing, computer networks, text-linking systems) can destabilize social hierarchies and promote broader definitions of authority in the informational workplace. Heim points out that under the influence of these technologies "psychic life will be redefined" (164). But if Hutcheon is correct in her observation that postmodernism is non-oppositional, then how will such a reconstruction of order and authority take place? How and by whom is psychic life—and more important, political life—going to be redefined?

These questions must ultimately be addressed not in theory but in practice; which is where the significance of Nelson's new Xanadu lies. With Xanadu, Nelson invalidates technological abjection, advancing an unabashedly millenarian vision of technological renaissance in which the system shall set us free. In its extensive ambitions, Xanadu transcends the hyperreal. It is not an opium vision but something stranger still, a business plan for the development of what Barthes called "the *social* space of writing" (81), a practical attempt to reconfigure literate culture. Xanadu is the most ambitious project ever proposed for hypertext or "non-sequential writing" (*Dream Machines* 29; *Literary Machines* 5/2). Hypertext systems exploit the interactive potential of computers to reconstruct text not as a fixed series of symbols, but as a variable-access database in which any discursive unit may possess multiple vectors of association (see Joyce; Landow; Slatin). A hypertext is a complex network of textual elements. It consists of units or "lexias," which may be analogous to pages, paragraphs, sections, or volumes. Lexias are connected by "links," which act like dynamic footnotes that automatically retrieve the material to which they refer. Because it is no longer book-bounded, hypertextual discourse may be modified at will as reader/writers forge new links within and among documents. Potentially this collectivity of linked text, which Nelson calls the "docuverse," can expand without limit.

As Nelson foresees it, Xanadu would embody this textual universe. The system would provide a central repository and distribution network for all writing: it would be the publishing house, communications medium, and great hypertextual Library of Babel. Yet for all its radical ambitions, Nelson's design preserves familiar proprieties. Local Xanadu outlets would be Silverstands™, retail access and consulting centers modeled after fast-food franchises and thus integrated with the present economy of information exchange. Xanadu would protect intellectual property through copyright. Users would pay per byte accessed and would receive royalties when others obtained proprietary material they had published in the system. The problems and complexities of this scheme are vast, and at the moment, the fulfilled Xanadu remains a "2020 Vision," a probe into the relatively near future. But it is a future with compelling and important implications for the postmodern present.

The future, as Disney and Spielberg have taught us, is a place we must come "back" to. The American tomorrow will be a heyday of nostalgia, an intensive pursuit of "lost" or "forgotten" values. Xanadu is no exception: Ted Nelson sees the history of writing in the 21st century as an epic of recovery. His "grand hope" lies in "a return to literacy, a cure for television stupor, a new Renaissance of ideas and generalist understanding, a grand posterity that does not lose the details which are the final substance of everything"

("How Hypertext (Un)does the Canon" 4). To a skeptical observer, this vision of Xanadu might suggest another domain of the postmodern theme park. Gentle readers, welcome to Literacyland!

But on the other hand, this vision might add up to more than just a sideshow attraction. Nelson foresees a renovation of culture, a unification of discourse, a reader-and-writer's paradise where all writing opens itself to/in the commerce of ideas. This is the world in which all "work" becomes "text," not substance but reference, not containment but connection (see Barthes; Landow; Zuboff). The magnitude of the change implied here is enormous. But what about the politics of that change? What community of interpretation—and beyond that, what social order—does this intertextual world presume? With the conviction of a true Enlightenment man, Nelson envisions "a new populitism that can make the deeper understandings of the few at last available to the many" ("How Hypertext (Un)does the Canon" 6).

What is *populitism?*—another of Nelson's infamous neologisms (e.g., "hypermedia," "cybercrud," "teledildonics"), in this case a portmanteau combining "populism" with "elite." The word suggests the society-of-text envisioned by theorists like Shoshana Zuboff and Jay David Bolter, a writing space in which traces of authority persist only as local and contingent effects, the social equivalent of the deconstructed author-function. A "populite" culture might mark the first step toward realization of Jean-François Lyotard's "game of perfect information" where all have equal access to the world of data, and where "[g]iven equal competence (no longer in the acquisition of knowledge, but in its production), what extra performativity depends on in the final analysis is 'imagination,' which allows one either to make a new move or change the rules of the game" (52). This is the utopia of information-in-process, the ultimate wetware dream of the clerisy: discourse converted with 100 percent efficiency into capital, the mechanism of that magical process being nomology or rule-making—admittedly a rather specialized form of "imagination."

At least two troubles lurk in this paradise. First, the prospect that social/textual order will devolve not unto the many but only to a very few; and more important, that those few will fail to recognize the terms of their splendid isolation. Consider the case of the reluctant computer dick Clifford Stoll, whose memoir, *The Cuckoo's Egg*, nicely illustrates these problems. Stoll excoriates "cyberpunks," electronic vandals who abuse the openness of scientific computing environments. Their unsportsmanlike conduct spoils the information game, necessitating cumbersome restrictions on the free flow of data. But Stoll's definition of informational "freedom" appears murky at best. He repeatedly refers to the mainframe whose system he monitors as "his" computer, likening cybernetic intrusions to burglaries. Digital information, as Stoll sees it, stands in strict analogy to material and private property.

Private in what sense? Stoll professes to believe that scientists must have easy access to research results, but only within their own communities. He is quick to condemn incursions by "unauthorized" outsiders. There is some sense in this argument: Stoll repeatedly points out that the intruder in the Stanford mainframe might have interfered with a lifesaving medical imaging system. But along with this concern comes an ideological danger. Who decides what information "belongs" to whom? Stoll's "popular elite" is restricted to academic scientists, a version of "the people" as *nomenklatura*, those whose need to know is defined by their professional affiliation. More disturbingly, Stoll seems unaware of the way this brotherhood is situated within larger political hierarchies. Describing a meeting with Pentagon brass, he reflects: "How far I'd come. A year ago, I would have viewed these officers as war-mongering puppets of the Wall Street capitalists. This, after all, was what I'd learned in college. Now things didn't seem so black and white. They seemed like smart people handling a serious problem" (278).

Here is elite populism at its scariest. Though he protests (too much) his political correctness, Stoll's sense of specialist community shifts to accommodate the demands of the moment. He observes repeatedly over the course of the memoir that he is finally "coming of age" as a working scientist. When in Fort Meade, Stoll does as the natives do, recognizing agents of Air Force Intelligence, the National Security Agency, even the CIA and FBI as brothers-in-craft. After all, they are "smart" (technologically adept) and "serious" (professional). Their immediate goal seems legitimate and laudable. They are just "handling" a problem, tracking down the intruder who has violated the electronic privacy of Stoll's community (and, not coincidentally, their own). They are the good policemen, the ones Who Are Your Friends, not really "Them" after all but just a quaint, braid-shouldered version of "Us."

Stoll is not troubled that these boon companions live at the heart of the military-industrial complex. He disregards the fact that they seem aware of domestic communications intercepts—in phone conversations, Stoll's CIA contact refers to the FBI as "the F entity," evidently to thwart a monitoring program (144). Stoll does task his agency buddies for sowing disinformation and managing dirty wars, but this critique never gets much past the stage of rhetorical questions. In fact Stoll seems increasingly comfortable in the intelligence community. If the data spooks turn out to be less interested in freedom of scientific speech than in quashing a security leak, Stoll has no real objection. His own ideals and interests are conveniently served in the process.

What leads to such regrettable blindness, and how might it have been prevented? These may be especially pertinent questions as we consider entrusting our literate culture to an automated information system. The spooks are not so easily conjured away. It is no longer sufficient to object that scientists and humanists form distinct communities, and that Stoll's seduction could not happen in our own elect company. The old "Two Cultures" paradigm has shifted out from under us, largely through catholic adoption of technologies like data networks and hypertext. Networks are networks, and we can assume that most if not all of them will eventually engender closed elites. Fascism, as Deleuze and Guattari instruct, is a matter of all-too-human desire (26). What can shield humanist networks, or even the "generalist" networks Nelson foresees, from the strategy of divide and co-opt? What might insulate Xanadu from those ancestral voices prophesying war?

The answer, as forecasters like Pamela McCorduck, K. Eric Drexler, and Andrew Ross point out, may lie in the hypertext concept itself—the operating principle of an open and dynamic medium, a consensual canon with a minimum of hierarchical impedances and a fundamental instability in those hierarchies it maintains. Visionary and problematic as it may seem, Nelson's idea of "populitism" has much to recommend it—not the least of which is its invitation to consider more carefully the likely social impact of advanced communication systems. In fact hypertext may well portend social change, a fundamental reshaping of text production and reception. The telos of the electronic society-of-text is anarchy in its true sense: local autonomy based on consensus, limited by a relentless disintegration of global authority. Since information is now virtually an equivalent of capital, and since textuality is our most powerful way of shaping information, it follows that Xanadu might indeed change the world. But to repeat the crucial question, how will this change come about? What actual social processes can translate the pragmatics of Nelson's business plan into the radicalism of a hypertext manifesto?

The complete answers lie with future history. In one respect, Ted Nelson's insistence that Xanadu become an economically viable enterprise is exemplary. We will discover the full implications of this technology only as we build, manage, and work in hypertextual communities, starting within the existing constraints of information capitalism. But while we wait on history, we can try a little augury. In trying to theorize a nascent medium, one is reduced to *playing* medium, eking out predictions with the odd message from the Other Side. Which brings us to the last work of Marshall McLuhan, a particularly important ancestral voice from whom to hear. At his death, McLuhan left behind notes for an enigmatic final project: the fourfold "Laws of Media" which form the framework for a semiotics of technology. The Laws proceed from four basic questions that can be asked about any invention:

· What does it enhance or intensify?

· What does it render obsolete or displace?

· What does it retrieve that was previously obsolete?

· What does it produce or become when taken to its limit?

As McLuhan demonstrates, these questions are particularly instructive when applied to pivotal or transforming technologies like printing or broadcasting. They are intended to discover the ways in which information systems affect the social text, rearranging sense ratios and rewriting theories of cultural value. They reveal the nature of the basic statement, the "uttering or 'outering'" that underlies mechanical extensions of human faculties. If we put Xanadu and hypertext to this series of questions, we may discover more about both the potential and the limits of hypertext as an agency of change.

## 1 What Does Hypertext Enhance or Intensify?

According to McLuhan's standard analysis, communications media adjust the balance or "ratio" of the senses by privileging one channel of perception over others. Print promotes sight over hearing, giving us an objectified, perspectival, symbolized world: "an eye for an ear" (*Understanding Media* 81). But this approach needs modification for our purposes. Hypertext differs from earlier media in that it is not a new thing at all but a return or *recursion* (of which more later) to an earlier form of symbolic discourse, namely print. The effect of hypertext thus falls not simply upon the sense channels but farther along the cognitive chain. As Vannevar Bush pointed out in the very first speculation on informational linking technologies, these mechanisms enhance the fundamental capacity of *pattern recognition* ("As We May Think," qtd. in *Literary Machines* 1/50).

Hypertext is all about connection, linkage, and affiliation. Formally speaking, its universe is the one Thomas Pynchon had in mind when he defined "paranoia" as "the realization that *everything is connected*, everything in the Creation—not yet blindingly one, but at least connected. . . ." (820). In hypertext systems, this ethos of connection is realized in technics: users do not passively rehearse or receive discourse, they explore and construct links (Joyce, 12). At the kernel of the hypertext concept lie ideas of affiliation, correspondence, and resonance. In this, as Nelson has argued from the start, hypertext is nothing more than an extension of what literature has always been (at least since "Tradition and the Individual Talent")—a temporally extended network of relations which successive generations of readers and writers perpetually make and unmake.

This redefinition of textuality gives rise to a number of questions. What does it mean to enhance our sensitivity to patterns in this shifting matrix, to become sensitized to what Pynchon calls "other orders behind the visible?" Does this mean that hypertext will turn us into "paranoids," anxious interpreters convinced that all structures are mysteriously organized against us? What does interpretive "resistance" mean in a hypertextual context? Can such a reading strategy be possible after poststructuralism, with the author-function reduced (like Pynchon himself) to quasi-anonymous disappearance, a voiceless occasion for deconstructive "writing" (McHoul and Wills, 9)?

Perverse though it may seem, hypertext does increase the agonistic element in reading. Early experience with hypertext narrative suggests that its readers may actually be more concerned with prior authority and design than are readers of conventional writing. The apparent "quickliming of the author" does not dispel the aura of intention in hypertext (Douglas, 100). The constantly repeated ritual of interaction, with its reminder of discursive alternatives, reveals the text as a made thing, not monologic perhaps but hardly indeterminate. The text gestures toward openness—*what options can you imagine?*—but then swiftly forecloses: some options are available but not others, and someone clearly did the defining long before you began interacting. The author persists, undead presence in the literary machine, the inevitable Hand that turns the time. Hypertextual writing—at least when considered as read-only or "exploratory" text (see Joyce)—may thus emphasize antithetical modes of reading, leading us to regard the deconstructed system-maker much in the way that Leo Bersani describes the author of *Gravity's Rainbow:* as "the enemy text" (108).

So perhaps we need a Psychiatrist General's Warning: Interacting With This Hypertext Can Make You Paranoid—indeed it must, since the root sense of paranoia, a parallel or parallax gnosis, happens to be a handy way to conceive of the meta-sense of pattern recognition that hypertext serves to enhance. But would such a distortion of our cognitive ratios necessarily constitute pathology? In dealing with vast and nebulous information networks—to say nothing of those corporate-sponsored "virtual realities" that may lie in our future—a certain "creative paranoia" may be a definite asset. In fact the paragnosticism implicit in hypertext may be the best way to keep the information game clean. Surrounded by filaments and tendrils of a network, the sojourner in Xanadu or other hypertext systems will always be reminded of her situation in a fabric of power arrangements. Her ability to build and pursue links should encourage her to subject those arrangements to inquiry. Which brings us to the second of McLuhan's key questions:

## 2 What Does Hypertext Displace or Render Obsolete?

Though it may be tempting to respond, *the book, stupid,* that answer is ineligible. The book is already "dead" (or superseded) if by "alive" you mean that the institution in question is essential to our continued commerce in ideas. True, the cultural indications are ambiguous. Irving Louis Horowitz argues that reports of the book's demise are exaggerated; even in an age of television and computers, we produce more books each year than ever before (20). Indeed, our information ecology seems likely to retain a mix of print

and electronic media for at least the next century. Yet as Alvin Kernan recently pointed out, the outlook for books in the long run is anything but happy (135–43). As the economic and ecological implications of dwindling forests come home, the cost of paper will rise precipitously. At the same time, acidic decay of existing books will enormously increase maintenance costs to libraries. Given these factors, some shift to electronic storage seems inevitable (though Kernan, an analogue man to the last, argues for microfilm).

Yet this change in the medium of print does not worry cultural conservatives like Kernan, Neil Postman, or E.D. Hirsch nearly so much as the prospect that the decline of the book may terminate the cultural dominance of print. The chief technological culprit in Kernan's "death of literature" is not the smart machine but the idiot box. "Such common culture as we still have," Kernan laments, "comes largely from television" (147). But the idiot box—or to be precise, the boxed idiot—is precisely the intellectual problem that hypertext seems excellently suited to address. In answer to McLuhan's second question—what does hypertext render obsolete?—the best answer is not *literacy* but rather *post-literacy*. As Nelson foresees, the development of hypertext systems implies a revival of typographic culture (albeit it in a dynamic, truly paperless environment). That forecast may seem recklessly naive or emptily prophetic, but it is quite likely valid. Hypertext means the end of the death of literature.

Here the voice of the skeptic must be heard: *a revival of literacy?—read my lips: not in a million years.* Even the most devoted champion of print is likely to resist the notion of a Gutenberg renaissance. In the West, genuine literacy—cultural, multicultural, or simply functional—can be found only among a well-defined managerial and professional class. At present that class is fairly large, but in the U.S. and U.K., world leaders in laissez-faire education, it is contracting noticeably. So it must seem foolish to imagine, as Ted Nelson does, a mass consumer market for typographic information, a growth industry based on the electronic equivalent of the local library.

Indeed, should Xanadu become a text-only system (which is not intended), its prospects would be poor in the long run. There are however other horizons for interactive textuality—not just hypertext but another Nelsonian coinage, "hypermedia." Print is not the only means of communication deliverable in a polysequential format articulated by software links. In trying to imagine the future of hypertext culture, we must also consider interactive multimedia "texts" that incorporate voice, music, animated graphics, and video along with alphabetic script (Lanham, 287). Hypertext is about connection—promiscuous, pervasive, and polymorphously perverse connection. It is a writing practice ideally suited to the irregular, the transgressive, and the carnivalesque (see Harpold). Culturally speaking, the *promiscuity* of hypertext (in the root sense of "a tendency to seek relations") knows no bounds of form, format, or cultural level. There is no reason to assume that hypertext or hypermedia should not support popular as well as elite culture, or indeed that it might not promote a "populite" miscegenation of discourses.

But what can this mean—talking books in homeboy jive? Street rap mixed over Eliotic scholia? Nintendo with delusions of cinema? Or worse, could we be thinking of yet more industrial light and magic, the disneyverse of eyephones and datagloves where YOU (insert userName) are IN THE FANTASY? Perhaps, as one critic of the computer industry recently put it, interactive multimedia must inevitably decay to its lowest common denominator, "hyper-MTV" (Levy "Multimedia," 52). According to this analysis, the linear and objectifying tendencies of any print content in a multimedium text would be overwhelmed by the subjective, irrational, and emotive influence of audio/video. This being the case, hypertext could hardly claim to represent "a cure for television stupor."

But Nelson's aspiration should not be so easily set aside as merely a vision in a dream. Hypertext does indeed have the power to recover print literacy—though not in quite the way that Nelson supposes; which brings us to the third of McLuhan's queries:

## 3 What Does Hypertext Retrieve That Was Previously Obsolete?

Xanadu and similar projects could invite large numbers of people to become reacquainted with the cultural power of typographic literacy. To assert this, of course, is to break with McLuhan's understanding of media history. It is hard to dispute the argument of *Understanding Media* and *The Gutenberg Galaxy* that the culture of the printing press has entered into dialectic contention with a different ethos based on the "cool" immediacy of broadcasting. But though that diagnosis remains tremendously important, McLuhan's

cultural prognosis for the West holds less value. McLuhan saw clearly the transforming impact of "electric" technologies, but perhaps because he did not live much beyond the onset of the personal computer boom, he failed to recognize the next step—the *recursion* to a new stage of typographic literacy through the syncretic medium of hypertext.

It is crucial to distinguish recursion from return or simple repetition, because this difference answers the objection that print literacy will be lost or suppressed in multimedia texts. Recursion is self-reference with the possibility of progressive self-modification (Hofstadter, 127). Considered for its recursive possibilities, "writing" means something radically different in linked interactive compositions than it does in a codex book or even a conventional electronic document. Literacy in hypertext encompasses two domains: the ordinary grammatical, rhetorical, and tropological space that we now know as "literature," and also a second province, stricter in its formalisms but much greater in its power to shape interactive discourse. This second domain has been called "writing space" (Bolter, 4); a case might be made (with apologies to those who insist that virtual reality is strictly a non-print phenomenon) that it also represents the true meaning of *cyberspace*.

Walter Benjamin observed with some regret that by the 1930's, any literate European could become an author, at least to the extent of publishing a letter or article in the newspapers (232). With no regrets at all, Ted Nelson envisions a similar extension of amateur literary production in Xanadu, where all readers of the system can potentially become writers, or at least editors and commentators. The First Amendment guarantee of free speech, Nelson points out, is a *personal* liberty: anyone may publish, and in Xanadu everyone can. Nelson bases his prediction of revived literacy on the promise of a broadly popular publishing franchise.

This vision is limited in one crucial regard. Nelson treats print essentially as the *content* of his system, which is taking a rather narrow view. In describing Xanadu as a more or less transparent medium for the transmission of text, Nelson overlooks the fact that alphabetic or alphanumeric representation also defines the *form* of Xanadu, and indeed of any hypertext system. This neglect is consistent with the generally broad focus of Nelson's vision, which has led him to dismiss details of user-interface design as "front-end functions" to be worked out by the user.

699

Design details, whether anterior or posterior to the system, cannot be passed over so easily. In fact the structure and specifications of the hypertext environment are themselves parts of the docuverse, arguably the most important parts. Beneath any hypertext document or system there exists a lower layer that we might call the *hypotext*. On this level, in the working implementations of its "protocols," Xanadu is a creature of print. The command structures that govern linkage, display, editing, accounting, and all the other functions of the system exist as digital impulses that may be translated into typographic text. They were written out, first in pseudo-English strings, then in a high-level programming language, finally as binary code. Therefore Xanadu at its most intimate level is governed by all those features of the typographic medium so familiar from McLuhan's analysis: singular sequentiality, objectivity, instrumentality, "left-brained" visual bias, and so on. The wonder of hypertext and hypermedia lies in their capacity to escape these limitations by using the microprocessor to turn linear, monologic typography recursively back upon itself—to create linear control structures that militate against absolute linear control.

In recognizing the recursive trick behind hypertextual writing, we come to a broader understanding of electronic literacy. Literacy under hypertext must extend not only to the "content" of a composition but to its hypotextual "form" as well—e.g., the way nodes are divided to accommodate data structures and display strategies, or the types of linkage available and the ways they are apparent to the reader. Practically speaking, this means that users of a hypertext system can be expected to understand print not only as the medium of traditional literary discourse, but also as a meta-tool, the key to power at the level of the system itself.

Ong and McLuhan have argued that television and radio introduce "secondary orality," a recursion to non-print forms of language and an "audile space" of cognition (*Orality and Literacy*, 135; *Laws of Media*, 57). By analogy, hypertext and hypermedia seem likely to instigate a *secondary literacy*— "secondary" in that this approach to reading and writing includes a self-consciousness about the technological mediation of those acts, a sensitivity to the way texts-below-the-text constitute another order behind the visible. This secondary literacy involves both rhetoric and technics: to read at the hypotextual level is to confront (paragnostically) the design of the system; to write at this level is to

reprogram, revising the work of the first maker. Thus this secondary literacy opens for its readers a *cyberspace* in the truest sense of the word, meaning a place of command and control where the written word has the power to remake appearances. This space has always been accessible to the programming elite, to system operators like Clifford Stoll and shady operators like his hacker adversary. But Nelson's 2020 Vision puts a Silverstand in every commercial strip right next to McDonald's and Videoland. Vice President Gore's information "Superhighway" would bring cyberspace even closer. If Xanadu succeeds in re-awakening primary literacy as a mass phenomenon, there is reason to believe that it will inculcate secondary literacy as well.

But like any grand hope, this technopiate dream of a new literacy ultimately has to confront its man from Porlock. Secondary literacy might well prove culturally disastrous. The idea of a general cyberspace franchise, in which all control structures are truly contingent and "consensual," does summon up visions of informatic chaos. "Chaos," however, is a concept we have recently begun to understand as something other than simply an absence of "order:" it is instead a condition of possibility in which new arrangements spontaneously assemble themselves (Prigogine and Stengers, 14).

Taking this neo-chaotic view, we might inquire into the positive effects of secondary literacy in a postmodern political context. In outlining a first move beyond our recent "depthless," ahistorical quiescence, Frederic Jameson calls for an "aesthetic of cognitive mapping," a "pedagogical political culture" in which we would begin to teach ourselves where we stand in the networks of transnational power (92). At this moment, as the West reconsiders its New World Order in the aftermath of a war for oil reserves, we seem in especially urgent need of such education. But a cultural pedagogy clearly needs something more than the evening war news, especially when reporters are confined to informational wading pools. We require not only a sensitivity to the complex textuality of power but an ability to intercept and manipulate that text—an advanced creative paranoia. This must ultimately be a human skill, independent of technological "utterance;" but the secondary literacy fostered by hypertext could help us at least to begin the enormous task of drawing our own cognitive maps. Here, however, we verge on the main question of hypertextual politics, which brings up the last question in the Toronto catechism:

## 4 What Does Hypertext Become When Taken to Its Limit?

Orthodox McLuhanite doctrine holds that "every form, pushed to the limit of its potential, reverses its characteristics" (*Laws of Media,* viii). Media evolution, in McLuhan's view, proceeds through sharply punctuated equilibriums. "Hot" media like print tend to increase their routinization and determinism until they reach a limit (say, the prose of the late 19th century). Beyond that point, the overheated medium turns paradoxical, passing almost instantly from hot to supercool, bombarding readers with such a plethora of codings that conventional interpretation collapses. Structure and hierarchy, the distinguishing features of a hot medium, reduce to indeterminacy. The plurality of codes overwhelms hermeneutic certainty, the "figure" of a univocal text reverses into polysemous "ground," and we reach the ultima thule of Gutenberg culture, *Finnegans Wake.*

But though McLuhan had much to say about the reversal of overheated media, he left the complementary possibility unexplored. What happens to already cool or participatory media when they reach their limits? True to the fourth law, their characteristics reverse, but here the effect is reactionary, not radical. Radio, for instance, begins in interactive orality (two-way transceiving) but decays into the hegemony of commercial broadcasting, where "talk radio" lingers as a reminder of how open the airwaves are not. Television too starts by shattering the rigid hierarchies of the Gutenberg nation-state, promising to bring anyplace into our living rooms; but its version of Global Village turns out to be homogenous and hegemonic, a planetary empire of signs (as we say in Atlanta, "Always Coca-Cola").

Hypertext and hypermedia are also interactively cool, so following this analysis we might conclude that they will undergo a similar implosion, becoming every bit as institutionalized and conservative as broadcast networks. Indeed, it doesn't take McLuhanite media theory to arrive at that forecast. According to the economic logic of late capitalism, wouldn't the Xanadu Operating Company ultimately sell out to Sony, Matsushita, Phillips, or some other wielder of multinational leverage?

Such a self-negating "reversal" may not be the only possible outcome, however. What if the corporate shogunate decide not to venture their capital? What if business leaders realize that truly interactive information networks do not make wise investments? This conclusion might be supported by memory of the nastiness Sears and IBM stirred up when they tried to curtail user autonomy on their Prodigy videotex system (see Levy, "In the Realm of the Censor"). This scenario of corporate rejection is not just speculative fabulation, but the basis for a proposed modification to McLuhan's fourth law. Media taken to their limits tend to reverse, but not all media reverse in the same way. The case of a complex, syncretic, and fundamentally interactive medium like hypertext may involve a "reversal" that does not bring us back to the same-as-it-ever-was—not a reversal in fact but a recursion (*déjà vu*) to a new cultural space.

We have entered into a period of change in reading and writing that Richard Lanham calls a "digital revolution" (268). As this revolution proceeds (if it is allowed to do so), its consequences will be enormous. The idea of hypertext as a figment of the capitalist imagination, an information franchise in both Nelson's and Lyotard's senses, could well break down. Though Xanadu may in fact open its Silverstands some day, hypertext might not long remain a commercial proposition. The type of literacy and the kind of social structure this medium supports stand fundamentally against absolute property and hierarchy. As we have hinted, hypertext and hypermedia peel back to reveal not just an aesthetics of cognitive mapping but nothing less than the simulacral map-as-territory itself: the real beginnings of cyberspace in the sense of a *domain of control.*

"Cyberspace. A consensual hallucination experienced daily by billions of legitimate operators, in every nation. . . . A graphic representation of data abstracted from the banks of every computer in the human system" (Gibson, 51). William Gibson's concept of a cybernetic workspace, laid out in his dystopian novel *Neuromancer,* represents the ultimate shared vision in the global dream of information commerce. For all its advancement beyond the age of nation-state capitalism, Gibson's world remains intensely competitive and hierarchical (for nation-state substitute the revived *zaibatsu*). *Neuromancer* is *Nineteen Eighty-Four* updated for 1984, the future somewhat gloomily surveyed from Reagan's America.

There is accordingly no trace of social "consensus" in Gibson's "consensual" infosphere. In his version of cyberspace, the shape of vision is imposed from without. "They" control the horizontal, "They" control the vertical. Of course there must be some elements of chaos, else Gibson would be out of business as a paperback writer; so he invents the "cyberspace cowboy," a hacker hero who plays the information game by what he likes to call his own rules. But though cowboys may attempt to unsettle the system, their incursions amount at best to harrassment and privateering. These forms of enterprise are deemed "illegal," though they are really just business by another name ("biz," in Gibson's parlance), inventiveness and competitive advantage being the only effective principles of operation.

Gibson's dark dream is one thing—in effect it is a realization of McLuhan's prophecy of reversal, an empowering technology turned into a mechanism of co-optation and enslavement. But perhaps Ted Nelson's 2020 Vision of hypertextual literacy is something else. If not a utopian alternative, Nelson's project may at least provide a heterotopia, an otherplace not zoned in the usual ways for property and performativity. Cyberspace as Gibson and others define it is a Cartesian territory where scientists of control define boundaries and power lines. The Xanadu model lets us conceive instead a decentered space of literacy and empowerment where each subject acts as *kubernetes* or as Timothy Leary says, "reality pilot," steering her way across the intertextual sea ("Reality Pilot" 247).

Nelson's visions of the future differ crucially from Gibson's. In Xanadu we find not consensual illusion but genuine, negotiated consensus. The pathways and connections among texts would be created on demand. According to Nelson's plans to date, only the most fundamental "back end" conventions would be strictly determined: users would be free to customize "front end" systems to access information more or less as they like. Xanadu thus possesses virtually no "canons" in the sense of a shelf of classics or a book of laws; the canons of Xanadu might come closer to the musical meaning of the word—congeries of connections and relationships that are recognizably orderly yet inexhaustibly various. The shifting networks of consensus and textual demand (or desire) in Xanadu would be constructed by users and for users. Their very multiplicity and promiscuity, one might argue, would militate powerfully against any slide from populitism back toward hierarchy.

Nelson's visionary optimism seems vindicated, then. Xanadu as currently conceived—even in its status as Nelson's scheme to get rich very slowly—opens the door to a true social revolution with implications beyond the world of literature or mass entertainment. Xanadu would remove economic and social gatekeeping functions from the current owners of the means of text production (editors, publishers,

managers of conglomerates). It would transfer control of cultural work to a broadly conceived population of culture workers: writers, artists, critics, "independent scholars," autodidacts, "generalists," fans, punks, cranks, hacks, hackers, and other non- or quasi-professionals. "Tomorrow's hypertext systems have immense political ramifications, and there are many struggles to come," Nelson warns (*Literary Machines* 3/19). This is an understatement of cosmic proportions.

But it would be a mistake to celebrate cybernetic May Day without performing a few reality checks. Along with all those visionary forecasts of "post-hierarchical" information exchange (Zuboff, 399), some hard facts need to be acknowledged. The era of the garage-born computer messiah has passed. Directly or indirectly, most development of hardware and software depends on heavily capitalized multinational companies that do a thriving business with the defense establishment. This affiliation clearly influences the development of new media—consider an influential paper on "The Rhetoric of Hypertext" which uses the requirements of a military training system to propose general standards of coherence and instrumental effectiveness for this medium (Carlson, 1990). Technological development does not happen in cyberspace, but in the more familiar universe of postindustrial capital. Thus to the clearheaded, any suggestion that computer technology might be anything but an instrument of this system must seem quixotic—or just plain stupid.

Before stepping off into cyberspace, we do well to peel off the futurist headgear and listen to some voices in the street. No one wants to read anymore: "books suck, Nintendo rules." Computers are either imperial business machines or head toys for yuppies. Anyone still interested in "mass" culture needs to check out the yawning gap between the rich and the debtpayers, not to mention the incipient splintering of Euro-America into warring ethnicities and "multicultural" tribes. And while we're at it, we might also do some thinking about our most recent global conflict, wargame-as-video-game with realistic third-world blood, a campaign in defense of economic imbalance and the West's right to determine political order in the Middle East. Perhaps we are using the word "revolution" far too loosely. Given the present state of political and cultural affairs, any vision of a "populite" future, or as John Perry Barlow has it, an "electronic frontier" (see Sterling), needs hard scrutiny. Revolution, as Tommie Lee Jones reminds us, is what you find *in your face*.

Do we really want a revolution? Are academic and corporate intellectuals truly prepared to dispense with the current means of text production and the advantages they afford in the present information economy? More to the point, *are we capable* of overturning these institutions, assuming we have the will to do so? Looking back from the seventies, Jean Baudrillard criticized the students of Paris '68 for assuming control of the national broadcast center only to reinstate one-to-many programming and the obscurantist focus of the "media event." The pre-revolutionary identity of television swiftly reasserted itself in the midst of radical action. The seizure was a sham, Baudrillard concludes: "Only total revolution, theoretical and practical, can restore the symbolic in the demise of the sign and of value. Even signs must burn" (*Political Economy of the Sign*, 163). Xanadu as Nelson imagines it does promise to immolate certain cultural icons: the entrepreneurial publishing house, the codex book, the idea of text as unified, self-contained utterance. Taken to its limits, hypertext could reverse/recourse into a general medium of control, a means of ensuring popular franchise in the new order of virtual space. Public-access Xanadu might be the last hope for consensual democracy in an age of global simulation.

Or it might not: we do well to remember that Ted Nelson's vision comes cleverly packaged with assurances that copyright and intellectual property shall not perish from the earth. Some signs would seem to be flame-resistant. The vision of Xanadu as cyberspatial New Jersusalem is conceivable and perhaps eligible, but by no stretch of the imagination is it inevitable. To live in the postmodern condition is to get along without the consolation of providential fictions or theories of historical necessity. This renunciation includes the "Laws of Media," whose force in the final analysis is theoretical and heuristic, not normative. As Linda Hutcheon observes, postmodernism undermines any attempt at binary distinction. To invoke the possibility of a "post-hierarchical" information order, one must assert the fact that all orders are contingent, the product of discursive formations and social contracts. But this postulate generates a fatally recursive paradox: if all order is consensual, then the social consensus may well express itself against revolution and in support of the old order. The term "post-hierarchical" may some day turn out to carry the same nasty irony as the words "postmodern" or "postwar" in the aftermath of Desert Storm: welcome back to the future, same as it ever was.

In the end it is impossible to dismiss Nelson's prophecies of cultural renovation in Xanadu; but it is equally hard to predict their easy fulfillment. Xanadu and the hypertext concept in general challenge humanists and information scientists to reconsider fundamental assumptions about the social space of writing. They may in fact open the way to a new textual order and a new politics of knowledge and expression. However, changes of this magnitude cannot come without major upheavals. Responsibility for the evolution of hypertext systems as genuine alternatives to the present information economy rests as much with software developers, social scientists, and literary theorists as it does with legislators and capitalists. If anything unites these diverse elites, it might be their allegiance to existing institutions of intellectual authority—the printed word, the book, the library, the university, the publishing house.

It may be, as Linda Hutcheon asserts, that though we are incapable of direct opposition to our native conditions, we can still criticize and undermine them through such postmodern strategies as deconstruction, parody, and pastiche (120–21). Secondary literacy might indeed find expression in a perverse turn about or within the primary body of literate culture. But it seems equally possible that our engagement with interactive media will follow the path of reaction, not revolution. The cultural mood at century's end seems anything but radical. Witness President Bush's attacks on cultural diversity (or as he saw it, "political correctness") in higher education. Or consider Camille Paglia's memorable "defense" of polyvalent, post-print ways of knowing, capped off by a bizarre reversal in which she decrees that children of the Tube must be force-fed "the logocentric and Apollonian side of our culture" (Postman and Paglia, 55). Given these signs and symptoms, the prospects for populite renaissance do not seem especially rosy. "It is time for the enlightened repression of the children," Paglia declares. Yet in the face of all this we can still find visionary souls who say they want a textual, social, cultural, intellectual revolution. In the words of Lennon:

> Well, you know . . .
> We all want to change your head.

The question remains: which heads do the changing, and which get the change?

Works Cited

Barthes, Roland. "From Work to Text." *Textual Strategies: Readings in Poststructuralist Criticism*. Ed. Josué Harari. Ithaca, NY: Cornell UP, 1979. 73–81.

Baudrillard, Jean. *For a Critique of the Political Economy of the Sign*. Trans. Charles Levin. St. Louis: Telos, 1981.

———. *Simulations*. Trans. Paul Foss, Paul Patton, and Philip Beitchman. New York: Semiotext(e), 1983.

Benjamin, Walter. "The Work of Art in the Age of Mechanical Reproduction." *Illuminations*. Ed. Hannah Arendt. New York: Schocken, 1969. 217–52.

Bersani, Leo. "Pynchon, Paranoia, and Literature." *Representations* 25 (1989): 99–118.

Bolter, Jay. *Writing Space: The Computer, Hypertext, and the History of Writing*. Fairlawn, N.J.: Lawrence Erlbaum Associates, 1990.

Bush, Vannevar. "As We May Think." *Atlantic Monthly* (July, 1945): 101–08.

Carlson, Patricia. "The Rhetoric of Hypertext." *Hypermedia* 2(1990): 109–31.

Conklin, Jeffrey. "Hypertext: An Introduction and Survey." *Computer* 20(1987): 17–41.

Coover, Robert. "The End of Books." *New York Times Book Review*, June 21, 1992. 1 ff.

Deleuze, Gilles and Félix Guattari. *Anti-Oedipus: Capitalism and Schizophrenia*. Trans. Robert Hurley, Mark Seem, Helen R. Lane. Minneapolis: University of Minnesota, 1977.

Dorfman, Ariel. *The Empire's Old Clothes*. New York: Pantheon, 1983.

Douglas, Jane Yellowlees. "Wandering through the Labyrinth: Encountering Interactive Fiction." *Computers and Composition* 6(1989): 93–103.

Drexler, K. Eric. *Engines of Creation: The Coming Era of Nanotechnology*. New York: Doubleday, 1987.

Eagleton, Terry. "Capitalism, Modernism and Postmodernism." *New Left Review* 152 (1985): 60–73.

Gibson, William. *Neuromancer*. New York: Ace, 1984.

Harpold, Terence. "The Grotesque Corpus: Hypertext as Carnival." *What's a Critic to Do?* Ed. G.P. Landow. Baltimore: Johns Hopkins UP [forthcoming].

Hassan, Ihab. *The Postmodern Turn: Essays in Postmodern Theory and Culture*. Columbus: Ohio State, 1987.

Heim, Michael. *Electric Language: a Philosophical Study of Word Processing*. New Haven: Yale UP, 1987.

Hofstadter, Douglas. *Gödel, Escher, Bach: An Eternal Golden Braid*. New York: Basic, 1979.

Horowitz, Irving Louis. *Communicating Ideas: The Crisis of Publishing in a Post-Industrial Society*. New York: Oxford UP, 1986.

Hutcheon, Linda. *A Poetics of Postmodernism: History, Theory, Fiction*. New York: Routledge, 1988.

Jameson, Frederic. "Postmodernism, or the Cultural Logic of Late Capitalism." *New Left Review* 146(1984): 53–92.

Joyce, Michael. "Siren Shapes: Exploratory and Constructive Hypertexts." *Academic Computing* (November, 1988): 11 ff.

Kernan, Alvin. *The Death of Literature*. New Haven: Yale UP, 1990.

Landow, George. *Hypertext: The Convergence of Contemporary Critical Theory and Technology*. Baltimore: Johns Hopkins UP, 1992.

Lanham, Richard. "The Electronic Word: Literary Study and the Digital Revolution." *New Literary History* 20(1989): 268–89.

Leary, Timothy. "The Cyberpunk: The Individual as Reality Pilot." *Storming the Reality Studio: A Casebook of Cyberpunk and Postmodern Fiction*. Ed. Larry McCaffery. Durham: Duke UP, 1992. 245–58.

Levy, Steven. *Hackers: Heroes of the Computer Revolution*. New York: Dell, 1984.

———. "The End of Literature: Multimedia is Television's Insidious Offspring." *Macworld* (June, 1990): 51+.

———. "In the Realm of the Censor: The Online Service Prodigy Tells its Users to Shut Up and Shop." *Macworld* (January, 1991): 69+.

Lyotard, Jean François. *The Postmodern Condition: A Report on Knowledge*. Trans. Geoff Bennington and Brian Massumi. Minneapolis: University of Minnesota, 1984.

McCorduck, Pamela. *The Universal Machine: Confessions of a Technological Optimist*. New York: McGraw-Hill, 1985.

McHoul, Alec and David Wills. *Writing Pynchon: Strategies in Fictional Analysis*. Urbana: University of Illinois, 1990.

McLuhan, H. Marshall. *Understanding Media: The Extensions of Man*. New York: McGraw-Hill, 1964.

McLuhan, H. Marshall and Eric McLuhan. *Laws of Media: The New Science*. Toronto: University of Toronto, 1988.

Nelson, Theodor Holm. *Computer Lib/Dream Machines*. Redmond, WA: Tempus Books, 1987.

———. *Literary Machines*. Sausalito, CA: Mindful, 1990.

———. "How Hypertext (Un)does the Canon." Paper delivered at the Modern Language Association Convention, Chicago, December 28, 1990.

Ong, Walter. *Orality and Literacy: The Technologizing of the Word*. New York: Methuen, 1982.

Pfeil, Fred. *Another Tale to Tell: Politics and Narrative in Postmodern Culture*. New York: Verso, 1990.

Postman, Neil and Camille Paglia. "She Wants Her TV! He Wants His Book!" *Harper's* 282(March, 1991): 44 ff.

Prigogine, Ilya and Isabelle Stengers. *Order out of Chaos: Man's New Dialogue with Nature*. New York: Bantam, 1984.

Pynchon, Thomas. *Gravity's Rainbow*. New York: Viking, 1973.

Ross, Andrew. *Strange Weather: Culture, Science, and Technology in the Age of Limits*. New York: Verso, 1991.

Slatin, John. "Reading Hypertext: Order and Coherence in a New Medium." *College English* 52(1990): 870–83.

Stansberry, Dominic. "Hyperfiction: Beyond the Garden of the Forking Paths." *New Media*. May, 1993. 52–55.

Sterling, Bruce. *The Hacker Crackdown: Law and Disorder on the Electronic Frontier*. New York: Bantam, 1992.

Stoll, Clifford. *The Cuckoo's Egg: Tracking a Spy Through the Maze of Computer Espionage*. New York: Doubleday, 1989.

Zuboff, Shoshana. *In the Age of the Smart Machine: The Future of Work and Power*. New York: Basic, 1988.

# 49. [Introduction]
# The End of Books

What is the end of books? Provocation, the communication of different perspectives, the pleasing rearrangement of thought through language and narrative—these are a few possible ends. They are certainly ones that Robert Coover has worked toward in his postmodern fiction, provided in codex format in *Pricksongs and Descants, The Universal Baseball Association, The Public Burning,* and *Briar Rose,* among others. What Coover found in teaching a hypertext writing workshop was that allowing students to write on the computer in this form actually furthered the end of books.

"Getting [writing students] to try out alternative or innovative forms is harder than talking them into chastity as a life style," Coover writes. "But confronted with hyperspace, they have no choice: all the comforting structures have been erased." What resulted from the confrontation between an unusual hypertext writing opportunity and a well-read, conservative student was, Coover found, high-quality and copious literary output. The benefits seen in this workshop came with the help of Brown's robust and well-supported systems for composition—and these systems were important, since students did not have the same access to programmers that collaborating artists did in earlier projects. They did have, within the environment provided in Coover's class, the ability to collaborate on the authorship of hypertext systems before the Web was invented, working on projects in groups that met in person and interacting with each other via online writing.

J. Yellowlees Douglas, in her post-"The End of Books" book which takes its name from this essay, calls this "the single article that arguably has made more readers aware of hypertext fiction and inflamed more critics than any other" (7). Coover has managed not only to provoke students into writing innovative fiction, but also to provoke critics into writing sweeping denunciations of the idea of electronic literature. These critical inflammations have resulted in heated humanist tracts but little illumination. Some have had difficulty getting beyond the title of this essay, at least emotionally; the alternate reading of the title described in the first paragraph may help, in this case.

Since this essay's 1992 appearance in the *New York Times Book Review,* Coover has declared that the Golden Age of literary hypertext has ended, and that this heavily textual era of innovation in the form has given way to the world of the Web. (Although many who weren't bothered by "The End of Books" have bemoaned this more recent declaration, Coover himself foresees, at the very least, an enjoyable Silver Age, and hopes that reading will continue to have a place in our computerized experiences.) If the sunlit afternoon of hypertext has ended, that can only mean that some of those comforting structures that were lacking in 1990's hypertext composition class do currently exist—and the system shock that hypertext writing produced in 1992 can no longer be administered in the same way. Perhaps the next way to stimulate students into literary creativity using the computer will involve something more novel than link-and-node hypertext?

—NM

## Further Reading

Coover, Robert. "Literary Hypertext: The Passing of the Golden Age." Keynote Address at Digital Arts and Culture 99, Atlanta, Georgia. 29 October 1999. <http://nickm.com/vox/golden_age.html>.

Birkerts, Sven. *The Gutenberg Elegies.* Boston: Faber and Faber, 1994.

Douglas, J. Yellowlees. *The End of Books—Or Books Without End?: Reading Interactive Narratives.* Ann Arbor: University of Michigan Press, 2000.

Landow, George. *Hypertext: The Convergence of Contemporary Critical Theory and Technology.* Baltimore: Johns Hopkins University Press, 1992.

Although it was radical for college writing students to compose hypertexts in 1990, the idea of providing the computer as a creative platform had been promoted for decades, often with younger students in mind, by Alan Kay (◊26), Seymour Papert (◊28), and Ted Nelson (◊21) among others.

Constructive hypertext systems were advocated by hypertext fiction's Homeric figure, Michael Joyce (◊42). Joyce wrote *Afternoon, a story,* as described in Coover's essay.

◊21
301

"Izme Pass" by Carolyn Guyer and Martha Petry (which Coover mentions here) is the first published collaborative hypertext ⊗.

◊25
377

◊26
391

◊28
413

Coover has already taken electronic writing in a different direction, or along a different dimension, by having writers in Spring 2002 create text for display in Brown University's CAVE (CAVE Automatic Virtual Environment, further described in the introduction to Myron Krueger's essay (◊25). These efforts bring writerly concerns and perspectives to shared virtual environments, where text has seldom had any place at all. The 3D display of text in space had been explored earlier in different types of systems by MIT's Visible Language Workshop under the direction of Muriel Cooper.

◊42
613

705

Original Publication

*The New York Times Book Review* 11, 23–25. 21 June 1992.

# The End of Books

## Robert Coover

In the real world nowadays, that is to say, in the world of video transmissions, cellular phones, fax machines, computer networks, and in particular out in the humming digitalized precincts of avant-garde computer hackers, cyberpunks and hyperspace freaks, you will often hear it said that the print medium is a doomed and outdated technology, a mere curiosity of bygone days destined soon to be consigned forever to those dusty unattended museums we now call libraries. Indeed, the very proliferation of books and other print-based media, so prevalent in this forest-harvesting, paper-wasting age, is held to be a sign of its feverish moribundity, the last futile gasp of a once vital form before it finally passes away forever, dead as God.

Which would mean of course that the novel, too, as we know it, has come to its end. Not that those announcing its demise are grieving. For all its passing charm, the traditional novel, which took center stage at the same time that industrial mercantile democracies arose—and which Hegel called "the epic of the middle-class world"—is perceived by its would-be executioners as the virulent carrier of the patriarchal, colonial, canonical, proprietary, hierarchical and authoritarian values of a past that is no longer with us.

Much of the novel's alleged power is embedded in the line, that compulsory author-directed movement from the beginning of a sentence to its period, from the top of the page to the bottom, from the first page to the last. Of course, through print's long history, there have been countless strategies to counter the line's power, from marginalia and footnotes to the creative innovations of novelists like Laurence Sterne, James Joyce, Raymond Queneau, Julio Cortázar, Italo Calvino and Milorad Pavić, not to exclude the form's father, Cervantes himself. But true freedom from the tyranny of the line is perceived as only really possible now at last with the advent of hypertext, written and read on the computer, where the line in fact does not exist unless one invents and implants it in the text.

"Hypertext" is not a system but a generic term, coined a quarter of a century ago by a computer populist named Ted Nelson to describe the writing done in the nonlinear or nonsequential space made possible by the computer. Moreover, unlike print text, hypertext provides multiple paths between text segments, now often called "lexias" in a borrowing from the pre-hypertextual but prescient Roland Barthes. With its webs of linked lexias, its networks of alternate routes (as opposed to print's fixed unidirectional page-turning) hypertext presents a radically divergent technology, interactive and polyvocal, favoring a plurality of discourses over definitive utterance and freeing the reader from domination by the author. Hypertext reader and writer are said to become co-learners or co-writers, as it were, fellow-travelers in the mapping and remapping of textual (and visual, kinetic and aural) components, not all of which are provided by what used to be called the author.

Though used at first primarily as a radically new teaching arena, by the mid-1980's hyperspace was drawing fiction writers into its intricate and infinitely expandable, infinitely alluring webs, its green-limned gardens of multiple forking paths, to allude to another author popular with hypertext buffs, Jorge Luis Borges.

Several systems support the configuring of this space for fiction writing. Some use simple randomized linking like the shuffling of cards, others (such as Guide and HyperCard) offer a kind of do-it-yourself basic tool set, and still others (more elaborate systems like Storyspace, which is currently the software of choice among fiction writers in this country, and Intermedia, developed at Brown University) provide a complete package of sophisticated structuring and navigational devices.

Although hypertext's champions often assail the arrogance of the novel, their own claims are hardly modest. You will often hear them proclaim, quite seriously, that there have been three great events in the history of literacy: the invention of writing, the invention of movable type and the invention of hypertext. As hyperspace-walker George P. Landow puts it in his recent book surveying the field, *Hypertext:* "Electronic text processing marks the next major shift in information technology after the development of the printed book. It promises (or threatens) to produce effects on our culture, particularly on our literature, education, criticism and scholarship, just as radical as those produced by Gutenberg's movable type."

Noting that the "movement from the tactile to the digital is the primary fact about the contemporary world," Mr. Landow observes that, whereas most writings of print-bound critics working in an exhausted technology are "models of scholarly solemnity, records of disillusionment and brave sacrifice of humanistic positions," writers in and on hypertext "are downright celebratory. . . . Most post-structuralists write from within the twilight of a wished-for coming day; most writers of hypertext write of many of the same things from within the dawn."

Dawn it is, to be sure. The granddaddy of full-length hypertext fictions is Michael Joyce's landmark *Afternoon*, first released on floppy disk in 1987 and moved into a new Storyspace "reader," partly developed by Mr. Joyce himself, in 1990.

Mr. Joyce, who is also the author of a printed novel, *The War Outside Ireland: A History of the Doyles in North America With an Account of their Migrations*, wrote in the on-line journal *Postmodern Culture* that hyperfiction "is the first instance of the true electronic text, what we will come to conceive as the natural form of multimodal, multisensual writing," but it is still so radically new it is hard to be certain just what it is. No fixed center, for starters—and no edges either, no ends or boundaries. The traditional narrative time line vanishes into a geographical landscape or exitless maze, with beginnings, middles and ends being no longer part of the immediate display. Instead: branching options, menus, link markers and mapped networks. There are no hierarchies in these topless (and bottomless) networks, as paragraphs, chapters and other conventional text divisions are replaced by evenly empowered and equally ephemeral window-sized blocks of text and graphics—soon to be supplemented with sound, animation, and film.

As Carolyn Guyer and Martha Petry put it in the opening "directions" to their hypertext fiction "Izme Pass," which was published (if "published" is the word) on a disk included in the spring 1991 issue of the magazine *Writing on the Edge:*

> This is a new kind of fiction, and a new kind of reading. The form of the text is rhythmic, looping on itself in patterns and layers that gradually accrete meaning, just as the passage of time and events does in one's lifetime. Trying the textlinks embedded within the work will bring the narrative together in new configurations, fluid constellations formed by the path of your interest. The difference between

reading hyperfiction and reading traditional printed fiction may be the difference between sailing the islands and standing on the dock watching the sea. One is not necessarily better than the other.

I must confess at this point that I am not myself an expert navigator of hyperspace, nor am I—as I am entering my seventh decade and thus rather committed, for better or for worse, to the obsolescent print technology—likely to engage in any major hypertext fictions of my own. But, interested as ever in the subversion of the traditional bourgeois novel and in fictions that challenge linearity, I felt that something was happening out (or in) there and that I ought to know what it was: if I were not going to sail the Guyer-Petry islands, I had at least better run to the shore with my field glasses. And what better way to learn than to teach a course in the subject?

Thus began the Brown University Hypertext Fiction Workshop, two spring semesters (and already as many software generations) old, a course devoted as much to the changing of reading habits as to the creation of new narratives.

Writing students are notoriously conservative creatures. They write stubbornly and hopefully within the tradition of what they have read. Getting them to try out alternative or innovative forms is harder than talking them into chastity as a life style. But confronted with hyperspace, they have no choice: all the comforting structures have been erased. It's improvise or go home. Some frantically rebuild those old structures, some just get lost and drift out of sight, most leap in fearlessly without even asking how deep it is (infinitely deep) and admit, even as they paddle for dear life, that this new arena is indeed an exciting, provocative if frequently frustrating medium for the creation of new narratives, a potentially revolutionary space, capable, exactly as advertised, of transforming the very art of fiction, even if it now remains somewhat at the fringe, remote still, in these very early days, from the mainstream.

With hypertext we focus, both as writers and as readers, on structure as much as on prose, for we are made aware suddenly of the shapes of narratives that are often hidden in print stories. The most radical new element that comes to the fore in hypertext is the system of multidirectional and often labyrinthine linkages we are invited or obliged to create. Indeed the creative imagination often becomes more preoccupied with linkage, routing and mapping than with statement or style, or with what we would call character or plot (two traditional narrative elements that are decidedly in jeopardy). We are always astonished to discover how much of the reading and writing experience occurs in the interstices and trajectories between text fragments. That is to say, the text fragments are like stepping stones, there for our safety, but the real current of the narratives runs between them.

"The great thing," as one young writer, Alvin Lu, put it in an on-line class essay, is "the degree to which narrative is completely destructed into its constituent bits. Bits of information convey knowledge, but the juxtaposition of bits creates narrative. The emphasis of a hypertext (narrative) should be the degree to which the reader is given power, not to read, but to organize the texts made available to her. Anyone can read, but not everyone has sophisticated methods of organization made available to them."

The fictions developed in the workshop, all of which are "still in progress," have ranged from geographically anchored narratives similar to *Our Town* and Choose-Your-Own-Adventure stories to parodies of the classics, nested narratives, spatial poems, interactive comedy, metamorphic dreams, irresolvable murder mysteries, moving comic books and Chinese sex manuals.

In hypertext, multivocalism is popular, graphic elements, both drawn and scanned, have been incorporated into the narratives, imaginative font changes have been employed to identify various voices or plot elements, and there has also been a very effective use of formal documents not typically used in fictions—statistical charts, song lyrics, newspaper articles, film scripts, doodles and photographs, baseball cards and box scores, dictionary entries, rock music album covers, astrological forecasts, board games, and medical and police reports.

At our weekly workshops, selected writers display, on an overhead projector, their developing narrative structures, then face the usual critique of their writing, design, development of character, emotional impact, attention to detail and so on, as appropriate. But they also engage in continuous on-line dialogue with one another, exchanging criticism, enthusiasm, doubts, speculations, theorizing, wisecracks. So much fun is all of this, so compelling this "downright celebratory" experience, as Mr. Landow would have it, that the creative output, so far anyway, has been much greater than that of ordinary undergraduate writing workshops, and certainly of as high a quality.

In addition to the individual fictions, which are more or less protected from tampering in the old proprietary way, we in the workshop have also played freely and often quite anarchically in a group fiction space called "Hotel." Here, writers are free to check in, to open up new rooms, new corridors, new intrigues, to unlink texts or create new links, to intrude upon or subvert the texts of others, to alter plot trajectories, manipulate time and space, to engage in dialogue through invented characters, then kill off one another's characters or even to sabotage the hotel's plumbing. Thus one day we might find a man and woman encountering each other in the hotel bar, working up some kind of sexual liaison, only to return a few days later and discover that one or both had sex changes. During one of my hypertext workshops, a certain reading tension was caused when we found that there was more than one bartender in our hotel: was this the same bar or not? One of the students—Alvin Lu again—responded by linking all the bartenders to Room 666, which he called the "Production Center," where some imprisoned alien monster was giving birth to full-grown bartenders on demand.

This space of essentially anonymous text fragments remains on line and each new set of workshop students is invited to check in there and continue the story of the Hypertext Hotel. I would like to see it stay open for a century or two.

However, as all of us have discovered, even though the basic technology of hypertext may be with us for centuries to come, perhaps even as long as the technology of the book, its hardware and software seem to be fragile and short-lived; whole new generations of equipment and programs arrive before we can finish reading the instructions of the old. Even as I write, Brown University's highly sophisticated Intermedia system, on which we have been writing our hypertext fictions, is being phased out because it is too expensive to maintain and incompatible with Apple's new operating-system software, System 7.0. A good portion of our last semester was spent transporting our documents from Intermedia to Storyspace (which Brown is now adopting) and adjusting to the new environment.

This problem of operating-system standards is being urgently addressed and debated now by hypertext writers; if interaction is to be a hallmark of the new technology, all its players must have a common and consistent language and all must be equally empowered in its use. There are other problems too. Navigational procedures: how do you move around in infinity without getting lost? The structuring of the space can be so compelling and confusing as to utterly absorb and neutralize the narrator and to exhaust the reader. And there is the related problem of filtering. With an unstable text that can be intruded upon by other author-readers, how do you, caught in the maze, avoid the trivial? How do you duck the garbage? Venerable novelistic values like unity, integrity, coherence, vision, voice seem to be in danger. Eloquence is being redefined. "Text" has lost its canonical certainty. How does one judge, analyze, write about a work that never reads the same way twice?

And what of narrative flow? There is still movement, but in hyperspace's dimensionless infinity, it is more like endless expansion ; it runs the risk of being so distended and slackly driven as to lose its centripetal force, to give way to a kind of static low-charged lyricism—that dreamy gravityless lost-in-space feeling of the early sci-fi films. How does one resolve the conflict between the reader's desire for coherence and closure and the text's desire for continuance, its fear of death? Indeed, what is closure in such an environment? If everything is middle, how do you know when you are done, either as reader or writer? If the author is free to take a story anywhere at any time and in as many directions as she or he wishes, does that not become the obligation to do so?

No doubt, this will be a major theme for narrative artists of the future, even those locked into the old print tech-

nologies. And that's nothing new. The problem of closure was a major theme—was it not?—of the *Epic of Gilgamesh* as it was chopped out in clay at the dawn of literacy, and of the Homeric rhapsodies as they were committed to papyrus by technologically innovative Greek literati some 26 centuries ago. There is continuity, after all, across the ages riven by shifting technologies.

Much of this I might have guessed—and in fact did guess—before entering hyperspace, before I ever picked up a mouse, and my thoughts have been tempered only slightly by on-line experience. What I had not clearly foreseen, however, was that this is a technology that both absorbs and totally displaces. Print documents may be read in hyperspace, but hypertext does not translate into print. It is not like film, which is really just the dead end of linear narrative, just as 12-tone music is the dead end of music by the stave.

Hypertext is truly a new and unique environment. Artists who work there must be read there. And they will probably be judged there as well: criticism, like fiction, is moving off the page and on line, and it is itself susceptible to continuous changes of mind and text. Fluidity, contingency, indeterminacy, plurality, discontinuity are the hypertext buzzwords of the day, and they seem to be fast becoming principles, in the same way that relativity not so long ago displaced the falling apple.

# 50. [Introduction]
# Time Frames

Scott McCloud is the Aristotle of comics, showing the way for contemporary thinkers who would seek to rigorously analyze emerging media.

What Aristotle did for Attic drama in the *Poetics,* McCloud has done for the neglected form of comics. He has explained what the most talented comic artists knew, although only Will Eisner had begun to articulate it—how the comic format works, and what its underlying structures and techniques are. He began by rigidly defining comics as "sequential art" (or, if further explication is necessary, "juxtaposed pictorial and other images in deliberate sequence"). McCloud then found that, based on this definition, comics are as old as the ancient Egyptians. From there, he went on to consider many of the important higher-level techniques of the comic artist: How does the variation between generic and specific representation of people work? What "happens" in between the panels of the comic images we read? What are the uses of color in the comic art form? And, as is discussed in the chapter excerpted here, how can time be represented in a medium which is (although it is read over a period of time) purely spatial? It is hardly necessary to even mention that McCloud's work has implcations for combining text and image, but it provides other lessons and examples.

Many of those involved with new media are pleased by McCloud's deft metacomic tricks, a number of which are represented in this chapter. Since McCloud uses a narrative medium suited to general exposition, he was able to write a comic about comics, and take advantage of this to illustrate (in every sense of the word) his points. Other similar attempts are not always as successful: although there have been buildings constructed mainly to comment on architecture, these are not usually popular or very habitable structures. While the first edition of George Landow's *Hypertext* was issued by Johns Hopkins on disk as *Hypertext in Hypertext,* this edition never gained wide scholarly currency—not being as widely cited as the book it was based upon—and Landow's *Hypertext 2.0* was not issued in a similar format. Some interest in hypertextual criticism of hypertext remains, as can be seen in the September 2002 special issue of the *Journal of Digital Information,* edited by Jill Walker and Susana Tosca. Perhaps this will build upon other nonfiction hypertext work to provide interesting results; it may also simply be dancing about dance.

Looking to *Understanding Comics* can provoke new media insight, but it's certainly not the case that all of McCloud's techniques can be easily dragged and dropped into the digital realm. What McCloud's work nevertheless shows is that new forms, even those that have not been studied seriously for centuries or even decades, do indeed have certain conventions and rules, and that if the form being studied is considered with care and thought, these rules can be determined, benefiting those who work in the form, who are striving to improve the practice of their art.
—NM

See Brenda Laurel's essay (◊38) for a direct application of Aristotelian dramatic ideas to new media.

Some new media practitioners have also begun to consider their own work as a type of sequential art. Given that thumbnails and storyboards are already used by many new media systems designers, perhaps viewing a particular path through such a system as a comics-like sequence is a logical next step. New media tends not to have the continual movement of the motion picture (storyboarding's most high-profile application), but rather periods of reading and navigation more closely aligned with the experience of comics. In *Reinventing Comics* McCloud has also considered how the specific form of comics may be transformed by new media and what forms might emerge. It's fitting, then, that Ted Nelson employed an underground comics format to communicate the user experience he wanted new media systems to have—an example of which appears in his 1974 *Computer Lib/Dream Machines.*

◊38
563

Further Reading

Eisner, Will. *Comics & Sequential Art.* Tamarac, Florida: Poorhouse Press, 1985.

Landow, George P. *Hypertext in Hypertext.* 2 3.5" disks; Macintosh and Windows versions. Baltimore: Johns Hopkins University Press, 1994.

McCloud, Scott. *Reinventing Comics.* New York: Harperperennial, 2000.

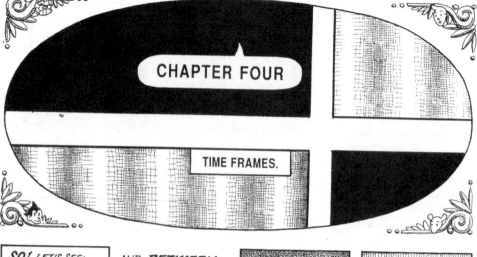

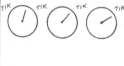

Original Publication

*Understanding Comics: The Invisible Art.* 94–117. Northhampton, MA: Kitchen Sink Press, 1993.

**BUT** HOW *COULD* THIS BE ANYTHING BUT A *SINGLE MOMENT*;? OUR EYES HAVE BEEN *WELL-TRAINED* BY THE *PHOTOGRAPH* AND BY *REPRESENTATIONAL ART* TO SEE ANY SINGLE CONTINUOUS IMAGE AS A *SINGLE INSTANT IN TIME.*

BUT THE ACTIONS THAT WE SEE OCCURRING SEEMINGLY AT THE SAME TIME OBVIOUSLY *CAN'T BE!*

ANOTHER WAY TO LOOK AT IT: LET'S THINK OF TIME AS A *ROPE.*

EACH INCH REPRESENTS A *SECOND.*

SUCH A ROPE MIGHT BE SAID TO WIND SOME-THING LIKE *THIS* THROUGH OUR PANEL.

*SIMPLIFIED* OF COURSE, SINCE EACH BALLOON HAS ITS OWN *TWISTS AND TURNS.*

AND SINCE EACH FACE AND FIGURE IS DRAWN TO MATCH HIS/HER OWN *WORDS--*

*SMILE!*

*PAF!*

*AAGH!* THAT FLASH IS *BLINDING,* UNCLE HENRY!

HEE-HEE

-- THOSE FIGURES, FACES AND WORDS ARE MATCHED IN *TIME* AS WELL.

THE PROPERTIES OF THE SINGLE CONTINUOUS *IMAGE*, MEANWHILE, TEND TO MATCH EACH FIGURE WITH EVERY *OTHER* FIGURE.

SINGLE *IMAGE*.

SINGLE *MOMENT*.

PORTRAYING TIME ON A LINE MOVING *LEFT TO RIGHT*, THIS PUTS ALL THE *IMAGES* ON THE SAME VERTICAL AXIS.

AND *TANGLES UP TIME* BEYOND *ALL RECOGNITION!*

SNAP!

SNAP!

CRASH!

PERHAPS WE'VE BEEN TOO CONDITIONED BY PHOTOGRAPHY TO PERCEIVE SINGLE IMAGES AS *SINGLE MOMENTS*. AFTER ALL, IT DOES TAKE AN EYE *TIME* TO MOVE ACROSS SCENES IN *REAL LIFE!*

EACH FIGURE IS ARRANGED FROM *LEFT TO RIGHT* IN THE SEQUENCE WE WILL "*READ*" THEM, EACH OCCUPYING A DISTINCT *TIME SLOT*.

IN SOME RESPECTS THIS PANEL BY ITSELF ACTUALLY *FITS* OUR *DEFINITION* OF COMICS! ALL IT NEEDS IS A FEW *GUTTERS* THROWN IN TO *CLARIFY THE SEQUENCE*.

SMILE!

PA...

AAGH! THAT FLASH IS *BLINDING*, UNCLE HENRY!

HEE-HEE!

OH, *HENRY!* PUT THAT CAMERA *AWAY*, WILL YOU?

AWW, LET HIM *BE*, MOM. HE'S JUST *HAVING FUN*.

WELL, IF OL' HENRY IS GONNA HAVE MUCH *MORE* FUN, WE MAY HAFTA LOCK UP THE *WINE CELLAR*.

*CHECK!*

HMMM...

SURE YOU WANT TO MOVE *THERE*, JED?

THUMP!

*ONE* PANEL, OPERATING AS *SEVERAL* PANELS.

715

NOT *ALL* PANELS ARE LIKE THAT, OF COURSE.

A SILENT PANEL SUCH AS THIS COULD *INDEED* BE SAID TO DEPICT A *SINGLE MOMENT!*

HE'S GIVING IT HIS *ALL,* FOLKS!

IF *SOUND* IS INTRODUCED, THIS CEASES TO BE TRUE--

--*BUT,* IN AN OTHERWISE SILENT *CAPTIONED* PANEL, THE SINGLE MOMENT CAN ACTUALLY BE *HELD.*

HE WAS GIVING IT HIS *ALL,* WHEN--

THESE VARIOUS SHAPES WE CALL *PANELS* HOLD IN THEIR BORDERS ALL OF THE ICONS THAT ADD UP TO THE *VOCABULARY OF COMICS.*

ALL EXCEPT *ONE.*

FOR JUST AS THE BODY'S LARGEST ORGAN --OUR *SKIN*-- IS SELDOM *THOUGHT OF* AS AN ORGAN--

--SO TOO IS THE PANEL *ITSELF* OVERLOOKED AS COMICS' MOST IMPORTANT *ICON!*

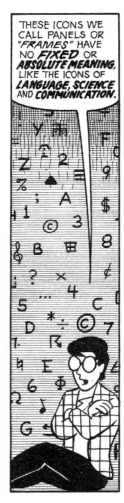

THESE ICONS WE CALL PANELS OR *"FRAMES"* HAVE NO *FIXED* OR *ABSOLUTE MEANING,* LIKE THE ICONS OF *LANGUAGE, SCIENCE* AND *COMMUNICATION.*

NOR IS THEIR MEANING AS *FLUID* AND *MALLEABLE* AS THE SORTS OF ICONS WE CALL *PICTURES.*

THE PANEL ACTS AS A SORT OF *GENERAL INDICATOR* THAT *TIME* OR *SPACE* IS BEING *DIVIDED.*

THE *DURATIONS* OF THAT *TIME* AND THE *DIMENSIONS* OF THAT *SPACE* ARE DEFINED MORE BY THE *CONTENTS* OF THE PANEL THAN BY THE PANEL *ITSELF.* *

HE'S GIVING IT HIS *ALL,* FOLKS!

HE WAS GIVING IT HIS *ALL,* WHEN--

PANEL *SHAPES* VARY *CONSIDERABLY* THOUGH, AND WHILE DIFFERENCES OF SHAPE DON'T AFFECT THE SPECIFIC *"MEANINGS"* OF THOSE PANELS VIS-A-VIS TIME, THEY *CAN* AFFECT THE READING *EXPERIENCE.*

WHICH BRINGS US TO THE STRANGE RELATIONSHIP BETWEEN TIME AS *DEPICTED* IN COMICS AND TIME AS *PERCEIVED* BY THE READER.

\* EISNER DISCUSSES THIS UNDER THE HEADING *"FRAMING TIME"* IN COMICS AND SEQUENTIAL ART.

IN LEARNING TO READ COMICS WE ALL LEARNED TO PERCEIVE TIME *SPATIALLY*, FOR IN THE WORLD OF COMICS, *TIME AND SPACE* ARE *ONE AND THE SAME.*

THE PROBLEM IS *THERE'S NO CONVERSION CHART!*

THE FEW CENTIMETERS WHICH TRANSPORT US FROM *SECOND TO SECOND* IN *ONE* SEQUENCE COULD TAKE US A *HUNDRED MILLION YEARS* IN *ANOTHER*.

SO, AS *READERS*, WE'RE LEFT WITH ONLY A *VAGUE SENSE* THAT AS OUR EYES ARE MOVING THROUGH *SPACE*, THEY'RE ALSO MOVING THROUGH *TIME*-- WE JUST DON'T KNOW BY *HOW MUCH!*

IN MOST CASES IT'S NOT HARD TO MAKE AN EDUCATED GUESS AS TO THE DURATION OF A GIVEN SEQUENCE, SO LONG AS THE *ELEMENTS* OF THAT SEQUENCE ARE *FAMILIAR* TO US.

I ALWAYS FIGURED MARY-ANNE WOULD GO FOR GILLIGAN.

I GUESS.

FROM A *LIFETIME OF CONVERSATIONS*, WE CAN BE SURE THAT A *"PAUSE"* PANEL LIKE THIS LASTS FOR NO MORE THAN SEVERAL *SECONDS*.

BUT IF THE CREATOR OF THIS SCENE WANTED TO *LENGTHEN* THAT PAUSE, HOW COULD HE OR SHE DO SO? ONE OBVIOUS SOLUTION WOULD BE TO ADD MORE PANELS, BUT IS THAT THE ONLY WAY?

D'YA THINK THE SOX COULD FINALLY DO IT THIS YEAR?

I GUESS.

IS THERE ANY WAY TO MAKE A SINGLE SILENT PANEL LIKE THIS ONE SEEM *LONGER?* HOW ABOUT WIDENING THE SPACE *BETWEEN PANELS?* ANY *DIFFERENCE?*

HEY, I *DESERVE* A BETTER JOB! I COULD BE A *BRAIN SURGEON!*

I GUESS.

WE'VE SEEN HOW TIME CAN BE CONTROLLED THROUGH THE *CONTENT* OF PANELS, THE *NUMBER* OF PANELS AND CLOSURE *BETWEEN* PANELS, BUT THERE'S STILL *ONE MORE.*

AS UNLIKELY AS IT SOUNDS, THE PANEL *SHAPE* CAN ACTUALLY MAKE A *DIFFERENCE* IN OUR *PERCEPTION* OF TIME. EVEN THOUGH THIS LONG PANEL HAS THE SAME BASIC "MEANING" AS ITS SHORTER VERSIONS, STILL IT HAS THE *FEELING* OF GREATER LENGTH!

THAT *MADONNA,* MAN, SHE'S ONE *HOT* BABE!

I GUESS.

EVER NOTICED HOW THE WORDS *"SHORT"* OR *"LONG"* CAN REFER EITHER TO THE *FIRST* DIMENSION OR TO THE *FOURTH?*

IN A MEDIUM WHERE TIME AND SPACE *MERGE* SO *COMPLETELY,* THE DISTINCTION OFTEN *VANISHES!*

THE *PANEL BORDER* IS OUR *GUIDE* THROUGH *TIME AND SPACE,* BUT IT WILL ONLY GUIDE US *SO FAR.*

AS MENTIONED, PANELS COME IN MANY SHAPES AND SIZES, THOUGH THE *CLASSIC RECTANGLE* IS USED MOST *OFTEN.*

MOST OF US ARE SO USED TO THE STANDARD *RECTANGULAR* FORMAT THAT A *"BORDERLESS"* PANEL SUCH AS THIS CAN TAKE ON A *TIMELESS QUALITY.*

HEY, ARE YOU EVEN *LISTENING* TO ME?!

I GUESS.

WHEN THE *CONTENT* OF A SILENT PANEL OFFERS NO CLUES AS TO ITS *DURATION,* IT CAN ALSO PRODUCE A SENSE OF *TIMELESSNESS.*

BECAUSE OF ITS *UNRESOLVED NATURE,* SUCH A PANEL MAY *LINGER* IN THE READER'S MIND.

AND ITS PRESENCE MAY BE FELT IN THE PANELS WHICH *FOLLOW* IT.

WHEN *"BLEEDS"* ARE USED -- I.E., WHEN A PANEL RUNS OFF THE EDGE OF THE *PAGE* -- THIS EFFECT IS *COMPOUNDED.*

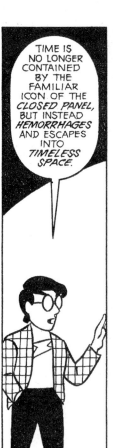

TIME IS NO LONGER CONTAINED BY THE FAMILIAR ICON OF THE *CLOSED PANEL,* BUT INSTEAD *HEMORRHAGES* AND ESCAPES INTO *TIMELESS SPACE.*

SUCH IMAGES CAN *SET THE MOOD* OR A *SENSE OF PLACE* FOR *WHOLE SCENES* THROUGH THEIR *LINGERING TIMELESS PRESENCE.*

ONCE AGAIN, THIS IS A TECHNIQUE USED MOST OFTEN IN JAPAN AND ONLY RECENTLY ADOPTED HERE IN THE WEST.

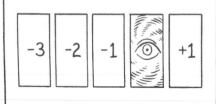

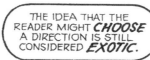

AS MENTIONED EARLIER, *TIME* AND *SPACE* IN THE WORLD OF COMICS ARE *CLOSELY LINKED.*

AS A RESULT, SO TOO ARE THE ISSUES OF *TIME* AND *MOTION.*

AS DISCUSSED IN CHAPTER *THREE,* MOTION IN COMICS IS PRODUCED *BETWEEN* PANELS BY THE MENTAL PROCESS CALLED *CLOSURE*--

--USUALLY BY TRANSITION TYPES *ONE TWO*...BUT LET'S NOT GET INTO *THAT* AGAIN!

DESPITE COMICS' *THREE THOUSAND YEAR HISTORY,* IT WASN'T UNTIL TÖPFFER'S *MID-1800's DOODLINGS* THAT *SPECIFIC* MOTIONS WERE PORTRAYED IN COMICS IN THE NOW-FAMILIAR *PANEL-TO-PANEL* FORM.

HOW, IN BRIGHT AND WITTY SOCIETY, ONE SHOULD BE SEATED IN ORDER TO TALK THEATRES, CASINOS, AND THE LATEST NON-SENSE IN GENERAL.

HOW, IF A SUPERIOR MAKES A JOKE, ONE JUMPS UP WITH A ROAR OF LAUGHTER.

WITHIN A FEW YEARS, HOWEVER, MOTION WAS A *HOT TOPIC INDEED!*

IN THE LAST QUARTER OF THE *NINETEENTH CENTURY* IT SEEMED LIKE *EVERYONE* WAS TRYING TO CAPTURE MOTION THROUGH *SCIENCE!*

BY *1880,* INVENTORS THE *WORLD OVER* KNEW THAT *"MOVING PICTURES"* WERE JUST AROUND THE CORNER. *EVERYONE* WANTED TO BE *FIRST!*

MY *STROBOSCOPE* IS SUPERIOR IN EVERY WAY TO THE OBSOLETE *ZOËTROPE!*

BAH! MY *PRAXINOSCOPE* IS BETTER!

FOOLS! MY *KINEMATOSCOPE* WILL SHOW YOU!

HA! CHILD'S PLAY! THEY ARE BUT *MERE TOYS* NEXT TO THE AWESOME *PHANTASMATROPE!*

FRAUDS *ALL!* MY *ZOÖPRAXINOSCOPE* WILL--!

EVENTUALLY *THOMAS EDISON,* THAT OLD SCALLYWAG, FILED THE FIRST *PATENT* ON A PROCESS USING STRIPS OF *CLEAR PLASTIC PHOTOS* AND *FILM* WAS *OFF AND RUNNING!*

AS THE *MOVING PICTURE* BEGAN ITS SPECTACULAR RISE, A FEW OF THE MORE RADICAL *PAINTERS* OF THE DAY EXPLORED THE IDEA THAT MOTION COULD BE DEPICTED BY A *SINGLE* IMAGE ON *CANVAS.*

*THE FUTURISTS* IN ITALY AND *MARCEL DUCHAMP* IN FRANCE BEGAN THE *SYSTEMATIC DECOMPOSITION OF MOVING IMAGES* IN A *STATIC MEDIUM.*

IT WASN'T A BAD IDEA!

Girl Running on a Balcony by Balla

Nude Descending a Staircase #2 by Duchamp

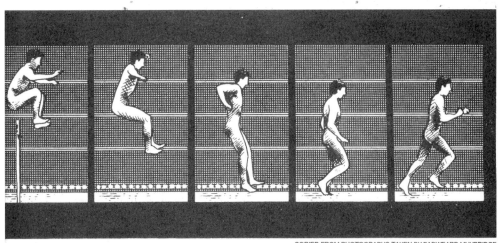

COPIED FROM PHOTOGRAPHS TAKEN BY EADWEARD MUYBRIDGE

IF YOU'RE GOING TO PAINT A WORLD--

--FILLED WITH MOTION--

--THEN BE PREPARED TO PAINT *MOTION!*

DUCHAMP, MORE CONCERNED WITH THE *IDEA* OF MOTION THAN THE *SENSATION*, WOULD EVENTUALLY REDUCE SUCH CONCEPTS AS MOTION TO A *SINGLE LINE.*

DUCHAMP SOON MOVED ON, THE FUTURISTS *DISBANDED* AND FINE ARTISTS GENERALLY *LOST INTEREST* IN THIS *OTHER* TYPE OF *"MOVING PICTURE."*

BUT THROUGHOUT THIS SAME PERIOD *ANOTHER* MEDIUM, LESS *CONSPICUOUSLY,* HAD BEEN INVESTIGATING THIS SAME AREA.

I'M SURE YOU CAN ALL GUESS WHICH MEDIUM I MEAN!

FROM ITS *EARLIEST DAYS*, THE MODERN COMIC HAS GRAPPLED WITH THE PROBLEM OF SHOWING MOTION IN A *STATIC* MEDIUM.

HOW DO YOU SHOW THIS ASPECT OF TIME IN AN ART WHERE *TIME STANDS STILL?*

AND IN COMICS, UNLIKE PAINTING, IT WAS MORE THAN JUST A *THEORETICAL QUESTION!*

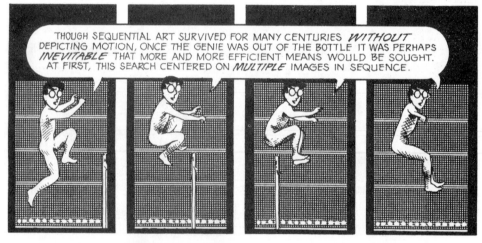

THOUGH SEQUENTIAL ART SURVIVED FOR MANY CENTURIES *WITHOUT* DEPICTING MOTION, ONCE THE GENIE WAS OUT OF THE BOTTLE IT WAS PERHAPS *INEVITABLE* THAT MORE AND MORE EFFICIENT MEANS WOULD BE SOUGHT. AT FIRST, THIS SEARCH CENTERED ON *MULTIPLE* IMAGES IN SEQUENCE.

BUT JUST AS A SINGLE PANEL CAN REPRESENT A *SPAN* OF TIME THROUGH *SOUND*--

--SO TOO CAN A SINGLE PANEL REPRESENT A SPAN OF TIME THROUGH *PICTURES!*

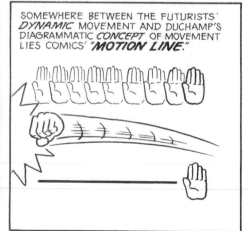

SOMEWHERE BETWEEN THE FUTURISTS' *DYNAMIC* MOVEMENT AND DUCHAMP'S DIAGRAMMATIC *CONCEPT* OF MOVEMENT LIES COMICS' *"MOTION LINE."*

IN THE BEGINNING, MOTION LINES--OR *"ZIP-RIBBONS"* AS SOME CALL THEM-- WERE *WILD, MESSY,* ALMOST *DESPERATE* ATTEMPTS TO REPRESENT THE PATHS OF *MOVING OBJECTS* THROUGH *SPACE.*

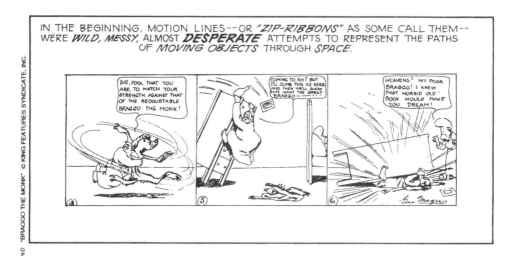

OVER THE YEARS, THESE LINES BECAME MORE *REFINED* AND *STYLIZED,* EVEN *DIAGRAMMATIC.*

EVENTUALLY, IN THE HANDS OF *HEROIC FANTASY* ARTISTS LIKE *BILL EVERETT* AND *JACK KIRBY*--

--THOSE SAME LINES BECAME *SO* STYLIZED AS TO ALMOST HAVE A *LIFE* AND *PHYSICAL PRESENCE* **ALL THEIR OWN,**!

729

* MULTIPLE IMAGES CAN BE FOUND IN THE WORK OF KRIGSTEIN, INFANTINO AND OTHERS.

COLAN, WHO WAS ALSO A *FILM-BUFF*, WAS OF COURSE AWARE THAT WHEN A CAMERA'S SHUTTER SPEED IS TOO SLOW TO FULLY FREEZE A MOVING OBJECT'S IMAGE, AN INTERESTING *BLURRING* EFFECT OCCURS.

A CAR GOING AT *60 MPH* MIGHT LOOK LIKE *THIS*.

*BUT* IF THE CAMERA MOVES *WITH* THE MOVING OBJECT, THAT OBJECT WILL REMAIN *FOCUSED* WHILE THE *BACKGROUND* WILL NOW BE *STREAKED*.

*AMERICAN* COMICS ARTISTS TOOK LITTLE OR NO INTEREST IN THIS KIND OF *PHOTOGRAPHIC TRICKERY*.

AND IN *EUROPE* WHERE MOTION LINES WERE USED ONLY *SPARINGLY*, IT WAS LIKEWISE IGNORED.

BUT IN *JAPAN*, ONCE AGAIN, A VERY *DIFFERENT* COMICS CULTURE EMBRACED THIS VERY DIFFERENT CONCEPT OF MOTION AS *THEIR OWN!*

IN A MEDIUM WHERE TIME AND SPACE *MERGE*--

--THE STORYTELLER HAS SOME UNUSUAL TOOLS AT HIS/HER DISPOSAL--

--SUCH AS THE *POLYPTYCH*, WHERE A MOVING FIGURE OR FIGURES--

--IS IMPOSED OVER A *CONTINUOUS BACKGROUND.*

IN COMICS, *COMPOSITION* FOLLOWS A VERY DIFFERENT SET OF RULES THAN IN MOST *GRAPHIC ARTS.*

BY INTRODUCING *TIME* INTO THE EQUATION, COMICS ARTISTS ARE ARRANGING THE PAGE IN WAYS NOT ALWAYS CONDUCIVE TO TRADITIONAL PICTURE-MAKING.

HERE, THE COMPOSITION OF THE *PICTURE* IS JOINED BY THE COMPOSITION OF *CHANGE*, THE COMPOSITION OF *DRAMA*--

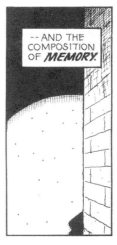

-- AND THE COMPOSITION OF *MEMORY.*

IF THE COMPOSITION OF A SINGLE PANEL IS TRULY *"PERFECT,"* DOESN'T THAT IMPLY THAT IT CAN--OR EVEN SHOULD--STAND *ALONE?*

THE *NATURAL* WORLD CREATES *GREAT BEAUTY* EVERY DAY, YET THE ONLY RULES OF COMPOSITION IT FOLLOWS ARE THOSE OF *FUNCTION* AND *CHANCE.*

COMICS, AT ITS BEST, SHOULD DO NO LESS.

AS WE'VE SEEN, THE INTERACTION OF *TIME* AND *COMICS* GENERALLY LEADS US TO ONE OF TWO SUBJECTS: *SOUND* OR *MOTION.*

SOUND BREAKS DOWN INTO *TWO SUBSETS*: *WORD BALLOONS* AND *SOUND EFFECTS.*

BOTH TYPES ADD TO THE *DURATION* OF A PANEL, PARTIALLY THROUGH THE NATURE OF SOUND *ITSELF* AND BY INTRODUCING ISSUES OF *ACTION* AND *REACTION.*

MOTION ALSO BREAKS DOWN INTO TWO SUBSETS. THE *FIRST* TYPE-- PANEL-TO-PANEL *CLOSURE* -- WAS IMPORTANT ENOUGH TO MERIT ITS OWN *CHAPTER.*

THE *OTHER* TYPE -- MOTION *WITHIN* PANELS -- CAN BE *FURTHER* DIVIDED INTO SEVERAL DISTINCT *STYLES.* I'VE COVERED THE ONES *I* KNOW, BUT THERE MAY BE MANY *OTHERS*. TIME WILL TELL.

THE WORKINGS OF *TIME IN COMICS* SHOULD BE AS SIMPLE AS--

ONE-- --TWO-- --THREE--

--BUT THEY'RE *NOT.*

TICK TICK TICK

# 51. [Introduction]
# Surveillance and Capture
## Two Models of Privacy

The police get search warrants to allow them to gather information about the people they suspect of wrongdoing—at least, on TV shows like *Law and Order*. If the judge doesn't think they have enough reason to suspect the person, the request for a warrant is denied. In a dystopia, however—the canonical example is that of *1984*—there is total surveillance. Information is gathered about everyone, and the analysis of this information is used to decide who to suspect. Visions of total surveillance have often been dismissed as pure fantasy. Enzensberger's essay (◊18) presents the standard objection: "The monitoring of all telephone conversations, for instance, postulates an apparatus which would need to be *n* times more extensive and more complicated than that of the present telephone system. A censor's office, which carried out its work extensively, would of necessity become the largest branch of industry in its society."

Michel Foucault's influential concept of *panopticism* presents a scenario in which this is not the case. Panopticism gets its name from a thought experiment about prison design from a time before electronic surveillance. In the *panopticon*, conceived by Jeremy Bentham, the prison's guards sit in a central tower, ringed by a building containing cells. The cells are constructed so that light shines through them, toward the tower. This "backlights" the inmates in their individual cells, making each prisoner's every move visible to a guard in the tower. The tower is constructed so that prisoners can never tell if they are being watched. As Foucault writes, "the major effect of the Panopticon" is "to induce in the inmate a state of conscious and permanent visibility that assures the automatic functioning of power. So to arrange things that the surveillance is permanent in its effects, even if it is discontinuous in its action; that the perfection of power should tend to render its actual exercise unnecessary; that this architectural apparatus should be a machine for creating and sustaining a power relation independent of the person who exercises it; in short, that the inmates should be caught up in a power situation of which they are themselves the bearers" (201). The inmates know that they may be monitored at any time, so they will act at all times as though they are being monitored, becoming their own surveillance.

This *surveillance model* of privacy, especially in the terminology of Foucault's panopticon, has been the dominant model for most discourse about privacy in the new media field. This model fails to highlight certain aspects of the technical elements of new media—glossing over ways in which the institutional practices of computer system design may be antithetical to privacy, as well as ways that the tools of computer science may be able to provide effective privacy-enhancing technologies.

In the essay reprinted here, Phil Agre grapples with the questions of institutional practice, presenting a different metaphor for privacy, the *capture model*, drawn from an awareness of the current methods of computer systems design. Following the standard computer science practices in order to design or deploy a new media system that captures (collects through effort) information about its use, privacy considerations inevitably arise. Agre also demonstrates that looking through the lens of capture can show us ways in which our activities are themselves restructured. Just as the inmate of the panopticon changes his behavior, internalizing his surveillance, so the "informated organization" internalizes capture—reordering behavior so that it is more amenable to capture models (which were likely developed under the fiction that they transparently represented the prior state of behavior).

◊18
259

The Web's opportunities for creative self-surveillance have not been overlooked by the owners of autopanoptic Web cams, many of whom have been happy to broadcast video of their working and Web-surfing selves to the world.

The capture of private information is accelerating as computing becomes ever more integrated with our life processes and spaces, whether in the guise of Web forms, swipe cards, or the implanting of computers and tracking devices under the rubric of "ubiquitous computing." For this integration to be effective, the computer must "know" about the situation into which it is integrated. That is, the computer system must be designed to contain a model of the activities taking place. The standard computer systems design methodology is to analyze these processes at ever more fine-grained levels of detail. In the capture model, the more detailed the information, the more computational processes can analyze and augment the activity, and therefore the more potentially fruitful the results of introducing computing into the situation. The information provided through capture in systems development may have quite positive results, and—as is not the case with the surveillance model—is seldom considered as harmful to the party whose information is captured.

In a further difference from the surveillance model, which imagines the results of all information collection destined for the central repository of a "Big Brother," the capture model understands information to go in many directions, and for many purposes. A delivery service may capture information about drivers, handlers, senders, receivers, the packages that pass through their hands, and the vehicles in which they are transported. A bank may capture information about tellers, borrowers, depositors, loan officers, and the money that (virtually) passes through their hands. An individual may use a handheld computer and personal information management (PIM) software to organize and categorize interactions with work, family, and friends. The capture model helps to explain, more clearly than a surveillance concept might, how the gathering of such information has benefits as well as privacy implications and work-restructuring implications, even if the individual in question is not continually under observation. A delivery driver may also use PIM software to schedule a deposit of money at the bank, and the three "captured" events (vehicle movement, PIM task completion, bank account activity) will not immediately be correlated, because the three pieces of information do not initially exist in the same context. Increasing correlation of this sort is, however, an acknowledged corporate goal.

Controversies over Web site cookies are one topic that has highlighted how the new media environment is filled with corporate attempts to build profiles of customers and other visitors from captured data—which are then used to target-market, and are sold and traded. Such tracking has generally been discussed in terms of "surveillance-style" monitoring of shopping activity. Web users aren't particularly happy about the situation, considered either way. Unlike many capture subjects discussed by Agre, neither users nor their employers see these actions, whether viewed as capture or surveillance, to be particularly beneficial. For example, the company DoubleClick received strong protest in response to its public plans to merge a large consumer database it had purchased with the information it has collected by serving advertisements (and cookies) on many Web sites. Such practices, however, are quietly continuing. The issue is hard to understand in terms of the "Big Brother" surveillance of *1984* or the self-surveillance encouraged by the panoptic model. It can be seen, instead, as the organization of personal information as a commodity. As Roger Clarke and others have explicated, such organization is objectionable not simply because we don't like calls from telemarketers, or because we like to keep some things about ourselves to ourselves. It is also objectionable because of the way we exist as social beings—managing our personae in the public world by deciding what to disclose, and to whom. Cookies don't simply threaten the security of our credit card data, they also compromise our ability to manage how we present and define ourselves.

Organizations such as the NSA acquire vast amounts of information about our society. The Echelon system, as the ACLU's *Echelon Watch* reports, monitors "as many as 3 billion communications everyday, including phone calls, e-mail messages, Internet downloads, [and] satellite transmissions" in the United States, the United Kingdom, Canada, Australia, and New Zealand. After such data is collected it is scanned for unusual flows, pre-defined keywords, or emergent patterns. The information found is used not only against targets chosen in advance (which reportedly include

Agre's description of the capture model greatly contributes to understanding privacy issues, but as he emphasizes in this selection, the capture model does not render surveillance an outmoded idea. Different scenarios with implications for privacy are now playing out—some best understood through the surveillance model and some best understood as capture—in the use and development of new media.

suspected terrorists and international charities, as well as foreign companies who are bidding for business against domestic ones), but also to *identify new suspects*. When "panopticism" is used to refer to this phenomenon, it is no longer referring to the knowledge of possible surveillance that leads to self-surveillance. It is *also* referring to attempts to actually create the total surveillance state of *1984*. While Enzensberger argued that such a total collapse of privacy was impossible, he made this argument from the perspective of human surveillance, writing before it was practical to employ computer analysis for processing massive amounts of intercepted communications.

A 1997 collection edited by Agre and Marc Rotenberg takes up the question of where privacy is headed in the online era. Privacy-enhancing technologies are one important area of development. For example, the widespread use of strong cryptography is one way of enhancing privacy—not because it would be strong enough to prevent the NSA or its counterparts from accessing the contents of a message in which they were particularly interested, but because their access would require the use of a certain amount of computer power, enough to make the continual monitoring of all intercepted messages, suspect or not, impractical.

Cryptography has been a primary example of how computers are not, as they have sometimes been characterized in the humanities, a force somehow by their design aligned with surveillance and authoritarianism. In the 1990s, as pro-cryptography sentiment grew, many governments actively opposed the use of strong cryptography by their citizens, at the least demanding "key escrow" or other measures to aid state surveillance. But as electronic commerce became increasingly important to visions of future economic growth, and as it became clear that only strong encryption would lead to consumers feeling comfortable about sending credit card data over the Internet, these government objections diminished.

The availability of cryptography is only an initial, tentative step. Encrypted email is now rare enough to draw attention, and infrequent enough for the government to open and search in its entirety, if it cares to. Only once the use of cryptography for new media communications has become as standard as the use of envelopes for paper communications will the easy ability of the government to violate privacy—whether considered as surveillance or capture—cease to hang over every electronic movement and data exchange. What will remain will be continual capture of private data by mega-corporations, tracking employees, customers, and passersby though every glimpse, transaction, and workplace activity. Already, corporations may monitor all casual conversation by users that passes through their software, and even do so under the shroud of legality. As of this writing, the Microsoft Instant Messenger license agreement specifies that all communications in that system are the property of Microsoft; the company may choose to do anything it likes with them, including publishing them with attribution. In space, perhaps, no one can hear you scream. But in cyberspace, someone—perhaps the richest man on the planet—can indeed hear you, whether you scream, cry, or whisper, even in a "private" conversation.

—NWF

Further Reading

Agre, Philip E., and Marc Rotenberg, eds. *Technology and Privacy: The New Landscape.* Cambridge: MIT Press, 1997.

Agre, Philip E. *Computation and Human Experience.* Cambridge University Press, 1997.

Cornford, James. "The Virtual University Is . . . the University Made Concrete?," *Information, Communication, and Society,* 3(4):508–525, 2001.

Clarke, Roger. "The Digital Persona and Its Application to Data Surveillance." *Information Society* 10(2):77–92. April–June 1994.

Foucault, Michel. "Panopticism," from *Discipline and Punish: The Birth of the Prison,* trans. by Alan Sheridan. New York: Pantheon, 1977. From the French *Surveiller et Punir: Naissance de la Prison,* 1975.

Zuboff, Soshana. "Panoptic Power and the Social Text," *In the Age of the Smart Machine: The Future of Work and Power,* 362–386. New York: Basic Books, 1988.

Original Publication
*Information Society* 10(2):101–127. April–June 1994.

# Surveillance and Capture

## Two Models of Privacy

Philip E. Agre

## 1 Introduction

Ideas about privacy are, among other things, cultural phenomena. They are shaped through historical experience, they condition perceptions of newly arising phenomena, and they are reproduced or transformed in all of the same complicated ways as other elements of culture. Cultural ideas about privacy are particularly significant right now, given the rapid emergence of new technologies and new policy issues around privacy. In this paper I propose to contrast two cultural models of privacy:

> The "surveillance model," currently dominant in the public discourse of at least the English-speaking world, is built upon visual metaphors and derives from historical experiences of secret police surveillance.

> A less familiar alternative, the "capture model," has manifested itself principally in the practices of information technologists; it is built upon linguistic metaphors and takes as its prototype the deliberate reorganization of industrial work activities to allow computers to track them in real time.

These two models are not mutually exclusive. By emphasizing the contrasts between them, I hope to make evident their contingent nature. Privacy issues take different forms in different institutional settings and historical periods, and no single model suffices to fully characterize all of the forms that privacy issues can take.

> Section 2 motivates this study by discussing a set of emerging technologies for tracking people and materials. Consideration of these technologies within existing concepts of privacy reveals certain previously unfocalized elements, most particularly the reorganization of activity to accommodate the tracking process.

Section 3 takes up this observation more formally by introducing and defining the surveillance model and the capture model of privacy issues.

Section 4 discusses the capture model in more depth, relating it to deeply ingrained aspects of applied computing as a professional practice. It introduces the concept of a "grammar of action" and provides several examples. It then describes an idealized five-stage cycle for the development of capture systems and reflects on certain computer-supported cooperative work systems in this light.

Section 5 describes some trade-offs inherent in the concept of capture, and consequently in the very design of computer systems as they are currently understood.

Section 6 introduces the general question of capture as a social phenomenon, insisting that capture be studied against the background of the larger institutional dynamics in which it is embedded.

Section 7 offers a provisional analysis of the political economy of capture, starting with a discussion of the role of information technology in reducing economic transaction costs.

Section 8 concludes by returning to the comparison between the surveillance and capture models and assessing some of the possible futures to which they point.

## 2 Tracking

This reexamination of privacy was originally motivated by the emergence of new technologies for the tracking of people, automobiles, packages, materials, and so forth. In the "active badge" project at Olivetti (Want *et al.* 1992) and Xerox (Weiser 1993), for example, employees wear on their clothing a black plastic rectangle called a "badge" that uses infrared light to indicate its location to devices mounted on walls and ceilings, which in turn are connected to a database. Several experiments have explored various uses of the badges, for example to determine a colleague's location in the building or to automatically direct a given individual's calls to the physically closest telephone. This research has been viewed as a step toward "ubiquitous computing," in which computational machinery is distributed throughout the physical environment (e.g., Gold 1993). For example, several groups (Elrod *et al.* 1993, Mill *et al.* 1992) are creating "smart buildings" in which climate controls are integrated with networked digital systems.

Active badges may be the best-known tracking technology, but they are hardly unique. Other tracking schemes involve radio-frequency beacons installed on materials in manufacturing and distribution (Fales 1992, Sabetti 1993). And the trade press has reported on numerous implementations of tracking systems:

> • UPS uses bar-codes and a customized electronic clipboard to track the movements of packages; when a package is delivered, the clipboard digitally records the recipient's signature and sends information about the package's status to a central computer through a nationwide cellular telephone network (Duffy 1993, Eckerson 1991).

> • The Canadian Ministry of Transportation uses a wireless packet radio network and a national database to keep track of commercial vehicles in Toronto. Police and inspectors use information provided by the system to check drivers' speed and watch for unlicensed vehicles, and they can call up a complete history of any vehicle in a few seconds (Loudermilk 1993).

> • A trucking firm called Americana Inc. uses wireless communications and the US military's Global Positioning System (GPS) to allow dispatchers to automatically track its trucks. Each truck carries an Apple Macintosh that periodically takes a reading from a GPS device and sends it to headquarters by electronic mail (Lawton 1992).

> • Computer networks are increasingly making possible automatic real-time data collection and analysis for large-scale accounting and control systems, and this development is revolutionizing (if belatedly) the field of management accounting (Johnson and Kaplan 1987: 5–6 ff.).

> • A system called VoiceFrame is used to monitor people who have been convicted of crimes. Each offender wears a bracelet that notifies the authorities if it passes outside a certain boundary (Leibowitz 1992).

> • In a wide range of "virtual reality" and "telepresence" systems, some mechanism continually informs a computer about the locations of certain parts of a person's body. The locations might be computed and transmitted by devices that are physically attached to the relevant body parts, or they might be computed

by a stationary device that observes the body's motion, perhaps through a video camera (Meyer, Applewhite, and Biocca 1992).

> • One division of NCR has integrated its just-in-time manufacturing systems with a plant-wide system of bar-code readers. The status of each job is available from computer terminals throughout the organization (Anonymous 1990).

> • Fast food chains are rapidly integrating their operations through point-of-sale (POS) terminals and bookkeeping systems for tracking individual stores' activities by interconnecting their local computers with mainframes at headquarters, which performs intensive analysis of the resulting data (McPartlin 1992, Simpson 1989). Items captured and stored in the database include "product mix, sales statistics, labor information, food costs," "bank deposits, cash register information, sales totals, average order amounts at different points in the day," and customer traffic (Baum 1992). Most such systems have replaced branch managers' functions with centralized control (Walton 1989: 42 ff.), a pattern found throughout mass retailing (Smith 1988).

> • Numerous projects are currently building systems for "design rationale capture" (DRC) (Carroll and Moran 1991). The idea is that design changes in large engineering projects are often made difficult by inadequate institutional memory about the reasoning behind previous design decisions. A DRC system fills this gap by allowing designers to maintain a running account of their reasoning during the design process, using a taxonomy of types of reasoning and a complex system of datastructures for representing them all. This material is then stored for later reference. For Carroll (1992), design rationale capture is the culmination of an underlying logic of computer design activities. Design practice, he argues, can be viewed as reifying a particular work practice, and design rationale capture similarly involves the reification of the design process itself, with all of its elements of hermeneutic inquiry.

> • Several vendors have built software systems for tracking job applicants through the whole application and interview process. The systems can keep track of each individual's paperwork, generate routine letters, and maintain a database of applicants that can be searched in a wide variety of ways, including generating documents for affirmative action

reporting and the like. Employees participating in the hiring process update the database upon each step of the process (Romei 1991).

• In Thailand, the Ministry of the Interior is developing a centralized database to maintain information on each of the country's citizens. Each individual will have a unique identification number recorded on a card with a magnetic strip (Hoffman 1990).

The cases vary among themselves in several ways. Although each system keeps track of significant changes in a tracked entity's state, the nature of these changes varies. In some cases the changes are simply changes in physical location, reckoned against some kind of stationary coordinate grid; the system may well place some kind of interpretation on these locations, perhaps relative to a street map. In other cases the changes are defined in institutional terms, for example whether a package has been formally received or whether someone has been formally offered or turned down for a job. In the former case, the term "tracking" takes on a more literal sense of tracking through space. In the latter case, the term "tracking" is a metaphor; the entity in question traces a trajectory through a more abstract space which might have numerous "dimensions."

One might further distinguish between systems that track human beings and systems that track physical objects. Such a distinction would be misleading, though. Systems are indeed found at each extreme—for example radio transmitters attached to shipping crates or fastened to prisoners' limbs. But many of the systems track both people and objects, and others track objects as stand-ins for people. A system that tracks people by means of identification cards, for example, is really tracking the cards; any connection between the card and person will have to be made in some other way, such as an official or supervisor checking each individual's appearance against a photograph upon each significant event. Similarly, a system that tracks trucks can generally depend on a stable correspondence, at least over short periods, between trucks and their drivers.

Systems that track physical objects, for their part, vary considerably in the means by which they detect significant state changes. Some depend on complex schemes for reckoning absolute or relative location; these systems may only require an approximate location, and thus may only receive a periodic update from a location measuring device.

Other systems depend on a distributed system of passive sensors. Yet others might involve sensors that actively seek out the entities being tracked. But a large number of systems involve human intervention: a human being executes some physical action that closes a causal chain between the tracked entity and the centralized system, thereby signifying that such-and-such a state-change has taken place.

In general, the various tracking systems vary widely in the way they divide their computational labor between the moving entity, some stationary computer system, and various human or mechanical intermediaries. A GPS device, for example, performs all of the necessary computation at the location of the object being tracked. At another extreme, a tracking system might employ an algorithm to locate the tracked entity within each successive video image it receives from a stationary camera. And in the middle ground between these extremes lie numerous schemes for splitting the burden of tracking, for example by placing bar codes or LEDs on the entity being tracked, or by restricting the entity's movements so that it necessarily comes into contact with relatively simple sensors (Udoka 1991). (For a general treatment of this trade-off in the design of robots, see Donald (forthcoming).)

Despite all of these variations, the various tracking systems have a great deal in common. In each case, some entity changes state, a computer internally represents those states, and certain technical and social means are provided for (intendedly at least) maintaining the correspondence between the representation and the reality. The computer may maintain a centralized database (this is the usual case) or it may be more widely distributed. Each entity has a definite identity that remains stable over time, and if several entities are being tracked then the tracking system has some means of consistently "attaching" a given entity to its corresponding representation. This representation will be expressed within some mathematically definable representation scheme, which is capable of expressing a certain formal space of states of affairs. The computer maintains a representation only of certain aspects of the entity. In particular, the representation scheme recognizes certain specific kinds of changes of state, namely those which correspond to changes in the stored representation. A system for tracking an object's location, for example, should be unaffected by changes in its color; the recognized state-changes will all take the form of transitions from, say, one sequence of coordinates to another. As the entity's corresponding representation changes, records may well be kept of its state transitions, yielding a "history" of its trajectory through time. And this trajectory, of course, can be either literal or metaphorical, depending on what aspects of the entity are represented.

In addition to the continual updating of a representation, each tracking system is capable of closing a causal loop between the entity and the computer. That is, information does not simply flow from the entity to the computer; in addition, certain human or mechanical agents, faced with a given entity in a prescribed type of situation, are capable of determining its identity and "calling up" the information in its "file." (These agents' activities may, of course, be tracked as well.) Again, the causal means that provide for this loop-closing vary widely, from bar codes to identification cards to license plates to keys to paperwork of all sorts, and the computational division of labor among the entity, agent, central computer, and so forth varies widely as well.

Tracking systems like these can obviously be used for good or ill. Other things being equal, it is probably a good idea to track hazardous materials, government money, and so forth. At the same time, research on computers and privacy has emphasized the fear, often perfectly justified, that the accumulated information about a tracked person might be used for abusive purposes, for example stalking by a would-be assailant, irresponsible publication of embarrassing facts, or oppressively detailed control of work activities. In particular, this research has focused on the element of data-collection; its question is what becomes of the data once it is collected. Yet tracking schemes have another side: the practical arrangements through which the data is collected in the first place, including the arrangements that make human activities and physical processes trackable. As human activities become intertwined with the mechanisms of computerized tracking, the notion of human interactions with a "computer"—understood as a discrete, physically localized entity—begins to lose its force; in its place we encounter activity-systems that are .thoroughly integrated with distributed computational processes. It is this deeper implication of tracking that forms the central motivation for this paper.

## 3 Surveillance and capture

Let us, then, formally introduce the surveillance model and the capture model of privacy issues. A "model," for present purposes, is a way of looking at things; specifically, it is a set of metaphors. Distinct models do not divide the world's sociotechnical phenomena into nonoverlapping classes; instead, they simply point out some potentially significant features of the phenomena—features that may call for more concrete analysis.

The surveillance model has five components:

> (1) visual metaphors, as in Orwell's "Big Brother is watching you" or Bentham's Panopticon;
>
> (2) the assumption that this "watching" is nondisruptive and surreptitious (except perhaps when going astray or issuing a threat);
>
> (3) territorial metaphors, as in the "invasion" of a "private" personal space, prototypically the family home, marked out by "rights" and the opposition between "coercion" and "consent";
>
> (4) centralized orchestration by means of a bureaucracy with a unified set of "files"; and
>
> (5) identification with the state, and in particular with consciously planned-out malevolent aims of a specifically political nature.

When stated in this way, it becomes evident that the surveillance model is a cultural phenomenon. Although its earliest genealogy deserves further research, its modern history is clearly rooted in the historical experience of secret police organizations and their networks of listening devices and informers, most prominently in the totalitarian states of Nazi Germany and the Soviet Union, and to a lesser but still significant extent in the United States. George Orwell's *1984* gave these symbols their most vivid literary form, but the cultural legacy of this history is also evident in, for example, the unpleasant connotations associated with certain uses of a word like "files." Moreover, philosophers and cultural critics have generally held vision and visual metaphors in low esteem through much of this century, as Jay (1993) has documented in the case of France. In any case, it is important to keep in mind that the surveillance model is a system of metaphors; in applying the surveillance model to a private company, for example, one is simply *likening* it to a malevolent state organization, and it will be important to explore the limits of this comparison.

The surveillance model is by far the most prevalent in the literature on privacy. It is found, for example, in definitions of privacy in terms of the right to be left alone, or in concerns over information being used for unintended purposes. Indeed, the vast majority of the existing literature on computers and privacy employs the surveillance model without critically analyzing it or considering alternatives, indexing it through the term "surveillance" or references to "Big Brother" and other themes from Orwell (Burnham 1983, Clarke 1989, *The Economist* 1993, Flaherty 1989, Flynn 1993, Gandy 1993, Larson 1992, Piller 1993, Rabel 1993, Robins and Webster 1988, Rule 1974, Smith 1979, Ware 1993). My point is not that this work is wrong, but rather that alternative models might draw different, but equally important, elements into the foreground.

One such alternative metaphor-system is the capture model. In naming this model, I have employed a common term of art among computing people, the verb "to capture." Computationalists' discourse rarely brings to the surface the connotations of violence in the metaphor of "capture"; captured information is not spoken of as fleeing, escaping, or resenting its imprisonment. The term has two uses. The first and most frequent refers to a computer system's (figurative) act of acquiring certain data as input, whether from a human operator or from an electronic or electromechanical device. Thus one might refer to a cash register in a fast-food restaurant as "capturing" a patron's order, the implication being that the information is not simply used on the spot, but is also passed along to a database. The second use of "capture," which is more common in artificial intelligence research, refers to a representation scheme's ability to fully, accurately, or "cleanly" express particular semantic notions or distinctions, without reference to the actual taking-in of data. Thus one might refer to the object classes of an object-oriented computer program as "capturing" the distinction between standing orders and particular occasions on which goods are delivered. This ambiguity between an epistemological idea (acquiring the data) and an ontological idea (modeling the reality it reflects) is remarkably common in the vocabulary of computing. (AI researchers, for example, apply the word "epistemological" in the *second* sense of "capture," not the first.)

The capture model can be contrasted point-by-point with the surveillance model. It comprises:

(1) linguistic metaphors for human activities, assimilating them to the constructs of a computer system's representation languages;

(2) the assumption that the linguistic "parsing" of human activities involves active intervention in and reorganization of those activities;

(3) structural metaphors; the captured activity is figuratively assembled from a "catalog" of parts provided as part of its institutional setting;

(4) decentralized and heterogeneous organization; the process is normally conducted within particular, local practices which involve people in the workings of larger social formations; and

(5) the driving aims are not political but philosophical, as activity is reconstructed through assimilation to a transcendent ("virtual") order of mathematical formalism.

Since the capture model is less familiar than the surveillance model, the next four sections will be devoted to explaining it. The capture model, like the surveillance model, is a metaphor-system and not a literal description. It can, for example, be applied equally well to public or private organizations (or to the many activity-systems that cross the increasingly permeable boundaries between these two domains), although my analysis will focus on workplace settings. It is important to make clear, with regard to point (5), that the capture model is a philosophical metaphor in the same sense as the surveillance model is a political metaphor. The actual institutional sites to which the capture model might be applied presumably have their political aspects; the point is simply that the capture model suggests using certain philosophical projects as models for understanding the activities in these sites.

The two sets of metaphors have significantly different origins. Whereas the surveillance model originates in the classically political sphere of state action, the capture model has deep roots in the practical application of computer systems. As such, technical developments such as the tracking schemes described in Section 2 do not bring the capture model into existence; rather, they express in a clear way something that has long been implicit in applied computer work, whether or not its relevance to privacy issues has been recognized.

## 4 Grammars of action

Computers are frequently said to store and transmit "information." The term, though, conceals a significant ambiguity. On one hand, information can be defined (as per Shannon and Weaver) as a purely mathematical measure of information and information-carrying capacity, without regard for the content. On the other hand, information is information also *about* something. (A similar point applies to customary uses of the term "data.") Although it makes sense to speak of false information (for example, in a faulty credit database), the tacit assumption is most commonly that information is true—that it corresponds in some transparent way to certain people, places, and things in the world. This assumption does not, strictly speaking, derive from any inherent property of computers. It is, rather, a theory of representation that is embedded in the way that computers have customarily been used.

To see this, consider a textbook of information management such as Martin (1989). Martin's goal is to instruct MIS managers on the principled construction of information systems, and specifically on the principled selection of what ought to be represented. In doing this, he describes an ontology of entities and relations and functions and activities, along with a set of procedures for systematically representing the existing organization in these terms. Having prepared this self-representation, the next step is to implement it on a computer. The purpose of this computer will be to *model* the organization—that is, to maintain a set of datastructures that mirror the day-to-day activities of the organization's members. In philosophical terms, the resulting computer will embody a correspondence theory of representation: the machine's internal states will be "true" (so far as this theory is concerned) because they maintain a certain fixed set of relation-preserving mappings to the external states of affairs in the world.

The practice of constructing systematic representations of organizational activities is not at all new, of course, nor is it inherently tied to computer systems development. Indeed, Martin emphasizes that it can be valuable in itself, even without any computers being installed, simply for the redundancies and other inefficient patterns of activity it can bring to management's notice. As such, it clearly stands in a line of descent that includes the elaborate representational schemes of industrial time and motion studies (Gilbreth 1912, Holmes 1938) and other forms of systematic rationalization of work activities (Lichtner 1924). When applied to the tracking of organizational processes, of course, these schemes relied heavily on paperwork (Yates 1989) or on the intrinsic controls built into the movements of machinery (Edwards 1979).

Besides the creation of tracking systems, systematic activity-mapping schemes have also been applied to the automation of activities. Couger (1973), for example, surveys a variety of such schemes from the early days of computing, each based on tracing the flows of information within a business. A map of these information-flows, and of the information-processing operations that take place along the way, could be treated as a blueprint for a computer program that automated those same operations.

Yet another analogous representation practice is found in research on "knowledge representation" in the field of artificial intelligence. Several of the entity-relationship diagrams in Martin (1989: 168 ff.) resemble nothing so much as the "semantic networks" employed in AI knowledge representation research (Brachman and Levesque 1985). AI researchers, more than their counterparts in other kinds of applied computer science, set about explicitly searching for ontological systems that would allow a computer to represent cleanly and accurately a wide range of human knowledge—including knowledge about human activities and social organizations.

Despite their varied surface forms, these lines of research together constitute a coherent genealogy—a tradition of applied representational work that has informed organizational practice the world over. Its underlying approach is organized and reproduced largely through its practical conduct: its methods, its language, its paradigms of good practice, its training regimens, and so forth. Although it has become deeply identified with organizational applications of information technology, it is (at least in principle) neither a necessary nor a sufficient condition for the use of computers. At the same time, it has grown such deep roots in computational practice that it is hard to imagine what any alternative computational practice would be like.

Among the many attributes shared by these representation schemes, perhaps the most significant for present purposes is their use of linguistic metaphors: they each employ formal "languages" for representing human activities. Human activity is thus effectively treated as a kind of language itself, for which a good representation scheme provides an accurate grammar. This grammar specifies a set of unitary actions—the "words" or "lexical items" of action, which AI people call "primitives" and which Quinn (1993: 103–109 ff.) calls "minimum replicable units." It also specifies certain means by which actions might be compounded—most commonly by arranging them into a sequence, although various languages provide more sophisticated means of combination (for example, conditional and iterated sequences).

These *grammars of action* are central to the capture model. Grammars of action have many and varied manifestations.

- Accounting systems, for example, are based on grammars of action; in order to keep a set of books, it is necessary to organize one's financial activities with a view to categorizing every move as one of the action-types that one's particular accounting scheme recognizes.

- Telemarketers and many types of telephone-based customer service personnel employ scripts that are based on a set of standard moves, many of whose names are drawn from the structured patter of sales people (e.g., "assumptive close"). Some grammars of sales interaction are extraordinarily complex (Miller and Heiman 1987).

- A limited-access highway (such as the roads in the American interstate highway system) enforces, through both physical and legal means, a simple grammar of action whose elements are entrances, discrete continuous segments of traveled roadway, and exits. Toll-collection systems for such roads often employ a keypunch card which contains a table for mapping "grammatical" trips to collectible tolls.

- The user interfaces of many (if not all) computers are readily understood as supplying their users with grammars of action. The permissible unitary actions are ASCII keystrokes, menu selections, shell commands, and so forth. Some projects have attempted to formalize the interaction-patterns discovered in empirical study of human conversations, and then to build computer programs that can engage in these patterns (Luff, Gilbert, and Frohlich 1990).

- Waiters in large restaurants frequently employ an automated system for passing orders to the kitchen and keeping track of tabs (Rule and Attewell 1989, Quinn 1992: 142–145). The waiter might interact with the system by swiping a card through a reader on the cash register and entering commands on a touch-sensitive display.

- "Enterprise integration" (EI) systems draw an organization's computer systems together on a global network with a standardized set of communications protocols and data models. One proposal for an EI architecture (Pan and Tenenbaum 1991) breaks an organization's work activities down into "tasks," each represented within a common language, and automatically evaluates which tasks should be assigned to computational "agents" and which should be assigned to human workers.

What matters in each case is not the sequences of "inputs" to or "outputs" from a given machine, but rather the ways in which human activities have been structured. The capture model describes the situation that results when grammars of action are imposed upon human activities, and when the newly reorganized activities are represented by computers in real time. It is convenient to subdivide this process into a five-stage cycle. This division is, of course, a great oversimplification: the phases frequently operate concurrently, advances in one phase may force revision of the work done in an earlier phase, and work in each stage draws on a wide range of sociotechnical advances not necessarily related to the other stages.

**Analysis.** Somebody studies an existing form of activity and identifies its fundamental units in terms of some ontology (e.g., entities, relations, functions, primitive actions, and so forth). This ontology might draw on the participants' terms for things, or it might not. Programming languages and systems analysis methodologies frequently supply basic ontologies (objects, variables, relations) upon which domain-specific ontologies can be built. The resulting ontologies are sometimes standardized across whole institutions, industries, or markets.

**Articulation.** Somebody articulates a grammar of the ways in which those units can be strung together to form actual sensible stretches of activity. This process can be complicated, and it often requires revision of the preceding ontological analysis. It is typically guided by an almost aesthetic criterion of obtaining a complete, closed, formally specified picture of the activity.

**Imposition.** The resulting grammar is then given a normative force. The people who engage in the articulated activity are somehow induced to organize their actions so that they are readily "parseable" in terms of the grammar. The "somehow" is typically both social (explicit procedures backed up by certain relations of authority) and technical (whether through machinery or simply through physical barriers); participants in the activity may or may not participate in the process and may or may not resist it. Institutions frequently impose grammars on activities for reasons other than real-time capture—for example, for security, efficiency, protection from liability, and simple control.

**Instrumentation.** Social and technical means are provided, whether through paperwork or machinery, and potentially with a complex division of labor, for maintaining a running parse of the ongoing activity. This phase may coincide with the imposition phase, or it may follow by years or decades. Afterward, the participants begin, of necessity, to orient their activities toward the capture machinery and its institutional consequences.

**Elaboration.** The captured activity records, which are in economic terms among the products of the reorganized activity, can now be stored, inspected, audited, merged with other records, subjected to statistical analysis, employed as the basis of Pareto optimization, and so forth. Likewise, concurrent computational processes can use captured records to "watch" the ongoing activities for purposes of error detection, advice giving, performance measurement, quality control, and so forth. These additional processes might arise simultaneously with the instrumentation phase, or they may accumulate long afterward.

This cycle is normally attended by a kind of mythology, according to which the newly constructed grammar of action has not been "invented" but "discovered." The activity in question, in other words, is said to have *already* been organized according to the grammar. Of course this is not wholly false; imposing a grammar that radically and arbitrarily misrepresents the activity will probably lead to calamity. But even when a grammar of action is relatively "good" in this sense, its imposition will generally require hard work, both for the people who are imposing the grammar and the people upon whom the grammar is imposed. The work of these latter participants consists in part of finding ways to organize one's activities, even in the tricky and exceptional cases, so that they can be parsed within such-and-such a vocabulary of discrete units.

Indeed, it is crucial to appreciate the senses in which the imposition and instrumentation phases constitute a reorganization of the existing activity, as opposed to simply a representation of it. Let us distinguish eight such senses, in increasing order of significance for the current argument:

(1) The introduction of new technologies, whether they involve the capture of activities or not, is frequently the occasion for a wide variety of other kinds of changes to the activity, for example due to extrinsic economic changes (e.g., Iacono and Kling 1987). Indeed technological change is generally inseparable from broader social changes.

(2) The representations constructed in the articulation phase (based to some extent on empirical study of the activity, but mostly on informal speculation and scenario-making) and then in the elaboration phase (based on the newly accumulated database of parsed activity) frequently suggest rearrangements of the activity (Quinn 1992, Taylor 1923). Some of these rearrangements may be designed in part to facilitate the capture process, as in Hammer's (1990: 112) dictum, "Capture information once and at the source."

(3) Grammars of action frequently oversimplify the activities they are intended to represent, if only because the people who articulate the grammars are only superficially acquainted with its actual complexities and the actual social forces that determine its form (Suchman and Jordan 1989). The ontology may fail to make enough distinctions, or else whole subcategories of "invisible" activity might go unrepresented. The grammar might impose overly restrictive ordering constraints on the unitary actions, it might neglect the interleaving of distinct forms of activity, or it might mistake prescribed procedures for an accurate descriptive account (or at least a practicable form) of the activity (Suchman 1983). As a result, the participants in the newly instrumented activity will find it necessary to evolve a system of "work-arounds" to keep things going (Gasser 1986).

(4) Grammars of action can be "mistaken" in other ways. Most especially, they can encode a systematically distorted conception of the activity. For example, Kling (1991) argues that extant computer-supported cooperative work (CSCW) systems are based on ontologies that recognize cooperation but

not conflict, and collaboration but not competition (cf. Orlikowski 1993). The imposition of a distorted grammar on an activity can have a wide range of consequences.

(5) When the practical circumstances of an activity are instrumented, the resulting machinery rarely takes its measurements without human cooperation, interpretation, categorization, data entry, report writing, displaying of identification, swiping of cards through readers, aiming of sensors at bar codes, and so forth. The real-time accumulation of data on the activity, in other words, introduces new elements into the activity itself. When these elements are not anticipated in the design, the potential for disruption is great. Medical settings, for example, often report backlogs of unentered data (Hawker 1991, Walton 1989: 20).

(6) The people whose activities are being captured will probably adjust their conduct based on their understanding of what will become of the data and what this entails for their own lives. For example, they might work faster, choose easier (or otherwise advantageous) tasks, conduct certain aspects of the activity out of the reach of the instrumentation, change course depending on patterns that might emerge from already-captured data, and so on. In general, as Suchman (1992) suggests, they will maintain an orientation to the "image" they project to whoever is making use of the captured information, be it a boss, a colleague, an auditor, a regulatory agency, an insurance company, or whatever. On Suchman's analysis, the compliance between system records and ongoing events is an interpreted or negotiated correspondence rather than a literal one. The relation of records to events involves organization members' judgement calls about what is a close enough fit "for all practical purposes." Thus, inasmuch as the captured actions are addressed to an "audience" via computer-mediated representation, they take on a "performative" quality (cf. Dourish 1993) that belies the intendedly objective character of the representational process (cf. Garfinkel 1984 [1967]).

(7) Given this human intervention in the capture process, the process often becomes the site of more overtly political conflicts. The participants may adjust the timing and contents of the various data-capture events to their advantage. They might interpret and categorize events in sympathetic ways, bias

judgement calls in one direction or another, or choose action-sequences that include or exclude certain elements. They might attempt to minimize use of the computer or use tracking data to coerce or influence others in the organization. They might falsify certain information, they might delay entering it, or they might neglect entering it altogether.

(8) The newly introduced system might bring new institutional dynamics, not least because the designers' ontologies and grammars will normally be oblivious to the political dimensions of activity (Kling 1980). These new dynamics might range from manipulation of the institutional procedures around the system's use to lobbying for technical changes to overtly political campaigns to regulate uses of the technology.

The picture that emerges is at odds with the mythology of transparent representation. The phenomena listed in (1) and (2), to be sure, only conflict with the mythology to the extent that the imposition of a grammar cannot be distinguished from the other ways in which activities change. One might argue, moreover, that the phenomena listed in (3) and (4) can be mitigated through more sophisticated analysis and articulation. And the phenomena listed in (5) through (7) can often be mitigated to some degree through increasingly rigid sociotechnical means of instrumentation (an instance of (8)). But no matter how thoroughly the capture process is controlled, it is impossible, short perhaps of total mechanization of a given form of activity, to remove the elements of interpretation, strategy, and institutional dynamics. This is not to say that capture is impossible; to the contrary, numerous impressive examples already exist. The point, rather, is that capture is never purely technical but always *sociotechnical* in nature. If a capture system "works" then what is working is a larger sociopolitical structure, not just a technical system (Bowers 1992). And if the capture process is guided by some notion of the "discovery" of a preexisting grammar, then this notion and its functioning should be understood in political terms as an ideology.

A good example of the five-stage capture cycle is found in the research of Winograd and Flores et al. on CSCW systems. In their original research on The Coordinator (Flores et al. 1988), they made explicit the methodological principle that system design should begin with an ontology that clarifies the underlying structure of existing practices. Although this assertion is far from novel in itself, their contribution was to radicalize it through the application of philosophical concepts (Winograd and Flores 1986). The idea is that a deeper-than-normal ontology can provide a firmer and more accurate basis for system-building. Winograd and Flores take their inspiration for this project from the existential hermeneutics of Martin Heidegger's *Being and Time* (1961 [1927]). Heidegger's project was to employ successive cycles of phenomenological description to uncover successively deeper layers of ontological structure in human experience, eventually yielding some kind of authentic engagement with the ultimate ontological category of Being itself.

For Winograd and Flores, this method promises a kind of ultimate authority to their project of *a priori* clarification (Suchman 1993). Human activities, they argue, go astray when they depart from the essential structures that rigorous phenomenological analysis reveals, and computer-mediated tools can prevent such mistakes by imposing particular grammars of action upon their users. Although this idea is altogether natural within the traditions of computer science, and while Winograd and Flores' philosophy is alert to some of the oversimplifications implicit in conventional computational practices, Heidegger would have been aghast at the idea of formalizing ontological categories in computational (or otherwise mathematical) terms, much less employing machinery to enforce compliance with them.

Winograd and Flores' ontology, moreover, has little to do with Heidegger's, being drawn principally from the quite un-Heideggerian theory of speech acts (Searle 1969). In their design for The Coordinator, they provide a grammar of linguistic action in conventional state-graph notation. Users exchange electronic messages in conducting their work, and they are supposed to label each message with a particular speech act. The system, meanwhile, can capture the speech-act structure of each sequence of interactions. Although some research groups have presented equivocal evaluations of The Coordinator's success in practice (e.g., Bullen and Bennett 1990), it is not my purpose to argue that such systems cannot work. Quite the contrary, I wish to portray The Coordinator and its more sophisticated successors (Marshak 1993, Medina-Mora et al. 1992) as deeply rooted in a social and technical tradition. Although computer-supported cooperative work systems such as The Coordinator require their designers to perform particularly rigorous ontological work in the analysis and articulation phases (cf. Clawson and Bostrom 1993), this work is no different in kind from the generations of systems analysis that have gone before it.

To summarize, the phenomenon of capture is deeply ingrained in the practice of computer system design through a metaphor of human activity as a kind of language. Within this practice, a computer system is made to capture an ongoing activity through the imposition of a grammar of action that has been articulated through a project of empirical and ontological inquiry. Advances in computer science have thus gone hand-in-hand with ontological advances. Furthermore, the phenomenon of capture also underlies the tracking systems discussed in Section 2. Tracking is impossible without a grammar of states and state-changes and the technical means to detect the states (or the state-changes) when they occur. Except in the simplest cases, this will require that the grammar be imposed through one means or another: location tracking devices, paperwork, identity cards, and so forth. The resulting "technology" of tracking is not a simple matter of machinery: it also includes the empirical project of analysis, the ontological project of articulation, and the social project of imposition.

## 5 Capture and functionality

A variety of projects, particularly in the participatory design movement (Schuler and Namioka 1993), have sought alternatives to the engineering strategy of thoroughgoing capture, through schemes that allow people to record information in the form of computerized text (and in other computerized media as well) without imposing any detailed grammar on it. The stored materials can later be retrieved and interpreted by others. Simple electronic mail and hypertext systems work this way, as do certain more sophisticated systems (MacLean, Young, and Moran 1989).

But these systems all participate in a trade-off that goes to the core of computing: a computer—at least as computers are currently understood—can only compute with what it captures; so the less a system captures, the less functionality it can provide to its users. To understand this trade-off, consider the contrast between voice mail and electronic mail. Both media are routinely employed to convey stretches of language from one person to another, as well as a variety of other functions: storing the messages, reviewing them later, replying to them, attaching timestamps and labels to them, and so on. Nonetheless, they capture different aspects of the language: whereas voice mail captures spoken language at the level of sampled frequency spectra, electronic mail captures written language at the level of ASCII keystrokes. Each medium thus has capacities that the other does not: voice mail, unlike e-mail, can transmit singing and languages without Latin orthographies, and e-mail archives, unlike voice mail, can be searched by keyword. Finally, neither medium captures the grammatical structure of the messages it transmits, much less anything about the content of those messages. Thus neither medium can offer features based on automatic recognition of agrammaticality, urgency, or relevance to a given topic. (It may be possible to heuristically *infer* such matters from e-mail messages, but systems for doing so are far from practical at this moment.) Some analogous examples include the contrast between painting and drawing programs, and between ASCII-based text editors and WYSIWYG word processors.

This trade-off is also found in systems for tracking human activities through automatic capture. Simply put, a system can only track what it can capture, and it can only capture information that can be expressed within a grammar of action that has been imposed upon the activity. Numerous systems, including many of the examples in Section 2, reside toward the minimal end of this trade-off since they only track simple position information. Systems like these are not particularly convincing cases of the capture model since they do not usually require much imposition beyond the installation of the tracking instruments themselves. But position tracking is frequently a precursor to more qualitatively complex kinds of capture, for example when positional information is stored along with other events or transactions that might be captured: arrival at a certain destination, crossing a certain boundary, changes in the status of materials or participants, encounters with other participants, and so forth.

The inherent trade-off of computer systems for capturing human activities underlies the most significant technical trend in their ongoing historical development: the tendency toward ever "deeper" articulation and capture of activities. As Quinn (1992: 104 ff.) has put it in the case of businesses in service industries, the "minimum replicable unit" has gotten steadily smaller:

> Early in the life cycle of many service industries, the smallest truly replicable unit seemed to be an individual office, store, or franchise location. Later, as

volume increased, it often became possible for the headquarters to develop and replicate greater efficiencies within locations by managing and measuring critical performance variables at individual departmental, sales counter, activity, or stock-keeping unit (SKU) levels. Then the successful reduction of key activities to their most refined elements allowed McDonald's, Federal Express, Wal-Mart, Citicorp, Mrs. Fields, Pizza Hut, and even the New York Stock Exchange (NYSE) to push the repeatability unit to even smaller "micro management" levels. Replicating precisely measured activity cycles, delivery times, customer query sequences, personal selling approaches, customer data, inventory control patterns, ingredients, freshness and cooking cycles, counter display techniques, cleanliness and maintenance procedures, and so on, in detail became keys to service and financial success. Lapses led to difficulties.

Each step in this process of ontological refinement requires designers to revisit each of the five stages of the capture cycle, formulating ever more refined ontologies and grammars of activity and then imposing, instrumenting, and elaborating these through work reorganization and new technology. The remainder of the paper considers certain aspects of the social organization of this process.

## 6 Capture in society

The previous section has described the capture model largely as something internal to the engineering and scientific traditions of computer work. And indeed, considered simply as a set of ideas, the capture model is very much a creature of computing research and its intellectual genealogy. The systems that result from the application of these ideas, though, are sociotechnical phenomena of considerable magnitude whose analysis requires us to consider numerous factors beyond the ideas themselves. It is far too early to make any final assessment of capture as a social phenomenon. Instead, I would like simply to sketch some general analytical considerations that might be helpful in guiding future research and activism.

Ideas about computers and privacy, Section 2 has argued, are, among other things, cultural phenomena. As such, they routinely structure writing and thinking on the subject without anyone necessarily being aware of them. They do so in many ways: through metaphors and other literary figures, through more or less conventionalized genres of writing, and through habits of selective perception and inquiry. As Kling and Dunlop (1993) have pointed out, analysis of the place of computer technology in society has often been impoverished through a bifurcation into two structurally opposed genres, which they call utopian and anti-utopian. The utopian genre, as its name suggests, emphasizes good things: efficiency, the amplification of various professions' powers, and other beneficial consequences of computing. The anti-utopian genre, for its part, draws on a stock of cultural images of class conflict and totalitarian domination. Both genres are prevalent in journalistic and academic writing alike.

In the particular area of workplace computing, one strand of anti-utopian writing is found in union-oriented criticisms of managerial control imperatives (Garson 1989, Howard 1985, Shaiken 1985; cf. Rule and Attewell 1989). The argument, first formalized by Braverman (1974) but possessing deeper historical roots in the American union movement, was originally motivated by real historical conflicts over production knowledge, which consisted of the appropriation of craft knowledge through scientific management and the replacement of craft work-ways with fragmented and rationalized forms of work enforced through direct surveillance and control. An extensive school of thought has generalized this experience into a theory of the historical development of work.

Just as the utopians are often accurate in reporting the benefits of computing, these critics are surely not hallucinating the instances of computer-mediated domination they describe, particularly in certain manufacturing and distribution industries with long histories of organized workplace conflict. But a considerable body of empirical research has demonstrated that the picture, at least in the present day, is more complex than this single-factor theory can explain (Thompson 1989). In particular, Kling and Iacono (1984) argue against reducing the managerial strategies and organizational dynamics around computing to simple hierarchical control. Their goal is not simply to find a compromise or halfway position between the utopian and anti-utopian genres, but rather to develop a multi-dimensional model that elucidates a variety of interactions. In particular, they argue for an institutional model based on complex patterns of negotiation and control that operate in all directions, not just from the top down. Allen (1994), in particular, describes some emerging patterns of lateral control relations in increasingly integrated firms.

Attewell (1991) broadens the scope of analysis even further, arguing that an adequate model of organizational computing must integrate several disparate factors: an organization's environment, culture, business strategy, work organization, and labor market conditions.

When applied as the sole framework of computing and privacy, the surveillance model contributes to the near-inevitability of oversimplified analysis. For example, it has directed several authors' attention to the rise of computer-mediated schemes for detailed monitoring of work activities (e.g., Clement 1988), the idea being that distributed computer systems have the potential to establish a regime of total visibility through real-time digital representation of work activities. But while numerous workers have justly resented their experiences with such systems, the systems themselves are evolving, and the evidence is equivocal on their ubiquity, their effectiveness, and the degree of resentment they have provoked (Grant, Higgins, and Irving 1988; Kling 1989; Kling and Dunlop 1993). Again, the point is not to identify a halfway position between extreme views, but to come to a more complicated appreciation of the actual dynamics of such developments. Unfortunately, all the surveillance model offers is a metaphor of bureaucratically organized state terror that often seems disproportionate to the actual experience of corporate life. The rhetoric of "Big Brother technologies" is easily—and frequently—ridiculed through paraphrase in terms of "sinister conspiracies" and the like. The paradoxical result is that genuinely worrisome developments can seem "not so bad" simply for lacking the overt horrors of Orwell's dystopia.

To be sure, the capture model is compatible with some perfectly conventional utopian and anti-utopian scenarios. And it is worth asking, what would a total reorganization of all spheres of life in accord with the capture model be like? Some guidance on the question is available simply from the capture model's definition: grammars of action would have to be articulated for every domain of human activity (work, consumption, travel, politics medicine, and so forth), and these grammars would have to be imposed on their respective domains, with the result that sociotechnical machinery of numerous types would register every state-change of any significance in real time.

What would become of the data in this imaginary world? Whereas the surveillance model suggests that the resulting masses of data would be gathered and stored in some central location, the capture model is agnostic on this matter. Indeed, the capture model emphasizes that capture, as a specifically social process, is not a unitary phenomenon. To the contrary, every domain of activity has its own historical logic, its own vocabulary of actions, and its own distinctive social relations of representation. As a result, information gathered through capture in one domain of activity may or may not be commensurable with information captured in another domain. Even without this element of unification and centralization, though, this picture of a totally captured society offers plenty of opportunity for utopian and anti-utopian speculation. In particular, it has a millenarian flavor of perfect transparency of correspondence between digital representations and the now fully ordered affairs of embodied activity.

Nonetheless, this picture is wholly unsatisfactory, since it provides no notion of the larger social dynamics that capture processes will participate in or interact with. Indeed, without a worked-out conception of how real activities might actually be reorganized during the various phases of the capture cycle, this sketch of a hypothetical world of total capture is hard to distinguish in any convincing way from the utopias and dystopias associated with the surveillance model.

Any serious analysis of capture, then, will require an understanding of the social relations within which the sociotechnical phenomenon of computing is embedded. In particular, it does not suffice to postulate a historical trend toward ever-more-thorough capture of human activities without providing some way to analyze the social forces that structure the social relationships around capture in any given setting. Far from portraying "capture" as a social actor in its own right, a nuanced understanding of the capture model sketches out the landscape of possibilities and alternatives upon which particular concrete instances of capture will be contested.

In considering the institutional context of the capture model, it will help to distinguish the general concept of capture from two specific applications of grammars of action, automation and Taylorism. While "automation" has a broad meaning, referring to any introduction of new technology, it also refers more specifically to the systematic replacement of human activities with the operation of machinery. This process often involves the representation of existing forms of activity by means of grammars of action, for example by systems analysts who map out the information flows in an

organization with the aim of reproducing them all in software. In such a project, the intention is not to instrument the activity but simply to replace it. In work rationalization according to Taylor and his followers, engineers represent existing forms of activity with the goal of reorganizing them according to principles of efficiency. Again, the resulting activity is probably not instrumented, for the simple reason that its precise structure and speed are already known.

Automation and Taylorism are both extremely restrictive approaches to work reorganization. In particular, they both address the twin imperatives of efficiency and control in the same fashion: by legislating the precise sequence of actions in advance. As a result, they are both highly inflexible. This inflexibility is reflected, in turn, in the wide range of sociological theories of organization that are based on a simple opposition between "routines" and "non-routine" (i.e., "skilled") activities (Cyert and March 1963, Nelson and Winter 1982, Sabel 1982, Stinchcombe 1990). Capture, by contrast, permits efficiency and control to be treated separately, so that people who engage in heavily captured activity have a certain kind of freedom not enjoyed by people in Taylorized work. Inasmuch as capture is based on a linguistic metaphor, this freedom is precisely the type ascribed to language users by linguistic theories of grammar—for example in Chomsky's (1971: 50) notion of "free creation within a system of rule." That is, just as the speakers of English can produce a potentially infinite variety of grammatical sentences from the finite means of English vocabulary and grammar, people engaged in captured activity can engage in an infinite variety of sequences of action, provided these sequences are composed of the unitary elements and means of combination prescribed by the grammar of action.

It is thus that captured work activities are often connected with the corporate discourse of "empowerment" (Agre forthcoming). In particular, capture is compatible with modes of work reorganization that increase the skill level of jobs, as well as with "de-skilling," since capture does not require that control be exercised through the fragmentation of jobs and the *a priori* specification of their forms. Instead, capture permits work activities to be disciplined through aggregate measures derived from captured information. Taylorite time-and-motion studies might be performed as well, but their purpose is now to ensure that highly efficient sequences of action exist in the first place. The general picture of empowerment and measurement is consistent with a wide range of power relations, from the intensive production pressures placed on fast food workers by centralized monitoring of captured information to the relatively gentle bureaucratic negotiations experienced by doctors dealing with the medical-activity capture schemes of hospitals, health maintenance organizations, and insurance companies. In particular, the measurements that are derived from representations of captured work can be put to a variety of uses, including piece-rate pay and periodic adjustments of work methods. The ultimate use of such measurements is the establishment of bidding for services in real-time markets, whereby the control function previously provided by bureaucracy is transferred to the inherent discipline of the market. A useful theory of the capture model's place in society would provide a way of understanding when the capture model is employed, how it is employed, and how its employment affects relationships among people. A great deal of work is required before such a theory can be formulated, but at least some plausible starting points are available.

## 7 The political economy of capture

These general considerations provide the background for an analysis of capture as an institutional phenomenon. While institutions deserve analysis on numerous levels, I propose to focus on Ciborra's (1983, 1987) economic model of the institutional effects of information technology. The analysis in this section will be considerably more speculative than in previous sections, and should be understood as the outline of a research agenda.

Ciborra's model is based on Coase's (1937) notion of "transaction costs." Coase begins by looking at all productive human interactions as economic exchanges, and then he asks why some such relations are organized through market mechanisms and others are organized within the authority relationships of hierarchical firms. His answer, roughly speaking, is that the boundaries of firms are drawn around transactions which are less costly to perform within a hierarchy than they are to perform in a market. Transaction costs, which are the costs associated with the use of market exchange, include the costs of locating and evaluating the various goods and services for sale in the market, defining the precise nature of the goods and services to be exchanged,

and negotiating and enforcing the contracts that govern the exchange. (For the subsequent history of the theory of transaction costs, see Williamson and Winter (1991).)

Markets work over time to reduce transaction costs, for the simple reason that competition tends to reduce all costs of production. For example, improved computing and communications technologies make it easier to collect and analyze information on offerings available in the market. As technological changes permit decreases in transaction costs, the theory predicts that the boundaries of firms and the contractual basis of various economic arrangements will change as well in particular ways. For example, firms may begin to purchase certain goods and services on the open market instead of organizing their production in-house, and patterns of vertical integration may change as it becomes more efficient to coordinate certain institutional interfaces through market mechanisms rather than bureaucratic organization.

Ciborra (1987: 258–260) applies this theory to the role of information technology in organizational change. Following Ouchi (1979), he extends Coase's framework slightly by distinguishing three organizational types—markets, bureaucracies, and clans—depending on the degree of ambiguity or uncertainty present in a given way of producing and selling a given product or service, and on the degree of congruence among the interests of the various parties to the interaction. According to this analysis, an economic relationship will be organized as a market (with completely separate transactions on every occasion of exchange) when ambiguity and uncertainty are low and the interests of the parties are in conflict; it will be organized as a rule-bound bureaucratic organization when ambiguity and congruity of interests are moderate; and it will be a closely knit, informal "clan" when ambiguity and congruity of interests are high. (Numerous intermediate and hybrid forms are found as well.) Formulated in this way, the theory specifically predicts that, as transaction costs are reduced, industries will demonstrate a historical trajectory in the direction from clans to hierarchies to markets.

If true, this theory ought to be invaluable to managers faced with planning the organizational concomitants of technological change. With the transition from clan to hierarchy, or hierarchy to market, or with other significant transitions in work-organization within each of these categories, the theory of transaction costs prescribes in some detail the economically most efficient and stable contractual form that can be given to the social relationships in the new form of work. In particular, Ciborra (1987) argues, strategies for designing and managing information technology ought to depend on which category of economic relationships is present (that is, the relationships that *will be* present once the system is working).

When applied in accordance with the capture model, information technology reduces transaction costs by imposing more clearly defined—less ambiguous and less uncertain—relationships upon the parties to economic interactions, thereby decreasing the overhead associated with coordination of various individuals' activities. More specifically, once a grammar of action has been imposed upon an activity, the discrete units and individual episodes of the activity are more readily identified, verified, counted, measured, compared, represented, rearranged, contracted for, and evaluated in terms of economic efficiency. This is a particularly simple matter when the interactions in question are already organized by market relationships, and Ciborra conjectures (1987: 263) that "market transactions rather than bureaucratic firms are at present the main field of application of DP technology, since the structured and standardized nature of those transactions make them more suitable to automation." Indeed some of the most spectacular applications of information technology are found in the operation of global markets in stocks, commodities, currencies, and derivatives built upon these things (Kurtzman 1993), and this increasingly includes generalized markets in debt streams of all sorts (Lenzner and Heuslein 1993).

But information technology can also reduce information costs when applied to work activities in bureaucracies and clans, perhaps leading these activities to change their economic organization. When designed and introduced in accord with the capture model, through the use of an ontology and grammar of social interaction, computer-supported cooperative work (CSCW) tools are particularly well suited to this purpose. The grammars which such tools impose upon an organization's activities necessarily structure, to some substantial extent, the relationships among the organization's members (Ciborra and Olson 1988). In particular, Ciborra (1987: 263) recommends for this purpose the framework of speech acts and commitments (Flores and Ludlow 1981) later employed by

the Coordinator (see above, Section 4). (As a general matter, of course, such systems are more readily implemented when supporting activities that are already organized through a grammar of action. The point is simply that they may prove suitable for less structured activities as well.) Once these qualitative structures of work interactions have been formalized and successfully submitted to automatic tracking and enforcement, it costs less to coordinate them all.

The analysis of transaction costs has political consequences for the design of computer systems that support cooperative work. For example, Ciborra and Olson (1988) assert that, in reducing transaction costs, new technologies can be designed to reinforce clan-like structures as opposed to creating economic pressures for a transition to hierarchical or market structures. But this is contrary to Coase's (1937) original argument, which is that the use of markets or hierarchies (or, by extension, clans) is determined by their relative costs, with non-market organizations' savings in transaction costs being balanced against their comparative economic inefficiencies. (Incidentally, clans should not be confused with the contemporary phenomenon of frequently reorganized multifunctional "teams," which are, economically speaking, really a kind of internal labor market.) By this logic, technologies that reduce transaction costs will, other things being equal, necessarily shift the balance in the direction of market relations. But, as Coase points out, new technologies can also reduce the costs of organizing (he cites the telegraph and telephone, though the point clearly applies to computer networks as well), thus potentially preserving or even extending the economic scope of firms even in the face of reduced transaction costs. The broader point has considerable significance for designers who wish to encourage clan-like forms of social relations as opposed to market or hierarchical relations: a focus on the reduction of transaction costs will not serve this goal.

These propositions on transaction cost economics, together with the foregoing analysis of capture, suggest a rudimentary theory of the political economy of captured information. To place this theory in perspective, it will help to consider Schiller's (1988) analysis of information as a commodity. Schiller argues against deriving the economic properties of information simply from its inherent qualities (its lack of inherent physical form, ease of duplication, and so forth). Instead, he asserts that the specific historical form of information depends on its embedding in a particular set of social relationships. Information, in particular, has increasingly become a commodity, that is, something produced, exchanged, and used within the framework of a market economy. Indeed, as a rapidly expanding sector of the market, information has become "a fundamental source of growth for the market economy as a whole (1988: 27)." Information, though, has not always been a commodity in this strict sense, and Schiller points to the historical process by which the production of information has become a market-based industry largely comparable to any other, a process that has involved the progressive reorganization of the human activities through which information is produced and used.

The economic theory of capture presented here makes it possible to extend Schiller's analysis in the case of one considerable category of information commodities, namely captured information. Regardless of its particular content, captured information is distinguished by its dual relationship—both product and representation—to the human activities upon which particular grammars of action have been imposed. In particular, the capture process makes "visible" a great deal of information-creating activity which had formerly been left implicit in the production of other, historically prior commodities. Moreover, the phenomenon of capture extends market relations not simply through the commodification of the captured information itself (if in fact that information is marketed), but also through the movement toward market relations, through a reduction in transaction costs, of the human activities that the information represents. In other words, by imposing a mathematically precise form upon previously unformalized activities, capture standardizes those activities and their component elements and thereby prepares them (again, other things being equal) for an eventual transition to market-based relationships. This transition is not a mechanical process, to be sure; attempts to impose grammars of action upon existing forms of activity are themselves forms of activity pursued by fully blown human agents, and they regularly fall prey to technical or economic miscalculations, or to the resistance of the participants. The tendency of information technology to contribute to the spread of market relations into previously hierarchical or informal territories of activity should thus be understood as the historically contingent confluence of a disciplinary practice and an economic "law," on the same basis

as the mutual accommodation of supply and demand in perfect markets.

That said, the role of information technology in the generalization and extension of market relations is formidable and not to be underestimated. The process is extraordinarily systematic. At the level of the professional practice of computer people it takes the form of a kind of representational crusade—the conscious formulation of a thoroughgoing system of ontological categories for the full range of productive activities, at every level from the global economy as a whole to the most refined unitary action. No matter how forbidding their discursive forms may be and no matter how esoteric much of their specific content routinely is, these ontological schemes must nonetheless be understood fundamentally not as "technical" but as "social." In other words, the practice of formulating these ontologies is, all disciplinary insularity aside, and regardless of anyone's conscious understandings of the process, a form of social theorization. And this theorizing is not simply a scholastic exercise but is part of a much larger material process through which these new social ontologies, in a certain specific sense, become real.

The relevant sense of "reality" must be defined with care, since, as Section 4 has argued at length, the articulation and imposition of grammars of action routinely involves a kind of mythology: the idea that the activity in question has already been organized in accord with the grammar, and that the subsequent capture scheme simply reads off, in real time, a representation of this preexisting formal structure. This kind of mythology is frequently associated with the constitution of novel commodities, and may even help define the commodity-form as a social phenomenon. Indeed, the theory of transaction costs exhibits the same form of mythology, inasmuch as it presupposes that the entire world of productive activities can be conceptualized, *a priori,* in terms of extremely numerous episodes of exchanges among economic actors.

The truth, of course, is more complicated. The introduction of capture systems into existing activities requires a great deal of effort, including not simply the technical work of building and installing the system but the social work of imposing the system and then living with it. In particular, the work of imposing a capture system frequently involves conflict, as the affected parties organize resistance to it and its beneficiaries organize to overcome, dissolve, or circumvent this resistance (Agre in press). Normally these conflicts take place within the context of existing organizational structures, but if the transaction cost analysis is any guide then many of these conflicts will become largely moot as the contested social relationships move increasingly toward the market. The growth in temporary employment (Negrey 1993, Sacco 1993) and the trend toward outsourcing of non-core functions (Quinn 1992) may be, at least in part, one reflection of this movement. Be this as it may, a rapidly growing literature is exploring the potentially considerable structural changes to firms and markets in which information technology may participate (Davis 1987, Quinn 1992, Scott Morton 1991).

The analysis in this section, once again, should not be understood as a finished theory but as a conjectural outline of a program of research. Lest the theory be overgeneralized, several qualifying points, already implicit in the argument above, should be emphasized. Information technology is not synonymous with the capture model (at least not in principle), the application of information technology can have other consequences besides the reduction of transaction costs, and reductions in transaction costs do not necessarily induce transitions to market relations if other, countervailing factors are present. Changes that reduce the costs of some transactions may be accompanied by, even linked to, other changes that simultaneously increase the costs of other transactions. (Indeed, Allen (1994) suggests that increased integration of production processes requires new, less routinized kinds of relationships among the people involved.) Applications of information technology are invariably accompanied by other developments and other agendas that can influence the shape and consequences of narrowly technological changes. Finally, all of these phenomena are subject to contestation on a wide variety of fronts.

These qualifications having been stated, the hypothesis seeking validation can be formulated in the largest possible terms: the computer practitioner's practice of capture is instrumental to a process by which economic actors reduce their transaction costs and thereby help transform productive activities along a trajectory towards an increasingly detailed reliance upon (or subjection to) market relations. The result is a generalized acceleration of economic activity whose social benefits in terms of productive efficiency are clear enough but whose social costs ought to be a matter of concern.

## 8 Conclusion

The previous sections have outlined a political economy of workplace privacy, building on an analysis of the professional practice of computer people. This discussion provides some resources for a more careful consideration of the relationship between the two models of privacy, the surveillance model and the capture model, that I introduced at the outset. Let us review these models' respective definitions, recalling once again that they are intended as metaphor-systems and not as mutually exclusive categories:

> (1) The surveillance model employs visual metaphors, most famously Orwell's "Big Brother is watching you"; the capture model employs linguistic metaphors by means of various grammars of action.

> (2) The surveillance model emphasizes nondisruptive, surreptitious data collection; the capture model describes the readily apparent instrumentation that entails the reorganization of existing activities.

> (3) The surveillance model is concerned to mark off a "private" region by means of territorial metaphors of "invasion" and the like; the capture model portrays captured activities as being constructed in real-time from a set of institutionally standardized parts specified by the captured ontology.

> (4) The surveillance model depicts the monitoring of activity as centrally organized and presumes that the resulting information is centrally stored; the capture model emphasizes the locally organized nature of contests over the capture process and their structuring within particular institutional contexts.

> (5) The surveillance model takes as its prototype the malevolent political activities of state organizations; the capture model takes as its prototype the quasi-philosophical project of ontological reconstruction undertaken by computer professionals in private organizations.

The body of the paper has introduced a reasonably substantive theory of capture as part of the historical dynamics of a market economy. This theory does not pretend to cover all uses of commodified information, and it would be worth exploring the possibilities of a parallel theory of information formed into commodities through processes better understood through the surveillance model. Such a theory is available in the work of Gandy (1993), who emphasizes the now vast market machinery around the personal information that people leave behind in a wide range of public records and economic transactions. Much of this information, no doubt, arises in the first place through the capture of activities of various kinds. One possibility is that market pressures of various sorts tend to induce a transition in the manner in which information is collected, away from the surveillance model and toward the capture model. Such a trend, if it exists, will presumably be most marked in workplaces, where the relations of power necessary to impose grammars of action are the most fully developed. But the accumulation of personal information through medical care, the contractual conditions of insurance coverage, and driving on increasingly instrumented public roads (Bender 1991, Jurgen 1991) also provides promising sites of investigation along these lines.

Some additional topics invite further research. It would be valuable to catalog the kinds of organizational transformations that can accompany the imposition of grammars of action. Capture, and particularly the sharing and standardization of ontologies, may provide a vocabulary for exploring some of the interlocking, overlapping, and cross-fertilization among various forms of computer-mediated work that are evolving within the global economy (Rosenberg 1982). The processes of articulation and imposition should be studied empirically in a variety of settings, particularly with regard to the forms of "participation" that they exhibit. The genealogy of the capture model should be sought in the history of ideas and in the historical development of the computer profession and its practices. The transaction cost model of capture economics should be evaluated and extended with reference to detailed case studies.

The analysis of the capture model has significant implications for designers. It provides some tools for placing technical design-styles in larger political and economic contexts, and thereby for more consciously setting research priorities in accordance with democratic goals. This analysis might also provide some impetus for investigations of the underlying structures of design practices, and it might provide a prototype for research into the political and economic dimensions of various specific formations of design. Finally, it would seem important to articulate various counter-traditions of design and their associated counter-visions of human activity, keeping in mind the trade-offs that are stubbornly inherent in computers and computational design as these things are currently constituted.

Acknowledgements

This paper originated in comments that I prepared as a discussant at the Symposium on Basic Research Topics at the Conference on Computer-Human Interaction in May 1992 in Monterey, California. Thanks to John Carroll and Jim Hollan for their roles in organizing this meeting. I presented a subsequent version at the Third Conference on Computers, Freedom, and Privacy in March 1993 in San Francisco. Thanks to numerous participants in this conference for their useful comments. The paper has also benefitted from comments by Jonathan Allen, Rick Crawford, Bruce Donald, Mike Robinson, Dan Schiller, Lucy Suchman, and Randy Trigg.

Bibliography

Philip E. Agre, From high tech to human tech: Empowerment, measurement, and social studies of computing, in Geof Bowker, Leigh Star, Les Gasser, and Bill Turner, eds *Social Science Research, Technical Systems and Cooperative Work,* forthcoming.

Philip E. Agre, Conceptions of the user in computer system design, in Peter Thomas, ed., *Social and Interactional Dimensions of Human-Computer Interfaces,* Cambridge: Cambridge University Press, in press.

Jonathan Allen, Mutual control in the newly integrated work environments, *The Information Society* 10(3), 1994, this issue.

Anonymous, Bar code data collection is the key in the success of NCR's JIT processes, *Industrial Engineering* 22(9), 1990, pages 30–32.

Paul Attewell, Big brother and the sweatshop: Computer surveillance in the automated office, Sociological Theory 5(1), 1987, 87–89. Reprinted in Charles Dunlop and Rob Kling, eds., *Computerization and Controversy: Value Conflicts and Social Choices,* Boston: Academic Press, 1991.

David Baum, Au Bon Pain gains quick access to sales data: Unix-based cooperative processing system gives restaurants a competitive advantage, *InfoWorld* 14(32), 10 August 1992, page 46.

Jacob G. Bender, An overview of systems studies of automated highway systems, *IEEE Transactions on Vehicular Technology* 40(1), 1991, pages 82–99.

John Bowers, The politics of formalism, in Martin Lea, ed., *Contexts of Computer-Mediated Communication,* New York: Harvester Wheatsheaf, 1992.

Ronald J. Brachman and Hector J. Levesque, *Readings in Knowledge Representation,* Los Altos, CA: Morgan Kaufmann, 1985.

Harry Braverman, *Labor and Monopoly Capital: The Degradation of Work in the Twentieth Century,* New York: Monthly Review Press, 1974.

Christine Bullen and John Bennett, Learning from user experiences with groupware, in *Proceedings of the ACM Conference on Computer-Supported Cooperative Work,* Portland, Oregon, 1988, pages 125–139.

David Burnham, *The Rise of the Computer State,* New York: Random House, 1983.

John M. Carroll and Thomas P. Moran, Introduction to this special issue on design rationale, *Human-Computer Interaction* 6(3–4), 1991, pages 197–200.

John M. Carroll, Creating a design science of human-computer interaction, in Alain Bensoussan and Jean-Pierre Verjus, eds., *Future Tendencies in Computer Science, Control, and Applied Mathematics: 25th Anniversary of INRIA,* New York: Springer Verlag, 1992.

Noam Chomsky, *Problems of Knowledge and Freedom: The Russell Lectures,* New York: Pantheon, 1971.

Claudio U. Ciborra, Information systems and transactions architecture, *International Journal of Policy Analysis and Information Systems* 21(3), 1983, pages 145–160.

Claudio U. Ciborra, Research agenda for a transaction cost approach to information systems, in Richard J. Boland, Jr. and Rudy A. Hirschheim, eds., *Critical Issues in Information Systems Research,* Chichester, UK: Wiley, 1987.

Claudio U. Ciborra and Margrethe H. Olson, Encountering electronic work groups: A transaction costs perspective, *Proceedings of the Conference on Computer-Supported Cooperative Work,* September 26–29, 1988, Portland, Oregon, pages 94–101.

Roger A. Clarke, Information technology and dataveillance, *Communications of the ACM* 31(5), 1989, pages 498–512.

Victoria K. Clawson and Robert P. Bostrom, *Facilitation: The human side of groupware,* Paper presented at the Groupware '93 Conference, San Jose, California, 1993.

Andrew Clement, Office automation and the technical control of information workers, in Vincent Mosco and Janet Wasko, eds., *The Political Economy of Information,* Madison: University of Wisconsin Press, 1988.

Ronald H. Coase, The nature of the firm, *Economica* NS 4, 1937, pages 385–405.

J. Daniel Couger, Evolution of business system development techniques, *Computing Surveys* 5(3), 1973, pages 167–198.

Richard M. Cyert and James G. March, *A Behavioral Theory of the Firm,* Englewood Cliffs, NJ: Prentice-Hall, 1963.

Stanley M. Davis, *Future Perfect,* Reading, MA: Addison-Wesley, 1987.

Bruce Donald, On information invariants in robots, unpublished manuscript.

Paul Dourish, Culture and control in a media space, in Georgio de Michelis, Carla Simone and Kjeld Schmidt, eds., *Proceedings of the Third European Conference on Computer-Supported Cooperative Work: ECSCW'93,* Dordrecht, The Netherlands: Kluwer, 1993.

Caroline A. Duffy, UPS toes the line with its package-tracking technologies, *PC Week* 10(25), 28 June 1993, page 211.

Wayne Eckerson, Hand-held computers will help UPS track packages; tablets will let drivers capture electronic signatures, *Network World* 8(18), 6 May 1991, pages 15–16.

The Economist, Big Brother is clocking you: The technology that promised fewer traffic jams may damage your civil liberties, *The Economist,* 7 August 1993, pages 71–72.

Richard Edwards, *Contested Terrain: The Transformation of the Workplace in the Twentieth Century,* New York: Basic Books, 1979.

Scott Elrod, Gene Hall, Rick Costanza, Michael Dixon, and Jim des Rivieres, Responsive office environments, *Communications of the ACM* 36(7), 1993, pages 84–85.

James F. Fales, Exciting times for new developments in tracking systems, *Industrial Engineering* 24(5), 1992, page 14.

David H. Flaherty, *Protecting Privacy in Surveillance Societies: The Federal Republic of Germany, Sweden, France, Canada, and the United States,* Chapel Hill: University of North Carolina Press, 1989.

Fernando Flores and J. J. Ludlow, Doing and speaking in the office, in Goran Fick, Ralph H. Sprague, eds., Decision support systems: Issues and challenges, Oxford: Pergamon Press, 1980.

Fernando Flores, Michael Graves, Brad Hartfield, and Terry Winograd, Computer systems and the design of organizational interaction, ACM Transactions on Office Information Systems 6(2), 1988, pages 153–172.

Laurie Flynn, They're watching you: Electronic surveillance of workers raises privacy concerns, *San Jose Mercury News,* 13 June 1993, page 1F.

Oscar H. Gandy, Jr., *The Panoptic Sort: A Political Economy of Personal Information,* Boulder: Westview Press, 1993.

Harold Garfinkel, "Good" organizational reasons for "bad" clinic records, in *Studies in Ethnomethodology,* Polity Press, 1984. Originally published in 1967.

Barbara Garson, *The Electronic Sweatshop: How Computers are Transforming the Office of the Future into the Factory of the Past,* New York: Penguin, 1989.

Les Gasser, The integration of computing and routine work, *ACM Transactions on Office Information Systems* 4(3), 1986, pages 205–225.

Frank B. Gilbreth, *Primer of Scientific Management,* New York: Van Nostrand, 1912.

Rich Gold, This is not a pipe, *Communications of the ACM* 36(7), 1993, page 72.

Rebecca A. Grant, Christopher A. Higgins, and Richard H. Irving, Computerized performance monitors: Are they costing you customers?, *Sloan Management Review* 29(3), 1988, pages 39–45.

Michael Hammer, Reengineering work: Don't automate, obliterate, *Harvard Business Review* 68(4), July-August 1990, pages 104–112.

A. Hawker, Not standard practice, *Health Service Journal* 101, 28 March 1991, pages 31, 33.

Martin Heidegger, *Being and Time,* translated by John Macquarrie and Edward Robinson, Harper and Row, 1961. Originally published in German in 1927.

Thomas Hoffman, Database control, *Information Week* 277, 9 July 1990, page 26.

Walter G. Holmes, *Applied Time and Motion Study,* New York: Ronald Press, 1938.

Robert Howard, *Brave New Workplace,* New York: Penguin, 1985.

Martin Jay, *Downcast Eyes: The Denigration of Vision in Twentieth-

*Century French Thought,* Berkeley: University of California Press, 1993.

H. Thomas Johnson and Robert S. Kaplan, *Relevance Lost: The Rise and Fall of Management Accounting,* Boston: Harvard Business School Press, 1987.

Ronald K. Jurgen, Smart cars and highways go global, *IEEE Spectrum* 28(5), 1991, pages 26–36.

Rob Kling, Social analyses of computing: Theoretical perspectives in recent empirical research, *Computing Surveys* 12(1), 1980, pages 61–110.

Rob Kling and Suzanne Iacono, Computing as an occasion for social control, *Journal of Social Issues* 40(3), 1984, pages 77–96.

Rob Kling, Theoretical perspectives in social analysis of computerization, in Zenon W. Pylyshyn and Liam J. Bannon, *Perspectives on the Computer Revolution,* second edition, Norwood, NJ: Ablex, 1989.

Rob Kling, Cooperation, coordination and control in computer-supported work, *Communications of the ACM* 34(12), 1991, pages 83–88.

Rob Kling and Charles Dunlop, Controversies about computerization and the character of white collar worklife, *The Information Society* 9(1), 1993, pages 1–30.

Joel Kurtzman, *The Death of Money,* New York: Simon and Schuster, 1993.

Erik Larson, *The Naked Consumer: How Our Private Lives Become Public Commodities,* New York: Henry Holt, 1992.

George Lawton, Macs hit the road to keep trucks on track, help cut costs, *MacWEEK* 6(41), 16 November 1992, pages 32–33.

Ed Leibowitz, Halt: Open architecture detains prisoners under house arrest and keeps tabs on parolees, *Teleconnect* 10(11), 1992, pages 36–38.

Robert Lenzner and William Heuslein, How derivatives are transforming Wall Street, *Forbes* 151(7), 29 March 1993, pages 62–72.

William O. Lichtner, *Planned Control in Manufacturing,* New York: Ronald Press, 1924.

Stephen Loudermilk, Toronto tracks vehicles over wireless net, *PC Week* 10(6), 15 February 1993, pages 47–48.

Paul Luff, Nigel Gilbert, and David Frohlich, eds., *Computers and Conversation,* London: Academic Press, 1990.

Ronni T. Marshak, Action Technologies' workflow products, *Workflow Computing Report* 16(5), 1993, pages 1–20.

James Martin, *Strategic Information Planning Methodologies,* second edition, Englewood Cliffs, NJ: Prentice Hall, 1989.

John P. McPartlin, Press 1 for cheeseburger: IS chiefs scramble for advantage in the fast food fracas, *Information Week* 374, 18 May 1992, page 78.

Raul Medina-Mora, Terry Winograd, Rodrigo Flores, and Fernando Flores, The action workflow approach to workflow management technology, *Proceedings of CSCW–92,* Toronto, Ontario, 1992, pages 281–288.

Kenneth Meyer, Hugh L. Applewhite, and Frank A. Biocca, A survey of position trackers, *Presence* 1(2), 1992, pages 173–200.

Peter A. D. Mill, Volker Hartkopf, Vivan Loftness, and Pleasantine Drake, The challenge to smart buildings: User-controlled ecological environments for productivity, in David V. Gibson, George Kozmetsky, and Raymond W. Smilor, eds., *The Technopolis Phenomenon: Smart Cities, Fast Systems, Global Networks,* Lanham, MD: Rowman and Littlefield, 1992.

Robert B. Miller and Stephen E. Heiman, Conceptual Selling, New York: Warner, 1987.

Cynthia Negrey, *Gender, Time, and Reduced Work,* Albany: State University of New York Press, 1993.

Richard R. Nelson and Sidney G. Winter, An Evolutionary Theory of Economic Change, Cambridge: Harvard University Press, 1982.

Wanda J. Orlikowski, Learning from Notes: Organizational issues in groupware implementation, *The Information Society* 9(3), 1993, pages 237–250.

William G. Ouchi, A conceptual framework for the design of organizational control mechanisms, *Management Science* 25(9), 1979, pages 838–848.

Jeff Y.-C. Pan and J. Marty Tenenbaum, An intelligent agent framework for enterprise integration, *IEEE Transactions on Systems, Man and Cybernetics* 21(6), 1991, pages 1391–408.

Charles Piller, Privacy in peril: how computers are making private life a thing of the past, *Macworld* 10(7), 1993, pages 124–130.

James Brian Quinn, *Intelligent Enterprise: A Knowledge and Service Based Paradigm for Industry,* New York: Free Press, 1992.

Timothy R. Rabel, Software and privacy: revising Orwell, IEEE Software 10(3), 1993, pages 92–93.

Kevin Robins and Frank Webster, Cybernetic capitalism: Information, technology, everyday life, in Vincent Mosco and Janet Wasko, eds., *The Political Economy of Information,* Madison: University of Wisconsin Press, 1988.

Lura K. Romei, Software helps find the applicants you need, *Modern Office Technology* 36(8), 1991, pages 52–53.

Nathan Rosenberg, *Technological interdependence in the American economy, Inside the Black Box: Technology and Economics,* Cambridge: Cambridge University Press, 1982.

James B. Rule, Private Lives and Public Surveillance: Social Control in the Computer Age, New York: Schocken Books, 1974.

James Rule and Paul Attewell, What do computers do?, *Social Problems* 36(3), 1989, pages 225–241.

Charles F. Sabel, *Work and Politics: The Division of Labor in Industry,* Cambridge: Cambridge University Press, 1982.

Tony Sabetti, RF/ID creates dynamic links between people, objects, and processes, *I&CS (Instrumentation & Control Systems) 66(10),* 1993, pages 41–44.

Samuel R. Sacco, All employment relationships are changing, *Modern Office Technology* 38(5), 1993, pages 47–48.

Dan Schiller, How to think about information, in Vincent Mosco and Janet Wasko, eds., T*he Political Economy of Information,*

Madison: University of Wisconsin Press, 1988.

Douglas Schuler and Aki Namioka, eds., *Participatory Design: Principles and Practices,* Hillsdale, NJ: Erlbaum, 1993.

Michael S. Scott Morton, ed., *The Corporation of the 1990s: Information Technology and Organizational Transformation,* New York: Oxford University Press, 1991.

John R. Searle, *Speech Acts: An Essay in the Philosophy of Language,* Cambridge: Cambridge University Press, 1969.

Harley Shaiken, *Work Transformed: Automation and Labor in the Computer Age,* New York: Holt, Rinehart, and Winston, 1985.

Robert Ellis Smith, *Privacy: How to Protect What's Left of It,* New York: Anchor Press, 1979.

Steve Smith, How much change at the store?: The impact of new technologies and labour process on managers and staffs in retail distribution, in David Knights and Hugh Willmott, eds., *New Technology and the Labour Process,* London: Macmillan, 1988.

Arthur L. Stinchcombe, *Information and Organizations,* Berkeley: University of California Press, 1990.

Lucy A. Suchman, Office procedure as practical action: Models of work and system design, *ACM Transactions on Office Information Systems* 1(4), 1983, pages 320–328.

Lucy Suchman and Brigitte Jordan, Computerization and women's knowledge, in Kea Tijdens, Mary Jennings, Ina Wagner, and Margaret Weggelaar, eds., *Women, Work and Computerization: Forming New Alliances,* Amsterdam: North-Holland, 1989.

Lucy Suchman, Technologies of accountability: Of lizards and aeroplanes, in Graham Button, ed., *Technology in Working Order: Studies of Work, Interaction, and Technology,* London: Routledge, 1992.

Lucy Suchman, Do categories have politics?: The language/action perspective reconsidered, in Georgio de Michelis, Carla Simone and Kjeld Schmidt, eds., *Proceedings of the Third European Conference on Computer-Supported Cooperative Work: ECSCW'93,* Dordrecht, The Netherlands: Kluwer, 1993.

Frederick Winslow Taylor, *The Principles of Scientific Management,* New York: Harper, 1923.

Paul Thompson, *The Nature of Work: An Introduction to Debates on the Labour Process,* second edition, London: Macmillan, 1989.

S. J. Udoka, Automated data capture techniques: A prerequisite for effective integrated manufacturing systems, *Computers and Industrial Engineering* 21, 1991, pages 217–222.

Charles Von Simpson, Food fight: Business strategies, Computerworld 23(40), 2 October 1989, pages S22–26.

Richard E. Walton, *Up and Running: Integrating Information Technology and the Organization,* Boston: Harvard Business School Press, 1989.

Roy Want, Andy Hopper, Veronica Falcao, and Jonathan Gibbons, The active badge location system, *ACM Transactions on Information Systems* 10(1), 1992, pages 91–102.

Willis H. Ware, The new faces of privacy, *The Information Society* 9(3), 1993, pages 195–212.

Mark Weiser, Ubiquitous computing, *Computer* 26(10), 1993, pages 71–72.

Oliver E. Williamson and Sidney G. Winter, *The Nature of the Firm: Origins, Evolution, and Development,* Oxford: Oxford University Press, 1991.

Terry Winograd and Fernando Flores, *Understanding Computers and Cognition: A New Foundation for Design,* Norwood, NJ: Ablex, 1986.

JoAnne Yates, *Control through Communication: The Rise of System in American Management,* Baltimore: Johns Hopkins University Press, 1989.

# 52. [Introduction]
# Nonlinearity and Literary Theory

Espen Aarseth's essay is neither about hypertext nor about some other type of text that is specific to the computer. How, then, did such a document insinuate itself into a book called *Hyper/Text/Theory*, and how did it manage to also work its way into one called *The New Media Reader*?

Aarseth noticed, during readings of texts that are presented or generated through computer software (such as Michael Joyce's *Afternoon*) that many of the interesting qualities of electronic literature stem not from its representation on a phosphor-lined vacuum tube (or a grid of liquid crystal) rather than a page, but from its nonlinear nature. He also noted that this quality of nonlinearity is neither insisted upon by the computer nor precluded by print. Rather than attempting to apply existing literary theory to try to explain unusual computer literary artifacts, Aarseth has developed general and yet powerful theories, theories which apply outside of new media but are based largely upon the study of new media works and those unusual aspects of text that they highlight.

The allure of the screen causes many enthusiasts to see computer literature as its own entirely new category, a view that Robert Coover considers, but does not fully embrace, in his essay (◊49). Yet just as film and print literature have common structures and influence one another, new media art and writing relate to works that are non-digital. One of the signs of the maturity of new media scholarship is that it has started to generate approaches that apply to objects outside the field.

In addition to describing a typology for nonlinear texts, Aarseth's essay makes an important contribution by discussing hypertext fiction in depth alongside interactive fiction works (a.k.a. text adventure games) such as *Adventure* and alongside conversational characters such as *Eliza/Doctor*. By going outside the boundaries of hypertext—not only to refer to print works such as *Hopscotch* but also to consider other computer software for presenting texts—Aarseth was able to identify and categorize the most salient features of nonlinear texts, rather than basing his conclusions on a group of homogeneously hypertextual works, all created—although perhaps by authors with different goals—under similar assumptions.

Another important point made in this essay is that today's electronic textual systems are not so new when systems like the telegraph are considered. Although *The New Media Reader* includes only writings from the middle of the century up through the ascendance of the Web, consideration of the history of new media certainly should not be restricted to the period after World War II.

Aarseth's *Cybertext* offers an excellent study of what are called, in this essay, nonlinear texts. It is widely cited in recent work, has been the starting point for an involved discussion on *ebr (Electronic Book Review)* and has inspired a series of edited volumes beginning with *The Cybertext Yearbook 2000*. While Aarseth has provided many insights in this essay and in *Cybertext*, one of his most important contributions has been to suggest a new ontology of texts, or textonomy, as he calls it, and to line out a category, and enumerate a set of independent features, that seem to be of both theoretical and critical interest.
—NM

Michael Joyce's essay "Siren Shapes" is ◊42.

That the study of new media can inform our understanding of the old is sometimes overlooked by enthusiasts for new technologies, but it was noted by Marshall McLuhan (◊13). It has been taken up recently in the concept of media ecology, the comparative media studies approach of Henry Jenkins, and by Jay David Bolter (◊47) and Richard Grusin in their book *Remediation*.

Tom Standage's *The Victorian Internet* explores the telegraphic heritage of today's networks.

Further Reading

Aarseth, Espen. *Cybertext: Perspectives on Ergodic Literature*. Baltimore: Johns Hopkins University Press, 1997.
Bolter, Jay David and Richard Grusin. *Remediation: Understanding New Media*. Cambridge: MIT Press. 1999.
Standage, Tom. *The Victorian Internet*. New York: Walker and Company, 1998.

Original Publication
*Hyper/Text/Theory,* 51–86. Ed. George Landow. Baltimore: Johns
Hopkins University Press, 1994.

# Nonlinearity and Literary Theory

## Espen J. Aarseth

Electronic writing will require a simpler, more positive
literary theory.
—J. David Bolter

The future can only be anticipated in the form of an
absolute danger.
—Jacques Derrida

In this essay I outline a theory of nonlinear texts and
investigate some of its possible implications for the practice
of literary theory and criticism. A nonlinear text is an object
of verbal communication that is not simply one fixed
sequence of letters, words, and sentences but one in which
the words or sequence of words may differ from reading to
reading because of the shape, conventions, or mechanisms of
the text. Nonlinear texts can be very different from each
other, at least as different as they are from the linear texts.
In the conceptual framework presented here, the linear text
may be seen as a special case of the nonlinear in which the
convention is to read word by word from beginning to end.
Recently, because of the computer, certain types of nonlinear
texts have received attention from educational, technological,
and theoretical circles. Now may be the time to broaden the
scope of interest and to examine textual nonlinearity from a
general point of view.

Over the past two decades, the spread and radical
development of the computer as a means of cultural and
aesthetic expression has created a challenge to the
paradigms of cultural theory that has not yet been
systematically answered. Studies of specific computer-
mediated phenomena often suffer from a lack of insight
into neighboring phenomena, again caused by a missing
frame of reference, a general theoretical overview based on a
broad comparative study, and a dialectic between
neighboring fields. This is not least the case in literary
theory, in which technological issues traditionally have been

met with very little interest. During the past decade,
however, such issues have seen a marked increase of
attention, perhaps not totally independent of the successful
introduction of electronic word processing as an academic
tool. The word processor has served to familiarize the
literary scholar with *some* aspects of the new text
technologies; but, due to its collaborative and emulative
nature (the way electronic word processing assumes the
goals of the earlier technologies), the more radical potential
of textual computing is easily ignored, and the computer is
gratefully perceived as less threatening than it actually is.

This essay, unlike the others in this book [*Hyper/Text/
Theory*], is not primarily concerned with hypertext. Instead,
I shall try to take a step back, to investigate the larger
repertoire of textual forms of which hypertext can be said to
be one. Hypertext, when regarded as a type of text, shares
with a variety of other textual types a fundamental trait,
which we defined as nonlinearity. It must immediately be
pointed out that this concept refers only to the physico-
logical form (or arrangement, appearance) of the texts, and
not to any fictional meaning or external reference they might
have. Thus, it is not the plot, or the narrative, or any other
well-known poetic unit that will be our definitive agency but
the shape or structure of the text itself. A narrative may be
perfectly nonlinear (for example describing a sequence of
events in a repetitive or nonsequential way) and yet be
represented in a totally linear text.

The advent of computer-mediated textuality seems to have
left many of those theorists and critics who noticed it in a
terminological vacuum. In their eagerness to describe the
brave new reality, they let a few words like *electronic* and
*hypertext* cover many different phenomena. Behind the
electronic text there is a large and heterogeneous variety of
phenomena, and, as we shall see, a computer-mediated text
may have more in common with a paper-based one than
with one of its electronic brethren.

After considering some fundamental problems with the
concept of textuality, I shall propose a typology of nonlinear
texts based on principles extracted from various samples, and
then I shall outline the main forms of nonlinearity. Since the
paradigms and practice of literary theory cannot remain
unaffected by its encounter with nonlinear literature, except
by pretending it never happened, I both discuss new
applications of literary theory and suggest some possible
new departures.

## Behind the Lines: What Is a Text, Anyway?

> The text as a whole and as a singular whole may be compared to an object, which may be viewed from several sides, but never from all sides at once.
> —Paul Ricoeur

To present nonlinear textuality as a phenomenon relevant to textual theory, one must rethink the concept of textuality to comprise linear as well as nonlinear texts. "The text," as it is commonly perceived, entails a set of powerful metaphysics that I have no hope of dispersing here. The three most important ones are those of *reading, writing,* and *stability.* Regardless of mutual contradiction, these three work together to control our notion of what a text is. For our purpose, they can be summed up as follows: (1) A text is what you read, the words and phrases that you see before your eyes and the meanings they produce in your head. (2) A text is a message, imbued with the values and intentions of a specific writer/genre/culture. (3) A text is a fixed sequence of constituents (beginning, middle, end) that cannot change, although its interpretations might. In opposition to these notions, I argue that the lessons of nonlinear literature show us a textuality different from our readings (and our readings of "reading"), more fundamental than our messages, and, through the evolving rituals and technologies of use and distribution, subject to many types of change. I do not for a moment believe that my constructed binarism of the nonlinear text and the linear text or any of the other perspectives in this essay are any more free of a metaphysics than any previous textual theory, but I hope they are better suited to identifying some of the relevant issues of textual communication.

My use of the word *text* is seemingly at odds with that of certain schools of textual theory that regard the text as a semantic network of symbolic relations, loosely attached to the notion of the literary work. I do not intend to challenge that idea; I believe that it belongs to a different aspect or level of the same object. We then have two perspectives: the text as a technical, historical, and social object and the text as it is individually received and understood. These aspects, which we might call the *informative* and the *interpretable,* are governed by different rules, but they are interdependent and influence (and sometimes intrude on) each other in many ways.

The informative aspect of the text is usually the harder to see, because it is the most obvious. In addition to its visible words and spaces, which we may call the *script,* a text includes a practice, a structure or ritual of use. Different practices adhere to different texts; we do not read *Peanuts* (the comic strip) the way we read the Bible. Of course, a rich text such as the Bible has many uses and is perused in many ways. I am not talking of interpretation here, just the algorithm and choreography that conducts the script from the text to the mind of the beholder. This may be compared (carefully) to the concept of genre, except that genre is seen prior to the text, and revered or betrayed by it; here it is the other way around.

The relationship between the text and the script requires closer attention. There is, of course, not *one* such relationship but as many as there are technologies and conventions of reading and writing. A simplistic model might depict two of the most common relationships as the following: text subordinate to script (the handwritten letter, the electronic word-processing document) and script subordinate to text (the mass-produced paper copy, the read-only CD-ROM). In the first case, whatever you do to the script affects the text; in the second, it does not. When we look for ways to describe differences between types of text, the word *electronic* usually does not get us very far.

The interpretable aspect of the text is that which makes it different; to be blunt, it is that which makes it worth reading. Formal as well as semantic elements come into play: if a text has an unusual shape, that alone arouses our interest. Most texts, however, are boringly familiar in their shape; we already know how to read them. I intend to deal with the interpretable aspect only insofar as it is affected by my discussion of the informative; to engage it fully here would be (at best) a pointless historic review of the highlights of linguistic and literary theory.

There is a problem here that goes back to a flaw at the heart of my definition of nonlinear text. When I said that a text can be nonlinear by convention, the definition is laid open to interference from the interpretable level. What if a text simply insists on its nonlinearity? Should we take its word for it? There are many such texts; Milorad Pavić's *Landscape Painted with Tea* (1990) comes to mind. From the second half, it can be read as a crossword puzzle, either "across" or "down," following the explicit instructions given on pages 100–101. But what if a text gives us such instructions at the start, then cancels them later on? Or worse, what if the text starts by warning us against possible attacks of illegitimate nonlinearities, then proceeds to order us to go at once to page 50 for further instructions and skip the intervening pages that, we are told, have been contaminated by subversive directions? These hypothetical cases, which are far from impossible, illustrate a peculiar semiotic power of the linear text over the nonlinear: the linear can flirt with nonlinearity, but the nonlinear cannot lie and pretend to be linear.

But let us return to our metaphysical question, which really is a serious one: What is a text? Or, to rephrase it, Which elements and effects belong to the text and which do not? The poststructuralists are fond of discussing this question in (and in relation to) the preface or the foreword, but since I do not have such places at my disposal in this book, but only a chapter, I shall not argue with them. Instead, consider this: does the author's name belong to a text? It is usually only found outside the text—on the cover, in the catalogue, in the book review, and in some cases in the top or bottom margins of the page; but it can be argued that, along with the text's title, which is also found outside the text proper (not "enclosed" in it), the words that make up the author's name are the single most meaningful phrase of the text. Of the text, but not in the text. Imagine the difference between a text by P. G. Wodehouse and a text by Agatha Christie; no problem there. It does not even have to be any specific books; we know the difference anyway. The fact that we may know something about the authors behind these names is not anywhere near as important as what we know about a text, once we know it is by one of them. Once I pick up a book by Ken Follett, I have already started the interpretation of it, long before I have started on the first page. Even if the name itself is unknown to us, its hints of gender and cultural background are meaningful.

Authors have always known these things. In antiquity and the early Middle Ages, some writers would use the name of a famous author to get their ideas read and spread—not as a villainous forgery with the goal of short-term benefit but as a way to enhance the endurance and position of their work. Think of it as a kind of benevolent computer virus. In more recent times, female writers used male pseudonyms: the fiction was even better if a fictitious author could be constructed. Still, "serious" authors use pseudonyms for their less serious work; that way the weight of their "true" name will not mislead their readers' expectations and interpretations. This shift works well even if the connection

between the two names is known; it is the name, not the person behind it, that is important. The name belongs to the text, the writer (as in ghostwriter) does not.

Our distinction between the text and the script in the case of mass-produced and -distributed copies leads to the fundamental question of in what sense the script-independent text (the so-called real text behind all the copies) can be said to exist. This distinction may seem so much quaint and unnecessary contentiousness, but as part of the textual ontology—or, to coin a name for our field, *textonomy*—presented in this essay, it helps us to show that the stability of paper-based documents is as much a product of our metaphysical belief in a transcendental text as an inherent quality of the physical object.

Imagine a book in which some of the pages appear to be missing, or the print is unreadable every 16 pages, or some of the pages are repeated while an equal number omitted. Even if this copy is the only one we ever see, we automatically assume that it is not supposed to be this way and that a more correct version exists. It may never have been printed; but to us, who can imagine it perfectly (except for the missing words, of course), it is still more real than the one we are holding. For instance, in Terry Eagleton's *Literary Theory*, there are two chapters bearing the number one; the first titled "Introduction: What is Literature" (p.1), and the other "The Rise of English" (p.17).[1] Since my copy is from the eighth printing (1990) and the book was first published in 1983, it is unlikely that there is a version with only one first chapter, but we nevertheless assume that this is what the text meant, and that the introduction got numbered by mistake. We do this out of lack of respect for the copy; it appears to misrepresent the "real" text, even if such a thing may never have existed. In short, we prefer the imagined integrity of a metaphysical object to the stable version that we observe. Which one is more real than the other? As long as we are able to imagine and reconstruct an ideal version, everything appears to be fine, and our metaphysics remains intact. But what if the flawed version interferes so deeply with our sense of reception that it, in more than a manner of speaking, steals the show? Following our metaphysical logic, we would have to say that a new text had been created, since the alternative would be a script without a text. But, because of its unintentional origin, this new text cannot be metaphysically equal to the text it replaces, and so we are left with a paradox: some texts are metaphysical, some are not, and if we do not know their origins, we have no way to tell the difference.

The alternative, of course, is to abandon the concept of a real text-behind-the-text altogether. On Saturday, February the 7th, 1987, I saw John Boorman's *Zardoz* (1974) at the Bergen Film Club. *Or did I?* As it happened, somehow the reels got mixed up and were projected in the sequence 1, 2, 4, 3, 5. The film is a weird, allegorical adventure, from a barbaric future in which technology has become inexplicable and supernatural to everyone but a secluded group of very bored immortals. The title is an anagramatic allusion to *The Wizard of Oz*, and the story contains many surreal and fantastic elements—not least, it seemed to me, the sudden jump in the narrative, followed after a while by a just as strange flashback. When the fifth reel came on, however, I slowly started to suspect that this rather crude montage technique was neither Boorman nor his film company's doing, but most likely a mistake in "reel time." By then the damage was done, and I had had the confusing privilege of being lost in the materiality of a film—a strangely appropriate experience, somewhat parallel to that of the main character, played by Sean Connery, a barbarian who manages to get into the secret place, the Vortex of the immortals, to see their strange customs and technology (and their eventual destruction) from the inside.

By virtue of the altered sequence, an unintended cinematic experience, a new expression, was created. But was it a new film? I am tempted to answer, *no*. Not because I feel that a film (or any other artistic "work") has to be the intended and consecutive design of a conscious, creative operator, but because both the original and the heretical sequences are based on the same material potential. In this sense, a text or a film is like a limited language in which all the parts are known, but the full potential of their combinations is not. The mutation of *Zardoz* was created by a hidden possibility in its channel, not by the introduction of a new code or principle.

There are many scales of change in a text's metamorphosis: unintentional (the blunders of a typesetter or projectionist in the dark), usurpatory (a re-mix of samples from a musical recording, a hacked version of a computer game), plagiary (one composer's unacknowledged variations on a theme of another), and subversive or estranging (the "cut up" textual experiments of William Burroughs and John Cage), to suggest a few. Some of the results of some of these

operations we might accept as authentic new works, others not, according to the cultural legitimacy of their method of construction or their operator; or, in the case of a new aesthetic system, depending on contemporary empathy with the perceived political symbolism of the mode of mutation.

Textual integrity and the border between two works of art—this is hardly a startlingly original conclusion—is a cultural construct. More importantly, as I have tried to show, so is our notion of what constitutes the text itself—not only our conception of its function, meaning, or metaphysical reliability but also what it appears to be made of and what conditions have to be met for us to acknowledge its existence. What remains to be investigated, then, is the possibility that textuality exists beyond metaphysics, through location, anatomy, and temporality.

There is no sense in denying that this crisis of the text (if so pretentious a denotation must be used) is brought about by the digital wonders of the information age—or rather, by the somewhat eschatological claims of the proponents of the so-called new media: "the book is dead," "this is the Late Age of Print," "the electronic text will free us from the tyranny of paper," and "in the future, everyone will be a writer." No doubt, these are interesting times. The problem with terms such as the *electronic text* and the *printed book* is that they are, to borrow a phrase from Clifford Geertz, too "dangerously unfocused" to sustain a precise analysis. Nevertheless, this enthusiastic eschatology forces us to see dusty old things in a new light and perhaps learn a thing or two in the process.

And so the computer—that old, mythological beast—has become instrumental in everyone's quest for a new understanding of the text. The danger of turning this quest into just another metaphysics comes mainly from two sides, both of which it is impossible to avoid altogether: the vigorous rhetoric of the current generation of media prophets urging us to believe in their electronic text; and, more fundamentally, that there *is* such a thing as *the text*, a theoretical entity that defines the sufficient and necessary conditions of textuality, with no regard for practice, history, or technology. (There are also the problems of translation, transcript, pastiche, theft, censorship, editing, variorum editions, incomplete manuscripts, and oral narratives, which will not be discussed here.)

One of the most important ideological aspects of the effects on verbal communication of the present and earlier information technologies is that the transcendental concept of text seems to survive. It does not come to mean something else, like "electronic book," "computer novel," or "virtual document": the electronic text, for all its hype and naiveté, is still a text. If we accept this claim, then it seems clear that textuality cannot be defined in terms of location, anatomy, or temporality. What is the difference, in terms of script, between *Don Quixote* on paper and *Don Quixote* on a screen? I believe they are the same, although I "know" that the ink-cellulose relationship promotes and impedes different rituals of use than does the electron-phosphor relationship.

To clarify the fundamental mechanisms of texts, we should study text as information. This simple and perhaps anticlimactic injunction does not leave the eternal questions of rhetoric and poetics in the hands of the information theorists any more than the fundamental problems of semantics can be solved by phoneticians, but it might give us a more stable object to work with in a time when our old paper-based paradigms seem to disperse on the winds of the rhetoric of the new technologies. Under these circumstances it might seem a suspect move to link our concept of textuality to the very scientific ideology that causes our crisis, the theories of cybernetics and information as conceived by Norbert Wiener, Claude Shannon, and others in the 1940s.[2] However, this is hardly a controversial connection in itself, for the influence of this paradigm on literary theory can be found throughout structuralism and beyond, in the hegemonic works of Roman Jakobson and Umberto Eco, for example. Where this new adaptation might prove to be a radical departure is in the way we shall use it to define textuality independent of its traditional associates, the reader/receiver/audience and writer/sender/author. This move, which might be seen as self-defense, serves two practical purposes: to avoid the rather silly idea that the reader and author are becoming the same person; and to free the text from being identified with its readings and its writings. A text is not what we may read out of it, nor is it identical with what someone once wrote into it. It is something more, a potential that can be realized only partially and only through its script. Furthermore, texts (whether they exist or not), like electrons, can never be experienced directly, only by the signs of their behavior. Texts are cross products between a set of matrices— linguistic (the script), technological (the mechanical conditions), and historical (the socio-political context); and because of the temporal instability of all of these variables,

texts are processes impossible to terminate and reduce. This perspective lets us include nonlinear texts, many of which have no author (or even reader) in the traditional sense.

After the tensions and misunderstandings caused by the intrusions of new computer-mediated textualities and the inevitable resistance to them have been absorbed into literary theory, new textual paradigms will eventually emerge. They will no doubt be very different from the perspective presented here, but with a little luck their metaphysics might be informed by the principles behind the lines of the textual technologies, as well as by the metaphors of the latest interfaces.

## A Typology of Nonlinear Textuality

The use of the term *nonlinearity* in this essay is grounded in mathematics and not inspired by the modern physical sciences. I emphasize this point not because I want to distance myself from the claims of literary critics, like Katherine Hayles, who employ the term in its latter sense, but because the influence of nonlinear dynamics on recent literary theory should not be confused with the present formal concept of nonlinear textuality.[3] Insights promoted by the metaphors of nonlinear physics aid understanding of nonlinear texts as well as linear ones, but reading a nonlinear text is not the same as a reading informed by research in fractal geometry or chaos theory. The behavior of some kinds of nonlinear texts can certainly be described in terms of unpredictability, self-organization, and turbulence, but for the definition and basic understanding of nonlinear literature we need not look that far.

For a formal definition of our concept, the mathematical branch of topology will suffice. According to my copy of *Webster's New Twentieth-Century Dictionary*, this is the theory of "those properties of geometric figures that remain unchanged even when under distortion, so long as no surfaces are torn." Without too much discordance, I hope, the textonomical version of topology may be described as "the study of the ways in which the various sections of a text are connected, disregarding the physical properties of the channel (paper, stone, electromagnetic, and so on), by means of which the text is transmitted." The original mathematical meaning is transposed from geometry to textonomy rather than metaphorized, because the formalism is left intact. Textual topology describes the formal structures that govern the sequence and accessibility of the script, whether the process is conducted manually (for example, by convention) or mechanically (for example, by computer).

If texts are to be described in topological terms, they must be shown to consist of a set of smaller units and the connections between them. Further, the function of these units must be relevant to our notion of nonlinearity. It is not difficult to partition any text into graphemes (letters), lexemes (words), or syntagms (phrases or sentences), but none of these elements indicates nonlinearity by its presence. As later examples reveal, the position of a single letter or the position of many syntagms strung together can make a text nonlinear. Therefore, the unit for which we are looking is clearly not defined by linguistic form. This unit, which is best conceived as an arbitrarily long string of graphemes, is identified by its relation to the other units as constrained and separated by the conventions or mechanisms of their mother text. It should be noted that these textual units usually do not upset the laws of grammatical language, but that is of no importance to our definition.

As a suitable name for such a unit I suggest *texton*, which denotes a basic element of textuality. In accordance with the concept of textuality developed in the previous section, a more logical name might seem to be *scripton*, but this term posits that the textual unit belongs to the reading process rather than that it inheres in the textual structure as a strategic potential. A scripton, then, is an unbroken sequence of one or more textons as they are projected by the text. Another alternative to *texton* might be *lexie*, after Roland Barthes's *"unités de lecture"* ("units of reading") in *S/Z*.[4] This candidate, adopted by George P. Landow (1992) from an English translation as "lexia," I want to avoid because of Barthes's emphasis on seriality (*"fragments contigu"*) and the destructive process of its separation (*"découpé"*) from the text.[5] For Barthes, lexies are not the building blocks of textuality but a violent and powerful demonstration of "reading." In sharp contrast to the playful combinatorics of textual nonlinearity, Barthes's motto is clearly *divide et impera*.

In addition to its textons, a text consists of one or more *traversal functions,* the conventions and mechanisms that combine and project textons as scriptons to the *user* (or reader) of the text. We use these functions to distinguish between the variants in our textual typology. A traversal function might be a simple act of accessing a text (for example "pick a random card" or *"Ecc* 12:12b") or it might be a complex set of instructions (for example a computer program such as *Eliza*) that compiles a scripton from textons. Since there is an infinite set of traversal functions, I shall not try to make an inventory of them here but instead describe a set of basic variates that together defines a multidimensional coordinate system into which the functions can be plotted. This proposed matrix, which is clearly incomplete, may be expanded or changed as new traversal functions are discovered, or as existing ones are better understood. The categories I intend to extract are pragmatic and tentative, and will hopefully yield to a more concise model as the research progresses.

Below is a list of the variates, slightly adapted from my *Texts of Change,* in which they are developed and discussed at length and applied to a set of nonlinear texts.[6] Then, by the exploratory data-analysis method known as correspondence analysis, a two-dimensional plot was produced in which the texts formed groups that provided a basis for general classification.[7]

**Topology.** The fundamental difference is that between the *linear* and the *nonlinear.* A nonlinear text is a work that does not present its scriptons in one fixed sequence, whether temporal or spatial. Instead, through cybernetic agency (the user[s], the text, or both), an arbitrary sequence emerges.

**Dynamics.** Then there is the difference between the *static* and the *dynamic* text. In a static text the scriptons are constant, whereas in a dynamic text the contents of scriptons may change while the number of textons remains fixed (*intratextonic* dynamics), or the number of textons may vary as well (*textonic* dynamics).

**Determinability** concerns the stability of the traversal function; a text is *determinate* if the adjacent scriptons of every scripton are always the same, and *indeterminate* if not.

**Transiency.** If the mere passing of the user's time causes scriptons to appear, it is *transient,* if not, it is *intransient.* If the transiency has the nature of "real time" it is *synchronous*; if the relationship between the user's time and the passing of fictional time is arbitrary, we call it *asynchronous.*

**Maneuverability.** The question of how easy it is to access the scriptons of a text can be described in terms of traversal functions and their combinations. The most open (or weak) we call *random access to all scriptons*; then there is the standard hypertext traversal function—the *link, explicit access to all scriptons*; the *hidden* link; the *conditional* or *complex* link; and, finally, the arbitrary or *completely controlled access.*

**User-functionality.** Besides the *interpretative function* of the user, which of course is present in the use of both linear and nonlinear textuality, the use of nonlinear texts may be described in terms of four active feedback functions: the *explorative function*, in which the user decides which "path" to take; the *role-playing function*, in which the user assumes strategic responsibility for a "character" in a "world" described by the text; the *configurative function*, in which textons and/or traversal functions are in part chosen and/or designed by the user; and the *poetic function*, in which the user's actions, dialogue, or design are aesthetically motivated.

Any type of text can be discussed according to these categories; I avoid the primitive and theoretically uninteresting division between electronic and hard copy texts as well as the nebulous concept of interactive fiction. The model is equally applicable to a child's interrogation of a storyteller and a researcher's conversation with an artificial intelligence program, or a radio broadcast of *The Wind in the Willows*.

The best way to test a model is to see how well it stands up to new data. Since I developed mine in 1991, a new text type has appeared, invented by the science fiction author William Gibson. His *Agrippa: A Book of the Dead* (1992) displays its script at a fixed scrolling pace on the screen and then encrypts it by a technique cryptically known as RSA, rendering it effectively unreadable after that one projection.[8] Leaving the more obvious jokes aside (better make reservations down at the library, quick!), this is clearly one more of those one-of-a-kind texts for which "the medium is the message" seems to have been intended. But that should not stop the empirical literary critic. I must admit to a curious feeling of unease here. *Agrippa* perversely obeys the logic of cultural capitalism beyond the wildest dreams of publishers: it is the non-reusable book. At the same time it obviously subverts the metaphysics of textual mass production. How? By being a copy that destroys its text, or a text which destroys its copy? *Agrippa* is a unique lesson in textual ontology, a linear text that seems to flirt with nonlinearity, not through its convention or mechanism but through the difference between its used and unused copies. The individual copy-as-text is linear, because there is only one sequence: first, the decrypted scripton once, then the re-encrypted one for ever after; but the text-as-copy may turn out to be either of the scriptons and is therefore nonlinear. Rather than accept that this paradoxical result undermines

my linear-nonlinear distinction, I contend that by destroying its traversal function it exposes the inherent instability of the metaphysical concept of "the text itself." Thus, *Agrippa* becomes nonlinear only if we choose to accept the "text-behind-the-text" as more real than the physical object that can refuse to be read. As for the rest of our categories, *Agrippa* is a rather unusual combination of a static, determinate, and transient text with completely controlled access to scriptons.

As a simplified synthesis of this model I now propose four pragmatic categories, or degrees, of nonlinearity: (1) the simple nonlinear text, whose textons are totally static, open and explorable by the user; (2) the discontinuous nonlinear text, or hypertext, which may be traversed by "jumps" (explicit links) between textons; (3) the determinate "cybertext," in which the behavior of textons is predictable but conditional and with the element of role-playing; and (4) the indeterminate cybertext in which textons are dynamic and unpredictable. The weakness of this simplified model is that some nonlinear texts, such as those that are both static and indeterminate, fall between the generalized categories. However, it is not uncommon in cultural theory that generalization means loss of precision, and it should always be weighed against the usefulness and convenience of the simplification and the fact that a more rigorous and unmitigated model exists.

The rest of this essay discusses each of these four categories, some of the texts that can be said to belong to them, their attributes and peculiarities, and their importance to literary theories and to the practice of literary criticism.

## The Readerless Text

Nonlinearity can be achieved in many ways, the simplest of which is a script forking out in two directions on a surface, forcing its witness (the user) to choose one path in preference to another. In such a case (for example, the "dream maps" in Kathy Acker's *Blood and Guts in High School*), the user can immediately afterwards take the other path and thus eventually view all parts of the script simultaneously.[9] The verbal oscillation created by two equally possible combinations, the choice of which is entirely up to the user, produces an ambiguity different from the usual poetic double meaning of a word or phrase, because there seem to be two different versions, neither of which can exist alongside the other, and both obviously different from the text itself. Like optical illusions, we can imagine first one, then the other, but not both at the same time. When we look at the whole of such a nonlinear text, we cannot read it; and when we read it, we cannot see the whole text. Something has come between us and the text, and that is ourselves, trying to read. This self-consciousness forces us to take responsibility for what we read and to accept that it can never be the text itself. The text, far from yielding its riches to our critical gaze, appears to seduce us, but it remains immaculate, recedes, and we are left with our partial and impure thoughts, like unworthy pilgrims beseeching an absent deity.

However, if a text cannot be conquered, it is all the better suited for worship. The wall-inscriptions of the temples in ancient Egypt were often connected two-dimensionally (on one wall) or three-dimensionally (from wall to wall and from room to room), and this layout allowed a nonlinear arrangement of the religious text in accordance with the symbolic architectural layout of the temple.[10]

Without doubt, the most prominent and popular nonlinear text in history must be the famous Chinese work of oracular wisdom, *I Ching* or *Book of Changes*, one of the great classics of antiquity, which was used for thousands of years for meditation and as an oracle. It is not, as is sometimes stated, the oldest text in Chinese and world literary history, but it is well over three thousand years old and originates from the symbol system said to have been invented over five thousand years ago by the legendary Fu Hsi.[11] Other notables, among them King Wen, the Duke of Chou, and Confucius, have developed and annotated the text down through the ages; and the text is still being rewritten and mutating, adapting to modern society and its paradigms.[12]

*I Ching* is made up of sixty-four symbols or hexagrams, which are the binary combinations of six whole or broken ("changing") lines ($64 = 2^6$). A hexagram (such as nr. 49:☲ *Ko/Revolution*) contains a main texton and six small ones, one for each line. By manipulating three coins or forty-nine yarrow stalks according to a randomizing principle, textons from two hexagrams are combined, producing one out of 4096 possible scriptons. This scripton contains the answer to a question the user wrote down in advance. The extremely clever openness of the formulations, the sense of ritual involved in throwing the coins or stalks, and the strangely personal communication between the user and the book almost always make an answer extracted from *I Ching* seem relevant and sometimes even divinely inspired.

Unlike historic texts with a fixed expression, such as *Beowulf*, *I Ching* seems to speak uniquely to us across the millennia, not as a distant mirror that can be understood in a philological or romantic sense but as an entity that somehow understands us and exists for us. This almost religious effect can be partly explained by the repeated updates and the fact that the text was intended to be useful and directly relevant to events in people's lives, but it seems to me that it is the explicit and elaborate ritual, largely unchanged through the ages, that creates the textual *presence* that allows us to be naive users—not readers but agents of the text, closely related to the users of three thousand years ago, despite the epistemological interventions of time and culture. *The Book of Changes* may not be the world's first text, but it is certainly the first expert system based on the principles of binary computing that very much later became automated by electricity and the vacuum tube.

Both types of text discussed so far seem to reject the presence of the traditional reader figure, as it is implied and applied in the theories of literature. As an individual, this pale and uncontroversial character never mattered much to us critics anyway, and then only as a construct on which to hang the baser pleasures of the text; he is our poor and predictable cousin, slave to the rhythm, lost in the textual pleasure dome like the ball in a pinball machine. Later, for the reader-response theorists, he became a thumbtack with which to pin down the variable of literary meaning when it could no longer be located in the text. Active or passive, the reader is always portrayed as a receiver of the text, going quietly about the business of consuming, constructing *meaning only*, a fixed but evolving character at the end of the text's production line, defined by the conventions and strategies of reading. Of course, it can be argued that this relationship is no different for nonlinear texts, once the shock of an alien form is gone and the particular convention is understood and mastered. This counterpoint, which may be called the *Verfremdung*-argument, has much merit, but it ignores the fact that the understanding (beyond trivial) of a nonlinear text can never be a consummate understanding, because the realization of its script (and not just its meaning) belongs to the individual user, who is acutely aware of his or her own constructive participation. Since the object is unstable both in a syntactic and semantic sense, it cannot be read, only glimpsed and guessed at. Much of the initial discomfort felt by the user of a nonlinear text is caused by its not behaving as a real text should; once the strangeness is gone, the user knows what to expect, which is not to expect everything. The users learn to accept their position as agents of the text, sometimes happily, as in the case of the *Book of Changes*, and sometimes unhappily, as with the forking directions texts. The difference between these two types of experience can be explained by the presence or absence of an established (meaningful) ritual, which must absolve the user from the burden of reading, which in the case of nonlinearity may be defined as the frustrating attempt to harmonize contradictory scriptons from the same text. The user of *I Ching* relates the scripton directly to his or her individual situation, and the interpretation, following the ritual of producing the hexagram, can only be done by the individual.

This fall from readership should not be confused with the clever destabilization effects of so-called metafictions, in which the opposite point—readership confirmed—is made. Even (and especially) the famously "unreadable" texts subversively observe the metaphysics of the general reader: the door would not be locked if the owner did not believe in thieves.

Few texts drive home the point of the readerless text more abundantly than Raymond Queneau's *Cent Mille Milliards de Poèmes* (1961).[13] In this short book, ten pages are cut into fourteen one-line strips, and the user is invited to flip the strips individually, to form 100,000,000,000,000 different combinations. As it turns out, each of the 140 strips (or textons) is a sonnet line, and the result of any combination is a scripton in the form of a formally perfect sonnet. Here is sonnet number 65 957 658 052 316:

> Quand l'un aveque l'autre aussitôt sympathise
> que convoitait c'est sûr une horde d'escrocs
> des êtres indécis vous parlent sans franchise
> il ne trouve aussi sec qu'un sac de vieux fayots
>
> L'un et l'autre a raison non la foule insoumise
> qui clochard devenant jetait ses oripeaux
> aller à la grand ville est bien une entreprise
> l'enfant pur aux yeux bleus aime les berlingots
>
> Du pôle à Rosario fait une belle trotte
> on giffle le marmot qui plonge sa menotte
> lorsqu'on revient au port en essuyant un grain
>
> Ne fallait pas si loin agiter ses breloques
> on transports et le marbre et débris et défroques
> la gémellité vraie accuse son destin.

This may not be the most exciting of lyrical poetry, but it is unique in a very special sense: I have never read it before, and chances are that neither has anybody else. Who wrote it? Was it me, or Queneau (and if so, in 1961 or 1992?), or perhaps the text itself? Will anybody ever read number 65 957 658 052 317? For one person to read all the sonnets is clearly impossible, and even a very small fraction—say ten million—would take at least one hundred years. *Cent Mille Milliards de Poèmes* effectively mocks the theoretical notions of writer and reader, while the power of the text is cleverly demonstrated. (What it does to our notion of the sonnet is perhaps better left unsaid.) "Obviously the possibilities of the book as format are being strained to the limit," comments William Paulson, who goes on to propose *Poèmes* as "an ideal candidate for a computerized version."[14] Contrary to Paulson, I suggest that the fact that it *is* a book is just as significant; and if it seems easy to implement as a computer program, that is because of the simple and unstrained elegance of its idea.

The difference between these experiences and my experience with Boorman's *Zardoz* is that in the latter case I could, based on my cultural competence, deduce the actual existence of a version that was independent of me and the possibility of a proper reading that could be conducted by an easily imagined proper reader, but not by me. In other words, I rejected my reading because it told me that I was not a real reader, since what I was reading was not the real text. The shock of discovering that one is not a reader can only happen (and only accidentally) with a linear text, because that is the only text in which the metaphysics of a real reader has any credibility and the only text in which the reader can exist as a reducible, accountable figure. In addition, *reader* has—until now—always been defined by literary theorists with only the linear text in mind. If we want to know what is going on between nonlinear texts and their users, we must come up with a concept that implies both more and less than reading and redefines literary satisfaction as well as hermeneutic behavior.

## Hypertext Is Not What You (May) Think

Hypertext, for all its packaging and theories, is an amazingly simple concept. It is merely a direct connection from one position in a text to another. However, when we speak of hypertext, it can signify at least three different things: (1) the general concept, as outlined above; (2) an implementation of the concept, usually a computer application called a hypertext system, with idiosyncrasies and enhancements that make it different from other systems; and (3) a text embedded in (and defined by) such a system. As an unfortunate result, many assumptions made about the general concept of hypertext are really about a specific implementation. Added to that are the political conjectures about the benevolent effects on the structures of power between writers and readers, teachers and students, government and the public, in which the good guys seem to be winning, at least in theory. Only the first of these relationships will be discussed here, and only because of the assumptions about the effects of hypertext upon the figures of author and reader.[15] (Of course, implicit in the term *hypertext* is a sphere of meanings beyond the operational. Those who would play on this potential cannot completely escape its dark side: the excessive, the abnormal, the sickly.)

Although the term *hypertext* was first used by Theodor H. Nelson in 1965 (compare Nelson 1987), the modern origin of the idea is generally accepted to stem from Vannevar Bush, whose article "As We May Think" (1945) described a possible solution to the scientist's problem of keeping up with the "growing mountain of research," in the form of a "sort of mechanized private file and library," a machine for storing, annotating, retrieving, and linking information: the *memex*.[16] Although Bush emphasizes the "trail"—the linear ordering of interesting items from the "maze of materials available"—he allows his user to go off on little side excursions. Bush was no techno-pessimist (at the end of the article he even envisions the neural jack of the 1980s cyberpunk science fiction!), and we can hardly blame him for not coming up with a complete "web view" on hypertextuality in 1945. But it should be pointed out that in his fascinating vision—his *poetics*— nonlinearity is as much a problem (the "maze") as a solution (the "trail"). Where he clearly concurs with his apostles is in his focus on user-created links and annotations. This may seem more radical than it actually is, with subversive political consequences for the world of literature and art; but Bush's user is clearly modeled on the traditional academic author, who can carry out his critical comparisons and annotations of sources with the same serene distance as before, only much more efficiently.

The principle of hypertext should not be linked to a particular ideology or poetics because it can be used (and of

course misused) by many. Moreover, when as literary critics we examine a hypertextual text, we should take care not to confuse its interpretation with the author-reader relationship made possible by the ideology of its hypertext system and then assign the conclusions to a general theory of literary hypertext.

Hypertext theorists frequently employ spatial imagery to describe the relations made possible by links and textons: maps, three-dimensionality, textual landscapes, navigation, topography, and the like. This rhetoric fails to hide the fact that the main feature of hypertext is discontinuity—the jump—the sudden displacement of the user's position in the text. Pure hypertext is actually among the least topographical modes of nonlinearity. To ease this situation, hypertext systems often introduce additional features: overviews, index views, web views, texton lists, and so on. Some would undoubtedly argue that these instruments are also hypertext, but since we would recognize a text as hypertext without any of them, we should also endeavor to discuss the literary ramifications of hypertext without them. When they are included in a literary hypertext, they substantially affect the textual ritual, usually to a point at which it is difficult to speak about the same text.

A text that already has become canonical in the discussions of literary hypertext is Michael Joyce's *Afternoon, a story*.[17] Comprising (according to the information supplied at startup) 539 textons and 950 links, *Afternoon* both celebrates and subverts hypertext structure. The first of its kind, it intriguingly demonstrates the potential of hypertextuality for literary experiment and explores the effects of nonlinearity on narration.

There are no visible links in *Afternoon*, and the user may click on any word in the scriptons to see if they yield (link to) something special. If they do not, or the user presses the return key, the next default scripton in the present chain occupies the screen. In addition, the user may call up a menu with explicit links, but this can be a disruptive element in the otherwise suggestive and enigmatic ride on the link stream. To complicate matters, some links are conditional; they are available only if the user has earlier traversed certain unspecified scriptons. As anyone familiar with hypertext programs knows, this interface is very unusual: an invisible link is as unheard of as a newspaper article without a headline. The conditional link is just as uncanny and makes the text "seem to have a mind of its own."[18] Thus *Afternoon*, arguably the first literary hypertext, turns out to be something more: a cybertext disguised in hypertext's clothing.

It is hard to classify *Afternoon* as a narrative (or "a story," as the text paradoxically titles itself). Although within most of the individual scriptons the voice of a first person narrator relates events to a narratee in a traditional manner, the unpredictable changing of scenes (as one trail of related scriptons abruptly stops and another begins) constantly undermines the would-be reader's attempt to identify with the narratee, as well as the identification of the narrator and the (implied) author or exo-narrator, as it were. In *Afternoon* there seems to be an anti-narrator at work, giving the narrator (and me) a hard time. In linear experimental texts the subversive effect is sometimes achieved by a "distance between narrator and narratee" and sometimes by the "loss of narratee"—the narrator as solipsist.[19] In *Afternoon*, however, the relation between narrator and narratee appears relatively normal; while the distance between the user and narratee on one side and narrator and author on the other is stretched to the limit by the unreliable links. Far from feeling like Landow's "reader-author" (117), who has no problem constructing "meaning and narrative from fragments provided by someone else," I felt constantly sidetracked, turning and turning in the dilating text, dead sure that important things were being whispered just beyond my hearing. I cannot deny that it was a very fascinating literary experience.

It can be argued that the text I encountered was (in more than one sense) not the same as the one discussed by Stuart Moulthrop, J. David Bolter, and Landow. From their accounts it appears that they used a different and more advanced version of *Afternoon*'s hypertext system, the "author version" of Storyspace, which allows writing and adding links, and most significantly contains a global view, a graphical representation of the topological relations between all textons and links. My version was in Readingspace, the stand-alone reader program that *Afternoon*'s publisher distributes. Consequently, my encounter, "one scripton at a time," with *Afternoon* was very different from theirs; for the global view, even if they did not use it, gave them a safety net that I lacked. While I was lost in the labyrinth, they could be "up there" with its creator—but only up to a point. Whatever changes they might impose, it would only be on their own copies; Joyce's text

would stand unchanged. In this, hypertext is not different from paper-based linear texts. The balance of power between readers and writers is not changed by hypertext alone, nor by its enhancements, but by the political and economic logic of society (to use some slightly inaccurate clichés). This may change, under the influence of technological change and other things; but until it does, hypertext is just one more "instrument in some representational enterprise," to borrow a phrase from Samuel Delany.

To expand the notion of hypertext by subsuming other computer-mediated textual communication phenomena such as Usenet (see Bolter, 29) or intertextual allusion (see Landow, 10) will only render the concept useless for critical discourse. Landow's term "implicit hypertext" implies that an allusion and a link are essentially the same, but we only need a hypertext with both links and allusions to see that they work differently and must be considered two separate literary instruments. Bolter, eager to proclaim the end of "the printed book," plays along with the metaphysics of logocentrism and reduces print on paper to barely a corner of its multiform nature: "A printed book generally speaks with a single voice and assumes a consistent character, a persona, before its audience."[20] For "the electronic text," however, this no longer applies, because "it is not a physical artifact." To go against Bolter's rhetoric, I would say that instead of having two sets of opposed attributes, one connected to the "printed" and one to the "electronic" text, we have a number of different text types, some paper based and some digital, with the greater variety among the digital ones, and the paper based most centrally placed. Thus, there may be more difference between two digital texts than between either of those and a paper text. Allusion, reference, quotation, and linking are all *different* functions of intertextuality, just as Usenet newsgroups, electronic mailing lists, hypertext systems, paperback bestsellers, and flysheets represent different modes of textuality.

As the analysis of *Afternoon* indicates, literary hypertexts seem to pose interesting perspectives for students of literature. The question of nonlinear narrative versus anti-narrative should not be decided by the evidence from only one text (even if it exists in two versions), and perhaps we need a new terminology that lets us name the representation and composition principle that relates to nonlinearity as narrative relates to linearity.

However, one traditional term seems almost perfect to describe literary hypertexts. *Afternoon* does not represent a break with the *novel*. On the contrary, it finds its place in a long tradition of experimental literature in which one of the main strategies is to subvert and resist narrative. The novel ("the new"), from Cervantes to the *Roman Nouveau*, has always been an anti-genre, and *Afternoon* is but its latest confirmation.

## Death and Cybernetics in the Ever-ending Text

> I'm not sure that I have a story. And if I do, I'm not
> sure that everything isn't my story.
> —Michael Joyce, *Afternoon, a story*

If literary hypertext is a new form of computer-mediated textuality, cybertext is a fairly old one, going back to the 1960s if not longer. *Cyber* is derived from *cybernetics*, the name of Norbert Wiener's science of "control and communication in the animal and the machine," again derived from the Greek *kybernêtês, steersman* (compare governor). A cybertext is a self-changing text, in which scriptons and traversal functions are controlled by an immanent cybernetic agent, either mechanical or human. There are many species of cybertext, and my distinction between determinate and indeterminate tries to set up an important division between two main groups: those that can be predicted (for example, one set of user actions will always yield the same set of scriptons) and those that cannot. The second group will be discussed in the next section.

The history of computer-mediated cybertexts can be traced to two different sources, both originating from fields of computer science, and both with their memorable ur-texts. The first, *Eliza*, created by Joseph Weizenbaum in 1966, was an early success in the field called artificial intelligence. The mother of all dialogue programs (*Parry, SHRDLU, Racter*, and countless others), *Eliza* played the part of a psychotherapist, asking the user questions and constructing further questions using information from the answers. Usually, dialogues turned rather Pinteresque as soon as the users discovered *Eliza's very* mechanical nature; but Weizenbaum's invention effectively demonstrated man's needs for communication, no matter with whom (or indeed *what*), and an important literary genre—the artificial conversationalist—was born.

The other source is known as the classic game *Adventure*, the first of the highly popular computer game genre of adventure games. According to Jon Lanestedt, *Adventure* was first a landscape simulation of Colossal Cave in Kentucky, topographed as a Fortran program by William Crowther at the end of the 1960s, then enhanced by Don Woods to attain its adventure form, and later modified and ported by others to countless computer platforms as the home-computer explosion started at the end of the 1970s.[21] Its technical structure became the paradigm for a very large number of similar games, even after more advanced types, such as Infocom's *Zork*, became commercially available.

The basic structure of *Adventure* can be described not as a topography but as an *ergography*, the textually represented laborious progress of the main character/narratee/user; the text's "you." *You's* task is to find all the treasure and kill the appropriate monsters while avoiding getting killed or stuck or lost in the topographical maze. The user controls *you* by typing commands, such as "kill troll," or "grab gold," that are interpreted by a simple verb-object parser. Directions can be specified by simple letters: "n" for "north," "d" for "down" etc. Depending on the user's input, the text will issue short scriptons describing the landscape, possible exits to the next room, any objects lying about, or the result of the user's last command. Here is a short sample of the start of a session with *Adventure* (my commands are in capital letters):

```
Welcome to Adventure!! Would you like instructions?
N
Please answer the question!
NO
You are standing at the end of a road before a small
brick building. Around you is a forest. A small stream
flows out of the building and down a gully.
BUILDING
You are inside a building, a well house for a large
spring.
There are some keys on the ground here.
There is a shiny brass lamp nearby.
There is food here.
There is a bottle of water here.
TAKE KEYS
Ok.

. . . .

LEAVE
You are at end of road again.
```

DOWN
You are in a valley in the forest beside a stream
tumbling along a rocky bed.
DOWN
At your feet all the water of the stream splashes into a
2-inch slit in the rock. Downstream the streambed is
bare rock.
DOWNSTREAM
You don't fit through a two-inch slit!
You're at slit in streambed.

*Adventure* and most texts like it are determinate, intransient, and intratextonically dynamic, with completely controlled access to scriptons. The user's function takes the form of role-playing, since the user assumes strategic responsibility for the narratee. As with *Afternoon,* these texts often give me a feeling of being lost, the feeling that the real action is taking place elsewhere in the text; but in adventure games the ennui is usually replaced by death, when the *you* has reached a dead end in the topography or invoked some deadly response by a wrong action. Death in the cybertext is a strange kind of death, however, in relation to death both in fiction and in real life. Rather than signifying closure—the end—"cyberdeath" signifies a sort of reincarnation of the main character: death implies beginning. This phenomenon most clearly establishes the difference between main character, narratee, and user. The main character is simply dead, erased, and must begin again. The narratee, on the other hand, is explicitly told what happened, usually in a sarcastic manner, and offered the chance to start anew. The user, aware of all this in a way denied to the narratee, learns from the mistakes and previous experience and is able to play a different game.

Just as death in the determinate cybertext is a kind of unend, the end of the cybertext is a kind of undeath also contrary to fiction. The end of a cybertext (when the user quits) can be either successful (the user wins) or unsuccessful (the game is not solved). The first case denies the satisfaction that can be experienced at the end of a good, traditional epic, since the *you* remains in the text after completing the adventures, but there is nothing more to do. Even when the text includes some sort of ceremony of victory, it cannot provide the traditional build-up and release of tension that the readers of fiction normally expect. In Aristotelian terms, the end is marked by peripety not catharsis. If the end is unsuccessful, this too means abandonment of the *you,* which

then remains in the text as a ghost in the machine: not living, not properly buried, and with a cause left unfinished.

If the absent structure of narrative is the key problem in literary hypertext, in determinate cybertext the absent structure is the plot. Since without a user there can be no action (*praxis*) in a determinate cybertext, the concept of story (*fabula*) is meaningless. In fiction the story determines and hides behind the plot, which produces the action, whereas in cybertext the plot itself is hidden, and so the discursive causality is reversed: action determines (or seeks in vain for) the plot, which if found does not produce anything interesting, only (barely) closure. Although there is a narrator, because of the narratee's significant interruptions there can be no narrative, only narration. The goal of this dialogue is to try out possible plots until the shoe fits: the user is playing for the plot.

Anthony Niesz and Norman Holland, in their early article on what they called "interactive fiction" (a concept that corresponds to determinate cybertext, if one disregards their definition of it), contend that "Interactive fiction has become possible only with the advent of high-speed digital computers that are capable of handling words."[22] However, when they compare computer-based adventure games to paper-based ones, the only difference they can find is that the latter do "not yield the sense of true dialogue that one gets from computerized interactive fiction." What they mean is that the user does not type words on the screen and watch the response. (The "sense of true dialogue" is hard to take seriously.) In fact, a game book such as *The Money Spider* (of the type that instructs, "If you want to hear about Schmidt, turn to 270, and if you want to hear about Popper, turn to 90") tells the user to write on its pages to map progress.[23] When classified by the categories of the variate model, *The Money Spider*, just like *Adventure*, is determinate, intransient, and intratextonically dynamic (since the user by writing changes at least one texton), with completely controlled access to scriptons (it is possible to cheat, of course, but that can be done in *Afternoon* too). This is no coincidence, because the game book genre was in part inspired by and adapted from the computer-mediated adventure game: an interesting example of how "the printed book" can subsume "the electronic text," if the market demands it.

## "The Lingo of the Cable": Travels in Cybertextuality

As the field of artificial intelligence expanded, it soon overlapped with that of topography and world simulation and produced story generators and models for representing actions and characters.[24] Later, research took an explicit interest in the adventure game, developing complex models of the interaction between a user-controlled character and artificial persons within a simulated world, for example, the Oz Project of the Simulated Realities Group at Carnegie Mellon University.[25] Such systems can be classified as indeterminate cybertexts, since the level of complexity and the flexibility of user input, like explicitly programmed random behavior, make scriptons unpredictable. Interestingly, a main goal of adventure game theorists such as Brenda Laurel and others is to be able to control what they call the plot. The user-character will be allowed some leeway, but by use of Playwright, an expert system with knowledge of dramatic structure (perhaps not totally unlike an intelligent version of *Afternoon's* anti-narrator), the situations and actions would be carefully orchestrated to fit its model of appropriate drama. Although this aesthetically motivated poetics has the goal of creating well-formed dramatic unity, it is hard not to see the potential for conflict between the user and this *deus in machina*. As the history of the novel has shown, the forces of carnivalism will work centrifugally against the law of genre in any simulated social situation. At last, in the cybertext, the user can become a little akin to an author—*not,* I hasten to add, to the author of the cybertext (and perhaps the conception of author should not be stretched this far), but perhaps, say, to a novelist of the nineteenth century.

The early determinate texts, such as *Adventure* and *Eliza,* seemingly invited the user to participate, but soon revealed that this was impossible, and that subordination was the name of the game. The user could only fill, or more typically fail to fill the narrow track of the text's hidden "plot"; and the texts evolved to play on this failure, as testified by the often (and sometimes unintended) ironic and humorous response to the user's contra-generic activities (for example, "drop dead"—"You're not carrying that!").

Indeterminate cybertext should be seen as a movement not against, but *beyond* genre. As the simulation of social structure becomes richer, plot control becomes increasingly difficult; and it is easy to predict the decentered cybertext in which stories, plots, and counterplots arise "naturally" from the autonomous movements of the cybernetic constructs. Already free of narrative, this Baudrillardian nightmare—if that is what it is (compare Moulthrop, "Hypertext and 'the Hyperreal'")—promises many more escapes: from plot and plotters (authors and author-machines), from genre and contra-generity, and from the social self. If it succeeds, the textual pleasure machine could be said to have escaped even from simulation and become an emulation, a "supplement" as dangerous as they come.

As always, we do not have to wait for the textual machines to catch up. They already have. The telegraph, "the singing wire," is a conspicuously unsung hero in most histories of communication.[26] Invented in 1793 by Claude Chappe, the first modern telegraph was optical, not electric, implemented as a chain of semaphore towers in France. Later the American Samuel Morse constructed his electromagnetic telegraph, and in 1844 set up a line between Baltimore and Washington, thus redefining the meaning of the word communication. A reason for media theorists' omission of the telegraph could be that it is categorically unclean, depending equally on material and immaterial technologies, and therefore an embarrassment to the great divide between print and electronic media.

From the start, the electric telegraph was used for textual fun and games. Marshall McLuhan tells this story: "When a group of Oxford undergraduates heard that Rudyard Kipling received ten shillings for every word he wrote, they sent him ten shillings by telegram during their meeting: 'Please send us one of your very best words.' Back came the word a few minutes later: 'Thanks.'"[27]

This is not the place to retrace the fundamental changes to society, time, and space brought about by the telegraph, but it should be noted that telegraph and later the telex was *the* method of instant global textual communication during a period of more than a hundred years, before digital computer networks came into being in the 1960s and '70s. However, with the computer's ability to handle more than two communicators simultaneously, new types of nonlocal textual fora were made possible. First there were the mainframe computers with their user communities sending messages to each other and so forth, then communication between computers (and their users) over a distance, by telephone wire or dedicated cable networks. With the emergence of the networks and the use of modems, many different kinds of textual communication evolved, from e-mail via mailing lists and newsgroups to so-called on-line chat, such as the interesting phenomenon Internet Relay Chat.[28]

At the end of the 1970s, with the spread of the highly popular *Adventure* over the networks, it was to be expected that someone should combine instant textual communication and adventure gaming. In the fall of 1979 at Essex University, Roy Trubshaw started the development of the Multi-User Dungeon (MUD) on a DEC System-10 mainframe, a task taken over by Richard Bartle in the summer of 1980.[29] The first MUD was a successful game, with users scoring points by killing each others' characters or finding hidden treasures and eventually reaching the powerful status of wizard, but it was also much more than a game; it was a cyberplace where people could enjoy complete anonymity and freedom from their social and physical selves and take on any persona they could think of, doing things with words that they would normally never do. Thus a new mode of textual expression was initiated, different even from the telegraph: the user had to be very quick, and formulate short, unretractable sentences in seconds, or die. Dorothy Parker and Ernest Hemingway would have loved it.

Like *Adventure* before it, MUD spread out globally on the academic computer networks, was soon copied, and changed into other types of multi-user texts. In the summer of 1989 at Carnegie Mellon University, James Aspnes programmed a MUD with a significant new feature: in addition to creating their own characters, the users were allowed to expand the MUD's textual descriptions, adding their own landscapes to the topography of the MUD. This MUD, known as TinyMUD and reachable from any computer linked to the global Internet, emphasized social interaction and building. There was no merit system; if your character was killed, it simply got an insurance fee of 50 pennies. The co-creativity of the users was a very anarchic step from the first MUDs. TinyMUD lasted from August 19, 1989, to April 28, 1990, when its data base of descriptions became too big to handle, filled up by more than 132,000 user-defined objects, each of which could contain several textons.

When regarded as literary objects, MUDs seem to defy every concept of literary theory. Every user has a different (or several different) and partial perspective(s), and the users bombard each other with textons meant only to last as long as they are not scrolled off the screen. MUDs are like constantly meandering rivers, developing new courses that

cross and re-cross each other and are filled with all sorts of peculiar flotsam and jetsam. And suddenly, in the middle of chaos, a group of characters may start singing in unison the Yoyodyne song from Thomas Pynchon's *The Crying of Lot 49*: "High above the LA freeways, / And the traffic's whine, / Stands the well-known Galactonics / Branch of Yoyodyne."[30] Strange things happen at sea.

Compared to a nineteenth-century novel, TinyMUD appears totally different: transient, dynamic, indeterminate, with explorative, role-playing, configurative, and poetic user-functionality. And yet, this is literature: letters, words, and sentences are selected, arranged and disseminated to delight, impress, or enrage an unknown audience. The scriptons, which can be funny, poignant, sleazy, silly, obnoxious, or noisy, usually come in a heterogeneous mix. With more than twenty characters in the same room, it takes a hardened "MUDder" to keep track of what is going on. Special-purpose MUD-client programs that have been developed to run on the user's local machine and ease communication provide functionality that is not part of the MUD itself, such as filtering out noisy characters and automating often-used commands. Not all characters one meets on a MUD have real persons behind them, and several characters might be played by the same person. An early automatic character (so-called bot) on TinyMUD was called Terminator, had its own office, and was, like its cinematic namesake, programmed to kill. If you paid it 200 pennies it would go and pester any character you specified. Bots were simply external programs built using various artificial intelligence techniques and logged on by their creators to TinyMUD just like human players, but usually recognized by their somewhat poor communication skills.

A discussion of MUDs in terms of authors and readers is irrelevant: a MUD cannot be read, only experienced from the very narrow perspective of one or more of the user's characters, with a lot of simultaneous scriptons being beyond reach; and the user cannot be sure that a particular contribution will ever be experienced by more than a few people, or, since the other characters might all be artificial persons or controlled by the same real person, by anyone at all.

## The Limits of Fiction

An important issue raised by both determinate and indeterminate cybertexts is their relation to the ontological categories of textuality: fiction, nonfiction, poetry, drama, etc. In the case of cybertexts such as *Adventure* and

TinyMUD, the most obvious choice, fiction, is not obvious enough. *Adventure* invites a belief from the user, but this is not the same belief or suspension of disbelief that must be sustained by the user of realistic or fantastic novels. Cybertextuality has an empirical element that is not found in fiction and that necessitates an ontological category of its own, which might as well be called simulation.

In fiction the user must construct mental images that somehow correspond to the world described in the text. The user is responsible for the images, but the text is in control and can dictate changes without any deference to external logic. From the user's perspective, fictions are neither logical nor illogical. If the fiction claims that elephants are pink, then in the fiction they are, because nobody is "there" to contradict it. A fiction, then, is not about something that does not exist but about something that it is meaningless to contradict.

In *Adventure*, the responsibility for coherence is shared between the user and the text. If the you-character drops a sword in one place, leaves, and comes back, the sword is still there. In other words, there is a systematic contract between text and user, like the causal one that exists in the real world and which, unlike fictions, can be empirically tested. In TinyMUD the simulation of reality is even closer to the real thing, since the conversations the user's character conducts with other characters often have the signs of real conversations.

Simulations are somewhere in between reality and fiction: they are not obliged to represent reality, but they do have an empirical logic of their own, and therefore they should not be called fictions. Unlike fictions, which simply present something else, cybertexts *represent* something beyond themselves.

## The Rhetoric of Nonlinearity

As we have seen, the profound challenge of nonlinear texts to the basic concepts of literary theory makes it difficult to discuss them in common literary terms. Even to the extent it is still possible, it should be done with caution; and if we can be sure of nothing else, we may be certain that contradiction will be the uninvited master trope of our discourse. But still—what kind of (literary? semiotic?) phenomenon is nonlinear textuality? Is there a name or recognized class for the device (or better, set of devices) of nonlinearity? Do some domains of literary theory lend their vocabularies more easily to its description than others? (If so, those are the ones most worthy of suspicion.)

As the advocates of hypertext enthusiastically remind us, it can be found as fiction, poetry, textbooks, encyclopedias, and so on; so nonlinearity as the superset of hypertext is clearly not a literary genre, or a type of poetic expression or discourse. This problem of classification can also be described in semiotic terms, but mainly to the effect that a text type (in our nongeneric sense) is a signification system, "an autonomous semiotic construct that has an abstract mode of existence independent of any communicative act it makes possible," which does not really answer the question.[31] To semiotics, texts are *chains* of signs, and therefore linear by definition.[32]

If we turn to rhetoric, we see that nonlinearity is clearly not a trope, since it works on the level of words, not meaning; but it could be classified as a type of figure, following Pierre Fontanier's taxonomy of tropes and figures. In the second part of his classic inventory of rhetorical figures, *Figures du Discours*, Fontanier defines *"les Figures non-Tropes"*—the figures other than tropes.[33] These he divides into several classes: construction-figures, elocution-figures, style-figures, and thought-figures, with various subclasses including inversion, apposition, ellipsis, and repetition. Among these classes we could place the figures of nonlinearity, with the following set of subclasses: *forking, linking/jumping, permutation, computation,* and *polygenesis.* These subclasses can be further divided, of course; and more importantly, instances from different subclasses (and from traditional ones such as repetition and topography) can combine to constitute a text type.

Compared to the textual typology presented earlier, this perspective has the advantage of connecting to a traditional concept of literary theory, the figure. In this, however, the idea of rhetoric is even farther removed from its origin as a theory of speech. But since the non-tropic figure is the concept for unusual positionings of words, it might not be totally unjustified.

In terms of the simplified hierarchy of nonlinear texts, these classes of figures belong to the following levels: forking, found in the spatially nonlinear text; linking/ jumping, belonging to the stratum of hypertext; permutation, computation, and polygenesis, all found in both determinate and indeterminate cybertext. Whereas a user-created permutation is determinate (for example, Queneau's *Poèmes*), a computed permutation may be determinate or indeterminate (for example, *I Ching*). A computation may be determinate or contain a random function that makes it indeterminate. Polygenesis can be determinate (for example, when the user types a sentence to *Eliza*, its response can be predicted) or indeterminate (as in the MUDs). A further classification of the figures of nonlinearity, such as distinguishing between different types of forks, links, random functions, polygenetic modes, and so on, will not be undertaken here.

## The Corruption of the Critic

How can literary theory attack the textualities of nonlinearity? How can we cut them up, read into them, describe them so they fit in our narratives? How can we link them to our totems and control their hidden mechanisms? Hypertext seems already well on its way into the canon. Is this a good sign? Conquests, unlike discoveries, are seldom accidental. On the other hand, there is no such thing as literary theory; there are only theories and theorists. And texts. Literary theory, more than most academic disciplines, has always been uncentered and fragmented, a widening gyre of readings and interests linked to countless philosophies, like a true Barthesian *texte scriptible*. So if hypertext should find a home, why not here?

This essay will not answer any of the big questions: What will hypertext do to the ways we think about texts? How will it resist the ways we are going to think about it, and be remembered as something other than an in-house pet, a dead tradition of literary experiment, explained and packaged from the start? How will the powerful but extremely primitive logic of the link affect our discursive methods?

If hypertext has connected well with literary studies, cybertext, a much older textual phenomenon, has gone by largely unnoticed. An article or two, a few doctoral dissertations; the lack of interest is significant, and may have several causes. One is obvious: adventure games are *games*, and that is not our department. Neither is the similarity between *I Ching*, Queneau's *Poèmes,* and *Adventure* too striking at first sight. Perhaps, also, the adventure game, for all its trivia and popular appeal, is too radical to be recognized, because it disfigures not only the reading process but also the reader. Literary critics have generally scorned prosaic texts that too openly captured their users—in which the relationship between reader and narratee became too intimate, lacking ironic distance or *Verfremdung.* Like the telegraph, such texts fall between accepted categories, in this case between lyrical poetry and prose. *Afternoon* on the other hand, with its subversive anti-narrator, has seemingly no problem with this, and can be welcomed and configured into literature and the literary.

The key difference between *Afternoon* and cybertexts such as *Adventure* and TinyMUD is what the virtual reality researchers call immersion: the user's convinced sense that the artificial environment is not just a main agent with whom they can identify but surrounds the user.[34] In cybertextual terms we could say that the user assumes the strategic and emotional responsibility of the character, or that the distances between the positions of main character, narratee, and user have collapsed.

To the critical institution, this ontological embarrassment becomes an ethical one. How can we be critics if we can no longer read? How can reviewers of cybertexts face the fact they probably missed large numbers of scriptons? And worse, not only will we have to admit that we barely made it to first base, but in the exploration of indeterminate cybertexts we will be reviewing the results of our own strategic and creative investments.[35]

## Problems of "Textual Anthropology"

This crisis in criticism might not amount to anything terrible, but it could be used as a new departure for literary hermeneutics. After the celebrated deaths of the author, the work, and reading, the text is now giving up the spirit, betrayed by its most trusted companion, the signifier. What is left is linear and nonlinear textuality, or better, linear and nonlinear textualities. This empirical evolution makes possible a shift in method from a philological to an anthropological approach in which the object of study is a process (the changing text) rather than a project (the static text). On-line phenomena and particularly the MUDs, with their fluid exchanges of textual praxis, offer unique opportunities for the study of rhetoric, semiotics, and cultural communication in general.

MUDs and similar nonlocal forms of instant textual communication can be studied from many perspectives in the human sciences; psychological, sociological, anthropological, linguistic, philosophical, historical, etc. Shades of these will inevitably find their way into the literary and textual perspectives that we might expect from our own discipline. If literary theorists and critics do engage in the study of indeterminate cybertexts, it should be with an awareness that the old role of *a posteriori* investigator no longer suffices. Like the user, the critic must be there when it happens. Not only that but, like the participant observer of social anthropology, he or she must make it happen—improvise, mingle with the natives, play roles, provoke response.

What, may we ask, will then be the difference between this literary anthropology and a real anthropologist's investigation of on-line phenomena? In other words, what keeps criticism from changing into a sub-discipline of traditional social anthropology? First, it must be noted that social anthropology and literary theory already have several perspectives and goals in common, and a recent history of mutual influence. In cultural anthropology, cultures are treated as texts to be interpreted and subjected to critique,[36] and even the problem of anthropological method as a literary process has become a concern.[37]

In the transient social textualities, the ontologies of the two traditions might seem to converge, and the boundaries between cultural anthropology and literary theory may appear fuzzier than ever. It could therefore be useful to explore some problems and conflicts of perspective that might await eventual partnerships of the two fields. Since MUDs and other indeterminate cybertexts are closed signification systems, that is, textual types, they should not be analyzed as traditional cultures or subcultures. The postorganic anthropology solicited in a recent essay on the phenomenon known as cyberspace is perhaps just another term for what literary critics have been doing since Plato.[38] To be analyzed and defined, a culture must be shown to exist independently of any one signification system. When a science starts to confuse its metaphors with its empirical substratum (for example when "texts" become texts), it is dangerously close to becoming a mythology. An anthropology of MUDs, for instance, should not see as its primary object the rituals and interactions between the characters inside; but rather the relation between the outside participants (the users) and their inside symbolic actions. Literary theory, on the other hand, should not focus on the social behavior made possible by textual symbols, but on how the sign system is used to construct and explore the possibility of a text-based representation of identity. If a cooperation between anthropology and textual criticism is to be achieved, the two disciplines should not try to do each other's work, or mistake the other's ontology for its own.

After these speculations the question remains: What will the study of nonlinearity and cybertextuality do to literary theory? At this point there can be no clear answer. Between the blurry promises of technology and the sharp edges of political reality there is, in the words of Jacques Derrida, "as yet no exergue." This essay has attempted to create a usable terminology for the study of a wider range of textualities than has hitherto been acknowledged by the field of literary study and to point to some current problems and challenges in the study of computer-mediated textualities. As we have seen, fundamental structural terms like *story, plot, fiction*, and *narrative* are not always suitable to describe the nonlinear textualities. To use them without qualification is clearly irresponsible. The figures of nonlinearity suggest that one must revise literary terminology and poetics in order to avoid further confusion and unnecessary ambiguity. Some of my reconfigurations of these literary and theoretical concepts might turn out to be unnecessary, and others are probably not radical enough. As I have shown, in addition to hypertext there is a wealth of nonlinear text types, from ancient inscriptions to sophisticated computer programs based on the latest semantic research. I have not tried to present an exhaustive empirical survey of such types or to give a detailed historical exposition of the development and spread of textual nonlinearity. Others are very welcome to either of these tasks; I have no intention of taking them on. Nor do I believe that there is any need to construct a historical tradition of nonlinear literature, as the specimens I have seen so far seem to be different from and isolated from each other rather than belong to anything that can reasonably be characterized as a common genre. There are undoubtedly local traditions, but nonlinear strategies appear to rise out of a prevalent and trans-historic need to compose a practical effect, perpendicular to linear textuality, but usually with a specific and constructive or subversive rather than sensationalistic or frivolous objective.

When confronted with new data that is recognized as relevant but unusual, an academic discipline such as literary studies can employ at least two different tactics to harmonize the situation. The existing theories may be used to grasp and focus the new material (the intruder is tamed), or the new material can be used to reevaluate and modify the old perspectives (the field is changed). Here I have focused not on the effects and insights produced by the various branches of literary theory when applied to nonlinear texts but on the potential for new perspectives on literature in general that the study of nonlinear textuality might bring us. Nonlinear texts and literary theories may have a lot to say to each other, but we should not let only one side do all the talking.

## Notes

1. Terry Eagleton, *Literary Theory: An Introduction* (Minneapolis: University of Minnesota Press, 1983).

2. Norbert Wiener, *Cybernetics; Or, Control and Communication in the Animal and the Machine* (New York: Technology, 1948).

3. N. Katherine Hayles, *Chaos Bound: Orderly Disorder in Contemporary Literature and Science* (Ithaca: Cornell University Press, 1990).

4. Roland Barthes, *S/Z* (Paris: Seuil, 1970), 20.

5. George P. Landow, *Hypertext: The Convergence of Contemporary Critical Theory and Technology* (Baltimore: Johns Hopkins University Press, 1992).

6. Espen Aarseth, *Texts of Change: Towards a Poetics of Nonlinearity* (c.phil. diss., unpublished, University of Bergen, Department of Comparative Literature, 1991).

7. See Michael J. Greenacre, *Theory and Applications of Correspondence Analysis* (London: Academic Press, 1984).

8. William Gibson, *Agrippa: A Book of the Dead* (New York: Kevin Begos, 1992).

9. Kathy Acker, *Blood and Guts in High School* (New York: Grove Press, 1978), 46–51.

10. Rolf Gundlach, "Tempelrelief," in *Lexicon der Ägyptologie* (Wiesbaden: Otto Harrassowitz, 1985), 6:407–11.

11. James Legge, *I Ching: Book of Changes* (1888; Secaucus, N.J.: Citadel Press, 1964), 7.

12. C. G. Jung, foreword to *I Ching or Book of Changes,* trans. Cary F. Baynes from a German translation by Richard Wilhelm (1950; London: Arkana/Penguin, 1989), lvii–lxi.

13. Raymond Queneau, *Cent Mille Milliards de Poèmes* (Paris: Gallimard, 1961).

14 .William Paulson, "Computers, Minds, and Texts: Preliminary Reflections," *New Literary History* 20 (1989): 297.

15. For critical views of political claims about electronic media in general, see James W. Carey, *Communication As Culture: Essays on Media and Society* (Boston: Unwin Hyman, 1988), especially "The Mythos of the Electronic Revolution," and about hypertext, Stuart Moulthrop, "You Say You Want a Revolution?: Hypertext and the Laws of Media," *Postmodern Culture* 1 (May 1991).

16. Theodor Holm Nelson, *Literary Machines, ed. 87.1* (Swarthmore, Pa.: Theodor H. Nelson, 1987), and Vannevar Bush, "As We May Think," *Atlantic Monthly* 176 (July 1945): 101–8.

17. Michael Joyce, *Afternoon, a story* (Cambridge, Mass.: Eastgate Systems, 1990). For discussions of *Afternoon,* see Stuart Moulthrop, "Hypertext and 'the Hyperreal,'" *Hypertext '89* (New York: Association of Computing Machinery, 1989), 259–67; J. David Bolter, *Writing Space: The Computer, Hypertext, and the History of Writing* (Hillsdale, N.J.: Lawrence Erlbaum, 1991); and Landow, *Hypertext.*

18. Moulthrop, "Hypertext and 'the Hyperreal,'" 239.

19. Inger Christensen, *The Meaning of Metafiction: A Critical Study of Selected Novels by Sterne, Nabokov, Barth, and Becket* (Bergen: Universitetsforlaget, 1981), 141–43.

20. Bolter, *Writing Space,* 7.

21. Jon Lanestedt, *Episk Programvare—En Litterœr Teksttype?* [*Epic Software—A Literary Text Type?*] (c.phil. diss., University of Oslo, 1989). William Crowther and Don Woods, *Adventure,* this version implemented by Gordon Letwin (IBM/Microsoft, 1981).

22. Anthony J. Niesz and Norman N. Holland, "Interactive Fiction," *Critical Inquiry* 11 (1984): 113.

23. Robin Waterfield and Wilfred Davies, *The Money Spider* (London: Penguin 1988).

24. See James Richard Meehan, *The Metanovel: Writing Stories by Computer* (Ph.D. diss., Yale University, University Microfilms International, 1976); Roger C. Schank and Peter Childers, *The Cognitive Computer: On Language, Learning, and Artificial Intelligence* (Reading, Mass.: Addison-Wesley, 1984); and Michael Lebowitz, "Creating Characters in a Story-telling Universe," *Poetics* 13 (1984): 171–94.

25. Brenda Laurel, *Computers as Theatre* (Reading, Mass.: Addison-Wesley, 1991).

26. Cf. Carey, *Communication As Culture,* ch. 8.

27. Marshall McLuhan, *Understanding Media: The Extensions of Man* (New York: Penguin Books/Mentor, 1964), 225.

28. Elizabeth M. Reid, *Electropolis: Communication and Community on Internet Relay Chat* (honors thesis, University of Melbourne, 1991).

29. Richard Bartle, *Interactive Multi-User Computer Games* (parts from a research report commissioned by British Telecom, disseminated by the author, 1990).

30. Thomas Pynchon, *The Crying of Lot 49* (London: Picador, 1967).

31.Umberto Eco, *A Theory of Semiotics* (Bloomington: Indiana University Press, 1979), 9.

32. Louis Hjelmslev, *Prolegomena to a Theory of Language* (1943), trans. Francis J. Whitfield (Madison: University of Wisconsin Press, 1961), 30.

33. Pierre Fontanier, *Les Figures du Discours* (1821–30; Paris: Flammarion, 1968), 271.

34. Howard Rheingold, *Virtual Reality* (New York: Summit Books, 1991).

35. See also Richard Ziegfeld, "Interactive Fiction: A New Literary Genre?" *New Literary History* 20 (1989): 341–72.

36. George E. Marcus and Michael M. J. Fischer, *Anthropology as Cultural Critique: An Experimental Moment in the Human Sciences* (Chicago: University of Chicago Press, 1986).

37. Clifford Geertz, *Works and Lives: The Anthropologist as Author* (Stanford: Stanford University Press, 1988).

38. David Tomas, "Old Rituals for New Space," in *Cyberspace: First Steps,* ed. Michael Benedikt (Cambridge: MIT Press, 1991), 31–47.

# 53. [Introduction]
# Nomadic Power and Cultural Resistance

The Critical Art Ensemble turned the rhizome on its root. The figures of the rhizome and nomadology, fashioned by Gilles Deleuze and Félix Guattari (◊27), have been a worldwide inspiration for culture workers—from the net.art mailing list at rhizome.org to Homi K. Bhabha's postcolonial critique. Rhizome language has been adopted as a language of liberation, as an alternative to the New Left that in retrospect seems to have died in the streets in 1968. Yet in this essay the CAE posits the rhizome and nomad—as used by many new media writers to discuss network and hypertextual technologies—as figures of corporate power, rather than of liberation.

That the applications of rhizome language to new media technologies may have sprouted from a misreading of Deleuze and Guattari is of little importance in this context; language achieves meaning through use. By co-opting the language of the rhizome and nomad from the technoliberationists, CAE cut to the heart of the argument that new media networks are inherently incompatible with the power relations of the industrial revolution. They demolished the idea that it is impossible for power to co-opt network and hypertext technologies, that such technologies have a manifest destiny of freedom.

The CAE argued: that the power elite are now the primary beneficiaries of network technologies; that these technologies allow them, as well as the sites of industrial production, to be so mobile as to make resistance in physical space ineffectual; that the communication and control functions of the elite are now fully cyberspatial, so cyberspace becomes the only effective site of resistance; and that the only potentially effective cyberspace resistance is "disturbance" via the sabotage of information technologies and the potential panic created by the cutoff of information flow (and resulting destabilization of the privatized safe harbors created by the powerful for those they employ).

Since the mid–1990s, significant flaws have been found in these arguments. The most telling of these is that corporate power continues to feel a need to press for greater mobility (e.g., via the World Trade Organization), and continues to have its meetings about this matter in physical space. Meanwhile, protest movements have found effective means to use cyberspatial technologies for their own communication, and have developed the nomadic ability to meet corporate power on the street wherever it chooses to gather. The power elite have found themselves unexpectedly trapped in meeting-room bunkers, rather than free to move as they please.

Yet the question of how, or whether, to use new media technologies for taking (virtual) action, rather than organizing and reporting (physical) action, remains open. The most attention-getting work that positions the network as a space for action has been the "virtual sit-ins" of "hacktivists" and "cyberhippies." But is unclear whether this work is actually more like a physical sit-in or like gathering signatures on a petition. It does not close down spaces of power or have an undeniable public presence the way physical sit-ins have. It does provide a way for relatively large numbers of people to express personal dissatisfaction with power, as petitions do, and it involves a similar level of personal (physical) risk. Yet this work goes beyond the petition in its theatrical dimensions, which exist both for the participants and for their audience—the press, and the sit-in targets.

CAE, for their part, have weighed in to the debate by declaring that, at this historical moment, even the physical sit-in has almost no tactical value, and that hacktivist virtual actions are in the main tactically negative (even if they may possess small pedagogical value, which might eventually

From "Electronic Civil Disobedience, Simulation, and the Public Sphere":

In an addendum written in 1995 for *ECD and Other Unpopular Ideas*, CAE noted that there was growing paranoia among U.S. security agencies about controlling the electronic resistance. Oddly enough, these agencies scared themselves with their own constructions of electronic criminality. It was much like [Orson] Welles being scared of his own broadcast. In that comic moment, CAE ironically suggested that ECD was successful without ever having been tried . . . This is a comment that CAE wishes it had never made, as some activists have come to take it seriously and are trying to act on it, primarily by using the Web to produce hyperreal activist threats to fan the flames of corporate-state paranoia. Again, this is a media battle that will be lost. State panic and paranoia will be transformed through mass media into public paranoia, which in turn will only reinforce state power. In the U.S., the voting public consistently supports harsher sentencing for "criminals," more jails, and more police, and it is this hyperreal paranoia that gets law-and-order politicians the votes needed to turn these directives into legislation or government order. How many times must we see this happen? From McCarthyism to Reagan's fear of the Evil Empire to the War on Drugs, the result in each case has been more funds for military, security, and disciplinary agencies . . .

◊27
405

781

partially motivate tactically positive action). This objection to the virtual sit-in comes because, for CAE, Electronic Civil Disobedience is not a form of traditional Civil Disobedience, but an inversion of it. Rather than "the people united" of CD, ECD imagines many independently-acting cells. Rather than CD's aiming for media manipulation through which public pressure will be brought to bear on an institution to change its policies, ECD aims to bring the pressure for change *directly* (arguing that there is now no corporate or governmental instutition who is not amply prepared to do battle in the media, to reverse the spin of any publicly-applied pressure). For ECD to be effective, CAE argues in "Electronic Civil Disobedience, Simulation, and the Public Sphere," action should not only be non-theatrical—it should be conducted in secret.

The Hacktivismo group of cDc (Cult of the Dead Cow) is an organization that partially shares CAE's belief in the value of secrecy, but disagrees both with CAE and many hacktivists on the subject of disobedience. The cDc model is, instead, one of *disruptive compliance*. Their work focuses on the development of software that enables actions forbidden by repression, rather than enabling (private or public) attacks on repressors. An example is software for allowing political dissidents to, as safely as possible, share information while behind the Great Firewall of China (which was, of course, constructed with the help of U.S. corporations). For such software to be effective the details of its operation may be, in some cases, best kept secret. However, in general cDc hopes that open code can become the *lingua franca* of a hacktivism that seeks to wage peace, not war. While the term isn't used, the software described in cDc's "Waging Peace on the Internet" would create a set of connections between dissidents that sound, in technoliberationist terms, rhizomatic.
—NWF

*From "Waging Peace on the Internet":*

For the past four years the cDc has been talking about hacktivism. It's a chic word, beloved among journalists and appropriators alike. Yet the meaning is serious. Our definition of hacktivism is, "using technology to advance human rights through electronic media." Many on-line activists claim to be hacktivists, but their tactics are often at odds with what we consider hacktivism to be.

From the cDc's perspective, creation is good; destruction is bad. Hackers should promote the free flow of information, and causing anything to disrupt, prevent, or retard that flow is improper. For instance, cDc does not consider Web defacements or Denial of Service (DoS) attacks to be legitimate hacktivist actions. The former is nothing more than hi-tech vandalism, and the latter, an assault on free speech. . . .

There is no such thing as electronic civil disobedience. Body mass and large numbers don't count as they do on the street. On the Internet, it's the code that counts, specifically code and programmers with conscience.

We need to start thinking in terms of disruptive compliance rather than civil disobedience if we want to be effective on-line. Disruptive compliance has no meaning outside of cyberspace. Disruptive, of course, refers to disruptive technology, a radically new way of doing things; compliance refers back to the Internet and its original intent of constructive free-flow and openness. . . .

Here is where the Napster analogy breaks down. Trust was never a paramount factor in using the application. It was a fun loving network developed on the free side of the firewall, where users' greatest worries were, a) Can I find what I want? b) How long will it take to download? c) Is it of good quality? and, d) Do I have time to download four more tunes before I go to the keg party?

No one ever had to ask, a) If I'm caught using this, will I be arrested? b) Is this application good for ten years in jail?

Having millions of students on the Napster network made sense because the more users there are on-line, the larger the lending library becomes. Users behind national firewalls cannot be so casual. Having millions of users on a network may be one thing, but only a fool would trust more than his or her closest friends when the consequences of entrapment are so high. Thus, carefree peer-to-peer networks are replaced by careful hacktivist-to-hacktivist (H2H) networks.

Further Readings

Critical Art Ensemble. "Electronic Civil Disobedience, Simulation, and the Public Sphere." Originally posted on the nettime email list. <http://www.nettime.org/nettime.w3archive/199901/msg00033.html>

Critical Art Ensemble. <http://www.critical-art.net>

Hacktivism: When Politics Meets Technology. Web site. <http://hacktivism.openflows.org>

Khalilzad, Zalmay, John P. White, and Andrew W. Marshall, eds. *Strategic Appraisal: The Changing Role of Information in Warfare.* Santa Monica, Calif.: Rand Publications, 1999. <http://www.rand.org/publications/MR/MR1016>

Ruffin, Oxblood. "Waging Peace on the Internet." *The Register.* 19 April 2002. <http://www.theregister.co.uk/content/6/24946.html>

Original Publication

*The Electronic Disturbance,* 11–30. New York: Autonomedia, 1994.

# Nomadic Power and Cultural Resistance

## Critical Art Ensemble

The term that best describes the present social condition is liquescence. The once unquestioned markers of stability, such as God or Nature, have dropped into the black hole of scepticism, dissolving positioned identification of subject or object. Meaning simultaneously flows through a process of proliferation and condensation, at once drifting, slipping, speeding into the antinomies of apocalypse and utopia. The location of power—and the site of resistance—rest in an ambiguous zone without borders. How could it be otherwise, when the traces of power flow in transition between nomadic dynamics and sedentary structures—between hyperspeed and hyperinertia? It is perhaps utopian to begin with the claim that resistance begins (and ends?) with a Nietzschean casting-off of the yoke of catatonia inspired by the postmodern condition, and yet the disruptive nature of consciousness leaves little choice.

Treading water in the pool of liquid power need not be an image of acquiescence and complicity. In spite of their awkward situation, the political activist and the cultural activist (anachronistically known as the artist) can still produce disturbances. Although such action may more closely resemble the gestures of a drowning person, and it is uncertain just what is being disturbed, in this situation the postmodern roll of the dice favors the act of disturbance.

After all, what other chance is there? It is for this reason that former strategies of "subversion" (a word which in critical discourse has about as much meaning as the word "community"), or camouflaged attack, have come under a cloud of suspicion. Knowing what to subvert assumes that forces of oppression are stable and can be identified and separated—an assumption that is just too fantastic in an age of dialectics in ruins. Knowing how to subvert presupposes an understanding of the opposition that rests in the realm of certitude, or (at least) high probability. The rate at which strategies of subversion are co-opted indicates that the adaptability of power is too often underestimated; however, credit should be given to the resisters, to the extent that the subversive act or product is not co-optively reinvented as quickly as the bourgeois aesthetic of efficiency might dictate. The peculiar entwinement of the cynical and the utopian in the concept of disturbance as a necessary gamble is a heresy to those who still adhere to 19th-century narratives in which the mechanisms and class(es) of oppression, as well as the tactics needed to overcome them, are clearly identified. After all, the wager is deeply connected to conservative apologies for Christianity, and the attempt to appropriate rationalist rhetoric and models to persuade the fallen to return to traditional eschatology. A renounced Cartesian like Pascal, or a renounced revolutionary like Dostoyevsky, typify its use. Yet it must be realized that the promise of a better future, whether secular or spiritual, has always presupposed the economy of the wager. The connection between history and necessity is cynically humorous when one looks back over the trail of political and cultural debris of revolution and near-revolution in ruins. The French revolutions from 1789 to 1968 never stemmed the obscene tide of the commodity (they seem to have helped pave the way), while the Russian and Cuban revolutions merely replaced the commodity with the totalizing anachronism of the bureaucracy. At best, all that is derived from these disruptions is a structure for a nostalgic review of reconstituted moments of temporary autonomy.

The cultural producer has not fared any better. Mallarmé brought forth the concept of the wager in *A Roll of the Dice,* and perhaps unwittingly liberated invention from the bunker of transcendentalism that he hoped to defend, as well as releasing the artist from the myth of the poetic subject. (It is reasonable to suggest that de Sade had already accomplished these tasks at a much earlier date). Duchamp (the attack on essentialism), Cabaret Voltaire (the methodology of random production), and Berlin dada (the disappearance of art into political action) all disturbed the cultural waters, and yet opened one of the cultural passages for the resurgence of transcendentalism in late Surrealism. By way of reaction to the above three, a channel was also opened for formalist domination (still to this day the demon of the culture-text) that locked the culture-object into the luxury market of late capital. However, the gamble of these forerunners of disturbance reinjected the dream of autonomy with the amphetamine of hope that gives contemporary cultural producers and activists the energy to step up to the electronic gaming table to roll the dice again.

In *The Persian Wars,* Herodotus describes a feared people known as the Scythians, who maintained a horticultural-nomadic society unlike the sedentary empires in the "cradle of civilization." The homeland of the Scythians on the Northern Black Sea was inhospitable both climatically and geographically, but resisted colonization less for these natural reasons than because there was no economic or military means by which to colonize or subjugate it. With no fixed cities or territories, this "wandering horde" could never really be located. Consequently, they could never be put on the defensive and conquered. They maintained their autonomy through movement, making it seem to outsiders that they were always present and poised for attack even when absent. The fear inspired by the Scythians was quite justified, since they were often on the military offensive, although no one knew where until the time of their instant appearance, or until traces of their power were discovered. A floating border was maintained in their homeland, but Power was not a matter of spatial occupation for the Scythians. They wandered, taking territory and tribute as needed, in whatever area they found themselves. In so doing, they constructed an invisible empire that dominated "Asia" for

twenty-seven years, and extended as far south as Egypt. The empire itself was not sustainable, since their nomadic nature denied the need or value of holding territories. (Garrisons were not left in defeated territories). They were free to wander, since it was quickly realized by their adversaries that even when victory seemed probable, for practicality's sake it was better not to engage them, and to instead concentrate military and economic effort on other sedentary societies— that is, on societies in which an infrastructure could be located and destroyed. This policy was generally reinforced, because an engagement with the Scythians required the attackers to allow themselves to found by the Scythians. It was extraordinarily rare for the Scythians to be caught in a defensive posture. Should the Scythians not like the terms of engagement, they always had the option of remaining invisible, and thereby preventing the enemy from constructing a theater of operations.

This archaic model of power distribution and predatory strategy has been reinvented by the power elite of late capital for much the same ends. Its reinvention is predicated upon the technological opening of cyberspace, where speed/absence and inertia/presence collide in hyperreality. The archaic model of nomadic power, once a means to an unstable empire, has evolved into a sustainable means of domination. In a state of double signification, the contemporary society of nomads becomes both a diffuse power field without location, and a fixed sight machine appearing as spectacle. The former privilege allows for the appearance of global economy, while the latter acts as a garrison in various territories, maintaining the order of the commodity with an ideology specific to the given area.

Although both the diffuse power field and the sight machine are integrated through technology, and are necessary parts for global empire, it is the former that has fully realized the Scythian myth. The shift from archaic space to an electronic network offers the full complement of nomadic power advantages: The militarized nomads are always on the offensive. The obscenity of spectacle and the terror of speed are their constant companions. In most cases sedentary populations submit to the obscenity of spectacle, and contentedly pay the tribute demanded, in the form of labor, material, and profit. First world, third world, nation or tribe, all must give tribute. The differentiated and hierarchical nations, classes, races, and genders of sedentary modern society all blend under nomadic domination into the role of its service workers—into caretakers of the cyberelite. This separation, mediated by spectacle, offers tactics that are beyond the archaic nomadic model. Rather than a hostile plundering of an adversary, there is a friendly pillage, seductively and ecstatically conducted against the passive. Hostility from the oppressed is rechanneled into the bureaucracy, which misdirects antagonism away from the nomadic power field. The retreat into the invisibility of nonlocation prevents those caught in the panoptic spatial lock-down from defining a site of resistance (a theater of operations), and they are instead caught in a historical tape loop of resisting the monuments of dead capital. (Abortion rights? Demonstrate on the steps of the Supreme Court. For the release of drugs which slow the development of HIV, storm the NIH). No longer needing to take a defensive posture is the nomads' greatest strength.

As the electronic information-cores overflow with files of electronic people (those transformed into credit histories, consumer types, patterns and tendencies, etc.), electronic research, electronic money, and other forms of information power, the nomad is free to wander the electronic net, able to cross national boundaries with minimal resistance from national bureaucracies. The privileged realm of electronic space controls the physical logistics of manufacture, since the release of raw materials and manufactured goods requires electronic consent and direction. Such power must be relinquished to the cyber realm, or the efficiency (and thereby the profitability) of complex manufacture, distribution, and consumption would collapse into a communication gap. Much the same is true of the military; there is cyberelite control of information resources and dispersal. Without command and control, the military becomes immobile, or at best limited to chaotic dispersal in localized space. In this manner all sedentary structures become servants of the nomads.

The nomadic elite itself is frustratingly difficult to grasp. Even in 1956, when C. Wright Mills wrote *The Power Elite*, it was clear that the sedentary elite already understood the importance of invisibility. (This was quite a shift from the looming spatial markers of power used by the feudal aristocracy). Mills found it impossible to get any direct information on the elite, and was left with speculations drawn from questionable empirical categories (for example,

the social register). As the contemporary elite moves from centralized urban areas to decentralized and deterritorialized cyberspace, Mills' dilemma becomes increasingly aggravated. How can a subject be critically assessed that cannot be located, examined, or even seen? Class analysis reaches a point of exhaustion. Subjectively there is a feeling of oppression, and yet it is difficult to locate, let alone assume, an oppressor. In all likelihood, this group is not a class at all—that is, an aggregate of people with common political and economic interests—but a downloaded elite military consciousness. The cyberelite is now a transcendent entity that can only be imagined. Whether they have integrated programmed motives is unknown. Perhaps so, or perhaps their predatory actions fragment their solidarity, leaving shared electronic pathways and stores of information as the only basis of unity. The paranoia of imagination is the foundation for a thousand conspiracy theories—all of which are true. Roll the dice.

The development of an absent and potentially unassailable nomadic power, coupled with the rear vision of revolution in ruins, has nearly muted the contestational voice. Traditionally, during times of disillusionment, strategies of retreatism begin to dominate. For the cultural producer, numerous examples of cynical participation populate the landscape of resistance. The experience of Baudelaire comes to mind. In 1848 Paris he fought on the barricades, guided by the notion that "property is theft," only to turn to cynical nihilism after the revolution's failure. (Baudelaire was never able to completely surrender. His use of plagiarism as an inverted colonial strategy forcefully recalls the notion that property is theft). André Breton's early surrealist project— synthesizing the liberation of desire with the liberation of the worker—unraveled when faced with the rise of fascism. (Breton's personal arguments with Louis Aragon over the function of the artist as revolutionary agent should also be noted. Breton never could abandon the idea of poetic self as a privileged narrative). Breton increasingly embraced mysticism in the 30s, and ended by totally retreating into transcendentalism. The tendency of the disillusioned cultural worker to retreat toward introspection to sidestep the Enlightenment question of "What is to be done with the social situation in light of sadistic power?" is the representation of life through denial. It is not that interior liberation is undesirable and unnecessary, only that it cannot become singular or privileged. To turn away from the revolution of everyday life, and place cultural resistance under the authority of the poetic self, has always led to cultural production that is the easiest to commodify and bureaucratize.

From the American postmodern viewpoint, the 19th-century category of the poetic self (as delineated by the Decadents, the Symbolists, the Nabis School, etc.) has come to represent complicity and acquiescence when presented as pure. The culture of appropriation has eliminated this option in and of itself. (It still has some value as a point of intersection. For example, bell hooks uses it well as an entrance point to other discourses). Though in need of revision, Asger Jorn's modernist motto "The avant-garde never gives up!" still has some relevance. Revolution in ruins and the labyrinth of appropriation have emptied the comforting certitude of the dialectic. The Marxist watershed, during which the means of oppression had a clear identity, and the route of resistance was unilinear, has disappeared into the void of scepticism. However, this is no excuse for surrender. The ostracized surrealist, Georges Bataille, presents an option still not fully explored: In everyday life, rather than confronting the aesthetic of utility, attack from the rear through the nonrational economy of the perverse and sacrificial. Such a strategy offers the possibility for intersecting exterior and interior disturbance.

The significance of the movement of disillusionment from Baudelaire to Artaud is that its practitioners imagined sacrificial economy. However, their conception of if was too often limited to an elite theater of tragedy, thus reducing it to a resource for "artistic" exploitation. To complicate matters further, the artistic presentation of the perverse was always so serious that sites of application were often consequently overlooked. Artaud's stunning realization that the body without organs had appeared, although he seemed uncertain as to what it might be, was limited to tragedy and apocalypse. Signs and traces of the body without organs appear throughout mundane experience. The body without organs is Ronald McDonald, not an esoteric aesthetic; after all, there is a critical place for comedy and humor as a means of resistance. Perhaps this is the Situationist International's greatest contribution to the postmodern aesthetic. The dancing Nietzsche lives.

In addition to aestheticized retreatism, a more sociological variety appeals to romantic resisters—a primitive version of nomadic disappearance. This is the disillusioned retreat to fixed areas that elude surveillance. Typically, the retreat is to the most culturally negating rural areas, or to deterritorialized urban neighborhoods. The basic principle is to achieve autonomy by hiding from social authority. As in band societies whose culture cannot be touched because it cannot be found, freedom is enhanced for those participating in the project. However, unlike band societies, which emerged within a given territory, these transplanted communities are always susceptible to infections from spectacle, language, and even nostalgia for former environments, rituals, and habits. These communities are inherently unstable (which is not necessarily negative). Whether these communities can be transformed from campgrounds for the disillusioned and defeated (as in late 60s-early 70s America) to effective bases for resistance remains to be seen. One has to question, however, whether an effective sedentary base of resistance will not be quickly exposed and undermined, so that it will not last long enough to have an effect.

Another 19th-century narrative that persists beyond its natural life is the labor movement—i.e., the belief that the key to resistance is to have an organized body of workers stop production. Like revolution, the idea of the union has been shattered, and perhaps never existed in everyday life. The ubiquity of broken strikes, give-backs, and lay-offs attests that what is called a union is no more than a labor bureaucracy. The fragmentation of the world—intonations, regions, first and third worlds, etc., as a means of discipline by nomadic power—has anachronized national labor movements. Production sites are too mobile and management techniques too flexible for labor action to be effective. If labor in one area resists corporate demands, an alternative labor pool is quickly found. The movement of Dupont's and General Motors' production plants into Mexico, for example, demonstrates this nomadic ability. Mexico as labor colony also allows reduction of unit cost, by eliminating first world "wage standards" and employee benefits. The speed of the corporate world is paid for by the intensification of exploitation; sustained fragmentation of time and of space makes it possible. The size and desperation of the third world labor pool, in conjunction with complicit political systems, provide organized labor no base from which to bargain.

The Situationists attempted to contend with this problem by rejecting the value of both labor and capital. All should quit work—proles, bureaucrats, service workers, everyone. Although it is easy to sympathize with the concept, it presupposes an impractical unity. The notion of a general strike was much too limited; it got bogged down in national struggles, never moving beyond Paris, and in the end it did little damage to the global machine. The hope of a more elite strike manifesting itself in the occupation movement was a strategy that was also dead on arrival, for much the same reason.

The Situationist delight in occupation is interesting to the extent that it was an inversion of the aristocratic right to property, although this very fact makes it suspect from its inception, since even modern strategies should not merely seek to invert feudal institutions. The relationship between occupation and ownership, as presented in conservative social thought, was appropriated by revolutionaries in the first French revolution. The liberation and occupation of the Bastille was significant less for the few prisoners released, than to signal that obtaining property through occupation is a double-edged sword. This inversion made the notion of property into a conservatively viable justification for genocide. In the Irish genocide of the 1840s, English landowners realized that it would be more profitable to use their estates for raising grazing animals than to leave the tenant farmers there who traditionally occupied the land. When the potato blight struck, destroying the tenant farmers' crops and leaving them unable to pay rent, an opening was perceived for mass eviction. English landlords requested and received military assistance from London to remove the farmers and to ensure they did not reoccupy the land. Of course the farmers believed they had the right to be on the land due to their long-standing occupation of it, regardless of their failure to pay rent. Unfortunately, the farmers were transformed into a pure excess population since their right to property by occupation was not recognized. Laws were passed denying them the right to immigrate to England, leaving thousands to die without food or shelter in the Irish winter. Some were able to immigrate to the US, and remained alive, but only as abject refugees. Meanwhile, in the US itself, the genocide of Native Americans was well underway, justified in part by the belief that since the native tribes did not own land, all territories were open, and once

occupied (invested with sedentary value), they could be "defended." Occupation theory has been more bitter than heroic.

In the postmodern period of nomadic power, labor and occupation movements have not been relegated to the historical scrap heap, but neither have they continued to exercise the potency that they once did. Elite power, having rid itself of its national and urban bases to wander in absence on the electronic pathways, can no longer be disrupted by strategies predicated upon the contestation of sedentary forces. The architectural monuments of power are hollow and empty, and function now only as bunkers for the complicit and those who acquiesce. They are secure places revealing mere traces of power. As with all monumental architecture, they silence resistance and resentment by the signs of resolution, continuity, commodification, and nostalgia. These places can be occupied, but to do so will not disrupt the nomadic flow. At best such an occupation is a disturbance that can be made invisible through media manipulation; a particularly valued bunker (such as a bureaucracy) can be easily reoccupied by the postmodern war machine. The electronic valuables inside the bunker, of course, cannot be taken by physical measures.

The web connecting the bunkers—the street—is of such little value to nomadic power that it has been left to the underclass. (One exception is the greatest monument to the war machine ever constructed: The Interstate Highway System. Still valued and well defended, that location shows almost no sign of disturbance.) Giving the street to the most alienated of classes ensures that only profound alienation can occur there. Not just the police, but criminals, addicts, and even the homeless are being used as disrupters of public space. The underclass' actual appearance, in conjunction with media spectacle, has allowed the forces of order to construct the hysterical perception that the streets are unsafe, unwholesome, and useless. The promise of safety and familiarity lures hordes of the unsuspecting into privatized public spaces such as malls. The price of this protectionism is the relinquishment of individual sovereignty. No one but the commodity has rights in the mall. The streets in particular and public spaces in general are in ruins. Nomadic power speaks to its followers through the autoexperience of electronic media. The smaller the public, the greater the order.

The avant-garde never gives up, and yet the limitations of antiquated models and the sites of resistance tend to push resistance into the void of disillusionment. It is important to keep the bunkers under siege; however, the vocabulary of resistance must be expanded to include means of electronic disturbance. Just as authority located in the street was once met by demonstrations and barricades, the authority that locates itself in the electronic field must be met with electronic resistance. Spatial strategies may not be key in this endeavor, but they are necessary for support, at least in the case of broad spectrum disturbance. These older strategies of physical challenge are also better developed, while the electronic strategies are not. It is time to turn attention to the electronic resistance, both in terms of the bunker and the nomadic field. The electronic field is an area where little is known; in such a gamble, one should be ready to face the ambiguous and unpredictable hazards of an untried resistance. Preparations for the double-edged sword should be made.

Nomadic power must be resisted in cyberspace rather than in physical space. The postmodern gambler is an electronic player. A small but coordinated group of hackers could introduce electronic viruses, worms, and bombs into the data banks, programs, and networks of authority, possibly bringing the destructive force of inertia into the nomadic realm. Prolonged inertia equals the collapse of nomadic authority on a global level. Such a strategy does not require a unified class action, nor does it require simultaneous action in numerous geographic areas. The less nihilistic could resurrect the strategy of occupation by holding data as hostage instead of property. By whatever means electronic authority is disturbed, the key is to totally disrupt command and control. Under such conditions, all dead capital in the military/corporate entwinement becomes an economic drain—material, equipment, and labor power all would be left without a means of deployment. Late capital would collapse under its own excessive weight.

Even though this suggestion is but a science-fiction scenario, this narrative does reveal problems which must be addressed. Most obvious is that those who have engaged cyberreality are generally a depoliticized group. Most infiltration into cyberspace has either been playful vandalism (as with Robert Morris' rogue program, or the string of PC viruses like Michaelangelo), politically misguided espionage (Markus Hess' hacking of military computers, which was possibly done for the benefit of the KGB), or personal revenge against a particular source of authority. The hacker* code of ethics discourages any act of disturbance in cyberspace. Even the Legion of Doom (a group of young hackers that put the fear into the Secret Service) claims to have never damaged a system. Their activities were motivated by curiosity about computer systems, and belief in free access to information. Beyond these very focused concerns with decentralized information, political thought or action has never really entered the group's consciousness. Any trouble that they have had with the law (and only a few members break the law) stemmed either from credit fraud or electronic trespass. The problem is much the same as politicizing scientists whose research leads to weapons development. It must be asked, How can this class be asked to destabilize or crash its own world? To complicate matters further, only a few understand the specialized knowledge necessary for such action. Deep cyberreality is the least democratized of all frontiers. As mentioned above, cyberworkers as a professional class do not have to be fully unified, but how can enough members of this class be enlisted to stage a disruption, especially when cyberreality is under state-of-the-art self-surveillance?

These problems have drawn many "artists" to electronic media, and this has made some contemporary electronic art so politically charged. Since it is unlikely that scientific or techno-workers will generate a theory of electronic disturbance, artists-activists (as well as other concerned groups) have been left with the responsibility to help provide a critical discourse on just what is at stake in the development of this new frontier. By appropriating the legitimized authority of "artistic creation," and using it as a means to establish a public forum for speculation on a model of resistance within emerging techno-culture, the cultural producer can contribute to the perpetual fight against authoritarianism. Further, concrete strategies of image/text communication, developed through the use of technology that has fallen through the cracks in the war machine, will better enable those concerned to invent explosive material to toss into the political-economic bunkers. Postering, pamphleteering, street theater, public art—all were useful in the past. But as mentioned above, where is the "public"; who is on the street? Judging from the number of hours that the average person watches television, it seems that the public is electronically engaged. The electronic world, however, is by no means fully established, and it is time to take advantage of this fluidity through invention, before we are left with only critique as a weapon.

Bunkers have already been described as privatized public spaces which serve various particularized functions, such as political continuity (government offices or national monuments), or areas for consumption frenzy (malls). In line with the feudal tradition of the fortress mentality, the bunker guarantees safety and familiarity in exchange for the relinquishment of individual sovereignty. It can act as a seductive agent offering the credible illusion of consumptive choice and ideological peace for the complicit, or it can act as an aggressive force demanding acquiescence for the resistant. The bunker brings nearly all to its interior with the exception of those left to guard the streets. After all, nomadic power does not offer the choice not to work or not to consume. The bunker is such an all-embracing feature of everyday life that even the most resistant cannot always approach it critically. Alienation, in part, stems from this uncontrollable entrapment in the bunker.

Bunkers vary in appearance as much as they do in function. The nomadic bunker—the product of "the global village"—has both an electronic and an architectural form. The electronic form is witnessed as media; as such it attempts to colonize the private residence. Informative distraction flows in an unceasing stream of fictions produced by Hollywood, Madison Avenue, and CNN. The economy of desire can be safely viewed through the familiar window of screenal space. Secure in the electronic bunker, a life of alienated autoexperience (a loss of the social) can continue in quiet acquiescence and deep privation. The viewer is brought to the world, the world to the viewer, all mediated through the ideology of the screen. This is virtual life in a virtual world.

Like the electronic bunker, the architectural bunker is another site where hyperspeed and hyperinertia intersect. Such bunkers are not restricted to national boundaries; in fact, they span the globe. Although they cannot actually move through physical space, they simulate the appearance of being everywhere at once. The architecture itself may vary considerably, even in terms of particular types; however, the logo or totem of a particular type is universal, as are its consumables. In a general sense, it is its redundant

* "Hacker" refers here to a generic class of computer sophisticates who often, but not always, operate counter to the needs of the military/corporate structure. As used here the term includes crackers, phreakers, hackers proper, and cypherpunks.

participation in these characteristics that make it so seductive.

This type of bunker was typical of capitalist power's first attempt to go nomadic. During the Counterreformation, when the Catholic Church realized during the Council of Trent (1545–63) that universal presence was a key to power in the age of colonization, this type of bunker came of age. (It took the full development of the capitalist system to produce the technology necessary to return to power through absence). The appearance of the church in frontier areas both East and West, the universalization of ritual, the maintenance of relative grandeur in its architecture, and the ideological marker of the crucifix, all conspired to present a reliable place of familiarity and security. Wherever a person was, the homeland of the church was waiting.

In more contemporary times, the gothic arches have transformed themselves into golden arches. McDonald's is global. Wherever an economic frontier is opening, so is a McDonald's. Travel where you might, that same hamburger and coke are waiting. Like Bernini's piazza at St. Peters, the golden arches reach out to embrace their clients—so long as they consume, and leave when they are finished. While in the bunker, national boundaries are a thing of the past, in fact you are at home. Why travel at all? After all, wherever you go, you are already there.

There are also sedentary bunkers. This type is clearly nationalized, and hence is the bunker of choice for governments. It is the oldest type, appearing at the dawn of complex society, and reaching a peak in modern society with conglomerates of bunkers spread throughout the urban sprawl. These bunkers are in some cases the last trace of centralized national power (the White House), or in others, they are locations to manufacture a complicit cultural elite (the university), or sites of manufactured continuity (historical monuments). These are sites most vulnerable to electronic disturbance, as their images and mythologies are the easiest to appropriate.

In any bunker (along with its associated geography, territory, and ecology) the resistant cultural producer can best achieve disturbance. There is enough consumer technology available to at least temporarily reinscribe the bunker with image and language that reveal its sacrificial intent, as well as the obscenity of its bourgeois utilitarian aesthetic. Nomadic power has created panic in the streets, with its mythologies of political subversion, economic deterioration, and biological infection, which in turn produce a fortress ideology, and hence a demand for bunkers. It is now necessary to bring panic into the bunker, thus disturbing the illusion of security and leaving no place to hide. The incitement of panic in all sites is the postmodern gamble.

# 54. [Introduction]
# The World-Wide Web

The Web is a relatively primitive hypertext system, but it has certainly fulfilled its goal of being a pool of human knowledge—in fact, it has overflowed this original goal to become a vast sea of human knowledge. The Web demonstrates, as Donald Norman has said, that the technologies that prevail don't have to be the best ones—they just have to be good enough. Other factors, including availability, price, and the openness of standards can allow a technology which is inferior in many specific ways to dominate. That is just what has happened with the hypertext technologies of the Web—inferior to those conceptualized in Ted Nelson's Xanadu, inferior to those proposed in the Dexter hypertext standard, and inferior to a host of earlier local-area or stand-alone hypertext systems—and also overwhelmingly successful in linking and making accessible a world-wide wealth of information, more than has ever been contained in any physical library. The ACM Hypertext conference was probably right to reject Tim Berners-Lee's paper about the Web in 1991, reducing the announcement of this earth-shattering system to a poster session, just as it was probably right for the technologically inferior Web to eat alive those "superior" hypertext systems talked about at the ACM Hypertext conference.

The power of the Web is evident today, and should have been in 1994 when considered not against other hypertext systems but against its real competitors, then-popular Internet services such as Gopher and WAIS. (The most useful and most widely used Internet service today continues to be email, the less glamorous workhorse of the network.) Now, of course, it is television and video games that are seen as the Web's competition, at least within the media industries. But while the Web was well-suited to the information-publication tasks that had been the primary use of Gopher, the television-like "shows" and console-like games launched on the Web by well-funded companies in the 1990s found little traction. (A particularly spectacular failure that pursued this analogy was the high-rolling, show-based incarnation of the Microsoft Network, also known as MSN.) Instead, the Web's "killer app" was, and still is, simply the fast, ubiquitous, and not always flashy type of publication it has reveled in since the mid-1990s. These publications often are not much more elaborate than the pure textual format that email has used for decades. The true triumph of the Web is seen in the fulfillment of urgent public desire in *The Starr Report,* first released on the Web after the investigation was provoked by a textual Web publication; the banter and rehashed news of a new sort of community on *Slashdot;* the tense reloading of pages as a nation waited to see who prevailed in the 2000 presidential election; obsessively-updated personal diaries and Web logs; an almost infinite and rewriteable encyclopedia of academic discourse, organized and disorganized resistance, chessboards shared between distant opponents, labyrinths of literature, voyeurism of the ordinary, daily and sporadic expressions of desire; a pool that is murky and profound, teeming with the useless and the indispensable; a body of text we can surf in playfully or sail through with resolve on voyages of many sorts—religious missions or commercial journeys or attempts at conquest or exploration that aim to grow the great record of knowledge and give voice to, or change forever, who we are.
—NM & NWF

Further Reading

Berners-Lee, Tim. With Mark Fishetti. *Weaving the Web: The Original Design and Ultimate Destiny of the World Wide Web, by Its Inventor.* Harper San Francisco: 1999.

Google. <http://www.google.com>

Open Directory Project. <http://www.dmoz.org>

World Wide Web Consortium. <http://www.w3.org>

Original Publication

*Communications of the ACM,* 37(8):907–912. August 1994.

# The World-Wide Web
## Tim Berners-Lee, Robert Cailliau, Ari Luotonen, Henrik Frystyk Nielsen, and Arthur Secret

The World-Wide Web (W3) was developed to be a pool of human knowledge, which would allow collaborators in remote sites to share their ideas and all aspects of a common project. Physicists and engineers at CERN, the European Particle Physics Laboratory in Geneva, Switzerland, collaborate with many other institutes to build the software and hardware for high-energy physics research. The idea of the Web was prompted by positive experience of a small "home-brew" personal hypertext system used for keeping track of personal information on a distributed project. The Web was designed so that if it was used independently for two projects, and later relationships were found between the projects, then no major or centralized changes would have to be made, but the information could smoothly reshape to represent the new state of knowledge. This property of scaling has allowed the Web to expand rapidly from its origins at CERN across the Internet irrespective of boundaries of nations or disciplines.

If you haven't yet experienced the Web, the best way to find out about it is to try it. An Appendix to this article gives some recipes for getting hold of W3 clients. Given one of these, you will quickly find out all you need to know, and much more. For hard copy to read on the plane, or if you don't have Internet access from your desktop machine, refer to our paper in *Electronic Networking* (see "Glossary and Further Reading") for an overview of the project, material which we will not repeat but will summarize here.

A W3 "client" program runs on your computer. When it starts, it displays an object, normally a document with text and possibly images. Some of the phrases and images are highlighted: in blue, or boxed, or perhaps numbered, depending on what sort of a display you have and how your preferences have been set. Clicking the mouse on the

highlighted area ("anchor") causes the client program to retrieve another object from some other computer, a "server." The retrieved object is normally also in a hypertext format, so the process of navigation continues (see Figure 54.1).

When viewing some documents, the reader can request a search, by typing in plain text (or complex commands) to send to the server, rather than following a link. In either case, the client sends a request off to the server, often a completely different machine in some other part of the world, and within (typically) a second, the related information, in either hypertext, plain text or multimedia format, is presented. This is done repeatedly, and by a sequence of selections and searches one can find anything that is "out there." Some important things to note are:

- Whatever type of server, the user interface is the same, so users do not need to understand the differences between the many protocols in common use. Before W3, access to networked information typically involved knowledge of many different access "recipes" for different systems, and a different command language for each. The model of hypertext with text input has proved sufficiently powerful to express all the user interfaces, while being sufficiently simple to require no training for a computer user.

- Links can point to anything that can be displayed, including search result lists. (When a query is applied to an object, the resulting object has an address, defined to be the address of the queried object concatenated with the text of the query. As the result object has an address, one can make links to it. Following the link later leads to a reevaluation of the query.)

- While menus and directories are available, the extra option of hypertext provides a more powerful communications tool. In simple cases, the server program can generate a hypertext view representing (for example) the directory structure of an existing file store. This allows existing data to be put "on the Web" without further human effort.

- There is a very extendable system for introducing new formats for multimedia data.

- There are many W3 client programs. As hypertext information is transmitted on the network in logical (mark-up) form, each client can interpret this in a way natural for the given platform, making optimal use of fonts, colors, and other human interface resources available on that platform.

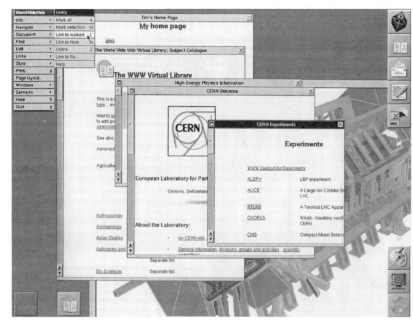

Figure 54.1. Using the World-Wide Web. Shown here is the authors' prototype World-Wide Web application for NextStep machines. The application initially displays the user's "home" page (top) of personal notes and links (top). Clicking on underlined text takes the reader to new documents. In this case, the user visited the Virtual Library, and, in the high energy physics department, found a link to CERN. Linked to CERN was the "Atlas" collaboration's web including an engineering drawing (background). To save having to follow the same path again, the link menu (shown) allows a new link to be made, for example from text typed into the home page, directly to the Atlas information.

## What Does W3 Define?

W3 has come to stand for a number of things, which should be distinguished. These include

- The idea of a boundless information world in which all items have a reference by which they can be retrieved;

- The address system (URI) which the project implemented to make this world possible, despite many different protocols;

- A network protocol (HTTP) used by native W3 servers giving performance and features not otherwise available;

- A markup language (HTML) which every W3 client is required to understand, and is used for the transmission of basic things such as text, menus and simple on-line help information across the net;

- The body of data available on the Internet using all or some of the preceding listed items.

The client-server architecture of the Web is illustrated in Figure 54.2.

## Universal Resource Identifiers

Universal Resource Identifiers[1] (URIs) are the strings used as addresses of objects (e.g., menus, documents, images) on the Web. For example, the URI of the main page for the WWW project happens to be

http://info.cern.ch/hypertext/WWW/TheProject.html
[As of summer 2002, http://www.w3.org/ ]

URIs are "Universal" in that they encode members of the universal set of network addresses. For a new network protocol that has some concept of object, one can form an address for any object as the set of protocol parameters necessary to access the object. If these parameters are encoded into a concise string, with a prefix to identify the protocol and encoding, one has a new URI scheme. There are URIs for Internet news articles and newsgroups (the NNTP protocol), and for FTP archives, for telnet destinations, email addresses, and so on. The same can be done for names of objects in a given name space.

The prefix "http" in the preceding example indicates the address space, and defines the interpretation of the rest of the string. The HTTP protocol is to be used, so the string contains the address of the server to be contacted, and a substring to be passed to the server. Different protocols use different syntaxes, but there is a small amount of common syntax. For example, the common URI syntax reserves the "/" as a way of representing a hierarchical space, and "?" as a separator between the address of an object and a query operation applied to it. As these forms recur in several information systems, to allow expression of them in the common syntax allows the features to be retained in the common model, where appropriate. Hierarchical forms are useful for hypertext, where one "work" may be split up into many interlinked documents. Relative names exploit the

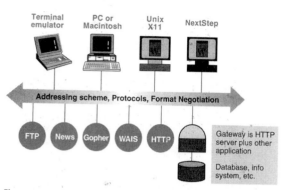

Figure 54.2. The World-Wide Web client-server architecture. For published information to be universally available, W3 relies on a common addressing syntax, a set of common protocols, and negotiation of data formats.

hierarchical structure and allow links to be made within the work independent of the higher parts of the URI such as the server name.

URI syntax allows objects to be addressed not only using HTTP, but also using the other common networked information protocols in use today (FTP, NNTP, Gopher, and WAIS), and will allow extension when new protocols are developed.

URIs are central to the W3 architecture. The fact that it is easy to address an object anywhere on the Internet is essential for the system to scale, and for the information space to be independent of the network and server topology.

## Hypertext Transfer Protocol

Perhaps misnamed, rather than being a protocol for transferring hypertext, HTTP is a protocol for transferring information with the efficiency necessary for making hypertext jumps. The data transferred may be plain text, hypertext, images, or anything else.

When a user browses the Web, objects are retrieved in rapid succession from often widely dispersed servers. For small documents, the limitations to the response time stem mainly from the number of round trip delays across the network necessary before the rendition of the object can be started. HTTP is therefore a simple request/response protocol.

HTTP does not only transfer HTML documents. Although HTML comprehension is required of W3 clients, HTTP is used for retrieving documents in an unbounded and extensible set of formats. To achieve this, the client sends a (weighted) list of the formats it can handle, and the server replies with data in any of those formats that it can produce.

This allows proprietary formats to be used between consenting programs in private, without the need for standardization of those formats. This is important both for high-end users who share data in sophisticated forms, and also as a hook for formats that have yet to be invented. The same negotiation system is used for natural language (English, French, for example) where available, as well as for compression forms.

HTTP is an Internet protocol. It is similar in its readable, text-based style to the File Transfer (FTP) and Network News (NNTP) Protocols that have been used to transfer files and news on the Internet for many years. Unlike these protocols, however, HTTP, is stateless. (That is, it runs over a TCP connection that is held only for the duration of one operation.) The stateless model is efficient when a link from one object may lead equally well to an object stored on the same server, or to another distant server. The purpose of a reference such as a URI is that it should always refer to the "same" (in some sense) object. This also makes a stateless protocol appropriate, as it returns results based on the URI but irrelevant of any previous operations performed by the client.

The HTTP request from the client starts with an operation code (known as the method, in conformance with object-oriented terminology) and the URI of the object. The "GET" method used by all browsers is defined to be idempotent in that it should preserve the state of the Web (apart from billing for the information transfer, and statistics). A "PUT" method is defined for front-end update, and a "POST" method for the attachment of a new document to the Web, or submission of a filled-in form or other object to some processor. Use of PUT and POST is currently limited, partly due to scarcity of hypertext editors. The extension to other methods is a subject of study.

When objects are transferred over the network, information about them ("metainformation") is transferred in HTTP headers. The set of headers is an extension of the Multipurpose Internet Mail Extensions (MIME) set. This design decision was taken to open the door to integration of hypermedia mail, news, and information access. Unlike in email, transfer in binary, and transfer in nonstandard but mutually agreed document formats is possible. This allows, for example, servers to indicate links from, and titles of, documents (such as bit-map images) whose data format does not otherwise include such information.

The convention that unrecognized HTTP headers and parameters are ignored has made it easy to try new ideas on working production servers. This has allowed the protocol definition to evolve in a controlled way by the incorporation of tested ideas.

## Hypertext Markup Language (HTML)

Despite the ability of HTTP to negotiate formats, W3 needed a common basic language of interchange for hypertext. HTML is that language, and much of the fabric of the Web is constructed out of it. It was designed to be sufficiently simple so as to be easily produced by both people and programs, but also to adhere to the SGML standard in that a valid HTML document, if attached to SGML declarations including the HTML "DTD," may be parsed by an SGML parser. HTML is a markup language that does not have to be used with HTTP. It can be used in hypertext email (it is proposed as a format for MIME), news, and anywhere basic hypertext is needed. It includes simple structure elements, such as several levels of headings, bulleted lists, menus and compact lists, all of which are useful when presenting choices, and in on-line documents.

Under development is a much enriched version of HTML known has HTML+. This includes features for more sophisticated on-line documentation, form templates for the entry of data by users, tables and mathematical formulae.

Currently many browsers support a subset of the HTML+ features in addition to the core HTML set.

HTML is defined to be a language of communication, which actually flows over the network. There is no requirement that files are stored in HTML. Servers may store files in other formats, or in variations on HTML that include extra information of local interest only, and then generate HTML on the fly with each request.

## W3 and Other Systems

Two other systems, WAIS (from Thinking Machines Corporation and now WAIS, Inc.) and Gopher (from the University of Minnesota), share W3's client-server architecture and a certain amount of its functionality. Table 54.1 indicates some of the differences.

The WAIS protocol is influenced largely by the z39.50 protocol designed for networking library catalogs. It allows a text-based search, and retrieval following a search. Indexes to be searched are found by searching in a master index. This two-stage search has been demonstrated to be sufficiently powerful to cover the current world of WAIS data. There are no navigational tools to allow the reader to be shown the available resources, however, or guided through the data: the reader is "parachuted in" to a hopefully relevant spot in the information world, but left without context.

Gopher provides a free text search mechanism, but principally uses menus. A menu is a list of titles, from which

| | WAIS | Gopher | World-Wide Web |
|---|---|---|---|
| **Original target application** | Text-based information retrieval | Campus-wide information (CWIS) | Collaborative work |
| **Typical objects** | | | |
| Text | YES | YES | YES |
| Menus, Graphics | NO | YES | YES |
| Hypertext | NO | NO | YES |
| **Search functions** | | | |
| Text search | YES | YES | YES |
| Relevance feedback | YES | NO | NO |
| Reference to other servers | NO | YES | YES |
| **Registered servers** | | | |
| April 1993 | 113 | 455 | 62 |
| April 1994 | 137 | 1410 | 829 |

Table 54.1. A comparison of three popular network information projects.

Registered server figures taken April 27, 1993 and April 15, 1994. WAIS: from Thinking Machines Corporation directory, number of distinct hosts. Gopher: from "All the Gophers in the world" register at the University of Minnesota. W3: from Geographical registry at CERN. In all cases many more servers exist which are not directly registered, so these are a very rough guide with no indication of quantity or quality of information at each host.

the user may pick one. While gopher space is in fact a web containing many loops, the menu system gives the user the impression of a tree. The Veronica server provides a master index for gopher space.

The W3 data model is similar to the gopher model, except that menus are generalized to hypertext documents. In both cases, simple file servers generate the menus or hypertext directly from the file structure of a server. The W3 hypertext model gives the program more power to communicate the options available to the reader, as it can include headings and various forms of list structure, for example, within the hypertext.

All three systems allow for the provision of graphics, sound and video, although because the WAIS system only has access by text search, text has to be associated with graphics files to allow them to be found.

W3 clients provide access to servers of all types, as a single simple interface to the whole Web is considered very important. Unknown to the user, several protocols are in use behind the scenes. A common code library "libwww" put into the public domain by CERN has promoted this uniformity. Whereas one would not wish to see greater proliferation of protocols, the existence of more than one protocol probably allows for the most rapid progress during this phase in the development of the field. It also allows a certain limited confidence that, if an architecture can encompass older systems and allow transition to current systems, it will, by induction, be able to provide a transition to newer and better ideas as they are invented.

## Recent W3 Developments

This article, like others in this issue, was derived from material written in April 1993 for the INET'93 conference. Growth of the Web since that time has been so great that this section has been completely rewritten. There are now 829 (May: 1,248) rather than 62 registered HTTP servers, and many more client programs available as then.

The initial prototype W3 client was a "wysiwyg" hypertext browser/editor using NeXTStep. We developed a line mode browser, and were encouraging the developments of a good browser for X workstations. One year ago, NCSA's Mosaic W3 browser was in wide use on X workstations. Its easy installation and use was a major reason for the spread of the Web. Today there are many browsers available for workstations, Macintosh and IBM/PC compatible machines, and for users with

character-based terminals. Of the latter category, "Lynx" from the University of Kansas provides full-screen access to the Web for users with character terminals or emulators running on personal computers. Since new software is appearing frequently, readers are advised to check the lists on the Web for those most suited to their needs.

The availability of browsers and the availability of quality information have provoked each other. One available indicator of growth has been Merit Inc.'s count of the traffic of various different protocols across the NSF T3 backbone in the U.S. (see Figure 54.3).

An indicator of the uptake rate of clients is the load on the *info.cern.ch* W3 server at CERN, which provides information about the Web itself, which more than doubled every 4 months over the three years between April 1991 and April 1994.

Information providers have also blossomed. Some of these provide simple overviews of what is available at particular institutes or in particular fields. Others use the power of the W3 model to provide a virtual world of great richness.

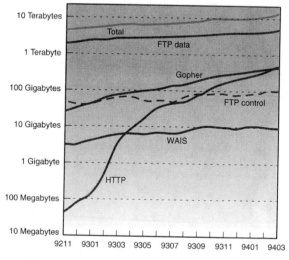

Figure 54.3. Traffic in bytes per month across the NSF T3 backbone in the U.S. File Transfer Protocol (FTP) was traditionally used to access archives of software. FTP uses separate connections for control and data flow. WAIS arose as an interface to text retrieval systems, Gopher protocol with menu-style interfaces, and W3's HTTP with hypertext and multimedia. W3 clients handle many protocols to access all these worlds of data as a seamless continuum, but new W3 servers use HTTP by preference. Each vertical division represents a tenfold increase in traffic. The horizontal divisions are months. Data: Merit <ftp://ftp.merit.edu/statistics/nsfnet>. [As of summer 2002, http://www.ifla.org/documents/internet/nsf-hist.txt ]

Examples of servers that use hypertext in interesting ways are the RAL-Durham Particle Database, and the Legal Information Institute's hypertexts of several great tomes of American law. Franz Hoesel's hypertext version of the Vatican's Renaissance Culture exhibit at the Library of Congress set an example that was followed by many collections of art, history and other fields. The Palo Alto town hall runs a server with everything from building regulations to restaurants. As an example of the increasing use of the Web for commerce, a user-friendly virtual clothing store prompts for one's size, and points to a virtual store containing only those clothes that are the right size and also in stock.

## The Future

The W3 initiative occupies the meeting point of many fields of technology. Users put pressure and effort into bringing about the adoption of W3 in new areas. Apart from being a place of communication and learning, and a new market place, the Web is a show ground for new developments in information technology. Some of the developments that we look forward to in the next few years include

- The implementation of a name service that will allow documents to be referenced by name, independent of their location;

- Hypertext editors allowing nonexpert users to make hypertext links to organize published information. This will bring the goal of computer-supported collaboration closer, with front-end update, and annotation;

- More sophisticated document type definitions providing for the needs of commercial publishers of on-line material;

- The development of a common format for hypertext links from two- and three-dimensional images giving more exciting interface possibilities;

- Integration with concurrent editors and other real-time features such as teleconferencing and virtual reality;

- Easy-to-use servers for low-end machines to ease publication of information by small groups and individuals;

- Evolution of objects from being principally human-readable documents to contain more machine-oriented semantic information, allowing more sophisticated processing;

- Conventions on the Internet for charging and commercial use to allow direct access to for-profit services.

## Conclusion

It is intended that after reading this article you will have an idea of what W3 is, where it fits in with other systems in the field, and where it is going. There is much more to be said, especially about providing information, but this is described on the Web itself. Also in the "Web about the Web" are lists of contributed research and development work and ideas, and pointers to work in progress, so that those interested can work together.

The Web does not yet meet its design goal as being a pool of knowledge that is as easy to update as to read. That level of immediacy of knowledge sharing waits for easy-to-use hypertext editors to be generally available on most platforms. Most information has in fact passed through publishers or system managers of one sort or another. However, the incredible diversity of information available gives great credit to the creativity and ingenuity of information providers, and points to a very exciting future.

## Appendix: Getting Started

If you have a vt100 terminal, you can try out a full-screen interface by telnet to ukanaix.cc.ukans.edu[†] and logging in as www. With any terminal, you can telnet to info.cern.ch[†] for the simplest interface. These browsers are also available in source and in some cases binary form. Details of status and coordinates of about 20 different browsers are available on the Web—just follow a link to World-Wide Web, and select "software available."

The kernel W3 code (a common code library, and basic server and clients) from CERN is in the public domain. (All protocols and specifications are public domain.) It is available by anonymous FTP from info.cern.ch.[†]

NCSA's "Mosaic" browser for W3 is available for X, Mac or PC/Windows by anonymous FTP from ftp.ncsa.uiuc.edu, currently without charge for academic users. [As of summer 2002, ftp.ncsa.uiuc.edu is still online; Mosaic is available for free from there by ftp. Hosts marked † are no longer online.]

Note
1. The Internet Engineering Task Force (IETF) is currently defining a similar and derived syntax known as a Uniform Resource Locator (URL). As this work is not complete, and there is no guarantee that URLs will have the same syntax or properties as URIs, we use the term URI here to avoid confusion.

Glossary and Further Reading

FTP: File Transfer Protocol. Postel, J. and Reynolds, J. File Transfer Protocol. Internet RFC 959, October 1985. <ftp://ds.internic.net/rfc/rfc959.txt>

Gopher: The Internet Gopher. Anklesaria, F. et. al. The Internet Gopher Protocol. Internet RFC 1436, March 1993. <ftp://ds.internic.net/rfc/rfc1436.txt>

HTML: Hypertext Markup Language. Berners-Lee, T., and Connolly, D. Hypertext Markup Language Protocol. <ftp://info.cern.ch/pub/www/doc/html-spec.ps,.txt>

HTTP: Hypertext Transfer Protocol. Berners-Lee, T. Hypertext Transfer Protocol. <ftp://info.cern.ch/pub/www/doc/http-spec.ps,.txt>

MIME: Multipurpose Internet Mail Extensions. Borenstein, N., and Freed, N. MIME (Multipurpose Internet Mail Extensions): Mechanisms for Specifying and Describing the Format of Internet Message Bodies. Internet RFC 1341, June 1992.

NNTP: Network News Transfer Protocol. Kantor, B. and Lapsley, P. A proposed standard for the transmission of news. Internet RFC 977, 1986.

URI: Universal Resource Identifier. Berners-Lee, T. Universal Resource Identifiers for the World-Wide Web. Submitted as an Internet RFC as yet unnumbered. See <http://info.cern.ch/hypertext/WWW/Addressing/Addressing.html> for pointers to information on this area.

WAIS: Wide Area Information Servers. See Addyman, T. WAIS: Strengths, Weaknesses and Opportunities. In *Proceedings of Information Networking 93* (London, May 1993), Meckler, London.

W3: Berners-Lee, T.J., Cailliau, R., Groff, J-F., Pollermann, B. World-Wide Web: The Information universe. *Electronic Networking: Research, Applications and Policy,* (Spring 1992), 52–58. See also documents in <ftp://info.cern.ch/pub/www/ doc> and information referenced by <http://info.cern.ch/hypertext/WWW/ TheProject.html>

[As of summer 2002, for files formerly available at info.cern.ch, see <http://www.w3.org/>. For RFCs, see <http://www.faqs.org/rfcs/>.]

# Permissions

"The Endless Chain" by Ben Bagdikian. *The Media Monopoly*. Boston: Beacon Press, 1983. With updated information from the 6th edition, 2000. Reprinted by permission of the author.

"Direct Manipulation: A Step Beyond Programming Languages" by Ben Shneiderman. © 1983 IEEE. Reprinted, with permission, from *IEEE Computer* 16(8):57–69. August 1983. Reprinted by permission of the author and the IEEE.

"Video Games and Computer Holding Power" by Sherry Turkle. *The Second Self: Computers and the Human Spirit*, 64–92. New York: Simon & Schuster, 1984. Reprinted by permission of the author.

"A Cyborg Manifesto" by Donna Haraway. *Socialist Review* 80:65–108. 1985. Reprinted by permission of the author.

"The GNU Manifesto" by Richard Stallman. Free Software Foundation Web Site, <http://www.fsf.org>, accessed 2001. Permission has been granted for anyone to reprint unmodified versions.

"Using Computers: A Direction for Design" by Terry Winograd and Fernando Flores. *Understanding Computers and Cognition: A New Foundation for Design*. 163–179. Norwood, N.J.: Ablex Publishing, 1986. Reprinted with permission of Terry Winograd.

"The Six Elements and the Causal Relations Among Them" by Brenda Laurel. *Computers as Theatre*, 49–65. 2nd edition. Reading, Mass.: Addison–Wesley, 1993. Reprinted by permission of the author.

"Star Raiders: Dramatic Interaction in a Small World" by Brenda Laurel. "Toward the Design of a Computer-Based Interactive Fantasy System," 81–86. Ph.D. Thesis, Ohio State University, 1986. Reprinted by permission of the author.

"Towards a New Classification of Tele-Information Services" by Jan L. Bordewijk and Ben van Kaam. *Intermedia* 34(1):16–21. January 1986.

"Mythinformation" by Langdon Winner. From *The Whale and the Reactor: A Search for Limits in an Age of High Technology*, 1986. Reprinted by permission of the University of Chicago Press.

From *Plans and Situated Actions: The Problem of Human-Machine Communications* by Lucy Suchman. vii–x, 5–26. Cambridge: Cambridge University Press, 1987. Reprinted with permission of Cambridge University Press.

"Siren Shapes: Exploratory and Constructive Hypertexts" by Michael Joyce. *Academic Computing* 3:10–14, 37–42. 1988. Reprinted by permission of the author.

"The Work of Culture in the Age of Cybernetic Systems" by Bill Nichols. *Screen* 21(1):22–46. Winter 1998. Reprinted by permission of the author.

"The Fantasy Beyond Control" © 1990 Lynn Hershman. Reprinted by permission of the author.

"Cardboard Computers: Mocking-It-Up or Hands-On the Future" by Pelle Ehn and Morten Kyng. *Design at Work: Cooperative Design of Computer Systems*, 169–195. Edited by Joan Greenbaum and Morten Kyng. Hillsdale, N.J.: Lawrence Erlbaum Associates, 1991. Reprinted by permission of Pelle Ehn and Lawrence Erlbaum Associates.

"The Lessons of Lucasfilm's Habitat" by Chip Morningstar and F. Randall Farmer. *Cyberspace: First Steps*, 273–301. Edited by Michael Benedikt. Cambridge: MIT Press, 1991.

"Seeing and Writing" by J. David Bolter. *Writing Space: The Computer, Hypertext, and the History of Writing*, 63–81. Hillsdale, J.J. Lawrence Erlbaum Associates, 1991. Reprinted by permission of Lawrence Erlbaum Associates.

"You Say You Want a Revolution? Hypertext and the Laws of Media" by Stuart Moulthrop. *Postmodern Culture*, 1(3). May 1991. Reprinted by permission of the author.

"The End of Books" by Robert Coover. © 1992 by Robert Coover. Originally appeared in *The New York Times Book Review*. Reprinted by permission of Georges Borchardt, Inc., Literary Agency.

# Index